WALT WHITMAN

WALT WHITMAN

POETRY AND PROSE

Leaves of Grass (1855)

Leaves of Grass (1891–92)

Supplementary Poems

Complete Prose Works (1892)

Supplementary Prose

THE LIBRARY OF AMERICA

Distributed in the United States
by Penguin Books USA Inc
and in Canada by Penguin Books Canada Ltd.

Library of Congress Catalog Card Number: 52466
For cataloging information, see end of volume.
ISBN 1–883011–35–3

Originally published in hardcover, in a somewhat different form,
by The Library of America in 1982

First Library of America College Edition
May 1996

Manufactured in the United States of America

Justin Kaplan

wrote the notes and chronology
and selected the texts
for this volume

The publishers wish to thank the New York Public Library and the Library of Congress for their assistance.

Contents

Each section has its own table of contents.

LEAVES OF GRASS

[1855]

Contents

These poems had no titles in 1855, and no titles appear in the text of the present edition. Whitman eventually gave the poems the titles shown here.

AMERICA does not repel the past or what it has produced under its forms or amid other politics or the idea of castes or the old religions . . . . accepts the lesson with calmness . . . is not so impatient as has been supposed that the slough still sticks to opinions and manners and literature while the life which served its requirements has passed into the new life of the new forms . . . perceives that the corpse is slowly borne from the eating and sleeping rooms of the house . . . perceives that it waits a little while in the door . . . that it was fittest for its days . . . that its action has descended to the stalwart and wellshaped heir who approaches . . . and that he shall be fittest for his days.

The Americans of all nations at any time upon the earth have probably the fullest poetical nature. The United States themselves are essentially the greatest poem. In the history of the earth hitherto the largest and most stirring appear tame and orderly to their ampler largeness and stir. Here at last is something in the doings of man that corresponds with the broadcast doings of the day and night. Here is not merely a nation but a teeming nation of nations. Here is action untied from strings necessarily blind to particulars and details magnificently moving in vast masses. Here is the hospitality which forever indicates heroes . . . . Here are the roughs and beards and space and ruggedness and nonchalance that the soul loves. Here the performance disdaining the trivial unapproached in the tremendous audacity of its crowds and groupings and the push of its perspective spreads with crampless and flowing breadth and showers its prolific and splendid extravagance. One sees it must indeed own the riches of the summer and winter, and need never be bankrupt while corn grows from the ground or the orchards drop apples or the bays contain fish or men beget children upon women.

Other states indicate themselves in their deputies . . . . but the genius of the United States is not best or most in its executives or legislatures, nor in its ambassadors or authors or colleges or churches or parlors, nor even in its newspapers or inventors . . . but always most in the common people. Their manners speech dress friendships—the freshness and candor of their physiognomy—the picturesque looseness of their carriage . . . their deathless attachment to freedom—their aversion to anything indecorous or soft or mean—the practical acknowledgment of the citizens of one state by the citizens of all other states—the fierceness of their roused resentment—their curiosity and welcome of novelty—their self-esteem and wonderful sympathy—their susceptibility to a slight—the air they have of persons who never knew how it felt to stand in the presence of superiors—the fluency of their speech—their delight in music, the sure symptom of manly tenderness and native elegance of soul . . . their good temper and openhandedness—the terrible significance of their elections—the President's taking off his hat to them not they to him—these too are unrhymed poetry. It awaits the gigantic and generous treatment worthy of it.

The largeness of nature or the nation were monstrous without a corresponding largeness and generosity of the spirit of the citizen. Not nature nor swarming states nor streets and steamships nor prosperous business nor farms nor capital nor learning may suffice for the ideal of man . . . nor suffice the poet. No reminiscences may suffice either. A live nation can always cut a deep mark and can have the best authority the cheapest . . . namely from its own soul. This is the sum of the profitable uses of individuals or states and of present action and grandeur and of the subjects of poets.—As if it were necessary to trot back generation after generation to the eastern records! As if the beauty and sacredness of the demonstrable must fall behind that of the mythical! As if men do not make their mark out of any times! As if the opening of the western continent by discovery and what has transpired since in North and South America were less than the small theatre of the antique or the aimless sleepwalking of the middle ages! The pride of the United States leaves the wealth and finesse of the cities and all returns of commerce and agriculture and all the magnitude of geography or shows of exterior victory to enjoy the breed of fullsized men or one fullsized man unconquerable and simple.

The American poets are to enclose old and new for America is the race of races. Of them a bard is to be commensurate with a people. To him the other continents arrive as contributions . . . he gives them reception for their sake and his own sake. His spirit responds to his country's spirit . . . . he incarnates its geography and natural life and rivers and lakes. Mississippi with annual freshets and changing chutes, Missouri and Columbia and Ohio and Saint Lawrence with the falls and beautiful masculine Hudson, do not embouchure where they spend themselves more than they embouchure into him. The blue breadth over the inland sea of Virginia and Maryland and the sea off Massachusetts and Maine and over Manhattan bay and over Champlain and Erie and over Ontario and Huron and Michigan and Superior, and over the Texan and Mexican and Floridian and Cuban seas and over the seas off California and Oregon, is not tallied by the blue breadth of the waters below more than the breadth of above and below is tallied by him. When the long Atlantic coast stretches longer and the Pacific coast stretches longer he easily stretches with them north or south. He spans between them also from east to west and reflects what is between them. On him rise solid growths that offset the growths of pine and cedar and hemlock and liveoak and locust and chestnut and cypress and hickory and limetree and cottonwood and tuliptree and cactus and wildvine and tamarind and persimmon . . . . and tangles as tangled as any canebrake or swamp . . . . and forests coated with transparent ice and icicles hanging from the boughs and crackling in the wind . . . . and sides and peaks of mountains . . . . and pasturage sweet and free as savannah or upland or prairie . . . . with flights and songs and screams that answer those of the wildpigeon and highhold and orchard-oriole and coot and surf-duck and redshouldered-hawk and fish-hawk and white-ibis and indianhen and cat-owl and water-pheasant and qua-bird and piedsheldrake and blackbird and mockingbird and buzzard and condor and night-heron and eagle. To him the hereditary countenance descends both mother's and father's. To him enter the essences of the real things and past and present events—of the enormous diversity of temperature and agriculture and mines—the tribes of red aborigines—the weatherbeaten vessels entering new ports or making landings on rocky coasts—the first settlements north or south—the rapid stature and muscle—the haughty defiance of '76, and the war and peace and formation of the constitution . . . . the union always surrounded by blatherers and always calm and impregnable—the perpetual coming of immigrants—the wharfhem'd cities and superior marine—the unsurveyed interior—the loghouses and clearings and wild animals and hunters and trappers . . . . the free commerce—the fisheries and whaling and gold-digging—the endless gestation of new states—the convening of Congress every December, the members duly coming up from all climates and the uttermost parts . . . . the noble character of the young mechanics and of all free American workmen and workwomen . . . . the general ardor and friendliness and enterprise—the perfect equality of the female with the male . . . . the large amativeness—the fluid movement of the population—the factories and mercantile life and laborsaving machinery—the Yankee swap—the New-York firemen and the target excursion—the southern plantation life—the character of the northeast and of the northwest and southwest—slavery and the tremulous spreading of hands to protect it, and the stern opposition to it which shall never cease till it ceases or the speaking of tongues and the moving of lips cease. For such the expression of the American poet is to be transcendant and new. It is to be indirect and not direct or descriptive or epic. Its quality goes through these to much more. Let the age and wars of other nations be chanted and their eras and characters be illustrated and that finish the verse. Not so the great psalm of the republic. Here the theme is creative and has vista. Here comes one among the wellbeloved stonecutters and plans with decision and science and sees the solid and beautiful forms of the future where there are now no solid forms.

Of all nations the United States with veins full of poetical stuff most need poets and will doubtless have the greatest and use them the greatest. Their Presidents shall not be their common referee so much as their poets shall. Of all mankind the great poet is the equable man. Not in him but off from him things are grotesque or eccentric or fail of their sanity. Nothing out of its place is good and nothing in its place is bad. He bestows on every object or quality its fit proportions neither more nor less. He is the arbiter of the diverse and he is the key. He is the equalizer of his age and land . . . . he supplies what wants supplying and checks what wants checking. If peace is the routine out of him speaks the spirit of peace, large, rich, thrifty, building vast and populous cities, encouraging agriculture and the arts and commerce—lighting the study of man, the soul, immortality—federal, state or municipal government, marriage, health, freetrade, intertravel by land and sea . . . . nothing too close, nothing too far off . . . the stars not too far off. In war he is the most deadly force of the war. Who recruits him recruits horse and foot . . . he fetches parks of artillery the best that engineer ever knew. If the time becomes slothful and heavy he knows how to arouse it . . . he can make every word he speaks draw blood. Whatever stagnates in the flat of custom or obedience or legislation he never stagnates. Obedience does not master him, he masters it. High up out of reach he stands turning a concentrated light . . . he turns the pivot with his finger . . . he baffles the swiftest runners as he stands and easily overtakes and envelops them. The time straying toward infidelity and confections and persiflage he withholds by his steady faith . . . he spreads out his dishes . . . he offers the sweet firmfibred meat that grows men and women. His brain is the ultimate brain. He is no arguer . . . he is judgment. He judges not as the judge judges but as the sun falling around a helpless thing. As he sees the farthest he has the most faith. His thoughts are the hymns of the praise of things. In the talk on the soul and eternity and God off of his equal plane he is silent. He sees eternity less like a play with a prologue and denouement . . . . he sees eternity in men and women . . . he does not see men and women as dreams or dots. Faith is the antiseptic of the soul . . . it pervades the common people and preserves them . . . they never give up believing and expecting and trusting. There is that indescribable freshness and unconsciousness about an illiterate person that humbles and mocks the power of the noblest expressive genius. The poet sees for a certainty how one not a great artist may be just as sacred and perfect as the greatest artist. . . . . . The power to destroy or remould is freely used by him but never the power of attack. What is past is past. If he does not expose superior models and prove himself by every step he takes he is not what is wanted. The presence of the greatest poet conquers . . . not parleying or struggling or any prepared attempts. Now he has passed that way see after him! there is not left any vestige of despair or misanthropy or cunning or exclusiveness or the ignominy of a nativity or color or delusion of hell or the necessity of hell . . . . . and no man thenceforward shall be degraded for ignorance or weakness or sin.

The greatest poet hardly knows pettiness or triviality. If he breathes into any thing that was before thought small it dilates with the grandeur and life of the universe. He is a seer . . . . he is individual . . . he is complete in himself . . . . the others are as good as he, only he sees it and they do not. He is not one of the chorus . . . . he does not stop for any regulation . . . he is the president of regulation. What the eyesight does to the rest he does to the rest. Who knows the curious mystery of the eyesight? The other senses corroborate themselves, but this is removed from any proof but its own and foreruns the identities of the spiritual world. A single glance of it mocks all the investigations of man and all the instruments and books of the earth and all reasoning. What is marvellous? what is unlikely? what is impossible or baseless or vague? after you have once just opened the space of a peachpit and given audience to far and near and to the sunset and had all things enter with electric swiftness softly and duly without confusion or jostling or jam.

The land and sea, the animals fishes and birds, the sky of heaven and the orbs, the forests mountains and rivers, are not small themes . . . but folks expect of the poet to indicate more than the beauty and dignity which always attach to dumb real objects . . . . they expect him to indicate the path between reality and their souls. Men and women perceive the beauty well enough . . probably as well as he. The passionate tenacity of hunters, woodmen, early risers, cultivators of gardens and orchards and fields, the love of healthy women for the manly form, seafaring persons, drivers of horses, the passion for light and the open air, all is an old varied sign of the unfailing perception of beauty and of a residence of the poetic in outdoor people. They can never be assisted by poets to perceive . . . some may but they never can. The poetic quality is not marshalled in rhyme or uniformity or abstract addresses to things nor in melancholy complaints or good precepts, but is the life of these and much else and is in the soul. The profit of rhyme is that it drops seeds of a sweeter and more luxuriant rhyme, and of uniformity that it conveys itself into its own roots in the ground out of sight. The rhyme and uniformity of perfect poems show the free growth of metrical laws and bud from them as unerringly and loosely as lilacs or roses on a bush, and take shapes as compact as the shapes of chestnuts and oranges and melons and pears, and shed the perfume impalpable to form. The fluency and ornaments of the finest poems or music or orations or recitations are not independent but dependent. All beauty comes from beautiful blood and a beautiful brain. If the greatnesses are in conjunction in a man or woman it is enough . . . . the fact will prevail through the universe . . . . but the gaggery and gilt of a million years will not prevail. Who troubles himself about his ornaments or fluency is lost. This is what you shall do: Love the earth and sun and the animals, despise riches, give alms to every one that asks, stand up for the stupid and crazy, devote your income and labor to others, hate tyrants, argue not concerning God, have patience and indulgence toward the people, take off your hat to nothing known or unknown or to any man or number of men, go freely with powerful uneducated persons and with the young and with the mothers of families, read these leaves in the open air every season of every year of your life, re-examine all you have been told at school or church or in any book, dismiss whatever insults your own soul, and your very flesh shall be a great poem and have the richest fluency not only in its words but in the silent lines of its lips and face and between the lashes of your eyes and in every motion and joint of your body. . . . . The poet shall not spend his time in unneeded work. He shall know that the ground is always ready ploughed and manured . . . . others may not know it but he shall. He shall go directly to the creation. His trust shall master the trust of everything he touches . . . . and shall master all attachment.

The known universe has one complete lover and that is the greatest poet. He consumes an eternal passion and is indifferent which chance happens and which possible contingency of fortune or misfortune and persuades daily and hourly his delicious pay. What balks or breaks others is fuel for his burning progress to contact and amorous joy. Other proportions of the reception of pleasure dwindle to nothing to his proportions. All expected from heaven or from the highest he is rapport with in the sight of the daybreak or a scene of the winter woods or the presence of children playing or with his arm round the neck of a man or woman. His love above all love has leisure and expanse . . . . he leaves room ahead of himself. He is no irresolute or suspicious lover . . . he is sure . . . he scorns intervals. His experience and the showers and thrills are not for nothing. Nothing can jar him . . . . suffering and darkness cannot—death and fear cannot. To him complaint and jealousy and envy are corpses buried and rotten in the earth . . . . he saw them buried. The sea is not surer of the shore or the shore of the sea than he is of the fruition of his love and of all perfection and beauty.

The fruition of beauty is no chance of hit or miss . . . it is inevitable as life . . . . it is exact and plumb as gravitation. From the eyesight proceeds another eyesight and from the hearing proceeds another hearing and from the voice proceeds another voice eternally curious of the harmony of things with man. To these respond perfections not only in the committees that were supposed to stand for the rest but in the rest themselves just the same. These understand the law of perfection in masses and floods . . . that its finish is to each for itself and onward from itself . . . that it is profuse and impartial . . . that there is not a minute of the light or dark nor an acre of the earth or sea without it—nor any direction of the sky nor any trade or employment nor any turn of events. This is the reason that about the proper expression of beauty there is precision and balance . . . one part does not need to be thrust above another. The best singer is not the one who has the most lithe and powerful organ . . . the pleasure of poems is not in them that take the handsomest measure and similes and sound.

Without effort and without exposing in the least how it is done the greatest poet brings the spirit of any or all events and passions and scenes and persons some more and some less to bear on your individual character as you hear or read. To do this well is to compete with the laws that pursue and follow time. What is the purpose must surely be there and the clue of it must be there . . . . and the faintest indication is the indication of the best and then becomes the clearest indication. Past and present and future are not disjoined but joined. The greatest poet forms the consistence of what is to be from what has been and is. He drags the dead out of their coffins and stands them again on their feet . . . . he says to the past, Rise and walk before me that I may realize you. He learns the lesson . . . . he places himself where the future becomes present. The greatest poet does not only dazzle his rays over character and scenes and passions . . . he finally ascends and finishes all . . . he exhibits the pinnacles that no man can tell what they are for or what is beyond . . . . he glows a moment on the extremest verge. He is most wonderful in his last half-hidden smile or frown . . . by that flash of the moment of parting the one that sees it shall be encouraged or terrified afterward for many years. The greatest poet does not moralize or make applications of morals . . . he knows the soul. The soul has that measureless pride which consists in never acknowledging any lessons but its own. But it has sympathy as measureless as its pride and the one balances the other and neither can stretch too far while it stretches in company with the other. The inmost secrets of art sleep with the twain. The greatest poet has lain close betwixt both and they are vital in his style and thoughts.

The art of art, the glory of expression and the sunshine of the light of letters is simplicity. Nothing is better than simplicity . . . . nothing can make up for excess or for the lack of definiteness. To carry on the heave of impulse and pierce intellectual depths and give all subjects their articulations are powers neither common nor very uncommon. But to speak in literature with the perfect rectitude and insousiance of the movements of animals and the unimpeachableness of the sentiment of trees in the woods and grass by the roadside is the flawless triumph of art. If you have looked on him who has achieved it you have looked on one of the masters of the artists of all nations and times. You shall not contemplate the flight of the graygull over the bay or the mettlesome action of the blood horse or the tall leaning of sunflowers on their stalk or the appearance of the sun journeying through heaven or the appearance of the moon afterward with any more satisfaction than you shall contemplate him. The greatest poet has less a marked style and is more the channel of thoughts and things without increase or diminution, and is the free channel of himself. He swears to his art, I will not be meddlesome, I will not have in my writing any elegance or effect or originality to hang in the way between me and the rest like curtains. I will have nothing hang in the way, not the richest curtains. What I tell I tell for precisely what it is. Let who may exalt or startle or fascinate or soothe I will have purposes as health or heat or snow has and be as regardless of observation. What I experience or portray shall go from my composition without a shred of my composition. You shall stand by my side and look in the mirror with me.

The old red blood and stainless gentility of great poets will be proved by their unconstraint. A heroic person walks at his ease through and out of that custom or precedent or authority that suits him not. Of the traits of the brotherhood of writers savans musicians inventors and artists nothing is finer than silent defiance advancing from new free forms. In the need of poems philosophy politics mechanism science behaviour, the craft of art, an appropriate native grand-opera, shipcraft, or any craft, he is greatest forever and forever who contributes the greatest original practical example. The cleanest expression is that which finds no sphere worthy of itself and makes one.

The messages of great poets to each man and woman are, Come to us on equal terms, Only then can you understand us, We are no better than you, What we enclose you enclose, What we enjoy you may enjoy. Did you suppose there could be only one Supreme? We affirm there can be unnumbered Supremes, and that one does not countervail another any more than one eyesight countervails another . . and that men can be good or grand only of the consciousness of their supremacy within them. What do you think is the grandeur of storms and dismemberments and the deadliest battles and wrecks and the wildest fury of the elements and the power of the sea and the motion of nature and of the throes of human desires and dignity and hate and love? It is that something in the soul which says, Rage on, Whirl on, I tread master here and everywhere, Master of the spasms of the sky and of the shatter of the sea, Master of nature and passion and death, And of all terror and all pain.

The American bards shall be marked for generosity and affection and for encouraging competitors . . They shall be kosmos . . without monopoly or secrecy . . glad to pass any thing to any one . . hungry for equals night and day. They shall not be careful of riches and privilege . . . . they shall be riches and privilege . . . . they shall perceive who the most affluent man is. The most affluent man is he that confronts all the shows he sees by equivalents out of the stronger wealth of himself. The American bard shall delineate no class of persons nor one or two out of the strata of interests nor love most nor truth most nor the soul most nor the body most . . . . and not be for the eastern states more than the western or the northern states more than the southern.

Exact science and its practical movements are no checks on the greatest poet but always his encouragement and support. The outset and remembrance are there . . there the arms that lifted him first and brace him best . . . . there he returns after all his goings and comings. The sailor and traveler . . the anatomist chemist astronomer geologist phrenologist spiritualist mathematician historian and lexicographer are not poets, but they are the lawgivers of poets and their construction underlies the structure of every perfect poem. No matter what rises or is uttered they sent the seed of the conception of it . . . of them and by them stand the visible proofs of souls . . . . . always of their fatherstuff must be begotten the sinewy races of bards. If there shall be love and content between the father and the son and if the greatness of the son is the exuding of the greatness of the father there shall be love between the poet and the man of demonstrable science. In the beauty of poems are the tuft and final applause of science.

Great is the faith of the flush of knowledge and of the investigation of the depths of qualities and things. Cleaving and circling here swells the soul of the poet yet is president of itself always. The depths are fathomless and therefore calm.

The innocence and nakedness are resumed . . . they are neither modest nor immodest. The whole theory of the special and supernatural and all that was twined with it or educed out of it departs as a dream. What has ever happened . . . . what happens and whatever may or shall happen, the vital laws enclose all . . . . they are sufficient for any case and for all cases . . . none to be hurried or retarded . . . . any miracle of affairs or persons inadmissible in the vast clear scheme where every motion and every spear of grass and the frames and spirits of men and women and all that concerns them are unspeakably perfect miracles all referring to all and each distinct and in its place. It is also not consistent with the reality of the soul to admit that there is anything in the known universe more divine than men and women.

Men and women and the earth and all upon it are simply to be taken as they are, and the investigation of their past and present and future shall be unintermitted and shall be done with perfect candor. Upon this basis philosophy speculates ever looking toward the poet, ever regarding the eternal tendencies of all toward happiness never inconsistent with what is clear to the senses and to the soul. For the eternal tendencies of all toward happiness make the only point of sane philosophy. Whatever comprehends less than that . . . whatever is less than the laws of light and of astronomical motion . . . or less than the laws that follow the thief the liar the glutton and the drunkard through this life and doubtless afterward . . . . . . or less than vast stretches of time or the slow formation of density or the patient upheaving of strata—is of no account. Whatever would put God in a poem or system of philosophy as contending against some being or influence is also of no account. Sanity and ensemble characterise the great master . . . spoilt in one principle all is spoilt. The great master has nothing to do with miracles. He sees health for himself in being one of the mass . . . . he sees the hiatus in singular eminence. To the perfect shape comes common ground. To be under the general law is great for that is to correspond with it. The master knows that he is unspeakably great and that all are unspeakably great . . . . that nothing for instance is greater than to conceive children and bring them up well . . . that to be is just as great as to perceive or tell.

In the make of the great masters the idea of political liberty is indispensible. Liberty takes the adherence of heroes wherever men and women exist . . . . but never takes any adherence or welcome from the rest more than from poets. They are the voice and exposition of liberty. They out of ages are worthy the grand idea . . . . to them it is confided and they must sustain it. Nothing has precedence of it and nothing can warp or degrade it. The attitude of great poets is to cheer up slaves and horrify despots. The turn of their necks, the sound of their feet, the motions of their wrists, are full of hazard to the one and hope to the other. Come nigh them awhile and though they neither speak or advise you shall learn the faithful American lesson. Liberty is poorly served by men whose good intent is quelled from one failure or two failures or any number of failures, or from the casual indifference or ingratitude of the people, or from the sharp show of the tushes of power, or the bringing to bear soldiers and cannon or any penal statutes. Liberty relies upon itself, invites no one, promises nothing, sits in calmness and light, is positive and composed, and knows no discouragement. The battle rages with many a loud alarm and frequent advance and retreat . . . . the enemy triumphs . . . . the prison, the handcuffs, the iron necklace and anklet, the scaffold, garrote and leadballs do their work . . . . the cause is asleep . . . . the strong throats are choked with their own blood . . . . the young men drop their eyelashes toward the ground when they pass each other . . . . and is liberty gone out of that place? No never. When liberty goes it is not the first to go nor the second or third to go . . it waits for all the rest to go . . it is the last. . . When the memories of the old martyrs are faded utterly away . . . . when the large names of patriots are laughed at in the public halls from the lips of the orators . . . . when the boys are no more christened after the same but christened after tyrants and traitors instead . . . . when the laws of the free are grudgingly permitted and laws for informers and blood-money are sweet to the taste of the people . . . . when I and you walk abroad upon the earth stung with compassion at the sight of numberless brothers answering our equal friendship and calling no man master—and when we are elated with noble joy at the sight of slaves . . . . when the soul retires in the cool communion of the night and surveys its experience and has much extasy over the word and deed that put back a helpless innocent person into the gripe of the gripers or into any cruel inferiority . . . . when those in all parts of these states who could easier realize the true American character but do not yet—when the swarms of cringers, suckers, doughfaces, lice of politics, planners of sly involutions for their own preferment to city offices or state legislatures or the judiciary or congress or the presidency, obtain a response of love and natural deference from the people whether they get the offices or no . . . . when it is better to be a bound booby and rogue in office at a high salary than the poorest free mechanic or farmer with his hat unmoved from his head and firm eyes and a candid and generous heart . . . . and when servility by town or state or the federal government or any oppression on a large scale or small scale can be tried on without its own punishment following duly after in exact proportion against the smallest chance of escape . . . . or rather when all life and all the souls of men and women are discharged from any part of the earth—then only shall the instinct of liberty be discharged from that part of the earth.

As the attributes of the poets of the kosmos concentre in the real body and soul and in the pleasure of things they possess the superiority of genuineness over all fiction and romance. As they emit themselves facts are showered over with light . . . . the daylight is lit with more volatile light . . . . also the deep between the setting and rising sun goes deeper many fold. Each precise object or condition or combination or process exhibits a beauty . . . . the multiplication table its—old age its—the carpenter's trade its—the grand-opera its . . . . the hugehulled cleanshaped New-York clipper at sea under steam or full sail gleams with unmatched beauty . . . . the American circles and large harmonies of government gleam with theirs . . . . and the commonest definite intentions and actions with theirs. The poets of the kosmos advance through all interpositions and coverings and turmoils and stratagems to first principles. They are of use . . . . they dissolve poverty from its need and riches from its conceit. You large proprietor they say shall not realize or perceive more than any one else. The owner of the library is not he who holds a legal title to it having bought and paid for it. Any one and every one is owner of the library who can read the same through all the varieties of tongues and subjects and styles, and in whom they enter with ease and take residence and force toward paternity and maternity, and make supple and powerful and rich and large. . . . . These American states strong and healthy and accomplished shall receive no pleasure from violations of natural models and must not permit them. In paintings or mouldings or carvings in mineral or wood, or in the illustrations of books or newspapers, or in any comic or tragic prints, or in the patterns of woven stuffs or any thing to beautify rooms or furniture or costumes, or to put upon cornices or monuments or on the prows or sterns of ships, or to put anywhere before the human eye indoors or out, that which distorts honest shapes or which creates unearthly beings or places or contingencies is a nuisance and revolt. Of the human form especially it is so great it must never be made ridiculous. Of ornaments to a work nothing outre can be allowed . . but those ornaments can be allowed that conform to the perfect facts of the open air and that flow out of the nature of the work and come irrepressibly from it and are necessary to the completion of the work. Most works are most beautiful without ornament. . . Exaggerations will be revenged in human physiology. Clean and vigorous children are jetted and conceived only in those communities where the models of natural forms are public every day. . . . . Great genius and the people of these states must never be demeaned to romances. As soon as histories are properly told there is no more need of romances.

The great poets are also to be known by the absence in them of tricks and by the justification of perfect personal candor. Then folks echo a new cheap joy and a divine voice leaping from their brains: How beautiful is candor! All faults may be forgiven of him who has perfect candor. Henceforth let no man of us lie, for we have seen that openness wins the inner and outer world and that there is no single exception, and that never since our earth gathered itself in a mass have deceit or subterfuge or prevarication attracted its smallest particle or the faintest tinge of a shade—and that through the enveloping wealth and rank of a state or the whole republic of states a sneak or sly person shall be discovered and despised . . . . and that the soul has never been once fooled and never can be fooled . . . . and thrift without the loving nod of the soul is only a fœtid puff . . . . and there never grew up in any of the continents of the globe nor upon any planet or satellite or star, nor upon the asteroids, nor in any part of ethereal space, nor in the midst of density, nor under the fluid wet of the sea, nor in that condition which precedes the birth of babes, nor at any time during the changes of life, nor in that condition that follows what we term death, nor in any stretch of abeyance or action afterward of vitality, nor in any process of formation or reformation anywhere, a being whose instinct hated the truth.

Extreme caution or prudence, the soundest organic health, large hope and comparison and fondness for women and children, large alimentiveness and destructiveness and causality, with a perfect sense of the oneness of nature and the propriety of the same spirit applied to human affairs . . these are called up of the float of the brain of the world to be parts of the greatest poet from his birth out of his mother's womb and from her birth out of her mother's. Caution seldom goes far enough. It has been thought that the prudent citizen was the citizen who applied himself to solid gains and did well for himself and his family and completed a lawful life without debt or crime. The greatest poet sees and admits these economies as he sees the economies of food and sleep, but has higher notions of prudence than to think he gives much when he gives a few slight attentions at the latch of the gate. The premises of the prudence of life are not the hospitality of it or the ripeness and harvest of it. Beyond the independence of a little sum laid aside for burial-money, and of a few clapboards around and shingles overhead on a lot of American soil owned, and the easy dollars that supply the year's plain clothing and meals, the melancholy prudence of the abandonment of such a great being as a man is to the toss and pallor of years of moneymaking with all their scorching days and icy nights and all their stifling deceits and underhanded dodgings, or infinitessimals of parlors, or shameless stuffing while others starve . . and all the loss of the bloom and odor of the earth and of the flowers and atmosphere and of the sea and of the true taste of the women and men you pass or have to do with in youth or middle age, and the issuing sickness and desperate revolt at the close of a life without elevation or naivete, and the ghastly chatter of a death without serenity or majesty, is the great fraud upon modern civilization and forethought, blotching the surface and system which civilization undeniably drafts, and moistening with tears the immense features it spreads and spreads with such velocity before the reached kisses of the soul. . . Still the right explanation remains to be made about prudence. The prudence of the mere wealth and respectability of the most esteemed life appears too faint for the eye to observe at all when little and large alike drop quietly aside at the thought of the prudence suitable for immortality. What is wisdom that fills the thinness of a year or seventy or eighty years to wisdom spaced out by ages and coming back at a certain time with strong reinforcements and rich presents and the clear faces of wedding-guests as far as you can look in every direction running gaily toward you? Only the soul is of itself . . . . all else has reference to what ensues. All that a person does or thinks is of consequence. Not a move can a man or woman make that affects him or her in a day or a month or any part of the direct lifetime or the hour of death but the same affects him or her onward afterward through the indirect lifetime. The indirect is always as great and real as the direct. The spirit receives from the body just as much as it gives to the body. Not one name of word or deed . . not of venereal sores or discolorations . . not the privacy of the onanist . . not of the putrid veins of gluttons or rumdrinkers . . . not peculation or cunning or betrayal or murder . . no serpentine poison of those that seduce women . . not the foolish yielding of women . . not prostitution . . not of any depravity of young men . . not of the attainment of gain by discreditable means . . not any nastiness of appetite . . not any harshness of officers to men or judges to prisoners or fathers to sons or sons to fathers or of husbands to wives or bosses to their boys . . not of greedy looks or malignant wishes . . . nor any of the wiles practised by people upon themselves . . . ever is or ever can be stamped on the programme but it is duly realized and returned, and that returned in further performances . . . and they returned again. Nor can the push of charity or personal force ever be any thing else than the profoundest reason, whether it bring arguments to hand or no. No specification is necessary . . to add or subtract or divide is in vain. Little or big, learned or unlearned, white or black, legal or illegal, sick or well, from the first inspiration down the windpipe to the last expiration out of it, all that a male or female does that is vigorous and benevolent and clean is so much sure profit to him or her in the unshakable order of the universe and through the whole scope of it forever. If the savage or felon is wise it is well . . . . if the greatest poet or savan is wise it is simply the same . . if the President or chief justice is wise it is the same . . . if the young mechanic or farmer is wise it is no more or less . . if the prostitute is wise it is no more nor less. The interest will come round . . all will come round. All the best actions of war and peace . . . all help given to relatives and strangers and the poor and old and sorrowful and young children and widows and the sick, and to all shunned persons . . all furtherance of fugitives and of the escape of slaves . . all the self-denial that stood steady and aloof on wrecks and saw others take the seats of the boats . . . all offering of substance or life for the good old cause, or for a friend's sake or opinion's sake . . . all pains of enthusiasts scoffed at by their neighbors . . all the vast sweet love and precious suffering of mothers . . . all honest men baffled in strifes recorded or unrecorded . . . . all the grandeur and good of the few ancient nations whose fragments of annals we inherit . . and all the good of the hundreds of far mightier and more ancient nations unknown to us by name or date or location . . . . all that was ever manfully begun, whether it succeeded or no . . . . all that has at any time been well suggested out of the divine heart of man or by the divinity of his mouth or by the shaping of his great hands . . and all that is well thought or done this day on any part of the surface of the globe . . or on any of the wandering stars or fixed stars by those there as we are here . . or that is henceforth to be well thought or done by you whoever you are, or by any one—these singly and wholly inured at their time and inure now and will inure always to the identities from which they sprung or shall spring. . . Did you guess any of them lived only its moment? The world does not so exist . . no parts palpable or impalpable so exist . . . no result exists now without being from its long antecedent result, and that from its antecedent, and so backward without the farthest mentionable spot coming a bit nearer the beginning than any other spot. . . . . Whatever satisfies the soul is truth. The prudence of the greatest poet answers at last the craving and glut of the soul, is not contemptuous of less ways of prudence if they conform to its ways, puts off nothing, permits no let-up for its own case or any case, has no particular sabbath or judgment-day, divides not the living from the dead or the righteous from the unrighteous, is satisfied with the present, matches every thought or act by its correlative, knows no possible forgiveness or deputed atonement . . knows that the young man who composedly periled his life and lost it has done exceeding well for himself, while the man who has not periled his life and retains it to old age in riches and ease has perhaps achieved nothing for himself worth mentioning . . and that only that person has no great prudence to learn who has learnt to prefer real longlived things, and favors body and soul the same, and perceives the indirect assuredly following the direct, and what evil or good he does leaping onward and waiting to meet him again—and who in his spirit in any emergency whatever neither hurries or avoids death.

The direct trial of him who would be the greatest poet is today. If he does not flood himself with the immediate age as with vast oceanic tides . . . . . and if he does not attract his own land body and soul to himself and hang on its neck with incomparable love and plunge his semitic muscle into its merits and demerits . . . and if he be not himself the age transfigured . . . . and if to him is not opened the eternity which gives similitude to all periods and locations and processes and animate and inanimate forms, and which is the bond of time, and rises up from its inconceivable vagueness and infiniteness in the swimming shape of today, and is held by the ductile anchors of life, and makes the present spot the passage from what was to what shall be, and commits itself to the representation of this wave of an hour and this one of the sixty beautiful children of the wave—let him merge in the general run and wait his development. . . . . Still the final test of poems or any character or work remains. The prescient poet projects himself centuries ahead and judges performer or performance after the changes of time. Does it live through them? Does it still hold on untired? Will the same style and the direction of genius to similar points be satisfactory now? Has no new discovery in science or arrival at superior planes of thought and judgment and behaviour fixed him or his so that either can be looked down upon? Have the marches of tens and hundreds and thousands of years made willing detours to the right hand and the left hand for his sake? Is he beloved long and long after he is buried? Does the young man think often of him? and the young woman think often of him? and do the middleaged and the old think of him?

A great poem is for ages and ages in common and for all degrees and complexions and all departments and sects and for a woman as much as a man and a man as much as a woman. A great poem is no finish to a man or woman but rather a beginning. Has any one fancied he could sit at last under some due authority and rest satisfied with explanations and realize and be content and full? To no such terminus does the greatest poet bring . . . he brings neither cessation or sheltered fatness and ease. The touch of him tells in action. Whom he takes he takes with firm sure grasp into live regions previously unattained . . . . thenceforward is no rest . . . . they see the space and ineffable sheen that turn the old spots and lights into dead vacuums. The companion of him beholds the birth and progress of stars and learns one of the meanings. Now there shall be a man cohered out of tumult and chaos . . . . the elder encourages the younger and shows him how . . . they two shall launch off fearlessly together till the new world fits an orbit for itself and looks unabashed on the lesser orbits of the stars and sweeps through the ceaseless rings and shall never be quiet again.

There will soon be no more priests. Their work is done. They may wait awhile . . perhaps a generation or two . . dropping off by degrees. A superior breed shall take their place . . . . the gangs of kosmos and prophets en masse shall take their place. A new order shall arise and they shall be the priests of man, and every man shall be his own priest. The churches built under their umbrage shall be the churches of men and women. Through the divinity of themselves shall the kosmos and the new breed of poets be interpreters of men and women and of all events and things. They shall find their inspiration in real objects today, symptoms of the past and future . . . . They shall not deign to defend immortality or God or the perfection of things or liberty or the exquisite beauty and reality of the soul. They shall arise in America and be responded to from the remainder of the earth.

The English language befriends the grand American expression . . . . it is brawny enough and limber and full enough. On the tough stock of a race who through all change of circumstance was never without the idea of political liberty, which is the animus of all liberty, it has attracted the terms of daintier and gayer and subtler and more elegant tongues. It is the powerful language of resistance . . . it is the dialect of common sense. It is the speech of the proud and melancholy races and of all who aspire. It is the chosen tongue to express growth faith self-esteem freedom justice equality friendliness amplitude prudence decision and courage. It is the medium that shall well nigh express the inexpressible.

No great literature nor any like style of behaviour or oratory or social intercourse or household arrangements or public institutions or the treatment by bosses of employed people, nor executive detail or detail of the army or navy, nor spirit of legislation or courts or police or tuition or architecture or songs or amusements or the costumes of young men, can long elude the jealous and passionate instinct of American standards. Whether or no the sign appears from the mouths of the people, it throbs a live interrogation in every freeman's and freewoman's heart after that which passes by or this built to remain. Is it uniform with my country? Are its disposals without ignominious distinctions? Is it for the evergrowing communes of brothers and lovers, large, well-united, proud beyond the old models, generous beyond all models? Is it something grown fresh out of the fields or drawn from the sea for use to me today here? I know that what answers for me an American must answer for any individual or nation that serves for a part of my materials. Does this answer? or is it without reference to universal needs? or sprung of the needs of the less developed society of special ranks? or old needs of pleasure overlaid by modern science and forms? Does this acknowledge liberty with audible and absolute acknowledgement, and set slavery at nought for life and death? Will it help breed one goodshaped and wellhung man, and a woman to be his perfect and independent mate? Does it improve manners? Is it for the nursing of the young of the republic? Does it solve readily with the sweet milk of the nipples of the breasts of the mother of many children? Has it too the old ever-fresh forbearance and impartiality? Does it look with the same love on the last born and on those hardening toward stature, and on the errant, and on those who disdain all strength of assault outside of their own?

The poems distilled from other poems will probably pass away. The coward will surely pass away. The expectation of the vital and great can only be satisfied by the demeanor of the vital and great. The swarms of the polished deprecating and reflectors and the polite float off and leave no remembrance. America prepares with composure and goodwill for the visitors that have sent word. It is not intellect that is to be their warrant and welcome. The talented, the artist, the ingenious, the editor, the statesman, the erudite . . they are not unappreciated . . they fall in their place and do their work. The soul of the nation also does its work. No disguise can pass on it . . no disguise can conceal from it. It rejects none, it permits all. Only toward as good as itself and toward the like of itself will it advance half-way. An individual is as superb as a nation when he has the qualities which make a superb nation. The soul of the largest and wealthiest and proudest nation may well go half-way to meet that of its poets. The signs are effectual. There is no fear of mistake. If the one is true the other is true. The proof of a poet is that his country absorbs him as affectionately as he has absorbed it.

I CELEBRATE myself,
And what I assume you shall assume,
For every atom belonging to me as good belongs to you.

I loafe and invite my soul,
I lean and loafe at my ease . . . . observing a spear of
summer grass.

Houses and rooms are full of perfumes . . . . the shelves
are crowded with perfumes,
I breathe the fragrance myself, and know it and like it,
The distillation would intoxicate me also, but I shall not let it.

The atmosphere is not a perfume . . . . it has no taste of
the distillation . . . . it is odorless,
It is for my mouth forever . . . . I am in love with it,
I will go to the bank by the wood and become undisguised
and naked,
I am mad for it to be in contact with me.

The smoke of my own breath,
Echos, ripples, and buzzed whispers . . . . loveroot,
silkthread, crotch and vine,
My respiration and inspiration . . . . the beating of my heart
. . . . the passing of blood and air through my lungs,
The sniff of green leaves and dry leaves, and of the shore
and darkcolored sea-rocks, and of hay in the barn,
The sound of the belched words of my voice . . . . words
loosed to the eddies of the wind,
A few light kisses . . . . a few embraces . . . . a reaching
around of arms,
The play of shine and shade on the trees as the supple
boughs wag,
The delight alone or in the rush of the streets, or along the
fields and hillsides,
The feeling of health . . . . the full-noon trill . . . . the
song of me rising from bed and meeting the sun.

Have you reckoned a thousand acres much? Have you reckoned the earth much?
Have you practiced so long to learn to read?
Have you felt so proud to get at the meaning of poems?

Stop this day and night with me and you shall possess the origin of all poems,
You shall possess the good of the earth and sun . . . . there are millions of suns left,
You shall no longer take things at second or third hand . . . . nor look through the eyes of the dead . . . . nor feed on the spectres in books,
You shall not look through my eyes either, nor take things from me,
You shall listen to all sides and filter them from yourself.

I have heard what the talkers were talking . . . . the talk of the beginning and the end,
But I do not talk of the beginning or the end.

There was never any more inception than there is now,
Nor any more youth or age than there is now;
And will never be any more perfection than there is now,
Nor any more heaven or hell than there is now.

Urge and urge and urge,
Always the procreant urge of the world.

Out of the dimness opposite equals advance . . . . Always substance and increase,
Always a knit of identity . . . . always distinction . . . . always a breed of life.

To elaborate is no avail . . . . Learned and unlearned feel that it is so.

Sure as the most certain sure . . . . plumb in the uprights, well entretied, braced in the beams,
Stout as a horse, affectionate, haughty, electrical,
I and this mystery here we stand.

Clear and sweet is my soul . . . . and clear and sweet is all
that is not my soul.

Lack one lacks both . . . . and the unseen is proved by the
seen,
Till that becomes unseen and receives proof in its turn.

Showing the best and dividing it from the worst, age vexes
age,
Knowing the perfect fitness and equanimity of things, while
they discuss I am silent, and go bathe and admire myself.

Welcome is every organ and attribute of me, and of any
man hearty and clean,
Not an inch nor a particle of an inch is vile, and none shall
be less familiar than the rest.

I am satisfied . . . . I see, dance, laugh, sing;
As God comes a loving bedfellow and sleeps at my side all
night and close on the peep of the day,
And leaves for me baskets covered with white towels
bulging the house with their plenty,
Shall I postpone my acceptation and realization and scream
at my eyes,
That they turn from gazing after and down the road,
And forthwith cipher and show me to a cent,
Exactly the contents of one, and exactly the contents of
two, and which is ahead?

Trippers and askers surround me,
People I meet . . . . . the effect upon me of my early life
. . . . of the ward and city I live in . . . . of the nation,
The latest news . . . . discoveries, inventions, societies
. . . . authors old and new,
My dinner, dress, associates, looks, business, compliments,
dues,
The real or fancied indifference of some man or woman I
love,
The sickness of one of my folks—or of myself . . . . or ill-

doing . . . . or loss or lack of money . . . . or depressions or exaltations,
They come to me days and nights and go from me again,
But they are not the Me myself.

Apart from the pulling and hauling stands what I am,
Stands amused, complacent, compassionating, idle, unitary,
Looks down, is erect, bends an arm on an impalpable certain rest,
Looks with its sidecurved head curious what will come next,
Both in and out of the game, and watching and wondering at it.

Backward I see in my own days where I sweated through fog with linguists and contenders,
I have no mockings or arguments . . . . I witness and wait.

I believe in you my soul . . . . the other I am must not abase itself to you,
And you must not be abased to the other.

Loafe with me on the grass . . . . loose the stop from your throat,
Not words, not music or rhyme I want . . . . not custom or lecture, not even the best,
Only the lull I like, the hum of your valved voice.

I mind how we lay in June, such a transparent summer morning;
You settled your head athwart my hips and gently turned over upon me,
And parted the shirt from my bosom-bone, and plunged your tongue to my barestript heart,
And reached till you felt my beard, and reached till you held my feet.

Swiftly arose and spread around me the peace and joy and knowledge that pass all the art and argument of the earth;
And I know that the hand of God is the elderhand of my own,

And I know that the spirit of God is the eldest brother of my own,
And that all the men ever born are also my brothers . . . . and the women my sisters and lovers,
And that a kelson of the creation is love;
And limitless are leaves stiff or drooping in the fields,
And brown ants in the little wells beneath them,
And mossy scabs of the wormfence, and heaped stones, and elder and mullen and pokeweed.

A child said, What is the grass? fetching it to me with full hands;
How could I answer the child? . . . . I do not know what it is any more than he.

I guess it must be the flag of my disposition, out of hopeful green stuff woven.

Or I guess it is the handkerchief of the Lord,
A scented gift and remembrancer designedly dropped,
Bearing the owner's name someway in the corners, that we may see and remark, and say Whose?

Or I guess the grass is itself a child . . . . the produced babe of the vegetation.

Or I guess it is a uniform hieroglyphic,
And it means, Sprouting alike in broad zones and narrow zones,
Growing among black folks as among white,
Kanuck, Tuckahoe, Congressman, Cuff, I give them the same, I receive them the same.

And now it seems to me the beautiful uncut hair of graves.

Tenderly will I use you curling grass,
It may be you transpire from the breasts of young men,
It may be if I had known them I would have loved them;
It may be you are from old people and from women, and from offspring taken soon out of their mothers' laps,
And here you are the mothers' laps.

This grass is very dark to be from the white heads of old mothers,
Darker than the colorless beards of old men,
Dark to come from under the faint red roofs of mouths.

O I perceive after all so many uttering tongues!
And I perceive they do not come from the roofs of mouths for nothing.

I wish I could translate the hints about the dead young men and women,
And the hints about old men and mothers, and the offspring taken soon out of their laps.

What do you think has become of the young and old men?
And what do you think has become of the women and children?

They are alive and well somewhere;
The smallest sprout shows there is really no death,
And if ever there was it led forward life, and does not wait at the end to arrest it,
And ceased the moment life appeared.

All goes onward and outward . . . . and nothing collapses,
And to die is different from what any one supposed, and luckier.

Has any one supposed it lucky to be born?
I hasten to inform him or her it is just as lucky to die, and I know it.

I pass death with the dying, and birth with the new-washed babe . . . . and am not contained between my hat and boots,
And peruse manifold objects, no two alike, and every one good,
The earth good, and the stars good, and their adjuncts all good.

I am not an earth nor an adjunct of an earth,
I am the mate and companion of people, all just as immortal and fathomless as myself;
They do not know how immortal, but I know.

Every kind for itself and its own . . . . for me mine male and female,
For me all that have been boys and that love women,
For me the man that is proud and feels how it stings to be slighted,
For me the sweetheart and the old maid . . . . for me mothers and the mothers of mothers,
For me lips that have smiled, eyes that have shed tears,
For me children and the begetters of children.

Who need be afraid of the merge?
Undrape . . . . you are not guilty to me, nor stale nor discarded,
I see through the broadcloth and gingham whether or no,
And am around, tenacious, acquisitive, tireless . . . . and can never be shaken away.

The little one sleeps in its cradle,
I lift the gauze and look a long time, and silently brush away flies with my hand.

The youngster and the redfaced girl turn aside up the bushy hill,
I peeringly view them from the top.

The suicide sprawls on the bloody floor of the bedroom.
It is so . . . . I witnessed the corpse . . . . there the pistol had fallen.

The blab of the pave . . . . the tires of carts and sluff of bootsoles and talk of the promenaders,
The heavy omnibus, the driver with his interrogating thumb, the clank of the shod horses on the granite floor,
The carnival of sleighs, the clinking and shouted jokes and pelts of snowballs;

The hurrahs for popular favorites . . . . the fury of roused mobs,
The flap of the curtained litter—the sick man inside, borne to the hospital,
The meeting of enemies, the sudden oath, the blows and fall,
The excited crowd—the policeman with his star quickly working his passage to the centre of the crowd;
The impassive stones that receive and return so many echoes,
The souls moving along . . . . are they invisible while the least atom of the stones is visible?
What groans of overfed or half-starved who fall on the flags sunstruck or in fits,
What exclamations of women taken suddenly, who hurry home and give birth to babes,
What living and buried speech is always vibrating here . . . . what howls restrained by decorum,
Arrests of criminals, slights, adulterous offers made, acceptances, rejections with convex lips,
I mind them or the resonance of them . . . . I come again and again.

The big doors of the country-barn stand open and ready,
The dried grass of the harvest-time loads the slow-drawn wagon,
The clear light plays on the brown gray and green intertinged,
The armfuls are packed to the sagging mow:
I am there . . . . I help . . . . I came stretched atop of the load,
I felt its soft jolts . . . . one leg reclined on the other,
I jump from the crossbeams, and seize the clover and timothy,
And roll head over heels, and tangle my hair full of wisps.

Alone far in the wilds and mountains I hunt,
Wandering amazed at my own lightness and glee,
In the late afternoon choosing a safe spot to pass the night,
Kindling a fire and broiling the freshkilled game,
Soundly falling asleep on the gathered leaves, my dog and gun by my side.

The Yankee clipper is under her three skysails . . . . she
cuts the sparkle and scud,
My eyes settle the land . . . . I bend at her prow or shout
joyously from the deck.

The boatmen and clamdiggers arose early and stopped for me,
I tucked my trowser-ends in my boots and went and had a
good time,
You should have been with us that day round the chowder-
kettle.

I saw the marriage of the trapper in the open air in the far-
west . . . . the bride was a red girl,
Her father and his friends sat near by crosslegged and
dumbly smoking . . . . they had moccasins to their feet
and large thick blankets hanging from their shoulders;
On a bank lounged the trapper . . . . he was dressed mostly
in skins . . . . his luxuriant beard and curls protected
his neck,
One hand rested on his rifle . . . . the other hand held
firmly the wrist of the red girl,
She had long eyelashes . . . . her head was bare . . . . her
coarse straight locks descended upon her voluptuous
limbs and reached to her feet.

The runaway slave came to my house and stopped outside,
I heard his motions crackling the twigs of the woodpile,
Through the swung half-door of the kitchen I saw him
limpsey and weak,
And went where he sat on a log, and led him in and assured
him,
And brought water and filled a tub for his sweated body
and bruised feet,
And gave him a room that entered from my own, and gave
him some coarse clean clothes,
And remember perfectly well his revolving eyes and his
awkwardness,
And remember putting plasters on the galls of his neck and
ankles;

He staid with me a week before he was recuperated and passed north,
I had him sit next me at table . . . . my firelock leaned in the corner.

Twenty-eight young men bathe by the shore,
Twenty-eight young men, and all so friendly,
Twenty-eight years of womanly life, and all so lonesome.

She owns the fine house by the rise of the bank,
She hides handsome and richly drest aft the blinds of the window.

Which of the young men does she like the best?
Ah the homeliest of them is beautiful to her.

Where are you off to, lady? for I see you,
You splash in the water there, yet stay stock still in your room.

Dancing and laughing along the beach came the twenty-ninth bather,
The rest did not see her, but she saw them and loved them.

The beards of the young men glistened with wet, it ran from their long hair,
Little streams passed all over their bodies.

An unseen hand also passed over their bodies,
It descended tremblingly from their temples and ribs.

The young men float on their backs, their white bellies swell to the sun . . . . they do not ask who seizes fast to them,
They do not know who puffs and declines with pendant and bending arch,
They do not think whom they souse with spray.

The butcher-boy puts off his killing-clothes, or sharpens his knife at the stall in the market,
I loiter enjoying his repartee and his shuffle and breakdown.

Blacksmiths with grimed and hairy chests environ the anvil,
Each has his main-sledge . . . . they are all out . . . . there is a great heat in the fire.

From the cinder-strewed threshold I follow their movements,
The lithe sheer of their waists plays even with their massive arms,
Overhand the hammers roll—overhand so slow—overhand so sure,
They do not hasten, each man hits in his place.

The negro holds firmly the reins of his four horses . . . . the block swags underneath on its tied-over chain,
The negro that drives the huge dray of the stoneyard . . . . steady and tall he stands poised on one leg on the stringpiece,
His blue shirt exposes his ample neck and breast and loosens over his hipband,
His glance is calm and commanding . . . . he tosses the slouch of his hat away from his forehead,
The sun falls on his crispy hair and moustache . . . . falls on the black of his polish'd and perfect limbs.

I behold the picturesque giant and love him . . . . and I do not stop there,
I go with the team also.

In me the caresser of life wherever moving . . . . backward as well as forward slueing,
To niches aside and junior bending.

Oxen that rattle the yoke or halt in the shade, what is that you express in your eyes?
It seems to me more than all the print I have read in my life.

My tread scares the wood-drake and wood-duck on my distant and daylong ramble,
They rise together, they slowly circle around.
. . . . I believe in those winged purposes,
And acknowledge the red yellow and white playing within me,

And consider the green and violet and the tufted crown intentional;
And do not call the tortoise unworthy because she is not something else,
And the mockingbird in the swamp never studied the gamut, yet trills pretty well to me,
And the look of the bay mare shames silliness out of me.

The wild gander leads his flock through the cool night,
Ya-honk! he says, and sounds it down to me like an invitation;
The pert may suppose it meaningless, but I listen closer,
I find its purpose and place up there toward the November sky.

The sharphoofed moose of the north, the cat on the housesill, the chickadee, the prairie-dog,
The litter of the grunting sow as they tug at her teats,
The brood of the turkeyhen, and she with her halfspread wings,
I see in them and myself the same old law.

The press of my foot to the earth springs a hundred affections,
They scorn the best I can do to relate them.

I am enamoured of growing outdoors,
Of men that live among cattle or taste of the ocean or woods,
Of the builders and steerers of ships, of the wielders of axes and mauls, of the drivers of horses,
I can eat and sleep with them week in and week out.

What is commonest and cheapest and nearest and easiest is Me,
Me going in for my chances, spending for vast returns,
Adorning myself to bestow myself on the first that will take me,
Not asking the sky to come down to my goodwill,
Scattering it freely forever.

The pure contralto sings in the organloft,
The carpenter dresses his plank . . . . the tongue of his
    foreplane whistles its wild ascending lisp,
The married and unmarried children ride home to their
    thanksgiving dinner,
The pilot seizes the king-pin, he heaves down with a strong
    arm,
The mate stands braced in the whaleboat, lance and
    harpoon are ready,
The duck-shooter walks by silent and cautious stretches,
The deacons are ordained with crossed hands at the altar,
The spinning-girl retreats and advances to the hum of the
    big wheel,
The farmer stops by the bars of a Sunday and looks at the
    oats and rye,
The lunatic is carried at last to the asylum a confirmed case,
He will never sleep any more as he did in the cot in his
    mother's bedroom;
The jour printer with gray head and gaunt jaws works at
    his case,
He turns his quid of tobacco, his eyes get blurred with the
    manuscript;
The malformed limbs are tied to the anatomist's table,
What is removed drops horribly in a pail;
The quadroon girl is sold at the stand . . . . the drunkard
    nods by the barroom stove,
The machinist rolls up his sleeves . . . . the policeman
    travels his beat . . . . the gate-keeper marks who pass,
The young fellow drives the express-wagon . . . . I love
    him though I do not know him;
The half-breed straps on his light boots to compete in
    the race,
The western turkey-shooting draws old and young . . . .
    some lean on their rifles, some sit on logs,
Out from the crowd steps the marksman and takes his
    position and levels his piece;
The groups of newly-come immigrants cover the wharf
    or levee,
The woollypates hoe in the sugarfield, the overseer views
    them from his saddle;

The bugle calls in the ballroom, the gentlemen run for their partners, the dancers bow to each other;
The youth lies awake in the cedar-roofed garret and harks to the musical rain,
The Wolverine sets traps on the creek that helps fill the Huron,
The reformer ascends the platform, he spouts with his mouth and nose,
The company returns from its excursion, the darkey brings up the rear and bears the well-riddled target,
The squaw wrapt in her yellow-hemmed cloth is offering moccasins and beadbags for sale,
The connoisseur peers along the exhibition-gallery with halfshut eyes bent sideways,
The deckhands make fast the steamboat, the plank is thrown for the shoregoing passengers,
The young sister holds out the skein, the elder sister winds it off in a ball and stops now and then for the knots,
The one-year wife is recovering and happy, a week ago she bore her first child,
The cleanhaired Yankee girl works with her sewing-machine or in the factory or mill,
The nine months' gone is in the parturition chamber, her faintness and pains are advancing;
The pavingman leans on his twohanded rammer—the reporter's lead flies swiftly over the notebook—the signpainter is lettering with red and gold,
The canal-boy trots on the towpath—the bookkeeper counts at his desk—the shoemaker waxes his thread,
The conductor beats time for the band and all the performers follow him,
The child is baptised—the convert is making the first professions,
The regatta is spread on the bay . . . . how the white sails sparkle!
The drover watches his drove, he sings out to them that would stray,
The pedlar sweats with his pack on his back—the purchaser higgles about the odd cent,

The camera and plate are prepared, the lady must sit for her daguerreotype,
The bride unrumples her white dress, the minutehand of the clock moves slowly,
The opium eater reclines with rigid head and just-opened lips,
The prostitute draggles her shawl, her bonnet bobs on her tipsy and pimpled neck,
The crowd laugh at her blackguard oaths, the men jeer and wink to each other,
(Miserable! I do not laugh at your oaths nor jeer you,)
The President holds a cabinet council, he is surrounded by the great secretaries,
On the piazza walk five friendly matrons with twined arms;
The crew of the fish-smack pack repeated layers of halibut in the hold,
The Missourian crosses the plains toting his wares and his cattle,
The fare-collector goes through the train—he gives notice by the jingling of loose change,
The floormen are laying the floor—the tinners are tinning the roof—the masons are calling for mortar,
In single file each shouldering his hod pass onward the laborers;
Seasons pursuing each other the indescribable crowd is gathered . . . . it is the Fourth of July . . . . what salutes of cannon and small arms!
Seasons pursuing each other the plougher ploughs and the mower mows and the wintergrain falls in the ground;
Off on the lakes the pikefisher watches and waits by the hole in the frozen surface,
The stumps stand thick round the clearing, the squatter strikes deep with his axe,
The flatboatmen make fast toward dusk near the cottonwood or pekantrees,
The coon-seekers go now through the regions of the Red river, or through those drained by the Tennessee, or through those of the Arkansas,
The torches shine in the dark that hangs on the Chattahoochee or Altamahaw;

Patriarchs sit at supper with sons and grandsons and great grandsons around them,
In walls of adobe, in canvass tents, rest hunters and trappers after their day's sport.
The city sleeps and the country sleeps,
The living sleep for their time . . . . the dead sleep for their time,
The old husband sleeps by his wife and the young husband sleeps by his wife;
And these one and all tend inward to me, and I tend outward to them,
And such as it is to be of these more or less I am.

I am of old and young, of the foolish as much as the wise,
Regardless of others, ever regardful of others,
Maternal as well as paternal, a child as well as a man,
Stuffed with the stuff that is coarse, and stuffed with the stuff that is fine,
One of the great nation, the nation of many nations—the smallest the same and the largest the same,
A southerner soon as a northerner, a planter nonchalant and hospitable,
A Yankee bound my own way . . . . ready for trade . . . . my joints the limberest joints on earth and the sternest joints on earth,
A Kentuckian walking the vale of the Elkhorn in my deerskin leggings,
A boatman over the lakes or bays or along coasts . . . . a Hoosier, a Badger, a Buckeye,
A Louisianian or Georgian, a poke-easy from sandhills and pines,
At home on Canadian snowshoes or up in the bush, or with fishermen off Newfoundland,
At home in the fleet of iceboats, sailing with the rest and tacking,
At home on the hills of Vermont or in the woods of Maine or the Texan ranch,
Comrade of Californians . . . . comrade of free northwesterners, loving their big proportions,

Comrade of raftsmen and coalmen—comrade of all who
shake hands and welcome to drink and meat;
A learner with the simplest, a teacher of the thoughtfulest,
A novice beginning experient of myriads of seasons,
Of every hue and trade and rank, of every caste and religion,
Not merely of the New World but of Africa Europe or Asia
. . . . a wandering savage,
A farmer, mechanic, or artist . . . . a gentleman, sailor,
lover or quaker,
A prisoner, fancy-man, rowdy, lawyer, physician or priest.

I resist anything better than my own diversity,
And breathe the air and leave plenty after me,
And am not stuck up, and am in my place.

The moth and the fisheggs are in their place,
The suns I see and the suns I cannot see are in their place,
The palpable is in its place and the impalpable is in its place.

These are the thoughts of all men in all ages and lands, they
are not original with me,
If they are not yours as much as mine they are nothing or
next to nothing,
If they do not enclose everything they are next to nothing,
If they are not the riddle and the untying of the riddle they
are nothing,
If they are not just as close as they are distant they are
nothing.

This is the grass that grows wherever the land is and the
water is,
This is the common air that bathes the globe.

This is the breath of laws and songs and behaviour,
This is the tasteless water of souls . . . . this is the true
sustenance,
It is for the illiterate . . . . it is for the judges of the supreme
court . . . . it is for the federal capitol and the state
capitols,

It is for the admirable communes of literary men and composers and singers and lecturers and engineers and savans,
It is for the endless races of working people and farmers and seamen.

This is the trill of a thousand clear cornets and scream of the octave flute and strike of triangles.

I play not a march for victors only . . . . I play great marches for conquered and slain persons.

Have you heard that it was good to gain the day?
I also say it is good to fall . . . . battles are lost in the same spirit in which they are won.

I sound triumphal drums for the dead . . . . I fling through my embouchures the loudest and gayest music to them,
Vivas to those who have failed, and to those whose war-vessels sank in the sea, and those themselves who sank in the sea,
And to all generals that lost engagements, and all overcome heroes, and the numberless unknown heroes equal to the greatest heroes known.

This is the meal pleasantly set . . . . this is the meat and drink for natural hunger,
It is for the wicked just the same as the righteous . . . . I make appointments with all,
I will not have a single person slighted or left away,
The keptwoman and sponger and thief are hereby invited . . . . the heavy-lipped slave is invited . . . . the venerealee is invited,
There shall be no difference between them and the rest.

This is the press of a bashful hand . . . . this is the float and odor of hair,
This is the touch of my lips to yours . . . . this is the murmur of yearning,
This is the far-off depth and height reflecting my own face,
This is the thoughtful merge of myself and the outlet again.

Do you guess I have some intricate purpose?
Well I have . . . . for the April rain has, and the mica on
the side of a rock has.

Do you take it I would astonish?
Does the daylight astonish? or the early redstart twittering
through the woods?
Do I astonish more than they?

This hour I tell things in confidence,
I might not tell everybody but I will tell you.

Who goes there! hankering, gross, mystical, nude?
How is it I extract strength from the beef I eat?

What is a man anyhow? What am I? and what are you?
All I mark as my own you shall offset it with your own,
Else it were time lost listening to me.

I do not snivel that snivel the world over,
That months are vacuums and the ground but wallow
and filth,
That life is a suck and a sell, and nothing remains at the end
but threadbare crape and tears.

Whimpering and truckling fold with powders for invalids
. . . . conformity goes to the fourth-removed,
I cock my hat as I please indoors or out.

Shall I pray? Shall I venerate and be ceremonious?

I have pried through the strata and analyzed to a hair,
And counselled with doctors and calculated close and found
no sweeter fat than sticks to my own bones.

In all people I see myself, none more and not one a
barleycorn less,
And the good or bad I say of myself I say of them.

And I know I am solid and sound,
To me the converging objects of the universe perpetually flow,

All are written to me, and I must get what the writing means.

And I know I am deathless,
I know this orbit of mine cannot be swept by a carpenter's compass,
I know I shall not pass like a child's carlacue cut with a burnt stick at night.

I know I am august,
I do not trouble my spirit to vindicate itself or be understood,
I see that the elementary laws never apologize,
I reckon I behave no prouder than the level I plant my house by after all.

I exist as I am, that is enough,
If no other in the world be aware I sit content,
And if each and all be aware I sit content.

One world is aware, and by far the largest to me, and that is myself,
And whether I come to my own today or in ten thousand or ten million years,
I can cheerfully take it now, or with equal cheerfulness I can wait.

My foothold is tenoned and mortised in granite,
I laugh at what you call dissolution,
And I know the amplitude of time.

I am the poet of the body,
And I am the poet of the soul.

The pleasures of heaven are with me, and the pains of hell are with me,
The first I graft and increase upon myself . . . . the latter I translate into a new tongue.

I am the poet of the woman the same as the man,
And I say it is as great to be a woman as to be a man,
And I say there is nothing greater than the mother of men.

I chant a new chant of dilation or pride,
We have had ducking and deprecating about enough,
I show that size is only developement.

Have you outstript the rest? Are you the President?
It is a trifle . . . . they will more than arrive there every
 one, and still pass on.

I am he that walks with the tender and growing night;
I call to the earth and sea half-held by the night.

Press close barebosomed night! Press close magnetic
 nourishing night!
Night of south winds! Night of the large few stars!
Still nodding night! Mad naked summer night!

Smile O voluptuous coolbreathed earth!
Earth of the slumbering and liquid trees!
Earth of departed sunset! Earth of the mountains misty-topt!
Earth of the vitreous pour of the full moon just tinged
 with blue!
Earth of shine and dark mottling the tide of the river!
Earth of the limpid gray of clouds brighter and clearer for
 my sake!
Far-swooping elbowed earth! Rich apple-blossomed earth!
Smile, for your lover comes!

Prodigal! you have given me love! . . . . therefore I to you
 give love!
O unspeakable passionate love!

Thruster holding me tight and that I hold tight!
We hurt each other as the bridegroom and the bride hurt
 each other.

You sea! I resign myself to you also . . . . I guess what
 you mean,
I behold from the beach your crooked inviting fingers,
I believe you refuse to go back without feeling of me;

We must have a turn together . . . . I undress . . . . hurry
me out of sight of the land,
Cushion me soft . . . . rock me in billowy drowse,
Dash me with amorous wet . . . . I can repay you.

Sea of stretched ground-swells!
Sea breathing broad and convulsive breaths!
Sea of the brine of life! Sea of unshovelled and always-ready
graves!
Howler and scooper of storms! Capricious and dainty sea!
I am integral with you . . . . I too am of one phase and of
all phases.

Partaker of influx and efflux . . . . extoler of hate and
conciliation,
Extoler of amies and those that sleep in each others' arms.

I am he attesting sympathy;
Shall I make my list of things in the house and skip the
house that supports them?

I am the poet of commonsense and of the demonstrable and
of immortality;
And am not the poet of goodness only . . . . I do not
decline to be the poet of wickedness also.

Washes and razors for foofoos . . . . for me freckles and a
bristling beard.

What blurt is it about virtue and about vice?
Evil propels me, and reform of evil propels me . . . . I stand
indifferent,
My gait is no faultfinder's or rejecter's gait,
I moisten the roots of all that has grown.

Did you fear some scrofula out of the unflagging pregnancy?
Did you guess the celestial laws are yet to be worked over
and rectified?

I step up to say that what we do is right and what we affirm
is right . . . . and some is only the ore of right,

Witnesses of us . . . . one side a balance and the antipodal
side a balance,
Soft doctrine as steady help as stable doctrine,
Thoughts and deeds of the present our rouse and early start.

This minute that comes to me over the past decillions,
There is no better than it and now.

What behaved well in the past or behaves well today is not
such a wonder,
The wonder is always and always how there can be a mean
man or an infidel.

Endless unfolding of words of ages!
And mine a word of the modern . . . . a word en masse.

A word of the faith that never balks,
One time as good as another time . . . . here or
henceforward it is all the same to me.

A word of reality . . . . materialism first and last imbueing.

Hurrah for positive science! Long live exact demonstration!
Fetch stonecrop and mix it with cedar and branches of lilac;
This is the lexicographer or chemist . . . . this made a
grammar of the old cartouches,
These mariners put the ship through dangerous unknown seas,
This is the geologist, and this works with the scalpel, and
this is a mathematician.

Gentlemen I receive you, and attach and clasp hands with you,
The facts are useful and real . . . . they are not my dwelling
. . . . I enter by them to an area of the dwelling.

I am less the reminder of property or qualities, and more
the reminder of life,
And go on the square for my own sake and for others' sakes,
And make short account of neuters and geldings, and favor
men and women fully equipped,

And beat the gong of revolt, and stop with fugitives and
them that plot and conspire.

Walt Whitman, an American, one of the roughs, a kosmos,
Disorderly fleshy and sensual . . . . eating drinking and
breeding,
No sentimentalist . . . . no stander above men and women or
apart from them . . . . no more modest than immodest.

Unscrew the locks from the doors!
Unscrew the doors themselves from their jambs!

Whoever degrades another degrades me . . . . and whatever
is done or said returns at last to me,
And whatever I do or say I also return.

Through me the afflatus surging and surging . . . . through
me the current and index.

I speak the password primeval . . . . I give the sign of
democracy;
By God! I will accept nothing which all cannot have their
counterpart of on the same terms.

Through me many long dumb voices,
Voices of the interminable generations of slaves,
Voices of prostitutes and of deformed persons,
Voices of the diseased and despairing, and of thieves and
dwarfs,
Voices of cycles of preparation and accretion,
And of the threads that connect the stars—and of wombs,
and of the fatherstuff,
And of the rights of them the others are down upon,
Of the trivial and flat and foolish and despised,
Of fog in the air and beetles rolling balls of dung.

Through me forbidden voices,
Voices of sexes and lusts . . . . voices veiled, and I remove
the veil,
Voices indecent by me clarified and transfigured.

I do not press my finger across my mouth,
I keep as delicate around the bowels as around the head and
heart,
Copulation is no more rank to me than death is.

I believe in the flesh and the appetites,
Seeing hearing and feeling are miracles, and each part and
tag of me is a miracle.

Divine am I inside and out, and I make holy whatever I
touch or am touched from;
The scent of these arm-pits is aroma finer than prayer,
This head is more than churches or bibles or creeds.

If I worship any particular thing it shall be some of the
spread of my body;
Translucent mould of me it shall be you,
Shaded ledges and rests, firm masculine coulter, it shall be you,
Whatever goes to the tilth of me it shall be you,
You my rich blood, your milky stream pale strippings of my
life;
Breast that presses against other breasts it shall be you,
My brain it shall be your occult convolutions,
Root of washed sweet-flag, timorous pond-snipe, nest of
guarded duplicate eggs, it shall be you,
Mixed tussled hay of head and beard and brawn it shall be you,
Trickling sap of maple, fibre of manly wheat, it shall be you;
Sun so generous it shall be you,
Vapors lighting and shading my face it shall be you,
You sweaty brooks and dews it shall be you,
Winds whose soft-tickling genitals rub against me it shall
be you,
Broad muscular fields, branches of liveoak, loving lounger in
my winding paths, it shall be you,
Hands I have taken, face I have kissed, mortal I have ever
touched, it shall be you.

I dote on myself . . . . there is that lot of me, and all so
luscious,
Each moment and whatever happens thrills me with joy.

I cannot tell how my ankles bend . . . . nor whence the
cause of my faintest wish,
Nor the cause of the friendship I emit . . . . nor the cause
of the friendship I take again.

To walk up my stoop is unaccountable . . . . I pause to
consider if it really be,
That I eat and drink is spectacle enough for the great
authors and schools,
A morning-glory at my window satisfies me more than the
metaphysics of books.

To behold the daybreak!
The little light fades the immense and diaphanous shadows,
The air tastes good to my palate.

Hefts of the moving world at innocent gambols, silently
rising, freshly exuding,
Scooting obliquely high and low.

Something I cannot see puts upward libidinous prongs,
Seas of bright juice suffuse heaven.

The earth by the sky staid with . . . . the daily close of
their junction,
The heaved challenge from the east that moment over my
head,
The mocking taunt, See then whether you shall be master!

Dazzling and tremendous how quick the sunrise would kill me,
If I could not now and always send sunrise out of me.

We also ascend dazzling and tremendous as the sun,
We found our own my soul in the calm and cool of the
daybreak.

My voice goes after what my eyes cannot reach,
With the twirl of my tongue I encompass worlds and
volumes of worlds.

Speech is the twin of my vision . . . . it is unequal to
measure itself.

It provokes me forever,
It says sarcastically, Walt, you understand enough . . . .
why don't you let it out then?

Come now I will not be tantalized . . . . you conceive too
much of articulation.

Do you not know how the buds beneath are folded?
Waiting in gloom protected by frost,
The dirt receding before my prophetical screams,
I underlying causes to balance them at last,
My knowledge my live parts . . . . it keeping tally with the
meaning of things,
Happiness . . . . which whoever hears me let him or her set
out in search of this day.

My final merit I refuse you . . . . I refuse putting from me
the best I am.

Encompass worlds but never try to encompass me,
I crowd your noisiest talk by looking toward you.

Writing and talk do not prove me,
I carry the plenum of proof and every thing else in my face,
With the hush of my lips I confound the topmost skeptic.

I think I will do nothing for a long time but listen,
And accrue what I hear into myself . . . . and let sounds
contribute toward me.

I hear the bravuras of birds . . . . the bustle of growing
wheat . . . . gossip of flames . . . . clack of sticks
cooking my meals.

I hear the sound of the human voice . . . . a sound I love,
I hear all sounds as they are tuned to their uses . . . .

sounds of the city and sounds out of the city . . . . sounds of the day and night;
Talkative young ones to those that like them . . . . the recitative of fish-pedlars and fruit-pedlars . . . . the loud laugh of workpeople at their meals,
The angry base of disjointed friendship . . . . the faint tones of the sick,
The judge with hands tight to the desk, his shaky lips pronouncing a death-sentence,
The heave'e'yo of stevedores unlading ships by the wharves . . . . the refrain of the anchor-lifters;
The ring of alarm-bells . . . . the cry of fire . . . . the whirr of swift-streaking engines and hose-carts with premonitory tinkles and colored lights,
The steam-whistle . . . . the solid roll of the train of approaching cars;
The slow-march played at night at the head of the association,
They go to guard some corpse . . . . the flag-tops are draped with black muslin.

I hear the violincello or man's heart's complaint,
And hear the keyed cornet or else the echo of sunset.

I hear the chorus . . . . it is a grand-opera . . . . this indeed is music!

A tenor large and fresh as the creation fills me,
The orbic flex of his mouth is pouring and filling me full.

I hear the trained soprano . . . . she convulses me like the climax of my love-grip;
The orchestra whirls me wider than Uranus flies,
It wrenches unnamable ardors from my breast,
It throbs me to gulps of the farthest down horror,
It sails me . . . . I dab with bare feet . . . . they are licked by the indolent waves,
I am exposed . . . . cut by bitter and poisoned hail,
Steeped amid honeyed morphine . . . . my windpipe squeezed in the fakes of death,

Let up again to feel the puzzle of puzzles,
And that we call Being.

To be in any form, what is that?
If nothing lay more developed the quahaug and its callous
shell were enough.

Mine is no callous shell,
I have instant conductors all over me whether I pass or stop,
They seize every object and lead it harmlessly through me.

I merely stir, press, feel with my fingers, and am happy,
To touch my person to some one else's is about as much as
I can stand.

Is this then a touch? . . . . quivering me to a new identity,
Flames and ether making a rush for my veins,
Treacherous tip of me reaching and crowding to help them,
My flesh and blood playing out lightning, to strike what is
hardly different from myself,
On all sides prurient provokers stiffening my limbs,
Straining the udder of my heart for its withheld drip,
Behaving licentious toward me, taking no denial,
Depriving me of my best as for a purpose,
Unbuttoning my clothes and holding me by the bare waist,
Deluding my confusion with the calm of the sunlight and
pasture fields,
Immodestly sliding the fellow-senses away,
They bribed to swap off with touch, and go and graze at
the edges of me,
No consideration, no regard for my draining strength or my
anger,
Fetching the rest of the herd around to enjoy them awhile,
Then all uniting to stand on a headland and worry me.

The sentries desert every other part of me,
They have left me helpless to a red marauder,
They all come to the headland to witness and assist against me.

I am given up by traitors;
I talk wildly . . . . I have lost my wits . . . . I and nobody else am the greatest traitor,
I went myself first to the headland . . . . my own hands carried me there.

You villain touch! what are you doing? . . . . my breath is tight in its throat;
Unclench your floodgates! you are too much for me.

Blind loving wrestling touch! Sheathed hooded sharptoothed touch!
Did it make you ache so leaving me?

Parting tracked by arriving . . . . perpetual payment of the perpetual loan,
Rich showering rain, and recompense richer afterward.

Sprouts take and accumulate . . . . stand by the curb prolific and vital,
Landscapes projected masculine full-sized and golden.

All truths wait in all things,
They neither hasten their own delivery nor resist it,
They do not need the obstetric forceps of the surgeon,
The insignificant is as big to me as any,
What is less or more than a touch?

Logic and sermons never convince,
The damp of the night drives deeper into my soul.

Only what proves itself to every man and woman is so,
Only what nobody denies is so.

A minute and a drop of me settle my brain;
I believe the soggy clods shall become lovers and lamps,
And a compend of compends is the meat of a man or woman,
And a summit and flower there is the feeling they have for each other,

And they are to branch boundlessly out of that lesson until it becomes omnific,
And until every one shall delight us, and we them.

I believe a leaf of grass is no less than the journeywork of the stars,
And the pismire is equally perfect, and a grain of sand, and the egg of the wren,
And the tree-toad is a chef-d'ouvre for the highest,
And the running blackberry would adorn the parlors of heaven,
And the narrowest hinge in my hand puts to scorn all machinery,
And the cow crunching with depressed head surpasses any statue,
And a mouse is miracle enough to stagger sextillions of infidels,
And I could come every afternoon of my life to look at the farmer's girl boiling her iron tea-kettle and baking shortcake.

I find I incorporate gneiss and coal and long-threaded moss and fruits and grains and esculent roots,
And am stucco'd with quadrupeds and birds all over,
And have distanced what is behind me for good reasons,
And call any thing close again when I desire it.

In vain the speeding or shyness,
In vain the plutonic rocks send their old heat against my approach,
In vain the mastadon retreats beneath its own powdered bones,
In vain objects stand leagues off and assume manifold shapes,
In vain the ocean settling in hollows and the great monsters lying low,
In vain the buzzard houses herself with the sky,
In vain the snake slides through the creepers and logs,
In vain the elk takes to the inner passes of the woods,
In vain the razorbilled auk sails far north to Labrador,

I follow quickly . . . . I ascend to the nest in the fissure of the cliff.

I think I could turn and live awhile with the animals . . . . they are so placid and self-contained,
I stand and look at them sometimes half the day long.

They do not sweat and whine about their condition,
They do not lie awake in the dark and weep for their sins,
They do not make me sick discussing their duty to God,
Not one is dissatisfied . . . . not one is demented with the mania of owning things,
Not one kneels to another nor to his kind that lived thousands of years ago,
Not one is respectable or industrious over the whole earth.

So they show their relations to me and I accept them;
They bring me tokens of myself . . . . they evince them plainly in their possession.

I do not know where they got those tokens,
I must have passed that way untold times ago and negligently dropt them,
Myself moving forward then and now and forever,
Gathering and showing more always and with velocity,
Infinite and omnigenous and the like of these among them;
Not too exclusive toward the reachers of my remembrancers,
Picking out here one that shall be my amie,
Choosing to go with him on brotherly terms.

A gigantic beauty of a stallion, fresh and responsive to my caresses,
Head high in the forehead and wide between the ears,
Limbs glossy and supple, tail dusting the ground,
Eyes well apart and full of sparkling wickedness . . . . ears finely cut and flexibly moving.

His nostrils dilate . . . . my heels embrace him . . . . his well built limbs tremble with pleasure . . . . we speed around and return.

I but use you a moment and then I resign you stallion . . . . and do not need your paces, and outgallop them,
And myself as I stand or sit pass faster than you.

Swift wind! Space! My Soul! Now I know it is true what I guessed at;
What I guessed when I loafed on the grass,
What I guessed while I lay alone in my bed . . . . and again as I walked the beach under the paling stars of the morning.

My ties and ballasts leave me . . . . I travel . . . . I sail . . . . my elbows rest in the sea-gaps,
I skirt the sierras . . . . my palms cover continents,
I am afoot with my vision.

By the city's quadrangular houses . . . . in log-huts, or camping with lumbermen,
Along the ruts of the turnpike . . . . along the dry gulch and rivulet bed,
Hoeing my onion-patch, and rows of carrots and parsnips . . . . crossing savannas . . . trailing in forests,
Prospecting . . . . gold-digging . . . . girdling the trees of a new purchase,
Scorched ankle-deep by the hot sand . . . . hauling my boat down the shallow river;
Where the panther walks to and fro on a limb overhead . . . . where the buck turns furiously at the hunter,
Where the rattlesnake suns his flabby length on a rock . . . . where the otter is feeding on fish,
Where the alligator in his tough pimples sleeps by the bayou,
Where the black bear is searching for roots or honey . . . . where the beaver pats the mud with his paddle-tail;
Over the growing sugar . . . . over the cottonplant . . . . over the rice in its low moist field;
Over the sharp-peaked farmhouse with its scalloped scum and slender shoots from the gutters;
Over the western persimmon . . . . over the longleaved corn and the delicate blueflowered flax;

Over the white and brown buckwheat, a hummer and a
buzzer there with the rest,
Over the dusky green of the rye as it ripples and shades in
the breeze;
Scaling mountains . . . . pulling myself cautiously up . . . .
holding on by low scragged limbs,
Walking the path worn in the grass and beat through the
leaves of the brush;
Where the quail is whistling betwixt the woods and the
wheatlot,
Where the bat flies in the July eve . . . . where the great
goldbug drops through the dark;
Where the flails keep time on the barn floor,
Where the brook puts out of the roots of the old tree and
flows to the meadow,
Where cattle stand and shake away flies with the tremulous
shuddering of their hides,
Where the cheese-cloth hangs in the kitchen, and andirons
straddle the hearth-slab, and cobwebs fall in festoons
from the rafters;
Where triphammers crash . . . . where the press is whirling
its cylinders;
Wherever the human heart beats with terrible throes out of
its ribs;
Where the pear-shaped balloon is floating aloft . . . .
floating in it myself and looking composedly down;
Where the life-car is drawn on the slipnoose . . . . where
the heat hatches pale-green eggs in the dented sand,
Where the she-whale swims with her calves and never
forsakes them,
Where the steamship trails hindways its long pennant
of smoke,
Where the ground-shark's fin cuts like a black chip out of
the water,
Where the half-burned brig is riding on unknown currents,
Where shells grow to her slimy deck, and the dead are
corrupting below;
Where the striped and starred flag is borne at the head of
the regiments;
Approaching Manhattan, up by the long-stretching island,

Under Niagara, the cataract falling like a veil over my countenance;
Upon a door-step . . . . upon the horse-block of hard wood outside,
Upon the race-course, or enjoying pic-nics or jigs or a good game of base-ball,
At he-festivals with blackguard jibes and ironical license and bull-dances and drinking and laughter,
At the cider-mill, tasting the sweet of the brown sqush . . . . sucking the juice through a straw,
At apple-pealings, wanting kisses for all the red fruit I find,
At musters and beach-parties and friendly bees and huskings and house-raisings;
Where the mockingbird sounds his delicious gurgles, and cackles and screams and weeps,
Where the hay-rick stands in the barnyard, and the dry-stalks are scattered, and the brood cow waits in the hovel,
Where the bull advances to do his masculine work, and the stud to the mare, and the cock is treading the hen,
Where the heifers browse, and the geese nip their food with short jerks;
Where the sundown shadows lengthen over the limitless and lonesome prairie,
Where the herds of buffalo make a crawling spread of the square miles far and near;
Where the hummingbird shimmers . . . . where the neck of the longlived swan is curving and winding;
Where the laughing-gull scoots by the slappy shore and laughs her near-human laugh;
Where beehives range on a gray bench in the garden half-hid by the high weeds;
Where the band-necked partridges roost in a ring on the ground with their heads out;
Where burial coaches enter the arched gates of a cemetery;
Where winter wolves bark amid wastes of snow and icicled trees;
Where the yellow-crowned heron comes to the edge of the marsh at night and feeds upon small crabs;
Where the splash of swimmers and divers cools the warm noon;

Where the katydid works her chromatic reed on the walnut-tree over the well;
Through patches of citrons and cucumbers with silver-wired leaves,
Through the salt-lick or orange glade . . . . or under conical firs;
Through the gymnasium . . . . through the curtained saloon . . . . through the office or public hall;
Pleased with the native and pleased with the foreign . . . . pleased with the new and old,
Pleased with women, the homely as well as the handsome,
Pleased with the quakeress as she puts off her bonnet and talks melodiously,
Pleased with the primitive tunes of the choir of the whitewashed church,
Pleased with the earnest words of the sweating Methodist preacher, or any preacher . . . . looking seriously at the camp-meeting;
Looking in at the shop-windows in Broadway the whole forenoon . . . . pressing the flesh of my nose to the thick plate-glass,
Wandering the same afternoon with my face turned up to the clouds;
My right and left arms round the sides of two friends and I in the middle;
Coming home with the bearded and dark-cheeked bush-boy . . . . riding behind him at the drape of the day;
Far from the settlements studying the print of animals' feet, or the moccasin print;
By the cot in the hospital reaching lemonade to a feverish patient,
By the coffined corpse when all is still, examining with a candle;
Voyaging to every port to dicker and adventure;
Hurrying with the modern crowd, as eager and fickle as any,
Hot toward one I hate, ready in my madness to knife him;
Solitary at midnight in my back yard, my thoughts gone from me a long while,
Walking the old hills of Judea with the beautiful gentle god by my side;

Speeding through space . . . . speeding through heaven
and the stars,
Speeding amid the seven satellites and the broad ring and
the diameter of eighty thousand miles,
Speeding with tailed meteors . . . . throwing fire-balls like
the rest,
Carrying the crescent child that carries its own full mother
in its belly;
Storming enjoying planning loving cautioning,
Backing and filling, appearing and disappearing,
I tread day and night such roads.

I visit the orchards of God and look at the spheric product,
And look at quintillions ripened, and look at quintillions
green.

I fly the flight of the fluid and swallowing soul,
My course runs below the soundings of plummets.

I help myself to material and immaterial,
No guard can shut me off, no law can prevent me.

I anchor my ship for a little while only,
My messengers continually cruise away or bring their returns
to me.

I go hunting polar furs and the seal . . . . leaping chasms
with a pike-pointed staff . . . . clinging to topples of
brittle and blue.

I ascend to the foretruck . . . . I take my place late at night
in the crow's nest . . . . we sail through the arctic sea
. . . . it is plenty light enough,
Through the clear atmosphere I stretch around on the
wonderful beauty,
The enormous masses of ice pass me and I pass them . . . .
the scenery is plain in all directions,
The white-topped mountains point up in the distance . . . .
I fling out my fancies toward them;

We are about approaching some great battlefield in which
we are soon to be engaged,
We pass the colossal outposts of the encampments . . . .
we pass with still feet and caution;
Or we are entering by the suburbs some vast and ruined city
. . . . the blocks and fallen architecture more than all
the living cities of the globe.

I am a free companion . . . . I bivouac by invading
watchfires.

I turn the bridegroom out of bed and stay with the bride
myself,
And tighten her all night to my thighs and lips.

My voice is the wife's voice, the screech by the rail of the
stairs,
They fetch my man's body up dripping and drowned.

I understand the large hearts of heroes,
The courage of present times and all times;
How the skipper saw the crowded and rudderless wreck of the
steamship, and death chasing it up and down the storm,
How he knuckled tight and gave not back one inch, and
was faithful of days and faithful of nights,
And chalked in large letters on a board, Be of good cheer,
We will not desert you;
How he saved the drifting company at last,
How the lank loose-gowned women looked when boated
from the side of their prepared graves,
How the silent old-faced infants, and the lifted sick, and the
sharp-lipped unshaved men;
All this I swallow and it tastes good . . . . I like it well, and
it becomes mine,
I am the man . . . . I suffered . . . . I was there.

The disdain and calmness of martyrs,
The mother condemned for a witch and burnt with dry
wood, and her children gazing on;

The hounded slave that flags in the race and leans by the fence, blowing and covered with sweat,
The twinges that sting like needles his legs and neck,
The murderous buckshot and the bullets,
All these I feel or am.

I am the hounded slave . . . . I wince at the bite of the dogs,
Hell and despair are upon me . . . . crack and again crack the marksmen,
I clutch the rails of the fence . . . . my gore dribs thinned with the ooze of my skin,
I fall on the weeds and stones,
The riders spur their unwilling horses and haul close,
They taunt my dizzy ears . . . . they beat me violently over the head with their whip-stocks.

Agonies are one of my changes of garments;
I do not ask the wounded person how he feels . . . . I myself become the wounded person,
My hurt turns livid upon me as I lean on a cane and observe.

I am the mashed fireman with breastbone broken . . . . tumbling walls buried me in their debris,
Heat and smoke I inspired . . . . I heard the yelling shouts of my comrades,
I heard the distant click of their picks and shovels;
They have cleared the beams away . . . . they tenderly lift me forth.

I lie in the night air in my red shirt . . . . the pervading hush is for my sake,
Painless after all I lie, exhausted but not so unhappy,
White and beautiful are the faces around me . . . . the heads are bared of their fire-caps,
The kneeling crowd fades with the light of the torches.

Distant and dead resuscitate,
They show as the dial or move as the hands of me . . . . and I am the clock myself.

I am an old artillerist, and tell of some fort's bombardment
. . . . and am there again.

Again the reveille of drummers . . . . again the attacking
cannon and mortars and howitzers,
Again the attacked send their cannon responsive.

I take part . . . . I see and hear the whole,
The cries and curses and roar . . . . the plaudits for well
aimed shots,
The ambulanza slowly passing and trailing its red drip,
Workmen searching after damages and to make indispensible
repairs,
The fall of grenades through the rent roof . . . . the fan-
shaped explosion,
The whizz of limbs heads stone wood and iron high in the air.

Again gurgles the mouth of my dying general . . . . he
furiously waves with his hand,
He gasps through the clot . . . . Mind not me . . . . mind
. . . . the entrenchments.

I tell not the fall of Alamo . . . . not one escaped to tell
the fall of Alamo,
The hundred and fifty are dumb yet at Alamo.

Hear now the tale of a jetblack sunrise,
Hear of the murder in cold blood of four hundred and
twelve young men.

Retreating they had formed in a hollow square with their
baggage for breastworks,
Nine hundred lives out of the surrounding enemy's nine
times their number was the price they took in advance,
Their colonel was wounded and their ammunition gone,
They treated for an honorable capitulation, received writing
and seal, gave up their arms, and marched back
prisoners of war.

They were the glory of the race of rangers,
Matchless with a horse, a rifle, a song, a supper or a courtship,
Large, turbulent, brave, handsome, generous, proud and affectionate,
Bearded, sunburnt, dressed in the free costume of hunters,
Not a single one over thirty years of age.

The second Sunday morning they were brought out in squads and massacred . . . . it was beautiful early summer,
The work commenced about five o'clock and was over by eight.

None obeyed the command to kneel,
Some made a mad and helpless rush . . . . some stood stark and straight,
A few fell at once, shot in the temple or heart . . . . the living and dead lay together,
The maimed and mangled dug in the dirt . . . . the new-comers saw them there;
Some half-killed attempted to crawl away,
These were dispatched with bayonets or battered with the blunts of muskets;
A youth not seventeen years old seized his assassin till two more came to release him,
The three were all torn, and covered with the boy's blood.

At eleven o'clock began the burning of the bodies;
And that is the tale of the murder of the four hundred and twelve young men,
And that was a jetblack sunrise.

Did you read in the seabooks of the oldfashioned frigate-fight?
Did you learn who won by the light of the moon and stars?

Our foe was no skulk in his ship, I tell you,
His was the English pluck, and there is no tougher or truer, and never was, and never will be;
Along the lowered eve he came, horribly raking us.

We closed with him . . . . the yards entangled . . . . the cannon touched,
My captain lashed fast with his own hands.

We had received some eighteen-pound shots under the water,
On our lower-gun-deck two large pieces had burst at the first fire, killing all around and blowing up overhead.

Ten o'clock at night, and the full moon shining and the leaks on the gain, and five feet of water reported,
The master-at-arms loosing the prisoners confined in the after-hold to give them a chance for themselves.

The transit to and from the magazine was now stopped by the sentinels,
They saw so many strange faces they did not know whom to trust.

Our frigate was afire . . . . the other asked if we demanded quarters? if our colors were struck and the fighting done?

I laughed content when I heard the voice of my little captain,
We have not struck, he composedly cried, We have just begun our part of the fighting.

Only three guns were in use,
One was directed by the captain himself against the enemy's mainmast,
Two well-served with grape and canister silenced his musketry and cleared his decks.

The tops alone seconded the fire of this little battery, especially the maintop,
They all held out bravely during the whole of the action.

Not a moment's cease,
The leaks gained fast on the pumps . . . . the fire eat toward the powder-magazine,
One of the pumps was shot away . . . . it was generally thought we were sinking.

Serene stood the little captain,
He was not hurried . . . . his voice was neither high nor low,
His eyes gave more light to us than our battle-lanterns.

Toward twelve at night, there in the beams of the moon they surrendered to us.

Stretched and still lay the midnight,
Two great hulls motionless on the breast of the darkness,
Our vessel riddled and slowly sinking . . . . preparations to pass to the one we had conquered,
The captain on the quarter deck coldly giving his orders through a countenance white as a sheet,
Near by the corpse of the child that served in the cabin,
The dead face of an old salt with long white hair and carefully curled whiskers,
The flames spite of all that could be done flickering aloft and below,
The husky voices of the two or three officers yet fit for duty,
Formless stacks of bodies and bodies by themselves . . . . dabs of flesh upon the masts and spars,
The cut of cordage and dangle of rigging . . . . the slight shock of the soothe of waves,
Black and impassive guns, and litter of powder-parcels, and the strong scent,
Delicate sniffs of the seabreeze . . . . smells of sedgy grass and fields by the shore . . . death-messages given in charge to survivors,
The hiss of the surgeon's knife and the gnawing teeth of his saw,
The wheeze, the cluck, the swash of falling blood . . . . the short wild scream, the long dull tapering groan,
These so . . . . these irretrievable.

O Christ! My fit is mastering me!
What the rebel said gaily adjusting his throat to the rope-noose,
What the savage at the stump, his eye-sockets empty, his mouth spirting whoops and defiance,
What stills the traveler come to the vault at Mount Vernon,

What sobers the Brooklyn boy as he looks down the shores of the Wallabout and remembers the prison ships,
What burnt the gums of the redcoat at Saratoga when he surrendered his brigades,
These become mine and me every one, and they are but little,
I become as much more as I like.

I become any presence or truth of humanity here,
And see myself in prison shaped like another man,
And feel the dull unintermitted pain.

For me the keepers of convicts shoulder their carbines and keep watch,
It is I let out in the morning and barred at night.

Not a mutineer walks handcuffed to the jail, but I am handcuffed to him and walk by his side,
I am less the jolly one there, and more the silent one with sweat on my twitching lips.

Not a youngster is taken for larceny, but I go up too and am tried and sentenced.

Not a cholera patient lies at the last gasp, but I also lie at the last gasp,
My face is ash-colored, my sinews gnarl . . . . away from me people retreat.

Askers embody themselves in me, and I am embodied in them,
I project my hat and sit shamefaced and beg.

I rise extatic through all, and sweep with the true gravitation,
The whirling and whirling is elemental within me.

Somehow I have been stunned. Stand back!
Give me a little time beyond my cuffed head and slumbers and dreams and gaping,
I discover myself on a verge of the usual mistake.

That I could forget the mockers and insults!
That I could forget the trickling tears and the blows of the bludgeons and hammers!

That I could look with a separate look on my own
crucifixion and bloody crowning!

I remember . . . . I resume the overstaid fraction,
The grave of rock multiplies what has been confided to it
. . . . or to any graves,
The corpses rise . . . . the gashes heal . . . . the fastenings
roll away.

I troop forth replenished with supreme power, one of an
average unending procession,
We walk the roads of Ohio and Massachusetts and Virginia
and Wisconsin and New York and New Orleans and
Texas and Montreal and San Francisco and Charleston
and Savannah and Mexico,
Inland and by the seacoast and boundary lines . . . . and
we pass the boundary lines.

Our swift ordinances are on their way over the whole earth,
The blossoms we wear in our hats are the growth of two
thousand years.

Eleves I salute you,
I see the approach of your numberless gangs . . . . I see
you understand yourselves and me,
And know that they who have eyes are divine, and the blind
and lame are equally divine,
And that my steps drag behind yours yet go before them,
And are aware how I am with you no more than I am with
everybody.

The friendly and flowing savage . . . . Who is he?
Is he waiting for civilization or past it and mastering it?

Is he some southwesterner raised outdoors? Is he Canadian?
Is he from the Mississippi country? or from Iowa, Oregon
or California? or from the mountains? or prairie life or
bush-life? or from the sea?

Wherever he goes men and women accept and desire him,
They desire he should like them and touch them and speak
to them and stay with them.

Behaviour lawless as snow-flakes . . . . words simple as grass
. . . . uncombed head and laughter and naivete;
Slowstepping feet and the common features, and the
common modes and emanations,
They descend in new forms from the tips of his fingers,
They are wafted with the odor of his body or breath . . . .
they fly out of the glance of his eyes.

Flaunt of the sunshine I need not your bask . . . . lie over,
You light surfaces only . . . . I force the surfaces and the
depths also.

Earth! you seem to look for something at my hands,
Say old topknot! what do you want?

Man or woman! I might tell how I like you, but cannot,
And might tell what it is in me and what it is in you, but
cannot,
And might tell the pinings I have . . . . the pulse of my
nights and days.

Behold I do not give lectures or a little charity,
What I give I give out of myself.

You there, impotent, loose in the knees, open your scarfed
chops till I blow grit within you,
Spread your palms and lift the flaps of your pockets,
I am not to be denied . . . . I compel . . . . I have stores
plenty and to spare,
And any thing I have I bestow.

I do not ask who you are . . . . that is not important to me,
You can do nothing and be nothing but what I will infold you.

To a drudge of the cottonfields or emptier of privies I lean
. . . . on his right cheek I put the family kiss,
And in my soul I swear I never will deny him.

On women fit for conception I start bigger and nimbler babes,
This day I am jetting the stuff of far more arrogant republics.

To any one dying . . . . thither I speed and twist the knob
of the door,
Turn the bedclothes toward the foot of the bed,
Let the physician and the priest go home.

I seize the descending man . . . . I raise him with resistless
will.

O despairer, here is my neck,
By God! you shall not go down! Hang your whole weight
upon me.

I dilate you with tremendous breath . . . . I buoy you up;
Every room of the house do I fill with an armed force . . . .
lovers of me, bafflers of graves:
Sleep! I and they keep guard all night;
Not doubt, not decease shall dare to lay finger upon you,
I have embraced you, and henceforth possess you to myself,
And when you rise in the morning you will find what I tell
you is so.

I am he bringing help for the sick as they pant on their backs,
And for strong upright men I bring yet more needed help.

I heard what was said of the universe,
Heard it and heard of several thousand years;
It is middling well as far as it goes . . . . but is that all?

Magnifying and applying come I,
Outbidding at the start the old cautious hucksters,
The most they offer for mankind and eternity less than a
spirt of my own seminal wet,
Taking myself the exact dimensions of Jehovah and laying
them away,
Lithographing Kronos and Zeus his son, and Hercules his
grandson,

Buying drafts of Osiris and Isis and Belus and Brahma and Adonai,
In my portfolio placing Manito loose, and Allah on a leaf, and the crucifix engraved,
With Odin, and the hideous-faced Mexitli, and all idols and images,
Honestly taking them all for what they are worth, and not a cent more,
Admitting they were alive and did the work of their day,
Admitting they bore mites as for unfledged birds who have now to rise and fly and sing for themselves,
Accepting the rough deific sketches to fill out better in myself . . . . bestowing them freely on each man and woman I see,
Discovering as much or more in a framer framing a house,
Putting higher claims for him there with his rolled-up sleeves, driving the mallet and chisel;
Not objecting to special revelations . . . . considering a curl of smoke or a hair on the back of my hand as curious as any revelation;
Those ahold of fire-engines and hook-and-ladder ropes more to me than the gods of the antique wars,
Minding their voices peal through the crash of destruction,
Their brawny limbs passing safe over charred laths . . . . their white foreheads whole and unhurt out of the flames;
By the mechanic's wife with her babe at her nipple interceding for every person born;
Three scythes at harvest whizzing in a row from three lusty angels with shirts bagged out at their waists;
The snag-toothed hostler with red hair redeeming sins past and to come,
Selling all he possesses and traveling on foot to fee lawyers for his brother and sit by him while he is tried for forgery:
What was strewn in the amplest strewing the square rod about me, and not filling the square rod then;
The bull and the bug never worshipped half enough,
Dung and dirt more admirable than was dreamed,
The supernatural of no account . . . . myself waiting my time to be one of the supremes,

The day getting ready for me when I shall do as much good
as the best, and be as prodigious,
Guessing when I am it will not tickle me much to receive
puffs out of pulpit or print;
By my life-lumps! becoming already a creator!
Putting myself here and now to the ambushed womb of the
shadows!

. . . . A call in the midst of the crowd,
My own voice, orotund sweeping and final.

Come my children,
Come my boys and girls, and my women and household
and intimates,
Now the performer launches his nerve . . . . he has passed
his prelude on the reeds within.

Easily written loosefingered chords! I feel the thrum of their
climax and close.

My head evolves on my neck,
Music rolls, but not from the organ . . . . folks are around
me, but they are no household of mine.

Ever the hard and unsunk ground,
Ever the eaters and drinkers . . . . ever the upward and
downward sun . . . . ever the air and the ceaseless tides,
Ever myself and my neighbors, refreshing and wicked
and real,
Ever the old inexplicable query . . . . ever that thorned
thumb—that breath of itches and thirsts,
Ever the vexer's hoot! hoot! till we find where the sly one
hides and bring him forth;
Ever love . . . . ever the sobbing liquid of life,
Ever the bandage under the chin . . . . ever the tressels
of death.

Here and there with dimes on the eyes walking,
To feed the greed of the belly the brains liberally spooning,

Tickets buying or taking or selling, but in to the feast never
once going;
Many sweating and ploughing and thrashing, and then the
chaff for payment receiving,
A few idly owning, and they the wheat continually claiming.

This is the city . . . . and I am one of the citizens;
Whatever interests the rest interests me . . . . politics,
churches, newspapers, schools,
Benevolent societies, improvements, banks, tariffs, steamships,
factories, markets,
Stocks and stores and real estate and personal estate.

They who piddle and patter here in collars and tailed coats
. . . . I am aware who they are . . . . and that they
are not worms or fleas,
I acknowledge the duplicates of myself under all the scrape-
lipped and pipe-legged concealments.

The weakest and shallowest is deathless with me,
What I do and say the same waits for them,
Every thought that flounders in me the same flounders in
them.

I know perfectly well my own egotism,
And know my omniverous words, and cannot say any less,
And would fetch you whoever you are flush with myself.

My words are words of a questioning, and to indicate reality;
This printed and bound book . . . . but the printer and the
printing-office boy?
The marriage estate and settlement . . . . but the body and
mind of the bridegroom? also those of the bride?
The panorama of the sea . . . . but the sea itself?
The well-taken photographs . . . . but your wife or friend
close and solid in your arms?
The fleet of ships of the line and all the modern
improvements . . . . but the craft and pluck of the
admiral?

The dishes and fare and furniture . . . . but the host and
hostess, and the look out of their eyes?
The sky up there . . . . yet here or next door or across the
way?
The saints and sages in history . . . . but you yourself?
Sermons and creeds and theology . . . . but the human
brain, and what is called reason, and what is called love,
and what is called life?

I do not despise you priests;
My faith is the greatest of faiths and the least of faiths,
Enclosing all worship ancient and modern, and all between
ancient and modern,
Believing I shall come again upon the earth after five
thousand years,
Waiting responses from oracles . . . . honoring the gods
. . . . saluting the sun,
Making a fetish of the first rock or stump . . . . powowing
with sticks in the circle of obis,
Helping the lama or brahmin as he trims the lamps of
the idols,
Dancing yet through the streets in a phallic procession . . . .
rapt and austere in the woods, a gymnosophist,
Drinking mead from the skull-cup . . . . to shasta and
vedas admirant . . . . minding the koran,
Walking the teokallis, spotted with gore from the stone and
knife—beating the serpent-skin drum;
Accepting the gospels, accepting him that was crucified,
knowing assuredly that he is divine,
To the mass kneeling—to the puritan's prayer rising—sitting
patiently in a pew,
Ranting and frothing in my insane crisis—waiting dead-like
till my spirit arouses me;
Looking forth on pavement and land, and outside of
pavement and land,
Belonging to the winders of the circuit of circuits.

One of that centripetal and centrifugal gang,
I turn and talk like a man leaving charges before a journey.

Down-hearted doubters, dull and excluded,
Frivolous sullen moping angry affected disheartened
atheistical,
I know every one of you, and know the unspoken
interrogatories,
By experience I know them.

How the flukes splash!
How they contort rapid as lightning, with spasms and
spouts of blood!

Be at peace bloody flukes of doubters and sullen mopers,
I take my place among you as much as among any;
The past is the push of you and me and all precisely the same,
And the night is for you and me and all,
And what is yet untried and afterward is for you and me
and all.

I do not know what is untried and afterward,
But I know it is sure and alive, and sufficient.

Each who passes is considered, and each who stops is
considered, and not a single one can it fail.

It cannot fail the young man who died and was buried,
Nor the young woman who died and was put by his side,
Nor the little child that peeped in at the door and then
drew back and was never seen again,
Nor the old man who has lived without purpose, and feels it
with bitterness worse than gall,
Nor him in the poorhouse tubercled by rum and the bad
disorder,
Nor the numberless slaughtered and wrecked . . . . nor the
brutish koboo, called the ordure of humanity,
Nor the sacs merely floating with open mouths for food to
slip in,
Nor any thing in the earth, or down in the oldest graves of
the earth,
Nor any thing in the myriads of spheres, nor one of the
myriads of myriads that inhabit them,
Nor the present, nor the least wisp that is known.

It is time to explain myself . . . . let us stand up.

What is known I strip away . . . . I launch all men and women forward with me into the unknown.

The clock indicates the moment . . . . but what does eternity indicate?

Eternity lies in bottomless reservoirs . . . . its buckets are rising forever and ever,
They pour and they pour and they exhale away.

We have thus far exhausted trillions of winters and summers;
There are trillions ahead, and trillions ahead of them.

Births have brought us richness and variety,
And other births will bring us richness and variety.

I do not call one greater and one smaller,
That which fills its period and place is equal to any.

Were mankind murderous or jealous upon you my brother or my sister?
I am sorry for you . . . . they are not murderous or jealous upon me;
All has been gentle with me . . . . . . I keep no account with lamentation;
What have I to do with lamentation?

I am an acme of things accomplished, and I an encloser of things to be.

My feet strike an apex of the apices of the stairs,
On every step bunches of ages, and larger bunches between the steps,
All below duly traveled—and still I mount and mount.

Rise after rise bow the phantoms behind me,
Afar down I see the huge first Nothing, the vapor from the nostrils of death,

I know I was even there . . . . I waited unseen and always,
And slept while God carried me through the lethargic mist,
And took my time . . . . and took no hurt from the fœtid
carbon.

Long I was hugged close . . . . long and long.

Immense have been the preparations for me,
Faithful and friendly the arms that have helped me.

Cycles ferried my cradle, rowing and rowing like cheerful
boatmen;
For room to me stars kept aside in their own rings,
They sent influences to look after what was to hold me.

Before I was born out of my mother generations guided me,
My embryo has never been torpid . . . . nothing could
overlay it;
For it the nebula cohered to an orb . . . . the long slow
strata piled to rest it on . . . . vast vegetables gave it
sustenance,
Monstrous sauroids transported it in their mouths and
deposited it with care.

All forces have been steadily employed to complete and
delight me,
Now I stand on this spot with my soul.

Span of youth! Ever-pushed elasticity! Manhood balanced
and florid and full!

My lovers suffocate me!
Crowding my lips, and thick in the pores of my skin,
Jostling me through streets and public halls . . . . coming
naked to me at night,
Crying by day Ahoy from the rocks of the river . . . .
swinging and chirping over my head,
Calling my name from flowerbeds or vines or tangled
underbrush,
Or while I swim in the bath . . . . or drink from the pump

at the corner . . . . or the curtain is down at the opera . . . . or I glimpse at a woman's face in the railroad car;
Lighting on every moment of my life,
Bussing my body with soft and balsamic busses,
Noiselessly passing handfuls out of their hearts and giving them to be mine.

Old age superbly rising! Ineffable grace of dying days!

Every condition promulges not only itself . . . . it promulges what grows after and out of itself,
And the dark hush promulges as much as any.

I open my scuttle at night and see the far-sprinkled systems,
And all I see, multiplied as high as I can cipher, edge but the rim of the farther systems.

Wider and wider they spread, expanding and always expanding,
Outward and outward and forever outward.

My sun has his sun, and round him obediently wheels,
He joins with his partners a group of superior circuit,
And greater sets follow, making specks of the greatest inside them.

There is no stoppage, and never can be stoppage;
If I and you and the worlds and all beneath or upon their surfaces, and all the palpable life, were this moment reduced back to a pallid float, it would not avail in the long run,
We should surely bring up again where we now stand,
And as surely go as much farther, and then farther and farther.

A few quadrillions of eras, a few octillions of cubic leagues, do not hazard the span, or make it impatient,
They are but parts . . . . any thing is but a part.

See ever so far . . . . there is limitless space outside of that,
Count ever so much . . . . there is limitless time around that.

Our rendezvous is fitly appointed . . . . God will be there
and wait till we come.

I know I have the best of time and space—and that I was
never measured, and never will be measured.

I tramp a perpetual journey,
My signs are a rain-proof coat and good shoes and a staff
cut from the woods;
No friend of mine takes his ease in my chair,
I have no chair, nor church nor philosophy;
I lead no man to a dinner-table or library or exchange,
But each man and each woman of you I lead upon a knoll,
My left hand hooks you round the waist,
My right hand points to landscapes of continents, and a
plain public road.

Not I, not any one else can travel that road for you,
You must travel it for yourself.

It is not far . . . . it is within reach,
Perhaps you have been on it since you were born, and did
not know,
Perhaps it is every where on water and on land.

Shoulder your duds, and I will mine, and let us hasten forth;
Wonderful cities and free nations we shall fetch as we go.

If you tire, give me both burdens, and rest the chuff of your
hand on my hip,
And in due time you shall repay the same service to me;
For after we start we never lie by again.

This day before dawn I ascended a hill and looked at the
crowded heaven,
And I said to my spirit, When we become the enfolders of
those orbs and the pleasure and knowledge of every
thing in them, shall we be filled and satisfied then?
And my spirit said No, we level that lift to pass and
continue beyond.

You are also asking me questions, and I hear you;
I answer that I cannot answer . . . . you must find out for
yourself.

Sit awhile wayfarer,
Here are biscuits to eat and here is milk to drink,
But as soon as you sleep and renew yourself in sweet clothes
I will certainly kiss you with my goodbye kiss and open
the gate for your egress hence.

Long enough have you dreamed contemptible dreams,
Now I wash the gum from your eyes,
You must habit yourself to the dazzle of the light and of
every moment of your life

Long have you timidly waded, holding a plank by the shore,
Now I will you to be a bold swimmer,
To jump off in the midst of the sea, and rise again and nod
to me and shout, and laughingly dash with your hair.

I am the teacher of athletes,
He that by me spreads a wider breast than my own proves
the width of my own,
He most honors my style who learns under it to destroy the
teacher.

The boy I love, the same becomes a man not through derived
power but in his own right,
Wicked, rather than virtuous out of conformity or fear,
Fond of his sweetheart, relishing well his steak,
Unrequited love or a slight cutting him worse than a wound
cuts,
First rate to ride, to fight, to hit the bull's eye, to sail a
skiff, to sing a song or play on the banjo,
Preferring scars and faces pitted with smallpox over all
latherers and those that keep out of the sun.

I teach straying from me, yet who can stray from me?
I follow you whoever you are from the present hour;
My words itch at your ears till you understand them.

I do not say these things for a dollar, or to fill up the time
while I wait for a boat;
It is you talking just as much as myself . . . . I act as the
tongue of you,
It was tied in your mouth . . . . in mine it begins to be
loosened.

I swear I will never mention love or death inside a house,
And I swear I never will translate myself at all, only to him
or her who privately stays with me in the open air.

If you would understand me go to the heights or water-shore,
The nearest gnat is an explanation and a drop or the motion
of waves a key,
The maul the oar and the handsaw second my words.

No shuttered room or school can commune with me,
But roughs and little children better than they.

The young mechanic is closest to me . . . . he knows me
pretty well,
The woodman that takes his axe and jug with him shall take
me with him all day,
The farmboy ploughing in the field feels good at the sound
of my voice,
In vessels that sail my words must sail . . . . I go with
fishermen and seamen, and love them,
My face rubs to the hunter's face when he lies down alone
in his blanket,
The driver thinking of me does not mind the jolt of his
wagon,
The young mother and old mother shall comprehend me,
The girl and the wife rest the needle a moment and forget
where they are,
They and all would resume what I have told them.

I have said that the soul is not more than the body,
And I have said that the body is not more than the soul,
And nothing, not God, is greater to one than one's-self is,

And whoever walks a furlong without sympathy walks to his own funeral, dressed in his shroud,
And I or you pocketless of a dime may purchase the pick of the earth,
And to glance with an eye or show a bean in its pod confounds the learning of all times,
And there is no trade or employment but the young man following it may become a hero,
And there is no object so soft but it makes a hub for the wheeled universe,
And any man or woman shall stand cool and supercilious before a million universes.

And I call to mankind, Be not curious about God,
For I who am curious about each am not curious about God,
No array of terms can say how much I am at peace about God and about death.

I hear and behold God in every object, yet I understand God not in the least,
Nor do I understand who there can be more wonderful than myself.

Why should I wish to see God better than this day?
I see something of God each hour of the twenty-four, and each moment then,
In the faces of men and women I see God, and in my own face in the glass;
I find letters from God dropped in the street, and every one is signed by God's name,
And I leave them where they are, for I know that others will punctually come forever and ever.

And as to you death, and you bitter hug of mortality . . . . it is idle to try to alarm me.

To his work without flinching the accoucheur comes,
I see the elderhand pressing receiving supporting,
I recline by the sills of the exquisite flexible doors . . . . and mark the outlet, and mark the relief and escape.

And as to you corpse I think you are good manure, but that
does not offend me,
I smell the white roses sweetscented and growing,
I reach to the leafy lips . . . . I reach to the polished
breasts of melons.

And as to you life, I reckon you are the leavings of many
deaths,
No doubt I have died myself ten thousand times before.

I hear you whispering there O stars of heaven,
O suns . . . . O grass of graves . . . . O perpetual transfers
and promotions . . . . if you do not say anything how
can I say anything?

Of the turbid pool that lies in the autumn forest,
Of the moon that descends the steeps of the soughing twilight,
Toss, sparkles of day and dusk . . . . toss on the black
stems that decay in the muck,
Toss to the moaning gibberish of the dry limbs.

I ascend from the moon . . . . I ascend from the night,
And perceive of the ghastly glitter the sunbeams reflected,
And debouch to the steady and central from the offspring
great or small.

There is that in me . . . . I do not know what it is . . . .
but I know it is in me.

Wrenched and sweaty . . . . calm and cool then my body
becomes;
I sleep . . . . I sleep long.

I do not know it . . . . it is without name . . . . it is a
word unsaid,
It is not in any dictionary or utterance or symbol.

Something it swings on more than the earth I swing on,
To it the creation is the friend whose embracing awakes me.

Perhaps I might tell more . . . . Outlines! I plead for my
brothers and sisters.

Do you see O my brothers and sisters?
It is not chaos or death . . . . it is form and union and plan
. . . . it is eternal life . . . . it is happiness.

The past and present wilt . . . . I have filled them and
emptied them,
And proceed to fill my next fold of the future.

Listener up there! Here you . . . . what have you to
confide to me?
Look in my face while I snuff the sidle of evening,
Talk honestly, for no one else hears you, and I stay only a
minute longer.

Do I contradict myself?
Very well then . . . . I contradict myself;
I am large . . . . I contain multitudes.

I concentrate toward them that are nigh . . . . I wait on
the door-slab.

Who has done his day's work and will soonest be through
with his supper?
Who wishes to walk with me?

Will you speak before I am gone? Will you prove already
too late?

The spotted hawk swoops by and accuses me . . . . he
complains of my gab and my loitering.

I too am not a bit tamed . . . . I too am untranslatable,
I sound my barbaric yawp over the roofs of the world.

The last scud of day holds back for me,
It flings my likeness after the rest and true as any on the
shadowed wilds,
It coaxes me to the vapor and the dusk.

I depart as air . . . . I shake my white locks at the runaway
sun,
I effuse my flesh in eddies and drift it in lacy jags.

I bequeath myself to the dirt to grow from the grass I love,
If you want me again look for me under your bootsoles.

You will hardly know who I am or what I mean,
But I shall be good health to you nevertheless,
And filter and fibre your blood.

Failing to fetch me at first keep encouraged,
Missing me one place search another,
I stop some where waiting for you

Leaves of Grass

COME closer to me,
Push close my lovers and take the best I possess,
Yield closer and closer and give me the best you possess.

This is unfinished business with me . . . . how is it with you?
I was chilled with the cold types and cylinder and wet paper between us.

I pass so poorly with paper and types . . . . I must pass with the contact of bodies and souls.

I do not thank you for liking me as I am, and liking the touch of me . . . . I know that it is good for you to do so.

Were all educations practical and ornamental well displayed out of me, what would it amount to?
Were I as the head teacher or charitable proprietor or wise statesman, what would it amount to?
Were I to you as the boss employing and paying you, would that satisfy you?

The learned and virtuous and benevolent, and the usual terms;
A man like me, and never the usual terms.

Neither a servant nor a master am I,
I take no sooner a large price than a small price . . . . I will have my own whoever enjoys me,
I will be even with you, and you shall be even with me.

If you are a workman or workwoman I stand as nigh as the nighest that works in the same shop,
If you bestow gifts on your brother or dearest friend, I demand as good as your brother or dearest friend,
If your lover or husband or wife is welcome by day or night, I must be personally as welcome;

If you have become degraded or ill, then I will become so for your sake;
If you remember your foolish and outlawed deeds, do you think I cannot remember my foolish and outlawed deeds?
If you carouse at the table I say I will carouse at the opposite side of the table;
If you meet some stranger in the street and love him or her, do I not often meet strangers in the street and love them?
If you see a good deal remarkable in me I see just as much remarkable in you.

Why what have you thought of yourself?
Is it you then that thought yourself less?
Is it you that thought the President greater than you? or the rich better off than you? or the educated wiser than you?

Because you are greasy or pimpled—or that you was once drunk, or a thief, or diseased, or rheumatic, or a prostitute—or are so now—or from frivolity or impotence—or that you are no scholar, and never saw your name in print . . . . do you give in that you are any less immortal?

Souls of men and women! it is not you I call unseen, unheard, untouchable and untouching;
It is not you I go argue pro and con about, and to settle whether you are alive or no;
I own publicly who you are, if nobody else owns . . . . and see and hear you, and what you give and take;
What is there you cannot give and take?

I see not merely that you are polite or whitefaced . . . . married or single . . . . citizens of old states or citizens of new states . . . . eminent in some profession . . . . a lady or gentleman in a parlor . . . . or dressed in the jail uniform . . . . or pulpit uniform,
Not only the free Utahan, Kansian, or Arkansian . . . . not only the free Cuban . . . not merely the slave . . . . not Mexican native, or Flatfoot, or negro from Africa,
Iroquois eating the warflesh—fishtearer in his lair of rocks

and sand . . . . Esquimaux in the dark cold snowhouse . . . . Chinese with his transverse eyes . . . . Bedowee—or wandering nomad—or tabounschik at the head of his droves,
Grown, half-grown, and babe—of this country and every country, indoors and outdoors I see . . . . and all else is behind or through them.

The wife—and she is not one jot less than the husband,
The daughter—and she is just as good as the son,
The mother—and she is every bit as much as the father.

Offspring of those not rich—boys apprenticed to trades,
Young fellows working on farms and old fellows working on farms;
The naive . . . . the simple and hardy . . . . he going to the polls to vote . . . . he who has a good time, and he who has a bad time;
Mechanics, southerners, new arrivals, sailors, mano'warsmen, merchantmen, coasters,
All these I see . . . . but nigher and farther the same I see;
None shall escape me, and none shall wish to escape me.

I bring what you much need, yet always have,
I bring not money or amours or dress or eating . . . . but I bring as good;
And send no agent or medium . . . . and offer no representative of value—but offer the value itself.

There is something that comes home to one now and perpetually,
It is not what is printed or preached or discussed . . . . it eludes discussion and print,
It is not to be put in a book . . . . it is not in this book,
It is for you whoever you are . . . . it is no farther from you than your hearing and sight are from you,
It is hinted by nearest and commonest and readiest . . . . it is not them, though it is endlessly provoked by them . . . . What is there ready and near you now?

You may read in many languages and read nothing about it;
You may read the President's message and read nothing about it there,
Nothing in the reports from the state department or treasury department . . . . or in the daily papers, or the weekly papers,
Or in the census returns or assessors' returns or prices current or any accounts of stock.

The sun and stars that float in the open air . . . . the appleshaped earth and we upon it . . . . surely the drift of them is something grand;
I do not know what it is except that it is grand, and that it is happiness,
And that the enclosing purport of us here is not a speculation, or bon-mot or reconnoissance,
And that it is not something which by luck may turn out well for us, and without luck must be a failure for us,
And not something which may yet be retracted in a certain contingency.

The light and shade—the curious sense of body and identity—the greed that with perfect complaisance devours all things—the endless pride and outstretching of man—unspeakable joys and sorrows,
The wonder every one sees in every one else he sees . . . . and the wonders that fill each minute of time forever and each acre of surface and space forever,
Have you reckoned them as mainly for a trade or farmwork? or for the profits of a store? or to achieve yourself a position? or to fill a gentleman's leisure or a lady's leisure?

Have you reckoned the landscape took substance and form that it might be painted in a picture?
Or men and women that they might be written of, and songs sung?
Or the attraction of gravity and the great laws and harmonious combinations and the fluids of the air as subjects for the savans?
Or the brown land and the blue sea for maps and charts?

Or the stars to be put in constellations and named fancy
names?
Or that the growth of seeds is for agricultural tables or
agriculture itself?

Old institutions . . . . these arts libraries legends collections—
and the practice handed along in manufactures . . . .
will we rate them so high?
Will we rate our prudence and business so high? I
have no objection,
I rate them as high as the highest . . . . but a child born of
a woman and man I rate beyond all rate.

We thought our Union grand and our Constitution grand;
I do not say they are not grand and good—for they are,
I am this day just as much in love with them as you,
But I am eternally in love with you and with all my fellows
upon the earth.

We consider the bibles and religions divine . . . . I do not
say they are not divine,
I say they have all grown out of you and may grow out of
you still,
It is not they who give the life . . . . it is you who give the
life;
Leaves are not more shed from the trees or trees from the
earth than they are shed out of you.

The sum of all known value and respect I add up in you
whoever you are;
The President is up there in the White House for you . . . .
it is not you who are here for him,
The Secretaries act in their bureaus for you . . . . not you
here for them,
The Congress convenes every December for you,
Laws, courts, the forming of states, the charters of cities, the
going and coming of commerce and mails are all for you.

All doctrines, all politics and civilization exurge from you,
All sculpture and monuments and anything inscribed
anywhere are tallied in you,

The gist of histories and statistics as far back as the records reach is in you this hour—and myths and tales the same;
If you were not breathing and walking here where would they all be?
The most renowned poems would be ashes . . . . orations and plays would be vacuums.

All architecture is what you do to it when you look upon it;
Did you think it was in the white or gray stone? or the lines of the arches and cornices?

All music is what awakens from you when you are reminded by the instruments,
It is not the violins and the cornets . . . . it is not the oboe nor the beating drums—nor the notes of the baritone singer singing his sweet romanza . . . . nor those of the men's chorus, nor those of the women's chorus,
It is nearer and farther than they.

Will the whole come back then?
Can each see the signs of the best by a look in the lookingglass? Is there nothing greater or more?
Does all sit there with you and here with me?

The old forever new things . . . . you foolish child! . . . . the closest simplest things—this moment with you,
Your person and every particle that relates to your person,
The pulses of your brain waiting their chance and encouragement at every deed or sight;
Anything you do in public by day, and anything you do in secret betweendays,
What is called right and what is called wrong . . . . what you behold or touch . . . . what causes your anger or wonder,
The anklechain of the slave, the bed of the bedhouse, the cards of the gambler, the plates of the forger;
What is seen or learned in the street, or intuitively learned,
What is learned in the public school—spelling, reading, writing and ciphering . . . . the blackboard and the teacher's diagrams:

The panes of the windows and all that appears through them . . . . the going forth in the morning and the aimless spending of the day;
(What is it that you made money? what is it that you got what you wanted?)
The usual routine . . . . the workshop, factory, yard, office, store, or desk;
The jaunt of hunting or fishing, or the life of hunting or fishing,
Pasturelife, foddering, milking and herding, and all the personnel and usages;
The plum-orchard and apple-orchard . . . . gardening . . seedlings, cuttings, flowers and vines,
Grains and manures . . marl, clay, loam . . the subsoil plough . . the shovel and pick and rake and hoe . . irrigation and draining;
The currycomb . . the horse-cloth . . the halter and bridle and bits . . the very wisps of straw,
The barn and barn-yard . . the bins and mangers . . the mows and racks:
Manufactures . . commerce . . engineering . . the building of cities, and every trade carried on there . . and the implements of every trade,
The anvil and tongs and hammer . . the axe and wedge . . the square and mitre and jointer and smoothingplane;
The plumbob and trowel and level . . the wall-scaffold, and the work of walls and ceilings . . or any mason-work:
The ship's compass . . the sailor's tarpaulin . . the stays and lanyards, and the ground-tackle for anchoring or mooring,
The sloop's tiller . . the pilot's wheel and bell . . the yacht or fish-smack . . the great gay-pennanted three-hundred-foot steamboat under full headway, with her proud fat breasts and her delicate swift-flashing paddles;
The trail and line and hooks and sinkers . . the seine, and hauling the seine;
Smallarms and rifles . . . . the powder and shot and caps and wadding . . . . the ordnance for war . . . . the carriages:
Everyday objects . . . . the housechairs, the carpet, the bed

and the counterpane of the bed, and him or her sleeping at night, and the wind blowing, and the indefinite noises:
The snowstorm or rainstorm . . . . the tow-trowsers . . . . the lodge-hut in the woods, and the still-hunt:
City and country . . fireplace and candle . . gaslight and heater and aqueduct;
The message of the governor, mayor, or chief of police . . . . the dishes of breakfast or dinner or supper;
The bunkroom, the fire-engine, the string-team, and the car or truck behind;
The paper I write on or you write on . . and every word we write . . and every cross and twirl of the pen . . and the curious way we write what we think . . . . yet very faintly;
The directory, the detector, the ledger . . . . the books in ranks or the bookshelves . . . . the clock attached to the wall,
The ring on your finger . . the lady's wristlet . . the hammers of stonebreakers or coppersmiths . . the druggist's vials and jars;
The etui of surgical instruments, and the etui of oculist's or aurist's instruments, or dentist's instruments;
Glassblowing, grinding of wheat and corn . . casting, and what is cast . . tinroofing, shingledressing,
Shipcarpentering, flagging of sidewalks by flaggers . . dockbuilding, fishcuring, ferrying;
The pump, the piledriver, the great derrick . . the coalkiln and brickkiln,
Ironworks or whiteleadworks . . the sugarhouse . . steam-saws, and the great mills and factories;
The cottonbale . . the stevedore's hook . . the saw and buck of the sawyer . . the screen of the coalscreener . . the mould of the moulder . . the workingknife of the butcher;
The cylinder press . . the handpress . . the frisket and tympan . . the compositor's stick and rule,
The implements for daguerreotyping . . . . the tools of the rigger or grappler or sailmaker or blockmaker,

Goods of guttapercha or papiermache . . . . colors and
brushes . . . . glaziers' implements,
The veneer and gluepot . . the confectioner's ornaments . .
the decanter and glasses . . the shears and flatiron;
The awl and kneestrap . . the pint measure and quart
measure . . the counter and stool . . the writingpen of
quill or metal;
Billiards and tenpins . . . . the ladders and hanging ropes of
the gymnasium, and the manly exercises;
The designs for wallpapers or oilcloths or carpets . . . . the
fancies for goods for women . . . . the bookbinder's
stamps;
Leatherdressing, coachmaking, boilermaking, ropetwisting,
distilling, signpainting, limeburning, coopering,
cottonpicking,
The walkingbeam of the steam-engine . . the throttle and
governors, and the up and down rods,
Stavemachines and plainingmachines . . . . the cart of the
carman . . the omnibus . . the ponderous dray;
The snowplough and two engines pushing it . . . . the ride
in the express train of only one car . . . . the swift go
through a howling storm:
The bearhunt or coonhunt . . . . the bonfire of shavings in
the open lot in the city . . the crowd of children watching;
The blows of the fighting-man . . the upper cut and one-
two-three;
The shopwindows . . . . the coffins in the sexton's
wareroom . . . . the fruit on the fruitstand . . . . the
beef on the butcher's stall,
The bread and cakes in the bakery . . . . the white and red
pork in the pork-store;
The milliner's ribbons . . the dressmaker's patterns . . . .
the tea-table . . the homemade sweetmeats:
The column of wants in the one-cent paper . . the news by
telegraph . . . . the amusements and operas and shows:
The cotton and woolen and linen you wear . . . . the money
you make and spend;
Your room and bedroom . . . . your piano-forte . . . . the
stove and cookpans,

The house you live in . . . . the rent . . . . the other tenants . . . . the deposite in the savings-bank . . . . the trade at the grocery,
The pay on Saturday night . . . . the going home, and the purchases;
In them the heft of the heaviest . . . . in them far more than you estimated, and far less also,
In them, not yourself . . . . you and your soul enclose all things, regardless of estimation,
In them your themes and hints and provokers . . if not, the whole earth has no themes or hints or provokers, and never had.

I do not affirm what you see beyond is futile . . . . I do not advise you to stop,
I do not say leadings you thought great are not great,
But I say that none lead to greater or sadder or happier than those lead to.

Will you seek afar off? You surely come back at last,
In things best known to you finding the best or as good as the best,
In folks nearest to you finding also the sweetest and strongest and lovingest,
Happiness not in another place, but this place . . not for another hour, but this hour,
Man in the first you see or touch . . . . always in your friend or brother or nighest neighbor . . . . Woman in your mother or lover or wife,
And all else thus far known giving place to men and women.

When the psalm sings instead of the singer,
When the script preaches instead of the preacher,
When the pulpit descends and goes instead of the carver that carved the supporting desk,
When the sacred vessels or the bits of the eucharist, or the lath and plast, procreate as effectually as the young silversmiths or bakers, or the masons in their overalls,
When a university course convinces like a slumbering woman and child convince,

When the minted gold in the vault smiles like the
nightwatchman's daughter,
When warrantee deeds loafe in chairs opposite and are my
friendly companions,
I intend to reach them my hand and make as much of them
as I do of men and women.

Leaves of Grass

TO think of time . . . . to think through the retrospection,
To think of today . . and the ages continued henceforward.

Have you guessed you yourself would not continue? Have you dreaded those earth-beetles?
Have you feared the future would be nothing to you?

Is today nothing? Is the beginningless past nothing?
If the future is nothing they are just as surely nothing.

To think that the sun rose in the east . . . . . that men and women were flexible and real and alive . . . . that every thing was real and alive;
To think that you and I did not see feel think nor bear our part,
To think that we are now here and bear our part.

Not a day passes . . not a minute or second without an accouchement;
Not a day passes . . not a minute or second without a corpse.

When the dull nights are over, and the dull days also,
When the soreness of lying so much in bed is over,
When the physician, after long putting off, gives the silent and terrible look for an answer,
When the children come hurried and weeping, and the brothers and sisters have been sent for,
When medicines stand unused on the shelf, and the camphor-smell has pervaded the rooms,
When the faithful hand of the living does not desert the hand of the dying,
When the twitching lips press lightly on the forehead of the dying,
When the breath ceases and the pulse of the heart ceases,

Then the corpse-limbs stretch on the bed, and the living
look upon them,
They are palpable as the living are palpable.

The living look upon the corpse with their eyesight,
But without eyesight lingers a different living and looks
curiously on the corpse.

To think that the rivers will come to flow, and the snow
fall, and fruits ripen . . and act upon others as upon us
now . . . . yet not act upon us;
To think of all these wonders of city and country . . and
others taking great interest in them . . and we taking
small interest in them.

To think how eager we are in building our houses,
To think others shall be just as eager . . and we quite
indifferent.

I see one building the house that serves him a few years
. . . . or seventy or eighty years at most;
I see one building the house that serves him longer than that.

Slowmoving and black lines creep over the whole earth . . . .
they never cease . . . . they are the burial lines,
He that was President was buried, and he that is now
President shall surely be buried.

Cold dash of waves at the ferrywharf,
Posh and ice in the river . . . . half-frozen mud in the streets,
A gray discouraged sky overhead . . . . the short last
daylight of December,
A hearse and stages . . . . other vehicles give place,
The funeral of an old stagedriver . . . . the cortege mostly
drivers.

Rapid the trot to the cemetery,
Duly rattles the deathbell . . . . the gate is passed . . . .
the grave is halted at . . . . the living alight . . . . the
hearse uncloses,

The coffin is lowered and settled . . . . the whip is laid on the coffin,
The earth is swiftly shovelled in . . . . a minute . . no one moves or speaks . . . . it is done,
He is decently put away . . . . is there anything more?

He was a goodfellow,
Freemouthed, quicktempered, not badlooking, able to take his own part,
Witty, sensitive to a slight, ready with life or death for a friend,
Fond of women, . . played some . . eat hearty and drank hearty,
Had known what it was to be flush . . grew lowspirited toward the last . . sickened . . was helped by a contribution,
Died aged forty-one years . . and that was his funeral.

Thumb extended or finger uplifted,
Apron, cape, gloves, strap . . . . wetweather clothes . . . . whip carefully chosen . . . . boss, spotter, starter, and hostler,
Somebody loafing on you, or you loafing on somebody . . . . headway . . . . man before and man behind,
Good day's work or bad day's work . . . . pet stock or mean stock . . . . first out or last out . . . . turning in at night,
To think that these are so much and so nigh to other drivers . . and he there takes no interest in them.

The markets, the government, the workingman's wages . . . . to think what account they are through our nights and days;
To think that other workingmen will make just as great account of them . . yet we make little or no account.

The vulgar and the refined . . . . what you call sin and what you call goodness . . to think how wide a difference;

To think the difference will still continue to others, yet we
lie beyond the difference.

To think how much pleasure there is!
Have you pleasure from looking at the sky? Have you
pleasure from poems?
Do you enjoy yourself in the city? or engaged in business?
or planning a nomination and election? or with your
wife and family?
Or with your mother and sisters? or in womanly housework?
or the beautiful maternal cares?

These also flow onward to others . . . . you and I flow
onward;
But in due time you and I shall take less interest in them.

Your farm and profits and crops . . . . to think how
engrossed you are;
To think there will still be farms and profits and crops . .
yet for you of what avail?

What will be will be well—for what is is well,
To take interest is well, and not to take interest shall be well.

The sky continues beautiful . . . . the pleasure of men with
women shall never be sated . . nor the pleasure of
women with men . . nor the pleasure from poems;
The domestic joys, the daily housework or business, the
building of houses—they are not phantasms . . they
have weight and form and location;
The farms and profits and crops . . the markets and wages
and government . . they also are not phantasms;
The difference between sin and goodness is no apparition;
The earth is not an echo . . . . man and his life and all the
things of his life are well-considered.

You are not thrown to the winds . . you gather certainly
and safely around yourself,
Yourself! Yourself! Yourself forever and ever!

It is not to diffuse you that you were born of your mother
and father—it is to identify you,
It is not that you should be undecided, but that you should
be decided;
Something long preparing and formless is arrived and
formed in you,
You are thenceforth secure, whatever comes or goes.

The threads that were spun are gathered . . . . the weft
crosses the warp . . . . the pattern is systematic.

The preparations have every one been justified;
The orchestra have tuned their instruments sufficiently . . . .
the baton has given the signal.

The guest that was coming . . . . he waited long for
reasons . . . . he is now housed,
He is one of those who are beautiful and happy . . . . he is
one of those that to look upon and be with is enough.

The law of the past cannot be eluded.
The law of the present and future cannot be eluded,
The law of the living cannot be eluded . . . . it is eternal,
The law of promotion and transformation cannot be eluded,
The law of heroes and good-doers cannot be eluded,
The law of drunkards and informers and mean persons
cannot be eluded.

Slowmoving and black lines go ceaselessly over the earth,
Northerner goes carried and southerner goes carried . . . .
and they on the Atlantic side and they on the Pacific,
and they between, and all through the Mississippi
country . . . . and all over the earth.

The great masters and kosmos are well as they go . . . . the
heroes and good-doers are well,
The known leaders and inventors and the rich owners and
pious and distinguished may be well,
But there is more account than that . . . . there is strict
account of all.

The interminable hordes of the ignorant and wicked are not nothing,
The barbarians of Africa and Asia are not nothing,
The common people of Europe are not nothing . . . . the American aborigines are not nothing,
A zambo or a foreheadless Crowfoot or a Camanche is not nothing,
The infected in the immigrant hospital are not nothing . . . . the murderer or mean person is not nothing,
The perpetual succession of shallow people are not nothing as they go,
The prostitute is not nothing . . . . the mocker of religion is not nothing as he goes.

I shall go with the rest . . . . we have satisfaction:
I have dreamed that we are not to be changed so much . . . . nor the law of us changed;
I have dreamed that heroes and good-doers shall be under the present and past law,
And that murderers and drunkards and liars shall be under the present and past law;
For I have dreamed that the law they are under now is enough.

And I have dreamed that the satisfaction is not so much changed . . . . and that there is no life without satisfaction;
What is the earth? what are body and soul without satisfaction?

I shall go with the rest,
We cannot be stopped at a given point . . . . that is no satisfaction;
To show us a good thing or a few good things for a space of time—that is no satisfaction;
We must have the indestructible breed of the best, regardless of time.

If otherwise, all these things came but to ashes of dung;
If maggots and rats ended us, then suspicion and treachery and death.

Do you suspect death? If I were to suspect death I should
die now,
Do you think I could walk pleasantly and well-suited toward
annihilation?

Pleasantly and well-suited I walk,
Whither I walk I cannot define, but I know it is good,
The whole universe indicates that it is good,
The past and the present indicate that it is good.

How beautiful and perfect are the animals! How perfect is
my soul!
How perfect the earth, and the minutest thing upon it!
What is called good is perfect, and what is called sin is just
as perfect;
The vegetables and minerals are all perfect . . and the
imponderable fluids are perfect;
Slowly and surely they have passed on to this, and slowly
and surely they will yet pass on.

O my soul! if I realize you I have satisfaction,
Animals and vegetables! if I realize you I have satisfaction,
Laws of the earth and air! if I realize you I have satisfaction.

I cannot define my satisfaction . . yet it is so,
I cannot define my life . . yet it is so.

I swear I see now that every thing has an eternal soul!
The trees have, rooted in the ground . . . . the weeds of
the sea have . . . . the animals.

I swear I think there is nothing but immortality!
That the exquisite scheme is for it, and the nebulous float is
for it, and the cohering is for it,
And all preparation is for it . . and identity is for it . . and
life and death are for it.

Leaves of Grass

I WANDER all night in my vision,
Stepping with light feet . . . . swiftly and noiselessly stepping and stopping,
Bending with open eyes over the shut eyes of sleepers;
Wandering and confused . . . . lost to myself . . . . ill-assorted . . . . contradictory,
Pausing and gazing and bending and stopping.

How solemn they look there, stretched and still;
How quiet they breathe, the little children in their cradles.

The wretched features of ennuyees, the white features of corpses, the livid faces of drunkards, the sick-gray faces of onanists,
The gashed bodies on battlefields, the insane in their strong-doored rooms, the sacred idiots,
The newborn emerging from gates and the dying emerging from gates,
The night pervades them and enfolds them.

The married couple sleep calmly in their bed, he with his palm on the hip of the wife, and she with her palm on the hip of the husband,
The sisters sleep lovingly side by side in their bed,
The men sleep lovingly side by side in theirs,
And the mother sleeps with her little child carefully wrapped.

The blind sleep, and the deaf and dumb sleep,
The prisoner sleeps well in the prison . . . . the runaway son sleeps,
The murderer that is to be hung next day . . . . how does he sleep?
And the murdered person . . . . how does he sleep?

The female that loves unrequited sleeps,
And the male that loves unrequited sleeps;
The head of the moneymaker that plotted all day sleeps,
And the enraged and treacherous dispositions sleep.

I stand with drooping eyes by the worstsuffering and restless,
I pass my hands soothingly to and fro a few inches from them;
The restless sink in their beds . . . . they fitfully sleep.

The earth recedes from me into the night,
I saw that it was beautiful . . . . and I see that what is not the earth is beautiful.

I go from bedside to bedside . . . . I sleep close with the other sleepers, each in turn;
I dream in my dream all the dreams of the other dreamers,
And I become the other dreamers.

I am a dance . . . . Play up there! the fit is whirling me fast.

I am the everlaughing . . . . it is new moon and twilight,
I see the hiding of douceurs . . . . I see nimble ghosts whichever way I look,
Cache and cache again deep in the ground and sea, and where it is neither ground or sea.

Well do they do their jobs, those journeymen divine,
Only from me can they hide nothing and would not if they could;
I reckon I am their boss, and they make me a pet besides,
And surround me, and lead me and run ahead when I walk,
And lift their cunning covers and signify me with stretched arms, and resume the way;
Onward we move, a gay gang of blackguards with mirthshouting music and wildflapping pennants of joy.

I am the actor and the actress . . . . the voter . . the politician,

The emigrant and the exile . . the criminal that stood in the box,
He who has been famous, and he who shall be famous after today,
The stammerer . . . . the wellformed person . . the wasted or feeble person.

I am she who adorned herself and folded her hair expectantly,
My truant lover has come and it is dark.

Double yourself and receive me darkness,
Receive me and my lover too . . . . he will not let me go without him.

I roll myself upon you as upon a bed . . . . I resign myself to the dusk.

He whom I call answers me and takes the place of my lover,
He rises with me silently from the bed.

Darkness you are gentler than my lover . . . . his flesh was sweaty and panting,
I feel the hot moisture yet that he left me.

My hands are spread forth . . I pass them in all directions,
I would sound up the shadowy shore to which you are journeying.

Be careful, darkness . . . . already, what was it touched me?
I thought my lover had gone . . . . else darkness and he are one,
I hear the heart-beat . . . . I follow . . I fade away.

O hotcheeked and blushing! O foolish hectic!
O for pity's sake, no one must see me now! . . . . my clothes were stolen while I was abed,
Now I am thrust forth, where shall I run?

Pier that I saw dimly last night when I looked from the windows,

Pier out from the main, let me catch myself with you and
stay . . . . I will not chafe you;
I feel ashamed to go naked about the world,
And am curious to know where my feet stand . . . . and
what is this flooding me, childhood or manhood . . . .
and the hunger that crosses the bridge between.

The cloth laps a first sweet eating and drinking,
Laps life-swelling yolks . . . . laps ear of rose-corn, milky
and just ripened:
The white teeth stay, and the boss-tooth advances in darkness,
And liquor is spilled on lips and bosoms by touching
glasses, and the best liquor afterward.

I descend my western course . . . . my sinews are flaccid,
Perfume and youth course through me, and I am their wake.

It is my face yellow and wrinkled instead of the old woman's,
I sit low in a strawbottom chair and carefully darn my
grandson's stockings.

It is I too . . . . the sleepless widow looking out on the
winter midnight,
I see the sparkles of starshine on the icy and pallid earth.

A shroud I see—and I am the shroud . . . . I wrap a body
and lie in the coffin;
It is dark here underground . . . . it is not evil or pain here
. . . . it is blank here, for reasons.

It seems to me that everything in the light and air ought to
be happy;
Whoever is not in his coffin and the dark grave, let him
know he has enough.

I see a beautiful gigantic swimmer swimming naked through
the eddies of the sea,
His brown hair lies close and even to his head . . . . he
strikes out with courageous arms . . . . he urges
himself with his legs.

I see his white body . . . . I see his undaunted eyes;
I hate the swift-running eddies that would dash him headforemost on the rocks.

What are you doing you ruffianly red-trickled waves?
Will you kill the courageous giant? Will you kill him in the prime of his middle age?

Steady and long he struggles;
He is baffled and banged and bruised . . . . he holds out while his strength holds out,
The slapping eddies are spotted with his blood . . . . they bear him away . . . . they roll him and swing him and turn him:
His beautiful body is borne in the circling eddies . . . . it is continually bruised on rocks,
Swiftly and out of sight is borne the brave corpse.

I turn but do not extricate myself;
Confused . . . . a pastreading . . . . another, but with darkness yet.

The beach is cut by the razory ice-wind . . . . the wreck-guns sound,
The tempest lulls and the moon comes floundering through the drifts.

I look where the ship helplessly heads end on . . . . I hear the burst as she strikes . . I hear the howls of dismay . . . . they grow fainter and fainter.

I cannot aid with my wringing fingers;
I can but rush to the surf and let it drench me and freeze upon me.

I search with the crowd . . . . not one of the company is washed to us alive;
In the morning I help pick up the dead and lay them in rows in a barn.

Now of the old war-days . . the defeat at Brooklyn;
Washington stands inside the lines . . he stands on the entrenched hills amid a crowd of officers,
His face is cold and damp . . . . he cannot repress the weeping drops . . . . he lifts the glass perpetually to his eyes . . . . the color is blanched from his cheeks,
He sees the slaughter of the southern braves confided to him by their parents.

The same at last and at last when peace is declared,
He stands in the room of the old tavern . . . . the wellbeloved soldiers all pass through,
The officers speechless and slow draw near in their turns,
The chief encircles their necks with his arm and kisses them on the cheek,
He kisses lightly the wet cheeks one after another . . . . he shakes hands and bids goodbye to the army.

Now I tell what my mother told me today as we sat at dinner together,
Of when she was a nearly grown girl living home with her parents on the old homestead.

A red squaw came one breakfasttime to the old homestead,
On her back she carried a bundle of rushes for rushbottoming chairs;
Her hair straight shiny coarse black and profuse halfenveloped her face,
Her step was free and elastic . . . . her voice sounded exquisitely as she spoke.

My mother looked in delight and amazement at the stranger,
She looked at the beauty of her tallborne face and full and pliant limbs,
The more she looked upon her she loved her,
Never before had she seen such wonderful beauty and purity;
She made her sit on a bench by the jamb of the fireplace . . . . she cooked food for her,

She had no work to give her but she gave her remembrance
and fondness.

The red squaw staid all the forenoon, and toward the
middle of the afternoon she went away;
O my mother was loth to have her go away,
All the week she thought of her . . . . she watched for her
many a month,
She remembered her many a winter and many a summer,
But the red squaw never came nor was heard of there again.

Now Lucifer was not dead . . . . or if he was I am his
sorrowful terrible heir;
I have been wronged . . . . I am oppressed . . . . I hate
him that oppresses me,
I will either destroy him, or he shall release me.

Damn him! how he does defile me,
How he informs against my brother and sister and takes pay
for their blood,
How he laughs when I look down the bend after the
steamboat that carries away my woman.

Now the vast dusk bulk that is the whale's bulk . . . . it
seems mine,
Warily, sportsman! though I lie so sleepy and sluggish, my
tap is death.

A show of the summer softness . . . . a contact of something
unseen . . . . an amour of the light and air;
I am jealous and overwhelmed with friendliness,
And will go gallivant with the light and the air myself,
And have an unseen something to be in contact with them
also.

O love and summer! you are in the dreams and in me,
Autumn and winter are in the dreams . . . . the farmer
goes with his thrift,
The droves and crops increase . . . . the barns are wellfilled.

Elements merge in the night . . . . ships make tacks in the
dreams . . . . the sailor sails . . . . the exile returns
home,
The fugitive returns unharmed . . . . the immigrant is back
beyond months and years;
The poor Irishman lives in the simple house of his childhood,
with the wellknown neighbors and faces,
They warmly welcome him . . . . he is barefoot again . . . .
he forgets he is welloff;
The Dutchman voyages home, and the Scotchman and
Welchman voyage home . . and the native of the
Mediterranean voyages home;
To every port of England and France and Spain enter
wellfilled ships;
The Swiss foots it toward his hills . . . . the Prussian goes
his way, and the Hungarian his way, and the Pole goes
his way,
The Swede returns, and the Dane and Norwegian return.

The homeward bound and the outward bound,
The beautiful lost swimmer, the ennuyee, the onanist, the
female that loves unrequited, the moneymaker,
The actor and actress . . those through with their parts and
those waiting to commence,
The affectionate boy, the husband and wife, the voter, the
nominee that is chosen and the nominee that has failed,
The great already known, and the great anytime after to day,
The stammerer, the sick, the perfectformed, the homely,
The criminal that stood in the box, the judge that sat and
sentenced him, the fluent lawyers, the jury, the
audience,
The laugher and weeper, the dancer, the midnight widow,
the red squaw,
The consumptive, the erysipalite, the idiot, he that is
wronged,
The antipodes, and every one between this and them in the
dark,
I swear they are averaged now . . . . one is no better than
the other,
The night and sleep have likened them and restored them.

I swear they are all beautiful,
Every one that sleeps is beautiful . . . . every
dim night is beautiful,
The wildest and bloodiest is over and all is peace

Peace is always beautiful,
The myth of heaven indicates peace and night.

The myth of heaven indicates the soul;
The soul is always beautiful . . . . it appears more or it
appears less . . . . it comes or lags behind,
It comes from its embowered garden and looks pleasantly
on itself and encloses the world;
Perfect and clean the genitals previously jetting, and perfect
and clean the womb cohering,
The head wellgrown and proportioned and plumb, and the
bowels and joints proportioned and plumb.

The soul is always beautiful,
The universe is duly in order . . . . every thing is in its place,
What is arrived is in its place, and what waits is in its place;
The twisted skull waits . . . . the watery or rotten blood
waits,
The child of the glutton or venerealee waits long, and the
child of the drunkard waits long, and the drunkard
himself waits long,
The sleepers that lived and died wait . . . . the far advanced
are to go on in their turns, and the far behind are to
go on in their turns,
The diverse shall be no less diverse, but they shall flow and
unite . . . . they unite now.

The sleepers are very beautiful as they lie unclothed,
They flow hand in hand over the whole earth from east to
west as they lie unclothed;
The Asiatic and African are hand in hand . . . . the European
and American are hand in hand,
Learned and unlearned are hand in hand . . and male and
female are hand in hand;

The bare arm of the girl crosses the bare breast of her lover . . . . they press close without lust . . . . his lips press her neck,
The father holds his grown or ungrown son in his arms with measureless love . . . . and the son holds the father in his arms with measureless love,
The white hair of the mother shines on the white wrist of the daughter,
The breath of the boy goes with the breath of the man . . . . friend is inarmed by friend,
The scholar kisses the teacher and the teacher kisses the scholar . . . . the wronged is made right,
The call of the slave is one with the master's call . . and the master salutes the slave,
The felon steps forth from the prison . . . . the insane becomes sane . . . . the suffering of sick persons is relieved,
The sweatings and fevers stop . . the throat that was unsound is sound . . the lungs of the consumptive are resumed . . the poor distressed head is free,
The joints of the rheumatic move as smoothly as ever, and smoother than ever,
Stiflings and passages open . . . . the paralysed become supple,
The swelled and convulsed and congested awake to themselves in condition,
They pass the invigoration of the night and the chemistry of the night and awake.

I too pass from the night;
I stay awhile away O night, but I return to you again and love you;
Why should I be afraid to trust myself to you?
I am not afraid . . . . I have been well brought forward by you;
I love the rich running day, but I do not desert her in whom I lay so long;
I know not how I came of you, and I know not where I go with you . . . . but I know I came well and shall go well.

I will stop only a time with the night . . . . and rise betimes.

I will duly pass the day O my mother and duly return to you;
Not you will yield forth the dawn again more surely than you will yield forth me again,
Not the womb yields the babe in its time more surely than I shall be yielded from you in my time.

Leaves of Grass

THE bodies of men and women engirth me, and I engirth them,
They will not let me off nor I them till I go with them and respond to them and love them.

Was it dreamed whether those who corrupted their own live bodies could conceal themselves?
And whether those who defiled the living were as bad as they who defiled the dead?

The expression of the body of man or woman balks account,
The male is perfect and that of the female is perfect.

The expression of a wellmade man appears not only in his face,
It is in his limbs and joints also . . . . it is curiously in the joints of his hips and wrists,
It is in his walk . . the carriage of his neck . . the flex of his waist and knees . . . . dress does not hide him,
The strong sweet supple quality he has strikes through the cotton and flannel;
To see him pass conveys as much as the best poem . . perhaps more,
You linger to see his back and the back of his neck and shoulderside.

The sprawl and fulness of babes . . . . the bosoms and heads of women . . . . the folds of their dress . . . . their style as we pass in the street . . . . the contour of their shape downwards;
The swimmer naked in the swimmingbath . . seen as he swims through the salt transparent greenshine, or lies on his back and rolls silently with the heave of the water;
Framers bare-armed framing a house . . hoisting the beams in their places . . or using the mallet and mortising-chisel,

The bending forward and backward of rowers in rowboats . . . . the horseman in his saddle;
Girls and mothers and housekeepers in all their exquisite offices,
The group of laborers seated at noontime with their open dinnerkettles, and their wives waiting,
The female soothing a child . . . . the farmer's daughter in the garden or cowyard,
The woodman rapidly swinging his axe in the woods . . . . the young fellow hoeing corn . . . . the sleighdriver guiding his six horses through the crowd,
The wrestle of wrestlers . . two apprentice-boys, quite grown, lusty, goodnatured, nativeborn, out on the vacant lot at sundown after work,
The coats vests and caps thrown down . . the embrace of love and resistance,
The upperhold and underhold—the hair rumpled over and blinding the eyes;
The march of firemen in their own costumes—the play of the masculine muscle through cleansetting trowsers and waistbands,
The slow return from the fire . . . . the pause when the bell strikes suddenly again—the listening on the alert,
The natural perfect and varied attitudes . . . . the bent head, the curved neck, the counting:
Suchlike I love . . . . I loosen myself and pass freely . . . . and am at the mother's breast with the little child,
And swim with the swimmer, and wrestle with wrestlers, and march in line with the firemen, and pause and listen and count.

I knew a man . . . . he was a common farmer . . . . he was the father of five sons . . . and in them were the fathers of sons . . . and in them were the fathers of sons.

This man was of wonderful vigor and calmness and beauty of person;
The shape of his head, the richness and breadth of his

manners, the pale yellow and white of his hair and beard, the immeasurable meaning of his black eyes,
These I used to go and visit him to see . . . . He was wise also,
He was six feet tall . . . . he was over eighty years old . . . . his sons were massive clean bearded tanfaced and handsome,
They and his daughters loved him . . . . all who saw him loved him . . . . they did not love him by allowance . . . they loved him with personal love;
He drank water only . . . . the blood showed like scarlet through the clear brown skin of his face;
He was a frequent gunner and fisher . . . . he sailed his boat himself . . . he had a fine one presented to him by a shipjoiner . . . . he had fowling-pieces, presented to him by men that loved him;
When he went with his five sons and many grandsons to hunt or fish you would pick him out as the most beautiful and vigorous of the gang,
You would wish long and long to be with him . . . . you would wish to sit by him in the boat that you and he might touch each other.

I have perceived that to be with those I like is enough,
To stop in company with the rest at evening is enough,
To be surrounded by beautiful curious breathing laughing flesh is enough,
To pass among them . . to touch any one . . . . to rest my arm ever so lightly round his or her neck for a moment . . . . what is this then?
I do not ask any more delight . . . . I swim in it as in a sea.

There is something in staying close to men and women and looking on them and in the contact and odor of them that pleases the soul well,
All things please the soul, but these please the soul well.

This is the female form,
A divine nimbus exhales from it from head to foot,
It attracts with fierce undeniable attraction,

I am drawn by its breath as if I were no more than a helpless vapor . . . . all falls aside but myself and it,
Books, art, religion, time . . the visible and solid earth . . the atmosphere and the fringed clouds . . what was expected of heaven or feared of hell are now consumed,
Mad filaments, ungovernable shoots play out of it . . the response likewise ungovernable,
Hair, bosom, hips, bend of legs, negligent falling hands—all diffused . . . . mine too diffused,
Ebb stung by the flow, and flow stung by the ebb . . . . loveflesh swelling and deliciously aching,
Limitless limpid jets of love hot and enormous . . . . quivering jelly of love . . . white-blow and delirious juice,
Bridegroom-night of love working surely and softly into the prostrate dawn,
Undulating into the willing and yielding day,
Lost in the cleave of the clasping and sweetfleshed day.

This is the nucleus . . . after the child is born of woman the man is born of woman,
This is the bath of birth . . . this is the merge of small and large and the outlet again.

Be not ashamed women . . your privilege encloses the rest . . it is the exit of the rest,
You are the gates of the body and you are the gates of the soul.

The female contains all qualities and tempers them . . . . she is in her place . . . . she moves with perfect balance,
She is all things duly veiled . . . . she is both passive and active . . . . she is to conceive daughters as well as sons and sons as well as daughters.

As I see my soul reflected in nature . . . . as I see through a mist one with inexpressible completeness and beauty . . . . see the bent head and arms folded over the breast . . . . the female I see,

I see the bearer of the great fruit which is immortality . . . . the good thereof is not tasted by roues, and never can be.

The male is not less the soul, nor more . . . . he too is in his place,
He too is all qualities . . . . he is action and power . . . . the flush of the known universe is in him,
Scorn becomes him well and appetite and defiance become him well,
The fiercest largest passions . . bliss that is utmost and sorrow that is utmost become him well . . . . pride is for him,
The fullspread pride of man is calming and excellent to the soul;
Knowledge becomes him . . . . he likes it always . . . . he brings everything to the test of himself,
Whatever the survey . . whatever the sea and the sail, he strikes soundings at last only here,
Where else does he strike soundings except here?

The man's body is sacred and the woman's body is sacred . . . . it is no matter who,
Is it a slave? Is it one of the dullfaced immigrants just landed on the wharf?

Each belongs here or anywhere just as much as the welloff . . . . just as much as you,
Each has his or her place in the procession.

All is a procession,
The universe is a procession with measured and beautiful motion.

Do you know so much that you call the slave or the dullface ignorant?
Do you suppose you have a right to a good sight . . . and he or she has no right to a sight?
Do you think matter has cohered together from its diffused float, and the soil is on the surface and water runs and vegetation sprouts for you . . and not for him and her?

A slave at auction!
I help the auctioneer . . . . the sloven does not half know his business.

Gentlemen look on this curious creature,
Whatever the bids of the bidders they cannot be high enough for him,
For him the globe lay preparing quintillions of years without one animal or plant,
For him the revolving cycles truly and steadily rolled.

In that head the allbaffling brain,
In it and below it the making of the attributes of heroes.

Examine these limbs, red black or white . . . . they are very cunning in tendon and nerve;
They shall be stript that you may see them.

Exquisite senses, lifelit eyes, pluck, volition,
Flakes of breastmuscle, pliant backbone and neck, flesh not flabby, goodsized arms and legs,
And wonders within there yet.

Within there runs his blood . . . . the same old blood . . the same red running blood;
There swells and jets his heart . . . . There all passions and desires . . all reachings and aspirations:
Do you think they are not there because they are not expressed in parlors and lecture-rooms?

This is not only one man . . . . he is the father of those who shall be fathers in their turns,
In him the start of populous states and rich republics,
Of him countless immortal lives with countless embodiments and enjoyments.

How do you know who shall come from the offspring of his offspring through the centuries?
Who might you find you have come from yourself if you could trace back through the centuries?

A woman at auction,
She too is not only herself . . . . she is the teeming mother of mothers,
She is the bearer of them that shall grow and be mates to the mothers.

Her daughters or their daughters' daughters . . who knows who shall mate with them?
Who knows through the centuries what heroes may come from them?

In them and of them natal love . . . . in them the divine mystery . . . . the same old beautiful mystery.

Have you ever loved a woman?
Your mother . . . . is she living? . . . . Have you been much with her? and has she been much with you?
Do you not see that these are exactly the same to all in all nations and times all over the earth?

If life and the soul are sacred the human body is sacred;
And the glory and sweet of a man is the token of manhood untainted,
And in man or woman a clean strong firmfibred body is beautiful as the most beautiful face.

Have you seen the fool that corrupted his own live body? or the fool that corrupted her own live body?
For they do not conceal themselves, and cannot conceal themselves.

Who degrades or defiles the living human body is cursed,
Who degrades or defiles the body of the dead is not more cursed.

Leaves of Grass

SAUNTERING the pavement or riding the country byroad here then are faces,
Faces of friendship, precision, caution, suavity, ideality,
The spiritual prescient face, the always welcome common benevolent face,
The face of the singing of music, the grand faces of natural lawyers and judges broad at the backtop,
The faces of hunters and fishers, bulged at the brows . . . . the shaved blanched faces of orthodox citizens,
The pure extravagant yearning questioning artist's face,
The welcome ugly face of some beautiful soul . . . . the handsome detested or despised face,
The sacred faces of infants . . . . the illuminated face of the mother of many children,
The face of an amour . . . . the face of veneration,
The face as of a dream . . . . the face of an immobile rock,
The face withdrawn of its good and bad . . a castrated face,
A wild hawk . . his wings clipped by the clipper,
A stallion that yielded at last to the thongs and knife of the gelder.

Sauntering the pavement or crossing the ceaseless ferry, here then are faces;
I see them and complain not and am content with all.

Do you suppose I could be content with all if I thought them their own finale?

This now is too lamentable a face for a man;
Some abject louse asking leave to be . . cringing for it,
Some milknosed maggot blessing what lets it wrig to its hole.

This face is a dog's snout sniffing for garbage;
Snakes nest in that mouth . . I hear the sibilant threat.

This face is a haze more chill than the arctic sea,
Its sleepy and wobbling icebergs crunch as they go.

This is a face of bitter herbs . . . . this an emetic . . . . they need no label,
And more of the drugshelf . . laudanum, caoutchouc, or hog's lard.

This face is an epilepsy advertising and doing business . . . . its wordless tongue gives out the unearthly cry,
Its veins down the neck distend . . . . its eyes roll till they show nothing but their whites,
Its teeth grit . . the palms of the hands are cut by the turned-in nails,
The man falls struggling and foaming to the ground while he speculates well.

This face is bitten by vermin and worms,
And this is some murderer's knife with a halfpulled scabbard.

This face owes to the sexton his dismalest fee,
An unceasing deathbell tolls there.

Those are really men! . . . . the bosses and tufts of the great round globe.

Features of my equals, would you trick me with your creased and cadaverous march?
Well then you cannot trick me.

I see your rounded never-erased flow,
I see neath the rims of your haggard and mean disguises.

Splay and twist as you like . . . . poke with the tangling fores of fishes or rats,
You'll be unmuzzled . . . . you certainly will.

I saw the face of the most smeared and slobbering idiot they had at the asylum,
And I knew for my consolation what they knew not;

I knew of the agents that emptied and broke my brother,
The same wait to clear the rubbish from the fallen tenement;
And I shall look again in a score or two of ages,
And I shall meet the real landlord perfect and unharmed,
every inch as good as myself.

The Lord advances and yet advances:
Always the shadow in front . . . . always the reached hand
bringing up the laggards.

Out of this face emerge banners and horses . . . . O superb!
. . . . I see what is coming,
I see the high pioneercaps . . . . I see the staves of runners
clearing the way,
I hear victorious drums.

This face is a lifeboat;
This is the face commanding and bearded . . . . it asks no
odds of the rest;
This face is flavored fruit ready for eating;
This face of a healthy honest boy is the programme of
all good.

These faces bear testimony slumbering or awake,
They show their descent from the Master himself.

Off the word I have spoken I except not one . . . . red
white or black, all are deific,
In each house is the ovum . . . . it comes forth after a
thousand years.

Spots or cracks at the windows do not disturb me,
Tall and sufficient stand behind and make signs to me;
I read the promise and patiently wait.

This is a fullgrown lily's face,
She speaks to the limber-hip'd man near the garden pickets,
Come here, she blushingly cries . . . . Come nigh to me
limber-hip'd man and give me your finger and thumb,
Stand at my side till I lean as high as I can upon you,

Fill me with albescent honey . . . . bend down to me,
Rub to me with your chafing beard . . rub to my breast and shoulders.

The old face of the mother of many children:
Whist! I am fully content.

Lulled and late is the smoke of the Sabbath morning,
It hangs low over the rows of trees by the fences,
It hangs thin by the sassafras, the wildcherry and the catbrier under them.

I saw the rich ladies in full dress at the soiree,
I heard what the run of poets were saying so long,
Heard who sprang in crimson youth from the white froth and the water-blue.

Behold a woman!
She looks out from her quaker cap . . . . her face is clearer and more beautiful than the sky.

She sits in an armchair under the shaded porch of the farmhouse,
The sun just shines on her old white head.

Her ample gown is of creamhued linen,
Her grandsons raised the flax, and her granddaughters spun it with the distaff and the wheel.

The melodious character of the earth!
The finish beyond which philosophy cannot go and does not wish to go!
The justified mother of men!

A YOUNG man came to me with a message from his brother,
How should the young man know the whether and when of his brother?
Tell him to send me the signs.

And I stood before the young man face to face, and took his right hand in my left hand and his left hand in my right hand,
And I answered for his brother and for men . . . . and I answered for the poet, and sent these signs.

Him all wait for . . . . him all yield up to . . . . his word is decisive and final,
Him they accept . . . . in him lave . . . . in him perceive themselves as amid light,
Him they immerse, and he immerses them.

Beautiful women, the haughtiest nations, laws, the landscape, people and animals,
The profound earth and its attributes, and the unquiet ocean,
All enjoyments and properties, and money, and whatever money will buy,
The best farms . . . . others toiling and planting, and he unavoidably reaps,
The noblest and costliest cities . . . . others grading and building, and he domiciles there;
Nothing for any one but what is for him . . . . near and far are for him,
The ships in the offing . . . . the perpetual shows and marches on land are for him if they are for any body.

He puts things in their attitudes,
He puts today out of himself with plasticity and love,
He places his own city, times, reminiscences, parents,

brothers and sisters, associations employment and politics, so that the rest never shame them afterward, nor assume to command them.

He is the answerer,
What can be answered he answers, and what cannot be answered he shows how it cannot be answered.

A man is a summons and challenge,
It is vain to skulk . . . . Do you hear that mocking and laughter? Do you hear the ironical echoes?

Books friendships philosophers priests action pleasure pride beat up and down seeking to give satisfaction;
He indicates the satisfaction, and indicates them that beat up and down also.

Whichever the sex . . . whatever the season or place he may go freshly and gently and safely by day or by night,
He has the passkey of hearts . . . . to him the response of the prying of hands on the knobs.

His welcome is universal . . . . the flow of beauty is not more welcome or universal than he is,
The person he favors by day or sleeps with at night is blessed.

Every existence has its idiom . . . . every thing has an idiom and tongue;
He resolves all tongues into his own, and bestows it upon men . . and any man translates . . and any man translates himself also:
One part does not counteract another part . . . . He is the joiner . . he sees how they join.

He says indifferently and alike, How are you friend? to the President at his levee,
And he says Good day my brother, to Cudge that hoes in the sugarfield;
And both understand him and know that his speech is right.

He walks with perfect ease in the capitol,
He walks among the Congress . . . . and one representative says to another, Here is our equal appearing and new.

Then the mechanics take him for a mechanic,
And the soldiers suppose him to be a captain . . . . and the sailors that he has followed the sea,
And the authors take him for an author . . . . and the artists for an artist,
And the laborers perceive he could labor with them and love them;
No matter what the work is, that he is one to follow it or has followed it,
No matter what the nation, that he might find his brothers and sisters there.

The English believe he comes of their English stock,
A Jew to the Jew he seems . . . . a Russ to the Russ . . . . usual and near . . removed from none.

Whoever he looks at in the traveler's coffeehouse claims him,
The Italian or Frenchman is sure, and the German is sure, and the Spaniard is sure . . . . and the island Cuban is sure.

The engineer, the deckhand on the great lakes or on the Mississippi or St Lawrence or Sacramento or Hudson or Delaware claims him.

The gentleman of perfect blood acknowledges his perfect blood,
The insulter, the prostitute, the angry person, the beggar, see themselves in the ways of him . . . . he strangely transmutes them,
They are not vile any more . . . . they hardly know themselves, they are so grown.

You think it would be good to be the writer of melodious verses,
Well it would be good to be the writer of melodious verses;

But what are verses beyond the flowing character you could have? . . . . or beyond beautiful manners and behaviour?
Or beyond one manly or affectionate deed of an apprenticeboy? . . or old woman? . . or man that has been in prison or is likely to be in prison?

SUDDENLY out of its stale and drowsy lair, the lair of slaves,
Like lightning Europe le'pt forth . . . . half startled at itself,
Its feet upon the ashes and the rags . . . . Its hands tight to the throats of kings.

O hope and faith! O aching close of lives! O many a sickened heart!
Turn back unto this day, and make yourselves afresh.

And you, paid to defile the People . . . . you liars mark:
Not for numberless agonies, murders, lusts,
For court thieving in its manifold mean forms,
Worming from his simplicity the poor man's wages;
For many a promise sworn by royal lips, And broken, and laughed at in the breaking,
Then in their power not for all these did the blows strike of personal revenge . . or the heads of the nobles fall;
The People scorned the ferocity of kings.

But the sweetness of mercy brewed bitter destruction, and the frightened rulers come back:
Each comes in state with his train . . . . hangman, priest and tax-gatherer . . . . soldier, lawyer, jailer and sycophant.

Yet behind all, lo, a Shape,
Vague as the night, draped interminably, head front and form in scarlet folds,
Whose face and eyes none may see,
Out of its robes only this . . . . the red robes, lifted by the arm,
One finger pointed high over the top, like the head of a snake appears.

Meanwhile corpses lie in new-made graves . . . . bloody corpses of young men:

The rope of the gibbet hangs heavily . . . . the bullets of
princes are flying . . . . the creatures of power laugh
aloud,
And all these things bear fruits . . . . and they are good.

Those corpses of young men,
Those martyrs that hang from the gibbets . . . those hearts
pierced by the gray lead,
Cold and motionless as they seem . . live elsewhere with
unslaughter'd vitality.

They live in other young men, O kings,
They live in brothers, again ready to defy you:
They were purified by death . . . . They were taught and
exalted.

Not a grave of the murdered for freedom but grows seed
for freedom . . . . in its turn to bear seed,
Which the winds carry afar and re-sow, and the rains and
the snows nourish.

Not a disembodied spirit can the weapons of tyrants let loose,
But it stalks invisibly over the earth . . whispering
counseling cautioning.

Liberty let others despair of you . . . . I never despair of you.

Is the house shut? Is the master away?
Nevertheless be ready . . . . be not weary of watching,
He will soon return . . . . his messengers come anon.

CLEAR the way there Jonathan!
Way for the President's marshal! Way for the government cannon!
Way for the federal foot and dragoons . . . . and the phantoms afterward.

I rose this morning early to get betimes in Boston town;
Here's a good place at the corner . . . . I must stand and see the show.

I love to look on the stars and stripes . . . . I hope the fifes will play Yankee Doodle.

How bright shine the foremost with cutlasses,
Every man holds his revolver . . . . marching stiff through Boston town.

A fog follows . . . . antiques of the same come limping,
Some appear wooden-legged and some appear bandaged and bloodless.

Why this is a show! It has called the dead out of the earth,
The old graveyards of the hills have hurried to see;
Uncountable phantoms gather by flank and rear of it,
Cocked hats of mothy mould and crutches made of mist,
Arms in slings and old men leaning on young men's shoulders.

What troubles you, Yankee phantoms? What is all this chattering of bare gums?
Does the ague convulse your limbs? Do you mistake your crutches for firelocks, and level them?

If you blind your eyes with tears you will not see the President's marshal,

If you groan such groans you might balk the government
cannon.

For shame old maniacs! . . . . Bring down those tossed
arms, and let your white hair be;
Here gape your smart grandsons . . . . their wives gaze at
them from the windows,
See how well-dressed . . . . see how orderly they conduct
themselves.

Worse and worse . . . . Can't you stand it? Are you
retreating?
Is this hour with the living too dead for you?

Retreat then! Pell-mell! . . . . Back to the hills, old limpers!
I do not think you belong here anyhow.

But there is one thing that belongs here . . . . Shall I tell
you what it is, gentlemen of Boston?

I will whisper it to the Mayor . . . . he shall send a
committee to England,
They shall get a grant from the Parliament, and go with a
cart to the royal vault,
Dig out King George's coffin . . . . unwrap him quick from
the graveclothes . . . . box up his bones for a journey:
Find a swift Yankee clipper . . . . here is freight for you
blackbellied clipper,
Up with your anchor! shake out your sails! . . . . steer
straight toward Boston bay.

Now call the President's marshal again, and bring out the
government cannon,
And fetch home the roarers from Congress, and make
another procession and guard it with foot and
dragoons.

Here is a centrepiece for them:
Look! all orderly citizens . . . . look from the windows
women.

The committee open the box and set up the regal ribs and
glue those that will not stay,
And clap the skull on top of the ribs, and clap a crown on
top of the skull.

You have got your revenge old buster! . . . . The crown is
come to its own and more than its own.

Stick your hands in your pockets Jonathan . . . . you are a
made man from this day,
You are mighty cute . . . . and here is one of your bargains.

THERE was a child went forth every day,
And the first object he looked upon and received with wonder or pity or love or dread, that object he became,
And that object became part of him for the day or a certain part of the day . . . . or for many years or stretching cycles of years.

The early lilacs became part of this child,
And grass, and white and red morningglories, and white and red clover, and the song of the phœbe-bird,
And the March-born lambs, and the sow's pink-faint litter, and the mare's foal, and the cow's calf, and the noisy brood of the barnyard or by the mire of the pond-side . . and the fish suspending themselves so curiously below there . . and the beautiful curious liquid . . and the water-plants with their graceful flat heads . . all became part of him.

And the field-sprouts of April and May became part of him . . . . wintergrain sprouts, and those of the light-yellow corn, and of the esculent roots of the garden,
And the appletrees covered with blossoms, and the fruit afterward . . . . and woodberries . . and the commonest weeds by the road;
And the old drunkard staggering home from the outhouse of the tavern whence he had lately risen,
And the schoolmistress that passed on her way to the school . . and the friendly boys that passed . . and the quarrelsome boys . . and the tidy and freshcheeked girls . . and the barefoot negro boy and girl,
And all the changes of city and country wherever he went.

His own parents . . he that had propelled the fatherstuff at night, and fathered him . . and she that conceived him in her womb and birthed him . . . . they gave this child more of themselves than that,
They gave him afterward every day . . . . they and of them became part of him.

The mother at home quietly placing the dishes on the suppertable,
The mother with mild words . . . . clean her cap and gown . . . . a wholesome odor falling off her person and clothes as she walks by:
The father, strong, selfsufficient, manly, mean, angered, unjust,
The blow, the quick loud word, the tight bargain, the crafty lure,
The family usages, the language, the company, the furniture . . . . the yearning and swelling heart,
Affection that will not be gainsayed . . . . The sense of what is real . . . . the thought if after all it should prove unreal,
The doubts of daytime and the doubts of nighttime . . . the curious whether and how,
Whether that which appears so is so . . . . Or is it all flashes and specks?
Men and women crowding fast in the streets . . if they are not flashes and specks what are they?
The streets themselves, and the facades of houses . . . . the goods in the windows,
Vehicles . . teams . . the tiered wharves, and the huge crossing at the ferries;
The village on the highland seen from afar at sunset . . . . the river between,
Shadows . . aureola and mist . . light falling on roofs and gables of white or brown, three miles off,
The schooner near by sleepily dropping down the tide . . the little boat slacktowed astern,
The hurrying tumbling waves and quickbroken crests and slapping;
The strata of colored clouds . . . . the long bar of maroontint away solitary by itself . . . . the spread of purity it lies motionless in,
The horizon's edge, the flying seacrow, the fragrance of saltmarsh and shoremud;
These became part of that child who went forth every day, and who now goes and will always go forth every day,
And these become of him or her that peruses them now.

WHO learns my lesson complete?
Boss and journeyman and apprentice? . . . . churchman and atheist?
The stupid and the wise thinker . . . . parents and offspring . . . . merchant and clerk and porter and customer . . . . editor, author, artist and schoolboy?

Draw nigh and commence,
It is no lesson . . . . it lets down the bars to a good lesson,
And that to another . . . . and every one to another still.

The great laws take and effuse without argument,
I am of the same style, for I am their friend,
I love them quits and quits . . . . I do not halt and make salaams.

I lie abstracted and hear beautiful tales of things and the reasons of things,
They are so beautiful I nudge myself to listen.

I cannot say to any person what I hear . . . . I cannot say it to myself . . . . it is very wonderful.

It is no little matter, this round and delicious globe, moving so exactly in its orbit forever and ever, without one jolt or the untruth of a single second;
I do not think it was made in six days, nor in ten thousand years, nor ten decillions of years,
Nor planned and built one thing after another, as an architect plans and builds a house.

I do not think seventy years is the time of a man or woman,
Nor that seventy millions of years is the time of a man or woman,
Nor that years will ever stop the existence of me or any one else.

Is it wonderful that I should be immortal? as every one is immortal,
I know it is wonderful . . . . but my eyesight is equally wonderful . . . . and how I was conceived in my mother's womb is equally wonderful,
And how I was not palpable once but am now . . . . and was born on the last day of May 1819 . . . . and passed from a babe in the creeping trance of three summers and three winters to articulate and walk . . . . are all equally wonderful.

And that I grew six feet high . . . . and that I have become a man thirty-six years old in 1855 . . . . and that I am here anyhow—are all equally wonderful;
And that my soul embraces you this hour, and we affect each other without ever seeing each other, and never perhaps to see each other, is every bit as wonderful:
And that I can think such thoughts as these is just as wonderful,
And that I can remind you, and you think them and know them to be true is just as wonderful,
And that the moon spins round the earth and on with the earth is equally wonderful,
And that they balance themselves with the sun and stars is equally wonderful.

Come I should like to hear you tell me what there is in yourself that is not just as wonderful,
And I should like to hear the name of anything between Sunday morning and Saturday night that is not just as wonderful.

GREAT are the myths . . . . I too delight in them,
Great are Adam and Eve . . . . I too look back and accept them;
Great the risen and fallen nations, and their poets, women, sages, inventors, rulers, warriors and priests.

Great is liberty! Great is equality! I am their follower,
Helmsmen of nations, choose your craft . . . . where you sail I sail,
Yours is the muscle of life or death . . . . yours is the perfect science . . . . in you I have absolute faith.

Great is today, and beautiful,
It is good to live in this age . . . . there never was any better.

Great are the plunges and throes and triumphs and falls of democracy,
Great the reformers with their lapses and screams,
Great the daring and venture of sailors on new explorations.

Great are yourself and myself,
We are just as good and bad as the oldest and youngest or any,
What the best and worst did we could do,
What they felt . . do not we feel it in ourselves?
What they wished . . do we not wish the same?

Great is youth, and equally great is old age . . . . great are the day and night;
Great is wealth and great is poverty . . . . great is expression and great is silence.

Youth large lusty and loving . . . . youth full of grace and force and fascination,
Do you know that old age may come after you with equal grace and force and fascination?

Day fullblown and splendid . . . . day of the immense sun,
and action and ambition and laughter,
The night follows close, with millions of suns, and sleep and
restoring darkness.

Wealth with the flush hand and fine clothes and hospitality:
But then the soul's wealth—which is candor and knowledge
and pride and enfolding love:
Who goes for men and women showing poverty richer than
wealth?

Expression of speech . . in what is written or said forget not
that silence is also expressive,
That anguish as hot as the hottest and contempt as cold as
the coldest may be without words,
That the true adoration is likewise without words and
without kneeling.

Great is the greatest nation . . the nation of clusters of
equal nations.

Great is the earth, and the way it became what it is,
Do you imagine it is stopped at this? . . . . and the increase
abandoned?
Understand then that it goes as far onward from this as this
is from the times when it lay in covering waters and gases.

Great is the quality of truth in man,
The quality of truth in man supports itself through all
changes,
It is inevitably in the man . . . . He and it are in love, and
never leave each other.

The truth in man is no dictum . . . . it is vital as eyesight,
If there be any soul there is truth . . . . if there be man or
woman there is truth . . . . If there be physical or
moral there is truth,
If there be equilibrium or volition there is truth . . . . if
there be things at all upon the earth there is truth.

O truth of the earth! O truth of things! I am determined to press the whole way toward you,
Sound your voice! I scale mountains or dive in the sea after you.

Great is language . . . . it is the mightiest of the sciences,
It is the fulness and color and form and diversity of the earth . . . . and of men and women . . . . and of all qualities and processes;
It is greater than wealth . . . . it is greater than buildings or ships or religions or paintings or music.

Great is the English speech . . . . What speech is so great as the English?
Great is the English brood . . . . What brood has so vast a destiny as the English?
It is the mother of the brood that must rule the earth with the new rule,
The new rule shall rule as the soul rules, and as the love and justice and equality that are in the soul rule.

Great is the law . . . . Great are the old few landmarks of the law . . . . they are the same in all times and shall not be disturbed.

Great are marriage, commerce, newspapers, books, freetrade, railroads, steamers, international mails and telegraphs and exchanges.

Great is Justice;
Justice is not settled by legislators and laws . . . . it is in the soul,
It cannot be varied by statutes any more than love or pride or the attraction of gravity can,
It is immutable . . it does not depend on majorities . . . . majorities or what not come at last before the same passionless and exact tribunal.

For justice are the grand natural lawyers and perfect judges . . . . it is in their souls,

It is well assorted . . . . they have not studied for nothing
. . . . the great includes the less,
They rule on the highest grounds . . . . they oversee all
eras and states and administrations.

The perfect judge fears nothing . . . . he could go front to
front before God,
Before the perfect judge all shall stand back . . . . life and
death shall stand back . . . . heaven and hell shall
stand back.

Great is goodness;
I do not know what it is any more than I know what health
is . . . . but I know it is great.

Great is wickedness . . . . I find I often admire it just as
much as I admire goodness:
Do you call that a paradox? It certainly is a paradox.

The eternal equilibrium of things is great, and the eternal
overthrow of things is great,
And there is another paradox.

Great is life . . and real and mystical . . wherever and
whoever,
Great is death . . . . Sure as life holds all parts together,
death holds all parts together;
Sure as the stars return again after they merge in the light,
death is great as life.

LEAVES OF GRASS

[1891–92]

COME, said my Soul,
Such verses for my Body let us write, (for we are one,)
That should I after death invisibly return,
Or, long, long hence, in other spheres,
There to some group of mates the chants resuming,
(Tallying Earth's soil, trees, winds, tumultuous waves,)
Ever with pleas'd smile I may keep on,
Ever and ever yet the verses owning—as, first, I here and now,
Signing for Soul and Body, set to them my name,

Walt Whitman

As there are now several editions of L. of G., different texts and dates, I wish to say that I prefer and recommend this present one, complete, for future printing, if there should be any; a copy and a fac-simile, indeed, of the text of these 426 pages. The subsequent adjusting interval which is so important to form'd and launch'd work, books especially, has pass'd; and waiting till fully after that, I have given (pages 656–672) my concluding words.

W. W.

Contents

(With dates of first appearance and final revision)

DRUM-TAPS

WHISPERS OF HEAVENLY DEATH

FROM NOON TO STARRY NIGHT

FIRST ANNEX: SANDS AT SEVENTY

SECOND ANNEX: GOOD-BYE MY FANCY

Inscriptions

One's-Self I Sing

One's-Self I sing, a simple separate person,
Yet utter the word Democratic, the word En-Masse.

Of physiology from top to toe I sing,
Not physiognomy alone nor brain alone is worthy for the
Muse, I say the Form complete is worthier far,
The Female equally with the Male I sing.

Of Life immense in passion, pulse, and power,
Cheerful, for freest action form'd under the laws divine,
The Modern Man I sing.

As I Ponder'd in Silence

As I ponder'd in silence,
Returning upon my poems, considering, lingering long,
A Phantom arose before me with distrustful aspect,
Terrible in beauty, age, and power,
The genius of poets of old lands,
As to me directing like flame its eyes,
With finger pointing to many immortal songs,
And menacing voice, *What singest thou?* it said,
Know'st thou not there is but one theme for ever-enduring bards?
And that is the theme of War, the fortune of battles,
The making of perfect soldiers.

Be it so, then I answer'd,
I too haughty Shade also sing war, and a longer and greater one than any,
Waged in my book with varying fortune, with flight, advance and retreat, victory deferr'd and wavering,
(Yet methinks certain, or as good as certain, at the last,) the field the world,
For life and death, for the Body and for the eternal Soul,
Lo, I too am come, chanting the chant of battles,
I above all promote brave soldiers.

In Cabin'd Ships at Sea

IN cabin'd ships at sea,
The boundless blue on every side expanding,
With whistling winds and music of the waves, the large imperious waves,
Or some lone bark buoy'd on the dense marine,
Where joyous full of faith, spreading white sails,
She cleaves the ether mid the sparkle and the foam of day, or under many a star at night,
By sailors young and old haply will I, a reminiscence of the land, be read,
In full rapport at last.

Here are our thoughts, voyagers' thoughts,
Here not the land, firm land, alone appears, may then by them be said,
The sky o'erarches here, we feel the undulating deck beneath our feet,
We feel the long pulsation, ebb and flow of endless motion,
The tones of unseen mystery, the vague and vast suggestions of the briny world, the liquid-flowing syllables,
The perfume, the faint creaking of the cordage, the melancholy rhythm,
The boundless vista and the horizon far and dim are all here,
And this is ocean's poem.

Then falter not O book, fulfil your destiny,
You not a reminiscence of the land alone,
You too as a lone bark cleaving the ether, purpos'd I know not whither, yet ever full of faith,
Consort to every ship that sails, sail you!
Bear forth to them folded my love, (dear mariners, for you I fold it here in every leaf;)
Speed on my book! spread your white sails my little bark athwart the imperious waves,
Chant on, sail on, bear o'er the boundless blue from me to every sea,
This song for mariners and all their ships.

To Foreign Lands

I HEARD that you ask'd for something to prove this puzzle
the New World,
And to define America, her athletic Democracy,
Therefore I send you my poems that you behold in them
what you wanted.

To a Historian

YOU who celebrate bygones,
Who have explored the outward, the surfaces of the races,
the life that has exhibited itself,
Who have treated of man as the creature of politics,
aggregates, rulers and priests,
I, habitan of the Alleghanies, treating of him as he is in
himself in his own rights,
Pressing the pulse of the life that has seldom exhibited itself,
(the great pride of man in himself,)
Chanter of Personality, outlining what is yet to be,
I project the history of the future.

To Thee Old Cause

TO thee old cause!
Thou peerless, passionate, good cause,
Thou stern, remorseless, sweet idea,
Deathless throughout the ages, races, lands,
After a strange sad war, great war for thee,
(I think all war through time was really fought, and ever
will be really fought, for thee,)
These chants for thee, the eternal march of thee.

(A war O soldiers not for itself alone,
Far, far more stood silently waiting behind, now to advance
in this book.)

Thou orb of many orbs!
Thou seething principle! thou well-kept, latent germ! thou
centre!

Around the idea of thee the war revolving,
With all its angry and vehement play of causes,
(With vast results to come for thrice a thousand years,)
These recitatives for thee,—my book and the war are one,
Merged in its spirit I and mine, as the contest hinged on thee,
As a wheel on its axis turns, this book unwitting to itself,
Around the idea of thee.

Eidólons

I MET a seer,
Passing the hues and objects of the world,
The fields of art and learning, pleasure, sense,
To glean eidólons.

Put in thy chants said he,
No more the puzzling hour nor day, nor segments, parts, put in,
Put first before the rest as light for all and entrance-song of all,
That of eidólons.

Ever the dim beginning,
Ever the growth, the rounding of the circle,
Ever the summit and the merge at last, (to surely start again,)
Eidólons! eidólons!

Ever the mutable,
Ever materials, changing, crumbling, re-cohering,
Ever the ateliers, the factories divine,
Issuing eidólons.

Lo, I or you,
Or woman, man, or state, known or unknown,
We seeming solid wealth, strength, beauty build,
But really build eidólons.

The ostent evanescent,
The substance of an artist's mood or savan's studies long,

Or warrior's, martyr's, hero's toils,
To fashion his eidólon.

Of every human life,
(The units gather'd, posted, not a thought, emotion, deed, left out,)
The whole or large or small summ'd, added up,
In its eidólon.

The old, old urge,
Based on the ancient pinnacles, lo, newer, higher pinnacles,
From science and the modern still impell'd,
The old, old urge, eidólons.

The present now and here,
America's busy, teeming, intricate whirl,
Of aggregate and segregate for only thence releasing,
To-day's eidólons.

These with the past,
Of vanish'd lands, of all the reigns of kings across the sea,
Old conquerors, old campaigns, old sailors' voyages,
Joining eidólons.

Densities, growth, façades,
Strata of mountains, soils, rocks, giant trees,
Far-born, far-dying, living long, to leave,
Eidólons everlasting.

Exaltè, rapt, ecstatic,
The visible but their womb of birth,
Of orbic tendencies to shape and shape and shape,
The mighty earth-eidólon.

All space, all time,
(The stars, the terrible perturbations of the suns,
Swelling, collapsing, ending, serving their longer, shorter use,)
Fill'd with eidólons only.

The noiseless myriads,
The infinite oceans where the rivers empty,

The separate countless free identities, like eyesight,
The true realities, eidólons.

Not this the world,
Nor these the universes, they the universes,
Purport and end, ever the permanent life of life,
Eidólons, eidólons.

Beyond thy lectures learn'd professor,
Beyond thy telescope or spectroscope observer keen, beyond all mathematics,
Beyond the doctor's surgery, anatomy, beyond the chemist with his chemistry,
The entities of entities, eidólons.

Unfix'd yet fix'd,
Ever shall be, ever have been and are,
Sweeping the present to the infinite future,
Eidólons, eidólons, eidólons.

The prophet and the bard,
Shall yet maintain themselves, in higher stages yet,
Shall mediate to the Modern, to Democracy, interpret yet to them,
God and eidólons.

And thee my soul,
Joys, ceaseless exercises, exaltations,
Thy yearning amply fed at last, prepared to meet,
Thy mates, eidólons.

Thy body permanent,
The body lurking there within thy body,
The only purport of the form thou art, the real I myself,
An image, an eidólon.

Thy very songs not in thy songs,
No special strains to sing, none for itself,
But from the whole resulting, rising at last and floating,
A round full-orb'd eidólon.

For Him I Sing

FOR him I sing,
I raise the present on the past,
(As some perennial tree out of its roots, the present on the
    past,)
With time and space I him dilate and fuse the immortal laws,
To make himself by them the law unto himself.

When I Read the Book

WHEN I read the book, the biography famous,
And is this then (said I) what the author calls a man's life?
And so will some one when I am dead and gone write my life?
(As if any man really knew aught of my life,
Why even I myself I often think know little or nothing of
    my real life,
Only a few hints, a few diffused faint clews and indirections
I seek for my own use to trace out here.)

Beginning My Studies

BEGINNING my studies the first step pleas'd me so much,
The mere fact consciousness, these forms, the power of
    motion,
The least insect or animal, the senses, eyesight, love,
The first step I say awed me and pleas'd me so much,
I have hardly gone and hardly wish'd to go any farther,
But stop and loiter all the time to sing it in ecstatic songs.

Beginners

How they are provided for upon the earth, (appearing at
    intervals,)
How dear and dreadful they are to the earth,
How they inure to themselves as much as to any—what a
    paradox appears their age,
How people respond to them, yet know them not,
How there is something relentless in their fate all times,
How all times mischoose the objects of their adulation and
    reward,

And how the same inexorable price must still be paid for the
same great purchase.

To The States

To the States or any one of them, or any city of the States,
Resist much, obey little,
Once unquestioning obedience, once fully enslaved,
Once fully enslaved, no nation, state, city of this earth, ever
afterward resumes its liberty.

On Journeys through the States

On journeys through the States we start,
(Ay through the world, urged by these songs,
Sailing henceforth to every land, to every sea,)
We willing learners of all, teachers of all, and lovers of all.

We have watch'd the seasons dispensing themselves and
passing on,
And have said, Why should not a man or woman do as
much as the seasons, and effuse as much?

We dwell a while in every city and town,
We pass through Kanada, the North-east, the vast valley of
the Mississippi, and the Southern States,
We confer on equal terms with each of the States,
We make trial of ourselves and invite men and women to hear,
We say to ourselves, Remember, fear not, be candid,
promulge the body and the soul,
Dwell a while and pass on, be copious, temperate, chaste,
magnetic,
And what you effuse may then return as the seasons return,
And may be just as much as the seasons.

To a Certain Cantatrice

Here, take this gift,
I was reserving it for some hero, speaker, or general,

One who should serve the good old cause, the great idea,
the progress and freedom of the race,
Some brave confronter of despots, some daring rebel;
But I see that what I was reserving belongs to you just as
much as to any.

Me Imperturbe

ME imperturbe, standing at ease in Nature,
Master of all or mistress of all, aplomb in the midst of
irrational things,
Imbued as they, passive, receptive, silent as they,
Finding my occupation, poverty, notoriety, foibles, crimes,
less important than I thought,
Me toward the Mexican sea, or in the Mannahatta or the
Tennessee, or far north or inland,
A river man, or a man of the woods or of any farm-life of
these States or of the coast, or the lakes or Kanada,
Me wherever my life is lived, O to be self-balanced for
contingencies,
To confront night, storms, hunger, ridicule, accidents,
rebuffs, as the trees and animals do.

Savantism

THITHER as I look I see each result and glory retracing
itself and nestling close, always obligated,
Thither hours, months, years—thither trades, compacts,
establishments, even the most minute,
Thither every-day life, speech, utensils, politics, persons,
estates;
Thither we also, I with my leaves and songs, trustful,
admirant,
As a father to his father going takes his children along with
him.

The Ship Starting

LO, the unbounded sea,
On its breast a ship starting, spreading all sails, carrying even
her moonsails,

The pennant is flying aloft as she speeds she speeds so
stately—below emulous waves press forward,
They surround the ship with shining curving motions and
foam.

I Hear America Singing

I HEAR America singing, the varied carols I hear,
Those of mechanics, each one singing his as it should be
blithe and strong,
The carpenter singing his as he measures his plank or beam,
The mason singing his as he makes ready for work, or leaves
off work,
The boatman singing what belongs to him in his boat, the
deckhand singing on the steamboat deck,
The shoemaker singing as he sits on his bench, the hatter
singing as he stands,
The wood-cutter's song, the ploughboy's on his way in the
morning, or at noon intermission or at sundown,
The delicious singing of the mother, or of the young wife at
work, or of the girl sewing or washing,
Each singing what belongs to him or her and to none else,
The day what belongs to the day—at night the party of
young fellows, robust, friendly,
Singing with open mouths their strong melodious songs.

What Place Is Besieged?

WHAT place is besieged, and vainly tries to raise the siege?
Lo, I send to that place a commander, swift, brave, immortal,
And with him horse and foot, and parks of artillery,
And artillery-men, the deadliest that ever fired gun.

Still Though the One I Sing

STILL though the one I sing,
(One, yet of contradictions made,) I dedicate to Nationality,
I leave in him revolt, (O latent right of insurrection! O
quenchless, indispensable fire!)

Shut Not Your Doors

SHUT not your doors to me proud libraries,
For that which was lacking on all your well-fill'd shelves, yet needed most, I bring,
Forth from the war emerging, a book I have made,
The words of my book nothing, the drift of it every thing,
A book separate, not link'd with the rest nor felt by the intellect,
But you ye untold latencies will thrill to every page.

Poets to Come

POETS to come! orators, singers, musicians to come!
Not to-day is to justify me and answer what I am for,
But you, a new brood, native, athletic, continental, greater than before known,
Arouse! for you must justify me.

I myself but write one or two indicative words for the future,
I but advance a moment only to wheel and hurry back in the darkness.

I am a man who, sauntering along without fully stopping, turns a casual look upon you and then averts his face,
Leaving it to you to prove and define it,
Expecting the main things from you.

To You

STRANGER, if you passing meet me and desire to speak to me, why should you not speak to me?
And why should I not speak to you?

Thou Reader

THOU reader throbbest life and pride and love the same as I,
Therefore for thee the following chants.

Starting from Paumanok

1

Starting from fish-shape Paumanok where I was born,
Well-begotten, and rais'd by a perfect mother,
After roaming many lands, lover of populous pavements,
Dweller in Mannahatta my city, or on southern savannas,
Or a soldier camp'd or carrying my knapsack and gun, or a miner in California,
Or rude in my home in Dakota's woods, my diet meat, my drink from the spring,
Or withdrawn to muse and meditate in some deep recess,
Far from the clank of crowds intervals passing rapt and happy,
Aware of the fresh free giver the flowing Missouri, aware of mighty Niagara,
Aware of the buffalo herds grazing the plains, the hirsute and strong-breasted bull,
Of earth, rocks, Fifth-month flowers experienced, stars, rain, snow, my amaze,
Having studied the mocking-bird's tones and the flight of the mountain-hawk,
And heard at dawn the unrivall'd one, the hermit thrush from the swamp-cedars,
Solitary, singing in the West, I strike up for a New World.

2

Victory, union, faith, identity, time,
The indissoluble compacts, riches, mystery,
Eternal progress, the kosmos, and the modern reports.

This then is life,
Here is what has come to the surface after so many throes and convulsions.

How curious! how real!
Underfoot the divine soil, overhead the sun.

See revolving the globe,
The ancestor-continents away group'd together,

The present and future continents north and south, with the
isthmus between.

See, vast trackless spaces,
As in a dream they change, they swiftly fill,
Countless masses debouch upon them,
They are now cover'd with the foremost people, arts,
institutions, known.

See, projected through time,
For me an audience interminable.

With firm and regular step they wend, they never stop,
Successions of men, Americanos, a hundred millions,
One generation playing its part and passing on,
Another generation playing its part and passing on in its
turn,
With faces turn'd sideways or backward towards me to listen,
With eyes retrospective towards me.

3

Americanos! conquerors! marches humanitarian!
Foremost! century marches! Libertad! masses!
For you a programme of chants.

Chants of the prairies,
Chants of the long-running Mississippi, and down to the
Mexican sea,
Chants of Ohio, Indiana, Illinois, Iowa, Wisconsin and
Minnesota,
Chants going forth from the centre from Kansas, and thence
equidistant,
Shooting in pulses of fire ceaseless to vivify all.

4

Take my leaves America, take them South and take them
North,
Make welcome for them everywhere, for they are your own
offspring,
Surround them East and West, for they would surround you,

And you precedents, connect lovingly with them, for they
connect lovingly with you.

I conn'd old times,
I sat studying at the feet of the great masters,
Now if eligible O that the great masters might return and
study me.

In the name of these States shall I scorn the antique?
Why these are the children of the antique to justify it.

5

Dead poets, philosophs, priests,
Martyrs, artists, inventors, governments long since,
Language-shapers on other shores,
Nations once powerful, now reduced, withdrawn, or desolate,
I dare not proceed till I respectfully credit what you have
left wafted hither,
I have perused it, own it is admirable, (moving awhile
among it,)
Think nothing can ever be greater, nothing can ever deserve
more than it deserves,
Regarding it all intently a long while, then dismissing it,
I stand in my place with my own day here.

Here lands female and male,
Here the heir-ship and heiress-ship of the world, here the
flame of materials,
Here spirituality the translatress, the openly-avow'd,
The ever-tending, the finalè of visible forms,
The satisfier, after due long-waiting now advancing,
Yes here comes my mistress the soul.

6

The soul,
Forever and forever—longer than soil is brown and solid—
longer than water ebbs and flows.

I will make the poems of materials, for I think they are to
be the most spiritual poems,

And I will make the poems of my body and of mortality,
For I think I shall then supply myself with the poems of my soul and of immortality.

I will make a song for these States that no one State may under any circumstances be subjected to another State,
And I will make a song that there shall be comity by day and by night between all the States, and between any two of them,
And I will make a song for the ears of the President, full of weapons with menacing points,
And behind the weapons countless dissatisfied faces;
And a song make I of the One form'd out of all,
The fang'd and glittering One whose head is over all,
Resolute warlike One including and over all,
(However high the head of any else that head is over all.)

I will acknowledge contemporary lands,
I will trail the whole geography of the globe and salute courteously every city large and small,
And employments! I will put in my poems that with you is heroism upon land and sea,
And I will report all heroism from an American point of view.

I will sing the song of companionship,
I will show what alone must finally compact these,
I believe these are to found their own ideal of manly love, indicating it in me,
I will therefore let flame from me the burning fires that were threatening to consume me,
I will lift what has too long kept down those smouldering fires,
I will give them complete abandonment,
I will write the evangel-poem of comrades and of love,
For who but I should understand love with all its sorrow and joy?
And who but I should be the poet of comrades?

7

I am the credulous man of qualities, ages, races,
I advance from the people in their own spirit,
Here is what sings unrestricted faith.

Omnes! omnes! let others ignore what they may,
I make the poem of evil also, I commemorate that part also,
I am myself just as much evil as good, and my nation is—
and I say there is in fact no evil,
(Or if there is I say it is just as important to you, to the
land or to me, as any thing else.)

I too, following many and follow'd by many, inaugurate a
religion, I descend into the arena,
(It may be I am destin'd to utter the loudest cries there, the
winner's pealing shouts,
Who knows? they may rise from me yet, and soar above
every thing.)

Each is not for its own sake,
I say the whole earth and all the stars in the sky are for
religion's sake.

I say no man has ever yet been half devout enough,
None has ever yet adored or worship'd half enough,
None has begun to think how divine he himself is, and how
certain the future is.

I say that the real and permanent grandeur of these States
must be their religion,
Otherwise there is no real and permanent grandeur;
(Nor character nor life worthy the name without religion,
Nor land nor man or woman without religion.)

8

What are you doing young man?
Are you so earnest, so given up to literature, science, art,
amours?
These ostensible realities, politics, points?
Your ambition or business whatever it may be?

It is well—against such I say not a word, I am their poet also,
But behold! such swiftly subside, burnt up for religion's sake,

For not all matter is fuel to heat, impalpable flame, the
essential life of the earth,
Any more than such are to religion.

9

What do you seek so pensive and silent?
What do you need camerado?
Dear son do you think it is love?

Listen dear son—listen America, daughter or son,
It is a painful thing to love a man or woman to excess, and
yet it satisfies, it is great,
But there is something else very great, it makes the whole
coincide,
It, magnificent, beyond materials, with continuous hands
sweeps and provides for all.

10

Know you, solely to drop in the earth the germs of a greater
religion,
The following chants each for its kind I sing.

My comrade!
For you to share with me two greatnesses, and a third one
rising inclusive and more resplendent,
The greatness of Love and Democracy, and the greatness of
Religion.

Melange mine own, the unseen and the seen,
Mysterious ocean where the streams empty,
Prophetic spirit of materials shifting and flickering around me,
Living beings, identities now doubtless near us in the air
that we know not of,
Contact daily and hourly that will not release me,
These selecting, these in hints demanded of me.

Not he with a daily kiss onward from childhood kissing me,
Has winded and twisted around me that which holds me
to him,

Any more than I am held to the heavens and all the spiritual world,
After what they have done to me, suggesting themes.

O such themes—equalities! O divine average!
Warblings under the sun, usher'd as now, or at noon, or setting,
Strains musical flowing through ages, now reaching hither,
I take to your reckless and composite chords, add to them, and cheerfully pass them forward.

11

As I have walk'd in Alabama my morning walk,
I have seen where the she-bird the mocking-bird sat on her nest in the briers hatching her brood.

I have seen the he-bird also,
I have paus'd to hear him near at hand inflating his throat and joyfully singing.

And while I paus'd it came to me that what he really sang for was not there only,
Nor for his mate nor himself only, nor all sent back by the echoes,
But subtle, clandestine, away beyond,
A charge transmitted and gift occult for those being born.

12

Democracy! near at hand to you a throat is now inflating itself and joyfully singing.

Ma femme! for the brood beyond us and of us,
For those who belong here and those to come,
I exultant to be ready for them will now shake out carols stronger and haughtier than have ever yet been heard upon earth.

I will make the songs of passion to give them their way,
And your songs outlaw'd offenders, for I scan you with kindred eyes, and carry you with me the same as any.

I will make the true poem of riches,
To earn for the body and the mind whatever adheres and goes forward and is not dropt by death;
I will effuse egotism and show it underlying all, and I will be the bard of personality,
And I will show of male and female that either is but the equal of the other,
And sexual organs and acts! do you concentrate in me, for I am determin'd to tell you with courageous clear voice to prove you illustrious,
And I will show that there is no imperfection in the present, and can be none in the future,
And I will show that whatever happens to anybody it may be turn'd to beautiful results,
And I will show that nothing can happen more beautiful than death,
And I will thread a thread through my poems that time and events are compact,
And that all the things of the universe are perfect miracles, each as profound as any.

I will not make poems with reference to parts,
But I will make poems, songs, thoughts, with reference to ensemble,
And I will not sing with reference to a day, but with reference to all days,
And I will not make a poem nor the least part of a poem but has reference to the soul,
Because having look'd at the objects of the universe, I find there is no one nor any particle of one but has reference to the soul.

13

Was somebody asking to see the soul?
See, your own shape and countenance, persons, substances, beasts, the trees, the running rivers, the rocks and sands.

All hold spiritual joys and afterwards loosen them;
How can the real body ever die and be buried?

Of your real body and any man's or woman's real body,
Item for item it will elude the hands of the corpse-cleaners
and pass to fitting spheres,
Carrying what has accrued to it from the moment of birth
to the moment of death.

Not the types set up by the printer return their impression,
the meaning, the main concern,
Any more than a man's substance and life or a woman's
substance and life return in the body and the soul,
Indifferently before death and after death.

Behold, the body includes and is the meaning, the main
concern, and includes and is the soul;
Whoever you are, how superb and how divine is your body,
or any part of it!

14

Whoever you are, to you endless announcements!

Daughter of the lands did you wait for your poet?
Did you wait for one with a flowing mouth and indicative
hand?
Toward the male of the States, and toward the female of the
States,
Exulting words, words to Democracy's lands.

Interlink'd, food-yielding lands!
Land of coal and iron! land of gold! land of cotton, sugar, rice!
Land of wheat, beef, pork! land of wool and hemp! land of
the apple and the grape!
Land of the pastoral plains, the grass-fields of the world!
land of those sweet-air'd interminable plateaus!
Land of the herd, the garden, the healthy house of adobie!
Lands where the north-west Columbia winds, and where the
south-west Colorado winds!
Land of the eastern Chesapeake! land of the Delaware!
Land of Ontario, Erie, Huron, Michigan!
Land of the Old Thirteen! Massachusetts land! land of
Vermont and Connecticut!

Land of the ocean shores! land of sierras and peaks!
Land of boatmen and sailors! fishermen's land!
Inextricable lands! the clutch'd together! the passionate ones!
The side by side! the elder and younger brothers! the bony-
limb'd!
The great women's land! the feminine! the experienced
sisters and the inexperienced sisters!
Far breath'd land! Arctic braced! Mexican breez'd! the
diverse! the compact!
The Pennsylvanian! the Virginian! the double Carolinian!
O all and each well-loved by me! my intrepid nations! O I
at any rate include you all with perfect love!
I cannot be discharged from you! not from one any sooner
than another!
O death! O for all that, I am yet of you unseen this hour
with irrepressible love,
Walking New England, a friend, a traveler,
Splashing my bare feet in the edge of the summer ripples on
Paumanok's sands,
Crossing the prairies, dwelling again in Chicago, dwelling in
every town,
Observing shows, births, improvements, structures, arts,
Listening to orators and oratresses in public halls,
Of and through the States as during life, each man and
woman my neighbor,
The Louisianian, the Georgian, as near to me, and I as near
to him and her,
The Mississippian and Arkansian yet with me, and I yet with
any of them,
Yet upon the plains west of the spinal river, yet in my house
of adobie,
Yet returning eastward, yet in the Seaside State or in
Maryland,
Yet Kanadian cheerily braving the winter, the snow and ice
welcome to me,
Yet a true son either of Maine or of the Granite State, or
the Narragansett Bay State, or the Empire State,
Yet sailing to other shores to annex the same, yet
welcoming every new brother,

Hereby applying these leaves to the new ones from the hour
 they unite with the old ones,
Coming among the new ones myself to be their companion
 and equal, coming personally to you now,
Enjoining you to acts, characters, spectacles, with me.

15

With me with firm holding, yet haste, haste on.

For your life adhere to me,
(I may have to be persuaded many times before I consent to
 give myself really to you, but what of that?
Must not Nature be persuaded many times?)

No dainty dolce affettuoso I,
Bearded, sun-burnt, gray-neck'd, forbidding, I have arrived,
To be wrestled with as I pass for the solid prizes of the
 universe,
For such I afford whoever can persevere to win them.

16

On my way a moment I pause,
Here for you! and here for America!
Still the present I raise aloft, still the future of the States I
 harbinge glad and sublime,
And for the past I pronounce what the air holds of the red
 aborigines.

The red aborigines,
Leaving natural breaths, sounds of rain and winds, calls as of
 birds and animals in the woods, syllabled to us for
 names,
Okonee, Koosa, Ottawa, Monongahela, Sauk, Natchez,
 Chattahoochee, Kaqueta, Oronoco,
Wabash, Miami, Saginaw, Chippewa, Oshkosh, Walla-Walla,
Leaving such to the States they melt, they depart, charging
 the water and the land with names.

17

Expanding and swift, henceforth,
Elements, breeds, adjustments, turbulent, quick and audacious,

A world primal again, vistas of glory incessant and branching,
A new race dominating previous ones and grander far, with new contests,
New politics, new literatures and religions, new inventions and arts.

These, my voice announcing—I will sleep no more but arise,
You oceans that have been calm within me! how I feel you, fathomless, stirring, preparing unprecedented waves and storms.

18

See, steamers steaming through my poems,
See, in my poems immigrants continually coming and landing,
See, in arriere, the wigwam, the trail, the hunter's hut, the flat-boat, the maize-leaf, the claim, the rude fence, and the backwoods village,
See, on the one side the Western Sea and on the other the Eastern Sea, how they advance and retreat upon my poems as upon their own shores,
See, pastures and forests in my poems—see, animals wild and tame—see, beyond the Kaw, countless herds of buffalo feeding on short curly grass,
See, in my poems, cities, solid, vast, inland, with paved streets, with iron and stone edifices, ceaseless vehicles, and commerce,
See, the many-cylinder'd steam printing-press—see, the electric telegraph stretching across the continent,
See, through Atlantica's depths pulses American Europe reaching, pulses of Europe duly return'd,
See, the strong and quick locomotive as it departs, panting, blowing the steam-whistle,
See, ploughmen ploughing farms—see, miners digging mines—see, the numberless factories,
See, mechanics busy at their benches with tools—see from among them superior judges, philosophs, Presidents, emerge, drest in working dresses,
See, lounging through the shops and fields of the States, me well-belov'd, close-held by day and night,

Hear the loud echoes of my songs there—read the hints
come at last.

19

O camerado close! O you and me at last, and us two only.

O a word to clear one's path ahead endlessly!
O something ecstatic and undemonstrable! O music wild!
O now I triumph—and you shall also;
O hand in hand—O wholesome pleasure—O one more
desirer and lover!
O to haste firm holding—to haste, haste on with me.

Song of Myself

1

I CELEBRATE myself, and sing myself,
And what I assume you shall assume,
For every atom belonging to me as good belongs to you.

I loafe and invite my soul,
I lean and loafe at my ease observing a spear of summer grass.

My tongue, every atom of my blood, form'd from this soil,
this air,
Born here of parents born here from parents the same, and
their parents the same,
I, now thirty-seven years old in perfect health begin,
Hoping to cease not till death.

Creeds and schools in abeyance,
Retiring back a while sufficed at what they are, but never
forgotten,
I harbor for good or bad, I permit to speak at every hazard,
Nature without check with original energy.

2

Houses and rooms are full of perfumes, the shelves are
crowded with perfumes,

I breathe the fragrance myself and know it and like it,
The distillation would intoxicate me also, but I shall not
let it.

The atmosphere is not a perfume, it has no taste of the
distillation, it is odorless,
It is for my mouth forever, I am in love with it,
I will go to the bank by the wood and become undisguised
and naked,
I am mad for it to be in contact with me.

The smoke of my own breath,
Echoes, ripples, buzz'd whispers, love-root, silk-thread,
crotch and vine,
My respiration and inspiration, the beating of my heart, the
passing of blood and air through my lungs,
The sniff of green leaves and dry leaves, and of the shore
and dark-color'd sea-rocks, and of hay in the barn,
The sound of the belch'd words of my voice loos'd to the
eddies of the wind,
A few light kisses, a few embraces, a reaching around of arms,
The play of shine and shade on the trees as the supple
boughs wag,
The delight alone or in the rush of the streets, or along the
fields and hill-sides,
The feeling of health, the full-noon trill, the song of me
rising from bed and meeting the sun.

Have you reckon'd a thousand acres much? have you
reckon'd the earth much?
Have you practis'd so long to learn to read?
Have you felt so proud to get at the meaning of poems?

Stop this day and night with me and you shall possess the
origin of all poems,
You shall possess the good of the earth and sun, (there are
millions of suns left,)
You shall no longer take things at second or third hand, nor
look through the eyes of the dead, nor feed on the
spectres in books,

You shall not look through my eyes either, nor take things
from me,
You shall listen to all sides and filter them from your self.

3

I have heard what the talkers were talking, the talk of the
beginning and the end,
But I do not talk of the beginning or the end.

There was never any more inception than there is now,
Nor any more youth or age than there is now,
And will never be any more perfection than there is now,
Nor any more heaven or hell than there is now.

Urge and urge and urge,
Always the procreant urge of the world.

Out of the dimness opposite equals advance, always
substance and increase, always sex,
Always a knit of identity, always distinction, always a breed
of life.

To elaborate is no avail, learn'd and unlearn'd feel that it is so.

Sure as the most certain sure, plumb in the uprights, well
entretied, braced in the beams,
Stout as a horse, affectionate, haughty, electrical,
I and this mystery here we stand.

Clear and sweet is my soul, and clear and sweet is all that is
not my soul.

Lack one lacks both, and the unseen is proved by the seen,
Till that becomes unseen and receives proof in its turn.

Showing the best and dividing it from the worst age vexes age,
Knowing the perfect fitness and equanimity of things, while
they discuss I am silent, and go bathe and admire myself.

Welcome is every organ and attribute of me, and of any
man hearty and clean,

Not an inch nor a particle of an inch is vile, and none shall
be less familiar than the rest.

I am satisfied—I see, dance, laugh, sing;
As the hugging and loving bed-fellow sleeps at my side
through the night, and withdraws at the peep of the
day with stealthy tread,
Leaving me baskets cover'd with white towels swelling the
house with their plenty,
Shall I postpone my acceptation and realization and scream
at my eyes,
That they turn from gazing after and down the road,
And forthwith cipher and show me to a cent,
Exactly the value of one and exactly the value of two, and
which is ahead?

4

Trippers and askers surround me,
People I meet, the effect upon me of my early life or the
ward and city I live in, or the nation,
The latest dates, discoveries, inventions, societies, authors
old and new,
My dinner, dress, associates, looks, compliments, dues,
The real or fancied indifference of some man or woman I
love,
The sickness of one of my folks or of myself, or ill-doing or
loss or lack of money, or depressions or exaltations,
Battles, the horrors of fratricidal war, the fever of doubtful
news, the fitful events;
These come to me days and nights and go from me again,
But they are not the Me myself.

Apart from the pulling and hauling stands what I am,
Stands amused, complacent, compassionating, idle, unitary,
Looks down, is erect, or bends an arm on an impalpable
certain rest,
Looking with side-curved head curious what will come next,
Both in and out of the game and watching and wondering
at it.

Backward I see in my own days where I sweated through
fog with linguists and contenders,
I have no mockings or arguments, I witness and wait.

5

I believe in you my soul, the other I am must not abase
itself to you,
And you must not be abased to the other.

Loafe with me on the grass, loose the stop from your throat,
Not words, not music or rhyme I want, not custom or
lecture, not even the best,
Only the lull I like, the hum of your valvèd voice.

I mind how once we lay such a transparent summer morning,
How you settled your head athwart my hips and gently
turn'd over upon me,
And parted the shirt from my bosom-bone, and plunged
your tongue to my bare-stript heart,
And reach'd till you felt my beard, and reach'd till you held
my feet.

Swiftly arose and spread around me the peace and knowledge
that pass all the argument of the earth,
And I know that the hand of God is the promise of my own,
And I know that the spirit of God is the brother of my own,
And that all the men ever born are also my brothers, and
the women my sisters and lovers,
And that a kelson of the creation is love,
And limitless are leaves stiff or drooping in the fields,
And brown ants in the little wells beneath them,
And mossy scabs of the worm fence, heap'd stones, elder,
mullein and poke-weed.

6

A child said *What is the grass?* fetching it to me with full
hands;
How could I answer the child? I do not know what it is any
more than he.

I guess it must be the flag of my disposition, out of hopeful
green stuff woven.

Or I guess it is the handkerchief of the Lord,
A scented gift and remembrancer designedly dropt,
Bearing the owner's name someway in the corners, that we
may see and remark, and say *Whose?*

Or I guess the grass is itself a child, the produced babe of
the vegetation.

Or I guess it is a uniform hieroglyphic,
And it means, Sprouting alike in broad zones and narrow
zones,
Growing among black folks as among white,
Kanuck, Tuckahoe, Congressman, Cuff, I give them the
same, I receive them the same.

And now it seems to me the beautiful uncut hair of graves.

Tenderly will I use you curling grass,
It may be you transpire from the breasts of young men,
It may be if I had known them I would have loved them,
It may be you are from old people, or from offspring taken
soon out of their mothers' laps,
And here you are the mothers' laps.

This grass is very dark to be from the white heads of old
mothers,
Darker than the colorless beards of old men,
Dark to come from under the faint red roofs of mouths.

O I perceive after all so many uttering tongues,
And I perceive they do not come from the roofs of mouths
for nothing.

I wish I could translate the hints about the dead young men
and women,
And the hints about old men and mothers, and the
offspring taken soon out of their laps.

What do you think has become of the young and old men?
And what do you think has become of the women and
children?

They are alive and well somewhere,
The smallest sprout shows there is really no death,
And if ever there was it led forward life, and does not wait
at the end to arrest it,
And ceas'd the moment life appear'd.

All goes onward and outward, nothing collapses,
And to die is different from what any one supposed, and
luckier.

7

Has any one supposed it lucky to be born?
I hasten to inform him or her it is just as lucky to die, and I
know it.

I pass death with the dying and birth with the new-wash'd
babe, and am not contain'd between my hat and boots,
And peruse manifold objects, no two alike and every one good,
The earth good and the stars good, and their adjuncts all
good.

I am not an earth nor an adjunct of an earth,
I am the mate and companion of people, all just as
immortal and fathomless as myself,
(They do not know how immortal, but I know.)

Every kind for itself and its own, for me mine male and
female,
For me those that have been boys and that love women,
For me the man that is proud and feels how it stings to be
slighted,
For me the sweet-heart and the old maid, for me mothers
and the mothers of mothers,
For me lips that have smiled, eyes that have shed tears,
For me children and the begetters of children.

Undrape! you are not guilty to me, nor stale nor discarded,
I see through the broadcloth and gingham whether or no,
And am around, tenacious, acquisitive, tireless, and cannot
be shaken away.

8

The little one sleeps in its cradle,
I lift the gauze and look a long time, and silently brush
away flies with my hand.

The youngster and the red-faced girl turn aside up the
bushy hill,
I peeringly view them from the top.

The suicide sprawls on the bloody floor of the bedroom,
I witness the corpse with its dabbled hair, I note where the
pistol has fallen.

The blab of the pave, tires of carts, sluff of boot-soles, talk
of the promenaders,
The heavy omnibus, the driver with his interrogating thumb,
the clank of the shod horses on the granite floor,
The snow-sleighs, clinking, shouted jokes, pelts of snow-balls,
The hurrahs for popular favorites, the fury of rous'd mobs,
The flap of the curtain'd litter, a sick man inside borne to
the hospital,
The meeting of enemies, the sudden oath, the blows and fall,
The excited crowd, the policeman with his star quickly
working his passage to the centre of the crowd,
The impassive stones that receive and return so many echoes,
What groans of over-fed or half-starv'd who fall sunstruck or
in fits,
What exclamations of women taken suddenly who hurry
home and give birth to babes,
What living and buried speech is always vibrating here, what
howls restrain'd by decorum,
Arrests of criminals, slights, adulterous offers made,
acceptances, rejections with convex lips,
I mind them or the show or resonance of them—I come
and I depart.

9

The big doors of the country barn stand open and ready,
The dried grass of the harvest-time loads the slow-drawn
wagon,
The clear light plays on the brown gray and green intertinged,
The armfuls are pack'd to the sagging mow.

I am there, I help, I came stretch'd atop of the load,
I felt its soft jolts, one leg reclined on the other,
I jump from the cross-beams and seize the clover and timothy,
And roll head over heels and tangle my hair full of wisps.

10

Alone far in the wilds and mountains I hunt,
Wandering amazed at my own lightness and glee,
In the late afternoon choosing a safe spot to pass the night,
Kindling a fire and broiling the fresh-kill'd game,
Falling asleep on the gather'd leaves with my dog and gun
by my side.

The Yankee clipper is under her sky-sails, she cuts the
sparkle and scud,
My eyes settle the land, I bend at her prow or shout
joyously from the deck.

The boatmen and clam-diggers arose early and stopt for me,
I tuck'd my trowser-ends in my boots and went and had a
good time;
You should have been with us that day round the chowder-
kettle.

I saw the marriage of the trapper in the open air in the far
west, the bride was a red girl,
Her father and his friends sat near cross-legged and dumbly
smoking, they had moccasins to their feet and large
thick blankets hanging from their shoulders,
On a bank lounged the trapper, he was drest mostly in
skins, his luxuriant beard and curls protected his neck,
he held his bride by the hand,

She had long eyelashes, her head was bare, her coarse straight
locks descended upon her voluptuous limbs and reach'd
to her feet.

The runaway slave came to my house and stopt outside,
I heard his motions crackling the twigs of the woodpile,
Through the swung half-door of the kitchen I saw him
limpsy and weak,
And went where he sat on a log and led him in and assured
him,
And brought water and fill'd a tub for his sweated body and
bruis'd feet,
And gave him a room that enter'd from my own, and gave
him some coarse clean clothes,
And remember perfectly well his revolving eyes and his
awkwardness,
And remember putting plasters on the galls of his neck and
ankles;
He staid with me a week before he was recuperated and
pass'd north,
I had him sit next me at table, my fire-lock lean'd in the
corner.

11

Twenty-eight young men bathe by the shore,
Twenty-eight young men and all so friendly;
Twenty-eight years of womanly life and all so lonesome.

She owns the fine house by the rise of the bank,
She hides handsome and richly drest aft the blinds of the
window.

Which of the young men does she like the best?
Ah the homeliest of them is beautiful to her.

Where are you off to, lady? for I see you,
You splash in the water there, yet stay stock still in your room.

Dancing and laughing along the beach came the twenty-
ninth bather,
The rest did not see her, but she saw them and loved them.

The beards of the young men glisten'd with wet, it ran from
their long hair,
Little streams pass'd all over their bodies.

An unseen hand also pass'd over their bodies,
It descended tremblingly from their temples and ribs.

The young men float on their backs, their white bellies bulge
to the sun, they do not ask who seizes fast to them,
They do not know who puffs and declines with pendant and
bending arch,
They do not think whom they souse with spray.

12

The butcher-boy puts off his killing-clothes, or sharpens his
knife at the stall in the market,
I loiter enjoying his repartee and his shuffle and break-down.

Blacksmiths with grimed and hairy chests environ the anvil,
Each has his main-sledge, they are all out, there is a great
heat in the fire.

From the cinder-strew'd threshold I follow their movements,
The lithe sheer of their waists plays even with their massive
arms,
Overhand the hammers swing, overhand so slow, overhand
so sure,
They do not hasten, each man hits in his place.

13

The negro holds firmly the reins of his four horses, the
block swags underneath on its tied-over chain,
The negro that drives the long dray of the stone-yard, steady
and tall he stands pois'd on one leg on the string-piece,
His blue shirt exposes his ample neck and breast and loosens
over his hip-band,
His glance is calm and commanding, he tosses the slouch of
his hat away from his forehead,
The sun falls on his crispy hair and mustache, falls on the
black of his polish'd and perfect limbs.

I behold the picturesque giant and love him, and I do not
stop there,
I go with the team also.

In me the caresser of life wherever moving, backward as well
as forward sluing,
To niches aside and junior bending, not a person or object
missing,
Absorbing all to myself and for this song.

Oxen that rattle the yoke and chain or halt in the leafy
shade, what is that you express in your eyes?
It seems to me more than all the print I have read in my life.

My tread scares the wood-drake and wood-duck on my
distant and day-long ramble,
They rise together, they slowly circle around.

I believe in those wing'd purposes,
And acknowledge red, yellow, white, playing within me,
And consider green and violet and the tufted crown
intentional,
And do not call the tortoise unworthy because she is not
something else,
And the jay in the woods never studied the gamut, yet trills
pretty well to me,
And the look of the bay mare shames silliness out of me.

14

The wild gander leads his flock through the cool night,
Ya-honk he says, and sounds it down to me like an
invitation,
The pert may suppose it meaningless, but I listening close,
Find its purpose and place up there toward the wintry sky.

The sharp-hoof'd moose of the north, the cat on the house-
sill, the chickadee, the prairie-dog,
The litter of the grunting sow as they tug at her teats,
The brood of the turkey-hen and she with her half-spread
wings,
I see in them and myself the same old law.

The press of my foot to the earth springs a hundred affections,
They scorn the best I can do to relate them.

I am enamour'd of growing out-doors,
Of men that live among cattle or taste of the ocean or woods,
Of the builders and steerers of ships and the wielders of axes
and mauls, and the drivers of horses,
I can eat and sleep with them week in and week out.

What is commonest, cheapest, nearest, easiest, is Me,
Me going in for my chances, spending for vast returns,
Adorning myself to bestow myself on the first that will take me,
Not asking the sky to come down to my good will,
Scattering it freely forever.

15

The pure contralto sings in the organ loft,
The carpenter dresses his plank, the tongue of his foreplane
whistles its wild ascending lisp,
The married and unmarried children ride home to their
Thanksgiving dinner,
The pilot seizes the king-pin, he heaves down with a strong
arm,
The mate stands braced in the whale-boat, lance and harpoon
are ready,
The duck-shooter walks by silent and cautious stretches,
The deacons are ordain'd with cross'd hands at the altar,
The spinning-girl retreats and advances to the hum of the
big wheel,
The farmer stops by the bars as he walks on a First-day loafe
and looks at the oats and rye,
The lunatic is carried at last to the asylum a confirm'd case,
(He will never sleep any more as he did in the cot in his
mother's bed-room;)
The jour printer with gray head and gaunt jaws works at his
case,
He turns his quid of tobacco while his eyes blurr with the
manuscript;
The malform'd limbs are tied to the surgeon's table,

What is removed drops horribly in a pail;
The quadroon girl is sold at the auction-stand, the drunkard nods by the bar-room stove,
The machinist rolls up his sleeves, the policeman travels his beat, the gate-keeper marks who pass,
The young fellow drives the express-wagon, (I love him, though I do not know him;)
The half-breed straps on his light boots to compete in the race,
The western turkey-shooting draws old and young, some lean on their rifles, some sit on logs,
Out from the crowd steps the marksman, takes his position, levels his piece;
The groups of newly-come immigrants cover the wharf or levee,
As the woolly-pates hoe in the sugar-field, the overseer views them from his saddle,
The bugle calls in the ball-room, the gentlemen run for their partners, the dancers bow to each other,
The youth lies awake in the cedar-roof'd garret and harks to the musical rain,
The Wolverine sets traps on the creek that helps fill the Huron,
The squaw wrapt in her yellow-hemm'd cloth is offering moccasins and bead-bags for sale,
The connoisseur peers along the exhibition-gallery with half-shut eyes bent sideways,
As the deck-hands make fast the steamboat the plank is thrown for the shore-going passengers,
The young sister holds out the skein while the elder sister winds it off in a ball, and stops now and then for the knots,
The one-year wife is recovering and happy having a week ago borne her first child,
The clean-hair'd Yankee girl works with her sewing-machine or in the factory or mill,
The paving-man leans on his two-handed rammer, the reporter's lead flies swiftly over the note-book, the sign-painter is lettering with blue and gold,

The canal boy trots on the tow-path, the book-keeper
counts at his desk, the shoemaker waxes his thread,
The conductor beats time for the band and all the performers
follow him,
The child is baptized, the convert is making his first
professions,
The regatta is spread on the bay, the race is begun, (how
the white sails sparkle!)
The drover watching his drove sings out to them that would
stray,
The pedler sweats with his pack on his back, (the purchaser
higgling about the odd cent;)
The bride unrumples her white dress, the minute-hand of
the clock moves slowly,
The opium-eater reclines with rigid head and just-open'd lips,
The prostitute draggles her shawl, her bonnet bobs on her
tipsy and pimpled neck,
The crowd laugh at her blackguard oaths, the men jeer and
wink to each other,
(Miserable! I do not laugh at your oaths nor jeer you;)
The President holding a cabinet council is surrounded by
the great Secretaries,
On the piazza walk three matrons stately and friendly with
twined arms,
The crew of the fish-smack pack repeated layers of halibut in
the hold,
The Missourian crosses the plains toting his wares and his
cattle,
As the fare-collector goes through the train he gives notice
by the jingling of loose change,
The floor-men are laying the floor, the tinners are tinning
the roof, the masons are calling for mortar,
In single file each shouldering his hod pass onward the
laborers;
Seasons pursuing each other the indescribable crowd is
gather'd, it is the fourth of Seventh-month, (what
salutes of cannon and small arms!)
Seasons pursuing each other the plougher ploughs, the
mower mows, and the winter-grain falls in the ground;

Off on the lakes the pike-fisher watches and waits by the
hole in the frozen surface,
The stumps stand thick round the clearing, the squatter
strikes deep with his axe,
Flatboatmen make fast towards dusk near the cotton-wood
or pecan-trees,
Coon-seekers go through the regions of the Red river or
through those drain'd by the Tennessee, or through
those of the Arkansas,
Torches shine in the dark that hangs on the Chattahooche
or Altamahaw,
Patriarchs sit at supper with sons and grandsons and great-
grandsons around them,
In walls of adobie, in canvas tents, rest hunters and trappers
after their day's sport,
The city sleeps and the country sleeps,
The living sleep for their time, the dead sleep for their time,
The old husband sleeps by his wife and the young husband
sleeps by his wife;
And these tend inward to me, and I tend outward to them,
And such as it is to be of these more or less I am,
And of these one and all I weave the song of myself.

16

I am of old and young, of the foolish as much as the wise,
Regardless of others, ever regardful of others,
Maternal as well as paternal, a child as well as a man,
Stuff'd with the stuff that is coarse and stuff'd with the stuff
that is fine,
One of the Nation of many nations, the smallest the same
and the largest the same,
A Southerner soon as a Northerner, a planter nonchalant
and hospitable down by the Oconee I live,
A Yankee bound my own way ready for trade, my joints the
limberest joints on earth and the sternest joints on earth,
A Kentuckian walking the vale of the Elkhorn in my deer-
skin leggings, a Louisianian or Georgian,
A boatman over lakes or bays or along coasts, a Hoosier,
Badger, Buckeye;

At home on Kanadian snow-shoes or up in the bush, or with fishermen off Newfoundland,
At home in the fleet of ice-boats, sailing with the rest and tacking,
At home on the hills of Vermont or in the woods of Maine, or the Texan ranch,
Comrade of Californians, comrade of free North-Westerners, (loving their big proportions,)
Comrade of raftsmen and coalmen, comrade of all who shake hands and welcome to drink and meat,
A learner with the simplest, a teacher of the thoughtfullest,
A novice beginning yet experient of myriads of seasons,
Of every hue and caste am I, of every rank and religion,
A farmer, mechanic, artist, gentleman, sailor, quaker,
Prisoner, fancy-man, rowdy, lawyer, physician, priest.

I resist any thing better than my own diversity,
Breathe the air but leave plenty after me,
And am not stuck up, and am in my place.

(The moth and the fish-eggs are in their place,
The bright suns I see and the dark suns I cannot see are in their place,
The palpable is in its place and the impalpable is in its place.)

17

These are really the thoughts of all men in all ages and lands, they are not original with me,
If they are not yours as much as mine they are nothing, or next to nothing,
If they are not the riddle and the untying of the riddle they are nothing,
If they are not just as close as they are distant they are nothing.

This is the grass that grows wherever the land is and the water is,
This the common air that bathes the globe.

18

With music strong I come, with my cornets and my drums,
I play not marches for accepted victors only, I play marches for conquer'd and slain persons.

Have you heard that it was good to gain the day?
I also say it is good to fall, battles are lost in the same spirit in which they are won.

I beat and pound for the dead,
I blow through my embouchures my loudest and gayest for them.

Vivas to those who have fail'd!
And to those whose war-vessels sank in the sea!
And to those themselves who sank in the sea!
And to all generals that lost engagements, and all overcome heroes!
And the numberless unknown heroes equal to the greatest heroes known!

19

This is the meal equally set, this the meat for natural hunger,
It is for the wicked just the same as the righteous, I make appointments with all,
I will not have a single person slighted or left away,
The kept-woman, sponger, thief, are hereby invited,
The heavy-lipp'd slave is invited, the venerealee is invited;
There shall be no difference between them and the rest.

This is the press of a bashful hand, this the float and odor of hair,
This the touch of my lips to yours, this the murmur of yearning,
This the far-off depth and height reflecting my own face,
This the thoughtful merge of myself, and the outlet again.

Do you guess I have some intricate purpose?
Well I have, for the Fourth-month showers have, and the mica on the side of a rock has.

Do you take it I would astonish?
Does the daylight astonish? does the early redstart twittering through the woods?
Do I astonish more than they?

This hour I tell things in confidence,
I might not tell everybody, but I will tell you.

20

Who goes there? hankering, gross, mystical, nude;
How is it I extract strength from the beef I eat?

What is a man anyhow? what am I? what are you?

All I mark as my own you shall offset it with your own,
Else it were time lost listening to me.

I do not snivel that snivel the world over,
That months are vacuums and the ground but wallow and filth.

Whimpering and truckling fold with powders for invalids, conformity goes to the fourth-remov'd,
I wear my hat as I please indoors or out.

Why should I pray? why should I venerate and be ceremonious?

Having pried through the strata, analyzed to a hair, counsel'd with doctors and calculated close,
I find no sweeter fat than sticks to my own bones.

In all people I see myself, none more and not one a barley-corn less,
And the good or bad I say of myself I say of them.

I know I am solid and sound,
To me the converging objects of the universe perpetually flow,
All are written to me, and I must get what the writing means.

I know I am deathless,
I know this orbit of mine cannot be swept by a carpenter's compass,
I know I shall not pass like a child's carlacue cut with a burnt stick at night.

I know I am august,
I do not trouble my spirit to vindicate itself or be understood,
I see that the elementary laws never apologize,
(I reckon I behave no prouder than the level I plant my
house by, after all.)

I exist as I am, that is enough,
If no other in the world be aware I sit content,
And if each and all be aware I sit content.

One world is aware and by far the largest to me, and that is
myself,
And whether I come to my own to-day or in ten thousand
or ten million years,
I can cheerfully take it now, or with equal cheerfulness I
can wait.

My foothold is tenon'd and mortis'd in granite,
I laugh at what you call dissolution,
And I know the amplitude of time.

21

I am the poet of the Body and I am the poet of the Soul,
The pleasures of heaven are with me and the pains of hell
are with me,
The first I graft and increase upon myself, the latter I
translate into a new tongue.

I am the poet of the woman the same as the man,
And I say it is as great to be a woman as to be a man,
And I say there is nothing greater than the mother of men.

I chant the chant of dilation or pride,
We have had ducking and deprecating about enough,
I show that size is only development.

Have you outstript the rest? are you the President?
It is a trifle, they will more than arrive there every one, and
still pass on.

I am he that walks with the tender and growing night,
I call to the earth and sea half-held by the night.

Press close bare-bosom'd night—press close magnetic
nourishing night!
Night of south winds—night of the large few stars!
Still nodding night—mad naked summer night.

Smile O voluptuous cool-breath'd earth!
Earth of the slumbering and liquid trees!
Earth of departed sunset—earth of the mountains misty-topt!
Earth of the vitreous pour of the full moon just tinged with
blue!
Earth of shine and dark mottling the tide of the river!
Earth of the limpid gray of clouds brighter and clearer for
my sake!
Far-swooping elbow'd earth—rich apple-blossom'd earth!
Smile, for your lover comes.

Prodigal, you have given me love—therefore I to you give
love!
O unspeakable passionate love.

22

You sea! I resign myself to you also—I guess what you mean,
I behold from the beach your crooked inviting fingers,
I believe you refuse to go back without feeling of me,
We must have a turn together, I undress, hurry me out of
sight of the land,
Cushion me soft, rock me in billowy drowse,
Dash me with amorous wet, I can repay you.

Sea of stretch'd ground-swells,
Sea breathing broad and convulsive breaths,
Sea of the brine of life and of unshovell'd yet always-ready
graves,
Howler and scooper of storms, capricious and dainty sea,
I am integral with you, I too am of one phase and of all
phases.

Partaker of influx and efflux I, extoller of hate and conciliation,
Extoller of amies and those that sleep in each others' arms.

I am he attesting sympathy,
(Shall I make my list of things in the house and skip the
house that supports them?)

I am not the poet of goodness only, I do not decline to be
the poet of wickedness also.

What blurt is this about virtue and about vice?
Evil propels me and reform of evil propels me, I stand
indifferent,
My gait is no fault-finder's or rejecter's gait,
I moisten the roots of all that has grown.

Did you fear some scrofula out of the unflagging pregnancy?
Did you guess the celestial laws are yet to be work'd over
and rectified?

I find one side a balance and the antipodal side a balance,
Soft doctrine as steady help as stable doctrine,
Thoughts and deeds of the present our rouse and early start.

This minute that comes to me over the past decillions,
There is no better than it and now.

What behaved well in the past or behaves well to-day is not
such a wonder,
The wonder is always and always how there can be a mean
man or an infidel.

23

Endless unfolding of words of ages!
And mine a word of the modern, the word En-Masse.

A word of the faith that never balks,
Here or henceforward it is all the same to me, I accept
Time absolutely.

It alone is without flaw, it alone rounds and completes all,
That mystic baffling wonder alone completes all.

I accept Reality and dare not question it,
Materialism first and last imbuing.

Hurrah for positive science! long live exact demonstration!
Fetch stonecrop mixt with cedar and branches of lilac,
This is the lexicographer, this the chemist, this made a grammar of the old cartouches,
These mariners put the ship through dangerous unknown seas.
This is the geologist, this works with the scalpel, and this is a mathematician.

Gentlemen, to you the first honors always!
Your facts are useful, and yet they are not my dwelling,
I but enter by them to an area of my dwelling.

Less the reminders of properties told my words,
And more the reminders they of life untold, and of freedom and extrication,
And make short account of neuters and geldings, and favor men and women fully equipt,
And beat the gong of revolt, and stop with fugitives and them that plot and conspire.

24

Walt Whitman, a kosmos, of Manhattan the son,
Turbulent, fleshy, sensual, eating, drinking and breeding,
No sentimentalist, no stander above men and women or apart from them,
No more modest than immodest.

Unscrew the locks from the doors!
Unscrew the doors themselves from their jambs!

Whoever degrades another degrades me,
And whatever is done or said returns at last to me.

Through me the afflatus surging and surging, through me
the current and index.

I speak the pass-word primeval, I give the sign of democracy,
By God! I will accept nothing which all cannot have their
counterpart of on the same terms.

Through me many long dumb voices,
Voices of the interminable generations of prisoners and slaves,
Voices of the diseas'd and despairing and of thieves and
dwarfs,
Voices of cycles of preparation and accretion,
And of the threads that connect the stars, and of wombs
and of the father-stuff,
And of the rights of them the others are down upon,
Of the deform'd, trivial, flat, foolish, despised,
Fog in the air, beetles rolling balls of dung.

Through me forbidden voices,
Voices of sexes and lusts, voices veil'd and I remove the veil,
Voices indecent by me clarified and transfigur'd.

I do not press my fingers across my mouth,
I keep as delicate around the bowels as around the head and
heart,
Copulation is no more rank to me than death is.

I believe in the flesh and the appetites,
Seeing, hearing, feeling, are miracles, and each part and tag
of me is a miracle.

Divine am I inside and out, and I make holy whatever I
touch or am touch'd from,
The scent of these arm-pits aroma finer than prayer,
This head more than churches, bibles, and all the creeds.

If I worship one thing more than another it shall be the
spread of my own body, or any part of it,
Translucent mould of me it shall be you!
Shaded ledges and rests it shall be you!

Firm masculine colter it shall be you!
Whatever goes to the tilth of me it shall be you!
You my rich blood! your milky stream pale strippings of
my life!
Breast that presses against other breasts it shall be you!
My brain it shall be your occult convolutions!
Root of wash'd sweet-flag! timorous pond-snipe! nest of
guarded duplicate eggs! it shall be you!
Mix'd tussled hay of head, beard, brawn, it shall be you!
Trickling sap of maple, fibre of manly wheat, it shall be you!
Sun so generous it shall be you!
Vapors lighting and shading my face it shall be you!
You sweaty brooks and dews it shall be you!
Winds whose soft-tickling genitals rub against me it shall
be you!
Broad muscular fields, branches of live oak, loving lounger
in my winding paths, it shall be you!
Hands I have taken, face I have kiss'd, mortal I have ever
touch'd, it shall be you.

I dote on myself, there is that lot of me and all so luscious,
Each moment and whatever happens thrills me with joy,
I cannot tell how my ankles bend, nor whence the cause of
my faintest wish,
Nor the cause of the friendship I emit, nor the cause of the
friendship I take again.

That I walk up my stoop, I pause to consider if it really be,
A morning-glory at my window satisfies me more than the
metaphysics of books.

To behold the day-break!
The little light fades the immense and diaphanous shadows,
The air tastes good to my palate.

Hefts of the moving world at innocent gambols silently
rising freshly exuding,
Scooting obliquely high and low.

Something I cannot see puts upward libidinous prongs,
Seas of bright juice suffuse heaven.

The earth by the sky staid with, the daily close of their
junction,
The heav'd challenge from the east that moment over my head,
The mocking taunt. See then whether you shall be master!

25

Dazzling and tremendous how quick the sun-rise would kill
me,
If I could not now and always send sun-rise out of me.

We also ascend dazzling and tremendous as the sun,
We found our own O my soul in the calm and cool of the
day-break.

My voice goes after what my eyes cannot reach,
With the twirl of my tongue I encompass worlds and
volumes of worlds.

Speech is the twin of my vision, it is unequal to measure itself,
It provokes me forever, it says sarcastically,
Walt you contain enough, why don't you let it out then?

Come now I will not be tantalized, you conceive too much
of articulation,
Do you not know O speech how the buds beneath you are
folded?
Waiting in gloom, protected by frost,
The dirt receding before my prophetical screams,
I underlying causes to balance them at last,
My knowledge my live parts, it keeping tally with the
meaning of all things,
Happiness, (which whoever hears me let him or her set out
in search of this day.)

My final merit I refuse you, I refuse putting from me what I
really am,
Encompass worlds, but never try to encompass me,
I crowd your sleekest and best by simply looking toward you.

Writing and talk do not prove me,
I carry the plenum of proof and every thing else in my face,
With the hush of my lips I wholly confound the skeptic.

26

Now I will do nothing but listen,
To accrue what I hear into this song, to let sounds contribute toward it.

I hear bravuras of birds, bustle of growing wheat, gossip of flames, clack of sticks cooking my meals,
I hear the sound I love, the sound of the human voice,
I hear all sounds running together, combined, fused or following,
Sounds of the city and sounds out of the city, sounds of the day and night,
Talkative young ones to those that like them, the loud laugh of work-people at their meals,
The angry base of disjointed friendship, the faint tones of the sick,
The judge with hands tight to the desk, his pallid lips pronouncing a death-sentence,
The heave'e'yo of stevedores unlading ships by the wharves, the refrain of the anchor-lifters,
The ring of alarm-bells, the cry of fire, the whirr of swift-streaking engines and hose-carts with premonitory tinkles and color'd lights,
The steam-whistle, the solid roll of the train of approaching cars,
The slow march play'd at the head of the association marching two and two,
(They go to guard some corpse, the flag-tops are draped with black muslin.)

I hear the violoncello, ('tis the young man's heart's complaint,)
I hear the key'd cornet, it glides quickly in through my ears,
It shakes mad-sweet pangs through my belly and breast.

I hear the chorus, it is a grand opera,
Ah this indeed is music—this suits me.

A tenor large and fresh as the creation fills me,
The orbic flex of his mouth is pouring and filling me full.

I hear the train'd soprano (what work with hers is this?)
The orchestra whirls me wider than Uranus flies,
It wrenches such ardors from me I did not know I possess'd
them,
It sails me, I dab with bare feet, they are lick'd by the
indolent waves,
I am cut by bitter and angry hail, I lose my breath,
Steep'd amid honey'd morphine, my windpipe throttled in
fakes of death,
At length let up again to feel the puzzle of puzzles,
And that we call Being.

27

To be in any form, what is that?
(Round and round we go, all of us, and ever come back
thither,)
If nothing lay more develop'd the quahaug in its callous
shell were enough.

Mine is no callous shell,
I have instant conductors all over me whether I pass or stop,
They seize every object and lead it harmlessly through me.

I merely stir, press, feel with my fingers, and am happy,
To touch my person to some one else's is about as much as
I can stand.

28

Is this then a touch? quivering me to a new identity,
Flames and ether making a rush for my veins,
Treacherous tip of me reaching and crowding to help them,
My flesh and blood playing out lightning to strike what is
hardly different from myself,
On all sides prurient provokers stiffening my limbs,
Straining the udder of my heart for its withheld drip,
Behaving licentious toward me, taking no denial,
Depriving me of my best as for a purpose,

Unbuttoning my clothes, holding me by the bare waist,
Deluding my confusion with the calm of the sunlight and pasture-fields,
Immodestly sliding the fellow-senses away,
They bribed to swap off with touch and go and graze at the edges of me,
No consideration, no regard for my draining strength or my anger,
Fetching the rest of the herd around to enjoy them a while,
Then all uniting to stand on a headland and worry me.

The sentries desert every other part of me,
They have left me helpless to a red marauder,
They all come to the headland to witness and assist against me.

I am given up by traitors,
I talk wildly, I have lost my wits, I and nobody else am the greatest traitor,
I went myself first to the headland, my own hands carried me there.

You villain touch! what are you doing? my breath is tight in its throat,
Unclench your floodgates, you are too much for me.

29

Blind loving wrestling touch, sheath'd hooded sharp-tooth'd touch!
Did it make you ache so, leaving me?

Parting track'd by arriving, perpetual payment of perpetual loan,
Rich showering rain, and recompense richer afterward.

Sprouts take and accumulate, stand by the curb prolific and vital,
Landscapes projected masculine, full-sized and golden.

30

All truths wait in all things,
They neither hasten their own delivery nor resist it,

They do not need the obstetric forceps of the surgeon,
The insignificant is as big to me as any,
(What is less or more than a touch?)

Logic and sermons never convince,
The damp of the night drives deeper into my soul.

(Only what proves itself to every man and woman is so,
Only what nobody denies is so.)

A minute and a drop of me settle my brain,
I believe the soggy clods shall become lovers and lamps,
And a compend of compends is the meat of a man or woman,
And a summit and flower there is the feeling they have for each other,
And they are to branch boundlessly out of that lesson until it becomes omnific,
And until one and all shall delight us, and we them.

31

I believe a leaf of grass is no less than the journey-work of the stars,
And the pismire is equally perfect, and a grain of sand, and the egg of the wren,
And the tree-toad is a chef-d'œuvre for the highest,
And the running blackberry would adorn the parlors of heaven,
And the narrowest hinge in my hand puts to scorn all machinery,
And the cow crunching with depress'd head surpasses any statue,
And a mouse is miracle enough to stagger sextillions of infidels.

I find I incorporate gneiss, coal, long-threaded moss, fruits, grains, esculent roots,
And am stucco'd with quadrupeds and birds all over,
And have distanced what is behind me for good reasons,
But call any thing back again when I desire it.

In vain the speeding or shyness,
In vain the plutonic rocks send their old heat against my
approach,
In vain the mastodon retreats beneath its own powder'd
bones,
In vain objects stand leagues off and assume manifold shapes,
In vain the ocean settling in hollows and the great monsters
lying low,
In vain the buzzard houses herself with the sky,
In vain the snake slides through the creepers and logs,
In vain the elk takes to the inner passes of the woods,
In vain the razor-bill'd auk sails far north to Labrador,
I follow quickly, I ascend to the nest in the fissure of the cliff.

32

I think I could turn and live with animals, they are so placid
and self-contain'd,
I stand and look at them long and long.

They do not sweat and whine about their condition,
They do not lie awake in the dark and weep for their sins,
They do not make me sick discussing their duty to God,
Not one is dissatisfied, not one is demented with the mania
of owning things,
Not one kneels to another, nor to his kind that lived
thousands of years ago,
Not one is respectable or unhappy over the whole earth.

So they show their relations to me and I accept them,
They bring me tokens of myself, they evince them plainly in
their possession.

I wonder where they get those tokens,
Did I pass that way huge times ago and negligently drop
them?

Myself moving forward then and now and forever,
Gathering and showing more always and with velocity,
Infinite and omnigenous, and the like of these among them,
Not too exclusive toward the reachers of my
remembrancers,

Picking out here one that I love, and now go with him on
brotherly terms.

A gigantic beauty of a stallion, fresh and responsive to my
caresses,
Head high in the forehead, wide between the ears,
Limbs glossy and supple, tail dusting the ground,
Eyes full of sparkling wickedness, ears finely cut, flexibly
moving.

His nostrils dilate as my heels embrace him,
His well-built limbs tremble with pleasure as we race around
and return.

I but use you a minute, then I resign you, stallion,
Why do I need your paces when I myself out-gallop them?
Even as I stand or sit passing faster than you.

33

Space and Time! now I see it is true, what I guess'd at,
What I guess'd when I loaf'd on the grass,
What I guess'd while I lay alone in my bed,
And again as I walk'd the beach under the paling stars of
the morning.

My ties and ballasts leave me, my elbows rest in sea-gaps,
I skirt sierras, my palms cover continents,
I am afoot with my vision.

By the city's quadrangular houses—in log huts, camping
with lumbermen,
Along the ruts of the turnpike, along the dry gulch and
rivulet bed,
Weeding my onion-patch or hoeing rows of carrots and
parsnips, crossing savannas, trailing in forests,
Prospecting, gold-digging, girdling the trees of a new
purchase,
Scorch'd ankle-deep by the hot sand, hauling my boat down
the shallow river,

Where the panther walks to and fro on a limb overhead,
where the buck turns furiously at the hunter,
Where the rattlesnake suns his flabby length on a rock,
where the otter is feeding on fish,
Where the alligator in his tough pimples sleeps by the bayou,
Where the black bear is searching for roots or honey, where
the beaver pats the mud with his paddle-shaped tail;
Over the growing sugar, over the yellow-flower'd cotton
plant, over the rice in its low moist field,
Over the sharp-peak'd farm house, with its scallop'd scum
and slender shoots from the gutters,
Over the western persimmon, over the long-leav'd corn,
over the delicate blue-flower flax,
Over the white and brown buckwheat, a hummer and
buzzer there with the rest,
Over the dusky green of the rye as it ripples and shades in
the breeze;
Scaling mountains, pulling myself cautiously up, holding on
by low scragged limbs,
Walking the path worn in the grass and beat through the
leaves of the brush,
Where the quail is whistling betwixt the woods and the
wheat-lot,
Where the bat flies in the Seventh-month eve, where the
great goldbug drops through the dark,
Where the brook puts out of the roots of the old tree and
flows to the meadow,
Where cattle stand and shake away flies with the tremulous
shuddering of their hides,
Where the cheese-cloth hangs in the kitchen, where
andirons straddle the hearth-slab, where cobwebs fall in
festoons from the rafters;
Where trip-hammers crash, where the press is whirling its
cylinders,
Wherever the human heart beats with terrible throes under
its ribs,
Where the pear-shaped balloon is floating aloft, (floating in
it myself and looking composedly down,)
Where the life-car is drawn on the slip-noose, where the
heat hatches pale-green eggs in the dented sand,

Where the she-whale swims with her calf and never forsakes it,
Where the steam-ship trails hind-ways its long pennant of
smoke,
Where the fin of the shark cuts like a black chip out of the
water,
Where the half-burn'd brig is riding on unknown currents,
Where shells grow to her slimy deck, where the dead are
corrupting below;
Where the dense-starr'd flag is borne at the head of the
regiments,
Approaching Manhattan up by the long-stretching island,
Under Niagara, the cataract falling like a veil over my
countenance,
Upon a door-step, upon the horse-block of hard wood
outside,
Upon the race-course, or enjoying picnics or jigs or a good
game of base-ball,
At he-festivals, with blackguard gibes, ironical license, bull-
dances, drinking, laughter,
At the cider-mill tasting the sweets of the brown mash,
sucking the juice through a straw,
At apple-peelings wanting kisses for all the red fruit I find,
At musters, beach-parties, friendly bees, huskings, house-
raisings;
Where the mocking-bird sounds his delicious gurgles,
cackles, screams, weeps,
Where the hay-rick stands in the barn-yard, where the dry-
stalks are scatter'd, where the brood-cow waits in the
hovel,
Where the bull advances to do his masculine work, where
the stud to the mare, where the cock is treading the
hen,
Where the heifers browse, where geese nip their food with
short jerks,
Where sun-down shadows lengthen over the limitless and
lonesome prairie,
Where herds of buffalo make a crawling spread of the square
miles far and near,
Where the humming-bird shimmers, where the neck of the
long-lived swan is curving and winding,

Where the laughing-gull scoots by the shore, where she
laughs her near-human laugh,
Where bee-hives range on a gray bench in the garden half
hid by the high weeds,
Where band-neck'd partridges roost in a ring on the ground
with their heads out,
Where burial coaches enter the arch'd gates of a cemetery,
Where winter wolves bark amid wastes of snow and icicled
trees,
Where the yellow-crown'd heron comes to the edge of the
marsh at night and feeds upon small crabs,
Where the splash of swimmers and divers cools the warm
noon,
Where the katy-did works her chromatic reed on the
walnut-tree over the well,
Through patches of citrons and cucumbers with silver-wired
leaves,
Through the salt-lick or orange glade, or under conical firs,
Through the gymnasium, through the curtain'd saloon,
through the office or public hall;
Pleas'd with the native and pleas'd with the foreign, pleas'd
with the new and old,
Pleas'd with the homely woman as well as the handsome,
Pleas'd with the quakeress as she puts off her bonnet and
talks melodiously,
Pleas'd with the tune of the choir of the whitewash'd
church,
Pleas'd with the earnest words of the sweating Methodist
preacher, impress'd seriously at the camp-meeting;
Looking in at the shop-windows of Broadway the whole
forenoon, flatting the flesh of my nose on the thick
plate glass,
Wandering the same afternoon with my face turn'd up to
the clouds, or down a lane or along the beach,
My right and left arms round the sides of two friends, and I
in the middle;
Coming home with the silent and dark-cheek'd bush-boy,
(behind me he rides at the drape of the day,)
Far from the settlements studying the print of animals' feet,
or the moccasin print,

By the cot in the hospital reaching lemonade to a feverish
patient,
Nigh the coffin'd corpse when all is still, examining with a
candle;
Voyaging to every port to dicker and adventure,
Hurrying with the modern crowd as eager and fickle as any,
Hot toward one I hate, ready in my madness to knife him,
Solitary at midnight in my back yard, my thoughts gone
from me a long while,
Walking the old hills of Judæa with the beautiful gentle God
by my side,
Speeding through space, speeding through heaven and the
stars,
Speeding amid the seven satellites and the broad ring, and
the diameter of eighty thousand miles,
Speeding with tail'd meteors, throwing fire-balls like the rest,
Carrying the crescent child that carries its own full mother
in its belly,
Storming, enjoying, planning, loving, cautioning,
Backing and filling, appearing and disappearing,
I tread day and night such roads.

I visit the orchards of spheres and look at the product,
And look at quintillions ripen'd and look at quintillions green.

I fly those flights of a fluid and swallowing soul,
My course runs below the soundings of plummets.

I help myself to material and immaterial,
No guard can shut me off, no law prevent me.

I anchor my ship for a little while only,
My messengers continually cruise away or bring their returns
to me.

I go hunting polar furs and the seal, leaping chasms with a
pike-pointed staff, clinging to topples of brittle and blue.

I ascend to the foretruck,
I take my place late at night in the crow's-nest,

We sail the arctic sea, it is plenty light enough,
Through the clear atmosphere I stretch around on the
wonderful beauty,
The enormous masses of ice pass me and I pass them, the
scenery is plain in all directions,
The white-topt mountains show in the distance, I fling out
my fancies toward them,
We are approaching some great battle-field in which we are
soon to be engaged,
We pass the colossal outposts of the encampment, we pass
with still feet and caution,
Or we are entering by the suburbs some vast and ruin'd city,
The blocks and fallen architecture more than all the living
cities of the globe.

I am a free companion, I bivouac by invading watchfires,
I turn the bridegroom out of bed and stay with the bride
myself,
I tighten her all night to my thighs and lips.

My voice is the wife's voice, the screech by the rail of the
stairs,
They fetch my man's body up dripping and drown'd.

I understand the large hearts of heroes,
The courage of present times and all times,
How the skipper saw the crowded and rudderless wreck of
the steam-ship, and Death chasing it up and down the
storm,
How he knuckled tight and gave not back an inch, and was
faithful of days and faithful of nights,
And chalk'd in large letters on a board, *Be of good cheer, we
will not desert you;*
How he follow'd with them and tack'd with them three
days and would not give it up,
How he saved the drifting company at last,
How the lank loose-gown'd women look'd when boated
from the side of their prepared graves,

How the silent old-faced infants and the lifted sick, and the
sharp-lipp'd unshaved men;
All this I swallow, it tastes good, I like it well, it becomes
mine,
I am the man, I suffer'd, I was there.

The disdain and calmness of martyrs,
The mother of old, condemn'd for a witch, burnt with dry
wood, her children gazing on,
The hounded slave that flags in the race, leans by the fence,
blowing, cover'd with sweat,
The twinges that sting like needles his legs and neck, the
murderous buckshot and the bullets,
All these I feel or am.

I am the hounded slave, I wince at the bite of the dogs,
Hell and despair are upon me, crack and again crack the
marksmen,
I clutch the rails of the fence, my gore dribs, thinn'd with
the ooze of my skin,
I fall on the weeds and stones,
The riders spur their unwilling horses, haul close,
Taunt my dizzy ears and beat me violently over the head
with whip-stocks.

Agonies are one of my changes of garments,
I do not ask the wounded person how he feels, I myself
become the wounded person,
My hurts turn livid upon me as I lean on a cane and observe.

I am the mash'd fireman with breast-bone broken,
Tumbling walls buried me in their debris,
Heat and smoke I inspired, I heard the yelling shouts of my
comrades,
I heard the distant click of their picks and shovels,
They have clear'd the beams away, they tenderly lift me forth.

I lie in the night air in my red shirt, the pervading hush is
for my sake,
Painless after all I lie exhausted but not so unhappy,

White and beautiful are the faces around me, the heads are
bared of their fire-caps,
The kneeling crowd fades with the light of the torches.

Distant and dead resuscitate,
They show as the dial or move as the hands of me, I am the
clock myself.

I am an old artillerist, I tell of my fort's bombardment,
I am there again.

Again the long roll of the drummers,
Again the attacking cannon, mortars,
Again to my listening ears the cannon responsive.

I take part, I see and hear the whole,
The cries, curses, roar, the plaudits for well-aim'd shots,
The ambulanza slowly passing trailing its red drip,
Workmen searching after damages, making indispensable
repairs,
The fall of grenades through the rent roof, the fan-shaped
explosion,
The whizz of limbs, heads, stone, wood, iron, high in the air.

Again gurgles the mouth of my dying general, he furiously
waves with his hand,
He gasps through the clot *Mind not me—mind—the
entrenchments.*

34

Now I tell what I knew in Texas in my early youth,
(I tell not the fall of Alamo,
Not one escaped to tell the fall of Alamo,
The hundred and fifty are dumb yet at Alamo,)
'Tis the tale of the murder in cold blood of four hundred
and twelve young men.

Retreating they had form'd in a hollow square with their
baggage for breastworks,

Nine hundred lives out of the surrounding enemy's, nine
times their number, was the price they took in advance,
Their colonel was wounded and their ammunition gone,
They treated for an honorable capitulation, receiv'd writing
and seal, gave up their arms and march'd back prisoners
of war.

They were the glory of the race of rangers,
Matchless with horse, rifle, song, supper, courtship,
Large, turbulent, generous, handsome, proud, and
affectionate,
Bearded, sunburnt, drest in the free costume of hunters,
Not a single one over thirty years of age.

The second First-day morning they were brought out in
squads and massacred, it was beautiful early summer,
The work commenced about five o'clock and was over by
eight.

None obey'd the command to kneel,
Some made a mad and helpless rush, some stood stark and
straight,
A few fell at once, shot in the temple or heart, the living
and dead lay together,
The maim'd and mangled dug in the dirt, the new-comers
saw them there,
Some half-kill'd attempted to crawl away,
These were despatch'd with bayonets or batter'd with the
blunts of muskets,
A youth not seventeen years old seiz'd his assassin till two
more came to release him,
The three were all torn and cover'd with the boy's blood.

At eleven o'clock began the burning of the bodies;
That is the tale of the murder of the four hundred and
twelve young men.

35

Would you hear of an old-time sea-fight?
Would you learn who won by the light of the moon and
stars?

List to the yarn, as my grandmother's father the sailor told
it to me.

Our foe was no skulk in his ship I tell you, (said he,)
His was the surly English pluck, and there is no tougher or
truer, and never was, and never will be;
Along the lower'd eve he came horribly raking us.

We closed with him, the yards entangled, the cannon touch'd,
My captain lash'd fast with his own hands.

We had receiv'd some eighteen pound shots under the water,
On our lower-gun-deck two large pieces had burst at the
first fire, killing all around and blowing up overhead.

Fighting at sun-down, fighting at dark,
Ten o'clock at night, the full moon well up, our leaks on
the gain, and five feet of water reported,
The master-at-arms loosing the prisoners confined in the
after-hold to give them a chance for themselves.

The transit to and from the magazine is now stopt by the
sentinels,
They see so many strange faces they do not know whom to
trust.

Our frigate takes fire,
The other asks if we demand quarter?
If our colors are struck and the fighting done?

Now I laugh content, for I hear the voice of my little captain,
We have not struck, he composedly cries, *we have just begun
our part of the fighting.*

Only three guns are in use,
One is directed by the captain himself against the enemy's
mainmast,
Two well serv'd with grape and canister silence his musketry
and clear his decks.

The tops alone second the fire of this little battery,
especially the main-top,
They hold out bravely during the whole of the action.

Not a moment's cease,
The leaks gain fast on the pumps, the fire eats toward the
powder-magazine.

One of the pumps has been shot away, it is generally thought
we are sinking.

Serene stands the little captain,
He is not hurried, his voice is neither high nor low,
His eyes give more light to us than our battle-lanterns.

Toward twelve there in the beams of the moon they
surrender to us.

36

Stretch'd and still lies the midnight,
Two great hulls motionless on the breast of the darkness,
Our vessel riddled and slowly sinking, preparations to pass
to the one we have conquer'd,
The captain on the quarter-deck coldly giving his orders
through a countenance white as a sheet,
Near by the corpse of the child that serv'd in the cabin,
The dead face of an old salt with long white hair and
carefully curl'd whiskers,
The flames spite of all that can be done flickering aloft and
below,
The husky voices of the two or three officers yet fit for duty,
Formless stacks of bodies and bodies by themselves, dabs of
flesh upon the masts and spars,
Cut of cordage, dangle of rigging, slight shock of the
soothe of waves,
Black and impassive guns, litter of powder-parcels, strong
scent,
A few large stars overhead, silent and mournful shining,
Delicate sniffs of sea-breeze, smells of sedgy grass and fields
by the shore, death-messages given in charge to survivors,

The hiss of the surgeon's knife, the gnawing teeth of his saw,
Wheeze, cluck, swash of falling blood, short wild scream,
and long, dull, tapering groan,
These so, these irretrievable.

37

You laggards there on guard! look to your arms!
In at the conquer'd doors they crowd! I am possess'd!
Embody all presences outlaw'd or suffering,
See myself in prison shaped like another man,
And feel the dull unintermitted pain.

For me the keepers of convicts shoulder their carbines and
keep watch,
It is I let out in the morning and barr'd at night.

Not a mutineer walks handcuff'd to jail but I am handcuff'd
to him and walk by his side,
(I am less the jolly one there, and more the silent one with
sweat on my twitching lips.)

Not a youngster is taken for larceny but I go up too, and
am tried and sentenced.

Not a cholera patient lies at the last gasp but I also lie at
the last gasp,
My face is ash-color'd, my sinews gnarl, away from me
people retreat.

Askers embody themselves in me and I am embodied in them,
I project my hat, sit shame-faced, and beg.

38

Enough! enough! enough!
Somehow I have been stunn'd. Stand back!
Give me a little time beyond my cuff'd head, slumbers,
dreams, gaping,
I discover myself on the verge of a usual mistake.

That I could forget the mockers and insults!
That I could forget the trickling tears and the blows of the
bludgeons and hammers!
That I could look with a separate look on my own crucifixion
and bloody crowning.

I remember now,
I resume the overstaid fraction,
The grave of rock multiplies what has been confided to it,
or to any graves,
Corpses rise, gashes heal, fastenings roll from me.

I troop forth replenish'd with supreme power, one of an
average unending procession,
Inland and sea-coast we go, and pass all boundary lines,
Our swift ordinances on their way over the whole earth,
The blossoms we wear in our hats the growth of thousands
of years.

Eleves, I salute you! come forward!
Continue your annotations, continue your questionings.

39

The friendly and flowing savage, who is he?
Is he waiting for civilization, or past it and mastering it?

Is he some Southwesterner rais'd out-doors? is he Kanadian?
Is he from the Mississippi country? Iowa, Oregon, California?
The mountains? prairie-life, bush-life? or sailor from the sea?

Wherever he goes men and women accept and desire him,
They desire he should like them, touch them, speak to
them, stay with them.

Behavior lawless as snow-flakes, words simple as grass,
uncomb'd head, laughter, and naivetè,
Slow-stepping feet, common features, common modes and
emanations,
They descend in new forms from the tips of his fingers,
They are wafted with the odor of his body or breath, they
fly out of the glance of his eyes.

40

Flaunt of the sunshine I need not your bask—lie over!
You light surfaces only, I force surfaces and depths also.

Earth! you seem to look for something at my hands,
Say, old top-knot, what do you want?

Man or woman, I might tell how I like you, but cannot,
And might tell what it is in me and what it is in you, but
cannot,
And might tell that pining I have, that pulse of my nights
and days.

Behold, I do not give lectures or a little charity,
When I give I give myself.

You there, impotent, loose in the knees,
Open your scarf'd chops till I blow grit within you,
Spread your palms and lift the flaps of your pockets,
I am not to be denied, I compel, I have stores plenty and
to spare,
And any thing I have I bestow.

I do not ask who you are, that is not important to me,
You can do nothing and be nothing but what I will
infold you.

To cotton-field drudge or cleaner of privies I lean,
On his right cheek I put the family kiss,
And in my soul I swear I never will deny him.

On women fit for conception I start bigger and nimbler babes,
(This day I am jetting the stuff of far more arrogant republics.)

To any one dying, thither I speed and twist the knob of the
door,
Turn the bed-clothes toward the foot of the bed,
Let the physician and the priest go home.

I seize the descending man and raise him with resistless will,
O despairer, here is my neck,
By God, you shall not go down! hang your whole weight
upon me.

I dilate you with tremendous breath, I buoy you up,
Every room of the house do I fill with an arm'd force,
Lovers of me, bafflers of graves.

Sleep—I and they keep guard all night,
Not doubt, not decease shall dare to lay finger upon you,
I have embraced you, and henceforth possess you to myself,
And when you rise in the morning you will find what I tell
you is so.

41

I am he bringing help for the sick as they pant on their backs,
And for strong upright men I bring yet more needed help.

I heard what was said of the universe,
Heard it and heard it of several thousand years;
It is middling well as far as it goes—but is that all?

Magnifying and applying come I,
Outbidding at the start the old cautious hucksters,
Taking myself the exact dimensions of Jehovah,
Lithographing Kronos, Zeus his son, and Hercules his
grandson,
Buying drafts of Osiris, Isis, Belus, Brahma, Buddha,
In my portfolio placing Manito loose, Allah on a leaf, the
crucifix engraved,
With Odin and the hideous-faced Mexitli and every idol
and image,
Taking them all for what they are worth and not a cent more,
Admitting they were alive and did the work of their days,
(They bore mites as for unfledg'd birds who have now to
rise and fly and sing for themselves,)
Accepting the rough deific sketches to fill out better in myself,
bestowing them freely on each man and woman I see,
Discovering as much or more in a framer framing a house,

Putting higher claims for him there with his roll'd-up sleeves
driving the mallet and chisel,
Not objecting to special revelations, considering a curl of
smoke or a hair on the back of my hand just as curious
as any revelation,
Lads ahold of fire-engines and hook-and-ladder ropes no
less to me than the gods of the antique wars,
Minding their voices peal through the crash of destruction,
Their brawny limbs passing safe over charr'd laths, their
white foreheads whole and unhurt out of the flames;
By the mechanic's wife with her babe at her nipple interceding
for every person born,
Three scythes at harvest whizzing in a row from three lusty
angels with shirts bagg'd out at their waists,
The snag-tooth'd hostler with red hair redeeming sins past
and to come,
Selling all he possesses, traveling on foot to fee lawyers for
his brother and sit by him while he is tried for forgery;
What was strewn in the amplest strewing the square rod
about me, and not filling the square rod then,
The bull and the bug never worshipp'd half enough,
Dung and dirt more admirable than was dream'd,
The supernatural of no account, myself waiting my time to
be one of the supremes,
The day getting ready for me when I shall do as much good
as the best, and be as prodigious;
By my life-lumps! becoming already a creator,
Putting myself here and now to the ambush'd womb of the
shadows.

42

A call in the midst of the crowd,
My own voice, orotund sweeping and final.

Come my children,
Come my boys and girls, my women, household and
intimates,
Now the performer launches his nerve, he has pass'd his
prelude on the reeds within.

Easily written loose-finger'd chords—I feel the thrum of
your climax and close.

My head slues round on my neck,
Music rolls, but not from the organ,
Folks are around me, but they are no household of mine.

Ever the hard unsunk ground,
Ever the eaters and drinkers, ever the upward and downward
sun, ever the air and the ceaseless tides,
Ever myself and my neighbors, refreshing, wicked, real,
Ever the old inexplicable query, ever that thorn'd thumb,
that breath of itches and thirsts,
Ever the vexer's *hoot! hoot!* till we find where the sly one
hides and bring him forth,
Ever love, ever the sobbing liquid of life,
Ever the bandage under the chin, ever the trestles of death.

Here and there with dimes on the eyes walking,
To feed the greed of the belly the brains liberally spooning,
Tickets buying, taking, selling, but in to the feast never
once going.
Many sweating, ploughing, thrashing, and then the chaff for
payment receiving,
A few idly owning, and they the wheat continually claiming.

This is the city and I am one of the citizens,
Whatever interests the rest interests me, politics, wars,
markets, newspapers, schools,
The mayor and councils, banks, tariffs, steamships, factories,
stocks, stores, real estate and personal estate.

The little plentiful manikins skipping around in collars and
tail'd coats,
I am aware who they are, (they are positively not worms or
fleas,)
I acknowledge the duplicates of myself, the weakest and
shallowest is deathless with me,
What I do and say the same waits for them,
Every thought that flounders in me the same flounders in
them.

I know perfectly well my own egotism,
Know my omnivorous lines and must not write any less,
And would fetch you whoever you are flush with myself.

Not words of routine this song of mine,
But abruptly to question, to leap beyond yet nearer bring;
This printed and bound book—but the printer and the printing-office boy?
The well-taken photographs—but your wife or friend close and solid in your arms?
The black ship mail'd with iron, her mighty guns in her turrets—but the pluck of the captain and engineers?
In the houses the dishes and fare and furniture—but the host and hostess, and the look out of their eyes?
The sky up there—yet here or next door, or across the way?
The saints and sages in history—but you yourself?
Sermons, creeds, theology—but the fathomless human brain,
And what is reason? and what is love? and what is life?

43

I do not despise you priests, all time, the world over,
My faith is the greatest of faiths and the least of faiths,
Enclosing worship ancient and modern and all between ancient and modern,
Believing I shall come again upon the earth after five thousand years,
Waiting responses from oracles, honoring the gods, saluting the sun,
Making a fetich of the first rock or stump, powowing with sticks in the circle of obis,
Helping the llama or brahmin as he trims the lamps of the idols,
Dancing yet through the streets in a phallic procession, rapt and austere in the woods a gymnosophist,
Drinking mead from the skull-cup, to Shastas and Vedas admirant, minding the Koran,
Walking the teokallis, spotted with gore from the stone and knife, beating the serpent-skin drum,

Accepting the Gospels, accepting him that was crucified,
knowing assuredly that he is divine,
To the mass kneeling or the puritan's prayer rising, or
sitting patiently in a pew,
Ranting and frothing in my insane crisis, or waiting dead-
like till my spirit arouses me,
Looking forth on pavement and land, or outside of pavement
and land,
Belonging to the winders of the circuit of circuits.

One of that centripetal and centrifugal gang I turn and talk
like a man leaving charges before a journey.

Down-hearted doubters dull and excluded,
Frivolous, sullen, moping, angry, affected, dishearten'd,
atheistical,
I know every one of you, I know the sea of torment, doubt,
despair and unbelief.

How the flukes splash!
How they contort rapid as lightning, with spasms and spouts
of blood!

Be at peace bloody flukes of doubters and sullen mopers,
I take my place among you as much as among any,
The past is the push of you, me, all, precisely the same,
And what is yet untried and afterward is for you, me, all,
precisely the same.

I do not know what is untried and afterward,
But I know it will in its turn prove sufficient, and cannot fail.

Each who passes is consider'd, each who stops is consider'd,
not a single one can it fail.

It cannot fail the young man who died and was buried,
Nor the young woman who died and was put by his side,
Nor the little child that peep'd in at the door, and then
drew back and was never seen again,

Nor the old man who has lived without purpose, and feels it with bitterness worse than gall,
Nor him in the poor house tubercled by rum and the bad disorder,
Nor the numberless slaughter'd and wreck'd, nor the brutish koboo call'd the ordure of humanity,
Nor the sacs merely floating with open mouths for food to slip in,
Nor any thing in the earth, or down in the oldest graves of the earth,
Nor any thing in the myriads of spheres, nor the myriads of myriads that inhabit them,
Nor the present, nor the least wisp that is known.

44

It is time to explain myself—let us stand up.

What is known I strip away,
I launch all men and women forward with me into the Unknown.

The clock indicates the moment—but what does eternity indicate?

We have thus far exhausted trillions of winters and summers,
There are trillions ahead, and trillions ahead of them.

Births have brought us richness and variety,
And other births will bring us richness and variety.

I do not call one greater and one smaller,
That which fills its period and place is equal to any.

Were mankind murderous or jealous upon you, my brother, my sister?
I am sorry for you, they are not murderous or jealous upon me,
All has been gentle with me, I keep no account with lamentation,
(What have I to do with lamentation?)

I am an acme of things accomplish'd, and I an encloser of
things to be.

My feet strike an apex of the apices of the stairs,
On every step bunches of ages, and larger bunches between
the steps,
All below duly travel'd, and still I mount and mount.

Rise after rise bow the phantoms behind me,
Afar down I see the huge first Nothing, I know I was even
there,
I waited unseen and always, and slept through the lethargic
mist,
And took my time, and took no hurt from the fetid carbon.

Long I was hugg'd close—long and long.

Immense have been the preparations for me,
Faithful and friendly the arms that have help'd me.

Cycles ferried my cradle, rowing and rowing like cheerful
boatmen,
For room to me stars kept aside in their own rings,
They sent influences to look after what was to hold me.

Before I was born out of my mother generations guided me,
My embryo has never been torpid, nothing could overlay it.

For it the nebula cohered to an orb,
The long slow strata piled to rest it on,
Vast vegetables gave it sustenance,
Monstrous sauroids transported it in their mouths and
deposited it with care.

All forces have been steadily employ'd to complete and
delight me,
Now on this spot I stand with my robust soul.

45

O span of youth! ever-push'd elasticity!
O manhood, balanced, florid and full.

My lovers suffocate me,
Crowding my lips, thick in the pores of my skin,
Jostling me through streets and public halls, coming naked
to me at night,
Crying by day *Ahoy!* from the rocks of the river, swinging
and chirping over my head,
Calling my name from flower-beds, vines, tangled underbrush,
Lighting on every moment of my life,
Bussing my body with soft balsamic busses,
Noiselessly passing handfuls out of their hearts and giving
them to be mine.

Old age superbly rising! O welcome, ineffable grace of
dying days!

Every condition promulges not only itself, it promulges what
grows after and out of itself,
And the dark hush promulges as much as any.

I open my scuttle at night and see the far-sprinkled systems,
And all I see multiplied as high as I can cipher edge but the
rim of the farther systems.

Wider and wider they spread, expanding, always expanding,
Outward and outward and forever outward.

My sun has his sun and round him obediently wheels,
He joins with his partners a group of superior circuit,
And greater sets follow, making specks of the greatest inside
them.

There is no stoppage and never can be stoppage,
If I, you, and the worlds, and all beneath or upon their
surfaces, were this moment reduced back to a pallid
float, it would not avail in the long run,
We should surely bring up again where we now stand,
And surely go as much farther, and then farther and farther.

A few quadrillions of eras, a few octillions of cubic leagues,
do not hazard the span or make it impatient,
They are but parts, any thing is but a part.

See ever so far, there is limitless space outside of that,
Count ever so much, there is limitless time around that.

My rendezvous is appointed, it is certain,
The Lord will be there and wait till I come on perfect terms,
The great Camerado, the lover true for whom I pine will be there.

46

I know I have the best of time and space, and was never measured and never will be measured.

I tramp a perpetual journey, (come listen all!)
My signs are a rain-proof coat, good shoes, and a staff cut from the woods,
No friend of mine takes his ease in my chair,
I have no chair, no church, no philosophy,
I lead no man to a dinner-table, library, exchange,
But each man and each woman of you I lead upon a knoll,
My left hand hooking you round the waist,
My right hand pointing to landscapes of continents and the public road.

Not I, not any one else can travel that road for you,
You must travel it for yourself.

It is not far, it is within reach,
Perhaps you have been on it since you were born and did not know,
Perhaps it is everywhere on water and on land.

Shoulder your duds dear son, and I will mine, and let us hasten forth,
Wonderful cities and free nations we shall fetch as we go.

If you tire, give me both burdens, and rest the chuff of your hand on my hip,
And in due time you shall repay the same service to me,
For after we start we never lie by again.

This day before dawn I ascended a hill and look'd at the
crowded heaven,
And I said to my spirit *When we become the enfolders of those orbs, and the pleasure and knowledge of every thing in them, shall we be fill'd and satisfied then?*
And my spirit said *No, we but level that lift to pass and continue beyond.*

You are also asking me questions and I hear you,
I answer that I cannot answer, you must find out for yourself.

Sit a while dear son,
Here are biscuits to eat and here is milk to drink,
But as soon as you sleep and renew yourself in sweet
clothes, I kiss you with a good-by kiss and open the
gate for your egress hence.

Long enough have you dream'd contemptible dreams,
Now I wash the gum from your eyes,
You must habit yourself to the dazzle of the light and of
every moment of your life.

Long have you timidly waded holding a plank by the shore,
Now I will you to be a bold swimmer,
To jump off in the midst of the sea, rise again, nod to me,
shout, and laughingly dash with your hair.

47

I am the teacher of athletes,
He that by me spreads a wider breast than my own proves
the width of my own,
He most honors my style who learns under it to destroy the
teacher.

The boy I love, the same becomes a man not through
derived power, but in his own right,
Wicked rather than virtuous out of conformity or fear,
Fond of his sweetheart, relishing well his steak,
Unrequited love or a slight cutting him worse than sharp
steel cuts,

First-rate to ride, to fight, to hit the bull's eye, to sail a skiff, to sing a song or play on the banjo,
Preferring scars and the beard and faces pitted with small-pox over all latherers,
And those well-tann'd to those that keep out of the sun.

I teach straying from me, yet who can stray from me?
I follow you whoever you are from the present hour,
My words itch at your ears till you understand them.

I do not say these things for a dollar or to fill up the time while I wait for a boat,
(It is you talking just as much as myself, I act as the tongue of you,
Tied in your mouth, in mine it begins to be loosen'd.)

I swear I will never again mention love or death inside a house,
And I swear I will never translate myself at all, only to him or her who privately stays with me in the open air.

If you would understand me go to the heights or water-shore,
The nearest gnat is an explanation, and a drop or motion of waves a key,
The maul, the oar, the hand-saw, second my words.

No shutter'd room or school can commune with me,
But roughs and little children better than they.

The young mechanic is closest to me, he knows me well,
The woodman that takes his axe and jug with him shall take me with him all day,
The farm-boy ploughing in the field feels good at the sound of my voice,
In vessels that sail my words sail, I go with fishermen and seamen and love them.

The soldier camp'd or upon the march is mine,
On the night ere the pending battle many seek me, and I do not fail them,
On that solemn night (it may be their last) those that know me seek me.

My face rubs to the hunter's face when he lies down alone
in his blanket,
The driver thinking of me does not mind the jolt of his
wagon,
The young mother and old mother comprehend me,
The girl and the wife rest the needle a moment and forget
where they are,
They and all would resume what I have told them.

48

I have said that the soul is not more than the body,
And I have said that the body is not more than the soul,
And nothing, not God, is greater to one than one's self is,
And whoever walks a furlong without sympathy walks to his
own funeral drest in his shroud,
And I or you pocketless of a dime may purchase the pick of
the earth,
And to glance with an eye or show a bean in its pod
confounds the learning of all times,
And there is no trade or employment but the young man
following it may become a hero,
And there is no object so soft but it makes a hub for the
wheel'd universe,
And I say to any man or woman, Let your soul stand cool
and composed before a million universes.

And I say to mankind, Be not curious about God,
For I who am curious about each am not curious about God,
(No array of terms can say how much I am at peace about
God and about death.)

I hear and behold God in every object, yet understand God
not in the least,
Nor do I understand who there can be more wonderful
than myself.

Why should I wish to see God better than this day?
I see something of God each hour of the twenty-four, and
each moment then,

In the faces of men and women I see God, and in my own face in the glass,
I find letters from God dropt in the street, and every one is sign'd by God's name,
And I leave them where they are, for I know that wheresoe'er I go,
Others will punctually come for ever and ever.

49

And as to you Death, and you bitter hug of mortality, it is idle to try to alarm me.

To his work without flinching the accoucheur comes,
I see the elder-hand pressing receiving supporting,
I recline by the sills of the exquisite flexible doors,
And mark the outlet, and mark the relief and escape.

And as to you Corpse I think you are good manure, but that does not offend me,
I smell the white roses sweet-scented and growing,
I reach to the leafy lips, I reach to the polish'd breasts of melons.

And as to you Life I reckon you are the leavings of many deaths,
(No doubt I have died myself ten thousand times before.)

I hear you whispering there O stars of heaven,
O suns—O grass of graves—O perpetual transfers and promotions,
If you do not say any thing how can I say any thing?

Of the turbid pool that lies in the autumn forest,
Of the moon that descends the steeps of the soughing twilight,
Toss, sparkles of day and dusk—toss on the black stems that decay in the muck,
Toss to the moaning gibberish of the dry limbs.

I ascend from the moon, I ascend from the night,
I perceive that the ghastly glimmer is noonday sunbeams reflected,
And debouch to the steady and central from the offspring great or small.

50

There is that in me—I do not know what it is—but I know it is in me.

Wrench'd and sweaty—calm and cool then my body becomes,
I sleep—I sleep long.

I do not know it—it is without name—it is a word unsaid,
It is not in any dictionary, utterance, symbol.

Something it swings on more than the earth I swing on,
To it the creation is the friend whose embracing awakes me.

Perhaps I might tell more. Outlines! I plead for my brothers and sisters.

Do you see O my brothers and sisters?
It is not chaos or death—it is form, union, plan—it is eternal life—it is Happiness.

51

The past and present wilt—I have fill'd them, emptied them.
And proceed to fill my next fold of the future.

Listener up there! what have you to confide to me?
Look in my face while I snuff the sidle of evening,
(Talk honestly, no one else hears you, and I stay only a minute longer.)

Do I contradict myself?
Very well then I contradict myself,
(I am large, I contain multitudes.)

I concentrate toward them that are nigh, I wait on the
door-slab.

Who has done his day's work? who will soonest be through
with his supper?
Who wishes to walk with me?

Will you speak before I am gone? will you prove already
too late?

52

The spotted hawk swoops by and accuses me, he complains
of my gab and my loitering.

I too am not a bit tamed, I too am untranslatable,
I sound my barbaric yawp over the roofs of the world.

The last scud of day holds back for me,
It flings my likeness after the rest and true as any on the
shadow'd wilds,
It coaxes me to the vapor and the dusk.

I depart as air, I shake my white locks at the runaway sun,
I effuse my flesh in eddies, and drift it in lacy jags.

I bequeath myself to the dirt to grow from the grass I love,
If you want me again look for me under your boot-soles.

You will hardly know who I am or what I mean,
But I shall be good health to you nevertheless,
And filter and fibre your blood.

Failing to fetch me at first keep encouraged,
Missing me one place search another,
I stop somewhere waiting for you.

Children of Adam

To the Garden the World

To the garden the world anew ascending,
Potent mates, daughters, sons, preluding,
The love, the life of their bodies, meaning and being,
Curious here behold my resurrection after slumber,
The revolving cycles in their wide sweep having brought me
again,
Amorous, mature, all beautiful to me, all wondrous,
My limbs and the quivering fire that ever plays through
them, for reasons, most wondrous,
Existing I peer and penetrate still,
Content with the present, content with the past,
By my side or back of me Eve following,
Or in front, and I following her just the same.

From Pent-up Aching Rivers

From pent-up aching rivers,
From that of myself without which I were nothing,
From what I am determin'd to make illustrious, even if I
stand sole among men,
From my own voice resonant, singing the phallus,
Singing the song of procreation,
Singing the need of superb children and therein superb
grown people,
Singing the muscular urge and the blending,
Singing the bedfellow's song, (O resistless yearning!
O for any and each the body correlative attracting!
O for you whoever you are your correlative body! O it,
more than all else, you delighting!)
From the hungry gnaw that eats me night and day,
From native moments, from bashful pains, singing them,
Seeking something yet unfound though I have diligently
sought it many a long year,
Singing the true song of the soul fitful at random,

Renascent with grossest Nature or among animals,
Of that, of them and what goes with them my poems
informing,
Of the smell of apples and lemons, of the pairing of birds,
Of the wet of woods, of the lapping of waves,
Of the mad pushes of waves upon the land, I them chanting,
The overture lightly sounding, the strain anticipating,
The welcome nearness, the sight of the perfect body,
The swimmer swimming naked in the bath, or motionless
on his back lying and floating,
The female form approaching, I pensive, love-flesh
tremulous aching,
The divine list for myself or you or for any one making,
The face, the limbs, the index from head to foot, and what
it arouses,
The mystic deliria, the madness amorous, the utter
abandonment,
(Hark close and still what I now whisper to you,
I love you, O you entirely possess me,
O that you and I escape from the rest and go utterly off,
free and lawless,
Two hawks in the air, two fishes swimming in the sea not
more lawless than we;)
The furious storm through me careering, I passionately
trembling.
The oath of the inseparableness of two together, of the
woman that loves me and whom I love more than my
life, that oath swearing,
(O I willingly stake all for you,
O let me be lost if it must be so!
O you and I! what is it to us what the rest do or think?
What is all else to us? only that we enjoy each other and
exhaust each other if it must be so;)
From the master, the pilot I yield the vessel to,
The general commanding me, commanding all, from him
permission taking,
From time the programme hastening, (I have loiter'd too
long as it is,)
From sex, from the warp and from the woof,
From privacy, from frequent repinings alone,

From plenty of persons near and yet the right person not near,
From the soft sliding of hands over me and thrusting of
fingers through my hair and beard,
From the long sustain'd kiss upon the mouth or bosom,
From the close pressure that makes me or any man drunk,
fainting with excess,
From what the divine husband knows, from the work of
fatherhood,
From exultation, victory and relief, from the bedfellow's
embrace in the night,
From the act-poems of eyes, hands, hips and bosoms,
From the cling of the trembling arm,
From the bending curve and the clinch,
From side by side the pliant coverlet off-throwing,
From the one so unwilling to have me leave, and me just as
unwilling to leave,
(Yet a moment O tender waiter, and I return,)
From the hour of shining stars and dropping dews,
From the night a moment I emerging flitting out,
Celebrate you act divine and you children prepared for,
And you stalwart loins.

I Sing the Body Electric

1

I SING the body electric,
The armies of those I love engirth me and I engirth them,
They will not let me off till I go with them, respond to them,
And discorrupt them, and charge them full with the charge
of the soul.

Was it doubted that those who corrupt their own bodies
conceal themselves?
And if those who defile the living are as bad as they who
defile the dead?
And if the body does not do fully as much as the soul?
And if the body were not the soul, what is the soul?

2

The love of the body of man or woman balks account, the
body itself balks account,
That of the male is perfect, and that of the female is perfect.

The expression of the face balks account,
But the expression of a well-made man appears not only in
his face,
It is in his limbs and joints also, it is curiously in the joints
of his hips and wrists,
It is in his walk, the carriage of his neck, the flex of his waist
and knees, dress does not hide him,
The strong sweet quality he has strikes through the cotton
and broadcloth,
To see him pass conveys as much as the best poem, perhaps
more,
You linger to see his back, and the back of his neck and
shoulder-side.

The sprawl and fulness of babes, the bosoms and heads of
women, the folds of their dress, their style as we pass in
the street, the contour of their shape downwards,
The swimmer naked in the swimming-bath, seen as he swims
through the transparent green-shine, or lies with his face
up and rolls silently to and fro in the heave of the water,
The bending forward and backward of rowers in row-boats,
the horseman in his saddle,
Girls, mothers, house-keepers, in all their performances,
The group of laborers seated at noon-time with their open
dinner-kettles, and their wives waiting,
The female soothing a child, the farmer's daughter in the
garden or cow-yard,
The young fellow hoeing corn, the sleigh-driver driving his
six horses through the crowd,
The wrestle of wrestlers, two apprentice-boys, quite grown,
lusty, good-natured, native-born, out on the vacant lot
at sundown after work,
The coats and caps thrown down, the embrace of love and
resistance,

The upper-hold and under-hold, the hair rumpled over and blinding the eyes;
The march of firemen in their own costumes, the play of masculine muscle through clean-setting trowsers and waist-straps,
The slow return from the fire, the pause when the bell strikes suddenly again, and the listening on the alert,
The natural, perfect, varied attitudes, the bent head, the curv'd neck and the counting;
Such-like I love—I loosen myself, pass freely, am at the mother's breast with the little child,
Swim with the swimmers, wrestle with wrestlers, march in line with the firemen, and pause, listen, count.

3

I knew a man, a common farmer, the father of five sons,
And in them the fathers of sons, and in them the fathers of sons.
This man was of wonderful vigor, calmness, beauty of person,
The shape of his head, the pale yellow and white of his hair and beard, the immeasurable meaning of his black eyes, the richness and breadth of his manners,
These I used to go and visit him to see, he was wise also,
He was six feet tall, he was over eighty years old, his sons were massive, clean, bearded, tan-faced, handsome,
They and his daughters loved him, all who saw him loved him,
They did not love him by allowance, they loved him with personal love,
He drank water only, the blood show'd like scarlet through the clear-brown skin of his face,
He was a frequent gunner and fisher, he sail'd his boat himself, he had a fine one presented to him by a ship-joiner, he had fowling-pieces presented to him by men that loved him,
When he went with his five sons and many grand-sons to hunt or fish, you would pick him out as the most beautiful and vigorous of the gang,

You would wish long and long to be with him, you would
wish to sit by him in the boat that you and he might
touch each other.

4

I have perceiv'd that to be with those I like is enough,
To stop in company with the rest at evening is enough,
To be surrounded by beautiful, curious, breathing, laughing
flesh is enough,
To pass among them or touch any one, or rest my arm ever
so lightly round his or her neck for a moment, what is
this then?
I do not ask any more delight, I swim in it as in a sea.

There is something in staying close to men and women and
looking on them, and in the contact and odor of them,
that pleases the soul well,
All things please the soul, but these please the soul well.

5

This is the female form,
A divine nimbus exhales from it from head to foot,
It attracts with fierce undeniable attraction,
I am drawn by its breath as if I were no more than a helpless
vapor, all falls aside but myself and it,
Books, art, religion, time, the visible and solid earth, and
what was expected of heaven or fear'd of hell, are now
consumed,
Mad filaments, ungovernable shoots play out of it, the
response likewise ungovernable,
Hair, bosom, hips, bend of legs, negligent falling hands all
diffused, mine too diffused,
Ebb stung by the flow and flow stung by the ebb, love-flesh
swelling and deliciously aching,
Limitless limpid jets of love hot and enormous, quivering
jelly of love, white-blow and delirious juice,
Bridegroom night of love working surely and softly into the
prostrate dawn,
Undulating into the willing and yielding day,
Lost in the cleave of the clasping and sweet-flesh'd day.

This the nucleus—after the child is born of woman, man is born of woman,
This the bath of birth, this the merge of small and large, and the outlet again.

Be not ashamed women, your privilege encloses the rest, and is the exit of the rest,
You are the gates of the body, and you are the gates of the soul.

The female contains all qualities and tempers them,
She is in her place and moves with perfect balance,
She is all things duly veil'd, she is both passive and active,
She is to conceive daughters as well as sons, and sons as well as daughters.

As I see my soul reflected in Nature,
As I see through a mist, One with inexpressible completeness, sanity, beauty,
See the bent head and arms folded over the breast, the Female I see.

6

The male is not less the soul nor more, he too is in his place,
He too is all qualities, he is action and power,
The flush of the known universe is in him,
Scorn becomes him well, and appetite and defiance become him well,
The wildest largest passions, bliss that is utmost, sorrow that is utmost become him well, pride is for him,
The full-spread pride of man is calming and excellent to the soul,
Knowledge becomes him, he likes it always, he brings every thing to the test of himself,
Whatever the survey, whatever the sea and the sail he strikes soundings at last only here,
(Where else does he strike soundings except here?)

The man's body is sacred and the woman's body is sacred,
No matter who it is, it is sacred—is it the meanest one in the laborers' gang?

Is it one of the dull-faced immigrants just landed on the wharf?
Each belongs here or anywhere just as much as the well-off, just as much as you,
Each has his or her place in the procession.

(All is a procession,
The universe is a procession with measured and perfect motion.)

Do you know so much yourself that you call the meanest ignorant?
Do you suppose you have a right to a good sight, and he or she has no right to a sight?
Do you think matter has cohered together from its diffuse float, and the soil is on the surface, and water runs and vegetation sprouts,
For you only, and not for him and her?

7

A man's body at auction,
(For before the war I often go to the slave-mart and watch the sale,)
I help the auctioneer, the sloven does not half know his business.

Gentlemen look on this wonder,
Whatever the bids of the bidders they cannot be high enough for it,
For it the globe lay preparing quintillions of years without one animal or plant,
For it the revolving cycles truly and steadily roll'd.

In this head the all-baffling brain,
In it and below it the makings of heroes.

Examine these limbs, red, black, or white, they are cunning in tendon and nerve,
They shall be stript that you may see them.

Exquisite senses, life-lit eyes, pluck, volition,
Flakes of breast-muscle, pliant backbone and neck, flesh not flabby, good-sized arms and legs,
And wonders within there yet.

Within there runs blood,
The same old blood! the same red-running blood!
There swells and jets a heart, there all passions, desires, reachings, aspirations,
(Do you think they are not there because they are not express'd in parlors and lecture-rooms?)

This is not only one man, this the father of those who shall be fathers in their turns,
In him the start of populous states and rich republics,
Of him countless immortal lives with countless embodiments and enjoyments.

How do you know who shall come from the offspring of his offspring through the centuries?
(Who might you find you have come from yourself, if you could trace back through the centuries?)

8

A woman's body at auction,
She too is not only herself, she is the teeming mother of mothers,
She is the bearer of them that shall grow and be mates to the mothers.

Have you ever loved the body of a woman?
Have you ever loved the body of a man?
Do you not see that these are exactly the same to all in all nations and times all over the earth?

If any thing is sacred the human body is sacred,
And the glory and sweet of a man is the token of manhood untainted,
And in man or woman a clean, strong, firm-fibred body, is more beautiful than the most beautiful face.

Have you seen the fool that corrupted his own live body? or
the fool that corrupted her own live body?
For they do not conceal themselves, and cannot conceal
themselves.

9

O my body! I dare not desert the likes of you in other men
and women, nor the likes of the parts of you,
I believe the likes of you are to stand or fall with the likes of
the soul, (and that they are the soul,)
I believe the likes of you shall stand or fall with my poems,
and that they are my poems,
Man's, woman's, child's, youth's, wife's, husband's,
mother's, father's, young man's, young woman's poems,
Head, neck, hair, ears, drop and tympan of the ears,
Eyes, eye-fringes, iris of the eye, eyebrows, and the waking
or sleeping of the lids,
Mouth, tongue, lips, teeth, roof of the mouth, jaws, and the
jaw-hinges,
Nose, nostrils of the nose, and the partition,
Cheeks, temples, forehead, chin, throat, back of the neck,
neck-slue,
Strong shoulders, manly beard, scapula, hind-shoulders, and
the ample side-round of the chest,
Upper-arm, armpit, elbow-socket, lower-arm, arm-sinews,
arm-bones,
Wrist and wrist-joints, hand, palm, knuckles, thumb,
forefinger, finger-joints, finger-nails,
Broad breast-front, curling hair of the breast, breast-bone,
breast-side,
Ribs, belly, backbone, joints of the backbone,
Hips, hip-sockets, hip-strength, inward and outward round,
man-balls, man-root,
Strong set of thighs, well carrying the trunk above,
Leg-fibres, knee, knee-pan, upper-leg, under-leg,
Ankles, instep, foot-ball, toes, toe-joints, the heel;
All attitudes, all the shapeliness, all the belongings of my or
your body or of any one's body, male or female,
The lung-sponges, the stomach-sac, the bowels sweet and
clean,

The brain in its folds inside the skull-frame,
Sympathies, heart-valves, palate-valves, sexuality, maternity,
Womanhood, and all that is a woman, and the man that comes from woman,
The womb, the teats, nipples, breast-milk, tears, laughter, weeping, love-looks, love-perturbations and risings,
The voice, articulation, language, whispering, shouting aloud,
Food, drink, pulse, digestion, sweat, sleep, walking, swimming,
Poise on the hips, leaping, reclining, embracing, arm-curving and tightening,
The continual changes of the flex of the mouth, and around the eyes,
The skin, the sunburnt shade, freckles, hair,
The curious sympathy one feels when feeling with the hand the naked meat of the body,
The circling rivers the breath, and breathing it in and out,
The beauty of the waist, and thence of the hips, and thence downward toward the knees,
The thin red jellies within you or within me, the bones and the marrow in the bones,
The exquisite realization of health;
O I say these are not the parts and poems of the body only, but of the soul,
O I say now these are the soul!

A Woman Waits for Me

A WOMAN waits for me, she contains all, nothing is lacking,
Yet all were lacking if sex were lacking, or if the moisture of the right man were lacking.

Sex contains all, bodies, souls,
Meanings, proofs, purities, delicacies, results, promulgations,
Songs, commands, health, pride, the maternal mystery, the seminal milk,
All hopes, benefactions, bestowals, all the passions, loves, beauties, delights of the earth,

All the governments, judges, gods, follow'd persons of the earth,
These are contain'd in sex as parts of itself and justifications of itself.

Without shame the man I like knows and avows the deliciousness of his sex,
Without shame the woman I like knows and avows hers.

Now I will dismiss myself from impassive women,
I will go stay with her who waits for me, and with those women that are warm-blooded and sufficient for me,
I see that they understand me and do not deny me,
I see that they are worthy of me, I will be the robust husband of those women.

They are not one jot less than I am,
They are tann'd in the face by shining suns and blowing winds,
Their flesh has the old divine suppleness and strength,
They know how to swim, row, ride, wrestle, shoot, run, strike, retreat, advance, resist, defend themselves,
They are ultimate in their own right—they are calm, clear, well-possess'd of themselves.

I draw you close to me, you women,
I cannot let you go, I would do you good,
I am for you, and you are for me, not only for our own sake, but for others' sakes,
Envelop'd in you sleep greater heroes and bards,
They refuse to awake at the touch of any man but me.

It is I, you women, I make my way,
I am stern, acrid, large, undissuadable, but I love you,
I do not hurt you any more than is necessary for you,
I pour the stuff to start sons and daughters fit for these States, I press with slow rude muscle,
I brace myself effectually, I listen to no entreaties,
I dare not withdraw till I deposit what has so long accumulated within me.

Through you I drain the pent-up rivers of myself,
In you I wrap a thousand onward years,
On you I graft the grafts of the best-beloved of me and America,
The drops I distil upon you shall grow fierce and athletic girls, new artists, musicians, and singers,
The babes I beget upon you are to beget babes in their turn,
I shall demand perfect men and women out of my love-spendings,
I shall expect them to interpenetrate with others, as I and you interpenetrate now,
I shall count on the fruits of the gushing showers of them, as I count on the fruits of the gushing showers I give now,
I shall look for loving crops from the birth, life, death, immortality, I plant so lovingly now.

Spontaneous Me

SPONTANEOUS me, Nature,
The loving day, the mounting sun, the friend I am happy with,
The arm of my friend hanging idly over my shoulder,
The hillside whiten'd with blossoms of the mountain ash,
The same late in autumn, the hues of red, yellow, drab, purple, and light and dark green,
The rich coverlet of the grass, animals and birds, the private untrimm'd bank, the primitive apples, the pebble-stones,
Beautiful dripping fragments, the negligent list of one after another as I happen to call them to me or think of them,
The real poems, (what we call poems being merely pictures,)
The poems of the privacy of the night, and of men like me,
This poem drooping shy and unseen that I always carry, and that all men carry,
(Know once for all, avow'd on purpose, wherever are men like me, are our lusty lurking masculine poems,)
Love-thoughts, love-juice, love-odor, love-yielding, love-climbers, and the climbing sap,

Arms and hands of love, lips of love, phallic thumb of love,
breasts of love, bellies press'd and glued together with
love,
Earth of chaste love, life that is only life after love,
The body of my love, the body of the woman I love, the
body of the man, the body of the earth,
Soft forenoon airs that blow from the south-west,
The hairy wild-bee that murmurs and hankers up and down,
that gripes the full-grown lady-flower, curves upon her
with amorous firm legs, takes his will of her, and holds
himself tremulous and tight till he is satisfied;
The wet of woods through the early hours,
Two sleepers at night lying close together as they sleep, one
with an arm slanting down across and below the waist
of the other,
The smell of apples, aromas from crush'd sage-plant, mint,
birch-bark,
The boy's longings, the glow and pressure as he confides to
me what he was dreaming,
The dead leaf whirling its spiral whirl and falling still and
content to the ground,
The no-form'd stings that sights, people, objects, sting me
with,
The hubb'd sting of myself, stinging me as much as it ever
can any one,
The sensitive, orbic, underlapp'd brothers, that only privileged
feelers may be intimate where they are,
The curious roamer the hand roaming all over the body, the
bashful withdrawing of flesh where the fingers soothingly
pause and edge themselves,
The limpid liquid within the young man,
The vex'd corrosion so pensive and so painful,
The torment, the irritable tide that will not be at rest,
The like of the same I feel, the like of the same in others,
The young man that flushes and flushes, and the young
woman that flushes and flushes,
The young man that wakes deep at night, the hot hand seek-
ing to repress what would master him,
The mystic amorous night, the strange half-welcome pangs,
visions, sweats,

The pulse pounding through palms and trembling encircling
fingers, the young man all color'd, red, ashamed, angry;
The souse upon me of my lover the sea, as I lie willing and
naked,
The merriment of the twin babes that crawl over the grass in
the sun, the mother never turning her vigilant eyes from
them,
The walnut-trunk, the walnut-husks, and the ripening or
ripen'd long-round walnuts,
The continence of vegetables, birds, animals,
The consequent meanness of me should I skulk or find
myself indecent, while birds and animals never once
skulk or find themselves indecent,
The great chastity of paternity, to match the great chastity of
maternity,
The oath of procreation I have sworn, my Adamic and fresh
daughters,
The greed that eats me day and night with hungry gnaw, till
I saturate what shall produce boys to fill my place when
I am through,
The wholesome relief, repose, content,
And this bunch pluck'd at random from myself,
It has done its work—I toss it carelessly to fall where it
may.

One Hour to Madness and Joy

One hour to madness and joy! O furious! O confine me not!
(What is this that frees me so in storms?
What do my shouts amid lightnings and raging winds mean?)

O to drink the mystic deliria deeper than any other man!
O savage and tender achings! (I bequeath them to you my
children,
I tell them to you, for reasons, O bridegroom and bride.)

O to be yielded to you whoever you are, and you to be
yielded to me in defiance of the world!
O to return to Paradise! O bashful and feminine!

O to draw you to me, to plant on you for the first time the
lips of a determin'd man.

O the puzzle, the thrice-tied knot, the deep and dark pool,
all untied and illumin'd!
O to speed where there is space enough and air enough at last!
To be absolv'd from previous ties and conventions, I from
mine and you from yours!
To find a new unthought-of nonchalance with the best of
Nature!
To have the gag remov'd from one's mouth!
To have the feeling to-day or any day I am sufficient as I am.

O something unprov'd! something in a trance!
To escape utterly from others' anchors and holds!
To drive free! to love free! to dash reckless and dangerous!
To court destruction with taunts, with invitations!
To ascend, to leap to the heavens of the love indicated to me!
To rise thither with my inebriate soul!
To be lost if it must be so!
To feed the remainder of life with one hour of fulness and
freedom!
With one brief hour of madness and joy.

Out of the Rolling Ocean the Crowd

OUT of the rolling ocean the crowd came a drop gently
to me,
Whispering *I love you, before long I die,*
I have travel'd a long way merely to look on you to touch you,
For I could not die till I once look'd on you,
For I fear'd I might afterward lose you.

Now we have met, we have look'd, we are safe,
Return in peace to the ocean my love,
I too am part of that ocean my love, we are not so much
separated,
Behold the great rondure, the cohesion of all, how perfect!
But as for me, for you, the irresistible sea is to separate us,

As for an hour carrying us diverse, yet cannot carry us
diverse forever;
Be not impatient—a little space—know you I salute the air,
the ocean and the land,
Every day at sundown for your dear sake my love.

Ages and Ages Returning at Intervals

AGES and ages returning at intervals,
Undestroy'd, wandering immortal,
Lusty, phallic, with the potent original loins, perfectly sweet,
I, chanter of Adamic songs,
Through the new garden the West, the great cities calling,
Deliriate, thus prelude what is generated, offering these,
offering myself,
Bathing myself, bathing my songs in Sex,
Offspring of my loins.

We Two, How Long We Were Fool'd

WE two, how long we were fool'd,
Now transmuted, we swiftly escape as Nature escapes,
We are Nature, long have we been absent, but now we return,
We become plants, trunks, foliage, roots, bark,
We are bedded in the ground, we are rocks,
We are oaks, we grow in the openings side by side,
We browse, we are two among the wild herds spontaneous
as any,
We are two fishes swimming in the sea together,
We are what locust blossoms are, we drop scent around
lanes mornings and evenings,
We are also the coarse smut of beasts, vegetables, minerals,
We are two predatory hawks, we soar above and look down,
We are two resplendent suns, we it is who balance ourselves
orbic and stellar, we are as two comets,
We prowl fang'd and four-footed in the woods, we spring
on prey,
We are two clouds forenoons and afternoons driving overhead,
We are seas mingling, we are two of those cheerful waves
rolling over each other and interwetting each other,

We are what the atmosphere is, transparent, receptive,
pervious, impervious,
We are snow, rain, cold, darkness, we are each product and
influence of the globe,
We have circled and circled till we have arrived home again,
we two,
We have voided all but freedom and all but our own joy.

O Hymen! O Hymenee!

O HYMEN! O hymenee! why do you tantalize me thus?
O why sting me for a swift moment only?
Why can you not continue? O why do you now cease?
Is it because if you continued beyond the swift moment you
would soon certainly kill me?

I Am He that Aches with Love

I AM he that aches with amorous love;
Does the earth gravitate? does not all matter, aching, attract
all matter?
So the body of me to all I meet or know.

Native Moments

NATIVE moments—when you come upon me—ah you are
here now,
Give me now libidinous joys only,
Give me the drench of my passions, give me life coarse and
rank,
To-day I go consort with Nature's darlings, to-night too,
I am for those who believe in loose delights, I share the
midnight orgies of young men,
I dance with the dancers and drink with the drinkers,
The echoes ring with our indecent calls, I pick out some
low person for my dearest friend,
He shall be lawless, rude, illiterate, he shall be one condemn'd
by others for deeds done,
I will play a part no longer, why should I exile myself from
my companions?

O you shunn'd persons, I at least do not shun you,
I come forthwith in your midst, I will be your poet,
I will be more to you than to any of the rest.

Once I Pass'd through a Populous City

ONCE I pass'd through a populous city imprinting my brain for future use with its shows, architecture, customs, traditions,
Yet now of all that city I remember only a woman I casually met there who detain'd me for love of me,
Day by day and night by night we were together—all else has long been forgotten by me,
I remember I say only that woman who passionately clung to me,
Again we wander, we love, we separate again,
Again she holds me by the hand, I must not go,
I see her close beside me with silent lips sad and tremulous.

I Heard You Solemn-Sweet Pipes of the Organ

I HEARD you solemn-sweet pipes of the organ as last Sunday morn I pass'd the church,
Winds of autumn, as I walk'd the woods at dusk I heard your long-stretch'd sighs up above so mournful,
I heard the perfect Italian tenor singing at the opera, I heard the soprano in the midst of the quartet singing;
Heart of my love! you too I heard murmuring low through one of the wrists around my head,
Heard the pulse of you when all was still ringing little bells last night under my ear.

Facing West from California's Shores

FACING west from California's shores,
Inquiring, tireless, seeking what is yet unfound,
I, a child, very old, over waves, towards the house of maternity, the land of migrations, look afar,
Look off the shores of my Western sea, the circle almost circled;

For starting westward from Hindustan, from the vales of
Kashmere,
From Asia, from the north, from the God, the sage, and the
hero,
From the south, from the flowery peninsulas and the spice
islands,
Long having wander'd since, round the earth having wander'd,
Now I face home again, very pleas'd and joyous,
(But where is what I started for so long ago?
And why is it yet unfound?)

As Adam Early in the Morning

As Adam early in the morning,
Walking forth from the bower refresh'd with sleep,
Behold me where I pass, hear my voice, approach,
Touch me, touch the palm of your hand to my body as I pass,
Be not afraid of my body.

Calamus

In Paths Untrodden

In paths untrodden,
In the growth by margins of pond-waters,
Escaped from the life that exhibits itself,
From all the standards hitherto publish'd, from the pleasures,
profits, conformities,
Which too long I was offering to feed my soul,
Clear to me now standards not yet publish'd, clear to me
that my soul,
That the soul of the man I speak for rejoices in comrades,
Here by myself away from the clank of the world,
Tallying and talk'd to here by tongues aromatic,
No longer abash'd, (for in this secluded spot I can respond
as I would not dare elsewhere,)
Strong upon me the life that does not exhibit itself, yet
contains all the rest,
Resolv'd to sing no songs to-day but those of manly
attachment,
Projecting them along that substantial life,
Bequeathing hence types of athletic love,
Afternoon this delicious Ninth-month in my forty-first year,
I proceed for all who are or have been young men,
To tell the secret of my nights and days,
To celebrate the need of comrades.

Scented Herbage of My Breast

Scented herbage of my breast,
Leaves from you I glean, I write, to be perused best
afterwards,
Tomb-leaves, body-leaves growing up above me above death,
Perennial roots, tall leaves, O the winter shall not freeze you
delicate leaves,
Every year shall you bloom again, out from where you
retired you shall emerge again;
O I do not know whether many passing by will discover you
or inhale your faint odor, but I believe a few will;

O slender leaves! O blossoms of my blood! I permit you to tell in your own way of the heart that is under you,
O I do not know what you mean there underneath yourselves, you are not happiness,
You are often more bitter than I can bear, you burn and sting me,
Yet you are beautiful to me you faint tinged roots, you make me think of death,
Death is beautiful from you, (what indeed is finally beautiful except death and love?)
O I think it is not for life I am chanting here my chant of lovers, I think it must be for death,
For how calm, how solemn it grows to ascend to the atmosphere of lovers,
Death or life I am then indifferent, my soul declines to prefer,
(I am not sure but the high soul of lovers welcomes death most,)
Indeed O death, I think now these leaves mean precisely the same as you mean,
Grow up taller sweet leaves that I may see! grow up out of my breast!
Spring away from the conceal'd heart there!
Do not fold yourself so in your pink-tinged roots timid leaves!
Do not remain down there so ashamed, herbage of my breast!
Come I am determin'd to unbare this broad breast of mine, I have long enough stifled and choked;
Emblematic and capricious blades I leave you, now you serve me not,
I will say what I have to say by itself,
I will sound myself and comrades only, I will never again utter a call only their call,
I will raise with it immortal reverberations through the States,
I will give an example to lovers to take permanent shape and will through the States,
Through me shall the words be said to make death exhilarating,
Give me your tone therefore O death, that I may accord with it,
Give me yourself, for I see that you belong to me now above all, and are folded inseparably together, you love and death are,

Nor will I allow you to balk me any more with what I was calling life,
For now it is convey'd to me that you are the purports essential,
That you hide in these shifting forms of life, for reasons, and that they are mainly for you,
That you beyond them come forth to remain, the real reality,
That behind the mask of materials you patiently wait, no matter how long,
That you will one day perhaps take control of all,
That you will perhaps dissipate this entire show of appearance,
That may-be you are what it is all for, but it does not last so very long,
But you will last very long.

Whoever You Are Holding Me Now in Hand

WHOEVER you are holding me now in hand,
Without one thing all will be useless,
I give you fair warning before you attempt me further,
I am not what you supposed, but far different.

Who is he that would become my follower?
Who would sign himself a candidate for my affections?

The way is suspicious, the result uncertain, perhaps destructive,
You would have to give up all else, I alone would expect to be your sole and exclusive standard,
Your novitiate would even then be long and exhausting,
The whole past theory of your life and all conformity to the lives around you would have to be abandon'd,
Therefore release me now before troubling yourself any further, let go your hand from my shoulders,
Put me down and depart on your way.

Or else by stealth in some wood for trial,
Or back of a rock in the open air,
(For in any roof'd room of a house I emerge not, nor in company,

And in libraries I lie as one dumb, a gawk, or unborn, or
dead,)
But just possibly with you on a high hill, first watching lest
any person for miles around approach unawares,
Or possibly with you sailing at sea, or on the beach of the
sea or some quiet island,
Here to put your lips upon mine I permit you,
With the comrade's long-dwelling kiss or the new
husband's kiss,
For I am the new husband and I am the comrade.

Or if you will, thrusting me beneath your clothing,
Where I may feel the throbs of your heart or rest upon
your hip,
Carry me when you go forth over land or sea;
For thus merely touching you is enough, is best,
And thus touching you would I silently sleep and be carried
eternally.

But these leaves conning you con at peril,
For these leaves and me you will not understand,
They will elude you at first and still more afterward, I will
certainly elude you,
Even while you should think you had unquestionably caught
me, behold!
Already you see I have escaped from you.

For it is not for what I have put into it that I have written
this book,
Nor is it by reading it you will acquire it,
Nor do those know me best who admire me and vauntingly
praise me,
Nor will the candidates for my love (unless at most a very
few) prove victorious,
Nor will my poems do good only, they will do just as much
evil, perhaps more,
For all is useless without that which you may guess at many
times and not hit, that which I hinted at;
Therefore release me and depart on your way.

For You O Democracy

COME, I will make the continent indissoluble,
I will make the most splendid race the sun ever shone upon,
I will make divine magnetic lands,
With the love of comrades,
With the life-long love of comrades.

I will plant companionship thick as trees along all the rivers of America, and along the shores of the great lakes, and all over the prairies,
I will make inseparable cities with their arms about each other's necks,
By the love of comrades,
By the manly love of comrades.

For you these from me, O Democracy, to serve you ma femme!
For you, for you I am trilling these songs.

These I Singing in Spring

THESE I singing in spring collect for lovers,
(For who but I should understand lovers and all their sorrow and joy?
And who but I should be the poet of comrades?)
Collecting I traverse the garden the world, but soon I pass the gates,
Now along the pond-side, now wading in a little, fearing not the wet,
Now by the post-and-rail fences where the old stones thrown there, pick'd from the fields, have accumulated,
(Wild-flowers and vines and weeds come up through the stones and partly cover them, beyond these I pass,)
Far, far in the forest, or sauntering later in summer, before I think where I go,
Solitary, smelling the earthy smell, stopping now and then in the silence,
Alone I had thought, yet soon a troop gathers around me,
Some walk by my side and some behind, and some embrace my arms or neck,

They the spirits of dear friends dead or alive, thicker they
come, a great crowd, and I in the middle,
Collecting, dispensing, singing, there I wander with them,
Plucking something for tokens, tossing toward whoever is
near me,
Here, lilac, with a branch of pine,
Here, out of my pocket, some moss which I pull'd off a
live-oak in Florida as it hung trailing down,
Here, some pinks and laurel leaves, and a handful of sage,
And here what I now draw from the water, wading in the
pond-side,
(O here I last saw him that tenderly loves me, and returns
again never to separate from me,
And this, O this shall henceforth be the token of comrades,
this calamus-root shall,
Interchange it youths with each other! let none render it
back!)
And twigs of maple and a bunch of wild orange and
chestnut,
And stems of currants and plum-blows, and the aromatic
cedar,
These I compass'd around by a thick cloud of spirits,
Wandering, point to or touch as I pass, or throw them
loosely from me,
Indicating to each one what he shall have, giving something
to each;
But what I drew from the water by the pond-side, that I
reserve,
I will give of it, but only to them that love as I myself am
capable of loving.

Not Heaving from My Ribb'd Breast Only

NOT heaving from my ribb'd breast only,
Not in sighs at night in rage dissatisfied with myself,
Not in those long-drawn, ill-suppresst sighs,
Not in many an oath and promise broken,
Not in my wilful and savage soul's volition,
Not in the subtle nourishment of the air,
Not in this beating and pounding at my temples and wrists,

Not in the curious systole and diastole within which will
one day cease,
Not in many a hungry wish told to the skies only,
Not in cries, laughter, defiances, thrown from me when
alone far in the wilds,
Not in husky pantings through clinch'd teeth,
Not in sounded and resounded words, chattering words,
echoes, dead words,
Not in the murmurs of my dreams while I sleep,
Nor the other murmurs of these incredible dreams of every
day,
Nor in the limbs and senses of my body that take you and
dismiss you continually—not there,
Not in any or all of them O adhesiveness! O pulse of my life!
Need I that you exist and show yourself any more than in
these songs.

Of the Terrible Doubt of Appearances

Of the terrible doubt of appearances,
Of the uncertainty after all, that we may be deluded,
That may-be reliance and hope are but speculations after all,
That may-be identity beyond the grave is a beautiful fable
only,
May-be the things I perceive, the animals, plants, men, hills,
shining and flowing waters,
The skies of day and night, colors, densities, forms, may-be
these are (as doubtless they are) only apparitions, and
the real something has yet to be known,
(How often they dart out of themselves as if to confound
me and mock me!
How often I think neither I know, nor any man knows,
aught of them,)
May-be seeming to me what they are (as doubtless they
indeed but seem) as from my present point of view,
and might prove (as of course they would) nought of
what they appear, or nought anyhow, from entirely
changed points of view;
To me these and the like of these are curiously answer'd by
my lovers, my dear friends,

When he whom I love travels with me or sits a long while
holding me by the hand,
When the subtle air, the impalpable, the sense that words
and reason hold not, surround us and pervade us,
Then I am charged with untold and untellable wisdom, I
am silent, I require nothing further,
I cannot answer the question of appearances or that of
identity beyond the grave,
But I walk or sit indifferent, I am satisfied,
He ahold of my hand has completely satisfied me.

The Base of All Metaphysics

AND now gentlemen,
A word I give to remain in your memories and minds,
As base and finalè too for all metaphysics.

(So to the students the old professor,
At the close of his crowded course.)

Having studied the new and antique, the Greek and
Germanic systems,
Kant having studied and stated, Fichte and Schelling and
Hegel,
Stated the lore of Plato, and Socrates greater than Plato,
And greater than Socrates sought and stated, Christ divine
having studied long,
I see reminiscent to-day those Greek and Germanic systems,
See the philosophies all, Christian churches and tenets see,
Yet underneath Socrates clearly see, and underneath Christ
the divine I see,
The dear love of man for his comrade, the attraction of
friend to friend,
Of the well-married husband and wife, of children and parents,
Of city for city and land for land.

Recorders Ages Hence

RECORDERS ages hence,
Come, I will take you down underneath this impassive
exterior, I will tell you what to say of me,

Publish my name and hang up my picture as that of the tenderest lover,
The friend the lover's portrait, of whom his friend his lover was fondest,
Who was not proud of his songs, but of the measureless ocean of love within him, and freely pour'd it forth,
Who often walk'd lonesome walks thinking of his dear friends, his lovers,
Who pensive away from one he lov'd often lay sleepless and dissatisfied at night,
Who knew too well the sick, sick dread lest the one he lov'd might secretly be indifferent to him,
Whose happiest days were far away through fields, in woods, on hills, he and another wandering hand in hand, they twain apart from other men,
Who oft as he saunter'd the streets curv'd with his arm the shoulder of his friend, while the arm of his friend rested upon him also.

When I Heard at the Close of the Day

WHEN I heard at the close of the day how my name had been receiv'd with plaudits in the capitol, still it was not a happy night for me that follow'd,
And else when I carous'd, or when my plans were accomplish'd, still I was not happy,
But the day when I rose at dawn from the bed of perfect health, refresh'd, singing, inhaling the ripe breath of autumn,
When I saw the full moon in the west grow pale and disappear in the morning light,
When I wander'd alone over the beach, and undressing bathed, laughing with the cool waters, and saw the sun rise,
And when I thought how my dear friend my lover was on his way coming, O then I was happy,
O then each breath tasted sweeter, and all that day my food nourish'd me more, and the beautiful day pass'd well,
And the next came with equal joy, and with the next at evening came my friend,

And that night while all was still I heard the waters roll
slowly continually up the shores,
I heard the hissing rustle of the liquid and sands as directed
to me whispering to congratulate me,
For the one I love most lay sleeping by me under the same
cover in the cool night,
In the stillness in the autumn moonbeams his face was
inclined toward me,
And his arm lay lightly around my breast—and that night I
was happy.

Are You the New Person Drawn toward Me?

ARE you the new person drawn toward me?
To begin with take warning, I am surely far different from
what you suppose;
Do you suppose you will find in me your ideal?
Do you think it so easy to have me become your lover?
Do you think the friendship of me would be unalloy'd
satisfaction?
Do you think I am trusty and faithful?
Do you see no further than this façade, this smooth and
tolerant manner of me?
Do you suppose yourself advancing on real ground toward a
real heroic man?
Have you no thought O dreamer that it may be all maya,
illusion?

Roots and Leaves Themselves Alone

ROOTS and leaves themselves alone are these,
Scents brought to men and women from the wild woods
and pond-side,
Breast-sorrel and pinks of love, fingers that wind around
tighter than vines,
Gushes from the throats of birds hid in the foliage of trees
as the sun is risen,
Breezes of land and love set from living shores to you on
the living sea, to you O sailors!
Frost-mellow'd berries and Third-month twigs offer'd fresh

to young persons wandering out in the fields when the winter breaks up,
Love-buds put before you and within you whoever you are,
Buds to be unfolded on the old terms,
If you bring the warmth of the sun to them they will open and bring form, color, perfume, to you,
If you become the aliment and the wet they will become flowers, fruits, tall branches and trees.

Not Heat Flames up and Consumes

NOT heat flames up and consumes,
Not sea-waves hurry in and out,
Not the air delicious and dry, the air of ripe summer, bears lightly along white down-balls of myriads of seeds,
Wafted, sailing gracefully, to drop where they may;
Not these, O none of these more than the flames of me, consuming, burning for his love whom I love,
O none more than I hurrying in and out;
Does the tide hurry, seeking something, and never give up? O I the same,
O nor down-balls nor perfumes, nor the high rain-emitting clouds, are borne through the open air,
Any more than my soul is borne through the open air,
Wafted in all directions O love, for friendship, for you.

Trickle Drops

TRICKLE drops! my blue veins leaving!
O drops of me! trickle, slow drops,
Candid from me falling, drip, bleeding drops,
From wounds made to free you whence you were prison'd,
From my face, from my forehead and lips,
From my breast, from within where I was conceal'd, press forth red drops, confession drops,
Stain every page, stain every song I sing, every word I say, bloody drops,
Let them know your scarlet heat, let them glisten,
Saturate them with yourself all ashamed and wet,
Glow upon all I have written or shall write, bleeding drops,
Let it all be seen in your light, blushing drops.

City of Orgies

CITY of orgies, walks and joys,
City whom that I have lived and sung in your midst will one day make you illustrious,
Not the pageants of you, not your shifting tableaus, your spectacles, repay me,
Not the interminable rows of your houses, nor the ships at the wharves,
Nor the processions in the streets, nor the bright windows with goods in them,
Nor to converse with learn'd persons, or bear my share in the soiree or feast;
Not those, but as I pass O Manhattan, your frequent and swift flash of eyes offering me love,
Offering response to my own—these repay me,
Lovers, continual lovers, only repay me.

Behold This Swarthy Face

BEHOLD this swarthy face, these gray eyes,
This beard, the white wool unclipt upon my neck,
My brown hands and the silent manner of me without charm;
Yet comes one a Manhattanese and ever at parting kisses me lightly on the lips with robust love,
And I on the crossing of the street or on the ship's deck give a kiss in return,
We observe that salute of American comrades land and sea,
We are those two natural and nonchalant persons.

I Saw in Louisiana a Live-Oak Growing

I SAW in Louisiana a live-oak growing,
All alone stood it and the moss hung down from the branches,
Without any companion it grew there uttering joyous leaves of dark green,
And its look, rude, unbending, lusty, made me think of myself,
But I wonder'd how it could utter joyous leaves standing alone there without its friend near, for I knew I could not,

And I broke off a twig with a certain number of leaves upon
it, and twined around it a little moss,
And brought it away, and I have placed it in sight in my
room,
It is not needed to remind me as of my own dear friends,
(For I believe lately I think of little else than of them,)
Yet it remains to me a curious token, it makes me think of
manly love;
For all that, and though the live-oak glistens there in
Louisiana solitary in a wide flat space,
Uttering joyous leaves all its life without a friend a lover near,
I know very well I could not.

To a Stranger

PASSING stranger! you do not know how longingly I look
upon you,
You must be he I was seeking, or she I was seeking, (it
comes to me as of a dream,)
I have somewhere surely lived a life of joy with you,
All is recall'd as we flit by each other, fluid, affectionate,
chaste, matured,
You grew up with me, were a boy with me or a girl with me,
I ate with you and slept with you, your body has become
not yours only nor left my body mine only,
You give me the pleasure of your eyes, face, flesh, as we
pass, you take of my beard, breast, hands, in return,
I am not to speak to you, I am to think of you when I sit
alone or wake at night alone,
I am to wait, I do not doubt I am to meet you again,
I am to see to it that I do not lose you.

This Moment Yearning and Thoughtful

THIS moment yearning and thoughtful sitting alone,
It seems to me there are other men in other lands yearning
and thoughtful,
It seems to me I can look over and behold them in Germany,
Italy, France, Spain,

Or far, far away, in China, or in Russia or Japan, talking other dialects,
And it seems to me if I could know those men I should become attached to them as I do to men in my own lands,
O I know we should be brethren and lovers,
I know I should be happy with them.

I Hear It Was Charged against Me

I HEAR it was charged against me that I sought to destroy institutions,
But really I am neither for nor against institutions,
(What indeed have I in common with them? or what with the destruction of them?)
Only I will establish in the Mannahatta and in every city of these States inland and seaboard,
And in the fields and woods, and above every keel little or large that dents the water,
Without edifices or rules or trustees or any argument,
The institution of the dear love of comrades.

The Prairie-Grass Dividing

THE prairie-grass dividing, its special odor breathing,
I demand of it the spiritual corresponding,
Demand the most copious and close companionship of men,
Demand the blades to rise of words, acts, beings,
Those of the open atmosphere, coarse, sunlit, fresh, nutritious,
Those that go their own gait, erect, stepping with freedom and command, leading not following,
Those with a never-quell'd audacity, those with sweet and lusty flesh clear of taint,
Those that look carelessly in the faces of Presidents and governors, as to say *Who are you?*
Those of earth-born passion, simple, never constrain'd, never obedient,
Those of inland America.

When I Peruse the Conquer'd Fame

When I peruse the conquer'd fame of heroes and the victories of mighty generals, I do not envy the generals,
Nor the President in his Presidency, nor the rich in his great house,
But when I hear of the brotherhood of lovers, how it was with them,
How together through life, through dangers, odium, unchanging, long and long,
Through youth and through middle and old age, how unfaltering, how affectionate and faithful they were,
Then I am pensive—I hastily walk away fill'd with the bitterest envy.

We Two Boys Together Clinging

We two boys together clinging,
One the other never leaving,
Up and down the roads going, North and South excursions making,
Power enjoying, elbows stretching, fingers clutching,
Arm'd and fearless, eating, drinking, sleeping, loving,
No law less than ourselves owning, sailing, soldiering, thieving, threatening,
Misers, menials, priests alarming, air breathing, water drinking, on the turf or the sea-beach dancing,
Cities wrenching, ease scorning, statutes mocking, feebleness chasing,
Fulfilling our foray.

A Promise to California

A promise to California,
Or inland to the great pastoral Plains, and on to Puget sound and Oregon;
Sojourning east a while longer, soon I travel toward you, to remain, to teach robust American love,
For I know very well that I and robust love belong among you, inland, and along the Western sea;

For these States tend inland and toward the Western sea,
and I will also.

Here the Frailest Leaves of Me

HERE the frailest leaves of me and yet my strongest lasting,
Here I shade and hide my thoughts, I myself do not expose
them,
And yet they expose me more than all my other poems.

No Labor-Saving Machine

NO labor-saving machine,
Nor discovery have I made,
Nor will I be able to leave behind me any wealthy bequest
to found a hospital or library,
Nor reminiscence of any deed of courage for America,
Nor literary success nor intellect, nor book for the book-shelf,
But a few carols vibrating through the air I leave,
For comrades and lovers.

A Glimpse

A GLIMPSE through an interstice caught,
Of a crowd of workmen and drivers in a bar-room around
the stove late of a winter night, and I unremark'd
seated in a corner,
Of a youth who loves me and whom I love, silently
approaching and seating himself near, that he may hold
me by the hand,
A long while amid the noises of coming and going, of
drinking and oath and smutty jest,
There we two, content, happy in being together, speaking
little, perhaps not a word.

A Leaf for Hand in Hand

A LEAF for hand in hand;
You natural persons old and young!
You on the Mississippi and on all the branches and bayous
of the Mississippi!

You friendly boatmen and mechanics! you roughs!
You twain! and all processions moving along the streets!
I wish to infuse myself among you till I see it common for
you to walk hand in hand.

Earth, My Likeness

Earth, my likeness,
Though you look so impassive, ample and spheric there,
I now suspect that is not all;
I now suspect there is something fierce in you eligible to
burst forth,
For an athlete is enamour'd of me, and I of him,
But toward him there is something fierce and terrible in me
eligible to burst forth,
I dare not tell it in words, not even in these songs.

I Dream'd in a Dream

I dream'd in a dream I saw a city invincible to the attacks
of the whole of the rest of the earth,
I dream'd that was the new city of Friends,
Nothing was greater there than the quality of robust love, it
led the rest,
It was seen every hour in the actions of the men of that
city,
And in all their looks and words.

What Think You I Take My Pen in Hand?

What think you I take my pen in hand to record?
The battle-ship, perfect-model'd, majestic, that I saw pass
the offing to-day under full sail?
The splendors of the past day? or the splendor of the night
that envelops me?
Or the vaunted glory and growth of the great city spread
around me?—no;
But merely of two simple men I saw to-day on the pier in the
midst of the crowd, parting the parting of dear friends,

The one to remain hung on the other's neck and passionately
kiss'd him,
While the one to depart tightly prest the one to remain in
his arms.

To the East and to the West

To the East and to the West,
To the man of the Seaside State and of Pennsylvania,
To the Kanadian of the north, to the Southerner I love,
These with perfect trust to depict you as myself, the germs
are in all men,
I believe the main purport of these States is to found a
superb friendship, exaltè, previously unknown,
Because I perceive it waits, and has been always waiting,
latent in all men.

Sometimes with One I Love

SOMETIMES with one I love I fill myself with rage for fear I
effuse unreturn'd love,
But now I think there is no unreturn'd love, the pay is
certain one way or another,
(I loved a certain person ardently and my love was not
return'd,
Yet out of that I have written these songs.)

To a Western Boy

MANY things to absorb I teach to help you become eleve of
mine;
Yet if blood like mine circle not in your veins,
If you be not silently selected by lovers and do not silently
select lovers,
Of what use is it that you seek to become eleve of mine?

Fast Anchor'd Eternal O Love!

FAST-ANCHOR'D eternal O love! O woman I love!
O bride! O wife! more resistless than I can tell, the thought
of you!

Then separate, as disembodied or another born,
Ethereal, the last athletic reality, my consolation,
I ascend, I float in the regions of your love O man,
O sharer of my roving life.

Among the Multitude

AMONG the men and women the multitude,
I perceive one picking me out by secret and divine signs,
Acknowledging none else, not parent, wife, husband,
brother, child, any nearer than I am,
Some are baffled, but that one is not—that one knows me.

Ah lover and perfect equal,
I meant that you should discover me so by faint indirections,
And I when I meet you mean to discover you by the like
in you.

O You Whom I Often and Silently Come

O YOU whom I often and silently come where you are that
I may be with you,
As I walk by your side or sit near, or remain in the same
room with you,
Little you know the subtle electric fire that for your sake is
playing within me.

That Shadow My Likeness

THAT shadow my likeness that goes to and fro seeking a
livelihood, chattering, chaffering,
How often I find myself standing and looking at it where it
flits,
How often I question and doubt whether that is really me;
But among my lovers and caroling these songs,
O I never doubt whether that is really me.

Full of Life Now

FULL of life now, compact, visible,
I, forty years old the eighty-third year of the States,
To one a century hence or any number of centuries hence,
To you yet unborn these, seeking you.

When you read these I that was visible am become invisible,
Now it is you, compact, visible, realizing my poems,
seeking me,
Fancying how happy you were if I could be with you and
become your comrade;
Be it as if I were with you. (Be not too certain but I am
now with you.)

SALUT AU MONDE!

1

O TAKE my hand Walt Whitman!
Such gliding wonders! such sights and sounds!
Such join'd unended links, each hook'd to the next,
Each answering all, each sharing the earth with all.

What widens within you Walt Whitman?
What waves and soils exuding?
What climes? what persons and cities are here?
Who are the infants, some playing, some slumbering?
Who are the girls? who are the married women?
Who are the groups of old men going slowly with their
arms about each other's necks?
What rivers are these? what forests and fruits are these?
What are the mountains call'd that rise so high in the mists?
What myriads of dwellings are they fill'd with dwellers?

2

Within me latitude widens, longitude lengthens,
Asia, Africa, Europe, are to the east—America is provided
for in the west,
Banding the bulge of the earth winds the hot equator,

Curiously north and south turn the axis-ends,
Within me is the longest day, the sun wheels in slanting
rings, it does not set for months,
Stretch'd in due time within me the midnight sun just rises
above the horizon and sinks again,
Within me zones, seas, cataracts, forests, volcanoes, groups,
Malaysia, Polynesia, and the great West Indian islands.

3

What do you hear Walt Whitman?

I hear the workman singing and the farmer's wife singing,
I hear in the distance the sounds of children and of animals
early in the day,
I hear emulous shouts of Australians pursuing the wild horse,
I hear the Spanish dance with castanets in the chestnut
shade, to the rebeck and guitar,
I hear continual echoes from the Thames,
I hear fierce French liberty songs,
I hear of the Italian boat-sculler the musical recitative of old
poems,
I hear the locusts in Syria as they strike the grain and grass
with the showers of their terrible clouds,
I hear the Coptic refrain toward sundown, pensively falling
on the breast of the black venerable vast mother the Nile,
I hear the chirp of the Mexican muleteer, and the bells of
the mule,
I hear the Arab muezzin calling from the top of the mosque,
I hear the Christian priests at the altars of their churches, I
hear the responsive base and soprano,
I hear the cry of the Cossack, and the sailor's voice putting
to sea at Okotsk,
I hear the wheeze of the slave-coffle as the slaves march on,
as the husky gangs pass on by twos and threes, fasten'd
together with wrist-chains and ankle-chains,
I hear the Hebrew reading his records and psalms,
I hear the rhythmic myths of the Greeks, and the strong
legends of the Romans,
I hear the tale of the divine life and bloody death of the
beautiful God the Christ,

I hear the Hindoo teaching his favorite pupil the loves,
wars, adages, transmitted safely to this day from poets
who wrote three thousand years ago.

4

What do you see Walt Whitman?
Who are they you salute, and that one after another salute you?

I see a great round wonder rolling through space,
I see diminute farms, hamlets, ruins, graveyards, jails,
factories, palaces, hovels, huts of barbarians, tents of
nomads upon the surface,
I see the shaded part on one side where the sleepers are
sleeping, and the sunlit part on the other side,
I see the curious rapid change of the light and shade,
I see distant lands, as real and near to the inhabitants of
them as my land is to me.

I see plenteous waters,
I see mountain peaks, I see the sierras of Andes where they
range,
I see plainly the Himalayas, Chian Shahs, Altays, Ghauts,
I see the giant pinnacles of Elbruz, Kazbek, Bazardjusi,
I see the Styrian Alps, and the Karnac Alps,
I see the Pyrenees, Balks, Carpathians, and to the north the
Dofrafields, and off at sea mount Hecla,
I see Vesuvius and Etna, the mountains of the Moon, and
the Red mountains of Madagascar,
I see the Lybian, Arabian, and Asiatic deserts,
I see huge dreadful Arctic and Antarctic icebergs,
I see the superior oceans and the inferior ones, the Atlantic
and Pacific, the sea of Mexico, the Brazilian sea, and
the sea of Peru,
The waters of Hindustan, the China sea, and the gulf of
Guinea,
The Japan waters, the beautiful bay of Nagasaki land-lock'd
in its mountains,
The spread of the Baltic, Caspian, Bothnia, the British
shores, and the bay of Biscay,

The clear-sunn'd Mediterranean, and from one to another
of its islands,
The White sea, and the sea around Greenland.

I behold the mariners of the world,
Some are in storms, some in the night with the watch on
the look-out,
Some drifting helplessly, some with contagious diseases.

I behold the sail and steamships of the world, some in
clusters in port, some on their voyages,
Some double the cape of Storms, some cape Verde, others
capes Guardafui, Bon, or Bajadore,
Others Dondra head, others pass the straits of Sunda, others
cape Lopatka, others Behring's straits,
Others cape Horn, others sail the gulf of Mexico or along
Cuba or Hayti, others Hudson's bay or Baffin's bay,
Others pass the straits of Dover, others enter the Wash,
others the firth of Solway, others round cape Clear,
others the Land's End,
Others traverse the Zuyder Zee or the Scheld,
Others as comers and goers at Gibraltar or the Dardanelles,
Others sternly push their way through the northern winter-
packs,
Others descend or ascend the Obi or the Lena,
Others the Niger or the Congo, others the Indus, the
Burampooter and Cambodia,
Others wait steam'd up ready to start in the ports of Australia,
Wait at Liverpool, Glasgow, Dublin, Marseilles, Lisbon,
Naples, Hamburg, Bremen, Bordeaux, the Hague,
Copenhagen,
Wait at Valparaiso, Rio Janeiro, Panama.

5

I see the tracks of the railroads of the earth,
I see them in Great Britain, I see them in Europe,
I see them in Asia and in Africa.

I see the electric telegraphs of the earth,
I see the filaments of the news of the wars, deaths, losses,
gains, passions, of my race.

I see the long river-stripes of the earth,
I see the Amazon and the Paraguay,
I see the four great rivers of China, the Amour, the Yellow River, the Yiang-tse, and the Pearl,
I see where the Seine flows, and where the Danube, the Loire, the Rhone, and the Guadalquiver flow,
I see the windings of the Volga, the Dnieper, the Oder,
I see the Tuscan going down the Arno, and the Venetian along the Po,
I see the Greek seaman sailing out of Egina bay.

6

I see the site of the old empire of Assyria, and that of Persia, and that of India,
I see the falling of the Ganges over the high rim of Saukara.

I see the place of the idea of the Deity incarnated by avatars in human forms,
I see the spots of the successions of priests on the earth, oracles, sacrificers, brahmins, sabians, llamas, monks, muftis, exhorters,
I see where druids walk'd the groves of Mona, I see the mistletoe and vervain,
I see the temples of the deaths of the bodies of Gods, I see the old signifiers.

I see Christ eating the bread of his last supper in the midst of youths and old persons,
I see where the strong divine young man the Hercules toil'd faithfully and long and then died,
I see the place of the innocent rich life and hapless fate of the beautiful nocturnal son, the full-limb'd Bacchus,
I see Kneph, blooming, drest in blue, with the crown of feathers on his head,
I see Hermes, unsuspected, dying, well-belov'd, saying to the people *Do not weep for me,*
This is not my true country, I have lived banish'd from my true country, I now go back there,
I return to the celestial sphere where every one goes in his turn.

7

I see the battle-fields of the earth, grass grows upon them
and blossoms and corn,
I see the tracks of ancient and modern expeditions.

I see the nameless masonries, venerable messages of the
unknown events, heroes, records of the earth.

I see the places of the sagas,
I see pine-trees and fir-trees torn by northern blasts,
I see granite bowlders and cliffs, I see green meadows and
lakes,
I see the burial-cairns of Scandinavian warriors,
I see them raised high with stones by the marge of restless
oceans, that the dead men's spirits when they wearied
of their quiet graves might rise up through the mounds
and gaze on the tossing billows, and be refresh'd by
storms, immensity, liberty, action.

I see the steppes of Asia,
I see the tumuli of Mongolia, I see the tents of Kalmucks
and Baskirs,
I see the nomadic tribes with herds of oxen and cows,
I see the table-lands notch'd with ravines, I see the jungles
and deserts,
I see the camel, the wild steed, the bustard, the fat-tail'd
sheep, the antelope, and the burrowing wolf.

I see the highlands of Abyssinia,
I see flocks of goats feeding, and see the fig-tree, tamarind,
date,
And see fields of teff-wheat and places of verdure and gold.

I see the Brazilian vaquero,
I see the Bolivian ascending mount Sorata,
I see the Wacho crossing the plains, I see the incomparable
rider of horses with his lasso on his arm,
I see over the pampas the pursuit of wild cattle for their hides.

8

I see the regions of snow and ice,
I see the sharp-eyed Samoiede and the Finn,
I see the seal-seeker in his boat poising his lance,
I see the Siberian on his slight-built sledge drawn by dogs,
I see the porpoise-hunters, I see the whale-crews of the south Pacific and the north Atlantic,
I see the cliffs, glaciers, torrents, valleys, of Switzerland—I mark the long winters and the isolation.

I see the cities of the earth and make myself at random a part of them,
I am a real Parisian,
I am a habitan of Vienna, St. Petersburg, Berlin, Constantinople,
I am of Adelaide, Sidney, Melbourne,
I am of London, Manchester, Bristol, Edinburgh, Limerick,
I am of Madrid, Cadiz, Barcelona, Oporto, Lyons, Brussels, Berne, Frankfort, Stuttgart, Turin, Florence,
I belong in Moscow, Cracow, Warsaw, or northward in Christiania or Stockholm, or in Siberian Irkutsk, or in some street in Iceland,
I descend upon all those cities, and rise from them again.

10

I see vapors exhaling from unexplored countries,
I see the savage types, the bow and arrow, the poison'd splint, the fetich, and the obi.

I see African and Asiatic towns,
I see Algiers, Tripoli, Derne, Mogadore, Timbuctoo, Monrovia,
I see the swarms of Pekin, Canton, Benares, Delhi, Calcutta, Tokio,
I see the Kruman in his hut, and the Dahoman and Ashantee-man in their huts,
I see the Turk smoking opium in Aleppo,
I see the picturesque crowds at the fairs of Khiva and those of Herat,

I see Teheran, I see Muscat and Medina and the intervening
sands, I see the caravans toiling onward,
I see Egypt and the Egyptians, I see the pyramids and
obelisks,
I look on chisell'd histories, records of conquering kings,
dynasties, cut in slabs of sand-stone, or on granite-blocks,
I see at Memphis mummy-pits containing mummies embalm'd,
swathed in linen cloth, lying there many centuries,
I look on the fall'n Theban, the large-ball'd eyes, the side-
drooping neck, the hands folded across the breast.

I see all the menials of the earth, laboring,
I see all the prisoners in the prisons,
I see the defective human bodies of the earth,
The blind, the deaf and dumb, idiots, hunchbacks, lunatics,
The pirates, thieves, betrayers, murderers, slave-makers of
the earth,
The helpless infants, and the helpless old men and women.

I see male and female everywhere,
I see the serene brotherhood of philosophs,
I see the constructiveness of my race,
I see the results of the perseverance and industry of my race,
I see ranks, colors, barbarisms, civilizations, I go among
them, I mix indiscriminately,
And I salute all the inhabitants of the earth.

11

You whoever you are!
You daughter or son of England!
You of the mighty Slavic tribes and empires! you Russ in
Russia!
You dim-descended, black, divine-soul'd African, large, fine-
headed, nobly-form'd, superbly destin'd, on equal terms
with me!
You Norwegian! Swede! Dane! Icelander! you Prussian!
You Spaniard of Spain! you Portuguese!
You Frenchwoman and Frenchman of France!
You Belge! you liberty-lover of the Netherlands! (you stock
whence I myself have descended;)

You sturdy Austrian! you Lombard! Hun! Bohemian! farmer
of Styria!
You neighbor of the Danube!
You working-man of the Rhine, the Elbe, or the Weser! you
working-woman too!
You Sardinian! you Bavarian! Swabian! Saxon! Wallachian!
Bulgarian!
You Roman! Neapolitan! you Greek!
You lithe matador in the arena at Seville!
You mountaineer living lawlessly on the Taurus or Caucasus!
You Bokh horse-herd watching your mares and stallions
feeding!
You beautiful-bodied Persian at full speed in the saddle
shooting arrows to the mark!
You Chinaman and Chinawoman of China! You Tartar of
Tartary!
You women of the earth subordinated at your tasks!
You Jew journeying in your old age through every risk to
stand once on Syrian ground!
You other Jews waiting in all lands for your Messiah!
You thoughtful Armenian pondering by some stream of the
Euphrates! you peering amid the ruins of Nineveh! you
ascending mount Ararat!
You foot-worn pilgrim welcoming the far-away sparkle of
the minarets of Mecca!
You sheiks along the stretch from Suez to Bab-el-mandeb
ruling your families and tribes!
You olive-grower tending your fruit on fields of Nazareth,
Damascus, or lake Tiberias!
You Thibet trader on the wide inland or bargaining in the
shops of Lassa!
You Japanese man or woman! you liver in Madagascar,
Ceylon, Sumatra, Borneo!
All you continentals of Asia, Africa, Europe, Australia,
indifferent of place!
All you on the numberless islands of the archipelagoes of
the sea!
And you of centuries hence when you listen to me!
And you each and everywhere whom I specify not, but
include just the same!

Health to you! good will to you all, from me and America
sent!

Each of us inevitable,
Each of us limitless—each of us with his or her right upon
the earth,
Each of us allow'd the eternal purports of the earth,
Each of us here as divinely as any is here.

12

You Hottentot with clicking palate! you woolly-hair'd hordes!
You own'd persons dropping sweat-drops or blood-drops!
You human forms with the fathomless ever-impressive
countenances of brutes!
You poor koboo whom the meanest of the rest look down
upon for all your glimmering language and spirituality!
You dwarf'd Kamtschatkan, Greenlander, Lapp!
You Austral negro, naked, red, sooty, with protrusive lip,
groveling, seeking your food!
You Caffre, Berber, Soudanese!
You haggard, uncouth, untutor'd Bedowee!
You plague-swarms in Madras, Nankin, Kaubul, Cairo!
You benighted roamer of Amazonia! you Patagonian! you
Feejeeman!
I do not prefer others so very much before you either,
I do not say one word against you, away back there where
you stand,
(You will come forward in due time to my side.)

13

My spirit has pass'd in compassion and determination
around the whole earth,
I have look'd for equals and lovers and found them ready
for me in all lands,
I think some divine rapport has equalized me with them.

You vapors, I think I have risen with you, moved away to
distant continents, and fallen down there, for reasons,
I think I have blown with you you winds;
You waters I have finger'd every shore with you,

I have run through what any river or strait of the globe has
run through,
I have taken my stand on the bases of peninsulas and on the
high embedded rocks, to cry thence:

Salut au monde!
What cities the light or warmth penetrates I penetrate those
cities myself,
All islands to which birds wing their way I wing my way
myself.

Toward you all, in America's name,
I raise high the perpendicular hand, I make the signal,
To remain after me in sight forever,
For all the haunts and homes of men.

Song of the Open Road

I

Afoot and light-hearted I take to the open road,
Healthy, free, the world before me,
The long brown path before me leading wherever I choose.

Henceforth I ask not good-fortune, I myself am good-fortune,
Henceforth I whimper no more, postpone no more, need
nothing,
Done with indoor complaints, libraries, querulous criticisms,
Strong and content I travel the open road.

The earth, that is sufficient,
I do not want the constellations any nearer,
I know they are very well where they are,
I know they suffice for those who belong to them.

(Still here I carry my old delicious burdens,
I carry them, men and women, I carry them with me
wherever I go,
I swear it is impossible for me to get rid of them,
I am fill'd with them, and I will fill them in return.)

2

You road I enter upon and look around, I believe you are
not all that is here,
I believe that much unseen is also here.

Here the profound lesson of reception, nor preference nor
denial,
The black with his woolly head, the felon, the diseas'd, the
illiterate person, are not denied;
The birth, the hasting after the physician, the beggar's tramp,
the drunkard's stagger, the laughing party of mechanics,
The escaped youth, the rich person's carriage, the fop, the
eloping couple,
The early market-man, the hearse, the moving of furniture
into the town, the return back from the town,
They pass, I also pass, any thing passes, none can be
interdicted,
None but are accepted, none but shall be dear to me.

3

You air that serves me with breath to speak!
You objects that call from diffusion my meanings and give
them shape!
You light that wraps me and all things in delicate equable
showers!
You paths worn in the irregular hollows by the roadsides!
I believe you are latent with unseen existences, you are so
dear to me.

You flagg'd walks of the cities! you strong curbs at the
edges!
You ferries! you planks and posts of wharves! you timber-
lined sides! you distant ships!
You rows of houses! you window-pierc'd façades! you roofs!
You porches and entrances! you copings and iron guards!
You windows whose transparent shells might expose so much!
You doors and ascending steps! you arches!
You gray stones of interminable pavements! you trodden
crossings!

From all that has touch'd you I believe you have imparted to
yourselves, and now would impart the same secretly to me,
From the living and the dead you have peopled your
impassive surfaces, and the spirits thereof would be
evident and amicable with me.

4

The earth expanding right hand and left hand,
The picture alive, every part in its best light,
The music falling in where it is wanted, and stopping where
it is not wanted,
The cheerful voice of the public road, the gay fresh sentiment
of the road.

O highway I travel, do you say to me *Do not leave me?*
Do you say *Venture not—if you leave me you are lost?*
Do you say *I am already prepared, I am well-beaten and
undenied, adhere to me?*

O public road, I say back I am not afraid to leave you, yet I
love you,
You express me better than I can express myself,
You shall be more to me than my poem.

I think heroic deeds were all conceiv'd in the open air, and
all free poems also,
I think I could stop here myself and do miracles,
I think whatever I shall meet on the road I shall like, and
whoever beholds me shall like me,
I think whoever I see must be happy.

5

From this hour I ordain myself loos'd of limits and
imaginary lines,
Going where I list, my own master total and absolute,
Listening to others, considering well what they say,
Pausing, searching, receiving, contemplating,
Gently, but with undeniable will, divesting myself of the
holds that would hold me.

I inhale great draughts of space,
The east and the west are mine, and the north and the south are mine.

I am larger, better than I thought,
I did not know I held so much goodness.

All seems beautiful to me,
I can repeat over to men and women You have done such good to me I would do the same to you,
I will recruit for myself and you as I go,
I will scatter myself among men and women as I go,
I will toss a new gladness and roughness among them,
Whoever denies me it shall not trouble me,
Whoever accepts me he or she shall be blessed and shall bless me.

6

Now if a thousand perfect men were to appear it would not amaze me,
Now if a thousand beautiful forms of women appear'd it would not astonish me.

Now I see the secret of the making of the best persons,
It is to grow in the open air and to eat and sleep with the earth.

Here a great personal deed has room,
(Such a deed seizes upon the hearts of the whole race of men,
Its effusion of strength and will overwhelms law and mocks all authority and all argument against it.)

Here is the test of wisdom,
Wisdom is not finally tested in schools,
Wisdom cannot be pass'd from one having it to another not having it,
Wisdom is of the soul, is not susceptible of proof, is its own proof,
Applies to all stages and objects and qualities and is content,

Is the certainty of the reality and immortality of things, and
the excellence of things;
Something there is in the float of the sight of things that
provokes it out of the soul.

Now I re-examine philosophies and religions,
They may prove well in lecture-rooms, yet not prove at all
under the spacious clouds and along the landscape and
flowing currents.

Here is realization,
Here is a man tallied—he realizes here what he has in him,
The past, the future, majesty, love—if they are vacant of
you, you are vacant of them.

Only the kernel of every object nourishes;
Where is he who tears off the husks for you and me?
Where is he that undoes stratagems and envelopes for you
and me?

Here is adhesiveness, it is not previously fashion'd, it is
apropos;
Do you know what it is as you pass to be loved by strangers?
Do you know the talk of those turning eye-balls?

7

Here is the efflux of the soul,
The efflux of the soul comes from within through embower'd
gates, ever provoking questions,
These yearnings why are they? these thoughts in the darkness
why are they?
Why are there men and women that while they are nigh me
the sunlight expands my blood?
Why when they leave me do my pennants of joy sink flat
and lank?
Why are there trees I never walk under but large and
melodious thoughts descend upon me?
(I think they hang there winter and summer on those trees
and always drop fruit as I pass;)
What is it I interchange so suddenly with strangers?

What with some driver as I ride on the seat by his side?
What with some fisherman drawing his seine by the shore as I walk by and pause?
What gives me to be free to a woman's and man's good-will? what gives them to be free to mine?

8

The efflux of the soul is happiness, here is happiness,
I think it pervades the open air, waiting at all times,
Now it flows unto us, we are rightly charged.

Here rises the fluid and attaching character,
The fluid and attaching character is the freshness and sweetness of man and woman,
(The herbs of the morning sprout no fresher and sweeter every day out of the roots of themselves, than it sprouts fresh and sweet continually out of itself.)

Toward the fluid and attaching character exudes the sweat of the love of young and old,
From it falls distill'd the charm that mocks beauty and attainments,
Toward it heaves the shuddering longing ache of contact.

9

Allons! whoever you are come travel with me!
Traveling with me you find what never tires.

The earth never tires,
The earth is rude, silent, incomprehensible at first, Nature is rude and incomprehensible at first,
Be not discouraged, keep on, there are divine things well envelop'd,
I swear to you there are divine things more beautiful than words can tell.

Allons! we must not stop here,
However sweet these laid-up stores, however convenient this dwelling we cannot remain here,

However shelter'd this port and however calm these waters
we must not anchor here,
However welcome the hospitality that surrounds us we are
permitted to receive it but a little while.

10

Allons! the inducements shall be greater,
We will sail pathless and wild seas,
We will go where winds blow, waves dash, and the Yankee
clipper speeds by under full sail.

Allons! with power, liberty, the earth, the elements,
Health, defiance, gayety, self-esteem, curiosity;
Allons! from all formules!
From your formules, O bat-eyed and materialistic priests.

The stale cadaver blocks up the passage—the burial waits no
longer.

Allons! yet take warning!
He traveling with me needs the best blood, thews, endurance,
None may come to the trial till he or she bring courage and
health,
Come not here if you have already spent the best of yourself,
Only those may come who come in sweet and determin'd
bodies,
No diseas'd person, no rum-drinker or venereal taint is
permitted here.

(I and mine do not convince by arguments, similes, rhymes,
We convince by our presence.)

11

Listen! I will be honest with you,
I do not offer the old smooth prizes, but offer rough new
prizes,
These are the days that must happen to you:
You shall not heap up what is call'd riches,
You shall scatter with lavish hand all that you earn or achieve,
You but arrive at the city to which you were destin'd, you

hardly settle yourself to satisfaction before you are call'd
by an irresistible call to depart,
You shall be treated to the ironical smiles and mockings of
those who remain behind you,
What beckonings of love you receive you shall only answer
with passionate kisses of parting,
You shall not allow the hold of those who spread their
reach'd hands toward you.

12

Allons! after the great Companions, and to belong to them!
They too are on the road—they are the swift and majestic
men—they are the greatest women,
Enjoyers of calms of seas and storms of seas,
Sailors of many a ship, walkers of many a mile of land,
Habituès of many distant countries, habituès of far-distant
dwellings,
Trusters of men and women, observers of cities, solitary
toilers,
Pausers and contemplators of tufts, blossoms, shells of the
shore,
Dancers at wedding-dances, kissers of brides, tender helpers
of children, bearers of children,
Soldiers of revolts, standers by gaping graves, lowerers-down
of coffins,
Journeyers over consecutive seasons, over the years, the
curious years each emerging from that which preceded it,
Journeyers as with companions, namely their own diverse
phases,
Forth-steppers from the latent unrealized baby-days,
Journeyers gayly with their own youth, journeyers with their
bearded and well-grain'd manhood,
Journeyers with their womanhood, ample, unsurpass'd,
content,
Journeyers with their own sublime old age of manhood or
womanhood,
Old age, calm, expanded, broad with the haughty breadth
of the universe,
Old age, flowing free with the delicious near-by freedom of
death.

13

Allons! to that which is endless as it was beginningless,
To undergo much, tramps of days, rests of nights,
To merge all in the travel they tend to, and the days and nights they tend to,
Again to merge them in the start of superior journeys,
To see nothing anywhere but what you may reach it and pass it,
To conceive no time, however distant, but what you may reach it and pass it,
To look up or down no road but it stretches and waits for you, however long but it stretches and waits for you,
To see no being, not God's or any, but you also go thither,
To see no possession, but you may possess it, enjoying all without labor or purchase, abstracting the feast yet not abstracting one particle of it,
To take the best of the farmer's farm and the rich man's elegant villa, and the chaste blessings of the well-married couple, and the fruits of orchards and flowers of gardens,
To take to your use out of the compact cities as you pass through,
To carry buildings and streets with you afterward wherever you go,
To gather the minds of men out of their brains as you encounter them, to gather the love out of their hearts,
To take your lovers on the road with you, for all that you leave them behind you,
To know the universe itself as a road, as many roads, as roads for traveling souls.

All parts away for the progress of souls,
All religion, all solid things, arts, governments—all that was or is apparent upon this globe or any globe, falls into niches and corners before the procession of souls along the grand roads of the universe.

Of the progress of the souls of men and women along the grand roads of the universe, all other progress is the needed emblem and sustenance.

Forever alive, forever forward,
Stately, solemn, sad, withdrawn, baffled, mad, turbulent, feeble, dissatisfied,
Desperate, proud, fond, sick, accepted by men, rejected by men,
They go! they go! I know that they go, but I know not where they go,
But I know that they go toward the best—toward something great.

Whoever you are, come forth! or man or woman come forth!
You must not stay sleeping and dallying there in the house, though you built it, or though it has been built for you.

Out of the dark confinement! out from behind the screen!
It is useless to protest, I know all and expose it.

Behold through you as bad as the rest,
Through the laughter, dancing, dining, supping, of people,
Inside of dresses and ornaments, inside of those wash'd and trimm'd faces,
Behold a secret silent loathing and despair.

No husband, no wife, no friend, trusted to hear the confession,
Another self, a duplicate of every one, skulking and hiding it goes,
Formless and wordless through the streets of the cities, polite and bland in the parlors,
In the cars of railroads, in steamboats, in the public assembly,
Home to the houses of men and women, at the table, in the bedroom, everywhere,
Smartly attired, countenance smiling, form upright, death under the breast-bones, hell under the skull-bones,
Under the broadcloth and gloves, under the ribbons and artificial flowers,
Keeping fair with the customs, speaking not a syllable of itself,
Speaking of any thing else but never of itself.

14

Allons! through struggles and wars!
The goal that was named cannot be countermanded.

Have the past struggles succeeded?
What has succeeded? yourself? your nation? Nature?
Now understand me well—it is provided in the essence of things that from any fruition of success, no matter what, shall come forth something to make a greater struggle necessary.

My call is the call of battle, I nourish active rebellion,
He going with me must go well arm'd,
He going with me goes often with spare diet, poverty, angry enemies, desertions.

15

Allons! the road is before us!
It is safe—I have tried it—my own feet have tried it well—be not detain'd!

Let the paper remain on the desk unwritten, and the book on the shelf unopen'd!
Let the tools remain in the workshop! let the money remain unearn'd!
Let the school stand! mind not the cry of the teacher!
Let the preacher preach in his pulpit! let the lawyer plead in the court, and the judge expound the law.

Camerado, I give you my hand!
I give you my love more precious than money,
I give you myself before preaching or law;
Will you give me yourself? will you come travel with me?
Shall we stick by each other as long as we live?

Crossing Brooklyn Ferry

1

Flood-tide below me! I see you face to face!
Clouds of the west—sun there half an hour high—I see you also face to face.

Crowds of men and women attired in the usual costumes, how curious you are to me!
On the ferry-boats the hundreds and hundreds that cross, returning home, are more curious to me than you suppose,
And you that shall cross from shore to shore years hence are more to me, and more in my meditations, than you might suppose.

2

The impalpable sustenance of me from all things at all hours of the day,
The simple, compact, well-join'd scheme, myself disintegrated, every one disintegrated yet part of the scheme,
The similitudes of the past and those of the future,
The glories strung like beads on my smallest sights and hearings, on the walk in the street and the passage over the river,
The current rushing so swiftly and swimming with me far away,
The others that are to follow me, the ties between me and them,
The certainty of others, the life, love, sight, hearing of others.

Others will enter the gates of the ferry and cross from shore to shore,
Others will watch the run of the flood-tide,
Others will see the shipping of Manhattan north and west, and the heights of Brooklyn to the south and east,
Others will see the islands large and small;
Fifty years hence, others will see them as they cross, the sun half an hour high,
A hundred years hence, or ever so many hundred years hence, others will see them,
Will enjoy the sunset, the pouring-in of the flood-tide, the falling-back to the sea of the ebb-tide.

3

It avails not, time nor place—distance avails not,
I am with you, you men and women of a generation, or ever so many generations hence,

Just as you feel when you look on the river and sky, so I felt,
Just as any of you is one of a living crowd, I was one of a crowd,
Just as you are refresh'd by the gladness of the river and the bright flow, I was refresh'd,
Just as you stand and lean on the rail, yet hurry with the swift current, I stood yet was hurried,
Just as you look on the numberless masts of ships and the thick-stemm'd pipes of steamboats, I look'd.

I too many and many a time cross'd the river of old,
Watched the Twelfth-month sea-gulls, saw them high in the air floating with motionless wings, oscillating their bodies,
Saw how the glistening yellow lit up parts of their bodies and left the rest in strong shadow,
Saw the slow-wheeling circles and the gradual edging toward the south,
Saw the reflection of the summer sky in the water,
Had my eyes dazzled by the shimmering track of beams,
Look'd at the fine centrifugal spokes of light round the shape of my head in the sunlit water,
Look'd on the haze on the hills southward and south-westward,
Look'd on the vapor as it flew in fleeces tinged with violet,
Look'd toward the lower bay to notice the vessels arriving,
Saw their approach, saw aboard those that were near me,
Saw the white sails of schooners and sloops, saw the ships at anchor,
The sailors at work in the rigging or out astride the spars,
The round masts, the swinging motion of the hulls, the slender serpentine pennants,
The large and small steamers in motion, the pilots in their pilot-houses,
The white wake left by the passage, the quick tremulous whirl of the wheels,
The flags of all nations, the falling of them at sunset,
The scallop-edged waves in the twilight, the ladled cups, the frolicsome crests and glistening,

The stretch afar growing dimmer and dimmer, the gray
walls of the granite storehouses by the docks,
On the river the shadowy group, the big steam-tug closely
flank'd on each side by the barges, the hay-boat, the
belated lighter,
On the neighboring shore the fires from the foundry
chimneys burning high and glaringly into the night,
Casting their flicker of black contrasted with wild red and
yellow light over the tops of houses, and down into the
clefts of streets.

4

These and all else were to me the same as they are to you,
I loved well those cities, loved well the stately and rapid river,
The men and women I saw were all near to me,
Others the same—others who look back on me because I
look'd forward to them,
(The time will come, though I stop here to-day and to-night.)

5

What is it then between us?
What is the count of the scores or hundreds of years
between us?

Whatever it is, it avails not—distance avails not, and place
avails not,
I too lived, Brooklyn of ample hills was mine,
I too walk'd the streets of Manhattan island, and bathed in
the waters around it,
I too felt the curious abrupt questionings stir within me,
In the day among crowds of people sometimes they came
upon me,
In my walks home late at night or as I lay in my bed they
came upon me,
I too had been struck from the float forever held in solution,
I too had receiv'd identity by my body,
That I was I knew was of my body, and what I should be I
knew I should be of my body.

6

It is not upon you alone the dark patches fall,
The dark threw its patches down upon me also,
The best I had done seem'd to me blank and suspicious,
My great thoughts as I supposed them, were they not in reality meagre?
Nor is it you alone who know what it is to be evil,
I am he who knew what it was to be evil,
I too knotted the old knot of contrariety,
Blabb'd, blush'd, resented, lied, stole, grudg'd,
Had guile, anger, lust, hot wishes I dared not speak,
Was wayward, vain, greedy, shallow, sly, cowardly, malignant,
The wolf, the snake, the hog, not wanting in me,
The cheating look, the frivolous word, the adulterous wish, not wanting,
Refusals, hates, postponements, meanness, laziness, none of these wanting,
Was one with the rest, the days and haps of the rest,
Was call'd by my nighest name by clear loud voices of young men as they saw me approaching or passing,
Felt their arms on my neck as I stood, or the negligent leaning of their flesh against me as I sat,
Saw many I loved in the street or ferry-boat or public assembly, yet never told them a word,
Lived the same life with the rest, the same old laughing, gnawing, sleeping,
Play'd the part that still looks back on the actor or actress,
The same old role, the role that is what we make it, as great as we like,
Or as small as we like, or both great and small.

7

Closer yet I approach you,
What thought you have of me now, I had as much of you—I laid in my stores in advance,
I consider'd long and seriously of you before you were born.

Who was to know what should come home to me?
Who knows but I am enjoying this?

Who knows, for all the distance, but I am as good as looking
at you now, for all you cannot see me?

8

Ah, what can ever be more stately and admirable to me than
mast-hemm'd Manhattan?
River and sunset and scallop-edg'd waves of flood-tide?
The sea-gulls oscillating their bodies, the hay-boat in the
twilight, and the belated lighter?
What gods can exceed these that clasp me by the hand, and
with voices I love call me promptly and loudly by my
nighest name as I approach?
What is more subtle than this which ties me to the woman
or man that looks in my face?
Which fuses me into you now, and pours my meaning into
you?

We understand then do we not?
What I promis'd without mentioning it, have you not
accepted?
What the study could not teach—what the preaching could
not accomplish is accomplish'd, is it not?

9

Flow on, river! flow with the flood-tide, and ebb with the
ebb-tide!
Frolic on, crested and scallop-edg'd waves!
Gorgeous clouds of the sunset! drench with your splendor
me, or the men and women generations after me!
Cross from shore to shore, countless crowds of passengers!
Stand up, tall masts of Mannahatta! stand up, beautiful hills
of Brooklyn!
Throb, baffled and curious brain! throw out questions and
answers!
Suspend here and everywhere, eternal float of solution!
Gaze, loving and thirsting eyes, in the house or street or
public assembly!
Sound out, voices of young men! loudly and musically call
me by my nighest name!

Live, old life! play the part that looks back on the actor or
actress!
Play the old role, the role that is great or small according as
one makes it!
Consider, you who peruse me, whether I may not in
unknown ways be looking upon you;
Be firm, rail over the river, to support those who lean idly,
yet haste with the hasting current;
Fly on, sea-birds! fly sideways, or wheel in large circles high
in the air;
Receive the summer sky, you water, and faithfully hold it till
all downcast eyes have time to take it from you!
Diverge, fine spokes of light, from the shape of my head, or
any one's head, in the sunlit water!
Come on, ships from the lower bay! pass up or down,
white-sail'd schooners, sloops, lighters!
Flaunt away, flags of all nations! be duly lower'd at sunset!
Burn high your fires, foundry chimneys! cast black shadows
at nightfall! cast red and yellow light over the tops of
the houses!
Appearances, now or henceforth, indicate what you are,
You necessary film, continue to envelop the soul,
About my body for me, and your body for you, be hung
out divinest aromas,
Thrive, cities—bring your freight, bring your shows, ample
and sufficient rivers,
Expand, being than which none else is perhaps more spiritual,
Keep your places, objects than which none else is more lasting.

You have waited, you always wait, you dumb, beautiful
ministers,
We receive you with free sense at last, and are insatiate
henceforward,
Not you any more shall be able to foil us, or withhold
yourselves from us,
We use you, and do not cast you aside—we plant you
permanently within us,
We fathom you not—we love you—there is perfection in
you also,
You furnish your parts toward eternity,
Great or small, you furnish your parts toward the soul.

Song of the Answerer

I

Now list to my morning's romanza, I tell the signs of the Answerer,
To the cities and farms I sing as they spread in the sunshine before me.

A young man comes to me bearing a message from his brother,
How shall the young man know the whether and when of his brother?
Tell him to send me the signs.

And I stand before the young man face to face, and take his right hand in my left hand and his left hand in my right hand,
And I answer for his brother and for men, and I answer for him that answers for all, and send these signs.

Him all wait for, him all yield up to, his word is decisive and final,
Him they accept, in him lave, in him perceive themselves as amid light,
Him they immerse and he immerses them.

Beautiful women, the haughtiest nations, laws, the landscape, people, animals,
The profound earth and its attributes and the unquiet ocean, (so tell I my morning's romanza,)
All enjoyments and properties and money, and whatever money will buy,
The best farms, others toiling and planting and he unavoidably reaps,
The noblest and costliest cities, others grading and building and he domiciles there,
Nothing for any one but what is for him, near and far are for him, the ships in the offing,
The perpetual shows and marches on land are for him if they are for anybody.

He puts things in their attitudes,
He puts to-day out of himself with plasticity and love,
He places his own times, reminiscences, parents, brothers and sisters, associations, employment, politics, so that the rest never shame them afterward, nor assume to command them.

He is the Answerer,
What can be answer'd he answers, and what cannot be answer'd he shows how it cannot be answer'd.

A man is a summons and challenge,
(It is vain to skulk—do you hear that mocking and laughter? do you hear the ironical echoes?)

Books, friendships, philosophers, priests, action, pleasure, pride, beat up and down seeking to give satisfaction,
He indicates the satisfaction, and indicates them that beat up and down also.

Whichever the sex, whatever the season or place, he may go freshly and gently and safely by day or by night,
He has the pass-key of hearts, to him the response of the prying of hands on the knobs.

His welcome is universal, the flow of beauty is not more welcome or universal than he is,
The person he favors by day or sleeps with at night is blessed.

Every existence has its idiom, every thing has an idiom and tongue,
He resolves all tongues into his own and bestows it upon men, and any man translates, and any man translates himself also,
One part does not counteract another part, he is the joiner, he sees how they join.

He says indifferently and alike *How are you friend?* to the President at his levee,

And he says *Good-day my brother,* to Cudge that hoes in the sugar-field,
And both understand him and know that his speech is right.

He walks with perfect ease in the capitol,
He walks among the Congress, and one Representative says to another, *Here is our equal appearing and new.*

Then the mechanics take him for a mechanic,
And the soldiers suppose him to be a soldier, and the sailors that he has follow'd the sea,
And the authors take him for an author, and the artists for an artist,
And the laborers perceive he could labor with them and love them,
No matter what the work is, that he is the one to follow it or has follow'd it,
No matter what the nation, that he might find his brothers and sisters there.

The English believe he comes of their English stock,
A Jew to the Jew he seems, a Russ to the Russ, usual and near, removed from none.

Whoever he looks at in the traveler's coffee-house claims him,
The Italian or Frenchman is sure, the German is sure, the Spaniard is sure, and the island Cuban is sure,
The engineer, the deck-hand on the great lakes, or on the Mississippi or St. Lawrence or Sacramento, or Hudson or Paumanok sound, claims him.

The gentleman of perfect blood acknowledges his perfect blood,
The insulter, the prostitute, the angry person, the beggar, see themselves in the ways of him, he strangely transmutes them,
They are not vile any more, they hardly know themselves they are so grown.

2

The indications and tally of time,
Perfect sanity shows the master among philosophs,
Time, always without break, indicates itself in parts,
What always indicates the poet is the crowd of the pleasant company of singers, and their words,
The words of the singers are the hours or minutes of the light or dark, but the words of the maker of poems are the general light and dark,
The maker of poems settles justice, reality, immortality,
His insight and power encircle things and the human race,
He is the glory and extract thus far of things and of the human race.

The singers do not beget, only the Poet begets,
The singers are welcom'd, understood, appear often enough, but rare has the day been, likewise the spot, of the birth of the maker of poems, the Answerer,
(Not every century nor every five centuries has contain'd such a day, for all its names.)

The singers of successive hours of centuries may have ostensible names, but the name of each of them is one of the singers,
The name of each is, eye-singer, ear-singer, head-singer, sweet-singer, night-singer, parlor-singer, love-singer, weird-singer, or something else.

All this time and at all times wait the words of true poems,
The words of true poems do not merely please,
The true poets are not followers of beauty but the august masters of beauty;
The greatness of sons is the exuding of the greatness of mothers and fathers,
The words of true poems are the tuft and final applause of science.

Divine instinct, breadth of vision, the law of reason, health, rudeness of body, withdrawnness,
Gayety, sun-tan, air-sweetness, such are some of the words of poems.

The sailor and traveler underlie the makers of poems, the
Answerer,
The builder, geometer, chemist, anatomist, phrenologist,
artist, all these underlie the maker of poems, the
Answerer.

The words of the true poems give you more than poems,
They give you to form for yourself poems, religions, politics,
war, peace, behavior, histories, essays, daily life, and
every thing else,
They balance ranks, colors, races, creeds, and the sexes,
They do not seek beauty, they are sought,
Forever touching them or close upon them follows beauty,
longing, fain, love-sick.

They prepare for death, yet are they not the finish, but
rather the outset,
They bring none to his or her terminus or to be content
and full,
Whom they take they take into space to behold the birth of
stars, to learn one of the meanings,
To launch off with absolute faith, to sweep through the
ceaseless rings and never be quiet again.

Our Old Feuillage

Always our old feuillage!
Always Florida's green peninsula—always the priceless delta
of Louisiana—always the cotton-fields of Alabama and
Texas,
Always California's golden hills and hollows, and the silver
mountains of New Mexico—always soft-breath'd Cuba,
Always the vast slope drain'd by the Southern sea, inseparable
with the slopes drain'd by the Eastern and Western seas,
The area the eighty-third year of these States, the three and
a half millions of square miles,
The eighteen thousand miles of sea-coast and bay-coast on
the main, the thirty thousand miles of river navigation,
The seven millions of distinct families and the same number

of dwellings—always these, and more, branching forth into numberless branches,
Always the free range and diversity—always the continent of Democracy;
Always the prairies, pastures, forests, vast cities, travelers, Kanada, the snows;
Always these compact lands tied at the hips with the belt stringing the huge oval lakes;
Always the West with strong native persons, the increasing density there, the habitans, friendly, threatening, ironical, scorning invaders;
All sights, South, North, East—all deeds, promiscuously done at all times,
All characters, movements, growths, a few noticed, myriads unnoticed,
Through Mannahatta's streets I walking, these things gathering,
On interior rivers by night in the glare of pine knots, steamboats wooding up,
Sunlight by day on the valley of the Susquehanna, and on the valleys of the Potomac and Rappahannock, and the valleys of the Roanoke and Delaware,
In their northerly wilds beasts of prey haunting the Adirondacks the hills, or lapping the Saginaw waters to drink,
In a lonesome inlet a sheldrake lost from the flock, sitting on the water rocking silently,
In farmers' barns oxen in the stable, their harvest labor done, they rest standing, they are too tired,
Afar on arctic ice the she-walrus lying drowsily while her cubs play around,
The hawk sailing where men have not yet sail'd, the farthest polar sea, ripply, crystalline, open, beyond the floes,
White drift spooning ahead where the ship in the tempest dashes,
On solid land what is done in cities as the bells strike midnight together,
In primitive woods the sounds there also sounding, the howl of the wolf, the scream of the panther, and the hoarse bellow of the elk,

In winter beneath the hard blue ice of Moosehead lake, in summer visible through the clear waters, the great trout swimming,
In lower latitudes in warmer air in the Carolinas the large black buzzard floating slowly high beyond the tree tops,
Below, the red cedar festoon'd with tylandria, the pines and cypresses growing out of the white sand that spreads far and flat,
Rude boats descending the big Pedee, climbing plants, parasites with color'd flowers and berries enveloping huge trees,
The waving drapery on the live-oak trailing long and low, noiselessly waved by the wind,
The camp of Georgia wagoners just after dark, the supper-fires and the cooking and eating by whites and negroes,
Thirty or forty great wagons, the mules, cattle, horses, feeding from troughs,
The shadows, gleams, up under the leaves of the old sycamore-trees, the flames with the black smoke from the pitch-pine curling and rising;
Southern fishermen fishing, the sounds and inlets of North Carolina's coast, the shad-fishery and the herring-fishery, the large sweep-seines, the windlasses on shore work'd by horses, the clearing, curing, and packing-houses;
Deep in the forest in piney woods turpentine dropping from the incisions in the trees, there are the turpentine works,
There are the negroes at work in good health, the ground in all directions is cover'd with pine straw;
In Tennessee and Kentucky slaves busy in the coalings, at the forge, by the furnace-blaze, or at the corn-shucking,
In Virginia, the planter's son returning after a long absence, joyfully welcom'd and kiss'd by the aged mulatto nurse,
On rivers boatmen safely moor'd at nightfall in their boats under shelter of high banks,
Some of the younger men dance to the sound of the banjo or fiddle, others sit on the gunwale smoking and talking;
Late in the afternoon the mocking-bird, the American mimic, singing in the Great Dismal Swamp,
There are the greenish waters, the resinous odor, the plenteous moss, the cypress-tree, and the juniper-tree;

Northward, young men of Mannahatta, the target company
from an excursion returning home at evening, the musket-
muzzles all bear bunches of flowers presented by women;
Children at play, or on his father's lap a young boy fallen
asleep, (how his lips move! how he smiles in his sleep!)
The scout riding on horseback over the plains west of the
Mississippi, he ascends a knoll and sweeps his eyes around;
California life, the miner, bearded, dress'd in his rude costume,
the stanch California friendship, the sweet air, the graves
one in passing meets solitary just aside the horse-path;
Down in Texas the cotton-field, the negro-cabins, drivers
driving mules or oxen before rude carts, cotton bales
piled on banks and wharves;
Encircling all, vast-darting up and wide, the American Soul,
with equal hemispheres, one Love, one Dilation or Pride;
In arriere the peace-talk with the Iroquois the aborigines,
the calumet, the pipe of good-will, arbitration, and
indorsement,
The sachem blowing the smoke first toward the sun and
then toward the earth,
The drama of the scalp-dance enacted with painted faces
and guttural exclamations,
The setting out of the war-party, the long and stealthy march,
The single file, the swinging hatchets, the surprise and
slaughter of enemies;
All the acts, scenes, ways, persons, attitudes of these States,
reminiscences, institutions,
All these States compact, every square mile of these States
without excepting a particle;
Me pleas'd, rambling in lanes and country fields,
Paumanok's fields,
Observing the spiral flight of two little yellow butterflies
shuffling between each other, ascending high in the air,
The darting swallow, the destroyer of insects, the fall traveler
southward but returning northward early in the spring,
The country boy at the close of the day driving the herd of
cows and shouting to them as they loiter to browse by
the road-side,
The city wharf, Boston, Philadelphia, Baltimore, Charleston,
New Orleans, San Francisco,

The departing ships when the sailors heave at the capstan;
Evening—me in my room—the setting sun,
The setting summer sun shining in my open window, showing the swarm of flies, suspended, balancing in the air in the centre of the room, darting athwart, up and down, casting swift shadows in specks on the opposite wall where the shine is;
The athletic American matron speaking in public to crowds of listeners,
Males, females, immigrants, combinations, the copiousness, the individuality of the States, each for itself—the money-makers,
Factories, machinery, the mechanical forces, the windlass, lever, pulley, all certainties,
The certainty of space, increase, freedom, futurity,
In space the sporades, the scatter'd islands, the stars—on the firm earth, the lands, my lands,
O lands! all so dear to me—what you are, (whatever it is,) I putting it at random in these songs, become a part of that, whatever it is,
Southward there, I screaming, with wings slow flapping, with the myriads of gulls wintering along the coasts of Florida,
Otherways there atwixt the banks of the Arkansaw, the Rio Grande, the Nueces, the Brazos, the Tombigbee, the Red River, the Saskatchawan or the Osage, I with the spring waters laughing and skipping and running,
Northward, on the sands, on some shallow bay of Paumanok, I with parties of snowy herons wading in the wet to seek worms and aquatic plants,
Retreating, triumphantly twittering, the king-bird, from piercing the crow with its bill, for amusement—and I triumphantly twittering,
The migrating flock of wild geese alighting in autumn to refresh themselves, the body of the flock feed, the sentinels outside move around with erect heads watching, and are from time to time reliev'd by other sentinels—and I feeding and taking turns with the rest,
In Kanadian forests the moose, large as an ox, corner'd by hunters, rising desperately on his hind-feet, and plunging with his fore-feet, the hoofs as sharp as knives—

and I, plunging at the hunters, corner'd and desperate,
In the Mannahatta, streets, piers, shipping, store-houses, and
the countless workmen working in the shops,
And I too of the Mannahatta, singing thereof—and no less
in myself than the whole of the Mannahatta in itself,
Singing the song of These, my ever-united lands—my body
no more inevitably united, part to part, and made out
of a thousand diverse contributions one identity, any
more than my lands are inevitably united and made
ONE IDENTITY;
Nativities, climates, the grass of the great pastoral Plains,
Cities, labors, death, animals, products, war, good and
evil—these me,
These affording, in all their particulars, the old feuillage to
me and to America, how can I do less than pass the
clew of the union of them, to afford the like to you?
Whoever you are! how can I but offer you divine leaves,
that you also be eligible as I am?
How can I but as here chanting, invite you for yourself to
collect bouquets of the incomparable feuillage of these
States?

A SONG OF JOYS

O TO make the most jubilant song!
Full of music—full of manhood, womanhood, infancy!
Full of common employments—full of grain and trees.

O for the voices of animals—O for the swiftness and balance
of fishes!
O for the dropping of raindrops in a song!
O for the sunshine and motion of waves in a song!

O the joy of my spirit—it is uncaged—it darts like lightning!
It is not enough to have this globe or a certain time,
I will have thousands of globes and all time.

O the engineer's joys! to go with a locomotive!
To hear the hiss of steam, the merry shriek, the steam-
whistle, the laughing locomotive!
To push with resistless way and speed off in the distance.

O the gleesome saunter over fields and hillsides!
The leaves and flowers of the commonest weeds, the moist
fresh stillness of the woods,
The exquisite smell of the earth at daybreak, and all through
the forenoon.

O the horseman's and horsewoman's joys!
The saddle, the gallop, the pressure upon the seat, the cool
gurgling by the ears and hair.

O the fireman's joys!
I hear the alarm at dead of night,
I hear bells, shouts! I pass the crowd, I run!
The sight of the flames maddens me with pleasure.

O the joy of the strong-brawn'd fighter, towering in the
arena in perfect condition, conscious of power, thirsting
to meet his opponent.

O the joy of that vast elemental sympathy which only the
human soul is capable of generating and emitting in
steady and limitless floods.

O the mother's joys!
The watching, the endurance, the precious love, the
anguish, the patiently yielded life.

O the joy of increase, growth, recuperation,
The joy of soothing and pacifying, the joy of concord and
harmony.

O to go back to the place where I was born,
To hear the birds sing once more,
To ramble about the house and barn and over the fields
once more,
And through the orchard and along the old lanes once more.

O to have been brought up on bays, lagoons, creeks, or
along the coast,
To continue and be employ'd there all my life,

The briny and damp smell, the shore, the salt weeds exposed
at low water,
The work of fishermen, the work of the eel-fisher and clam-
fisher;
I come with my clam-rake and spade, I come with my eel-spear,
Is the tide out? I join the group of clam-diggers on the flats,
I laugh and work with them, I joke at my work like a
mettlesome young man;
In winter I take my eel-basket and eel-spear and travel out on
foot on the ice—I have a small axe to cut holes in the ice,
Behold me well-clothed going gayly or returning in the
afternoon, my brood of tough boys accompanying me,
My brood of grown and part-grown boys, who love to be
with no one else so well as they love to be with me,
By day to work with me, and by night to sleep with me.

Another time in warm weather out in a boat, to lift the
lobster-pots where they are sunk with heavy stones, (I
know the buoys,)
O the sweetness of the Fifth-month morning upon the
water as I row just before sunrise toward the buoys,
I pull the wicker pots up slantingly, the dark green lobsters
are desperate with their claws as I take them out, I
insert wooden pegs in the joints of their pincers,
I go to all the places one after another, and then row back
to the shore,
There in a huge kettle of boiling water the lobsters shall be
boil'd till their color becomes scarlet.

Another time mackerel-taking,
Voracious, mad for the hook, near the surface, they seem to
fill the water for miles;
Another time fishing for rock-fish in Chesapeake bay, I one
of the brown-faced crew;
Another time trailing for blue-fish off Paumanok, I stand
with braced body,
My left foot is on the gunwale, my right arm throws far out
the coils of slender rope,
In sight around me the quick veering and darting of fifty
skiffs, my companions.

O boating on the rivers,
The voyage down the St. Lawrence, the superb scenery, the steamers,
The ships sailing, the Thousand Islands, the occasional timber-raft and the raftsmen with long-reaching sweep-oars,
The little huts on the rafts, and the stream of smoke when they cook supper at evening.

(O something pernicious and dread!
Something far away from a puny and pious life!
Something unproved! something in a trance!
Something escaped from the anchorage and driving free.)

O to work in mines, or forging iron,
Foundry casting, the foundry itself, the rude high roof, the ample and shadow'd space,
The furnace, the hot liquid pour'd out and running.

O to resume the joys of the soldier!
To feel the presence of a brave commanding officer—to feel his sympathy!
To behold his calmness—to be warm'd in the rays of his smile!
To go to battle—to hear the bugles play and the drums beat!
To hear the crash of artillery—to see the glittering of the bayonets and musket-barrels in the sun!
To see men fall and die and not complain!
To taste the savage taste of blood—to be so devilish!
To gloat so over the wounds and deaths of the enemy.

O the whaleman's joys! O I cruise my old cruise again!
I feel the ship's motion under me, I feel the Atlantic breezes fanning me,
I hear the cry again sent down from the mast-head, *There—she blows!*
Again I spring up the rigging to look with the rest—we descend, wild with excitement,
I leap in the lower'd boat, we row toward our prey where he lies,

We approach stealthy and silent, I see the mountainous
mass, lethargic, basking,
I see the harpooneer standing up, I see the weapon dart
from his vigorous arm;
O swift again far out in the ocean the wounded whale,
settling, running to windward, tows me,
Again I see him rise to breathe, we row close again,
I see a lance driven through his side, press'd deep, turn'd in
the wound,
Again we back off, I see him settle again, the life is leaving
him fast,
As he rises he spouts blood, I see him swim in circles
narrower and narrower, swiftly cutting the water—I see
him die,
He gives one convulsive leap in the centre of the circle, and
then falls flat and still in the bloody foam.

O the old manhood of me, my noblest joy of all!
My children and grand-children, my white hair and beard,
My largeness, calmness, majesty, out of the long stretch of
my life.

O ripen'd joy of womanhood! O happiness at last!
I am more than eighty years of age, I am the most
venerable mother,
How clear is my mind—how all people draw nigh to me!
What attractions are these beyond any before? what bloom
more than the bloom of youth?
What beauty is this that descends upon me and rises out of me?

O the orator's joys!
To inflate the chest, to roll the thunder of the voice out
from the ribs and throat,
To make the people rage, weep, hate, desire, with yourself,
To lead America—to quell America with a great tongue.

O the joy of my soul leaning pois'd on itself, receiving
identity through materials and loving them, observing
characters and absorbing them,
My soul vibrated back to me from them, from sight,

hearing, touch, reason, articulation, comparison, memory, and the like,
The real life of my senses and flesh transcending my senses and flesh,
My body done with materials, my sight done with my material eyes,
Proved to me this day beyond cavil that it is not my material eyes which finally see,
Nor my material body which finally loves, walks, laughs, shouts, embraces, procreates.

O the farmer's joys!
Ohioan's, Illinoisian's, Wisconsinese', Kanadian's, Iowan's, Kansian's, Missourian's, Oregonese' joys!
To rise at peep of day and pass forth nimbly to work,
To plough land in the fall for winter-sown crops,
To plough land in the spring for maize,
To train orchards, to graft the trees, to gather apples in the fall.

O to bathe in the swimming-bath, or in a good place along shore,
To splash the water! to walk ankle-deep, or race naked along the shore.

O to realize space!
The plenteousness of all, that there are no bounds,
To emerge and be of the sky, of the sun and moon and flying clouds, as one with them.

O the joy of a manly self-hood!
To be servile to none, to defer to none, not to any tyrant known or unknown,
To walk with erect carriage, a step springy and elastic,
To look with calm gaze or with a flashing eye,
To speak with a full and sonorous voice out of a broad chest,
To confront with your personality all the other personalities of the earth.

Know'st thou the excellent joys of youth?
Joys of the dear companions and of the merry word and
laughing face?
Joy of the glad light-beaming day, joy of the wide-breath'd
games?
Joy of sweet music, joy of the lighted ball-room and the
dancers?
Joy of the plenteous dinner, strong carouse and drinking?

Yet O my soul supreme!
Know'st thou the joys of pensive thought?
Joys of the free and lonesome heart, the tender, gloomy heart?
Joys of the solitary walk, the spirit bow'd yet proud, the
suffering and the struggle?
The agonistic throes, the ecstasies, joys of the solemn
musings day or night?
Joys of the thought of Death, the great spheres Time and
Space?
Prophetic joys of better, loftier love's ideals, the divine wife,
the sweet, eternal, perfect comrade?
Joys all thine own undying one, joys worthy thee O soul.

O while I live to be the ruler of life, not a slave,
To meet life as a powerful conqueror,
No fumes, no ennui, no more complaints or scornful
criticisms,
To these proud laws of the air, the water and the ground,
proving my interior soul impregnable,
And nothing exterior shall ever take command of me.

For not life's joys alone I sing, repeating—the joy of death!
The beautiful touch of Death, soothing and benumbing a
few moments, for reasons,
Myself discharging my excrementitious body to be burn'd,
or render'd to powder, or buried,
My real body doubtless left to me for other spheres,
My voided body nothing more to me, returning to the
purifications, further offices, eternal uses of the earth.

O to attract by more than attraction!
How it is I know not—yet behold! the something which
obeys none of the rest,
It is offensive, never defensive—yet how magnetic it draws.

O to struggle against great odds, to meet enemies undaunted!
To be entirely alone with them, to find how much one can
stand!
To look strife, torture, prison, popular odium, face to face!
To mount the scaffold, to advance to the muzzles of guns
with perfect nonchalance!
To be indeed a God!

O to sail to sea in a ship!
To leave this steady unendurable land,
To leave the tiresome sameness of the streets, the sidewalks
and the houses,
To leave you O you solid motionless land, and entering a ship,
To sail and sail and sail!

O to have life henceforth a poem of new joys!
To dance, clap hands, exult, shout, skip, leap, roll on, float on!
To be a sailor of the world bound for all ports,
A ship itself, (see indeed these sails I spread to the sun
and air,)
A swift and swelling ship full of rich words, full of joys.

Song of the Broad-Axe

1

Weapon shapely, naked, wan,
Head from the mother's bowels drawn,
Wooded flesh and metal bone, limb only one and lip only one,
Gray-blue leaf by red-heat grown, helve produced from a
little seed sown,
Resting the grass amid and upon,
To be lean'd and to lean on.

Strong shapes and attributes of strong shapes, masculine
trades, sights and sounds,

Long varied train of an emblem, dabs of music,
Fingers of the organist skipping staccato over the keys of the
great organ.

2

Welcome are all earth's lands, each for its kind,
Welcome are lands of pine and oak,
Welcome are lands of the lemon and fig,
Welcome are lands of gold,
Welcome are lands of wheat and maize, welcome those of
the grape,
Welcome are lands of sugar and rice,
Welcome the cotton-lands, welcome those of the white
potato and sweet potato,
Welcome are mountains, flats, sands, forests, prairies,
Welcome the rich borders of rivers, table-lands, openings,
Welcome the measureless grazing-lands, welcome the
teeming soil of orchards, flax, honey, hemp;
Welcome just as much the other more hard-faced lands,
Lands rich as lands of gold or wheat and fruit lands,
Lands of mines, lands of the manly and rugged ores,
Lands of coal, copper, lead, tin, zinc,
Lands of iron—lands of the make of the axe.

3

The log at the wood-pile, the axe supported by it,
The sylvan hut, the vine over the doorway, the space clear'd
for a garden,
The irregular tapping of rain down on the leaves after the
storm is lull'd,
The wailing and moaning at intervals, the thought of the sea,
The thought of ships struck in the storm and put on their
beam ends, and the cutting away of masts,
The sentiment of the huge timbers of old-fashion'd houses
and barns,
The remember'd print or narrative, the voyage at a venture
of men, families, goods,
The disembarkation, the founding of a new city,
The voyage of those who sought a New England and found
it, the outset anywhere,

The settlements of the Arkansas, Colorado, Ottawa,
Willamette,
The slow progress, the scant fare, the axe, rifle, saddle-bags;
The beauty of all adventurous and daring persons,
The beauty of wood-boys and wood-men with their clear
untrimm'd faces,
The beauty of independence, departure, actions that rely on
themselves,
The American contempt for statutes and ceremonies, the
boundless impatience of restraint,
The loose drift of character, the inkling through random
types, the solidification;
The butcher in the slaughter-house, the hands aboard
schooners and sloops, the raftsman, the pioneer,
Lumbermen in their winter camp, daybreak in the woods,
stripes of snow on the limbs of trees, the occasional
snapping,
The glad clear sound of one's own voice, the merry song,
the natural life of the woods, the strong day's work,
The blazing fire at night, the sweet taste of supper, the talk,
the bed of hemlock-boughs and the bear-skin;
The house-builder at work in cities or anywhere,
The preparatory jointing, squaring, sawing, mortising,
The hoist-up of beams, the push of them in their places,
laying them regular,
Setting the studs by their tenons in the mortises according
as they were prepared,
The blows of mallets and hammers, the attitudes of the
men, their curv'd limbs,
Bending, standing, astride the beams, driving in pins,
holding on by posts and braces,
The hook'd arm over the plate, the other arm wielding
the axe,
The floor-men forcing the planks close to be nail'd,
Their postures bringing their weapons downward on the
bearers,
The echoes resounding through the vacant building;
The huge storehouse carried up in the city well under way,

The six framing-men, two in the middle and two at each end, carefully bearing on their shoulders a heavy stick for a cross-beam,
The crowded line of masons with trowels in their right hands rapidly laying the long side-wall, two hundred feet from front to rear,
The flexible rise and fall of backs, the continual click of the trowels striking the bricks,
The bricks one after another each laid so workmanlike in its place, and set with a knock of the trowel-handle,
The piles of materials, the mortar on the mortar-boards, and the steady replenishing by the hod-men;
Spar-makers in the spar-yard, the swarming row of well-grown apprentices,
The swing of their axes on the square-hew'd log shaping it toward the shape of a mast,
The brisk short crackle of the steel driven slantingly into the pine,
The butter-color'd chips flying off in great flakes and slivers,
The limber motion of brawny young arms and hips in easy costumes,
The constructor of wharves, bridges, piers, bulk-heads, floats, stays against the sea;
The city fireman, the fire that suddenly bursts forth in the close-pack'd square,
The arriving engines, the hoarse shouts, the nimble stepping and daring,
The strong command through the fire-trumpets, the falling in line, the rise and fall of the arms forcing the water,
The slender, spasmic, blue-white jets, the bringing to bear of the hooks and ladders and their execution,
The crash and cut away of connecting wood-work, or through floors if the fire smoulders under them,
The crowd with their lit faces watching, the glare and dense shadows;
The forger at his forge-furnace and the user of iron after him,
The maker of the axe large and small, and the welder and temperer,
The chooser breathing his breath on the cold steel and trying the edge with his thumb,

The one who clean-shapes the handle and sets it firmly in
the socket;
The shadowy processions of the portraits of the past users also,
The primal patient mechanics, the architects and engineers,
The far-off Assyrian edifice and Mizra edifice,
The Roman lictors preceding the consuls,
The antique European warrior with his axe in combat,
The uplifted arm, the clatter of blows on the helmeted head,
The death-howl, the limpsy tumbling body, the rush of
friend and foe thither,
The siege of revolted lieges determin'd for liberty,
The summons to surrender, the battering at castle gates, the
truce and parley,
The sack of an old city in its time,
The bursting in of mercenaries and bigots tumultuously and
disorderly,
Roar, flames, blood, drunkenness, madness,
Goods freely rifled from houses and temples, screams of
women in the gripe of brigands,
Craft and thievery of camp-followers, men running, old
persons despairing,
The hell of war, the cruelties of creeds,
The list of all executive deeds and words just or unjust,
The power of personality just or unjust.

4

Muscle and pluck forever!
What invigorates life invigorates death,
And the dead advance as much as the living advance,
And the future is no more uncertain than the present,
For the roughness of the earth and of man encloses as much
as the delicatesse of the earth and of man,
And nothing endures but personal qualities.

What do you think endures?
Do you think a great city endures?
Or a teeming manufacturing state? or a prepared constitution?
or the best built steamships?
Or hotels of granite and iron? or any chef-d'œuvres of
engineering, forts, armaments?

Away! these are not to be cherish'd for themselves,
They fill their hour, the dancers dance, the musicians play
for them,
The show passes, all does well enough of course,
All does very well till one flash of defiance.

A great city is that which has the greatest men and women,
If it be a few ragged huts it is still the greatest city in the
whole world.

5

The place where a great city stands is not the place of
stretch'd wharves, docks, manufactures, deposits of
produce merely,
Nor the place of ceaseless salutes of new-comers or the
anchor-lifters of the departing,
Nor the place of the tallest and costliest buildings or shops
selling goods from the rest of the earth,
Nor the place of the best libraries and schools, nor the place
where money is plentiest,
Nor the place of the most numerous population.

Where the city stands with the brawniest breed of orators
and bards,
Where the city stands that is belov'd by these, and loves
them in return and understands them,
Where no monuments exist to heroes but in the common
words and deeds,
Where thrift is in its place, and prudence is in its place,
Where the men and women think lightly of the laws,
Where the slave ceases, and the master of slaves ceases,
Where the populace rise at once against the never-ending
audacity of elected persons,
Where fierce men and women pour forth as the sea to the
whistle of death pours its sweeping and unript waves,
Where outside authority enters always after the precedence
of inside authority,
Where the citizen is always the head and ideal, and President,
Mayor, Governor and what not, are agents for pay,

Where children are taught to be laws to themselves, and to
 depend on themselves,
Where equanimity is illustrated in affairs,
Where speculations on the soul are encouraged,
Where women walk in public processions in the streets the
 same as the men,
Where they enter the public assembly and take places the
 same as the men;
Where the city of the faithfulest friends stands,
Where the city of the cleanliness of the sexes stands,
Where the city of the healthiest fathers stands,
Where the city of the best-bodied mothers stands,
There the great city stands.

6

How beggarly appear arguments before a defiant deed!
How the floridness of the materials of cities shrivels before a
 man's or woman's look!

All waits or goes by default till a strong being appears;
A strong being is the proof of the race and of the ability of
 the universe,
When he or she appears materials are overaw'd,
The dispute on the soul stops,
The old customs and phrases are confronted, turn'd back, or
 laid away.

What is your money-making now? what can it do now?
What is your respectability now?
What are your theology, tuition, society, traditions, statute-
 books, now?
Where are your jibes of being now?
Where are your cavils about the soul now?

7

A sterile landscape covers the ore, there is as good as the
 best for all the forbidding appearance,
There is the mine, there are the miners,
The forge-furnace is there, the melt is accomplish'd, the
 hammersmen are at hand with their tongs and hammers,
What always served and always serves is at hand.

Than this nothing has better served, it has served all,
Served the fluent-tongued and subtle-sensed Greek, and
 long ere the Greek,
Served in building the buildings that last longer than any,
Served the Hebrew, the Persian, the most ancient Hindustanee,
Served the mound-raiser on the Mississippi, served those
 whose relics remain in Central America,
Served Albic temples in woods or on plains, with unhewn
 pillars and the druids,
Served the artificial clefts, vast, high, silent, on the snow-
 cover'd hills of Scandinavia,
Served those who time out of mind made on the granite
 walls rough sketches of the sun, moon, stars, ships,
 ocean waves,
Served the paths of the irruptions of the Goths, served the
 pastoral tribes and nomads,
Served the long distant Kelt, served the hardy pirates of the
 Baltic,
Served before any of those the venerable and harmless men
 of Ethiopia,
Served the making of helms for the galleys of pleasure and
 the making of those for war,
Served all great works on land and all great works on the sea,
For the mediæval ages and before the mediæval ages,
Served not the living only then as now, but served the dead.

8

I see the European headsman,
He stands mask'd, clothed in red, with huge legs and strong
 naked arms,
And leans on a ponderous axe.

(Whom have you slaughter'd lately European headsman?
Whose is that blood upon you so wet and sticky?)

I see the clear sunsets of the martyrs,
I see from the scaffolds the descending ghosts,
Ghosts of dead lords, uncrown'd ladies, impeach'd ministers,
 rejected kings,
Rivals, traitors, poisoners, disgraced chieftains and the rest.

I see those who in any land have died for the good cause,
The seed is spare, nevertheless the crop shall never run out,
(Mind you O foreign kings, O priests, the crop shall never run out.)

I see the blood wash'd entirely away from the axe,
Both blade and helve are clean,
They spirt no more the blood of European nobles, they clasp no more the necks of queens.

I see the headsman withdraw and become useless,
I see the scaffold untrodden and mouldy, I see no longer any axe upon it,
I see the mighty and friendly emblem of the power of my own race, the newest, largest race.

9

(America! I do not vaunt my love for you,
I have what I have.)

The axe leaps!
The solid forest gives fluid utterances,
They tumble forth, they rise and form,
Hut, tent, landing, survey,
Flail, plough, pick, crowbar, spade,
Shingle, rail, prop, wainscot, jamb, lath, panel, gable,
Citadel, ceiling, saloon, academy, organ, exhibition-house, library,
Cornice, trellis, pilaster, balcony, window, turret, porch,
Hoe, rake, pitchfork, pencil, wagon, staff, saw, jack-plane, mallet, wedge, rounce,
Chair, tub, hoop, table, wicket, vane, sash, floor,
Work-box, chest, string'd instrument, boat, frame, and what not,
Capitols of States, and capitol of the nation of States,
Long stately rows in avenues, hospitals for orphans or for the poor or sick,
Manhattan steamboats and clippers taking the measure of all seas.

The shapes arise!
Shapes of the using of axes anyhow, and the users and all that neighbors them,
Cutters down of wood and haulers of it to the Penobscot or Kennebec,
Dwellers in cabins among the Californian mountains or by the little lakes, or on the Columbia,
Dwellers south on the banks of the Gila or Rio Grande, friendly gatherings, the characters and fun,
Dwellers along the St. Lawrence, or north in Kanada, or down by the Yellowstone, dwellers on coasts and off coasts,
Seal-fishers, whalers, arctic seamen breaking passages through the ice.

The shapes arise!
Shapes of factories, arsenals, foundries, markets,
Shapes of the two-threaded tracks of railroads,
Shapes of the sleepers of bridges, vast frameworks, girders, arches,
Shapes of the fleets of barges, tows, lake and canal craft, river craft,
Ship-yards and dry-docks along the Eastern and Western seas, and in many a bay and by-place,
The live-oak kelsons, the pine planks, the spars, the hackmatack-roots for knees,
The ships themselves on their ways, the tiers of scaffolds, the workmen busy outside and inside,
The tools lying around, the great auger and little auger, the adze, bolt, line, square, gouge, and bead-plane.

10

The shapes arise!
The shape measur'd, saw'd, jack'd, join'd, stain'd,
The coffin-shape for the dead to lie within in his shroud,
The shape got out in posts, in the bedstead posts, in the posts of the bride's bed,
The shape of the little trough, the shape of the rockers beneath, the shape of the babe's cradle,

The shape of the floor-planks, the floor-planks for dancers' feet,
The shape of the planks of the family home, the home of the friendly parents and children,
The shape of the roof of the home of the happy young man and woman, the roof over the well-married young man and woman,
The roof over the supper joyously cook'd by the chaste wife, and joyously eaten by the chaste husband, content after his day's work.

The shapes arise!
The shape of the prisoner's place in the court-room, and of him or her seated in the place,
The shape of the liquor-bar lean'd against by the young rum-drinker and the old rum-drinker,
The shape of the shamed and angry stairs trod by sneaking footsteps,
The shape of the sly settee, and the adulterous unwholesome couple,
The shape of the gambling-board with its devilish winnings and losings,
The shape of the step-ladder for the convicted and sentenced murderer, the murderer with haggard face and pinion'd arms,
The sheriff at hand with his deputies, the silent and white-lipp'd crowd, the dangling of the rope.

The shapes arise!
Shapes of doors giving many exits and entrances,
The door passing the dissever'd friend flush'd and in haste,
The door that admits good news and bad news,
The door whence the son left home confident and puff'd up,
The door he enter'd again from a long and scandalous absence, diseas'd, broken down, without innocence, without means.

11

Her shape arises,
She less guarded than ever, yet more guarded than ever,

The gross and soil'd she moves among do not make her
gross and soil'd,
She knows the thoughts as she passes, nothing is conceal'd
from her,
She is none the less considerate or friendly therefor,
She is the best belov'd, it is without exception, she has no
reason to fear and she does not fear,
Oaths, quarrels, hiccupp'd songs, smutty expressions, are
idle to her as she passes,
She is silent, she is possess'd of herself, they do not offend her,
She receives them as the laws of Nature receive them, she is
strong,
She too is a law of Nature—there is no law stronger than
she is.

12

The main shapes arise!
Shapes of Democracy total, result of centuries,
Shapes ever projecting other shapes,
Shapes of turbulent manly cities,
Shapes of the friends and home-givers of the whole earth,
Shapes bracing the earth and braced with the whole earth.

Song of the Exposition

1

(Ah little recks the laborer,
How near his work is holding him to God,
The loving Laborer through space and time.)

After all not to create only, or found only,
But to bring perhaps from afar what is already founded,
To give it our own identity, average, limitless, free,
To fill the gross the torpid bulk with vital religious fire,
Not to repel or destroy so much as accept, fuse, rehabilitate,
To obey as well as command, to follow more than to lead,
These also are the lessons of our New World;
While how little the New after all, how much the Old, Old
World!

Long and long has the grass been growing,
Long and long has the rain been falling,
Long has the globe been rolling round.

2

Come Muse migrate from Greece and Ionia,
Cross out please those immensely overpaid accounts,
That matter of Troy and Achilles' wrath, and Æneas',
Odysseus' wanderings,
Placard "Removed" and "To Let" on the rocks of your
snowy Parnassus,
Repeat at Jerusalem, place the notice high on Jaffa's gate
and on Mount Moriah,
The same on the walls of your German, French and Spanish
castles, and Italian collections,
For know a better, fresher, busier sphere, a wide, untried
domain awaits, demands you.

3

Responsive to our summons,
Or rather to her long-nurs'd inclination,
Join'd with an irresistible, natural gravitation,
She comes! I hear the rustling of her gown,
I scent the odor of her breath's delicious fragrance,
I mark her step divine, her curious eyes a-turning, rolling,
Upon this very scene.

The dame of dames! can I believe then,
Those ancient temples, sculptures classic, could none of
them retain her?
Nor shades of Virgil and Dante, nor myriad memories,
poems, old associations, magnetize and hold on to her?
But that she's left them all—and here?

Yes, if you will allow me to say so,
I, my friends, if you do not, can plainly see her,
The same undying soul of earth's, activity's, beauty's,
heroism's expression,

Out from her evolutions hither come, ended the strata of
her former themes,
Hidden and cover'd by to-day's, foundation of to-day's,
Ended, deceas'd through time, her voice by Castaly's fountain,
Silent the broken-lipp'd Sphynx in Egypt, silent all those
century-baffling tombs,
Ended for aye the epics of Asia's, Europe's helmeted
warriors, ended the primitive call of the muses,
Calliope's call forever closed, Clio, Melpomene, Thalia dead,
Ended the stately rhythmus of Una and Oriana, ended the
quest of the holy Graal,
Jerusalem a handful of ashes blown by the wind, extinct,
The Crusaders' streams of shadowy midnight troops sped
with the sunrise,
Amadis, Tancred, utterly gone, Charlemagne, Roland,
Oliver gone,
Palmerin, ogre, departed, vanish'd the turrets that Usk from
its waters reflected,
Arthur vanish'd with all his knights, Merlin and Lancelot and
Galahad, all gone, dissolv'd utterly like an exhalation;
Pass'd! pass'd! for us, forever pass'd, that once so mighty
world, now void, inanimate, phantom world,
Embroider'd, dazzling, foreign world, with all its gorgeous
legends, myths,
Its kings and castles proud, its priests and warlike lords and
courtly dames,
Pass'd to its charnel vault, coffin'd with crown and armor on,
Blazon'd with Shakspere's purple page,
And dirged by Tennyson's sweet sad rhyme.

I say I see, my friends, if you do not, the illustrious emigré,
(having it is true in her day, although the same,
changed, journey'd considerable,)
Making directly for this rendezvous, vigorously clearing a
path for herself, striding through the confusion,
By thud of machinery and shrill steam-whistle undismay'd,
Bluff'd not a bit by drain-pipe, gasometers, artificial fertilizers,
Smiling and pleas'd with palpable intent to stay,
She's here, install'd amid the kitchen ware!

4

But hold—don't I forget my manners?
To introduce the stranger, (what else indeed do I live to chant for?) to thee Columbia;
In liberty's name welcome immortal! clasp hands,
And ever henceforth sisters dear be both.

Fear not O Muse! truly new ways and days receive, surround you,
I candidly confess a queer, queer race, of novel fashion,
And yet the same old human race, the same within, without,
Faces and hearts the same, feelings the same, yearnings the same,
The same old love, beauty and use the same.

5

We do not blame thee elder World, nor really separate ourselves from thee,
(Would the son separate himself from the father?)
Looking back on thee, seeing thee to thy duties, grandeurs, through past ages bending, building,
We build to ours to-day.

Mightier than Egypt's tombs,
Fairer than Grecia's, Roma's temples,
Prouder than Milan's statued, spired cathedral,
More picturesque than Rhenish castle-keeps,
We plan even now to raise, beyond them all,
Thy great cathedral sacred industry, no tomb,
A keep for life for practical invention.

As in a waking vision,
E'en while I chant I see it rise, I scan and prophesy outside and in,
Its manifold ensemble.

Around a palace, loftier, fairer, ampler than any yet,
Earth's modern wonder, history's seven outstripping,
High rising tier on tier with glass and iron façades,

Gladdening the sun and sky, enhued in cheerfulest hues,
Bronze, lilac, robin's-egg, marine and crimson,
Over whose golden roof shall flaunt, beneath thy banner
Freedom,
The banners of the States and flags of every land,
A brood of lofty, fair, but lesser palaces shall cluster.

Somewhere within their walls shall all that forwards perfect
human life be started,
Tried, taught, advanced, visibly exhibited.

Not only all the world of works, trade, products,
But all the workmen of the world here to be represented.

Here shall you trace in flowing operation,
In every state of practical, busy movement, the rills of
civilization,
Materials here under your eye shall change their shape as if
by magic,
The cotton shall be pick'd almost in the very field,
Shall be dried, clean'd, ginn'd, baled, spun into thread and
cloth before you,
You shall see hands at work at all the old processes and all
the new ones,
You shall see the various grains and how flour is made and
then bread baked by the bakers,
You shall see the crude ores of California and Nevada
passing on and on till they become bullion,
You shall watch how the printer sets type, and learn what a
composing-stick is,
You shall mark in amazement the Hoe press whirling its
cylinders, shedding the printed leaves steady and fast,
The photograph, model, watch, pin, nail, shall be created
before you.

In large calm halls, a stately museum shall teach you the
infinite lessons of minerals,
In another, woods, plants, vegetation shall be illustrated—in
another animals, animal life and development.

One stately house shall be the music house,
Others for other arts—learning, the sciences, shall all be here,
None shall be slighted, none but shall here be honor'd,
help'd, exampled.

6

(This, this and these, America, shall be *your* pyramids and
obelisks,
Your Alexandrian Pharos, gardens of Babylon,
Your temple at Olympia.)

The male and female many laboring not,
Shall ever here confront the laboring many,
With precious benefits to both, glory to all,
To thee America, and thee eternal Muse.

And here shall ye inhabit powerful Matrons!
In your vast state vaster than all the old,
Echoed through long, long centuries to come,
To sound of different, prouder songs, with stronger themes,
Practical, peaceful life, the people's life, the People themselves,
Lifted, illumin'd, bathed in peace—elate, secure in peace.

7

Away with themes of war! away with war itself!
Hence from my shuddering sight to never more return that
show of blacken'd, mutilated corpses!
That hell unpent and raid of blood, fit for wild tigers or for
lop-tongued wolves, not reasoning men,
And in its stead speed industry's campaigns,
With thy undaunted armies, engineering,
Thy pennants labor, loosen'd to the breeze,
Thy bugles sounding loud and clear.

Away with old romance!
Away with novels, plots and plays of foreign courts,
Away with love-verses sugar'd in rhyme, the intrigues,
amours of idlers,
Fitted for only banquets of the night where dancers to late
music slide,

The unhealthy pleasures, extravagant dissipations of the few,
With perfumes, heat and wine, beneath the dazzling
chandeliers.

To you ye reverent sane sisters,
I raise a voice for far superber themes for poets and for art,
To exalt the present and the real,
To teach the average man the glory of his daily walk and
trade,
To sing in songs how exercise and chemical life are never to
be baffled,
To manual work for each and all, to plough, hoe, dig,
To plant and tend the tree, the berry, vegetables, flowers,
For every man to see to it that he really do something, for
every woman too;
To use the hammer and the saw, (rip, or cross-cut,)
To cultivate a turn for carpentering, plastering, painting,
To work as tailor, tailoress, nurse, hostler, porter,
To invent a little, something ingenious, to aid the washing,
cooking, cleaning,
And hold it no disgrace to take a hand at them themselves.

I say I bring thee Muse to-day and here,
All occupations, duties broad and close,
Toil, healthy toil and sweat, endless, without cessation,
The old, old practical burdens, interests, joys,
The family, parentage, childhood, husband and wife,
The house-comforts, the house itself and all its belongings,
Food and its preservation, chemistry applied to it,
Whatever forms the average, strong, complete, sweet-blooded
man or woman, the perfect longeve personality,
And helps its present life to health and happiness, and
shapes its soul,
For the eternal real life to come.

With latest connections, works, the inter-transportation of
the world,
Steam-power, the great express lines, gas, petroleum,
These triumphs of our time, the Atlantic's delicate cable,

The Pacific railroad, the Suez canal, the Mont Cenis and
Gothard and Hoosac tunnels, the Brooklyn bridge,
This earth all spann'd with iron rails, with lines of steamships
threading every sea,
Our own rondure, the current globe I bring.

8

And thou America,
Thy offspring towering e'er so high, yet higher Thee above
all towering,
With Victory on thy left, and at thy right hand Law;
Thou Union holding all, fusing, absorbing, tolerating all,
Thee, ever thee, I sing.

Thou, also thou, a World,
With all thy wide geographies, manifold, different, distant,
Rounded by thee in one—one common orbic language,
One common indivisible destiny for All.

And by the spells which ye vouchsafe to those your
ministers in earnest,
I here personify and call my themes, to make them pass
before ye.

Behold, America! (and thou, ineffable guest and sister!)
For thee come trooping up thy waters and thy lands;
Behold! thy fields and farms, thy far-off woods and mountains,
As in procession coming.

Behold, the sea itself,
And on its limitless, heaving breast, the ships;
See, where their white sails, bellying in the wind, speckle the
green and blue,
See, the steamers coming and going, steaming in or out of
port,
See, dusky and undulating, the long pennants of smoke.

Behold, in Oregon, far in the north and west,
Or in Maine, far in the north and east, thy cheerful axemen,
Wielding all day their axes.

Behold, on the lakes, thy pilots at their wheels, thy oarsmen,
How the ash writhes under those muscular arms!

There by the furnace, and there by the anvil,
Behold thy sturdy blacksmiths swinging their sledges,
Overhand so steady, overhand they turn and fall with joyous
clank,
Like a tumult of laughter.

Mark the spirit of invention everywhere, thy rapid patents,
Thy continual workshops, foundries, risen or rising,
See, from their chimneys how the tall flame-fires stream.

Mark, thy interminable farms, North, South,
Thy wealthy daughter-states, Eastern and Western,
The varied products of Ohio, Pennsylvania, Missouri,
Georgia, Texas, and the rest,
Thy limitless crops, grass, wheat, sugar, oil, corn, rice,
hemp, hops,
Thy barns all fill'd, the endless freight-train and the bulging
storehouse,
Thy grapes that ripen on thy vines, the apples in thy orchards,
Thy incalculable lumber, beef, pork, potatoes, thy coal, thy
gold and silver,
The inexhaustible iron in thy mines.

All thine O sacred Union!
Ships, farms, shops, barns, factories, mines,
City and State, North, South, item and aggregate,
We dedicate, dread Mother, all to thee!

Protectress absolute, thou! bulwark of all!
For well we know that while thou givest each and all,
(generous as God,)
Without thee neither all nor each, nor land, home,
Nor ship, nor mine, nor any here this day secure,
Nor aught, nor any day secure.

9

And thou, the Emblem waving over all!
Delicate beauty, a word to thee, (it may be salutary,)

Remember thou hast not always been as here to-day so
comfortably ensovereign'd,
In other scenes than these have I observ'd thee flag,
Not quite so trim and whole and freshly blooming in folds
of stainless silk,
But I have seen thee bunting, to tatters torn upon thy
splinter'd staff,
Or clutch'd to some young color-bearer's breast with
desperate hands,
Savagely struggled for, for life or death, fought over long,
'Mid cannons' thunder-crash and many a curse and groan
and yell, and rifle-volleys cracking sharp,
And moving masses as wild demons surging, and lives as
nothing risk'd,
For thy mere remnant grimed with dirt and smoke and
sopp'd in blood,
For sake of that, my beauty, and that thou might'st dally as
now secure up there,
Many a good man have I seen go under.

Now here and these and hence in peace, all thine O Flag!
And here and hence for thee, O universal Muse! and thou
for them!
And here and hence O Union, all the work and workmen
thine!
None separate from thee—henceforth One only, we and thou,
(For the blood of the children, what is it, only the blood
maternal?
And lives and works, what are they all at last, except the
roads to faith and death?)

While we rehearse our measureless wealth, it is for thee,
dear Mother,
We own it all and several to-day indissoluble in thee;
Think not our chant, our show, merely for products gross or
lucre—it is for thee, the soul in thee, electric, spiritual!
Our farms, inventions, crops, we own in thee! cities and
States in thee!
Our freedom all in thee! our very lives in thee!

Song of the Redwood-Tree

I

A California song,
A prophecy and indirection, a thought impalpable to breathe as air,
A chorus of dryads, fading, departing, or hamadryads departing,
A murmuring, fateful, giant voice, out of the earth and sky,
Voice of a mighty dying tree in the redwood forest dense.

Farewell my brethren,
Farewell O earth and sky, farewell ye neighboring waters,
My time has ended, my term has come.

Along the northern coast,
Just back from the rock-bound shore and the caves,
In the saline air from the sea in the Mendocino country,
With the surge for base and accompaniment low and hoarse,
With crackling blows of axes sounding musically driven by strong arms,
Riven deep by the sharp tongues of the axes, there in the redwood forest dense,
I heard the mighty tree its death-chant chanting.

The choppers heard not, the camp shanties echoed not,
The quick-ear'd teamsters and chain and jack-screw men heard not,
As the wood-spirits came from their haunts of a thousand years to join the refrain,
But in my soul I plainly heard.

Murmuring out of its myriad leaves,
Down from its lofty top rising two hundred feet high,
Out of its stalwart trunk and limbs, out of its foot-thick bark,
That chant of the seasons and time, chant not of the past only but the future.

You untold life of me,
And all you venerable and innocent joys,

Perennial hardy life of me with joys 'mid rain and many a summer sun,
And the white snows and night and the wild winds;
O the great patient rugged joys, my soul's strong joys unreck'd by man,
(For know I bear the soul befitting me, I too have consciousness, identity,
And all the rocks and mountains have, and all the earth,)
Joys of the life befitting me and brothers mine,
Our time, our term has come.

Nor yield we mournfully majestic brothers,
We who have grandly fill'd our time;
With Nature's calm content, with tacit huge delight,
We welcome what we wrought for through the past,
And leave the field for them.

For them predicted long,
For a superber race, they too to grandly fill their time,
For them we abdicate, in them ourselves ye forest kings!
In them these skies and airs, these mountain peaks, Shasta, Nevadas,
These huge precipitous cliffs, this amplitude, these valleys, far Yosemite,
To be in them absorb'd, assimilated.

Then to a loftier strain,
Still prouder, more ecstatic rose the chant,
As if the heirs, the deities of the West,
Joining with master-tongue bore part.

Not wan from Asia's fetiches,
Nor red from Europe's old dynastic slaughter-house,
(Area of murder-plots of thrones, with scent left yet of wars and scaffolds everywhere,)
But come from Nature's long and harmless throes, peacefully builded thence,
These virgin lands, lands of the Western shore,
To the new culminating man, to you, the empire new,
You promis'd long, we pledge, we dedicate.

You occult deep volitions,
You average spiritual manhood, purpose of all, pois'd on yourself, giving not taking law,
You womanhood divine, mistress and source of all, whence life and love and aught that comes from life and love,
You unseen moral essence of all the vast materials of America, (age upon age working in death the same as life,)
You that, sometimes known, oftener unknown, really shape and mould the New World, adjusting it to Time and Space,
You hidden national will lying in your abysms, conceal'd but ever alert,
You past and present purposes tenaciously pursued, may-be unconscious of yourselves,
Unswerv'd by all the passing errors, perturbations of the surface;
You vital, universal, deathless germs, beneath all creeds, arts, statutes, literatures,
Here build your homes for good, establish here, these areas entire, lands of the Western shore,
We pledge, we dedicate to you.

For man of you, your characteristic race,
Here may he hardy, sweet, gigantic grow, here tower proportionate to Nature,
Here climb the vast pure spaces unconfined, uncheck'd by wall or roof,
Here laugh with storm or sun, here joy, here patiently inure,
Here heed himself, unfold himself, (not others' formulas heed,) here fill his time,
To duly fall, to aid, unreck'd at last,
To disappear, to serve.

Thus on the northern coast,
In the echo of teamsters' calls and the clinking chains, and the music of choppers' axes,
The falling trunk and limbs, the crash, the muffled shriek, the groan,
Such words combined from the redwood-tree, as of voices ecstatic, ancient and rustling,
The century-lasting, unseen dryads, singing, withdrawing,
All their recesses of forests and mountains leaving,

From the Cascade range to the Wahsatch, or Idaho far, or
Utah,
To the deities of the modern henceforth yielding,
The chorus and indications, the vistas of coming humanity,
the settlements, features all,
In the Mendocino woods I caught.

2

The flashing and golden pageant of California,
The sudden and gorgeous drama, the sunny and ample lands,
The long and varied stretch from Puget sound to Colorado
south,
Lands bathed in sweeter, rarer, healthier air, valleys and
mountain cliffs,
The fields of Nature long prepared and fallow, the silent,
cyclic chemistry,
The slow and steady ages plodding, the unoccupied surface
ripening, the rich ores forming beneath;
At last the New arriving, assuming, taking possession,
A swarming and busy race settling and organizing everywhere,
Ships coming in from the whole round world, and going
out to the whole world,
To India and China and Australia and the thousand island
paradises of the Pacific,
Populous cities, the latest inventions, the steamers on the rivers,
the railroads, with many a thrifty farm, with machinery,
And wool and wheat and the grape, and diggings of yellow
gold.

3

But more in you than these, lands of the Western shore,
(These but the means, the implements, the standing-ground,)
I see in you, certain to come, the promise of thousands of
years, till now deferr'd,
Promis'd to be fulfill'd, our common kind, the race.

The new society at last, proportionate to Nature,
In man of you, more than your mountain peaks or stalwart
trees imperial,

In woman more, far more, than all your gold or vines, or
even vital air.

Fresh come, to a new world indeed, yet long prepared,
I see the genius of the modern, child of the real and ideal,
Clearing the ground for broad humanity, the true America,
heir of the past so grand,
To build a grander future.

A Song for Occupations

1

A SONG for occupations!
In the labor of engines and trades and the labor of fields I
find the developments,
And find the eternal meanings.

Workmen and Workwomen!
Were all educations practical and ornamental well display'd
out of me, what would it amount to?
Were I as the head teacher, charitable proprietor, wise
statesman, what would it amount to?
Were I to you as the boss employing and paying you, would
that satisfy you?

The learn'd, virtuous, benevolent, and the usual terms,
A man like me and never the usual terms.

Neither a servant nor a master I,
I take no sooner a large price than a small price, I will have
my own whoever enjoys me,
I will be even with you and you shall be even with me.

If you stand at work in a shop I stand as nigh as the nighest
in the same shop,
If you bestow gifts on your brother or dearest friend I
demand as good as your brother or dearest friend,
If your lover, husband, wife, is welcome by day or night, I
must be personally as welcome,

If you become degraded, criminal, ill, then I become so for your sake,
If you remember your foolish and outlaw'd deeds, do you think I cannot remember my own foolish and outlaw'd deeds?
If you carouse at the table I carouse at the opposite side of the table,
If you meet some stranger in the streets and love him or her, why I often meet strangers in the street and love them.

Why what have you thought of yourself?
Is it you then that thought yourself less?
Is it you that thought the President greater than you?
Or the rich better off than you? or the educated wiser than you?

(Because you are greasy or pimpled, or were once drunk, or a thief,
Or that you are diseas'd, or rheumatic, or a prostitute,
Or from frivolity or impotence, or that you are no scholar and never saw your name in print,
Do you give in that you are any less immortal?)

2

Souls of men and women! it is not you I call unseen, unheard, untouchable and untouching,
It is not you I go argue pro and con about, and to settle whether you are alive or no,
I own publicly who you are, if nobody else owns.

Grown, half-grown and babe, of this country and every country, in-doors and out-doors, one just as much as the other, I see,
And all else behind or through them.

The wife, and she is not one jot less than the husband,
The daughter, and she is just as good as the son,
The mother, and she is every bit as much as the father.

Offspring of ignorant and poor, boys apprenticed to trades,
Young fellows working on farms and old fellows working on farms,
Sailor-men, merchant-men, coasters, immigrants,
All these I see, but nigher and farther the same I see,
None shall escape me and none shall wish to escape me.

I bring what you much need yet always have,
Not money, amours, dress, eating, erudition, but as good,
I send no agent or medium, offer no representative of value, but offer the value itself.

There is something that comes to one now and perpetually,
It is not what is printed, preach'd, discussed, it eludes discussion and print,
It is not to be put in a book, it is not in this book,
It is for you whoever you are, it is no farther from you than your hearing and sight are from you,
It is hinted by nearest, commonest, readiest, it is ever provoked by them.

You may read in many languages, yet read nothing about it,
You may read the President's message and read nothing about it there,
Nothing in the reports from the State department or Treasury department, or in the daily papers or weekly papers,
Or in the census or revenue returns, prices current, or any accounts of stock.

3

The sun and stars that float in the open air,
The apple-shaped earth and we upon it, surely the drift of them is something grand,
I do not know what it is except that it is grand, and that it is happiness,
And that the enclosing purport of us here is not a speculation or bon-mot or reconnoissance,
And that it is not something which by luck may turn out well for us, and without luck must be a failure for us,
And not something which may yet be retracted in a certain contingency.

The light and shade, the curious sense of body and identity, the greed that with perfect complaisance devours all things,
The endless pride and outstretching of man, unspeakable joys and sorrows,
The wonder every one sees in every one else he sees, and the wonders that fill each minute of time forever,
What have you reckon'd them for, camerado?
Have you reckon'd them for your trade or farm-work? or for the profits of your store?
Or to achieve yourself a position? or to fill a gentleman's leisure, or a lady's leisure?

Have you reckon'd that the landscape took substance and form that it might be painted in a picture?
Or men and women that they might be written of, and songs sung?
Or the attraction of gravity, and the great laws and harmonious combinations and the fluids of the air, as subjects for the savans?
Or the brown land and the blue sea for maps and charts?
Or the stars to be put in constellations and named fancy names?
Or that the growth of seeds is for agricultural tables, or agriculture itself?

Old institutions, these arts, libraries, legends, collections, and the practice handed along in manufactures, will we rate them so high?
Will we rate our cash and business high? I have no objection,
I rate them as high as the highest—then a child born of a woman and man I rate beyond all rate.

We thought our Union grand, and our Constitution grand,
I do not say they are not grand and good, for they are,
I am this day just as much in love with them as you,
Then I am in love with You, and with all my fellows upon the earth.

We consider bibles and religions divine—I do not say they are not divine,
I say they have all grown out of you, and may grow out of you still,
It is not they who give the life, it is you who give the life,
Leaves are not more shed from the trees, or trees from the earth, than they are shed out of you.

4

The sum of all known reverence I add up in you whoever you are,
The President is there in the White House for you, it is not you who are here for him,
The Secretaries act in their bureaus for you, not you here for them,
The Congress convenes every Twelfth-month for you,
Laws, courts, the forming of States, the charters of cities, the going and coming of commerce and mails, are all for you.

List close my scholars dear,
Doctrines, politics and civilization exurge from you,
Sculpture and monuments and any thing inscribed anywhere are tallied in you,
The gist of histories and statistics as far back as the records reach is in you this hour, and myths and tales the same,
If you were not breathing and walking here, where would they all be?
The most renown'd poems would be ashes, orations and plays would be vacuums.

All architecture is what you do to it when you look upon it,
(Did you think it was in the white or gray stone? or the lines of the arches and cornices?)

All music is what awakes from you when you are reminded by the instruments,
It is not the violins and the cornets, it is not the oboe nor the beating drums, nor the score of the baritone singer singing his sweet romanza, nor that of the men's chorus, nor that of the women's chorus,
It is nearer and farther than they.

5

Will the whole come back then?
Can each see signs of the best by a look in the looking-
glass? is there nothing greater or more?
Does all sit there with you, with the mystic unseen soul?

Strange and hard that paradox true I give,
Objects gross and the unseen soul are one.

House-building, measuring, sawing the boards,
Blacksmithing, glass-blowing, nail-making, coopering, tinroofing, shingle-dressing,
Ship-joining, dock-building, fish-curing, flagging of sidewalks
by flaggers,
The pump, the pile-driver, the great derrick, the coal-kiln
and brick-kiln,
Coal-mines and all that is down there, the lamps in the
darkness, echoes, songs, what meditations, what vast
native thoughts looking through smutch'd faces,
Iron-works, forge-fires in the mountains or by river-banks,
men around feeling the melt with huge crowbars, lumps
of ore, the due combining of ore, limestone, coal,
The blast-furnace and the puddling-furnace, the loup-lump
at the bottom of the melt at last, the rolling-mill, the
stumpy bars of pig-iron, the strong clean-shaped T-rail
for railroads,
Oil-works, silk-works, white-lead-works, the sugar-house,
steam-saws, the great mills and factories,
Stone-cutting, shapely trimmings for façades or window or
door-lintels, the mallet, the tooth-chisel, the jib to
protect the thumb,
The calking-iron, the kettle of boiling vault-cement, and the
fire under the kettle,
The cotton-bale, the stevedore's hook, the saw and buck of
the sawyer, the mould of the moulder, the working-knife
of the butcher, the ice-saw, and all the work with ice,
The work and tools of the rigger, grappler, sail-maker,
block-maker,
Goods of gutta-percha, papier-maché, colors, brushes,
brush-making, glazier's implements,

The veneer and glue-pot, the confectioner's ornaments, the decanter and glasses, the shears and flat-iron,
The awl and knee-strap, the pint measure and quart measure, the counter and stool, the writing-pen of quill or metal, the making of all sorts of edged tools,
The brewery, brewing, the malt, the vats, every thing that is done by brewers, wine-makers, vinegar-makers,
Leather-dressing, coach-making, boiler-making, rope-twisting, distilling, sign-painting, lime-burning, cotton-picking, electroplating, electrotyping, stereotyping,
Stave-machines, planing-machines, reaping-machines, ploughing-machines, thrashing-machines, steam wagons,
The cart of the carman, the omnibus, the ponderous dray,
Pyrotechny, letting off color'd fireworks at night, fancy figures and jets;
Beef on the butcher's stall, the slaughter-house of the butcher, the butcher in his killing-clothes,
The pens of live pork, the killing-hammer, the hog-hook, the scalder's tub, gutting, the cutter's cleaver, the packer's maul, and the plenteous winterwork of pork-packing,
Flour-works, grinding of wheat, rye, maize, rice, the barrels and the half and quarter barrels, the loaded barges, the high piles on wharves and levees,
The men and the work of the men on ferries, railroads, coasters, fish-boats, canals;
The hourly routine of your own or any man's life, the shop, yard, store, or factory,
These shows all near you by day and night—workman! whoever you are, your daily life!
In that and them the heft of the heaviest—in that and them far more than you estimated, (and far less also,)
In them realities for you and me, in them poems for you and me,
In them, not yourself—you and your soul enclose all things, regardless of estimation,
In them the development good—in them all themes, hints, possibilities.

I do not affirm that what you see beyond is futile, I do not advise you to stop,

I do not say leadings you thought great are not great,
But I say that none lead to greater than these lead to.

6

Will you seek afar off? you surely come back at last,
In things best known to you finding the best, or as good as the best,
In folks nearest to you finding the sweetest, strongest, lovingest,
Happiness, knowledge, not in another place but this place, not for another hour but this hour,
Man in the first you see or touch, always in friend, brother, nighest neighbor—woman in mother, sister, wife,
The popular tastes and employments taking precedence in poems or anywhere,
You workwomen and workmen of these States having your own divine and strong life,
And all else giving place to men and women like you.

When the psalm sings instead of the singer,
When the script preaches instead of the preacher,
When the pulpit descends and goes instead of the carver that carved the supporting desk,
When I can touch the body of books by night or by day, and when they touch my body back again,
When a university course convinces like a slumbering woman and child convince,
When the minted gold in the vault smiles like the night-watchman's daughter,
When warrantee deeds loafe in chairs opposite and are my friendly companions,
I intend to reach them my hand, and make as much of them as I do of men and women like you.

A Song of the Rolling Earth

1

A SONG of the rolling earth, and of words according,
Were you thinking that those were the words, those upright lines? those curves, angles, dots?

No, those are not the words, the substantial words are in the ground and sea,
They are in the air, they are in you.

Were you thinking that those were the words, those delicious sounds out of your friends' mouths?
No, the real words are more delicious than they.

Human bodies are words, myriads of words,
(In the best poems re-appears the body, man's or woman's, well-shaped, natural, gay,
Every part able, active, receptive, without shame or the need of shame.)

Air, soil, water, fire—those are words,
I myself am a word with them—my qualities interpenetrate with theirs—my name is nothing to them,
Though it were told in the three thousand languages, what would air, soil, water, fire, know of my name?

A healthy presence, a friendly or commanding gesture, are words, sayings, meanings,
The charms that go with the mere looks of some men and women, are sayings and meanings also.

The workmanship of souls is by those inaudible words of the earth,
The masters know the earth's words and use them more than audible words.

Amelioration is one of the earth's words,
The earth neither lags nor hastens,
It has all attributes, growths, effects, latent in itself from the jump,
It is not half beautiful only, defects and excrescences show just as much as perfections show.

The earth does not withhold, it is generous enough,
The truths of the earth continually wait, they are not so conceal'd either,

They are calm, subtle, untransmissible by print,
They are imbued through all things conveying themselves
willingly,
Conveying a sentiment and invitation, I utter and utter,
I speak not, yet if you hear me not of what avail am I to you?
To bear, to better, lacking these of what avail am I?

(Accouche! accouchez!
Will you rot your own fruit in yourself there?
Will you squat and stifle there?)

The earth does not argue,
Is not pathetic, has no arrangements,
Does not scream, haste, persuade, threaten, promise,
Makes no discriminations, has no conceivable failures,
Closes nothing, refuses nothing, shuts none out,
Of all the powers, objects, states, it notifies, shuts none out.

The earth does not exhibit itself nor refuse to exhibit itself,
possesses still underneath,
Underneath the ostensible sounds, the august chorus of
heroes, the wail of slaves,
Persuasions of lovers, curses, gasps of the dying, laughter of
young people, accents of bargainers,
Underneath these possessing words that never fail.

To her children the words of the eloquent dumb great
mother never fail,
The true words do not fail, for motion does not fail and
reflection does not fail,
Also the day and night do not fail, and the voyage we pursue
does not fail.

Of the interminable sisters,
Of the ceaseless cotillons of sisters,
Of the centripetal and centrifugal sisters, the elder and
younger sisters,
The beautiful sister we know dances on with the rest.

With her ample back towards every beholder,
With the fascinations of youth and the equal fascinations of age,
Sits she whom I too love like the rest, sits undisturb'd,
Holding up in her hand what has the character of a mirror, while her eyes glance back from it,
Glance as she sits, inviting none, denying none,
Holding a mirror day and night tirelessly before her own face.

Seen at hand or seen at a distance,
Duly the twenty-four appear in public every day,
Duly approach and pass with their companions or a companion,
Looking from no countenances of their own, but from the countenances of those who are with them,
From the countenances of children or women or the manly countenance,
From the open countenances of animals or from inanimate things,
From the landscape or waters or from the exquisite apparition of the sky,
From our countenances, mine and yours, faithfully returning them,
Every day in public appearing without fail, but never twice with the same companions.

Embracing man, embracing all, proceed the three hundred and sixty-five resistlessly round the sun;
Embracing all, soothing, supporting, follow close three hundred and sixty-five offsets of the first, sure and necessary as they.

Tumbling on steadily, nothing dreading,
Sunshine, storm, cold, heat, forever withstanding, passing, carrying,
The soul's realization and determination still inheriting,
The fluid vacuum around and ahead still entering and dividing,
No balk retarding, no anchor anchoring, on no rock striking,

Swift, glad, content, unbereav'd, nothing losing,
Of all able and ready at any time to give strict account,
The divine ship sails the divine sea.

2

Whoever you are! motion and reflection are especially for you,
The divine ship sails the divine sea for you.

Whoever you are! you are he or she for whom the earth is solid and liquid,
You are he or she for whom the sun and moon hang in the sky,
For none more than you are the present and the past,
For none more than you is immortality.

Each man to himself and each woman to herself, is the word of the past and present, and the true word of immortality;
No one can acquire for another—not one,
Not one can grow for another—not one.

The song is to the singer, and comes back most to him,
The teaching is to the teacher, and comes back most to him,
The murder is to the murderer, and comes back most to him,
The theft is to the thief, and comes back most to him,
The love is to the lover, and comes back most to him,
The gift is to the giver, and comes back most to him—it cannot fail,
The oration is to the orator, the acting is to the actor and actress not to the audience,
And no man understands any greatness or goodness but his own, or the indication of his own.

3

I swear the earth shall surely be complete to him or her who shall be complete,
The earth remains jagged and broken only to him or her who remains jagged and broken.

I swear there is no greatness or power that does not emulate
those of the earth,
There can be no theory of any account unless it corroborate
the theory of the earth,
No politics, song, religion, behavior, or what not, is of
account, unless it compare with the amplitude of the
earth,
Unless it face the exactness, vitality, impartiality, rectitude of
the earth.

I swear I begin to see love with sweeter spasms than that
which responds love,
It is that which contains itself, which never invites and never
refuses.

I swear I begin to see little or nothing in audible words,
All merges toward the presentation of the unspoken meanings
of the earth,
Toward him who sings the songs of the body and of the
truths of the earth,
Toward him who makes the dictionaries of words that print
cannot touch.

I swear I see what is better than to tell the best,
It is always to leave the best untold.

When I undertake to tell the best I find I cannot,
My tongue is ineffectual on its pivots,
My breath will not be obedient to its organs,
I become a dumb man.

The best of the earth cannot be told anyhow, all or any is best,
It is not what you anticipated, it is cheaper, easier, nearer,
Things are not dismiss'd from the places they held before,
The earth is just as positive and direct as it was before,
Facts, religions, improvements, politics, trades, are as real as
before,
But the soul is also real, it too is positive and direct,
No reasoning, no proof has establish'd it,
Undeniable growth has establish'd it.

4

These to echo the tones of souls and the phrases of souls,
(If they did not echo the phrases of souls what were they then?
If they had not reference to you in especial what were they then?)

I swear I will never henceforth have to do with the faith that tells the best,
I will have to do only with that faith that leaves the best untold.

Say on, sayers! sing on, singers!
Delve! mould! pile the words of the earth!
Work on, age after age, nothing is to be lost,
It may have to wait long, but it will certainly come in use,
When the materials are all prepared and ready, the architects shall appear.

I swear to you the architects shall appear without fail,
I swear to you they will understand you and justify you,
The greatest among them shall be he who best knows you, and encloses all and is faithful to all,
He and the rest shall not forget you, they shall perceive that you are not an iota less than they,
You shall be fully glorified in them.

Youth, Day, Old Age and Night

Youth, large, lusty, loving—youth full of grace, force, fascination,
Do you know that Old Age may come after you with equal grace, force, fascination?

Day full-blown and splendid—day of the immense sun, action, ambition, laughter,
The Night follows close with millions of suns, and sleep and restoring darkness.

Birds of Passage

Song of the Universal

1

COME said the Muse,
Sing me a song no poet yet has chanted,
Sing me the universal.

In this broad earth of ours,
Amid the measureless grossness and the slag,
Enclosed and safe within its central heart,
Nestles the seed perfection.

By every life a share or more or less,
None born but it is born, conceal'd or unconceal'd the seed
is waiting.

2

Lo! keen-eyed towering science,
As from tall peaks the modern overlooking,
Successive absolute fiats issuing.

Yet again, lo! the soul, above all science,
For it has history gather'd like husks around the globe,
For it the entire star-myriads roll through the sky.

In spiral routes by long detours,
(As a much-tacking ship upon the sea,)
For it the partial to the permanent flowing,
For it the real to the ideal tends.

For it the mystic evolution,
Not the right only justified, what we call evil also justified.

Forth from their masks, no matter what,
From the huge festering trunk, from craft and guile and tears,
Health to emerge and joy, joy universal.

Out of the bulk, the morbid and the shallow,
Out of the bad majority, the varied countless frauds of men
and states,
Electric, antiseptic yet, cleaving, suffusing all,
Only the good is universal.

3

Over the mountain-growths disease and sorrow,
An uncaught bird is ever hovering, hovering,
High in the purer, happier air.

From imperfection's murkiest cloud,
Darts always forth one ray of perfect light,
One flash of heaven's glory.

To fashion's, custom's discord,
To the mad Babel-din, the deafening orgies,
Soothing each lull a strain is heard, just heard,
From some far shore the final chorus sounding.

O the blest eyes, the happy hearts,
That see, that know the guiding thread so fine,
Along the mighty labyrinth.

4

And thou America,
For the scheme's culmination, its thought and its reality,
For these (not for thyself) thou hast arrived.

Thou too surroundest all,
Embracing carrying welcoming all, thou too by pathways
broad and new,
To the ideal tendest.

The measur'd faiths of other lands, the grandeurs of the past,
Are not for thee, but grandeurs of thine own,
Deific faiths and amplitudes, absorbing, comprehending all,
All eligible to all.

All, all for immortality,
Love like the light silently wrapping all,

Nature's amelioration blessing all,
The blossoms, fruits of ages, orchards divine and certain,
Forms, objects, growths, humanities, to spiritual images
ripening.

Give me O God to sing that thought,
Give me, give him or her I love this quenchless faith,
In Thy ensemble, whatever else withheld withhold not
from us,
Belief in plan of Thee enclosed in Time and Space,
Health, peace, salvation universal.

Is it a dream?
Nay but the lack of it the dream,
And failing it life's lore and wealth a dream,
And all the world a dream.

Pioneers! O Pioneers!

COME my tan-faced children,
Follow well in order, get your weapons ready,
Have you your pistols? have you your sharp-edged axes?
Pioneers! O pioneers!

For we cannot tarry here,
We must march my darlings, we must bear the brunt of
danger,
We the youthful sinewy races, all the rest on us depend,
Pioneers! O pioneers!

O you youths, Western youths,
So impatient, full of action, full of manly pride and friendship,
Plain I see you Western youths, see you tramping with the
foremost,
Pioneers! O pioneers!

Have the elder races halted?
Do they droop and end their lesson, wearied over there
beyond the seas?
We take up the task eternal, and the burden and the lesson,
Pioneers! O pioneers!

All the past we leave behind,
We debouch upon a newer mightier world, varied world,
Fresh and strong the world we seize, world of labor and the march,
Pioneers! O pioneers!

We detachments steady throwing,
Down the edges, through the passes, up the mountains steep,
Conquering, holding, daring, venturing as we go the unknown ways,
Pioneers! O pioneers!

We primeval forests felling,
We the rivers stemming, vexing we and piercing deep the mines within,
We the surface broad surveying, we the virgin soil upheaving,
Pioneers! O pioneers!

Colorado men are we,
From the peaks gigantic, from the great sierras and the high plateaus,
From the mine and from the gully, from the hunting trail we come,
Pioneers! O pioneers!

From Nebraska, from Arkansas,
Central inland race are we, from Missouri, with the continental blood intervein'd,
All the hands of comrades clasping, all the Southern, all the Northern,
Pioneers! O pioneers!

O resistless restless race!
O beloved race in all! O my breast aches with tender love for all!
O I mourn and yet exult, I am rapt with love for all,
Pioneers! O pioneers!

Raise the mighty mother mistress,
Waving high the delicate mistress, over all the starry mistress, (bend your heads all,)

Raise the fang'd and warlike mistress, stern, impassive,
weapon'd mistress,
Pioneers! O pioneers!

See my children, resolute children,
By those swarms upon our rear we must never yield or falter,
Ages back in ghostly millions frowning there behind us urging,
Pioneers! O pioneers!

On and on the compact ranks,
With accessions ever waiting, with the places of the dead
quickly fill'd,
Through the battle, through defeat, moving yet and never
stopping,
Pioneers! O pioneers!

O to die advancing on!
Are there some of us to droop and die? has the hour come?
Then upon the march we fittest die, soon and sure the gap
is fill'd,
Pioneers! O pioneers!

All the pulses of the world,
Falling in they beat for us, with the Western movement beat,
Holding single or together, steady moving to the front, all
for us,
Pioneers! O pioneers!

Life's involv'd and varied pageants,
All the forms and shows, all the workmen at their work,
All the seamen and the landsmen, all the masters with their
slaves,
Pioneers! O pioneers!

All the hapless silent lovers,
All the prisoners in the prisons, all the righteous and the
wicked,
All the joyous, all the sorrowing, all the living, all the dying,
Pioneers! O pioneers!

I too with my soul and body,
We, a curious trio, picking, wandering on our way,
Through these shores amid the shadows, with the apparitions pressing,
Pioneers! O pioneers!

Lo, the darting bowling orb!
Lo, the brother orbs around, all the clustering suns and planets,
All the dazzling days, all the mystic nights with dreams,
Pioneers! O pioneers!

These are of us, they are with us,
All for primal needed work, while the followers there in embryo wait behind,
We to-day's procession heading, we the route for travel clearing,
Pioneers! O pioneers!

O you daughters of the West!
O you young and elder daughters! O you mothers and you wives!
Never must you be divided, in our ranks you move united,
Pioneers! O pioneers!

Minstrels latent on the prairies!
(Shrouded bards of other lands, you may rest, you have done your work,)
Soon I hear you coming warbling, soon you rise and tramp amid us,
Pioneers! O pioneers!

Not for delectations sweet,
Not the cushion and the slipper, not the peaceful and the studious,
Not the riches safe and palling, not for us the tame enjoyment,
Pioneers! O pioneers!

Do the feasters gluttonous feast?
Do the corpulent sleepers sleep? have they lock'd and bolted doors?

Still be ours the diet hard, and the blanket on the ground,
Pioneers! O pioneers!

Has the night descended?
Was the road of late so toilsome? did we stop discouraged nodding on our way?
Yet a passing hour I yield you in your tracks to pause oblivious,
Pioneers! O pioneers!

Till with sound of trumpet,
Far, far off the daybreak call—hark! how loud and clear I hear it wind,
Swift! to the head of the army!—swift! spring to your places,
Pioneers! O pioneers!

To You

WHOEVER you are, I fear you are walking the walks of dreams,
I fear these supposed realities are to melt from under your feet and hands,
Even now your features, joys, speech, house, trade, manners, troubles, follies, costume, crimes, dissipate away from you,
Your true soul and body appear before me,
They stand forth out of affairs, out of commerce, shops, work, farms, clothes, the house, buying, selling, eating, drinking, suffering, dying.

Whoever you are, now I place my hand upon you, that you be my poem,
I whisper with my lips close to your ear,
I have loved many women and men, but I love none better than you.

O I have been dilatory and dumb,
I should have made my way straight to you long ago,
I should have blabb'd nothing but you, I should have chanted nothing but you.

I will leave all and come and make the hymns of you,
None has understood you, but I understand you,
None has done justice to you, you have not done justice to yourself,
None but has found you imperfect, I only find no imperfection in you,
None but would subordinate you, I only am he who will never consent to subordinate you,
I only am he who places over you no master, owner, better, God, beyond what waits intrinsically in yourself.

Painters have painted their swarming groups and the centre-figure of all,
From the head of the centre-figure spreading a nimbus of gold-color'd light,
But I paint myriads of heads, but paint no head without its nimbus of gold-color'd light,
From my hand from the brain of every man and woman it streams, effulgently flowing forever.

O I could sing such grandeurs and glories about you!
You have not known what you are, you have slumber'd upon yourself all your life,
Your eyelids have been the same as closed most of the time,
What you have done returns already in mockeries,
(Your thrift, knowledge, prayers, if they do not return in mockeries, what is their return?)

The mockeries are not you,
Underneath them and within them I see you lurk,
I pursue you where none else has pursued you,
Silence, the desk, the flippant expression, the night, the accustom'd routine, if these conceal you from others or from yourself, they do not conceal you from me,
The shaved face, the unsteady eye, the impure complexion, if these balk others they do not balk me,
The pert apparel, the deform'd attitude, drunkenness, greed, premature death, all these I part aside.

There is no endowment in man or woman that is not tallied in you,

There is no virtue, no beauty in man or woman, but as
good is in you,
No pluck, no endurance in others, but as good is in you,
No pleasure waiting for others, but an equal pleasure waits
for you.

As for me, I give nothing to any one except I give the like
carefully to you,
I sing the songs of the glory of none, not God, sooner than
I sing the songs of the glory of you.

Whoever you are! claim your own at any hazard!
These shows of the East and West are tame compared to you,
These immense meadows, these interminable rivers, you are
immense and interminable as they,
These furies, elements, storms, motions of Nature, throes of
apparent dissolution, you are he or she who is master
or mistress over them,
Master or mistress in your own right over Nature, elements,
pain, passion, dissolution.

The hopples fall from your ankles, you find an unfailing
sufficiency,
Old or young, male or female, rude, low, rejected by the rest,
whatever you are promulges itself,
Through birth, life, death, burial, the means are provided,
nothing is scanted,
Through angers, losses, ambition, ignorance, ennui, what
you are picks its way.

France,

The 18th Year of these States.

A GREAT year and place,
A harsh discordant natal scream out-sounding, to touch the
mother's heart closer than any yet.

I walk'd the shores of my Eastern sea,
Heard over the waves the little voice,
Saw the divine infant where she woke mournfully wailing,

amid the roar of cannon, curses, shouts, crash of falling buildings,
Was not so sick from the blood in the gutters running, nor from the single corpses, nor those in heaps, nor those borne away in the tumbrils,
Was not so desperate at the battues of death—was not so shock'd at the repeated fusillades of the guns.

Pale, silent, stern, what could I say to that long-accrued retribution?
Could I wish humanity different?
Could I wish the people made of wood and stone?
Or that there be no justice in destiny or time?

O Liberty! O mate for me!
Here too the blaze, the grape-shot and the axe, in reserve, to fetch them out in case of need,
Here too, though long represt, can never be destroy'd,
Here too could rise at last murdering and ecstatic,
Here too demanding full arrears of vengeance.

Hence I sign this salute over the sea,
And I do not deny that terrible red birth and baptism,
But remember the little voice that I heard wailing, and wait with perfect trust, no matter how long,
And from to-day sad and cogent I maintain the bequeath'd cause, as for all lands,
And I send these words to Paris with my love,
And I guess some chansonniers there will understand them,
For I guess there is latent music yet in France, floods of it,
O I hear already the bustle of instruments, they will soon be drowning all that would interrupt them,
O I think the east wind brings a triumphal and free march,
It reaches hither, it swells me to joyful madness,
I will run transpose it in words, to justify it,
I will yet sing a song for you ma femme.

Myself and Mine

MYSELF and mine gymnastic ever,
To stand the cold or heat, to take good aim with a gun, to sail a boat, to manage horses, to beget superb children,

To speak readily and clearly, to feel at home among common
people,
And to hold our own in terrible positions on land and sea.

Not for an embroiderer,
(There will always be plenty of embroiderers, I welcome
them also,)
But for the fibre of things and for inherent men and women.

Not to chisel ornaments,
But to chisel with free stroke the heads and limbs of
plenteous supreme Gods, that the States may realize
them walking and talking.

Let me have my own way,
Let others promulge the laws, I will make no account of the
laws,
Let others praise eminent men and hold up peace, I hold up
agitation and conflict,
I praise no eminent man, I rebuke to his face the one that
was thought most worthy.

(Who are you? and what are you secretly guilty of all your life?
Will you turn aside all your life? will you grub and chatter
all your life?
And who are you, blabbing by rote, years, pages, languages,
reminiscences,
Unwitting to-day that you do not know how to speak
properly a single word?)

Let others finish specimens, I never finish specimens,
I start them by exhaustless laws as Nature does, fresh and
modern continually.

I give nothing as duties,
What others give as duties I give as living impulses,
(Shall I give the heart's action as a duty?)

Let others dispose of questions, I dispose of nothing, I
arouse unanswerable questions,

Who are they I see and touch, and what about them?
What about these likes of myself that draw me so close by
tender directions and indirections?

I call to the world to distrust the accounts of my friends,
but listen to my enemies, as I myself do,
I charge you forever reject those who would expound me,
for I cannot expound myself,
I charge that there be no theory or school founded out of me,
I charge you to leave all free, as I have left all free.

After me, vista!
O I see life is not short, but immeasurably long,
I henceforth tread the world chaste, temperate, an early
riser, a steady grower,
Every hour the semen of centuries, and still of centuries.

I must follow up these continual lessons of the air, water,
earth,
I perceive I have no time to lose.

Year of Meteors

(1859–60.)

YEAR of meteors! brooding year!
I would bind in words retrospective some of your deeds and
signs,
I would sing your contest for the 19th Presidentiad,
I would sing how an old man, tall, with white hair, mounted
the scaffold in Virginia,
(I was at hand, silent I stood with teeth shut close, I watch'd,
I stood very near you old man when cool and indifferent,
but trembling with age and your unheal'd wounds you
mounted the scaffold;)
I would sing in my copious song your census returns of the
States,
The tables of population and products, I would sing of your
ships and their cargoes,

The proud black ships of Manhattan arriving, some fill'd with immigrants, some from the isthmus with cargoes of gold,
Songs thereof would I sing, to all that hitherward comes would I welcome give,
And you would I sing, fair stripling! welcome to you from me, young prince of England!
(Remember you surging Manhattan's crowds as you pass'd with your cortege of nobles?
There in the crowds stood I, and singled you out with attachment;)
Nor forget I to sing of the wonder, the ship as she swam up my bay,
Well-shaped and stately the Great Eastern swam up my bay, she was 600 feet long,
Her moving swiftly surrounded by myriads of small craft I forget not to sing;
Nor the comet that came unannounced out of the north flaring in heaven,
Nor the strange huge meteor-procession dazzling and clear shooting over our heads,
(A moment, a moment long it sail'd its balls of unearthly light over our heads,
Then departed, dropt in the night, and was gone;)
Of such, and fitful as they, I sing—with gleams from them would I gleam and patch these chants,
Your chants, O year all mottled with evil and good—year of forebodings!
Year of comets and meteors transient and strange—lo! even here one equally transient and strange!
As I flit through you hastily, soon to fall and be gone, what is this chant,
What am I myself but one of your meteors?

With Antecedents

1

WITH antecedents,
With my fathers and mothers and the accumulations of past ages,

With all which, had it not been, I would not now be here,
as I am,
With Egypt, India, Phenicia, Greece and Rome,
With the Kelt, the Scandinavian, the Alb and the Saxon,
With antique maritime ventures, laws, artisanship, wars and
journeys,
With the poet, the skald, the saga, the myth, and the oracle,
With the sale of slaves, with enthusiasts, with the troubadour,
the crusader, and the monk,
With those old continents whence we have come to this
new continent,
With the fading kingdoms and kings over there,
With the fading religions and priests,
With the small shores we look back to from our own large
and present shores,
With countless years drawing themselves onward and arrived
at these years,
You and me arrived—America arrived and making this year,
This year! sending itself ahead countless years to come.

2

O but it is not the years—it is I, it is You,
We touch all laws and tally all antecedents,
We are the skald, the oracle, the monk and the knight, we
easily include them and more,
We stand amid time beginningless and endless, we stand
amid evil and good,
All swings around us, there is as much darkness as light,
The very sun swings itself and its system of planets around us,
Its sun, and its again, all swing around us.

As for me, (torn, stormy, amid these vehement days,)
I have the idea of all, and am all and believe in all,
I believe materialism is true and spiritualism is true, I reject
no part.

(Have I forgotten any part? any thing in the past?
Come to me whoever and whatever, till I give you
recognition.)

I respect Assyria, China, Teutonia, and the Hebrews,
I adopt each theory, myth, god, and demi-god,
I see that the old accounts, bibles, genealogies, are true,
without exception,
I assert that all past days were what they must have been,
And that they could no-how have been better than they were,
And that to-day is what it must be, and that America is,
And that to-day and America could no-how be better than
they are.

3

In the name of these States and in your and my name,
the Past,
And in the name of these States and in your and my name,
the Present time.

I know that the past was great and the future will be great,
And I know that both curiously conjoint in the present time,
(For the sake of him I typify, for the common average
man's sake, your sake if you are he,)
And that where I am or you are this present day, there is
the centre of all days, all races,
And there is the meaning to us of all that has ever come of
races and days, or ever will come.

A Broadway Pageant

1

Over the Western sea hither from Niphon come,
Courteous, the swart-cheek'd two-sworded envoys,
Leaning back in their open barouches, bare-headed, impassive,
Ride to-day through Manhattan.

Libertad! I do not know whether others behold what I
behold,
In the procession along with the nobles of Niphon, the
errand-bearers,
Bringing up the rear, hovering above, around, or in the
ranks marching,
But I will sing you a song of what I behold Libertad.

When million-footed Manhattan unpent descends to her
 pavements,
When the thunder-cracking guns arouse me with the proud
 roar I love,
When the round-mouth'd guns out of the smoke and smell
 I love spit their salutes,
When the fire-flashing guns have fully alerted me, and heaven-
 clouds canopy my city with a delicate thin haze,
When gorgeous the countless straight stems, the forests at
 the wharves, thicken with colors,
When every ship richly drest carries her flag at the peak,
When pennants trail and street-festoons hang from the
 windows,
When Broadway is entirely given up to foot-passengers and
 foot-standers, when the mass is densest,
When the façades of the houses are alive with people, when
 eyes gaze riveted tens of thousands at a time,
When the guests from the islands advance, when the
 pageant moves forward visible,
When the summons is made, when the answer that waited
 thousands of years answers,
I too arising, answering, descend to the pavements, merge
 with the crowd, and gaze with them.

2

Superb-faced Manhattan!
Comrade Americanos! to us, then at last the Orient comes.

To us, my city,
Where our tall-topt marble and iron beauties range on
 opposite sides, to walk in the space between,
To-day our Antipodes comes.

The Originatress comes,
The nest of languages, the bequeather of poems, the race
 of eld,
Florid with blood, pensive, rapt with musings, hot with
 passion,
Sultry with perfume, with ample and flowing garments,

With sunburnt visage, with intense soul and glittering eyes,
The race of Brahma comes.

See my cantabile! these and more are flashing to us from the procession,
As it moves changing, a kaleidoscope divine it moves changing before us.

For not the envoys nor the tann'd Japanee from his island only,
Lithe and silent the Hindoo appears, the Asiatic continent itself appears, the past, the dead,
The murky night-morning of wonder and fable inscrutable,
The envelop'd mysteries, the old and unknown hive-bees,
The north, the sweltering south, eastern Assyria, the Hebrews, the ancient of ancients,
Vast desolated cities, the gliding present, all of these and more are in the pageant-procession.

Geography, the world, is in it,
The Great Sea, the brood of islands, Polynesia, the coast beyond,
The coast you henceforth are facing—you Libertad! from your Western golden shores,
The countries there with their populations, the millions en-masse are curiously here,
The swarming market-places, the temples with idols ranged along the sides or at the end, bonze, brahmin, and llama,
Mandarin, farmer, merchant, mechanic, and fisherman,
The singing-girl and the dancing-girl, the ecstatic persons, the secluded emperors,
Confucius himself, the great poets and heroes, the warriors, the castes, all,
Trooping up, crowding from all directions, from the Altay mountains,
From Thibet, from the four winding and far-flowing rivers of China,
From the southern peninsulas and the demi-continental islands, from Malaysia,
These and whatever belongs to them palpable show forth to me, and are seiz'd by me,

And I am seiz'd by them, and friendlily held by them,
Till as here them all I chant, Libertad! for themselves and
for you.

For I too raising my voice join the ranks of this pageant,
I am the chanter, I chant aloud over the pageant,
I chant the world on my Western sea,
I chant copious the islands beyond, thick as stars in the sky,
I chant the new empire grander than any before, as in a
vision it comes to me,
I chant America the mistress, I chant a greater supremacy,
I chant projected a thousand blooming cities yet in time on
those groups of sea-islands,
My sail-ships and steam-ships threading the archipelagoes,
My stars and stripes fluttering in the wind,
Commerce opening, the sleep of ages having done its work,
races reborn, refresh'd,
Lives, works resumed—the object I know not—but the old,
the Asiatic renew'd as it must be,
Commencing from this day surrounded by the world.

3

And you Libertad of the world!
You shall sit in the middle well-pois'd thousands and
thousands of years,
As to-day from one side the nobles of Asia come to you,
As to-morrow from the other side the queen of England
sends her eldest son to you.

The sign is reversing, the orb is enclosed,
The ring is circled, the journey is done,
The box-lid is but perceptibly open'd, nevertheless the
perfume pours copiously out of the whole box.

Young Libertad! with the venerable Asia, the all-mother,
Be considerate with her now and ever hot Libertad, for you
are all,
Bend your proud neck to the long-off mother now sending
messages over the archipelagoes to you,
Bend your proud neck low for once, young Libertad.

Were the children straying westward so long? so wide the
tramping?
Were the precedent dim ages debouching westward from
Paradise so long?
Were the centuries steadily footing it that way, all the while
unknown, for you, for reasons?

They are justified, they are accomplish'd, they shall now be
turn'd the other way also, to travel toward you thence,
They shall now also march obediently eastward for your sake
Libertad.

Sea-Drift

Out of the Cradle Endlessly Rocking

OUT of the cradle endlessly rocking,
Out of the mocking-bird's throat, the musical shuttle,
Out of the Ninth-month midnight,
Over the sterile sands and the fields beyond, where the child
leaving his bed wander'd alone, bareheaded, barefoot,
Down from the shower'd halo,
Up from the mystic play of shadows twining and twisting as
if they were alive,
Out from the patches of briers and blackberries,
From the memories of the bird that chanted to me,
From your memories sad brother, from the fitful risings and
fallings I heard,
From under that yellow half-moon late-risen and swollen as
if with tears,
From those beginning notes of yearning and love there in
the mist,
From the thousand responses of my heart never to cease,
From the myriad thence-arous'd words,
From the word stronger and more delicious than any,
From such as now they start the scene revisiting,
As a flock, twittering, rising, or overhead passing,
Borne hither, ere all eludes me, hurriedly,
A man, yet by these tears a little boy again,
Throwing myself on the sand, confronting the waves,
I, chanter of pains and joys, uniter of here and hereafter,
Taking all hints to use them, but swiftly leaping beyond them,
A reminiscence sing.

Once Paumanok,
When the lilac-scent was in the air and Fifth-month grass
was growing,
Up this seashore in some briers,
Two feather'd guests from Alabama, two together,
And their nest, and four light-green eggs spotted with brown,
And every day the he-bird to and fro near at hand,

And every day the she-bird crouch'd on her nest, silent,
with bright eyes,
And every day I, a curious boy, never too close, never
disturbing them,
Cautiously peering, absorbing, translating.

Shine! shine! shine!
Pour down your warmth, great sun!
While we bask, we two together.

Two together!
Winds blow south, or winds blow north,
Day come white, or night come black,
Home, or rivers and mountains from home,
Singing all time, minding no time,
While we two keep together.

Till of a sudden,
May-be kill'd, unknown to her mate,
One forenoon the she-bird crouch'd not on the nest,
Nor return'd that afternoon, nor the next,
Nor ever appear'd again.

And thenceforward all summer in the sound of the sea,
And at night under the full of the moon in calmer weather,
Over the hoarse surging of the sea,
Or flitting from brier to brier by day,
I saw, I heard at intervals the remaining one, the he-bird,
The solitary guest from Alabama.

Blow! blow! blow!
Blow up sea-winds along Paumanok's shore;
I wait and I wait till you blow my mate to me.

Yes, when the stars glisten'd,
All night long on the prong of a moss-scallop'd stake,
Down almost amid the slapping waves,
Sat the lone singer wonderful causing tears.

He call'd on his mate,
He pour'd forth the meanings which I of all men know.

Yes my brother I know,
The rest might not, but I have treasur'd every note,
For more than once dimly down to the beach gliding,
Silent, avoiding the moonbeams, blending myself with the shadows,
Recalling now the obscure shapes, the echoes, the sounds and sights after their sorts,
The white arms out in the breakers tirelessly tossing,
I, with bare feet, a child, the wind wafting my hair,
Listen'd long and long.

Listen'd to keep, to sing, now translating the notes,
Following you my brother.

Soothe! soothe! soothe!
Close on its wave soothes the wave behind,
And again another behind embracing and lapping, every one close,
But my love soothes not me, not me.

Low hangs the moon, it rose late,
It is lagging—O I think it is heavy with love, with love.

O madly the sea pushes upon the land,
With love, with love.

O night! do I not see my love fluttering out among the breakers?
What is that little black thing I see there in the white?

Loud! loud! loud!
Loud I call to you, my love!

High and clear I shoot my voice over the waves,
Surely you must know who is here, is here,
You must know who I am, my love.

Low-hanging moon!
What is that dusky spot in your brown yellow?
O it is the shape, the shape of my mate!
O moon do not keep her from me any longer.

Land! land! O land!
Whichever way I turn, O I think you could give me my mate back again if you only would,
For I am almost sure I see her dimly whichever way I look.

O rising stars!
Perhaps the one I want so much will rise, will rise with some of you.

O throat! O trembling throat!
Sound clearer through the atmosphere!
Pierce the woods, the earth,
Somewhere listening to catch you must be the one I want.

Shake out carols!
Solitary here, the night's carols!
Carols of lonesome love! death's carols!
Carols under that lagging, yellow, waning moon!
O under that moon where she droops almost down into the sea!
O reckless despairing carols.

But soft! sink low!
Soft! let me just murmur,
And do you wait a moment you husky-nois'd sea,
For somewhere I believe I heard my mate responding to me,
So faint, I must be still, be still to listen,
But not altogether still, for then she might not come immediately to me.

Hither my love!
Here I am! here!
With this just-sustain'd note I announce myself to you,
This gentle call is for you my love, for you.

Do not be decoy'd elsewhere,
That is the whistle of the wind, it is not my voice,
That is the fluttering, the fluttering of the spray,
Those are the shadows of leaves.

O darkness! O in vain!
O I am very sick and sorrowful.

O brown halo in the sky near the moon, drooping upon the sea!
O troubled reflection in the sea!
O throat! O throbbing heart!
And I singing uselessly, uselessly all the night.

O past! O happy life! O songs of joy!
In the air, in the woods, over fields,
Loved! loved! loved! loved! loved!
But my mate no more, no more with me!
We two together no more.

The aria sinking,
All else continuing, the stars shining,
The winds blowing, the notes of the bird continuous echoing,
With angry moans the fierce old mother incessantly moaning,
On the sands of Paumanok's shore gray and rustling,
The yellow half-moon enlarged, sagging down, drooping,
the face of the sea almost touching,
The boy ecstatic, with his bare feet the waves, with his hair
the atmosphere dallying,
The love in the heart long pent, now loose, now at last
tumultuously bursting,
The aria's meaning, the ears, the soul, swiftly depositing,
The strange tears down the cheeks coursing,
The colloquy there, the trio, each uttering,
The undertone, the savage old mother incessantly crying,
To the boy's soul's questions sullenly timing, some drown'd
secret hissing,
To the outsetting bard.

Demon or bird! (said the boy's soul,)
Is it indeed toward your mate you sing? or is it really to me?
For I, that was a child, my tongue's use sleeping, now I
have heard you,
Now in a moment I know what I am for, I awake,
And already a thousand singers, a thousand songs, clearer,
louder and more sorrowful than yours,
A thousand warbling echoes have started to life within me,
never to die.

O you singer solitary, singing by yourself, projecting me,
O solitary me listening, never more shall I cease
 perpetuating you,
Never more shall I escape, never more the reverberations,
Never more the cries of unsatisfied love be absent from me,
Never again leave me to be the peaceful child I was before
 what there in the night,
By the sea under the yellow and sagging moon,
The messenger there arous'd, the fire, the sweet hell within,
The unknown want, the destiny of me.

O give me the clew! (it lurks in the night here somewhere,)
O if I am to have so much, let me have more!

A word then, (for I will conquer it,)
The word final, superior to all,
Subtle, sent up—what is it?—I listen;
Are you whispering it, and have been all the time, you sea-
 waves?
Is that it from your liquid rims and wet sands?

Whereto answering, the sea,
Delaying not, hurrying not,
Whisper'd me through the night, and very plainly before
 daybreak,
Lisp'd to me the low and delicious word death,
And again death, death, death, death,
Hissing melodious, neither like the bird nor like my arous'd
 child's heart,
But edging near as privately for me rustling at my feet,
Creeping thence steadily up to my ears and laving me softly
 all over,
Death, death, death, death, death.

Which I do not forget,
But fuse the song of my dusky demon and brother,
That he sang to me in the moonlight on Paumanok's gray
 beach,
With the thousand responsive songs at random,
My own songs awaked from that hour,

And with them the key, the word up from the waves,
The word of the sweetest song and all songs,
That strong and delicious word which, creeping to my feet,
(Or like some old crone rocking the cradle, swathed in
sweet garments, bending aside,)
The sea whisper'd me.

As I Ebb'd with the Ocean of Life

1

As I ebb'd with the ocean of life,
As I wended the shores I know,
As I walk'd where the ripples continually wash you Paumanok,
Where they rustle up hoarse and sibilant,
Where the fierce old mother endlessly cries for her castaways,
I musing late in the autumn day, gazing off southward,
Held by this electric self out of the pride of which I utter
poems,
Was seiz'd by the spirit that trails in the lines underfoot,
The rim, the sediment that stands for all the water and all
the land of the globe.

Fascinated, my eyes reverting from the south, dropt, to
follow those slender windrows,
Chaff, straw, splinters of wood, weeds, and the sea-gluten,
Scum, scales from shining rocks, leaves of salt-lettuce, left by
the tide,
Miles walking, the sound of breaking waves the other side
of me,
Paumanok there and then as I thought the old thought of
likenesses,
These you presented to me you fish-shaped island,
As I wended the shores I know,
As I walk'd with that electric self seeking types.

2

As I wend to the shores I know not,
As I list to the dirge, the voices of men and women wreck'd,
As I inhale the impalpable breezes that set in upon me,

As the ocean so mysterious rolls toward me closer and closer,
I too but signify at the utmost a little wash'd-up drift,
A few sands and dead leaves to gather,
Gather, and merge myself as part of the sands and drift.

O baffled, balk'd, bent to the very earth,
Oppress'd with myself that I have dared to open my mouth,
Aware now that amid all that blab whose echoes recoil upon
me I have not once had the least idea who or what I am,
But that before all my arrogant poems the real Me stands
yet untouch'd, untold, altogether unreach'd,
Withdrawn far, mocking me with mock-congratulatory signs
and bows,
With peals of distant ironical laughter at every word I have
written,
Pointing in silence to these songs, and then to the sand
beneath.

I perceive I have not really understood any thing, not a
single object, and that no man ever can,
Nature here in sight of the sea taking advantage of me to
dart upon me and sting me,
Because I have dared to open my mouth to sing at all.

3

You oceans both, I close with you,
We murmur alike reproachfully rolling sands and drift,
knowing not why,
These little shreds indeed standing for you and me and all.

You friable shore with trails of debris,
You fish-shaped island, I take what is underfoot,
What is yours is mine my father.

I too Paumanok,
I too have bubbled up, floated the measureless float, and
been wash'd on your shores,
I too am but a trail of drift and debris,
I too leave little wrecks upon you, you fish-shaped island.

I throw myself upon your breast my father,
I cling to you so that you cannot unloose me,
I hold you so firm till you answer me something.

Kiss me my father,
Touch me with your lips as I touch those I love,
Breathe to me while I hold you close the secret of the
 murmuring I envy.

4

Ebb, ocean of life, (the flow will return,)
Cease not your moaning you fierce old mother,
Endlessly cry for your castaways, but fear not, deny not me,
Rustle not up so hoarse and angry against my feet as I
 touch you or gather from you.

I mean tenderly by you and all,
I gather for myself and for this phantom looking down
 where we lead, and following me and mine.

Me and mine, loose windrows, little corpses,
Froth, snowy white, and bubbles,
(See, from my dead lips the ooze exuding at last,
See, the prismatic colors glistening and rolling,)
Tufts of straw, sands, fragments,
Buoy'd hither from many moods, one contradicting another,
From the storm, the long calm, the darkness, the swell,
Musing, pondering, a breath, a briny tear, a dab of liquid or
 soil,
Up just as much out of fathomless workings fermented and
 thrown,
A limp blossom or two, torn, just as much over waves
 floating, drifted at random,
Just as much for us that sobbing dirge of Nature,
Just as much whence we come that blare of the cloud-
 trumpets,
We, capricious, brought hither we know not whence, spread
 out before you,
You up there walking or sitting,
Whoever you are, we too lie in drifts at your feet.

Tears

TEARS! tears! tears!
In the night, in solitude, tears,
On the white shore dripping, dripping, suck'd in by the sand,
Tears, not a star shining, all dark and desolate,
Moist tears from the eyes of a muffled head;
O who is that ghost? that form in the dark, with tears?
What shapeless lump is that, bent, crouch'd there on the sand?
Streaming tears, sobbing tears, throes, choked with wild cries;
O storm, embodied, rising, careering with swift steps along
 the beach!
O wild and dismal night storm, with wind—O belching and
 desperate!
O shade so sedate and decorous by day, with calm
 countenance and regulated pace,
But away at night as you fly, none looking—O then the
 unloosen'd ocean,
Of tears! tears! tears!

To the Man-of-War-Bird

THOU who hast slept all night upon the storm,
Waking renew'd on thy prodigious pinions,
(Burst the wild storm? above it thou ascended'st,
And rested on the sky, thy slave that cradled thee,)
Now a blue point, far, far in heaven floating,
As to the light emerging here on deck I watch thee,
(Myself a speck, a point on the world's floating vast.)

Far, far at sea,
After the night's fierce drifts have strewn the shore with
 wrecks,
With re-appearing day as now so happy and serene,
The rosy and elastic dawn, the flashing sun,
The limpid spread of air cerulean,
Thou also re-appearest.

Thou born to match the gale, (thou art all wings,)
To cope with heaven and earth and sea and hurricane,

Thou ship of air that never furl'st thy sails,
Days, even weeks untired and onward, through spaces, realms gyrating,
At dusk that look'st on Senegal, at morn America,
That sport'st amid the lightning-flash and thunder-cloud,
In them, in thy experiences, had'st thou my soul,
What joys! what joys were thine!

Aboard at a Ship's Helm

ABOARD at a ship's helm,
A young steersman steering with care.

Through fog on a sea-coast dolefully ringing,
An ocean-bell—O a warning bell, rock'd by the waves.

O you give good notice indeed, you bell by the sea-reefs ringing,
Ringing, ringing, to warn the ship from its wreck-place.

For as on the alert O steersman, you mind the loud admonition,
The bows turn, the freighted ship tacking speeds away under her gray sails,
The beautiful and noble ship with all her precious wealth speeds away gayly and safe.

But O the ship, the immortal ship! O ship aboard the ship!
Ship of the body, ship of the soul, voyaging, voyaging, voyaging.

On the Beach at Night

ON the beach at night,
Stands a child with her father,
Watching the east, the autumn sky.

Up through the darkness,
While ravening clouds, the burial clouds, in black masses spreading,

Lower sullen and fast athwart and down the sky,
Amid a transparent clear belt of ether yet left in the east,
Ascends large and calm the lord-star Jupiter,
And nigh at hand, only a very little above,
Swim the delicate sisters the Pleiades.

From the beach the child holding the hand of her father,
Those burial-clouds that lower victorious soon to devour all,
Watching, silently weeps.

Weep not, child,
Weep not, my darling,
With these kisses let me remove your tears,
The ravening clouds shall not long be victorious,
They shall not long possess the sky, they devour the stars
only in apparition,
Jupiter shall emerge, be patient, watch again another night,
the Pleiades shall emerge,
They are immortal, all those stars both silvery and golden
shall shine out again,
The great stars and the little ones shall shine out again, they
endure,
The vast immortal suns and the long-enduring pensive moons
shall again shine.

Then dearest child mournest thou only for Jupiter?
Considerest thou alone the burial of the stars?

Something there is,
(With my lips soothing thee, adding I whisper,
I give thee the first suggestion, the problem and indirection,)
Something there is more immortal even than the stars,
(Many the burials, many the days and night, passing away,)
Something that shall endure longer even than lustrous Jupiter,
Longer than sun or any revolving satellite,
Or the radiant sisters the Pleiades.

The World below the Brine

THE world below the brine,
Forests at the bottom of the sea, the branches and leaves,

Sea-lettuce, vast lichens, strange flowers and seeds, the thick tangle, openings, and pink turf,
Different colors, pale gray and green, purple, white, and gold, the play of light through the water,
Dumb swimmers there among the rocks, coral, gluten, grass, rushes, and the aliment of the swimmers,
Sluggish existences grazing there suspended, or slowly crawling close to the bottom,
The sperm-whale at the surface blowing air and spray, or disporting with his flukes,
The leaden-eyed shark, the walrus, the turtle, the hairy sea-leopard, and the sting-ray,
Passions there, wars, pursuits, tribes, sight in those ocean-depths, breathing that thick-breathing air, as so many do,
The change thence to the sight here, and to the subtle air breathed by beings like us who walk this sphere,
The change onward from ours to that of beings who walk other spheres.

On the Beach at Night Alone

On the beach at night alone,
As the old mother sways her to and fro singing her husky song,
As I watch the bright stars shining, I think a thought of the clef of the universes and of the future.

A vast similitude interlocks all,
All spheres, grown, ungrown, small, large, suns, moons, planets,
All distances of place however wide,
All distances of time, all inanimate forms,
All souls, all living bodies though they be ever so different, or in different worlds,
All gaseous, watery, vegetable, mineral processes, the fishes, the brutes,
All nations, colors, barbarisms, civilizations, languages,
All identities that have existed or may exist on this globe, or any globe,
All lives and deaths, all of the past, present, future,

This vast similitude spans them, and always has spann'd,
And shall forever span them and compactly hold and enclose
them.

Song for All Seas, All Ships

1

To-day a rude brief recitative,
Of ships sailing the seas, each with its special flag or ship-
signal,
Of unnamed heroes in the ships—of waves spreading and
spreading far as the eye can reach,
Of dashing spray, and the winds piping and blowing,
And out of these a chant for the sailors of all nations,
Fitful, like a surge.

Of sea-captains young or old, and the mates, and of all
intrepid sailors,
Of the few, very choice, taciturn, whom fate can never
surprise nor death dismay,
Pick'd sparingly without noise by thee old ocean, chosen by
thee,
Thou sea that pickest and cullest the race in time, and
unitest nations,
Suckled by thee, old husky nurse, embodying thee,
Indomitable, untamed as thee.

(Ever the heroes on water or on land, by ones or twos
appearing,
Ever the stock preserv'd and never lost, though rare,
enough for seed preserv'd.)

2

Flaunt out O sea your separate flags of nations!
Flaunt out visible as ever the various ship-signals!
But do you reserve especially for yourself and for the soul of
man one flag above all the rest,
A spiritual woven signal for all nations, emblem of man elate
above death,

Token of all brave captains and all intrepid sailors and mates,
And all that went down doing their duty,
Reminiscent of them, twined from all intrepid captains
young or old,
A pennant universal, subtly waving all time, o'er all brave
sailors,
All seas, all ships.

Patroling Barnegat

WILD, wild the storm, and the sea high running,
Steady the roar of the gale, with incessant undertone
muttering,
Shouts of demoniac laughter fitfully piercing and pealing,
Waves, air, midnight, their savagest trinity lashing,
Out in the shadows there milk-white combs careering,
On beachy slush and sand spirts of snow fierce slanting,
Where through the murk the easterly death-wind breasting,
Through cutting swirl and spray watchful and firm advancing,
(That in the distance! is that a wreck? is the red signal flaring?)
Slush and sand of the beach tireless till daylight wending,
Steadily, slowly, through hoarse roar never remitting,
Along the midnight edge by those milk-white combs careering,
A group of dim, weird forms, struggling, the night
confronting,
That savage trinity warily watching.

After the Sea-Ship

AFTER the sea-ship, after the whistling winds,
After the white-gray sails taut to their spars and ropes,
Below, a myriad myriad waves hastening, lifting up their
necks,
Tending in ceaseless flow toward the track of the ship,
Waves of the ocean bubbling and gurgling, blithely prying,
Waves, undulating waves, liquid, uneven, emulous waves,
Toward that whirling current, laughing and buoyant, with
curves,
Where the great vessel sailing and tacking displaced the surface,

Larger and smaller waves in the spread of the ocean
yearnfully flowing,
The wake of the sea-ship after she passes, flashing and
frolicsome under the sun,
A motley procession with many a fleck of foam and many
fragments,
Following the stately and rapid ship, in the wake following.

By the Roadside

A Boston Ballad

(1854.)

To get betimes in Boston town I rose this morning early,
Here's a good place at the corner, I must stand and see the show.

Clear the way there Jonathan!
Way for the President's marshal—way for the government cannon!
Way for the Federal foot and dragoons, (and the apparitions copiously tumbling.)

I love to look on the Stars and Stripes, I hope the fifes will play Yankee Doodle.
How bright shine the cutlasses of the foremost troops!
Every man holds his revolver, marching stiff through Boston town.

A fog follows, antiques of the same come limping,
Some appear wooden-legged, and some appear bandaged and bloodless.

Why this is indeed a show—it has called the dead out of the earth!
The old graveyards of the hills have hurried to see!
Phantoms! phantoms countless by flank and rear!
Cock'd hats of mothy mould—crutches made of mist!
Arms in slings—old men leaning on young men's shoulders.

What troubles you Yankee phantoms? what is all this chattering of bare gums?
Does the ague convulse your limbs? do you mistake your crutches for firelocks and level them?

If you blind your eyes with tears you will not see the President's marshal,
If you groan such groans you might balk the government cannon.

For shame old maniacs—bring down those toss'd arms, and let your white hair be,
Here gape your great grandsons, their wives gaze at them from the windows,
See how well dress'd, see how orderly they conduct themselves.

Worse and worse—can't you stand it? are you retreating?
Is this hour with the living too dead for you?

Retreat then—pell-mell!
To your graves—back—back to the hills old limpers!
I do not think you belong here anyhow.

But there is one thing that belongs here—shall I tell you what it is, gentlemen of Boston?

I will whisper it to the Mayor, he shall send a committee to England,
They shall get a grant from the Parliament, go with a cart to the royal vault,
Dig out King George's coffin, unwrap him quick from the grave-clothes, box up his bones for a journey,
Find a swift Yankee clipper—here is freight for you, black-bellied clipper,
Up with your anchor—shake out your sails—steer straight toward Boston bay.

Now call for the President's marshal again, bring out the government cannon,
Fetch home the roarers from Congress, make another procession, guard it with foot and dragoons.

This centre-piece for them;
Look, all orderly citizens—look from the windows, women!

The committee open the box, set up the regal ribs, glue
those that will not stay,
Clap the skull on top of the ribs, and clap a crown on top
of the skull.

You have got your revenge, old buster—the crown is come
to its own, and more than its own.

Stick your hands in your pockets, Jonathan—you are a made
man from this day,
You are mighty cute—and here is one of your bargains.

Europe,

The 72d and 73d Years of These States.

SUDDENLY out of its stale and drowsy lair, the lair of slaves,
Like lightning it le'pt forth half startled at itself,
Its feet upon the ashes and the rags, its hands tight to the
throats of kings.

O hope and faith!
O aching close of exiled patriots' lives!
O many a sicken'd heart!
Turn back unto this day and make yourselves afresh.

And you, paid to defile the People—you liars, mark!
Not for numberless agonies, murders, lusts,
For court thieving in its manifold mean forms, worming
from his simplicity the poor man's wages,
For many a promise sworn by royal lips and broken and
laugh'd at in the breaking,
Then in their power not for all these did the blows strike
revenge, or the heads of the nobles fall;
The People scorn'd the ferocity of kings.

But the sweetness of mercy brew'd bitter destruction, and
the frighten'd monarchs come back,
Each comes in state with his train, hangman, priest, tax-
gatherer,
Soldier, lawyer, lord, jailer, and sycophant.

Yet behind all lowering stealing, lo, a shape,
Vague as the night, draped interminably, head, front and
    form, in scarlet folds,
Whose face and eyes none may see,
Out of its robes only this, the red robes lifted by the arm,
One finger crook'd pointed high over the top, like the head
    of a snake appears.

Meanwhile corpses lie in new-made graves, bloody corpses
    of young men,
The rope of the gibbet hangs heavily, the bullets of princes
    are flying, the creatures of power laugh aloud,
And all these things bear fruits, and they are good.

Those corpses of young men,
Those martyrs that hang from the gibbets, those hearts
    pierc'd by the gray lead,
Cold and motionless as they seem live elsewhere with
    unslaughter'd vitality.

They live in other young men O kings!
They live in brothers again ready to defy you,
They were purified by death, they were taught and exalted.

Not a grave of the murder'd for freedom but grows seed for
    freedom, in its turn to bear seed,
Which the winds carry afar and re-sow, and the rains and
    the snows nourish.

Not a disembodied spirit can the weapons of tyrants let loose,
But it stalks invisibly over the earth, whispering, counseling,
    cautioning.

Liberty, let others despair of you—I never despair of you.

Is the house shut? is the master away?
Nevertheless, be ready, be not weary of watching,
He will soon return, his messengers come anon.

A Hand-Mirror

HOLD it up sternly—see this it sends back, (who is it? is
it you?)
Outside fair costume, within ashes and filth,
No more a flashing eye, no more a sonorous voice or
springy step,
Now some slave's eye, voice, hands, step,
A drunkard's breath, unwholesome eater's face, venerealee's
flesh,
Lungs rotting away piecemeal, stomach sour and cankerous,
Joints rheumatic, bowels clogged with abomination,
Blood circulating dark and poisonous streams,
Words babble, hearing and touch callous,
No brain, no heart left, no magnetism of sex;
Such from one look in this looking-glass ere you go hence,
Such a result so soon—and from such a beginning!

Gods

LOVER divine and perfect Comrade,
Waiting content, invisible yet, but certain,
Be thou my God.

Thou, thou, the Ideal Man,
Fair, able, beautiful, content, and loving,
Complete in body and dilate in spirit,
Be thou my God.

O Death, (for Life has served its turn,)
Opener and usher to the heavenly mansion,
Be thou my God.

Aught, aught of mightiest, best I see, conceive, or know,
(To break the stagnant tie—thee, thee to free, O soul,)
Be thou my God.

All great ideas, the races' aspirations,
All heroisms, deeds of rapt enthusiasts,
Be ye my Gods.

Or Time and Space,
Or shape of Earth divine and wondrous,
Or some fair shape I viewing, worship,
Or lustrous orb of sun or star by night,
Be ye my Gods.

Germs

FORMS, qualities, lives, humanity, language, thoughts,
The ones known, and the ones unknown, the ones on the
 stars,
The stars themselves, some shaped, others unshaped,
Wonders as of those countries, the soil, trees, cities,
 inhabitants, whatever they may be,
Splendid suns, the moons and rings, the countless
 combinations and effects,
Such-like, and as good as such-like, visible here or
 anywhere, stand provided for in a handful of space,
 which I extend my arm and half enclose with my hand,
That containing the start of each and all, the virtue, the
 germs of all.

Thoughts

OF ownership—as if one fit to own things could not at
 pleasure enter upon all, and incorporate them into
 himself or herself;
Of vista—suppose some sight in arriere through the
 formative chaos, presuming the growth, fulness, life,
 now attain'd on the journey,
(But I see the road continued, and the journey ever
 continued;)
Of what was once lacking on earth, and in due time has
 become supplied—and of what will yet be supplied,
Because all I see and know I believe to have its main
 purport in what will yet be supplied.

When I Heard the Learn'd Astronomer

WHEN I heard the learn'd astronomer,
When the proofs, the figures, were ranged in columns
 before me,

When I was shown the charts and diagrams, to add, divide, and measure them,
When I sitting heard the astronomer where he lectured with much applause in the lecture-room,
How soon unaccountable I became tired and sick,
Till rising and gliding out I wander'd off by myself,
In the mystical moist night-air, and from time to time,
Look'd up in perfect silence at the stars.

Perfections

ONLY themselves understand themselves and the like of themselves,
As souls only understand souls.

O Me! O Life!

O ME! O life! of the questions of these recurring,
Of the endless trains of the faithless, of cities fill'd with the foolish,
Of myself forever reproaching myself, (for who more foolish than I, and who more faithless?)
Of eyes that vainly crave the light, of the objects mean, of the struggle ever renew'd,
Of the poor results of all, of the plodding and sordid crowds I see around me,
Of the empty and useless years of the rest, with the rest me intertwined,
The question, O me! so sad, recurring—What good amid these, O me, O life?

Answer.

That you are here—that life exists and identity,
That the powerful play goes on, and you may contribute a verse.

To a President

ALL you are doing and saying is to America dangled mirages,
You have not learn'd of Nature—of the politics of Nature you have not learn'd the great amplitude, rectitude, impartiality,

You have not seen that only such as they are for these States,
And that what is less than they must sooner or later lift off
from these States.

I Sit and Look Out

I SIT and look out upon all the sorrows of the world, and
upon all oppression and shame,
I hear secret convulsive sobs from young men at anguish
with themselves, remorseful after deeds done,
I see in low life the mother misused by her children, dying,
neglected, gaunt, desperate,
I see the wife misused by her husband, I see the treacherous
seducer of young women,
I mark the ranklings of jealousy and unrequited love
attempted to be hid, I see these sights on the earth,
I see the workings of battle, pestilence, tyranny, I see martyrs
and prisoners,
I observe a famine at sea, I observe the sailors casting lots
who shall be kill'd to preserve the lives of the rest,
I observe the slights and degradations cast by arrogant persons
upon laborers, the poor, and upon negroes, and the like;
All these—all the meanness and agony without end I sitting
look out upon,
See, hear, and am silent.

To Rich Givers

WHAT you give me I cheerfully accept,
A little sustenance, a hut and garden, a little money, as I
rendezvous with my poems,
A traveler's lodging and breakfast as I journey through the
States,—why should I be ashamed to own such gifts?
why to advertise for them?
For I myself am not one who bestows nothing upon man
and woman,
For I bestow upon any man or woman the entrance to all
the gifts of the universe.

The Dalliance of the Eagles

SKIRTING the river road, (my forenoon walk, my rest,)
Skyward in air a sudden muffled sound, the dalliance of the eagles,
The rushing amorous contact high in space together,
The clinching interlocking claws, a living, fierce, gyrating wheel,
Four beating wings, two beaks, a swirling mass tight grappling,
In tumbling turning clustering loops, straight downward falling,
Till o'er the river pois'd, the twain yet one, a moment's lull,
A motionless still balance in the air, then parting, talons loosing,
Upward again on slow-firm pinions slanting, their separate diverse flight,
She hers, he his, pursuing.

Roaming in Thought

(*After reading* HEGEL.)

ROAMING in thought over the Universe, I saw the little that is Good steadily hastening towards immortality,
And the vast all that is call'd Evil I saw hastening to merge itself and become lost and dead.

A Farm Picture

THROUGH the ample open door of the peaceful country barn,
A sunlit pasture field with cattle and horses feeding,
And haze and vista, and the far horizon fading away.

A Child's Amaze

SILENT and amazed even when a little boy,
I remember I heard the preacher every Sunday put God in his statements,
As contending against some being or influence.

The Runner

On a flat road runs the well-train'd runner,
He is lean and sinewy with muscular legs,
He is thinly clothed, he leans forward as he runs,
With lightly closed fists and arms partially rais'd.

Beautiful Women

Women sit or move to and fro, some old, some young,
The young are beautiful—but the old are more beautiful than the young.

Mother and Babe

I see the sleeping babe nestling the breast of its mother,
The sleeping mother and babe—hush'd, I study them long and long.

Thought

Of obedience, faith, adhesiveness;
As I stand aloof and look there is to me something profoundly affecting in large masses of men following the lead of those who do not believe in men.

Visor'd

A mask, a perpetual natural disguiser of herself,
Concealing her face, concealing her form,
Changes and transformations every hour, every moment,
Falling upon her even when she sleeps.

Thought

Of Justice—as if Justice could be any thing but the same ample law, expounded by natural judges and saviors,
As if it might be this thing or that thing, according to decisions.

Gliding o'er All

GLIDING o'er all, through all,
Through Nature, Time, and Space,
As a ship on the waters advancing,
The voyage of the soul—not life alone,
Death, many deaths I'll sing.

Hast Never Come to Thee an Hour

HAST never come to thee an hour,
A sudden gleam divine, precipitating, bursting all these bubbles, fashions, wealth?
These eager business aims—books, politics, art, amours,
To utter nothingness?

Thought

OF Equality—as if it harm'd me, giving others the same chances and rights as myself—as if it were not indispensable to my own rights that others possess the same.

To Old Age

I SEE in you the estuary that enlarges and spreads itself grandly as it pours in the great sea.

Locations and Times

LOCATIONS and times—what is it in me that meets them all, whenever and wherever, and makes me at home?
Forms, colors, densities, odors—what is it in me that corresponds with them?

Offerings

A THOUSAND perfect men and women appear,
Around each gathers a cluster of friends, and gay children and youths, with offerings.

To the States,

To Identify the 16th, 17th, or 18th Presidentiad.

WHY reclining, interrogating? why myself and all drowsing?
What deepening twilight—scum floating atop of the waters,
Who are they as bats and night-dogs askant in the capitol?
What a filthy Presidentiad! (O South, your torrid suns! O
North, your arctic freezings!)
Are those really Congressmen? are those the great Judges? is
that the President?
Then I will sleep awhile yet, for I see that these States sleep,
for reasons;
(With gathering murk, with muttering thunder and lambent
shoots we all duly awake,
South, North, East, West, inland and seaboard, we will
surely awake.)

Drum-Taps

First O Songs for a Prelude

FIRST O songs for a prelude,
Lightly strike on the stretch'd tympanum pride and joy in my city,
How she led the rest to arms, how she gave the cue,
How at once with lithe limbs unwaiting a moment she sprang,
(O superb! O Manhattan, my own, my peerless!
O strongest you in the hour of danger, in crisis! O truer than steel!)
How you sprang—how you threw off the costumes of peace with indifferent hand,
How your soft opera-music changed, and the drum and fife were heard in their stead,
How you led to the war, (that shall serve for our prelude, songs of soldiers,)
How Manhattan drum-taps led.

Forty years had I in my city seen soldiers parading,
Forty years as a pageant, till unawares the lady of this teeming and turbulent city,
Sleepless amid her ships, her houses, her incalculable wealth,
With her million children around her, suddenly,
At dead of night, at news from the south,
Incens'd struck with clinch'd hand the pavement.

A shock electric, the night sustain'd it,
Till with ominous hum our hive at daybreak pour'd out its myriads.

From the houses then and the workshops, and through all the doorways,
Leapt they tumultuous, and lo! Manhattan arming.

To the drum-taps prompt,
The young men falling in and arming,

The mechanics arming, (the trowel, the jack-plane, the
blacksmith's hammer, tost aside with precipitation,)
The lawyer leaving his office and arming, the judge leaving
the court,
The driver deserting his wagon in the street, jumping down,
throwing the reins abruptly down on the horses' backs,
The salesman leaving the store, the boss, book-keeper,
porter, all leaving;
Squads gather everywhere by common consent and arm,
The new recruits, even boys, the old men show them how
to wear their accoutrements, they buckle the straps
carefully,
Outdoors arming, indoors arming, the flash of the musket-
barrels,
The white tents cluster in camps, the arm'd sentries around,
the sunrise cannon and again at sunset,
Arm'd regiments arrive every day, pass through the city, and
embark from the wharves,
(How good they look as they tramp down to the river,
sweaty, with their guns on their shoulders!
How I love them! how I could hug them, with their brown
faces and their clothes and knapsacks cover'd with
dust!)
The blood of the city up—arm'd! arm'd! the cry everywhere,
The flags flung out from the steeples of churches and from
all the public buildings and stores,
The tearful parting, the mother kisses her son, the son kisses
his mother,
(Loth is the mother to part, yet not a word does she speak
to detain him,)
The tumultuous escort, the ranks of policemen preceding,
clearing the way,
The unpent enthusiasm, the wild cheers of the crowd for
their favorites,
The artillery, the silent cannons bright as gold, drawn along,
rumble lightly over the stones,
(Silent cannons, soon to cease your silence,
Soon unlimber'd to begin the red business;)
All the mutter of preparation, all the determin'd arming,
The hospital service, the lint, bandages and medicines,

The women volunteering for nurses, the work begun for in earnest, no mere parade now;
War! an arm'd race is advancing! the welcome for battle, no turning away;
War! be it weeks, months, or years, an arm'd race is advancing to welcome it.

Mannahatta a-march—and it's O to sing it well!
It's O for a manly life in the camp.

And the sturdy artillery,
The guns bright as gold, the work for giants, to serve well the guns,
Unlimber them! (no more as the past forty years for salutes for courtesies merely,
Put in something now besides powder and wadding.)

And you lady of ships, you Mannahatta,
Old matron of this proud, friendly, turbulent city,
Often in peace and wealth you were pensive or covertly frown'd amid all your children,
But now you smile with joy exulting old Mannahatta.

Eighteen Sixty-One

Arm'd year—year of the struggle,
No dainty rhymes or sentimental love verses for you terrible year,
Not you as some pale poetling seated at a desk lisping cadenzas piano,
But as a strong man erect, clothed in blue clothes, advancing, carrying a rifle on your shoulder,
With well-gristled body and sunburnt face and hands, with a knife in the belt at your side,
As I heard you shouting loud, your sonorous voice ringing across the continent,
Your masculine voice O year, as rising amid the great cities,
Amid the men of Manhattan I saw you as one of the workmen, the dwellers in Manhattan,

Or with large steps crossing the prairies out of Illinois and Indiana,
Rapidly crossing the West with springy gait and descending the Alleghanies,
Or down from the great lakes or in Pennsylvania, or on deck along the Ohio river,
Or southward along the Tennessee or Cumberland rivers, or at Chattanooga on the mountain top,
Saw I your gait and saw I your sinewy limbs clothed in blue, bearing weapons, robust year,
Heard your determin'd voice launch'd forth again and again,
Year that suddenly sang by the mouths of the round-lipp'd cannon,
I repeat you, hurrying, crashing, sad, distracted year.

Beat! Beat! Drums!

BEAT! beat! drums!—blow! bugles! blow!
Through the windows—through doors—burst like a ruthless force,
Into the solemn church, and scatter the congregation,
Into the school where the scholar is studying;
Leave not the bridegroom quiet—no happiness must he have now with his bride,
Nor the peaceful farmer any peace, ploughing his field or gathering his grain,
So fierce you whirr and pound you drums—so shrill you bugles blow.

Beat! beat! drums!—blow! bugles! blow!
Over the traffic of cities—over the rumble of wheels in the streets;
Are beds prepared for sleepers at night in the houses? no sleepers must sleep in those beds,
No bargainers' bargains by day—no brokers or speculators—would they continue?
Would the talkers be talking? would the singer attempt to sing?
Would the lawyer rise in the court to state his case before the judge?

Then rattle quicker, heavier drums—you bugles wilder
blow.

Beat! beat! drums!—blow! bugles! blow!
Make no parley—stop for no expostulation,
Mind not the timid—mind not the weeper or prayer,
Mind not the old man beseeching the young man,
Let not the child's voice be heard, nor the mother's entreaties,
Make even the trestles to shake the dead where they lie
awaiting the hearses,
So strong you thump O terrible drums—so loud you bugles
blow.

From Paumanok Starting I Fly like a Bird

FROM Paumanok starting I fly like a bird,
Around and around to soar to sing the idea of all,
To the north betaking myself to sing there arctic songs,
To Kanada till I absorb Kanada in myself, to Michigan then,
To Wisconsin, Iowa, Minnesota, to sing their songs, (they
are inimitable;)
Then to Ohio and Indiana to sing theirs, to Missouri and
Kansas and Arkansas to sing theirs,
To Tennessee and Kentucky, to the Carolinas and Georgia
to sing theirs,
To Texas and so along up toward California, to roam
accepted everywhere;
To sing first, (to the tap of the war-drum if need be,)
The idea of all, of the Western world one and inseparable,
And then the song of each member of these States.

Song of the Banner at Daybreak

Poet.

O A new song, a free song,
Flapping, flapping, flapping, flapping, by sounds, by voices
clearer,
By the wind's voice and that of the drum,
By the banner's voice and child's voice and sea's voice and
father's voice,

Low on the ground and high in the air,
On the ground where father and child stand,
In the upward air where their eyes turn,
Where the banner at daybreak is flapping.

Words! book-words! what are you?
Words no more, for hearken and see,
My song is there in the open air, and I must sing,
With the banner and pennant a-flapping.

I'll weave the chord and twine in,
Man's desire and babe's desire, I'll twine them in, I'll put
in life,
I'll put the bayonet's flashing point, I'll let bullets and slugs
whizz,
(As one carrying a symbol and menace far into the future,
Crying with trumpet voice, *Arouse and beware! Beware and
arouse!*)
I'll pour the verse with streams of blood, full of volition, full
of joy,
Then loosen, launch forth, to go and compete,
With the banner and pennant a-flapping.

Pennant.

Come up here, bard, bard,
Come up here, soul, soul,
Come up here, dear little child,
To fly in the clouds and winds with me, and play with the
measureless light.

Child.

Father what is that in the sky beckoning to me with long
finger?
And what does it say to me all the while?

Father.

Nothing my babe you see in the sky,
And nothing at all to you it says—but look you my babe,
Look at these dazzling things in the houses, and see you the
money-shops opening,

And see you the vehicles preparing to crawl along the streets
with goods;
These, ah these, how valued and toil'd for these!
How envied by all the earth.

Poet.

Fresh and rosy red the sun is mounting high,
On floats the sea in distant blue careering through its channels,
On floats the wind over the breast of the sea setting in
toward land,
The great steady wind from west or west-by-south,
Floating so buoyant with milk-white foam on the waters.

But I am not the sea nor the red sun,
I am not the wind with girlish laughter,
Not the immense wind which strengthens, not the wind
which lashes,
Not the spirit that ever lashes its own body to terror and
death,
But I am that which unseen comes and sings, sings, sings,
Which babbles in brooks and scoots in showers on the land,
Which the birds know in the woods mornings and evenings,
And the shore-sands know and the hissing wave, and that
banner and pennant,
Aloft there flapping and flapping.

Child.

O father it is alive—it is full of people—it has children,
O now it seems to me it is talking to its children,
I hear it—it talks to me—O it is wonderful!
O it stretches—it spreads and runs so fast—O my father,
It is so broad it covers the whole sky.

Father.

Cease, cease, my foolish babe,
What you are saying is sorrowful to me, much it displeases me;
Behold with the rest again I say, behold not banners and
pennants aloft,
But the well-prepared pavements behold, and mark the
solid-wall'd houses.

Banner and Pennant.

Speak to the child O bard out of Manhattan,
To our children all, or north or south of Manhattan,
Point this day, leaving all the rest, to us over all—and yet
we know not why,
For what are we, mere strips of cloth profiting nothing,
Only flapping in the wind?

Poet.

I hear and see not strips of cloth alone,
I hear the tramp of armies, I hear the challenging sentry,
I hear the jubilant shouts of millions of men, I hear Liberty!
I hear the drums beat and the trumpets blowing,
I myself move abroad swift-rising flying then,
I use the wings of the land-bird and use the wings of the
sea-bird, and look down as from a height,
I do not deny the precious results of peace, I see populous
cities with wealth incalculable,
I see numberless farms, I see the farmers working in their
fields or barns,
I see mechanics working, I see buildings everywhere
founded, going up, or finish'd,
I see trains of cars swiftly speeding along railroad tracks
drawn by the locomotives,
I see the stores, depots, of Boston, Baltimore, Charleston,
New Orleans,
I see far in the West the immense area of grain, I dwell
awhile hovering,
I pass to the lumber forests of the North, and again to the
Southern plantation, and again to California;
Sweeping the whole I see the countless profit, the busy
gatherings, earn'd wages,
See the Identity formed out of thirty-eight spacious and
haughty States, (and many more to come,)
See forts on the shores of harbors, see ships sailing in and out;
Then over all, (aye! aye!) my little and lengthen'd pennant
shaped like a sword,
Runs swiftly up indicating war and defiance—and now the
halyards have rais'd it,

Side of my banner broad and blue, side of my starry banner,
Discarding peace over all the sea and land.

Banner and Pennant.

Yet louder, higher, stronger, bard! yet farther, wider cleave!
No longer let our children deem us riches and peace alone,
We may be terror and carnage, and are so now,
Not now are we any one of these spacious and haughty
 States, (nor any five, nor ten,)
Nor market nor depot we, nor money-bank in the city,
But these and all, and the brown and spreading land, and
 the mines below, are ours,
And the shores of the sea are ours, and the rivers great and
 small,
And the fields they moisten, and the crops and the fruits are
 ours,
Bays and channels and ships sailing in and out are ours—
 while we over all,
Over the area spread below, the three or four millions of
 square miles, the capitals,
The forty millions of people,—O bard! in life and death
 supreme,
We, even we, henceforth flaunt out masterful, high up
 above,
Not for the present alone, for a thousand years chanting
 through you,
This song to the soul of one poor little child.

Child.

O my father I like not the houses,
They will never to me be any thing, nor do I like money,
But to mount up there I would like, O father dear, that
 banner I like,
That pennant I would be and must be.

Father.

Child of mine you fill me with anguish,
To be that pennant would be too fearful,
Little you know what it is this day, and after this day, forever,
It is to gain nothing, but risk and defy every thing,

Forward to stand in front of wars—and O, such wars!—
what have you to do with them?
With passions of demons, slaughter, premature death?

Banner.

Demons and death then I sing,
Put in all, aye all will I, sword-shaped pennant for war,
And a pleasure new and ecstatic, and the prattled yearning
of children,
Blent with the sounds of the peaceful land and the liquid
wash of the sea,
And the black ships fighting on the sea envelop'd in smoke,
And the icy cool of the far, far north, with rustling cedars
and pines,
And the whirr of drums and the sound of soldiers marching,
and the hot sun shining south,
And the beach-waves combing over the beach on my
Eastern shore, and my Western shore the same,
And all between those shores, and my ever running
Mississippi with bends and chutes,
And my Illinois fields, and my Kansas fields, and my fields
of Missouri,
The Continent, devoting the whole identity without
reserving an atom,
Pour in! whelm that which asks, which sings, with all and
the yield of all,
Fusing and holding, claiming, devouring the whole,
No more with tender lip, nor musical labial sound,
But out of the night emerging for good, our voice
persuasive no more,
Croaking like crows here in the wind.

Poet.

My limbs, my veins dilate, my theme is clear at last,
Banner so broad advancing out of the night, I sing you
haughty and resolute,
I burst through where I waited long, too long, deafen'd and
blinded,
My hearing and tongue are come to me, (a little child
taught me,)

I hear from above O pennant of war your ironical call and
demand,
Insensate! insensate! (yet I at any rate chant you,) O banner!
Not houses of peace indeed are you, nor any nor all their
prosperity, (if need be, you shall again have every one
of those houses to destroy them,
You thought not to destroy those valuable houses, standing
fast, full of comfort, built with money,
May they stand fast, then? not an hour except you above
them and all stand fast;)
O banner, not money so precious are you, not farm produce
you, nor the material good nutriment,
Nor excellent stores, nor landed on wharves from the ships,
Not the superb ships with sail-power or steam-power,
fetching and carrying cargoes,
Nor machinery, vehicles, trade, nor revenues—but you as
henceforth I see you,
Running up out of the night, bringing your cluster of stars,
(ever-enlarging stars,)
Divider of daybreak you, cutting the air, touch'd by the sun,
measuring the sky,
(Passionately seen and yearn'd for by one poor little child,
While others remain busy or smartly talking, forever
teaching thrift, thrift;)
O you up there! O pennant! where you undulate like a
snake hissing so curious,
Out of reach, an idea only, yet furiously fought for, risking
bloody death, loved by me,
So loved—O you banner leading the day with stars brought
from the night!
Valueless, object of eyes, over all and demanding all—
(absolute owner of all)—O banner and pennant!
I too leave the rest—great as it is, it is nothing—houses,
machines are nothing—I see them not,
I see but you, O warlike pennant! O banner so broad, with
stripes, I sing you only,
Flapping up there in the wind.

Rise O Days from Your Fathomless Deeps

1

Rise O days from your fathomless deeps, till you loftier, fiercer sweep,
Long for my soul hungering gymnastic I devour'd what the earth gave me,
Long I roam'd the woods of the north, long I watch'd Niagara pouring,
I travel'd the prairies over and slept on their breast, I cross'd the Nevadas, I cross'd the plateaus,
I ascended the towering rocks along the Pacific, I sail'd out to sea,
I sail'd through the storm, I was refresh'd by the storm,
I watch'd with joy the threatening maws of the waves,
I mark'd the white combs where they career'd so high, curling over,
I heard the wind piping, I saw the black clouds,
Saw from below what arose and mounted, (O superb! O wild as my heart, and powerful!)
Heard the continuous thunder as it bellow'd after the lightning,
Noted the slender and jagged threads of lightning as sudden and fast amid the din they chased each other across the sky;
These, and such as these, I, elate, saw—saw with wonder, yet pensive and masterful,
All the menacing might of the globe uprisen around me,
Yet there with my soul I fed, I fed content, supercilious.

2

'Twas well, O soul—'twas a good preparation you gave me,
Now we advance our latent and ampler hunger to fill,
Now we go forth to receive what the earth and the sea never gave us,
Not through the mighty woods we go, but through the mightier cities,
Something for us is pouring now more than Niagara pouring,

Torrents of men, (sources and rills of the Northwest are you
indeed inexhaustible?)
What, to pavements and homesteads here, what were those
storms of the mountains and sea?
What, to passions I witness around me to-day? was the sea
risen?
Was the wind piping the pipe of death under the black clouds?
Lo! from deeps more unfathomable, something more deadly
and savage,
Manhattan rising, advancing with menacing front—
Cincinnati, Chicago, unchain'd;
What was that swell I saw on the ocean? behold what comes
here,
How it climbs with daring feet and hands—how it dashes!
How the true thunder bellows after the lightning—how
bright the flashes of lightning!
How Democracy with desperate vengeful port strides on,
shown through the dark by those flashes of lightning!
(Yet a mournful wail and low sob I fancied I heard through
the dark,
In a lull of the deafening confusion.)

3

Thunder on! stride on, Democracy! strike with vengeful stroke!
And do you rise higher than ever yet O days, O cities!
Crash heavier, heavier yet O storms! you have done me good,
My soul prepared in the mountains absorbs your immortal
strong nutriment,
Long had I walk'd my cities, my country roads through
farms, only half satisfied,
One doubt nauseous undulating like a snake, crawl'd on the
ground before me,
Continually preceding my steps, turning upon me oft,
ironically hissing low;
The cities I loved so well I abandon'd and left, I sped to
the certainties suitable to me,
Hungering, hungering, hungering, for primal energies and
Nature's dauntlessness,
I refresh'd myself with it only, I could relish it only,

I waited the bursting forth of the pent fire—on the water
and air I waited long;
But now I no longer wait, I am fully satisfied, I am glutted,
I have witness'd the true lightning, I have witness'd my
cities electric,
I have lived to behold man burst forth and warlike America
rise,
Hence I will seek no more the food of the northern solitary
wilds,
No more the mountains roam or sail the stormy sea.

Virginia—The West

THE noble sire fallen on evil days,
I saw with hand uplifted, menacing, brandishing,
(Memories of old in abeyance, love and faith in abeyance,)
The insane knife toward the Mother of All.

The noble son on sinewy feet advancing,
I saw, out of the land of prairies, land of Ohio's waters and
of Indiana,
To the rescue the stalwart giant hurry his plenteous offspring,
Drest in blue, bearing their trusty rifles on their shoulders.

Then the Mother of All with calm voice speaking,
As to you Rebellious, (I seemed to hear her say,) why strive
against me, and why seek my life?
When you yourself forever provide to defend me?
For you provided me Washington—and now these also.

City of Ships

CITY of ships!
(O the black ships! O the fierce ships!
O the beautiful sharp-bow'd steam-ships and sail-ships!)
City of the world! (for all races are here,
All the lands of the earth make contributions here;)
City of the sea! city of hurried and glittering tides!
City whose gleeful tides continually rush or recede, whirling
in and out with eddies and foam!

City of wharves and stores—city of tall façades of marble
and iron!
Proud and passionate city—mettlesome, mad, extravagant city!
Spring up O city—not for peace alone, but be indeed
yourself, warlike!
Fear not—submit to no models but your own O city!
Behold me—incarnate me as I have incarnated you!
I have rejected nothing you offer'd me—whom you adopted
I have adopted,
Good or bad I never question you—I love all—I do not
condemn any thing,
I chant and celebrate all that is yours—yet peace no more,
In peace I chanted peace, but now the drum of war is mine,
War, red war is my song through your streets, O city!

The Centenarian's Story

Volunteer of 1861–2, (at Washington Park, Brooklyn, assisting the Centenarian.)

GIVE me your hand old Revolutionary,
The hill-top is nigh, but a few steps, (make room
gentlemen,)
Up the path you have follow'd me well, spite of your
hundred and extra years,
You can walk old man, though your eyes are almost done,
Your faculties serve you, and presently I must have them
serve me.

Rest, while I tell what the crowd around us means,
On the plain below recruits are drilling and exercising,
There is the camp, one regiment departs to-morrow,
Do you hear the officers giving their orders?
Do you hear the clank of the muskets?

Why what comes over you now old man?
Why do you tremble and clutch my hand so convulsively?
The troops are but drilling, they are yet surrounded with
smiles,
Around them at hand the well-drest friends and the women,
While splendid and warm the afternoon sun shines down,

Green the midsummer verdure and fresh blows the dallying breeze,
O'er proud and peaceful cities and arm of the sea between.

But drill and parade are over, they march back to quarters,
Only hear that approval of hands! hear what a clapping!

As wending the crowds now part and disperse—but we old man,
Not for nothing have I brought you hither—we must remain,
You to speak in your turn, and I to listen and tell.

The Centenarian.

When I clutch'd your hand it was not with terror,
But suddenly pouring about me here on every side,
And below there where the boys were drilling, and up the slopes they ran,
And where tents are pitch'd, and wherever you see south and south-east and south-west,
Over hills, across lowlands, and in the skirts of woods,
And along the shores, in mire (now fill'd over) came again and suddenly raged,
As eighty-five years a-gone no mere parade receiv'd with applause of friends,
But a battle which I took part in myself—aye, long ago as it is, I took part in it,
Walking then this hilltop, this same ground.

Aye, this is the ground,
My blind eyes even as I speak behold it re-peopled from graves,
The years recede, pavements and stately houses disappear,
Rude forts appear again, the old hoop'd guns are mounted,
I see the lines of rais'd earth stretching from river to bay,
I mark the vista of waters, I mark the uplands and slopes;
Here we lay encamp'd, it was this time in summer also.

As I talk I remember all, I remember the Declaration,
It was read here, the whole army paraded, it was read to us here,

By his staff surrounded the General stood in the middle, he
held up his unsheath'd sword,
It glitter'd in the sun in full sight of the army.

'Twas a bold act then—the English war-ships had just arrived,
We could watch down the lower bay where they lay at anchor,
And the transports swarming with soldiers.

A few days more and they landed, and then the battle.

Twenty thousand were brought against us,
A veteran force furnish'd with good artillery.

I tell not now the whole of the battle,
But one brigade early in the forenoon order'd forward to
engage the red-coats,
Of that brigade I tell, and how steadily it march'd,
And how long and well it stood confronting death.

Who do you think that was marching steadily sternly
confronting death?
It was the brigade of the youngest men, two thousand strong,
Rais'd in Virginia and Maryland, and most of them known
personally to the General.

Jauntily forward they went with quick step toward
Gowanus' waters,
Till of a sudden unlook'd for by defiles through the woods,
gain'd at night,
The British advancing, rounding in from the east, fiercely
playing their guns,
That brigade of the youngest was cut off and at the enemy's
mercy.

The General watch'd them from this hill,
They made repeated desperate attempts to burst their
environment,
Then drew close together, very compact, their flag flying in
the middle,
But O from the hills how the cannon were thinning and
thinning them!

It sickens me yet, that slaughter!
I saw the moisture gather in drops on the face of the General.
I saw how he wrung his hands in anguish.

Meanwhile the British manœuvr'd to draw us out for a
    pitch'd battle,
But we dared not trust the chances of a pitch'd battle.

We fought the fight in detachments,
Sallying forth we fought at several points, but in each the
    luck was against us,
Our foe advancing, steadily getting the best of it, push'd us
    back to the works on this hill,
Till we turn'd menacing here, and then he left us.

That was the going out of the brigade of the youngest men,
    two thousand strong,
Few return'd, nearly all remain in Brooklyn.

That and here my General's first battle,
No women looking on nor sunshine to bask in, it did not
    conclude with applause,
Nobody clapp'd hands here then.

But in darkness in mist on the ground under a chill rain,
Wearied that night we lay foil'd and sullen,
While scornfully laugh'd many an arrogant lord off against
    us encamp'd,
Quite within hearing, feasting, clinking wineglasses together
    over their victory.

So dull and damp and another day,
But the night of that, mist lifting, rain ceasing,
Silent as a ghost while they thought they were sure of him,
    my General retreated.

I saw him at the river-side,
Down by the ferry lit by torches, hastening the embarcation;

My General waited till the soldiers and wounded were all
 pass'd over,
And then, (it was just ere sunrise,) these eyes rested on him
 for the last time.

Every one else seem'd fill'd with gloom,
Many no doubt thought of capitulation.

But when my General pass'd me,
As he stood in his boat and look'd toward the coming sun,
I saw something different from capitulation.

Terminus.

Enough, the Centenarian's story ends,
The two, the past and present, have interchanged,
I myself as connecter, as chansonnier of a great future, am
 now speaking.

And is this the ground Washington trod?
And these waters I listlessly daily cross, are these the waters
 he cross'd,
As resolute in defeat as other generals in their proudest
 triumphs?

I must copy the story, and send it eastward and westward,
I must preserve that look as it beam'd on you rivers of
 Brooklyn.

See—as the annual round returns the phantoms return,
It is the 27th of August and the British have landed,
The battle begins and goes against us, behold through the
 smoke Washington's face,
The brigade of Virginia and Maryland have march'd forth to
 intercept the enemy,
They are cut off, murderous artillery from the hills plays
 upon them,
Rank after rank falls, while over them silently droops the flag,
Baptized that day in many a young man's bloody wounds,
In death, defeat, and sisters', mothers' tears.

Ah, hills and slopes of Brooklyn! I perceive you are more
valuable than your owners supposed;
In the midst of you stands an encampment very old,
Stands forever the camp of that dead brigade.

Cavalry Crossing a Ford

A LINE in long array where they wind betwixt green islands,
They take a serpentine course, their arms flash in the sun—
hark to the musical clank,
Behold the silvery river, in it the splashing horses loitering
stop to drink,
Behold the brown-faced men, each group, each person a
picture, the negligent rest on the saddles,
Some emerge on the opposite bank, others are just entering
the ford—while,
Scarlet and blue and snowy white,
The guidon flags flutter gayly in the wind.

Bivouac on a Mountain Side

I SEE before me now a traveling army halting,
Below a fertile valley spread, with barns and the orchards of
summer,
Behind, the terraced sides of a mountain, abrupt, in places
rising high,
Broken, with rocks, with clinging cedars, with tall shapes
dingily seen,
The numerous camp-fires scatter'd near and far, some away
up on the mountain,
The shadowy forms of men and horses, looming, large-
sized, flickering,
And over all the sky—the sky! far, far out of reach, studded,
breaking out, the eternal stars.

An Army Corps on the March

WITH its cloud of skirmishers in advance,
With now the sound of a single shot snapping like a whip,
and now an irregular volley,

The swarming ranks press on and on, the dense brigades press on,
Glittering dimly, toiling under the sun—the dust-cover'd men,
In columns rise and fall to the undulations of the ground,
With artillery interspers'd—the wheels rumble, the horses sweat,
As the army corps advances.

By the Bivouac's Fitful Flame

By the bivouac's fitful flame,
A procession winding around me, solemn and sweet and slow—but first I note,
The tents of the sleeping army, the fields' and woods' dim outline,
The darkness lit by spots of kindled fire, the silence,
Like a phantom far or near an occasional figure moving,
The shrubs and trees, (as I lift my eyes they seem to be stealthily watching me,)
While wind in procession thoughts, O tender and wondrous thoughts,
Of life and death, of home and the past and loved, and of those that are far away;
A solemn and slow procession there as I sit on the ground,
By the bivouac's fitful flame.

Come Up from the Fields Father

Come up from the fields father, here's a letter from our Pete,
And come to the front door mother, here's a letter from thy dear son.

Lo, 'tis autumn,
Lo, where the trees, deeper green, yellower and redder,
Cool and sweeten Ohio's villages with leaves fluttering in the moderate wind,
Where apples ripe in the orchards hang and grapes on the trellis'd vines,
(Smell you the smell of the grapes on the vines?

Smell you the buckwheat where the bees were lately
buzzing?)

Above all, lo, the sky so calm, so transparent after the rain,
and with wondrous clouds,
Below too, all calm, all vital and beautiful, and the farm
prospers well.

Down in the fields all prospers well,
But now from the fields come father, come at the
daughter's call,
And come to the entry mother, to the front door come
right away.

Fast as she can she hurries, something ominous, her steps
trembling,
She does not tarry to smooth her hair nor adjust her cap.

Open the envelope quickly,
O this is not our son's writing, yet his name is sign'd,
O a strange hand writes for our dear son, O stricken
mother's soul!
All swims before her eyes, flashes with black, she catches the
main words only,
Sentences broken, *gunshot wound in the breast, cavalry
skirmish, taken to hospital,*
At present low, but will soon be better.

Ah now the single figure to me,
Amid all teeming and wealthy Ohio with all its cities and
farms,
Sickly white in the face and dull in the head, very faint,
By the jamb of a door leans.

Grieve not so, dear mother, (the just-grown daughter speaks
through her sobs,
The little sisters huddle around speechless and dismay'd,)
See, dearest mother, the letter says Pete will soon be better.

Alas poor boy, he will never be better, (nor may-be needs to
be better, that brave and simple soul,)
While they stand at home at the door he is dead already,
The only son is dead.

But the mother needs to be better,
She with thin form presently drest in black,
By day her meals untouch'd, then at night fitfully sleeping,
often waking,
In the midnight waking, weeping, longing with one deep
longing,
O that she might withdraw unnoticed, silent from life
escape and withdraw,
To follow, to seek, to be with her dear dead son.

Vigil Strange I Kept on the Field One Night

VIGIL strange I kept on the field one night;
When you my son and my comrade dropt at my side that day,
One look I but gave which your dear eyes return'd with a
look I shall never forget,
One touch of your hand to mine O boy, reach'd up as you
lay on the ground,
Then onward I sped in the battle, the even-contested battle,
Till late in the night reliev'd to the place at last again I
made my way,
Found you in death so cold dear comrade, found your body
son of responding kisses, (never again on earth
responding,)
Bared your face in the starlight, curious the scene, cool blew
the moderate night-wind,
Long there and then in vigil I stood, dimly around me the
battle-field spreading,
Vigil wondrous and vigil sweet there in the fragrant silent
night,
But not a tear fell, not even a long-drawn sigh, long, long I
gazed,
Then on the earth partially reclining sat by your side leaning
my chin in my hands,

Passing sweet hours, immortal and mystic hours with you
dearest comrade—not a tear, not a word,
Vigil of silence, love and death, vigil for you my son and my
soldier,
As onward silently stars aloft, eastward new ones upward
stole,
Vigil final for you brave boy, (I could not save you, swift
was your death,
I faithfully loved you and cared for you living, I think we
shall surely meet again,)
Till at latest lingering of the night, indeed just as the dawn
appear'd,
My comrade I wrapt in his blanket, envelop'd well his form,
Folded the blanket well, tucking it carefully over head and
carefully under feet,
And there and then and bathed by the rising sun, my son in
his grave, in his rude-dug grave I deposited,
Ending my vigil strange with that, vigil of night and battle-
field dim,
Vigil for boy of responding kisses, (never again on earth
responding,)
Vigil for comrade swiftly slain, vigil I never forget, how as
day brighten'd,
I rose from the chill ground and folded my soldier well in
his blanket,
And buried him where he fell.

A March in the Ranks Hard-Prest, and the Road Unknown

A MARCH in the ranks hard-prest, and the road unknown,
A route through a heavy wood with muffled steps in the
darkness,
Our army foil'd with loss severe, and the sullen remnant
retreating,
Till after midnight glimmer upon us the lights of a dim-
lighted building,
We come to an open space in the woods, and halt by the
dim-lighted building,

'Tis a large old church at the crossing roads, now an impromptu hospital,
Entering but for a minute I see a sight beyond all the pictures and poems ever made,
Shadows of deepest, deepest black, just lit by moving candles and lamps,
And by one great pitchy torch stationary with wild red flame and clouds of smoke,
By these, crowds, groups of forms vaguely I see on the floor, some in the pews laid down,
At my feet more distinctly a soldier, a mere lad, in danger of bleeding to death, (he is shot in the abdomen,)
I stanch the blood temporarily, (the youngster's face is white as a lily,)
Then before I depart I sweep my eyes o'er the scene fain to absorb it all,
Faces, varieties, postures beyond description, most in obscurity, some of them dead,
Surgeons operating, attendants holding lights, the smell of ether, the odor of blood,
The crowd, O the crowd of the bloody forms, the yard outside also fill'd,
Some on the bare ground, some on planks or stretchers, some in the death-spasm sweating,
An occasional scream or cry, the doctor's shouted orders or calls,
The glisten of the little steel instruments catching the glint of the torches,
These I resume as I chant, I see again the forms, I smell the odor,
Then hear outside the orders given, *Fall in, my men, fall in;*
But first I bend to the dying lad, his eyes open, a half-smile gives he me,
Then the eyes close, calmly close, and I speed forth to the darkness,
Resuming, marching, ever in darkness marching, on in the ranks,
The unknown road still marching.

A Sight in Camp in the Daybreak Gray and Dim

A SIGHT in camp in the daybreak gray and dim,
As from my tent I emerge so early sleepless,
As slow I walk in the cool fresh air the path near by the hospital tent,
Three forms I see on stretchers lying, brought out there untended lying,
Over each the blanket spread, ample brownish woolen blanket,
Gray and heavy blanket, folding, covering all.

Curious I halt and silent stand,
Then with light fingers I from the face of the nearest the first just lift the blanket;
Who are you elderly man so gaunt and grim, with well-gray'd hair, and flesh all sunken about the eyes?
Who are you my dear comrade?

Then to the second I step—and who are you my child and darling?
Who are you sweet boy with cheeks yet blooming?

Then to the third—a face nor child nor old, very calm, as of beautiful yellow-white ivory;
Young man I think I know you—I think this face is the face of the Christ himself,
Dead and divine and brother of all, and here again he lies.

As Toilsome I Wander'd Virginia's Woods

AS toilsome I wander'd Virginia's woods,
To the music of rustling leaves kick'd by my feet, (for 'twas autumn,)
I mark'd at the foot of a tree the grave of a soldier;
Mortally wounded he and buried on the retreat, (easily all could I understand,)
The halt of a mid-day hour, when up! no time to lose—yet this sign left,
On a tablet scrawl'd and nail'd on the tree by the grave,
Bold, cautious, true, and my loving comrade.

Long, long I muse, then on my way go wandering,
Many a changeful season to follow, and many a scene of life,
Yet at times through changeful season and scene, abrupt, alone, or in the crowded street,
Comes before me the unknown soldier's grave, comes the inscription rude in Virginia's woods,
Bold, cautious, true, and my loving comrade.

Not the Pilot

NOT the pilot has charged himself to bring his ship into port, though beaten back and many times baffled;
Not the pathfinder penetrating inland weary and long,
By deserts parch'd, snows chill'd, rivers wet, perseveres till he reaches his destination,
More than I have charged myself, heeded or unheeded, to compose a march for these States,
For a battle-call, rousing to arms if need be, years, centuries hence.

Year That Trembled and Reel'd Beneath Me

YEAR that trembled and reel'd beneath me!
Your summer wind was warm enough, yet the air I breathed froze me,
A thick gloom fell through the sunshine and darken'd me,
Must I change my triumphant songs? said I to myself,
Must I indeed learn to chant the cold dirges of the baffled?
And sullen hymns of defeat?

The Wound-Dresser

1

AN old man bending I come among new faces,
Years looking backward resuming in answer to children,
Come tell us old man, as from young men and maidens that love me,
(Arous'd and angry, I'd thought to beat the alarum, and urge relentless war,

But soon my fingers fail'd me, my face droop'd and I
resign'd myself,
To sit by the wounded and soothe them, or silently watch
the dead;)
Years hence of these scenes, of these furious passions, these
chances,
Of unsurpass'd heroes, (was one side so brave? the other
was equally brave;)
Now be witness again, paint the mightiest armies of earth,
Of those armies so rapid so wondrous what saw you to tell us?
What stays with you latest and deepest? of curious panics,
Of hard-fought engagements or sieges tremendous what
deepest remains?

2

O maidens and young men I love and that love me,
What you ask of my days those the strangest and sudden
your talking recalls,
Soldier alert I arrive after a long march cover'd with sweat
and dust,
In the nick of time I come, plunge in the fight, loudly
shout in the rush of successful charge,
Enter the captur'd works—yet lo, like a swift-running river
they fade,
Pass and are gone they fade—I dwell not on soldiers' perils
or soldier's joys,
(Both I remember well—many the hardships, few the joys,
yet I was content.)

But in silence, in dreams' projections,
While the world of gain and appearance and mirth goes on,
So soon what is over forgotten, and waves wash the imprints
off the sand,
With hinged knees returning I enter the doors, (while for
you up there,
Whoever you are, follow without noise and be of strong
heart.)

Bearing the bandages, water and sponge,
Straight and swift to my wounded I go,

Where they lie on the ground after the battle brought in,
Where their priceless blood reddens the grass the ground,
Or to the rows of the hospital tent, or under the roof'd
hospital,
To the long rows of cots up and down each side I return,
To each and all one after another I draw near, not one do
I miss,
An attendant follows holding a tray, he carries a refuse pail,
Soon to be fill'd with clotted rags and blood, emptied, and
fill'd again.

I onward go, I stop,
With hinged knees and steady hand to dress wounds,
I am firm with each, the pangs are sharp yet unavoidable,
One turns to me his appealing eyes—poor boy! I never
knew you,
Yet I think I could not refuse this moment to die for you, if
that would save you.

3

On, on I go, (open doors of time! open hospital doors!)
The crush'd head I dress, (poor crazed hand tear not the
bandage away,)
The neck of the cavalry-man with the bullet through and
through I examine,
Hard the breathing rattles, quite glazed already the eye, yet
life struggles hard,
(Come sweet death! be persuaded O beautiful death!
In mercy come quickly.)

From the stump of the arm, the amputated hand,
I undo the clotted lint, remove the slough, wash off the
matter and blood,
Back on his pillow the soldier bends with curv'd neck and
side-falling head,
His eyes are closed, his face is pale, he dares not look on
the bloody stump,
And has not yet look'd on it.

I dress a wound in the side, deep, deep,
But a day or two more, for see the frame all wasted and sinking,
And the yellow-blue countenance see.

I dress the perforated shoulder, the foot with the bullet-wound,
Cleanse the one with a gnawing and putrid gangrene, so sickening, so offensive,
While the attendant stands behind aside me holding the tray and pail.

I am faithful, I do not give out,
The fractur'd thigh, the knee, the wound in the abdomen,
These and more I dress with impassive hand, (yet deep in my breast a fire, a burning flame.)

4

Thus in silence in dreams' projections,
Returning, resuming, I thread my way through the hospitals,
The hurt and wounded I pacify with soothing hand,
I sit by the restless all the dark night, some are so young,
Some suffer so much, I recall the experience sweet and sad,
(Many a soldier's loving arms about this neck have cross'd and rested,
Many a soldier's kiss dwells on these bearded lips.)

Long, Too Long America

LONG, too long America,
Traveling roads all even and peaceful you learn'd from joys and prosperity only,
But now, ah now, to learn from crises of anguish, advancing, grappling with direst fate and recoiling not,
And now to conceive and show to the world what your children en-masse really are,
(For who except myself has yet conceiv'd what your children en-masse really are?)

Give Me the Splendid Silent Sun

1

GIVE me the splendid silent sun with all his beams full-dazzling,
Give me juicy autumnal fruit ripe and red from the orchard,
Give me a field where the unmow'd grass grows,
Give me an arbor, give me the trellis'd grape,
Give me fresh corn and wheat, give me serene-moving animals teaching content,
Give me nights perfectly quiet as on high plateaus west of the Mississippi, and I looking up at the stars,
Give me odorous at sunrise a garden of beautiful flowers where I can walk undisturb'd,
Give me for marriage a sweet-breath'd woman of whom I should never tire,
Give me a perfect child, give me away aside from the noise of the world a rural domestic life,
Give me to warble spontaneous songs recluse by myself, for my own ears only,
Give me solitude, give me Nature, give me again O Nature your primal sanities!

These demanding to have them, (tired with ceaseless excitement, and rack'd by the war-strife,)
These to procure incessantly asking, rising in cries from my heart,
While yet incessantly asking still I adhere to my city,
Day upon day and year upon year O city, walking your streets,
Where you hold me enchain'd a certain time refusing to give me up,
Yet giving to make me glutted, enrich'd of soul, you give me forever faces;
(O I see what I sought to escape, confronting, reversing my cries,
I see my own soul trampling down what it ask'd for.)

2

Keep your splendid silent sun,
Keep your woods O Nature, and the quiet places by the woods,

Keep your fields of clover and timothy, and your corn-fields and orchards,
Keep the blossoming buckwheat fields where the Ninth-month bees hum;
Give me faces and streets—give me these phantoms incessant and endless along the trottoirs!
Give me interminable eyes—give me women—give me comrades and lovers by the thousand!
Let me see new ones every day—let me hold new ones by the hand every day!
Give me such shows—give me the streets of Manhattan!
Give me Broadway, with the soldiers marching—give me the sound of the trumpets and drums!
(The soldiers in companies or regiments—some starting away, flush'd and reckless,
Some, their time up, returning with thinn'd ranks, young, yet very old, worn, marching, noticing nothing;)
Give me the shores and wharves heavy-fringed with black ships!
O such for me! O an intense life, full to repletion and varied!
The life of the theatre, bar-room, huge hotel, for me!
The saloon of the steamer! the crowded excursion for me! the torchlight procession!
The dense brigade bound for the war, with high piled military wagons following;
People, endless, streaming, with strong voices, passions, pageants,
Manhattan streets with their powerful throbs, with beating drums as now,
The endless and noisy chorus, the rustle and clank of muskets, (even the sight of the wounded,)
Manhattan crowds, with their turbulent musical chorus!
Manhattan faces and eyes forever for me.

Dirge for Two Veterans

THE last sunbeam
Lightly falls from the finish'd Sabbath,
On the pavement here, and there beyond it is looking,
Down a new-made double grave.

Lo, the moon ascending,
Up from the east the silvery round moon,
Beautiful over the house-tops, ghastly, phantom moon,
Immense and silent moon.

I see a sad procession,
And I hear the sound of coming full-key'd bugles,
All the channels of the city streets they're flooding,
As with voices and with tears.

I hear the great drums pounding,
And the small drums steady whirring,
And every blow of the great convulsive drums,
Strikes me through and through.

For the son is brought with the father,
(In the foremost ranks of the fierce assault they fell,
Two veterans son and father dropt together,
And the double grave awaits them.)

Now nearer blow the bugles,
And the drums strike more convulsive,
And the daylight o'er the pavement quite has faded,
And the strong dead-march enwraps me.

In the eastern sky up-buoying,
The sorrowful vast phantom moves illumin'd,
('Tis some mother's large transparent face,
In heaven brighter growing.)

O strong dead-march you please me!
O moon immense with your silvery face you soothe me!
O my soldiers twain! O my veterans passing to burial!
What I have I also give you.

The moon gives you light,
And the bugles and the drums give you music,
And my heart, O my soldiers, my veterans,
My heart gives you love.

Over the Carnage Rose Prophetic a Voice

OVER the carnage rose prophetic a voice,
Be not dishearten'd, affection shall solve the problems of freedom yet,
Those who love each other shall become invincible,
They shall yet make Columbia victorious.

Sons of the Mother of All, you shall yet be victorious,
You shall yet laugh to scorn the attacks of all the remainder of the earth.

No danger shall balk Columbia's lovers,
If need be a thousand shall sternly immolate themselves for one.

One from Massachusetts shall be a Missourian's comrade,
From Maine and from hot Carolina, and another an Oregonese, shall be friends triune,
More precious to each other than all the riches of the earth.

To Michigan, Florida perfumes shall tenderly come,
Not the perfumes of flowers, but sweeter, and wafted beyond death.

It shall be customary in the houses and streets to see manly affection,
The most dauntless and rude shall touch face to face lightly,
The dependence of Liberty shall be lovers,
The continuance of Equality shall be comrades.

These shall tie you and band you stronger than hoops of iron,
I, ecstatic, O partners! O lands! with the love of lovers tie you.

(Were you looking to be held together by lawyers?
Or by an agreement on a paper? or by arms?
Nay, nor the world, nor any living thing, will so cohere.)

I Saw Old General at Bay

I SAW old General at bay,
(Old as he was, his gray eyes yet shone out in battle like stars,)
His small force was now completely hemm'd in, in his works,
He call'd for volunteers to run the enemy's lines, a desperate emergency,
I saw a hundred and more step forth from the ranks, but two or three were selected,
I saw them receive their orders aside, they listen'd with care, the adjutant was very grave,
I saw them depart with cheerfulness, freely risking their lives.

The Artilleryman's Vision

WHILE my wife at my side lies slumbering, and the wars are over long,
And my head on the pillow rests at home, and the vacant midnight passes,
And through the stillness, through the dark, I hear, just hear, the breath of my infant,
There in the room as I wake from sleep this vision presses upon me;
The engagement opens there and then in fantasy unreal,
The skirmishers begin, they crawl cautiously ahead, I hear the irregular snap! snap!
I hear the sounds of the different missiles, the short *t-h-t! t-h-t!* of the rifle-balls,
I see the shells exploding leaving small white clouds, I hear the great shells shrieking as they pass,
The grape like the hum and whirr of wind through the trees, (tumultuous now the contest rages,)
All the scenes at the batteries rise in detail before me again,
The crashing and smoking, the pride of the men in their pieces,
The chief-gunner ranges and sights his piece and selects a fuse of the right time,
After firing I see him lean aside and look eagerly off to note the effect;

Elsewhere I hear the cry of a regiment charging, (the young colonel leads himself this time with brandish'd sword,)
I see the gaps cut by the enemy's volleys, (quickly fill'd up, no delay,)
I breathe the suffocating smoke, then the flat clouds hover low concealing all;
Now a strange lull for a few seconds, not a shot fired on either side,
Then resumed the chaos louder than ever, with eager calls and orders of officers,
While from some distant part of the field the wind wafts to my ears a shout of applause, (some special success,)
And ever the sound of the cannon far or near, (rousing even in dreams a devilish exultation and all the old mad joy in the depths of my soul,)
And ever the hastening of infantry shifting positions, batteries, cavalry, moving hither and thither,
(The falling, dying, I heed not, the wounded dripping and red I heed not, some to the rear are hobbling,)
Grime, heat, rush, aide-de-camps galloping by or on a full run,
With the patter of small arms, the warning *s-s-t* of the rifles, (these in my vision I hear or see,)
And bombs bursting in air, and at night the vari-color'd rockets.

Ethiopia Saluting the Colors

WHO are you dusky woman, so ancient hardly human,
With your woolly-white and turban'd head, and bare bony feet?
Why rising by the roadside here, do you the colors greet?

('Tis while our army lines Carolina's sands and pines,
Forth from thy hovel door thou Ethiopia com'st to me,
As under doughty Sherman I march toward the sea.)

Me master years a hundred since from my parents sunder'd,
A little child, they caught me as the savage beast is caught,
Then hither me across the sea the cruel slaver brought.

No further does she say, but lingering all the day,
Her high-borne turban'd head she wags, and rolls her
 darkling eye,
And courtesies to the regiments, the guidons moving by.

What is it fateful woman, so blear, hardly human?
Why wag your head with turban bound, yellow, red and
 green?
Are the things so strange and marvelous you see or have seen?

Not Youth Pertains to Me

NOT youth pertains to me,
Nor delicatesse, I cannot beguile the time with talk,
Awkward in the parlor, neither a dancer nor elegant,
In the learn'd coterie sitting constrain'd and still, for
 learning inures not to me,
Beauty, knowledge, inure not to me—yet there are two or
 three things inure to me,
I have nourish'd the wounded and sooth'd many a dying
 soldier,
And at intervals waiting or in the midst of camp,
Composed these songs.

Race of Veterans

RACE of veterans—race of victors!
Race of the soil, ready for conflict—race of the conquering
 march!
(No more credulity's race, abiding-temper'd race,)
Race henceforth owning no law but the law of itself,
Race of passion and the storm.

World Take Good Notice

WORLD take good notice, silver stars fading,
Milky hue ript, weft of white detaching,
Coals thirty-eight, baleful and burning,
Scarlet, significant, hands off warning,
Now and henceforth flaunt from these shores.

O Tan-Faced Prairie-Boy

O TAN-FACED prairie-boy,
Before you came to camp came many a welcome gift,
Praises and presents came and nourishing food, till at last
among the recruits,
You came, taciturn, with nothing to give—we but look'd on
each other,
When lo! more than all the gifts of the world you gave me.

Look Down Fair Moon

LOOK down fair moon and bathe this scene,
Pour softly down night's nimbus floods on faces ghastly,
swollen, purple,
On the dead on their backs with arms toss'd wide,
Pour down your unstinted nimbus sacred moon.

Reconciliation

WORD over all, beautiful as the sky,
Beautiful that war and all its deeds of carnage must in time
be utterly lost,
That the hands of the sisters Death and Night incessantly
softly wash again, and ever again, this soil'd world;
For my enemy is dead, a man divine as myself is dead,
I look where he lies white-faced and still in the coffin—I
draw near,
Bend down and touch lightly with my lips the white face in
the coffin.

How Solemn as One by One

(Washington City, 1865.)

HOW solemn as one by one,
As the ranks returning worn and sweaty, as the men file by
where I stand,
As the faces the masks appear, as I glance at the faces
studying the masks,

(As I glance upward out of this page studying you, dear
friend, whoever you are,)
How solemn the thought of my whispering soul to each in
the ranks, and to you,
I see behind each mask that wonder a kindred soul,
O the bullet could never kill what you really are, dear friend,
Nor the bayonet stab what you really are;
The soul! yourself I see, great as any, good as the best,
Waiting secure and content, which the bullet could never kill,
Nor the bayonet stab O friend.

As I Lay with My Head in Your Lap Camerado

As I lay with my head in your lap camerado,
The confession I made I resume, what I said to you and the
open air I resume,
I know I am restless and make others so,
I know my words are weapons full of danger, full of death,
For I confront peace, security, and all the settled laws, to
unsettle them,
I am more resolute because all have denied me than I could
ever have been had all accepted me,
I heed not and have never heeded either experience,
cautions, majorities, nor ridicule,
And the threat of what is call'd hell is little or nothing to
me,
And the lure of what is call'd heaven is little or nothing to
me;
Dear camerado! I confess I have urged you onward with
me, and still urge you, without the least idea what is
our destination,
Or whether we shall be victorious, or utterly quell'd and
defeated.

Delicate Cluster

DELICATE cluster! flag of teeming life!
Covering all my lands—all my seashores lining!
Flag of death! (how I watch'd you through the smoke of
battle pressing!

How I heard you flap and rustle, cloth defiant!)
Flag cerulean—sunny flag, with the orbs of night dappled!
Ah my silvery beauty—ah my woolly white and crimson!
Ah to sing the song of you, my matron mighty!
My sacred one, my mother.

To a Certain Civilian

DID you ask dulcet rhymes from me?
Did you seek the civilian's peaceful and languishing rhymes?
Did you find what I sang erewhile so hard to follow?
Why I was not singing erewhile for you to follow, to
understand—nor am I now;
(I have been born of the same as the war was born,
The drum-corps' rattle is ever to me sweet music, I love
well the martial dirge,
With slow wail and convulsive throb leading the officer's
funeral;)
What to such as you anyhow such a poet as I? therefore
leave my works,
And go lull yourself with what you can understand, and
with piano-tunes,
For I lull nobody, and you will never understand me.

Lo, Victress on the Peaks

LO, Victress on the peaks,
Where thou with mighty brow regarding the world,
(The world O Libertad, that vainly conspired against thee,)
Out of its countless beleaguering toils, after thwarting them
all,
Dominant, with the dazzling sun around thee,
Flauntest now unharm'd in immortal soundness and
bloom—lo, in these hours supreme,
No poem proud, I chanting bring to thee, nor mastery's
rapturous verse,
But a cluster containing night's darkness and blood-dripping
wounds,
And psalms of the dead.

Spirit Whose Work Is Done

(*Washington City, 1865.*)

SPIRIT whose work is done—spirit of dreadful hours!
Ere departing fade from my eyes your forests of bayonets;
Spirit of gloomiest fears and doubts, (yet onward ever unfaltering pressing,)
Spirit of many a solemn day and many a savage scene—electric spirit,
That with muttering voice through the war now closed, like a tireless phantom flitted,
Rousing the land with breath of flame, while you beat and beat the drum,
Now as the sound of the drum, hollow and harsh to the last, reverberates round me,
As your ranks, your immortal ranks, return, return from the battles,
As the muskets of the young men yet lean over their shoulders,
As I look on the bayonets bristling over their shoulders,
As those slanted bayonets, whole forests of them appearing in the distance, approach and pass on, returning homeward,
Moving with steady motion, swaying to and fro to the right and left,
Evenly lightly rising and falling while the steps keep time;
Spirit of hours I knew, all hectic red one day, but pale as death next day,
Touch my mouth ere you depart, press my lips close,
Leave me your pulses of rage—bequeath them to me—fill me with currents convulsive,
Let them scorch and blister out of my chants when you are gone,
Let them identify you to the future in these songs.

Adieu to a Soldier

ADIEU O soldier,
You of the rude campaigning, (which we shared,)
The rapid march, the life of the camp,

The hot contention of opposing fronts, the long manœuvre,
Red battles with their slaughter, the stimulus, the strong
terrific game,
Spell of all brave and manly hearts, the trains of time
through you and like of you all fill'd,
With war and war's expression.

Adieu dear comrade,
Your mission is fulfill'd—but I, more warlike,
Myself and this contentious soul of mine,
Still on our own campaigning bound,
Through untried roads with ambushes opponents lined,
Through many a sharp defeat and many a crisis, often baffled,
Here marching, ever marching on, a war fight out—aye here,
To fiercer, weightier battles give expression.

Turn O Libertad

TURN O Libertad, for the war is over,
From it and all henceforth expanding, doubting no more,
resolute, sweeping the world,
Turn from lands retrospective recording proofs of the past,
From the singers that sing the trailing glories of the past,
From the chants of the feudal world, the triumphs of kings,
slavery, caste,
Turn to the world, the triumphs reserv'd and to come—give
up that backward world,
Leave to the singers of hitherto, give them the trailing past,
But what remains remains for singers for you—wars to come
are for you,
(Lo, how the wars of the past have duly inured to you, and
the wars of the present also inure;)
Then turn, and be not alarm'd O Libertad—turn your
undying face,
To where the future, greater than all the past,
Is swiftly, surely preparing for you.

To the Leaven'd Soil They Trod

To the leaven'd soil they trod calling I sing for the last,
(Forth from my tent emerging for good, loosing, untying
the tent-ropes,)
In the freshness the forenoon air, in the far-stretching
circuits and vistas again to peace restored,
To the fiery fields emanative and the endless vistas beyond,
to the South and the North,
To the leaven'd soil of the general Western world to attest
my songs,
To the Alleghanian hills and the tireless Mississippi,
To the rocks I calling sing, and all the trees in the woods,
To the plains of the poems of heroes, to the prairies
spreading wide,
To the far-off sea and the unseen winds, and the sane
impalpable air;
And responding they answer all, (but not in words,)
The average earth, the witness of war and peace,
acknowledges mutely,
The prairie draws me close, as the father to bosom broad
the son,
The Northern ice and rain that began me nourish me to the
end,
But the hot sun of the South is to fully ripen my songs.

Memories of President Lincoln

When Lilacs Last in the Dooryard Bloom'd

1

WHEN lilacs last in the dooryard bloom'd,
And the great star early droop'd in the western sky in the night,
I mourn'd, and yet shall mourn with ever-returning spring.

Ever-returning spring, trinity sure to me you bring,
Lilac blooming perennial and drooping star in the west,
And thought of him I love.

2

O powerful western fallen star!
O shades of night—O moody, tearful night!
O great star disappear'd—O the black murk that hides the star!
O cruel hands that hold me powerless—O helpless soul of me!
O harsh surrounding cloud that will not free my soul.

3

In the dooryard fronting an old farm-house near the white-wash'd palings,
Stands the lilac-bush tall-growing with heart-shaped leaves of rich green,
With many a pointed blossom rising delicate, with the perfume strong I love,
With every leaf a miracle—and from this bush in the dooryard,
With delicate-color'd blossoms and heart-shaped leaves of rich green,
A sprig with its flower I break.

4

In the swamp in secluded recesses,
A shy and hidden bird is warbling a song.

Solitary the thrush,
The hermit withdrawn to himself, avoiding the settlements,
Sings by himself a song.

Song of the bleeding throat,
Death's outlet song of life, (for well dear brother I know,
If thou wast not granted to sing thou would'st surely die.)

5

Over the breast of the spring, the land, amid cities,
Amid lanes and through old woods, where lately the violets
 peep'd from the ground, spotting the gray debris,
Amid the grass in the fields each side of the lanes, passing
 the endless grass,
Passing the yellow-spear'd wheat, every grain from its
 shroud in the dark-brown fields uprisen,
Passing the apple-tree blows of white and pink in the
 orchards,
Carrying a corpse to where it shall rest in the grave,
Night and day journeys a coffin.

6

Coffin that passes through lanes and streets,
Through day and night with the great cloud darkening the
 land,
With the pomp of the inloop'd flags with the cities draped
 in black,
With the show of the States themselves as of crape-veil'd
 women standing,
With processions long and winding and the flambeaus of the
 night,
With the countless torches lit, with the silent sea of faces
 and the unbared heads,
With the waiting depot, the arriving coffin, and the sombre
 faces,
With dirges through the night, with the thousand voices
 rising strong and solemn,
With all the mournful voices of the dirges pour'd around
 the coffin,
The dim-lit churches and the shuddering organs—where
 amid these you journey,
With the tolling tolling bells' perpetual clang,
Here, coffin that slowly passes,
I give you my sprig of lilac.

7

(Nor for you, for one alone,
Blossoms and branches green to coffins all I bring,
For fresh as the morning, thus would I chant a song for you
O sane and sacred death.

All over bouquets of roses,
O death, I cover you over with roses and early lilies,
But mostly and now the lilac that blooms the first,
Copious I break, I break the sprigs from the bushes,
With loaded arms I come, pouring for you,
For you and the coffins all of you O death.)

8

O western orb sailing the heaven,
Now I know what you must have meant as a month since I
walk'd,
As I walk'd in silence the transparent shadowy night,
As I saw you had something to tell as you bent to me night
after night,
As you droop'd from the sky low down as if to my side,
(while the other stars all look'd on,)
As we wander'd together the solemn night, (for something I
know not what kept me from sleep,)
As the night advanced, and I saw on the rim of the west
how full you were of woe,
As I stood on the rising ground in the breeze in the cool
transparent night,
As I watch'd where you pass'd and was lost in the
netherward black of the night,
As my soul in its trouble dissatisfied sank, as where you
sad orb,
Concluded, dropt in the night, and was gone.

9

Sing on there in the swamp,
O singer bashful and tender, I hear your notes, I hear your
call,
I hear, I come presently, I understand you,

But a moment I linger, for the lustrous star has detain'd me,
The star my departing comrade holds and detains me.

10

O how shall I warble myself for the dead one there I loved?
And how shall I deck my song for the large sweet soul that
has gone?
And what shall my perfume be for the grave of him I love?

Sea-winds blown from east and west,
Blown from the Eastern sea and blown from the Western
sea, till there on the prairies meeting,
These and with these and the breath of my chant,
I'll perfume the grave of him I love.

11

O what shall I hang on the chamber walls?
And what shall the pictures be that I hang on the walls,
To adorn the burial-house of him I love?

Pictures of growing spring and farms and homes,
With the Fourth-month eve at sundown, and the gray
smoke lucid and bright,
With floods of the yellow gold of the gorgeous, indolent,
sinking sun, burning, expanding the air,
With the fresh sweet herbage under foot, and the pale green
leaves of the trees prolific,
In the distance the flowing glaze, the breast of the river,
with a wind-dapple here and there,
With ranging hills on the banks, with many a line against
the sky, and shadows,
And the city at hand with dwellings so dense, and stacks of
chimneys,
And all the scenes of life and the workshops, and the
workmen homeward returning.

12

Lo, body and soul—this land,
My own Manhattan with spires, and the sparkling and
hurrying tides, and the ships,

The varied and ample land, the South and the North in the
light, Ohio's shores and flashing Missouri,
And ever the far-spreading prairies cover'd with grass and corn.

Lo, the most excellent sun so calm and haughty,
The violet and purple morn with just-felt breezes,
The gentle soft-born measureless light,
The miracle spreading bathing all, the fulfill'd noon,
The coming eve delicious, the welcome night and the stars,
Over my cities shining all, enveloping man and land.

13

Sing on, sing on you gray-brown bird,
Sing from the swamps, the recesses, pour your chant from
the bushes,
Limitless out of the dusk, out of the cedars and pines.

Sing on dearest brother, warble your reedy song,
Loud human song, with voice of uttermost woe.

O liquid and free and tender!
O wild and loose to my soul—O wondrous singer!
You only I hear—yet the star holds me, (but will soon depart,)
Yet the lilac with mastering odor holds me.

14

Now while I sat in the day and look'd forth,
In the close of the day with its light and the fields of spring,
and the farmers preparing their crops,
In the large unconscious scenery of my land with its lakes
and forests,
In the heavenly aerial beauty, (after the perturb'd winds and
the storms,)
Under the arching heavens of the afternoon swift passing,
and the voices of children and women,
The many-moving sea-tides, and I saw the ships how they
sail'd,
And the summer approaching with richness, and the fields
all busy with labor,

And the infinite separate houses, how they all went on, each with its meals and minutia of daily usages,
And the streets how their throbbings throbb'd, and the cities pent—lo, then and there,
Falling upon them all and among them all, enveloping me with the rest,
Appear'd the cloud, appear'd the long black trail,
And I knew death, its thought, and the sacred knowledge of death.

Then with the knowledge of death as walking one side of me,
And the thought of death close-walking the other side of me,
And I in the middle as with companions, and as holding the hands of companions,
I fled forth to the hiding receiving night that talks not,
Down to the shores of the water, the path by the swamp in the dimness,
To the solemn shadowy cedars and ghostly pines so still.

And the singer so shy to the rest receiv'd me,
The gray-brown bird I know receiv'd us comrades three,
And he sang the carol of death, and a verse for him I love.

From deep secluded recesses,
From the fragrant cedars and the ghostly pines so still,
Came the carol of the bird.

And the charm of the carol rapt me,
As I held as if by their hands my comrades in the night,
And the voice of my spirit tallied the song of the bird.

Come lovely and soothing death,
Undulate round the world, serenely arriving, arriving,
In the day, in the night, to all, to each,
Sooner or later delicate death.

Prais'd be the fathomless universe,
For life and joy, and for objects and knowledge curious,
And for love, sweet love—but praise! praise! praise!
For the sure-enwinding arms of cool-enfolding death.

Dark mother always gliding near with soft feet,
Have none chanted for thee a chant of fullest welcome?
Then I chant it for thee, I glorify thee above all,
I bring thee a song that when thou must indeed come, come unfalteringly.

Approach strong deliveress,
When it is so, when thou hast taken them I joyously sing the dead,
Lost in the loving floating ocean of thee,
Laved in the flood of thy bliss O death.

From me to thee glad serenades,
Dances for thee I propose saluting thee, adornments and feastings for thee,
And the sights of the open landscape and the high-spread sky are fitting,
And life and the fields, and the huge and thoughtful night.

The night in silence under many a star,
The ocean shore and the husky whispering wave whose voice I know,
And the soul turning to thee O vast and well-veil'd death,
And the body gratefully nestling close to thee.

Over the tree-tops I float thee a song,
Over the rising and sinking waves, over the myriad fields and the prairies wide,
Over the dense-pack'd cities all and the teeming wharves and ways,
I float this carol with joy, with joy to thee O death.

15

To the tally of my soul,
Loud and strong kept up the gray-brown bird,
With pure deliberate notes spreading filling the night.

Loud in the pines and cedars dim,
Clear in the freshness moist and the swamp-perfume,
And I with my comrades there in the night.

While my sight that was bound in my eyes unclosed,
As to long panoramas of visions.

And I saw askant the armies,
I saw as in noiseless dreams hundreds of battle-flags,
Borne through the smoke of the battles and pierc'd with missiles I saw them,
And carried hither and yon through the smoke, and torn and bloody,
And at last but a few shreds left on the staffs, (and all in silence,)
And the staffs all splinter'd and broken.

I saw battle-corpses, myriads of them,
And the white skeletons of young men, I saw them,
I saw the debris and debris of all the slain soldiers of the war,
But I saw they were not as was thought,
They themselves were fully at rest, they suffer'd not,
The living remain'd and suffer'd, the mother suffer'd,
And the wife and the child and the musing comrade suffer'd,
And the armies that remain'd suffer'd.

16

Passing the visions, passing the night,
Passing, unloosing the hold of my comrades' hands,
Passing the song of the hermit bird and the tallying song of my soul,
Victorious song, death's outlet song, yet varying ever-altering song,
As low and wailing, yet clear the notes, rising and falling, flooding the night,
Sadly sinking and fainting, as warning and warning, and yet again bursting with joy,
Covering the earth and filling the spread of the heaven,
As that powerful psalm in the night I heard from recesses,
Passing, I leave thee lilac with heart-shaped leaves,
I leave thee there in the door-yard, blooming, returning with spring.

I cease from my song for thee,
From my gaze on thee in the west, fronting the west, communing with thee,
O comrade lustrous with silver face in the night.

Yet each to keep and all, retrievements out of the night,
The song, the wondrous chant of the gray-brown bird,
And the tallying chant, the echo arous'd in my soul,
With the lustrous and drooping star with the countenance
full of woe,
With the holders holding my hand nearing the call of the
bird,
Comrades mine and I in the midst, and their memory ever
to keep, for the dead I loved so well,
For the sweetest, wisest soul of all my days and lands—and
this for his dear sake,
Lilac and star and bird twined with the chant of my soul,
There in the fragrant pines and the cedars dusk and dim.

O Captain! My Captain!

O CAPTAIN! my Captain! our fearful trip is done,
The ship has weather'd every rack, the prize we sought is won,
The port is near, the bells I hear, the people all exulting,
While follow eyes the steady keel, the vessel grim and daring;
But O heart! heart! heart!
O the bleeding drops of red,
Where on the deck my Captain lies,
Fallen cold and dead.

O Captain! my Captain! rise up and hear the bells;
Rise up—for you the flag is flung—for you the bugle trills,
For you bouquets and ribbon'd wreaths—for you the shores
a-crowding,
For you they call, the swaying mass, their eager faces turning;
Here Captain! dear father!
This arm beneath your head!
It is some dream that on the deck,
You've fallen cold and dead.

My Captain does not answer, his lips are pale and still,
My father does not feel my arm, he has no pulse nor will,
The ship is anchor'd safe and sound, its voyage closed and done,
From fearful trip the victor ship comes in with object won;

Exult O shores, and ring O bells!
But I with mournful tread,
Walk the deck my Captain lies,
Fallen cold and dead.

Hush'd Be the Camps To-day

(*May 4, 1865.*)

HUSH'D be the camps to-day,
And soldiers let us drape our war-worn weapons,
And each with musing soul retire to celebrate,
Our dear commander's death.

No more for him life's stormy conflicts,
Nor victory, nor defeat—no more time's dark events,
Charging like ceaseless clouds across the sky.

But sing poet in our name,
Sing of the love we bore him—because you, dweller in
camps, know it truly.

As they invault the coffin there,
Sing—as they close the doors of earth upon him—one
verse,
For the heavy hearts of soldiers.

This Dust Was Once the Man

THIS dust was once the man,
Gentle, plain, just and resolute, under whose cautious hand,
Against the foulest crime in history known in any land or age,
Was saved the Union of these States.

BY BLUE ONTARIO'S SHORE

1

BY blue Ontario's shore,
As I mused of these warlike days and of peace return'd, and
the dead that return no more,

A Phantom gigantic superb, with stern visage accosted me,
Chant me the poem, it said, *that comes from the soul of America, chant me the carol of victory,*
And strike up the marches of Libertad, marches more powerful yet,
And sing me before you go the song of the throes of Democracy.

(Democracy, the destin'd conqueror, yet treacherous lip-smiles everywhere,
And death and infidelity at every step.)

2

A Nation announcing itself,
I myself make the only growth by which I can be appreciated,
I reject none, accept all, then reproduce all in my own forms.

A breed whose proof is in time and deeds,
What we are we are, nativity is answer enough to objections,
We wield ourselves as a weapon is wielded,
We are powerful and tremendous in ourselves,
We are executive in ourselves, we are sufficient in the variety of ourselves,
We are the most beautiful to ourselves and in ourselves,
We stand self-pois'd in the middle, branching thence over the world,
From Missouri, Nebraska, or Kansas, laughing attacks to scorn.

Nothing is sinful to us outside of ourselves,
Whatever appears, whatever does not appear, we are beautiful or sinful in ourselves only.

(O Mother—O Sisters dear!
If we are lost, no victor else has destroy'd us,
It is by ourselves we go down to eternal night.)

3

Have you thought there could be but a single supreme?
There can be any number of supremes—one does not countervail another any more than one eyesight countervails another, or one life countervails another.

All is eligible to all,
All is for individuals, all is for you,
No condition is prohibited, not God's or any.

All comes by the body, only health puts you rapport with
the universe.

Produce great Persons, the rest follows.

4

Piety and conformity to them that like,
Peace, obesity, allegiance, to them that like,
I am he who tauntingly compels men, women, nations,
Crying, Leap from your seats and contend for your lives!

I am he who walks the States with a barb'd tongue,
questioning every one I meet,
Who are you that wanted only to be told what you knew
before?
Who are you that wanted only a book to join you in your
nonsense?

(With pangs and cries as thine own O bearer of many children,
These clamors wild to a race of pride I give.)

O lands, would you be freer than all that has ever been
before?
If you would be freer than all that has been before, come
listen to me.

Fear grace, elegance, civilization, delicatesse,
Fear the mellow sweet, the sucking of honey-juice,
Beware the advancing mortal ripening of Nature,
Beware what precedes the decay of the ruggedness of states
and men.

5

Ages, precedents, have long been accumulating undirected
materials,
America brings builders, and brings its own styles.

The immortal poets of Asia and Europe have done their
work and pass'd to other spheres,
A work remains, the work of surpassing all they have done.

America, curious toward foreign characters, stands by its
own at all hazards,
Stands removed, spacious, composite, sound, initiates the
true use of precedents,
Does not repel them or the past or what they have
produced under their forms,
Takes the lesson with calmness, perceives the corpse slowly
borne from the house,
Perceives that it waits a little while in the door, that it was
fittest for its days,
That its life has descended to the stalwart and well-shaped
heir who approaches,
And that he shall be fittest for his days.

Any period one nation must lead,
One land must be the promise and reliance of the future.

These States are the amplest poem,
Here is not merely a nation but a teeming Nation of nations,
Here the doings of men correspond with the broadcast
doings of the day and night,
Here is what moves in magnificent masses careless of
particulars,
Here are the roughs, beards, friendliness, combativeness, the
soul loves,
Here the flowing trains, here the crowds, equality, diversity,
the soul loves.

6

Land of lands and bards to corroborate!
Of them standing among them, one lifts to the light a west-
bred face,
To him the hereditary countenance bequeath'd both
mother's and father's,
His first parts substances, earth, water, animals, trees,
Built of the common stock, having room for far and near,

Used to dispense with other lands, incarnating this land,
Attracting it body and soul to himself, hanging on its neck
with incomparable love,
Plunging his seminal muscle into its merits and demerits,
Making its cities, beginnings, events, diversities, wars, vocal
in him,
Making its rivers, lakes, bays, embouchure in him,
Mississippi with yearly freshets and changing chutes,
Columbia, Niagara, Hudson, spending themselves
lovingly in him,
If the Atlantic coast stretch or the Pacific coast stretch, he
stretching with them North or South,
Spanning between them East and West, and touching
whatever is between them,
Growths growing from him to offset the growths of pine,
cedar, hemlock, live-oak, locust, chestnut, hickory,
cottonwood, orange, magnolia,
Tangles as tangled in him as any canebrake or swamp,
He likening sides and peaks of mountains, forests coated
with northern transparent ice,
Off him pasturage sweet and natural as savanna, upland, prairie,
Through him flights, whirls, screams, answering those of the
fish-hawk, mocking-bird, night-heron, and eagle,
His spirit surrounding his country's spirit, unclosed to good
and evil,
Surrounding the essences of real things, old times and
present times,
Surrounding just found shores, islands, tribes of red
aborigines,
Weather-beaten vessels, landings, settlements, embryo
stature and muscle,
The haughty defiance of the Year One, war, peace, the
formation of the Constitution,
The separate States, the simple elastic scheme, the immigrants,
The Union always swarming with blatherers and always sure
and impregnable,
The unsurvey'd interior, log-houses, clearings, wild animals,
hunters, trappers,
Surrounding the multiform agriculture, mines, temperature,
the gestation of new States,

Congress convening every Twelfth-month, the members
duly coming up from the uttermost parts,
Surrounding the noble character of mechanics and farmers,
especially the young men,
Responding their manners, speech, dress, friendships, the
gait they have of persons who never knew how it felt to
stand in the presence of superiors,
The freshness and candor of their physiognomy, the
copiousness and decision of their phrenology,
The picturesque looseness of their carriage, their fierceness
when wrong'd,
The fluency of their speech, their delight in music, their
curiosity, good temper and open-handedness, the whole
composite make,
The prevailing ardor and enterprise, the large amativeness,
The perfect equality of the female with the male, the fluid
movement of the population,
The superior marine, free commerce, fisheries, whaling,
gold-digging,
Wharf-hemm'd cities, railroad and steamboat lines
intersecting all points,
Factories, mercantile life, labor-saving machinery, the
Northeast, Northwest, Southwest,
Manhattan firemen, the Yankee swap, southern plantation life,
Slavery—the murderous, treacherous conspiracy to raise it
upon the ruins of all the rest,
On and on to the grapple with it—Assassin! then your life
or ours be the stake, and respite no more.

7

(Lo, high toward heaven, this day,
Libertad, from the conqueress' field return'd,
I mark the new aureola around your head,
No more of soft astral, but dazzling and fierce,
With war's flames and the lambent lightnings playing,
And your port immovable where you stand,
With still the inextinguishable glance and the clinch'd and
lifted fist,
And your foot on the neck of the menacing one, the
scorner utterly crush'd beneath you,

The menacing arrogant one that strode and advanced with his senseless scorn, bearing the murderous knife,
The wide-swelling one, the braggart that would yesterday do so much,
To-day a carrion dead and damn'd, the despised of all the earth,
An offal rank, to the dunghill maggots spurn'd.)

8

Others take finish, but the Republic is ever constructive and ever keeps vista,
Others adorn the past, but you O days of the present, I adorn you,
O days of the future I believe in you—I isolate myself for your sake,
O America because you build for mankind I build for you,
O well-beloved stone-cutters, I lead them who plan with decision and science,
Lead the present with friendly hand toward the future.

(Bravas to all impulses sending sane children to the next age!
But damn that which spends itself with no thought of the stain, pains, dismay, feebleness, it is bequeathing.)

9

I listened to the Phantom by Ontario's shore,
I heard the voice arising demanding bards,
By them all native and grand, by them alone can these States be fused into the compact organism of a Nation.

To hold men together by paper and seal or by compulsion is no account,
That only holds men together which aggregates all in a living principle, as the hold of the limbs of the body or the fibres of plants.

Of all races and eras these States with veins full of poetical stuff most need poets, and are to have the greatest, and use them the greatest,
Their Presidents shall not be their common referee so much as their poets shall.

(Soul of love and tongue of fire!
Eye to pierce the deepest deeps and sweep the world!
Ah Mother, prolific and full in all besides, yet how long
barren, barren?)

10

Of these States the poet is the equable man,
Not in him but off from him things are grotesque,
eccentric, fail of their full returns,
Nothing out of its place is good, nothing in its place is bad,
He bestows on every object or quality its fit proportion,
neither more nor less,
He is the arbiter of the diverse, he is the key,
He is the equalizer of his age and land,
He supplies what wants supplying, he checks what wants
checking,
In peace out of him speaks the spirit of peace, large, rich,
thrifty, building populous towns, encouraging
agriculture, arts, commerce, lighting the study of man,
the soul, health, immortality, government,
In war he is the best backer of the war, he fetches artillery
as good as the engineer's, he can make every word he
speaks draw blood,
The years straying toward infidelity he withholds by his
steady faith,
He is no arguer, he is judgment, (Nature accepts him
absolutely,)
He judges not as the judge judges but as the sun falling
round a helpless thing,
As he sees the farthest he has the most faith,
His thoughts are the hymns of the praise of things,
In the dispute on God and eternity he is silent,
He sees eternity less like a play with a prologue and
denouement,
He sees eternity in men and women, he does not see men
and women as dreams or dots.

For the great Idea, the idea of perfect and free individuals,
For that, the bard walks in advance, leader of leaders,

The attitude of him cheers up slaves and horrifies foreign
despots.

Without extinction is Liberty, without retrograde is
Equality,
They live in the feelings of young men and the best women,
(Not for nothing have the indomitable heads of the earth
been always ready to fall for Liberty.)

11

For the great Idea,
That, O my brethren, that is the mission of poets.

Songs of stern defiance ever ready,
Songs of the rapid arming and the march,
The flag of peace quick-folded, and instead the flag we know,
Warlike flag of the great Idea.

(Angry cloth I saw there leaping!
I stand again in leaden rain your flapping folds saluting,
I sing you over all, flying beckoning through the fight—O
the hard-contested fight!
The cannons ope their rosy-flashing muzzles—the hurtled
balls scream,
The battle-front forms amid the smoke—the volleys pour
incessant from the line,
Hark, the ringing word *Charge!*—now the tussle and the
furious maddening yells,
Now the corpses tumble curl'd upon the ground,
Cold, cold in death, for precious life of you,
Angry cloth I saw there leaping.)

12

Are you he who would assume a place to teach or be a poet
here in the States?
The place is august, the terms obdurate.

Who would assume to teach here may well prepare himself
body and mind,

He may well survey, ponder, arm, fortify, harden, make lithe himself,
He shall surely be question'd beforehand by me with many and stern questions.

Who are you indeed who would talk or sing to America?
Have you studied out the land, its idioms and men?
Have you learn'd the physiology, phrenology, politics, geography, pride, freedom, friendship of the land? its substratums and objects?
Have you consider'd the organic compact of the first day of the first year of Independence, sign'd by the Commissioners, ratified by the States, and read by Washington at the head of the army?
Have you possess'd yourself of the Federal Constitution?
Do you see who have left all feudal processes and poems behind them, and assumed the poems and processes of Democracy?
Are you faithful to things? do you teach what the land and sea, the bodies of men, womanhood, amativeness, heroic angers, teach?
Have you sped through fleeting customs, popularities?
Can you hold your hand against all seductions, follies, whirls, fierce contentions? are you very strong? are you really of the whole People?
Are you not of some coterie? some school or mere religion?
Are you done with reviews and criticisms of life? animating now to life itself?
Have you vivified yourself from the maternity of these States?
Have you too the old ever-fresh forbearance and impartiality?
Do you hold the like love for those hardening to maturity? for the last-born? little and big? and for the errant?

What is this you bring my America?
Is it uniform with my country?
Is it not something that has been better told or done before?
Have you not imported this or the spirit of it in some ship?
Is it not a mere tale? a rhyme? a prettiness?—is the good old cause in it?

Has it not dangled long at the heels of the poets, politicians, literats, of enemies' lands?
Does it not assume that what is notoriously gone is still here?
Does it answer universal needs? will it improve manners?
Does it sound with trumpet-voice the proud victory of the Union in that secession war?
Can your performance face the open fields and the seaside?
Will it absorb into me as I absorb food, air, to appear again in my strength, gait, face?
Have real employments contributed to it? original makers, not mere amanuenses?
Does it meet modern discoveries, calibres, facts, face to face?
What does it mean to American persons, progresses, cities? Chicago, Kanada, Arkansas?
Does it see behind the apparent custodians the real custodians standing, menacing, silent, the mechanics, Manhattanese, Western men, Southerners, significant alike in their apathy, and in the promptness of their love?
Does it see what finally befalls, and has always finally befallen, each temporizer, patcher, outsider, partialist, alarmist, infidel, who has ever ask'd any thing of America?
What mocking and scornful negligence?
The track strew'd with the dust of skeletons,
By the roadside others disdainfully toss'd.

13

Rhymes and rhymers pass away, poems distill'd from poems pass away,
The swarms of reflectors and the polite pass, and leave ashes,
Admirers, importers, obedient persons, make but the soil of literature,
America justifies itself, give it time, no disguise can deceive it or conceal from it, it is impassive enough,
Only toward the likes of itself will it advance to meet them,
If its poets appear it will in due time advance to meet them, there is no fear of mistake,
(The proof of a poet shall be sternly deferr'd till his country absorbs him as affectionately as he has absorb'd it.)

He masters whose spirit masters, he tastes sweetest who
results sweetest in the long run,
The blood of the brawn beloved of time is unconstraint;
In the need of songs, philosophy, an appropriate native
grand-opera, shipcraft, any craft,
He or she is greatest who contributes the greatest original
practical example.

Already a nonchalant breed, silently emerging, appears on the
streets,
People's lips salute only doers, lovers, satisfiers, positive
knowers,
There will shortly be no more priests, I say their work is done,
Death is without emergencies here, but life is perpetual
emergencies here,
Are your body, days, manners, superb? after death you shall
be superb,
Justice, health, self-esteem, clear the way with irresistible
power;
How dare you place any thing before a man?

14

Fall behind me States!
A man before all—myself, typical, before all.

Give me the pay I have served for,
Give me to sing the songs of the great Idea, take all the rest,
I have loved the earth, sun, animals, I have despised riches,
I have given alms to every one that ask'd, stood up for the
stupid and crazy, devoted my income and labor to others,
Hated tyrants, argued not concerning God, had patience
and indulgence toward the people, taken off my hat to
nothing known or unknown,
Gone freely with powerful uneducated persons and with the
young, and with the mothers of families,
Read these leaves to myself in the open air, tried them by
trees, stars, rivers,
Dismiss'd whatever insulted my own soul or defiled my body,
Claim'd nothing to myself which I have not carefully claim'd
for others on the same terms,

Sped to the camps, and comrades found and accepted from every State,
(Upon this breast has many a dying soldier lean'd to breathe his last,
This arm, this hand, this voice, have nourish'd, rais'd, restored,
To life recalling many a prostrate form;)
I am willing to wait to be understood by the growth of the taste of myself,
Rejecting none, permitting all.

(Say O Mother, have I not to your thought been faithful?
Have I not through life kept you and yours before me?)

15

I swear I begin to see the meaning of these things,
It is not the earth, it is not America who is so great,
It is I who am great or to be great, it is You up there, or any one,
It is to walk rapidly through civilizations, governments, theories,
Through poems, pageants, shows, to form individuals.

Underneath all, individuals,
I swear nothing is good to me now that ignores individuals,
The American compact is altogether with individuals,
The only government is that which makes minute of individuals,
The whole theory of the universe is directed unerringly to one single individual—namely to You.

(Mother! with subtle sense severe, with the naked sword in your hand,
I saw you at last refuse to treat but directly with individuals.)

16

Underneath all, Nativity,
I swear I will stand by my own nativity, pious or impious so be it;

I swear I am charm'd with nothing except nativity,
Men, women, cities, nations, are only beautiful from nativity.

Underneath all is the Expression of love for men and women,
(I swear I have seen enough of mean and impotent modes
of expressing love for men and women,
After this day I take my own modes of expressing love for
men and women.)

I swear I will have each quality of my race in myself,
(Talk as you like, he only suits these States whose manners
favor the audacity and sublime turbulence of the States.)

Underneath the lessons of things, spirits, Nature,
governments, ownerships, I swear I perceive other lessons,
Underneath all to me is myself, to you yourself, (the same
monotonous old song.)

17

O I see flashing that this America is only you and me,
Its power, weapons, testimony, are you and me,
Its crimes, lies, thefts, defections, are you and me,
Its Congress is you and me, the officers, capitols, armies,
ships, are you and me,
Its endless gestations of new States are you and me,
The war, (that war so bloody and grim, the war I will
henceforth forget), was you and me,
Natural and artificial are you and me,
Freedom, language, poems, employments, are you and me,
Past, present, future, are you and me.

I dare not shirk any part of myself,
Not any part of America good or bad,
Not to build for that which builds for mankind,
Not to balance ranks, complexions, creeds, and the sexes,
Not to justify science nor the march of equality,
Nor to feed the arrogant blood of the brawn belov'd of time.

I am for those that have never been master'd,
For men and women whose tempers have never been master'd,

For those whom laws, theories, conventions, can never
master.

I am for those who walk abreast with the whole earth,
Who inaugurate one to inaugurate all.

I will not be outfaced by irrational things,
I will penetrate what it is in them that is sarcastic upon me,
I will make cities and civilizations defer to me,
This is what I have learnt from America—it is the amount,
and it I teach again.

(Democracy, while weapons were everywhere aim'd at your
breast,
I saw you serenely give birth to immortal children, saw in
dreams your dilating form,
Saw you with spreading mantle covering the world.)

18

I will confront these shows of the day and night,
I will know if I am to be less than they,
I will see if I am not as majestic as they,
I will see if I am not as subtle and real as they,
I will see if I am to be less generous than they,
I will see if I have no meaning, while the houses and ships
have meaning,
I will see if the fishes and birds are to be enough for
themselves, and I am not to be enough for myself.

I match my spirit against yours you orbs, growths,
mountains, brutes,
Copious as you are I absorb you all in myself, and become
the master myself,
America isolated yet embodying all, what is it finally except
myself?
These States, what are they except myself?

I know now why the earth is gross, tantalizing, wicked, it is
for my sake,
I take you specially to be mine, you terrible, rude forms.

(Mother, bend down, bend close to me your face,
I know not what these plots and wars and deferments are for,
I know not fruition's success, but I know that through war
and crime your work goes on, and must yet go on.)

19

Thus by blue Ontario's shore,
While the winds fann'd me and the waves came trooping
toward me,
I thrill'd with the power's pulsations, and the charm of my
theme was upon me,
Till the tissues that held me parted their ties upon me.

And I saw the free souls of poets,
The loftiest bards of past ages strode before me,
Strange large men, long unwaked, undisclosed, were
disclosed to me.

20

O my rapt verse, my call, mock me not!
Not for the bards of the past, not to invoke them have I
launch'd you forth,
Not to call even those lofty bards here by Ontario's shores,
Have I sung so capricious and loud my savage song.

Bards for my own land only I invoke,
(For the war the war is over, the field is clear'd,)
Till they strike up marches henceforth triumphant and
onward,
To cheer O Mother your boundless expectant soul.

Bards of the great Idea! bards of the peaceful inventions!
(for the war, the war is over!)
Yet bards of latent armies, a million soldiers waiting ever-
ready,
Bards with songs as from burning coals or the lightning's
fork'd stripes!
Ample Ohio's, Kanada's bards—bards of California! inland
bards—bards of the war!
You by my charm I invoke.

Reversals

Let that which stood in front go behind,
Let that which was behind advance to the front,
Let bigots, fools, unclean persons, offer new propositions,
Let the old propositions be postponed,
Let a man seek pleasure everywhere except in himself,
Let a woman seek happiness everywhere except in herself.

Autumn Rivulets

As Consequent, Etc.

As consequent from store of summer rains,
Or wayward rivulets in autumn flowing,
Or many a herb-lined brook's reticulations,
Or subterranean sea-rills making for the sea,
Songs of continued years I sing.

Life's ever-modern rapids first, (soon, soon to blend,
With the old streams of death.)

Some threading Ohio's farm-fields or the woods,
Some down Colorado's cañons from sources of perpetual snow,
Some half-hid in Oregon, or away southward in Texas,
Some in the north finding their way to Erie, Niagara, Ottawa,
Some to Atlantica's bays, and so to the great salt brine.

In you whoe'er you are my book perusing,
In I myself, in all the world, these currents flowing,
All, all toward the mystic ocean tending.

Currents for starting a continent new,
Overtures sent to the solid out of the liquid,
Fusion of ocean and land, tender and pensive waves,
(Not safe and peaceful only, waves rous'd and ominous too,
Out of the depths the storm's abysmic waves, who knows whence?
Raging over the vast, with many a broken spar and tatter'd sail.)

Or from the sea of Time, collecting vasting all, I bring,
A windrow-drift of weeds and shells.

O little shells, so curious-convolute, so limpid-cold and voiceless,

Will you not little shells to the tympans of temples held,
Murmurs and echoes still call up, eternity's music faint and far,
Wafted inland, sent from Atlantica's rim, strains for the soul
of the prairies,
Whisper'd reverberations, chords for the ear of the West
joyously sounding,
Your tidings old, yet ever new and untranslatable,
Infinitesimals out of my life, and many a life,
(For not my life and years alone I give—all, all I give,)
These waifs from the deep, cast high and dry,
Wash'd on America's shores?

The Return of the Heroes

1

For the lands and for these passionate days and for myself,
Now I awhile retire to thee O soil of autumn fields,
Reclining on thy breast, giving myself to thee,
Answering the pulses of thy sane and equable heart,
Tuning a verse for thee.

O earth that hast no voice, confide to me a voice,
O harvest of my lands—O boundless summer growths,
O lavish brown parturient earth—O infinite teeming womb,
A song to narrate thee.

2

Ever upon this stage,
Is acted God's calm annual drama,
Gorgeous processions, songs of birds,
Sunrise that fullest feeds and freshens most the soul,
The heaving sea, the waves upon the shore, the musical,
strong waves,
The woods, the stalwart trees, the slender, tapering trees,
The liliput countless armies of the grass,
The heat, the showers, the measureless pasturages,
The scenery of the snows, the winds' free orchestra,
The stretching light-hung roof of clouds, the clear cerulean
and the silvery fringes,

The high dilating stars, the placid beckoning stars,
The moving flocks and herds, the plains and emerald meadows,
The shows of all the varied lands and all the growths and
 products.

3

Fecund America—to-day,
Thou art all over set in births and joys!
Thou groan'st with riches, thy wealth clothes thee as a
 swathing-garment,
Thou laughest loud with ache of great possessions,
A myriad-twining life like interlacing vines binds all thy vast
 demesne,
As some huge ship freighted to water's edge thou ridest
 into port,
As rain falls from the heaven and vapors rise from earth, so
 have the precious values fallen upon thee and risen out
 of thee;
Thou envy of the globe! thou miracle!
Thou, bathed, choked, swimming in plenty,
Thou lucky Mistress of the tranquil barns,
Thou Prairie Dame that sittest in the middle and lookest
 out upon thy world, and lookest East and lookest West,
Dispensatress, that by a word givest a thousand miles, a
 million farms, and missest nothing,
Thou all-acceptress—thou hospitable, (thou only art
 hospitable as God is hospitable.)

4

When late I sang sad was my voice,
Sad were the shows around me with deafening noises of
 hatred and smoke of war;
In the midst of the conflict, the heroes, I stood,
Or pass'd with slow step through the wounded and dying.

But now I sing not war,
Nor the measur'd march of soldiers, nor the tents of camps,
Nor the regiments hastily coming up deploying in line of
 battle;
No more the sad, unnatural shows of war.

Ask'd room those flush'd immortal ranks, the first forth-
stepping armies?
Ask room alas the ghastly ranks, the armies dread that follow'd.

(Pass, pass, ye proud brigades, with your tramping sinewy legs,
With your shoulders young and strong, with your knapsacks
and your muskets;
How elate I stood and watch'd you, where starting off you
march'd.

Pass—then rattle drums again,
For an army heaves in sight, O another gathering army,
Swarming, trailing on the rear, O you dread accruing army,
O you regiments so piteous, with your mortal diarrhœa,
with your fever,
O my land's maim'd darlings, with the plenteous bloody
bandage and the crutch,
Lo, your pallid army follows.)

5

But on these days of brightness,
On the far-stretching beauteous landscape, the roads and
lanes, the high-piled farm-wagons, and the fruits and
barns,
Should the dead intrude?

Ah the dead to me mar not, they fit well in Nature,
They fit very well in the landscape under the trees and grass,
And along the edge of the sky in the horizon's far margin.

Nor do I forget you Departed,
Nor in winter or summer my lost ones,
But most in the open air as now when my soul is rapt and
at peace, like pleasing phantoms,
Your memories rising glide silently by me.

6

I saw the day the return of the heroes,
(Yet the heroes never surpass'd shall never return,
Them that day I saw not.)

I saw the interminable corps, I saw the processions of armies,
I saw them approaching, defiling by with divisions,
Streaming northward, their work done, camping awhile in
clusters of mighty camps.

No holiday soldiers—youthful, yet veterans,
Worn, swart, handsome, strong, of the stock of homestead
and workshop,
Harden'd of many a long campaign and sweaty march,
Inured on many a hard-fought bloody field.

A pause—the armies wait,
A million flush'd embattled conquerors wait,
The world too waits, then soft as breaking night and sure as
dawn,
They melt, they disappear.

Exult O lands! victorious lands!
Not there your victory on those red shuddering fields,
But here and hence your victory.

Melt, melt away ye armies—disperse ye blue-clad soldiers,
Resolve ye back again, give up for good your deadly arms,
Other the arms the fields henceforth for you, or South or
North,
With saner wars, sweet wars, life-giving wars.

7

Loud O my throat, and clear O soul!
The season of thanks and the voice of full-yielding,
The chant of joy and power for boundless fertility.

All till'd and untill'd fields expand before me,
I see the true arenas of my race, or first or last,
Man's innocent and strong arenas.

I see the heroes at other toils,
I see well-wielded in their hands the better weapons.

I see where the Mother of All,
With full-spanning eye gazes forth, dwells long,
And counts the varied gathering of the products.

Busy the far, the sunlit panorama,
Prairie, orchard, and yellow grain of the North,
Cotton and rice of the South and Louisianian cane,
Open unseeded fallows, rich fields of clover and timothy,
Kine and horses feeding, and droves of sheep and swine,
And many a stately river flowing and many a jocund brook,
And healthy uplands with herby-perfumed breezes,
And the good green grass, that delicate miracle the ever-
recurring grass.

8

Toil on heroes! harvest the products!
Not alone on those warlike fields the Mother of All,
With dilated form and lambent eyes watch'd you.

Toil on heroes! toil well! handle the weapons well!
The Mother of All, yet here as ever she watches you.

Well-pleased America thou beholdest,
Over the fields of the West those crawling monsters,
The human-divine inventions, the labor-saving implements;
Beholdest moving in every direction imbued as with life the
revolving hay-rakes,
The steam-power reaping-machines and the horse-power
machines,
The engines, thrashers of grain and cleaners of grain, well
separating the straw, the nimble work of the patent
pitchfork,
Beholdest the newer saw-mill, the southern cotton-gin, and
the rice-cleanser.

Beneath thy look O Maternal,
With these and else and with their own strong hands the
heroes harvest.

All gather and all harvest,
Yet but for thee O Powerful, not a scythe might swing as now in security,
Not a maize-stalk dangle as now its silken tassels in peace.

Under thee only they harvest, even but a wisp of hay under thy great face only,
Harvest the wheat of Ohio, Illinois, Wisconsin, every barbed spear under thee,
Harvest the maize of Missouri, Kentucky, Tennessee, each ear in its light-green sheath,
Gather the hay to its myriad mows in the odorous tranquil barns,
Oats to their bins, the white potato, the buckwheat of Michigan, to theirs;
Gather the cotton in Mississippi or Alabama, dig and hoard the golden the sweet potato of Georgia and the Carolinas,
Clip the wool of California or Pennsylvania,
Cut the flax in the Middle States, or hemp or tobacco in the Borders,
Pick the pea and the bean, or pull apples from the trees or bunches of grapes from the vines,
Or aught that ripens in all these States or North or South,
Under the beaming sun and under thee.

There Was a Child Went Forth

THERE was a child went forth every day,
And the first object he look'd upon, that object he became,
And that object became part of him for the day or a certain part of the day,
Or for many years or stretching cycles of years.

The early lilacs became part of this child,
And grass and white and red morning-glories, and white and red clover, and the song of the phœbe-bird,
And the Third-month lambs and the sow's pink-faint litter, and the mare's foal and the cow's calf,

And the noisy brood of the barnyard or by the mire of the pond-side,
And the fish suspending themselves so curiously below there, and the beautiful curious liquid,
And the water-plants with their graceful flat heads, all became part of him.

The field-sprouts of Fourth-month and Fifth-month became part of him,
Winter-grain sprouts and those of the light-yellow corn, and the esculent roots of the garden,
And the apple-trees cover'd with blossoms and the fruit afterward, and wood-berries, and the commonest weeds by the road,
And the old drunkard staggering home from the outhouse of the tavern whence he had lately risen,
And the schoolmistress that pass'd on her way to the school,
And the friendly boys that pass'd, and the quarrelsome boys,
And the tidy and fresh-cheek'd girls, and the barefoot negro boy and girl,
And all the changes of city and country wherever he went.

His own parents, he that had father'd him and she that had conceiv'd him in her womb and birth'd him,
They gave this child more of themselves than that,
They gave him afterward every day, they became part of him.

The mother at home quietly placing the dishes on the supper-table,
The mother with mild words, clean her cap and gown, a wholesome odor falling off her person and clothes as she walks by,
The father, strong, self-sufficient, manly, mean, anger'd, unjust,
The blow, the quick loud word, the tight bargain, the crafty lure,
The family usages, the language, the company, the furniture, the yearning and swelling heart,
Affection that will not be gainsay'd, the sense of what is real, the thought if after all it should prove unreal,

The doubts of day-time and the doubts of night-time, the
curious whether and how,
Whether that which appears so is so, or is it all flashes and
specks?
Men and women crowding fast in the streets, if they are not
flashes and specks what are they?
The streets themselves and the façades of houses, and goods
in the windows,
Vehicles, teams, the heavy-plank'd wharves, the huge
crossing at the ferries,
The village on the highland seen from afar at sunset, the
river between,
Shadows, aureola and mist, the light falling on roofs and
gables of white or brown two miles off,
The schooner near by sleepily dropping down the tide, the
little boat slack-tow'd astern,
The hurrying tumbling waves, quick-broken crests, slapping,
The strata of color'd clouds, the long bar of maroon-tint
away solitary by itself, the spread of purity it lies
motionless in,
The horizon's edge, the flying sea-crow, the fragrance of salt
marsh and shore mud,
These became part of that child who went forth every
day, and who now goes, and will always go forth
every day.

Old Ireland

FAR hence amid an isle of wondrous beauty,
Crouching over a grave an ancient sorrowful mother,
Once a queen, now lean and tatter'd seated on the ground,
Her old white hair drooping dishevel'd round her shoulders,
At her feet fallen an unused royal harp,
Long silent, she too long silent, mourning her shrouded
hope and heir,
Of all the earth her heart most full of sorrow because most
full of love.

Yet a word ancient mother,
You need crouch there no longer on the cold ground with
forehead between your knees,

O you need not sit there veil'd in your old white hair so dishevel'd,
For know you the one you mourn is not in that grave,
It was an illusion, the son you love was not really dead,
The Lord is not dead, he is risen again young and strong in another country,
Even while you wept there by your fallen harp by the grave,
What you wept for was translated, pass'd from the grave,
The winds favor'd and the sea sail'd it,
And now with rosy and new blood,
Moves to-day in a new country.

The City Dead-House

By the city dead-house by the gate,
As idly sauntering wending my way from the clangor,
I curious pause, for lo, an outcast form, a poor dead prostitute brought,
Her corpse they deposit unclaim'd, it lies on the damp brick pavement,
The divine woman, her body, I see the body, I look on it alone,
That house once full of passion and beauty, all else I notice not,
Nor stillness so cold, nor running water from faucet, nor odors morbific impress me,
But the house alone—that wondrous house—that delicate fair house—that ruin!
That immortal house more than all the rows of dwellings ever built!
Or white-domed capitol with majestic figure surmounted, or all the old high-spired cathedrals,
That little house alone more than them all—poor, desperate house!
Fair, fearful wreck—tenement of a soul—itself a soul,
Unclaim'd, avoided house—take one breath from my tremulous lips,
Take one tear dropt aside as I go for thought of you,
Dead house of love—house of madness and sin, crumbled, crush'd,

House of life, erewhile talking and laughing—but ah, poor
house, dead even then,
Months, years, an echoing, garnish'd house—but dead,
dead, dead.

This Compost

1

SOMETHING startles me where I thought I was safest,
I withdraw from the still woods I loved,
I will not go now on the pastures to walk,
I will not strip the clothes from my body to meet my lover
the sea,
I will not touch my flesh to the earth as to other flesh to
renew me.

O how can it be that the ground itself does not sicken?
How can you be alive you growths of spring?
How can you furnish health you blood of herbs, roots,
orchards, grain?
Are they not continually putting distemper'd corpses within
you?
Is not every continent work'd over and over with sour dead?

Where have you disposed of their carcasses?
Those drunkards and gluttons of so many generations?
Where have you drawn off all the foul liquid and meat?
I do not see any of it upon you to-day, or perhaps I am
deceiv'd,
I will run a furrow with my plough, I will press my spade
through the sod and turn it up underneath,
I am sure I shall expose some of the foul meat.

2

Behold this compost! behold it well!
Perhaps every mite has once form'd part of a sick person—
yet behold!
The grass of spring covers the prairies,
The bean bursts noiselessly through the mould in the garden,

The delicate spear of the onion pierces upward,
The apple-buds cluster together on the apple-branches,
The resurrection of the wheat appears with pale visage out
of its graves,
The tinge awakes over the willow-tree and the mulberry-tree,
The he-birds carol mornings and evenings while the she-
birds sit on their nests,
The young of poultry break through the hatch'd eggs,
The new-born of animals appear, the calf is dropt from the
cow, the colt from the mare,
Out of its little hill faithfully rise the potato's dark green leaves,
Out of its hill rises the yellow maize-stalk, the lilacs bloom
in the dooryards,
The summer growth is innocent and disdainful above all
those strata of sour dead.

What chemistry!
That the winds are really not infectious,
That this is no cheat, this transparent green-wash of the sea
which is so amorous after me,
That it is safe to allow it to lick my naked body all over
with its tongues,
That it will not endanger me with the fevers that have
deposited themselves in it,
That all is clean forever and forever,
That the cool drink from the well tastes so good,
That blackberries are so flavorous and juicy,
That the fruits of the apple-orchard and the orange-orchard,
that melons, grapes, peaches, plums, will none of them
poison me,
That when I recline on the grass I do not catch any disease,
Though probably every spear of grass rises out of what was
once a catching disease.

Now I am terrified at the Earth, it is that calm and patient,
It grows such sweet things out of such corruptions,
It turns harmless and stainless on its axis, with such endless
successions of diseas'd corpses,
It distills such exquisite winds out of such infused fetor,

It renews with such unwitting looks its prodigal, annual,
sumptuous crops,
It gives such divine materials to men, and accepts such
leavings from them at last.

To a Foil'd European Revolutionaire

COURAGE yet, my brother or my sister!
Keep on—Liberty is to be subserv'd whatever occurs;
That is nothing that is quell'd by one or two failures, or any
number of failures,
Or by the indifference or ingratitude of the people, or by
any unfaithfulness,
Or the show of the tushes of power, soldiers, cannon, penal
statutes.

What we believe in waits latent forever through all the
continents,
Invites no one, promises nothing, sits in calmness and light,
is positive and composed, knows no discouragement,
Waiting patiently, waiting its time.

(Not songs of loyalty alone are these,
But songs of insurrection also,
For I am the sworn poet of every dauntless rebel the world
over,
And he going with me leaves peace and routine behind him,
And stakes his life to be lost at any moment.)

The battle rages with many a loud alarm and frequent
advance and retreat,
The infidel triumphs, or supposes he triumphs,
The prison, scaffold, garroté, handcuffs, iron necklace and
lead-balls do their work,
The named and unnamed heroes pass to other spheres,
The great speakers and writers are exiled, they lie sick in
distant lands,
The cause is asleep, the strongest throats are choked with
their own blood,

The young men droop their eyelashes toward the ground
when they meet;
But for all this Liberty has not gone out of the place, nor
the infidel enter'd into full possession.

When liberty goes out of a place it is not the first to go, nor
the second or third to go,
It waits for all the rest to go, it is the last.

When there are no more memories of heroes and martyrs,
And when all life and all the souls of men and women are
discharged from any part of the earth,
Then only shall liberty or the idea of liberty be discharged
from that part of the earth,
And the infidel come into full possession.

Then courage European revolter, revoltress!
For till all ceases neither must you cease.

I do not know what you are for, (I do not know what I am
for myself, nor what any thing is for,)
But I will search carefully for it even in being foil'd,
In defeat, poverty, misconception, imprisonment—for they
too are great.

Did we think victory great?
So it is—but now it seems to me, when it cannot be help'd,
that defeat is great,
And that death and dismay are great.

Unnamed Lands

NATIONS ten thousand years before these States, and many
times ten thousand years before these States,
Garner'd clusters of ages that men and women like us grew
up and travel'd their course and pass'd on,
What vast-built cities, what orderly republics, what pastoral
tribes and nomads,
What histories, rulers, heroes, perhaps transcending all others,
What laws, customs, wealth, arts, traditions,

What sort of marriage, what costumes, what physiology and
phrenology,
What of liberty and slavery among them, what they thought
of death and the soul,
Who were witty and wise, who beautiful and poetic, who
brutish and undevelop'd,
Not a mark, not a record remains—and yet all remains.

O I know that those men and women were not for nothing,
any more than we are for nothing,
I know that they belong to the scheme of the world every
bit as much as we now belong to it.

Afar they stand, yet near to me they stand,
Some with oval countenances learn'd and calm,
Some naked and savage, some like huge collections of insects,
Some in tents, herdsmen, patriarchs, tribes, horsemen,
Some prowling through woods, some living peaceably on
farms, laboring, reaping, filling barns,
Some traversing paved avenues, amid temples, palaces,
factories, libraries, shows, courts, theatres, wonderful
monuments.

Are those billions of men really gone?
Are those women of the old experience of the earth gone?
Do their lives, cities, arts, rest only with us?
Did they achieve nothing for good for themselves?

I believe of all those men and women that fill'd the
unnamed lands, every one exists this hour here or
elsewhere, invisible to us,
In exact proportion to what he or she grew from in life, and
out of what he or she did, felt, became, loved, sinn'd,
in life.

I believe that was not the end of those nations or any
person of them, any more than this shall be the end of
my nation, or of me;

Of their languages, governments, marriage, literature,
products, games, wars, manners, crimes, prisons, slaves,
heroes, poets,
I suspect their results curiously await in the yet unseen
world, counterparts of what accrued to them in the
seen world,
I suspect I shall meet them there,
I suspect I shall there find each old particular of those
unnamed lands.

Song of Prudence

MANHATTAN'S streets I saunter'd pondering,
On Time, Space, Reality—on such as these, and abreast with
them Prudence.

The last explanation always remains to be made about
prudence,
Little and large alike drop quietly aside from the prudence
that suits immortality.

The soul is of itself,
All verges to it, all has reference to what ensues,
All that a person does, says, thinks, is of consequence,
Not a move can a man or woman make, that affects him or
her in a day, month, any part of the direct lifetime, or
the hour of death,
But the same affects him or her onward afterward through
the indirect lifetime.

The indirect is just as much as the direct,
The spirit receives from the body just as much as it gives to
the body, if not more.

Not one word or deed, not venereal sore, discoloration,
privacy of the onanist,
Putridity of gluttons or rum-drinkers, peculation, cunning,
betrayal, murder, seduction, prostitution,
But has results beyond death as really as before death.

Charity and personal force are the only investments worth
any thing.

No specification is necessary, all that a male or female does,
that is vigorous, benevolent, clean, is so much profit to
him or her,
In the unshakable order of the universe and through the
whole scope of it forever.

Who has been wise receives interest,
Savage, felon, President, judge, farmer, sailor, mechanic,
literat, young, old, it is the same,
The interest will come round—all will come round.

Singly, wholly, to affect now, affected their time, will forever
affect, all of the past and all of the present and all of
the future,
All the brave actions of war and peace,
All help given to relatives, strangers, the poor, old,
sorrowful, young children, widows, the sick, and to
shunn'd persons,
All self-denial that stood steady and aloof on wrecks, and
saw others fill the seats of the boats,
All offering of substance or life for the good old cause, or
for a friend's sake, or opinion's sake,
All pains of enthusiasts scoff"d at by their neighbors,
All the limitless sweet love and precious suffering of
mothers,
All honest men baffled in strifes recorded or unrecorded,
All the grandeur and good of ancient nations whose
fragments we inherit,
All the good of the dozens of ancient nations unknown to
us by name, date, location,
All that was ever manfully begun, whether it succeeded or no,
All suggestions of the divine mind of man or the divinity of
his mouth, or the shaping of his great hands,
All that is well thought or said this day on any part of the
globe, or on any of the wandering stars, or on any of
the fix'd stars, by those there as we are here,

All that is henceforth to be thought or done by you
whoever you are, or by any one,
These inure, have inured, shall inure, to the identities from
which they sprang, or shall spring.

Did you guess any thing lived only its moment?
The world does not so exist, no parts palpable or impalpable
so exist,
No consummation exists without being from some long
previous consummation, and that from some other,
Without the farthest conceivable one coming a bit nearer
the beginning than any.

Whatever satisfies souls is true;
Prudence entirely satisfies the craving and glut of souls,
Itself only finally satisfies the soul,
The soul has that measureless pride which revolts from every
lesson but its own.

Now I breathe the word of the prudence that walks abreast
with time, space, reality,
That answers the pride which refuses every lesson but its own.

What is prudence is indivisible,
Declines to separate one part of life from every part,
Divides not the righteous from the unrighteous or the living
from the dead,
Matches every thought or act by its correlative,
Knows no possible forgiveness or deputed atonement,
Knows that the young man who composedly peril'd his life
and lost it has done exceedingly well for himself
without doubt,
That he who never peril'd his life, but retains it to old age
in riches and ease, has probably achiev'd nothing for
himself worth mentioning,
Knows that only that person has really learn'd who has
learn'd to prefer results,
Who favors body and soul the same,
Who perceives the indirect assuredly following the direct,
Who in his spirit in any emergency whatever neither hurries
nor avoids death.

The Singer in the Prison

1

O sight of pity, shame and dole!
O fearful thought—a convict soul.

RANG the refrain along the hall, the prison,
Rose to the roof, the vaults of heaven above,
Pouring in floods of melody in tones so pensive sweet and
strong the like whereof was never heard,
Reaching the far-off sentry and the armed guards, who
ceas'd their pacing,
Making the hearer's pulses stop for ecstasy and awe.

2

The sun was low in the west one winter day,
When down a narrow aisle amid the thieves and outlaws of
the land,
(There by the hundreds seated, sear-faced murderers, wily
counterfeiters,
Gather'd to Sunday church in prison walls, the keepers round,
Plenteous, well-armed, watching with vigilant eyes,)
Calmly a lady walk'd holding a little innocent child by either
hand,
Whom seating on their stools beside her on the platform,
She, first preluding with the instrument a low and musical
prelude,
In voice surpassing all, sang forth a quaint old hymn.

A soul confined by bars and bands,
Cries, help! O help! and wrings her hands,
Blinded her eyes, bleeding her breast,
Nor pardon finds, nor balm of rest.

Ceaseless she paces to and fro,
O heart-sick days! O nights of woe!
Nor hand of friend, nor loving face,
Nor favor comes, nor word of grace.

It was not I that sinn'd the sin,
The ruthless body dragg'd me in;
Though long I strove courageously,
The body was too much for me.

Dear prison'd soul bear up a space,
For soon or late the certain grace;
To set thee free and bear thee home,
The heavenly pardoner death shall come.

Convict no more, nor shame, nor dole!
Depart—a God-enfranchis'd soul!

3

The singer ceas'd,
One glance swept from her clear calm eyes o'er all those
upturn'd faces,
Strange sea of prison faces, a thousand varied, crafty, brutal,
seam'd and beauteous faces,
Then rising, passing back along the narrow aisle between them,
While her gown touch'd them rustling in the silence,
She vanish'd with her children in the dusk.

While upon all, convicts and armed keepers ere they stirr'd,
(Convict forgetting prison, keeper his loaded pistol,)
A hush and pause fell down a wondrous minute,
With deep half-stifled sobs and sound of bad men bow'd
and moved to weeping,
And youth's convulsive breathings, memories of home,
The mother's voice in lullaby, the sister's care, the happy
childhood,
The long-pent spirit rous'd to reminiscence;
A wondrous minute then—but after in the solitary night, to
many, many there,
Years after, even in the hour of death, the sad refrain, the
tune, the voice, the words,
Resumed, the large calm lady walks the narrow aisle,
The wailing melody again, the singer in the prison sings,

O sight of pity, shame and dole!
O fearful thought—a convict soul.

Warble for Lilac-Time

WARBLE me now for joy of lilac-time, (returning in reminiscence,)
Sort me O tongue and lips for Nature's sake, souvenirs of earliest summer,
Gather the welcome signs, (as children with pebbles or stringing shells,)
Put in April and May, the hylas croaking in the ponds, the elastic air,
Bees, butterflies, the sparrow with its simple notes,
Blue-bird and darting swallow, nor forget the high-hole flashing his golden wings,
The tranquil sunny haze, the clinging smoke, the vapor,
Shimmer of waters with fish in them, the cerulean above,
All that is jocund and sparkling, the brooks running,
The maple woods, the crisp February days and the sugar-making,
The robin where he hops, bright-eyed, brown-breasted,
With musical clear call at sunrise, and again at sunset,
Or flitting among the trees of the apple-orchard, building the nest of his mate,
The melted snow of March, the willow sending forth its yellow-green sprouts,
For spring-time is here! the summer is here! and what is this in it and from it?
Thou, soul, unloosen'd—the restlessness after I know not what;
Come, let us lag here no longer, let us be up and away!
O if one could but fly like a bird!
O to escape, to sail forth as in a ship!
To glide with thee O soul, o'er all, in all, as a ship o'er the waters;
Gathering these hints, the preludes, the blue sky, the grass, the morning drops of dew,
The lilac-scent, the bushes with dark green heart-shaped leaves,
Wood-violets, the little delicate pale blossoms called innocence,

Samples and sorts not for themselves alone, but for their atmosphere,
To grace the bush I love—to sing with the birds,
A warble for joy of lilac-time, returning in reminiscence.

Outlines for a Tomb

(*G. P., Buried 1870.*)

1

WHAT may we chant, O thou within this tomb?
What tablets, outlines, hang for thee, O millionnaire?
The life thou lived'st we know not,
But that thou walk'dst thy years in barter, 'mid the haunts of brokers,
Nor heroism thine, nor war, nor glory.

2

Silent, my soul,
With drooping lids, as waiting, ponder'd,
Turning from all the samples, monuments of heroes.

While through the interior vistas,
Noiseless uprose, phantasmic, (as by night Auroras of the north,)
Lambent tableaus, prophetic, bodiless scenes,
Spiritual projections.

In one, among the city streets a laborer's home appear'd,
After his day's work done, cleanly, sweet-air'd, the gaslight burning,
The carpet swept and a fire in the cheerful stove.

In one, the sacred parturition scene,
A happy painless mother birth'd a perfect child.

In one, at a bounteous morning meal,
Sat peaceful parents with contented sons.

In one, by twos and threes, young people,
Hundreds concentring, walk'd the paths and streets and roads,
Toward a tall-domed school.

In one a trio beautiful,
Grandmother, loving daughter, loving daughter's daughter,
    sat,
Chatting and sewing.

In one, along a suite of noble rooms,
'Mid plenteous books and journals, paintings on the walls,
    fine statuettes,
Were groups of friendly journeymen, mechanics young and
    old,
Reading, conversing.

All, all the shows of laboring life,
City and country, women's, men's and children's,
Their wants provided for, hued in the sun and tinged for
    once with joy,
Marriage, the street, the factory, farm, the house-room,
    lodging-room,
Labor and toil, the bath, gymnasium, playground, library,
    college,
The student, boy or girl, led forward to be taught,
The sick cared for, the shoeless shod, the orphan father'd
    and mother'd,
The hungry fed, the houseless housed;
(The intentions perfect and divine,
The workings, details, haply human.)

3

O thou within this tomb,
From thee such scenes, thou stintless, lavish giver,
Tallying the gifts of earth, large as the earth,
Thy name an earth, with mountains, fields and tides.

Nor by your streams alone, you rivers,
By you, your banks Connecticut,
By you and all your teeming life old Thames,

By you Potomac laving the ground Washington trod, by
you Patapsco,
You Hudson, you endless Mississippi—nor you alone,
But to the high seas launch, my thought, his memory.

Out from Behind This Mask

(*To Confront a Portrait.*)

1

Out from behind this bending rough-cut mask,
These lights and shades, this drama of the whole,
This common curtain of the face contain'd in me for me, in
you for you, in each for each,
(Tragedies, sorrows, laughter, tears—O heaven!
The passionate teeming plays this curtain hid!)
This glaze of God's serenest purest sky,
This film of Satan's seething pit,
This heart's geography's map, this limitless small continent,
this soundless sea;
Out from the convolutions of this globe,
This subtler astronomic orb than sun or moon, than Jupiter,
Venus, Mars,
This condensation of the universe, (nay here the only
universe,
Here the idea, all in this mystic handful wrapt;)
These burin'd eyes, flashing to you to pass to future time,
To launch and spin through space revolving sideling, from
these to emanate,
To you whoe'er you are—a look.

2

A traveler of thoughts and years, of peace and war,
Of youth long sped and middle age declining,
(As the first volume of a tale perused and laid away, and this
the second,
Songs, ventures, speculations, presently to close,)
Lingering a moment here and now, to you I opposite turn,
As on the road or at some crevice door by chance, or
open'd window,

Pausing, inclining, baring my head, you specially I greet,
To draw and clinch your soul for once inseparably with mine,
Then travel travel on.

Vocalism

1

VOCALISM, measure, concentration, determination, and the divine power to speak words;
Are you full-lung'd and limber-lipp'd from long trial? from vigorous practice? from physique?
Do you move in these broad lands as broad as they?
Come duly to the divine power to speak words?
For only at last after many years, after chastity, friendship, procreation, prudence, and nakedness,
After treading ground and breasting river and lake,
After a loosen'd throat, after absorbing eras, temperaments, races, after knowledge, freedom, crimes,
After complete faith, after clarifyings, elevations, and removing obstructions,
After these and more, it is just possible there comes to a man, a woman, the divine power to speak words;
Then toward that man or that woman swiftly hasten all—none refuse, all attend,
Armies, ships, antiquities, libraries, paintings, machines, cities, hate, despair, amity, pain, theft, murder, aspiration, form in close ranks,
They debouch as they are wanted to march obediently through the mouth of that man or that woman.

2

O what is it in me that makes me tremble so at voices?
Surely whoever speaks to me in the right voice, him or her I shall follow,
As the water follows the moon, silently, with fluid steps, anywhere around the globe.

All waits for the right voices;
Where is the practis'd and perfect organ? where is the develop' d soul?
For I see every word utter'd thence has deeper, sweeter, new sounds, impossible on less terms.

I see brains and lips closed, tympans and temples unstruck,
Until that comes which has the quality to strike and to unclose,
Until that comes which has the quality to bring forth what lies slumbering forever ready in all words.

To Him That Was Crucified

My spirit to yours dear brother,
Do not mind because many sounding your name do not understand you,
I do not sound your name, but I understand you,
I specify you with joy O my comrade to salute you, and to salute those who are with you, before and since, and those to come also,
That we all labor together transmitting the same charge and succession,
We few equals indifferent of lands, indifferent of times,
We, enclosers of all continents, all castes, allowers of all theologies,
Compassionaters, perceivers, rapport of men,
We walk silent among disputes and assertions, but reject not the disputers nor any thing that is asserted,
We hear the bawling and din, we are reach'd at by divisions, jealousies, recriminations on every side,
They close peremptorily upon us to surround us, my comrade,
Yet we walk unheld, free, the whole earth over, journeying up and down till we make our ineffaceable mark upon time and the diverse eras,
Till we saturate time and eras, that the men and women of races, ages to come, may prove brethren and lovers as we are.

You Felons on Trial in Courts

You felons on trial in courts,
You convicts in prison-cells, you sentenced assassins chain'd
    and handcuff'd with iron,
Who am I too that I am not on trial or in prison?
Me ruthless and devilish as any, that my wrists are not
    chain'd with iron, or my ankles with iron?

You prostitutes flaunting over the trottoirs or obscene in
    your rooms,
Who am I that I should call you more obscene than myself?

O culpable! I acknowledge—I exposé!
(O admirers, praise not me—compliment not me—you
    make me wince,
I see what you do not—I know what you do not.)

Inside these breast-bones I lie smutch'd and choked,
Beneath this face that appears so impassive hell's tides
    continually run,
Lusts and wickedness are acceptable to me,
I walk with delinquents with passionate love,
I feel I am of them—I belong to those convicts and
    prostitutes myself,
And henceforth I will not deny them—for how can I deny
    myself?

Laws for Creations

Laws for creations,
For strong artists and leaders, for fresh broods of teachers
    and perfect literats for America,
For noble savans and coming musicians.

All must have reference to the ensemble of the world, and
    the compact truth of the world,
There shall be no subject too pronounced—all works shall
    illustrate the divine law of indirections.

What do you suppose creation is?
What do you suppose will satisfy the soul, except to walk free and own no superior?
What do you suppose I would intimate to you in a hundred ways, but that man or woman is as good as God?
And that there is no God any more divine than Yourself?
And that that is what the oldest and newest myths finally mean?
And that you or any one must approach creations through such laws?

To a Common Prostitute

Be composed—be at ease with me—I am Walt Whitman, liberal and lusty as Nature,
Not till the sun excludes you do I exclude you,
Not till the waters refuse to glisten for you and the leaves to rustle for you, do my words refuse to glisten and rustle for you.

My girl I appoint with you an appointment, and I charge you that you make preparation to be worthy to meet me,
And I charge you that you be patient and perfect till I come.

Till then I salute you with a significant look that you do not forget me.

I Was Looking a Long While

I was looking a long while for Intentions,
For a clew to the history of the past for myself, and for these chants—and now I have found it,
It is not in those paged fables in the libraries, (them I neither accept nor reject,)
It is no more in the legends than in all else,
It is in the present—it is this earth to-day,
It is in Democracy—(the purport and aim of all the past,)
It is the life of one man or one woman to-day—the average man of to-day,
It is in languages, social customs, literatures, arts,

It is in the broad show of artificial things, ships, machinery,
politics, creeds, modern improvements, and the
interchange of nations,
All for the modern—all for the average man of to-day.

Thought

Of persons arrived at high positions, ceremonies, wealth,
scholarships, and the like;
(To me all that those persons have arrived at sinks away
from them, except as it results to their bodies and souls,
So that often to me they appear gaunt and naked,
And often to me each one mocks the others, and mocks
himself or herself,
And of each one the core of life, namely happiness, is full of
the rotten excrement of maggots,
And often to me those men and women pass unwittingly
the true realities of life, and go toward false realities,
And often to me they are alive after what custom has served
them, but nothing more,
And often to me they are sad, hasty, unwaked sonnambules
walking the dusk.)

Miracles

Why, who makes much of a miracle?
As to me I know of nothing else but miracles,
Whether I walk the streets of Manhattan,
Or dart my sight over the roofs of houses toward the sky,
Or wade with naked feet along the beach just in the edge of
the water,
Or stand under trees in the woods,
Or talk by day with any one I love, or sleep in the bed at
night with any one I love,
Or sit at table at dinner with the rest,
Or look at strangers opposite me riding in the car,
Or watch honey-bees busy around the hive of a summer
forenoon,
Or animals feeding in the fields,
Or birds, or the wonderfulness of insects in the air,

Or the wonderfulness of the sundown, or of stars shining so
quiet and bright,
Or the exquisite delicate thin curve of the new moon in
spring;
These with the rest, one and all, are to me miracles,
The whole referring, yet each distinct and in its place.

To me every hour of the light and dark is a miracle,
Every cubic inch of space is a miracle,
Every square yard of the surface of the earth is spread with
the same,
Every foot of the interior swarms with the same.

To me the sea is a continual miracle,
The fishes that swim—the rocks—the motion of the waves—
the ships with men in them,
What stranger miracles are there?

Sparkles from the Wheel

WHERE the city's ceaseless crowd moves on the livelong
day,
Withdrawn I join a group of children watching, I pause
aside with them.

By the curb toward the edge of the flagging,
A knife-grinder works at his wheel sharpening a great knife,
Bending over he carefully holds it to the stone, by foot and
knee,
With measur'd tread he turns rapidly, as he presses with
light but firm hand,
Forth issue then in copious golden jets,
Sparkles from the wheel.

The scene and all its belongings, how they seize and affect me,
The sad sharp-chinn'd old man with worn clothes and broad
shoulder-band of leather,
Myself effusing and fluid, a phantom curiously floating, now
here absorb'd and arrested,
The group, (an unminded point set in a vast surrounding,)

The attentive, quiet children, the loud, proud, restive base
of the streets,
The low hoarse purr of the whirling stone, the light-press'd
blade,
Diffusing, dropping, sideways-darting, in tiny showers of gold,
Sparkles from the wheel.

To a Pupil

Is reform needed? is it through you?
The greater the reform needed, the greater the Personality
you need to accomplish it.

You! do you not see how it would serve to have eyes,
blood, complexion, clean and sweet?
Do you not see how it would serve to have such a body and
soul that when you enter the crowd an atmosphere of
desire and command enters with you, and every one is
impress'd with your Personality?

O the magnet! the flesh over and over!
Go, dear friend, if need be give up all else, and commence
to-day to inure yourself to pluck, reality, self-esteem,
definiteness, elevatedness,
Rest not till you rivet and publish yourself of your own
Personality.

Unfolded Out of the Folds

UNFOLDED out of the folds of the woman man comes
unfolded, and is always to come unfolded,
Unfolded only out of the superbest woman of the earth is
to come the superbest man of the earth,
Unfolded out of the friendliest woman is to come the
friendliest man,
Unfolded only out of the perfect body of a woman can a
man be form'd of perfect body,
Unfolded only out of the inimitable poems of woman can
come the poems of man, (only thence have my poems
come;)

Unfolded out of the strong and arrogant woman I love, only
thence can appear the strong and arrogant man I love,
Unfolded by brawny embraces from the well-muscled
woman I love, only thence come the brawny embraces
of the man,
Unfolded out of the folds of the woman's brain come all
the folds of the man's brain, duly obedient,
Unfolded out of the justice of the woman all justice is
unfolded,
Unfolded out of the sympathy of the woman is all
sympathy;
A man is a great thing upon the earth and through eternity,
but every jot of the greatness of man is unfolded out of
woman;
First the man is shaped in the woman, he can then be
shaped in himself.

What Am I After All

WHAT am I after all but a child, pleas'd with the sound of
my own name? repeating it over and over;
I stand apart to hear—it never tires me.

To you your name also;
Did you think there was nothing but two or three
pronunciations in the sound of your name?

Kosmos

WHO includes diversity and is Nature,
Who is the amplitude of the earth, and the coarseness and
sexuality of the earth, and the great charity of the earth,
and the equilibrium also,
Who has not look'd forth from the windows the eyes for
nothing, or whose brain held audience with messengers
for nothing,
Who contains believers and disbelievers, who is the most
majestic lover,
Who holds duly his or her triune proportion of realism,
spiritualism, and of the æsthetic or intellectual,

Who having consider'd the body finds all its organs and
parts good,
Who, out of the theory of the earth and of his or her body
understands by subtle analogies all other theories,
The theory of a city, a poem, and of the large politics of
these States;
Who believes not only in our globe with its sun and moon,
but in other globes with their suns and moons,
Who, constructing the house of himself or herself, not for a
day but for all time, sees races, eras, dates, generations,
The past, the future, dwelling there, like space, inseparable
together.

Others May Praise What They Like

OTHERS may praise what they like;
But I, from the banks of the running Missouri, praise
nothing in art or aught else,
Till it has well inhaled the atmosphere of this river, also the
western prairie-scent,
And exudes it all again.

Who Learns My Lesson Complete?

WHO learns my lesson complete?
Boss, journeyman, apprentice, churchman and atheist,
The stupid and the wise thinker, parents and offspring,
merchant, clerk, porter and customer,
Editor, author, artist, and schoolboy—draw nigh and
commence;
It is no lesson—it lets down the bars to a good lesson,
And that to another, and every one to another still.

The great laws take and effuse without argument,
I am of the same style, for I am their friend,
I love them quits and quits, I do not halt and make salaams.

I lie abstracted and hear beautiful tales of things and the
reasons of things,
They are so beautiful I nudge myself to listen.

I cannot say to any person what I hear—I cannot say it to myself—it is very wonderful.

It is no small matter, this round and delicious globe moving so exactly in its orbit for ever and ever, without one jolt or the untruth of a single second,
I do not think it was made in six days, nor in ten thousand years, nor ten billions of years,
Nor plann'd and built one thing after another as an architect plans and builds a house.

I do not think seventy years is the time of a man or woman,
Nor that seventy millions of years is the time of a man or woman,
Nor that years will ever stop the existence of me, or any one else.

Is it wonderful that I should be immortal? as every one is immortal;
I know it is wonderful, but my eyesight is equally wonderful, and how I was conceived in my mother's womb is equally wonderful,
And pass'd from a babe in the creeping trance of a couple of summers and winters to articulate and walk—all this is equally wonderful.

And that my soul embraces you this hour, and we affect each other without ever seeing each other, and never perhaps to see each other, is every bit as wonderful.

And that I can think such thoughts as these is just as wonderful,
And that I can remind you, and you think them and know them to be true, is just as wonderful.

And that the moon spins round the earth and on with the earth, is equally wonderful,
And that they balance themselves with the sun and stars is equally wonderful.

Tests

All submit to them where they sit, inner, secure,
unapproachable to analysis in the soul,
Not traditions, not the outer authorities are the judges,
They are the judges of outer authorities and of all traditions,
They corroborate as they go only whatever corroborates
themselves, and touches themselves;
For all that, they have it forever in themselves to
corroborate far and near without one exception.

The Torch

On my Northwest coast in the midst of the night a
fishermen's group stands watching,
Out on the lake that expands before them, others are
spearing salmon,
The canoe, a dim shadowy thing, moves across the black
water,
Bearing a torch ablaze at the prow.

O Star of France

1870–71.

O star of France,
The brightness of thy hope and strength and fame,
Like some proud ship that led the fleet so long,
Beseems to-day a wreck driven by the gale, a mastless hulk,
And 'mid its teeming madden'd half-drown'd crowds,
Nor helm nor helmsman.

Dim smitten star,
Orb not of France alone, pale symbol of my soul, its dearest
hopes,
The struggle and the daring, rage divine for liberty,
Of aspirations toward the far ideal, enthusiast's dreams of
brotherhood,
Of terror to the tyrant and the priest.

Star crucified—by traitors sold,
Star panting o'er a land of death, heroic land,
Strange, passionate, mocking, frivolous land.

Miserable! yet for thy errors, vanities, sins, I will not now
 rebuke thee,
Thy unexampled woes and pangs have quell'd them all,
And left thee sacred.

In that amid thy many faults thou ever aimedst highly,
In that thou wouldst not really sell thyself however great the
 price,
In that thou surely wakedst weeping from thy drugg'd
 sleep,
In that alone among thy sisters thou, giantess, didst rend
 the ones that shamed thee,
In that thou couldst not, wouldst not, wear the usual chains,
This cross, thy livid face, thy pierced hands and feet,
The spear thrust in thy side.

O star! O ship of France, beat back and baffled long!
Bear up O smitten orb! O ship continue on!

Sure as the ship of all, the Earth itself,
Product of deathly fire and turbulent chaos,
Forth from its spasms of fury and its poisons,
Issuing at last in perfect power and beauty,
Onward beneath the sun following its course,
So thee O ship of France!

Finish'd the days, the clouds dispel'd,
The travail o'er, the long-sought extrication,
When lo! reborn, high o'er the European world,
(In gladness answering thence, as face afar to face, reflecting
 ours Columbia,)
Again thy star O France, fair lustrous star,
In heavenly peace, clearer, more bright than ever,
Shall beam immortal.

The Ox-Tamer

In a far-away northern county in the placid pastoral region,
Lives my farmer friend, the theme of my recitative, a famous
tamer of oxen,
There they bring him the three-year-olds and the four-year-
olds to break them,
He will take the wildest steer in the world and break him
and tame him,
He will go fearless without any whip where the young
bullock chafes up and down the yard,
The bullock's head tosses restless high in the air with raging
eyes,
Yet see you! how soon his rage subsides—how soon this
tamer tames him;
See you! on the farms hereabout a hundred oxen young and
old, and he is the man who has tamed them,
They all know him, all are affectionate to him;
See you! some are such beautiful animals, so lofty looking;
Some are buff-color'd, some mottled, one has a white line
running along his back, some are brindled,
Some have wide flaring horns (a good sign)—see you! the
bright hides,
See, the two with stars on their foreheads—see, the round
bodies and broad backs,
How straight and square they stand on their legs—what fine
sagacious eyes!
How they watch their tamer—they wish him near them—
how they turn to look after him!
What yearning expression! how uneasy they are when he
moves away from them;
Now I marvel what it can be he appears to them, (books,
politics, poems, depart—all else departs,)
I confess I envy only his fascination—my silent, illiterate
friend,
Whom a hundred oxen love there in his life on farms,
In the northern county far, in the placid pastoral region.

An Old Man's Thought of School

For the Inauguration of a Public School, Camden, New Jersey, 1874.

AN old man's thought of school,
An old man gathering youthful memories and blooms that
youth itself cannot.

Now only do I know you,
O fair auroral skies—O morning dew upon the grass!

And these I see, these sparkling eyes,
These stores of mystic meaning, these young lives,
Building, equipping like a fleet of ships, immortal ships,
Soon to sail out over the measureless seas,
On the soul's voyage.

Only a lot of boys and girls?
Only the tiresome spelling, writing, ciphering classes?
Only a public school?

Ah more, infinitely more;
(As George Fox rais'd his warning cry, "Is it this pile of
brick and mortar, these dead floors, windows, rails, you
call the church?
Why this is not the church at all—the church is living, ever
living souls.")

And you America,
Cast you the real reckoning for your present?
The lights and shadows of your future, good or evil?
To girlhood, boyhood look, the teacher and the school.

Wandering at Morn

WANDERING at morn,
Emerging from the night from gloomy thoughts, thee in my
thoughts,
Yearning for thee harmonious Union! thee, singing bird
divine!

Thee coil'd in evil times my country, with craft and black
 dismay, with every meanness, treason thrust upon thee,
This common marvel I beheld—the parent thrush I watch'd
 feeding its young,
The singing thrush whose tones of joy and faith ecstatic,
Fail not to certify and cheer my soul.

There ponder'd, felt I,
If worms, snakes, loathsome grubs, may to sweet spiritual
 songs be turn'd,
If vermin so transposed, so used and bless'd may be,
Then may I trust in you, your fortunes, days, my country;
Who knows but these may be the lessons fit for you?
From these your future song may rise with joyous trills,
Destin'd to fill the world.

Italian Music in Dakota

[*"The Seventeenth—the finest Regimental Band I ever heard."*]

THROUGH the soft evening air enwinding all,
Rocks, woods, fort, cannon, pacing sentries, endless wilds,
In dulcet streams, in flutes' and cornets' notes,
Electric, pensive, turbulent, artificial,
(Yet strangely fitting even here, meanings unknown before,
Subtler than ever, more harmony, as if born here, related here,
Not to the city's fresco'd rooms, not to the audience of the
 opera house,
Sounds, echoes, wandering strains, as really here at home,
Sonnambula's innocent love, trios with *Norma's* anguish,
And thy ecstatic chorus *Poliuto;*)
Ray'd in the limpid yellow slanting sundown,
Music, Italian music in Dakota.

While Nature, sovereign of this gnarl'd realm,
Lurking in hidden barbaric grim recesses,
Acknowledging rapport however far remov'd,
(As some old root or soil of earth its last-born flower or
 fruit,)
Listens well pleas'd.

With All Thy Gifts

WITH all thy gifts America,
Standing secure, rapidly tending, overlooking the world,
Power, wealth, extent, vouchsafed to thee—with these and like of these vouchsafed to thee,
What if one gift thou lackest? (the ultimate human problem never solving,)
The gift of perfect women fit for thee—what if that gift of gifts thou lackest?
The towering feminine of thee? the beauty, health, completion, fit for thee?
The mothers fit for thee?

My Picture-Gallery

IN a little house keep I pictures suspended, it is not a fix'd house,
It is round, it is only a few inches from one side to the other;
Yet behold, it has room for all the shows of the world, all memories!
Here the tableaus of life, and here the groupings of death;
Here, do you know this? this is cicerone himself,
With finger rais'd he points to the prodigal pictures.

The Prairie States

A NEWER garden of creation, no primal solitude,
Dense, joyous, modern, populous millions, cities and farms,
With iron interlaced, composite, tied, many in one,
By all the world contributed—freedom's and law's and thrift's society,
The crown and teeming paradise, so far, of time's accumulations,
To justify the past.

Proud Music of the Storm

1

Proud music of the storm,
Blast that careers so free, whistling across the prairies,
Strong hum of forest tree-tops—wind of the mountains,
Personified dim shapes—you hidden orchestras,
You serenades of phantoms with instruments alert,
Blending with Nature's rhythmus all the tongues of nations;
You chords left as by vast composers—you choruses,
You formless, free, religious dances—you from the Orient,
You undertone of rivers, roar of pouring cataracts,
You sounds from distant guns with galloping cavalry,
Echoes of camps with all the different bugle-calls,
Trooping tumultuous, filling the midnight late, bending me
    powerless,
Entering my lonesome slumber-chamber, why have you
    seiz'd me?

2

Come forward O my soul, and let the rest retire,
Listen, lose not, it is toward thee they tend,
Parting the midnight, entering my slumber-chamber,
For thee they sing and dance O soul.

A festival song,
The duet of the bridegroom and the bride, a marriage-march,
With lips of love, and hearts of lovers fill'd to the brim with
    love,
The red-flush'd cheeks and perfumes, the cortege swarming
    full of friendly faces young and old,
To flutes' clear notes and sounding harps' cantabile.

Now loud approaching drums,
Victoria! see'st thou in powder-smoke the banners torn but
    flying? the rout of the baffled?
Hearest those shouts of a conquering army?

(Ah soul, the sobs of women, the wounded groaning in
    agony,

The hiss and crackle of flames, the blacken'd ruins, the
embers of cities,
The dirge and desolation of mankind.)

Now airs antique and mediæval fill me,
I see and hear old harpers with their harps at Welsh festivals,
I hear the minnesingers singing their lays of love,
I hear the minstrels, gleemen, troubadours, of the middle ages.

Now the great organ sounds,
Tremulous, while underneath, (as the hid footholds of the
earth,
On which arising rest, and leaping forth depend,
All shapes of beauty, grace and strength, all hues we know,
Green blades of grass and warbling birds, children that
gambol and play, the clouds of heaven above,)
The strong base stands, and its pulsations intermits not,
Bathing, supporting, merging all the rest, maternity of all
the rest,
And with it every instrument in multitudes,
The players playing, all the world's musicians,
The solemn hymns and masses rousing adoration,
All passionate heart-chants, sorrowful appeals,
The measureless sweet vocalists of ages,
And for their solvent setting earth's own diapason,
Of winds and woods and mighty ocean waves,
A new composite orchestra, binder of years and climes, ten-
fold renewer,
As of the far-back days the poets tell, the Paradiso,
The straying thence, the separation long, but now the
wandering done,
The journey done, the journeyman come home,
And man and art with Nature fused again.

Tutti! for earth and heaven;
(The Almighty leader now for once has signal'd with his wand.)

The manly strophe of the husbands of the world,
And all the wives responding.

The tongues of violins,
(I think O tongues ye tell this heart, that cannot tell itself,
This brooding yearning heart, that cannot tell itself.)

3

Ah from a little child,
Thou knowest soul how to me all sounds became music,
My mother's voice in lullaby or hymn,
(The voice, O tender voices, memory's loving voices,
Last miracle of all, O dearest mother's, sister's, voices;)
The rain, the growing corn, the breeze among the long-
leav'd corn,
The measur'd sea-surf beating on the sand,
The twittering bird, the hawk's sharp scream,
The wild-fowl's notes at night as flying low migrating north
or south,
The psalm in the country church or mid the clustering trees,
the open air camp-meeting,
The fiddler in the tavern, the glee, the long-strung sailor-song,
The lowing cattle, bleating sheep, the crowing cock at dawn.

All songs of current lands come sounding round me,
The German airs of friendship, wine and love,
Irish ballads, merry jigs and dances, English warbles,
Chansons of France, Scotch tunes, and o'er the rest,
Italia's peerless compositions.

Across the stage with pallor on her face, yet lurid passion,
Stalks Norma brandishing the dagger in her hand.

I see poor crazed Lucia's eyes' unnatural gleam,
Her hair down her back falls loose and dishevel'd.

I see where Ernani walking the bridal garden,
Amid the scent of night-roses, radiant, holding his bride by
the hand,
Hears the infernal call, the death-pledge of the horn.

To crossing swords and gray hairs bared to heaven,
The clear electric base and baritone of the world,
The trombone duo, Libertad forever!

From Spanish chestnut trees' dense shade,
By old and heavy convent walls a wailing song,

Song of lost love, the torch of youth and life quench'd in
despair,
Song of the dying swan, Fernando's heart is breaking.

Awaking from her woes at last retriev'd Amina sings,
Copious as stars and glad as morning light the torrents of
her joy.

(The teeming lady comes,
The lustrious orb, Venus contralto, the blooming mother,
Sister of loftiest gods, Alboni's self I hear.)

4

I hear those odes, symphonies, operas,
I hear in the *William Tell* the music of an arous'd and
angry people,
I hear Meyerbeer's *Huguenots,* the *Prophet,* or *Robert,*
Gounod's *Faust,* or Mozart's *Don Juan.*

I hear the dance-music of all nations,
The waltz, some delicious measure, lapsing, bathing me
in bliss,
The bolero to tinkling guitars and clattering castanets.

I see religious dances old and new,
I hear the sound of the Hebrew lyre,
I see the crusaders marching bearing the cross on high, to
the martial clang of cymbals,
I hear dervishes monotonously chanting, interspers'd with
frantic shouts, as they spin around turning always
towards Mecca,
I see the rapt religious dances of the Persians and the Arabs,
Again, at Eleusis, home of Ceres, I see the modern Greeks
dancing,
I hear them clapping their hands as they bend their bodies,
I hear the metrical shuffling of their feet.

I see again the wild old Corybantian dance, the performers
wounding each other,

I see the Roman youth to the shrill sound of flageolets
throwing and catching their weapons,
As they fall on their knees and rise again.

I hear from the Mussulman mosque the muezzin calling,
I see the worshippers within, nor form nor sermon,
argument nor word,
But silent, strange, devout, rais'd, glowing heads, ecstatic faces.

I hear the Egyptian harp of many strings,
The primitive chants of the Nile boatmen,
The sacred imperial hymns of China,
To the delicate sounds of the king, (the stricken wood and
stone,)
Or to Hindu flutes and the fretting twang of the vina,
A band of bayaderes.

5

Now Asia, Africa leave me, Europe seizing inflates me,
To organs huge and bands I hear as from vast concourses of
voices,
Luther's strong hymn, *Eine feste Burg ist unser Gott,*
Rossini's *Stabat Mater dolorosa,*
Or floating in some high cathedral dim with gorgeous
color'd windows,
The passionate *Agnus Dei* or *Gloria in Excelsis.*

Composers! mighty maestros!
And you, sweet singers of old lands, soprani, tenori, bassi!
To you a new bard caroling in the West,
Obeisant sends his love.

(Such led to thee O soul,
All senses, shows and objects, lead to thee,
But now it seems to me sound leads o'er all the rest.)

I hear the annual singing of the children in St. Paul's
cathedral,
Or, under the high roof of some colossal hall, the
symphonies, oratorios of Beethoven, Handel, or Haydn,
The *Creation* in billows of godhood laves me.

Give me to hold all sounds, (I madly struggling cry,)
Fill me with all the voices of the universe,
Endow me with their throbbings, Nature's also,
The tempests, waters, winds, operas and chants, marches
and dances,
Utter, pour in, for I would take them all!

6

Then I woke softly,
And pausing, questioning awhile the music of my dream,
And questioning all those reminiscences, the tempest in its
fury,
And all the songs of sopranos and tenors,
And those rapt oriental dances of religious fervor,
And the sweet varied instruments, and the diapason of
organs,
And all the artless plaints of love and grief and death,
I said to my silent curious soul out of the bed of the
slumber-chamber,
Come, for I have found the clew I sought so long,
Let us go forth refresh'd amid the day,
Cheerfully tallying life, walking the world, the real,
Nourish'd henceforth by our celestial dream.

And I said, moreover,
Haply what thou hast heard O soul was not the sound of
winds,
Nor dream of raging storm, nor sea-hawk's flapping wings
nor harsh scream,
Nor vocalism of sun-bright Italy,
Nor German organ majestic, nor vast concourse of voices,
nor layers of harmonies,
Nor strophes of husbands and wives, nor sound of marching
soldiers,
Nor flutes, nor harps, nor the bugle-calls of camps,
But to a new rhythmus fitted for thee,
Poems bridging the way from Life to Death, vaguely wafted
in night air, uncaught, unwritten,
Which let us go forth in the bold day and write.

Passage to India

I

Singing my days,
Singing the great achievements of the present,
Singing the strong light works of engineers,
Our modern wonders, (the antique ponderous Seven outvied,)
In the Old World the east the Suez canal,
The New by its mighty railroad spann'd,
The seas inlaid with eloquent gentle wires;
Yet first to sound, and ever sound, the cry with thee O soul,
The Past! the Past! the Past!

The Past—the dark unfathom'd retrospect!
The teeming gulf—the sleepers and the shadows!
The past—the infinite greatness of the past!
For what is the present after all but a growth out of the past?
(As a projectile form'd, impell'd, passing a certain line, still
keeps on,
So the present, utterly form'd, impell'd by the past.)

2

Passage O soul to India!
Eclaircise the myths Asiatic, the primitive fables.

Not you alone proud truths of the world,
Nor you alone ye facts of modern science,
But myths and fables of eld, Asia's, Africa's fables,
The far-darting beams of the spirit, the unloos'd dreams,
The deep diving bibles and legends,
The daring plots of the poets, the elder religions;
O you temples fairer than lilies pour'd over by the rising sun!
O you fables spurning the known, eluding the hold of the
known, mounting to heaven!
You lofty and dazzling towers, pinnacled, red as roses,
burnish'd with gold!
Towers of fables immortal fashion'd from mortal dreams!
You too I welcome and fully the same as the rest!
You too with joy I sing.

Passage to India!
Lo, soul, seest thou not God's purpose from the first?
The earth to be spann'd, connected by network,
The races, neighbors, to marry and be given in marriage,
The oceans to be cross'd, the distant brought near,
The lands to be welded together.

A worship new I sing,
You captains, voyagers, explorers, yours,
You engineers, you architects, machinists, yours,
You, not for trade or transportation only,
But in God's name, and for thy sake O soul.

3

Passage to India!
Lo soul for thee of tableaus twain,
I see in one the Suez canal initiated, open'd,
I see the procession of steamships, the Empress Eugenie's
    leading the van,
I mark from on deck the strange landscape, the pure sky,
    the level sand in the distance,
I pass swiftly the picturesque groups, the workmen gather'd,
The gigantic dredging machines.

In one again, different, (yet thine, all thine, O soul, the same,)
I see over my own continent the Pacific railroad
    surmounting every barrier,
I see continual trains of cars winding along the Platte
    carrying freight and passengers,
I hear the locomotives rushing and roaring, and the shrill
    steam-whistle,
I hear the echoes reverberate through the grandest scenery
    in the world,
I cross the Laramie plains, I note the rocks in grotesque
    shapes, the buttes,
I see the plentiful larkspur and wild onions, the barren,
    colorless, sage-deserts,
I see in glimpses afar or towering immediately above me the
    great mountains, I see the Wind river and the Wahsatch
    mountains,

I see the Monument mountain and the Eagle's Nest, I pass
    the Promontory, I ascend the Nevadas,
I scan the noble Elk mountain and wind around its base,
I see the Humboldt range, I thread the valley and cross the
    river,
I see the clear waters of lake Tahoe, I see forests of majestic
    pines,
Or crossing the great desert, the alkaline plains, I behold
    enchanting mirages of waters and meadows,
Marking through these and after all, in duplicate slender lines,
Bridging the three or four thousand miles of land travel,
Tying the Eastern to the Western sea,
The road between Europe and Asia.

(Ah Genoese thy dream! thy dream!
Centuries after thou art laid in thy grave,
The shore thou foundest verifies thy dream.)

4

Passage to India!
Struggles of many a captain, tales of many a sailor dead,
Over my mood stealing and spreading they come,
Like clouds and cloudlets in the unreach'd sky.

Along all history, down the slopes,
As a rivulet running, sinking now, and now again to the
    surface rising,
A ceaseless thought, a varied train—lo, soul, to thee, thy
    sight, they rise,
The plans, the voyages again, the expeditions;
Again Vasco de Gama sails forth,
Again the knowledge gain'd, the mariner's compass,
Lands found and nations born, thou born America,
For purpose vast, man's long probation fill'd,
Thou rondure of the world at last accomplish'd.

5

O vast Rondure, swimming in space,
Cover'd all over with visible power and beauty,
Alternate light and day and the teeming spiritual darkness,

Unspeakable high processions of sun and moon and
countless stars above,
Below, the manifold grass and waters, animals, mountains,
trees,
With inscrutable purpose, some hidden prophetic intention,
Now first it seems my thought begins to span thee.

Down from the gardens of Asia descending radiating,
Adam and Eve appear, then their myriad progeny after them,
Wandering, yearning, curious, with restless explorations,
With questionings, baffled, formless, feverish, with never-
happy hearts,
With that sad incessant refrain, *Wherefore unsatisfied soul?*
and *Whither O mocking life?*

Ah who shall soothe these feverish children?
Who justify these restless explorations?
Who speak the secret of impassive earth?
Who bind it to us? what is this separate Nature so unnatural?
What is this earth to our affections? (unloving earth,
without a throb to answer ours,
Cold earth, the place of graves.)

Yet soul be sure the first intent remains, and shall be carried
out,
Perhaps even now the time has arrived.

After the seas are all cross'd, (as they seem already cross'd,)
After the great captains and engineers have accomplish'd
their work,
After the noble inventors, after the scientists, the chemist,
the geologist, ethnologist,
Finally shall come the poet worthy that name,
The true son of God shall come singing his songs.

Then not your deeds only O voyagers, O scientists and
inventors, shall be justified,
All these hearts as of fretted children shall be sooth'd,
All affection shall be fully responded to, the secret shall be
told,

All these separations and gaps shall be taken up and hook'd
and link'd together,
The whole earth, this cold, impassive, voiceless earth, shall
be completely justified,
Trinitas divine shall be gloriously accomplish'd and
compacted by the true son of God, the poet,
(He shall indeed pass the straits and conquer the mountains,
He shall double the cape of Good Hope to some purpose,)
Nature and Man shall be disjoin'd and diffused no more,
The true son of God shall absolutely fuse them.

6

Year at whose wide-flung door I sing!
Year of the purpose accomplish'd!
Year of the marriage of continents, climates and oceans!
(No mere doge of Venice now wedding the Adriatic,)
I see O year in you the vast terraqueous globe given and
giving all,
Europe to Asia, Africa join'd, and they to the New World,
The lands, geographies, dancing before you, holding a
festival garland,
As brides and bridegrooms hand in hand.

Passage to India!
Cooling airs from Caucasus far, soothing cradle of man,
The river Euphrates flowing, the past lit up again.

Lo soul, the retrospect brought forward,
The old, most populous, wealthiest of earth's lands,
The streams of the Indus and the Ganges and their many
affluents,
(I my shores of America walking to-day behold, resuming all,)
The tale of Alexander on his warlike marches suddenly
dying,
On one side China and on the other side Persia and Arabia,
To the south the great seas and the bay of Bengal,
The flowing literatures, tremendous epics, religions, castes,
Old occult Brahma interminably far back, the tender and
junior Buddha,

Central and southern empires and all their belongings,
possessors,
The wars of Tamerlane, the reign of Aurungzebe,
The traders, rulers, explorers, Moslems, Venetians,
Byzantium, the Arabs, Portuguese,
The first travelers famous yet, Marco Polo, Batouta the
Moor,
Doubts to be solv'd, the map incognita, blanks to be fill'd,
The foot of man unstay'd, the hands never at rest,
Thyself O soul that will not brook a challenge.

The mediæval navigators rise before me,
The world of 1492, with its awaken'd enterprise,
Something swelling in humanity now like the sap of the
earth in spring,
The sunset splendor of chivalry declining.

And who art thou sad shade?
Gigantic, visionary, thyself a visionary,
With majestic limbs and pious beaming eyes,
Spreading around with every look of thine a golden world,
Enhuing it with gorgeous hues.

As the chief histrion,
Down to the footlights walks in some great scena,
Dominating the rest I see the Admiral himself,
(History's type of courage, action, faith,)
Behold him sail from Palos leading his little fleet,
His voyage behold, his return, his great fame,
His misfortunes, calumniators, behold him a prisoner,
chain'd,
Behold his dejection, poverty, death.

(Curious in time I stand, noting the efforts of heroes,
Is the deferment long? bitter the slander, poverty, death?
Lies the seed unreck'd for centuries in the ground? lo, to
God's due occasion,
Uprising in the night, it sprouts, blooms,
And fills the earth with use and beauty.)

7

Passage indeed O soul to primal thought,
Not lands and seas alone, thy own clear freshness,
The young maturity of brood and bloom,
To realms of budding bibles.

O soul, repressless, I with thee and thou with me,
Thy circumnavigation of the world begin,
Of man, the voyage of his mind's return,
To reason's early paradise,
Back, back to wisdom's birth, to innocent intuitions,
Again with fair creation.

8

O we can wait no longer,
We too take ship O soul,
Joyous we too launch out on trackless seas,
Fearless for unknown shores on waves of ecstasy to sail,
Amid the wafting winds, (thou pressing me to thee, I thee
to me, O soul,)
Caroling free, singing our song of God,
Chanting our chant of pleasant exploration.

With laugh and many a kiss,
(Let others deprecate, let others weep for sin, remorse,
humiliation,)
O soul thou pleasest me, I thee.

Ah more than any priest O soul we too believe in God,
But with the mystery of God we dare not dally.

O soul thou pleasest me, I thee,
Sailing these seas or on the hills, or waking in the night,
Thoughts, silent thoughts, of Time and Space and Death,
like waters flowing,
Bear me indeed as through the regions infinite,
Whose air I breathe, whose ripples hear, lave me all over,
Bathe me O God in thee, mounting to thee,
I and my soul to range in range of thee.

O Thou transcendent,
Nameless, the fibre and the breath,
Light of the light, shedding forth universes, thou centre of them,
Thou mightier centre of the true, the good, the loving,
Thou moral, spiritual fountain—affection's source—thou reservoir,
(O pensive soul of me—O thirst unsatisfied—waitest not there?
Waitest not haply for us somewhere there the Comrade perfect?)
Thou pulse—thou motive of the stars, suns, systems,
That, circling, move in order, safe, harmonious,
Athwart the shapeless vastnesses of space,
How should I think, how breathe a single breath, how speak, if, out of myself,
I could not launch, to those, superior universes?

Swiftly I shrivel at the thought of God,
At Nature and its wonders, Time and Space and Death,
But that I, turning, call to thee O soul, thou actual Me,
And lo, thou gently masterest the orbs,
Thou matest Time, smilest content at Death,
And fillest, swellest full the vastnesses of Space.

Greater than stars or suns,
Bounding O soul thou journeyest forth;
What love than thine and ours could wider amplify?
What aspirations, wishes, outvie thine and ours O soul?
What dreams of the ideal? what plans of purity, perfection, strength?
What cheerful willingness for others' sake to give up all?
For others' sake to suffer all?

Reckoning ahead O soul, when thou, the time achiev'd,
The seas all cross'd, weather'd the capes, the voyage done,
Surrounded, copest, frontest God, yieldest, the aim attain'd,
As fill'd with friendship, love complete, the Elder Brother found,
The Younger melts in fondness in his arms.

9

Passage to more than India!
Are thy wings plumed indeed for such far flights?
O soul, voyagest thou indeed on voyages like those?
Disportest thou on waters such as those?
Soundest below the Sanscrit and the Vedas?
Then have thy bent unleash'd.

Passage to you, your shores, ye aged fierce enigmas!
Passage to you, to mastership of you, ye strangling problems!
You, strew'd with the wrecks of skeletons, that, living, never
 reach'd you.

Passage to more than India!
O secret of the earth and sky!
Of you O waters of the sea! O winding creeks and rivers!
Of you O woods and fields! of you strong mountains of my
 land!
Of you O prairies! of you gray rocks!
O morning red! O clouds! O rain and snows!
O day and night, passage to you!

O sun and moon and all you stars! Sirius and Jupiter!
Passage to you!

Passage, immediate passage! the blood burns in my veins!
Away O soul! hoist instantly the anchor!
Cut the hawsers—haul out—shake out every sail!
Have we not stood here like trees in the ground long enough?
Have we not grovel'd here long enough, eating and
 drinking like mere brutes?
Have we not darken'd and dazed ourselves with books long
 enough?

Sail forth—steer for the deep waters only,
Reckless O soul, exploring, I with thee, and thou with me,
For we are bound where mariner has not yet dared to go,
And we will risk the ship, ourselves and all.

O my brave soul!
O farther farther sail!
O daring joy, but safe! are they not all the seas of God?
O farther, farther, farther sail!

Prayer of Columbus

A batter'd, wreck'd old man,
Thrown on this savage shore, far, far from home,
Pent by the sea and dark rebellious brows, twelve dreary months,
Sore, stiff with many toils, sicken'd and nigh to death,
I take my way along the island's edge,
Venting a heavy heart.

I am too full of woe!
Haply I may not live another day;
I cannot rest O God, I cannot eat or drink or sleep,
Till I put forth myself, my prayer, once more to Thee,
Breathe, bathe myself once more in Thee, commune with Thee,
Report myself once more to Thee.

Thou knowest my years entire, my life,
My long and crowded life of active work, not adoration merely;
Thou knowest the prayers and vigils of my youth,
Thou knowest my manhood's solemn and visionary meditations,
Thou knowest how before I commenced I devoted all to come to Thee,
Thou knowest I have in age ratified all those vows and strictly kept them,
Thou knowest I have not once lost nor faith nor ecstasy in Thee,
In shackles, prison'd, in disgrace, repining not,
Accepting all from Thee, as duly come from Thee.

All my emprises have been fill'd with Thee,
My speculations, plans, begun and carried on in thoughts of Thee,

Sailing the deep or journeying the land for Thee;
Intentions, purports, aspirations mine, leaving results to Thee.

O I am sure they really came from Thee,
The urge, the ardor, the unconquerable will,
The potent, felt, interior command, stronger than words,
A message from the Heavens whispering to me even in
sleep,
These sped me on.

By me and these the work so far accomplish'd,
By me earth's elder cloy'd and stifled lands uncloy'd,
unloos'd,
By me the hemispheres rounded and tied, the unknown to
the known.

The end I know not, it is all in Thee,
Or small or great I know not—haply what broad fields,
what lands,
Haply the brutish measureless human undergrowth I know,
Transplanted there may rise to stature, knowledge worthy
Thee,
Haply the swords I know may there indeed be turn'd to
reaping-tools,
Haply the lifeless cross I know, Europe's dead cross, may
bud and blossom there.

One effort more, my altar this bleak sand;
That Thou O God my life hast lighted,
With ray of light, steady, ineffable, vouchsafed of Thee,
Light rare untellable, lighting the very light,
Beyond all signs, descriptions, languages;
For that O God, be it my latest word, here on my knees,
Old, poor, and paralyzed, I thank Thee.

My terminus near,
The clouds already closing in upon me,
The voyage balk'd, the course disputed, lost,
I yield my ships to Thee.

My hands, my limbs grow nerveless,
My brain feels rack'd, bewilder'd,
Let the old timbers part, I will not part,
I will cling fast to Thee, O God, though the waves buffet me,
Thee, Thee at least I know.

Is it the prophet's thought I speak, or am I raving?
What do I know of life? what of myself?
I know not even my own work past or present,
Dim ever-shifting guesses of it spread before me,
Of newer better worlds, their mighty parturition,
Mocking, perplexing me.

And these things I see suddenly, what mean they?
As if some miracle, some hand divine unseal'd my eyes,
Shadowy vast shapes smile through the air and sky,
And on the distant waves sail countless ships,
And anthems in new tongues I hear saluting me.

The Sleepers

1

I WANDER all night in my vision,
Stepping with light feet, swiftly and noiselessly stepping and stopping,
Bending with open eyes over the shut eyes of sleepers,
Wandering and confused, lost to myself, ill-assorted, contradictory,
Pausing, gazing, bending, and stopping.

How solemn they look there, stretch'd and still,
How quiet they breathe, the little children in their cradles.

The wretched features of ennuyés, the white features of corpses, the livid faces of drunkards, the sick-gray faces of onanists,
The gash'd bodies on battle-fields, the insane in their strong-door'd rooms, the sacred idiots, the new-born emerging from gates, and the dying emerging from gates,
The night pervades them and infolds them.

The married couple sleep calmly in their bed, he with his
palm on the hip of the wife, and she with her palm on
the hip of the husband,
The sisters sleep lovingly side by side in their bed,
The men sleep lovingly side by side in theirs,
And the mother sleeps with her little child carefully wrapt.

The blind sleep, and the deaf and dumb sleep,
The prisoner sleeps well in the prison, the runaway son sleeps,
The murderer that is to be hung next day, how does he sleep?
And the murder'd person, how does he sleep?

The female that loves unrequited sleeps,
And the male that loves unrequited sleeps,
The head of the money-maker that plotted all day sleeps,
And the enraged and treacherous dispositions, all, all sleep.

I stand in the dark with drooping eyes by the worst-
suffering and the most restless,
I pass my hands soothingly to and fro a few inches from them,
The restless sink in their beds, they fitfully sleep.

Now I pierce the darkness, new beings appear,
The earth recedes from me into the night,
I saw that it was beautiful, and I see that what is not the
earth is beautiful.

I go from bedside to bedside, I sleep close with the other
sleepers each in turn,
I dream in my dream all the dreams of the other dreamers,
And I become the other dreamers.

I am a dance—play up there! the fit is whirling me fast!

I am the ever-laughing—it is new moon and twilight,
I see the hiding of douceurs, I see nimble ghosts whichever
way I look,
Cache and cache again deep in the ground and sea, and
where it is neither ground nor sea.

Well do they do their jobs those journeymen divine,
Only from me can they hide nothing, and would not if they
 could,
I reckon I am their boss and they make me a pet besides,
And surround me and lead me and run ahead when I walk,
To lift their cunning covers to signify me with stretch'd
 arms, and resume the way;
Onward we move, a gay gang of blackguards! with mirth-
 shouting music and wild-flapping pennants of joy!

I am the actor, the actress, the voter, the politician,
The emigrant and the exile, the criminal that stood in the box,
He who has been famous and he who shall be famous after
 to-day,
The stammerer, the well-form'd person, the wasted or feeble
 person.

I am she who adorn'd herself and folded her hair expectantly,
My truant lover has come, and it is dark.

Double yourself and receive me darkness,
Receive me and my lover too, he will not let me go without
 him.

I roll myself upon you as upon a bed, I resign myself to the
 dusk.

He whom I call answers me and takes the place of my lover,
He rises with me silently from the bed.

Darkness, you are gentler than my lover, his flesh was
 sweaty and panting,
I feel the hot moisture yet that he left me.

My hands are spread forth, I pass them in all directions,
I would sound up the shadowy shore to which you are
 journeying.

Be careful darkness! already what was it touch'd me?
I thought my lover had gone, else darkness and he are one,
I hear the heart-beat, I follow, I fade away.

2

I descend my western course, my sinews are flaccid,
Perfume and youth course through me and I am their wake.

It is my face yellow and wrinkled instead of the old woman's,
I sit low in a straw-bottom chair and carefully darn my
grandson's stockings.

It is I too, the sleepless widow looking out on the winter
midnight,
I see the sparkles of starshine on the icy and pallid earth.

A shroud I see and I am the shroud, I wrap a body and lie
in the coffin,
It is dark here under ground, it is not evil or pain here, it is
blank here, for reasons.

(It seems to me that every thing in the light and air ought
to be happy,
Whoever is not in his coffin and the dark grave let him
know he has enough.)

3

I see a beautiful gigantic swimmer swimming naked through
the eddies of the sea,
His brown hair lies close and even to his head, he strikes out
with courageous arms, he urges himself with his legs,
I see his white body, I see his undaunted eyes,
I hate the swift-running eddies that would dash him headforemost on the rocks.

What are you doing you ruffianly red-trickled waves?
Will you kill the courageous giant? will you kill him in the
prime of his middle age?

Steady and long he struggles,
He is baffled, bang'd, bruis'd, he holds out while his
strength holds out,
The slapping eddies are spotted with his blood, they bear
him away, they roll him, swing him, turn him,

His beautiful body is borne in the circling eddies, it is
continually bruis'd on rocks,
Swiftly and out of sight is borne the brave corpse.

4

I turn but do not extricate myself,
Confused, a past-reading, another, but with darkness yet.

The beach is cut by the razory ice-wind, the wreck-guns
sound,
The tempest lulls, the moon comes floundering through the
drifts.

I look where the ship helplessly heads end on, I hear the
burst as she strikes, I hear the howls of dismay, they
grow fainter and fainter.

I cannot aid with my wringing fingers,
I can but rush to the surf and let it drench me and freeze
upon me.

I search with the crowd, not one of the company is wash'd
to us alive,
In the morning I help pick up the dead and lay them in
rows in a barn.

5

Now of the older war-days, the defeat at Brooklyn,
Washington stands inside the lines, he stands on the
intrench'd hills amid a crowd of officers,
His face is cold and damp, he cannot repress the weeping
drops,
He lifts the glass perpetually to his eyes, the color is
blanch'd from his cheeks,
He sees the slaughter of the southern braves confided to
him by their parents.

The same at last and at last when peace is declared,
He stands in the room of the old tavern, the well-belov'd
soldiers all pass through,

The officers speechless and slow draw near in their turns,
The chief encircles their necks with his arm and kisses them
on the cheek,
He kisses lightly the wet cheeks one after another, he shakes
hands and bids good-by to the army.

6

Now what my mother told me one day as we sat at dinner
together,
Of when she was a nearly grown girl living home with her
parents on the old homestead.

A red squaw came one breakfast-time to the old homestead,
On her back she carried a bundle of rushes for rushbottoming chairs,
Her hair, straight, shiny, coarse, black, profuse, half-
envelop'd her face,
Her step was free and elastic, and her voice sounded
exquisitely as she spoke.

My mother look'd in delight and amazement at the stranger,
She look'd at the freshness of her tall-borne face and full
and pliant limbs,
The more she look'd upon her she loved her,
Never before had she seen such wonderful beauty and
purity,
She made her sit on a bench by the jamb of the fireplace,
she cook'd food for her,
She had no work to give her, but she gave her remembrance
and fondness.

The red squaw staid all the forenoon, and toward the
middle of the afternoon she went away,
O my mother was loth to have her go away,
All the week she thought of her, she watch'd for her many a
month,
She remember'd her many a winter and many a summer,
But the red squaw never came nor was heard of there again.

7

A show of the summer softness—a contact of something
 unseen—an amour of the light and air,
I am jealous and overwhelm'd with friendliness,
And will go gallivant with the light and air myself.

O love and summer, you are in the dreams and in me,
Autumn and winter are in the dreams, the farmer goes with
 his thrift,
The droves and crops increase, the barns are well-fill'd.

Elements merge in the night, ships make tacks in the dreams,
The sailor sails, the exile returns home,
The fugitive returns unharm'd, the immigrant is back
 beyond months and years,
The poor Irishman lives in the simple house of his
 childhood with the well-known neighbors and faces,
They warmly welcome him, he is barefoot again, he forgets
 he is well off,
The Dutchman voyages home, and the Scotchman and
 Welshman voyage home, and the native of the
 Mediterranean voyages home,
To every port of England, France, Spain, enter well-fill'd ships,
The Swiss foots it toward his hills, the Prussian goes his
 way, the Hungarian his way, and the Pole his way,
The Swede returns, and the Dane and Norwegian return.

The homeward bound and the outward bound,
The beautiful lost swimmer, the ennuyé, the onanist, the
 female that loves unrequited, the money-maker,
The actor and actress, those through with their parts and
 those waiting to commence,
The affectionate boy, the husband and wife, the voter, the
 nominee that is chosen and the nominee that has fail'd,
The great already known and the great any time after to-day,
The stammerer, the sick, the perfect-form'd, the homely,
The criminal that stood in the box, the judge that sat and
 sentenced him, the fluent lawyers, the jury, the audience,
The laugher and weeper, the dancer, the midnight widow,
 the red squaw,

The consumptive, the erysipalite, the idiot, he that is wrong'd,
The antipodes, and every one between this and them in the dark,
I swear they are averaged now—one is no better than the other,
The night and sleep have liken'd them and restored them.

I swear they are all beautiful,
Every one that sleeps is beautiful, every thing in the dim light is beautiful,
The wildest and bloodiest is over, and all is peace.

Peace is always beautiful,
The myth of heaven indicates peace and night.

The myth of heaven indicates the soul,
The soul is always beautiful, it appears more or it appears less, it comes or it lags behind,
It comes from its embower'd garden and looks pleasantly on itself and encloses the world,
Perfect and clean the genitals previously jetting, and perfect and clean the womb cohering,
The head well-grown proportion'd and plumb, and the bowels and joints proportion'd and plumb.

The soul is always beautiful,
The universe is duly in order, every thing is in its place,
What has arrived is in its place and what waits shall be in its place,
The twisted skull waits, the watery or rotten blood waits,
The child of the glutton or venerealee waits long, and the child of the drunkard waits long, and the drunkard himself waits long,
The sleepers that lived and died wait, the far advanced are to go on in their turns, and the far behind are to come on in their turns,
The diverse shall be no less diverse, but they shall flow and unite—they unite now.

8

The sleepers are very beautiful as they lie unclothed,
They flow hand in hand over the whole earth from east to west as they lie unclothed,
The Asiatic and African are hand in hand, the European and American are hand in hand,
Learn'd and unlearn'd are hand in hand, and male and female are hand in hand,
The bare arm of the girl crosses the bare breast of her lover, they press close without lust, his lips press her neck,
The father holds his grown or ungrown son in his arms with measureless love, and the son holds the father in his arms with measureless love,
The white hair of the mother shines on the white wrist of the daughter,
The breath of the boy goes with the breath of the man, friend is inarm'd by friend,
The scholar kisses the teacher and the teacher kisses the scholar, the wrong'd is made right,
The call of the slave is one with the master's call, and the master salutes the slave,
The felon steps forth from the prison, the insane becomes sane, the suffering of sick persons is reliev'd,
The sweatings and fevers stop, the throat that was unsound is sound, the lungs of the consumptive are resumed, the poor distress'd head is free,
The joints of the rheumatic move as smoothly as ever, and smoother than ever,
Stiflings and passages open, the paralyzed become supple,
The swell'd and convuls'd and congested awake to themselves in condition,
They pass the invigoration of the night and the chemistry of the night, and awake.

I too pass from the night,
I stay a while away O night, but I return to you again and love you.

Why should I be afraid to trust myself to you?
I am not afraid, I have been well brought forward by you,

I love the rich running day, but I do not desert her in
whom I lay so long,
I know not how I came of you and I know not where I go
with you, but I know I came well and shall go well.

I will stop only a time with the night, and rise betimes,
I will duly pass the day O my mother, and duly return to you.

Transpositions

Let the reformers descend from the stands where they are
forever bawling—let an idiot or insane person appear
on each of the stands;
Let judges and criminals be transposed—let the prison-
keepers be put in prison—let those that were prisoners
take the keys;
Let them that distrust birth and death lead the rest.

To Think of Time

I

To think of time—of all that retrospection,
To think of to-day, and the ages continued henceforward.

Have you guess'd you yourself would not continue?
Have you dreaded these earth-beetles?
Have you fear'd the future would be nothing to you?

Is to-day nothing? is the beginningless past nothing?
If the future is nothing they are just as surely nothing.

To think that the sun rose in the east—that men and
women were flexible, real, alive—that every thing was
alive,
To think that you and I did not see, feel, think, nor bear
our part,
To think that we are now here and bear our part.

2

Not a day passes, not a minute or second without an accouchement,
Not a day passes, not a minute or second without a corpse.

The dull nights go over and the dull days also,
The soreness of lying so much in bed goes over,
The physician after long putting off gives the silent and terrible look for an answer,
The children come hurried and weeping, and the brothers and sisters are sent for,
Medicines stand unused on the shelf, (the camphor-smell has long pervaded the rooms,)
The faithful hand of the living does not desert the hand of the dying,
The twitching lips press lightly on the forehead of the dying,
The breath ceases and the pulse of the heart ceases,
The corpse stretches on the bed and the living look upon it,
It is palpable as the living are palpable.

The living look upon the corpse with their eyesight,
But without eyesight lingers a different living and looks curiously on the corpse.

3

To think the thought of death merged in the thought of materials,
To think of all these wonders of city and country, and others taking great interest in them, and we taking no interest in them.

To think how eager we are in building our houses,
To think others shall be just as eager, and we quite indifferent.

(I see one building the house that serves him a few years, or seventy or eighty years at most,
I see one building the house that serves him longer than that.)

Slow-moving and black lines creep over the whole earth—
they never cease—they are the burial lines,
He that was President was buried, and he that is now
President shall surely be buried.

4

A reminiscence of the vulgar fate,
A frequent sample of the life and death of workmen,
Each after his kind.

Cold dash of waves at the ferry-wharf, posh and ice in the
river, half-frozen mud in the streets,
A gray discouraged sky overhead, the short last daylight of
December,
A hearse and stages, the funeral of an old Broadway stage-
driver, the cortege mostly drivers.

Steady the trot to the cemetery, duly rattles the death-bell,
The gate is pass'd, the new-dug grave is halted at, the living
alight, the hearse uncloses,
The coffin is pass'd out, lower'd and settled, the whip is laid
on the coffin, the earth is swiftly shovel'd in,
The mound above is flatted with the spades—silence,
A minute—no one moves or speaks—it is done,
He is decently put away—is there any thing more?

He was a good fellow, free-mouth'd, quick-temper'd, not
bad-looking,
Ready with life or death for a friend, fond of women,
gambled, ate hearty, drank hearty,
Had known what it was to be flush, grew low-spirited
toward the last, sicken'd, was help'd by a contribution,
Died, aged forty-one years—and that was his funeral.

Thumb extended, finger uplifted, apron, cape, gloves, strap,
wet-weather clothes, whip carefully chosen,
Boss, spotter, starter, hostler, somebody loafing on you, you
loafing on somebody, headway, man before and man
behind,

Good day's work, bad day's work, pet stock, mean stock, first out, last out, turning-in at night,
To think that these are so much and so nigh to other drivers, and he there takes no interest in them.

5

The markets, the government, the working-man's wages, to think what account they are through our nights and days,
To think that other working-men will make just as great account of them, yet we make little or no account.

The vulgar and the refined, what you call sin and what you call goodness, to think how wide a difference,
To think the difference will still continue to others, yet we lie beyond the difference.

To think how much pleasure there is,
Do you enjoy yourself in the city? or engaged in business? or planning a nomination and election? or with your wife and family?
Or with your mother and sisters? or in womanly housework? or the beautiful maternal cares?
These also flow onward to others, you and I flow onward,
But in due time you and I shall take less interest in them.

Your farm, profits, crops—to think how engross'd you are,
To think there will still be farms, profits, crops, yet for you of what avail?

6

What will be will be well, for what is is well,
To take interest is well, and not to take interest shall be well.

The domestic joys, the daily housework or business, the building of houses, are not phantasms, they have weight, form, location,
Farms, profits, crops, markets, wages, government, are none of them phantasms,
The difference between sin and goodness is no delusion,
The earth is not an echo, man and his life and all the things of his life are well-consider'd.

You are not thrown to the winds, you gather certainly and
safely around yourself,
Yourself! yourself! yourself, for ever and ever!

7

It is not to diffuse you that you were born of your mother
and father, it is to identify you,
It is not that you should be undecided, but that you should
be decided,
Something long preparing and formless is arrived and
form'd in you,
You are henceforth secure, whatever comes or goes.

The threads that were spun are gather'd, the weft crosses
the warp, the pattern is systematic.

The preparations have every one been justified,
The orchestra have sufficiently tuned their instruments, the
baton has given the signal.

The guest that was coming, he waited long, he is now housed,
He is one of those who are beautiful and happy, he is one
of those that to look upon and be with is enough.

The law of the past cannot be eluded,
The law of the present and future cannot be eluded,
The law of the living cannot be eluded, it is eternal,
The law of promotion and transformation cannot be eluded,
The law of heroes and good-doers cannot be eluded,
The law of drunkards, informers, mean persons, not one
iota thereof can be eluded.

8

Slow moving and black lines go ceaselessly over the earth,
Northerner goes carried and Southerner goes carried, and
they on the Atlantic side and they on the Pacific,
And they between, and all through the Mississippi country,
and all over the earth.

The great masters and kosmos are well as they go, the
heroes and good-doers are well,

The known leaders and inventors and the rich owners and
pious and distinguish'd may be well,
But there is more account than that, there is strict account
of all.

The interminable hordes of the ignorant and wicked are not
nothing,
The barbarians of Africa and Asia are not nothing,
The perpetual successions of shallow people are not nothing
as they go.

Of and in all these things,
I have dream'd that we are not to be changed so much, nor
the law of us changed,
I have dream'd that heroes and good-doers shall be under
the present and past law,
And that murderers, drunkards, liars, shall be under the
present and past law,
For I have dream'd that the law they are under now is
enough.

And I have dream'd that the purpose and essence of the
known life, the transient,
Is to form and decide identity for the unknown life, the
permanent.

If all came but to ashes of dung,
If maggots and rats ended us, then Alarum! for we are
betray'd,
Then indeed suspicion of death.

Do you suspect death? if I were to suspect death I should
die now,
Do you think I could walk pleasantly and well-suited toward
annihilation?

Pleasantly and well-suited I walk,
Whither I walk I cannot define, but I know it is good,
The whole universe indicates that it is good,
The past and the present indicate that it is good.

How beautiful and perfect are the animals!
How perfect the earth, and the minutest thing upon it!
What is called good is perfect, and what is called bad is just
as perfect,
The vegetables and minerals are all perfect, and the
imponderable fluids perfect;
Slowly and surely they have pass'd on to this, and slowly
and surely they yet pass on.

9

I swear I think now that every thing without exception has
an eternal soul!
The trees have, rooted in the ground! the weeds of the sea
have! the animals!

I swear I think there is nothing but immortality!
That the exquisite scheme is for it, and the nebulous float is
for it, and the cohering is for it!
And all preparation is for it—and identity is for it—and life
and materials are altogether for it!

Whispers of Heavenly Death

Darest Thou Now O Soul

DAREST thou now O soul,
Walk out with me toward the unknown region,
Where neither ground is for the feet nor any path to follow?

No map there, nor guide,
Nor voice sounding, nor touch of human hand,
Nor face with blooming flesh, nor lips, nor eyes, are in that land.

I know it not O soul,
Nor dost thou, all is a blank before us,
All waits undream'd of in that region, that inaccessible land.

Till when the ties loosen,
All but the ties eternal, Time and Space,
Nor darkness, gravitation, sense, nor any bounds bounding us.

Then we burst forth, we float,
In Time and Space O soul, prepared for them,
Equal, equipt at last, (O joy! O fruit of all!) them to fulfil O soul.

Whispers of Heavenly Death

WHISPERS of heavenly death murmur'd I hear,
Labial gossip of night, sibilant chorals,
Footsteps gently ascending, mystical breezes wafted soft and low,
Ripples of unseen rivers, tides of a current flowing, forever flowing,
(Or is it the plashing of tears? the measureless waters of human tears?)

I see, just see skyward, great cloud-masses,
Mournfully slowly they roll, silently swelling and mixing,

With at times a half-dimm'd sadden'd far-off star,
Appearing and disappearing.

(Some parturition rather, some solemn immortal birth;
On the frontiers to eyes impenetrable,
Some soul is passing over.)

Chanting the Square Deific

1

CHANTING the square deific, out of the One advancing, out of the sides,
Out of the old and new, out of the square entirely divine,
Solid, four-sided, (all the sides needed,) from this side Jehovah am I,
Old Brahm I, and I Saturnius am;
Not Time affects me—I am Time, old, modern as any,
Unpersuadable, relentless, executing righteous judgments,
As the Earth, the Father, the brown old Kronos, with laws,
Aged beyond computation, yet ever new, ever with those mighty laws rolling,
Relentless I forgive no man—whoever sins dies—I will have that man's life;
Therefore let none expect mercy—have the seasons, gravitation, the appointed days, mercy? no more have I,
But as the seasons and gravitation, and as all the appointed days that forgive not,
I dispense from this side judgments inexorable without the least remorse.

2

Consolator most mild, the promis'd one advancing,
With gentle hand extended, the mightier God am I,
Foretold by prophets and poets in their most rapt prophecies and poems,
From this side, lo! the Lord Christ gazes—lo! Hermes I—lo! mine is Hercules' face,
All sorrow, labor, suffering, I, tallying it, absorb in myself,
Many times have I been rejected, taunted, put in prison, and crucified, and many times shall be again,

All the world have I given up for my dear brothers' and
sisters' sake, for the soul's sake,
Wending my way through the homes of men, rich or poor,
with the kiss of affection,
For I am affection, I am the cheer-bringing God, with hope
and all-enclosing charity,
With indulgent words as to children, with fresh and sane
words, mine only,
Young and strong I pass knowing well I am destin'd myself
to an early death;
But my charity has no death—my wisdom dies not, neither
early nor late,
And my sweet love bequeath'd here and elsewhere never dies.

3

Aloof, dissatisfied, plotting revolt,
Comrade of criminals, brother of slaves,
Crafty, despised, a drudge, ignorant,
With sudra face and worn brow, black, but in the depths of
my heart, proud as any,
Lifted now and always against whoever scorning assumes to
rule me,
Morose, full of guile, full of reminiscences, brooding, with
many wiles,
(Though it was thought I was baffled and dispel'd, and my
wiles done, but that will never be,)
Defiant, I, Satan, still live, still utter words, in new lands
duly appearing, (and old ones also,)
Permanent here from my side, warlike, equal with any, real
as any,
Nor time nor change shall ever change me or my words.

4

Santa Spirita, breather, life,
Beyond the light, lighter than light,
Beyond the flames of hell, joyous, leaping easily above hell,
Beyond Paradise, perfumed solely with mine own perfume,
Including all life on earth, touching, including God,
including Saviour and Satan,

Ethereal, pervading all, (for without me what were all? what
were God?)
Essence of forms, life of the real identities, permanent,
positive, (namely the unseen,)
Life of the great round world, the sun and stars, and of
man, I, the general soul,
Here the square finishing, the solid, I the most solid,
Breathe my breath also through these songs.

Of Him I Love Day and Night

Of him I love day and night I dream'd I heard he was dead,
And I dream'd I went where they had buried him I love,
but he was not in that place,
And I dream'd I wander'd searching among burial-places to
find him,
And I found that every place was a burial-place;
The houses full of life were equally full of death, (this house
is now,)
The streets, the shipping, the places of amusement, the
Chicago, Boston, Philadelphia, the Mannahatta, were as
full of the dead as of the living,
And fuller, O vastly fuller of the dead than of the living;
And what I dream'd I will henceforth tell to every person
and age,
And I stand henceforth bound to what I dream'd,
And now I am willing to disregard burial-places and
dispense with them,
And if the memorials of the dead were put up indifferently
everywhere, even in the room where I eat or sleep, I
should be satisfied,
And if the corpse of any one I love, or if my own corpse, be
duly render'd to powder and pour'd in the sea, I shall
be satisfied,
Or if it be distributed to the winds I shall be satisfied.

Yet, Yet, Ye Downcast Hours

Yet, yet, ye downcast hours, I know ye also,
Weights of lead, how ye clog and cling at my ankles,

Earth to a chamber of mourning turns—I hear the
o'erweening, mocking voice,
Matter is conqueror—matter, triumphant only, continues onward.

Despairing cries float ceaselessly toward me,
The call of my nearest lover, putting forth, alarm'd, uncertain,
The sea I am quickly to sail, come tell me,
Come tell me where I am speeding, tell me my destination.

I understand your anguish, but I cannot help you,
I approach, hear, behold, the sad mouth, the look out of
the eyes, your mute inquiry,
Whither I go from the bed I recline on, come tell me;
Old age, alarm'd, uncertain—a young woman's voice,
appealing to me for comfort;
A young man's voice, *Shall I not escape?*

As If a Phantom Caress'd Me

As if a phantom caress'd me,
I thought I was not alone walking here by the shore;
But the one I thought was with me as now I walk by the
shore, the one I loved that caress'd me,
As I lean and look through the glimmering light, that one
has utterly disappear'd,
And those appear that are hateful to me and mock me.

Assurances

I NEED no assurances, I am a man who is pre-occupied of
his own soul;
I do not doubt that from under the feet and beside the
hands and face I am cognizant of, are now looking
faces I am not cognizant of, calm and actual faces,
I do not doubt but the majesty and beauty of the world are
latent in any iota of the world,
I do not doubt I am limitless, and that the universes are
limitless, in vain I try to think how limitless,
I do not doubt that the orbs and the systems of orbs play
their swift sports through the air on purpose, and that I

shall one day be eligible to do as much as they, and more than they,
I do not doubt that temporary affairs keep on and on millions of years,
I do not doubt interiors have their interiors, and exteriors have their exteriors, and that the eyesight has another eyesight, and the hearing another hearing, and the voice another voice,
I do not doubt that the passionately-wept deaths of young men are provided for, and that the deaths of young women and the deaths of little children are provided for,
(Did you think Life was so well provided for, and Death, the purport of all Life, is not well provided for?)
I do not doubt that wrecks at sea, no matter what the horrors of them, no matter whose wife, child, husband, father, lover, has gone down, are provided for, to the minutest points,
I do not doubt that whatever can possibly happen anywhere at any time, is provided for in the inherences of things,
I do not think Life provides for all and for Time and Space, but I believe Heavenly Death provides for all.

Quicksand Years

QUICKSAND years that whirl me I know not whither,
Your schemes, politics, fail, lines give way, substances mock and elude me,
Only the theme I sing, the great and strong-possess'd soul, eludes not,
One's-self must never give way—that is the final substance—that out of all is sure,
Out of politics, triumphs, battles, life, what at last finally remains?
When shows break up what but One's-Self is sure?

That Music Always Round Me

THAT music always round me, unceasing, unbeginning, yet long untaught I did not hear,

But now the chorus I hear and am elated,
A tenor, strong, ascending with power and health, with glad notes of daybreak I hear,
A soprano at intervals sailing buoyantly over the tops of immense waves,
A transparent base shuddering lusciously under and through the universe,
The triumphant tutti, the funeral wailings with sweet flutes and violins, all these I fill myself with,
I hear not the volumes of sound merely, I am moved by the exquisite meanings,
I listen to the different voices winding in and out, striving, contending with fiery vehemence to excel each other in emotion;
I do not think the performers know themselves—but now I think I begin to know them.

What Ship Puzzled at Sea

WHAT ship puzzled at sea, cons for the true reckoning?
Or coming in, to avoid the bars and follow the channel a perfect pilot needs?
Here, sailor! here, ship! take aboard the most perfect pilot,
Whom, in a little boat, putting off and rowing, I hailing you offer.

A Noiseless Patient Spider

A NOISELESS patient spider,
I mark'd where on a little promontory it stood isolated,
Mark'd how to explore the vacant vast surrounding,
It launch'd forth filament, filament, filament, out of itself,
Ever unreeling them, ever tirelessly speeding them.

And you O my soul where you stand,
Surrounded, detached, in measureless oceans of space,
Ceaselessly musing, venturing, throwing, seeking the spheres to connect them,
Till the bridge you will need be form'd, till the ductile anchor hold,

Till the gossamer thread you fling catch somewhere, O my soul.

O Living Always, Always Dying

O LIVING always, always dying!
O the burials of me past and present,
O me while I stride ahead, material, visible, imperious as ever;
O me, what I was for years, now dead, (I lament not, I am content;)
O to disengage myself from those corpses of me, which I turn and look at where I cast them,
To pass on, (O living! always living!) and leave the corpses behind.

To One Shortly to Die

FROM all the rest I single out you, having a message for you,
You are to die—let others tell you what they please, I cannot prevaricate,
I am exact and merciless, but I love you—there is no escape for you.

Softly I lay my right hand upon you, you just feel it,
I do not argue, I bend my head close and half envelop it,
I sit quietly by, I remain faithful,
I am more than nurse, more than parent or neighbor,
I absolve you from all except yourself spiritual bodily, that is eternal, you yourself will surely escape,
The corpse you will leave will be but excrementitious.

The sun bursts through in unlooked-for directions,
Strong thoughts fill you and confidence, you smile,
You forget you are sick, as I forget you are sick,
You do not see the medicines, you do not mind the weeping friends, I am with you,
I exclude others from you, there is nothing to be commiserated,
I do not commiserate, I congratulate you.

Night on the Prairies

NIGHT on the prairies,
The supper is over, the fire on the ground burns low,
The wearied emigrants sleep, wrapt in their blankets;
I walk by myself—I stand and look at the stars, which I
think now I never realized before.

Now I absorb immortality and peace,
I admire death and test propositions.

How plenteous! how spiritual! how resumé!
The same old man and soul—the same old aspirations, and
the same content.

I was thinking the day most splendid till I saw what the
not-day exhibited,
I was thinking this globe enough till there sprang out so
noiseless around me myriads of other globes.

Now while the great thoughts of space and eternity fill me I
will measure myself by them,
And now touch'd with the lives of other globes arrived as
far along as those of the earth,
Or waiting to arrive, or pass'd on farther than those of the
earth,
I henceforth no more ignore them than I ignore my own life,
Or the lives of the earth arrived as far as mine, or waiting to
arrive.

O I see now that life cannot exhibit all to me, as the day
cannot,
I see that I am to wait for what will be exhibited by death.

Thought

As I sit with others at a great feast, suddenly while the
music is playing,
To my mind, (whence it comes I know not,) spectral in
mist of a wreck at sea,

Of certain ships, how they sail from port with flying
streamers and wafted kisses, and that is the last of them,
Of the solemn and murky mystery about the fate of the
President,
Of the flower of the marine science of fifty generations
founder'd off the Northeast coast and going down—of
the steamship Arctic going down,
Of the veil'd tableau—women gather'd together on deck,
pale, heroic, waiting the moment that draws so close—
O the moment!
A huge sob—a few bubbles—the white foam spirting up—
and then the women gone,
Sinking there while the passionless wet flows on—and I now
pondering, Are those women indeed gone?
Are souls drown'd and destroy'd so?
Is only matter triumphant?

The Last Invocation

At the last, tenderly,
From the walls of the powerful fortress'd house,
From the clasp of the knitted locks, from the keep of the
well-closed doors,
Let me be wafted.

Let me glide noiselessly forth;
With the key of softness unlock the locks—with a whisper,
Set ope the doors O soul.

Tenderly—be not impatient,
(Strong is your hold O mortal flesh,
Strong is your hold O love.)

As I Watch'd the Ploughman Ploughing

As I watch'd the ploughman ploughing,
Or the sower sowing in the fields, or the harvester harvesting,
I saw there too, O life and death, your analogies;
(Life, life is the tillage, and Death is the harvest according.)

Pensive and Faltering

PENSIVE and faltering,
The words *the Dead* I write,
For living are the Dead,
(Haply the only living, only real,
And I the apparition, I the spectre.)

THOU MOTHER WITH THY EQUAL BROOD

1

THOU Mother with thy equal brood,
Thou varied chain of different States, yet one identity only,
A special song before I go I'd sing o'er all the rest,
For thee, the future.

I'd sow a seed for thee of endless Nationality,
I'd fashion thy ensemble including body and soul,
I'd show away ahead thy real Union, and how it may be
accomplish'd.

The paths to the house I seek to make,
But leave to those to come the house itself.

Belief I sing, and preparation;
As Life and Nature are not great with reference to the
present only,
But greater still from what is yet to come,
Out of that formula for thee I sing.

2

As a strong bird on pinions free,
Joyous, the amplest spaces heavenward cleaving,
Such be the thought I'd think of thee America,
Such be the recitative I'd bring for thee.

The conceits of the poets of other lands I'd bring thee not,
Nor the compliments that have served their turn so long,

Nor rhyme, nor the classics, nor perfume of foreign court or indoor library;
But an odor I'd bring as from forests of pine in Maine, or breath of an Illinois prairie,
With open airs of Virginia or Georgia or Tennessee, or from Texas uplands, or Florida's glades,
Or the Saguenay's black stream, or the wide blue spread of Huron,
With presentment of Yellowstone's scenes, or Yosemite,
And murmuring under, pervading all, I'd bring the rustling sea-sound,
That endlessly sounds from the two Great Seas of the world.

And for thy subtler sense subtler refrains dread Mother,
Preludes of intellect tallying these and thee, mind-formulas fitted for thee, real and sane and large as these and thee,
Thou! mounting higher, diving deeper than we knew, thou transcendental Union!
By thee fact to be justified, blended with thought,
Thought of man justified, blended with God,
Through thy idea, lo, the immortal reality!
Through thy reality, lo, the immortal idea!

3

Brain of the New World, what a task is thine,
To formulate the Modern—out of the peerless grandeur of the modern,
Out of thyself, comprising science, to recast poems, churches, art,
(Recast, may-be discard them, end them—may-be their work is done, who knows?)
By vision, hand, conception, on the background of the mighty past, the dead,
To limn with absolute faith the mighty living present.

And yet thou living present brain, heir of the dead, the Old World brain,
Thou that lay folded like an unborn babe within its folds so long,

Thou carefully prepared by it so long—haply thou but
unfoldest it, only maturest it,
It to eventuate in thee—the essence of the by-gone time
contain'd in thee,
Its poems, churches, arts, unwitting to themselves, destined
with reference to thee;
Thou but the apples, long, long, long a-growing,
The fruit of all the Old ripening to-day in thee.

4

Sail, sail thy best, ship of Democracy,
Of value is thy freight, 'tis not the Present only,
The Past is also stored in thee,
Thou holdest not the venture of thyself alone, not of the
Western continent alone,
Earth's *résumé* entire floats on thy keel O ship, is steadied
by thy spars,
With thee Time voyages in trust, the antecedent nations sink
or swim with thee,
With all their ancient struggles, martyrs, heroes, epics, wars,
thou bear'st the other continents,
Theirs, theirs as much as thine, the destination-port
triumphant;
Steer then with good strong hand and wary eye O
helmsman, thou carriest great companions,
Venerable priestly Asia sails this day with thee,
And royal feudal Europe sails with thee.

5

Beautiful world of new superber birth that rises to my eyes,
Like a limitless golden cloud filling the western sky,
Emblem of general maternity lifted above all,
Sacred shape of the bearer of daughters and sons,
Out of thy teeming womb thy giant babes in ceaseless
procession issuing,
Acceding from such gestation, taking and giving continual
strength and life,
World of the real—world of the twain in one,
World of the soul, born by the world of the real alone, led
to identity, body, by it alone,

Yet in beginning only, incalculable masses of composite
precious materials,
By history's cycles forwarded, by every nation, language,
hither sent,
Ready, collected here, a freer, vast, electric world, to be
constructed here,
(The true New World, the world of orbic science, morals,
literatures to come,)
Thou wonder world yet undefined, unform'd, neither do I
define thee,
How can I pierce the impenetrable blank of the future?
I feel thy ominous greatness evil as well as good,
I watch thee advancing, absorbing the present, transcending
the past,
I see thy light lighting, and thy shadow shadowing, as if the
entire globe,
But I do not undertake to define thee, hardly to
comprehend thee,
I but thee name, thee prophesy, as now,
I merely thee ejaculate!

Thee in thy future,
Thee in thy only permanent life, career, thy own unloosen'd
mind, thy soaring spirit,
Thee as another equally needed sun, radiant, ablaze, swift-
moving, fructifying all,
Thee risen in potent cheerfulness and joy, in endless great
hilarity,
Scattering for good the cloud that hung so long, that
weigh'd so long upon the mind of man,
The doubt, suspicion, dread, of gradual, certain decadence
of man;
Thee in thy larger, saner brood of female, male—thee in thy
athletes, moral, spiritual, South, North, West, East,
(To thy immortal breasts, Mother of All, thy every
daughter, son, endear'd alike, forever equal,)
Thee in thy own musicians, singers, artists, unborn yet, but
certain,
Thee in thy moral wealth and civilization, (until which thy
proudest material civilization must remain in vain,)

Thee in thy all-supplying, all-enclosing worship—thee in no single bible, saviour, merely,
Thy saviours countless, latent within thyself, thy bibles incessant within thyself, equal to any, divine as any,
(Thy soaring course thee formulating, not in thy two great wars, nor in thy century's visible growth,
But far more in these leaves and chants, thy chants, great Mother!)
Thee in an education grown of thee, in teachers, studies, students, born of thee,
Thee in thy democratic fêtes en-masse, thy high original festivals, operas, lecturers, preachers,
Thee in thy ultimata, (the preparations only now completed, the edifice on sure foundations tied,)
Thee in thy pinnacles, intellect, thought, thy topmost rational joys, thy love and godlike aspiration,
In thy resplendent coming literati, thy full-lung'd orators, thy sacerdotal bards, kosmic savans,
These! these in thee, (certain to come,) to-day I prophesy.

6

Land tolerating all, accepting all, not for the good alone, all good for thee,
Land in the realms of God to be a realm unto thyself,
Under the rule of God to be a rule unto thyself.

(Lo, where arise three peerless stars,
To be thy natal stars my country, Ensemble, Evolution, Freedom,
Set in the sky of Law.)

Land of unprecedented faith, God's faith,
Thy soil, thy very subsoil, all upheav'd,
The general inner earth so long so sedulously draped over, now hence for what it is boldly laid bare,
Open'd by thee to heaven's light for benefit or bale.

Not for success alone,
Not to fair-sail unintermitted always,

The storm shall dash thy face, the murk of war and worse
than war shall cover thee all over,
(Wert capable of war, its tug and trials? be capable of peace,
its trials,
For the tug and mortal strain of nations come at last in
prosperous peace, not war;)
In many a smiling mask death shall approach beguiling thee,
thou in disease shalt swelter,
The livid cancer spread its hideous claws, clinging upon thy
breasts, seeking to strike thee deep within,
Consumption of the worst, moral consumption, shall rouge
thy face with hectic,
But thou shalt face thy fortunes, thy diseases, and surmount
them all,
Whatever they are to-day and whatever through time they
may be,
They each and all shall lift and pass away and cease from
thee,
While thou, Time's spirals rounding, out of thyself, thyself
still extricating, fusing,
Equable, natural, mystical Union thou, (the mortal with
immortal blent,)
Shalt soar toward the fulfilment of the future, the spirit of
the body and the mind,
The soul, its destinies.

The soul, its destinies, the real real,
(Purport of all these apparitions of the real;)
In thee America, the soul, its destinies,
Thou globe of globes! thou wonder nebulous!
By many a throe of heat and cold convuls'd, (by these
thyself solidifying,)
Thou mental, moral orb—thou New, indeed new, Spiritual
World!
The Present holds thee not—for such vast growth as thine,
For such unparallel'd flight as thine, such brood as thine,
The FUTURE only holds thee and can hold thee.

A Paumanok Picture

Two boats with nets lying off the sea-beach, quite still,
Ten fishermen waiting—they discover a thick school of
mossbonkers—they drop the join'd seine-ends in the
water,
The boats separate and row off, each on its rounding course
to the beach, enclosing the mossbonkers,
The net is drawn in by a windlass by those who stop ashore,
Some of the fishermen lounge in their boats, others stand
ankle-deep in the water, pois'd on strong legs,
The boats partly drawn up, the water slapping against them,
Strew'd on the sand in heaps and windrows, well out from
the water, the green-back'd spotted mossbonkers.

From Noon to Starry Night

Thou Orb Aloft Full-Dazzling

THOU orb aloft full-dazzling! thou hot October noon!
Flooding with sheeny light the gray beach sand,
The sibilant near sea with vistas far and foam,
And tawny streaks and shades and spreading blue;
O sun of noon refulgent! my special word to thee.

Hear me illustrious!
Thy lover me, for always I have loved thee,
Even as basking babe, then happy boy alone by some wood
    edge, thy touching-distant beams enough,
Or man matured, or young or old, as now to thee I launch
    my invocation.

(Thou canst not with thy dumbness me deceive,
I know before the fitting man all Nature yields,
Though answering not in words, the skies, trees, hear his
    voice—and thou O sun,
As for thy throes, thy perturbations, sudden breaks and
    shafts of flame gigantic,
I understand them, I know those flames, those perturbations
    well.)

Thou that with fructifying heat and light,
O'er myriad farms, o'er lands and waters North and South,
O'er Mississippi's endless course, o'er Texas' grassy plains,
    Kanada's woods,
O'er all the globe that turns its face to thee shining in space,
Thou that impartially infoldest all, not only continents, seas,
Thou that to grapes and weeds and little wild flowers givest
    so liberally,
Shed, shed thyself on mine and me, with but a fleeting ray
    out of thy million millions,
Strike through these chants.

Nor only launch thy subtle dazzle and thy strength for these,
Prepare the later afternoon of me myself—prepare my
lengthening shadows,
Prepare my starry nights.

Faces

1

SAUNTERING the pavement or riding the country by-road,
lo, such faces!
Faces of friendship, precision, caution, suavity, ideality,
The spiritual-prescient face, the always welcome common
benevolent face,
The face of the singing of music, the grand faces of natural
lawyers and judges broad at the back-top,
The faces of hunters and fishers bulged at the brows, the
shaved blanch'd faces of orthodox citizens,
The pure, extravagant, yearning, questioning artist's face,
The ugly face of some beautiful soul, the handsome detested
or despised face,
The sacred faces of infants, the illuminated face of the
mother of many children,
The face of an amour, the face of veneration,
The face as of a dream, the face of an immobile rock,
The face withdrawn of its good and bad, a castrated face,
A wild hawk, his wings clipp'd by the clipper,
A stallion that yielded at last to the thongs and knife of the
gelder.

Sauntering the pavement thus, or crossing the ceaseless
ferry, faces and faces and faces,
I see them and complain not, and am content with all.

2

Do you suppose I could be content with all if I thought
them their own finalè?

This now is too lamentable a face for a man,
Some abject louse asking leave to be, cringing for it,
Some milk-nosed maggot blessing what lets it wrig to its hole.

This face is a dog's snout sniffing for garbage,
Snakes nest in that mouth, I hear the sibilant threat.

This face is a haze more chill than the arctic sea,
Its sleepy and wabbling icebergs crunch as they go.

This is a face of bitter herbs, this an emetic, they need no
label,
And more of the drug-shelf, laudanum, caoutchouc, or
hog's-lard.

This face is an epilepsy, its wordless tongue gives out the
unearthly cry,
Its veins down the neck distend, its eyes roll till they show
nothing but their whites,
Its teeth grit, the palms of the hands are cut by the turn'd-
in nails,
The man falls struggling and foaming to the ground, while
he speculates well.

This face is bitten by vermin and worms,
And this is some murderer's knife with a half-pull'd scabbard.

This face owes to the sexton his dismalest fee,
An unceasing death-bell tolls there.

3

Features of my equals would you trick me with your creas'd
and cadaverous march?
Well, you cannot trick me.

I see your rounded never-erased flow,
I see 'neath the rims of your haggard and mean disguises.

Splay and twist as you like, poke with the tangling fores of
fishes or rats,
You'll be unmuzzled, you certainly will.

I saw the face of the most smear'd and slobbering idiot they
had at the asylum,

And I knew for my consolation what they knew not,
I knew of the agents that emptied and broke my brother,
The same wait to clear the rubbish from the fallen tenement,
And I shall look again in a score or two of ages,
And I shall meet the real landlord perfect and unharm'd,
every inch as good as myself.

4

The Lord advances, and yet advances,
Always the shadow in front, always the reach'd hand
bringing up the laggards.

Out of this face emerge banners and horses—O superb! I
see what is coming,
I see the high pioneer-caps, see staves of runners clearing
the way,
I hear victorious drums.

This face is a life-boat,
This is the face commanding and bearded, it asks no odds
of the rest,
This face is flavor'd fruit ready for eating,
This face of a healthy honest boy is the programme of all good.

These faces bear testimony slumbering or awake,
They show their descent from the Master himself.

Off the word I have spoken I except not one—red, white,
black, are all deific,
In each house is the ovum, it comes forth after a thousand
years.

Spots or cracks at the windows do not disturb me,
Tall and sufficient stand behind and make signs to me,
I read the promise and patiently wait.

This is a full-grown lily's face,
She speaks to the limber-hipp'd man near the garden pickets,
Come here she blushingly cries, *Come nigh to me limber-
hipp'd man,*

Stand at my side till I lean as high as I can upon you,
Fill me with albescent honey, bend down to me,
Rub to me with your chafing beard, rub to my breast and shoulders.

5

The old face of the mother of many children,
Whist! I am fully content.

Lull'd and late is the smoke of the First-day morning,
It hangs low over the rows of trees by the fences,
It hangs thin by the sassafras and wild-cherry and cat-brier under them.

I saw the rich ladies in full dress at the soiree,
I heard what the singers were singing so long,
Heard who sprang in crimson youth from the white froth and the water-blue.

Behold a woman!
She looks out from her quaker cap, her face is clearer and more beautiful than the sky.

She sits in an armchair under the shaded porch of the farmhouse,
The sun just shines on her old white head.

Her ample gown is of cream-hued linen,
Her grandsons raised the flax, and her grand-daughters spun it with the distaff and the wheel.

The melodious character of the earth,
The finish beyond which philosophy cannot go and does not wish to go,
The justified mother of men.

The Mystic Trumpeter

1

HARK, some wild trumpeter, some strange musician,
Hovering unseen in air, vibrates capricious tunes to-night.

I hear thee trumpeter, listening alert I catch thy notes,
Now pouring, whirling like a tempest round me,
Now low, subdued, now in the distance lost.

2

Come nearer bodiless one, haply in thee resounds
Some dead composer, haply thy pensive life
Was fill'd with aspirations high, unform'd ideals,
Waves, oceans musical, chaotically surging,
That now ecstatic ghost, close to me bending, thy cornet
echoing, pealing,
Gives out to no one's ears but mine, but freely gives to mine,
That I may thee translate.

3

Blow trumpeter free and clear, I follow thee,
While at thy liquid prelude, glad, serene,
The fretting world, the streets, the noisy hours of day
withdraw,
A holy calm descends like dew upon me,
I walk in cool refreshing night the walks of Paradise,
I scent the grass, the moist air and the roses;
Thy song expands my numb'd imbonded spirit, thou freest,
launchest me,
Floating and basking upon heaven's lake.

4

Blow again trumpeter! and for my sensuous eyes,
Bring the old pageants, show the feudal world.

What charm thy music works! thou makest pass before me,
Ladies and cavaliers long dead, barons are in their castle
halls, the troubadours are singing,
Arm'd knights go forth to redress wrongs, some in quest of
the holy Graal;
I see the tournament, I see the contestants incased in heavy
armor seated on stately champing horses,
I hear the shouts, the sounds of blows and smiting steel;
I see the Crusaders' tumultuous armies—hark, how the
cymbals clang,

Lo, where the monks walk in advance, bearing the cross on
high.

5

Blow again trumpeter! and for thy theme,
Take now the enclosing theme of all, the solvent and the
setting,
Love, that is pulse of all, the sustenance and the pang,
The heart of man and woman all for love,
No other theme but love—knitting, enclosing, all-diffusing
love.

O how the immortal phantoms crowd around me!
I see the vast alembic ever working, I see and know the
flames that heat the world,
The glow, the blush, the beating hearts of lovers,
So blissful happy some, and some so silent, dark, and nigh
to death;
Love, that is all the earth to lovers—love, that mocks time
and space,
Love, that is day and night—love, that is sun and moon and
stars,
Love, that is crimson, sumptuous, sick with perfume,
No other words but words of love, no other thought but love.

6

Blow again trumpeter—conjure war's alarums.

Swift to thy spell a shuddering hum like distant thunder rolls,
Lo, where the arm'd men hasten—lo, mid the clouds of
dust the glint of bayonets,
I see the grime-faced cannoneers, I mark the rosy flash amid
the smoke, I hear the cracking of the guns;
Nor war alone—thy fearful music-song, wild player, brings
every sight of fear,
The deeds of ruthless brigands, rapine, murder—I hear the
cries for help!
I see ships foundering at sea, I behold on deck and below
deck the terrible tableaus.

7

O trumpeter, methinks I am myself the instrument thou
playest,
Thou melt'st my heart, my brain—thou movest, drawest,
changest them at will;
And now thy sullen notes send darkness through me,
Thou takest away all cheering light, all hope,
I see the enslaved, the overthrown, the hurt, the opprest of
the whole earth,
I feel the measureless shame and humiliation of my race, it
becomes all mine,
Mine too the revenges of humanity, the wrongs of ages,
baffled feuds and hatreds,
Utter defeat upon me weighs—all lost—the foe victorious,
(Yet 'mid the ruins Pride colossal stands unshaken to the
last,
Endurance, resolution to the last.)

8

Now trumpeter for thy close,
Vouchsafe a higher strain than any yet,
Sing to my soul, renew its languishing faith and hope,
Rouse up my slow belief, give me some vision of the future,
Give me for once its prophecy and joy.

O glad, exulting, culminating song!
A vigor more than earth's is in thy notes,
Marches of victory—man disenthral'd—the conqueror at
last,
Hymns to the universal God from universal man—all joy!
A reborn race appears—a perfect world, all joy!
Women and men in wisdom innocence and health—all joy!
Riotous laughing bacchanals fill'd with joy!
War, sorrow, suffering gone—the rank earth purged—
nothing but joy left!
The ocean fill'd with joy—the atmosphere all joy!
Joy! joy! in freedom, worship, love! joy in the ecstasy of life!
Enough to merely be! enough to breathe!
Joy! joy! all over joy!

To a Locomotive in Winter

THEE for my recitative,
Thee in the driving storm even as now, the snow, the winter-day declining,
Thee in thy panoply, thy measur'd dual throbbing and thy beat convulsive,
Thy black cylindric body, golden brass and silvery steel,
Thy ponderous side-bars, parallel and connecting rods, gyrating, shuttling at thy sides,
Thy metrical, now swelling pant and roar, now tapering in the distance,
Thy great protruding head-light fix'd in front,
Thy long, pale, floating vapor-pennants, tinged with delicate purple,
The dense and murky clouds out-belching from thy smoke-stack,
Thy knitted frame, thy springs and valves, the tremulous twinkle of thy wheels,
Thy train of cars behind, obedient, merrily following,
Through gale or calm, now swift, now slack, yet steadily careering;
Type of the modern—emblem of motion and power—pulse of the continent,
For once come serve the Muse and merge in verse, even as here I see thee,
With storm and buffeting gusts of wind and falling snow,
By day thy warning ringing bell to sound its notes,
By night thy silent signal lamps to swing.

Fierce-throated beauty!
Roll through my chant with all thy lawless music, thy swinging lamps at night,
Thy madly-whistled laughter, echoing, rumbling like an earth-quake, rousing all,
Law of thyself complete, thine own track firmly holding,
(No sweetness debonair of tearful harp or glib piano thine,)
Thy trills of shrieks by rocks and hills return'd,
Launch'd o'er the prairies wide, across the lakes,
To the free skies unpent and glad and strong.

O Magnet-South

O MAGNET-SOUTH! O glistening perfumed South! my South!
O quick mettle, rich blood, impulse and love! good and evil! O all dear to me!
O dear to me my birth-things—all moving things and the trees where I was born—the grains, plants, rivers,
Dear to me my own slow sluggish rivers where they flow, distant, over flats of silvery sands or through swamps,
Dear to me the Roanoke, the Savannah, the Altamahaw, the Pedee, the Tombigbee, the Santee, the Coosa and the Sabine,
O pensive, far away wandering, I return with my soul to haunt their banks again,
Again in Florida I float on transparent lakes, I float on the Okeechobee, I cross the hummock-land or through pleasant openings or dense forests,
I see the parrots in the woods, I see the papaw-tree and the blossoming titi;
Again, sailing in my coaster on deck, I coast off Georgia, I coast up the Carolinas,
I see where the live-oak is growing, I see where the yellow-pine, the scented bay-tree, the lemon and orange, the cypress, the graceful palmetto,
I pass rude sea-headlands and enter Pamlico sound through an inlet, and dart my vision inland;
O the cotton plant! the growing fields of rice, sugar, hemp!
The cactus guarded with thorns, the laurel-tree with large white flowers,
The range afar, the richness and barrenness, the old woods charged with mistletoe and trailing moss,
The piney odor and the gloom, the awful natural stillness, (here in these dense swamps the freebooter carries his gun, and the fugitive has his conceal'd hut;)
O the strange fascination of these half-known half-impassable swamps, infested by reptiles, resounding with the bellow of the alligator, the sad noises of the night-owl and the wild-cat, and the whirr of the rattlesnake,

The mocking-bird, the American mimic, singing all the
forenoon, singing through the moon-lit night,
The humming-bird, the wild turkey, the raccoon, the
opossum;
A Kentucky corn-field, the tall, graceful, long-leav'd corn,
slender, flapping, bright green, with tassels, with
beautiful ears each well-sheath'd in its husk;
O my heart! O tender and fierce pangs, I can stand them
not, I will depart;
O to be a Virginian where I grew up! O to be a Carolinian!
O longings irrepressible! O I will go back to old Tennessee
and never wander more.

Mannahatta

I WAS asking for something specific and perfect for my city,
Whereupon lo! upsprang the aboriginal name.

Now I see what there is in a name, a word, liquid, sane,
unruly, musical, self-sufficient,
I see that the word of my city is that word from of old,
Because I see that word nested in nests of water-bays,
superb,
Rich, hemm'd thick all around with sailships and steamships,
an island sixteen miles long, solid-founded,
Numberless crowded streets, high growths of iron, slender,
strong, light, splendidly uprising toward clear skies,
Tides swift and ample, well-loved by me, toward sundown,
The flowing sea-currents, the little islands, larger adjoining
islands, the heights, the villas,
The countless masts, the white shore-steamers, the lighters,
the ferry-boats, the black sea-steamers well-model'd,
The down-town streets, the jobbers' houses of business, the
houses of business of the ship-merchants and money-
brokers, the river-streets,
Immigrants arriving, fifteen or twenty thousand in a week,
The carts hauling goods, the manly race of drivers of horses,
the brown-faced sailors,
The summer air, the bright sun shining, and the sailing
clouds aloft,

The winter snows, the sleigh-bells, the broken ice in the river, passing along up or down with the flood-tide or ebb-tide,
The mechanics of the city, the masters, well-form'd, beautiful-faced, looking you straight in the eyes,
Trottoirs throng'd, vehicles, Broadway, the women, the shops and shows,
A million people—manners free and superb—open voices—hospitality—the most courageous and friendly young men,
City of hurried and sparkling waters! city of spires and masts!
City nested in bays! my city!

All Is Truth

O ME, man of slack faith so long,
Standing aloof, denying portions so long,
Only aware to-day of compact all-diffused truth,
Discovering to-day there is no lie or form of lie, and can be none, but grows as inevitably upon itself as the truth does upon itself,
Or as any law of the earth or any natural production of the earth does.

(This is curious and may not be realized immediately, but it must be realized,
I feel in myself that I represent falsehoods equally with the rest,
And that the universe does.)

Where has fail'd a perfect return indifferent of lies or the truth?
Is it upon the ground, or in water or fire? or in the spirit of man? or in the meat and blood?

Meditating among liars and retreating sternly into myself, I see that there are really no liars or lies after all,
And that nothing fails its perfect return, and that what are called lies are perfect returns,
And that each thing exactly represents itself and what has preceded it,

And that the truth includes all, and is compact just as much
as space is compact,
And that there is no flaw or vacuum in the amount of the
truth—but that all is truth without exception;
And henceforth I will go celebrate any thing I see or am,
And sing and laugh and deny nothing.

A Riddle Song

THAT which eludes this verse and any verse,
Unheard by sharpest ear, unform'd in clearest eye or
cunningest mind,
Nor lore nor fame, nor happiness nor wealth,
And yet the pulse of every heart and life throughout the
world incessantly,
Which you and I and all pursuing ever ever miss,
Open but still a secret, the real of the real, an illusion,
Costless, vouchsafed to each, yet never man the owner,
Which poets vainly seek to put in rhyme, historians in prose,
Which sculptor never chisel'd yet, nor painter painted,
Which vocalist never sung, nor orator nor actor ever utter'd,
Invoking here and now I challenge for my song.

Indifferently, 'mid public, private haunts, in solitude,
Behind the mountain and the wood,
Companion of the city's busiest streets, through the
assemblage,
It and its radiations constantly glide.

In looks of fair unconscious babes,
Or strangely in the coffin'd dead,
Or show of breaking dawn or stars by night,
As some dissolving delicate film of dreams,
Hiding yet lingering.

Two little breaths of words comprising it,
Two words, yet all from first to last comprised in it.

How ardently for it!
How many ships have sail'd and sunk for it!

How many travelers started from their homes and ne'er
return'd!
How much of genius boldly staked and lost for it!
What countless stores of beauty, love, ventur'd for it!
How all superbest deeds since Time began are traceable to
it—and shall be to the end!
How all heroic martyrdoms to it!
How, justified by it, the horrors, evils, battles of the earth!
How the bright fascinating lambent flames of it, in every
age and land, have drawn men's eyes,
Rich as a sunset on the Norway coast, the sky, the islands,
and the cliffs,
Or midnight's silent glowing northern lights unreachable.

Haply God's riddle it, so vague and yet so certain,
The soul for it, and all the visible universe for it,
And heaven at last for it.

Excelsior

WHO has gone farthest? for I would go farther,
And who has been just? for I would be the most just person
of the earth,
And who most cautious? for I would be more cautious,
And who has been happiest? O I think it is I—I think no
one was ever happier than I,
And who has lavish'd all? for I lavish constantly the best I
have,
And who proudest? for I think I have reason to be the
proudest son alive—for I am the son of the brawny and
tall-topt city,
And who has been bold and true? for I would be the
boldest and truest being of the universe,
And who benevolent? for I would show more benevolence
than all the rest,
And who has receiv'd the love of the most friends? for I
know what it is to receive the passionate love of many
friends,
And who possesses a perfect and enamour'd body? for I do

not believe any one possesses a more perfect or
enamour'd body than mine,
And who thinks the amplest thoughts? for I would surround
those thoughts,
And who has made hymns fit for the earth? for I am mad
with devouring ecstasy to make joyous hymns for the
whole earth.

Ah Poverties, Wincings, and Sulky Retreats

AH poverties, wincings, and sulky retreats,
Ah you foes that in conflict have overcome me,
(For what is my life or any man's life but a conflict with
foes, the old, the incessant war?)
You degradations, you tussle with passions and appetites,
You smarts from dissatisfied friendships, (ah wounds the
sharpest of all!)
You toil of painful and choked articulations, you meannesses,
You shallow tongue-talks at tables, (my tongue the
shallowest of any;)
You broken resolutions, you racking angers, you smother'd
ennuis!
Ah think not you finally triumph, my real self has yet to
come forth,
It shall yet march forth o'ermastering, till all lies beneath me,
It shall yet stand up the soldier of ultimate victory.

Thoughts

OF public opinion,
Of a calm and cool fiat sooner or later, (how impassive! how
certain and final!)
Of the President with pale face asking secretly to himself,
What will the people say at last?
Of the frivolous Judge—of the corrupt Congressman,
Governor, Mayor—of such as these standing helpless
and exposed,
Of the mumbling and screaming priest, (soon, soon deserted,)
Of the lessening year by year of venerableness, and of the
dicta of officers, statutes, pulpits, schools,

Of the rising forever taller and stronger and broader of the intuitions of men and women, and of Self-esteem and Personality;
Of the true New World—of the Democracies resplendent en-masse,
Of the conformity of politics, armies, navies, to them,
Of the shining sun by them—of the inherent light, greater than the rest,
Of the envelopment of all by them, and the effusion of all from them.

Mediums

THEY shall arise in the States,
They shall report Nature, laws, physiology, and happiness,
They shall illustrate Democracy and the kosmos,
They shall be alimentive, amative, perceptive,
They shall be complete women and men, their pose brawny and supple, their drink water, their blood clean and clear,
They shall fully enjoy materialism and the sight of products, they shall enjoy the sight of the beef, lumber, bread-stuffs, of Chicago the great city,
They shall train themselves to go in public to become orators and oratresses,
Strong and sweet shall their tongues be, poems and materials of poems shall come from their lives, they shall be makers and finders,
Of them and of their works shall emerge divine conveyers, to convey gospels,
Characters, events, retrospections, shall be convey'd in gospels, trees, animals, waters, shall be convey'd,
Death, the future, the invisible faith, shall all be convey'd.

Weave in, My Hardy Life

WEAVE in, weave in, my hardy life,
Weave yet a soldier strong and full for great campaigns to come,

Weave in red blood, weave sinews in like ropes, the senses, sight weave in,
Weave lasting sure, weave day and night the weft, the warp, incessant weave, tire not,
(We know not what the use O life, nor know the aim, the end, nor really aught we know,
But know the work, the need goes on and shall go on, the death-envelop'd march of peace as well as war goes on,)
For great campaigns of peace the same the wiry threads to weave,
We know not why or what, yet weave, forever weave.

Spain, 1873–74

OUT of the murk of heaviest clouds,
Out of the feudal wrecks and heap'd-up skeletons of kings,
Out of that old entire European debris, the shatter'd mummeries,
Ruin'd cathedrals, crumble of palaces, tombs of priests,
Lo, Freedom's features fresh undimm'd look forth—the same immortal face looks forth;
(A glimpse as of thy Mother's face Columbia,
A flash significant as of a sword,
Beaming towards thee.)

Nor think we forget thee maternal;
Lag'd'st thou so long? shall the clouds close again upon thee?
Ah, but thou hast thyself now appear'd to us—we know thee,
Thou hast given us a sure proof, the glimpse of thyself,
Thou waitest there as everywhere thy time.

By Broad Potomac's Shore

BY broad Potomac's shore, again old tongue,
(Still uttering, still ejaculating, canst never cease this babble?)
Again old heart so gay, again to you, your sense, the full flush spring returning,
Again the freshness and the odors, again Virginia's summer sky, pellucid blue and silver,
Again the forenoon purple of the hills,

Again the deathless grass, so noiseless soft and green,
Again the blood-red roses blooming.

Perfume this book of mine O blood-red roses!
Lave subtly with your waters every line Potomac!
Give me of you O spring, before I close, to put between its pages!
O forenoon purple of the hills, before I close, of you!
O deathless grass, of you!

From Far Dakota's Cañons

June 25, 1876.

FROM far Dakota's cañons,
Lands of the wild ravine, the dusky Sioux, the lonesome stretch, the silence,
Haply to-day a mournful wail, haply a trumpet-note for heroes.

The battle-bulletin,
The Indian ambuscade, the craft, the fatal environment,
The cavalry companies fighting to the last in sternest heroism,
In the midst of their little circle, with their slaughter'd horses for breastworks,
The fall of Custer and all his officers and men.

Continues yet the old, old legend of our race,
The loftiest of life upheld by death,
The ancient banner perfectly maintain'd,
O lesson opportune, O how I welcome thee!

As sitting in dark days,
Lone, sulky, through the time's thick murk looking in vain for light, for hope,
From unsuspected parts a fierce and momentary proof,
(The sun there at the centre though conceal'd,
Electric life forever at the centre,)
Breaks forth a lightning flash.

Thou of the tawny flowing hair in battle,
I erewhile saw, with erect head, pressing ever in front,
bearing a bright sword in thy hand,
Now ending well in death the splendid fever of thy deeds,
(I bring no dirge for it or thee, I bring a glad triumphal
sonnet,)
Desperate and glorious, aye in defeat most desperate, most
glorious,
After thy many battles in which never yielding up a gun or a
color,
Leaving behind thee a memory sweet to soldiers,
Thou yieldest up thyself.

Old War-Dreams

In midnight sleep of many a face of anguish,
Of the look at first of the mortally wounded, (of that
indescribable look,)
Of the dead on their backs with arms extended wide,
I dream, I dream, I dream.

Of scenes of Nature, fields and mountains,
Of skies so beauteous after a storm, and at night the moon
so unearthly bright,
Shining sweetly, shining down, where we dig the trenches
and gather the heaps,
I dream, I dream, I dream.

Long have they pass'd, faces and trenches and fields,
Where through the carnage I moved with a callous
composure, or away from the fallen,
Onward I sped at the time—but now of their forms at
night,
I dream, I dream, I dream.

Thick-Sprinkled Bunting

Thick-sprinkled bunting! flag of stars!
Long yet your road, fateful flag—long yet your road, and
lined with bloody death,

For the prize I see at issue at last is the world,
All its ships and shores I see interwoven with your threads greedy banner;
Dream'd again the flags of kings, highest borne, to flaunt unrival'd?
O hasten flag of man—O with sure and steady step, passing highest flags of kings,
Walk supreme to the heavens mighty symbol—run up above them all,
Flag of stars! thick-sprinkled bunting!

What Best I See in Thee

To U. S. G. return'd from his World's Tour.

WHAT best I see in thee,
Is not that where thou mov'st down history's great highways,
Ever undimm'd by time shoots warlike victory's dazzle,
Or that thou sat'st where Washington sat, ruling the land in peace,
Or thou the man whom feudal Europe feted, venerable Asia swarm'd upon,
Who walk'd with kings with even pace the round world's promenade;
But that in foreign lands, in all thy walks with kings,
Those prairie sovereigns of the West, Kansas, Missouri, Illinois,
Ohio's, Indiana's millions, comrades, farmers, soldiers, all to the front,
Invisibly with thee walking with kings with even pace the round world's promenade,
Were all so justified.

Spirit That Form'd This Scene

Written in Platte Cañon, Colorado.

SPIRIT that form'd this scene,
These tumbled rock-piles grim and red,
These reckless heaven-ambitious peaks,
These gorges, turbulent-clear streams, this naked freshness,

These formless wild arrays, for reasons of their own,
I know thee, savage spirit—we have communed together,
Mine too such wild arrays, for reasons of their own;
Was't charged against my chants they had forgotten art?
To fuse within themselves its rules precise and delicatesse?
The lyrist's measur'd beat, the wrought-out temple's grace—
column and polish'd arch forgot?
But thou that revelest here—spirit that form'd this scene,
They have remember'd thee.

As I Walk These Broad Majestic Days

As I walk these broad majestic days of peace,
(For the war, the struggle of blood finish'd, wherein, O
terrific Ideal,
Against vast odds erewhile having gloriously won,
Now thou stridest on, yet perhaps in time toward denser wars,
Perhaps to engage in time in still more dreadful contests,
dangers,
Longer campaigns and crises, labors beyond all others,)
Around me I hear that eclat of the world, politics, produce,
The announcements of recognized things, science,
The approved growth of cities and the spread of inventions.

I see the ships, (they will last a few years,)
The vast factories with their foremen and workmen,
And hear the indorsement of all, and do not object to it.

But I too announce solid things,
Science, ships, politics, cities, factories, are not nothing,
Like a grand procession to music of distant bugles pouring,
triumphantly moving, and grander heaving in sight,
They stand for realities—all is as it should be.

Then my realities;
What else is so real as mine?
Libertad and the divine average, freedom to every slave on
the face of the earth,
The rapt promises and luminè of seers, the spiritual world,
these centuries-lasting songs,

And our visions, the visions of poets, the most solid
announcements of any.

A Clear Midnight

THIS is thy hour O Soul, thy free flight into the wordless,
Away from books, away from art, the day erased, the lesson
done,
Thee fully forth emerging, silent, gazing, pondering the
themes thou lovest best,
Night, sleep, death and the stars.

Songs of Parting

As the Time Draws Nigh

As the time draws nigh glooming a cloud,
A dread beyond of I know not what darkens me.

I shall go forth,
I shall traverse the States awhile, but I cannot tell whither
or how long,
Perhaps soon some day or night while I am singing my
voice will suddenly cease.

O book, O chants! must all then amount to but this?
Must we barely arrive at this beginning of us?—and yet it is
enough, O soul;
O soul, we have positively appear'd—that is enough.

Years of the Modern

YEARS of the modern! years of the unperform'd!
Your horizon rises, I see it parting away for more august
dramas,
I see not America only, not only Liberty's nation but other
nations preparing,
I see tremendous entrances and exits, new combinations, the
solidarity of races,
I see that force advancing with irresistible power on the
world's stage,
(Have the old forces, the old wars, played their parts? are
the acts suitable to them closed?)
I see Freedom, completely arm'd and victorious and very
haughty, with Law on one side and Peace on the other,
A stupendous trio all issuing forth against the idea of caste;
What historic denouements are these we so rapidly
approach?
I see men marching and countermarching by swift millions,
I see the frontiers and boundaries of the old aristocracies
broken,

I see the landmarks of European kings removed,
I see this day the People beginning their landmarks, (all
others give way;)
Never were such sharp questions ask'd as this day,
Never was average man, his soul, more energetic, more like
a God,
Lo, how he urges and urges, leaving the masses no rest!
His daring foot is on land and sea everywhere, he colonizes
the Pacific, the archipelagoes,
With the steamship, the electric telegraph, the newspaper,
the wholesale engines of war,
With these and the world-spreading factories he interlinks all
geography, all lands;
What whispers are these O lands, running ahead of you,
passing under the seas?
Are all nations communing? is there going to be but one
heart to the globe?
Is humanity forming en-masse? for lo, tyrants tremble,
crowns grow dim,
The earth, restive, confronts a new era, perhaps a general
divine war,
No one knows what will happen next, such portents fill the
days and nights;
Years prophetical! the space ahead as I walk, as I vainly try
to pierce it, is full of phantoms,
Unborn deeds, things soon to be, project their shapes
around me,
This incredible rush and heat, this strange ecstatic fever of
dreams O years!
Your dreams O years, how they penetrate through me! (I
know not whether I sleep or wake;)
The perform'd America and Europe grow dim, retiring in
shadow behind me,
The unperform'd, more gigantic than ever, advance, advance
upon me.

Ashes of Soldiers

ASHES of soldiers South or North,
As I muse retrospective murmuring a chant in thought,

The war resumes, again to my sense your shapes,
And again the advance of the armies.

Noiseless as mists and vapors,
From their graves in the trenches ascending,
From cemeteries all through Virginia and Tennessee,
From every point of the compass out of the countless
graves,
In wafted clouds, in myriads large, or squads of twos or
threes or single ones they come,
And silently gather round me.

Now sound no note O trumpeters,
Not at the head of my cavalry parading on spirited horses,
With sabres drawn and glistening, and carbines by their
thighs, (ah my brave horsemen!
My handsome tan-faced horsemen! what life, what joy and
pride,
With all the perils were yours.)

Nor you drummers, neither at reveillé at dawn,
Nor the long roll alarming the camp, nor even the muffled
beat for a burial,
Nothing from you this time O drummers bearing my
warlike drums.

But aside from these and the marts of wealth and the
crowded promenade,
Admitting around me comrades close unseen by the rest and
voiceless,
The slain elate and alive again, the dust and debris alive,
I chant this chant of my silent soul in the name of all dead
soldiers.

Faces so pale with wondrous eyes, very dear, gather closer yet,
Draw close, but speak not.

Phantoms of countless lost,
Invisible to the rest henceforth become my companions,
Follow me ever—desert me not while I live.

Sweet are the blooming cheeks of the living—sweet are the
musical voices sounding,
But sweet, ah sweet, are the dead with their silent eyes.

Dearest comrades, all is over and long gone,
But love is not over—and what love, O comrades!
Perfume from battle-fields rising, up from the fœtor arising.

Perfume therefore my chant, O love, immortal love,
Give me to bathe the memories of all dead soldiers,
Shroud them, embalm them, cover them all over with
tender pride.

Perfume all—make all wholesome,
Make these ashes to nourish and blossom,
O love, solve all, fructify all with the last chemistry.

Give me exhaustless, make me a fountain,
That I exhale love from me wherever I go like a moist
perennial dew,
For the ashes of all dead soldiers South or North.

Thoughts

1

Of these years I sing,
How they pass and have pass'd through convuls'd pains, as
through parturitions,
How America illustrates birth, muscular youth, the promise,
the sure fulfilment, the absolute success, despite of
people—illustrates evil as well as good,
The vehement struggle so fierce for unity in one's-self;
How many hold despairingly yet to the models departed,
caste, myths, obedience, compulsion, and to infidelity,
How few see the arrived models, the athletes, the Western
States, or see freedom or spirituality, or hold any faith
in results,
(But I see the athletes, and I see the results of the war
glorious and inevitable, and they again leading to other
results.)

How the great cities appear—how the Democratic masses,
turbulent, wilful, as I love them,
How the whirl, the contest, the wrestle of evil with good,
the sounding and resounding, keep on and on,
How society waits unform'd, and is for a while between
things ended and things begun,
How America is the continent of glories, and of the triumph
of freedom and of the Democracies, and of the fruits of
society, and of all that is begun,
And how the States are complete in themselves—and how
all triumphs and glories are complete in themselves, to
lead onward,
And how these of mine and of the States will in their turn
be convuls'd, and serve other parturitions and
transitions,
And how all people, sights, combinations, the democratic
masses too, serve—and how every fact, and war itself,
with all its horrors, serves,
And how now or at any time each serves the exquisite
transition of death.

2

Of seeds dropping into the ground, of births,
Of the steady concentration of America, inland, upward, to
impregnable and swarming places,
Of what Indiana, Kentucky, Arkansas, and the rest, are to be,
Of what a few years will show there in Nebraska, Colorado,
Nevada, and the rest,
(Or afar, mounting the Northern Pacific to Sitka or Aliaska,)
Of what the feuillage of America is the preparation for—
and of what all sights, North, South, East and West,
are,
Of this Union welded in blood, of the solemn price paid, of
the unnamed lost ever present in my mind;
Of the temporary use of materials for identity's sake,
Of the present, passing, departing—of the growth of
completer men than any yet,
Of all sloping down there where the fresh free giver the
mother, the Mississippi flows,
Of mighty inland cities yet unsurvey'd and unsuspected,

Of the new and good names, of the modern developments,
of inalienable homesteads,
Of a free and original life there, of simple diet and clean and
sweet blood,
Of litheness, majestic faces, clear eyes, and perfect physique
there,
Of immense spiritual results future years far West, each side
of the Anahuacs,
Of these songs, well understood there, (being made for that
area,)
Of the native scorn of grossness and gain there,
(O it lurks in me night and day—what is gain after all to
savageness and freedom?)

Song at Sunset

SPLENDOR of ended day floating and filling me,
Hour prophetic, hour resuming the past,
Inflating my throat, you divine average,
You earth and life till the last ray gleams I sing.

Open mouth of my soul uttering gladness,
Eyes of my soul seeing perfection,
Natural life of me faithfully praising things,
Corroborating forever the triumph of things.

Illustrious every one!
Illustrious what we name space, sphere of unnumber'd
spirits,
Illustrious the mystery of motion in all beings, even the
tiniest insect,
Illustrious the attribute of speech, the senses, the body,
Illustrious the passing light—illustrious the pale reflection
on the new moon in the western sky,
Illustrious whatever I see or hear or touch, to the last.

Good in all,
In the satisfaction and aplomb of animals,
In the annual return of the seasons,
In the hilarity of youth,

In the strength and flush of manhood,
In the grandeur and exquisiteness of old age,
In the superb vistas of death.

Wonderful to depart!
Wonderful to be here!
The heart, to jet the all-alike and innocent blood!
To breathe the air, how delicious!
To speak—to walk—to seize something by the hand!
To prepare for sleep, for bed, to look on my rose-color'd flesh!
To be conscious of my body, so satisfied, so large!
To be this incredible God I am!
To have gone forth among other Gods, these men and women I love.

Wonderful how I celebrate you and myself!
How my thoughts play subtly at the spectacles around!
How the clouds pass silently overhead!
How the earth darts on and on! and how the sun, moon, stars, dart on and on!
How the water sports and sings! (surely it is alive!)
How the trees rise and stand up, with strong trunks, with branches and leaves!
(Surely there is something more in each of the trees, some living soul.)

O amazement of things—even the least particle!
O spirituality of things!
O strain musical flowing through ages and continents, now reaching me and America!
I take your strong chords, intersperse them, and cheerfully pass them forward.

I too carol the sun, usher'd or at noon, or as now, setting,
I too throb to the brain and beauty of the earth and of all the growths of the earth,
I too have felt the resistless call of myself.

As I steam'd down the Mississippi,
As I wander'd over the prairies,

As I have lived, as I have look'd through my windows my eyes,
As I went forth in the morning, as I beheld the light
breaking in the east,
As I bathed on the beach of the Eastern Sea, and again on
the beach of the Western Sea,
As I roam'd the streets of inland Chicago, whatever streets I
have roam'd,
Or cities or silent woods, or even amid the sights of war,
Wherever I have been I have charged myself with
contentment and triumph.

I sing to the last the equalities modern or old,
I sing the endless finalés of things,
I say Nature continues, glory continues,
I praise with electric voice,
For I do not see one imperfection in the universe,
And I do not see one cause or result lamentable at last in
the universe.

O setting sun! though the time has come,
I still warble under you, if none else does, unmitigated
adoration.

As at Thy Portals Also Death

As at thy portals also death,
Entering thy sovereign, dim, illimitable grounds,
To memories of my mother, to the divine blending,
maternity,
To her, buried and gone, yet buried not, gone not from me,
(I see again the calm benignant face fresh and beautiful still,
I sit by the form in the coffin,
I kiss and kiss convulsively again the sweet old lips, the
cheeks, the closed eyes in the coffin;)
To her, the ideal woman, practical, spiritual, of all of earth,
life, love, to me the best,
I grave a monumental line, before I go, amid these songs,
And set a tombstone here.

My Legacy

THE business man the acquirer vast,
After assiduous years surveying results, preparing for departure,
Devises houses and lands to his children, bequeaths stocks, goods, funds for a school or hospital,
Leaves money to certain companions to buy tokens, souvenirs of gems and gold.

But I, my life surveying, closing,
With nothing to show to devise from its idle years,
Nor houses nor lands, nor tokens of gems or gold for my friends,
Yet certain remembrances of the war for you, and after you,
And little souvenirs of camps and soldiers, with my love,
I bind together and bequeath in this bundle of songs.

Pensive on Her Dead Gazing

PENSIVE on her dead gazing I heard the Mother of All,
Desperate on the torn bodies, on the forms covering the battle-fields gazing,
(As the last gun ceased, but the scent of the powder-smoke linger'd,)
As she call'd to her earth with mournful voice while she stalk'd,
Absorb them well O my earth, she cried, I charge you lose not my sons, lose not an atom,
And you streams absorb them well, taking their dear blood,
And you local spots, and you airs that swim above lightly impalpable,
And all you essences of soil and growth, and you my rivers' depths,
And you mountain sides, and the woods where my dear children's blood trickling redden'd,
And you trees down in your roots to bequeath to all future trees,
My dead absorb or South or North—my young men's bodies absorb, and their precious precious blood,

Which holding in trust for me faithfully back again give me
many a year hence,
In unseen essence and odor of surface and grass, centuries
hence,
In blowing airs from the fields back again give me my
darlings, give my immortal heroes,
Exhale me them centuries hence, breathe me their breath,
let not an atom be lost,
O years and graves! O air and soil! O my dead, an aroma
sweet!
Exhale them perennial sweet death, years, centuries hence.

Camps of Green

Not alone those camps of white, old comrades of the wars,
When as order'd forward, after a long march,
Footsore and weary, soon as the light lessens we halt for the
night,
Some of us so fatigued carrying the gun and knapsack,
dropping asleep in our tracks,
Others pitching the little tents, and the fires lit up begin to
sparkle,
Outposts of pickets posted surrounding alert through the dark,
And a word provided for countersign, careful for safety,
Till to the call of the drummers at daybreak loudly beating
the drums,
We rise up refresh'd, the night and sleep pass'd over, and
resume our journey,
Or proceed to battle.

Lo, the camps of the tents of green,
Which the days of peace keep filling, and the days of war
keep filling,
With a mystic army, (is it too order'd forward? is it too only
halting awhile,
Till night and sleep pass over?)

Now in those camps of green, in their tents dotting the world,
In the parents, children, husbands, wives, in them, in the
old and young,

Sleeping under the sunlight, sleeping under the moonlight,
content and silent there at last,
Behold the mighty bivouac-field and waiting-camp of all,
Of the corps and generals all, and the President over the
corps and generals all,
And of each of us O soldiers, and of each and all in the
ranks we fought,
(There without hatred we all, all meet.)

For presently O soldiers, we too camp in our place in the
bivouac-camps of green,
But we need not provide for outposts, nor word for the
countersign,
Nor drummer to beat the morning drum.

The Sobbing of the Bells

(Midnight, Sept. 19–20, 1881.)

THE sobbing of the bells, the sudden death-news everywhere,
The slumberers rouse, the rapport of the People,
(Full well they know that message in the darkness,
Full well return, respond within their breasts, their brains,
the sad reverberations,)
The passionate toll and clang—city to city, joining,
sounding, passing,
Those heart-beats of a Nation in the night.

As They Draw to a Close

As they draw to a close,
Of what underlies the precedent songs—of my aims in
them,
Of the seed I have sought to plant in them,
Of joy, sweet joy, through many a year, in them,
(For them, for them have I lived, in them my work is done,)
Of many an aspiration fond, of many a dream and plan;
Through Space and Time fused in a chant, and the flowing
eternal identity,
To Nature encompassing these, encompassing God—to the
joyous, electric all,

To the sense of Death, and accepting exulting in Death in
its turn the same as life,
The entrance of man to sing;
To compact you, ye parted, diverse lives,
To put rapport the mountains and rocks and streams,
And the winds of the north, and the forests of oak and pine,
With you O soul.

Joy, Shipmate, Joy!

JOY, shipmate, joy!
(Pleas'd to my soul at death I cry,)
Our life is closed, our life begins,
The long, long anchorage we leave,
The ship is clear at last, she leaps!
She swiftly courses from the shore,
Joy, shipmate, joy.

The Untold Want

THE untold want by life and land ne'er granted,
Now voyager sail thou forth to seek and find.

Portals

WHAT are those of the known but to ascend and enter the
Unknown?
And what are those of life but for Death?

These Carols

THESE carols sung to cheer my passage through the world I
see,
For completion I dedicate to the Invisible World.

Now Finalè to the Shore

NOW finalè to the shore,
Now land and life finalè and farewell,
Now Voyager depart, (much, much for thee is yet in store,)

Often enough hast thou adventur'd o'er the seas,
Cautiously cruising, studying the charts,
Duly again to port and hawser's tie returning;
But now obey thy cherish'd secret wish,
Embrace thy friends, leave all in order,
To port and hawser's tie no more returning,
Depart upon thy endless cruise old Sailor.

So Long!

To conclude, I announce what comes after me.

I remember I said before my leaves sprang at all,
I would raise my voice jocund and strong with reference to
 consummations.

When America does what was promis'd,
When through these States walk a hundred millions of
 superb persons,
When the rest part away for superb persons and contribute
 to them,
When breeds of the most perfect mothers denote America,
Then to me and mine our due fruition.

I have press'd through in my own right,
I have sung the body and the soul, war and peace have I
 sung, and the songs of life and death,
And the songs of birth, and shown that there are many births.

I have offer'd my style to every one, I have journey'd with
 confident step;
While my pleasure is yet at the full I whisper *So long!*
And take the young woman's hand and the young man's
 hand for the last time.

I announce natural persons to arise,
I announce justice triumphant,
I announce uncompromising liberty and equality,
I announce the justification of candor and the justification
 of pride.

I announce that the identity of these States is a single
identity only,
I announce the Union more and more compact, indissoluble,
I announce splendors and majesties to make all the previous
politics of the earth insignificant.

I announce adhesiveness, I say it shall be limitless, unloosen'd,
I say you shall yet find the friend you were looking for.

I announce a man or woman coming, perhaps you are the
one, (*So long!*)
I announce the great individual, fluid as Nature, chaste,
affectionate, compassionate, fully arm'd.

I announce a life that shall be copious, vehement, spiritual,
bold,
I announce an end that shall lightly and joyfully meet its
translation.

I announce myriads of youths, beautiful, gigantic, sweet-
blooded,
I announce a race of splendid and savage old men.

O thicker and faster—(*So long!*)
O crowding too close upon me,
I foresee too much, it means more than I thought,
It appears to me I am dying.

Hasten throat and sound your last,
Salute me—salute the days once more. Peal the old cry
once more.

Screaming electric, the atmosphere using,
At random glancing, each as I notice absorbing,
Swiftly on, but a little while alighting,
Curious envelop'd messages delivering,
Sparkles hot, seed ethereal down in the dirt dropping,
Myself unknowing, my commission obeying, to question it
never daring,
To ages and ages yet the growth of the seed leaving,

To troops out of the war arising, they the tasks I have set
promulging,
To women certain whispers of myself bequeathing, their
affection me more clearly explaining,
To young men my problems offering—no dallier I—I the
muscle of their brains trying,
So I pass, a little time vocal, visible, contrary,
Afterward a melodious echo, passionately bent for, (death
making me really undying,)
The best of me then when no longer visible, for toward that
I have been incessantly preparing.

What is there more, that I lag and pause and crouch
extended with unshut mouth?
Is there a single final farewell?

My songs cease, I abandon them,
From behind the screen where I hid I advance personally
solely to you.

Camerado, this is no book,
Who touches this touches a man,
(Is it night? are we here together alone?)
It is I you hold and who holds you,
I spring from the pages into your arms—decease calls me
forth.

O how your fingers drowse me,
Your breath falls around me like dew, your pulse lulls the
tympans of my ears,
I feel immerged from head to foot,
Delicious, enough.

Enough O deed impromptu and secret,
Enough O gliding present—enough O summ'd-up past.

Dear friend whoever you are take this kiss,
I give it especially to you, do not forget me,
I feel like one who has done work for the day to retire awhile,

I receive now again of my many translations, from my
avataras ascending, while others doubtless await me,
An unknown sphere more real than I dream'd, more direct,
darts awakening rays about me, *So long!*
Remember my words, I may again return,
I love you, I depart from materials,
I am as one disembodied, triumphant, dead.

First Annex: Sands at Seventy

Mannahatta

My city's fit and noble name resumed,
Choice aboriginal name, with marvellous beauty, meaning,
A rocky founded island—shores where ever gayly dash the coming, going, hurrying sea waves.

Paumanok

Sea-beauty! stretch'd and basking!
One side thy inland ocean laving, broad, with copious commerce, steamers, sails,
And one the Atlantic's wind caressing, fierce or gentle—mighty hulls dark-gliding in the distance.
Isle of sweet brooks of drinking-water—healthy air and soil!
Isle of the salty shore and breeze and brine!

From Montauk Point

I stand as on some mighty eagle's beak,
Eastward the sea absorbing, viewing, (nothing but sea and sky,)
The tossing waves, the foam, the ships in the distance,
The wild unrest, the snowy, curling caps—that inbound urge and urge of waves,
Seeking the shores forever.

To Those Who've Fail'd

To those who've fail'd, in aspiration vast,
To unnam'd soldiers fallen in front on the lead,
To calm, devoted engineers—to over-ardent travelers—to pilots on their ships,
To many a lofty song and picture without recognition—I'd rear a laurel-cover'd monument,
High, high above the rest—To all cut off before their time,
Possess'd by some strange spirit of fire,
Quench'd by an early death.

A Carol Closing Sixty-Nine

A carol closing sixty-nine—a *résumé*—a repetition,
My lines in joy and hope continuing on the same,
Of ye, O God, Life, Nature, Freedom, Poetry;
Of you, my Land—your rivers, prairies, States—you,
  mottled Flag I love,
Your aggregate retain'd entire—Of north, south, east and
  west, your items all;
Of me myself—the jocund heart yet beating in my breast,
The body wreck'd, old, poor and paralyzed—the strange
  inertia falling pall-like round me,
The burning fires down in my sluggish blood not yet
  extinct,
The undiminish'd faith—the groups of loving friends.

The Bravest Soldiers

Brave, brave were the soldiers (high named to-day) who
  lived through the fight;
But the bravest press'd to the front and fell, unnamed,
  unknown.

A Font of Type

This latent mine—these unlaunch'd voices—passionate
  powers,
Wrath, argument, or praise, or comic leer, or prayer devout,
(Not nonpareil, brevier, bourgeois, long primer merely,)
These ocean waves arousable to fury and to death,
Or sooth'd to ease and sheeny sun and sleep,
Within the pallid slivers slumbering.

As I Sit Writing Here

As I sit writing here, sick and grown old,
Not my least burden is that dulness of the years, querilities,
Ungracious glooms, aches, lethargy, constipation,
  whimpering *ennui*,
May filter in my daily songs.

My Canary Bird

Did we count great, O soul, to penetrate the themes of
mighty books,
Absorbing deep and full from thoughts, plays, speculations?
But now from thee to me, caged bird, to feel thy joyous
warble,
Filling the air, the lonesome room, the long forenoon,
Is it not just as great, O soul?

Queries to My Seventieth Year

Approaching, nearing, curious,
Thou dim, uncertain spectre—bringest thou life or death?
Strength, weakness, blindness, more paralysis and heavier?
Or placid skies and sun? Wilt stir the waters yet?
Or haply cut me short for good? Or leave me here as now,
Dull, parrot-like and old, with crack'd voice harping,
screeching?

The Wallabout Martyrs

[*In Brooklyn, in an old vault, mark'd by no special recognition, lie huddled at this moment the undoubtedly authentic remains of the stanchest and earliest revolutionary patriots from the British prison ships and prisons of the times of 1776–83, in and around New York, and from all over Long Island; originally buried—many thousands of them—in trenches in the Wallabout sands.*]

Greater than memory of Achilles or Ulysses,
More, more by far to thee than tomb of Alexander,
Those cart loads of old charnel ashes, scales and splints of
mouldy bones,
Once living men—once resolute courage, aspiration, strength,
The stepping stones to thee to-day and here, America.

The First Dandelion

Simple and fresh and fair from winter's close emerging,
As if no artifice of fashion, business, politics, had ever been,
Forth from its sunny nook of shelter'd grass—innocent,
golden, calm as the dawn,
The spring's first dandelion shows its trustful face.

America

Centre of equal daughters, equal sons,
All, all alike endear'd, grown, ungrown, young or old,
Strong, ample, fair, enduring, capable, rich,
Perennial with the Earth, with Freedom, Law and Love,
A grand, sane, towering, seated Mother,
Chair'd in the adamant of Time.

Memories

How sweet the silent backward tracings!
The wanderings as in dreams—the meditation of old times
resumed—their loves, joys, persons, voyages.

To-day and Thee

The appointed winners in a long-stretch'd game;
The course of Time and nations—Egypt, India, Greece and
Rome;
The past entire, with all its heroes, histories, arts,
experiments,
Its store of songs, inventions, voyages, teachers, books,
Garner'd for now and thee—To think of it!
The heirdom all converged in thee!

After the Dazzle of Day

After the dazzle of day is gone,
Only the dark, dark night shows to my eyes the stars;
After the clangor of organ majestic, or chorus, or perfect
band,
Silent, athwart my soul, moves the symphony true.

Abraham Lincoln, Born Feb. 12, 1809

To-day, from each and all, a breath of prayer—a pulse of
thought,
To memory of Him—to birth of Him.

Publish'd Feb. 12, 1888.

Out of May's Shows Selected

Apple orchards, the trees all cover'd with blossoms;
Wheat fields carpeted far and near in vital emerald green;
The eternal, exhaustless freshness of each early morning;
The yellow, golden, transparent haze of the warm afternoon
    sun;
The aspiring lilac bushes with profuse purple or white flowers.

Halcyon Days

Not from successful love alone,
Nor wealth, nor honor'd middle age, nor victories of
    politics or war;
But as life wanes, and all the turbulent passions calm,
As gorgeous, vapory, silent hues cover the evening sky,
As softness, fulness, rest, suffuse the frame, like freshier,
    balmier air,
As the days take on a mellower light, and the apple at last
    hangs really finish'd and indolent-ripe on the tree,
Then for the teeming quietest, happiest days of all!
The brooding and blissful halcyon days!

Fancies at Navesink

THE PILOT IN THE MIST

Steaming the northern rapids—(an old St. Lawrence
    reminiscence,
A sudden memory-flash comes back, I know not why,
Here waiting for the sunrise, gazing from this hill;)*
Again 'tis just at morning—a heavy haze contends with
    daybreak,
Again the trembling, laboring vessel veers me—I press
    through foam-dash'd rocks that almost touch me,
Again I mark where aft the small thin Indian helmsman
Looms in the mist, with brow elate and governing hand.

*Navesink—a sea-side mountain, lower entrance of New York Bay.

HAD I THE CHOICE

Had I the choice to tally greatest bards,
To limn their portraits, stately, beautiful, and emulate at will,
Homer with all his wars and warriors—Hector, Achilles, Ajax,
Or Shakspere's woe-entangled Hamlet, Lear, Othello—
Tennyson's fair ladies,
Metre or wit the best, or choice conceit to wield in perfect
rhyme, delight of singers;
These, these, O sea, all these I'd gladly barter,
Would you the undulation of one wave, its trick to me
transfer,
Or breathe one breath of yours upon my verse,
And leave its odor there.

YOU TIDES WITH CEASELESS SWELL

You tides with ceaseless swell! you power that does this
work!
You unseen force, centripetal, centrifugal, through space's
spread,
Rapport of sun, moon, earth, and all the constellations,
What are the messages by you from distant stars to us? what
Sirius'? what Capella's?
What central heart—and you the pulse—vivifies all? what
boundless aggregate of all?
What subtle indirection and significance in you? what clue
to all in you? what fluid, vast identity,
Holding the universe with all its parts as one—as sailing
in a ship?

LAST OF EBB, AND DAYLIGHT WANING

Last of ebb, and daylight waning,
Scented sea-cool landward making, smells of sedge and salt
incoming,
With many a half-caught voice sent up from the eddies,
Many a muffled confession—many a sob and whisper'd
word,
As of speakers far or hid.

How they sweep down and out! how they mutter!
Poets unnamed—artists greatest of any, with cherish'd lost
designs,
Love's unresponse—a chorus of age's complaints—hope's
last words,
Some suicide's despairing cry, *Away to the boundless waste,
and never again return.*

On to oblivion then!
On, on, and do your part, ye burying, ebbing tide!
On for your time, ye furious debouché!

AND YET NOT YOU ALONE

And yet not you alone, twilight and burying ebb,
Nor you, ye lost designs alone—nor failures, aspirations;
I know, divine deceitful ones, your glamour's seeming;
Duly by you, from you, the tide and light again—duly the
hinges turning,
Duly the needed discord-parts offsetting, blending,
Weaving from you, from Sleep, Night, Death itself,
The rhythmus of Birth eternal.

PROUDLY THE FLOOD COMES IN

Proudly the flood comes in, shouting, foaming, advancing,
Long it holds at the high, with bosom broad outswelling,
All throbs, dilates—the farms, woods, streets of cities—
workmen at work,
Mainsails, topsails, jibs, appear in the offing—steamers'
pennants of smoke—and under the forenoon sun,
Freighted with human lives, gaily the outward bound, gaily
the inward bound,
Flaunting from many a spar the flag I love.

BY THAT LONG SCAN OF WAVES

By that long scan of waves, myself call'd back, resumed
upon myself,
In every crest some undulating light or shade—some
retrospect,

Joys, travels, studies, silent panoramas—scenes ephemeral,
The long past war, the battles, hospital sights, the wounded and the dead,
Myself through every by-gone phase—my idle youth—old age at hand,
My three-score years of life summ'd up, and more, and past,
By any grand ideal tried, intentionless, the whole a nothing,
And haply yet some drop within God's scheme's ensemble—some wave, or part of wave,
Like one of yours, ye multitudinous ocean.

THEN LAST OF ALL

Then last of all, caught from these shores, this hill,
Of you O tides, the mystic human meaning:
Only by law of you, your swell and ebb, enclosing me the same,
The brain that shapes, the voice that chants this song.

Election Day, November, 1884

If I should need to name, O Western World, your powerfulest scene and show,
'Twould not be you, Niagara—nor you, ye limitless prairies—nor your huge rifts of canyons, Colorado,
Nor you, Yosemite—nor Yellowstone, with all its spasmic geyser-loops ascending to the skies, appearing and disappearing,
Nor Oregon's white cones—nor Huron's belt of mighty lakes—nor Mississippi's stream:
—This seething hemisphere's humanity, as now, I'd name—*the still small voice* vibrating—America's choosing day,
(The heart of it not in the chosen—the act itself the main, the quadriennial choosing,)
The stretch of North and South arous'd—sea-board and inland—Texas to Maine—the Prairie States—Vermont, Virginia, California,
The final ballot-shower from East to West—the paradox and conflict,
The countless snow-flakes falling—(a swordless conflict,
Yet more than all Rome's wars of old, or modern

Napoleon's:) the peaceful choice of all,
Or good or ill humanity—welcoming the darker odds, the dross:
—Foams and ferments the wine? it serves to purify—while the heart pants, life glows:
These stormy gusts and winds waft precious ships,
Swell'd Washington's, Jefferson's, Lincoln's sails.

With Husky-Haughty Lips, O Sea!

With husky-haughty lips, O sea!
Where day and night I wend thy surf-beat shore,
Imaging to my sense thy varied strange suggestions,
(I see and plainly list thy talk and conference here,)
Thy troops of white-maned racers racing to the goal,
Thy ample, smiling face, dash'd with the sparkling dimples of the sun,
Thy brooding scowl and murk—thy unloos'd hurricanes,
Thy unsubduedness, caprices, wilfulness;
Great as thou art above the rest, thy many tears—a lack from all eternity in thy content,
(Naught but the greatest struggles, wrongs, defeats, could make thee greatest—no less could make thee,)
Thy lonely state—something thou ever seek'st and seek'st, yet never gain'st,
Surely some right withheld—some voice, in huge monotonous rage, of freedom-lover pent,
Some vast heart, like a planet's, chain'd and chafing in those breakers,
By lengthen'd swell, and spasm, and panting breath,
And rhythmic rasping of thy sands and waves,
And serpent hiss, and savage peals of laughter,
And undertones of distant lion roar,
(Sounding, appealing to the sky's deaf ear—but now, rapport for once,
A phantom in the night thy confidant for once,)
The first and last confession of the globe,
Outsurging, muttering from thy soul's abysms,
The tale of cosmic elemental passion,
Thou tellest to a kindred soul.

Death of General Grant

As one by one withdraw the lofty actors,
From that great play on history's stage eterne,
That lurid, partial act of war and peace—of old and new
contending,
Fought out through wrath, fears, dark dismays, and many a
long suspense;
All past—and since, in countless graves receding,
mellowing,
Victor's and vanquish'd—Lincoln's and Lee's—now thou
with them,
Man of the mighty days—and equal to the days!
Thou from the prairies!—tangled and many-vein'd and hard
has been thy part,
To admiration has it been enacted!

Red Jacket (from Aloft)

[*Impromptu on Buffalo City's monument to, and re-burial of the old Iroquois orator, October 9, 1884.*]

Upon this scene, this show,
Yielded to-day by fashion, learning, wealth,
(Nor in caprice alone—some grains of deepest meaning,)
Haply, aloft, (who knows?) from distant sky-clouds' blended
shapes,
As some old tree, or rock or cliff, thrill'd with its soul,
Product of Nature's sun, stars, earth direct—a towering
human form,
In hunting-shirt of film, arm'd with the rifle, a half-ironical
smile curving its phantom lips,
Like one of Ossian's ghosts looks down.

Washington's Monument, February, 1885

Ah, not this marble, dead and cold:
Far from its base and shaft expanding—the round zones
circling, comprehending,
Thou, Washington, art all the world's, the continents'
entire—not yours alone, America,

Europe's as well, in every part, castle of lord or laborer's cot,
Or frozen North, or sultry South—the African's—the Arab's
in his tent,
Old Asia's there with venerable smile, seated amid her ruins;
(Greets the antique the hero new? 'tis but the same—the
heir legitimate, continued ever,
The indomitable heart and arm—proofs of the never-broken
line,
Courage, alertness, patience, faith, the same—e'en in defeat
defeated not, the same:)
Wherever sails a ship, or house is built on land, or day or
night,
Through teeming cities' streets, indoors or out, factories or
farms,
Now, or to come, or past—where patriot wills existed or
exist,
Wherever Freedom, pois'd by Toleration, sway'd by Law,
Stands or is rising thy true monument.

Of That Blithe Throat of Thine

[*More than eighty-three degrees north—about a good day's steaming distance to the Pole by one of our fast oceaners in clear water—Greely the explorer heard the song of a single snow-bird merrily sounding over the desolation.*]

Of that blithe throat of thine from arctic bleak and blank,
I'll mind the lesson, solitary bird—let me too welcome
chilling drifts,
E'en the profoundest chill, as now—a torpid pulse, a brain
unnerv'd,
Old age land-lock'd within its winter bay—(cold, cold, O
cold!)
These snowy hairs, my feeble arm, my frozen feet,
For them thy faith, thy rule I take, and grave it to the last;
Not summer's zones alone—not chants of youth, or south's
warm tides alone,
But held by sluggish floes, pack'd in the northern ice, the
cumulus of years,
These with gay heart I also sing.

Broadway

What hurrying human tides, or day or night!
What passions, winnings, losses, ardors, swim thy waters!
What whirls of evil, bliss and sorrow, stem thee!
What curious questioning glances—glints of love!
Leer, envy, scorn, contempt, hope, aspiration!
Thou portal—thou arena—thou of the myriad long-drawn lines and groups!
(Could but thy flagstones, curbs, façades, tell their inimitable tales;
Thy windows rich, and huge hotels—thy side-walks wide;)
Thou of the endless sliding, mincing, shuffling feet!
Thou, like the parti-colored world itself—like infinite, teeming, mocking life!
Thou visor'd, vast, unspeakable show and lesson!

To Get the Final Lilt of Songs

To get the final lilt of songs,
To penetrate the inmost lore of poets—to know the mighty ones,
Job, Homer, Eschylus, Dante, Shakspere, Tennyson, Emerson;
To diagnose the shifting-delicate tints of love and pride and doubt—to truly understand,
To encompass these, the last keen faculty and entrance-price,
Old age, and what it brings from all its past experiences.

Old Salt Kossabone

Far back, related on my mother's side,
Old Salt Kossabone, I'll tell you how he died:
(Had been a sailor all his life—was nearly 90—lived with his married grandchild, Jenny;
House on a hill, with view of bay at hand, and distant cape, and stretch to open sea;)
The last of afternoons, the evening hours, for many a year his regular custom,
In his great arm chair by the window seated,

(Sometimes, indeed, through half the day,)
Watching the coming, going of the vessels, he mutters to
himself—And now the close of all:
One struggling outbound brig, one day, baffled for long—
cross-tides and much wrong going,
At last at nightfall strikes the breeze aright, her whole luck
veering,
And swiftly bending round the cape, the darkness proudly
entering, cleaving, as he watches,
"She's free—she's on her destination"—these the last
words—when Jenny came, he sat there dead,
Dutch Kossabone, Old Salt, related on my mother's side, far
back.

The Dead Tenor

As down the stage again,
With Spanish hat and plumes, and gait inimitable,
Back from the fading lessons of the past, I'd call, I'd tell
and own,
How much from thee! the revelation of the singing voice
from thee!
(So firm—so liquid-soft—again that tremulous, manly
timbre!
The perfect singing voice—deepest of all to me the lesson—
trial and test of all:)
How through those strains distill'd—how the rapt ears, the
soul of me, absorbing
Fernando's heart, *Manrico's* passionate call, *Ernani's,* sweet
Gennaro's,
I fold thenceforth, or seek to fold, within my chants
transmuting,
Freedom's and Love's and Faith's unloos'd cantabile,
(As perfume's, color's, sunlight's correlation:)
From these, for these, with these, a hurried line, dead tenor,
A wafted autumn leaf, dropt in the closing grave, the
shovel'd earth,
To memory of thee.

Continuities

[*From a talk I had lately with a German spiritualist.*]

Nothing is ever really lost, or can be lost,
No birth, identity, form—no object of the world.
Nor life, nor force, nor any visible thing;
Appearance must not foil, nor shifted sphere confuse thy brain.
Ample are time and space—ample the fields of Nature.
The body, sluggish, aged, cold—the embers left from earlier fires,
The light in the eye grown dim, shall duly flame again;
The sun now low in the west rises for mornings and for noons continual;
To frozen clods ever the spring's invisible law returns,
With grass and flowers and summer fruits and corn.

Yonnondio

[*The sense of the word is* lament for the aborigines. *It is an Iroquois term; and has been used for a personal name.*]

A song, a poem of itself—the word itself a dirge,
Amid the wilds, the rocks, the storm and wintry night,
To me such misty, strange tableaux the syllables calling up;
Yonnondio—I see, far in the west or north, a limitless ravine, with plains and mountains dark,
I see swarms of stalwart chieftains, medicine-men, and warriors,
As flitting by like clouds of ghosts, they pass and are gone in the twilight,
(Race of the woods, the landscapes free, and the falls!
No picture, poem, statement, passing them to the future:)
Yonnondio! Yonnondio!—unlimn'd they disappear;
To-day gives place, and fades—the cities, farms, factories fade;
A muffled sonorous sound, a wailing word is borne through the air for a moment,
Then blank and gone and still, and utterly lost.

Life

EVER the undiscouraged, resolute, struggling soul of man;
(Have former armies fail'd? then we send fresh armies—and fresh again;)
Ever the grappled mystery of all earth's ages old or new;
Ever the eager eyes, hurrahs, the welcome-clapping hands, the loud applause;
Ever the soul dissatisfied, curious, unconvinced at last;
Struggling to-day the same—battling the same.

"Going Somewhere"

MY science-friend, my noblest woman-friend,
(Now buried in an English grave—and this a memory-leaf for her dear sake,)
Ended our talk—"The sum, concluding all we know of old or modern learning, intuitions deep,
"Of all Geologies—Histories—of all Astronomy—of Evolution, Metaphysics all,
"Is, that we all are onward, onward, speeding slowly, surely bettering,
"Life, life an endless march, an endless army, (no halt, but it is duly over,)
"The world, the race, the soul—in space and time the universes,
"All bound as is befitting each—all surely going somewhere."

Small the Theme of My Chant

From the 1869 edition L. of G.

SMALL the theme of my Chant, yet the greatest—namely, One's-Self—a simple, separate person. That, for the use of the New World, I sing.
Man's physiology complete, from top to toe, I sing. Not physiognomy alone, nor brain alone, is worthy for the Muse;—I say the Form complete is worthier far. The Female equally with the Male, I sing.

Nor cease at the theme of One's-Self. I speak the word of the modern, the word En-Masse.
My Days I sing, and the Lands—with interstice I knew of hapless War.
(O friend, whoe'er you are, at last arriving hither to commence, I feel through every leaf the pressure of your hand, which I return.
And thus upon our journey, footing the road, and more than once, and link'd together let us go.)

True Conquerors

Old farmers, travelers, workmen (no matter how crippled or bent,)
Old sailors, out of many a perilous voyage, storm and wreck,
Old soldiers from campaigns, with all their wounds, defeats and scars;
Enough that they've survived at all—long life's unflinching ones!
Forth from their struggles, trials, fights, to have emerged at all—in that alone,
True conquerors o'er all the rest.

The United States to Old World Critics

Here first the duties of to-day, the lessons of the concrete,
Wealth, order, travel, shelter, products, plenty;
As of the building of some varied, vast, perpetual edifice,
Whence to arise inevitable in time, the towering roofs, the lamps,
The solid-planted spires tall shooting to the stars.

The Calming Thought of All

That coursing on, whate'er men's speculations,
Amid the changing schools, theologies, philosophies,
Amid the bawling presentations new and old,
The round earth's silent vital laws, facts, modes continue.

Thanks in Old Age

Thanks in old age—thanks ere I go,
For health, the midday sun, the impalpable air—for life, mere life,
For precious ever-lingering memories, (of you my mother dear—you, father—you, brothers, sisters, friends,)
For all my days—not those of peace alone—the days of war the same,
For gentle words, caresses, gifts from foreign lands,
For shelter, wine and meat—for sweet appreciation,
(You distant, dim unknown—or young or old—countless, unspecified, readers belov'd,
We never met, and ne'er shall meet—and yet our souls embrace, long, close and long;)
For beings, groups, love, deeds, words, books—for colors, forms,
For all the brave strong men—devoted, hardy men—who've forward sprung in freedom's help, all years, all lands,
For braver, stronger, more devoted men—(a special laurel ere I go, to life's war's chosen ones,
The cannoneers of song and thought—the great artillerists—the foremost leaders, captains of the soul:)
As soldier from an ended war return'd—As traveler out of myriads, to the long procession retrospective,
Thanks—joyful thanks!—a soldier's, traveler's thanks.

Life and Death

The two old, simple problems ever intertwined,
Close home, elusive, present, baffled, grappled.
By each successive age insoluble, pass'd on,
To ours to-day—and we pass on the same.

The Voice of the Rain

And who art thou? said I to the soft-falling shower,
Which, strange to tell, gave me an answer, as here translated:

I am the Poem of Earth, said the voice of the rain,
Eternal I rise impalpable out of the land and the bottomless sea,
Upward to heaven, whence, vaguely form'd, altogether changed, and yet the same,
I descend to lave the drouths, atomies, dust-layers of the globe,
And all that in them without me were seeds only, latent, unborn;
And forever, by day and night, I give back life to my own origin, and make pure and beautify it;
(For song, issuing from its birth-place, after fulfilment, wandering,
Reck'd or unreck'd, duly with love returns.)

Soon Shall the Winter's Foil Be Here

Soon shall the winter's foil be here;
Soon shall these icy ligatures unbind and melt—A little while,
And air, soil, wave, suffused shall be in softness, bloom and growth—a thousand forms shall rise
From these dead clods and chills as from low burial graves.
Thine eyes, ears—all thy best attributes—all that takes cognizance of natural beauty,
Shall wake and fill. Thou shalt perceive the simple shows, the delicate miracles of earth,
Dandelions, clover, the emerald grass, the early scents and flowers,
The arbutus under foot, the willow's yellow-green, the blossoming plum and cherry;
With these the robin, lark and thrush, singing their songs—the flitting bluebird;
For such the scenes the annual play brings on.

While Not the Past Forgetting

While not the past forgetting,
To-day, at least, contention sunk entire—peace, brotherhood uprisen;
For sign reciprocal our Northern, Southern hands,

Lay on the graves of all dead soldiers, North or South,
(Nor for the past alone—for meanings to the future,)
Wreaths of roses and branches of palm.

Publish'd May 30, 1888

The Dying Veteran

[*A Long Island incident—early part of the present century.*]

Amid these days of order, ease, prosperity,
Amid the current songs of beauty, peace, decorum,
I cast a reminiscence—(likely 'twill offend you,
I heard it in my boyhood;)—More than a generation since,
A queer old savage man, a fighter under Washington himself,
(Large, brave, cleanly, hot-blooded, no talker, rather spiritualistic,
Had fought in the ranks—fought well—had been all through the Revolutionary war,)
Lay dying—sons, daughters, church-deacons, lovingly tending him,
Sharping their sense, their ears, towards his murmuring, half-caught words:
"Let me return again to my war-days,
To the sights and scenes—to forming the line of battle,
To the scouts ahead reconnoitering,
To the cannons, the grim artillery,
To the galloping aids, carrying orders,
To the wounded, the fallen, the heat, the suspense,
The perfume strong, the smoke, the deafening noise;
Away with your life of peace!—your joys of peace!
Give me my old wild battle-life again!"

Stronger Lessons

Have you learn'd lessons only of those who admired you, and were tender with you, and stood aside for you?
Have you not learn'd great lessons from those who reject you, and brace themselves against you? or who treat you with contempt, or dispute the passage with you?

A Prairie Sunset

Shot gold, maroon and violet, dazzling silver, emerald, fawn,
The earth's whole amplitude and Nature's multiform power consign'd for once to colors;
The light, the general air possess'd by them—colors till now unknown,
No limit, confine—not the Western sky alone—the high meridian—North, South, all,
Pure luminous color fighting the silent shadows to the last.

Twenty Years

Down on the ancient wharf, the sand, I sit, with a new-comer chatting:
He shipp'd as green-hand boy, and sail'd away, (took some sudden, vehement notion;)
Since, twenty years and more have circled round and round,
While he the globe was circling round and round,—and now returns:
How changed the place—all the old land-marks gone—the parents dead;
(Yes, he comes back *to lay in port for good—to settle*—has a well-fill'd purse—no spot will do but this;)
The little boat that scull'd him from the sloop, now held in leash I see,
I hear the slapping waves, the restless keel, the rocking in the sand,
I see the sailor kit, the canvas bag, the great box bound with brass,
I scan the face all berry-brown and bearded—the stout-strong frame,
Dress'd in its russet suit of good Scotch cloth:
(Then what the told-out story of those twenty years? What of the future?)

Orange Buds by Mail from Florida

[*Voltaire closed a famous argument by claiming that a ship of war and the grand opera were proofs enough of civilization's and France's progress, in his day.*]

A lesser proof than old Voltaire's, yet greater,
Proof of this present time, and thee, thy broad expanse, America,

To my plain Northern hut, in outside clouds and snow,
Brought safely for a thousand miles o'er land and tide,
Some three days since on their own soil live-sprouting,
Now here their sweetness through my room unfolding,
A bunch of orange buds by mail from Florida.

Twilight

The soft voluptuous opiate shades,
The sun just gone, the eager light dispell'd—(I too will soon be gone, dispell'd,)
A haze—nirwana—rest and night—oblivion.

You Lingering Sparse Leaves of Me

You lingering sparse leaves of me on winter-nearing boughs,
And I some well-shorn tree of field or orchard-row;
You tokens diminute and lorn—(not now the flush of May, or July clover-bloom—no grain of August now;)
You pallid banner-staves—you pennants valueless—you overstay'd of time,
Yet my soul-dearest leaves confirming all the rest,
The faithfulest—hardiest—last.

Not Meagre, Latent Boughs Alone

Not meagre, latent boughs alone, O songs! (scaly and bare, like eagles' talons,)
But haply for some sunny day (who knows?) some future spring, some summer—bursting forth,
To verdant leaves, or sheltering shade—to nourishing fruit,
Apples and grapes—the stalwart limbs of trees emerging—the fresh, free, open air,
And love and faith, like scented roses blooming.

The Dead Emperor

To-day, with bending head and eyes, thou, too, Columbia,
Less for the mighty crown laid low in sorrow—less for the Emperor,

Thy true condolence breathest, sendest out o'er many a salt
sea mile,
Mourning a good old man—a faithful shepherd, patriot.

Publish'd March 10, 1888.

As the Greek's Signal Flame

[*For Whittier's eightieth birthday, December 17, 1887.*]

As the Greek's signal flame, by antique records told,
Rose from the hill-top, like applause and glory,
Welcoming in fame some special veteran, hero,
With rosy tinge reddening the land he'd served,
So I aloft from Mannahatta's ship-fringed shore,
Lift high a kindled brand for thee, Old Poet.

The Dismantled Ship

In some unused lagoon, some nameless bay,
On sluggish, lonesome waters, anchor'd near the shore,
An old, dismasted, gray and batter'd ship, disabled, done,
After free voyages to all the seas of earth, haul'd up at last
and hawser'd tight,
Lies rusting, mouldering.

Now Precedent Songs, Farewell

Now precedent songs, farewell—by every name farewell,
(Trains of a staggering line in many a strange procession,
waggons,
From ups and downs—with intervals—from elder years,
mid-age, or youth,)
"In Cabin'd Ships," or "Thee Old Cause" or "Poets to
Come"
Or "Paumanok," "Song of Myself," "Calamus," or "Adam,"
Or "Beat! Beat! Drums!" or "To the Leaven'd Soil they
Trod,"
Or "Captain! My Captain!" "Kosmos," "Quicksand Years,"
or "Thoughts,"
"Thou Mother with thy Equal Brood," and many, many
more unspecified,

From fibre heart of mine—from throat and tongue—(My life's hot pulsing blood,
The personal urge and form for me—not merely paper, automatic type and ink,)
Each song of mine—each utterance in the past—having its long, long history,
Of life or death, or soldier's wound, of country's loss or safety,
(O heaven! what flash and started endless train of all! compared indeed to that!
What wretched shred e'en at the best of all!)*

An Evening Lull

After a week of physical anguish,
Unrest and pain, and feverish heat,
Toward the ending day a calm and lull comes on,
Three hours of peace and soothing rest of brain.*

*The two songs on this page are eked out during an afternoon, June, 1888, in my seventieth year, at a critical spell of illness. Of course no reader and probably no human being at any time will ever have such phases of emotional and solemn action as these involve to me. I feel in them an end and close of all.

Old Age's Lambent Peaks

The touch of flame—the illuminating fire—the loftiest look at last,
O'er city, passion, sea—o'er prairie, mountain, wood—the earth itself;
The airy, different, changing hues of all, in falling twilight,
Objects and groups, bearings, faces, reminiscences;
The calmer sight—the golden setting, clear and broad:
So much i' the atmosphere, the points of view, the situations whence we scan,
Bro't out by them alone—so much (perhaps the best) unreck'd before;
The lights indeed from them—old age's lambent peaks.

After the Supper and Talk

After the supper and talk—after the day is done,
As a friend from friends his final withdrawal prolonging,
Good-bye and Good-bye with emotional lips repeating,
(So hard for his hand to release those hands—no more will
they meet,
No more for communion of sorrow and joy, of old and
young,
A far-stretching journey awaits him, to return no more,)
Shunning, postponing severance—seeking to ward off the
last word ever so little,
E'en at the exit-door turning—charges superfluous calling
back—e'en as he descends the steps,
Something to eke out a minute additional—shadows of
nightfall deepening,
Farewells, messages lessening—dimmer the forthgoer's
visage and form,
Soon to be lost for aye in the darkness—loth, O so loth to
depart!
Garrulous to the very last.

Second Annex: Good-Bye my Fancy

Preface Note to 2d Annex

Concluding L. of G.—1891.

HAD I not better withhold (in this old age and paralysis of me) such little tags and fringe-dots (maybe specks, stains,) as follow a long dusty journey, and witness it afterward? I have probably not been enough afraid of careless touches, from the first—and am not now—nor of parrot-like repetitions—nor platitudes and the commonplace. Perhaps I am too democratic for such avoidances. Besides, is not the verse-field, as originally plann'd by my theory, now sufficiently illustrated—and full time for me to silently retire?—(indeed amid no loud-call or market for my sort of poetic utterance.)

In answer, or rather defiance, to that kind of well-put interrogation, here comes this little cluster, and conclusion of my preceding clusters. Though not at all clear that, as here collated, it is worth printing (certainly I have nothing fresh to write)—I while away the hours of my 72d year—hours of forced confinement in my den—by putting in shape this small old age collation:

Last droplets of and after spontaneous rain,
From many limpid distillations and past showers;
(Will they germinate anything? mere exhalations as they all
  are—the land's and sea's—America's;
Will they filter to any deep emotion? any heart and brain?)

However that may be, I feel like improving to-day's opportunity and wind up. During the last two years I have sent out, in the lulls of illness and exhaustion, certain chirps—lingering-dying ones probably (undoubtedly)—which now I may as well gather and put in fair type while able to see correctly—(for my eyes plainly warn me they are dimming, and my brain more and more palpably neglects or refuses, month after month, even slight tasks or revisions.)

In fact, here I am these current years 1890 and '91, (each

successive fortnight getting stiffer and stuck deeper) much like some hard-cased dilapidated grim ancient shell-fish or time-bang'd conch (no legs, utterly non-locomotive) cast up high and dry on the shore-sands, helpless to move anywhere—nothing left but behave myself quiet, and while away the days yet assign'd, and discover if there is anything for the said grim and time-bang'd conch to be got at last out of inherited good spirits and primal buoyant centre-pulses down there deep somewhere within his gray-blurr'd old shell . . . . (Reader, you must allow a little fun here—for one reason there are too many of the following poemets about death, &c., and for another the passing hours (July 5, 1890) are so sunny-fine. And old as I am I feel to-day almost a part of some frolicsome wave, or for sporting yet like a kid or kitten—probably a streak of physical adjustment and perfection here and now. I believe I have it in me perennially anyhow.)

Then behind all, the deep-down consolation (it is a glum one, but I dare not be sorry for the fact of it in the past, nor refrain from dwelling, even vaunting here at the end) that this late-years palsied old shorn and shell-fish condition of me is the indubitable outcome and growth, now near for 20 years along, of too overzealous, over-continued bodily and emotional excitement and action through the times of 1862, '3, '4 and '5, visiting and waiting on wounded and sick army volunteers, both sides, in campaigns or contests, or after them, or in hospitals or fields south of Washington City, or in that place and elsewhere—those hot, sad, wrenching times—the army volunteers, all States,—or North or South—the wounded, suffering, dying—the exhausting, sweating summers, marches, battles, carnage—those trenches hurriedly heap'd by the corpse-thousands, mainly unknown—Will the America of the future—will this vast rich Union ever realize what itself cost, back there after all?—those hecatombs of battle-deaths—Those times of which, O far-off reader, this whole book is indeed finally but a reminiscent memorial from thence by me to you?

Sail Out for Good, Eidólon Yacht!

HEAVE the anchor short!
Raise main-sail and jib—steer forth,
O little white-hull'd sloop, now speed on really deep waters,
(I will not call it our concluding voyage,
But outset and sure entrance to the truest, best, maturest;)
Depart, depart from solid earth—no more returning to these
shores,
Now on for aye our infinite free venture wending,
Spurning all yet tried ports, seas, hawsers, densities,
gravitation,
Sail out for good, eidólon yacht of me!

Lingering Last Drops

AND whence and why come you?

We know not whence, (was the answer,)
We only know that we drift here with the rest,
That we linger'd and lagg'd—but were wafted at last, and
are now here,
To make the passing shower's concluding drops.

Good-Bye my Fancy

GOOD-BYE* my fancy—(I had a word to say,
But 'tis not quite the time—The best of any man's word
or say,
Is when its proper place arrives—and for its meaning,
I keep mine till the last.)

*Behind a Good-bye there lurks much of the salutation of another beginning—to me, Development, Continuity, Immortality, Transformation, are the chiefest life-meanings of Nature and Humanity, and are the *sine qua non* of all facts, and each fact.

Why do folks dwell so fondly on the last words, advice, appearance, of the departing? Those last words are not samples of the best, which involve vitality at its full, and balance, and perfect control and scope. But they are valuable beyond measure to confirm and endorse the varied train, facts, theories and faith of the whole preceding life.

On, On the Same, Ye Jocund Twain!

On, on the same, ye jocund twain!
My life and recitative, containing birth, youth, mid-age years,
Fitful as motley-tongues of flame, inseparably twined and merged in one—combining all,
My single soul—aims, confirmations, failures, joys—Nor single soul alone,
I chant my nation's crucial stage, (America's, haply humanity's)—the trial great, the victory great,
A strange *eclaircissement* of all the masses past, the eastern world, the ancient, medieval,
Here, here from wanderings, strayings, lessons, wars, defeats —here at the west a voice triumphant—justifying all,
A gladsome pealing cry—a song for once of utmost pride and satisfaction;
I chant from it the common bulk, the general average horde, (the best no sooner than the worst)—And now I chant old age,
(My verses, written first for forenoon life, and for the summer's, autumn's spread,
I pass to snow-white hairs the same, and give to pulses winter-cool'd the same;)
As here in careless trill, I and my recitatives, with faith and love,
Wafting to other work, to unknown songs, conditions,
On, on, ye jocund twain! continue on the same!

My 71st Year

After surmounting three-score and ten,
With all their chances, changes, losses, sorrows,
My parents' deaths, the vagaries of my life, the many tearing passions of me, the war of '63 and '4,
As some old broken soldier, after a long, hot, wearying march, or haply after battle,
To-day at twilight, hobbling, answering company roll-call, *Here,* with vital voice,
Reporting yet, saluting yet the Officer over all.

Apparitions

A VAGUE mist hanging 'round half the pages:
(Sometimes how strange and clear to the soul,
That all these solid things are indeed but apparitions,
concepts, non-realities.)

The Pallid Wreath

SOMEHOW I cannot let it go yet, funeral though it is,
Let it remain back there on its nail suspended,
With pink, blue, yellow, all blanch'd, and the white now
gray and ashy,
One wither'd rose put years ago for thee, dear friend;
But I do not forget thee. Hast thou then faded?
Is the odor exhaled? Are the colors, vitalities, dead?
No, while memories subtly play—the past vivid as ever;
For but last night I woke, and in that spectral ring saw thee,
Thy smile, eyes, face, calm, silent, loving as ever:
So let the wreath hang still awhile within my eye-reach,
It is not yet dead to me, nor even pallid.

An Ended Day

THE soothing sanity and blitheness of completion,
The pomp and hurried contest-glare and rush are done;
Now triumph! transformation! jubilate!*

*NOTE.—*Summer country life.—Several years.*—In my rambles and explorations I found a woody place near the creek, where for some reason the birds in happy mood seem'd to resort in unusual numbers. Especially at the beginning of the day, and again at the ending, I was sure to get there the most copious bird-concerts. I repair'd there frequently at sunrise—and also at sunset, or just before . . . Once the question arose in me: Which is the best singing, the first or the lattermost? The first always exhilarated, and perhaps seem'd more joyous and stronger; but I always felt the sunset or late afternoon sounds more penetrating and sweeter—seem'd to touch the soul—often the evening thrushes, two or three of them, responding and perhaps blending. Though I miss'd some of the mornings, I found myself getting to be quite strictly punctual at the evening utterances.

Old Age's Ship & Crafty Death's

FROM east and west across the horizon's edge,
Two mighty masterful vessels sailers steal upon us:
But we'll make race a-time upon the seas—a battle-contest
yet! bear lively there!
(Our joys of strife and derring-do to the last!)
Put on the old ship all her power to-day!
Crowd top-sail, top-gallant and royal studding-sails,
Out challenge and defiance—flags and flaunting pennants
added,
As we take to the open—take to the deepest, freest waters.

To the Pending Year

HAVE I no weapon-word for thee—some message brief and
fierce?
(Have I fought out and done indeed the battle?) Is there no
shot left,
For all thy affectations, lisps, scorns, manifold silliness?
Nor for myself—my own rebellious self in thee?

Down, down, proud gorge!—though choking thee;
Thy bearded throat and high-borne forehead to the gutter;
Crouch low thy neck to eleemosynary gifts.

ANOTHER NOTE.—"He went out with the tide and the sunset," was a phrase I heard from a surgeon describing an old sailor's death under peculiarly gentle conditions.

During the Secession War, 1863 and '4, visiting the Army Hospitals around Washington, I form'd the habit, and continued it to the end, whenever the ebb or flood tide began the latter part of day, of punctually visiting those at that time populous wards of suffering men. Somehow (or I thought so) the effect of the hour was palpable. The badly wounded would get some ease, and would like to talk a little, or be talk'd to. Intellectual and emotional natures would be at their best: Deaths were always easier; medicines seem'd to have better effect when given then, and a lulling atmosphere would pervade the wards.

Similar influences, similar circumstances and hours, day-close, after great battles, even with all their horrors. I had more than once the same experience on the fields cover'd with fallen or dead.

Shakspere-Bacon's Cipher

I DOUBT it not—then more, far more;
In each old song bequeath'd—in every noble page or text,
(Different—something unreck'd before—some unsuspected
author,)
In every object, mountain, tree, and star—in every birth and
life,
As part of each—evolv'd from each—meaning, behind the
ostent,
A mystic cipher waits infolded.

Long, Long Hence

AFTER a long, long course, hundreds of years, denials,
Accumulations, rous'd love and joy and thought,
Hopes, wishes, aspirations, ponderings, victories, myriads of
readers,
Coating, compassing, covering—after ages' and ages'
encrustations,
Then only may these songs reach fruition.

Bravo, Paris Exposition!

ADD to your show, before you close it, France,
With all the rest, visible, concrete, temples, towers, goods,
machines and ores,
Our sentiment wafted from many million heart-throbs,
ethereal but solid,
(We grand-sons and great-grand-sons do not forget your
grand-sires,)
From fifty Nations and nebulous Nations, compacted, sent
oversea to-day,
America's applause, love, memories and good-will.

*Interpolation Sounds**

[*General Philip Sheridan was buried at the Cathedral, Washington, D. C., August, 1888, with all the pomp, music and ceremonies of the Roman Catholic service.*]

OVER and through the burial chant,
Organ and solemn service, sermon, bending priests,
To me come interpolation sounds not in the show—plainly
to me, crowding up the aisle and from the window,
Of sudden battle's hurry and harsh noises—war's grim game
to sight and ear in earnest;
The scout call'd up and forward—the general mounted and
his aids around him—the new-brought word—the
instantaneous order issued;
The rifle crack—the cannon thud—the rushing forth of men
from their tents;
The clank of cavalry—the strange celerity of forming ranks—
the slender bugle note;
The sound of horses' hoofs departing—saddles, arms,
accoutrements.

To the Sun-set Breeze

AH, whispering, something again, unseen,
Where late this heated day thou enterest at my window, door,
Thou, laving, tempering all, cool-freshing, gently vitalizing
Me, old, alone, sick, weak-down, melted-worn with sweat;

*NOTE.—CAMDEN, N. J., August 7, 1888.—Walt Whitman asks the *New York Herald* "to add his tribute to Sheridan:"

"In the grand constellation of five or six names, under Lincoln's Presidency, that history will bear for ages in her firmament as marking the last life-throbs of secession, and beaming on its dying gasps, Sheridan's will be bright. One consideration rising out of the now dead soldier's example as it passes my mind, is worth taking notice of. If the war had continued any long time these States, in my opinion, would have shown and proved the most conclusive military talents ever evinced by any nation on earth. That they possess'd a rank and file ahead of all other known in points of quality and limitlessness of number are easily admitted. But we have, too, the eligibility of organizing, handling and officering equal to the other. These two, with modern arms, transportation, and inventive American genius, would make the United States, with earnestness, not only able to stand the whole world, but conquer that world united against us."

Thou, nestling, folding close and firm yet soft, companion
better than talk, book, art,
(Thou hast, O Nature! elements! utterance to my heart
beyond the rest—and this is of them,)
So sweet thy primitive taste to breathe within—thy soothing
fingers on my face and hands,
Thou, messenger-magical strange bringer to body and spirit
of me,
(Distances balk'd—occult medicines penetrating me from
head to foot,)
I feel the sky, the prairies vast—I feel the mighty northern
lakes,
I feel the ocean and the forest—somehow I feel the globe
itself swift-swimming in space;
Thou blown from lips so loved, now gone—haply from
endless store, God-sent,
(For thou art spiritual, Godly, most of all known to my
sense,)
Minister to speak to me, here and now, what word has
never told, and cannot tell,
Art thou not universal concrete's distillation? Law's, all
Astronomy's last refinement?
Hast thou no soul? Can I not know, identify thee?

Old Chants

An ancient song, reciting, ending,
Once gazing toward thee, Mother of All,
Musing, seeking themes fitted for thee,
Accept for me, thou saidst, *the elder ballads,*
And name for me before thou goest each ancient poet.

(Of many debts incalculable,
Haply our New World's chieftest debt is to old poems.)

Ever so far back, preluding thee, America,
Old chants, Egyptian priests, and those of Ethiopia,
The Hindu epics, the Grecian, Chinese, Persian,
The Biblic books and prophets, and deep idyls of the
Nazarene,

The Iliad, Odyssey, plots, doings, wanderings of Eneas,
Hesiod, Eschylus, Sophocles, Merlin, Arthur,
The Cid, Roland at Roncesvalles, the Nibelungen,
The troubadours, minstrels, minnesingers, skalds,
Chaucer, Dante, flocks of singing birds,
The Border Minstrelsy, the bye-gone ballads, feudal tales, essays, plays,
Shakspere, Schiller, Walter Scott, Tennyson,
As some vast wondrous weird dream-presences,
The great shadowy groups gathering around,
Darting their mighty masterful eyes forward at thee,
Thou! with as now thy bending neck and head, with courteous hand and word, ascending,
Thou! pausing a moment, drooping thine eyes upon them, blent with their music,
Well pleased, accepting all, curiously prepared for by them,
Thou enterest at thy entrance porch.

A Christmas Greeting

From a Northern Star-Group to a Southern, 1889–'90.

WELCOME, Brazilian brother—thy ample place is ready;
A loving hand—a smile from the north—a sunny instant hail!
(Let the future care for itself, where it reveals its troubles, impedimentas,
Ours, ours the present throe, the democratic aim, the acceptance and the faith;)
To thee to-day our reaching arm, our turning neck—to thee from us the expectant eye,
Thou cluster free! thou brilliant lustrous one! thou, learning well,
The true lesson of a nation's light in the sky,
(More shining than the Cross, more than the Crown,)
The height to be superb humanity.

Sounds of the Winter

SOUNDS of the winter too,
Sunshine upon the mountains—many a distant strain
From cheery railroad train—from nearer field, barn, house,

The whispering air—even the mute crops, garner'd apples, corn,
Children's and women's tones—rhythm of many a farmer and of flail,
An old man's garrulous lips among the rest, *Think not we give out yet,*
Forth from these snowy hairs we keep up yet the lilt.

A Twilight Song

As I sit in twilight late alone by the flickering oak-flame,
Musing on long-pass'd war-scenes—of the countless buried unknown soldiers,
Of the vacant names, as unindented air's and sea's—the unreturn'd,
The brief truce after battle, with grim burial-squads, and the deep-fill'd trenches
Of gather'd dead from all America, North, South, East, West, whence they came up,
From wooded Maine, New-England's farms, from fertile Pennsylvania, Illinois, Ohio,
From the measureless West, Virginia, the South, the Carolinas, Texas,
(Even here in my room-shadows and half-lights in the noiseless flickering flames,
Again I see the stalwart ranks on-filing, rising—I hear the rhythmic tramp of the armies;)
You million unwrit names all, all—you dark bequest from all the war,
A special verse for you—a flash of duty long neglected—your mystic roll strangely gather'd here,
Each name recall'd by me from out the darkness and death's ashes,
Henceforth to be, deep, deep within my heart recording, for many a future year,
Your mystic roll entire of unknown names, or North or South,
Embalm'd with love in this twilight song.

When the Full-Grown Poet Came

WHEN the full-grown poet came,
Out spake pleased Nature (the round impassive globe, with all its shows of day and night,) saying, *He is mine;*
But out spake too the Soul of man, proud, jealous and unreconciled, *Nay, he is mine alone;*
—Then the full-grown poet stood between the two, and took each by the hand;
And to-day and ever so stands, as blender, uniter, tightly holding hands,
Which he will never release until he reconciles the two,
And wholly and joyously blends them.

Osceola

[*When I was nearly grown to manhood in Brooklyn, New York, (middle of 1838,) I met one of the return'd U. S. Marines from Fort Moultrie, S. C., and had long talks with him—learn'd the occurrence below described—death of Osceola. The latter was a young, brave, leading Seminole in the Florida war of that time—was surrender'd to our troops, imprison'd and literally died of "a broken heart," at Fort Moultrie. He sicken'd of his confinement—the doctor and officers made every allowance and kindness possible for him; then the close:*]

WHEN his hour for death had come,
He slowly rais'd himself from the bed on the floor,
Drew on his war-dress, shirt, leggings, and girdled the belt around his waist,
Call'd for vermilion paint (his looking-glass was held before him,)
Painted half his face and neck, his wrists, and back-hands.
Put the scalp-knife carefully in his belt—then lying down, resting a moment,
Rose again, half sitting, smiled, gave in silence his extended hand to each and all,
Sank faintly low to the floor (tightly grasping the tomahawk handle,)
Fix'd his look on wife and little children—the last:
(And here a line in memory of his name and death.)

A Voice from Death

(The Johnstown, Penn., cataclysm, May 31, 1889.)

A VOICE from Death, solemn and strange, in all his sweep
and power,
With sudden, indescribable blow—towns drown'd—
humanity by thousands slain,
The vaunted work of thrift, goods, dwellings, forge, street,
iron bridge,
Dash'd pell-mell by the blow—yet usher'd life continuing on,
(Amid the rest, amid the rushing, whirling, wild debris,
A suffering woman saved—a baby safely born!)

Although I come and unannounc'd, in horror and in pang,
In pouring flood and fire, and wholesale elemental crash,
(this voice so solemn, strange,)
I too a minister of Deity.

Yea, Death, we bow our faces, veil our eyes to thee,
We mourn the old, the young untimely drawn to thee,
The fair, the strong, the good, the capable,
The household wreck'd, the husband and the wife, the
engulf'd forger in his forge,
The corpses in the whelming waters and the mud,
The gather'd thousands to their funeral mounds, and
thousands never found or gather'd.

Then after burying, mourning the dead,
(Faithful to them found or unfound, forgetting not, bearing
the past, here new musing,)
A day—a passing moment or an hour—America itself bends
low,
Silent, resign'd, submissive.

War, death, cataclysm like this, America,
Take deep to thy proud prosperous heart.

E'en as I chant, lo! out of death, and out of ooze and slime,
The blossoms rapidly blooming, sympathy, help, love,

From West and East, from South and North and over sea,
Its hot-spurr'd hearts and hands humanity to human aid moves on;
And from within a thought and lesson yet.

Thou ever-darting Globe! through Space and Air!
Thou waters that encompass us!
Thou that in all the life and death of us, in action or in sleep!
Thou laws invisible that permeate them and all,
Thou that in all, and over all, and through and under all, incessant!
Thou! thou! the vital, universal, giant force resistless, sleepless, calm,
Holding Humanity as in thy open hand, as some ephemeral toy,
How ill to e'er forget thee!

For I too have forgotten,
(Wrapt in these little potencies of progress, politics, culture, wealth, inventions, civilization,)
Have lost my recognition of your silent ever-swaying power, ye mighty, elemental throes,
In which and upon which we float, and every one of us is buoy'd.

A Persian Lesson

For his o'erarching and last lesson the greybeard sufi,
In the fresh scent of the morning in the open air,
On the slope of a teeming Persian rose-garden,
Under an ancient chestnut-tree wide spreading its branches,
Spoke to the young priests and students.

"Finally my children, to envelop each word, each part of the rest,
Allah is all, all, all—is immanent in every life and object,
May-be at many and many-a-more removes—yet Allah, Allah, Allah is there.

"Has the estray wander'd far? Is the reason-why strangely hidden?

Would you sound below the restless ocean of the entire world?
Would you know the dissatisfaction? the urge and spur of every life;
The something never still'd—never entirely gone? the invisible need of every seed?

"It is the central urge in every atom,
(Often unconscious, often evil, downfallen,)
To return to its divine source and origin, however distant,
Latent the same in subject and in object, without one exception."

The Commonplace

THE commonplace I sing;
How cheap is health! how cheap nobility!
Abstinence, no falsehood, no gluttony, lust;
The open air I sing, freedom, toleration,
(Take here the mainest lesson—less from books—less from the schools,)
The common day and night—the common earth and waters,
Your farm—your work, trade, occupation,
The democratic wisdom underneath, like solid ground for all.

"The Rounded Catalogue Divine Complete"

[*Sunday,—— — ——.—Went this forenoon to church. A college professor, Rev. Dr.———, gave us a fine sermon, during which I caught the above words; but the minister included in his "rounded catalogue" letter and spirit, only the esthetic things, and entirely ignored what I name in the following:*]

THE devilish and the dark, the dying and diseas'd,
The countless (nineteen-twentieths) low and evil, crude and savage,
The crazed, prisoners in jail, the horrible, rank, malignant,
Venom and filth, serpents, the ravenous sharks, liars, the dissolute;
(What is the part the wicked and the loathesome bear within earth's orbic scheme?)

Newts, crawling things in slime and mud, poisons,
The barren soil, the evil men, the slag and hideous rot.

Mirages

(Noted verbatim after a supper-talk out doors in Nevada with two old miners.)

MORE experiences and sights, stranger, than you'd think for;
Times again, now mostly just after sunrise or before sunset,
Sometimes in spring, oftener in autumn, perfectly clear
 weather, in plain sight,
Camps far or near, the crowded streets of cities and the
 shop-fronts,
(Account for it or not—credit or not—it is all true,
And my mate there could tell you the like—we have often
 confab'd about it,)
People and scenes, animals, trees, colors and lines, plain as
 could be,
Farms and dooryards of home, paths border'd with box,
 lilacs in corners,
Weddings in churches, thanksgiving dinners, returns of
 long-absent sons,
Glum funerals, the crape-veil'd mother and the daughters,
Trials in courts, jury and judge, the accused in the box,
Contestants, battles, crowds, bridges, wharves,
Now and then mark'd faces of sorrow or joy,
(I could pick them out this moment if I saw them again,)
Show'd to me just aloft to the right in the sky-edge,
Or plainly there to the left on the hill-tops.

L. of G.'s Purport

NOT to exclude or demarcate, or pick out evils from their
 formidable masses (even to expose them,)
But add, fuse, complete, extend—and celebrate the
 immortal and the good.

Haughty this song, its words and scope,
To span vast realms of space and time,
Evolution—the cumulative—growths and generations.

Begun in ripen'd youth and steadily pursued,
Wandering, peering, dallying with all—war, peace, day and night absorbing,
Never even for one brief hour abandoning my task,
I end it here in sickness, poverty, and old age.

I sing of life, yet mind me well of death:
To-day shadowy Death dogs my steps, my seated shape, and has for years—
Draws sometimes close to me, as face to face.

The Unexpress'd

How dare one say it?
After the cycles, poems, singers, plays,
Vaunted Ionia's, India's—Homer, Shakspere—the long, long times' thick dotted roads, areas,
The shining clusters and the Milky Ways of stars—Nature's pulses reap'd,
All retrospective passions, heroes, war, love, adoration,
All ages' plummets dropt to their utmost depths,
All human lives, throats, wishes, brains—all experiences' utterance;
After the countless songs, or long or short, all tongues, all lands,
Still something not yet told in poesy's voice or print—something lacking,
(Who knows? the best yet unexpress'd and lacking.)

Grand Is the Seen

GRAND is the seen, the light, to me—grand are the sky and stars,
Grand is the earth, and grand are lasting time and space,
And grand their laws, so multiform, puzzling, evolutionary;
But grander far the unseen soul of me, comprehending, endowing all those,
Lighting the light, the sky and stars, delving the earth, sailing the sea,

(What were all those, indeed, without thee, unseen soul? of
what amount without thee?)
More evolutionary, vast, puzzling, O my soul!
More multiform far—more lasting thou than they.

Unseen Buds

UNSEEN buds, infinite, hidden well,
Under the snow and ice, under the darkness, in every square
or cubic inch,
Germinal, exquisite, in delicate lace, microscopic, unborn,
Like babes in wombs, latent, folded, compact, sleeping;
Billions of billions, and trillions of trillions of them waiting,
(On earth and in the sea—the universe—the stars there in
the heavens,)
Urging slowly, surely forward, forming endless,
And waiting ever more, forever more behind.

Good-Bye my Fancy!

GOOD-BYE my Fancy!
Farewell dear mate, dear love!
I'm going away, I know not where,
Or to what fortune, or whether I may ever see you again,
So Good-bye my Fancy.

Now for my last—let me look back a moment;
The slower fainter ticking of the clock is in me,
Exit, nightfall, and soon the heart-thud stopping.

Long have we lived, joy'd, caress'd together;
Delightful!—now separation—Good-bye my Fancy.

Yet let me not be too hasty,
Long indeed have we lived, slept, filter'd, become really
blended into one;
Then if we die we die together, (yes, we'll remain one,)
If we go anywhere we'll go together to meet what happens,
May-be we'll be better off and blither, and learn something,

May-be it is yourself now really ushering me to the true
songs, (who knows?)
May-be it is you the mortal knob really undoing, turning—
so now finally,
Good-bye—and hail! my Fancy.

A Backward Glance o'er Travel'd Roads

PERHAPS the best of songs heard, or of any and all true love, or life's fairest episodes, or sailors', soldiers' trying scenes on land or sea, is the *résumé* of them, or any of them, long afterwards, looking at the actualities away back past, with all their practical excitations gone. How the soul loves to float amid such reminiscences!

So here I sit gossiping in the early candle-light of old age—I and my book—casting backward glances over our travel'd road. After completing, as it were, the journey—(a varied jaunt of years, with many halts and gaps of intervals—or some lengthen'd ship-voyage, wherein more than once the last hour had apparently arrived, and we seem'd certainly going down—yet reaching port in a sufficient way through all discomfitures at last)—After completing my poems, I am curious to review them in the light of their own (at the time unconscious, or mostly unconscious) intentions, with certain unfoldings of the thirty years they seek to embody. These lines, therefore, will probably blend the weft of first purposes and speculations, with the warp of that experience afterwards, always bringing strange developments.

Result of seven or eight stages and struggles extending through nearly thirty years, (as I nigh my three-score-and-ten I live largely on memory,) I look upon "Leaves of Grass," now finish'd to the end of its opportunities and powers, as my definitive *carte visite* to the coming generations of the New World,* if I may assume to say so. That I have not gain'd the acceptance of my own time, but have fallen back on fond dreams of the future—anticipations—("still lives the song, though Regnar dies")—That from a worldly and business point of view "Leaves of Grass" has been worse than a failure—that public criticism on the book and myself as author of it yet shows mark'd anger and contempt more than anything else—("I find a solid line of enemies to you every-

*When Champollion, on his death-bed, handed to the printer the revised proof of his "Egyptian Grammar," he said gayly, "Be careful of this—it is my *carte de visite* to posterity."

where,"—letter from W. S. K., Boston, May 28, 1884)—And that solely for publishing it I have been the object of two or three pretty serious special official buffetings—is all probably no more than I ought to have expected. I had my choice when I commenc'd. I bid neither for soft eulogies, big money returns, nor the approbation of existing schools and conventions. As fulfill'd, or partially fulfill'd, the best comfort of the whole business (after a small band of the dearest friends and upholders ever vouchsafed to man or cause—doubtless all the more faithful and uncompromising—this little phalanx!—for being so few) is that, unstopp'd and unwarp'd by any influence outside the soul within me, I have had my say entirely my own way, and put it unerringly on record—the value thereof to be decided by time.

In calculating that decision, William O'Connor and Dr. Bucke are far more peremptory than I am. Behind all else that can be said, I consider "Leaves of Grass" and its theory experimental—as, in the deepest sense, I consider our American republic itself to be, with its theory. (I think I have at least enough philosophy not to be too absolutely certain of any thing, or any results.) In the second place, the volume is a *sortie*—whether to prove triumphant, and conquer its field of aim and escape and construction, nothing less than a hundred years from now can fully answer. I consider the point that I have positively gain'd a hearing, to far more than make up for any and all other lacks and withholdings. Essentially, *that* was from the first, and has remain'd throughout, the main object. Now it seems to be achiev'd, I am certainly contented to waive any otherwise momentous drawbacks, as of little account. Candidly and dispassionately reviewing all my intentions, I feel that they were creditable—and I accept the result, whatever it may be.

After continued personal ambition and effort, as a young fellow, to enter with the rest into competition for the usual rewards, business, political, literary, &c.—to take part in the great *mèlée*, both for victory's prize itself and to do some good—After years of those aims and pursuits, I found myself remaining possess'd, at the age of thirty-one to thirty-three, with a special desire and conviction. Or rather, to be quite exact, a desire that had been flitting through my previous life, or hovering on the flanks, mostly indefinite hitherto, had steadily advanced to the front, defined itself, and finally dominated everything else. This was a feeling or ambition to articulate and faithfully express in literary or poetic form, and uncompromisingly, my own physical, emotional, moral, intellectual, and æsthetic Personality, in the midst of, and tallying, the momentous spirit and facts of its immediate days, and of current America—and to exploit that Personality, identified with place and date, in a far more candid and comprehensive sense than any hitherto poem or book.

Perhaps this is in brief, or suggests, all I have sought to do. Given the Nineteenth Century, with the United States, and what they furnish as area and points of view, "Leaves of Grass" is, or seeks to be, simply a faithful and doubtless self-will'd record. In the midst of all, it gives one man's—the author's—identity, ardors, observations, faiths, and thoughts, color'd hardly at all with any decided coloring from other & faiths or other identities. Plenty of songs had been sung—beautiful, matchless songs—adjusted to other lands than these—another spirit and stage of evolution; but I would sing, and leave out or put in, quite solely with reference to America and to-day. Modern science and democracy seem'd to be throwing out their challenge to poetry to put them in its statements in contradistinction to the songs and myths of the past. As I see it now (perhaps too late,) I have unwittingly taken up that challenge and made an attempt at such statements—which I certainly would not assume to do now, knowing more clearly what it means.

For grounds for "Leaves of Grass," as a poem, I abandon'd the conventional themes, which do not appear in it: none of the stock ornamentation, or choice plots of love or war, or high, exceptional personages of Old-World song; nothing, as I may say, for beauty's sake—no legend, or myth, or romance, nor euphemism, nor rhyme. But the broadest average of humanity and its identities in the now ripening Nineteenth Century, and especially in each of their countless examples and practical occupations in the United States to-day.

One main contrast of the ideas behind every page of my

verses, compared with establish'd poems, is their different relative attitude towards God, towards the objective universe, and still more (by reflection, confession, assumption, &c.) the quite changed attitude of the ego, the one chanting or talking, towards himself and towards his fellow-humanity. It is certainly time for America, above all, to begin this readjustment in the scope and basic point of view of verse; for everything else has changed. As I write, I see in an article on Wordsworth, in one of the current English magazines, the lines, "A few weeks ago an eminent French critic said that, owing to the special tendency to science and to its all-devouring force, poetry would cease to be read in fifty years." But I anticipate the very contrary. Only a firmer, vastly broader, new area begins to exist—nay, is already form'd—to which the poetic genius must emigrate. Whatever may have been the case in years gone by, the true use for the imaginative faculty of modern times is to give ultimate vivification to facts, to science, and to common lives, endowing them with the glows and glories and final illustriousness which belong to every real thing, and to real things only. Without that ultimate vivification—which the poet or other artist alone can give—reality would seem incomplete, and science, democracy, and life itself, finally in vain.

Few appreciate the moral revolutions, our age, which have been profounder far than the material or inventive or war-produced ones. The Nineteenth Century, now well towards its close (and ripening into fruit the seeds of the two preceding centuries*)—the uprisings of national masses and shiftings of boundary-lines—the historical and other prominent facts of the United States—the war of attempted Secession—the stormy rush and haste of nebulous forces—never can future years witness more excitement and din of action—never completer change of army front along the whole line, the

*The ferment and germination even of the United States to-day, dating back to, and in my opinion mainly founded on, the Elizabethan age in English history, the age of Francis Bacon and Shakspere. Indeed, when we pursue it, what growth or advent is there that does not date back, back, until lost—perhaps its most tantalizing clues lost—in the receded horizons of the past?

whole civilized world. For all these new and evolutionary facts, meanings, purposes, new poetic messages, new forms and expressions, are inevitable.

My Book and I—what a period we have presumed to span! those thirty years from 1850 to '80—and America in them! Proud, proud indeed may we be, if we have cull'd enough of that period in its own spirit to worthily waft a few live breaths of it to the future!

Let me not dare, here or anywhere, for my own purposes, or any purposes, to attempt the definition of Poetry, nor answer the question what it is. Like Religion, Love, Nature, while those terms are indispensable, and we all give a sufficiently accurate meaning to them, in my opinion no definition that has ever been made sufficiently encloses the name Poetry; nor can any rule or convention ever so absolutely obtain but some great exception may arise and disregard and overturn it.

Also it must be carefully remember'd that first-class literature does not shine by any luminosity of its own; nor do its poems. They grow of circumstances, and are evolutionary. The actual living light is always curiously from elsewhere—follows unaccountable sources, and is lunar and relative at the best. There are, I know, certain controling themes that seem endlessly appropriated to the poets—as war, in the past—in the Bible, religious rapture and adoration—always love, beauty, some fine plot, or pensive or other emotion. But, strange as it may sound at first, I will say there is something striking far deeper and towering far higher than those themes for the best elements of modern song.

Just as all the old imaginative works rest, after their kind, on long trains of presuppositions, often entirely unmention'd by themselves, yet supplying the most important bases of them, and without which they could have had no reason for being, so "Leaves of Grass," before a line was written, presupposed something different from any other, and, as it stands, is the result of such presupposition. I should say, indeed, it were useless to attempt reading the book without first carefully tallying that preparatory background and quality in the mind. Think of the United States to-day—the facts of these thirty-eight or forty empires solder'd in one—

sixty or seventy millions of equals, with their lives, their passions, their future—these incalculable, modern, American, seething multitudes around us, of which we are inseparable parts! Think, in comparison, of the petty environage and limited area of the poets of past or present Europe, no matter how great their genius. Think of the absence and ignorance, in all cases hitherto, of the multitudinousness, vitality, and the unprecedented stimulants of to-day and here. It almost seems as if a poetry with cosmic and dynamic features of magnitude and limitlessness suitable to the human soul, were never possible before. It is certain that a poetry of absolute faith and equality for the use of the democratic masses never was.

In estimating first-class song, a sufficient Nationality, or, on the other hand, what may be call'd the negative and lack of it, (as in Goethe's case, it sometimes seems to me,) is often, if not always, the first element. One needs only a little penetration to see, at more or less removes, the material facts of their country and radius, with the coloring of the moods of humanity at the time, and its gloomy or hopeful prospects, behind all poets and each poet, and forming their birth-marks. I know very well that my "Leaves" could not possibly have emerged or been fashion'd or completed, from any other era than the latter half of the Nineteenth Century, nor any other land than democratic America, and from the absolute triumph of the National Union arms.

And whether my friends claim it for me or not, I know well enough, too, that in respect to pictorial talent, dramatic situations, and especially in verbal melody and all the conventional technique of poetry, not only the divine works that to-day stand ahead in the world's reading, but dozens more, transcend (some of them immeasurably transcend) all I have done, or could do. But it seem'd to me, as the objects in Nature, the themes of æstheticism, and all special exploitations of the mind and soul, involve not only their own inherent quality, but the quality, just as inherent and important, of *their point of view,** the time had come to reflect all themes and things, old and new, in the lights thrown on them by the

*According to Immanuel Kant, the last essential reality, giving shape and significance to all the rest.

advent of America and democracy—to chant those themes through the utterance of one, not only the grateful and reverent legatee of the past, but the born child of the New World—to illustrate all through the genesis and ensemble of to-day; and that such illustration and ensemble are the chief demands of America's prospective imaginative literature. Not to carry out, in the approved style, some choice plot of fortune or misfortune, or fancy, or fine thoughts, or incidents, or courtesies—all of which has been done overwhelmingly and well, probably never to be excell'd—but that while in such æsthetic presentation of objects, passions, plots, thoughts, &c., our lands and days do not want, and probably will never have, anything better than they already possess from the bequests of the past, it still remains to be said that there is even towards all those a subjective and contemporary point of view appropriate to ourselves alone, and to our new genius and environments, different from anything hitherto; and that such conception of current or gone-by life and art is for us the only means of their assimilation consistent with the Western world.

Indeed, and anyhow, to put it specifically, has not the time arrived when, (if it must be plainly said, for democratic America's sake, if for no other) there must imperatively come a readjustment of the whole theory and nature of Poetry? The question is important, and I may turn the argument over and repeat it: Does not the best thought of our day and Republic conceive of a birth and spirit of song superior to anything past or present? To the effectual and moral consolidation of our lands (already, as materially establish'd, the greatest factors in known history, and far, far greater through what they prelude and necessitate, and are to be in future)—to conform with and build on the concrete realities and theories of the universe furnish'd by science, and henceforth the only irrefragable basis for anything, verse included—to root both influences in the emotional and imaginative action of the modern time, and dominate all that precedes or opposes them—is not either a radical advance and step forward, or a new verteber of the best song indispensable?

The New World receives with joy the poems of the antique, with European feudalism's rich fund of epics, plays, ballads—seeks not in the least to deaden or displace those voices from our ear and area—holds them indeed as indispensable studies, influences, records, comparisons. But though the dawn-dazzle of the sun of literature is in those poems for us of to-day—though perhaps the best parts of current character in nations, social groups, or any man's or woman's individuality, Old World or New, are from them—and though if I were ask'd to name the most precious bequest to current American civilization from all the hitherto ages, I am not sure but I would name those old and less old songs ferried hither from east and west—some serious words and debits remain; some acrid considerations demand a hearing. Of the great poems receiv'd from abroad and from the ages, and to-day enveloping and penetrating America, is there one that is consistent with these United States, or essentially applicable to them as they are and are to be? Is there one whose underlying basis is not a denial and insult to democracy? What a comment it forms, anyhow, on this era of literary fulfilment, with the splendid day-rise of science and resuscitation of history, that our chief religious and poetical works are not our own, nor adapted to our light, but have been furnish'd by far-back ages out of their arriere and darkness, or, at most, twilight dimness! What is there in those works that so imperiously and scornfully dominates all our advanced civilization, and culture?

Even Shakspere, who so suffuses current letters and art (which indeed have in most degrees grown out of him,) belongs essentially to the buried past. Only he holds the proud distinction for certain important phases of that past, of being the loftiest of the singers life has yet given voice to. All, however, relate to and rest upon conditions, standards, politics, sociologies, ranges of belief, that have been quite eliminated from the Eastern hemisphere, and never existed at all in the Western. As authoritative types of song they belong in America just about as much as the persons and institutes they depict. True, it may be said, the emotional, moral, and æsthetic natures of humanity have not radically changed—that in these the old poems apply to our times and all times, irrespective of date; and that they are of incalculable value as pictures of the past. I willingly make those admissions, and to their fullest extent; then advance the points herewith as of serious, even paramount importance.

I have indeed put on record elsewhere my reverence and eulogy for those never-to-be-excell'd poetic bequests, and their indescribable preciousness as heirlooms for America. Another and separate point must now be candidly stated. If I had not stood before those poems with uncover'd head, fully aware of their colossal grandeur and beauty of form and spirit, I could not have written "Leaves of Grass." My verdict and conclusions as illustrated in its pages are arrived at through the temper and inculcation of the old works as much as through anything else—perhaps more than through anything else. As America fully and fairly construed is the legitimate result and evolutionary outcome of the past, so I would dare to claim for my verse. Without stopping to qualify the averment, the Old World has had the poems of myths, fictions, feudalism, conquest, caste, dynastic wars, and splendid exceptional characters and affairs, which have been great; but the New World needs the poems of realities and science and of the democratic average and basic equality, which shall be greater. In the centre of all, and object of all, stands the Human Being, towards whose heroic and spiritual evolution poems and everything directly or indirectly tend, Old World or New.

Continuing the subject, my friends have more than once suggested—or may be the garrulity of advancing age is possessing me—some further embryonic facts of "Leaves of Grass," and especially how I enter'd upon them. Dr. Bucke has, in his volume, already fully and fairly described the preparation of my poetic field, with the particular and general plowing, planting, seeding, and occupation of the ground, till everything was fertilized, rooted, and ready to start its own way for good or bad. Not till after all this, did I attempt any serious acquaintance with poetic literature. Along in my sixteenth year I had become possessor of a stout, well-cramm'd one thousand page octavo volume (I have it yet,) containing Walter Scott's poetry entire—an inexhaustible mine and treasury of poetic forage (especially the endless forests and jungles of notes)—has been so to me for fifty years, and remains so to this day.*

Later, at intervals, summers and falls, I used to go off, sometimes for a week at a stretch, down in the country, or to Long Island's seashores—there, in the presence of outdoor influences, I went over thoroughly the Old and New Testaments, and absorb'd (probably to better advantage for me than in any library or indoor room—it makes such difference *where* you read,) Shakspere, Ossian, the best translated versions I could get of Homer, Eschylus, Sophocles, the old German Nibelungen, the ancient Hindoo poems, and one or two other masterpieces, Dante's among them. As it happen'd, I read the latter mostly in an old wood. The Iliad (Buckley's prose version,) I read first thoroughly on the peninsula of Orient, northeast end of Long Island, in a shelter'd hollow of rocks and sand, with the sea on each side. (I have wonder'd since why I was not overwhelm'd by those mighty masters. Likely because I read them, as described, in the full presence of Nature, under the sun, with the far-spreading landscape and vistas, or the sea rolling in.)

Toward the last I had among much else look'd over Edgar Poe's poems—of which I was not an admirer, tho' I always saw that beyond their limited range of melody (like perpetual chimes of music bells, ringing from lower *b* flat up to *g*) they were melodious expressions, and perhaps never excell'd ones, of certain pronounc'd phases of human morbidity. (The Poetic area is very spacious—has room for all—has so many mansions!) But I was repaid in Poe's prose by the idea that (at any rate for our occasions, our day) there can be no such thing as a long poem. The same thought had been haunting my mind before, but Poe's argument, though short, work'd the sum out and proved it to me.

*Sir Walter Scott's COMPLETE POEMS; especially including BORDER MINSTRELSY; then Sir Tristrem; Lay of the Last Minstrel; Ballads from the German; Marmion; Lady of the Lake; Vision of Don Roderick; Lord of the Isles; Rokeby; Bridal of Triermain; Field of Waterloo; Harold the Dauntless; all the Dramas; various Introductions, endless interesting Notes, and Essays on Poetry, Romance, &c.

Lockhart's 1833 (or '34) edition with Scott's latest and copious revisions and annotations. (All the poems were thoroughly read by me, but the ballads of the Border Minstrelsy over and over again.)

Another point had an early settlement, clearing the ground greatly. I saw, from the time my enterprise and questionings positively shaped themselves (how best can I express my own distinctive era and surroundings, America, Democracy?) that the trunk and centre whence the answer was to radiate, and to which all should return from straying however far a distance, must be an identical body and soul, a personality—which personality, after many considerations and ponderings I deliberately settled should be myself—indeed could not be any other. I also felt strongly (whether I have shown it or not) that to the true and full estimate of the Present both the Past and the Future are main considerations.

These, however, and much more might have gone on and come to naught (almost positively would have come to naught,) if a sudden, vast, terrible, direct and indirect stimulus for new and national declamatory expression had not been given to me. It is certain, I say, that, although I had made a start before, only from the occurrence of the Secession War, and what it show'd me as by flashes of lightning, with the emotional depths it sounded and arous'd (of course, I don't mean in my own heart only, I saw it just as plainly in others, in millions)—that only from the strong flare and provocation of that war's sights and scenes the final reasons-for-being of an autochthonic and passionate song definitely came forth.

I went down to the war fields in Virginia (end of 1862), lived thenceforward in camp—saw great battles and the days and nights afterward—partook of all the fluctuations, gloom, despair, hopes again arous'd, courage evoked—death readily risk'd—*the cause,* too—along and filling those agonistic and lurid following years, 1863–'64–'65—the real parturition years (more than 1776–'83) of this henceforth homogeneous Union. Without those three or four years and the experiences they gave, "Leaves of Grass" would not now be existing.

But I set out with the intention also of indicating or hinting some point-characteristics which I since see (though I did not then, at least not definitely) were bases and object-urgings toward those "Leaves" from the first. The word I myself put primarily for the description of them as they stand at last, is the word Suggestiveness. I round and finish little, if anything;

and could not, consistently with my scheme. The reader will always have his or her part to do, just as much as I have had mine. I seek less to state or display any theme or thought, and more to bring you, reader, into the atmosphere of the theme or thought—there to pursue your own flight. Another impetus-word is Comradeship as for all lands, and in a more commanding and acknowledg'd sense than hitherto. Other word-signs would be Good Cheer, Content, and Hope.

The chief trait of any given poet is always the spirit he brings to the observation of Humanity and Nature—the mood out of which he contemplates his subjects. What kind of temper and what amount of faith report these things? Up to how recent a date is the song carried? What the equipment, and special raciness of the singer—what his tinge of coloring? The last value of artistic expressers, past and present—Greek æsthetes, Shakspere—or in our own day Tennyson, Victor Hugo, Carlyle, Emerson—is certainly involv'd in such questions. I say the profoundest service that poems or any other writings can do for their reader is not merely to satisfy the intellect, or supply something polish'd and interesting, nor even to depict great passions, or persons or events, but to fill him with vigorous and clean manliness, religiousness, and give him *good heart* as a radical possession and habit. The educated world seems to have been growing more and more ennuyed for ages, leaving to our time the inheritance of it all. Fortunately there is the original inexhaustible fund of buoyancy, normally resident in the race, forever eligible to be appeal'd to and relied on.

As for native American individuality, though certain to come, and on a large scale, the distinctive and ideal type of Western character (as consistent with the operative political and even money-making features of United States' humanity in the Nineteenth Century as chosen knights, gentlemen and warriors were the ideals of the centuries of European feudalism) it has not yet appear'd. I have allow'd the stress of my poems from beginning to end to bear upon American individuality and assist it—not only because that is a great lesson in Nature, amid all her generalizing laws, but as counterpoise to the leveling tendencies of Democracy—and for other reasons. Defiant of ostensible literary and other conventions, I avowedly chant "the great pride of man in himself," and permit it to be more or less a *motif* of nearly all my verse. I think this pride indispensable to an American. I think it not inconsistent with obedience, humility, deference, and self-questioning.

Democracy has been so retarded and jeopardized by powerful personalities, that its first instincts are fain to clip, conform, bring in stragglers, and reduce everything to a dead level. While the ambitious thought of my song is to help the forming of a great aggregate Nation, it is, perhaps, altogether through the forming of myriads of fully develop'd and enclosing individuals. Welcome as are equality's and fraternity's doctrines and popular education, a certain liability accompanies them all, as we see. That primal and interior something in man, in his soul's abysms, coloring all, and, by exceptional fruitions, giving the last majesty to him—something continually touch'd upon and attain'd by the old poems and ballads of feudalism, and often the principal foundation of them—modern science and democracy appear to be endangering, perhaps eliminating. But that forms an appearance only; the reality is quite different. The new influences, upon the whole, are surely preparing the way for grander individualities than ever. To-day and here personal force is behind everything, just the same. The times and depictions from the Iliad to Shakspere inclusive can happily never again be realized—but the elements of courageous and lofty manhood are unchanged.

Without yielding an inch the working-man and working-woman were to be in my pages from first to last. The ranges of heroism and loftiness with which Greek and feudal poets endow'd their god-like or lordly born characters—indeed prouder and better based and with fuller ranges than those—I was to endow the democratic averages of America. I was to show that we, here and to-day, are eligible to the grandest and the best—more eligible now than any times of old were. I will also want my utterances (I said to myself before beginning) to be in spirit the poems of the morning. (They have been founded and mainly written in the sunny forenoon and early midday of my life.) I will want them to be the poems of women entirely as much as men. I have wish'd to put the complete Union of the States in my songs without any preference or partiality whatever. Henceforth, if they live and are read, it must be just as much South as North—just as much along the Pacific as Atlantic—in the valley of the Mississippi, in Canada, up in Maine, down in Texas, and on the shores of Puget Sound.

From another point of view "Leaves of Grass" is avowedly the song of Sex and Amativeness, and even Animality—though meanings that do not usually go along with those words are behind all, and will duly emerge; and all are sought to be lifted into a different light and atmosphere. Of this feature, intentionally palpable in a few lines, I shall only say the espousing principle of those lines so gives breath of life to my whole scheme that the bulk of the pieces might as well have been left unwritten were those lines omitted. Difficult as it will be, it has become, in my opinion, imperative to achieve a shifted attitude from superior men and women towards the thought and fact of sexuality, as an element in character, personality, the emotions, and a theme in literature. I am not going to argue the question by itself; it does not stand by itself. The vitality of it is altogether in its relations, bearings, significance—like the clef of a symphony. At last analogy the lines I allude to, and the spirit in which they are spoken, permeate all "Leaves of Grass," and the work must stand or fall with them, as the human body and soul must remain as an entirety.

Universal as are certain facts and symptoms of communities or individuals all times, there is nothing so rare in modern conventions and poetry as their normal recognizance. Literature is always calling in the doctor for consultation and confession, and always giving evasions and swathing suppressions in place of that "heroic nudity"* on which only a genuine diagnosis of serious cases can be built. And in respect to editions of "Leaves of Grass" in time to come (if there should be such) I take occasion now to confirm those lines with the settled convictions and deliberate renewals of thirty years, and to hereby prohibit, as far as word of mine can do so, any elision of them.

Then still a purpose enclosing all, and over and beneath all.

*"Nineteenth Century," July, 1883.

Ever since what might be call'd thought, or the budding of thought, fairly began in my youthful mind, I had had a desire to attempt some worthy record of that entire faith and acceptance ("to justify the ways of God to man" is Milton's well-known and ambitious phrase) which is the foundation of moral America. I felt it all as positively then in my young days as I do now in my old ones; to formulate a poem whose every thought or fact should directly or indirectly be or connive at an implicit belief in the wisdom, health, mystery, beauty of every process, every concrete object, every human or other existence, not only consider'd from the point of view of all, but of each.

While I can not understand it or argue it out, I fully believe in a clue and purpose in Nature, entire and several; and that invisible spiritual results, just as real and definite as the visible, eventuate all concrete life and all materialism, through Time. My book ought to emanate buoyancy and gladness legitimately enough, for it was grown out of those elements, and has been the comfort of my life since it was originally commenced.

One main genesis-motive of the "Leaves" was my conviction (just as strong to-day as ever) that the crowning growth of the United States is to be spiritual and heroic. To help start and favor that growth—or even to call attention to it, or the need of it—is the beginning, middle and final purpose of the poems. (In fact, when really cipher'd out and summ'd to the last, plowing up in earnest the interminable average fallows of humanity—not "good government" merely, in the common sense—is the justification and main purpose of these United States.)

Isolated advantages in any rank or grace or fortune—the direct or indirect threads of all the poetry of the past—are in my opinion distasteful to the republican genius, and offer no foundation for its fitting verse. Establish'd poems, I know, have the very great advantage of chanting the already perform'd, so full of glories, reminiscences dear to the minds of men. But my volume is a candidate for the future. "All original art," says Taine, anyhow, "is self-regulated, and no original art can be regulated from without; it carries its own counterpoise, and does not receive it from elsewhere—

lives on its own blood"—a solace to my frequent bruises and sulky vanity.

As the present is perhaps mainly an attempt at personal statement or illustration, I will allow myself as further help to extract the following anecdote from a book, "Annals of Old Painters," conn'd by me in youth. Rubens, the Flemish painter, in one of his wanderings through the galleries of old convents, came across a singular work. After looking at it thoughtfully for a good while, and listening to the criticisms of his suite of students, he said to the latter, in answer to their questions (as to what school the work implied or belong'd,) "I do not believe the artist, unknown and perhaps no longer living, who has given the world this legacy, ever belong'd to any school, or ever painted anything but this one picture, which is a personal affair—a piece out of a man's life."

"Leaves of Grass" indeed (I cannot too often reiterate) has mainly been the outcropping of my own emotional and other personal nature—an attempt, from first to last, to put *a Person,* a human being (myself, in the latter half of the Nineteenth Century, in America,) freely, fully and truly on record. I could not find any similar personal record in current literature that satisfied me. But it is not on "Leaves of Grass" distinctively as *literature,* or a specimen thereof, that I feel to dwell, or advance claims. No one will get at my verses who insists upon viewing them as a literary performance, or attempt at such performance, or as aiming mainly toward art or æstheticism.

I say no land or people or circumstances ever existed so needing a race of singers and poems differing from all others, and rigidly their own, as the land and people and circumstances of our United States need such singers and poems to-day, and for the future. Still further, as long as the States continue to absorb and be dominated by the poetry of the Old World, and remain unsupplied with autochthonous song, to express, vitalize and give color to and define their material and political success, and minister to them distinctively, so long will they stop short of first-class Nationality and remain defective.

In the free evening of my day I give to you, reader, the foregoing garrulous talk, thoughts, reminiscences,

As idly drifting down the ebb,
Such ripples, half-caught voices, echo from the shore.

Concluding with two items for the imaginative genius of the West, when it worthily rises—First, what Herder taught to the young Goethe, that really great poetry is always (like the Homeric or Biblical canticles) the result of a national spirit, and not the privilege of a polish'd and select few; Second, that the strongest and sweetest songs yet remain to be sung.

SUPPLEMENTARY POEMS

Contents

These poems, which do not appear in the 1855 or 1891–92 *Leaves of Grass*, are selected from the editions shown below. Some were untitled in the 1860 *Leaves of Grass.* In these cases no title appears in the text of the present edition. Titles in quotation marks, below, are those given by Whitman to other versions of the untitled poem; parenthetical quotations are from first lines if no title was ever given. Dates are of first appearance and last revision.

Leaves of Grass

[1860]

from *Chants Democratic and Native American*

2

33. HIS shape arises,
Arrogant, masculine, näive, rowdyish,
Laugher, weeper, worker, idler, citizen, countryman,
Saunterer of woods, stander upon hills, summer swimmer in rivers or by the sea,
Of pure American breed, of reckless health, his body perfect, free from taint from top to toe, free forever from headache and dyspepsia, clean-breathed,
Ample-limbed, a good feeder, weight a hundred and eighty pounds, full-blooded, six feet high, forty inches round the breast and back,
Countenance sun-burnt, bearded, calm, unrefined,
Reminder of animals, meeter of savage and gentleman on equal terms,
Attitudes lithe and erect, costume free, neck gray and open, of slow movement on foot,
Passer of his right arm round the shoulders of his friends, companion of the street,
Persuader always of people to give him their sweetest touches, and never their meanest,
A Manhattanese bred, fond of Brooklyn, fond of Broadway, fond of the life of the wharves and the great ferries,
Enterer everywhere, welcomed everywhere, easily understood after all,
Never offering others, always offering himself, corroborating his phrenology,
Voluptuous, inhabitive, combative, conscientious, alimentive, intuitive, of copious friendship, sublimity, firmness, self-esteem, comparison, individuality, form, locality, eventuality,
Avowing by life, manners, works, to contribute illustrations of results of The States,

Teacher of the unquenchable creed, namely, egotism,
Inviter of others continually henceforth to try their strength against his.

5

RESPONDEZ! Respondez!
Let every one answer! Let those who sleep be waked! Let none evade—not you, any more than others!
(If it really be as is pretended, how much longer must we go on with our affectations and sneaking?
Let me bring this to a close—I pronounce openly for a new distribution of roles,)
Let that which stood in front go behind! and let that which was behind advance to the front and speak!
Let murderers, thieves, bigots, fools, unclean persons, offer new propositions!
Let the old propositions be postponed!
Let faces and theories be turned inside out! Let meanings be freely criminal, as well as results!
Let there be no suggestion above the suggestion of drudgery!
Let none be pointed toward his destination! (Say! do you know your destination?)
Let trillions of men and women be mocked with bodies and mocked with Souls!
Let the love that waits in them, wait! Let it die, or pass still-born to other spheres!
Let the sympathy that waits in every man, wait! or let it also pass, a dwarf, to other spheres!
Let contradictions prevail! Let one thing contradict another! and let one line of my poems contradict another!
Let the people sprawl with yearning aimless hands! Let their tongues be broken! Let their eyes be discouraged! Let none descend into their hearts with the fresh lusciousness of love!
Let the theory of America be management, caste, comparison! (Say! what other theory would you?)
Let them that distrust birth and death lead the rest! (Say! why shall they not lead you?)

Let the crust of hell be neared and trod on! Let the days be darker than the nights! Let slumber bring less slumber than waking-time brings!
Let the world never appear to him or her for whom it was all made!
Let the heart of the young man exile itself from the heart of the old man! and let the heart of the old man be exiled from that of the young man!
Let the sun and moon go! Let scenery take the applause of the audience! Let there be apathy under the stars!
Let freedom prove no man's inalienable right! Every one who can tyrannize, let him tyrannize to his satisfaction!
Let none but infidels be countenanced!
Let the eminence of meanness, treachery, sarcasm, hate, greed, indecency, impotence, lust, be taken for granted above all! Let writers, judges, governments, households, religions, philosophies, take such for granted above all!
Let the worst men beget children out of the worst women!
Let priests still play at immortality!
Let Death be inaugurated!
Let nothing remain upon the earth except the ashes of teachers, artists, moralists, lawyers, and learned and polite persons!
Let him who is without my poems be assassinated!
Let the cow, the horse, the camel, the garden-bee—Let the mud-fish, the lobster, the mussel, eel, the sting-ray, and the grunting pig-fish—Let these, and the like of these, be put on a perfect equality with man and woman!
Let churches accommodate serpents, vermin, and the corpses of those who have died of the most filthy of diseases!
Let marriage slip down among fools, and be for none but fools!
Let men among themselves talk and think obscenely of women! and let women among themselves talk and think obscenely of men!
Let every man doubt every woman! and let every woman trick every man!
Let us all, without missing one, be exposed in public, naked, monthly, at the peril of our lives! Let our bodies be freely handled and examined by whoever chooses!

Let nothing but copies, pictures, statues, reminiscences, elegant works, be permitted to exist upon the earth!
Let the earth desert God, nor let there ever henceforth be mentioned the name of God!
Let there be no God!
Let there be money, business, imports, exports, custom, authority, precedents, pallor, dyspepsia, smut, ignorance, unbelief!
Let judges and criminals be transposed! Let the prison-keepers be put in prison! Let those that were prisoners take the keys! (Say! why might they not just as well be transposed?)
Let the slaves be masters! Let the masters become slaves!
Let the reformers descend from the stands where they are forever bawling! Let an idiot or insane person appear on each of the stands!
Let the Asiatic, the African, the European, the American and the Australian, go armed against the murderous stealthiness of each other! Let them sleep armed! Let none believe in good-will!
Let there be no unfashionable wisdom! Let such be scorned and derided off from the earth!
Let a floating cloud in the sky—Let a wave of the sea—Let one glimpse of your eye-sight upon the landscape or grass—Let growing mint, spinach, onions, tomatoes—Let these be exhibited as shows at a great price for admission!
Let all the men of These States stand aside for a few smouchers! Let the few seize on what they choose! Let the rest gawk, giggle, starve, obey!
Let shadows be furnished with genitals! Let substances be deprived of their genitals!
Let there be wealthy and immense cities—but through any of them, not a single poet, saviour, knower, lover!
Let the infidels of These States laugh all faith away! If one man be found who has faith, let the rest set upon him! Let them affright faith! Let them destroy the power of breeding faith!
Let the she-harlots and the he-harlots be prudent! Let

them dance on, while seeming lasts! (O seeming! seeming! seeming!)
Let the preachers recite creeds! Let them teach only what they have been taught!
Let the preachers of creeds never dare to go meditate candidly upon the hills, alone, by day or by night! (If one ever once dare, he is lost!)
Let insanity have charge of sanity!
Let books take the place of trees, animals, rivers, clouds!
Let the daubed portraits of heroes supersede heroes!
Let the manhood of man never take steps after itself! Let it take steps after eunuchs, and after consumptive and genteel persons!
Let the white person tread the black person under his heel! (Say! which is trodden under heel, after all?)
Let the reflections of the things of the world be studied in mirrors! Let the things themselves continue unstudied!
Let a man seek pleasure everywhere except in himself! Let a woman seek happiness everywhere except in herself! (Say! what real happiness have you had one single time through your whole life?)
Let the limited years of life do nothing for the limitless years of death! (Say! what do you suppose death will do, then?)

6

1. YOU just maturing youth! You male or female!
Remember the organic compact of These States,
Remember the pledge of the Old Thirteen thenceforward to the rights, life, liberty, equality of man,
Remember what was promulged by the founders, ratified by The States, signed in black and white by the Commissioners, and read by Washington at the head of the army,
Remember the purposes of the founders,—Remember Washington;
Remember the copious humanity streaming from every direction toward America;

Remember the hospitality that belongs to nations and men;
(Cursed be nation, woman, man, without hospitality!)
Remember, government is to subserve individuals,
Not any, not the President, is to have one jot more than you or me,
Not any habitan of America is to have one jot less than you or me.

2. Anticipate when the thirty or fifty millions, are to become the hundred, or two hundred millions, of equal freemen and freewomen, amicably joined.

3. Recall ages—One age is but a part—ages are but a part;
Recall the angers, bickerings, delusions, superstitions, of the idea of caste,
Recall the bloody cruelties and crimes.

4. Anticipate the best women;
I say an unnumbered new race of hardy and well-defined women are to spread through all These States,
I say a girl fit for These States must be free, capable, dauntless, just the same as a boy.

5. Anticipate your own life—retract with merciless power,
Shirk nothing—retract in time—Do you see those errors, diseases, weaknesses, lies, thefts?
Do you see that lost character?—Do you see decay, consumption, rum-drinking, dropsy, fever, mortal cancer or inflammation?
Do you see death, and the approach of death?

6. Think of the Soul;
I swear to you that body of yours gives proportions to your Soul somehow to live in other spheres,
I do not know how, but I know it is so.

7. Think of loving and being loved;
I swear to you, whoever you are, you can interfuse yourself with such things that everybody that sees you shall look longingly upon you.

8. Think of the past;
I warn you that in a little while, others will find their past in
you and your times.

9. The race is never separated—nor man nor woman escapes,
All is inextricable—things, spirits, nature, nations, you too—
from precedents you come.

10. Recall the ever-welcome defiers, (The mothers precede
them;)
Recall the sages, poets, saviours, inventors, lawgivers, of the
earth,
Recall Christ, brother of rejected persons—brother of slaves,
felons, idiots, and of insane and diseased persons.

11. Think of the time when you was not yet born,
Think of times you stood at the side of the dying,
Think of the time when your own body will be dying.

12. Think of spiritual results,
Sure as the earth swims through the heavens, does every one
of its objects pass into spiritual results.

13. Think of manhood, and you to be a man;
Do you count manhood, and the sweet of manhood,
nothing?

14. Think of womanhood, and you to be a woman;
The creation is womanhood,
Have I not said that womanhood involves all?
Have I not told how the universe has nothing better than
the best womanhood?

from *Leaves of Grass*

24

LIFT me close to your face till I whisper,
What you are holding is in reality no book, nor part
of a book,

It is a man, flushed and full-blooded—it is I—*So long!*
We must separate—Here! take from my lips this kiss,
Whoever you are, I give it especially to you;
So long—and I hope we shall meet again.

from *Calamus*

5

1. STATES!
Were you looking to be held together by the lawyers?
By an agreement on a paper? Or by arms?

2. Away!
I arrive, bringing these, beyond all the forces of courts and arms,
These! to hold you together as firmly as the earth itself is held together.

3. The old breath of life, ever new,
Here! I pass it by contact to you, America.

4. O mother! have you done much for me?
Behold, there shall from me be much done for you.

5. There shall from me be a new friendship—It shall be called after my name,
It shall circulate through The States, indifferent of place,
It shall twist and intertwist them through and around each other—Compact shall they be, showing new signs,
Affection shall solve every one of the problems of freedom,
Those who love each other shall be invincible,
They shall finally make America completely victorious, in my name.

6. One from Massachusetts shall be a comrade to a Missourian,
One from Maine or Vermont, and a Carolinian and an Oregonese, shall be friends triune, more precious to each other than all the riches of the earth.

7. To Michigan shall be wafted perfume from Florida,
To the Mannahatta from Cuba or Mexico,
Not the perfume of flowers, but sweeter, and wafted beyond death.

8. No danger shall balk Columbia's lovers,
If need be, a thousand shall sternly immolate themselves for one,
The Kanuck shall be willing to lay down his life for the Kansian, and the Kansian for the Kanuck, on due need.

9. It shall be customary in all directions, in the houses and streets, to see manly affection,
The departing brother or friend shall salute the remaining brother or friend with a kiss.

10. There shall be innovations,
There shall be countless linked hands—namely, the Northeasterner's, and the Northwesterner's, and the Southwesterner's, and those of the interior, and all their brood,
These shall be masters of the world under a new power,
They shall laugh to scorn the attacks of all the remainder of the world.

11. The most dauntless and rude shall touch face to face lightly,
The dependence of Liberty shall be lovers,
The continuance of Equality shall be comrades.

12. These shall tie and band stronger than hoops of iron,
I, extatic, O partners! O lands! henceforth with the love of lovers tie you.

13. I will make the continent indissoluble,
I will make the most splendid race the sun ever yet shone upon,
I will make divine magnetic lands.

14. I will plant companionship thick as trees along all the rivers of America, and along the shores of the great lakes, and all over the prairies,

I will make inseparable cities, with their arms about each
other's necks.

15. For you these, from me, O Democracy, to serve you, ma
femme!
For you! for you, I am trilling these songs.

8

LONG I thought that knowledge alone would suffice me—O
if I could but obtain knowledge!
Then my lands engrossed me—Lands of the prairies, Ohio's
land, the southern savannas, engrossed me—For them I
would live—I would be their orator;
Then I met the examples of old and new heroes—I heard of
warriors, sailors, and all dauntless persons—And it
seemed to me that I too had it in me to be as dauntless
as any—and would be so;
And then, to enclose all, it came to me to strike up the
songs of the New World—And then I believed my life
must be spent in singing;
But now take notice, land of the prairies, land of the south
savannas, Ohio's land,
Take notice, you Kanuck woods—and you Lake Huron—
and all that with you roll toward Niagara—and you
Niagara also,
And you, Californian mountains—That you each and all find
somebody else to be your singer of songs,
For I can be your singer of songs no longer—One who
loves me is jealous of me, and withdraws me from all
but love,
With the rest I dispense—I sever from what I thought
would suffice me, for it does not—it is now empty and
tasteless to me,
I heed knowledge, and the grandeur of The States, and the
example of heroes, no more,
I am indifferent to my own songs—I will go with him I
love,
It is to be enough for us that we are together—We never
separate again.

9

HOURS continuing long, sore and heavy-hearted,
Hours of the dusk, when I withdraw to a lonesome and unfrequented spot, seating myself, leaning my face in my hands;
Hours sleepless, deep in the night, when I go forth, speeding swiftly the country roads, or through the city streets, or pacing miles and miles, stifling plaintive cries;
Hours discouraged, distracted—for the one I cannot content myself without, soon I saw him content himself without me;
Hours when I am forgotten, (O weeks and months are passing, but I believe I am never to forget!)
Sullen and suffering hours! (I am ashamed—but it is useless—I am what I am;)
Hours of my torment—I wonder if other men ever have the like, out of the like feelings?
Is there even one other like me—distracted—his friend, his lover, lost to him?
Is he too as I am now? Does he still rise in the morning, dejected, thinking who is lost to him? and at night, awaking, think who is lost?
Does he too harbor his friendship silent and endless? harbor his anguish and passion?
Does some stray reminder, or the casual mention of a name, bring the fit back upon him, taciturn and deprest?
Does he see himself reflected in me? In these hours, does he see the face of his hours reflected?

16

1. WHO is now reading this?

2. May-be one is now reading this who knows some wrong-doing of my past life,
Or may-be a stranger is reading this who has secretly loved me,
Or may-be one who meets all my grand assumptions and egotisms with derision,
Or may-be one who is puzzled at me.

3. As if I were not puzzled at myself!
Or as if I never deride myself! (O conscience-struck! O self-convicted!)
Or as if I do not secretly love strangers! (O tenderly, a long time, and never avow it;)
Or as if I did not see, perfectly well, interior in myself, the stuff of wrong-doing,
Or as if it could cease transpiring from me until it must cease.

from *Messenger Leaves*

TO YOU

LET us twain walk aside from the rest;
Now we are together privately, do you discard ceremony,
Come! vouchsafe to me what has yet been vouchsafed to none—Tell me the whole story,
Tell me what you would not tell your brother, wife, husband, or physician.

from *Thoughts*

I

OF the visages of things—And of piercing through to the accepted hells beneath;
Of ugliness—To me there is just as much in it as there is in beauty—And now the ugliness of human beings is acceptable to me;
Of detected persons—To me, detected persons are not, in any respect, worse than undetected persons—and are not in any respect worse than I am myself;
Of criminals—To me, any judge, or any juror, is equally criminal—and any reputable person is also—and the President is also.

Says

1

I say whatever tastes sweet to the most perfect person, that
is finally right.

2

I say nourish a great intellect, a great brain;
If I have said anything to the contrary, I hereby retract it.

3

I say man shall not hold property in man;
I say the least developed person on earth is just as important
and sacred to himself or herself, as the most developed
person is to himself or herself.

4

I say where liberty draws not the blood out of slavery, there
slavery draws the blood out of liberty,
I say the word of the good old cause in These States, and
resound it hence over the world.

5

I say the human shape or face is so great, it must never be
made ridiculous;
I say for ornaments nothing outre can be allowed,
And that anything is most beautiful without ornament,
And that exaggerations will be sternly revenged in your own
physiology, and in other persons' physiology also;
And I say that clean-shaped children can be jetted and
conceived only where natural forms prevail in public,
and the human face and form are never caricatured;
And I say that genius need never more be turned to
romances,
(For facts properly told, how mean appear all romances.)

6

I say the word of lands fearing nothing—I will have no
other land;
I say discuss all and expose all—I am for every topic openly;

I say there can be no salvation for These States without innovators—without free tongues, and ears willing to hear the tongues;
And I announce as a glory of These States, that they respectfully listen to propositions, reforms, fresh views and doctrines, from successions of men and women,
Each age with its own growth.

7

I have said many times that materials and the Soul are great, and that all depends on physique;
Now I reverse what I said, and affirm that all depends on the æsthetic or intellectual,
And that criticism is great—and that refinement is greatest of all;
And I affirm now that the mind governs—and that all depends on the mind.

8

With one man or woman—(no matter which one—I even pick out the lowest,)
With him or her I now illustrate the whole law;
I say that every right, in politics or what-not, shall be eligible to that one man or woman, on the same terms as any.

Debris

*

He is wisest who has the most caution,
He only wins who goes far enough.

*

Any thing is as good as established, when that is established that will produce it and continue it.

*

What General has a good army in himself, has a good army;

He happy in himself, or she happy in herself, is happy,
But I tell you you cannot be happy by others, any more
than you can beget or conceive a child by others.

*

Have you learned lessons only of those who admired you,
and were tender with you, and stood aside for you?
Have you not learned the great lessons of those who
rejected you, and braced themselves against you? or
who treated you with contempt, or disputed the
passage with you?
Have you had no practice to receive opponents when they
come?

*

Despairing cries float ceaselessly toward me, day and night,
The sad voice of Death—the call of my nearest lover,
putting forth, alarmed, uncertain,
This sea I am quickly to sail, come tell me,
Come tell me where I am speeding—tell me my destination.

*

I understand your anguish, but I cannot help you,
I approach, hear, behold—the sad mouth, the look out of
the eyes, your mute inquiry,
Whither I go from the bed I now recline on, come tell me;
Old age, alarmed, uncertain—A young woman's voice
appealing to me, for comfort,
A young man's voice, *Shall I not escape?*

*

A thousand perfect men and women appear,
Around each gathers a cluster of friends, and gay children
and youths, with offerings.

*

A mask—a perpetual natural disguiser of herself,
Concealing her face, concealing her form,
Changes and transformations every hour, every moment,
Falling upon her even when she sleeps.

*

One sweeps by, attended by an immense train,
All emblematic of peace—not a soldier or menial among
them.

*

One sweeps by, old, with black eyes, and profuse white hair,
He has the simple magnificence of health and strength,
His face strikes as with flashes of lightning whoever it turns
toward.

*

Three old men slowly pass, followed by three others, and
they by three others,
They are beautiful—the one in the middle of each group
holds his companions by the hand,
As they walk, they give out perfume wherever they walk.

*

Women sit, or move to and fro—some old, some young,
The young are beautiful—but the old are more beautiful
than the young.

*

What weeping face is that looking from the window?
Why does it stream those sorrowful tears?
Is it for some burial place, vast and dry?
Is it to wet the soil of graves?

*

I will take an egg out of the robin's nest in the orchard,
I will take a branch of gooseberries from the old bush in the
garden, and go and preach to the world;
You shall see I will not meet a single heretic or scorner,
You shall see how I stump clergymen, and confound them,
You shall see me showing a scarlet tomato, and a white
pebble from the beach.

*

Behavior—fresh, native, copious, each one for himself or herself,
Nature and the Soul expressed—America and freedom expressed—In it the finest art,
In it pride, cleanliness, sympathy, to have their chance,
In it physique, intellect, faith—in it just as much as to manage an army or a city, or to write a book—perhaps more,
The youth, the laboring person, the poor person, rivalling all the rest—perhaps outdoing the rest,
The effects of the universe no greater than its;
For there is nothing in the whole universe that can be more effective than a man's or woman's daily behavior can be,
In any position, in any of These States.

*

Not the pilot has charged himself to bring his ship into port, though beaten back, and many times baffled,
Not the path-finder, penetrating inland, weary and long,
By deserts parched, snows chilled, rivers wet, perseveres till he reaches his destination,
More than I have charged myself, heeded or unheeded, to compose a free march for These States,
To be exhilarating music to them, years, centuries hence.

*

I thought I was not alone, walking here by the shore,
But the one I thought was with me, as now I walk by the shore,
As I lean and look through the glimmering light—that one has utterly disappeared,
And those appear that perplex me.

Drum-Taps

[1865]

Bathed in War's Perfume

BATHED in war's perfume—delicate flag!
O to hear you call the sailors and the soldiers! flag like a
beautiful woman!
O to hear the tramp, tramp, of a million answering men! O
the ships they arm with joy!
O to see you leap and beckon from the tall masts of ships!
O to see you peering down on the sailors on the decks!
Flag like the eyes of women.

Sequel to Drum-Taps

[1865–1866]

Not my Enemies Ever Invade Me

NOT my enemies ever invade me—no harm to my pride
from them I fear;
But the lovers I recklessly love—lo! how they master me!
Lo! me, ever open and helpless, bereft of my strength!
Utterly abject, grovelling on the ground before them.

Passage to India

[1871]

Lessons

THERE are who teach only the sweet lessons of peace and
safety;
But I teach lessons of war and death to those I love,
That they readily meet invasions, when they come.

Two Rivulets

[1876]

Or from that Sea of Time

1

Or, from that Sea of Time,
Spray, blown by the wind—a double winrow-drift of weeds and shells;
(O little shells, so curious-convolute! so limpid-cold and voiceless!
Yet will you not, to the tympans of temples held,
Murmurs and echoes still bring up—Eternity's music, faint and far,
Wafted inland, sent from Atlantica's rim—strains for the Soul of the Prairies,
Whisper'd reverberations—chords for the ear of the West, joyously sounding
Your tidings old, yet ever new and untranslatable;)
Infinitessimals out of my life, and many a life,
(For not my life and years alone I give—all, all I give;)
These thoughts and Songs—waifs from the deep—here, cast high and dry,
Wash'd on America's shores.

2

Currents of starting a Continent new,
Overtures sent to the solid out of the liquid,
Fusion of ocean and land—tender and pensive waves,
(Not safe and peaceful only—waves rous'd and ominous too,
Out of the depths, the storm's abysms—Who knows whence? Death's waves,
Raging over the vast, with many a broken spar and tatter'd sail.)

In Former Songs

In former songs Pride have I sung, and Love, and passionate, joyful Life,
But here I twine the strands of Patriotism and Death.

And now, Life, Pride, Love, Patriotism and Death,
To you, O Freedom, purport of all!
(You that elude me most—refusing to be caught in songs of mine,)
I offer all to you.

2

'Tis not for nothing, Death,
I sound out you, and words of you, with daring tone—embodying you,
In my new Democratic chants—keeping you for a close,
For last impregnable retreat—a citadel and tower,
For my last stand—my pealing final cry.

COMPLETE PROSE WORKS

[1892]

Contents

Specimen Days

COLLECT

Notes Left Over

Pieces in Early Youth

November Boughs

GOOD-BYE MY FANCY

SOME LAGGARDS YET

Specimen Days

A Happy Hour's Command

Down in the Woods, July 2d, 1882.—If I do it at all I must delay no longer. Incongruous and full of skips and jumps as is that huddle of diary-jottings, war-memoranda of 1862–'65, Nature-notes of 1877–'81, with Western and Canadian observations afterwards, all bundled up and tied by a big string, the resolution and indeed mandate comes to me this day, this hour,—(and what a day! what an hour just passing! the luxury of riant grass and blowing breeze, with all the shows of sun and sky and perfect temperature, never before so filling me body and soul)—to go home, untie the bundle, reel out diary-scraps and memoranda, just as they are, large or small, one after another, into print-pages,* and let the melange's lackings and wants of connection take care of themselves. It will illustrate one phase of humanity anyhow; how few of life's days and hours (and they not by relative value or proportion, but by chance) are ever noted. Probably another point too, how we give long preparations for some object, planning and delving and fashioning, and then, when the actual hour for doing arrives, find ourselves still quite un-

*The pages from 714 to 729 are nearly verbatim an off-hand letter of mine in January, 1882, to an insisting friend. Following, I give some gloomy experiences. The war of attempted secession has, of course, been the distinguishing event of my time. I commenced at the close of 1862, and continued steadily through '63, '64, and '65, to visit the sick and wounded of the army, both on the field and in the hospitals in and around Washington city. From the first I kept little note-books for impromptu jottings in pencil to refresh my memory of names and circumstances, and what was specially wanted, &c. In these I brief'd cases, persons, sights, occurrences in camp, by the bedside, and not seldom by the corpses of the dead. Some were scratch'd down from narratives I heard and itemized while watching, or waiting, or tending somebody amid those scenes. I have dozens of such little note-books left, forming a special history of those years, for myself alone, full of associations never to be possibly said or sung. I wish I could convey to the reader the associations that attach to these soil'd and creas'd livraisons, each composed of a sheet or two of paper, folded small to carry in the pocket, and fasten'd with a pin. I leave them just as I threw them by after the war, blotch'd here and there with more than one blood-stain, hurriedly written, sometimes at the clinique, not seldom

prepared, and tumble the thing together, letting hurry and crudeness tell the story better than fine work. At any rate I obey my happy hour's command, which seems curiously imperative. May-be, if I don't do anything else, I shall send out the most wayward, spontaneous, fragmentary book ever printed.

Answer to an Insisting Friend

You ask for items, details of my early life—of genealogy and parentage, particularly of the women of my ancestry, and of its far back Netherlands stock on the maternal side—of the region where I was born and raised, and my father and mother before me, and theirs before them—with a word about Brooklyn and New York cities, the times I lived there as lad and young man. You say you want to get at these details mainly as the go-befores and embryons of "Leaves of Grass." Very good; you shall have at least some specimens of them all. I have often thought of the meaning of such things—that one can only encompass and complete matters of that kind by exploring behind, perhaps very far behind, themselves directly, and so into their genesis, antecedents, and cumulative stages.

---

amid the excitement of uncertainty, or defeat, or of action, or getting ready for it, or a march. Most of the pages from 736 to 803 are verbatim copies of those lurid and blood-smutch'd little note-books.

Very different are most of the memoranda that follow. Sometime after the war ended I had a paralytic stroke, which prostrated me for several years. In 1876 I began to get over the worst of it. From this date, portions of several seasons, especially summers, I spent at a secluded haunt down in Camden county, New Jersey—Timber creek, quite a little river (it enters from the great Delaware, twelve miles away)—with primitive solitudes, winding stream, recluse and woody banks, sweet-feeding springs, and all the charms that birds, grass, wild-flowers, rabbits and squirrels, old oaks, walnut trees, &c., can bring. Through these times, and on these spots, the diary from page 805 onward was mostly written.

The Collect afterward gathers up the odds and ends of whatever pieces I can now lay hands on, written at various times past, and swoops all together like fish in a net.

I suppose I publish and leave the whole gathering, first, from that eternal tendency to perpetuate and preserve which is behind all Nature, authors included; second, to symbolize two or three specimen interiors, personal and other, out of the myriads of my time, the middle range of the Nineteenth century in the New World; a strange, unloosen'd, wondrous time. But the book is probably without any definite purpose that can be told in a statement.

Then as luck would have it, I lately whiled away the tedium of a week's half-sickness and confinement, by collating these very items for another (yet unfulfill'd, probably abandon'd,) purpose; and if you will be satisfied with them, authentic in date-occurrence and fact simply, and told my own way, garrulous-like, here they are. I shall not hesitate to make extracts, for I catch at any thing to save labor; but those will be the best versions of what I want to convey.

Genealogy—Van Velsor and Whitman

The later years of the last century found the Van Velsor family, my mother's side, living on their own farm at Cold Spring, Long Island, New York State, near the eastern edge of Queens county, about a mile from the harbor.* My father's side—probably the fifth generation from the first English arrivals in New England—were at the same time farmers on their own land—(and a fine domain it was, 500 acres, all good soil, gently sloping east and south, about one-tenth woods, plenty of grand old trees,) two or three miles off, at West Hills, Suffolk county. The Whitman name in the Eastern States, and so branching West and South, starts undoubtedly from one John Whitman, born 1602, in Old England, where he grew up, married, and his eldest son was born in 1629. He came over in the "True Love" in 1640 to America, and lived in Weymouth, Mass., which place became the mother-hive of the New-Englanders of the name: he died in 1692. His brother, Rev. Zechariah Whitman, also came over in the "True Love," either at that time or soon after, and lived at Milford, Conn. A son of this Zechariah, named Joseph, migrated to Huntington, Long Island, and permanently settled there. Savage's "Genealogical Dictionary" (vol. iv, p. 524) gets the Whitman family establish'd at Huntington, per this Joseph, before 1664. It is quite certain that from that beginning, and from Joseph, the West Hill Whitmans, and all others in Suffolk county, have since radiated, myself among the number. John and Zechariah both went to England and back again divers times; they had

*Long Island was settled first on the west end by the Dutch, from Holland, then on the east end by the English—the dividing line of the two nationalities being a little west of Huntington, where my father's folks lived, and where I was born.

large families, and several of their children were born in the old country. We hear of the father of John and Zechariah, Abijah Whitman, who goes over into the 1500's, but we know little about him, except that he also was for some time in America.

These old pedigree-reminiscences come up to me vividly from a visit I made not long since (in my 63d year) to West Hills, and to the burial grounds of my ancestry, both sides. I extract from notes of that visit, written there and then:

The Old Whitman and Van Velsor Cemeteries

July 29, *1881*.—After more than forty years' absence, (except a brief visit, to take my father there once more, two years before he died,) went down Long Island on a week's jaunt to the place where I was born, thirty miles from New York city. Rode around the old familiar spots, viewing and pondering and dwelling long upon them, everything coming back to me. Went to the old Whitman homestead on the upland and took a view eastward, inclining south, over the broad and beautiful farm lands of my grandfather (1780,) and my father. There was the new house (1810,) the big oak a hundred and fifty or two hundred years old; there the well, the sloping kitchen-garden, and a little way off even the well-kept remains of the dwelling of my great-grandfather (1750–'60) still standing, with its mighty timbers and low ceilings. Near by, a stately grove of tall, vigorous black-walnuts, beautiful, Apollo-like, the sons or grandsons, no doubt, of black-walnuts during or before 1776. On the other side of the road spread the famous apple orchard, over twenty acres, the trees planted by hands long mouldering in the grave (my uncle Jesse's,) but quite many of them evidently capable of throwing out their annual blossoms and fruit yet.

I now write these lines seated on an old grave (doubtless of a century since at least) on the burial hill of the Whitmans of many generations. Fifty and more graves are quite plainly traceable, and as many more decay'd out of all form—depress'd mounds, crumbled and broken stones, cover'd with moss—the gray and sterile hill, the clumps of chestnuts outside, the silence, just varied by the soughing wind. There is always the deepest eloquence of sermon or poem in any of these ancient graveyards of which Long Island has so many; so what must this one have been to me? My whole family history, with its succession of links, from the first settlement down to date, told here—three centuries concentrate on this sterile acre.

The next day, July 30, I devoted to the maternal locality, and if possible was still more penetrated and impress'd. I write this paragraph on the burial hill of the Van Velsors, near Cold Spring, the most significant depository of the dead that could be imagin'd, without the slightest help from art, but far ahead of it, soil sterile, a mostly bare plateau-flat of half an acre, the top of a hill, brush and well grown trees and dense woods bordering all around, very primitive, secluded, no visitors, no road (you cannot drive here, you have to bring the dead on foot, and follow on foot.) Two or three-score graves quite plain; as many more almost rubb'd out. My grandfather Cornelius and my grandmother Amy (Naomi) and numerous relatives nearer or remoter, on my mother's side, lie buried here. The scene as I stood or sat, the delicate and wild odor of the woods, a slightly drizzling rain, the emotional atmosphere of the place, and the inferr'd reminiscences, were fitting accompaniments.

The Maternal Homestead

I went down from this ancient grave place eighty or ninety rods to the site of the Van Velsor homestead, where my mother was born (1795,) and where every spot had been familiar to me as a child and youth (1825–'40.) Then stood there a long rambling, dark-gray, shingle-sided house, with sheds, pens, a great barn, and much open road-space. Now of all those not a vestige left; all had been pull'd down, erased, and the plough and harrow pass'd over foundations, road-spaces and everything, for many summers; fenced in at present, and grain and clover growing like any other fine fields. Only a big hole from the cellar, with some little heaps of broken stone, green with grass and weeds, identified the place. Even the copious old brook and spring seem'd to have mostly dwindled away. The whole scene, with what it arous'd, memories of my young days there half a century ago, the vast kitchen and ample fireplace and the sitting-room adjoining, the plain furniture, the meals, the house full of merry people, my grandmother Amy's sweet old face in its Quaker cap, my grandfather "the Major," jovial, red, stout, with sonorous voice and characteristic physiognomy, with the actual sights themselves, made the most pronounc'd half-day's experience of my whole jaunt.

For there with all those wooded, hilly, healthy surroundings, my dearest mother, Louisa Van Velsor, grew up—(her mother, Amy Williams, of the Friends' or Quakers' denomination—the Williams family, seven sisters and one brother—the father and brother sailors, both of whom met their deaths at sea.) The Van Velsor people were noted for fine horses, which the men bred and train'd from blooded stock. My mother, as a young woman, was a daily and daring rider. As to the head of the family himself, the old race of the Netherlands, so deeply grafted on Manhattan island and in Kings and Queens counties, never yielded a more mark'd and full Americanized specimen than Major Cornelius Van Velsor.

Two Old Family Interiors

Of the domestic and inside life of the middle of Long Island, at and just before that time, here are two samples:

"The Whitmans, at the beginning of the present century, lived in a long story-and-a-half farm-house, hugely timber'd, which is still standing. A great smoke-canopied kitchen, with vast hearth and chimney, form'd one end of the house. The existence of slavery in New York at that time, and the possession by the family of some twelve or fifteen slaves, house and field servants, gave things quite a patriarchal look. The very young darkies could be seen, a swarm of them, toward sundown, in this kitchen, squatted in a circle on the floor, eating their supper of Indian pudding and milk. In the house, and in food and furniture, all was rude, but substantial. No carpets or stoves were known, and no coffee, and tea or sugar only for the women. Rousing wood fires gave both warmth and light on winter nights. Pork, poultry, beef, and all the ordinary vegetables and grains were plentiful. Cider was the men's common drink, and used at meals. The clothes were mainly homespun. Journeys were made by both men and women on horseback. Both sexes labor'd with their own hands—the men on the farm—the women in the house and around it. Books were scarce. The annual copy of the almanac was a treat, and was pored over through the long winter evenings. I must not forget to mention that both these families were near enough to the sea to behold it from the high places, and to hear in still hours the roar of the surf; the latter, after a storm, giving a peculiar sound at night. Then all hands, male and female, went down frequently on beach and bathing parties, and the men on practical expeditions for cutting salt hay, and for clamming and fishing."—*John Burroughs's* NOTES.

"The ancestors of Walt Whitman, on both the paternal and maternal sides, kept a good table, sustain'd the hospitalities, decorums, and an excellent social reputation in the county, and they were often of mark'd individuality. If space permitted, I should consider some of the men worthy special description; and still more some of the women. His great-grandmother on the paternal side, for instance, was a large swarthy woman, who lived to a very old age. She smoked tobacco, rode on horseback like a man, managed the most vicious horse, and, becoming a widow in later life, went forth every day over her farm-lands, frequently in the saddle, directing the labor of her slaves, with language in which, on exciting occasions, oaths were not spared. The two immediate grandmothers were, in the best sense, superior women. The maternal one (Amy Williams before marriage) was a Friend, or Quakeress, of sweet, sensible character, housewifely proclivities, and deeply intuitive and spiritual. The other, (Hannah Brush,) was an equally noble, perhaps stronger character, lived to be very old, had quite a family of sons, was a natural lady, was in early life a school-mistress, and had great solidity of mind. W. W. himself makes much of the women of his ancestry."—*The same.*

Out from these arrieres of persons and scenes, I was born May 31, 1819. And now to dwell awhile on the locality itself—as the successive growth stages of my infancy, childhood, youth and manhood were all pass'd on Long Island, which I sometimes feel as if I had incorporated. I roam'd, as boy and man, and have lived in nearly all parts, from Brooklyn to Montauk point.

Paumanok, and My Life on It As Child and Young Man

Worth fully and particularly investigating indeed this Paumanok, (to give the spot its aboriginal name,*) stretching east through Kings, Queens and Suffolk counties, 120 miles altogether—on the north Long Island sound, a beautiful, varied and picturesque series of inlets, "necks" and sea-like expansions, for a hundred miles to Orient point. On the ocean side the great south bay dotted with countless hummocks, mostly small, some quite large, occasionally long bars of sand out two hundred rods to a mile-and-a-half from the shore. While now and then, as at Rockaway and far east along the Hamptons, the beach makes right on the island, the sea dashing up without intervention. Several light-houses on the shores east; a long history of wrecks tragedies, some even of late years. As a youngster, I was in the atmosphere and traditions of many of these wrecks—of one or two almost an observer. Off Hempstead beach for example, was the loss of the ship "Mexico" in 1840, (alluded to in "the Sleepers" in L. of G.) And at Hampton, some years later, the destruction of the brig "Elizabeth," a fearful affair, in one of the worst winter gales, where Margaret Fuller went down, with her husband and child.

Inside the outer bars or beach this south bay is everywhere comparatively shallow; of cold winters all thick ice on the surface. As a boy I often went forth with a chum or two, on those frozen fields, with hand-sled, axe and eel-spear, after messes of eels. We would cut holes in the ice, sometimes striking quite an eel-bonanza, and filling our baskets with great, fat, sweet, white-meated fellows. The scenes, the ice, drawing the hand-sled, cutting holes, spearing the eels, &c., were of

*"Paumanok, (or Paumanake, or Paumanack, the Indian name of Long Island,) over a hundred miles long; shaped like a fish—plenty of sea shore, sandy, stormy, uninviting, the horizon boundless, the air too strong for invalids, the bays a wonderful resort for aquatic birds, the south-side meadows cover'd with salt hay, the soil of the island generally tough, but good for the locust-tree, the apple orchard, and the blackberry, and with numberless springs of the sweetest water in the world. Years ago, among the bay-men—a strong, wild race, now extinct, or rather entirely changed—a native of Long Island was called a *Paumanacker*, or *Creole-Paumanacker*."—*John Burroughs.*

course just such fun as is dearest to boyhood. The shores of this bay, winter and summer, and my doings there in early life, are woven all through L. of G. One sport I was very fond of was to go on a bay-party in summer to gather sea-gull's eggs. (The gulls lay two or three eggs, more than half the size of hen's eggs, right on the sand, and leave the sun's heat to hatch them.)

The eastern end of Long Island, the Peconic bay region, I knew quite well too—sail'd more than once around Shelter island, and down to Montauk—spent many an hour on Turtle hill by the old light-house, on the extreme point, looking out over the ceaseless roll of the Atlantic. I used to like to go down there and fraternize with the blue-fishers, or the annual squads of sea-bass takers. Sometimes, along Montauk peninsula, (it is some 15 miles long, and good grazing,) met the strange, unkempt, half-barbarous herdsmen, at that time living there entirely aloof from society or civilization, in charge, on those rich pasturages, of vast droves of horses, kine or sheep, own'd by farmers of the eastern towns. Sometimes, too, the few remaining Indians, or half-breeds, at that period left on Montauk peninsula, but now I believe altogether extinct.

More in the middle of the island were the spreading Hempstead plains, then (1830–'40) quite prairie-like, open, uninhabited, rather sterile, cover'd with kill-calf and huckleberry bushes, yet plenty of fair pasture for the cattle, mostly milch-cows, who fed there by hundreds, even thousands, and at evening, (the plains too were own'd by the towns, and this was the use of them in common,) might be seen taking their way home, branching off regularly in the right places. I have often been out on the edges of these plains toward sundown, and can yet recall in fancy the interminable cow-processions, and hear the music of the tin or copper bells clanking far or near, and breathe the cool of the sweet and slightly aromatic evening air, and note the sunset.

Through the same region of the island, but further east, extended wide central tracts of pine and scrub-oak, (charcoal was largely made here,) monotonous and sterile. But many a good day or half-day did I have, wandering through those solitary cross-roads, inhaling the peculiar and wild aroma.

Here, and all along the island and its shores, I spent intervals many years, all seasons, sometimes riding, sometimes boating, but generally afoot, (I was always then a good walker,) absorbing fields, shores, marine incidents, characters, the baymen, farmers, pilots—always had a plentiful acquaintance with the latter, and with fishermen—went every summer on sailing trips—always liked the bare sea-beach, south side, and have some of my happiest hours on it to this day.

As I write, the whole experience comes back to me after the lapse of forty and more years—the soothing rustle of the waves, and the saline smell—boyhood's times, the clam-digging, barefoot, and with trowsers roll'd up—hauling down the creek—the perfume of the sedge-meadows—the hay-boat, and the chowder and fishing excursions;—or, of later years, little voyages down and out New York bay, in the pilot boats. Those same later years, also, while living in Brooklyn, (1836–'50) I went regularly every week in the mild seasons down to Coney island, at that time a long, bare unfrequented shore, which I had all to myself, and where I loved, after bathing, to race up and down the hard sand, and declaim Homer or Shakspere to the surf and sea-gulls by the hour. But I am getting ahead too rapidly, and must keep more in my traces.

My First Reading.—Lafayette

From 1824 to '28 our family lived in Brooklyn in Front, Cranberry and Johnson streets. In the latter my father built a nice house for a home, and afterwards another in Tillary street. We occupied them, one after the other, but they were mortgaged, and we lost them. I yet remember Lafayette's visit.* Most of these years I went to the public schools. It must have been about 1829 or '30 that I went with my father and mother

*"On the visit of General Lafayette to this country, in 1824, he came over to Brooklyn in state, and rode through the city. The children of the schools turn'd out to join in the welcome. An edifice for a free public library for youths was just then commencing, and Lafayette consented to stop on his way and lay the corner-stone. Numerous children arriving on the ground, where a huge irregular excavation for the building was already dug, surrounded with heaps of rough stone, several gentlemen assisted in lifting the children to safe or convenient spots to see the ceremony. Among the rest, Lafayette, also helping the children, took up the five-year-old Walt Whitman, and pressing the child a moment to his breast, and giving him a kiss, handed him down to a safe spot in the excavation."—*John Burroughs.*

to hear Elias Hicks preach in a ball-room on Brooklyn heights. At about the same time employ'd as a boy in an office, lawyers', father and two sons, Clarke's, Fulton Street, near Orange. I had a nice desk and window-nook to myself; Edward C. kindly help'd me at my handwriting and composition, and, (the signal event of my life up to that time,) subscribed for me to a big circulating library. For a time I now revel'd in romance-reading of all kinds; first, the "Arabian Nights," all the volumes, an amazing treat. Then, with sorties in very many other directions, took in Walter Scott's novels, one after another, and his poetry, (and continue to enjoy novels and poetry to this day.)

Printing Office.—Old Brooklyn

After about two years went to work in a weekly newspaper and printing office, to learn the trade. The paper was the "Long Island Patriot," owned by S. E. Clements, who was also postmaster. An old printer in the office, William Hartshorne, a revolutionary character, who had seen Washington, was a special friend of mine, and I had many a talk with him about long past times. The apprentices, including myself, boarded with his grand-daughter. I used occasionally to go out riding with the boss, who was very kind to us boys; Sundays he took us all to a great old rough, fortress-looking stone church, on Joralemon street, near where the Brooklyn city hall now is—(at that time broad fields and country roads everywhere around.*) Afterward I work'd on the "Long Island

*Of the Brooklyn of that time (1830–40) hardly anything remains, except the lines of the old streets. The population was then between ten and twelve thousand. For a mile Fulton street was lined with magnificent elm trees. The character of the place was thoroughly rural. As a sample of comparative values, it may be mention'd that twenty-five acres in what is now the most costly part of the city, bounded by Flatbush and Fulton avenues, were then bought by Mr. Parmentier, a French *emigré,* for $4000. Who remembers the old places as they were? Who remembers the old citizens of that time? Among the former were Smith & Wood's, Coe Downing's, and other public houses at the ferry, the old Ferry itself, Love lane, the Heights as then, the Wallabout with the wooden bridge, and the road out beyond Fulton street to the old toll-gate. Among the latter were the majestic and genial General Jeremiah Johnson, with others, Gabriel Furman, Rev. E. M. Johnson, Alden Spooner, Mr. Pierrepont, Mr. Joralemon, Samuel Willoughby, Jonathan Trotter, George Hall, Cyrus P. Smith, N. B. Morse, John Dikeman, Adrian Hegeman, William Udall, and old Mr. Duflon, with his military garden.

Star," Alden Spooner's paper. My father all these years pursuing his trade as carpenter and builder, with varying fortune. There was a growing family of children—eight of us—my brother Jesse the oldest, myself the second, my dear sisters Mary and Hannah Louisa, my brothers Andrew, George, Thomas Jefferson, and then my youngest brother, Edward, born 1835, and always badly crippled, as I am myself of late years.

Growth—Health—Work

I develop'd (1833–4–5) into a healthy, strong youth (grew too fast, though, was nearly as big as a man at 15 or 16.) Our family at this period moved back to the country, my dear mother very ill for a long time, but recover'd. All these years I was down Long Island more or less every summer, now east, now west, sometimes months at a stretch. At 16, 17, and so on, was fond of debating societies, and had an active membership with them, off and on, in Brooklyn and one or two country towns on the island. A most omnivorous novel-reader, these and later years, devour'd everything I could get. Fond of the theatre, also, in New York, went whenever I could—sometimes witnessing fine performances.

1836–7, work'd as compositor in printing offices in New York city. Then, when little more than eighteen, and for a while afterwards, went to teaching country schools down in Queens and Suffolk counties, Long Island, and "boarded round." (This latter I consider one of my best experiences and deepest lessons in human nature behind the scenes, and in the masses.) In '39, '40, I started and publish'd a weekly paper in my native town, Huntington. Then returning to New York city and Brooklyn, work'd on as printer and writer, mostly prose, but an occasional shy at "poetry."

My Passion for Ferries

Living in Brooklyn or New York city from this time forward, my life, then, and still more the following years, was curiously identified with Fulton ferry, already becoming the greatest of its sort in the world for general importance, volume, variety, rapidity, and picturesqueness. Almost daily, later,

('50 to '60,) I cross'd on the boats, often up in the pilot-houses where I could get a full sweep, absorbing shows, accompaniments, surroundings. What oceanic currents, eddies, underneath—the great tides of humanity also, with ever-shifting movements. Indeed, I have always had a passion for ferries; to me they afford inimitable, streaming, never-failing, living poems. The river and bay scenery, all about New York island, any time of a fine day—the hurrying, splashing sea-tides—the changing panorama of steamers, all sizes, often a string of big ones outward bound to distant ports—the myriads of white-sail'd schooners, sloops, skiffs, and the marvelously beautiful yachts—the majestic sound boats as they rounded the Battery and came along towards 5, afternoon, eastward bound—the prospect off towards Staten island, or down the Narrows, or the other way up the Hudson—what refreshment of spirit such sights and experiences gave me years ago (and many a time since.) My old pilot friends, the Balsirs, Johnny Cole, Ira Smith, William White, and my young ferry friend, Tom Gere—how well I remember them all.

Broadway Sights

Besides Fulton ferry, off and on for years, I knew and frequented Broadway—that noted avenue of New York's crowded and mixed humanity, and of so many notables. Here I saw, during those times, Andrew Jackson, Webster, Clay, Seward, Martin Van Buren, filibuster Walker, Kossuth, Fitz Greene Halleck, Bryant, the Prince of Wales, Charles Dickens, the first Japanese ambassadors, and lots of other celebrities of the time. Always something novel or inspiriting; yet mostly to me the hurrying and vast amplitude of those never-ending human currents. I remember seeing James Fenimore Cooper in a court-room in Chambers street, back of the city hall, where he was carrying on a law case—(I think it was a charge of libel he had brought against some one.) I also remember seeing Edgar A. Poe, and having a short interview with him, (it must have been in 1845 or '6,) in his office, second story of a corner building, (Duane or Pearl street.) He was editor and owner or part owner of "the Broadway Journal." The visit was about a piece of mine he had publish'd. Poe was very cordial, in a quiet way, appear'd well in person, dress, &c. I have a distinct and pleasing remembrance of his looks, voice, manner and matter; very kindly and human, but subdued, perhaps a little jaded. For another of my reminiscences, here on the west side, just below Houston street, I once saw (it must have been about 1832, of a sharp, bright January day) a bent, feeble but stout-built very old man, bearded, swathed in rich furs, with a great ermine cap on his head, led and assisted, almost carried, down the steps of his high front stoop (a dozen friends and servants, emulous, carefully holding, guiding him) and then lifted and tuck'd in a gorgeous sleigh, envelop'd in other furs, for a ride. The sleigh was drawn by as fine a team of horses as I ever saw. (You needn't think all the best animals are brought up nowadays; never was such horseflesh as fifty years ago on Long Island, or south, or in New York city; folks look'd for spirit and mettle in a nag, not tame speed merely.) Well, I, a boy of perhaps thirteen or fourteen, stopp'd and gazed long at the spectacle of that fur-swathed old man, surrounded by friends and servants, and the careful seating of him in the sleigh. I remember the spirited, champing horses, the driver with his whip, and a fellow-driver by his side, for extra prudence. The old man, the subject of so much attention, I can almost see now. It was John Jacob Astor.

The years 1846, '47, and there along, see me still in New York city, working as writer and printer, having my usual good health, and a good time generally.

Omnibus Jaunts and Drivers

One phase of those days must by no means go unrecorded—namely, the Broadway omnibuses, with their drivers. The vehicles still (I write this paragraph in 1881) give a portion of the character of Broadway—the Fifth avenue, Madison avenue, and Twenty-third street lines yet running. But the flush days of the old Broadway stages, characteristic and copious, are over. The Yellow-birds, the Red-birds, the original Broadway, the Fourth avenue, the Knickerbocker, and a dozen others of twenty or thirty years ago, are all gone.

And the men specially identified with them, and giving vitality and meaning to them—the drivers—a strange, natural, quick-eyed and wondrous race—(not only Rabelais and Cervantes would have gloated upon them, but Homer and Shakspere would)—how well I remember them, and must here give a word about them. How many hours, forenoons and afternoons—how many exhilarating night-times I have had—perhaps June or July, in cooler air—riding the whole length of Broadway, listening to some yarn, (and the most vivid yarns ever spun, and the rarest mimicry)—or perhaps I declaiming some stormy passage from Julius Cæsar or Richard, (you could roar as loudly as you chose in that heavy, dense, uninterrupted street-bass.) Yes, I knew all the drivers then, Broadway Jack, Dressmaker, Balky Bill, George Storms, Old Elephant, his brother Young Elephant (who came afterward,) Tippy, Pop Rice, Big Frank, Yellow Joe, Pete Callahan, Patsy Dee, and dozens more; for there were hundreds. They had immense qualities, largely animal—eating, drinking, women—great personal pride, in their way—perhaps a few slouches here and there, but I should have trusted the general run of them, in their simple good-will and honor, under all circumstances. Not only for comradeship, and sometimes affection—great studies I found them also. (I suppose the critics will laugh heartily, but the influence of those Broadway omnibus jaunts and drivers and declamations and escapades undoubtedly enter'd into the gestation of "Leaves of Grass.")

Plays and Operas Too

And certain actors and singers, had a good deal to do with the business. All through these years, off and on, I frequented the old Park, the Bowery, Broadway and Chatham-square theatres, and the Italian operas at Chambers-street, Astor-place or the Battery—many seasons was on the free list, writing for papers even as quite a youth. The old Park theatre—what names, reminiscences, the words bring back! Placide, Clarke, Mrs. Vernon, Fisher, Clara F., Mrs. Wood, Mrs. Seguin, Ellen Tree, Hackett, the younger Kean, Macready, Mrs. Richardson, Rice—singers, tragedians, comedians. What perfect acting! Henry Placide in "Napoleon's Old Guard" or

"Grandfather Whitehead,"—or "the Provoked Husband" of Cibber, with Fanny Kemble as Lady Townley—or Sheridan Knowles in his own "Virginius"—or inimitable Power in "Born to Good Luck." These, and many more, the years of youth and onward. Fanny Kemble—name to conjure up great mimic scenes withal—perhaps the greatest. I remember well her rendering of Bianca in "Fazio," and Marianna in "the Wife." Nothing finer did ever stage exhibit—the veterans of all nations said so, and my boyish heart and head felt it in every minute cell. The lady was just matured, strong, better than merely beautiful, born from the footlights, had had three years' practice in London and through the British towns, and then she came to give America that young maturity and roseate power in all their noon, or rather forenoon, flush. It was my good luck to see her nearly every night she play'd at the old Park—certainly in all her principal characters.

I heard, these years, well render'd, all the Italian and other operas in vogue, "Sonnambula," "the Puritans," "Der Freischutz," "Huguenots," "Fille d'Regiment," "Faust," "Etoile du Nord," "Poliuto," and others. Verdi's "Ernani," "Rigoletto," and "Trovatore," with Donnizetti's "Lucia" or "Favorita" or "Lucrezia," and Auber's "Massaniello," or Rossini's "William Tell" and "Gazza Ladra," were among my special enjoyments. I heard Alboni every time she sang in New York and vicinity—also Grisi, the tenor Mario, and the baritone Badiali, the finest in the world.

This musical passion follow'd my theatrical one. As boy or young man I had seen, (reading them carefully the day beforehand,) quite all Shakspere's acting dramas, play'd wonderfully well. Even yet I cannot conceive anything finer than old Booth in "Richard Third," or "Lear," (I don't know which was best,) or Iago, (or Pescara, or Sir Giles Overreach, to go outside of Shakspere)—or Tom Hamblin in "Macbeth"—or old Clarke, either as the ghost in "Hamlet," or as Prospero in "the Tempest," with Mrs. Austin as Ariel, and Peter Richings as Caliban. Then other dramas, and fine players in them, Forrest as Metamora or Damon or Brutus—John R. Scott as Tom Cringle or Rolla—or Charlotte Cushman's Lady Gay Spanker in "London Assurance." Then of some years later, at Castle Garden, Battery, I yet recall the splendid seasons of the Havana musical troupe under Maretzek—the fine band, the cool sea-breezes, the unsurpass'd vocalism—Steffanone, Bosio, Truffi, Marini in "Marino Faliero," "Don Pasquale," or "Favorita." No better playing or singing ever in New York. It was here too I afterward heard Jenny Lind. (The Battery—its past associations—what tales those old trees and walks and sea-walls could tell!)

Through Eight Years

In 1848, '49, I was occupied as editor of the "daily Eagle" newspaper, in Brooklyn. The latter year went off on a leisurely journey and working expedition (my brother Jeff with me) through all the middle States, and down the Ohio and Mississippi rivers. Lived awhile in New Orleans, and work'd there on the editorial staff of "daily Crescent" newspaper. After a time plodded back northward, up the Mississippi, and around to, and by way of the great lakes, Michigan, Huron, and Erie, to Niagara falls and lower Canada, finally returning through central New York and down the Hudson; traveling altogether probably 8000 miles this trip, to and fro. '51, '53, occupied in house-building in Brooklyn. (For a little of the first part of that time in printing a daily and weekly paper, "the Freeman.") '55, lost my dear father this year by death. Commenced putting "Leaves of Grass" to press for good, at the job printing office of my friends, the brothers Rome, in Brooklyn, after many MS. doings and undoings—(I had great trouble in leaving out the stock "poetical" touches, but succeeded at last.) I am now (1856–'7) passing through my 37th year.

Sources of Character—Results—1860

To sum up the foregoing from the outset (and, of course, far, far more unrecorded,) I estimate three leading sources and formative stamps to my own character, now solidified for good or bad, and its subsequent literary and other outgrowth—the maternal nativity-stock brought hither from faraway Netherlands, for one, (doubtless the best)—the subterranean tenacity and central bony structure (obstinacy, wilfulness) which I get from my paternal English elements, for another—and the combination of my Long Island birth-spot, sea-shores, childhood's scenes, absorptions, with teeming Brooklyn and New York—with, I suppose, my experiences afterward in the secession outbreak, for the third.

For, in 1862, startled by news that my brother George, an officer in the 51st New York volunteers, had been seriously wounded (first Fredericksburg battle, December 13th,) I hurriedly went down to the field of war in Virginia. But I must go back a little.

Opening of the Secession War

News of the attack on fort Sumter and *the flag* at Charleston harbor, S.C., was receiv'd in New York city late at night (13th April, 1861,) and was immediately sent out in extras of the newspapers. I had been to the opera in Fourteenth street that night, and after the performance was walking down Broadway toward twelve o'clock, on my way to Brooklyn, when I heard in the distance the loud cries of the newsboys, who came presently tearing and yelling up the street, rushing from side to side even more furiously than usual. I bought an extra and cross'd to the Metropolitan hotel (Niblo's) where the great lamps were still brightly blazing, and, with a crowd of others, who gather'd impromptu, read the news, which was evidently authentic. For the benefit of some who had no papers, one of us read the telegram aloud, while all listen'd silently and attentively. No remark was made by any of the crowd, which had increas'd to thirty or forty, but all stood a minute or two, I remember, before they dispers'd. I can almost see them there now, under the lamps at midnight again.

National Uprising and Volunteering

I have said somewhere that the three Presidentiads preceding 1861 show'd how the weakness and wickedness of rulers are just as eligible here in America under republican, as in Europe under dynastic influences. But what can I say of that prompt and splendid wrestling with secession slavery, the arch-enemy personified, the instant he unmistakably show'd his face? The volcanic upheaval of the nation, after that firing on the flag at Charleston, proved for certain something which had been previously in great doubt, and at once substantially settled the question of disunion. In my judgment it will remain as the grandest and most encouraging spectacle yet vouchsafed in any age, old or new, to political progress and democracy. It was not for what came to the surface merely—though that was important—but what it indicated below, which was of eternal importance. Down in the abysms of New World humanity there had form'd and harden'd a primal hard-pan of national Union will, determin'd and in the majority, refusing to be tamper'd with or argued against, confronting all emergencies, and capable at any time of bursting all surface bonds, and breaking out like an earthquake. It is, indeed, the best lesson of the century, or of America, and it is a mighty privilege to have been part of it. (Two great spectacles, immortal proofs of democracy, unequall'd in all the history of the past, are furnish'd by the secession war—one at the beginning, the other at its close. Those are, the general, voluntary, arm'd upheaval, and the peaceful and harmonious disbanding of the armies in the summer of 1865.)

Contemptuous Feeling

Even after the bombardment of Sumter, however, the gravity of the revolt, and the power and will of the slave States for a strong and continued military resistance to national authority, were not at all realized at the North, except by a few. Nine-tenths of the people of the free States look'd upon the rebellion, as started in South Carolina, from a feeling one-half of contempt, and the other half composed of anger and incredulity. It was not thought it would be join'd in by Virginia, North Carolina, or Georgia. A great and cautious national official predicted that it would blow over "in sixty days," and folks generally believ'd the prediction. I remember talking about it on a Fulton ferry-boat with the Brooklyn mayor, who said he only "hoped the Southern fire-eaters would commit some overt act of resistance, as they would then be at once so effectually squelch'd, we would never hear of secession again—but he was afraid they never would have the pluck to really do anything." I remember, too, that a couple of companies of the Thirteenth Brooklyn, who rendezvou'd at the city armory, and started thence as thirty days' men, were all provided with pieces of rope, conspicuously tied to their musket-barrels, with which to bring back each man a prisoner from the audacious South, to be led in a noose, on our men's early and triumphant return!

Battle of Bull Run, July, 1861

All this sort of feeling was destin'd to be arrested and revers'd by a terrible shock—the battle of first Bull Run—certainly, as we now know it, one of the most singular fights on record. (All battles, and their results, are far more matters of accident than is generally thought; but this was throughout a casualty, a chance. Each side supposed it had won, till the last moment. One had, in point of fact, just the same right to be routed as the other. By a fiction, or series of fictions, the national forces at the last moment exploded in a panic and fled from the field.) The defeated troops commenced pouring into Washington over the Long Bridge at daylight on Monday, 22d—day drizzling all through with rain. The Saturday and Sunday of the battle (20th, 21st,) had been parch'd and hot to an extreme—the dust, the grime and smoke, in layers, sweated in, follow'd by other layers again sweated in, absorb'd by those excited souls—their clothes all saturated with the clay-powder filling the air—stirr'd up everywhere on the dry roads and trodden fields by the regiments, swarming wagons, artillery, &c.—all the men with this coating of murk and sweat and rain, now recoiling back, pouring over the Long Bridge—a horrible march of twenty miles, returning to Washington baffled, humiliated, panic-struck. Where are the vaunts, and the proud boasts with which you went forth? Where are your banners, and your bands of music, and your ropes to bring back your prisoners? Well, there isn't a band playing—and there isn't a flag but clings ashamed and lank to its staff.

The sun rises, but shines not. The men appear, at first sparsely and shame-faced enough, then thicker, in the streets of Washington—appear in Pennsylvania avenue, and on the steps and basement entrances. They come along in disorderly mobs, some in squads, stragglers, companies. Occasionally, a rare regiment, in perfect order, with its officers (some gaps, dead, the true braves,) marching in silence, with lowering faces, stern, weary to sinking, all black and dirty, but every man with his musket, and stepping alive; but these are the exceptions. Sidewalks of Pennsylvania avenue, Fourteenth street, &c., crowded, jamm'd with citizens, darkies, clerks, everybody, lookers-on; women in the windows, curious expressions from faces, as those swarms of dirt-cover'd return'd soldiers there (will they never end?) move by; but nothing said, no comments; (half our lookers-on secesh of the most venomous kind—they say nothing; but the devil snickers in their faces.) During the forenoon Washington gets all over motley with these defeated soldiers—queer-looking objects, strange eyes and faces, drench'd (the steady rain drizzles on all day) and fearfully worn, hungry, haggard, blister'd in the feet. Good people (but not over-many of them either,) hurry up something for their grub. They put wash-kettles on the fire, for soup, for coffee. They set tables on the side-walks—wagon-loads of bread are purchas'd, swiftly cut in stout chunks. Here are two aged ladies, beautiful, the first in the city for culture and charm, they stand with store of eating and drink at an improvis'd table of rough plank, and give food, and have the store replenish'd from their house every half-hour all that day; and there in the rain they stand, active, silent, white-hair'd, and give food, though the tears stream down their cheeks, almost without intermission, the whole time. Amid the deep excitement, crowds and motion, and desperate eagerness, it seems strange to see many, very many, of the soldiers sleeping—in the midst of all, sleeping sound. They drop down anywhere, on the steps of houses, up close by the basements or fences, on the sidewalk, aside on some vacant lot, and deeply sleep. A poor seventeen or eighteen year old boy lies there, on the stoop of a grand house; he sleeps so calmly, so profoundly. Some clutch their muskets firmly even in sleep. Some in squads; comrades, brothers, close together—and on them, as they lay, sulkily drips the rain.

As afternoon pass'd, and evening came, the streets, the barrooms, knots everywhere, listeners, questioners, terrible yarns, bugaboo, mask'd batteries, our regiment all cut up, &c.—stories and story-tellers, windy, bragging, vain centres of street-crowds. Resolution, manliness, seem to have abandon'd Washington. The principal hotel, Willard's, is full of shoulder-straps—thick, crush'd, creeping with shoulder-straps. (I see them, and must have a word with them. There you are, shoulder-straps!—but where are your companies? where are your men? Incompetents! never tell me of chances of battle, of getting stray'd, and the like. I think this is your work, this retreat, after all. Sneak, blow, put on airs there in Willard's sumptuous parlors and bar-rooms, or anywhere—no explanation shall save you. Bull Run is your work; had you been half or one-tenth worthy your men, this would never have happen'd.)

Meantime, in Washington, among the great persons and their entourage, a mixture of awful consternation, uncertainty, rage, shame, helplessness, and stupefying disappointment. The worst is not only imminent, but already here. In a few hours—perhaps before the next meal—the secesh generals, with their victorious hordes, will be upon us. The dream of humanity, the vaunted Union we thought so strong, so impregnable—lo! it seems already smash'd like a china plate. One bitter, bitter hour—perhaps proud America will never again know such an hour. She must pack and fly—no time to spare. Those white palaces—the dome-crown'd capitol there on the hill, so stately over the trees—shall they be left—or destroy'd first? For it is certain that the talk among certain of the magnates and officers and clerks and officials everywhere, for twenty-four hours in and around Washington after Bull Run, was loud and undisguised for yielding out and out, and substituting the southern rule, and Lincoln promptly abdicating and departing. If the secesh officers and forces had immediately follow'd, and by a bold Napoleonic movement had enter'd Washington the first day, (or even the second,) they could have had things their own way, and a powerful faction north to back them. One of our returning colonels express'd in public that night, amid a swarm of officers and gentlemen in a crowded room, the opinion that it was useless to fight, that the southerners had made their title clear, and that the best course for the national government to pursue was to desist from any further attempt at stopping them, and admit them again to the lead, on the best terms they were willing to grant. Not a voice was rais'd against this judgment, amid that large crowd of officers and gentlemen. (The fact is, the hour was one of the three or four of those crises we had then and afterward, during the fluctuations of four years, when human eyes appear'd at least just as likely to see the last breath of the Union as to see it continue.)

The Stupor Passes—Something Else Begins

But the hour, the day, the night pass'd, and whatever returns, an hour, a day, a night like that can never again return. The President, recovering himself, begins that very night—sternly, rapidly sets about the task of reorganizing his forces, and placing himself in positions for future and surer work. If there were nothing else of Abraham Lincoln for history to stamp him with, it is enough to send him with his wreath to the memory of all future time, that he endured that hour, that day, bitterer than gall—indeed a crucifixion day—that it did not conquer him—that he unflinchingly stemm'd it, and resolv'd to lift himself and the Union out of it.

Then the great New York papers at once appear'd, (commencing that evening, and following it up the next morning, and incessantly through many days afterwards,) with leaders that rang out over the land with the loudest, most reverberating ring of clearest bugles, full of encouragement, hope, inspiration, unfaltering defiance. Those magnificent editorials! they never flagg'd for a fortnight. The "Herald" commenced them—I remember the articles well. The "Tribune" was equally cogent and inspiriting—and the "Times," "Evening Post," and other principal papers, were not a whit behind. They came in good time, for they were needed. For in the humiliation of Bull Run, the popular feeling north, from its extreme of superciliousness, recoil'd to the depth of gloom and apprehension.

(Of all the days of the war, there are two especially I can never forget. Those were the day following the news, in New York and Brooklyn, of that first Bull Run defeat, and the day of Abraham Lincoln's death. I was home in Brooklyn on both occasions. The day of the murder we heard the news very early in the morning. Mother prepared breakfast—and other meals afterward—as usual; but not a mouthful was eaten all day by either of us. We each drank half a cup of coffee; that was all. Little was said. We got every newspaper morning and evening, and the frequent extras of that period, and pass'd them silently to each other.)

Down at the Front

Falmouth, Va., *opposite Fredericksburgh, December 21, 1862.*—Begin my visits among the camp hospitals in the army of the Potomac. Spend a good part of the day in a large brick mansion on the banks of the Rappahannock, used as a hospital since the battle—seems to have receiv'd only the worst cases. Out doors, at the foot of a tree, within ten yards of the front of the house, I notice a heap of amputated feet, legs, arms, hands, &c., a full load for a one-horse cart. Several dead bodies lie near, each cover'd with its brown woolen blanket. In the door-yard, towards the river, are fresh graves, mostly of officers, their names on pieces of barrel-staves or broken boards, stuck in the dirt. (Most of these bodies were subsequently taken up and transported north to their friends.) The large mansion is quite crowded upstairs and down, everything impromptu, no system, all bad enough, but I have no doubt the best that can be done; all the wounds pretty bad, some frightful, the men in their old clothes, unclean and bloody. Some of the wounded are rebel soldiers and officers, prisoners. One, a Mississippian, a captain, hit badly in leg, I talk'd with some time; he ask'd me for papers, which I gave him. (I saw him three months afterward in Washington, with his leg amputated, doing well.) I went through the rooms, downstairs and up. Some of the men were dying. I had nothing to give at that visit, but wrote a few letters to folks home, mothers, &c. Also talk'd to three or four, who seem'd most susceptible to it, and needing it.

After First Fredericksburg

December 23 to 31.—The results of the late battle are exhibited everywhere about here in thousands of cases, (hundreds die every day,) in the camp, brigade, and division hospitals. These are merely tents, and sometimes very poor ones, the wounded lying on the ground, lucky if their blankets are spread on layers of pine or hemlock twigs, or small leaves. No cots; seldom even a mattress. It is pretty cold. The ground is frozen hard, and there is occasional snow. I go around from one case to another. I do not see that I do much good to these wounded and dying; but I cannot leave them. Once in a while some youngster holds on to me convulsively, and I do what I can for him; at any rate, stop with him and sit near him for hours, if he wishes it.

Besides the hospitals, I also go occasionally on long tours through the camps, talking with the men, &c. Sometimes at night among the groups around the fires, in their shebang enclosures of bushes. These are curious shows, full of characters and groups. I soon get acquainted anywhere in camp, with officers or men, and am always well used. Sometimes I go down on picket with the regiments I know best. As to rations, the army here at present seems to be tolerably well supplied, and the men have enough, such as it is, mainly salt pork and hard tack. Most of the regiments lodge in the flimsy little shelter-tents. A few have built themselves huts of logs and mud, with fire-places.

Back to Washington

January, '63.—Left camp at Falmouth, with some wounded, a few days since, and came here by Aquia creek railroad, and so on government steamer up the Potomac. Many wounded were with us on the cars and boat. The cars were just common platform ones. The railroad journey of ten or twelve miles was made mostly before sunrise. The soldiers guarding the road came out from their tents or shebangs of bushes with rumpled hair and half-awake look. Those on duty were walking their posts, some on banks over us, others down far below the level of the track. I saw large cavalry camps off the road. At Aquia creek landing were numbers of wounded going north. While I waited some three hours, I went around among them. Several wanted word sent home to parents, brothers, wives, &c., which I did for them, (by mail the next day from Washington.) On the boat I had my hands full. One poor fellow died going up.

I am now remaining in and around Washington, daily visiting the hospitals. Am much in Patent-office, Eighth street, H street, Armory-square, and others. Am now able to do a little good, having money, (as almoner of others home,) and getting experience. To-day, Sunday afternoon and till nine in the evening, visited Campbell hospital; attended specially to one case in ward 1, very sick with pleurisy and typhoid fever, young man, farmer's son, D. F. Russell, company E, 60th New York, downhearted and feeble; a long time before he would take any interest; wrote a letter home to his mother, in Malone, Franklin county, N. Y., at his request; gave him some fruit and one or two other gifts; envelop'd and directed his letter, &c. Then went thoroughly through ward 6, observ'd every case in the ward, without, I think, missing one; gave perhaps from twenty to thirty persons, each one some little gift, such as oranges, apples, sweet crackers, figs, &c.

Thursday, Jan. 21.—Devoted the main part of the day to Armory-square hospital; went pretty thoroughly through wards F, G, H, and I; some fifty cases in each ward. In ward F supplied the men throughout with writing paper and stamp'd envelope each; distributed in small portions, to proper subjects, a large jar of first-rate preserv'd berries, which had been donated to me by a lady—her own cooking. Found several cases I thought good subjects for small sums of money, which I furnish'd. (The wounded men often come up broke, and it helps their spirits to have even the small sum I give them.) My paper and envelopes all gone, but distributed a good lot of amusing reading matter; also, as I thought judicious, tobacco, oranges, apples, &c. Interesting cases in ward I; Charles Miller, bed 19, company D, 53d Pennsylvania, is only sixteen years of age, very bright, courageous boy, left leg amputated below the knee; next bed to him, another young lad very sick; gave each appropriate gifts. In the bed above, also, amputation of the left leg; gave him a little jar of raspberries; bed 1, this ward, gave a small sum; also to a soldier on crutches, sitting on his bed near. . . . (I am more and more surprised at the very great proportion of youngsters from fifteen to twenty-one in the army. I afterwards found a still greater proportion among the southerners.)

Evening, same day, went to see D. F. R., before alluded to;

found him remarkably changed for the better; up and dress'd—quite a triumph; he afterwards got well, and went back to his regiment. Distributed in the wards a quantity of note-paper, and forty or fifty stamp'd envelopes, of which I had recruited my stock, and the men were much in need.

Fifty Hours Left Wounded on the Field

Here is a case of a soldier I found among the crowded cots in the Patent-office. He likes to have some one to talk to, and we will listen to him. He got badly hit in his leg and side at Fredericksburgh that eventful Saturday, 13th of December. He lay the succeeding two days and nights helpless on the field, between the city and those grim terraces of batteries; his company and regiment had been compell'd to leave him to his fate. To make matters worse, it happen'd he lay with his head slightly down hill, and could not help himself. At the end of some fifty hours he was brought off, with other wounded, under a flag of truce. I ask him how the rebels treated him as he lay during those two days and nights within reach of them—whether they came to him—whether they abused him? He answers that several of the rebels, soldiers and others, came to him at one time and another. A couple of them, who were together, spoke roughly and sarcastically, but nothing worse. One middle-aged man, however, who seem'd to be moving around the field, among the dead and wounded, for benevolent purposes, came to him in a way he will never forget; treated our soldier kindly, bound up his wounds, cheer'd him, gave him a couple of biscuits and a drink of whiskey and water; asked him if he could eat some beef. This good secesh, however, did not change our soldier's position, for it might have caused the blood to burst from the wounds, clotted and stagnated. Our soldier is from Pennsylvania; has had a pretty severe time; the wounds proved to be bad ones. But he retains a good heart, and is at present on the gain. (It is not uncommon for the men to remain on the field this way, one, two, or even four or five days.)

Hospital Scenes and Persons

Letter Writing.—When eligible, I encourage the men to write, and myself, when called upon, write all sorts of letters for them, (including love letters, very tender ones.) Almost as I reel off these memoranda, I write for a new patient to his wife. M.de F., of the 17th Connecticut, company H, has just come up (February 17th) from Windmill point, and is received in ward H, Armory-square. He is an intelligent looking man, has a foreign accent, black-eyed and hair'd, a Hebraic appearance. Wants a telegraphic message sent to his wife, New Canaan, Conn. I agree to send the message—but to make things sure I also sit down and write the wife a letter, and despatch it to the post-office immediately, as he fears she will come on, and he does not wish her to, as he will surely get well.

Saturday, January 30th.—Afternoon, visited Campbell hospital. Scene of cleaning up the ward, and giving the men all clean clothes—through the ward (6) the patients dressing or being dress'd—the naked upper half of the bodies—the good-humor and fun—the shirts, drawers, sheets of beds, &c., and the general fixing up for Sunday. Gave J.L. 50 cents.

Wednesday, February 4th.—Visited Armory-square hospital, went pretty thoroughly through wards E and D. Supplied paper and envelopes to all who wish'd—as usual, found plenty of men who needed those articles. Wrote letters. Saw and talk'd with two or three members of the Brooklyn 14th regt. A poor fellow in ward D, with a fearful wound in a fearful condition, was having some loose splinters of bone taken from the neighborhood of the wound. The operation was long, and one of great pain—yet, after it was well commenced, the soldier bore it in silence. He sat up, propp'd—was much wasted—had lain a long time quiet in one position (not for days only but weeks,) a bloodless, brown-skinn'd face, with eyes full of determination—belong'd to a New York regiment. There was an unusual cluster of surgeons, medical cadets, nurses, &c., around his bed—I thought the whole thing was done with tenderness, and done well. In one case, the wife sat by the side of her husband, his sickness typhoid fever, pretty bad. In another, by the side of her son, a mother—she told me she had seven children, and this was the youngest. (A fine, kind, healthy, gentle mother, good-looking, not very old, with a cap on her head, and dress'd like home—what a charm it gave to the whole ward.) I liked the woman nurse in ward

E—I noticed how she sat a long time by a poor fellow who just had, that morning, in addition to his other sickness, bad hemorrhage—she gently assisted him, reliev'd him of the blood, holding a cloth to his mouth, as he coughed it up—he was so weak he could only just turn his head over on the pillow.

One young New York man, with a bright, handsome face, had been lying several months from a most disagreeable wound, receiv'd at Bull Run. A bullet had shot him right through the bladder, hitting him front, low in the belly, and coming out back. He had suffer'd much—the water came out of the wound, by slow but steady quantities, for many weeks—so that he lay almost constantly in a sort of puddle—and there were other disagreeable circumstances. He was of good heart, however. At present comparatively comfortable, had a bad throat, was delighted with a stick of horehound candy I gave him, with one or two other trifles.

Patent-Office Hospital

February 23.—I must not let the great hospital at the Patent-office pass away without some mention. A few weeks ago the vast area of the second story of that noblest of Washington buildings was crowded close with rows of sick, badly wounded and dying soldiers. They were placed in three very large apartments. I went there many times. It was a strange, solemn, and, with all its features of suffering and death, a sort of fascinating sight. I go sometimes at night to soothe and relieve particular cases. Two of the immense apartments are fill'd with high and ponderous glass cases, crowded with models in miniature of every kind of utensil, machine or invention, it ever enter'd into the mind of man to conceive; and with curiosities and foreign presents. Between these cases are lateral openings, perhaps eight feet wide and quite deep, and in these were placed the sick, besides a great long double row of them up and down through the middle of the hall. Many of them were very bad cases, wounds and amputations. Then there was a gallery running above the hall in which there were beds also. It was, indeed, a curious scene, especially at night when lit up. The glass cases, the beds, the forms lying there, the gallery above, and the marble pavement under foot—the suffering, and the fortitude to bear it in various degrees—occasionally, from some, the groan that could not be repress'd—sometimes a poor fellow dying, with emaciated face and glassy eye, the nurse by his side, the doctor also there, but no friend, no relative—such were the sights but lately in the Patent-office. (The wounded have since been removed from there, and it is now vacant again.)

The White House by Moonlight

February 24th.—A spell of fine soft weather. I wander about a good deal, sometimes at night under the moon. To-night took a long look at the President's house. The white portico—the palace-like, tall, round columns, spotless as snow—the walls also—the tender and soft moonlight, flooding the pale marble, and making peculiar faint languishing shades, not shadows—everywhere a soft transparent hazy, thin, blue moon-lace, hanging in the air—the brilliant and extra-plentiful clusters of gas, on and around the façade, columns, portico, &c.—everything so white, so marbly pure and dazzling, yet soft—the White House of future poems, and of dreams and dramas, there in the soft and copious moon—the gorgeous front, in the trees, under the lustrous flooding moon, full of reality, full of illusion—the forms of the trees, leafless, silent, in trunk and myriad-angles of branches, under the stars and sky—the White House of the land, and of beauty and night—sentries at the gates, and by the portico, silent, pacing there in blue overcoats—stopping you not at all, but eyeing you with sharp eyes, whichever way you move.

An Army Hospital Ward

Let me specialize a visit I made to the collection of barrack-like one-story edifices, Campbell hospital, out on the flats, at the end of the then horse railway route, on Seventh street. There is a long building appropriated to each ward. Let us go into ward 6. It contains to-day, I should judge, eighty or a hundred patients, half sick, half wounded. The edifice is nothing but boards, well whitewash'd inside, and the usual slender-framed iron bedsteads, narrow and plain. You walk down the central passage, with a row on either side, their feet towards you, and their heads to the wall. There are fires in large stoves, and the prevailing white of the walls is reliev'd by some ornaments, stars, circles, &c., made of evergreens. The view of the whole edifice and occupants can be taken at once, for there is no partition. You may hear groans or other sounds of unendurable suffering from two or three of the cots, but in the main there is quiet—almost a painful absence of demonstration; but the pallid face, the dull'd eye, and the moisture on the lip, are demonstration enough. Most of these sick or hurt are evidently young fellows from the country, farmers' sons, and such like. Look at the fine large frames, the bright and broad countenances, and the many yet lingering proofs of strong constitution and physique. Look at the patient and mute manner of our American wounded as they lie in such a sad collection; representatives from all New England, and from New York, and New Jersey, and Pennsylvania—indeed from all the States and all the cities—largely from the west. Most of them are entirely without friends or acquaintances here—no familiar face, and hardly a word of judicious sympathy or cheer, through their sometimes long and tedious sickness, or the pangs of aggravated wounds.

A Connecticut Case

This young man in bed 25 is H. D. B., of the 27th Connecticut, company B. His folks live at Northford, near New Haven. Though not more than twenty-one, or thereabouts, he has knock'd much around the world, on sea and land, and has seen some fighting on both. When I first saw him he was very sick, with no appetite. He declined offers of money—said he did not need anything. As I was quite anxious to do something, he confess'd that he had a hankering for a good home-made rice pudding—thought he could relish it better than anything. At this time his stomach was very weak. (The doctor, whom I consulted, said nourishment would do him more good than anything; but things in the hospital, though better than usual, revolted him.) I soon procured B. his rice-pudding. A Washington lady, (Mrs. O'C.), hearing his wish, made the pudding herself, and I took it up to him the next day. He subsequently told me he lived upon it for three or four days. This B. is a good sample of the American eastern young man—the typical Yankee. I took a fancy to him, and gave him a nice pipe, for a keepsake. He receiv'd afterwards a box of things from home, and nothing would do but I must take dinner with him, which I did, and a very good one it was.

Two Brooklyn Boys

Here in this same ward are two young men from Brooklyn, members of the 51st New York. I had known both the two as young lads at home, so they seem near to me. One of them, J. L., lies there with an amputated arm, the stump healing pretty well. (I saw him lying on the ground at Fredericksburgh last December, all bloody, just after the arm was taken off. He was very phlegmatic about it, munching away at a cracker in the remaining hand—made no fuss.) He will recover, and thinks and talks yet of meeting the Johnny Rebs.

A Secesh Brave

The grand soldiers are not comprised in those of one side, any more than the other. Here is a sample of an unknown southerner, a lad of seventeen. At the War department, a few days ago, I witness'd a presentation of captured flags to the Secretary. Among others a soldier named Gant, of the 104th Ohio volunteers, presented a rebel battle-flag, which one of the officers stated to me was borne to the mouth of our cannon and planted there by a boy but seventeen years of age, who actually endeavor'd to stop the muzzle of the gun with fence-rails. He was kill'd in the effort, and the flag-staff was sever'd by a shot from one of our men.

The Wounded from Chancellorsville

May, '63.—As I write this, the wounded have begun to arrive from Hooker's command from bloody Chancellorsville. I was down among the first arrivals. The men in charge told me the bad cases were yet to come. If that is so I pity them, for these are bad enough. You ought to see the scene of the wounded arriving at the landing here at the foot of Sixth street, at night. Two boat loads came about half-past seven last night. A little after eight it rain'd a long and violent shower. The pale, helpless soldiers had been debark'd, and lay around on the wharf and neighborhood anywhere. The rain was, probably, grateful to them; at any rate they were exposed to it. The few torches light up the spectacle. All around—on the wharf, on the ground, out on side places—the men are lying on blankets, old quilts, &c., with bloody rags bound round heads, arms, and legs. The attendants are few, and at night few outsiders also—only a few hard-work'd transportation men and drivers. (The wounded are getting to be common, and people grow callous.) The men, whatever their condition, lie there, and patiently wait till their turn comes to be taken up. Near by, the ambulances are now arriving in clusters, and one after another is call'd to back up and take its load. Extreme cases are sent off on stretchers. The men generally make little or no ado, whatever their sufferings. A few groans that cannot be suppress'd, and occasionally a scream of pain as they lift a man into the ambulance. To-day, as I write, hundreds more are expected, and to-morrow and the next day more, and so on for many days. Quite often they arrive at the rate of 1000 a day.

A Night Battle, Over a Week Since

May 12.—There was part of the late battle at Chancellorsville, (second Fredericksburgh,) a little over a week ago, Saturday, Saturday night and Sunday, under Gen. Joe Hooker, I would like to give just a glimpse of—(a moment's look in a terrible storm at sea—of which a few suggestions are enough, and full details impossible.) The fighting had been very hot during the day, and after an intermission the latter part, was resumed at night, and kept up with furious energy till 3 o'clock in the morning. That afternoon (Saturday) an attack sudden and strong by Stonewall Jackson had gain'd a great advantage to the southern army, and broken our lines, entering us like a wedge, and leaving things in that position at dark. But Hooker at 11 at night made a desperate push, drove the secesh forces back, restored his original lines, and resumed his plans. This night scrimmage was very exciting, and afforded countless strange and fearful pictures. The fighting had been general both at Chancellorsville and northeast at Fredericksburgh. (We heard of some poor fighting, episodes, skedaddling on our part. I think not of it. I think of the fierce bravery, the general rule.) One corps, the 6th, Sedgewick's, fights four dashing and bloody battles in thirty-six hours, retreating in great jeopardy, losing largely but maintaining itself, fighting with the sternest desperation under all circumstances, getting over the Rappahannock only by the skin of its teeth, yet getting over. It lost many, many brave men, yet it took vengeance, ample vengeance.

But it was the tug of Saturday evening, and through the night and Sunday morning, I wanted to make a special note of. It was largely in the woods, and quite a general engagement. The night was very pleasant, at times the moon shining out full and clear, all Nature so calm in itself, the early summer grass so rich, and foliage of the trees—yet there the battle raging, and many good fellows lying helpless, with new accessions to them, and every minute amid the rattle of muskets and crash of cannon, (for there was an artillery contest too,) the red life-blood oozing out from heads or trunks or limbs upon that green and dew-cool grass. Patches of the woods take fire, and several of the wounded, unable to move, are consumed—quite large spaces are swept over, burning the dead also—some of the men have their hair and beards singed—some, burns on their faces and hands—others holes burnt in their clothing. The flashes of fire from the cannon, the quick flaring flames and smoke, and the immense roar—the musketry so general, the light nearly bright enough for each side to see the other—the crashing, tramping of men—the yelling—close quarters—we hear the secesh yells—our men cheer loudly back, especially if Hooker is in sight—hand to hand conflicts, each side stands up to it, brave, determin'd as demons, they often charge upon us—a thousand deeds are done worth to write newer greater poems on—and still the woods on fire—still many are not only scorch'd—too many, unable to move, are burn'd to death.

Then the camps of the wounded—O heavens, what scene is this?—is this indeed *humanity*—these butchers' shambles?

There are several of them. There they lie, in the largest, in an open space in the woods, from 200 to 300 poor fellows—the groans and screams—the odor of blood, mixed with the fresh scent of the night, the grass, the trees—that slaughter-house! O well is it their mothers, their sisters cannot see them—cannot conceive, and never conceiv'd, these things. One man is shot by a shell, both in the arm and leg—both are amputated—there lie the rejected members. Some have their legs blown off—some bullets through the breast—some indescribably horrid wounds in the face or head, all mutilated, sickening, torn, gouged out—some in the abdomen—some mere boys—many rebels, badly hurt—they take their regular turns with the rest, just the same as any—the surgeons use them just the same. Such is the camp of the wounded—such a fragment, a reflection afar off of the bloody scene—while over all the clear, large moon comes out at times softly, quietly shining. Amid the woods, that scene of flitting souls—amid the crack and crash and yelling sounds—the impalpable perfume of the woods—and yet the pungent, stifling smoke—the radiance of the moon, looking from heaven at intervals so placid—the sky so heavenly—the clear-obscure up there, those buoyant upper oceans—a few large placid stars beyond, coming silently and languidly out, and then disappearing—the melancholy, draperied night above, around. And there, upon the roads, the fields, and in those woods, that contest, never one more desperate in any age or land—both parties now in force—masses—no fancy battle, no semi-play, but fierce and savage demons fighting there—courage and scorn of death the rule, exceptions almost none.

What history, I say, can ever give—for who can know—the mad, determin'd tussle of the armies, in all their separate large and little squads—as this—each steep'd from crown to toe in desperate, mortal purports? Who know the conflict, hand-to-hand—the many conflicts in the dark, those shadowy-tangled, flashing moonbeam'd woods—the writhing groups and squads—the cries, the din, the cracking guns and pistols—the distant cannon—the cheers and calls and threats and awful music of the oaths—the indescribable mix—the officers' orders, persuasions, encouragements—the devils fully rous'd in human hearts—the strong shout, *Charge, men, charge*—the flash of the naked sword, and rolling flame and smoke? And still the broken, clear and clouded heaven—and still again the moonlight pouring silvery soft its radiant patches over all. Who paint the scene, the sudden partial panic of the afternoon, at dusk? Who paint the irrepressible advance of the second division of the Third corps, under Hooker himself, suddenly order'd up—those rapid-filing phantoms through the woods? Who show what moves there in the shadows, fluid and firm—to save, (and it did save,) the army's name, perhaps the nation? as there the veterans hold the field. (Brave Berry falls not yet—but death has mark'd him—soon he falls.)

Unnamed Remains the Bravest Soldier

Of scenes like these, I say, who writes—whoe'er can write the story? Of many a score—aye, thousands, north and south, of unwrit heroes, unknown heroisms, incredible, impromptu, first-class desperations—who tells? No history ever—no poem sings, no music sounds, those bravest men of all—those deeds. No formal general's report, nor book in the library, nor column in the paper, embalms the bravest, north or south, east or west. Unnamed, unknown, remain, and still remain, the bravest soldiers. Our manliest—our boys—our hardy darlings; no picture gives them. Likely, the typic one of them (standing, no doubt, for hundreds, thousands,) crawls aside to some bush-clump, or ferny tuft, on receiving his death-shot—there sheltering a little while, soaking roots, grass and soil, with red blood—the battle advances, retreats, flits from the scene, sweeps by—and there, haply with pain and suffering (yet less, far less, than is supposed,) the last lethargy winds like a serpent round him—the eyes glaze in death—none recks—perhaps the burial-squads, in truce, a week afterwards, search not the secluded spot—and there, at last, the Bravest Soldier crumbles in mother earth, unburied and unknown.

Some Specimen Cases

June 18th.—In one of the hospitals I find Thomas Haley, company M, 4th New York cavalry—a regular Irish boy, a fine specimen of youthful physical manliness—shot through the lungs—inevitably dying—came over to this country from Ireland to enlist—has not a single friend or acquaintance here—is sleeping soundly at this moment, (but it is the sleep of death)—has a bullet-hole straight through the lung. I saw Tom when first brought here, three days since, and didn't suppose he could live twelve hours—(yet he looks well enough in the face to a casual observer.) He lies there with his frame exposed above the waist, all naked, for coolness, a fine built man, the tan not yet bleach'd from his cheeks and neck. It is useless to talk to him, as with his sad hurt, and the stimulants they give him, and the utter strangeness of every object, face, furniture, &c., the poor fellow, even when awake, is like some frighten'd, shy animal. Much of the time he sleeps, or half sleeps. (Sometimes I thought he knew more than he show'd.) I often come and sit by him in perfect silence; he will breathe for ten minutes as softly and evenly as a young babe asleep. Poor youth, so handsome, athletic, with profuse beautiful shining hair. One time as I sat looking at him while he lay asleep, he suddenly, without the least start, awaken'd, open'd his eyes, gave me a long steady look, turning his face very slightly to gaze easier—one long, clear, silent look—a slight sigh—then turn'd back and went into his doze again. Little he knew, poor death-stricken boy, the heart of the stranger that hover'd near.

W. H. E., Co. F., 2d N.J.—His disease is pneumonia. He lay sick at the wretched hospital below Aquia creek, for seven or eight days before brought here. He was detail'd from his regiment to go there and help as nurse, but was soon taken down himself. Is an elderly, sallow-faced, rather gaunt, gray-hair'd man, a widower, with children. He express'd a great desire for good, strong green tea. An excellent lady, Mrs. W., of Washington, soon sent him a package; also a small sum of money. The doctor said give him the tea at pleasure; it lay on the table by his side, and he used it every day. He slept a great deal; could not talk much, as he grew deaf. Occupied bed 15, ward I, Armory. (The same lady above, Mrs. W., sent the men a large package of tobacco.)

J. G. lies in bed 52, ward I; is of company B, 7th Pennsylvania. I gave him a small sum of money, some tobacco, and envelopes. To a man adjoining also gave twenty-five cents; he flush'd in the face when I offer'd it—refused at first, but as I found he had not a cent, and was very fond of having the daily papers to read, I prest it on him. He was evidently very grateful, but said little.

J. T. L., of company F., 9th New Hampshire, lies in bed 37, ward I. Is very fond of tobacco. I furnish him some; also with a little money. Has gangrene of the feet; a pretty bad case; will surely have to lose three toes. Is a regular specimen of an old-fashion'd, rude, hearty, New England countryman, impressing me with his likeness to that celebrated singed cat, who was better than she look'd.

Bed 3, ward E, Armory, has a great hankering for pickles, something pungent. After consulting the doctor, I gave him a small bottle of horse-radish; also some apples; also a book. Some of the nurses are excellent. The woman-nurse in this ward I like very much. (Mrs. Wright—a year afterwards I found her in Mansion house hospital, Alexandria—she is a perfect nurse.)

In one bed a young man, Marcus Small, company K, 7th Maine—sick with dysentery and typhoid fever—pretty critical case—I talk with him often—he thinks he will die—looks like it indeed. I write a letter for him home to East Livermore, Maine—I let him talk to me a little, but not much, advise him to keep very quiet—do most of the talking myself—stay quite a while with him, as he holds on to my hand—talk to him in a cheering, but slow, low and measured manner—talk about his furlough, and going home as soon as he is able to travel.

Thomas Lindly, 1st Pennsylvania cavalry, shot very badly through the foot—poor young man, he suffers horribly, has to be constantly dosed with morphine, his face ashy and glazed, bright young eyes—I give him a large handsome apple, lay it in sight, tell him to have it roasted in the morning, as he generally feels easier then, and can eat a little breakfast. I write two letters for him.

Opposite, an old Quaker lady is sitting by the side of her son, Amer Moore, 2d U.S. artillery—shot in the head two weeks since, very low, quite rational—from hips down paralyzed—he will surely die. I speak a very few words to him every day and evening—he answers pleasantly—wants nothing—(he told me soon after he came about his home affairs, his mother had been an invalid, and he fear'd to let her know his condition.) He died soon after she came.

My Preparations for Visits

In my visits to the hospitals I found it was in the simple matter of personal presence, and emanating ordinary cheer and magnetism, that I succeeded and help'd more than by medical nursing, or delicacies, or gifts of money, or anything else. During the war I possess'd the perfection of physical health. My habit, when practicable, was to prepare for starting out on one of those daily or nightly tours of from a couple to four or five hours, by fortifying myself with previous rest, the bath, clean clothes, a good meal, and as cheerful an appearance as possible.

Ambulance Processions

June 25, Sundown.—As I sit writing this paragraph I see a train of about thirty huge four-horse wagons, used as ambulances, fill'd with wounded, passing up Fourteenth street, on their way, probably, to Columbian, Carver, and mount Pleasant hospitals. This is the way the men come in now, seldom in small numbers, but almost always in these long, sad processions. Through the past winter, while our army lay opposite Fredericksburgh, the like strings of ambulances were of frequent occurrence along Seventh street, passing slowly up from the steamboat wharf, with loads from Aquia creek.

Bad Wounds—The Young

The soldiers are nearly all young men, and far more American than is generally supposed—I should say nine-tenths are native-born. Among the arrivals from Chancellorsville I find a large proportion of Ohio, Indiana, and Illinois men. As usual, there are all sorts of wounds. Some of the men fearfully burnt from the explosions of artillery caissons. One ward has a long row of officers, some with ugly hurts. Yesterday was perhaps worse than usual. Amputations are going on—the attendants are dressing wounds. As you pass by, you must be on your guard where you look. I saw the other day a gentleman, a visitor apparently from curiosity, in one of the wards, stop and turn a moment to look at an awful wound they were probing. He turn'd pale, and in a moment more he had fainted away and fallen on the floor.

The Most Inspiriting of All War's Shows

June 29.—Just before sundown this evening a very large cavalry force went by—a fine sight. The men evidently had seen service. First came a mounted band of sixteen bugles, drums and cymbals, playing wild martial tunes—made my heart jump. Then the principal officers, then company after company, with their officers at their heads, making of course the main part of the cavalcade; then a long train of men with led horses, lots of mounted negroes with special horses—and a long string of baggage-wagons, each drawn by four horses—and then a motley rear guard. It was a pronouncedly warlike and gay show; the sabres clank'd, the men look'd young and healthy and strong; the electric tramping of so many horses on the hard road, and the gallant bearing, fine seat, and bright faced appearance of a thousand and more handsome young American men, were so good to see. An hour later another troop went by, smaller in numbers, perhaps three hundred men. They too look'd like serviceable men, campaigners used to field and fight.

July 3.—This forenoon, for more than an hour, again long strings of cavalry, several regiments, very fine men and horses, four or five abreast. I saw them in Fourteenth street, coming in town from north. Several hundred extra horses, some of the mares with colts, trotting along. (Appear'd to be a number of prisoners too.) How inspiriting always the cavalry regiments. Our men are generally well mounted, feel good, are young, gay on the saddle, their blankets in a roll behind them, their sabres clanking at their sides. This noise and movement and the tramp of many horses' hoofs has a curious effect upon one. The bugles play—presently you hear them afar off, deaden'd, mix'd with other noises. Then just as they had all pass'd, a string of ambulances commenc'd from the other way, moving up Fourteenth street north, slowly wending along, bearing a large lot of wounded to the hospitals.

Battle of Gettysburg

July 4th.—The weather to-day, upon the whole, is very fine, warm, but from a smart rain last night, fresh enough, and no dust, which is a great relief for this city. I saw the parade about noon, Pennsylvania avenue, from Fifteenth street down toward the capitol. There were three regiments of infantry, (I suppose the ones doing patrol duty here,) two or three societies of Odd Fellows, a lot of children in barouches, and a squad of policemen. (A useless imposition upon the soldiers—they have work enough on their backs without piling the like of this.) As I went down the Avenue, saw a big flaring placard on the bulletin board of a newspaper office, announcing "Glorious Victory for the Union Army!" Meade had fought Lee at Gettysburg, Pennsylvania, yesterday and day before, and repuls'd him most signally, taken 3,000 prisoners, &c. (I afterwards saw Meade's despatch, very modest, and a sort of order of the day from the President himself, quite religious, giving thanks to the Supreme, and calling on the people to do the same.) I walk'd on to Armory hospital—took along with me several bottles of blackberry and cherry syrup, good and strong, but innocent. Went through several of the wards, announc'd to the soldiers the news from Meade, and gave them all a good drink of the syrups with ice water, quite refreshing—prepar'd it all myself, and serv'd it around. Meanwhile the Washington bells are ringing their sundown peals for Fourth of July, and the usual fusilades of boys' pistols, crackers, and guns.

A Cavalry Camp

I am writing this, nearly sundown, watching a cavalry company (acting Signal service,) just come in through a shower, making their night's camp ready on some broad, vacant ground, a sort of hill, in full view opposite my window. There are the men in their yellow-striped jackets. All are dismounted; the freed horses stand with drooping heads and wet sides; they are to be led off presently in groups, to water. The little wall-tents and shelter tents spring up quickly. I see the fires already blazing, and pots and kettles over them. Some among the men are driving in tent-poles, wielding their axes with strong, slow blows. I see great huddles of horses, bundles of hay, groups of men (some with unbuckled sabres yet on their sides,) a few officers, piles of wood, the flames of the fires, saddles, harness, &c. The smoke streams upward, additional men arrive and dismount—some drive in stakes, and tie their horses to them; some go with buckets for water, some are chopping wood, and so on.

July 6th.—A steady rain, dark and thick and warm. A train of six-mule wagons has just pass'd bearing pontoons, great square-end flat-boats, and the heavy planking for overlaying them. We hear that the Potomac above here is flooded, and are wondering whether Lee will be able to get back across again, or whether Meade will indeed break him to pieces. The cavalry camp on the hill is a ceaseless field of observation for me. This forenoon there stand the horses, tether'd together, dripping, steaming, chewing their hay. The men emerge from their tents, dripping also. The fires are half quench'd.

July 10th.—Still the camp opposite—perhaps fifty or sixty tents. Some of the men are cleaning their sabres (pleasant to-day,) some brushing boots, some laying off, reading, writing—some cooking, some sleeping. On long temporary cross-sticks back of the tents are cavalry accoutrements—blankets and overcoats are hung out to air—there are the squads of horses tether'd, feeding, continually stamping and whisking their tails to keep off flies. I sit long in my third story window and look at the scene—a hundred little things going on—peculiar objects connected with the camp that could not be described, any one of them justly, without much minute drawing and coloring in words.

A New York Soldier

This afternoon, July 22d, I have spent a long time with Oscar F. Wilber, company G, 154th New York, low with chronic diarrhœa, and a bad wound also. He asked me to read him a chapter in the New Testament. I complied, and ask'd him what I should read. He said, "Make your own choice."

I open'd at the close of one of the first books of the evangelists, and read the chapters describing the latter hours of Christ, and the scenes at the crucifixion. The poor, wasted young man ask'd me to read the following chapter also, how Christ rose again. I read very slowly, for Oscar was feeble. It pleased him very much, yet the tears were in his eyes. He ask'd me if I enjoy'd religion. I said, "Perhaps not, my dear, in the way you mean, and yet, may-be, it is the same thing." He said, "It is my chief reliance." He talk'd of death, and said he did not fear it. I said, "Why, Oscar, don't you think you will get well?" He said, "I may, but it is not probable." He spoke calmly of his condition. The wound was very bad, it discharg'd much. Then the diarrhœa had prostrated him, and I felt that he was even then the same as dying. He behaved very manly and affectionate. The kiss I gave him as I was about leaving he return'd fourfold. He gave me his mother's address, Mrs. Sally D. Wilber, Alleghany post-office, Cattaraugus county, N. Y. I had several such interviews with him. He died a few days after the one just described.

Home-Made Music

August 8th.—To-night, as I was trying to keep cool, sitting by a wounded soldier in Armory-square, I was attracted by some pleasant singing in an adjoining ward. As my soldier was asleep, I left him, and entering the ward where the music was, I walk'd half-way down and took a seat by the cot of a young Brooklyn friend, S. R., badly wounded in the hand at Chancellorsville, and who has suffer'd much, but at that moment in the evening was wide awake and comparatively easy. He had turn'd over on his left side to get a better view of the singers, but the mosquito-curtains of the adjoining cots obstructed the sight. I stept round and loop'd them all up, so that he had a clear show, and then sat down again by him, and look'd and listen'd. The principal singer was a young lady-nurse of one of the wards, accompanying on a melodeon, and join'd by the lady-nurses of other wards. They sat there, making a charming group, with their handsome, healthy faces, and standing up a little behind them were some ten or fifteen of the convalescent soldiers, young men, nurses, &c., with books in their hands, singing. Of course it was not such a performance as the great soloists at the New York opera house take a hand in, yet I am not sure but I receiv'd as much pleasure under the circumstances, sitting there, as I have had from the best Italian compositions, express'd by world-famous performers. The men lying up and down the hospital, in their cots, (some badly wounded—some never to rise thence,) the cots themselves, with their drapery of white curtains, and the shadows down the lower and upper parts of the ward; then the silence of the men, and the attitudes they took—the whole was a sight to look around upon again and again. And there sweetly rose those voices up to the high, whitewash'd wooden roof, and pleasantly the roof sent it all back again. They sang very well, mostly quaint old songs and declamatory hymns, to fitting tunes. Here, for instance:

My days are swiftly gliding by, and I a pilgrim stranger,
Would not detain them as they fly, those hours of toil and danger;
For O we stand on Jordan's strand, our friends are passing over,
And just before, the shining shore we may almost discover.

We'll gird our loins my brethren dear, our distant home discerning,
Our absent Lord has left us word, let every lamp be burning,
For O we stand on Jordan's strand, our friends are passing over,
And just before, the shining shore we may almost discover.

Abraham Lincoln

August 12th.—I see the President almost every day, as I happen to live where he passes to or from his lodgings out of town. He never sleeps at the White House during the hot season, but has quarters at a healthy location some three miles north of the city, the Soldiers' home, a United States military establishment. I saw him this morning about 8½ coming in to business, riding on Vermont avenue, near L street. He always has a company of twenty-five or thirty cavalry, with sabres drawn and held upright over their shoulders. They say this guard was against his personal wish, but he let his counselors have their way. The party makes no great show in uniform or horses. Mr. Lincoln on the saddle generally rides a good-sized, easy-going gray horse, is dress'd in plain black, somewhat rusty and dusty, wears a black stiff hat, and looks about as ordinary in attire, &c., as the commonest man. A lieutenant, with yellow straps, rides at his left, and following behind, two by two, come the cavalry men, in their yellow-striped jackets. They are generally going at a slow trot, as that is the pace set them by the one they wait upon. The sabres and accoutrements clank, and the entirely unornamental *cortège* as it trots towards Lafayette square arouses no sensation, only some curious stranger stops and gazes. I see very plainly ABRAHAM LINCOLN's dark brown face, with the deep-cut lines, the eyes, always to me with a deep latent sadness in the expression. We have got so that we exchange bows, and very cordial ones. Sometimes the President goes and comes in an open barouche. The cavalry always accompany him, with drawn sabres. Often I notice as he goes out evenings—and sometimes in the morning, when he returns early—he turns off and halts at the large and handsome residence of the Secretary of War, on K street, and holds conference there. If in his barouche, I can see from my window he does not alight, but sits in his vehicle, and Mr. Stanton comes out to attend him. Sometimes one of his sons, a boy of ten or twelve, accompanies him, riding at his right on a pony. Earlier in the summer I occasionally saw the President and his wife, toward the latter part of the afternoon, out in a barouche, on a pleasure ride through the city. Mrs. Lincoln was dress'd in complete black, with a long crape veil. The equipage is of the plainest kind, only two horses, and they nothing extra. They pass'd me once very close, and I saw the President in the face fully, as they were moving slowly, and his look, though abstracted, happen'd to be directed steadily in my eye. He bow'd and smiled, but far beneath his smile I noticed well the expression I have alluded to. None of the artists or pictures has caught the deep, though subtle and indirect expression of this man's face. There is something else there. One of the great portrait painters of two or three centuries ago is needed.

Heated Term

There has lately been much suffering here from heat; we have had it upon us now eleven days. I go around with an umbrella and a fan. I saw two cases of sun-stroke yesterday, one in Pennsylvania avenue, and another in Seventh street. The City railroad company loses some horses every day. Yet Washington is having a livelier August, and is probably putting in a more energetic and satisfactory summer, than ever before during its existence. There is probably more human electricity, more population to make it, more business, more light-heartedness, than ever before. The armies that swiftly circumambiated from Fredericksburgh—march'd, struggled, fought, had out their mighty clinch and hurl at Gettysburg—wheel'd, circumambiated again, return'd to their ways, touching us not, either at their going or coming. And Washington feels that she has pass'd the worst; perhaps feels that she is henceforth mistress. So here she sits with her surrounding hills spotted with guns, and is conscious of a character and identity different from what it was five or six short weeks ago, and very considerably pleasanter and prouder.

Soldiers and Talks

Soldiers, soldiers, soldiers, you meet everywhere about the city, often superb-looking men, though invalids dress'd in worn uniforms, and carrying canes or crutches. I often have talks with them, occasionally quite long and interesting. One, for instance, will have been all through the peninsula under McClellan—narrates to me the fights, the marches, the strange, quick changes of that eventful campaign, and gives glimpses of many things untold in any official reports or books or journals. These, indeed, are the things that are genuine and precious. The man was there, has been out two years, has been through a dozen fights, the superfluous flesh of talking is long work'd off him, and he gives me little but the hard meat and sinew. I find it refreshing, these hardy, bright, intuitive, American young men, (experienc'd soldiers with all their youth.) The vocal play and significance moves one more than books. Then there hangs something majestic about a man who has borne his part in battles, especially if he is very quiet regarding it when you desire him to unbosom. I am continually lost at the absence of blowing and blowers among these old-young American militaires. I have found some man or other who has been in every battle since the war began, and have talk'd with them about each one in every part of the United States, and many of the engagements on the rivers and harbors too. I find men here from every State in the Union, without exception. (There are more Southerners, especially border State men, in the Union army than is generally supposed.*) I now doubt whether one can get a fair idea of what this war practically is, or what genuine America is, and her character, without some such experience as this I am having.

Death of a Wisconsin Officer

Another characteristic scene of that dark and bloody 1863, from notes of my visit to Armory-square hospital, one hot but pleasant summer day. In ward H we approach the cot of a young lieutenant of one of the Wisconsin regiments. Tread the bare board floor lightly here, for the pain and panting of death are in this cot. I saw the lieutenant when he was first brought here from Chancellorsville, and have been with him occasionally from day to day and night to night. He had been getting along pretty well till night before last, when a sudden hemorrhage that could not be stopt came upon him, and to-day it still continues at intervals. Notice that water-pail by the side of the bed, with a quantity of blood and bloody pieces

*Mr. Garfield *(In the House of Representatives, April 15, '79.)* "Do gentlemen know that (leaving out all the border States) there were fifty regiments and seven companies of white men in our army fighting for the Union from the States that went into rebellion? Do they know that from the single State of Kentucky more Union soldiers fought under our flag than Napoleon took into the battle of Waterloo? more than Wellington took with all the allied armies against Napoleon? Do they remember that 186,000 color'd men fought under our flag against the rebellion and for the Union, and that of that number 90,000 were from the States which went into rebellion?"

of muslin, nearly full; that tells the story. The poor young man is struggling painfully for breath, his great dark eyes with a glaze already upon them, and the choking faint but audible in his throat. An attendant sits by him, and will not leave him till the last; yet little or nothing can be done. He will die here in an hour or two, without the presence of kith or kin. Meantime the ordinary chat and business of the ward a little way off goes on indifferently. Some of the inmates are laughing and joking, others are playing checkers or cards, others are reading, &c.

I have noticed through most of the hospitals that as long as there is any chance for a man, no matter how bad he may be, the surgeon and nurses work hard, sometimes with curious tenacity, for his life, doing everything, and keeping somebody by him to execute the doctor's orders, and minister to him every minute night and day. See that screen there. As you advance through the dusk of early candle-light, a nurse will step forth on tip-toe, and silently but imperiously forbid you to make any noise, or perhaps to come near at all. Some soldier's life is flickering there, suspended between recovery and death. Perhaps at this moment the exhausted frame has just fallen into a light sleep that a step might shake. You must retire. The neighboring patients must move in their stocking feet. I have been several times struck with such mark'd efforts—everything bent to save a life from the very grip of the destroyer. But when that grip is once firmly fix'd, leaving no hope or chance at all, the surgeon abandons the patient. If it is a case where stimulus is any relief, the nurse gives milk-punch or brandy, or whatever is wanted, *ad libitum*. There is no fuss made. Not a bit of sentimentalism or whining have I seen about a single death-bed in hospital or on the field, but generally impassive indifference. All is over, as far as any efforts can avail; it is useless to expend emotions or labors. While there is a prospect they strive hard—at least most surgeons do; but death certain and evident, they yield the field.

Hospitals Ensemble

Aug., Sep., and Oct., '63.—I am in the habit of going to all, and to Fairfax seminary, Alexandria, and over Long bridge to the great Convalescent camp. The journals publish a regular directory of them—a long list. As a specimen of almost any one of the larger of these hospitals, fancy to yourself a space of three to twenty acres of ground, on which are group'd ten or twelve very large wooden barracks, with, perhaps, a dozen or twenty, and sometimes more than that number, small buildings, capable altogether of accommodating from five hundred to a thousand or fifteen hundred persons. Sometimes these wooden barracks or wards, each of them perhaps from a hundred to a hundred and fifty feet long, are rang'd in a straight row, evenly fronting the street; others are plann'd so as to form an immense V; and others again are ranged around a hollow square. They make altogether a huge cluster, with the additional tents, extra wards for contagious diseases, guard-houses, sutler's stores, chaplain's house; in the middle will probably be an edifice devoted to the offices of the surgeon in charge and the ward surgeons, principal attaches, clerks, &c. The wards are either letter'd alphabetically, ward G, ward K, or else numerically, 1, 2, 3, &c. Each has its ward surgeon and corps of nurses. Of course, there is, in the aggregate, quite a muster of employés, and over all the surgeon in charge. Here in Washington, when these army hospitals are all fill'd, (as they have been already several times,) they contain a population more numerous in itself than the whole of the Washington of ten or fifteen years ago. Within sight of the capitol, as I write, are some thirty or forty such collections, at times holding from fifty to seventy thousand men. Looking from any eminence and studying the topography in my rambles, I use them as landmarks. Through the rich August verdure of the trees, see that white group of buildings off yonder in the outskirts; then another cluster half a mile to the left of the first; then another a mile to the right, and another a mile beyond, and still another between us and the first. Indeed, we can hardly look in any direction but these clusters are dotting the landscape and environs. That little town, as you might suppose it, off there on the brow of a hill, is indeed a town, but of wounds, sickness, and death. It is Finley hospital, northeast of the city, on Kendall green, as it used to be call'd. That other is Campbell hospital. Both are large establishments. I have known these two alone to have from two thousand to twenty five hundred inmates. Then there is Carver hospital, larger still, a wall'd and military city regularly laid out, and guarded by squads of sentries. Again, off east, Lincoln hospital, a still larger one; and half a mile further Emory hospital. Still sweeping the eye around down the river toward Alexandria, we see, to the right, the locality where the Convalescent camp stands, with its five, eight, or sometimes ten thousand inmates. Even all these are but a portion. The Harewood, Mount Pleasant, Armory-square, Judiciary hospitals, are some of the rest, and all large collections.

A Silent Night Ramble

October 20th.—To-night, after leaving the hospital at 10 o'clock, (I had been on self-imposed duty some five hours, pretty closely confined,) I wander'd a long time around Washington. The night was sweet, very clear, sufficiently cool, a voluptuous half-moon, slightly golden, the space near it of a transparent blue-gray tinge. I walk'd up Pennsylvania avenue, and then to Seventh street, and a long while around the Patent-office. Somehow it look'd rebukefully strong, majestic, there in the delicate moonlight. The sky, the planets, the constellations all so bright, so calm, so expressively silent, so soothing, after those hospital scenes. I wander'd to and fro till the moist moon set, long after midnight.

Spiritual Characters among the Soldiers

Every now and then, in hospital or camp, there are beings I meet—specimens of unworldliness, disinterestedness, and animal purity and heroism—perhaps some unconscious Indianian, or from Ohio or Tennessee—on whose birth the calmness of heaven seems to have descended, and whose gradual growing up, whatever the circumstances of work-life or change, or hardship, or small or no education that attended it, the power of a strange spiritual sweetness, fibre and inward health, have also attended. Something veil'd and abstracted is often a part of the manners of these beings. I have met them, I say, not seldom in the army, in camp, and in the hospitals. The Western regiments contain many of them. They are often young men, obeying the events and occasions about them, marching, soldiering, fighting, foraging, cooking, working on farms or at some trade before the war—unaware of their own nature, (as to that, who is aware of his own nature?) their companions only understanding that they are different from the rest, more silent, "something odd about them," and apt to go off and meditate and muse in solitude.

Cattle Droves about Washington

Among other sights are immense droves of cattle with their drivers, passing through the streets of the city. Some of the men have a way of leading the cattle by a peculiar call, a wild, pensive hoot, quite musical, prolong'd, indescribable, sounding something between the cooing of a pigeon and the hoot of an owl. I like to stand and look at the sight of one of these immense droves—a little way off—(as the dust is great.) There are always men on horseback, cracking their whips and shouting—the cattle low—some obstinate ox or steer attempts to escape—then a lively scene—the mounted men, always excellent riders and on good horses, dash after the recusant, and wheel and turn—a dozen mounted drovers, their great slouch'd, broad-brim'd hats, very picturesque—another dozen on foot—everybody cover'd with dust—long goads in their hands—an immense drove of perhaps 1000 cattle—the shouting, hooting, movement, &c.

Hospital Perplexity

To add to other troubles, amid the confusion of this great army of sick, it is almost impossible for a stranger to find any friend or relative, unless he has the patient's specific address to start upon. Besides the directory printed in the newspapers here, there are one or two general directories of the hospitals kept at provost's headquarters, but they are nothing like complete; they are never up to date, and, as things are, with the daily streams of coming and going and changing, cannot be. I have known cases, for instance such as a farmer coming here from northern New York to find a wounded brother, faithfully hunting round for a week, and then compell'd to leave and go home without getting any trace of him. When he got home he found a letter from the brother giving the right address.

Down at the Front

Culpepper, Va., *Feb. '64.*—Here I am pretty well down toward the extreme front. Three or four days ago General S., who is now in chief command, (I believe Meade is absent, sick,) moved a strong force southward from camp as if intending business. They went to the Rapidan; there has since been some manœuvring and a little fighting, but nothing of consequence. The telegraphic accounts given Monday morning last, make entirely too much of it, I should say. What General S. intended we here know not, but we trust in that competent commander. We were somewhat excited, (but not so very much either,) on Sunday, during the day and night, as orders were sent out to pack up and harness, and be ready to evacuate, to fall back towards Washington. But I was very sleepy and went to bed. Some tremendous shouts arousing me during the night, I went forth and found it was from the men above mention'd, who were returning. I talk'd with some of the men; as usual I found them full of gayety, endurance, and many fine little outshows, the signs of the most excellent good manliness of the world. It was a curious sight to see those shadowy columns moving through the night. I stood unobserv'd in the darkness and watch'd them long. The mud was very deep. The men had their usual burdens, overcoats, knapsacks, guns and blankets. Along and along they filed by me, with often a laugh, a song, a cheerful word, but never once a murmur. It may have been odd, but I never before so realized the majesty and reality of the American people *en masse.* It fell upon me like a great awe. The strong ranks moved neither fast nor slow. They had march'd seven or eight miles already through the slipping unctuous mud. The brave First corps stopt here. The equally brave Third corps moved on to Brandy station. The famous Brooklyn 14th are here, guarding the town. You see their red legs actively moving everywhere. Then they have a theatre of their own here. They give musical performances, nearly everything done capitally. Of course the audience is a jam. It is good sport to attend one of these entertainments of the 14th. I like to look around at the soldiers, and the general collection in front of the curtain, more than the scene on the stage.

Paying the Bounties

One of the things to note here now is the arrival of the paymaster with his strong box, and the payment of bounties to veterans re-enlisting. Major H. is here to-day, with a small mountain of greenbacks, rejoicing the hearts of the 2d division of the First corps. In the midst of a rickety shanty, behind a little table, sit the major and clerk Eldridge, with the rolls before them, and much moneys. A re-enlisted man gets in cash about $200 down, (and heavy instalments following, as the pay-days arrive, one after another.) The show of the men crowding around is quite exhilarating; I like to stand and look. They feel elated, their pockets full, and the ensuing furlough, the visit home. It is a scene of sparkling eyes and flush'd cheeks. The soldier has many gloomy and harsh experiences, and this makes up for some of them. Major H. is order'd to pay first all the re-enlisted men of the First corps their bounties and back pay, and then the rest. You hear the peculiar sound of the rustling of the new and crisp greenbacks by the hour, through the nimble fingers of the major and my friend clerk E.

Rumors, Changes, &c.

About the excitement of Sunday, and the orders to be ready to start, I have heard since that the said orders came from some cautious minor commander, and that the high principalities knew not and thought not of any such move; which is likely. The rumor and fear here intimated a long circuit by Lee, and flank attack on our right. But I cast my eyes at the mud, which was then at its deepest and palmiest condition, and retired composedly to rest. Still it is about time for Culpepper to have a change. Authorities have chased each other here like clouds in a stormy sky. Before the first Bull Run this was the rendezvous and camp of instruction of the secession troops. I am stopping at the house of a lady who has witness'd all the eventful changes of the war, along this route of contending armies. She is a widow, with a family of young children, and lives here with her sister in a large handsome house. A number of army officers board with them.

Virginia

Dilapidated, fenceless, and trodden with war as Virginia is, wherever I move across her surface, I find myself rous'd to surprise and admiration. What capacity for products, improvements, human life, nourishment and expansion. Everywhere that I have been in the Old Dominion, (the subtle mockery of that title now!) such thoughts have fill'd me. The soil is yet far above the average of any of the northern States. And how full of breadth the scenery, everywhere distant mountains, everywhere convenient rivers. Even yet prodigal in forest woods, and surely eligible for all the fruits, orchards, and flowers. The skies and atmosphere most luscious, as I feel certain, from more than a year's residence in the State, and movements hither and yon. I should say very healthy, as a general thing. Then a rich and elastic quality, by night and by day. The sun rejoices in his strength, dazzling and burning, and yet, to me, never unpleasantly weakening. It is not the panting tropical heat, but invigorates. The north tempers it. The nights are often unsurpassable. Last evening (Feb. 8,) I saw the first of the new moon, the outlined old moon clear along with it; the sky and air so clear, such transparent hues of color, it seem'd to me I had never really seen the new moon before. It was the thinnest cut crescent possible. It hung delicate just above the sulky shadow of the Blue mountains. Ah, if it might prove an omen and good prophecy for this unhappy State.

Summer of 1864

I am back again in Washington, on my regular daily and nightly rounds. Of course there are many specialties. Dotting a ward here and there are always cases of poor fellows, long-suffering under obstinate wounds, or weak and dishearten'd from typhoid fever, or the like; mark'd cases, needing special and sympathetic nourishment. These I sit down and either talk to, or silently cheer them up. They always like it hugely, (and so do I.) Each case has its peculiarities, and needs some new adaptation. I have learnt to thus conform—learnt a good deal of hospital wisdom. Some of the poor young chaps, away from home for the first time in their lives, hunger and thirst for affection; this is sometimes the only thing that will reach their condition. The men like to have a pencil, and something to write in. I have given them cheap pocket-diaries, and almanacs for 1864, interleav'd with blank paper. For reading I generally have some old pictorial magazines or story papers—they are always acceptable. Also the morning or evening papers of the day. The best books I do not give, but lend to read through the wards, and then take them to others, and so on; they are very punctual about returning the books. In these wards, or on the field, as I thus continue to go round, I have come to adapt myself to each emergency, after its kind or call, however trivial, however solemn, every one justified and made real under its circumstances—not only visits and cheering talk and little gifts—not only washing and dressing wounds, (I have some cases where the patient is unwilling any one should do this but me)—but passages from the Bible, expounding them, prayer at the bedside, explanations of doctrine, &c. (I think I see my friends smiling at this confession, but I was never more in earnest in my life.) In camp and everywhere, I was in the habit of reading or giving recitations to the men. They were very fond of it, and liked declamatory poetical pieces. We would gather in a large group by ourselves, after supper, and spend the time in such readings, or in talking, and occasionally by an amusing game called the game of twenty questions.

A New Army Organization Fit for America

It is plain to me out of the events of the war, north and south, and out of all considerations, that the current military theory, practice, rules and organization, (adopted from Europe from the feudal institutes, with, of course, the "modern improvements," largely from the French,) though tacitly follow'd, and believ'd in by the officers generally, are not at all consonant with the United States, nor our people, nor our days. What it will be I know not—but I know that as entire an abnegation of the present military system, and the naval too, and a building up from radically different root-bases and centres appropriate to us, must eventually result, as that our political system has resulted and become establish'd, different from feudal Europe, and built up on itself from original, perennial, democratic premises. We have undoubtedly in the United States the greatest military power—an exhaustless, intelligent, brave and reliable rank and file—in the world, any land, perhaps all lands. The problem is to organize this in the manner fully appropriate to it, to the principles of the republic, and to get the best service out of it. In the present struggle, as already seen and review'd, probably three-fourths of the losses, men, lives, &c., have been sheer superfluity, extravagance, waste.

Death of a Hero

I wonder if I could ever convey to another—to you, for instance, reader dear—the tender and terrible realities of such cases, (many, many happen'd,) as the one I am now going to mention. Stewart C. Glover, company E, 5th Wisconsin—was wounded May 5, in one of those fierce tussles of the Wilderness—died May 21—aged about 20. He was a small and beardless young man—a splendid soldier—in fact almost an ideal American, of his age. He had serv'd nearly three years, and would have been entitled to his discharge in a few days. He was in Hancock's corps. The fighting had about ceas'd for the day, and the general commanding the brigade rode by and call'd for volunteers to bring in the wounded. Glover responded among the first—went out gayly—but while in the act of bearing in a wounded sergeant to our lines, was shot in the knee by a rebel sharpshooter; consequence, amputation and death. He had resided with his father, John Glover, an aged and feeble man, in Batavia, Genesee county, N. Y., but was at school in Wisconsin, after the war broke out, and there enlisted—soon took to soldier-life, liked it, was very manly, was belov'd by officers and comrades. He kept a little diary, like so many of the soldiers. On the day of his death he wrote the following in it, *to-day the doctor says I must die—all is over with me—ah, so young to die.* On another blank leaf he pencill'd to his brother, *dear brother Thomas, I have been brave but wicked—pray for me.*

Hospital Scenes.—Incidents

It is Sunday afternoon, middle of summer, hot and oppressive, and very silent through the ward. I am taking care of a critical case, now lying in a half lethargy. Near where I sit is a suffering rebel, from the 8th Louisiana; his name is Irving. He has been here a long time, badly wounded, and lately had his leg amputated; it is not doing very well. Right opposite me is a sick soldier-boy, laid down with his clothes on, sleeping, looking much wasted, his pallid face on his arm. I see by the yellow trimming on his jacket that he is a cavalry boy. I step softly over and find by his card that he is named William Cone, of the 1st Maine cavalry, and his folks live in Skowhegan.

Ice Cream Treat.—One hot day toward the middle of June, I gave the inmates of Carver hospital a general ice cream treat, purchasing a large quantity, and, under convoy of the doctor or head nurse, going around personally through the wards to see to its distribution.

An Incident.—In one of the fights before Atlanta, a rebel soldier, of large size, evidently a young man, was mortally wounded top of the head, so that the brains partially exuded. He lived three days, lying on his back on the spot where he first dropt. He dug with his heel in the ground during that time a hole big enough to put in a couple of ordinary knapsacks. He just lay there in the open air, and with little intermission kept his heel going night and day. Some of our soldiers then moved him to a house, but he died in a few minutes.

Another.—After the battles at Columbia, Tennessee, where we repuls'd about a score of vehement rebel charges, they left a great many wounded on the ground, mostly within our range. Whenever any of these wounded attempted to move away by any means, generally by crawling off, our men without exception brought them down by a bullet. They let none crawl away, no matter what his condition.

A Yankee Soldier

As I turn'd off the Avenue one cool October evening into Thirteenth street, a soldier with knapsack and overcoat stood at the corner inquiring his way. I found he wanted to go part of the road in my direction, so we walk'd on together. We soon fell into conversation. He was small and not very young, and a tough little fellow, as I judged in the evening light, catching glimpses by the lamps we pass'd. His answers were short, but clear. His name was Charles Carroll; he belong'd to one of the Massachusetts regiments, and was born in or near Lynn. His parents were living, but were very old. There were four sons, and all had enlisted. Two had died of starvation and misery in the prison at Andersonville, and one had been kill'd in the west. He only was left. He was now going home, and by the way he talk'd I inferr'd that his time was nearly out. He made great calculations on being with his parents to comfort them the rest of their days.

Union Prisoners South

Michael Stansbury, 48 years of age, a sea-faring man, a southerner by birth and raising, formerly captain of U. S. light ship Long Shoal, station'd at Long Shoal point, Pamlico sound—though a southerner, a firm Union man—was captur'd Feb. 17, 1863, and has been nearly two years in the Confederate prisons; was at one time order'd releas'd by Governor Vance, but a rebel officer re-arrested him; then sent on to Richmond for exchange—but instead of being exchanged was sent down (as a southern citizen, not a soldier,) to Salisbury, N. C., where he remain'd until lately, when he escap'd among the exchang'd by assuming the name of a dead soldier, and coming up via Wilmington with the rest. Was about sixteen months in Salisbury. Subsequent to October, '64, there were about 11,000 Union prisoners in the stockade; about 100 of them southern unionists, 200 U. S. deserters. During the past winter 1500 of the prisoners, to save their lives, join'd the confederacy, on condition of being assign'd merely to guard duty. Out of the 11,000 not more than 2500 came out; 500 of these were pitiable, helpless wretches—the rest were in a condition to travel. There were often 60 dead bodies to be buried in the morning; the daily average would be about 40. The regular food was a meal of corn, the cob and husk ground together, and sometimes once a week a ration of sorghum molasses. A diminutive ration of meat might possibly come once a month, not oftener. In the stockade, containing the 11,000 men, there was a partial show of tents, not enough for 2000. A large proportion of the men lived in holes in the ground, in the utmost wretchedness. Some froze to death, others had their hands and feet frozen. The rebel guards would occasionally, and on the least pretence, fire into the prison from mere demonism and wantonness. All the horrors that can be named, starvation, lassitude, filth, vermin, despair, swift loss of self-respect, idiocy, insanity, and frequent murder, were there. Stansbury has a wife and child living in Newbern—has written to them from here—is in the U. S. light-house employ still—(had been home to Newbern to see his family, and on his return to the ship was captured in his boat.) Has seen men brought there to Salisbury as hearty as you ever see in your life—in a few weeks completely dead gone, much of it from thinking on their condition—hope all gone. Has himself a hard, sad, strangely deaden'd kind of look, as of one chill'd for years in the cold and dark, where his good manly nature had no room to exercise itself.

Deserters

Oct. 24.—Saw a large squad of our own deserters, (over 300) surrounded with a cordon of arm'd guards, marching along Pennsylvania avenue. The most motley collection I ever saw, all sorts of rig, all sorts of hats and caps, many fine-looking young fellows, some of them shame-faced, some sickly, most of them dirty, shirts very dirty and long worn, &c. They tramp'd along without order, a huge huddling mass, not in ranks. I saw some of the spectators laughing, but I felt like anything else but laughing. These deserters are far more numerous than would be thought. Almost every day I see squads of them, sometimes two or three at a time, with a small guard; sometimes ten or twelve, under a larger one. (I hear that desertions from the army now in the field have often averaged 10,000 a month. One of the commonest sights in Washington is a squad of deserters.)

A Glimpse of War's Hell-Scenes

In one of the late movements of our troops in the valley, (near Upperville, I think,) a strong force of Moseby's mounted guerillas attack'd a train of wounded, and the guard of cavalry convoying them. The ambulances contain'd about 60 wounded, quite a number of them officers of rank. The rebels were in strength, and the capture of the train and its partial guard after a short snap was effectually accomplish'd. No sooner had our men surrender'd, the rebels instantly commenced robbing the train and murdering their prisoners, even the wounded. Here is the scene or a sample of it, ten minutes after. Among the wounded officers in the ambulances were one, a lieutenant of regulars, and another of higher rank. These two were dragg'd out on the ground on their backs, and were now surrounded by the guerillas, a demoniac crowd, each member of which was stabbing them in different parts of their bodies. One of the officers had his feet pinn'd firmly to the ground by bayonets stuck through them and thrust into the ground. These two officers, as afterwards found on examination, had receiv'd about twenty such thrusts, some of them through the mouth, face, &c. The wounded had all been dragg'd (to give a better chance also for plunder,) out of their wagons; some had been effectually dispatch'd, and their bodies were lying there lifeless and bloody. Others, not yet dead, but horribly mutilated, were moaning or groaning. Of our men who surrender'd, most had been thus maim'd or slaughter'd.

At this instant a force of our cavalry, who had been following the train at some interval, charged suddenly upon the secesh captors, who proceeded at once to make the best escape they could. Most of them got away, but we gobbled two officers and seventeen men, in the very acts just described. The sight was one which admitted of little discussion, as may be imagined. The seventeen captur'd men and two officers were put under guard for the night, but it was decided there and then that they should die. The next morning the two officers were taken in the town, separate places, put in the centre of the street, and shot. The seventeen men were taken to an open ground, a little one side. They were placed in a hollow square, half-encompass'd by two of our cavalry regiments, one of which regiments had three days before found the bloody corpses of three of their men hamstrung and hung up by the heels to limbs of trees by Moseby's guerillas, and the other had not long before had twelve men, after surrendering, shot and then hung by the neck to limbs of trees, and jeering inscriptions pinn'd to the breast of one of the corpses, who had been a sergeant. Those three, and those twelve, had been found, I say, by these environing regiments. Now, with revolvers, they form'd the grim cordon of the seventeen prisoners. The latter were placed in the midst of the hollow square, unfasten'd, and the ironical remark made to them that they were now to be given "a chance for themselves." A few ran for it. But what use? From every side the deadly pills came. In a few minutes the seventeen corpses strew'd the hollow square. I was curious to know whether some of the Union soldiers, some few, (some one or two at least of the youngsters,) did not abstain from shooting on the helpless men. Not one. There was no exultation, very little said, almost nothing, yet every man there contributed his shot.

Multiply the above by scores, aye hundreds—verify it in all the forms that different circumstances, individuals, places, could afford—light it with every lurid passion, the wolf's, the lion's lapping thirst for blood—the passionate, boiling volcanoes of human revenge for comrades, brothers slain—with the light of burning farms, and heaps of smutting, smouldering black embers—and in the human heart everywhere black, worse embers—and you have an inkling of this war.

Gifts—Money—Discrimination

As a very large proportion of the wounded came up from the front without a cent of money in their pockets, I soon discover'd that it was about the best thing I could do to raise their spirits, and show them that somebody cared for them, and practically felt a fatherly or brotherly interest in them, to give them small sums in such cases, using tact and discretion about it. I am regularly supplied with funds for this purpose by good women and men in Boston, Salem, Providence, Brooklyn, and New York. I provide myself with a quantity of bright new ten-cent and five-cent bills, and, when I think it incumbent, I give 25 or 30 cents, or perhaps 50 cents, and occasionally a still larger sum to some particular case. As I have started this subject, I take opportunity to ventilate the financial question. My supplies, altogether voluntary, mostly confidential, often seeming quite Providential, were numerous and varied. For instance, there were two distant and wealthy ladies, sisters, who sent regularly, for two years, quite heavy sums, enjoining that their names should be kept secret. The same delicacy was indeed a frequent condition. From several I had *carte blanche*. Many were entire strangers. From these sources, during from two to three years, in the manner described, in the hospitals, I bestowed, as almoner for others, many, many thousands of dollars. I learn'd one thing conclusively—that beneath all the ostensible greed and heartlessness of our times there is no end to the generous benevolence of men and women in the United States, when once sure of their object. Another thing became clear to me—while *cash* is not amiss to bring up the rear, tact and magnetic sympathy and unction are, and ever will be, sovereign still.

Items from My Note Books

Some of the half-eras'd, and not over-legible when made, memoranda of things wanted by one patient or another, will convey quite a fair idea. D. S. G., bed 52, wants a good book; has a sore, weak throat; would like some horehound candy; is from New Jersey, 28th regiment. C. H. L., 145th Pennsylvania, lies in bed 6, with jaundice and erysipelas; also wounded; stomach easily nauseated; bring him some oranges, also a little tart jelly; hearty, full-blooded young fellow—(he got better in a few days, and is now home on a furlough.) J. H. G., bed 24, wants an undershirt, drawers, and socks; has not had a change for quite a while; is evidently a neat, clean boy from New England—(I supplied him; also with a comb, toothbrush, and some soap and towels; I noticed afterward he was the cleanest of the whole ward.) Mrs. G., lady-nurse, ward F, wants a bottle of brandy—has two patients imperatively requiring stimulus—low with wounds and exhaustion. (I supplied her with a bottle of first-rate brandy from the Christian commission rooms.)

A Case from Second Bull Run

Well, poor John Mahay is dead. He died yesterday. His was a painful and long-lingering case, (see p. 741 *ante*.) I have been with him at times for the past fifteen months. He belonged to company A, 101st New York, and was shot through the lower region of the abdomen at second Bull Run, August, '62. One scene at his bedside will suffice for the agonies of nearly two years. The bladder had been perforated by a bullet going entirely through him. Not long since I sat a good part of the morning by his bedside, ward E, Armory square. The water ran out of his eyes from the intense pain, and the muscles of his face were distorted, but he utter'd nothing except a low groan now and then. Hot moist cloths were applied, and reliev'd him somewhat. Poor Mahay, a mere boy in age, but old in misfortune. He never knew the love of parents, was placed in infancy in one of the New York charitable institutions, and subsequently bound out to a tyrannical master in Sullivan county, (the scars of whose cowhide and club remain'd yet on his back.) His wound here was a most disagreeable one, for he was a gentle, cleanly, and affectionate boy. He found friends in his hospital life, and, indeed, was a universal favorite. He had quite a funeral ceremony.

Army Surgeons—Aid Deficiencies

I must bear my most emphatic testimony to the zeal, manliness, and professional spirit and capacity, generally prevailing among the surgeons, many of them young men, in the hospitals and the army. I will not say much about the exceptions, for they are few; (but I have met some of those few, and very incompetent and airish they were.) I never ceas'd to find the best men, and the hardest and most disinterested workers, among the surgeons in the hospitals. They are full of genius, too. I have seen many hundreds of them and this is my testimony. There are, however, serious deficiencies, wastes, sad want of system, in the commissions, contributions, and in all the voluntary, and a great part of the governmental nursing, edibles, medicines, stores, &c. (I do not say surgical attendance, because the surgeons cannot do more than human endurance permits.) Whatever puffing accounts there may be in the papers of the North, this is the actual fact. No thorough previous preparation, no system, no foresight, no genius. Always plenty of stores, no doubt, but never where they are needed, and never the proper application. Of all harrowing experiences, none is greater than that of the days following a heavy battle. Scores, hundreds of the noblest men on earth, uncomplaining, lie helpless, mangled, faint, alone, and so bleed to death, or die from exhaustion, either actually untouch'd at all, or merely the laying of them down and leaving them, when there ought to be means provided to save them.

The Blue Everywhere

This city, its suburbs, the capitol, the front of the White House, the places of amusement, the Avenue, and all the main streets, swarm with soldiers this winter, more than ever before. Some are out from the hospitals, some from the neighboring camps, &c. One source or another, they pour plenteously, and make, I should say, the mark'd feature in the human movement and costume-appearance of our national city. Their blue pants and overcoats are everywhere. The clump of crutches is heard up the stairs of the paymasters' offices, and there are characteristic groups around the doors of the same, often waiting long and wearily in the cold. Toward the latter part of the afternoon, you see the furlough'd men, sometimes singly, sometimes in small squads, making their way to the Baltimore depot. At all times, except early in the morning, the patrol detachments are moving around, especially during the earlier hours of evening, examining passes, and arresting all soldiers without them. They do not question the one-legged, or men badly disabled or maim'd, but all others are stopt. They also go around evenings through the auditoriums of the theatres, and make officers and all show their passes, or other authority, for being there.

A Model Hospital

Sunday, January 29th, 1865.—Have been in Armory-square this afternoon. The wards are very comfortable, new floors and plaster walls, and models of neatness. I am not sure but this is a model hospital after all, in important respects. I found several sad cases of old lingering wounds. One Delaware soldier, William H. Millis, from Bridgeville, whom I had been with after the battles of the Wilderness, last May, where he receiv'd a very bad wound in the chest, with another in the left arm, and whose case was serious (pneumonia had set in) all last June and July, I now find well enough to do light duty. For three weeks at the time mention'd he just hovered between life and death.

Boys in the Army

As I walk'd home about sunset, I saw in Fourteenth street a very young soldier, thinly clad, standing near the house I was about to enter. I stopt a moment in front of the door and call'd him to me. I knew that an old Tennessee regiment, and also an Indiana regiment, were temporarily stopping in new barracks, near Fourteenth street. This boy I found belonged to the Tennessee regiment. But I could hardly believe he carried a musket. He was but 15 years old, yet had been twelve months a soldier, and had borne his part in several battles, even historic ones. I ask'd him if he did not suffer from the cold, and if he had no overcoat. No, he did not suffer from cold, and had no overcoat, but could draw one whenever he wish'd. His father was dead, and his mother living in some part of East Tennessee; all the men were from that part of the country. The next forenoon I saw the Tennessee and Indiana regiments marching down the Avenue. My boy was with the former, stepping along with the rest. There were many other boys no older. I stood and watch'd them as they tramp'd along with slow, strong, heavy, regular steps. There did not appear to be a man over 30 years of age, and a large proportion were from 15 to perhaps 22 or 23. They had all the look of veterans, worn, stain'd, impassive, and a certain unbent, lounging gait, carrying in addition to their regular arms and knapsacks, frequently a frying-pan, broom, &c. They were all of pleasant physiognomy; no refinement, nor blanch'd with intellect, but as my eye pick'd them, moving along, rank by rank, there did not seem to be a single repulsive, brutal or markedly stupid face among them.

Burial of a Lady Nurse

Here is an incident just occurr'd in one of the hospitals. A lady named Miss or Mrs. Billings, who has long been a practical friend of soldiers, and nurse in the army, and had become attached to it in a way that no one can realize but him or her who has had experience, was taken sick, early this winter, linger'd some time, and finally died in the hospital. It was her request that she should be buried among the soldiers, and after the military method. This request was fully carried out. Her coffin was carried to the grave by soldiers, with the usual escort, buried, and a salute fired over the grave. This was at Annapolis a few days since.

Female Nurses for Soldiers

There are many women in one position or another, among the hospitals, mostly as nurses here in Washington, and among the military stations; quite a number of them young ladies acting as volunteers. They are a help in certain ways, and deserve to be mention'd with respect. Then it remains to be distinctly said that few or no young ladies, under the irresistible conventions of society, answer the practical requirements of nurses for soldiers. Middle-aged or healthy and good condition'd elderly women, mothers of children, are always best. Many of the wounded must be handled. A hundred things which cannot be gainsay'd, must occur and must be done. The presence of a good middle-aged or elderly woman, the magnetic touch of hands, the expressive features of the mother, the silent soothing of her presence, her words, her knowledge and privileges arrived at only through having had children, are precious and final qualifications. It is a natural faculty that is required; it is not merely having a genteel young woman at a table in a ward. One of the finest nurses I met was a red-faced illiterate old Irish woman; I have seen her take the poor wasted naked boys so tenderly up in her arms. There are plenty of excellent clean old black women that would make tip-top nurses.

Southern Escapees

Feb. 23, '65.—I saw a large procession of young men from the rebel army, (deserters they are call'd, but the usual meaning of the word does not apply to them,) passing the Avenue to-day. There were nearly 200, come up yesterday by boat from James river. I stood and watch'd them as they shuffled along, in a slow, tired, worn sort of way; a large proportion of light-hair'd, blonde, light gray-eyed young men among them. Their costumes had a dirt-stain'd uniformity; most had been originally gray; some had articles of our uniform, pants on one, vest or coat on another; I think they were mostly Georgia and North Carolina boys. They excited little or no attention. As I stood quite close to them, several good looking enough youths, (but O what a tale of misery their appearance told,) nodded or just spoke to me, without doubt divining pity and fatherliness out of my face, for my heart was full enough of it. Several of the couples trudg'd along with their arms about each other, some probably brothers, as if they were afraid they might somehow get separated. They nearly all look'd what one might call simple, yet intelligent, too. Some had pieces of old carpet, some blankets, and others old bags around their shoulders. Some of them here and there had fine faces, still it was a procession of misery. The two hundred had with them about half a dozen arm'd guards. Along this week I saw some such procession, more or less in numbers, every day, as they were brought up by the boat. The government does what it can for them, and sends them north and west.

Feb. 27.—Some three or four hundred more escapees from the confederate army came up on the boat. As the day has been very pleasant indeed, (after a long spell of bad weather,) I have been wandering around a good deal, without any other object than to be out-doors and enjoy it; have met these escaped men in all directions. Their apparel is the same ragged, long-worn motley as before described. I talk'd with a number of the men. Some are quite bright and stylish, for all their poor clothes—walking with an air, wearing their old head-coverings on one side, quite saucily. I find the old, unquestionable proofs, as all along the past four years, of the unscrupulous tyranny exercised by the secession government in conscripting the common people by absolute force everywhere, and paying no attention whatever to the men's time being up—keeping them in military service just the same. One gigantic young fellow, a Georgian, at least six feet three inches high, broad-sized in proportion, attired in the dirtiest, drab, well-smear'd rags, tied with strings, his trousers at the knees all strips and streamers, was complacently standing eating some bread and meat. He appear'd contented enough. Then a few minutes after I saw him slowly walking along. It was plain he did not take anything to heart.

Feb. 28.—As I pass'd the military headquarters of the city, not far from the President's house, I stopt to interview some of the crowd of escapees who were lounging there. In appearance they were the same as previously mention'd. Two of them, one about 17, and the other perhaps 25 or '6, I talk'd with some time. They were from North Carolina, born and rais'd there, and had folks there. The elder had been in the rebel service four years. He was first conscripted for two years. He was then kept arbitrarily in the ranks. This is the case with a large proportion of the secession army. There was nothing downcast in these young men's manners; the younger had been soldiering about a year; he was conscripted; there were six brothers (all the boys of the family) in the army, part of them as conscripts, part as volunteers; three had been kill'd; one had escaped about four months ago, and now this one had got away; he was a pleasant and well-talking lad, with the peculiar North Carolina idiom (not at all disagreeable to my ears.) He and the elder one were of the same company, and escaped together—and wish'd to remain together. They thought of getting transportation away to Missouri, and working there; but were not sure it was judicious. I advised them rather to go to some of the directly northern

States, and get farm work for the present. The younger had made six dollars on the boat, with some tobacco he brought; he had three and a half left. The elder had nothing; I gave him a trifle. Soon after, met John Wormley, 9th Alabama, a West Tennessee rais'd boy, parents both dead—had the look of one for a long time on short allowance—said very little—chew'd tobacco at a fearful rate, spitting in proportion—large clear dark-brown eyes, very fine—didn't know what to make of me—told me at last he wanted much to get some clean underclothes, and a pair of decent pants. Didn't care about coat or hat fixings. Wanted a chance to wash himself well, and put on the underclothes. I had the very great pleasure of helping him to accomplish all those wholesome designs.

March 1st.—Plenty more butternut or clay-color'd escapees every day. About 160 came in to-day, a large portion South Carolinians. They generally take the oath of allegiance, and are sent north, west, or extreme south-west if they wish. Several of them told me that the desertions in their army, of men going home, leave or no leave, are far more numerous than their desertions to our side. I saw a very forlorn looking squad of about a hundred, late this afternoon, on their way to the Baltimore depot.

The Capitol by Gas-Light

To-night I have been wandering awhile in the capitol, which is all lit up. The illuminated rotunda looks fine. I like to stand aside and look a long, long while, up at the dome; it comforts me somehow. The House and Senate were both in session till very late. I look'd in upon them, but only a few moments; they were hard at work on tax and appropriation bills. I wander'd through the long and rich corridors and apartments under the Senate; an old habit of mine, former winters, and now more satisfaction than ever. Not many persons down there, occasionally a flitting figure in the distance.

The Inauguration

March 4.—The President very quietly rode down to the capitol in his own carriage, by himself, on a sharp trot, about noon, either because he wish'd to be on hand to sign bills, or to get rid of marching in line with the absurd procession, the muslin temple of liberty, and pasteboard monitor. I saw him on his return, at three o'clock, after the performance was over. He was in his plain two-horse barouche, and look'd very much worn and tired; the lines, indeed, of vast responsibilities, intricate questions, and demands of life and death, cut deeper than ever upon his dark brown face; yet all the old goodness, tenderness, sadness, and canny shrewdness, underneath the furrows. (I never see that man without feeling that he is one to become personally attach'd to, for his combination of purest, heartiest tenderness, and native western form of manliness.) By his side sat his little boy, of ten years. There were no soldiers, only a lot of civilians on horseback, with huge yellow scarfs over their shoulders, riding around the carriage. (At the inauguration four years ago, he rode down and back again surrounded by a dense mass of arm'd cavalrymen eight deep, with drawn sabres; and there were sharpshooters station'd at every corner on the route.) I ought to make mention of the closing levee of Saturday night last. Never before was such a compact jam in front of the White House—all the grounds fill'd, and away out to the spacious sidewalks. I was there, as I took a notion to go—was in the rush inside with the crowd—surged along the passage-ways, the blue and other rooms, and through the great east room. Crowds of country people, some very funny. Fine music from the Marine band, off in a side place. I saw Mr. Lincoln, drest all in black, with white kid gloves and a claw-hammer coat, receiving, as in duty bound, shaking hands, looking very disconsolate, and as if he would give anything to be somewhere else.

Attitude of Foreign Governments during the War

Looking over my scraps, I find I wrote the following during 1864. The happening to our America, abroad as well as at home, these years, is indeed most strange. The democratic republic has paid her to-day the terrible and resplendent compliment of the united wish of all the nations of the world that her union should be broken, her future cut off, and that she should be compell'd to descend to the level of kingdoms and empires ordinarily great. There is certainly not one government in Europe but is now watching the war in this country, with the ardent prayer that the United States may be effectually split, crippled, and dismember'd by it. There is not one but would help toward that dismemberment, if it dared. I say such is the ardent wish to-day of England and of France, as governments, and of all the nations of Europe, as governments. I think indeed it is to-day the real, heartfelt wish of all the nations of the world, with the single exception of Mexico—Mexico, the only one to whom we have ever really done wrong, and now the only one who prays for us and for our triumph, with genuine prayer. Is it not indeed strange? America, made up of all, cheerfully from the beginning opening her arms to all, the result and justifier of all, of Britain, Germany, France and Spain—all here—the accepter, the friend, hope, last resource and general house of all—she who has harm'd none, but been bounteous to so many, to millions, the mother of strangers and exiles, all nations—should now I say be paid this dread compliment of general governmental fear and hatred. Are we indignant? alarm'd? Do we feel jeopardized? No; help'd, braced, concentrated, rather. We are all too prone to wander from ourselves, to affect Europe, and watch her frowns and smiles. We need this hot lesson of general hatred, and henceforth must never forget it. Never again will we trust the moral sense nor abstract friendliness of a single *government* of the old world.

The Weather.—Does It Sympathize with These Times?

Whether the rains, the heat and cold, and what underlies them all, are affected with what affects man in masses, and follow his play of passionate action, strain'd stronger than usual, and on a larger scale than usual—whether this, or no, it is certain that there is now, and has been for twenty months or more, on this American continent north, many a remarkable, many an unprecedented expression of the subtile world of air above us and around us. There, since this war, and the wide and deep national agitation, strange analogies, different combinations, a different sunlight, or absence of it; different products even out of the ground. After every great battle, a great storm. Even civic events the same. On Saturday last, a forenoon like whirling demons, dark, with slanting rain, full of rage; and then the afternoon, so calm, so bathed with flooding splendor from heaven's most excellent sun, with atmosphere of sweetness; so clear, it show'd the stars, long, long before they were due. As the President came out on the capitol portico, a curious little white cloud, the only one in that part of the sky, appear'd like a hovering bird, right over him.

Indeed, the heavens, the elements, all the meteorological influences, have run riot for weeks past. Such caprices, abruptest alternation of frowns and beauty, I never knew. It is a common remark that (as last summer was different in its spells of intense heat from any preceding it,) the winter just completed has been without parallel. It has remain'd so down to the hour I am writing. Much of the daytime of the past month was sulky, with leaden heaviness, fog, interstices of bitter cold, and some insane storms. But there have been samples of another description. Nor earth nor sky ever knew spectacles of superber beauty than some of the nights lately here. The western star, Venus, in the earlier hours of evening, has never been so large, so clear; it seems as if it told something, as if it held rapport indulgent with humanity, with us Americans. Five or six nights since, it hung close by the moon, then a little past its first quarter. The star was wonderful, the moon like a young mother. The sky, dark blue, the transparent night, the planets, the moderate west wind, the elastic temperature, the miracle of that great star, and the young and swelling moon swimming in the west, suffused the soul. Then I heard, slow and clear, the deliberate notes of a bugle come up out of the silence, sounding so good through the night's mystery, no hurry, but firm and faithful, floating along, rising, falling leisurely, with here and there a long-drawn note; the bugle, well play'd, sounding tattoo, in one of the army hospitals near here, where the wounded (some of them personally so dear to me,) are lying in their cots, and many a sick boy come down to the war from Illinois, Michigan, Wisconsin, Iowa, and the rest.

Inauguration Ball

March 6.—I have been up to look at the dance and supper-rooms, for the inauguration ball at the Patent office; and I could not help thinking, what a different scene they presented to my view a while since, fill'd with a crowded mass of the worst wounded of the war, brought in from second Bull Run, Antietam, and Fredericksburgh. To-night, beautiful women, perfumes, the violins' sweetness, the polka and the waltz; then the amputation, the blue face, the groan, the glassy eye of the dying, the clotted rag, the odor of wounds and blood, and many a mother's son amid strangers, passing away untended there, (for the crowd of the badly hurt was great, and much for nurse to do, and much for surgeon.)

Scene at the Capitol

I must mention a strange scene at the capitol, the hall of Representatives, the morning of Saturday last, (March 4th.) The day just dawn'd, but in half-darkness, everything dim, leaden, and soaking. In that dim light, the members nervous from long drawn duty, exhausted, some asleep, and many half asleep. The gas-light, mix'd with the dingy day-break, produced an unearthly effect. The poor little sleepy, stumbling pages, the smell of the hall, the members with heads leaning on their desks, the sounds of the voices speaking, with unusual intonations—the general moral atmosphere also of the close of this important session—the strong hope that the war is approaching its close—the tantalizing dread lest the hope may be a false one—the grandeur of the hall itself, with its effect of vast shadows up toward the panels and spaces over the galleries—all made a mark'd combination.

In the midst of this, with the suddenness of a thunderbolt, burst one of the most angry and crashing storms of rain and hail ever heard. It beat like a deluge on the heavy glass roof of the hall, and the wind literally howl'd and roar'd. For a moment, (and no wonder,) the nervous and sleeping Representatives were thrown into confusion. The slumberers awaked with fear, some started for the doors, some look'd up with blanch'd cheeks and lips to the roof, and the little pages began to cry; it was a scene. But it was over almost as soon as the drowsied men were actually awake. They recover'd themselves; the storm raged on, beating, dashing, and with loud noises at times. But the House went ahead with its business then, I think, as calmly and with as much deliberation as at any time in its career. Perhaps the shock did it good. (One is not without impression, after all, amid these members of Congress, of both the Houses, that if the flat routine of their duties should ever be broken in upon by some great emergency involving real danger, and calling for first-class personal qualities, those qualities would be found generally forthcoming, and from men not now credited with them.)

A Yankee Antique

March 27, 1865.—Sergeant Calvin F. Harlowe, company C, 29th Massachusetts, 3d brigade, 1st division, Ninth corps—a mark'd sample of heroism and death, (some may say bravado, but I say *heroism,* of grandest, oldest order)—in the late attack by the rebel troops, and temporary capture by them, of fort Steadman, at night. The fort was surprised at dead of night. Suddenly awaken'd from their sleep, and rushing from their tents, Harlowe, with others, found himself in the hands of the secesh—they demanded his surrender—he answer'd, *Never while I live.* (Of course it was useless. The others surrender'd; the odds were too great.) Again he was ask'd to yield, this time by a rebel captain. Though surrounded, and quite calm, he again refused, call'd sternly to his comrades to fight on, and himself attempted to do so. The rebel captain then shot him—but at the same instant he shot the captain. Both fell together mortally wounded. Harlowe died almost instantly. The rebels were driven out in a very short time. The body was buried next day, but soon taken up and sent home, (Plymouth county, Mass.) Harlowe was only 22 years of age—was a tall, slim, dark-hair'd, blue-eyed young man—had come out originally with the 29th; and that is the way he met his death, after four years' campaign. He was in the Seven Days fight before Richmond, in second Bull Run, Antietam, first Fredericksburgh, Vicksburgh, Jackson, Wilderness, and the campaigns following—was as good a soldier as ever wore the blue, and every old officer in the regiment will bear that testimony. Though so young, and in a common rank, he had a spirit as resolute and brave as any hero in the books, ancient or modern—It was too great to say the words "I surrender"—and so he died. (When I think of such things, knowing them well, all the vast and complicated events of the war, on which history dwells and makes its volumes, fall aside, and for the moment at any rate I see nothing but young Calvin Harlowe's figure in the night, disdaining to surrender.)

Wounds and Diseases

The war is over, but the hospitals are fuller than ever, from former and current cases. A large majority of the wounds are in the arms and legs. But there is every kind of wound, in every part of the body. I should say of the sick, from my observation, that the prevailing maladies are typhoid fever and the camp fevers generally, diarrhœa, catarrhal affections and bronchitis, rheumatism and pneumonia. These forms of sickness lead; all the rest follow. There are twice as many sick as there are wounded. The deaths range from seven to ten per cent. of those under treatment.*

Death of President Lincoln

April 16, '65.—I find in my notes of the time, this passage on the death of Abraham Lincoln: He leaves for America's history and biography, so far, not only its most dramatic reminiscence—he leaves, in my opinion, the greatest, best, most characteristic, artistic, moral personality. Not but that he had faults, and show'd them in the Presidency; but honesty, goodness, shrewdness, conscience, and (a new virtue, unknown to other lands, and hardly yet really known here, but the foundation and tie of all, as the future will grandly develop,) UNIONISM, in its truest and amplest sense, form'd the hard-pan of his character. These he seal'd with his life. The tragic

*In the U.S. Surgeon-General's office since, there is a formal record and treatment of 253,142 cases of wounds by government surgeons. What must have been the number unofficial, indirect—to say nothing of the Southern armies?

splendor of his death, purging, illuminating all, throws round his form, his head, an aureole that will remain and will grow brighter through time, while history lives, and love of country lasts. By many has this Union been help'd; but if one name, one man, must be pick'd out, he, most of all, is the conservator of it, to the future. He was assassinated—but the Union is not assassinated—*ça ira!* One falls, and another falls. The soldier drops, sinks like a wave—but the ranks of the ocean eternally press on. Death does its work, obliterates a hundred, a thousand—President, general, captain, private—but the Nation is immortal.

Sherman's Army's Jubilation—Its Sudden Stoppage

When Sherman's armies, (long after they left Atlanta,) were marching through South and North Carolina—after leaving Savannah, the news of Lee's capitulation having been receiv'd—the men never mov'd a mile without from some part of the line sending up continued, inspiriting shouts. At intervals all day long sounded out the wild music of those peculiar army cries. They would be commenc'd by one regiment or brigade, immediately taken up by others, and at length whole corps and armies would join in these wild triumphant choruses. It was one of the characteristic expressions of the western troops, and became a habit, serving as a relief and outlet to the men—a vent for their feelings of victory, returning peace, &c. Morning, noon, and afternoon, spontaneous, for occasion or without occasion, these huge, strange cries, differing from any other, echoing through the open air for many a mile, expressing youth, joy, wildness, irrepressible strength, and the ideas of advance and conquest, sounded along the swamps and uplands of the South, floating to the skies. ('There never were men that kept in better spirits in danger or defeat—what then could they do in victory?'—said one of the 15th corps to me, afterwards.) This exuberance continued till the armies arrived at Raleigh. There the news of the President's murder was receiv'd. Then no more shouts or yells, for a week. All the marching was comparatively muffled. It was very significant—hardly a loud word or laugh in many of the regiments. A hush and silence pervaded all.

No Good Portrait of Lincoln

Probably the reader has seen physiognomies (often old farmers, sea-captains, and such) that, behind their homeliness, or even ugliness, held superior points so subtle, yet so palpable, making the real life of their faces almost as impossible to depict as a wild perfume or fruit-taste, or a passionate tone of the living voice—and such was Lincoln's face, the peculiar color, the lines of it, the eyes, mouth, expression. Of technical beauty it had nothing—but to the eye of a great artist it furnished a rare study, a feast and fascination. The current portraits are all failures—most of them caricatures.

Releas'd Union Prisoners from South

The releas'd prisoners of war are now coming up from the southern prisons. I have seen a number of them. The sight is worse than any sight of battle-fields, or any collection of wounded, even the bloodiest. There was, (as a sample,) one large boat load, of several hundreds, brought about the 25th, to Annapolis; and out of the whole number only three individuals were able to walk from the boat. The rest were carried ashore and laid down in one place or another. Can those be *men*—those little livid brown, ash-streak'd, monkey-looking dwarfs?—are they really not mummied, dwindled corpses? They lay there, most of them, quite still, but with a horrible look in their eyes and skinny lips (often with not enough flesh on the lips to cover their teeth.) Probably no more appalling sight was ever seen on this earth. (There are deeds, crimes, that may be forgiven; but this is not among them. It steeps its perpetrators in blackest, escapeless, endless damnation. Over 50,000 have been compell'd to die the death of starvation—reader, did you ever try to realize what *starvation* actually is?—in those prisons—and in a land of plenty.) An indescribable meanness, tyranny, aggravating course of insults, almost incredible—was evidently the rule of treatment through all the southern military prisons. The dead there are not to be pitied as much as some of the living that come from there—if they can be call'd living—many of them are mentally imbecile, and will never recuperate.*

* *From a review of* "ANDERSONVILLE, A STORY OF SOUTHERN MILITARY PRISONS," *published serially in the "Toledo Blade," in 1879, and afterwards in book form.*

"There is a deep fascination in the subject of Andersonville—for that Golgotha, in which lie the whitening bones of 13,000 gallant young men, represents the dearest and costliest sacrifice of the war for the preservation of our national unity. It is a type, too, of its class. Its more than hundred hecatombs of dead represent several times that number of their brethren, for whom the prison gates of Belle Isle, Danville, Salisbury, Florence, Columbia, and Cahaba open'd only in eternity. There are few families in the North who have not at least one dear relative or friend among these 60,000 whose sad fortune it was to end their service for the Union by lying down and dying for it in a southern prison pen. The manner of their death, the horrors that cluster'd thickly around every moment of their existence, the loyal, unfaltering steadfastness with which they endured all that fate had brought them, has never been adequately told. It was not with them as with their comrades in the field, whose every act was perform'd in the presence of those whose duty it was to observe such matters and report them to the world. Hidden from the view of their friends in the north by the impenetrable veil which the military operations of the rebels drew around the so-called confederacy, the people knew next to nothing of their career or their sufferings. Thousands died there less heeded even than the hundreds who perish'd on the battle-field. Grant did not lose as many men kill'd outright, in the terrible campaign from the Wilderness to the James river—43 days of desperate fighting—as died in July and August at Andersonville. Nearly twice as many died in that prison as fell from the day that Grant cross'd the Rapidan, till he settled down in the trenches before Petersburg. More than four times as many Union dead lie under the solemn soughing pines about that forlorn little village in southern Georgia, than mark the course of Sherman from Chattanooga to Atlanta. The nation stands aghast at the expenditure of life which attended the two bloody campaigns of 1864, which virtually crush'd the confederacy, but no one remembers that more Union soldiers died in the rear of the rebel lines than were kill'd in the front of them. The great military events which stamp'd out the rebellion drew attention away from the sad drama which starvation and disease play'd in those gloomy pens in the far recesses of sombre southern forests."

From a letter of "Johnny Bouquet," in N.Y. Tribune, March 27, '81.

"I visited at Salisbury, N. C., the prison pen or the site of it, from which nearly 12,000 victims of southern politicians were buried, being confined in a pen without shelter, exposed to all the elements could do, to all the disease herding animals together could create, and to all the starvation and cruelty an incompetent and intense caitiff government could accomplish. From the conversation and almost from the recollection of the northern people this place has dropp'd, but not so in the gossip of the Salisbury people, nearly all of

Death of a Pennsylvania Soldier

Frank H. Irwin, company E, 93d Pennsylvania—died May 1, '65—My letter to his mother.—Dear madam: No doubt you and Frank's friends have heard the sad fact of his death in hospital here, through his uncle, or the lady from Baltimore, who took his things. (I have not seen them, only heard of them visiting Frank.) I will write you a few lines—as a casual friend that sat by his death-bed. Your son, corporal Frank H. Irwin, was wounded near fort Fisher, Virginia, March 25th, 1865—the wound was in the left knee, pretty bad. He was sent up to Washington, was receiv'd in ward C, Armory-square hospital, March 28th—the wound became worse, and on the 4th of April the leg was amputated a little above the knee—the operation was perform'd by Dr. Bliss, one of the best surgeons in the army—he did the whole operation himself—there was a good deal of bad matter gather'd—the bullet was found in the knee. For a couple of weeks afterwards he was doing pretty well. I visited and sat by him frequently, as he was fond of having me. The last ten or twelve days of April I saw that his case was critical. He previously had some fever, with cold spells. The last week in April he was much of the time flighty—but always mild and gentle. He died first of May. The actual cause of death was pyæmia, (the absorption of the matter in the system instead of its discharge.) Frank, as far as I saw, had everything requisite in surgical treatment, nursing,

---

whom say that the half was never told; that such was the nature of habitual outrage here that when Federal prisoners escaped the townspeople harbor'd them in their barns, afraid the vengeance of God would fall on them, to deliver even their enemies back to such cruelty. Said one old man at the Boyden House, who join'd in the conversation one evening: 'There were often men buried out of that prison pen still alive. I have the testimony of a surgeon that he has seen them pull'd out of the dead cart with their eyes open and taking notice, but too weak to lift a finger. There was not the least excuse for such treatment, as the confederate government had seized every sawmill in the region, and could just as well have put up shelter for these prisoners as not, wood being plentiful here. It will be hard to make any honest man in Salisbury say that there was the slightest necessity for those prisoners having to live in old tents, caves and holes half-full of water. Representations were made to the Davis government against the officers in charge of it, but no attention was paid to them. Promotion was the punishment for cruelty there. The inmates were skeletons. Hell could have no terrors for any man who died there, except the inhuman keepers.' "

&c. He had watches much of the time. He was so good and well-behaved and affectionate, I myself liked him very much. I was in the habit of coming in afternoons and sitting by him, and soothing him, and he liked to have me—liked to put his arm out and lay his hand on my knee—would keep it so a long while. Toward the last he was more restless and flighty at night—often fancied himself with his regiment—by his talk sometimes seem'd as if his feelings were hurt by being blamed by his officers for something he was entirely innocent of—said, "I never in my life was thought capable of such a thing, and never was." At other times he would fancy himself talking as it seem'd to children or such like, his relatives I suppose, and giving them good advice; would talk to them a long while. All the time he was out of his head not one single bad word or idea escaped him. It was remark'd that many a man's conversation in his senses was not half as good as Frank's delirium. He seem'd quite willing to die—he had become very weak and had suffer'd a good deal, and was perfectly resign'd, poor boy. I do not know his past life, but I feel as if it must have been good. At any rate what I saw of him here, under the most trying circumstances, with a painful wound, and among strangers, I can say that he behaved so brave, so composed, and so sweet and affectionate, it could not be surpass'd. And now like many other noble and good men, after serving his country as a soldier, he has yielded up his young life at the very outset in her service. Such things are gloomy—yet there is a text, "God doeth all things well"—the meaning of which, after due time, appears to the soul.

I thought perhaps a few words, though from a stranger, about your son, from one who was with him at the last, might be worth while—for I loved the young man, though I but saw him immediately to lose him. I am merely a friend visiting the hospitals occasionally to cheer the wounded and sick.

W. W.

The Armies Returning

May 7.—Sunday.—To-day as I was walking a mile or two south of Alexandria, I fell in with several large squads of the returning Western army, (*Sherman's men* as they call'd themselves) about a thousand in all, the largest portion of them half sick, some convalescents, on their way to a hospital camp. These fragmentary excerpts, with the unmistakable Western physiognomy and idioms, crawling along slowly—after a great campaign, blown this way, as it were, out of their latitude—I mark'd with curiosity, and talk'd with off and on for over an hour. Here and there was one very sick; but all were able to walk, except some of the last, who had given out, and were seated on the ground, faint and despondent. These I tried to cheer, told them the camp they were to reach was only a little way further over the hill, and so got them up and started, accompanying some of the worst a little way, and helping them, or putting them under the support of stronger comrades.

May 21.—Saw General Sheridan and his cavalry to-day; a strong, attractive sight; the men were mostly young, (a few middle-aged,) superb-looking fellows, brown, spare, keen, with well-worn clothing, many with pieces of water-proof cloth around their shoulders, hanging down. They dash'd along pretty fast, in wide close ranks, all spatter'd with mud; no holiday soldiers; brigade after brigade. I could have watch'd for a week. Sheridan stood on a balcony, under a big tree, coolly smoking a cigar. His looks and manner impress'd me favorably.

May 22.—Have been taking a walk along Pennsylvania avenue and Seventh street north. The city is full of soldiers, running around loose. Officers everywhere, of all grades. All have the weather-beaten look of practical service. It is a sight I never tire of. All the armies are now here (or portions of them,) for to-morrow's review. You see them swarming like bees everywhere.

The Grand Review

For two days now the broad spaces of Pennsylvania avenue along to Treasury hill, and so by detour around to the President's house, and so up to Georgetown, and across the aqueduct bridge, have been alive with a magnificent sight, the returning armies. In their wide ranks stretching clear across the Avenue, I watch them march or ride along, at a brisk pace, through two whole days—infantry, cavalry, artillery—some 200,000 men. Some days afterwards one or two other corps; and then, still afterwards, a good part of Sherman's immense army, brought up from Charleston, Savannah, &c.

Western Soldiers

May 26–7.—The streets, the public buildings and grounds of Washington, still swarm with soldiers from Illinois, Indiana, Ohio, Missouri, Iowa, and all the Western States. I am continually meeting and talking with them. They often speak to me first, and always show great sociability, and glad to have a good interchange of chat. These Western soldiers are more slow in their movements, and in their intellectual quality also; have no extreme alertness. They are larger in size, have a more serious physiognomy, are continually looking at you as they pass in the street. They are largely animal, and handsomely so. During the war I have been at times with the Fourteenth, Fifteenth, Seventeenth, and Twentieth Corps. I always feel drawn toward the men, and like their personal contact when we are crowded close together, as frequently these days in the street-cars. They all think the world of General Sherman; call him "old Bill," or sometimes "uncle Billy."

A Soldier on Lincoln

May 28.—As I sat by the bedside of a sick Michigan soldier in hospital to-day, a convalescent from the adjoining bed rose and came to me, and presently we began talking. He was a middle-aged man, belonged to the 2d Virginia regiment, but lived in Racine, Ohio, and had a family there. He spoke of President Lincoln, and said: "The war is over, and many are lost. And now we have lost the best, the fairest, the truest man in America. Take him altogether, he was the best man this country ever produced. It was quite a while I thought very different; but some time before the murder, that's the way I have seen it." There was deep earnestness in the soldier. (I found upon further talk he had known Mr. Lincoln personally, and quite closely, years before.) He was a veteran; was now in the fifth year of his service; was a cavalry man, and had been in a good deal of hard fighting.

Two Brothers, One South, One North

May 28–9.—I staid to-night a long time by the bedside of a new patient, a young Baltimorean, aged about 19 years, W. S. P., (2d Maryland, southern,) very feeble, right leg amputated, can't sleep hardly at all—has taken a great deal of morphine, which, as usual, is costing more than it comes to. Evidently very intelligent and well bred—very affectionate—held on to my hand, and put it by his face, not willing to let me leave. As I was lingering, soothing him in his pain, he says to me suddenly, "I hardly think you know who I am—I don't wish to impose upon you—I am a rebel soldier." I said I did not know that, but it made no difference. Visiting him daily for about two weeks after that, while he lived, (death had mark'd him, and he was quite alone,) I loved him much, always kiss'd him, and he did me. In an adjoining ward I found his brother, an officer of rank, a Union soldier, a brave and religious man, (Col. Clifton K. Prentiss, sixth Maryland infantry, Sixth corps, wounded in one of the engagements at Petersburgh, April 2—linger'd, suffer'd much, died in Brooklyn, Aug. 20, '65.) It was in the same battle both were hit. One was a strong Unionist, the other Secesh; both fought on their respective sides, both badly wounded, and both brought together here after a separation of four years. Each died for his cause.

Some Sad Cases Yet

May 31.—James H. Williams, aged 21, 3d Virginia cavalry.—About as mark'd a case of a strong man brought low by a complication of diseases, (laryngitis, fever, debility and diarrhœa,) as I have ever seen—his superb physique, remains swarthy yet, and flushed and red with fever—is altogether flighty—flesh of his great breast and arms tremulous, and pulse pounding away with treble quickness—lies a good deal of the time in a partial sleep, but with low muttering and groans—a sleep in which there is no rest. Powerful as he is, and so young, he will not be able to stand many more days of the strain and sapping heat of yesterday and to-day. His throat is in a bad way, tongue and lips parch'd. When I ask him how he feels, he is able just to articulate, "I feel pretty bad yet, old man," and looks at me with his great bright eyes. Father, John Williams, Millensport, Ohio.

June 9–10.—I have been sitting late to-night by the bedside of a wounded captain, a special friend of mine, lying with a painful fracture of left leg in one of the hospitals, in a large ward partially vacant. The lights were put out, all but a little candle, far from where I sat. The full moon shone in through the windows, making long, slanting silvery patches on the floor. All was still, my friend too was silent, but could not sleep; so I sat there by him, slowly wafting the fan, and occupied with the musings that arose out of the scene, the long shadowy ward, the beautiful ghostly moonlight on the floor, the white beds, here and there an occupant with huddled form, the bed-clothes thrown off. The hospitals have a number of cases of sun-stroke and exhaustion by heat, from the late reviews. There are many such from the Sixth corps, from the hot parade of day before yesterday. (Some of these shows cost the lives of scores of men.)

Sunday, Sep. 10.—Visited Douglas and Stanton hospitals. They are quite full. Many of the cases are bad ones, lingering wounds, and old sickness. There is a more than usual look of despair on the countenances of many of the men; hope has left them. I went through the wards, talking as usual. There are several here from the confederate army whom I had seen in other hospitals, and they recognized me. Two were in a dying condition.

Calhoun's Real Monument

In one of the hospital tents for special cases, as I sat to-day tending a new amputation, I heard a couple of neighboring soldiers talking to each other from their cots. One down with fever, but improving, had come up belated from Charleston not long before. The other was what we now call an "old veteran," (*i.e.,* he was a Connecticut youth, probably of less than the age of twenty-five years, the four last of which he had spent in active service in the war in all parts of the country.) The two were chatting of one thing and another. The fever soldier spoke of John C. Calhoun's monument, which he had seen, and was describing it. The veteran said: "I have seen Calhoun's monument. That you saw is not the real monument. But I have seen it. It is the desolated, ruined south; nearly the whole generation of young men between seventeen and thirty destroyed or maim'd; all the old families used up—the rich impoverish'd, the plantations cover'd with weeds, the slaves unloos'd and become the masters, and the name of southerner blacken'd with every shame—all that is Calhoun's real monument."

Hospitals Closing

October 3.—There are two army hospitals now remaining. I went to the largest of these (Douglas) and spent the afternoon and evening. There are many sad cases, old wounds, incurable sickness, and some of the wounded from the March and April battles before Richmond. Few realize how sharp and bloody those closing battles were. Our men exposed themselves more than usual; press'd ahead without urging. Then the southerners fought with extra desperation. Both sides knew that with the successful chasing of the rebel cabal from Richmond, and the occupation of that city by the national troops, the game was up. The dead and wounded were unusually many. Of the wounded the last lingering driblets have been brought to hospital here. I find many rebel wounded here, and have been extra busy to-day 'tending to the worst cases of them with the rest.

Oct., Nov. and Dec., '65—Sundays.—Every Sunday of these months visited Harewood hospital out in the woods, pleasant and recluse, some two and a half or three miles north of the capitol. The situation is healthy, with broken ground, grassy slopes and patches of oak woods, the trees large and fine. It was one of the most extensive of the hospitals, now reduced to four or five partially occupied wards, the numerous others being vacant. In November, this became the last military hospital kept up by the government, all the others being closed.

Cases of the worst and most incurable wounds, obstinate illness, and of poor fellows who have no homes to go to, are found here.

Dec. 10—Sunday.—Again spending a good part of the day at Harewood. I write this about an hour before sundown. I have walk'd out for a few minutes to the edge of the woods to soothe myself with the hour and scene. It is a glorious, warm, golden-sunny, still afternoon. The only noise is from a crowd of cawing crows, on some trees three hundred yards distant. Clusters of gnats swimming and dancing in the air in all directions. The oak leaves are thick under the bare trees, and give a strong and delicious perfume. Inside the wards everything is gloomy. Death is there. As I enter'd, I was confronted by it the first thing; a corpse of a poor soldier, just dead, of typhoid fever. The attendants had just straighten'd the limbs, put coppers on the eyes, and were laying it out.

The roads.—A great recreation, the past three years, has been in taking long walks out from Washington, five, seven, perhaps ten miles and back; generally with my friend Peter Doyle, who is as fond of it as I am. Fine moonlight nights, over the perfect military roads, hard and smooth—or Sundays—we had these delightful walks, never to be forgotten. The roads connecting Washington and the numerous forts around the city, made one useful result, at any rate, out of the war.

Typical Soldiers

Even the typical soldiers I have been personally intimate with,—it seems to me if I were to make a list of them it would be like a city directory. Some few only have I mention'd in the foregoing pages—most are dead—a few yet living. There is Reuben Farwell, of Michigan, (little 'Mitch;') Benton H. Wilson, color-bearer, 185th New York; Wm. Stansberry; Manvill Winterstein, Ohio; Bethuel Smith; Capt. Simms, of 51st New York, (kill'd at Petersburgh mine explosion,) Capt. Sam. Pooley and Lieut. Fred. McReady, same reg't. Also, same reg't., my brother, George W. Whitman—in active service all through, four years, re-enlisting twice—was promoted, step by step, (several times immediately after battles,) lieutenant, captain, major and lieut. colonel—was in the actions at Roanoke, Newbern, 2d Bull Run, Chantilly, South Mountain, Antietam, Fredericksburgh, Vicksburgh, Jackson, the bloody conflicts of the Wilderness, and at Spottsylvania, Cold Harbor, and afterwards around Petersburgh; at one of these latter was taken prisoner, and pass'd four or five months in secesh military prisons, narrowly escaping with life, from a severe fever, from starvation and half-nakedness in the winter. (What a history that 51st New York had! Went out early—march'd, fought everywhere—was in storms at sea, nearly wreck'd—storm'd forts—tramp'd hither and yon in Virginia, night and day, summer of '62—afterwards Kentucky and Mississippi—re-enlisted—was in all the engagements and campaigns, as above.) I strengthen and comfort myself much with the certainty that the capacity for just such regiments, (hundreds, thousands of them) is inexhaustible in the United States, and that there isn't a county nor a township in the republic—nor a street in any city—but could turn out, and, on occasion, would turn out, lots of just such typical soldiers, whenever wanted.

"Convulsiveness"

As I have look'd over the proof-sheets of the preceding pages, I have once or twice fear'd that my diary would prove, at best, but a batch of convulsively written reminiscences. Well, be it so. They are but parts of the actual distraction, heat, smoke and excitement of those times. The war itself, with the temper of society preceding it, can indeed be best described by that very word *convulsiveness.*

Three Years Summ'd Up

During those three years in hospital, camp or field, I made over six hundred visits or tours, and went, as I estimate, counting all, among from eighty thousand to a hundred thousand of the wounded and sick, as sustainer of spirit and body in some degree, in time of need. These visits varied from an hour or two, to all day or night; for with dear or critical cases I generally watch'd all night. Sometimes I took up my quarters in the hospital, and slept or watch'd there several nights in succession. Those three years I consider the greatest privilege and satisfaction, (with all their feverish excitements and physical deprivations and lamentable sights,) and, of course, the most profound lesson of my life. I can say that in my ministerings I comprehended all, whoever came in my way, northern or southern, and slighted none. It arous'd and brought out and decided undream'd-of depths of emotion. It has given me my most fervent views of the true *ensemble* and extent of the States. While I was with wounded and sick in thousands of cases from the New England States, and from New York, New Jersey, and Pennsylvania, and from Michigan, Wisconsin, Ohio, Indiana, Illinois, and all the Western States, I was with more or less from all the States, North and South, without exception. I was with many from the border States, especially from Maryland and Virginia, and found, during those lurid years 1862–63, far more Union southerners, especially Tennesseans, than is supposed. I was with many rebel officers and men among our wounded, and gave them always what I had, and tried to cheer them the same as any. I was among the army teamsters considerably, and, indeed, always found myself drawn to them. Among the black soldiers, wounded or sick, and in the contraband camps, I also took my way whenever in their neighborhood, and did what I could for them.

The Million Dead, Too, Summ'd Up

The dead in this war—there they lie, strewing the fields and woods and valleys and battle-fields of the south—Virginia, the Peninsula—Malvern hill and Fair Oaks—the banks of the Chickahominy—the terraces of Fredericksburgh—Antietam bridge—the grisly ravines of Manassas—the bloody promenade of the Wilderness—the varieties of the *strayed* dead, (the estimate of the War department is 25,000 national soldiers kill'd in battle and never buried at all, 5,000 drown'd—15,000 inhumed by strangers, or on the march in haste, in hitherto unfound localities—2,000 graves cover'd by sand and mud by Mississippi freshets, 3,000 carried away by caving-in of banks, &c.,)—Gettysburgh, the West, Southwest—Vicksburgh—Chattanooga—the trenches of Petersburgh—the numberless battles, camps, hospitals everywhere—the crop reap'd by the mighty reapers, typhoid, dysentery, inflammations—and blackest and loathesomest of all, the dead and living burial-pits, the prison-pens of Andersonville, Salisbury, Belle-Isle, &c., (not Dante's pictured hell and all its woes, its degradations, filthy torments, excell'd those prisons)—the dead, the dead, the dead—*our* dead—or South or North, ours all, (all, all, all, finally dear to me)—or East or West—Atlantic coast or Mississippi valley—somewhere they crawl'd to die, alone, in bushes, low gullies, or on the sides of hills—(there, in secluded spots, their skeletons, bleach'd bones, tufts of hair, buttons, fragments of clothing, are occasionally found yet)—our young men once so handsome and so joyous, taken from us—the son from the mother, the husband from the wife, the dear friend from the dear friend—the clusters of camp graves, in Georgia, the Carolinas, and in Tennessee—the single graves left in the woods or by the road-side, (hundreds, thousands, obliterated)—the corpses floated down the rivers, and caught and lodged, (dozens, scores, floated down the upper Potomac, after the cavalry engagements, the pursuit of Lee, following Gettysburgh)—some lie at the bottom of the sea—the general million, and the special cemeteries in almost all the States—the infinite dead—(the land entire saturated, perfumed with their impalpable ashes' exhalation in Nature's chemistry distill'd, and shall be so forever, in every future grain of wheat and ear of corn, and every flower that grows, and every breath we draw)—not only Northern dead leavening Southern soil—thousands, aye tens of thousands, of Southerners, crumble to-day in Northern earth.

And everywhere among these countless graves—everywhere in the many soldier Cemeteries of the Nation, (there are now, I believe, over seventy of them)—as at the time in the vast trenches, the depositories of slain, Northern and Southern, after the great battles—not only where the scathing trail passed those years, but radiating since in all the peaceful quarters of the land—we see, and ages yet may see, on monuments and gravestones, singly or in masses, to thousands or tens of thousands, the significant word Unknown.

(In some of the cemeteries nearly *all* the dead are unknown. At Salisbury, N. C., for instance, the known are only 85, while the unknown are 12,027, and 11,700 of these are buried in trenches. A national monument has been put up here, by order of Congress, to mark the spot—but what visible, material monument can ever fittingly commemorate that spot?)

The Real War Will Never Get in the Books

And so good-bye to the war. I know not how it may have been, or may be, to others—to me the main interest I found, (and still, on recollection, find,) in the rank and file of the armies, both sides, and in those specimens amid the hospitals, and even the dead on the field. To me the points illustrating the latent personal character and eligibilities of these States, in the two or three millions of American young and middle-aged men, North and South, embodied in those armies—and especially the one-third or one-fourth of their number, stricken by wounds or disease at some time in the course of the contest—were of more significance even than the political interests involved. (As so much of a race depends on how it faces death, and how it stands personal anguish and sickness. As, in the glints of emotions under emergencies, and the indirect traits and asides in Plutarch, we get far profounder clues to the antique world than all its more formal history.)

Future years will never know the seething hell and the black infernal background of countless minor scenes and interiors, (not the official surface-courteousness of the Generals, not the few great battles) of the Secession war; and it is best they should not—the real war will never get in the books. In the mushy influences of current times, too, the fervid atmosphere and typical events of those years are in danger of being totally forgotten. I have at night watch'd by the side of a sick man in the hospital, one who could not live many hours. I have seen his eyes flash and burn as he raised himself and recurr'd to the cruelties of his surrender'd brother, and mutilations of the corpse afterward. (See, in the preceding pages, the incident at Upperville—the seventeen kill'd as in the description, were left there on the ground. After they dropt dead, no one touch'd them—all were made sure of, however.

The carcasses were left for the citizens to bury or not, as they chose.)

Such was the war. It was not a quadrille in a ball-room. Its interior history will not only never be written—its practicality, minutiæ of deeds and passions, will never be even suggested. The actual soldier of 1862–'65, North and South, with all his ways, his incredible dauntlessness, habits, practices, tastes, language, his fierce friendship, his appetite, rankness, his superb strength and animality, lawless gait, and a hundred unnamed lights and shades of camp, I say, will never be written—perhaps must not and should not be.

The preceding notes may furnish a few stray glimpses into that life, and into those lurid interiors, never to be fully convey'd to the future. The hospital part of the drama from '61 to '65, deserves indeed to be recorded. Of that many-threaded drama, with its sudden and strange surprises, its confounding of prophecies, its moments of despair, the dread of foreign interference, the interminable campaigns, the bloody battles, the mighty and cumbrous and green armies, the drafts and bounties—the immense money expenditure, like a heavy-pouring constant rain—with, over the whole land, the last three years of the struggle, an unending, universal mourning-wail of women, parents, orphans—the marrow of the tragedy concentrated in those Army Hospitals—(it seem'd sometimes as if the whole interest of the land, North and South, was one vast central hospital, and all the rest of the affair but flanges)—those forming the untold and unwritten history of the war—infinitely greater (like life's) than the few scraps and distortions that are ever told or written. Think how much, and of importance, will be—how much, civic and military, has already been—buried in the grave, in eternal darkness.

An Interregnum Paragraph

Several years now elapse before I resume my diary. I continued at Washington working in the Attorney-General's department through '66 and '67, and some time afterward. In February '73 I was stricken down by paralysis, gave up my desk, and migrated to Camden, New Jersey, where I lived during '74 and '75, quite unwell—but after that began to grow better; commenc'd going for weeks at a time, even for months, down in the country, to a charmingly recluse and rural spot along Timber creek, twelve or thirteen miles from where it enters the Delaware river. Domicil'd at the farm-house of my friends, the Staffords, near by, I lived half the time along this creek and its adjacent fields and lanes. And it is to my life here that I, perhaps, owe partial recovery (a sort of second wind, or semi-renewal of the lease of life) from the prostration of 1874–'75. If the notes of that outdoor life could only prove as glowing to you, reader dear, as the experience itself was to me. Doubtless in the course of the following, the fact of invalidism will crop out, (I call myself *a half-Paralytic* these days, and reverently bless the Lord it is no worse,) between some of the lines—but I get my share of fun and healthy hours, and shall try to indicate them. (The trick is, I find, to tone your wants and tastes low down enough, and make much of negatives, and of mere daylight and the skies.)

New Themes Entered Upon

1876, '77.—I find the woods in mid-May and early June my best places for composition.* Seated on logs or stumps there, or resting on rails, nearly all the following memoranda have been jotted down. Wherever I go, indeed, winter or summer, city or country, alone at home or traveling, I must take notes —(the ruling passion strong in age and disablement, and even the approach of—but I must not say it yet.) Then underneath the following excerpta—crossing the *t's* and dotting the *i's* of certain moderate movements of late years—I am fain to fancy the foundations of quite a lesson learn'd. After you have exhausted what there is in business, politics, conviviality, love,

*Without apology for the abrupt change of field and atmosphere—after what I have put in the preceding fifty or sixty pages—temporary episodes, thank heaven!—I restore my book to the bracing and buoyant equilibrium of concrete outdoor Nature, the only permanent reliance for sanity of book or human life.

Who knows, (I have it in my fancy, my ambition,) but the pages now ensuing may carry ray of sun, or smell of grass or corn, or call of bird, or gleam of stars by night, or snow-flakes falling fresh and mystic, to denizen of heated city house, or tired workman or workwoman?—or may-be in sick-room or prison—to serve as cooling breeze, or Nature's aroma, to some fever'd mouth or latent pulse.

and so on—have found that none of these finally satisfy, or permanently wear—what remains? Nature remains; to bring out from their torpid recesses, the affinities of a man or woman with the open air, the trees, fields, the changes of seasons—the sun by day and the stars of heaven by night. We will begin from these convictions. Literature flies so high and is so hotly spiced, that our notes may seem hardly more than breaths of common air, or draughts of water to drink. But that is part of our lesson.

Dear, soothing, healthy, restoration-hours—after three confining years of paralysis—after the long strain of the war, and its wounds and death.

Entering a Long Farm-Lane

As every man has his hobby-liking, mine is for a real farm-lane fenced by old chestnut-rails gray-green with dabs of moss and lichen, copious weeds and briers growing in spots athwart the heaps of stray-pick'd stones at the fence bases—irregular paths worn between, and horse and cow tracks—all characteristic accompaniments marking and scenting the neighborhood in their seasons—apple-tree blossoms in forward April—pigs, poultry, a field of August buckwheat, and in another the long flapping tassels of maize—and so to the pond, the expansion of the creek, the secluded-beautiful, with young and old trees, and such recesses and vistas.

To the Spring and Brook

So, still sauntering on, to the spring under the willows—musical as soft clinking glasses—pouring a sizeable stream, thick as my neck, pure and clear, out from its vent where the bank arches over like a great brown shaggy eyebrow or mouth-roof—gurgling, gurgling ceaselessly—meaning, saying something, of course (if one could only translate it)—always gurgling there, the whole year through—never giving out—oceans of mint, blackberries in summer—choice of light and shade—just the place for my July sun-baths and water-baths too—but mainly the inimitable soft sound-gurgles of it, as I sit there hot afternoons. How they and all grow into me, day after day—everything in keeping—the wild, just-palpable perfume, and the dapple of leaf-shadows, and all the natural-medicinal, elemental-moral influences of the spot.

Babble on, O brook, with that utterance of thine! I too will express what I have gather'd in my days and progress, native, subterranean, past—and now thee. Spin and wind thy way—I with thee, a little while, at any rate. As I haunt thee so often, season by season, thou knowest reckest not me, (yet why be so certain? who can tell?)—but I will learn from thee, and dwell on thee—receive, copy, print from thee.

An Early Summer Reveille

Away then to loosen, to unstring the divine bow, so tense, so long. Away, from curtain, carpet, sofa, book—from "society"—from city house, street, and modern improvements and luxuries—away to the primitive winding, aforementioned wooded creek, with its untrimm'd bushes and turfy banks—away from ligatures, tight boots, buttons, and the whole cast-iron civilizee life—from entourage of artificial store, machine, studio, office, parlor—from tailordom and fashion's clothes—from any clothes, perhaps, for the nonce, the summer heats advancing, there in those watery, shaded solitudes. Away, thou soul, (let me pick thee out singly, reader dear, and talk in perfect freedom, negligently, confidentially,) for one day and night at least, returning to the naked source-life of us all—to the breast of the great silent savage all-acceptive Mother. Alas! how many of us are so sodden—how many have wander'd so far away, that return is almost impossible.

But to my jottings, taking them as they come, from the heap, without particular selection. There is little consecutiveness in dates. They run any time within nearly five or six years. Each was carelessly pencilled in the open air, at the time and place. The printers will learn this to some vexation perhaps, as much of their copy is from those hastily-written first notes.

Birds Migrating at Midnight

Did you ever chance to hear the midnight flight of birds passing through the air and darkness overhead, in countless armies, changing their early or late summer habitat? It is something not to be forgotten. A friend called me up just after 12 last night to mark the peculiar noise of unusually immense flocks migrating north (rather late this year.) In the silence, shadow and delicious odor of the hour, (the natural perfume belonging to the night alone,) I thought it rare music. You could *hear* the characteristic motion—once or twice "the rush of mighty wings," but oftener a velvety rustle, long drawn out—sometimes quite near—with continual calls and chirps, and some song-notes. It all lasted from 12 till after 3. Once in a while the species was plainly distinguishable; I could make out the bobolink, tanager, Wilson's thrush, white-crown'd sparrow, and occasionally from high in the air came the notes of the plover.

Bumble-Bees

May-month—month of swarming, singing, mating birds—the bumble-bee month—month of the flowering lilac—(and then my own birth-month.) As I jot this paragraph, I am out just after sunrise, and down towards the creek. The lights, perfumes, melodies—the blue birds, grass birds and robins, in every direction—the noisy, vocal, natural concert. For undertones, a neighboring wood-pecker tapping his tree, and the distant clarion of chanticleer. Then the fresh earth smells—the colors, the delicate drabs and thin blues of the perspective. The bright green of the grass has receiv'd an added tinge from the last two days' mildness and moisture. How the sun silently mounts in the broad clear sky, on his day's journey! How the warm beams bathe all, and come streaming kissingly and almost hot on my face.

A while since the croaking of the pond-frogs and the first white of the dog-wood blossoms. Now the golden dandelions in endless profusion, spotting the ground everywhere. The white cherry and pear-blows—the wild violets, with their blue eyes looking up and saluting my feet, as I saunter the wood-edge—the rosy blush of budding apple-trees—the light-clear emerald hue of the wheat-fields—the darker green of the rye—a warm elasticity pervading the air—the cedar-bushes profusely deck'd with their little brown apples—the summer fully awakening—the convocation of black birds, garrulous flocks of them, gathering on some tree, and making the hour and place noisy as I sit near.

Later.—Nature marches in procession, in sections, like the corps of an army. All have done much for me, and still do. But for the last two days it has been the great wild bee, the humble-bee, or "bumble," as the children call him. As I walk, or hobble, from the farm-house down to the creek, I traverse the before-mention'd lane, fenced by old rails, with many splits, splinters, breaks, holes, &c., the choice habitat of those crooning, hairy insects. Up and down and by and between these rails, they swarm and dart and fly in countless myriads. As I wend slowly along, I am often accompanied with a moving cloud of them. They play a leading part in my morning, midday or sunset rambles, and often dominate the landscape in a way I never before thought of—fill the long lane, not by scores or hundreds only, but by thousands. Large and vivacious and swift, with wonderful momentum and a loud swelling perpetual hum, varied now and then by something almost like a shriek, they dart to and fro, in rapid flashes, chasing each other, and (little things as they are,) conveying to me a new and pronounc'd sense of strength, beauty, vitality and movement. Are they in their mating season? or what is the meaning of this plenitude, swiftness, eagerness, display? As I walk'd, I thought I was follow'd by a particular swarm, but upon observation I saw that it was a rapid succession of changing swarms, one after another.

As I write, I am seated under a big wild-cherry tree—the warm day temper'd by partial clouds and a fresh breeze, neither too heavy nor light—and here I sit long and long, envelop'd in the deep musical drone of these bees, flitting, balancing, darting to and fro about me by hundreds—big fellows with light yellow jackets, great glistening swelling bodies, stumpy heads and gauzy wings—humming their perpetual rich mellow boom. (Is there not a hint in it for a musical composition, of which it should be the back-ground? some bumble-bee symphony?) How it all nourishes, lulls me, in the way most needed; the open air, the rye-fields, the apple orchards. The last two days have been faultless in sun, breeze, temperature and everything; never two more perfect days, and

I have enjoy'd them wonderfully. My health is somewhat better, and my spirit at peace. (Yet the anniversary of the saddest loss and sorrow of my life is close at hand.)

Another jotting, another perfect day: forenoon, from 7 to 9, two hours envelop'd in sound of bumble-bees and bird-music. Down in the apple-trees and in a neighboring cedar were three or four russet-back'd thrushes, each singing his best, and roulading in ways I never heard surpass'd. Two hours I abandon myself to hearing them, and indolently absorbing the scene. Almost every bird I notice has a special time in the year—sometimes limited to a few days—when it sings its best; and now is the period of these russet-backs. Meanwhile, up and down the lane, the darting, droning, musical bumble-bees. A great swarm again for my entourage as I return home, moving along with me as before.

As I write this, two or three weeks later, I am sitting near the brook under a tulip tree, 70 feet high, thick with the fresh verdure of its young maturity—a beautiful object—every branch, every leaf perfect. From top to bottom, seeking the sweet juice in the blossoms, it swarms with myriads of these wild bees, whose loud and steady humming makes an undertone to the whole, and to my mood and the hour. All of which I will bring to a close by extracting the following verses from Henry A. Beers's little volume:

"As I lay yonder in tall grass
A drunken bumble-bee went past
Delirious with honey toddy.
The golden sash about his body
Scarce kept it in his swollen belly
Distent with honeysuckle jelly.
Rose liquor and the sweet-pea wine
Had fill'd his soul with song divine;
Deep had he drunk the warm night through,
His hairy thighs were wet with dew.
Full many an antic he had play'd
While the world went round through sleep and shade.
Oft had he lit with thirsty lip
Some flower-cup's nectar'd sweets to sip,
When on smooth petals he would slip,

Or over tangled stamens trip,
And headlong in the pollen roll'd,
Crawl out quite dusted o'er with gold;
Or else his heavy feet would stumble
Against some bud, and down he'd tumble
Amongst the grass; there lie and grumble
In low, soft bass—poor maudlin bumble!"

Cedar-Apples

As I journey'd to-day in a light wagon ten or twelve miles through the country, nothing pleas'd me more, in their homely beauty and novelty (I had either never seen the little things to such advantage, or had never noticed them before) than that peculiar fruit, with its profuse clear-yellow dangles of inch-long silk or yarn, in boundless profusion spotting the dark-green cedar bushes—contrasting well with their bronze tufts—the flossy shreds covering the knobs all over, like a shock of wild hair on elfin pates. On my ramble afterward down by the creek I pluck'd one from its bush, and shall keep it. These cedar-apples last only a little while however, and soon crumble and fade.

Summer Sights and Indolencies

June 10th.—As I write, 5½ P. M., here by the creek, nothing can exceed the quiet splendor and freshness around me. We had a heavy shower, with brief thunder and lightning, in the middle of the day; and since, overhead, one of those not uncommon yet indescribable skies (in quality, not details or forms) of limpid blue, with rolling silver-fringed clouds, and a pure-dazzling sun. For underlay, trees in fulness of tender foliage—liquid, reedy, long-drawn notes of birds—based by the fretful mewing of a querulous cat-bird, and the pleasant chippering-shriek of two kingfishers. I have been watching the latter the last half hour, on their regular evening frolic over and in the stream; evidently a spree of the liveliest kind. They pursue each other, whirling and wheeling around, with many a jocund downward dip, splashing the spray in jets of diamonds—and then off they swoop, with slanting wings and graceful flight, sometimes so near me I can plainly see their dark-gray feather-bodies and milk-white necks.

Sundown Perfume—Quail-Notes—The Hermit-Thrush

June 19th, 4 to 6½ P.M.—Sitting alone by the creek—solitude here, but the scene bright and vivid enough—the sun shining, and quite a fresh wind blowing (some heavy showers last night,) the grass and trees looking their best—the clare-obscure of different greens, shadows, half-shadows, and the dappling glimpses of the water, through recesses—the wild flageolet-note of a quail near by—the just-heard fretting of some hylas down there in the pond—crows cawing in the distance—a drove of young hogs rooting in soft ground near the oak under which I sit—some come sniffing near me, and then scamper away, with grunts. And still the clear notes of the quail—the quiver of leaf-shadows over the paper as I write—the sky aloft, with white clouds, and the sun well declining to the west—the swift darting of many sand-swallows coming and going, their holes in a neighboring marl-bank—the odor of the cedar and oak, so palpable, as evening approaches—perfume, color, the bronze-and-gold of nearly ripen'd wheat—clover-fields, with honey-scent—the well-up maize, with long and rustling leaves—the great patches of thriving potatoes, dusky green, fleck'd all over with white blossoms—the old, warty, venerable oak above me—and ever, mix'd with the dual notes of the quail, the soughing of the wind through some near-by pines.

As I rise for return, I linger long to a delicious song-epilogue (is it the hermit-thrush?) from some bushy recess off there in the swamp, repeated leisurely and pensively over and over again. This, to the circle-gambols of the swallows flying by dozens in concentric rings in the last rays of sunset, like flashes of some airy wheel.

A July Afternoon by the Pond

The fervent heat, but so much more endurable in this pure air—the white and pink pond-blossoms, with great heart-shaped leaves; the glassy waters of the creek, the banks, with dense bushery, and the picturesque beeches and shade and turf; the tremulous, reedy call of some bird from recesses, breaking the warm, indolent, half-voluptuous silence; an occasional wasp, hornet, honey-bee or bumble (they hover near my hands or face, yet annoy me not, nor I them, as they appear to examine, find nothing, and away they go)—the vast space of the sky overhead so clear, and the buzzard up there sailing his slow whirl in majestic spirals and discs; just over the surface of the pond, two large slate-color'd dragon-flies, with wings of lace, circling and darting and occasionally balancing themselves quite still, their wings quivering all the time, (are they not showing off for my amusement?)—the pond itself, with the sword-shaped calamus; the water snakes—occasionally a flitting blackbird, with red dabs on his shoulders, as he darts slantingly by—the sounds that bring out the solitude, warmth, light and shade—the quawk of some pond duck—(the crickets and grasshoppers are mute in the noon heat, but I hear the song of the first cicadas;)—then at some distance the rattle and whirr of a reaping machine as the horses draw it on a rapid walk through a rye field on the opposite side of the creek—(what was the yellow or light-brown bird, large as a young hen, with short neck and long-stretch'd legs I just saw, in flapping and awkward flight over there through the trees?)—the prevailing delicate, yet palpable, spicy, grassy, clovery perfume to my nostrils; and over all, encircling all, to my sight and soul, the free space of the sky, transparent and blue—and hovering there in the west, a mass of white-gray fleecy clouds the sailors call "shoals of mackerel"—the sky, with silver swirls like locks of toss'd hair, spreading, expanding—a vast voiceless, formless simulacrum—yet may-be the most real reality and formulator of everything—who knows?

Locusts and Katydids

Aug. 22.—Reedy monotones of locust, or sounds of katydid—I hear the latter at night, and the other both day and night. I thought the morning and evening warble of birds delightful; but I find I can listen to these strange insects with just as much pleasure. A single locust is now heard near noon from a tree two hundred feet off, as I write—a long whirring, continued, quite loud noise graded in distinct whirls, or swinging circles, increasing in strength and rapidity up to a certain point, and then a fluttering, quietly tapering fall. Each strain is continued from one to two minutes. The locust-song is very appropriate to the scene—gushes, has meaning, is masculine, is like some fine old wine, not sweet, but far better than sweet.

But the katydid—how shall I describe its piquant utterances? One sings from a willow-tree just outside my open bedroom window, twenty yards distant; every clear night for a fortnight past has sooth'd me to sleep. I rode through a piece of woods for a hundred rods the other evening, and heard the katydids by myriads—very curious for once; but I like better my single neighbor on the tree.

Let me say more about the song of the locust, even to repetition; a long, chromatic, tremulous crescendo, like a brass disk whirling round and round, emitting wave after wave of notes, beginning with a certain moderate beat or measure, rapidly increasing in speed and emphasis, reaching a point of great energy and significance, and then quickly and gracefully dropping down and out. Not the melody of the swinging-bird—far from it; the common musician might think without melody, but surely having to the finer ear a harmony of its own; monotonous—but what a swing there is in that brassy drone, round and round, cymballine—or like the whirling of brass quoits.

The Lesson of a Tree

Sept. 1.—I should not take either the biggest or the most picturesque tree to illustrate it. Here is one of my favorites now before me, a fine yellow poplar, quite straight, perhaps 90 feet high, and four thick at the butt. How strong, vital, enduring! how dumbly eloquent! What suggestions of imperturbability and *being,* as against the human trait of mere *seeming.* Then the qualities, almost emotional, palpably artistic, heroic, of a tree; so innocent and harmless, yet so savage. It *is*, yet says nothing. How it rebukes by its tough and equable serenity all weathers, this gusty-temper'd little whiffet, man, that runs indoors at a mite of rain or snow. Science (or rather half-way science) scoffs at reminiscence of dryad and hamadryad, and of trees speaking. But, if they don't, they do as well as most speaking, writing, poetry, sermons—or rather they do a great deal better. I should say indeed that those old dryad-reminiscences are quite as true as any, and profounder than most reminiscences we get. ("Cut this out," as the quack mediciners say, and keep by you.) Go and sit in a grove or woods, with one or more of those voiceless companions, and read the foregoing, and think.

One lesson from affiliating a tree—perhaps the greatest moral lesson anyhow from earth, rocks, animals, is that same lesson of inherency, of *what is*, without the least regard to what the looker on (the critic) supposes or says, or whether he likes or dislikes. What worse—what more general malady pervades each and all of us, our literature, education, attitude toward each other, (even toward ourselves,) than a morbid trouble about *seems*, (generally temporarily seems too,) and no trouble at all, or hardly any, about the sane, slow-growing, perennial, real parts of character, books, friendship, marriage—humanity's invisible foundations and hold-together? (As the all-basis, the nerve, the great-sympathetic, the plenum within humanity, giving stamp to everything, is necessarily invisible.)

Aug. 4, 6 P.M.—Lights and shades and rare effects on tree-foliage and grass—transparent greens, grays, &c., all in sunset pomp and dazzle. The clear beams are now thrown in many new places, on the quilted, seam'd, bronze-drab, lower tree-trunks, shadow'd except at this hour—now flooding their young and old columnar ruggedness with strong light, unfolding to my sense new amazing features of silent, shaggy charm, the solid bark, the expression of harmless impassiveness, with many a bulge and gnarl unreck'd before. In the revealings of such light, such exceptional hour, such mood, one does not wonder at the old story fables, (indeed, why fables?) of people falling into love-sickness with trees, seiz'd extatic with the mystic realism of the resistless silent strength in them—*strength*, which after all is perhaps the last, completest, highest beauty.

Trees I am familiar with here.

- Oaks, (many kinds—one sturdy old fellow, vital, green, bushy, five feet thick at the butt, I sit under every day.)
- Cedars, plenty.
- Tulip trees, (*Liriodendron,* is of the magnolia family—I have seen it in Michigan and southern Illinois, 140 feet high and 8 feet thick at the butt*; does not transplant well; best rais'd from seeds—the lumbermen call it yellow poplar.)
- Sycamores.
- Gum-trees, both sweet and sour.
- Beeches.
- Black-walnuts.
- Sassafras.
- Willows.
- Catalpas.
- Persimmons.
- Mountain-ash.
- Hickories.
- Maples, many kinds.
- Locusts.
- Birches.
- Dogwood.
- Pine.
- the Elm.
- Chestnut.
- Linden.
- Aspen.
- Spruce.
- Hornbeam.
- Laurel.
- Holly.

Autumn Side-Bits

Sept. 20.—Under an old black oak, glossy and green, exhaling aroma—amid a grove the Albic druids might have chosen—envelop'd in the warmth and light of the noonday sun, and swarms of flitting insects—with the harsh cawing of many crows a hundred rods away—here I sit in solitude, absorbing, enjoying all. The corn, stack'd in its cone-shaped stacks, russet-color'd and sere—a large field spotted thick with scarlet-gold pumpkins—an adjoining one of cabbages, showing well

*There is a tulip poplar within sight of Woodstown, which is twenty feet around, three feet from the ground, four feet across about eighteen feet up the trunk, which is broken off about three or four feet higher up. On the south side an arm has shot out from which rise two stems, each to about ninety-one or ninety-two feet from the ground. Twenty-five (or more) years since the cavity in the butt was large enough for, and nine men at one time, ate dinner therein. It is supposed twelve to fifteen men could now, at one time, stand within its trunk. The severe winds of 1877 and 1878 did not seem to damage it, and the two stems send out yearly many blossoms, scenting the air immediately about it with their sweet perfume. It is entirely unprotected by other trees, on a hill.—*Woodstown, N. J., "Register," April 15, '79.*

in their green and pearl, mottled by much light and shade—melon patches, with their bulging ovals, and great silver-streak'd, ruffled, broad-edged leaves—and many an autumn sight and sound beside—the distant scream of a flock of guinea-hens—and pour'd over all the September breeze, with pensive cadence through the tree tops.

Another Day.—The ground in all directions strew'd with *debris* from a storm. Timber creek, as I slowly pace its banks, has ebb'd low, and shows reaction from the turbulent swell of the late equinoctial. As I look around, I take account of stock—weeds and shrubs, knolls, paths, occasional stumps, some with smooth'd tops, (several I use as seats of rest, from place to place, and from one I am now jotting these lines,)—frequent wild-flowers, little white, star-shaped things, or the cardinal red of the lobelia, or the cherry-ball seeds of the perennial rose, or the many-threaded vines winding up and around trunks of trees.

Oct. 1, 2 and 3.—Down every day in the solitude of the creek. A serene autumn sun and westerly breeze to-day (3d) as I sit here, the water surface prettily moving in wind-ripples before me. On a stout old beech at the edge, decayed and slanting, almost fallen to the stream, yet with life and leaves in its mossy limbs, a gray squirrel, exploring, runs up and down, flirts his tail, leaps to the ground, sits on his haunches upright as he sees me, (a Darwinian hint?) and then races up the tree again.

Oct. 4.—Cloudy and coolish; signs of incipient winter. Yet pleasant here, the leaves thick-falling, the ground brown with them already; rich coloring, yellows of all hues, pale and dark-green, shades from lightest to richest red—all set in and toned down by the prevailing brown of the earth and gray of the sky. So, winter is coming; and I yet in my sickness. I sit here amid all these fair sights and vital influences, and abandon myself to that thought, with its wandering trains of speculation.

The Sky—Days and Nights—Happiness

Oct. 20.—A clear, crispy day—dry and breezy air, full of oxygen. Out of the sane, silent, beauteous miracles that envelope and fuse me—trees, water, grass, sunlight, and early frost—the one I am looking at most to-day is the sky. It has that delicate, transparent blue, peculiar to autumn, and the only clouds are little or larger white ones, giving their still and spiritual motion to the great concave. All through the earlier day (say from 7 to 11) it keeps a pure, yet vivid blue. But as noon approaches the color gets lighter, quite gray for two or three hours—then still paler for a spell, till sun-down—which last I watch dazzling through the interstices of a knoll of big trees—darts of fire and a gorgeous show of light-yellow, liver-color and red, with a vast silver glaze askant on the water—the transparent shadows, shafts, sparkle, and vivid colors beyond all the paintings ever made.

I don't know what or how, but it seems to me mostly owing to these skies, (every now and then I think, while I have of course seen them every day of my life, I never really saw the skies before,) I have had this autumn some wondrously contented hours—may I not say perfectly happy ones? As I've read, Byron just before his death told a friend that he had known but three happy hours during his whole existence. Then there is the old German legend of the king's bell, to the same point. While I was out there by the wood, that beautiful sunset through the trees, I thought of Byron's and the bell story, and the notion started in me that I was having a happy hour. (Though perhaps my best moments I never jot down; when they come I cannot afford to break the charm by inditing memoranda. I just abandon myself to the mood, and let it float on, carrying me in its placid extasy.)

What is happiness, anyhow? Is this one of its hours, or the like of it?—so impalpable—a mere breath, an evanescent tinge? I am not sure—so let me give myself the benefit of the doubt. Hast Thou, pellucid, in Thy azure depths, medicine for case like mine? (Ah, the physical shatter and troubled spirit of me the last three years.) And dost Thou subtly mystically now drip it through the air invisibly upon me?

Night of Oct. 28.—The heavens unusually transparent—the stars out by myriads—the great path of the Milky Way, with its branch, only seen of very clear nights—Jupiter, setting in the west, looks like a huge hap-hazard splash, and has a little star for companion.

Clothed in his white garments,
Into the round and clear arena slowly entered the brahmin,
Holding a little child by the hand,
Like the moon with the planet Jupiter in a cloudless night-
sky.

Old Hindu Poem.

Early in November.—At its farther end the lane already described opens into a broad grassy upland field of over twenty acres, slightly sloping to the south. Here I am accustom'd to walk for sky views and effects, either morning or sundown. To-day from this field my soul is calm'd and expanded beyond description, the whole forenoon by the clear blue arching over all, cloudless, nothing particular, only sky and daylight. Their soothing accompaniments, autumn leaves, the cool dry air, the faint aroma—crows cawing in the distance—two great buzzards wheeling gracefully and slowly far up there—the occasional murmur of the wind, sometimes quite gently, then threatening through the trees—a gang of farm-laborers loading corn-stalks in a field in sight, and the patient horses waiting.

Colors—A Contrast

Such a play of colors and lights, different seasons, different hours of the day—the lines of the far horizon where the faint-tinged edge of the landscape loses itself in the sky. As I slowly hobble up the lane toward day-close, an incomparable sunset shooting in molten sapphire and gold, shaft after shaft, through the ranks of the long-leaved corn, between me and the west.

Another day.—The rich dark green of the tulip-trees and the oaks, the gray of the swamp-willows, the dull hues of the sycamores and black-walnuts, the emerald of the cedars (after rain,) and the light yellow of the beeches.

November 8, '76

The forenoon leaden and cloudy, not cold or wet, but indicating both. As I hobble down here and sit by the silent pond, how different from the excitement amid which, in the cities, millions of people are now waiting news of yesterday's Presidential election, or receiving and discussing the result—in this secluded place uncared-for, unknown.

Crows and Crows

Nov. 14.—As I sit here by the creek, resting after my walk, a warm languor bathes me from the sun. No sound but a cawing of crows, and no motion but their black flying figures from overhead, reflected in the mirror of the pond below. Indeed a principal feature of the scene to-day is these crows, their incessant cawing, far or near, and their countless flocks and processions moving from place to place, and at times almost darkening the air with their myriads. As I sit a moment writing this by the bank, I see the black, clear-cut reflection of them far below, flying through the watery looking-glass, by ones, twos, or long strings. All last night I heard the noises from their great roost in a neighboring wood.

A Winter Day on the Sea-Beach

One bright December mid-day lately I spent down on the New Jersey sea-shore, reaching it by a little more than an hour's railroad trip over the old Camden and Atlantic. I had started betimes, fortified by nice strong coffee and a good breakfast (cook'd by the hands I love, my dear sister Lou's—how much better it makes the victuals taste, and then assimilate, strengthen you, perhaps make the whole day comfortable afterwards.) Five or six miles at the last, our track enter'd a broad region of salt grass meadows, intersected by lagoons, and cut up everywhere by watery runs. The sedgy perfume, delightful to my nostrils, reminded me of "the mash" and south bay of my native island. I could have journey'd contentedly till night through these flat and odorous sea-prairies. From half-past 11 till 2 I was nearly all the time along the beach, or in sight of the ocean, listening to its hoarse murmur, and inhaling the bracing and welcome breezes. First, a rapid five-mile drive over the hard sand—our carriage wheels hardly made dents in it. Then after dinner (as there were nearly two hours to spare) I walk'd off in another direction, (hardly met or saw a person,) and taking possession of what appear'd to have been the reception-room of an old bath-house range, had a broad expanse of view all to myself—quaint, refreshing, unimpeded—a dry area of sedge and Indian grass immediately before and around me—space, simple, unornamented space. Distant vessels, and the far-off, just visible trailing smoke of an inward bound steamer; more plainly, ships, brigs, schooners, in sight, most of them with every sail set to the firm and steady wind.

The attractions, fascinations there are in sea and shore! How one dwells on their simplicity, even vacuity! What is it in us, arous'd by those indirections and directions? That spread of waves and gray-white beach, salt, monotonous, senseless—such an entire absence of art, books, talk, elegance—so indescribably comforting, even this winter day—grim, yet so delicate-looking, so spiritual—striking emotional, impalpable depths, subtler than all the poems, paintings, music, I have ever read, seen, heard. (Yet let me be fair, perhaps it is because I have read those poems and heard that music.)

Sea-Shore Fancies

Even as a boy, I had the fancy, the wish, to write a piece, perhaps a poem, about the sea-shore—that suggesting, dividing line, contact, junction, the solid marrying the liquid—that curious, lurking something, (as doubtless every objective form finally becomes to the subjective spirit,) which means far more than its mere first sight, grand as that is—blending the real and ideal, and each made portion of the other. Hours, days, in my Long Island youth and early manhood, I haunted the shores of Rockaway or Coney island, or away east to the Hamptons or Montauk. Once, at the latter place, (by the old lighthouse, nothing but sea-tossings in sight in every direction as far as the eye could reach,) I remember well, I felt that I must one day write a book expressing this liquid, mystic theme. Afterward, I recollect, how it came to me that instead of any special lyrical or epical or literary attempt, the sea-shore should be an invisible *influence*, a pervading gauge and tally for me, in my composition. (Let me give a hint here to young writers. I am not sure but I have unwittingly follow'd out the same rule with other powers besides sea and shores—avoiding them, in the way of any dead set at poetizing them, as too big for formal handling—quite satisfied if I could indirectly show that we have met and fused, even if only once, but enough—that we have really absorb'd each other and understand each other.)

There is a dream, a picture, that for years at intervals, (sometimes quite long ones, but surely again, in time,) has come noiselessly up before me, and I really believe, fiction as it is, has enter'd largely into my practical life—certainly into my writings, and shaped and color'd them. It is nothing more or less than a stretch of interminable white-brown sand, hard and smooth and broad, with the ocean perpetually, grandly, rolling in upon it, with slow-measured sweep, with rustle and hiss and foam, and many a thump as of low bass drums. This scene, this picture, I say, has risen before me at times for years. Sometimes I wake at night and can hear and see it plainly.

In Memory of Thomas Paine

Spoken at Lincoln Hall, Philadelphia, Sunday, Jan. 28, '77, for 140th anniversary of T.P.'s birth-day.

Some thirty-five years ago, in New York city, at Tammany hall, of which place I was then a frequenter, I happen'd to become quite well acquainted with Thomas Paine's perhaps most intimate chum, and certainly his later years' very frequent companion, a remarkably fine old man, Col. Fellows, who may yet be remember'd by some stray relics of that period and spot. If you will allow me, I will first give a description of the Colonel himself. He was tall, of military bearing, aged about 78 I should think, hair white as snow, clean-shaved on the face, dress'd very neatly, a tail-coat of blue cloth with metal buttons, buff vest, pantaloons of drab color, and his neck, breast and wrists showing the whitest of linen. Under all circumstances, fine manners; a good but not profuse talker, his wits still fully about him, balanced and live and undimm'd as ever. He kept pretty fair health, though so old. For employment—for he was poor—he had a post as constable of some of the upper courts. I used to think him very picturesque on the fringe of a crowd holding a tall staff, with his erect form, and his superb, bare, thick-hair'd, closely-cropt white head. The judges and young lawyers, with whom he was ever a favorite, and the subject of respect, used to call him Aristides. It was the general opinion among them that if manly rectitude and the instincts of absolute justice remain'd vital anywhere about New York City Hall, or Tammany, they were to be found in Col. Fellows. He liked young men, and enjoy'd to leisurely talk with them over a social glass of toddy, after his day's work, (he on these occasions never drank but one glass,) and it was at reiterated meetings of this kind in old Tammany's back parlor of those days, that he told me much about Thomas Paine. At one of our interviews he gave me a minute account of Paine's sickness and death. In short, from those talks, I was and am satisfied that my old friend, with his mark'd advantages, had mentally, morally and emotionally gauged the author of "Common Sense," and besides giving me a good portrait of his appearance and manners, had taken the true measure of his interior character.

Paine's practical demeanor, and much of his theoretical belief, was a mixture of the French and English schools of a century ago, and the best of both. Like most old-fashion'd people, he drank a glass or two every day, but was no tippler, nor intemperate, let alone being a drunkard. He lived simply and economically, but quite well—was always cheery and courteous, perhaps occasionally a little blunt, having very positive opinions upon politics, religion, and so forth. That he labor'd well and wisely for the States in the trying period of their parturition, and in the seeds of their character, there seems to me no question. I dare not say how much of what our Union is owning and enjoying to-day—its independence—its ardent belief in, and substantial practice of, radical human rights—and the severance of its government from all ecclesiastical and superstitious dominion—I dare not say how much of all this is owing to Thomas Paine, but I am inclined to think a good portion of it decidedly is.

But I was not going either into an analysis or eulogium of the man. I wanted to carry you back a generation or two, and give you by indirection a moment's glance—and also to ventilate a very earnest and I believe authentic opinion, nay conviction, of that time, the fruit of the interviews I have mention'd, and of questioning and cross-questioning, clench'd by my best information since, that Thomas Paine had a noble personality, as exhibited in presence, face, voice, dress, manner, and what may be call'd his atmosphere and magnetism, especially the later years of his life. I am sure of it. Of the foul and foolish fictions yet told about the circumstances of his decease, the absolute fact is that as he lived a good life, after its kind, he died calmly and philosophically, as became him. He served the embryo Union with most precious service—a service that every man, woman and child in our thirty-eight States is to some extent receiving the benefit of to-day—and I for one here cheerfully, reverently throw my pebble on the cairn of his memory. As we all know, the season demands—or rather, will it ever be out of season?—that America learn to better dwell on her choicest possession, the legacy of her good and faithful men—that she well preserve their fame, if unquestion'd—or, if need be, that she fail not to dissipate what clouds have intruded on that fame, and burnish it newer, truer and brighter, continually.

A Two Hours' Ice-Sail

Feb. 3, '77.—From 4 to 6 P.M. crossing the Delaware, (back again at my Camden home,) unable to make our landing, through the ice; our boat stanch and strong and skilfully piloted, but old and sulky, and poorly minding her helm. (*Power*, so important in poetry and war, is also first point of all in a winter steamboat, with long stretches of ice-packs to tackle.) For over two hours we bump'd and beat about, the invisible ebb, sluggish but irresistible, often carrying us long distances against our will. In the first tinge of dusk, as I look'd around, I thought there could not be presented a more chilling, arctic, grim-extended, depressing scene. Everything was yet plainly visible; for miles north and south, ice, ice, ice, mostly broken, but some big cakes, and no clear water in sight. The shores, piers, surfaces, roofs, shipping, mantled with snow. A faint winter vapor hung a fitting accompaniment around and over the endless whitish spread, and gave it just a tinge of steel and brown.

Feb. 6.—As I cross home in the 6 P.M. boat again, the transparent shadows are filled everywhere with leisurely falling, slightly slanting, curiously sparse but very large, flakes of snow. On the shores, near and far, the glow of just-lit gas-clusters at intervals. The ice, sometimes in hummocks, sometimes floating fields, through which our boat goes crunching. The light permeated by that peculiar evening haze, right after sunset, which sometimes renders quite distant objects so distinctly.

Spring Overtures—Recreations

Feb. 10.—The first chirping, almost singing, of a bird today. Then I noticed a couple of honey-bees spirting and humming about the open window in the sun.

Feb. 11.—In the soft rose and pale gold of the declining light, this beautiful evening, I heard the first hum and preparation of awakening spring—very faint—whether in the earth or roots, or starting of insects, I know not—but it was audible, as I lean'd on a rail (I am down in my country quarters awhile,) and look'd long at the western horizon. Turning to the east, Sirius, as the shadows deepen'd, came forth in dazzling splendor. And great Orion; and a little to the north-east the big Dipper, standing on end.

Feb. 20.—A solitary and pleasant sundown hour at the pond, exercising arms, chest, my whole body, by a tough oak sapling thick as my wrist, twelve feet high—pulling and pushing, inspiring the good air. After I wrestle with the tree awhile, I can feel its young sap and virtue welling up out of the ground and tingling through me from crown to toe, like health's wine. Then for addition and variety I launch forth in my vocalism; shout declamatory pieces, sentiments, sorrow, anger, &c., from the stock poets or plays—or inflate my lungs and sing the wild tunes and refrains I heard of the blacks down south, or patriotic songs I learn'd in the army. I make the echoes ring, I tell you! As the twilight fell, in a pause of these ebullitions, an owl somewhere the other side of the creek sounded *too-oo-oo-oo-oo,* soft and pensive (and I fancied a little sarcastic) repeated four or five times. Either to applaud the negro songs—or perhaps an ironical comment on the sorrow, anger, or style of the stock poets.

One of the Human Kinks

How is it that in all the serenity and lonesomeness of solitude, away off here amid the hush of the forest, alone, or as I have found in prairie wilds, or mountain stillness, one is never entirely without the instinct of looking around, (I never am, and others tell me the same of themselves, confidentially,) for somebody to appear, or start up out of the earth, or from behind some tree or rock? Is it a lingering, inherited remains of man's primitive wariness, from the wild animals? or from his savage ancestry far back? It is not at all nervousness or fear. Seems as if something unknown were possibly lurking in those bushes, or solitary places. Nay, it is quite certain there is—some vital unseen presence.

An Afternoon Scene

Feb. 22.—Last night and to-day rainy and thick, till mid-afternoon, when the wind chopp'd round, the clouds swiftly drew off like curtains, the clear appear'd, and with it the fairest, grandest, most wondrous rainbow I ever saw, all complete, very vivid at its earth-ends, spreading vast effusions of illuminated haze, violet, yellow, drab-green, in all directions overhead, through which the sun beam'd—an indescribable utterance of color and light, so gorgeous yet so soft, such as I had never witness'd before. Then its continuance: a full hour pass'd before the last of those earth-ends disappear'd. The sky behind was all spread in translucent blue, with many little white clouds and edges. To these a sunset, filling, dominating the esthetic and soul senses, sumptuously, tenderly, full. I end this note by the pond, just light enough to see, through the evening shadows, the western reflections in its water-mirror surface, with inverted figures of trees. I hear now and then the *flup* of a pike leaping out, and rippling the water.

The Gates Opening

April 6.—Palpable spring indeed, or the indications of it. I am sitting in bright sunshine, at the edge of the creek, the surface just rippled by the wind. All is solitude, morning freshness, negligence. For companions my two kingfishers sailing, winding, darting, dipping, sometimes capriciously separate, then flying together. I hear their guttural twittering again and again; for awhile nothing but that peculiar sound. As noon approaches other birds warm up. The reedy notes of the robin, and a musical passage of two parts, one a clear delicious gurgle, with several other birds I cannot place. To which is join'd, (yes, I just hear it,) one low purr at intervals from some impatient hylas at the pond-edge. The sibilant murmur of a pretty stiff breeze now and then through the trees. Then a poor little dead leaf, long frost-bound, whirls from somewhere up aloft in one wild escaped freedom-spree in space and sunlight, and then dashes down to the waters, which hold it closely and soon drown it out of sight. The bushes and trees are yet bare, but the beeches have their wrinkled yellow leaves of last season's foliage largely left, frequent cedars and pines yet green, and the grass not without proofs of coming fulness. And over all a wonderfully fine dome of clear blue, the play of light coming and going, and great fleeces of white clouds swimming so silently.

The Common Earth, the Soil

The soil, too—let others pen-and-ink the sea, the air, (as I sometimes try)—but now I feel to choose the common soil for theme—naught else. The brown soil here, (just between winter-close and opening spring and vegetation)—the rain-shower at night, and the fresh smell next morning—the red worms wriggling out of the ground—the dead leaves, the incipient grass, and the latent life underneath—the effort to start something—already in shelter'd spots some little flowers—the distant emerald show of winter wheat and the rye-fields—the yet naked trees, with clear interstices, giving prospects hidden in summer—the tough fallow and the plow-team, and the stout boy whistling to his horses for encouragement—and there the dark fat earth in long slanting stripes upturn'd.

Birds and Birds and Birds

A little later—bright weather.—An unusual melodiousness, these days, (last of April and first of May) from the black-birds; indeed all sorts of birds, darting, whistling, hopping or perch'd on trees. Never before have I seen, heard, or been in the midst of, and got so flooded and saturated with them and their performances, as this current month. Such oceans, such successions of them. Let me make a list of those I find here:

Black birds (plenty,)
Ring doves,
Owls,
Woodpeckers,
King-birds,
Crows (plenty,)
Wrens,
Kingfishers,
Quails,
Turkey-buzzards,
Hen-hawks,
Yellow birds,
Thrushes,
Reed birds,
Meadow-larks (plenty,)
Cat-birds (plenty,)
Cuckoos,
Pond snipes (plenty,)
Cheewinks,
Quawks,
Ground robins,
Ravens,
Gray snipes,
Eagles,
High-holes,
Herons,
Tits,
Woodpigeons.

Early came the
Blue birds,
Killdeer,
Plover,
Robin,
Woodcock,
Meadow lark,
White-bellied swallow,
Sandpiper,
Wilson's thrush,
Flicker.

Full-Starr'd Nights

May 21.—Back in Camden. Again commencing one of those unusually transparent, full-starr'd, blue-black nights, as if to show that however lush and pompous the day may be, there is something left in the not-day that can outvie it. The rarest, finest sample of long-drawn-out clear-obscure, from sundown to 9 o'clock. I went down to the Delaware, and cross'd and cross'd. Venus like blazing silver well up in the west. The large pale thin crescent of the new moon, half an hour high, sinking languidly under a bar-sinister of cloud, and then emerging.

Arcturus right overhead. A faint fragrant sea-odor wafted up from the south. The gloaming, the temper'd coolness, with every feature of the scene, indescribably soothing and tonic—one of those hours that give hints to the soul, impossible to put in a statement. (Ah, where would be any food for spirituality without night and the stars?) The vacant spaciousness of the air, and the veil'd blue of the heavens, seem'd miracles enough.

As the night advanc'd it changed its spirit and garments to ampler stateliness. I was almost conscious of a definite presence, Nature silently near. The great constellation of the Water-Serpent stretch'd its coils over more than half the heavens. The Swan with outspread wings was flying down the Milky Way. The northern Crown, the Eagle, Lyra, all up there in their places. From the whole dome shot down points of light, rapport with me, through the clear blue-black. All the usual sense of motion, all animal life, seem'd discarded, seem'd a fiction; a curious power, like the placid rest of Egyptian gods, took possession, none the less potent for being impalpable. Earlier I had seen many bats, balancing in the luminous twilight, darting their black forms hither and yon over the river; but now they altogether disappear'd. The evening star and the moon had gone. Alertness and peace lay calmly couching together through the fluid universal shadows.

Aug. 26.—Bright has the day been, and my spirits an equal *forzando.* Then comes the night, different, inexpressibly pensive, with its own tender and temper'd splendor. Venus lingers in the west with a voluptuous dazzle unshown hitherto this summer. Mars rises early, and the red sulky moon, two days past her full; Jupiter at night's meridian, and the long curling-slanted Scorpion stretching full view in the south, Aretus-neck'd. Mars walks the heavens lord-paramount now; all through this month I go out after supper and watch for him; sometimes getting up at midnight to take another look at his unparallel'd lustre. (I see lately an astronomer has made out through the new Washington telescope that Mars has certainly one moon, perhaps two.) Pale and distant, but near in the heavens, Saturn precedes him.

Mulleins and Mulleins

Large, placid mulleins, as summer advances, velvety in texture, of a light greenish-drab color, growing everywhere in the fields—at first earth's big rosettes in their broad-leav'd low cluster-plants, eight, ten, twenty leaves to a plant—plentiful on the fallow twenty-acre lot, at the end of the lane, and especially by the ridge-sides of the fences—then close to the ground, but soon springing up—leaves as broad as my hand, and the lower ones twice as long—so fresh and dewy in the morning—stalks now four or five, even seven or eight feet high. The farmers, I find, think the mullein a mean unworthy weed, but I have grown to a fondness for it. Every object has its lesson, enclosing the suggestion of everything else—and lately I sometimes think all is concentrated for me in these hardy, yellow-flower'd weeds. As I come down the lane early in the morning, I pause before their soft wool-like fleece and stem and broad leaves, glittering with countless diamonds. Annually for three summers now, they and I have silently return'd together; at such long intervals I stand or sit among them, musing—and woven with the rest, of so many hours and moods of partial rehabilitation—of my sane or sick spirit, here as near at peace as it can be.

Distant Sounds

The axe of the wood-cutter, the measured thud of a single threshing-flail, the crowing of chanticleer in the barn-yard, (with invariable responses from other barn-yards,) and the lowing of cattle—but most of all, or far or near, the wind—through the high tree-tops, or through low bushes, laving one's face and hands so gently, this balmy-bright noon, the coolest for a long time, (Sept. 2)—I will not call it *sighing*, for to me it is always a firm, sane, cheery expression, though a monotone, giving many varieties, or swift or slow, or dense or delicate. The wind in the patch of pine woods off there—how sibilant. Or at sea, I can imagine it this moment, tossing the waves, with spirits of foam flying far, and the free whistle, and the scent of the salt—and that vast paradox somehow with all its action and restlessness conveying a sense of eternal rest.

Other adjuncts.—But the sun and moon here and these times. As never more wonderful by day, the gorgeous orb imperial, so vast, so ardently, lovingly hot—so never a more glorious moon of nights, especially the last three or four. The great planets too—Mars never before so flaming bright, so flashing-large, with slight yellow tinge, (the astronomers say —is it true?—nearer to us than any time the past century) —and well up, lord Jupiter, (a little while since close by the moon)—and in the west, after the sun sinks, voluptuous Venus, now languid and shorn of her beams, as if from some divine excess.

A Sun-Bath—Nakedness

Sunday, Aug. 27.—Another day quite free from mark'd prostration and pain. It seems indeed as if peace and nutriment from heaven subtly filter into me as I slowly hobble down these country lanes and across fields, in the good air— as I sit here in solitude with Nature—open, voiceless, mystic, far removed, yet palpable, eloquent Nature. I merge myself in the scene, in the perfect day. Hovering over the clear brook-water, I am sooth'd by its soft gurgle in one place, and the hoarser murmurs of its three-foot fall in another. Come, ye disconsolate, in whom any latent eligibility is left—come get the sure virtues of creek-shore, and wood and field. Two months (July and August, '77,) have I absorb'd them, and they begin to make a new man of me. Every day, seclusion—every day at least two or three hours of freedom, bathing, no talk, no bonds, no dress, no books, no *manners.*

Shall I tell you, reader, to what I attribute my already much-restored health? That I have been almost two years, off and on, without drugs and medicines, and daily in the open air. Last summer I found a particularly secluded little dell off one side by my creek, originally a large dug-out marl-pit, now abandon'd, fill'd with bushes, trees, grass, a group of willows, a straggling bank, and a spring of delicious water running right through the middle of it, with two or three little cascades. Here I retreated every hot day, and follow it up this summer. Here I realize the meaning of that old fellow who said he was seldom less alone than when alone. Never before did I get so close to Nature; never before did she come so close to me. By old habit, I pencill'd down from to time to time, almost automatically, moods, sights, hours, tints and outlines, on the spot. Let me specially record the satisfaction of this current forenoon, so serene and primitive, so conventionally exceptional, natural.

An hour or so after breakfast I wended my way down to the recesses of the aforesaid dell, which I and certain thrushes, cat-birds, &c., had all to ourselves. A light south-west wind was blowing through the tree-tops. It was just the place and time for my Adamic air-bath and flesh-brushing from head to foot. So hanging clothes on a rail nearby, keeping old broad-brim straw on head and easy shoes on feet, hav'n't I had a good time the last two hours! First with the stiff-elastic bristles rasping arms, breast, sides, till they turn'd scarlet—then partially bathing in the clear waters of the running brook—taking everything very leisurely, with many rests and pauses—stepping about barefooted every few minutes now and then in some neighboring black ooze, for unctuous mud-bath to my feet—a brief second and third rinsing in the crystal running waters—rubbing with the fragrant towel—slow negligent promenades on the turf up and down in the sun, varied with occasional rests, and further frictions of the bristle-brush—sometimes carrying my portable chair with me from place to place, as my range is quite extensive here, nearly a hundred rods, feeling quite secure from intrusion, (and that indeed I am not at all nervous about, if it accidentally happens.)

As I walk'd slowly over the grass, the sun shone out enough to show the shadow moving with me. Somehow I seem'd to get identity with each and every thing around me, in its condition. Nature was naked, and I was also. It was too lazy, soothing, and joyous-equable to speculate about. Yet I might have thought somehow in this vein: Perhaps the inner never lost rapport we hold with earth, light, air, trees, &c., is not to be realized through eyes and mind only, but through the whole corporeal body, which I will not have blinded or bandaged any more than the eyes. Sweet, sane, still Nakedness in

Nature!—ah if poor, sick, prurient humanity in cities might really know you once more! Is not nakedness then indecent? No, not inherently. It is your thought, your sophistication, your fear, your respectability, that is indecent. There come moods when these clothes of ours are not only too irksome to wear, but are themselves indecent. Perhaps indeed he or she to whom the free exhilarating extasy of nakedness in Nature has never been eligible (and how many thousands there are!) has not really known what purity is—nor what faith or art or health really is. (Probably the whole curriculum of first-class philosophy, beauty, heroism, form, illustrated by the old Hellenic race—the highest height and deepest depth known to civilization in those departments—came from their natural and religious idea of Nakedness.)

Many such hours, from time to time, the last two summers—I attribute my partial rehabilitation largely to them. Some good people may think it a feeble or half-crack'd way of spending one's time and thinking. May-be it is.

The Oaks and I

Sept. 5, '77.—I write this, 11 A.M., shelter'd under a dense oak by the bank, where I have taken refuge from a sudden rain. I came down here, (we had sulky drizzles all the morning, but an hour ago a lull,) for the before-mention'd daily and simple exercise I am fond of—to pull on that young hickory sapling out there—to sway and yield to its tough-limber upright stem—haply to get into my old sinews some of its elastic fibre and clear sap. I stand on the turf and take these health-pulls moderately and at intervals for nearly an hour, inhaling great draughts of fresh air. Wandering by the creek, I have three or four naturally favorable spots where I rest—besides a chair I lug with me and use for more deliberate occasions. At other spots convenient I have selected, besides the hickory just named, strong and limber boughs of beech or holly, in easy-reaching distance, for my natural gymnasia, for arms, chest, trunk-muscles. I can soon feel the sap and sinew rising through me, like mercury to heat. I hold on boughs or slender trees caressingly there in the sun and shade, wrestle with their innocent stalwartness—and *know* the virtue thereof passes from them into me. (Or may-be we inter-change—may-be the trees are more aware of it all than I ever thought.)

But now pleasantly imprison'd here under the big oak—the rain dripping, and the sky cover'd with leaden clouds—nothing but the pond on one side, and the other a spread of grass, spotted with the milky blossoms of the wild carrot—the sound of an axe wielded at some distant wood-pile—yet in this dull scene, (as most folks would call it,) why am I so (almost) happy here and alone? Why would any intrusion, even from people I like, spoil the charm? But am I alone? Doubtless there comes a time—perhaps it has come to me—when one feels through his whole being, and pronouncedly the emotional part, that identity between himself subjectively and Nature objectively which Schelling and Fichte are so fond of pressing. How it is I know not, but I often realize a presence here—in clear moods I am certain of it, and neither chemistry nor reasoning nor esthetics will give the least explanation. All the past two summers it has been strengthening and nourishing my sick body and soul, as never before. Thanks, invisible physician, for thy silent delicious medicine, thy day and night, thy waters and thy airs, the banks, the grass, the trees, and e'en the weeds!

A Quintette

While I have been kept by the rain under the shelter of my great oak, (perfectly dry and comfortable, to the rattle of the drops all around,) I have pencill'd off the mood of the hour in a little quintette, which I will give you:

At vacancy with Nature,
Acceptive and at ease,
Distilling the present hour,
Whatever, wherever it is,
And over the past, oblivion.

Can you get hold of it, reader dear? and how do you like it anyhow?

The First Frost—Mems

Where I was stopping I saw the first palpable frost, on my sunrise walk, October 6; all over the yet-green spread a light blue-gray veil, giving a new show to the entire landscape. I had but little time to notice it, for the sun rose cloudless and mellow-warm, and as I returned along the lane it had turn'd to glittering patches of wet. As I walk I notice the bursting pods of wild-cotton, (Indian hemp they call it here,) with flossy-silky contents, and dark red-brown seeds—a startled rabbit—I pull a handful of the balsamic life-everlasting and stuff it down in my trowsers-pocket for scent.

Three Young Men's Deaths

December 20.—Somehow I got thinking to-day of young men's deaths—not at all sadly or sentimentally, but gravely, realistically, perhaps a little artistically. Let me give the following three cases from budgets of personal memoranda, which I have been turning over, alone in my room, and resuming and dwelling on, this rainy afternoon. Who is there to whom the theme does not come home? Then I don't know how it may be to others, but to me not only is there nothing gloomy or depressing in such cases—on the contrary, as reminiscences, I find them soothing, bracing, tonic.

Erastus Haskell.—[I just transcribe verbatim from a letter written by myself in one of the army hospitals, 16 years ago, during the secession war.] *Washington, July 28, 1863.*—Dear M.,—I am writing this in the hospital, sitting by the side of a soldier, I do not expect to last many hours. His fate has been a hard one—he seems to be only about 19 or 20—Erastus Haskell, company K, 141st N. Y.—has been out about a year, and sick or half-sick more than half that time—has been down on the peninsula—was detail'd to go in the band as fifer-boy. While sick, the surgeon told him to keep up with the rest—(probably work'd and march'd too long.) He is a shy, and seems to me a very sensible boy—has fine manners—never complains—was sick down on the peninsula in an old storehouse—typhoid fever. The first week this July was brought up here—journey very bad, no accommodations, no nourishment, nothing but hard jolting, and exposure enough to make a well man sick; (these fearful journeys do the job for many)—arrived here July 11th—a silent dark-skinn'd Spanish-looking youth, with large very dark blue eyes, peculiar looking. Doctor F. here made light of his sickness—said he would recover soon, &c.; but I thought very different, and told F. so repeatedly; (I came near quarreling with him about it from the first)—but he laugh'd, and would not listen to me. About four days ago, I told Doctor he would in my opinion lose the boy without doubt—but F. again laugh'd at me. The next day he changed his opinion—I brought the head surgeon of the post—he said the boy would probably die, but they would make a hard fight for him.

The last two days he has been lying panting for breath—a pitiful sight. I have been with him some every day or night since he arrived. He suffers a great deal with the heat—says little or nothing—is flighty the last three days, at times—knows me always, however—calls me "Walter"—(sometimes calls the name over and over and over again, musingly, abstractedly, to himself.) His father lives at Breesport, Chemung county, N. Y., is a mechanic with large family—is a steady, religious man; his mother too is living. I have written to them, and shall write again to-day—Erastus has not receiv'd a word from home for months.

As I sit here writing to you, M., I wish you could see the whole scene. This young man lies within reach of me, flat on his back, his hands clasp'd across his breast, his thick black hair cut close; he is dozing, breathing hard, every breath a spasm—it looks so cruel. He is a noble youngster,—I consider him past all hope. Often there is no one with him for a long while. I am here as much as possible.

WILLIAM ALCOTT, fireman. *Camden, Nov., 1874.*—Last Monday afternoon his widow, mother, relatives, mates of the fire department, and his other friends, (I was one, only lately it is true, but our love grew fast and close, the days and nights of those eight weeks by the chair of rapid decline, and the bed of death,) gather'd to the funeral of this young man, who had grown up, and was well-known here. With nothing special, perhaps, to record, I would give a word or two to his memory. He seem'd to me not an inappropriate specimen in character and elements, of that bulk of the average good American race that ebbs and flows perennially beneath this scum of eructations on the surface. Always very quiet in manner, neat in person and dress, good temper'd—punctual and industrious at his work, till he could work no longer—he just lived his steady, square, unobtrusive life, in its own humble sphere, doubtless unconscious of itself. (Though I think there were currents of emotion and intellect undevelop'd beneath, far deeper than his acquaintances ever suspected—or than he himself ever did.) He was no talker. His troubles, when he had any, he kept to himself. As there was nothing querulous about him in life, he made no complaints during his last sickness. He was one of those persons that while his associates never thought of attributing any particular talent or grace to him, yet all insensibly, really, liked Billy Alcott.

I, too, loved him. At last, after being with him quite a good deal—after hours and days of panting for breath, much of the time unconscious, (for though the consumption that had been lurking in his system, once thoroughly started, made rapid progress, there was still great vitality in him, and indeed for four or five days he lay dying, before the close,) late on Wednesday night, Nov. 4th, where we surrounded his bed in silence, there came a lull—a longer drawn breath, a pause, a faint sigh—another—a weaker breath, another sigh—a pause again and just a tremble—and the face of the poor wasted young man (he was just 26,) fell gently over, in death, on my hand, on the pillow.

CHARLES CASWELL.—[I extract the following, verbatim, from a letter to me dated September 29, from my friend John Burroughs, at Esopus-on-Hudson, New York State.] S. was away when your picture came, attending his sick brother, Charles—who has since died—an event that has sadden'd me much. Charlie was younger than S., and a most attractive young fellow. He work'd at my father's, and had done so for two years. He was about the best specimen of a young country farm-hand I ever knew. You would have loved him. He was like one of your poems. With his great strength, his blond hair, his cheerfulness and contentment, his universal good will, and his silent manly ways, he was a youth hard to match. He was murder'd by an old doctor. He had typhoid fever, and the old fool bled him twice. He lived to wear out the fever, but had not strength to rally. He was out of his head nearly all the time. In the morning, as he died in the afternoon, S. was standing over him, when Charlie put up his arms around S.'s neck, and pull'd his face down and kiss'd him. S. said he knew then the end was near. (S. stuck to him day and night to the last.) When I was home in August, Charlie was cradling on the hill, and it was a picture to see him walk through the grain. All work seem'd play to him. He had no vices, any more than Nature has, and was belov'd by all who knew him.

I have written thus to you about him, for such young men belong to you; he was of your kind. I wish you could have known him. He had the sweetness of a child, and the strength and courage and readiness of a young Viking. His mother and father are poor; they have a rough, hard farm. His mother works in the field with her husband when the work presses. She has had twelve children.

February Days

February 7, 1878.—Glistening sun to-day, with slight haze, warm enough, and yet tart, as I sit here in the open air, down in my country retreat, under an old cedar. For two hours I have been idly wandering around the woods and pond, lugging my chair, picking out choice spots to sit awhile—then up and slowly on again. All is peace here. Of course, none of the summer noises or vitality; to-day hardly even the winter ones. I amuse myself by exercising my voice in recitations, and in ringing the changes on all the vocal and alphabetical sounds. Not even an echo; only the cawing of a solitary crow, flying at some distance. The pond is one bright, flat spread, without a ripple—a vast Claude Lorraine glass, in which I study the sky, the light, the leafless trees, and an occasional crow, with flapping wings, flying overhead. The brown fields have a few white patches of snow left.

Feb. 9.—After an hour's ramble, now retreating, resting, sitting close by the pond, in a warm nook, writing this, shelter'd from the breeze, just before noon. The *emotional* aspects and influences of Nature! I, too, like the rest, feel these modern tendencies (from all the prevailing intellections, literature and poems,) to turn everything to pathos, ennui, morbidity, dissatisfaction, death. Yet how clear it is to me that those are not the born results, influences of Nature at all, but of one's own distorted, sick or silly soul. Here, amid this wild, free scene, how healthy, how joyous, how clean and vigorous and sweet!

Mid-afternoon.—One of my nooks is south of the barn, and here I am sitting now, on a log, still basking in the sun, shielded from the wind. Near me are the cattle, feeding on corn-stalks. Occasionally a cow or the young bull (how handsome and bold he is!) scratches and munches the far end of the log on which I sit. The fresh milky odor is quite perceptible, also the perfume of hay from the barn. The perpetual rustle of dry corn-stalks, the low sough of the wind round the barn gables, the grunting of pigs, the distant whistle of a locomotive, and occasional crowing of chanticleers, are the sounds.

Feb. 19.—Cold and sharp last night—clear and not much wind—the full moon shining, and a fine spread of constellations and little and big stars—Sirius very bright, rising early, preceded by many-orb'd Orion, glittering, vast, sworded, and chasing with his dog. The earth hard frozen, and a stiff glare of ice over the pond. Attracted by the calm splendor of the night, I attempted a short walk, but was driven back by the cold. Too severe for me also at 9 o'clock, when I came out this morning, so I turn'd back again. But now, near noon, I have walk'd down the lane, basking all the way in the sun (this farm has a pleasant southerly exposure,) and here I am, seated under the lee of a bank, close by the water. There are blue-birds already flying about, and I hear much chirping and twittering and two or three real songs, sustain'd quite awhile, in the mid-day brilliance and warmth. (There! that is a true carol, coming out boldly and repeatedly, as if the singer meant it.) Then as the noon strengthens, the reedy trill of the robin—to my ear the most cheering of bird-notes. At intervals, like bars and breaks (out of the low murmur that in any scene, however quiet, is never entirely absent to a delicate ear,) the occasional crunch and cracking of the ice-glare congeal'd over the creek, as it gives way to the sunbeams—sometimes with low sigh—sometimes with indignant, obstinate tug and snort.

(Robert Burns says in one of his letters: "There is scarcely any earthly object gives me more—I do not know if I should call it pleasure—but something which exalts me—something which enraptures me—than to walk in the shelter'd side of a wood in a cloudy winter day, and hear the stormy wind howling among the trees, and raving over the plain. It is my best season of devotion." Some of his most characteristic poems were composed in such scenes and seasons.)

A Meadow Lark

March 16.—Fine, clear, dazzling morning, the sun an hour high, the air just tart enough. What a stamp in advance my whole day receives from the song of that meadow lark perch'd on a fence-stake twenty rods distant! Two or three liquid-simple notes, repeated at intervals, full of careless happiness and hope. With its peculiar shimmering slow progress and rapid-noiseless action of the wings, it flies on a ways, lights on another stake, and so on to another, shimmering and singing many minutes.

Sundown Lights

May 6, 5 P.M.—This is the hour for strange effects in light and shade—enough to make a colorist go delirious—long spokes of molten silver sent horizontally through the trees (now in their brightest tenderest green,) each leaf and branch of endless foliage a lit-up miracle, then lying all prone on the youthful-ripe, interminable grass, and giving the blades not only aggregate but individual splendor, in ways unknown to any other hour. I have particular spots where I get these effects in their perfection. One broad splash lies on the water, with many a rippling twinkle, offset by the rapidly deepening black-green murky-transparent shadows behind, and at intervals all along the banks. These, with great shafts of horizontal fire thrown among the trees and along the grass as the sun lowers, give effects more and more peculiar, more and more superb, unearthly, rich and dazzling.

Thoughts under an Oak—A Dream

June 2.—This is the fourth day of a dark northeast storm, wind and rain. Day before yesterday was my birthday. I have now enter'd on my 60th year. Every day of the storm, protected by overshoes and a waterproof blanket, I regularly come down to the pond, and ensconce myself under the lee of the great oak; I am here now writing these lines. The dark smoke-color'd clouds roll in furious silence athwart the sky; the soft green leaves dangle all round me; the wind steadily keeps up its hoarse, soothing music over my head—Nature's mighty whisper. Seated here in solitude I have been musing over my life—connecting events, dates, as links of a chain, neither sadly nor cheerily, but somehow, to-day here under the oak, in the rain, in an unusually matter-of-fact spirit.

But my great oak—sturdy, vital, green—five feet thick at the butt. I sit a great deal near or under him. Then the tulip tree near by—the Apollo of the woods—tall and graceful, yet robust and sinewy, inimitable in hang of foliage and throwing-out of limb; as if the beauteous, vital, leafy creature could walk, if it only would. (I had a sort of dream-trance the other day, in which I saw my favorite trees step out and promenade up, down and around, very curiously—with a whisper from one, leaning down as he pass'd me, *We do all this on the present occasion, exceptionally, just for you.*)

Clover and Hay Perfume

July 3d, 4th, 5th.—Clear, hot, favorable weather—has been a good summer—the growth of clover and grass now generally mow'd. The familiar delicious perfume fills the barns and lanes. As you go along you see the fields of grayish white slightly tinged with yellow, the loosely stack'd grain, the slow-moving wagons passing, and farmers in the fields with stout boys pitching and loading the sheaves. The corn is about beginning to tassel. All over the middle and southern states the spear-shaped battalia, multitudinous, curving, flaunting—long, glossy, dark-green plumes for the great horseman, earth. I hear the cheery notes of my old acquaintance Tommy quail; but too late for the whip-poor-will, (though I heard one solitary lingerer night before last.) I watch the broad majestic flight of a turkey-buzzard, sometimes high up, sometimes low enough to see the lines of his form, even his spread quills, in relief against the sky. Once or twice lately I have seen an eagle here at early candle-light flying low.

An Unknown

June 15.—To-day I noticed a new large bird, size of a nearly grown hen—a haughty, white-bodied dark-wing'd hawk—I suppose a hawk from his bill and general look—only he had a clear, loud, quite musical, sort of bell-like call, which he repeated again and again, at intervals, from a lofty dead tree-top, overhanging the water. Sat there a long time, and I on the opposite bank watching him. Then he darted down, skimming pretty close to the stream—rose slowly, a magnificent sight, and sail'd with steady wide-spread wings, no flapping at all, up and down the pond two or three times, near me, in circles in clear sight, as if for my delectation. Once he came quite close over my head; I saw plainly his hook'd bill and hard restless eyes.

Bird-Whistling

How much music (wild, simple, savage, doubtless, but so tart-sweet,) there is in mere whistling. It is four-fifths of the utterance of birds. There are all sorts and styles. For the last half-hour, now, while I have been sitting here, some feather'd fellow away off in the bushes has been repeating over and over again what I may call a kind of throbbing whistle. And now a bird about the robin size has just appear'd, all mulberry red, flitting among the bushes—head, wings, body, deep red, not very bright—no song, as I have heard. *4 o'clock:* There is a real concert going on around me—a dozen different birds pitching in with a will. There have been occasional rains, and the growths all show its vivifying influences. As I finish this, seated on a log close by the pond-edge, much chirping and trilling in the distance, and a feather'd recluse in the woods near by is singing deliciously—not many notes, but full of music of almost human sympathy—continuing for a long, long while.

Horse-Mint

Aug. 22.—Not a human being, and hardly the evidence of one, in sight. After my brief semi-daily bath, I sit here for a bit, the brook musically brawling, to the chromatic tones of a fretful cat-bird somewhere off in the bushes. On my walk hither two hours since, through fields and the old lane, I stopt to view, now the sky, now the mile-off woods on the hill, and now the apple orchards. What a contrast from New York's or Philadelphia's streets! Everywhere great patches of dingy-blossom'd horse-mint wafting a spicy odor through the air, (especially evenings.) Everywhere the flowering boneset, and the rose-bloom of the wild bean.

Three of Us

July 14.—My two kingfishers still haunt the pond. In the bright sun and breeze and perfect temperature of to-day, noon, I am sitting here by one of the gurgling brooks, dipping a French water-pen in the limpid crystal, and using it to write these lines, again watching the feather'd twain, as they fly and sport athwart the water, so close, almost touching into its surface. Indeed there seem to be three of us. For nearly an hour I indolently look and join them while they dart and turn and take their airy gambols, sometimes far up the creek disappearing for a few moments, and then surely returning again, and performing most of their flight within sight of me, as if they knew I appreciated and absorb'd their vitality, spirituality, faithfulness, and the rapid, vanishing, delicate lines of moving yet quiet electricity they draw for me across the spread of the grass, the trees, and the blue sky. While the brook babbles, babbles, and the shadows of the boughs dapple in the sunshine around me, and the cool west by-nor'-west wind faintly soughs in the thick bushes and tree tops.

Among the objects of beauty and interest now beginning to appear quite plentifully in this secluded spot, I notice the humming-bird, the dragon-fly with its wings of slate-color'd gauze, and many varieties of beautiful and plain butterflies, idly flapping among the plants and wild posies. The mullein has shot up out of its nest of broad leaves, to a tall stalk towering sometimes five or six feet high, now studded with knobs of golden blossoms. The milk-weed, (I see a great gorgeous creature of gamboge and black lighting on one as I write,) is in flower, with its delicate red fringe; and there are profuse clusters of a feathery blossom waving in the wind on taper stems. I see lots of these and much else in every direction, as I saunter or sit. For the last half hour a bird has persistently kept up a simple, sweet, melodious song, from the bushes. (I have a positive conviction that some of these birds sing, and others fly and flirt about here, for my especial benefit.)

Death of William Cullen Bryant

New York City.—Came on from West Philadelphia, June 13, in the 2 P.M. train to Jersey city, and so across and to my friends, Mr. and Mrs. J. H. J., and their large house, large family (and large hearts,) amid which I feel at home, at peace—away up on Fifth avenue, near Eighty-sixth street, quiet, breezy, overlooking the dense woody fringe of the park—plenty of space and sky, birds chirping, and air comparatively fresh and odorless. Two hours before starting, saw the announcement of William Cullen Bryant's funeral, and felt a strong desire to attend. I had known Mr. Bryant over thirty years ago, and he had been markedly kind to me. Off and on, along that time for years as they pass'd, we met and chatted together. I thought him very sociable in his way, and a man to become attach'd to. We were both walkers, and when I work'd in Brooklyn he several times came over, middle of afternoons, and we took rambles miles long, till dark, out towards Bedford or Flatbush, in company. On these occasions he gave me clear accounts of scenes in Europe—the cities, looks, architecture, art, especially Italy—where he had travel'd a good deal.

June 14.—The Funeral.—And so the good, stainless, noble old citizen and poet lies in the closed coffin there—and this is his funeral. A solemn, impressive, simple scene, to spirit and senses. The remarkable gathering of gray heads, celebrities—the finely render'd anthem, and other music—the church, dim even now at approaching noon, in its light from the mellow-stain'd windows—the pronounc'd eulogy on the bard who loved Nature so fondly, and sung so well her shows and seasons—ending with these appropriate well-known lines:

> I gazed upon the glorious sky,
>   And the green mountains round,
> And thought that when I came to lie
>   At rest within the ground,
> 'Twere pleasant that in flowery June,
> When brooks send up a joyous tune,
>   And groves a cheerful sound,
> The sexton's hand, my grave to make,
> The rich green mountain turf should break.

Jaunt up the Hudson

June 20th.—On the "Mary Powell," enjoy'd everything beyond precedent. The delicious tender summer day, just warm enough—the constantly changing but ever beautiful panorama on both sides of the river—(went up near a hundred miles)—the high straight walls of the stony Palisades—beautiful Yonkers, and beautiful Irvington—the never-ending hills, mostly in rounded lines, swathed with verdure,—the distant turns, like great shoulders in blue veils—the frequent gray and brown of the tall-rising rocks—the river itself, now narrowing, now expanding—the white sails of the many sloops, yachts, &c., some near, some in the distance—the rapid succession of handsome villages and cities, (our boat is a swift traveler, and makes few stops)—the Race—picturesque West Point, and indeed all along—the costly and often turreted mansions forever showing in some cheery light color, through the woods—make up the scene.

Happiness and Raspberries

June 21.—Here I am, on the west bank of the Hudson, 80 miles north of New York, near Esopus, at the handsome, roomy, honeysuckle-and-rose-embower'd cottage of John Burroughs. The place, the perfect June days and nights, (leaning toward crisp and cool,) the hospitality of J. and Mrs. B., the air, the fruit, (especially my favorite dish, currants and raspberries, mixed, sugar'd, fresh and ripe from the bushes—I pick 'em myself)—the room I occupy at night, the perfect bed, the window giving an ample view of the Hudson and the opposite shores, so wonderful toward sunset, and the rolling music of the RR. trains, far over there—the peaceful rest—the early Venus-heralded dawn—the noiseless splash of sunrise, the light and warmth indescribably glorious, in which, (soon as the sun is well up,) I have a capital rubbing and rasping with the flesh-brush—with an extra scour on the back by Al. J., who is here with us—all inspiriting my invalid frame with new life, for the day. Then, after some whiffs of morning air, the delicious coffee of Mrs. B., with the cream, strawberries, and many substantials, for breakfast.

A Specimen Tramp Family

June 22.—This afternoon we went out (J. B., Al. and I) on quite a drive around the country. The scenery, the perpetual stone fences, (some venerable old fellows, dark-spotted with lichens)—the many fine locust-trees—the runs of brawling water, often over descents of rock—these, and lots else. It is lucky the roads are first-rate here, (as they are,) for it is up or down hill everywhere, and sometimes steep enough. B. has a tip-top horse, strong, young, and both gentle and fast. There is a great deal of waste land and hills on the river edge of Ulster county, with a wonderful luxuriance of wild flowers and bushes—and it seems to me I never saw more vitality of trees—eloquent hemlocks, plenty of locusts and fine maples, and the balm of Gilead, giving out aroma. In the fields and along the road-sides unusual crops of the tall-stemm'd wild daisy, white as milk and yellow as gold.

We pass'd quite a number of tramps, singly or in couples—one squad, a family in a rickety one-horse wagon, with some baskets evidently their work and trade—the man seated on a low board, in front, driving—the gauntish woman by his side, with a baby well bundled in her arms, its little red feet and lower legs sticking out right towards us as we pass'd—and in the wagon behind, we saw two (or three) crouching little children. It was a queer, taking, rather sad picture. If I had been alone and on foot, I should have stopp'd and held confab. But on our return nearly two hours afterward, we found them a ways further along the same road, in a lonesome open spot, haul'd aside, unhitch'd, and evidently going to camp for the night. The freed horse was not far off, quietly cropping the grass. The man was busy at the wagon, the boy had gather'd some dry wood, and was making a fire—and as we went a little further we met the woman afoot. I could not see her face, in its great sun-bonnet, but somehow her figure and gait told misery, terror, destitution. She had the rag-bundled, half-starv'd infant still in her arms, and in her hands held two or three baskets, which she had evidently taken to the next house for sale. A little barefoot five-year old girl-child, with fine eyes, trotted behind her, clutching her gown. We stopp'd, asking about the baskets, which we bought. As we paid the money, she kept her face hidden in the recesses of her bonnet. Then as we started, and stopp'd again, Al., (whose sympathies were evidently arous'd,) went back to the camping group to get another basket. He caught a look of her face, and talk'd with her a little. Eyes, voice and manner were those of a corpse, animated by electricity. She was quite young—the man she was traveling with, middle-aged. Poor woman—what story was it, out of her fortunes, to account for that inexpressibly scared way, those glassy eyes, and that hollow voice?

Manhattan from the Bay

June 25.—Returned to New York last night. Out to-day on the waters for a sail in the wide bay, southeast of Staten island—a rough, tossing ride, and a free sight—the long stretch of Sandy Hook, the highlands of Navesink, and the many vessels outward and inward bound. We came up through the midst of all, in the full sun. I especially enjoy'd the last hour or two. A moderate sea-breeze had set in; yet over the city, and the waters adjacent, was a thin haze, concealing nothing, only adding to the beauty. From my point of view, as I write amid the soft breeze, with a sea-temperature, surely nothing on earth of its kind can go beyond this show. To the left the North river with its far vista—nearer, three or four war-ships, anchor'd peacefully—the Jersey side, the banks of Weehawken, the Palisades, and the gradually receding blue, lost in the distance—to the right the East river—the mast-hemm'd shores—the grand obelisk-like towers of the bridge, one on either side, in haze, yet plainly defin'd, giant brothers twain, throwing free graceful interlinking loops high across the tumbled tumultuous current below—(the tide is just changing to its ebb)—the broad water-spread everywhere crowded—no, not crowded, but thick as stars in the sky—with all sorts and sizes of sail and steam vessels, plying ferry-boats, arriving and departing coasters, great ocean Dons, iron-black, modern, magnificent in size and power, fill'd with their incalculable value of human life and precious merchandise—with here and there, above all, those daring, careening things of grace and wonder, those white and shaded swift-darting fish-birds, (I wonder if shore or sea elsewhere can outvie them,) ever with their slanting spars, and fierce, pure, hawk-like beauty and motion—first-class New York sloop or schooner yachts, sailing, this fine day, the free sea in a good wind. And rising out of the midst, tall-topt, ship-hemm'd, modern, American, yet strangely oriental, V-shaped Manhattan, with its compact mass, its spires, its cloud-touching edifices group'd at the centre—the green of the trees, and all the white, brown and gray of the architecture well blended, as I see it, under a miracle of limpid sky, delicious light of heaven above, and June haze on the surface below.

Human and Heroic New York

The general subjective view of New York and Brooklyn—(will not the time hasten when the two shall be municipally united in one, and named Manhattan?)—what I may call the human interior and exterior of these great seething oceanic populations, as I get it in this visit, is to me best of all. After an absence of many years, (I went away at the outbreak of the secession war, and have never been back to stay since,) again I resume with curiosity the crowds, the streets I knew so well, Broadway, the ferries, the west side of the city, democratic Bowery—human appearances and manners as seen in all these, and along the wharves, and in the perpetual travel of the horse-cars, or the crowded excursion steamers, or in Wall and Nassau streets by day—in the places of amusement at night—

bubbling and whirling and moving like its own environment of waters—endless humanity in all phases—Brooklyn also—taken in for the last three weeks. No need to specify minutely—enough to say that (making all allowances for the shadows and side-streaks of a million-headed-city) the brief total of the impressions, the human qualities, of these vast cities, is to me comforting, even heroic, beyond statement. Alertness, generally fine physique, clear eyes that look straight at you, a singular combination of reticence and self-possession, with good nature and friendliness—a prevailing range of according manners, taste and intellect, surely beyond any elsewhere upon earth—and a palpable outcropping of that personal comradeship I look forward to as the subtlest, strongest future hold of this many-item'd Union—are not only constantly visible here in these mighty channels of men, but they form the rule and average. To-day, I should say—defiant of cynics and pessimists, and with a full knowledge of all their exceptions—an appreciative and perceptive study of the current humanity of New York gives the directest proof yet of successful Democracy, and of the solution of that paradox, the eligibility of the free and fully developed individual with the paramount aggregate. In old age, lame and sick, pondering for years on many a doubt and danger for this republic of ours—fully aware of all that can be said on the other side—I find in this visit to New York, and the daily contact and rapport with its myriad people, on the scale of the oceans and tides, the best, most effective medicine my soul has yet partaken—the grandest physical habitat and surroundings of land and water the globe affords—namely, Manhattan island and Brooklyn, which the future shall join in one city—city of superb democracy, amid superb surroundings.

Hours for the Soul

July 22d, 1878.—Living down in the country again. A wonderful conjunction of all that goes to make those sometime miracle-hours after sunset—so near and yet so far. Perfect, or nearly perfect days, I notice, are not so very uncommon; but the combinations that make perfect nights are few, even in a life time. We have one of those perfections to-night. Sunset left things pretty clear; the larger stars were visible soon as the shades allow'd. A while after 8, three or four great black clouds suddenly rose, seemingly from different points, and sweeping with broad swirls of wind but no thunder, underspread the orbs from view everywhere, and indicated a violent heat-storm. But without storm, clouds, blackness and all, sped and vanish'd as suddenly as they had risen; and from a little after 9 till 11 the atmosphere and the whole show above were in that state of exceptional clearness and glory just alluded to. In the northwest turned the Great Dipper with its pointers round the Cynosure. A little south of east the constellation of the Scorpion was fully up, with red Antares glowing in its neck; while dominating, majestic Jupiter swam, an hour and a half risen, in the east—(no moon till after 11.) A large part of the sky seem'd just laid in great splashes of phosphorus. You could look deeper in, farther through, than usual; the orbs thick as heads of wheat in a field. Not that there was any special brilliancy either—nothing near as sharp as I have seen of keen winter nights, but a curious general luminousness throughout to sight, sense, and soul. The latter had much to do with it. (I am convinced there are hours of Nature, especially of the atmosphere, mornings and evenings, address'd to the soul. Night transcends, for that purpose, what the proudest day can do.) Now, indeed, if never before, the heavens declared the glory of God. It was to the full the sky of the Bible, of Arabia, of the prophets, and of the oldest poems. There, in abstraction and stillness, (I had gone off by myself to absorb the scene, to have the spell unbroken,) the copiousness, the removedness, vitality, loose-clear-crowdedness, of that stellar concave spreading overhead, softly absorb'd into me, rising so free, interminably high, stretching east, west, north, south—and I, though but a point in the centre below, embodying all.

As if for the first time, indeed, creation noiselessly sank into and through me its placid and untellable lesson, beyond—O, so infinitely beyond !—anything from art, books, sermons, or from science, old or new. The spirit's hour—religion's hour—the visible suggestion of God in space and time—now once definitely indicated, if never again. The untold pointed at—the heavens all paved with it. The Milky Way, as if some superhuman symphony, some ode of universal vagueness, disdaining syllable and sound—a flashing glance of Deity, address'd to the soul. All silently—the indescribable night and stars—far off and silently.

THE DAWN.—*July 23.*—This morning, between one and two hours before sunrise, a spectacle wrought on the same background, yet of quite different beauty and meaning. The moon well up in the heavens, and past her half, is shining brightly—the air and sky of that cynical-clear, Minerva-like quality, virgin cool—not the weight of sentiment or mystery, or passion's ecstasy indefinable—not the religious sense, the varied All, distill'd and sublimated into one, of the night just described. Every star now clear-cut, showing for just what it is, there in the colorless ether. The character of the heralded morning, ineffably sweet and fresh and limpid, but for the esthetic sense alone, and for purity without sentiment. I have itemized the night—but dare I attempt the cloudless dawn? (What subtle tie is this between one's soul and the break of day? Alike, and yet no two nights or morning shows ever exactly alike.) Preceded by an immense star, almost unearthly in its effusion of white splendor, with two or three long unequal spoke-rays of diamond radiance, shedding down through the fresh morning air below—an hour of this, and then the sunrise.

THE EAST.—What a subject for a poem! Indeed, where else a more pregnant, more splendid one? Where one more idealistic-real, more subtle, more sensuous-delicate? The East, answering all lands, all ages, peoples; touching all senses, here, immediate, now—and yet so indescribably far off—such retrospect! The East—long-stretching—so losing itself—the orient, the gardens of Asia, the womb of history and song—forth-issuing all those strange, dim cavalcades—

> Florid with blood, pensive, rapt with musings, hot with passion,
> Sultry with perfume, with ample and flowing garments,
> With sunburnt visage, intense soul and glittering eyes.

Always the East—old, how incalculably old! And yet here the same—ours yet, fresh as a rose, to every morning, every life, to-day—and always will be.

Sept. 17.—Another presentation—same theme—just before sunrise again, (a favorite hour with me.) The clear gray sky, a faint glow in the dull liver-color of the east, the cool fresh odor and the moisture—the cattle and horses off there grazing in the fields—the star Venus again, two hours high. For sounds, the chirping of crickets in the grass, the clarion of chanticleer, and the distant cawing of an early crow. Quietly over the dense fringe of cedars and pines rises that dazzling, red, transparent disk of flame, and the low sheets of white vapor roll and roll into dissolution.

THE MOON.—*May 18.*—I went to bed early last night, but found myself waked shortly after 12, and, turning awhile sleepless and mentally feverish, I rose, dress'd myself, sallied forth and walk'd down the lane. The full moon, some three or four hours up—a sprinkle of light and less-light clouds just lazily moving—Jupiter an hour high in the east, and here and there throughout the heavens a random star appearing and disappearing. So, beautifully veil'd and varied—the air, with that early-summer perfume, not at all damp or raw—at times Luna languidly emerging in richest brightness for minutes, and then partially envelop'd again. Far off a whip-poor-will plied his notes incessantly. It was that silent time between 1 and 3.

The rare nocturnal scene, how soon it sooth'd and pacified me! Is there not something about the moon, some relation or reminder, which no poem or literature has yet caught? (In very old and primitive ballads I have come across lines or asides that suggest it.) After a while the clouds mostly clear'd, and as the moon swam on, she carried, shimmering and shifting, delicate color-effects of pellucid green and tawny vapor. Let me conclude this part with an extract, (some writer in the "Tribune," May 16, 1878:)

> No one ever gets tired of the moon. Goddess that she is by dower of her eternal beauty, she is a true woman by her tact—knows the charm of being seldom seen, of coming by surprise and staying but a little while; never wears the same dress two nights running, nor all night the same way; commends herself to the matter-of-fact people by her usefulness, and makes her uselessness adored by poets, artists, and

all lovers in all lands; lends herself to every symbolism and to every emblem; is Diana's bow and Venus's mirror and Mary's throne; is a sickle, a scarf, an eyebrow, his face or her face, as look'd at by her or by him; is the madman's hell, the poet's heaven, the baby's toy, the philosopher's study; and while her admirers follow her footsteps, and hang on her lovely looks, she knows how to keep her woman's secret—her other side—unguess'd and unguessable.

Furthermore.—February 19, 1880.—Just before 10 P.M. cold and entirely clear again, the show overhead, bearing southwest, of wonderful and crowded magnificence. The moon in her third quarter—the clusters of the Hyades and Pleiades, with the planet Mars between—in full crossing sprawl in the sky the great Egyptian X, (Sirius, Procyon, and the main stars in the constellations of the Ship, the Dove, and of Orion;) just north of east Bootes, and in his knee Arcturus, an hour high, mounting the heaven, ambitiously large and sparkling, as if he meant to challenge with Sirius the stellar supremacy.

With the sentiment of the stars and moon such nights I get all the free margins and indefiniteness of music or poetry, fused in geometry's utmost exactness.

Straw-Color'd and Other Psyches

Aug. 4.—A pretty sight! Where I sit in the shade—a warm day, the sun shining from cloudless skies, the forenoon well advanc'd—I look over a ten-acre field of luxuriant clover-hay, (the second crop)—the livid-ripe red blossoms and dabs of August brown thickly spotting the prevailing dark-green. Over all flutter myriads of light-yellow butterflies, mostly skimming along the surface, dipping and oscillating, giving a curious animation to the scene. The beautiful, spiritual insects! straw-color'd Psyches! Occasionally one of them leaves his mates, and mounts, perhaps spirally, perhaps in a straight line in the air, fluttering up, up, till literally out of sight. In the lane as I came along just now I noticed one spot, ten feet square or so, where more than a hundred had collected, holding a revel, a gyration-dance, or butterfly good-time, winding and circling, down and across, but always keeping within the limits.

The little creatures have come out all of a sudden the last few days, and are now very plentiful. As I sit outdoors, or walk, I hardly look around without somewhere seeing two (always two) fluttering through the air in amorous dalliance. Then their inimitable color, their fragility, peculiar motion—and that strange, frequent way of one leaving the crowd and mounting up, up in the free ether, and apparently never returning. As I look over the field, these yellow-wings everywhere mildly sparkling, many snowy blossoms of the wild carrot gracefully bending on their tall and taper stems—while for sounds, the distant guttural screech of a flock of guinea-hens comes shrilly yet somehow musically to my ears. And now a faint growl of heat-thunder in the north—and ever the low rising and falling wind-purr from the tops of the maples and willows.

Aug. 20.—Butterflies and butterflies, (taking the place of the bumble-bees of three months since, who have quite disappear'd,) continue to flit to and fro, all sorts, white, yellow, brown, purple—now and then some gorgeous fellow flashing lazily by on wings like artists' palettes dabb'd with every color. Over the breast of the pond I notice many white ones, crossing, pursuing their idle capricious flight. Near where I sit grows a tall-stemm'd weed topt with a profusion of rich scarlet blossoms, on which the snowy insects alight and dally, sometimes four or five of them at a time. By-and-by a humming-bird visits the same, and I watch him coming and going, daintily balancing and shimmering about. These white butterflies give new beautiful contrasts to the pure greens of the August foliage, (we have had some copious rains lately,) and over the glistening bronze of the pond-surface. You can tame even such insects; I have one big and handsome moth down here, knows and comes to me, likes me to hold him up on my extended hand.

Another Day, later.—A grand twelve-acre field of ripe cabbages with their prevailing hue of malachite green, and floating-flying over and among them in all directions myriads of these same white butterflies. As I came up the lane to-day I saw a living globe of the same, two to three feet in diameter, many scores cluster'd together and rolling along in the air, adhering to their ball-shape, six or eight feet above the ground.

A Night Remembrance

Aug. 25, 9–10 a.m.—I sit by the edge of the pond, everything quiet, the broad polish'd surface spread before me—the blue of the heavens and the white clouds reflected from it—and flitting across, now and then, the reflection of some flying bird. Last night I was down here with a friend till after midnight; everything a miracle of splendor—the glory of the stars, and the completely rounded moon—the passing clouds, silver and luminous-tawny—now and then masses of vapory illuminated scud—and silently by my side my dear friend. The shades of the trees, and patches of moonlight on the grass—the softly blowing breeze, and just-palpable odor of the neighboring ripening corn—the indolent and spiritual night, inexpressibly rich, tender, suggestive—something altogether to filter through one's soul, and nourish and feed and soothe the memory long afterwards.

Wild Flowers

This has been and is yet a great season for wild flowers; oceans of them line the roads through the woods, border the edges of the water-runlets, grow all along the old fences, and are scatter'd in profusion over the fields. An eight-petal'd blossom of gold-yellow, clear and bright, with a brown tuft in the middle, nearly as large as a silver half-dollar, is very common; yesterday on a long drive I noticed it thickly lining the borders of the brooks everywhere. Then there is a beautiful weed cover'd with blue flowers, (the blue of the old Chinese teacups treasur'd by our grand-aunts,) I am continually stopping to admire—a little larger than a dime, and very plentiful. White, however, is the prevailing color. The wild carrot I have spoken of; also the fragrant life-everlasting. But there are all hues and beauties, especially on the frequent tracts of half-open scrub-oak and dwarf-cedar hereabout—wild asters of all colors. Notwithstanding the frost-touch the hardy little chaps maintain themselves in all their bloom. The tree-leaves, too, some of them are beginning to turn yellow or drab or dull green. The deep wine-color of the sumachs and gum-trees is already visible, and the straw-color of the dog-wood and beech. Let me give the names of some of these perennial blossoms and friendly weeds I have made acquaintance with hereabout one season or another in my walks:

wild azalea,
wild honeysuckle,
wild roses,
golden rod,
larkspur,
early crocus,
sweet flag, (great patches of it,)
creeper, trumpet-flower,
scented marjoram,
snakeroot,
Solomon's seal,
sweet balm,
mint, (great plenty,)
wild geranium,
wild heliotrope,
burdock,
dandelions,
yarrow,
coreopsis,
wild pea,
woodbine,
elderberry,
poke-weed,
sun-flower,
chamomile,
violets,
clematis,
bloodroot,
swamp magnolia,
milk-weed,
wild daisy, (plenty,)
wild chrysanthemum.

A Civility Too Long Neglected

The foregoing reminds me of something. As the individualities I would mainly portray have certainly been slighted by folks who make pictures, volumes, poems, out of them—as a faint testimonial of my own gratitude for many hours of peace and comfort in half-sickness, (and not by any means sure but they will somehow get wind of the compliment,) I hereby dedicate the last half of these Specimen Days to the

bees,
black-birds,
dragon-flies,
pond-turtles,
mulleins, tansy, peppermint,
moths (great and little, some splendid fellows,)
glow-worms, (swarming millions of them indescribably strange and beautiful at night over the pond and creek,)
water-snakes,
crows,
millers,
mosquitoes,
butterflies,
wasps and hornets,
cat birds (and all other birds,)
cedars,
tulip-trees (and all other trees,)
and to the spots and memories of those days, and of the creek.

Delaware River—Days and Nights

April 5, 1879.—With the return of spring to the skies, airs, waters of the Delaware, return the sea-gulls. I never tire of watching their broad and easy flight, in spirals, or as they oscillate with slow unflapping wings, or look down with curved beak, or dipping to the water after food. The crows, plenty enough all through the winter, have vanish'd with the ice. Not one of them now to be seen. The steamboats have again come forth—bustling up, handsome, freshly painted, for summer work—the Columbia, the Edwin Forrest, (the Republic not yet out,) the Reybold, the Nelly White, the Twilight, the Ariel, the Warner, the Perry, the Taggart, the Jersey Blue—even the hulky old Trenton—not forgetting those saucy little bull-pups of the current, the steamtugs.

But let me bunch and catalogue the affair—the river itself, all the way from the sea—cape Island on one side and Henlopen light on the other—up the broad bay north, and so to Philadelphia, and on further to Trenton;—the sights I am most familiar with, (as I live a good part of the time in Camden, I view matters from that outlook)—the great arrogant, black, full-freighted ocean steamers, inward or outward bound—the ample width here between the two cities, intersected by Windmill island—an occasional man-of-war, sometimes a foreigner, at anchor, with her guns and portholes, and the boats, and the brown-faced sailors, and the regular oar-strokes, and the gay crowds of "visiting day"—the frequent large and handsome three-masted schooners, (a favorite style of marine build, hereabout of late years,) some of them new and very jaunty, with their white-gray sails and yellow pine spars—the sloops dashing along in a fair wind—(I see one now, coming up, under broad canvas, her gaff-topsail shining in the sun, high and picturesque—what a thing of beauty amid the sky and waters!)—the crowded wharf-slips along the city—the flags of different nationalities, the sturdy English cross on its ground of blood, the French tricolor, the banner of the great North German empire, and the Italian and the Spanish colors—sometimes, of an afternoon, the whole scene enliven'd by a fleet of yachts, in a half calm, lazily returning from a race down at Gloucester;—the neat, rakish, revenue steamer "Hamilton" in mid-stream, with her perpendicular stripes flaunting aft—and, turning the eyes north, the long ribands of fleecy-white steam, or dingy-black smoke, stretching far, fan-shaped, slanting diagonally across from the Kensington or Richmond shores, in the west-by-south-west wind.

Scenes on Ferry and River—Last Winter's Nights

Then the Camden ferry. What exhilaration, change, people, business, by day. What soothing, silent, wondrous hours, at night, crossing on the boat, most all to myself—pacing the deck, alone, forward or aft. What communion with the waters, the air, the exquisite *chiaroscuro*— the sky and stars, that speak no word, nothing to the intellect, yet so eloquent, so communicative to the soul. And the ferry men—little they know how much they have been to me, day and night—how many spells of listlessness, ennui, debility, they and their hardy ways have dispell'd. And the pilots—captains Hand, Walton, and Giberson by day, and captain Olive at night; Eugene Crosby, with his strong young arm so often supporting, circling, convoying me over the gaps of the bridge, through impediments, safely aboard. Indeed all my ferry friends—captain Frazee the superintendent, Lindell, Hiskey, Fred Rauch, Price, Watson, and a dozen more. And the ferry itself, with its queer scenes—sometimes children suddenly born in the waiting-houses (an actual fact—and more than once)—sometimes a masquerade party, going over at night, with a band of music, dancing and whirling like mad on the broad deck, in their fantastic dresses; sometimes the astronomer, Mr. Whitall, (who posts me up in points about the stars by a living lesson there and then, and answering every question)—sometimes a prolific family group, eight, nine, ten, even twelve! (Yesterday, as I cross'd, a mother, father, and eight children, waiting in the ferry-house, bound westward somewhere.)

I have mention'd the crows. I always watch them from the boats. They play quite a part in the winter scenes on the river, by day. Their black splatches are seen in relief against the snow and ice everywhere at that season—sometimes flying and flapping—sometimes on little or larger cakes, sailing up or down the stream. One day the river was mostly clear—only a single long ridge of broken ice making a narrow stripe by itself, running along down the current for over a mile, quite rapidly. On this white stripe the crows were congregated, hundreds of them—a funny procession—("half mourning" was the comment of some one.)

Then the reception room, for passengers waiting—life illustrated thoroughly. Take a March picture I jotted there two or three weeks since. Afternoon, about 3½ o'clock, it begins snow. There has been a matinee performance at the theater—from 4¼ to 5 comes a stream of homeward bound ladies. I never knew the spacious room to present a gayer, more lively scene—handsome, well-drest Jersey women and girls, scores of them, streaming in for nearly an hour—the bright eyes and glowing faces, coming in from the air—a sprinkling of snow on bonnets or dresses as they enter—the five or ten minutes' waiting—the chatting and laughing—(women can have capital times among themselves, with plenty of wit, lunches, jovial abandon)—Lizzie, the pleasant-manner'd waiting room woman—for sound, the bell-taps and steam-signals of the departing boats with their rhythmic break and undertone—the domestic pictures, mothers with bevies of daughters, (a charming sight)—children, countrymen—the railroad men in their blue clothes and caps—all the various characters of city and country represented or suggested. Then outside some belated passenger frantically running, jumping after the boat. Towards six o'clock the human stream gradually thickening—now a pressure of vehicles, drays, piled railroad crates—now a drove of cattle, making quite an excitement, the drovers with heavy sticks, belaboring the steaming sides of the frighten'd brutes. Inside the reception room, business bargains, flirting, love-making, *eclaircissements,* proposals—pleasant, sober-faced Phil coming in with his burden of afternoon papers—or Jo, or Charley (who jump'd in the dock last week, and saved a stout lady from drowning,) to replenish the stove, after clearing it with long crow-bar poker.

Besides all this "comedy human," the river affords nutriment of a higher order. Here are some of my memoranda of the past winter, just as pencill'd down on the spot.

A January Night.—Fine trips across the wide Delaware to-night. Tide pretty high, and a strong ebb. River, a little after 8, full of ice, mostly broken, but some large cakes making our strong-timber'd steamboat hum and quiver as she strikes them. In the clear moonlight they spread, strange, unearthly, silvery, faintly glistening, as far as I can see. Bumping, trembling, sometimes hissing like a thousand snakes, the tide-procession, as we wend with or through it, affording a grand undertone, in keeping with the scene. Overhead, the splendor indescribable; yet something haughty, almost supercilious, in the night. Never did I realize more latent sentiment, almost *passion*, in those silent interminable stars up there. One can understand, such a night, why, from the days of the Pharaohs or Job, the dome of heaven, sprinkled with planets, has supplied the subtlest, deepest criticism on human pride, glory, ambition.

Another Winter Night.—I don't know anything more *filling* than to be on the wide firm deck of a powerful boat, a clear, cool, extra-moonlight night, crushing proudly and resistlessly through this thick, marbly, glistening ice. The whole river is now spread with it—some immense cakes. There is such weirdness about the scene—partly the quality of the light, with its tinge of blue, the lunar twilight—only the large stars holding their own in the radiance of the moon. Temperature sharp, comfortable for motion, dry, full of oxygen. But the sense of power—the steady, scornful, imperious urge of our strong new engine, as she ploughs her way through the big and little cakes.

Another.—For two hours I cross'd and recross'd, merely for pleasure—for a still excitement. Both sky and river went through several changes. The first for awhile held two vast fan-shaped echelons of light clouds, through which the moon waded, now radiating, carrying with her an aureole of tawny transparent brown, and now flooding the whole vast with clear vapory light-green, through which, as through an illuminated veil, she moved with measur'd womanly motion. Then, another trip, the heavens would be absolutely clear, and Luna in all her effulgence. The big Dipper in the north, with the double star in the handle much plainer than common. Then the sheeny track of light in the water, dancing and rippling. Such transformations; such pictures and poems, inimitable.

Another.—I am studying the stars, under advantages, as I cross to-night. (It is late in February, and again extra clear.) High toward the west, the Pleiades, tremulous with delicate sparkle, in the soft heavens. Aldebaran, leading the V-shaped Hyades—and overhead Capella and her kids. Most majestic of all, in full display in the high south, Orion, vast-spread, roomy, chief histrion of the stage, with his shiny yellow rosette on his shoulder, and his three Kings—and a little to the east, Sirius, calmly arrogant, most wondrous single star. Going late ashore, (I couldn't give up the beauty and soothingness of the night,) as I staid around, or slowly wander'd, I heard the echoing calls of the railroad men in the West Jersey depot yard, shifting and switching trains, engines, &c.; amid the general silence otherways, and something in the acoustic quality of the air, musical, emotional effects, never thought of before. I linger'd long and long, listening to them.

Night of March 18, '79.—One of the calm, pleasantly cool, exquisitely clear and cloudless, early spring nights—the atmosphere again that rare vitreous blue-black, welcom'd by astronomers. Just at 8, evening, the scene overhead of certainly solemnest beauty, never surpass'd. Venus nearly down in the west, of a size and lustre as if trying to outshow herself, before departing. Teeming, maternal orb—I take you again to myself. I am reminded of that spring preceding Abraham Lincoln's murder, when I, restlessly haunting the Potomac banks, around Washington city, watch'd you, off there, aloof, moody as myself:

> As we walk'd up and down in the dark blue so mystic,
> As we walk'd in silence the transparent shadowy night,
> As I saw you had something to tell, as you bent to
> me night after night,
> As you droop from the sky low down, as if to my
> side, (while the other stars all look'd on,)
> As we wander'd together the solemn night.

With departing Venus, large to the last, and shining even to the edge of the horizon, the vast dome presents at this moment, such a spectacle! Mercury was visible just after sunset—a rare sight. Arcturus is now risen, just north of east. In calm glory all the stars of Orion hold the place of honor, in meridian, to the south—with the Dog-star a little to the left. And now, just rising, Spica, late, low, and slightly veil'd. Castor, Regulus and the rest, all shining unusually clear, (no Mars or Jupiter or moon till morning.) On the edges of the river, many lamps twinkling—with two or three huge chimneys, a couple of miles up, belching forth molten, steady flames, volcano-like, illuminating all around—and sometimes an electric or calcium, its Dante-Inferno gleams, in far shafts, terrible, ghastly-powerful. Of later May nights, crossing, I like to watch the fishermen's little buoy-lights—so pretty, so dreamy—like corpse candles—undulating delicate and lonesome on the surface of the shadowy waters, floating with the current.

The First Spring Day on Chestnut Street

Winter relaxing its hold, has already allow'd us a foretaste of spring. As I write, yesterday afternoon's softness and brightness, (after the morning fog, which gave it a better setting, by contrast,) show'd Chestnut street—say between Broad and Fourth—to more advantage in its various asides, and all its stores, and gay-dress'd crowds generally, than for three months past. I took a walk there between one and two. Doubtless, there were plenty of hard-up folks along the pavements, but nine-tenths of the myriad-moving human panorama to all appearance seem'd flush, well-fed, and fully-provided. At all events it was good to be on Chestnut street yesterday. The peddlers on the sidewalk—("sleeve-buttons, three for five cents")—the handsome little fellow with canary-bird whistles—the cane men, toy men, toothpick men—the old woman squatted in a heap on the cold stone flags, with her basket of matches, pins and tape—the young negro mother, sitting, begging, with her two little coffee-color'd twins on her lap—the beauty of the cramm'd conservatory of rare flowers, flaunting reds, yellows, snowy lilies, incredible orchids, at the Baldwin mansion near Twelfth street—the show of fine poultry, beef, fish, at the restaurants—the china stores, with glass and statuettes—the luscious tropical fruits—the street cars plodding along, with their tintinnabulating bells—the fat, cab-looking, rapidly driven one-horse vehicles of the post-office, squeez'd full of coming or going letter-carriers, so healthy and handsome and manly-looking, in their gray uniforms—the costly books, pictures, curiosities, in the windows—the gigantic policemen at most of the corners—will all be readily remember'd and recognized as features of this principal avenue of Philadelphia. Chestnut street, I have discover'd, is not without individuality, and its own points, even when compared with the great promenade-streets of other cities. I have never been in Europe, but acquired years' familiar experience with New York's, (perhaps the world's,) great thoroughfare, Broadway, and possess to some extent a personal and saunterer's knowledge of St. Charles street in New Orleans, Tremont street in Boston, and the broad trottoirs of Pennsylvania avenue in Washington. Of course it is a pity that Chestnut were not two or three times wider; but the street, any fine day, shows vividness, motion, variety, not easily to be surpass'd. (Sparkling eyes, human faces, magnetism, well-dress'd women, ambulating to and fro—with lots of fine things in the windows—are they not about the same, the civilized world over?)

> How fast the flitting figures come!
> The mild, the fierce, the stony face;
> Some bright with thoughtless smiles—and some
> Where secret tears have left their trace.

A few days ago one of the six-story clothing stores along here had the space inside its plate-glass show-window partition'd into a little corral, and litter'd deeply with rich clover and hay, (I could smell the odor outside,) on which reposed two magnificent fat sheep, full-sized but young—the handsomest creatures of the kind I ever saw. I stopp'd long and long, with the crowd, to view them—one lying down chewing the cud, and one standing up, looking out, with dense-fringed patient eyes. Their wool, of a clear tawny color, with streaks of glistening black—altogether a queer sight amidst that crowded promenade of dandies, dollars and drygoods.

Up the Hudson to Ulster County

April 23.—Off to New York on a little tour and visit. Leaving the hospitable, home-like quarters of my valued friends,

Mr. and Mrs. J. H. Johnston—took the 4 P.M. boat, bound up the Hudson, 100 miles or so. Sunset and evening fine. Especially enjoy'd the hour after we passed Cozzens's landing—the night lit by the crescent moon and Venus, now swimming in tender glory, and now hid by the high rocks and hills of the western shore, which we hugg'd close. (Where I spend the next ten days is in Ulster county and its neighborhood, with frequent morning and evening drives, observations of the river, and short rambles.)

April 24—Noon.—A little more and the sun would be oppressive. The bees are out gathering their bread from willows and other trees. I watch them returning, darting through the air or lighting on the hives, their thighs covered with the yellow forage. A solitary robin sings near. I sit in my shirt sleeves and gaze from an open bay-window on the indolent scene—the thin haze, the Fishkill hills in the distance—off on the river, a sloop with slanting mainsail, and two or three little shad-boats. Over on the railroad opposite, long freight trains, sometimes weighted by cylinder-tanks of petroleum, thirty, forty, fifty cars in a string, panting and rumbling along in full view, but the sound soften'd by distance.

Days at J. B.'s—Turf-Fires—Spring Songs

April 26.—At sunrise, the pure clear sound of the meadow lark. An hour later, some notes, few and simple, yet delicious and perfect, from the bush-sparrow—towards noon the reedy trill of the robin. To-day is the fairest, sweetest yet—penetrating warmth—a lovely veil in the air, partly heat-vapor and partly from the turf-fires everywhere in patches on the farms. A group of soft maples near by silently bursts out in crimson tips, buzzing all day with busy bees. The white sails of sloops and schooners glide up or down the river; and long trains of cars, with ponderous roll, or faint bell notes, almost constantly on the opposite shore. The earliest wild flowers in the woods and fields, spicy arbutus, blue liverwort, frail anemone, and the pretty white blossoms of the bloodroot. I launch out in slow rambles, discovering them. As I go along the roads I like to see the farmers' fires in patches, burning the dry brush, turf, debris. How the smoke crawls along, flat to the ground, slanting, slowly rising, reaching away, and at last dissipating.

I like its acrid smell—whiffs just reaching me—welcomer than French perfume.

The birds are plenty; of any sort, or of two or three sorts, curiously, not a sign, till suddenly some warm, gushing, sunny April (or even March) day—lo! there they are, from twig to twig, or fence to fence, flirting, singing, some mating, preparing to build. But most of them *en passant*—a fortnight, a month in these parts, and then away. As in all phases, Nature keeps up her vital, copious, eternal procession. Still, plenty of the birds hang around all or most of the season—now their love-time, and era of nest-building. I find flying over the river, crows, gulls and hawks. I hear the afternoon shriek of the latter, darting about, preparing to nest. The oriole will soon be heard here, and the twanging *meoeow* of the cat-bird; also the king-bird, cuckoo and the warblers. All along, there are three peculiarly characteristic spring songs—the meadow-lark's, so sweet, so alert and remonstrating (as if he said, "don't you see?" or, "can't you understand?")—the cheery, mellow, human tones of the robin—(I have been trying for years to get a brief term, or phrase, that would identify and describe that robin-call)—and the amorous whistle of the high-hole. Insects are out plentifully at midday.

April 29.—As we drove lingering along the road we heard, just after sundown, the song of the wood-thrush. We stopp'd without a word, and listen'd long. The delicious notes—a sweet, artless, voluntary, simple anthem, as from the flute-stops of some organ, wafted through the twilight—echoing well to us from the perpendicular high rock, where, in some thick young trees' recesses at the base, sat the bird—fill'd our senses, our souls.

Meeting a Hermit

I found in one of my rambles up the hills a real hermit, living in a lonesome spot, hard to get at, rocky, the view fine, with a little patch of land two rods square. A man of youngish middle age, city born and raised, had been to school, had travel'd in Europe and California. I first met him once or twice on the road, and pass'd the time of day, with some small talk; then, the third time, he ask'd me to go along a bit and rest in his hut (an almost unprecedented compliment, as I heard from others afterwards.) He was of Quaker stock, I think; talk'd with ease and moderate freedom, but did not unbosom his life, or story, or tragedy, or whatever it was.

An Ulster County Waterfall

I jot this mem. in a wild scene of woods and hills, where we have come to visit a waterfall. I never saw finer or more copious hemlocks, many of them large, some old and hoary. Such a sentiment to them, secretive, shaggy—what I call weather-beaten and let-alone—a rich underlay of ferns, yew sprouts and mosses, beginning to be spotted with the early summer wild-flowers. Enveloping all, the monotone and liquid gurgle from the hoarse impetuous copious fall—the greenish-tawny, darkly transparent waters, plunging with velocity down the rocks, with patches of milk-white foam—a stream of hurrying amber, thirty feet wide, risen far back in the hills and woods, now rushing with volume—every hundred rods a fall, and sometimes three or four in that distance. A primitive forest, druidical, solitary and savage—not ten visitors a year—broken rocks everywhere—shade overhead, thick underfoot with leaves—a just palpable wild and delicate aroma.

Walter Dumont and His Medal

As I saunter'd along the high road yesterday, I stopp'd to watch a man near by, ploughing a rough stony field with a yoke of oxen. Usually there is much geeing and hawing, excitement, and continual noise and expletives, about a job of this kind. But I noticed how different, how easy and wordless, yet firm and sufficient, the work of this young ploughman. His name was Walter Dumont, a farmer, and son of a farmer, working for their living. Three years ago, when the steamer "Sunnyside" was wreck'd of a bitter icy night on the west bank here, Walter went out in his boat—was the first man on hand with assistance—made a way through the ice to shore, connected a line, perform'd work of first-class readiness, daring, danger, and saved numerous lives. Some weeks after, one evening when he was up at Esopus, among the usual loafing crowd at the country store and post-office, there arrived the gift of an unexpected official gold medal for the quiet hero. The impromptu presentation was made to him on the spot, but he blush'd, hesitated as he took it, and had nothing to say.

Hudson River Sights

It was a happy thought to build the Hudson river railroad right along the shore. The grade is already made by nature; you are sure of ventilation one side—and you are in nobody's way. I see, hear, the locomotives and cars, rumbling, roaring, flaming, smoking, constantly, away off there, night and day—less than a mile distant, and in full view by day. I like both sight and sound. Express trains thunder and lighten along; of freight trains, most of them very long, there cannot be less than a hundred a day. At night far down you see the headlight approaching, coming steadily on like a meteor. The river at night has its special character-beauties. The shad fishermen go forth in their boats and pay out their nets—one sitting forward, rowing, and one standing up aft dropping it properly—marking the line with little floats bearing candles, conveying, as they glide over the water, an indescribable sentiment and doubled brightness. I like to watch the tows at night, too, with their twinkling lamps, and hear the husky panting of the steamers; or catch the sloops' and schooners' shadowy forms, like phantoms, white, silent, indefinite, out there. Then the Hudson of a clear moonlight night.

But there is one sight the very grandest. Sometimes in the fiercest driving storm of wind, rain, hail or snow, a great eagle will appear over the river, now soaring with steady and now overhended wings—always confronting the gale, or perhaps cleaving into, or at times literally *sitting* upon it. It is like reading some first-class natural tragedy or epic, or hearing martial trumpets. The splendid bird enjoys the hubbub—is adjusted and equal to it—finishes it so artistically. His pinions just oscillating—the position of his head and neck—his resistless, occasionally varied flight—now a swirl, now an upward movement—the black clouds driving—the angry wash below—the hiss of rain, the wind's piping (perhaps the ice colliding, grunting)—he tacking or jibing—now, as it were, for a change, abandoning himself to the gale, moving with it with such velocity—and now, resuming control, he comes up against it, lord of the situation and the storm—lord, amid it, of power and savage joy.

Sometimes (as at present writing,) middle of sunny afternoon, the old "Vanderbilt" steamer stalking ahead—I plainly hear her rhythmic, slushing paddles—drawing by long hawsers an immense and varied following string, ("an old sow and pigs," the river folks call it.) First comes a big barge, with a house built on it, and spars towering over the roof; then canal boats, a lengthen'd, clustering train, fasten'd and link'd together—the one in the middle, with high staff, flaunting a broad and gaudy flag—others with the almost invariable lines of new-wash'd clothes, drying; two sloops and a schooner aside the tow—little wind, and that adverse—with three long, dark, empty barges bringing up the rear. People are on the boats: men lounging, women in sun-bonnets, children, stovepipes with streaming smoke.

Two City Areas, Certain Hours

New York, *May 24, '79.*—Perhaps no quarters of this city (I have return'd again for awhile,) make more brilliant, animated, crowded, spectacular human presentations these fine May afternoons than the two I am now going to describe from personal observation. First: that area comprising Fourteenth street (especially the short range between Broadway and Fifth avenue) with Union square, its adjacencies, and so retro-stretching down Broadway for half a mile. All the walks here are wide, and the spaces ample and free—now flooded with liquid gold from the last two hours of powerful sunshine. The whole area at 5 o'clock, the days of my observations, must have contain'd from thirty to forty thousand finely-dress'd people, all in motion, plenty of them good-looking, many beautiful women, often youths and children, the latter in groups with their nurses—the trottoirs everywhere close-spread, thick-tangled, (yet no collision, no trouble,) with masses of bright color, action, and tasty toilets; (surely the women dress better than ever before, and the men do too.)

As if New York would show these afternoons what it can do in its humanity, its choicest physique and physiognomy, and its countless prodigality of locomotion, dry goods, glitter, magnetism, and happiness.

Second: also from 5 to 7 P.M. the stretch of Fifth avenue, all the way from the Central Park exits at Fifty-ninth street, down to Fourteenth, especially along the high grade by Fortieth street, and down the hill. A Mississippi of horses and rich vehicles, not by dozens and scores, but hundreds and thousands—the broad avenue filled and cramm'd with them—a moving, sparkling, hurrying crush, for more than two miles. (I wonder they don't get block'd, but I believe they never do.) Altogether it is to me the marvel sight of New York. I like to get in one of the Fifth avenue stages and ride up, stemming the swift-moving procession. I doubt if London or Paris or any city in the world can show such a carriage carnival as I have seen here five or six times these beautiful May afternoons.

Central Park Walks and Talks

May 16 to 22.—I visit Central Park now almost every day, sitting, or slowly rambling, or riding around. The whole place presents its very best appearance this current month—the full flush of the trees, the plentiful white and pink of the flowering shrubs, the emerald green of the grass spreading everywhere, yellow dotted still with dandelions—the specialty of the plentiful gray rocks, peculiar to these grounds, cropping out, miles and miles—and over all the beauty and purity, three days out of four, of our summer skies. As I sit, placidly, early afternoon, off against Ninetieth street, the policeman, C. C., a well-form'd sandy-complexion'd young fellow, comes over and stands near me. We grow quite friendly and chatty forthwith. He is a New Yorker born and raised, and in answer to my questions tells me about the life of a New York Park policeman, (while he talks keeping his eyes and ears vigilantly open, occasionally pausing and moving where he can get full views of the vistas of the road, up and down, and the spaces around.) The pay is $2.40 a day (seven days to a week)—the men come on and work eight hours straight ahead, which is all that is required of them out of the twenty-four. The position has more risks than one might suppose—for instance if a team or horse runs away (which happens daily) each man is expected not only to be prompt, but to waive safety and stop wildest nag or nags—(*do it*, and don't be thinking of your bones or face)—give the alarm-whistle too, so that other guards may repeat, and the vehicles up and down the tracks be warn'd. Injuries to the men are continually happening. There is much alertness and quiet strength. (Few appreciate, I have often thought, the Ulyssean capacity, derring do, quick readiness in emergencies, practicality, unwitting devotion and heroism, among our American young men and working-people—the firemen, the railroad employés, the steamer and ferry men, the police, the conductors and drivers—the whole splendid average of native stock, city and country.) It is good work, though; and upon the whole, the Park force members like it. They see life, and the excitement keeps them up. There is not so much difficulty as might be supposed from tramps, roughs, or in keeping people "off the grass." The worst trouble of the regular Park employé is from malarial fever, chills, and the like.

A Fine Afternoon, 4 to 6

Ten thousand vehicles careering through the Park this perfect afternoon. Such a show! and I have seen all—watch'd it narrowly, and at my leisure. Private barouches, cabs and coupés, some fine horseflesh—lapdogs, footmen, fashions, foreigners, cockades on hats, crests on panels—the full oceanic tide of New York's wealth and "gentility." It was an impressive, rich, interminable circus on a grand scale, full of action and color in the beauty of the day, under the clear sun and moderate breeze. Family groups, couples, single drivers—of course dresses generally elegant—much "style," (yet perhaps little or nothing, even in that direction, that fully justified itself.) Through the windows of two or three of the richest carriages I saw faces almost corpse-like, so ashy and listless. Indeed the whole affair exhibited less of sterling America, either in spirit or countenance, than I had counted on from such a select mass-spectacle. I suppose, as a proof of limitless wealth, leisure, and the aforesaid "gentility," it was tremendous. Yet what I saw those hours (I took two other occasions, two other afternoons to watch the same scene,) confirms a thought that haunts me every additional glimpse I get of our top-loftical general or rather exceptional phases of wealth and fashion in this country—namely, that they are ill at ease, much too conscious, cased in too many cerements, and far from happy—that there is nothing in them which we who are poor and plain need at all envy, and that instead of the perennial smell of the grass and woods and shores, their typical redolence is of soaps and essences, very rare may be, but suggesting the barber shop—something that turns stale and musty in a few hours anyhow.

Perhaps the show on the horseback road was prettiest. Many groups (threes a favorite number,) some couples, some singly—many ladies—frequently horses or parties dashing along on a full run—fine riding the rule—a few really first-class animals. As the afternoon waned, the wheel'd carriages grew less, but the saddle-riders seemed to increase. They linger'd long—and I saw some charming forms and faces.

Departing of the Big Steamers

May 15.—A three hours' bay-trip from 12 to 3 this afternoon, accompanying "the City of Brussels" down as far as the Narrows, in behoof of some Europe-bound friends, to give them a good send off. Our spirited little tug, the "Seth Low," kept close to the great black "Brussels," sometimes one side, sometimes the other, always up to her, or even pressing ahead, (like the blooded pony accompanying the royal elephant.) The whole affair, from the first, was an animated, quick-passing, characteristic New York scene; the large, good-looking, well dress'd crowd on the wharf-end—men and women come to see their friends depart, and bid them God-speed—the ship's sides swarming with passengers—groups of bronze-faced sailors, with uniform'd officers at their posts—the quiet directions, as she quickly unfastens and moves out, prompt to a minute—the emotional faces, adieus and fluttering handkerchiefs, and many smiles and some tears on the wharf—the answering faces, smiles, tears and fluttering handkerchiefs, from the ship—(what can be subtler and finer than this play of faces on such occasions in these responding crowds?—what go more to one's heart?)—the proud, steady, noiseless cleaving of the grand oceaner down the bay—we speeding by her side a few miles, and then turning, wheeling, amid a babel of wild hurrahs, shouted partings, ear-splitting steam whistles, kissing of hands and waving of handkerchiefs.

This departing of the big steamers, noons or afternoons—there is no better medicine when one is listless or vapory. I am fond of going down Wednesdays and Saturdays—their more special days—to watch them and the crowds on the wharves, the arriving passengers, the general bustle and activity, the eager looks from the faces, the clear-toned voices, (a travel'd foreigner, a musician, told me the other day she thinks an American crowd has the finest voices in the world,) the whole look of the great, shapely black ships themselves, and their groups and lined sides—in the setting of our bay with the blue sky overhead. Two days after the above I saw the "Britannic," the "Donau," the "Helvetia" and the "Schiedam" steam out, all off for Europe—a magnificent sight.

Two Hours on the Minnesota

From 7 to 9, aboard the United States school-ship Minnesota, lying up the North river. Captain Luce sent his gig for us about sundown, to the foot of Twenty-third street, and receiv'd us aboard with officer-like hospitality and sailor heartiness. There are several hundred youths on the Minnesota to be train'd for efficiently manning the government navy. I like the idea much; and, so far as I have seen to-night, I like the way it is carried out on this huge vessel. Below, on the gun-deck, were gather'd nearly a hundred of the boys, to give us some of their singing exercises, with a melodeon accompaniment, play'd by one of their number. They sang with a will. The best part, however, was the sight of the young fellows themselves. I went over among them before the singing began, and talk'd a few minutes informally. They are from all the States; I asked for the Southerners, but could only find one, a lad from Baltimore. In age, apparently, they range from about fourteen years to nineteen or twenty. They are all of

American birth, and have to pass a rigid medical examination; well-grown youths, good flesh, bright eyes, looking straight at you, healthy, intelligent, not a slouch among them, nor a menial—in every one the promise of a man. I have been to many public aggregations of young and old, and of schools and colleges, in my day, but I confess I have never been so near satisfied, so comforted, (both from the fact of the school itself, and the splendid proof of our country, our composite race, and the sample-promises of its good average capacities, its future,) as in the collection from all parts of the United States on this navy training ship. ("Are there going to be *any men* there?" was the dry and pregnant reply of Emerson to one who had been crowding him with the rich material statistics and possibilities of some western or Pacific region.)

May 26.—Aboard the Minnesota again. Lieut. Murphy kindly came for me in his boat. Enjoy'd specially those brief trips to and fro—the sailors, tann'd, strong, so bright and able-looking, pulling their oars in long side-swing, man-of-war style, as they row'd me across. I saw the boys in companies drilling with small arms; had a talk with Chaplain Rawson. At 11 o'clock all of us gathered to breakfast around a long table in the great ward room—I among the rest—a genial, plentiful, hospitable affair every way—plenty to eat, and of the best; became acquainted with several new officers. This second visit, with its observations, talks, (two or three at random with the boys,) confirm'd my first impressions.

Mature Summer Days and Nights

Aug. 4.—Forenoon—as I sit under the willow shade, (have retreated down in the country again,) a little bird is leisurely dousing and flirting himself amid the brook almost within reach of me. He evidently fears me not—takes me for some concomitant of the neighboring earthy banks, free bushery and wild weeds. 6 *p.m.*—The last three days have been perfect ones for the season, (four nights ago copious rains, with vehement thunder and lightning.) I write this sitting by the creek watching my two kingfishers at their sundown sport. The strong, beautiful, joyous creatures! Their wings glisten in the slanted sunbeams as they circle and circle around, occasionally dipping and dashing the water, and making long stretches up and down the creek. Wherever I go over fields, through lanes, in by-places, blooms the white-flowering wild-carrot, its delicate pat of snow-flakes crowning its slender stem, gracefully oscillating in the breeze.

Exposition Building—New City Hall—River Trip

PHILADELPHIA, *Aug. 26.*—Last night and to-night of unsurpass'd clearness, after two days' rain; moon splendor and star splendor. Being out toward the great Exposition building, West Philadelphia, I saw it lit up, and thought I would go in. There was a ball, democratic but nice; plenty of young couples waltzing and quadrilling—music by a good string-band. To the sight and hearing of these—to moderate strolls up and down the roomy spaces—to getting off aside, resting in an arm-chair and looking up a long while at the grand high roof with its graceful and multitudinous work of iron rods, angles, gray colors, plays of light and shade, receding into dim outlines—to absorbing (in the intervals of the string band,) some capital voluntaries and rolling caprices from the big organ at the other end of the building—to sighting a shadow'd figure or group or couple of lovers every now and then passing some near or farther aisle—I abandon'd myself for over an hour.

Returning home, riding down Market street in an open summer car, something detain'd us between Fifteenth and Broad, and I got out to view better the new, three-fifths-built marble edifice, the City Hall, of magnificent proportions—a majestic and lovely show there in the moonlight—flooded all over, façades, myriad silver-white lines and carv'd heads and mouldings, with the soft dazzle—silent, weird, beautiful—well, I know that never when finish'd will that magnificent pile impress one as it impress'd me those fifteen minutes.

To-night, since, I have been long on the river. I watch the C-shaped Northern Crown, (with the star Alshacca that blazed out so suddenly, alarmingly, one night a few years ago.) The moon in her third quarter, and up nearly all night. And there, as I look eastward, my long-absent Pleiades, welcome again to sight. For an hour I enjoy the soothing and vital scene to the low splash of waves—new stars steadily, noiselessly rising in the east.

As I cross the Delaware, one of the deck-hands, F. R., tells me how a woman jump'd overboard and was drown'd a couple of hours since. It happen'd in mid-channel—she leap'd from the forward part of the boat, which went over her. He saw her rise on the other side in the swift running water, throw her arms and closed hands high up, (white hands and bare forearms in the moonlight like a flash,) and then she sank. (I found out afterwards that this young fellow had promptly jump'd in, swam after the poor creature, and made, though unsuccessfully, the bravest efforts to rescue her; but he didn't mention that part at all in telling me the story.)

Swallows on the River

Sept. 3.—Cloudy and wet, and wind due east; air without palpable fog, but very heavy with moisture—welcome for a change. Forenoon, crossing the Delaware, I noticed unusual numbers of swallows in flight, circling, darting, graceful beyond description, close to the water. Thick, around the bows of the ferry-boat as she lay tied in her slip, they flew; and as we went out I watch'd beyond the pier-heads, and across the broad stream, their swift-winding loop-ribands of motion, down close to it, cutting and intersecting. Though I had seen swallows all my life, seem'd as though I never before realized their peculiar beauty and character in the landscape. (Some time ago, for an hour, in a huge old country barn, watching these birds flying, recall'd the 22d book of the Odyssey, where Ulysses slays the suitors, bringing things to *eclaircissement,* and Minerva, swallow-bodied, darts up through the spaces of the hall, sits high on a beam, looks complacently on the show of slaughter, and feels in her element, exulting, joyous.)

Begin a Long Jaunt West

The following three or four months (Sept. to Dec. '79) I made quite a western journey, fetching up at Denver, Colorado, and penetrating the Rocky Mountain region enough to get a good notion of it all. Left West Philadelphia after 9 o'clock one night, middle of September, in a comfortable sleeper. Oblivious of the two or three hundred miles across Pennsylvania; at Pittsburgh in the morning to breakfast. Pretty good view of the city and Birmingham—fog and damp, smoke, coke-furnaces, flames, discolor'd wooden houses, and vast collections of coal-barges. Presently a bit of fine region, West Virginia, the Panhandle, and crossing the river, the Ohio. By day through the latter State—then Indiana—and so rock'd to slumber for a second night, flying like lightning through Illinois.

In the Sleeper

What a fierce weird pleasure to lie in my berth at night in the luxurious palace-car, drawn by the mighty Baldwin—embodying, and filling me, too, full of the swiftest motion, and most resistless strength! It is late, perhaps midnight or after—distances join'd like magic—as we speed through Harrisburg, Columbus, Indianapolis. The element of danger adds zest to it all. On we go, rumbling and flashing, with our loud whinnies thrown out from time to time, or trumpet-blasts, into the darkness. Passing the homes of men, the farms, barns, cattle—the silent villages. And the car itself, the sleeper, with curtains drawn and lights turn'd down—in the berths the slumberers, many of them women and children—as on, on, on, we fly like lightning through the night—how strangely sound and sweet they sleep! (They say the French Voltaire in his time designated the grand opera and a ship of war the most signal illustrations of the growth of humanity's and art's advance beyond primitive barbarism. Perhaps if the witty philosopher were here these days, and went in the same car with perfect bedding and feed from New York to San Francisco, he would shift his type and sample to one of our American sleepers.)

Missouri State

We should have made the run of 960 miles from Philadelphia to St. Louis in thirty-six hours, but we had a collision and bad locomotive smash about two-thirds of the way, which set us back. So merely stopping over night that time in St. Louis, I sped on westward. As I cross'd Missouri State the whole distance by the St. Louis and Kansas City Northern Railroad, a fine early autumn day, I thought my eyes had never looked on scenes of greater pastoral beauty. For over two hundred miles successive rolling prairies, agriculturally perfect view'd by Pennsylvania and New Jersey eyes, and dotted here and there with fine timber. Yet fine as the land is, it isn't the finest portion; (there is a bed of impervious clay and hard-pan beneath this section that holds water too firmly, "drowns the land in wet weather, and bakes it in dry," as a cynical farmer told me.) South are some richer tracts, though perhaps the beauty-spots of the State are the northwestern counties. Altogether, I am clear, (now, and from what I have seen and learn'd since,) that Missouri, in climate, soil, relative situation, wheat, grass, mines, railroads, and every important materialistic respect, stands in the front rank of the Union. Of Missouri averaged politically and socially I have heard all sorts of talk, some pretty severe—but I should have no fear myself of getting along safely and comfortably anywhere among the Missourians. They raise a good deal of tobacco. You see at this time quantities of the light greenish-gray leaves pulled and hanging out to dry on temporary frameworks or rows of sticks. Looks much like the mullein familiar to eastern eyes.

Lawrence and Topeka, Kansas

We thought of stopping in Kansas City, but when we got there we found a train ready and a crowd of hospitable Kansians to take us on to Lawrence, to which I proceeded. I shall not soon forget my good days in L., in company with Judge Usher and his sons, (especially John and Linton,) true westerners of the noblest type. Nor the similar days in Topeka. Nor the brotherly kindness of my RR. friends there, and the city and State officials. Lawrence and Topeka are large, bustling, half-rural, handsome cities. I took two or three long drives about the latter, drawn by a spirited team over smooth roads.

The Prairies

And an Undeliver'd Speech.

At a large popular meeting at Topeka—the Kansas State Silver Wedding, fifteen or twenty thousand people—I had been erroneously bill'd to deliver a poem. As I seem'd to be made much of, and wanted to be good-natured, I hastily pencill'd out the following little speech. Unfortunately, (or fortunately,) I had such a good time and rest, and talk and dinner, with the U. boys, that I let the hours slip away and didn't drive over to the meeting and speak my piece. But here it is just the same:

"My friends, your bills announce me as giving a poem; but I have no poem—have composed none for this occasion. And I can honestly say I am now glad of it. Under these skies resplendent in September beauty—amid the peculiar landscape you are used to, but which is new to me—these interminable and stately prairies—in the freedom and vigor and sane enthusiasm of this perfect western air and autumn sunshine—it seems to me a poem would be almost an impertinence. But if you care to have a word from me, I should speak it about these very prairies; they impress me most, of all the objective shows I see or have seen on this, my first real visit to the West. As I have roll'd rapidly hither for more than a thousand miles, through fair Ohio, through bread-raising Indiana and Illinois—through ample Missouri, that contains and raises everything; as I have partially explor'd your charming city during the last two days, and, standing on Oread hill, by the university, have launch'd my view across broad expanses of living green, in every direction—I have again been most impress'd, I say, and shall remain for the rest of my life most impress'd, with that feature of the topography of your western central world—that vast Something, stretching out on its own unbounded scale, unconfined, which there is in these prairies, combining the real and ideal, and beautiful as dreams.

"I wonder indeed if the people of this continental inland West know how much of first-class *art* they have in these prairies—how original and all your own—how much of the influences of a character for your future humanity, broad, patriotic, heroic and new? how entirely they tally on land the grandeur and superb monotony of the skies of heaven, and the ocean with its waters? how freeing, soothing, nourishing they are to the soul?

"Then is it not subtly they who have given us our leading modern Americans, Lincoln and Grant?—vast-spread, average men—their foregrounds of character altogether practical and real, yet (to those who have eyes to see) with finest backgrounds of the ideal, towering high as any. And do we not see, in them, foreshadowings of the future races that shall fill these prairies?

"Not but what the Yankee and Atlantic States, and every other part—Texas, and the States flanking the south-east and the Gulf of Mexico—the Pacific shore empire—the Territories and Lakes, and the Canada line (the day is not yet, but it will come, including Canada entire)—are equally and integrally and indissolubly this Nation, the *sine qua non* of the human, political and commercial New World. But this favor'd central area of (in round numbers) two thousand miles square seems fated to be the home both of what I would call America's distinctive ideas and distinctive realities."

On to Denver—A Frontier Incident

The jaunt of five or six hundred miles from Topeka to Denver took me through a variety of country, but all unmistakably prolific, western, American, and on the largest scale. For a long distance we follow the line of the Kansas river, (I like better the old name, Kaw,) a stretch of very rich, dark soil, famed for its wheat, and call'd the Golden Belt—then plains and plains, hour after hour—Ellsworth county, the centre of the State—where I must stop a moment to tell a characteristic story of early days—scene the very spot where I am passing—time 1868. In a scrimmage at some public gathering in the town, A. had shot B. quite badly, but had not kill'd him. The sober men of Ellsworth conferr'd with one another and decided that A. deserv'd punishment. As they wished to set a good example and establish their reputation the reverse of a Lynching town, they open an informal court and bring both men before them for deliberate trial. Soon as this trial begins the wounded man is led forward to give his testimony. Seeing his enemy in durance and unarm'd, B. walks suddenly up in a fury and shoots A. through the head—shoots him dead. The court is instantly adjourn'd, and its unanimous members, without a word of debate, walk the murderer B. out, wounded as he is, and hang him.

In due time we reach Denver, which city I fall in love with from the first, and have that feeling confirm'd, the longer I stay there. One of my pleasantest days was a jaunt, via Platte cañon, to Leadville.

An Hour on Kenosha Summit

Jottings from the Rocky Mountains, mostly pencill'd during a day's trip over the South Park RR., returning from Leadville, and especially the hour we were detain'd, (much to my satisfaction,) at Kenosha summit. As afternoon advances, novelties, far-reaching splendors, accumulate under the bright sun in this pure air. But I had better commence with the day.

The confronting of Platte cañon just at dawn, after a ten miles' ride in early darkness on the rail from Denver—the seasonable stoppage at the entrance of the cañon, and good breakfast of eggs, trout, and nice griddle-cakes—then as we travel on, and get well in the gorge, all the wonders, beauty, savage power of the scene—the wild stream of water, from sources of snows, brawling continually in sight one side—the dazzling sun, and the morning lights on the rocks—such turns and grades in the track, squirming around corners, or up and down hills—far glimpses of a hundred peaks, titanic necklaces, stretching north and south—the huge rightly-named Dome-rock—and as we dash along, others similar, simple, monolithic, elephantine.

An Egotistical "Find"

"I have found the law of my own poems," was the unspoken but more-and-more decided feeling that came to me as I pass'd, hour after hour, amid all this grim yet joyous elemental abandon—this plenitude of material, entire absence of art, untrammel'd play of primitive Nature—the chasm, the gorge, the crystal mountain stream, repeated scores, hundreds of miles—the broad handling and absolute uncrampedness—the fantastic forms, bathed in transparent browns, faint reds and grays, towering sometimes a thousand, sometimes two or three thousand feet high—at their tops now and then huge masses pois'd, and mixing with the clouds, with only their outlines, hazed in misty lilac, visible. ("In Nature's grandest shows," says an old Dutch writer, an ecclesiastic, "amid the ocean's depth, if so might be, or countless worlds rolling above at night, a man thinks of them, weighs all, not for themselves or the abstract, but with reference to his own personality, and how they may affect him or color his destinies.")

New Senses—New Joys

We follow the stream of amber and bronze brawling along its bed, with its frequent cascades and snow-white foam. Through the cañon we fly—mountains not only each side, but seemingly, till we get near, right in front of us—every rood a new view flashing, and each flash defying description—on the almost perpendicular sides, clinging pines, cedars, spruces, crimson sumach bushes, spots of wild grass—but dominating all, those towering rocks, rocks, rocks, bathed in delicate vari-colors, with the clear sky of autumn overhead. New senses, new joys, seem develop'd. Talk as you like, a typical Rocky Mountain cañon, or a limitless sea-like stretch of the great Kansas or Colorado plains, under favoring circumstances, tallies, perhaps expresses, certainly awakes, those grandest and subtlest element emotions in the human soul, that all the marble temples and sculptures from Phidias to Thorwaldsen—all paintings, poems, reminiscences, or even music, probably never can.

Steam-Power, Telegraphs, &c.

I get out on a ten minutes' stoppage at Deer creek, to enjoy the unequal'd combination of hill, stone and wood. As we speed again, the yellow granite in the sunshine, with natural spires, minarets, castellated perches far aloft—then long stretches of straight-upright palisades, rhinoceros color—then gamboge and tinted chromos. Ever the best of my pleasures the cool-fresh Colorado atmosphere, yet sufficiently warm. Signs of man's restless advent and pioneerage, hard as Nature's face is—deserted dug-outs by dozens in the side-hills—the scantling hut, the telegraph-pole, the smoke of some impromptu chimney or outdoor fire—at intervals little settlements of log-houses, or parties of surveyors or telegraph builders, with their comfortable tents. Once, a canvas office where you could send a message by electricity anywhere around the world! Yes, pronounc'd signs of the man of latest dates, dauntlessly grappling with these grisliest shows of the old kosmos. At several places steam saw-mills, with their piles of logs and boards, and the pipes puffing. Occasionally Platte cañon expanding into a grassy flat of a few acres. At one such place, toward the end, where we stop, and I get out to stretch my legs, as I look skyward, or rather mountain-topward, a huge hawk or eagle (a rare sight here) is idly soaring, balancing along the ether, now sinking low and coming quite near, and then up again in stately-languid circles—then higher, higher, slanting to the north, and gradually out of sight.

America's Back-Bone

I jot these lines literally at Kenosha summit, where we return, afternoon, and take a long rest, 10,000 feet above sea-level. At this immense height the South Park stretches fifty miles before me. Mountainous chains and peaks in every variety of perspective, every hue of vista, fringe the view, in nearer, or middle, or far-dim distance, or fade on the horizon. We have now reach'd, penetrated the Rockies, (Hayden calls it the Front Range,) for a hundred miles or so; and though these chains spread away in every direction, specially north and south, thousands and thousands farther, I have seen specimens of the utmost of them, and know henceforth at least what they are, and what they look like. Not themselves alone, for they typify stretches and areas of half the globe—are, in fact, the vertebræ or back-bone of our hemisphere. As the anatomists say a man is only a spine, topp'd, footed, breasted and radiated, so the whole Western world is, in a sense, but an expansion of these mountains. In South America they are the Andes, in Central America and Mexico the Cordilleras, and in our States they go under different names—in California the Coast and Cascade ranges—thence more eastwardly the Sierra Nevadas—but mainly and more centrally here the Rocky Mountains proper, with many an elevation such as Lincoln's, Grey's, Harvard's, Yale's, Long's and Pike's peaks, all over 14,000 feet high. (East, the highest peaks of the Alleghanies, the Adirondacks, the Cattskills, and the White Mountains, range from 2000 to 5500 feet—only Mount Washington, in the latter, 6300 feet.)

The Parks

In the midst of all here, lie such beautiful contrasts as the sunken basins of the North, Middle, and South Parks, (the latter I am now on one side of, and overlooking,) each the size of a large, level, almost quandrangular, grassy, western county, wall'd in by walls of hills, and each park the source of a river. The ones I specify are the largest in Colorado, but the whole of that State, and of Wyoming, Utah, Nevada and western California, through their sierras and ravines, are copiously mark'd by similar spreads and openings, many of the small ones of paradisiac loveliness and perfection, with their offsets of mountains, streams, atmosphere and hues beyond compare.

Art Features

Talk, I say again, of going to Europe, of visiting the ruins of feudal castles, or Coliseum remains, or kings' palaces—when you can come *here.* The alternations one gets, too; after the Illinois and Kansas prairies of a thousand miles—smooth and easy areas of the corn and wheat of ten million democratic farms in the future—here start up in every conceivable presentation of shape, these non-utilitarian piles, coping the skies, emanating a beauty, terror, power, more than Dante or Angelo ever knew. Yes, I think the chyle of not only poetry and painting, but oratory, and even the metaphysics and music fit for the New World, before being finally assimilated, need first and feeding visits here.

Mountain streams.—The spiritual contrast and etheriality of the whole region consist largely to me in its never-absent peculiar streams—the snows of inaccessible upper areas melting and running down through the gorges continually. Nothing like the water of pastoral plains, or creeks with wooded banks and turf, or anything of the kind elsewhere. The shapes that element takes in the shows of the globe cannot be fully understood by an artist until he has studied these unique rivulets.

Aerial effects.—But perhaps as I gaze around me the rarest sight of all is in atmospheric hues. The prairies—as I cross'd them in my journey hither—and these mountains and parks, seem to me to afford new lights and shades. Everywhere the aerial gradations and sky-effects inimitable; nowhere else such perspectives, such transparent lilacs and grays. I can conceive of some superior landscape painter, some fine colorist, after sketching awhile out here, discarding all his previous work, delightful to stock exhibition amateurs, as muddy, raw and artificial. Near one's eye ranges an infinite variety; high up, the bare whitey-brown, above timber line; in certain spots afar patches of snow any time of year; (no trees, no flowers, no birds, at those chilling altitudes.) As I write I see the Snowy Range through the blue mist, beautiful and far off. I plainly see the patches of snow.

Denver Impressions

Through the long-lingering half-light of the most superb of evenings we return'd to Denver, where I staid several days leisurely exploring, receiving impressions, with which I may as well taper off this memorandum, itemizing what I saw there. The best was the men, three-fourths of them large, able, calm, alert, American. And cash! why they create it here. Out in the smelting works, (the biggest and most improv'd ones, for the precious metals, in the world,) I saw long rows of vats, pans, cover'd by bubbling-boiling water, and fill'd with pure silver, four or five inches thick, many thousand dollars' worth in a pan. The foreman who was showing me shovel'd it carelessly up with a little wooden shovel, as one might toss beans. Then large silver bricks, worth $2000 a brick, dozens of piles, twenty in a pile. In one place in the mountains, at a mining camp, I had a few days before seen rough bullion on the ground in the open air, like the confectioner's pyramids at some swell dinner in New York. (Such a sweet morsel to roll over with a poor author's pen and ink—and appropriate to slip in here—that the silver product of Colorado and Utah, with the gold product of California, New Mexico, Nevada and Dakota, foots up an addition to the world's coin of considerably over a hundred millions every year.)

A city, this Denver, well-laid out—Laramie street, and 15th and 16th and Champa streets, with others, particularly fine—some with tall storehouses of stone or iron, and windows of plate-glass—all the streets with little canals of mountain water running along the sides—plenty of people, "business," modernness—yet not without a certain racy wild smack, all its own. A place of fast horses, (many mares with their colts,) and I saw lots of big greyhounds for antelope hunting. Now and then groups of miners, some just come in, some starting out, very picturesque.

One of the papers here interview'd me, and reported me as saying off-hand: "I have lived in or visited all the great cities on the Atlantic third of the republic—Boston, Brooklyn with its hills, New Orleans, Baltimore, stately Washington, broad Philadelphia, teeming Cincinnati and Chicago, and for thirty years in that wonder, wash'd by hurried and glittering tides, my own New York, not only the New World's but the world's city—but, newcomer to Denver as I am, and threading its streets, breathing its air, warm'd by its sunshine, and having what there is of its human as well as aerial ozone flash'd upon me now for only three or four days, I am very much like a man feels sometimes toward certain people he meets with, and warms to, and hardly knows why. I, too, can hardly tell why, but as I enter'd the city in the slight haze of a late September afternoon, and have breath'd its air, and slept well o' nights, and have roam'd or rode leisurely, and watch'd the comers and goers at the hotels, and absorb'd the climatic magnetism of this curiously attractive region, there has steadily grown upon me a feeling of affection for the spot, which, sudden as it is, has become so definite and strong that I must put it on record."

So much for my feeling toward the Queen city of the plains and peaks, where she sits in her delicious rare atmosphere, over 5000 feet above sea-level, irrigated by mountain streams, one way looking east over the prairies for a thousand miles, and having the other, westward, in constant view by day, draped in their violet haze, mountain tops innumerable. Yes, I fell in love with Denver, and even felt a wish to spend my declining and dying days there.

I Turn South—and Then East Again

Leave Denver at 8 A.M. by the Rio Grande RR. going south. Mountains constantly in sight in the apparently near distance, veil'd slightly, but still clear and very grand—their cones, colors, sides, distinct against the sky—hundreds, it seem'd thousands, interminable necklaces of them, their tops and slopes hazed more or less slightly in that blue-gray, under the autumn sun, for over a hundred miles—the most spiritual show of objective Nature I ever beheld, or ever thought possible. Occasionally the light strengthens, making a contrast of yellow-tinged silver on one side, with dark and shaded gray on the other. I took a long look at Pike's peak, and was a little disappointed. (I suppose I had expected something stunning.) Our view over plains to the left stretches amply, with corrals here and there, the frequent cactus and wild ange, and herds of cattle feeding. Thus about 120 miles to Pueblo. At that town we board the comfortable and well-equipt Atchison, Topeka and Santa Fe RR., now striking east.

Unfulfill'd Wants—The Arkansas River

I had wanted to go to the Yellowstone river region—wanted specially to see the National Park, and the geysers and the "hoo-doo" or goblin land of that country; indeed, hesitated a little at Pueblo, the turning point—wanted to thread the Veta pass—wanted to go over the Santa Fe trail away southwestward to New Mexico—but turn'd and set my face eastward—leaving behind me whetting glimpse-tastes of southeastern Colorado, Pueblo, Bald mountain, the Spanish peaks, Sangre de Christos, Mile-Shoe-curve (which my veteran friend on the locomotive told me was "the boss railroad curve of the universe,") fort Garland on the plains, Veta, and the three great peaks of the Sierra Blancas.

The Arkansas river plays quite a part in the whole of this region—I see it, or its high-cut rocky northern shore, for miles, and cross and recross it frequently, as it winds and squirms like a snake. The plains vary here even more than usual—sometimes a long sterile stretch of scores of miles—then green, fertile and grassy, an equal length. Some very large herds of sheep. (One wants new words in writing about these plains, and all the inland American West—the terms, *far, large, vast,* &c., are insufficient.)

A Silent Little Follower—The Coreopsis

Here I must say a word about a little follower, present even now before my eyes. I have been accompanied on my whole journey from Barnegat to Pike's Peak by a pleasant floricultural friend, or rather millions of friends—nothing more or less than a hardy little yellow five petal'd September and October wild flower, growing I think everywhere in the middle and northern United States. I had seen it on the Hudson and over Long Island, and along the banks of the Delaware and through New Jersey, (as years ago up the Connecticut, and one fall by Lake Champlain.) This trip it follow'd me regularly, with its slender stem and eyes of gold, from Cape May to the Kaw valley, and so through the cañons and to these plains. In Missouri I saw immense fields all bright with it. Toward western Illinois I woke up one morning in the sleeper and the first thing when I drew the curtain of my berth and look'd out was its pretty countenance and bending neck.

Sept. 25th.—Early morning—still going east after we leave Sterling, Kansas, where I stopp'd a day and night. The sun up about half an hour; nothing can be fresher or more beautiful than this time, this region. I see quite a field of my yellow flower in full bloom. At intervals dots of nice two-story houses, as we ride swiftly by. Over the immense area, flat as a floor, visible for twenty miles in every direction in the clear air, a prevalence of autumn-drab and reddish-tawny herbage—sparse stacks of hay and enclosures, breaking the landscape—as we rumble by, flocks of prairie-hens starting up. Between Sterling and Florence a fine country. (Remembrances to E. L., my old-young soldier friend of war times, and his wife and boy at S.)

The Prairies and Great Plains in Poetry

(After traveling Illinois, Missouri, Kansas and Colorado.)

Grand as the thought that doubtless the child is already born who will see a hundred millions of people, the most prosperous and advanc'd of the world, inhabiting these Prairies, the great Plains, and the valley of the Mississippi, I could not help thinking it would be grander still to see all those inimitable American areas fused in the alembic of a perfect poem, or other esthetic work, entirely western, fresh and limitless—altogether our own, without a trace or taste of Europe's soil, reminiscence, technical letter or spirit. My days and nights, as I travel here—what an exhilaration!—not the air alone, and the sense of vastness, but every local sight and feature. Everywhere something characteristic—the cactuses, pinks, buffalo grass, wild sage—the receding perspective, and the far circle-line of the horizon all times of day, especially forenoon—the clear, pure, cool, rarefied nutriment for the lungs, previously quite unknown—the black patches and streaks left by surface-conflagrations—the deep-plough'd furrow of the "fire-guard"—the slanting snow-racks built all along to shield the railroad from winter drifts—the prairie-dogs and the herds of antelope—the curious "dry rivers"—occasionally a "dug-out" or corral—Fort Riley and Fort Wallace—those towns of the northern plains, (like ships on the sea,) Eagle-Tail, Coyotè, Cheyenne, Agate, Monotony, Kit Carson—with ever the ant-hill and the buffalo-wallow—ever the herds of cattle and the cow-boys ("cow-punchers") to me a strangely interesting class, bright-eyed as hawks, with their swarthy complexions and their broad-brimm'd hats—apparently always on horseback, with loose arms slightly raised and swinging as they ride.

The Spanish Peaks—Evening on the Plains

Between Pueblo and Bent's fort, southward, in a clear afternoon sun-spell I catch exceptionally good glimpses of the

Spanish peaks. We are in southeastern Colorado—pass immense herds of cattle as our first-class locomotive rushes us along—two or three times crossing the Arkansas, which we follow many miles, and of which river I get fine views, sometimes for quite a distance, its stony, upright, not very high, palisade banks, and then its muddy flats. We pass Fort Lyon—lots of adobie houses—limitless pasturage, appropriately fleck'd with those herds of cattle—in due time the declining sun in the west—a sky of limpid pearl over all—and so evening on the great plains. A calm, pensive, boundless landscape—the perpendicular rocks of the north Arkansas, hued in twilight—a thin line of violet on the southwestern horizon—the palpable coolness and slight aroma—a belated cowboy with some unruly member of his herd—an emigrant wagon toiling yet a little further, the horses slow and tired—two men, apparently father and son, jogging along on foot—and around all the indescribable *chiaroscuro* and sentiment, (profounder than anything at sea,) athwart these endless wilds.

America's Characteristic Landscape

Speaking generally as to the capacity and sure future destiny of that plain and prairie area (larger than any European kingdom) it is the inexhaustible land of wheat, maize, wool, flax, coal, iron, beef and pork, butter and cheese, apples and grapes—land of ten million virgin farms—to the eye at present wild and unproductive—yet experts say that upon it when irrigated may easily be grown enough wheat to feed the world. Then as to scenery (giving my own thought and feeling,) while I know the standard claim is that Yosemite, Niagara falls, the upper Yellowstone and the like, afford the greatest natural shows, I am not so sure but the Prairies and Plains, while less stunning at first sight, last longer, fill the esthetic sense fuller, precede all the rest, and make North America's characteristic landscape.

Indeed through the whole of this journey, with all its shows and varieties, what most impress'd me, and will longest remain with me, are these same prairies. Day after day, and night after night, to my eyes, to all my senses—the esthetic one most of all—they silently and broadly unfolded. Even their simplest statistics are sublime.

Earth's Most Important Stream

The valley of the Mississippi river and its tributaries, (this stream and its adjuncts involve a big part of the question,) comprehends more than twelve hundred thousand square miles, the greater part prairies. It is by far the most important stream on the globe, and would seem to have been marked out by design, slow-flowing from north to south, through a dozen climates, all fitted for man's healthy occupancy, its outlet unfrozen all the year, and its line forming a safe, cheap continental avenue for commerce and passage from the north temperate to the torrid zone. Not even the mighty Amazon (though larger in volume) on its line of east and west—not the Nile in Africa, nor the Danube in Europe, nor the three great rivers of China, compare with it. Only the Mediterranean sea has play'd some such part in history, and all through the past, as the Mississippi is destined to play in the future. By its demesnes, water'd and welded by its branches, the Missouri, the Ohio, the Arkansas, the Red, the Yazoo, the St. Francis and others, it already compacts twenty-five millions of people, not merely the most peaceful and money-making, but the most restless and warlike on earth. Its valley, or reach, is rapidly concentrating the political power of the American Union. One almost thinks it *is* the Union—or soon will be. Take it out, with its radiations, and what would be left? From the car windows through Indiana, Illinois, Missouri, or stopping some days along the Topeka and Santa Fe road, in southern Kansas, and indeed wherever I went, hundreds and thousands of miles through this region, my eyes feasted on primitive and rich meadows, some of them partially inhabited, but far, immensely far more untouch'd, unbroken—and much of it more lovely and fertile in its unplough'd innocence than the fair and valuable fields of New York's, Pennsylvania's, Maryland's or Virginia's richest farms.

Prairie Analogies—The Tree Question

The word Prairie is French, and means literally meadow. The cosmical analogies of our North American plains are the

Steppes of Asia, the Pampas and Llanos of South America, and perhaps the Saharas of Africa. Some think the plains have been originally lake-beds; others attribute the absence of forests to the fires that almost annually sweep over them—(the cause, in vulgar estimation, of Indian summer.) The tree question will soon become a grave one. Although the Atlantic slope, the Rocky mountain region, and the southern portion of the Mississippi valley, are well wooded, there are here stretches of hundreds and thousands of miles where either not a tree grows, or often useless destruction has prevail'd; and the matter of the cultivation and spread of forests may well be press'd upon thinkers who look to the coming generations of the prairie States.

Mississippi Valley Literature

Lying by one rainy day in Missouri to rest after quite a long exploration—first trying a big volume I found there of "Milton, Young, Gray, Beattie and Collins," but giving it up for a bad job—enjoying however for awhile, as often before, the reading of Walter Scott's poems, "Lay of the Last Minstrel," "Marmion," and so on—I stopp'd and laid down the book, and ponder'd the thought of a poetry that should in due time express and supply the teeming region I was in the midst of, and have briefly touch'd upon. One's mind needs but a moment's deliberation anywhere in the United States to see clearly enough that all the prevalent book and library poets, either as imported from Great Britain, or follow'd and *doppelgang'd* here, are foreign to our States, copiously as they are read by us all. But to fully understand not only how absolutely in opposition to our times and lands, and how little and cramp'd, and what anachronisms and absurdities many of their pages are, for American purposes, one must dwell or travel awhile in Missouri, Kansas and Colorado, and get rapport with their people and country.

Will the day ever come—no matter how long deferr'd—when those models and lay-figures from the British islands—and even the precious traditions of the classics—will be reminiscences, studies only? The pure breath, primitiveness, boundless prodigality and amplitude, strange mixture of delicacy and power, of continence, of real and ideal, and of all original and first-class elements, of these prairies, the Rocky mountains, and of the Mississippi and Missouri rivers—will they ever appear in, and in some sort form a standard for our poetry and art? (I sometimes think that even the ambition of my friend Joaquin Miller to put them in, and illustrate them, places him ahead of the whole crowd.)

Not long ago I was down New York bay, on a steamer, watching the sunset over the dark green heights of Navesink, and viewing all that inimitable spread of shore, shipping and sea, around Sandy hook. But an intervening week or two, and my eyes catch the shadowy outlines of the Spanish peaks. In the more than two thousand miles between, though of infinite and paradoxical variety, a curious and absolute fusion is doubtless steadily annealing, compacting, identifying all. But subtler and wider and more solid, (to produce such compaction,) than the laws of the States, or the common ground of Congress or the Supreme Court, or the grim welding of our national wars, or the steel ties of railroads, or all the kneading and fusing processes of our material and business history, past or present, would in my opinion be a great throbbing, vital, imaginative work, or series of works, or literature, in constructing which the Plains, the Prairies, and the Mississippi river, with the demesnes of its varied and ample valley, should be the concrete background, and America's humanity, passions, struggles, hopes, there and now—an *eclaircissement* as it is and is to be, on the stage of the New World, of all Time's hitherto drama of war, romance and evolution—should furnish the lambent fire, the ideal.

An Interviewer's Item

Oct. 17, '79.—To-day one of the newspapers of St. Louis prints the following informal remarks of mine on American, especially Western literature: "We called on Mr. Whitman yesterday and after a somewhat desultory conversation abruptly asked him: 'Do you think we are to have a distinctively American literature?' 'It seems to me,' said he, 'that our work at present is to lay the foundations of a great nation in products, in agriculture, in commerce, in networks of intercommunication, and in all that relates to the comforts of vast masses of men and families, with freedom of speech, ecclesiasticism, &c. These we have founded and are carrying out on a grander scale than ever hitherto, and Ohio, Illinois, Indiana, Missouri, Kansas and Colorado, seem to me to be the seat and field of these very facts and ideas. Materialistic prosperity in all its varied forms, with those other points that I mentioned, intercommunication and freedom, are first to be attended to. When those have their results and get settled, then a literature worthy of us will begin to be defined. Our American superiority and vitality are in the bulk of our people, not in a gentry like the old world. The greatness of our army during the secession war, was in the rank and file, and so with the nation. Other lands have their vitality in a few, a class, but we have it in the bulk of the people. Our leading men are not of much account and never have been, but the average of the people is immense, beyond all history. Sometimes I think in all departments, literature and art included, that will be the way our superiority will exhibit itself. We will not have great individuals or great leaders, but a great average bulk, unprecedentedly great.' "

The Women of the West

Kansas City.—I am not so well satisfied with what I see of the women of the prairie cities. I am writing this where I sit leisurely in a store in Main street, Kansas city, a streaming crowd on the sidewalks flowing by. The ladies (and the same in Denver) are all fashionably drest, and have the look of "gentility" in face, manner and action, but they do *not* have, either in physique or the mentality appropriate to them, any high native originality of spirit or body, (as the men certainly have, appropriate to them.) They are "intellectual" and fashionable, but dyspeptic-looking and generally doll-like; their ambition evidently is to copy their eastern sisters. Something far different and in advance must appear, to tally and complete the superb masculinity of the West, and maintain and continue it.

The Silent General

Sept. 28, '79.—So General Grant, after circumambiating the world, has arrived home again—landed in San Francisco yesterday, from the ship City of Tokio from Japan. What a man he is! what a history! what an illustration—his life—of the capacities of that American individuality common to us all. Cynical critics are wondering "what the people can see in Grant" to make such a hubbub about. They aver (and it is no doubt true) that he has hardly the average of our day's literary and scholastic culture, and absolutely no pronounc'd genius or conventional eminence of any sort. Correct: but he proves how an average western farmer, mechanic, boatman, carried by tides of circumstances, perhaps caprices, into a position of incredible military or civic responsibilities, (history has presented none more trying, no born monarch's, no mark more shining for attack or envy,) may steer his way fitly and steadily through them all, carrying the country and himself with credit year after year—command over a million armed men—fight more than fifty pitch'd battles—rule for eight years a land larger than all the kingdoms of Europe combined—and then, retiring, quietly (with a cigar in his mouth) make the promenade of the whole world, through its courts and coteries, and kings and czars and mikados, and splendidest glitters and etiquettes, as phlegmatically as he ever walk'd the portico of a Missouri hotel after dinner. I say all this is what people like—and I am sure I like it. Seems to me it transcends Plutarch. How those old Greeks, indeed, would have seized on him! A mere plain man—no art, no poetry—only practical sense, ability to do, or try his best to do, what devolv'd upon him. A common trader, money-maker, tanner, farmer of Illinois—general for the republic, in its terrific struggle with itself, in the war of attempted secession—President following, (a task of peace, more difficult than the war itself)—nothing heroic, as the authorities put it—and yet the greatest hero. The gods, the destinies, seem to have concentrated upon him.

President Hayes's Speeches

Sept. 30.—I see President Hayes has come out West, passing quite informally from point to point, with his wife and a small cortege of big officers, receiving ovations, and making daily and sometimes double-daily addresses to the people. To these addresses—all impromptu, and some would call them ephemeral—I feel to devote a memorandum. They are shrewd, good-natur'd, face-to-face speeches, on easy topics not too deep; but they give me some revised ideas of oratory—of a new, opportune theory and practice of that art, quite changed from the classic rules, and adapted to our days, our occasions, to American democracy, and to the swarming populations of the West. I hear them criticised as wanting in dignity, but to me they are just what they should be, considering all the circumstances, who they come from, and who they are address'd to. Underneath, his objects are to compact and fraternize the States, encourage their materialistic and industrial development, soothe and expand their self-poise, and tie all and each with resistless double ties not only of inter-trade barter, but human comradeship.

From Kansas city I went on to St. Louis, where I remain'd nearly three months, with my brother T. J. W., and my dear nieces.

St. Louis Memoranda

Oct., Nov., and Dec., '79.—The points of St. Louis are its position, its absolute wealth, (the long accumulations of time and trade, solid riches, probably a higher average thereof than any city,) the unrivall'd amplitude of its well-laid out environage of broad plateaus, for future expansion—and the great State of which it is the head. It fuses northern and southern qualities, perhaps native and foreign ones, to perfection, rendezvous the whole stretch of the Mississippi and Missouri rivers, and its American electricity goes well with its German phlegm. Fourth, Fifth and Third streets are store-streets, showy, modern, metropolitan, with hurrying crowds, vehicles, horse-cars, hubbub, plenty of people, rich goods, plate-glass windows, iron fronts often five or six stories high. You can purchase anything in St. Louis (in most of the big western cities for the matter of that) just as readily and cheaply as in the Atlantic marts. Often in going about the town you see reminders of old, even decay'd civilization. The water of the west, in some places, is not good, but they make it up here by plenty of very fair wine, and inexhaustible quantities of the best beer in the world. There are immense establishments for slaughtering beef and pork—and I saw flocks of sheep, 5000 in a flock. (In Kansas city I had visited a packing establishment that kills and packs an average of 2500 hogs a day the whole year round, for export. Another in Atchison, Kansas, same extent; others nearly equal elsewhere. And just as big ones here.)

Nights on the Mississippi

Oct. 29th, 30th, and 31st.—Wonderfully fine, with the full harvest moon, dazzling and silvery. I have haunted the river every night lately, where I could get a look at the bridge by moonlight. It is indeed a structure of perfection and beauty unsurpassable, and I never tire of it. The river at present is very low; I noticed to-day it had much more of a blue-clear look than usual. I hear the slight ripples, the air is fresh and cool, and the view, up or down, wonderfully clear, in the moonlight. I am out pretty late: it is so fascinating, dreamy. The cool night-air, all the influences, the silence, with those far-off eternal stars, do me good. I have been quite ill of late. And so, well-near the centre of our national demesne, these night views of the Mississippi.

Upon Our Own Land

"Always, after supper, take a walk half a mile long," says an old proverb, dryly adding, "and if convenient let it be upon your own land." I wonder does any other nation but ours afford opportunity for such a jaunt as this? Indeed has any previous period afforded it? No one, I discover, begins to know the real geographic, democratic, indissoluble American Union in the present, or suspect it in the future, until he explores these Central States, and dwells awhile observantly on their prairies, or amid their busy towns, and the mighty father of waters. A ride of two or three thousand miles, "on one's own land," with hardly a disconnection, could certainly be had in no other place than the United States, and at no period before this. If you want to see what the railroad is, and how civilization and progress date from it—how it is the conqueror of crude nature, which it turns to man's use, both on small scales and on the largest—come hither to inland America.

I return'd home, east, Jan. 5, 1880, having travers'd, to and fro and across, 10,000 miles and more. I soon resumed my seclusions down in the woods, or by the creek, or gaddings about cities, and an occasional disquisition, as will be seen following.

Edgar Poe's Significance

Jan. 1, '80.—In diagnosing this disease called humanity—to assume for the nonce what seems a chief mood of the personality and writings of my subject—I have thought that poets, somewhere or other on the list, present the most mark'd indications. Comprehending artists in a mass, musicians, painters, actors, and so on, and considering each and all of them as radiations or flanges of that furious whirling wheel, poetry, the centre and axis of the whole, where else indeed may we so well investigate the causes, growths, tally-marks of the time—the age's matter and malady?

By common consent there is nothing better for man or woman than a perfect and noble life, morally without flaw, happily balanced in activity, physically sound and pure, giving its due proportion, and no more, to the sympathetic, the human emotional element—a life, in all these, unhasting, unresting, untiring to the end. And yet there is another shape of personality dearer far to the artist-sense, (which likes the play of strongest lights and shades,) where the perfect character, the good, the heroic, although never attain'd, is never lost sight of, but through failures, sorrows, temporary downfalls, is return'd to again and again, and while often violated, is passionately adhered to as long as mind, muscles, voice, obey the power we call volition. This sort of personality we see more or less in Burns, Byron, Schiller, and George Sand. But we do not see it in Edgar Poe. (All this is the result of reading at intervals the last three days a new volume of his poems—I took it on my rambles down by the pond, and by degrees read it all through there.) While to the character first outlined the service Poe renders is certainly that entire contrast and contradiction which is next best to fully exemplifying it.

Almost without the first sign of moral principle, or of the concrete or its heroisms, or the simpler affections of the heart, Poe's verses illustrate an intense faculty for technical and abstract beauty, with the rhyming art to excess, an incorrigible propensity toward nocturnal themes, a demoniac undertone behind every page—and, by final judgment, probably belong among the electric lights of imaginative literature, brilliant and dazzling, but with no heat. There is an indescribable magnetism about the poet's life and reminiscences, as well as the poems. To one who could work out their subtle retracing and retrospect, the latter would make a close tally no doubt between the author's birth and antecedents, his childhood and youth, his physique, his so-call'd education, his studies and associates, the literary and social Baltimore, Richmond, Philadelphia and New York, of those times—not only the places and circumstances in themselves, but often, very often, in a strange spurning of, and reaction from them all.

The following from a report in the Washington "Star" of November 16, 1875, may afford those who care for it something further of my point of view toward this interesting figure and influence of our era. There occurr'd about that date in Baltimore a public reburial of Poe's remains, and dedication of a monument over the grave:

> "Being in Washington on a visit at the time, 'the old gray' went over to Baltimore, and though ill from paralysis, consented to hobble up and silently take a seat on the platform, but refused to make any speech, saying, 'I have felt a strong impulse to come over and be here to-day myself in memory of Poe, which I have obey'd, but not the slightest impulse to make a speech, which, my dear friends, must also be obeyed.' In an informal circle, however, in conversation after the ceremonies, Whitman said: 'For a long while, and until lately, I had a distaste for Poe's writings. I wanted, and still want for poetry, the clear sun shining, and fresh air blowing—the strength and power of health, not of delirium, even amid the stormiest passions—with always the background of the eternal moralities. Non-complying with

these requirements, Poe's genius has yet conquer'd a special recognition for itself, and I too have come to fully admit it, and appreciate it and him.

" 'In a dream I once had, I saw a vessel on the sea, at midnight, in a storm. It was no great full-rigg'd ship, nor majestic steamer, steering firmly through the gale, but seem'd one of those superb little schooner yachts I had often seen lying anchor'd, rocking so jauntily, in the waters around New York, or up Long Island sound—now flying uncontroll'd with torn sails and broken spars through the wild sleet and winds and waves of the night. On the deck was a slender, slight, beautiful figure, a dim man, apparently enjoying all the terror, the murk, and the dislocation of which he was the centre and the victim. That figure of my lurid dream might stand for Edgar Poe, his spirit, his fortunes, and his poems—themselves all lurid dreams.' "

Much more may be said, but I most desired to exploit the idea put at the beginning. By its popular poets the calibres of an age, the weak spots of its embankments, its sub-currents, (often more significant than the biggest surface ones,) are unerringly indicated. The lush and the weird that have taken such extraordinary possession of Nineteenth century verse-lovers—what mean they? The inevitable tendency of poetic culture to morbidity, abnormal beauty—the sickliness of all technical thought or refinement in itself—the abnegation of the perennial and democratic concretes at first hand, the body, the earth and sea, sex and the like—and the substitution of something for them at second or third hand—what bearings have they on current pathological study?

Beethoven's Septette

Feb. 11, '80.—At a good concert to-night in the foyer of the opera house, Philadelphia—the band a small but first-rate one. Never did music more sink into and soothe and fill me—never so prove its soul-rousing power, its impossibility of statement. Especially in the rendering of one of Beethoven's master septettes by the well-chosen and perfectly-combined instruments (violins, viola, clarionet, horn, 'cello and contra-bass,) was I carried away, seeing, absorbing many wonders.

Dainty abandon, sometimes as if Nature laughing on a hill-side in the sunshine; serious and firm monotonies, as of winds; a horn sounding through the tangle of the forest, and the dying echoes; soothing floating of waves, but presently rising in surges, angrily lashing, muttering, heavy; piercing peals of laughter, for interstices; now and then weird, as Nature herself is in certain moods—but mainly spontaneous, easy, careless—often the sentiment of the postures of naked children playing or sleeping. It did me good even to watch the violinists drawing their bows so masterly—every motion a study. I allow'd myself, as I sometimes do, to wander out of myself. The conceit came to me of a copious grove of singing birds, and in their midst a simple harmonic duo, two human souls, steadily asserting their own pensiveness, joyousness.

A Hint of Wild Nature

Feb. 13.—As I was crossing the Delaware to-day, saw a large flock of wild geese, right overhead, not very high up, ranged in V-shape, in relief against the noon clouds of light smoke-color. Had a capital though momentary view of them, and then of their course on and on southeast, till gradually fading—(my eyesight yet first rate for the open air and its distances, but I use glasses for reading.) Queer thoughts melted into me the two or three minutes, or less, seeing these creatures cleaving the sky—the spacious, airy realm—even the prevailing smoke-gray color everywhere, (no sun shining)—the waters below—the rapid flight of the birds, appearing just for a minute—flashing to me such a hint of the whole spread of Nature, with her eternal unsophisticated freshness, her never-visited recesses of sea, sky, shore—and then disappearing in the distance.

Loafing in the Woods

March 8.—I write this down in the country again, but in a new spot, seated on a log in the woods, warm, sunny, midday. Have been loafing here deep among the trees, shafts of tall pines, oak, hickory, with a thick undergrowth of laurels and grapevines—the ground cover'd everywhere by debris, dead leaves, breakage, moss—everything solitary, ancient, grim. Paths (such as they are) leading hither and yon—(how made I know not, for nobody seems to come here, nor man nor cattle-kind.) Temperature to-day about 60, the wind through the pine-tops; I sit and listen to its hoarse sighing above (and to the *stillness*) long and long, varied by aimless rambles in the old roads and paths, and by exercise-pulls at the young saplings, to keep my joints from getting stiff. Blue-birds, robins, meadow-larks begin to appear.

Next day, 9th.—A snowstorm in the morning, and continuing most of the day. But I took a walk over two hours, the same woods and paths, amid the falling flakes. No wind, yet the musical low murmur through the pines, quite pronounced, curious, like waterfalls, now still'd, now pouring again. All the senses, sight, sound, smell, delicately gratified. Every snowflake lay where it fell on the evergreens, holly-trees, laurels, &c., the multitudinous leaves and branches piled, bulging-white, defined by edge-lines of emerald—the tall straight columns of the plentiful bronze-topt pines—a slight resinous odor blending with that of the snow. (For there is a scent to everything, even the snow, if you can only detect it—no two places, hardly any two hours, anywhere, exactly alike. How different the odor of noon from midnight, or winter from summer, or a windy spell from a still one.)

A Contralto Voice

May 9, Sunday.—Visit this evening to my friends the J.'s—good supper, to which I did justice—lively chat with Mrs. J. and I. and J. As I sat out front on the walk afterward, in the evening air, the church-choir and organ on the corner opposite gave Luther's hymn, *Ein feste berg,* very finely. The air was borne by a rich contralto. For nearly half an hour there in the dark, (there was a good string of English stanzas,) came the music, firm and unhurried, with long pauses. The full silver star-beams of Lyra rose silently over the church's dim roof-ridge. Varicolor'd lights from the stain'd glass windows broke through the tree-shadows. And under all—under the Northern Crown up there, and in the fresh breeze below, and the *chiaroscuro* of the night, that liquid-full contralto.

Seeing Niagara to Advantage

June 4, '80.—For really seizing a great picture or book, or piece of music, or architecture, or grand scenery—or perhaps for the first time even the common sunshine, or landscape, or may be even the mystery of identity, most curious mystery of all—there comes some lucky five minutes of a man's life, set amid a fortuitous concurrence of circumstances, and bringing in a brief flash the culmination of years of reading and travel and thought. The present case about two o'clock this afternoon, gave me Niagara, its superb severity of action and color and majestic grouping, in one short, indescribable show. We were very slowly crossing the Suspension bridge—not a full stop anywhere, but next to it—the day clear, sunny, still—and I out on the platform. The falls were in plain view about a mile off, but very distinct, and no roar—hardly a murmur. The river tumbling green and white, far below me; the dark high banks, the plentiful umbrage, many bronze cedars, in shadow; and tempering and arching all the immense materiality, a clear sky overhead, with a few white clouds, limpid, spiritual, silent. Brief, and as quiet as brief, that picture—a remembrance always afterwards. Such are the things, indeed, I lay away with my life's rare and blessed bits of hours, reminiscent, past—the wild sea-storm I once saw one winter day, off Fire island—the elder Booth in Richard, that famous night forty years ago in the old Bowery—or Alboni in the children's scene in Norma—or night-views, I remember, on the field, after battles in Virginia—or the peculiar sentiment of moonlight and stars over the great Plains, western Kansas—or scooting up New York bay, with a stiff breeze and a good yacht, off Navesink. With these, I say, I henceforth place that view, that afternoon, that combination complete, that five minutes' perfect absorption of Niagara—not the great majestic gem alone by itself, but set complete in all its varied, full, indispensable surroundings.

Jaunting to Canada

To go back a little, I left Philadelphia, 9th and Green streets, at 8 o'clock P. M., June 3, on a first-class sleeper, by the Lehigh Valley (North Pennsylvania) route, through Bethlehem, Wilkesbarre, Waverly, and so (by Erie) on through Corning to Hornellsville, where we arrived at 8, morning, and had a bounteous breakfast. I must say I never put in such a good night on any railroad track—smooth, firm, the minimum of jolting, and all the swiftness compatible with safety. So without change to Buffalo, and thence to Clifton, where we arrived early afternoon; then on to London, Ontario, Canada, in four more—less than twenty-two hours altogether. I am domiciled at the hospitable house of my friends Dr. and Mrs. Bucke, in the ample and charming garden and lawns of the asylum.

Sunday with the Insane

June 6.—Went over to the religious services (Episcopal) main Insane asylum, held in a lofty, good-sized hall, third story. Plain boards, whitewash, plenty of cheap chairs, no ornament or color, yet all scrupulously clean and sweet. Some three hundred persons present, mostly patients. Everything, the prayers, a short sermon, the firm, orotund voice of the minister, and most of all, beyond any portraying or suggesting, *that audience,* deeply impress'd me. I was furnish'd with an arm-chair near the pulpit, and sat facing the motley, yet perfectly well-behaved and orderly congregation. The quaint dresses and bonnets of some of the women, several very old and gray, here and there like the heads in old pictures. O the looks that came from those faces! There were two or three I shall probably never forget. Nothing at all markedly repulsive or hideous—strange enough I did not see one such. Our common humanity, mine and yours, everywhere:

> "The same old blood—the same red, running blood;"

yet behind most, an inferr'd arriere of such storms, such wrecks, such mysteries, fires, love, wrong, greed for wealth, religious problems, crosses—mirror'd from those crazed faces (yet now temporarily so calm, like still waters,) all the woes and sad happenings of life and death—now from every one the devotional element radiating—was it not, indeed, *the peace of God that passeth all understanding,* strange as it may sound? I can only say that I took long and searching eye-sweeps as I sat there, and it seem'd so, rousing unprecedented thoughts, problems unanswerable. A very fair choir, and melodeon accompaniment. They sang "Lead, kindly light," after the sermon. Many join'd in the beautiful hymn, to which the minister read the introductory text, *"In the daytime also He led them with a cloud, and all the night with a light of fire."* Then the words:

Lead, kindly light, amid the encircling gloom,
Lead thou me on.
The night is dark, and I am far from home;
Lead thou me on.
Keep thou my feet; I do not ask to see
The distant scene; one step enough for me.

I was not ever thus, nor pray'd that thou
Should'st lead me on;
I lov'd to choose and see my path; but now
Lead thou me on.
I loved the garish day, and spite of fears
Pride ruled my will; remember not past years.

A couple of days after, I went to the "Refractory building," under special charge of Dr. Beemer, and through the wards pretty thoroughly, both the men's and women's. I have since made many other visits of the kind through the asylum, and around among the detach'd cottages. As far as I could see, this is among the most advanced, perfected, and kindly and rationally carried on, of all its kind in America. It is a town in itself, with many buildings and a thousand inhabitants.

I learn that Canada, and especially this ample and populous province, Ontario, has the very best and plentiest benevolent institutions in all departments.

Reminiscence of Elias Hicks

June 8.—To-day a letter from Mrs. E. S. L., Detroit, accompanied in a little post-office roll by a rare old engraved head of Elias Hicks, (from a portrait in oil by Henry Inman, painted for J. V. S., must have been 60 years or more ago, in

New York)—among the rest the following excerpt about E. H. in the letter:

> "I have listen'd to his preaching so often when a child, and sat with my mother at social gatherings where he was the centre, and every one so pleas'd and stirr'd by his conversation. I hear that you contemplate writing or speaking about him, and I wonder'd whether you had a picture of him. As I am the owner of two, I send you one."

Grand Native Growth

In a few days I go to lake Huron, and may have something to say of that region and people. From what I already see, I should say the young native population of Canada was growing up, forming a hardy, democratic, intelligent, radically sound, and just as American, good-natured and *individualistic* race, as the average range of best specimens among us. As among us, too, I please myself by considering that this element, though it may not be the majority, promises to be the leaven which must eventually leaven the whole lump.

A Zollverein Between the U. S. and Canada

Some of the more liberal of the presses here are discussing the question of a zollverein between the United States and Canada. It is proposed to form a union for commercial purposes—to altogether abolish the frontier tariff line, with its double sets of custom house officials now existing between the two countries, and to agree upon one tariff for both, the proceeds of this tariff to be divided between the two governments on the basis of population. It is said that a large proportion of the merchants of Canada are in favor of this step, as they believe it would materially add to the business of the country, by removing the restrictions that now exist on trade between Canada and the States. Those persons who are opposed to the measure believe that it would increase the material welfare of the country, but it would loosen the bonds between Canada and England; and this sentiment overrides the desire for commercial prosperity. Whether the sentiment can continue to bear the strain put upon it is a question. It is thought by many that commercial considerations must in the end prevail. It seems also to be generally agreed that such a zollverein, or common customs union, would bring practically more benefits to the Canadian provinces than to the United States. (It seems to me a certainty of time, sooner or later, that Canada shall form two or three grand States, equal and independent, with the rest of the American Union. The St. Lawrence and lakes are not for a frontier line, but a grand interior or mid-channel.)

The St. Lawrence Line

August 20.—Premising that my three or four months in Canada were intended, among the rest, as an exploration of the line of the St. Lawrence, from lake Superior to the sea, (the engineers here insist upon considering it as one stream, over 2000 miles long, including lakes and Niagara and all)—that I have only partially carried out my programme; but for the seven or eight hundred miles so far fulfill'd, I find that the *Canada question* is absolutely control'd by this vast water line, with its first-class features and points of trade, humanity, and many more—here I am writing this nearly a thousand miles north of my Philadelphia starting-point (by way of Montreal and Quebec) in the midst of regions that go to a further extreme of grimness, wildness of beauty, and a sort of still and pagan *scaredness,* while yet Christian, inhabitable, and partially fertile, than perhaps any other on earth. The weather remains perfect; some might call it a little cool, but I wear my old gray overcoat and find it just right. The days are full of sunbeams and oxygen. Most of the forenoons and afternoons I am on the forward deck of the steamer.

The Savage Saguenay

Up these black waters, over a hundred miles—always strong, deep, (hundreds of feet, sometimes thousands,) ever with high, rocky hills for banks, green and gray—at times a little like some parts of the Hudson, but much more pronounc'd and defiant. The hills rise higher—keep their ranks more unbroken. The river is straighter and of more resolute flow, and its hue, though dark as ink, exquisitely polish'd and sheeny under the August sun. Different, indeed, this Saguenay from all other rivers—different effects—a bolder, more vehement play of lights and shades. Of a rare charm of singleness and simplicity. (Like the organ-chant at midnight from the old Spanish convent, in "Favorita"—one strain only, simple and monotonous and unornamented—but indescribably penetrating and grand and masterful.) Great place for echoes: while our steamer was tied at the wharf at Tadousac (taj-oo-sac) waiting, the escape-pipe letting off steam, I was sure I heard a band at the hotel up in the rocks—could even make out some of the tunes. Only when our pipe stopp'd, I knew what caused it. Then at cape Eternity and Trinity rock, the pilot with his whistle producing similar marvellous results, echoes indescribably weird, as we lay off in the still bay under their shadows.

Capes Eternity and Trinity

But the great, haughty, silent capes themselves; I doubt if any crack points, or hills, or historic places of note, or anything of the kind elsewhere in the world, outvies these objects—(I write while I am before them face to face.) They are very simple, they do not startle—at least they did not me—but they linger in one's memory forever. They are placed very near each other, side by side, each a mountain rising flush out of the Saguenay. A good thrower could throw a stone on each in passing—at least it seems so. Then they are as distinct in form as a perfect physical man or a perfect physical woman. Cape Eternity is bare, rising, as just said, sheer out of the water, rugged and grim (yet with an indescribable beauty) nearly two thousand feet high. Trinity rock, even a little higher, also rising flush, top-rounded like a great head with close-cut verdure of hair. I consider myself well repaid for coming my thousand miles to get the sight and memory of the unrivall'd duo. They have stirr'd me more profoundly than anything of the kind I have yet seen. If Europe or Asia had them, we should certainly hear of them in all sorts of sent-back poems, rhapsodies, &c., a dozen times a year through our papers and magazines.

Chicoutimi and Ha-ha Bay

No indeed—life and travel and memory have offer'd and will preserve to me no deeper-cut incidents, panorama, or sights to cheer my soul, than these at Chicoutimi and Ha-ha bay, and my days and nights up and down this fascinating savage river—the rounded mountains, some bare and gray, some dull red, some draped close all over with matted green verdure or vines—the ample, calm, eternal rocks everywhere—the long streaks of motley foam, a milk-white curd on the glistening breast of the stream—the little two-masted schooner, dingy yellow, with patch'd sails, set wing-and-wing, nearing us, coming saucily up the water with a couple of swarthy, black-hair'd men aboard—the strong shades falling on the light gray or yellow outlines of the hills all through the forenoon, as we steam within gunshot of them—while ever the pure and delicate sky spreads over all. And the splendid sunsets, and the sights of evening—the same old stars, (relatively a little different, I see, so far north) Arcturus and Lyra, and the Eagle, and great Jupiter like a silver globe, and the constellation of the Scorpion. Then northern lights nearly every night.

The Inhabitants—Good Living

Grim and rocky and black-water'd as the demesne hereabout is, however; you must not think genial humanity, and comfort, and good-living are not to be met. Before I began this memorandum I made a first-rate breakfast of sea-trout, finishing off with wild raspberries. I find smiles and courtesy everywhere—physiognomies in general curiously like those in the United States—(I was astonish'd to find the same resemblance all through the province of Quebec.) In general the inhabitants of this rugged country (Charlevoix, Chicoutimi and Tadousac counties, and lake St. John region) a simple, hardy population, lumbering, trapping furs, boating, fishing, berry-picking and a little farming. I was watching a group of young boatmen eating their early dinner—nothing but an immense loaf of bread, had apparently been the size of a bushel measure, from which they cut chunks with a jack-knife. Must be a tremendous winter country this, when the solid frost and ice fully set in.

Cedar-Plums Like—Names

(Back again in Camden and down in Jersey.)

One time I thought of naming this collection "Cedar-Plums Like" (which I still fancy wouldn't have been a bad name, nor inappropriate.) A melange of loafing, looking, hobbling, sitting, traveling—a little thinking thrown in for salt, but very little—not only summer but all seasons—not only days but nights—some literary meditations—books, authors examined, Carlyle, Poe, Emerson tried, (always under my cedar-tree, in the open air, and never in the library)—mostly the scenes everybody sees, but some of my own caprices, meditations, egotism—truly an open air and mainly summer formation—singly, or in clusters—wild and free and somewhat acrid—indeed more like cedar-plums than you might guess at first glance.

But do you know what they are? (To city man, or some sweet parlor lady, I now talk.) As you go along roads, or barrens, or across country, anywhere through these States, middle, eastern, western, or southern, you will see, certain seasons of the year, the thick woolly tufts of the cedar mottled with bunches of china-blue berries, about as big as fox-grapes. But first a special word for the tree itself: everybody knows that the cedar is a healthy, cheap, democratic wood, streak'd red and white—an evergreen—that it is not a *cultivated* tree—that it keeps away moths—that it grows inland or seaboard, all climates, hot or cold, any soil—in fact rather prefers sand and bleak side spots—content if the plough, the fertilizer and the trimming-axe, will but keep away and let it alone. After a long rain, when everything looks bright, often have I stopt in my wood-saunters, south or north, or far west, to take in its dusky green, wash'd clean and sweet, and speck'd copiously with its fruit of clear, hardy blue. The wood of the cedar is of use—but what profit on earth are those sprigs of acrid plums? A question impossible to answer satisfactorily.

True, some of the herb doctors give them for stomachic affections, but the remedy is as bad as the disease. Then in my rambles down in Camden county I once found an old crazy woman gathering the clusters with zeal and joy. She show'd, as I was told afterward, a sort of infatuation for them, and every year placed and kept profuse bunches high and low about her room. They had a strange charm on her uneasy head, and effected docility and peace. (She was harmless, and lived near by with her well-off married daughter.) Whether there is any connection between those bunches, and being out of one's wits, I cannot say, but I myself entertain a weakness for them. Indeed, I love the cedar, anyhow—its naked ruggedness, its just palpable odor, (so different from the perfumer's best,) its silence, its equable acceptance of winter's cold and summer's heat, of rain or drouth—its shelter to me from those, at times—its associations—(well, I never could explain *why* I love anybody, or anything.) The service I now specially owe to the cedar is, while I cast around for a name for my proposed collection, hesitating, puzzled—after rejecting a long, long string, I lift my eyes, and lo! the very term I want. At any rate, I go no further—I tire in the search. I take what some invisible kind spirit has put before me. Besides, who shall say there is not affinity enough between (at least the bundle of sticks that produced) many of these pieces, or granulations, and those blue berries? their uselessness growing wild—a certain aroma of Nature I would so like to have in my pages—the thin soil whence they come—their content in being let alone—their stolid and deaf repugnance to answering questions, (this latter the nearest, dearest trait affinity of all.)

Then reader dear, in conclusion, as to the point of the name for the present collection, let us be satisfied to *have* a name—something to identify and bind it together, to concrete all its vegetable, mineral, personal memoranda, abrupt raids of criticism, crude gossip of philosophy, varied sands clumps—without bothering ourselves because certain pages do not present themselves to you or me as coming under their own name with entire fitness or amiability. (It is a profound, vexatious, never-explicable matter—this of names.

I have been exercised deeply about it my whole life.*)

After all of which the name "Cedar-Plums Like" got its nose put out of joint; but I cannot afford to throw away what I pencill'd down the lane there, under the shelter of my old friend, one warm October noon. Besides, it wouldn't be civil to the cedar tree.

Death of Thomas Carlyle

Feb. 10, '81.—And so the flame of the lamp, after long wasting and flickering, has gone out entirely.

As a representative author, a literary figure, no man else will bequeath to the future more significant hints of our stormy era, its fierce paradoxes, its din, and its struggling parturition periods, than Carlyle. He belongs to our own branch of the stock too; neither Latin nor Greek, but altogether Gothic. Rugged, mountainous, volcanic, he was himself more a French revolution than any of his volumes. In some respects,

*In the pocket of my receptacle-book I find a list of suggested and rejected names for this volume, or parts of it—such as the following:

As the wild bee hums in May,
& August mulleins grow,
& Winter snow-flakes fall,
& stars in the sky roll round.

Away from Books—away from Art,
Now for the Day and Night—the lesson done,
Now for the Sun and Stars.

Notes of a half-Paralytic,
Week in and Week out,
Embers of Ending Days,
Ducks and Drakes,
Flood Tide and Ebb,
Gossip at Early Candle-light,
Echoes and Escapades,
Such as I . . . . . Evening Dews,
Notes after Writing a Book,
Far and Near at 63,
Drifts and Cumulus,
Maize-Tassels. . . . .tindlings,
Fore and Aft. . . . .Vestibules,
Scintilla at 60 and after,
Sands on the Shores of 64,
As Voices in the Dusk, from Speakers far or hid,
Autochthons. . . . .Embryons,
Wing-and-Wing,
Notes and Recallés,
Only Mulleins and Bumble-Bees,
Pond-Babble. . . . . Tête-a-Têtes,
Echoes of a Life in the 19th Century in the New World,
Flanges of Fifty Years,
Abandons. . . . .Œurry Notes,
A Life-Mosaic. . . . .–ative Moments,
Types and Semi-Tones,
Oddments. . . . .Sand-Drifts,
Again and Again.

so far in the Nineteenth century, the best equipt, keenest mind, even from the college point of view, of all Britain; only he had an ailing body. Dyspepsia is to be traced in every page, and now and then fills the page. One may include among the lessons of his life—even though that life stretch'd to amazing length—how behind the tally of genius and morals stands the stomach, and gives a sort of casting vote.

Two conflicting agonistic elements seem to have contended in the man, sometimes pulling him different ways like wild horses. He was a cautious, conservative Scotchman, fully aware what a fœtid gas-bag much of modern radicalism is; but then his great heart demanded reform, demanded change—often terribly at odds with his scornful brain. No author ever put so much wailing and despair into his books, sometimes palpable, oftener latent. He reminds me of that passage in Young's poems where as death presses closer and closer for his prey, the soul rushes hither and thither, appealing, shrieking, berating, to escape the general doom.

Of short-comings, even positive blur-spots, from an American point of view, he had serious share.

Not for his merely literary merit, (though that was great)—not as "maker of books," but as launching into the self-complacent atmosphere of our days a rasping, questioning, dislocating agitation and shock, is Carlyle's final value. It is time the English-speaking peoples had some true idea about the verteber of genius, namely power. As if they must always have it cut and bias'd to the fashion, like a lady's cloak! What a needed service he performs! How he shakes our comfortable reading circles with a touch of the old Hebraic anger and prophecy—and indeed it is just the same. Not Isaiah himself more scornful, more threatening: "The crown of pride, the drunkards of Ephraim, shall be trodden under feet: And the glorious beauty which is on the head of the fat valley shall be a fading flower." (The word prophecy is much misused; it seems narrow'd to prediction merely. That is not the main sense of the Hebrew word translated "prophet;" it means one whose mind bubbles up and pours forth as a fountain, from inner, divine spontaneities revealing God. Prediction is a very minor part of prophecy. The great matter is to reveal and outpour the God-like suggestions pressing for birth in the soul. This is briefly the doctrine of the Friends or Quakers.)

Then the simplicity and amid ostensible frailty the towering strength of this man—a hardy oak knot, you could never wear out—an old farmer dress'd in brown clothes, and not handsome—his very foibles fascinating. Who cares that he wrote about Dr. Francia, and "Shooting Niagara"—and "the Nigger Question,"—and didn't at all admire our United States? (I doubt if he ever thought or said half as bad words about us as we deserve.) How he splashes like leviathan in the seas of modern literature and politics! Doubtless, respecting the latter, one needs first to realize, from actual observation, the squalor, vice and doggedness ingrain'd in the bulk-population of the British Islands, with the red tape, the fatuity, the flunkeyism everywhere, to understand the last meaning in his pages. Accordingly, though he was no chartist or radical, I consider Carlyle's by far the most indignant comment or protest anent the fruits of feudalism to-day in Great Britain—the increasing poverty and degradation of the homeless, landless twenty millions, while a few thousands, or rather a few hundreds, possess the entire soil, the money, and the fat berths. Trade and shipping, and clubs and culture, and prestige, and guns, and a fine select class of gentry and aristocracy, with every modern improvement, cannot begin to salve or defend such stupendous hoggishness.

The way to test how much he has left his country were to consider, or try to consider, for a moment, the array of British thought, the resultant *ensemble* of the last fifty years, as existing to-day, *but with Carlyle left out.* It would be like an army with no artillery. The show were still a gay and rich one—Byron, Scott, Tennyson, and many more—horsemen and rapid infantry, and banners flying—but the last heavy roar so dear to the ear of the train'd soldier, and that settles fate and victory, would be lacking.

For the last three years we in America have had transmitted glimpses of a thin-bodied, lonesome, wifeless, childless, very old man, lying on a sofa, kept out of bed by indomitable will, but, of late, never well enough to take the open air. I have noted this news from time to time in brief descriptions in the papers. A week ago I read such an item just before I started out for my customary evening stroll between eight and nine. In the fine cold night, unusually clear, (Feb. 5, '81,) as I walk'd some open grounds adjacent, the condition of Carlyle, and his approaching—perhaps even then actual—death, filled me with thoughts eluding statement, and curiously blending with the scene. The planet Venus, an hour high in the west, with all her volume and lustre recover'd, (she has been shorn and languid for nearly a year,) including an additional sentiment I never noticed before—not merely voluptuous, Paphian, steeping, fascinating—now with calm commanding seriousness and hauteur—the Milo Venus now. Upward to the zenith, Jupiter, Saturn, and the moon past her quarter, trailing in procession, with the Pleiades following, and the constellation Taurus, and red Aldebaran. Not a cloud in heaven. Orion strode through the southeast, with his glittering belt—and a trifle below hung the sun of the night, Sirius. Every star dilated, more vitreous, nearer than usual. Not as in some clear nights when the larger stars entirely outshine the rest. Every little star or cluster just as distinctly visible, and just as nigh. Berenice's hair showing every gem, and new ones. To the northeast and north the Sickle, the Goat and kids, Cassiopea, Castor and Pollux, and the two Dippers. While through the whole of this silent indescribable show, inclosing and bathing my whole receptivity, ran the thought of Carlyle dying. (To soothe and spiritualize, and, as far as may be, solve the mysteries of death and genius, consider them under the stars at midnight.)

And now that he has gone hence, can it be that Thomas Carlyle, soon to chemically dissolve in ashes and by winds, remains an identity still? In ways perhaps eluding all the statements, lore and speculations of ten thousand years—eluding all possible statements to mortal sense—does he yet exist, a definite, vital being, a spirit, an individual—perhaps now wafted in space among those stellar systems, which, suggestive and limitless as they are, merely edge more limitless, far more suggestive systems? I have no doubt of it. In silence, of a fine night, such questions are answer'd to the soul, the best answers that can be given. With me, too, when depress'd by some specially sad event, or tearing problem, I wait till I go out under the stars for the last voiceless satisfaction.

Carlyle from American Points of View

Later Thoughts and Jottings.

There is surely at present an inexplicable *rapport* (all the more piquant from its contradictoriness) between that deceas'd author and our United States of America—no matter whether it lasts or not.* As we Westerners assume definite shape, and result in formations and fruitage unknown before, it is curious with what a new sense our eyes turn to representative outgrowths of crises and personages in the Old World. Beyond question, since Carlyle's death, and the publication of Froude's memoirs, not only the interest in his books, but every personal bit regarding the famous Scotchman—his dyspepsia, his buffetings, his parentage, his paragon of a wife, his career in Edinburgh, in the lonesome nest on Craigenputtock moor, and then so many years in London—is probably wider and livelier to-day in this country than in his own land. Whether I succeed or no, I, too, reaching across the Atlantic and taking the man's dark fortune-telling of humanity and politics, would offset it all, (such is the fancy that comes to me,) by a far more profound horoscope-casting of those themes—G. F. Hegel's.†

*It will be difficult for the future—judging by his books, personal dissympathies, &c.,—to account for the deep hold this author has taken on the present age, and the way he has color'd its method and thought. I am certainly at a loss to account for it all as affecting myself. But there could be no view, or even partial picture, of the middle and latter part of our Nineteenth century, that did not markedly include Thomas Carlyle. In his case (as so many others, literary productions, works of art, personal identities, events,) there has been an impalpable something more effective than the palpable. Then I find no better text, (it is always important to have a definite, special, even oppositional, living man to start from,) for sending out certain speculations and comparisons for home use. Let us see what they amount to—those reactionary doctrines, fears, scornful analyses of democracy—even from the most erudite and sincere mind of Europe.

†Not the least mentionable part of the case, (a streak, it may be, of that humor with which history and fate love to contrast their gravity,) is that although neither of my great authorities during their lives consider'd the United States worthy of serious mention, all the principal works of both might not inappropriately be this day collected and bound up under the conspicuous title: *"Speculations for the use of North America, and Democracy there, with the relations of the same to Metaphysics, including Lessons and Warnings (encouragements too, and of the vastest,) from the Old World to the New."*

First, about a chance, a never-fulfill'd vacuity of this pale cast of thought—this British Hamlet from Cheyne row, more puzzling than the Danish one, with his contrivances for settling the broken and spavin'd joints of the world's government, especially its democratic dislocation. Carlyle's grim fate was cast to live and dwell in, and largely embody, the parturition agony and qualms of the old order, amid crowded accumulations of ghastly morbidity, giving birth to the new. But conceive of him (or his parents before him) coming to America, recuperated by the cheering realities and activity of our people and country—growing up and delving face-to-face resolutely among us here, especially at the West—inhaling and exhaling our limitless air and eligibilities—devoting his mind to the theories and developments of this Republic amid its practical facts as exemplified in Kansas, Missouri, Illinois, Tennessee, or Louisiana. I say *facts,* and face-to-face confrontings—so different from books, and all those quiddities and mere reports in the libraries, upon which the man (it was wittily said of him at the age of thirty, that there was no one in Scotland who had glean'd so much and seen so little,) almost wholly fed, and which even his sturdy and vital mind but reflected at best.

Something of the sort narrowly escaped happening. In 1835, after more than a dozen years of trial and non-success, the author of "Sartor Resartus" removing to London, very poor, a confirmed hypochondriac, "Sartor" universally scoffed at, no literary prospects ahead, deliberately settled on one last casting-throw of the literary dice—resolv'd to compose and launch forth a book on the subject of *the French Revolution*—and if that won no higher guerdon or prize than hitherto, to sternly abandon the trade of author forever, and emigrate for good to America. But the venture turn'd out a lucky one, and there was no emigration.

Carlyle's work in the sphere of literature as he commenced and carried it out, is the same in one or two leading respects that Immanuel Kant's was in speculative philosophy. But the Scotchman had none of the stomachic phlegm and never-perturb'd placidity of the Konigsberg sage, and did not, like the latter, understand his own limits, and stop when he got to the end of them. He clears away jungle and poison-vines and underbrush—at any rate hacks valiantly at them, smiting hip and thigh. Kant did the like in his sphere, and it was all he profess'd to do; his labors have left the ground fully prepared ever since—and greater service was probably never perform'd by mortal man. But the pang and hiatus of Carlyle seem to me to consist in the evidence everywhere that amid a whirl of fog and fury and cross-purposes, he firmly believ'd he had a clue to the medication of the world's ills, and that his bounden mission was to exploit it.*

There were two anchors, or sheet-anchors, for steadying, as a last resort, the Carlylean ship. One will be specified presently. The other, perhaps the main, was only to be found in some mark'd form of personal force, an extreme degree of competent urge and will, a man or men "born to command." Probably there ran through every vein and current of the Scotchman's blood something that warm'd up to this kind of trait and character above aught else in the world, and which makes him in my opinion the chief celebrater and promulger of it in literature—more than Plutarch, more than Shakspere. The great masses of humanity stand for nothing—at least nothing but nebulous raw material; only the big planets and shining suns for him. To ideas almost invariably languid or cold, a number-one forceful personality was sure to rouse his eulogistic passion and savage joy. In such case, even the standard of duty hereinafter rais'd, was to be instantly lower'd and vail'd. All that is comprehended under the terms republicanism and democracy were distasteful to him from the first, and as he grew older they became hateful and contemptible. For an undoubtedly candid and penetrating faculty such as his, the bearings he persistently ignored were marvellous. For instance, the promise, nay certainty of the democratic principle, to each and every State of the current world, not so much of helping it to perfect legislators and executives, but as the only effectual method for surely, however slowly, training people

*I hope I shall not myself fall into the error I charge upon him, of prescribing a specific for indispensable evils. My utmost pretension is probably but to offset that old claim of the exclusively curative power of first-class individual men, as leaders and rulers, by the claims, and general movement and result, of ideas. Something of the latter kind seems to me the distinctive theory of America, of democracy, and of the modern—or rather, I should say, it *is* democracy, and *is* the modern.

on a large scale toward voluntarily ruling and managing themselves (the ultimate aim of political and all other development)—to gradually reduce the fact of *governing* to its minimum, and to subject all its staffs and their doings to the telescopes and microscopes of committees and parties—and greatest of all, to afford (not stagnation and obedient content, which went well enough with the feudalism and ecclesiasticism of the antique and medieval world, but) a vast and sane and recurrent ebb and tide action for those floods of the great deep that have henceforth palpably burst forever their old bounds—seem never to have enter'd Carlyle's thought. It was splendid how he refus'd any compromise to the last. He was curiously antique. In that harsh, picturesque, most potent voice and figure, one seems to be carried back from the present of the British islands more than two thousand years, to the range between Jerusalem and Tarsus. His fullest best biographer justly says of him:

> "He was a teacher and a prophet, in the Jewish sense of the word. The prophecies of Isaiah and Jeremiah have become a part of the permanent spiritual inheritance of mankind, because events proved that they had interpreted correctly the signs of their own times, and their prophecies were fulfill'd. Carlyle, like them, believ'd that he had a special message to deliver to the present age. Whether he was correct in that belief, and whether his message was a true message, remains to be seen. He has told us that our most cherish'd ideas of political liberty, with their kindred corollaries, are mere illusions, and that the progress which has seem'd to go along with them is a progress towards anarchy and social dissolution. If he was wrong, he has misused his powers. The principles of his teachings are false. He has offer'd himself as a guide upon a road of which he had no knowledge; and his own desire for himself would be the speediest oblivion both of his person and his works. If, on the other hand, he has been right; if, like his great predecessors, he has read truly the tendencies of this modern age of ours, and his teaching is authenticated by facts, then Carlyle, too, will take his place among the inspired seers."

To which I add an amendment that under no circumstances, and no matter how completely time and events disprove his lurid vaticinations, should the English-speaking world forget this man, nor fail to hold in honor his unsurpass'd conscience, his unique method, and his honest fame. Never were convictions more earnest and genuine. Never was there less of a flunkey or temporizer. Never had political progressivism a foe it could more heartily respect.

The second main point of Carlyle's utterance was the idea of *duty being done.* (It is simply a new codicil—if it be particularly new, which is by no means certain—on the time-honor'd bequest of dynasticism, the mould-eaten rules of legitimacy and kings.) He seems to have been impatient sometimes to madness when reminded by persons who thought at least as deeply as himself, that this formula, though precious, is rather a vague one, and that there are many other considerations to a philosophical estimate of each and every department either in general history or individual affairs.

Altogether, I don't know anything more amazing than these persistent strides and throbbings so far through our Nineteenth century of perhaps its biggest, sharpest, and most erudite brain, in defiance and discontent with everything; contemptuously ignoring, (either from constitutional inaptitude, ignorance itself, or more likely because he demanded a definite cure-all here and now,) the only solace and solvent to be had.

There is, apart from mere intellect, in the make-up of every superior human identity, (in its moral completeness, considered as *ensemble,* not for that moral alone, but for the whole being, including physique,) a wondrous something that realizes without argument, frequently without what is called education, (though I think it the goal and apex of all education deserving the name)—an intuition of the absolute balance, in time and space, of the whole of this multifarious, mad chaos of fraud, frivolity, hoggishness—this revel of fools, and incredible make-believe and general unsettledness, we call *the world;* a soul-sight of that divine clue and unseen thread which holds the whole congeries of things, all history and time, and all events, however trivial, however momentous, like a leash'd dog in the hand of the hunter. Such soul-sight and root-centre for the mind—mere optimism explains only the surface or fringe of it—Carlyle was mostly, perhaps entirely without. He seems instead to have been haunted in the play of his mental action by a spectre, never entirely laid from first to last, (Greek scholars, I believe, find the same mocking and fantastic apparition attending Aristophanes, his comedies,)—the spectre of world-destruction.

How largest triumph or failure in human life, in war or peace, may depend on some little hidden centrality, hardly more than a drop of blood, a pulse-beat, or a breath of air! It is certain that all these weighty matters, democracy in America, Carlyleism, and the temperament for deepest political or literary exploration, turn on a simple point in speculative philosophy.

The most profound theme that can occupy the mind of man—the problem on whose solution science, art, the bases and pursuits of nations, and everything else, including intelligent human happiness, (here to-day, 1882, New York, Texas, California, the same as all times, all lands,) subtly and finally resting, depends for competent outset and argument, is doubtless involved in the query: What is the fusing explanation and tie—what the relation between the (radical, democratic) Me, the human identity of understanding, emotions, spirit, &c., on the one side, of and with the (conservative) Not Me, the whole of the material objective universe and laws, with what is behind them in time and space, on the other side? Immanuel Kant, though he explain'd, or partially explain'd, as may be said, the laws of the human understanding, left this question an open one. Schelling's answer, or suggestion of answer, is (and very valuable and important, as far as it goes,) that the same general and particular intelligence, passion, even the standards of right and wrong, which exist in a conscious and formulated state in man, exist in an unconscious state, or in perceptible analogies, throughout the entire universe of external Nature, in all its objects large or small, and all its movements and processes—thus making the impalpable human mind, and concrete Nature, notwithstanding their duality and separation, convertible, and in centrality and essence one. But G. F. Hegel's fuller statement of the matter probably remains the last best word that has been said upon it, up to date. Substantially adopting the scheme just epitomized, he so carries it out and fortifies it and merges everything in it, with certain serious gaps now for the first time fill'd, that it becomes a coherent metaphysical system, and substantial answer (as far as there can be any answer) to the foregoing question—a system which, while I distinctly admit that the brain of the future may add to, revise, and even entirely reconstruct, at any rate beams forth to-day, in its entirety, illuminating the thought of the universe, and satisfying the mystery thereof to the human mind, with a more consoling scientific assurance than any yet.

According to Hegel the whole earth, (an old nucleus-thought, as in the Vedas, and no doubt before, but never hitherto brought so absolutely to the front, fully surcharged with modern scientism and facts, and made the sole entrance to each and all,) with its infinite variety, the past, the surroundings of to-day, or what may happen in the future, the contrarieties of material with spiritual, and of natural with artificial, are all, to the eye of the *ensemblist,* but necessary sides and unfoldings, different steps or links, in the endless process of Creative thought, which, amid numberless apparent failures and contradictions, is held together by central and never-broken unity—not contradictions or failures at all, but radiations of one consistent and eternal purpose; the whole mass of everything steadily, unerringly tending and flowing toward the permanent *utile* and *morale,* as rivers to oceans. As life is the whole law and incessant effort of the visible universe, and death only the other or invisible side of the same, so the *utile,* so truth, so health, are the continuous-immutable laws of the moral universe, and vice and disease, with all their perturbations, are but transient, even if ever so prevalent expressions.

To politics throughout, Hegel applies the like catholic standard and faith. Not any one party, or any one form of government, is absolutely and exclusively true. Truth consists in the just relations of objects to each other. A majority or democracy may rule as outrageously and do as great harm as an oligarchy or despotism—though far less likely to do so. But the great evil is either a violation of the relations just referr'd to, or of the moral law. The specious, the unjust, the cruel, and what is called the unnatural, though not only permitted but in a certain sense, (like shade to light,) inevitable in the divine scheme, are by the whole constitution of that scheme, partial, inconsistent, temporary, and though having ever so great an ostensible majority, are certainly destin'd to failure, after causing great suffering.

Theology, Hegel translates into science.* All apparent contradictions in the statement of the Deific nature by different ages, nations, churches, points of view, are but fractional and imperfect expressions of one essential unity, from which they all proceed—crude endeavors or distorted parts, to be regarded both as distinct and united. In short (to put it in our own form, or summing up,) that thinker or analyzer or overlooker who by an inscrutable combination of train'd wisdom and natural intuition most fully accepts in perfect faith the moral unity and sanity of the creative scheme, in history, science, and all life and time, present and future, is both the truest cosmical devotee or religioso, and the profoundest philosopher. While he who, by the spell of himself and his circumstances, sees darkness and despair in the sum of the workings of God's providence, and who, in that, denies or prevaricates, is, no matter how much piety plays on his lips, the most radical sinner and infidel.

I am the more assured in recounting Hegel a little freely here,† not only for offsetting the Carlylean letter and spirit—cutting it out all and several from the very roots, and below the roots—but to counterpoise, since the late death and deserv'd apotheosis of Darwin, the tenets of the evolutionists. Unspeakably precious as those are to biology, and henceforth indispensable to a right aim and estimate in study, they neither comprise or explain everything—and the last word or whisper

*I am much indebted to J. Gostick's abstract.

†I have deliberately repeated it all, not only in offset to Carlyle's ever-lurking pessimism and world-decadence, but as presenting the most thoroughly *American points of view* I know. In my opinion the above formulas of Hegel are an essential and crowning justification of New World democracy in the creative realms of time and space. There is that about them which only the vastness, the multiplicity and the vitality of America would seem able to comprehend, to give scope and illustration to, or to be fit for, or even originate. It is strange to me that they were born in Germany, or in the old world at all. While a Carlyle, I should say, is quite the legitimate European product to be expected.

still remains to be breathed, after the utmost of those claims, floating high and forever above them all, and above technical metaphysics. While the contributions which German Kant and Fichte and Schelling and Hegel have bequeath'd to humanity—and which English Darwin has also in his field—are indispensable to the erudition of America's future, I should say that in all of them, and the best of them, when compared with the lightning flashes and flights of the old prophets and *exaltès,* the spiritual poets and poetry of all lands, (as in the Hebrew Bible,) there seems to be, nay certainly is, something lacking—something cold, a failure to satisfy the deepest emotions of the soul—a want of living glow, fondness, warmth, which the old *exaltès* and poets supply, and which the keenest modern philosophers so far do not.

Upon the whole, and for our purposes, this man's name certainly belongs on the list with the just-specified, first-class moral physicians of our current era—and with Emerson and two or three others—though his prescription is drastic, and perhaps destructive, while theirs is assimilating, normal and tonic. Feudal at the core, and mental offspring and radiation of feudalism as are his books, they afford ever-valuable lessons and affinities to democratic America. Nations or individuals, we surely learn deepest from unlikeness, from a sincere opponent, from the light thrown even scornfully on dangerous spots and liabilities. (Michel Angelo invoked heaven's special protection against his friends and affectionate flatterers; palpable foes he could manage for himself.) In many particulars Carlyle was indeed, as Froude terms him, one of those far-off Hebraic utterers, a new Micah or Habbakuk. His words at times bubble forth with abysmic inspiration. Always precious, such men; as precious now as any time. His rude, rasping, taunting, contradictory tones—what ones are more wanted amid the supple, polish'd, money-worshipping, Jesus-and-Judas-equalizing, suffrage-sovereignty echoes of current America? He has lit up our Nineteenth century with the light of a powerful, penetrating, and perfectly honest intellect of the first-class, turn'd on British and European politics, social life, literature, and representative personages—thoroughly dissatisfied with all, and mercilessly exposing the illness of all.

But while he announces the malady, and scolds and raves about it, he himself, born and bred in the same atmosphere, is a mark'd illustration of it.

A Couple of Old Friends—A Coleridge Bit

Latter April.—Have run down in my country haunt for a couple of days, and am spending them by the pond. I had already discover'd my kingfisher here (but only one—the mate not here yet.) This fine bright morning, down by the creek, he has come out for a spree, circling, flirting, chirping at a round rate. While I am writing these lines he is disporting himself in scoots and rings over the wider parts of the pond, into whose surface he dashes, once or twice making a loud *souse*—the spray flying in the sun—beautiful! I see his white and dark-gray plumage and peculiar shape plainly, as he has deign'd to come very near me. The noble, graceful bird! Now he is sitting on the limb of an old tree, high up, bending over the water—seems to be looking at me while I memorandize. I almost fancy he knows me. *Three days later.*—My second kingfisher is here with his (or her) mate. I saw the two together flying and whirling around. I had heard, in the distance, what I thought was the clear rasping staccato of the birds several times already—but I couldn't be sure the notes came from both until I saw them together. To-day at noon they appear'd, but apparently either on business, or for a little limited exercise only. No wild frolic now, full of free fun and motion, up and down for an hour. Doubtless, now they have cares, duties, incubation responsibilities. The frolics are deferr'd till summer-close.

I don't know as I can finish to-day's memorandum better than with Coleridge's lines, curiously appropriate in more ways than one:

> "All Nature seems at work—slugs leave their lair,
> The bees are stirring—birds are on the wing,
> And winter, slumbering in the open air,
> Wears on his smiling face a dream of spring;
> And I, the while, the sole unbusy thing,
> Nor honey make, nor pair, nor build, nor sing."

A Week's Visit to Boston

May 1, '81.—Seems as if all the ways and means of American travel to-day had been settled, not only with reference to speed and directness, but for the comfort of women, children, invalids, and old fellows like me. I went on by a through train that runs daily from Washington to the Yankee metropolis without change. You get in a sleeping-car soon after dark in Philadelphia, and after ruminating an hour or two, have your bed made up if you like, draw the curtains, and go to sleep in it—fly on through Jersey to New York—hear in your half-slumbers a dull jolting and bumping sound or two—are unconsciously toted from Jersey city by a midnight steamer around the Battery and under the big bridge to the track of the New Haven road—resume your flight eastward, and early the next morning you wake up in Boston. All of which was my experience. I wanted to go to the Revere house. A tall unknown gentleman, (a fellow-passenger on his way to Newport he told me, I had just chatted a few moments before with him,) assisted me out through the depot crowd, procured a hack, put me in it with my traveling bag, saying smilingly and quietly, "Now I want you to let this be *my* ride," paid the driver, and before I could remonstrate bow'd himself off.

The occasion of my jaunt, I suppose I had better say here, was for a public reading of "the death of Abraham Lincoln" essay, on the sixteenth anniversary of that tragedy; which reading duly came off, night of April 15. Then I linger'd a week in Boston—felt pretty well (the mood propitious, my paralysis lull'd)—went around everywhere, and saw all that was to be seen, especially human beings. Boston's immense material growth—commerce, finance, commission stores, the plethora of goods, the crowded streets and sidewalks—made of course the first surprising show. In my trip out West, last year, I thought the wand of future prosperity, future empire, must soon surely be wielded by St. Louis, Chicago, beautiful Denver, perhaps San Francisco; but I see the said wand stretch'd out just as decidedly in Boston, with just as much certainty of staying; evidences of copious capital—indeed no centre of the New World ahead of it, (half the big railroads in the West are built with Yankees' money, and they take the dividends.) Old Boston with its zigzag streets and multitudinous angles, (crush up a sheet of letter-paper in your hand, throw it down, stamp it flat, and that is a map of old Boston)—new Boston with its miles upon miles of large and costly houses—Beacon street, Commonwealth avenue, and a hundred others. But the best new departures and expansions of Boston, and of all the cities of New England, are in another direction.

The Boston of To-day

In the letters we get from Dr. Schliemann (interesting but fishy) about his excavations there in the far-off Homeric area, I notice cities, ruins, &c., as he digs them out of their graves, are certain to be in layers—that is to say, upon the foundation of an old concern, very far down indeed, is always another city or set of ruins, and upon that another superadded—and sometimes upon that still another—each representing either a long or rapid stage of growth and development, different from its predecessor, but unerringly growing out of and resting on it. In the moral, emotional, heroic, and human growths, (the main of a race in my opinion,) something of this kind has certainly taken place in Boston. The New England metropolis of to-day may be described as sunny, (there is something else that makes warmth, mastering even winds and meteorologies, though those are not to be sneez'd at,) joyous, receptive, full of ardor, sparkle, a certain element of yearning, magnificently tolerant, yet not to be fool'd; fond of good eating and drinking—costly in costume as its purse can buy; and all through its best average of houses, streets, people, that subtle something (generally thought to be climate, but it is not—it is something indefinable in *the race*, the turn of its development) which effuses behind the whirl of animation, study, business, a happy and joyous public spirit, as distinguish'd from a sluggish and saturnine one. Makes me think of the glints we get (as in Symonds's books) of the jolly old Greek cities. Indeed there is a good deal of the Hellenic in B., and the people are getting handsomer too—padded out, with freer motions, and with color in their faces. I never saw (although this is not Greek) so many *fine-looking gray hair'd women.* At my lecture I caught myself pausing more than once to look at them, plentiful everywhere through the audience—healthy and wifely and motherly, and wonderfully charming and beautiful—I think such as no time or land but ours could show.

My Tribute to Four Poets

April 16.—A short but pleasant visit to Longfellow. I am not one of the calling kind, but as the author of "Evangeline" kindly took the trouble to come and see me three years ago in Camden, where I was ill, I felt not only the impulse of my own pleasure on that occasion, but a duty. He was the only particular eminence I called on in Boston, and I shall not soon forget his lit-up face and glowing warmth and courtesy, in the modes of what is called the old school.

And now just here I feel the impulse to interpolate something about the mighty four who stamp this first American century with its birth-marks of poetic literature. In a late magazine one of my reviewers, who ought to know better, speaks of my "attitude of contempt and scorn and intolerance" toward the leading poets—of my "deriding" them, and preaching their "uselessness." If anybody cares to know what I think—and have long thought and avow'd—about them, I am entirely willing to propound. I can't imagine any better luck befalling these States for a poetical beginning and initiation than has come from Emerson, Longfellow, Bryant, and Whittier. Emerson, to me, stands unmistakably at the head, but for the others I am at a loss where to give any precedence. Each illustrious, each rounded, each distinctive. Emerson for his sweet, vital-tasting melody, rhym'd philosophy, and poems as amber-clear as the honey of the wild bee he loves to sing. Longfellow for rich color, graceful forms and incidents—all that makes life beautiful and love refined—competing with the singers of Europe on their own ground, and, with one exception, better and finer work than that of any of them. Bryant pulsing the first interior verse-throbs of a mighty world—bard of the river and the wood, ever conveying a taste of open air, with scents as from hayfields, grapes, birch-borders—always lurkingly fond of threnodies—

beginning and ending his long career with chants of death, with here and there through all, poems, or passages of poems, touching the highest universal truths, enthusiasms, duties—morals as grim and eternal, if not as stormy and fateful, as anything in Eschylus. While in Whittier, with his special themes—(his outcropping love of heroism and war, for all his Quakerdom, his verses at times like the measur'd step of Cromwell's old veterans)—in Whittier lives the zeal, the moral energy, that founded New England—the splendid rectitude and ardor of Luther, Milton, George Fox—I must not, dare not, say the wilfulness and narrowness—though doubtless the world needs now, and always will need, almost above all, just such narrowness and wilfulness.

Millet's Pictures—Last Items

April 18.—Went out three or four miles to the house of Quincy Shaw, to see a collection of J. F. Millet's pictures. Two rapt hours. Never before have I been so penetrated by this kind of expression. I stood long and long before "the Sower." I believe what the picture-men designate "the first Sower," as the artist executed a second copy, and a third, and, some think, improved in each. But I doubt it. There is something in this that could hardly be caught again—a sublime murkiness and original pent fury. Besides this masterpiece, there were many others, (I shall never forget the simple evening scene, "Watering the Cow,") all inimitable, all perfect as pictures, works of mere art; and then it seem'd to me, with that last impalpable ethic purpose from the artist (most likely unconscious to himself) which I am always looking for. To me all of them told the full story of what went before and necessitated the great French revolution—the long precedent crushing of the masses of a heroic people into the earth, in abject poverty, hunger—every right denied, humanity attempted to be put back for generations—yet Nature's force, titanic here, the stronger and hardier for that repression—waiting terribly to break forth, revengeful—the pressure on the dykes, and the bursting at last—the storming of the Bastile—the execution of the king and queen—the tempest of massacres and blood. Yet who can wonder?

Could we wish humanity different?
Could we wish the people made of wood or stone?
Or that there be no justice in destiny or time?

The true France, base of all the rest, is certainly in these pictures. I comprehend "Field-People Reposing," "the Diggers," and "the Angelus" in this opinion. Some folks always think of the French as a small race, five or five and a half feet high, and ever frivolous and smirking. Nothing of the sort. The bulk of the personnel of France, before the revolution, was large-sized, serious, industrious as now, and simple. The revolution and Napoleon's wars dwarf'd the standard of human size, but it will come up again. If for nothing else, I should dwell on my brief Boston visit for opening to me the new world of Millet's pictures. Will America ever have such an artist out of her own gestation, body, soul?

Sunday, April 17.—An hour and a half, late this afternoon, in silence and half light, in the great nave of Memorial hall, Cambridge, the walls thickly cover'd with mural tablets, bearing the names of students and graduates of the university who fell in the secession war.

April 23.—It was well I got away in fair order, for if I had staid another week I should have been killed with kindness, and with eating and drinking.

Birds—and a Caution

May 14.—Home again; down temporarily in the Jersey woods. Between 8 and 9 A.M. a full concert of birds, from different quarters, in keeping with the fresh scent, the peace, the naturalness all around me. I am lately noticing the russet-back, size of the robin or a trifle less, light breast and shoulders, with irregular dark stripes—tail long—sits hunch'd up by the hour these days, top of a tall bush, or some tree, singing blithely. I often get near and listen, as he seems tame; I like to watch the working of his bill and throat, the quaint sidle of his body, and flex of his long tail. I hear the woodpecker, and night and early morning the shuttle of the whip-poor-will—noons, the gurgle of thrush delicious, and *meo-o-ow* of the cat-bird. Many I cannot name; but I do not very particularly seek information. (You must not know too much, or be too precise or scientific about birds and trees and flowers and water-craft; a certain free margin, and even vagueness—perhaps ignorance, credulity—helps your enjoyment of these things, and of the sentiment of feather'd, wooded, river, or marine Nature generally. I repeat it—don't want to know too exactly, or the reasons why. My own notes have been written off-hand in the latitude of middle New Jersey. Though they describe what I saw—what appear'd to me—I dare say the expert ornithologist, botanist or entomologist will detect more than one slip in them.)

Samples of My Common-Place Book

I ought not to offer a record of these days, interests, recuperations, without including a certain old, well-thumb'd common-place book,* filled with favorite excerpts, I carried in my pocket for three summers, and absorb'd over and over again, when the mood invited. I find so much in having a poem or fine suggestion sink into me (a little then goes a great ways) prepar'd by these vacant-sane and natural influences.

* *Samples of my common-place book down at the creek:*

I have—says old Pindar—many swift arrows in my quiver which speak to the wise, though they need an interpreter to the thoughtless.

Such a man as it takes ages to make, and ages to understand.—*H. D. Thoreau.*

If you hate a man, don't kill him, but let him live.—*Buddhistic.*

Famous swords are made of refuse scraps, thought worthless.

Poetry is the only verity—the expression of a sound mind speaking after the ideal—and not after the apparent.—*Emerson.*

The form of oath among the Shoshone Indians is, "The earth hears me. The sun hears me. Shall I lie?"

The true test of civilization is not the census, nor the size of cities, nor the crops—no, but the kind of a man the country turns out.—*Emerson.*

The whole wide ether is the eagle's sway:
The whole earth is a brave man's fatherland.—*Euripides.*

Spices crush'd, their pungence yield,
  Trodden scents their sweets respire;
Would you have its strength reveal'd?
  Cast the incense in the fire.

My Native Sand and Salt Once More

July 25, '81.—Far Rockaway, L. I.—A good day here, on a jaunt, amid the sand and salt, a steady breeze setting in from the sea, the sun shining, the sedge-odor, the noise of the surf, a mixture of hissing and booming, the milk-white crests curling over. I had a leisurely bath and naked ramble as of old, on the warm-gray shore-sands, my companions off in a boat in deeper water—(I shouting to them Jupiter's menaces against the gods, from Pope's Homer.)

July 28—to Long Branch.—8½ A.M., on the steamer "Plymouth Rock," foot of 23d street, New York, for Long Branch. Another fine day, fine sights, the shores, the shipping and bay—everything comforting to the body and spirit of me. (I find the human and objective atmosphere of New York city and Brooklyn more affiliative to me than any other.) *An hour later*—Still on the steamer, now sniffing the salt very plainly—the long pulsating *swash* as our boat steams seaward—the hills of Navesink and many passing vessels—the

---

Matthew Arnold speaks of "the huge Mississippi of falsehood called History."

> The wind blows north, the wind blows south,
> The wind blows east and west;
> No matter how the free wind blows,
> Some ship will find it best.

Preach not to others what they should eat, but eat as becomes you, and be silent.—*Epictetus.*

Victor Hugo makes a donkey meditate and apostrophize thus:

> My brother, man, if you would know the truth,
> We both are by the same dull walls shut in;
> The gate is massive and the dungeon strong.
> But you look through the key-hole out beyond,
> And call this knowledge; yet have not at hand
> The key wherein to turn the fatal lock.

"William Cullen Bryant surprised me once," relates a writer in a New York paper, "by saying that prose was the natural language of composition, and he wonder'd how anybody came to write poetry."

> Farewell! I did not know thy worth;
> But thou art gone, and now 'tis prized:
> So angels walk'd unknown on earth,
> But when they flew were recognized.—*Hood.*

air the best part of all. At Long Branch the bulk of the day, stopt at a good hotel, took all very leisurely, had an excellent dinner, and then drove for over two hours about the place, especially Ocean avenue, the finest drive one can imagine, seven or eight miles right along the beach. In all directions costly villas, palaces, millionaires—(but few among them I opine like my friend George W. Childs, whose personal integrity, generosity, unaffected simplicity, go beyond all worldly wealth.)

Hot Weather New York

August.—In the big city awhile. Even the height of the dog-days, there is a good deal of fun about New York, if you only avoid fluster, and take all the buoyant wholesomeness that offers. More comfort, too, than most folks think. A middle-aged man, with plenty of money in his pocket, tells me that he has been off for a month to all the swell places, has dis-

---

John Burroughs, writing of Thoreau, says: "He improves with age—in fact requires age to take off a little of his asperity, and fully ripen him. The world likes a good hater and refuser almost as well as it likes a good lover and accepter—only it likes him farther off."

Louise Michel at the burial of Blanqui, (1881.)

Blanqui drill'd his body to subjection to his grand conscience and his noble passions, and commencing as a young man, broke with all that is sybaritish in modern civilization. Without the power to sacrifice self, great ideas will never bear fruit.

Out of the leaping furnace flame
A mass of molten silver came;
Then, beaten into pieces three,
Went forth to meet its destiny.
The first a crucifix was made,
Within a soldier's knapsack laid;
The second was a locket fair,
Where a mother kept her dead child's hair;
The third—a bangle, bright and warm,
Around a faithless woman's arm.

A mighty pain to love it is,
And 'tis a pain that pain to miss;
But of all pain the greatest pain,
It is to love, but love in vain.

burs'd a small fortune, has been hot and out of kilter everywhere, and has return'd home and lived in New York city the last two weeks quite contented and happy. People forget when it is hot here, it is generally hotter still in other places. New York is so situated, with the great ozonic brine on both sides, it comprises the most favorable health-chances in the world. (If only the suffocating crowding of some of its tenement houses could be broken up.) I find I never sufficiently realized how beautiful are the upper two-thirds of Manhattan island. I am stopping at Mott Haven, and have been familiar now for ten days with the region above One-hundredth street, and along the Harlem river and Washington heights. Am dwelling a few days with my friends, Mr. and Mrs. J. H. J., and a merry housefull of young ladies. Am putting the last touches on the printer's copy of my new volume of "Leaves of Grass"—the completed book at last. Work at it two or three hours, and then go down and loaf along the Harlem river; have just had a good spell of this recreation. The sun sufficiently veil'd, a soft south breeze, the river full of small or large shells (light

---

Maurice F. Egan on De Guérin.

A pagan heart, a Christian soul had he,
He follow'd Christ, yet for dead Pan he sigh'd,
Till earth and heaven met within his breast:
As if Theocritus in Sicily
Had come upon the Figure crucified,
And lost his gods in deep, Christ-given rest.

And if I pray, the only prayer
That moves my lips for me,
Is, leave the mind that now I bear,
And give me Liberty.—*Emily Brontë.*

I travel on not knowing,
I would not if I might;
I would rather walk with God in the dark,
Than go alone in the light;
I would rather walk with Him by faith
Than pick my way by sight.

Prof. Huxley in a late lecture.

I myself agree with the sentiment of Thomas Hobbes, of Malmesbury, that "the scope of all speculation is the performance of some action or thing to be done." I have not any very great respect for, or interest in, mere "knowing," as such.

taper boats) darting up and down, some singly, now and then long ones with six or eight young fellows practicing—very inspiriting sights. Two fine yachts lie anchor'd off the shore. I linger long, enjoying the sundown, the glow, the streak'd sky, the heights, distances, shadows.

Aug. 10.—As I haltingly ramble an hour or two this forenoon by the more secluded parts of the shore, or sit under an old cedar half way up the hill, the city near in view, many young parties gather to bathe or swim, squads of boys, generally twos or threes, some larger ones, along the sand-bottom, or off an old pier close by. A peculiar and pretty carnival—at its height a hundred lads or young men, very democratic, but all decent behaving. The laughter, voices, calls, responses—the springing and diving of the bathers from the great string-piece of the decay'd pier, where climb or stand long ranks of them, naked, rose-color'd, with movements, postures ahead of any sculpture. To all this, the sun, so bright, the dark-green shadow of the hills the other side, the amber-rolling waves, changing as the tide comes in to a transparent tea-color—the frequent splash of the playful boys, sousing—the glittering drops sparkling, and the good western breeze blowing.

"Custer's Last Rally"

Went to-day to see this just-finish'd painting by John Mulvany, who has been out in far Dakota, on the spot, at the forts, and among the frontiersmen, soldiers and Indians, for the last two years, on purpose to sketch it in from reality, or the best that could be got of it. Sat for over an hour before

---

Prince Metternich.

Napoleon was of all men in the world the one who most profoundly despised the race. He had a marvellous insight into the weaker sides of human nature, (and all our passions are either foibles themselves, or the cause of foibles.) He was a very small man of imposing character. He was ignorant, as a sub-lieutenant generally is: a remarkable instinct supplied the lack of knowledge. From his mean opinion of men, he never had any anxiety lest he should go wrong. He ventur'd everything, and gain'd thereby an immense step toward success. Throwing himself upon a prodigious arena, he amaz'd the world, and made himself master of it, while others cannot even get so far as being masters of their own hearth. Then he went on and on, until he broke his neck.

the picture, completely absorb'd in the first view. A vast canvas, I should say twenty or twenty-two feet by twelve, all crowded, and yet not crowded, conveying such a vivid play of color, it takes a little time to get used to it. There are no tricks; there is no throwing of shades in masses; it is all at first painfully real, overwhelming, needs good nerves to look at it. Forty or fifty figures, perhaps more, in full finish and detail in the mid-ground, with three times that number, or more, through the rest—swarms upon swarms of savage Sioux, in their war-bonnets, frantic, mostly on ponies, driving through the background, through the smoke, like a hurricane of demons. A dozen of the figures are wonderful. Altogether a western, autochthonic phase of America, the frontiers, culminating, typical, deadly, heroic to the uttermost—nothing in the books like it, nothing in Homer, nothing in Shakspere; more grim and sublime than either, all native, all our own, and all a fact. A great lot of muscular, tan-faced men, brought to bay under terrible circumstances—death ahold of them, yet every man undaunted, not one losing his head, wringing out every cent of the pay before they sell their lives. Custer (his hair cut short) stands in the middle, with dilated eye and extended arm, aiming a huge cavalry pistol. Captain Cook is there, partially wounded, blood on the white handkerchief around his head, aiming his carbine coolly, half kneeling—(his body was afterwards found close by Custer's). The slaughter'd or half-slaughter'd horses, for breastworks, make a peculiar feature. Two dead Indians, herculean, lie in the foreground, clutching their Winchester rifles, very characteristic. The many soldiers, their faces and attitudes, the carbines, the broad-brimm'd western hats, the powder-smoke in puffs, the dying horses with their rolling eyes almost human in their agony, the clouds of war-bonneted Sioux in the background, the figures of Custer and Cook—with indeed the whole scene, dreadful, yet with an attraction and beauty that will remain in my memory. With all its color and fierce action, a certain Greek continence pervades it. A sunny sky and clear light envelop all. There is an almost entire absence of the stock traits of European war pictures. The physiognomy of the work is realistic and Western. I only saw it for an hour or so; but it needs to be seen many times—needs to be studied over and over again. I could look on such a work at brief intervals all my life without tiring; it is very tonic to me; then it has an ethic purpose below all, as all great art must have. The artist said the sending of the picture abroad, probably to London, had been talk'd of. I advised him if it went abroad to take it to Paris. I think they might appreciate it there—nay, they certainly would. Then I would like to show Messieur Crapeau that some things can be done in America as well as others.

Some Old Acquaintances—Memories

Aug. 16.—"Chalk a big mark for to-day," was one of the sayings of an old sportsman-friend of mine, when he had had unusually good luck—come home thoroughly tired, but with satisfactory results of fish or birds. Well, to-day might warrant such a mark for me. Everything propitious from the start. An hour's fresh stimulation, coming down ten miles of Manhattan island by railroad and 8 o'clock stage. Then an excellent breakfast at Pfaff's restaurant, 24th street. Our host himself, an old friend of mine, quickly appear'd on the scene to welcome me and bring up the news, and, first opening a big fat bottle of the best wine in the cellar, talk about ante-bellum times, '59 and '60, and the jovial suppers at his then Broadway place, near Bleecker street. Ah, the friends and names and frequenters, those times, that place. Most are dead—Ada Clare, Wilkins, Daisy Sheppard, O'Brien, Henry Clapp, Stanley, Mullin, Wood, Brougham, Arnold—all gone. And there Pfaff and I, sitting opposite each other at the little table, gave a remembrance to them in a style they would have themselves fully confirm'd, namely, big, brimming, fill'd-up champagne-glasses, drain'd in abstracted silence, very leisurely, to the last drop. (Pfaff is a generous German *restaurateur,* silent, stout, jolly, and I should say the best selecter of champagne in America.)

A Discovery of Old Age

Perhaps the best is always cumulative. One's eating and drinking one wants fresh, and for the nonce, right off, and have done with it—but I would not give a straw for that person or poem, or friend, or city, or work of art, that was not more grateful the second time than the first—and more still the third. Nay, I do not believe any grandest eligibility ever comes forth at first. In my own experience, (persons, poems, places, characters,) I discover the best hardly ever at first, (no absolute rule about it, however,) sometimes suddenly bursting forth, or stealthily opening to me, perhaps after years of unwitting familiarity, unappreciation, usage.

A Visit, at the Last, to R. W. Emerson

Concord, Mass.—Out here on a visit—elastic, mellow, Indian-summery weather. Came to-day from Boston, (a pleasant ride of 40 minutes by steam, through Somerville, Belmont, Waltham, Stony Brook, and other lively towns,) convoy'd by my friend F. B. Sanborn, and to his ample house, and the kindness and hospitality of Mrs. S. and their fine family. Am writing this under the shade of some old hickories and elms, just after 4 P.M., on the porch, within a stone's throw of the Concord river. Off against me, across stream, on a meadow and side-hill, haymakers are gathering and wagoning-in probably their second or third crop. The spread of emerald-green and brown, the knolls, the score or two of little haycocks dotting the meadow, the loaded-up wagons, the patient horses, the slow-strong action of the men and pitch-forks—all in the just-waning afternoon, with patches of yellow sun-sheen, mottled by long shadows—a cricket shrilly chirping, herald of the dusk—a boat with two figures noiselessly gliding along the little river, passing under the stone bridge-arch—the slight settling haze of aerial moisture, the sky and the peacefulness expanding in all directions and overhead—fill and soothe me.

Same evening.—Never had I a better piece of luck befall me: a long and blessed evening with Emerson, in a way I couldn't have wish'd better or different. For nearly two hours he has been placidly sitting where I could see his face in the best light, near me. Mrs. S.'s back-parlor well fill'd with people, neighbors, many fresh and charming faces, women, mostly young, but some old. My friend A. B. Alcott and his daughter Louisa were there early. A good deal of talk, the subject Henry Thoreau—some new glints of his life and fortunes, with letters to and from him—one of the best by Margaret Fuller, others by Horace Greeley, Channing, &c.—one from Thoreau himself, most quaint and interesting. (No doubt I seem'd very stupid to the room-full of company, taking hardly any part in the conversation; but I had "my own pail to milk in," as the Swiss proverb puts it.) My seat and the relative arrangement were such that, without being rude, or anything of the kind, I could just look squarely at E., which I did a good part of the two hours. On entering, he had spoken very briefly and politely to several of the company, then settled himself in his chair, a trifle push'd back, and, though a listener and apparently an alert one, remain'd silent through the whole talk and discussion. A lady friend quietly took a seat next him, to give special attention. A good color in his face, eyes clear, with the well-known expression of sweetness, and the old clear-peering aspect quite the same.

Next Day.—Several hours at E.'s house, and dinner there. An old familiar house, (he has been in it thirty-five years,) with surroundings, furnishment, roominess, and plain elegance and fullness, signifying democratic ease, sufficient opulence, and an admirable old-fashioned simplicity—modern luxury, with its mere sumptuousness and affection, either touch'd lightly upon or ignored altogether. Dinner the same. Of course the best of the occasion (Sunday, September 18, '81) was the sight of E. himself. As just said, a healthy color in the cheeks, and good light in the eyes, cheery expression, and just the amount of talking that best suited, namely, a word or short phrase only where needed, and almost always with a smile. Besides Emerson himself, Mrs. E., with their daughter Ellen, the son Edward and his wife, with my friend F. S. and Mrs. S., and others, relatives and intimates. Mrs. Emerson, resuming the subject of the evening before, (I sat next to her,) gave me further and fuller information about Thoreau, who, years ago, during Mr. E.'s absence in Europe, had lived for some time in the family, by invitation.

Other Concord Notations

Though the evening at Mr. and Mrs. Sanborn's, and the memorable family dinner at Mr. and Mrs. Emerson's, have most pleasantly and permanently fill'd my memory, I must not slight other notations of Concord. I went to the old Manse, walk'd through the ancient garden, enter'd the rooms, noted the quaintness, the unkempt grass and bushes, the little panes in the windows, the low ceilings, the spicy smell, the creepers embowering the light. Went to the Concord battle ground, which is close by, scann'd French's statue, "the Minute Man," read Emerson's poetic inscription on the base, linger'd a long while on the bridge, and stopp'd by the grave of the unnamed British soldiers buried there the day after the fight in April '75. Then riding on, (thanks to my friend Miss M. and her spirited white ponies, she driving them,) a half hour at Hawthorne's and Thoreau's graves. I got out and went up of course on foot, and stood a long while and ponder'd. They lie close together in a pleasant wooded spot well up the cemetery hill, "Sleepy Hollow." The flat surface of the first was densely cover'd by myrtle, with a border of arbor-vitæ, and the other had a brown headstone, moderately elaborate, with inscriptions. By Henry's side lies his brother John, of whom much was expected, but he died young. Then to Walden pond, that beautifully embower'd sheet of water, and spent over an hour there. On the spot in the woods where Thoreau had his solitary house is now quite a cairn of stones, to mark the place; I too carried one and deposited on the heap. As we drove back, saw the "School of Philosophy," but it was shut up, and I would not have it open'd for me. Near by stopp'd at the house of W. T. Harris, the Hegelian, who came out, and we had a pleasant chat while I sat in the wagon. I shall not soon forget those Concord drives, and especially that charming Sunday forenoon one with my friend Miss M., and the white ponies.

Boston Common—More of Emerson

Oct. 10–13.—I spend a good deal of time on the Common, these delicious days and nights—every mid-day from 11.30 to about 1—and almost every sunset another hour. I know all the big trees, especially the old elms along Tremont and Beacon streets, and have come to a sociable-silent understanding with most of them, in the sunlit air, (yet crispy-cool enough,) as I saunter along the wide unpaved walks. Up and down this breadth by Beacon street, between these same old elms, I walk'd for two hours, of a bright sharp February mid-day twenty-one years ago, with Emerson, then in his prime, keen, physically and morally magnetic, arm'd at every point, and when he chose, wielding the emotional just as well as the intellectual. During those two hours he was the talker and I the listener. It was an argument-statement, reconnoitring, review, attack, and pressing home, (like an army corps in order, artillery, cavalry, infantry,) of all that could be said against that part (and a main part) in the construction of my poems, "Children of Adam." More precious than gold to me that dissertation—it afforded me, ever after, this strange and paradoxical lesson; each point of E.'s statement was unanswerable, no judge's charge ever more complete or convincing, I could never hear the points better put—and then I felt down in my soul the clear and unmistakable conviction to disobey all, and pursue my own way. "What have you to say then to such things?" said E., pausing in conclusion. "Only that while I can't answer them at all, I feel more settled than ever to adhere to my own theory, and exemplify it," was my candid response. Whereupon we went and had a good dinner at the American House. And thenceforward I never waver'd or was touch'd with qualms, (as I confess I had been two or three times before).

An Ossianic Night—Dearest Friends

Nov., '81.—Again back in Camden. As I cross the Delaware in long trips to-night, between 9 and 11, the scene overhead is a peculiar one—swift sheets of flitting vapor-gauze, follow'd by dense clouds throwing an inky pall on everything. Then a spell of that transparent steel-gray black sky I have noticed under similar circumstances, on which the moon would beam for a few moments with calm lustre, throwing down a broad dazzle of highway on the waters; then the mists careering again. All silently, yet driven as if by the furies they sweep along, sometimes quite thin, sometimes thicker—a real Ossianic night—amid the whirl, absent or dead friends, the old, the past, somehow tenderly suggested—while the Gael-strains chant themselves from the mists—["Be thy soul blest, O Carril! in the midst of thy eddying winds. O that thou woulds't come to my hall when I am alone by night! And thou dost come, my friend. I hear often thy light hand on my harp, when it hangs on the distant wall, and the feeble sound touches my ear. Why dost thou not speak to me in my grief, and tell me when I shall behold my friends? But thou passest away in thy murmuring blast; the wind whistles through the gray hairs of Ossian."]

But most of all, those changes of moon and sheets of hurrying vapor and black clouds, with the sense of rapid action in weird silence, recall the far-back Erse belief that such above were the preparations for receiving the wraiths of just-slain warriors—["We sat that night in Selma, round the strength of the shell. The wind was abroad in the oaks. The spirit of the mountain roar'd. The blast came rustling through the hall, and gently touch'd my harp. The sound was mournful and low, like the song of the tomb. Fingal heard it the first. The crowded sighs of his bosom rose. Some of my heroes are low, said the gray-hair'd king of Morven. I hear the sound of death on the harp. Ossian, touch the trembling string. Bid the sorrow rise, that their spirits may fly with joy to Morven's woody hills. I touch'd the harp before the king; the sound was mournful and low. Bend forward from your clouds, I said, ghosts of my fathers! bend. Lay by the red terror of your course. Receive the falling chief; whether he comes from a distant land, or rises from the rolling sea. Let his robe of mist be near; his spear that is form'd of a cloud. Place a half-extinguish'd meteor by his side, in the form of a hero's sword. And oh! let his countenance be lovely, that his friends may delight in his presence. Bend from your clouds, I said, ghosts of my fathers, bend. Such was my song in Selma, to the lightly trembling harp."]

How or why I know not, just at the moment, but I too muse and think of my best friends in their distant homes—of William O'Connor, of Maurice Bucke, of John Burroughs, and of Mrs. Gilchrist—friends of my soul—stanchest friends of my other soul, my poems.

Only a New Ferry Boat

Jan. 12, '82.—Such a show as the Delaware presented an hour before sundown yesterday evening, all along between Philadelphia and Camden, is worth weaving into an item. It was full tide, a fair breeze from the southwest, the water of a pale tawny color, and just enough motion to make things frolicsome and lively. Add to these an approaching sunset of unusual splendor, a broad tumble of clouds, with much golden haze and profusion of beaming shaft and dazzle. In the midst of all, in the clear drab of the afternoon light, there steam'd up the river the large, new boat, "the Wenonah," as pretty an object as you could wish to see, lightly and swiftly skimming along, all trim and white, cover'd with flags, transparent red and blue, streaming out in the breeze. Only a new ferry-boat, and yet in its fitness comparable with the prettiest product of Nature's cunning, and rivaling it. High up in the transparent ether gracefully balanced and circled four or five great sea hawks, while here below, amid the pomp and picturesqueness of sky and river, swam this creation of artificial beauty and motion and power, in its way no less perfect.

Death of Longfellow

Camden, April 3, '82.—I have just return'd from an old forest haunt, where I love to go occasionally away from parlors, pavements, and the newspapers and magazines—and where, of a clear forenoon, deep in the shade of pines and cedars and a tangle of old laurel-trees and vines, the news of Longfellow's death first reach'd me. For want of anything better, let me lightly twine a sprig of the sweet ground-ivy trailing so plentifully through the dead leaves at my feet, with reflections of that half hour alone, there in the silence, and lay it as my contribution on the dead bard's grave.

Longfellow in his voluminous works seems to me not only to be eminent in the style and forms of poetical expression that mark the present age, (an idiosyncrasy, almost a sickness, of verbal melody,) but to bring what is always dearest as poetry to the general human heart and taste, and probably must be so in the nature of things. He is certainly the sort of bard and counteractant most needed for our materialistic, self-assertive, money-worshipping, Anglo-Saxon races, and especially for the present age in America—an age tyrannically regulated with reference to the manufacturer, the merchant, the financier, the politician and the day workman—for whom and among whom he comes as the poet of melody, courtesy, deference—poet of the mellow twilight of the past in Italy, Germany, Spain, and in Northern Europe—poet of all sympathetic gentleness—and universal poet of women and young people. I should have to think long if I were ask'd to name the man who has done more, and in more valuable directions, for America.

I doubt if there ever was before such a fine intuitive judge and selecter of poems. His translations of many German and Scandinavian pieces are said to be better than the vernaculars. He does not urge or lash. His influence is like good drink or air. He is not tepid either, but always vital, with flavor, motion, grace. He strikes a splendid average, and does not sing exceptional passions, or humanity's jagged escapades. He is not revolutionary, brings nothing offensive or new, does not deal hard blows. On the contrary, his songs soothe and heal, or if they excite, it is a healthy and agreeable excitement. His very anger is gentle, is at second hand, (as in the "Quadroon Girl" and the "Witnesses.")

There is no undue element of pensiveness in Longfellow's strains. Even in the early translation, the Manrique, the movement is as of strong and steady wind or tide, holding up and buoying. Death is not avoided through his many themes, but there is something almost winning in his original verses and renderings on that dread subject—as, closing "the Happiest Land" dispute,

> And then the landlord's daughter
> Up to heaven rais'd her hand,
> And said, "Ye may no more contend,
> There lies the happiest land."

To the ungracious complaint-charge of his want of racy nativity and special originality, I shall only say that America and the world may well be reverently thankful—can never be thankful enough—for any such singing-bird vouchsafed out of the centuries, without asking that the notes be different from those of other songsters; adding what I have heard Longfellow himself say, that ere the New World can be worthily original, and announce herself and her own heroes, she must be well saturated with the originality of others, and respectfully consider the heroes that lived before Agamemnon.

Starting Newspapers

Reminiscences—(From the "Camden Courier.")—As I sat taking my evening sail across the Delaware in the staunch ferry-boat "Beverly," a night or two ago, I was join'd by two young reporter friends. "I have a message for you," said one of them; "the C. folks told me to say they would like a piece sign'd by your name, to go in their first number. Can you do it for them?" "I guess so," said I; "what might it be about?" "Well, anything on newspapers, or perhaps what you've done yourself, starting them." And off the boys went, for we had reach'd the Philadelphia side. The hour was fine and mild, the bright half-moon shining; Venus, with excess of splendor, just setting in the west, and the great Scorpion rearing its length more than half up in the southeast. As I cross'd leisurely for an hour in the pleasant night-scene, my young friend's words brought up quite a string of reminiscences.

I commenced when I was but a boy of eleven or twelve writing sentimental bits for the old "Long Island Patriot," in Brooklyn; this was about 1832. Soon after, I had a piece or two in George P. Morris's then celebrated and fashionable "Mirror," of New York city. I remember with what half-suppress'd excitement I used to watch for the big, fat, red-faced, slow-moving, very old English carrier who distributed the "Mirror" in Brooklyn; and when I got one, opening and cutting the leaves with trembling fingers. How it made my heart double-beat to see *my piece* on the pretty white paper, in nice type.

My first real venture was the "Long Islander," in my own beautiful town of Huntington, in 1839. I was about twenty years old. I had been teaching country school for two or three years in various parts of Suffolk and Queens counties, but liked printing; had been at it while a lad, learn'd the trade of compositor, and was encouraged to start a paper in the region where I was born. I went to New York, bought a press and types, hired some little help, but did most of the work myself, including the press-work. Everything seem'd turning out well; (only my own restlessness prevented me gradually establishing a permanent property there.) I bought a good horse, and every week went all round the country serving my papers, devoting one day and night to it. I never had happier jaunts—going over to south side, to Babylon, down the south road, across to Smithtown and Comac, and back home. The experiences of those jaunts, the dear old-fashion'd farmers and their wives, the stops by the hay-fields, the hospitality, nice dinners, occasional evenings, the girls, the rides through the brush, come up in my memory to this day.

I next went to the "Aurora" daily in New York city—a sort of free lance. Also wrote regularly for the "Tattler," an evening paper. With these and a little outside work I was occupied off and on, until I went to edit the "Brooklyn Eagle," where for two years I had one of the pleasantest sits of my life—a good owner, good pay, and easy work and hours. The troubles in the Democratic party broke forth about those times (1848–'49) and I split off with the radicals, which led to rows with the boss and "the party," and I lost my place.

Being now out of a job, I was offer'd impromptu, (it happen'd between the acts one night in the lobby of the old Broadway theatre near Pearl street, New York city,) a good chance to go down to New Orleans on the staff of the "Crescent," a daily to be started there with plenty of capital behind it. One of the owners, who was north buying material, met me walking in the lobby, and though that was our first acquaintance, after fifteen minutes' talk (and a drink) we made a formal bargain, and he paid me two hundred dollars down to bind the contract and bear my expenses to New Orleans. I started two days afterwards; had a good leisurely time, as the paper wasn't to be out in three weeks. I enjoy'd my journey and Louisiana life much. Returning to Brooklyn a year or two afterward I started the "Freeman," first as a weekly, then daily. Pretty soon the secession war broke out, and I, too, got drawn in the current southward, and spent the following three years there, (as memorandized preceding.)

Besides starting them as aforementioned, I have had to do,

one time or another, during my life, with a long list of papers, at divers places, sometimes under queer circumstances. During the war, the hospitals at Washington, among other means of amusement, printed a little sheet among themselves, surrounded by wounds and death, the "Armory Square Gazette," to which I contributed. The same long afterward, casually, to a paper—I think it was call'd the "Jimplecute"—out in Colorado where I stopp'd at the time. When I was in Quebec province, in Canada, in 1880, I went into the queerest little old French printing office near Tadousac. It was far more primitive and ancient than my Camden friend William Kurtz's place up on Federal street. I remember, as a youngster, several characteristic old printers of a kind hard to be seen these days.

The Great Unrest of Which We Are Part

My thoughts went floating on vast and mystic currents as I sat to-day in solitude and half-shade by the creek—returning mainly to two principal centres. One of my cherish'd themes for a never-achiev'd poem has been the two impetuses of man and the universe—in the latter, creation's incessant unrest,* exfoliation, (Darwin's evolution, I suppose.) Indeed, what is Nature but change, in all its visible, and still more its invisible processes? Or what is humanity in its faith, love, heroism, poetry, even morals, but *emotion*?

By Emerson's Grave

May 6, '82.—We stand by Emerson's new-made grave without sadness—indeed a solemn joy and faith, almost hauteur—our soul-benison no mere

*"Fifty thousand years ago the constellation of the Great Bear or Dipper was a starry cross; a hundred thousand years hence the imaginary Dipper will be upside down, and the stars which form the bowl and handle will have changed places. The misty nebulæ are moving, and besides are whirling around in great spirals, some one way, some another. Every molecule of matter in the whole universe is swinging to and fro; every particle of ether which fills space is in jelly-like vibration. Light is one kind of motion, heat another, electricity another, magnetism another, sound another. Every human sense is the result of motion; every perception, every thought is but motion of the molecules of the brain translated by that incomprehensible thing we call mind. The processes of growth, of existence, of decay, whether in worlds, or in the minutest organisms, are but motion."

"Warrior, rest, thy task is done,"

for one beyond the warriors of the world lies surely symboll'd here. A just man, poised on himself, all-loving, all-inclosing, and sane and clear as the sun. Nor does it seem so much Emerson himself we are here to honor—it is conscience, simplicity, culture, humanity's attributes at their best, yet applicable if need be to average affairs, and eligible to all. So used are we to suppose a heroic death can only come from out of battle or storm, or mighty personal contest, or amid dramatic incidents or danger, (have we not been taught so for ages by all the plays and poems?) that few even of those who most sympathizingly mourn Emerson's late departure will fully appreciate the ripen'd grandeur of that event, with its play of calm and fitness, like evening light on the sea.

How I shall henceforth dwell on the blessed hours when, not long since, I saw that benignant face, the clear eyes, the silently smiling mouth, the form yet upright in its great age—to the very last, with so much spring and cheeriness, and such an absence of decrepitude, that even the term *venerable* hardly seem'd fitting.

Perhaps the life now rounded and completed in its mortal development, and which nothing can change or harm more, has its most illustrious halo, not in its splendid intellectual or esthetic products, but as forming in its entirety one of the few, (alas! how few!) perfect and flawless excuses for being, of the entire literary class.

We can say, as Abraham Lincoln at Gettysburg, It is not we who come to consecrate the dead—we reverently come to receive, if so it may be, some consecration to ourselves and daily work from him.

At Present Writing—Personal

A letter to a German friend—extract.

May 31, '82.—"From to-day I enter upon my 64th year. The paralysis that first affected me nearly ten years ago, has since remain'd, with varying course—seems to have settled quietly down, and will probably continue. I easily tire, am very clumsy, cannot walk far; but my spirits are first-rate. I go around in public almost every day—now and then take long trips, by railroad or boat, hundreds of miles—live largely in the open air—am sunburnt and stout, (weigh 190)—keep up my activity and interest in life, people, progress, and the questions of the day. About two-thirds of the time I am quite comfortable. What mentality I ever had remains entirely unaffected; though physically I am a half-paralytic, and likely to be so, long as I live. But the principal object of my life seems to have been accomplish'd—I have the most devoted and ardent of friends, and affectionate relatives—and of enemies I really make no account."

After Trying a Certain Book

I tried to read a beautifully printed and scholarly volume on "the Theory of Poetry," received by mail this morning from England—but gave it up at last for a bad job. Here are some capricious pencillings that follow'd, as I find them in my notes:

In youth and maturity Poems are charged with sunshine and varied pomp of day; but as the soul more and more takes precedence, (the sensuous still included,) the Dusk becomes the poet's atmosphere. I too have sought, and ever seek, the brilliant sun, and make my songs according. But as I grow old, the half-lights of evening are far more to me.

The play of Imagination, with the sensuous objects of Nature for symbols, and Faith—with Love and Pride as the unseen impetus and moving-power of all, make up the curious chess-game of a poem.

Common teachers or critics are always asking "What does it mean?" Symphony of fine musician, or sunset, or sea-waves rolling up the beach—what do they mean? Undoubtedly in the most subtle-elusive sense they mean something—as love does, and religion does, and the best poem;—but who shall fathom and define those meanings? (I do not intend this as a warrant for wildness and frantic escapades—but to justify the soul's frequent joy in what cannot be defined to the intellectual part, or to calculation.)

At its best, poetic lore is like what may be heard of conversation in the dusk, from speakers far or hid, of which we get only a few broken murmurs. What is not gather'd is far more—perhaps the main thing.

Grandest poetic passages are only to be taken at free removes, as we sometimes look for stars at night, not by gazing directly toward them, but off one side.

(*To a poetic student and friend.*)—I only seek to put you in rapport. Your own brain, heart, evolution, must not only understand the matter, but largely supply it.

Final Confessions—Literary Tests

So draw near their end these garrulous notes. There have doubtless occurr'd some repetitions, technical errors in the consecutiveness of dates, in the minutiæ of botanical, astronomical, &c., exactness, and perhaps elsewhere;—for in gathering up, writing, peremptorily dispatching copy, this hot weather, (last of July and through August, '82,) and delaying not the printers, I have had to hurry along, no time to spare. But in the deepest veracity of all—in reflections of objects, scenes, Nature's outpourings, to my senses and receptivity, as they seem'd to me—in the work of giving those who care for it, some authentic glints, specimen-days of my life—and in the *bona fide* spirit and relations, from author to reader, on all the subjects design'd, and as far as they go, I feel to make unmitigated claims.

The synopsis of my early life, Long Island, New York city, and so forth, and the diary-jottings in the Secession war, tell their own story. My plan in starting what constitutes most of the middle of the book, was originally for hints and data of a Nature-poem that should carry one's experiences a few hours, commencing at noon-flush, and so through the after-part of the day—I suppose led to such idea by my own life-afternoon now arrived. But I soon found I could move at more ease, by giving the narrative at first hand. (Then there is a humiliating lesson one learns, in serene hours, of a fine day or night. Nature seems to look on all fixed-up poetry and art as something almost impertinent.)

Thus I went on, years following, various seasons and areas, spinning forth my thought beneath the night and stars, (or as I was confined to my room by half-sickness,) or at midday looking out upon the sea, or far north steaming over the Saguenay's black breast, jotting all down in the loosest sort of chronological order, and here printing from my impromptu notes, hardly even the seasons group'd together, or anything corrected—so afraid of dropping what smack of outdoors or sun or starlight might cling to the lines, I dared not try to meddle with or smooth them. Every now and then, (not often, but for a foil,) I carried a book in my pocket—or perhaps tore out from some broken or cheap edition a bunch of loose leaves; most always had something of the sort ready, but only took it out when the mood demanded. In that way, utterly out of reach of literary conventions, I re-read many authors.

I cannot divest my appetite of literature, yet I find myself eventually trying it all by Nature—*first premises* many call it, but really the crowning results of all, laws, tallies and proofs. (Has it never occurr'd to any one how the last deciding tests applicable to a book are entirely outside of technical and grammatical ones, and that any truly first-class production has little or nothing to do with the rules and calibres of ordinary critics? or the bloodless chalk of Allibone's Dictionary? I have fancied the ocean and the daylight, the mountain and the forest, putting their spirit in a judgment on our books. I have fancied some disembodied human soul giving its verdict.)

Nature and Democracy—Morality

Democracy most of all affiliates with the open air, is sunny and hardy and sane only with Nature—just as much as Art is. Something is required to temper both—to check them, restrain them from excess, morbidity. I have wanted, before departure, to bear special testimony to a very old lesson and requisite. American Democracy, in its myriad personalities, in factories, work-shops, stores, offices—through the dense streets and houses of cities, and all their manifold sophisticated life—must either be fibred, vitalized, by regular contact with out-door light and air and growths, farm-scenes, animals,

fields, trees, birds, sun-warmth and free skies, or it will certainly dwindle and pale. We cannot have grand races of mechanics, work people, and commonalty, (the only specific purpose of America,) on any less terms. I conceive of no flourishing and heroic elements of Democracy in the United States, or of Democracy maintaining itself at all, without the Nature-element forming a main part—to be its health-element and beauty-element—to really underlie the whole politics, sanity, religion and art of the New World.

Finally, the morality: "Virtue," said Marcus Aurelius, "what is it, only a living and enthusiastic sympathy with Nature?" Perhaps indeed the efforts of the true poets, founders, religions, literatures, all ages, have been, and ever will be, our time and times to come, essentially the same—to bring people back from their persistent strayings and sickly abstractions, to the costless average, divine, original concrete.

Collect

One or Two Index Items

THOUGH the ensuing COLLECT and preceding SPECIMEN DAYS are both largely from memoranda already existing, the hurried peremptory needs of copy for the printers, already referr'd to—(the musicians' story of a composer up in a garret rushing the middle body and last of his score together, while the fiddlers are playing the first parts down in the concert-room)—of this haste, while quite willing to get the consequent stimulus of life and motion, I am sure there must have resulted sundry technical errors. If any are too glaring they will be corrected in a future edition.

A special word about "PIECES IN EARLY YOUTH," at the end. On jaunts over Long Island, as boy and young fellow, nearly half a century ago, I heard of, or came across in my own experience, characters, true occurrences, incidents, which I tried my 'prentice hand at recording—(I was then quite an "abolitionist" and advocate of the "temperance" and "anti-capital-punishment" causes)—and publish'd during occasional visits to New York city. A majority of the sketches appear'd first in the "Democratic Review," others in the "Columbian Magazine," or the "American Review," of that period. My serious wish were to have all those crude and boyish pieces quietly dropp'd in oblivion—but to avoid the annoyance of their surreptitious issue, (as lately announced, from outsiders,) I have, with some qualms, tack'd them on here. *A Dough-Face Song* came out first in the "Evening Post"—*Blood-Money,* and *Wounded in the House of Friends,* in the "Tribune."

Poetry To-Day in America, &c., first appear'd (under the name of *"The Poetry of the Future,"*) in "The North American Review" for February, 1881. *A Memorandum at a Venture,* in same periodical, some time afterward.

Several of the convalescent out-door scenes and literary items, preceding, originally appear'd in the fortnightly "Critic," of New York.

Democratic Vistas

As the greatest lessons of Nature through the universe are perhaps the lessons of variety and freedom, the same present the greatest lessons also in New World politics and progress. If a man were ask'd, for instance, the distinctive points contrasting modern European and American political and other life with the old Asiatic cultus, as lingering-bequeath'd yet in China and Turkey, he might find the amount of them in John Stuart Mill's profound essay on Liberty in the future, where he demands two main constituents, or sub-strata, for a truly grand nationality—1st, a large variety of character—and 2d, full play for human nature to expand itself in numberless and even conflicting directions—(seems to be for general humanity much like the influences that make up, in their limitless field, that perennial health-action of the air we call the weather—an infinite number of currents and forces, and contributions, and temperatures, and cross purposes, whose ceaseless play of counterpart upon counterpart brings constant restoration and vitality.) With this thought—and not for itself alone, but all it necessitates, and draws after it—let me begin my speculations.

America, filling the present with greatest deeds and problems, cheerfully accepting the past, including feudalism, (as, indeed, the present is but the legitimate birth of the past, including feudalism,) counts, as I reckon, for her justification and success, (for who, as yet, dare claim success?) almost entirely on the future. Nor is that hope unwarranted. To-day, ahead, though dimly yet, we see, in vistas, a copious, sane, gigantic offspring. For our New World I consider far less important for what it has done, or what it is, than for results to come. Sole among nationalities, these States have assumed the task to put in forms of lasting power and practicality, on areas of amplitude rivaling the operations of the physical kosmos, the moral political speculations of ages, long, long deferr'd, the democratic republican principle, and the theory of development and perfection by voluntary standards, and self-reliance. Who else, indeed, except the United States, in history, so far, have accepted in unwitting faith, and, as we now see, stand, act upon, and go security for, these things?

church?

But preluding no longer, let me strike the key-note of the following strain. First premising that, though the passages of it have been written at widely different times, (it is, in fact, a collection of memoranda, perhaps for future designers, comprehenders,) and though it may be open to the charge of one part contradicting another—for there are opposite sides to the great question of democracy, as to every great question—I feel the parts harmoniously blended in my own realization and convictions, and present them to be read only in such oneness, each page and each claim and assertion modified and temper'd by the others. Bear in mind, too, that they are not the result of studying up in political economy, but of the ordinary sense, observing, wandering among men, these States, these stirring years of war and peace. I will not gloss over the appaling dangers of universal suffrage in the United States. In fact, it is to admit and face these dangers I am writing. To him or her within whose thought rages the battle, advancing, retreating, between democracy's convictions, aspirations, and the people's crudeness, vice, caprices, I mainly write this essay. I shall use the words America and democracy as convertible terms. Not an ordinary one is the issue. The United States are destined either to surmount the gorgeous history of feudalism, or else prove the most tremendous failure of time. Not the least doubtful am I on any prospects of their material success. The triumphant future of their business, geographic and productive departments, on larger scales and in more varieties than ever, is certain. In those respects the republic must soon (if she does not already) outstrip all examples hitherto afforded, and dominate the world.*

*"From a territorial area of less than nine hundred thousand square miles, the Union has expanded into over four millions and a half—fifteen times larger than that of Great Britain and France combined—with a shore-line, including Alaska, equal to the entire circumference of the earth, and with a domain within these lines far wider than that of the Romans in their proudest days of conquest and renown. With a river, lake, and coastwise commerce estimated at over two thousand millions of dollars per year; with a railway traffic of four to six thousand millions per year, and the annual domestic exchanges of the country running up to nearly ten thousand millions per year; with over two thousand millions of dollars invested in manufacturing, mechanical, and mining industry; with over five hundred millions of acres of land in actual occupancy, valued, with their appurtenances, at over seven thousand millions of dollars, and producing annually crops valued at over three thousand millions

Admitting all this, with the priceless value of our political institutions, general suffrage, (and fully acknowledging the latest, widest opening of the doors,) I say that, far deeper than these, what finally and only is to make of our western world a nationality superior to any hither known, and outtopping the past, must be vigorous, yet unsuspected Literatures, perfect personalities and sociologies, original, transcendental, and expressing (what, in highest sense, are not yet express'd at all,) democracy and the modern. With these, and out of these, I promulge new races of Teachers, and of perfect Women, indispensable to endow the birth-stock of a New World. For feudalism, caste, the ecclesiastic traditions, though palpably retreating from political institutions, still hold essentially, by their spirit, even in this country, entire possession of the more important fields, indeed the very subsoil, of education, and of social standards and literature.

I say that democracy can never prove itself beyond cavil, until it founds and luxuriantly grows its own forms of art, poems, schools, theology, displacing all that exists, or that has

---

of dollars; with a realm which, if the density of Belgium's population were possible, would be vast enough to include all the present inhabitants of the world; and with equal rights guaranteed to even the poorest and humblest of our forty millions of people—we can, with a manly pride akin to that which distinguish'd the palmiest days of Rome, claim," &c., &c., &c.—*Vice-President Colfax's Speech, July 4, 1870.*

LATER—*London "Times," (Weekly,) June 23, '82.*

"The wonderful wealth-producing power of the United States defies and sets at naught the grave drawbacks of a mischievous protective tariff, and has already obliterated, almost wholly, the traces of the greatest of modern civil wars. What is especially remarkable in the present development of American energy and success is its wide and equable distribution. North and south, east and west, on the shores of the Atlantic and the Pacific, along the chain of the great lakes, in the valley of the Mississippi, and on the coasts of the gulf of Mexico, the creation of wealth and the increase of population are signally exhibited. It is quite true, as has been shown by the recent apportionment of population in the House of Representatives, that some sections of the Union have advanced, relatively to the rest, in an extraordinary and unexpected degree. But this does not imply that the States which have gain'd no additional representatives or have actually lost some have been stationary or have receded. The fact is that the present tide of prosperity has risen so high that it has overflow'd all barriers, and has fill'd up the back-waters, and establish'd something like an approach to uniform success."

been produced anywhere in the past, under opposite influences. It is curious to me that while so many voices, pens, minds, in the press, lecture-rooms, in our Congress, &c., are discussing intellectual topics, pecuniary dangers, legislative problems, the suffrage, tariff and labor questions, and the various business and benevolent needs of America, with propositions, remedies, often worth deep attention, there is one need, a hiatus the profoundest, that no eye seems to perceive, no voice to state. Our fundamental want to-day in the United States, with closest, amplest reference to present conditions, and to the future, is of a class, and the clear idea of a class, of native authors, literatures, far different, far higher in grade than any yet known, sacerdotal, modern, fit to cope with our occasions, lands, permeating the whole mass of American mentality, taste, belief, breathing into it a new breath of life, giving it decision, affecting politics far more than the popular superficial suffrage, with results inside and underneath the elections of Presidents or Congresses—radiating, begetting appropriate teachers, schools, manners, and, as its grandest result, accomplishing, (what neither the schools nor the churches and their clergy have hitherto accomplish'd, and without which this nation will no more stand, permanently, soundly, than a house will stand without a substratum,) a religious and moral character beneath the political and productive and intellectual bases of the States. For know you not, dear, earnest reader, that the people of our land may all read and write, and may all possess the right to vote—and yet the main things may be entirely lacking?—(and this to suggest them.)

View'd, to-day, from a point of view sufficiently over-arching, the problem of humanity all over the civilized world is social and religious, and is to be finally met and treated by literature. The priest departs, the divine literatus comes. Never was anything more wanted than, to-day, and here in the States, the poet of the modern is wanted, or the great literatus of the modern. At all times, perhaps, the central point in any nation, and that whence it is itself really sway'd the most, and whence it sways others, is its national literature, especially its archetypal poems. Above all previous lands, a great original literature is surely to become the justification and reliance, (in some respects the sole reliance,) of American democracy.

Few are aware how the great literature penetrates all, gives hue to all, shapes aggregates and individuals, and, after subtle ways, with irresistible power, constructs, sustains, demolishes at will. Why tower, in reminiscence, above all the nations of the earth, two special lands, petty in themselves, yet inexpressibly gigantic, beautiful, columnar? Immortal Judah lives, and Greece immortal lives, in a couple of poems.

Nearer than this. It is not generally realized, but it is true, as the genius of Greece, and all the sociology, personality, politics and religion of those wonderful states, resided in their literature or esthetics, that what was afterwards the main support of European chivalry, the feudal, ecclesiastical, dynastic world over there—forming its osseous structure, holding it together for hundreds, thousands of years, preserving its flesh and bloom, giving it form, decision, rounding it out, and so saturating it in the conscious and unconscious blood, breed, belief, and intuitions of men, that it still prevails powerful to this day, in defiance of the mighty changes of time—was its literature, permeating to the very marrow, especially that major part, its enchanting songs, ballads, and poems.*

To the ostent of the senses and eyes, I know, the influences which stamp the world's history are wars, uprisings or downfalls of dynasties, changeful movements of trade, important inventions, navigation, military or civil governments, advent of powerful personalities, conquerors, &c. These of course play their part; yet, it may be, a single new thought, imagination, abstract principle, even literary style, fit for the time,

*See, for hereditaments, specimens, Walter Scott's Border Minstrelsy, Percy's collection, Ellis's early English Metrical Romances, the European continental poems of Walter of Aquitania, and the Nibelungen, of pagan stock, but monkish-feudal redaction; the history of the Troubadours, by Fauriel; even the far-back cumbrous old Hindu epics, as indicating the Asian eggs out of which European chivalry was hatch'd; Ticknor's chapters on the Cid, and on the Spanish poems and poets of Calderon's time. Then always, and, of course, as the superbest poetic culmination-expression of feudalism, the Shaksperean dramas, in the attitudes, dialogue, characters, &c., of the princes, lords and gentlemen, the pervading atmosphere, the implied and express'd standard of manners, the high port and proud stomach, the regal embroidery of style, &c.

put in shape by some great literatus, and projected among mankind, may duly cause changes, growths, removals, greater than the longest and bloodiest war, or the most stupendous merely political, dynastic, or commercial overturn.

In short, as, though it may not be realized, it is strictly true, that a few first-class poets, philosophs, and authors, have substantially settled and given status to the entire religion, education, law, sociology, &c., of the hitherto civilized world, by tinging and often creating the atmospheres out of which they have arisen, such also must stamp, and more than ever stamp, the interior and real democratic construction of this American continent, to-day, and days to come. Remember also this fact of difference, that, while through the antique and through the mediæval ages, highest thoughts and ideals realized themselves, and their expression made its way by other arts, as much as, or even more than by, technical literature, (not open to the mass of persons, or even to the majority of eminent persons,) such literature in our day and for current purposes, is not only more eligible than all the other arts put together, but has become the only general means of morally influencing the world. Painting, sculpture, and the dramatic theatre, it would seem, no longer play an indispensable or even important part in the workings and mediumship of intellect, utility, or even high esthetics. Architecture remains, doubtless with capacities, and a real future. Then music, the combiner, nothing more spiritual, nothing more sensuous, a god, yet completely human, advances, prevails, holds highest place; supplying in certain wants and quarters what nothing else could supply. Yet in the civilization of to-day it is undeniable that, over all the arts, literature dominates, serves beyond all—shapes the character of church and school—or, at any rate, is capable of doing so. Including the literature of science, its scope is indeed unparallel'd.

Before proceeding further, it were perhaps well to discriminate on certain points. Literature tills its crops in many fields, and some may flourish, while others lag. What I say in these Vistas has its main bearing on imaginative literature, especially poetry, the stock of all. In the department of science, and the specialty of journalism, there appear, in these States, promises, perhaps fulfilments, of highest earnestness, reality, and life. These, of course, are modern. But in the region of imaginative, spinal and essential attributes, something equivalent to creation is, for our age and lands, imperatively demanded. For not only is it not enough that the new blood, new frame of democracy shall be vivified and held together merely by political means, superficial suffrage, legislation, &c., but it is clear to me that, unless it goes deeper, gets at least as firm and as warm a hold in men's hearts, emotions and belief, as, in their days, feudalism or ecclesiasticism, and inaugurates its own perennial sources, welling from the centre forever, its strength will be defective, its growth doubtful, and its main charm wanting. I suggest, therefore, the possibility, should some two or three really original American poets, (perhaps artists or lecturers,) arise, mounting the horizon like planets, stars of the first magnitude, that, from their eminence, fusing contributions, races, far localities, &c., together they would give more compaction and more moral identity, (the quality to-day most needed,) to these States, than all its Constitutions, legislative and judicial ties, and all its hitherto political, warlike, or materialistic experiences. As, for instance, there could hardly happen anything that would more serve the States, with all their variety of origins, their diverse climes, cities, standards, &c., than possessing an aggregate of heroes, characters, exploits, sufferings, prosperity or misfortune, glory or disgrace, common to all, typical of all—no less, but even greater would it be to possess the aggregation of a cluster of mighty poets, artists, teachers, fit for us, national expressers, comprehending and effusing for the men and women of the States, what is universal, native, common to all, inland and seaboard, northern and southern. The historians say of ancient Greece, with her ever-jealous autonomies, cities, and states, that the only positive unity she ever own'd or receiv'd, was the sad unity of a common subjection, at the last, to foreign conquerors. Subjection, aggregation of that sort, is impossible to America; but the fear of conflicting and irreconcilable interiors, and the lack of a common skeleton, knitting all close, continually haunts me. Or, if it does not, nothing is plainer than the need, a long period to come, of a fusion of the States into the only reliable identity, the moral and artistic one. For, I say, the true nationality of the

States, the genuine union, when we come to a mortal crisis, is, and is to be, after all, neither the written law, nor, (as is generally supposed,) either self-interest, or common pecuniary or material objects—but the fervid and tremendous IDEA, melting everything else with resistless heat, and solving all lesser and definite distinctions in vast, indefinite, spiritual, emotional power.

It may be claim'd, (and I admit the weight of the claim,) that common and general worldly prosperity, and a populace well-to-do, and with all life's material comforts, is the main thing, and is enough. It may be argued that our republic is, in performance, really enacting to-day the grandest arts, poems, &c., by beating up the wilderness into fertile farms, and in her railroads, ships, machinery, &c. And it may be ask'd, Are these not better, indeed, for America, than any utterances even of greatest rhapsode, artist, or literatus?

I too hail those achievements with pride and joy: then answer that the soul of man will not with such only—nay, not with such at all—be finally satisfied; but needs what, (standing on these and on all things, as the feet stand on the ground,) is address'd to the loftiest, to itself alone.

Out of such considerations, such truths, arises for treatment in these Vistas the important question of character, of an American stock-personality, with literatures and arts for outlets and return-expressions, and, of course, to correspond, within outlines common to all. To these, the main affair, the thinkers of the United States, in general so acute, have either given feeblest attention, or have remain'd, and remain, in a state of somnolence.

For my part, I would alarm and caution even the political and business reader, and to the utmost extent, against the prevailing delusion that the establishment of free political institutions, and plentiful intellectual smartness, with general good order, physical plenty, industry, &c., (desirable and precious advantages as they all are,) do, of themselves, determine and yield to our experiment of democracy the fruitage of success. With such advantages at present fully, or almost fully, possess'd—the Union just issued, victorious, from the struggle with the only foes it need ever fear, (namely, those within itself, the interior ones,) and with unprecedented materialistic advancement—society, in these States, is canker'd, crude, superstitious, and rotten. Political, or law-made society is, and private, or voluntary society, is also. In any vigor, the element of the moral conscience, the most important, the verteber to State or man, seems to me either entirely lacking, or seriously enfeebled or ungrown.

I say we had best look our times and lands searchingly in the face, like a physician diagnosing some deep disease. Never was there, perhaps, more hollowness at heart than at present, and here in the United States. Genuine belief seems to have left us. The underlying principles of the States are not honestly believ'd in, (for all this hectic glow, and these melo-dramatic screamings,) nor is humanity itself believ'd in. What penetrating eye does not everywhere see through the mask? The spectacle is appaling. We live in an atmosphere of hypocrisy throughout. The men believe not in the women, nor the women in the men. A scornful superciliousness rules in literature. The aim of all the *littérateurs* is to find something to make fun of. A lot of churches, sects, &c., the most dismal phantasms I know, usurp the name of religion. Conversation is a mass of badinage. From deceit in the spirit, the mother of all false deeds, the offspring is already incalculable. An acute and candid person, in the revenue department in Washington, who is led by the course of his employment to regularly visit the cities, north, south and west, to investigate frauds, has talk'd much with me about his discoveries. The depravity of the business classes of our country is not less than has been supposed, but infinitely greater. The official services of America, national, state, and municipal, in all their branches and departments, except the judiciary, are saturated in corruption, bribery, falsehood, mal-administration; and the judiciary is tainted. The great cities reek with respectable as much as non-respectable robbery and scoundrelism. In fashionable life, flippancy, tepid amours, weak infidelism, small aims, or no aims at all, only to kill time. In business, (this all-devouring modern word, business,) the one sole object is, by any means, pecuniary gain. The magician's serpent in the fable ate up all the other serpents; and money-making is our magician's serpent, remaining to-day sole master of the field. The best class we show, is but a mob of fashionably dress'd speculators and vulgarians. True, indeed, behind this fantastic farce, enacted on the visible stage of society, solid things and stupendous labors are to be discover'd, existing crudely and going on in the background, to advance and tell themselves in time. Yet the truths are none the less terrible. I say that our New World democracy, however great a success in uplifting the masses out of their sloughs, in materialistic development, products, and in a certain highly-deceptive superficial popular intellectuality, is, so far, an almost complete failure in its social aspects, and in really grand religious, moral, literary, and esthetic results. In vain do we march with unprecedented strides to empire so colossal, outvying the antique, beyond Alexander's, beyond the proudest sway of Rome. In vain have we annex'd Texas, California, Alaska, and reach north for Canada and south for Cuba. It is as if we were somehow being endow'd with a vast and more and more thoroughly-appointed body, and then left with little or no soul.

Let me illustrate further, as I write, with current observations, localities, &c. The subject is important, and will bear repetition. After an absence, I am now again (September, 1870) in New York city and Brooklyn, on a few weeks' vacation. The splendor, picturesqueness, and oceanic amplitude and rush of these great cities, the unsurpass'd situation, rivers and bay, sparkling sea-tides, costly and lofty new buildings, façades of marble and iron, of original grandeur and elegance of design, with the masses of gay color, the preponderance of white and blue, the flags flying, the endless ships, the tumultuous streets, Broadway, the heavy, low, musical roar, hardly ever intermitted, even at night; the jobbers' houses, the rich shops, the wharves, the great Central Park, and the Brooklyn Park of hills, (as I wander among them this beautiful fall weather, musing, watching, absorbing)—the assemblages of the citizens in their groups, conversations, trades, evening amusements, or along the by-quarters—these, I say, and the like of these, completely satisfy my senses of power, fulness, motion, &c., and give me, through such senses and appetites, and through my esthetic conscience, a continued exaltation and absolute fulfilment. Always and more and more, as I cross the East and North rivers, the ferries, or with the pilots in their pilot-houses, or pass an hour in Wall street, or the gold exchange, I realize, (if we must admit such partialisms,) that not Nature alone is great in her fields of freedom and the open air, in her storms, the shows of night and day, the mountains, forests, seas—but in the artificial, the work of man too is equally great—in this profusion of teeming humanity—in these ingenuities, streets, goods, houses, ships—these hurrying, feverish, electric crowds of men, their complicated business genius, (not least among the geniuses,) and all this mighty, many-threaded wealth and industry concentrated here.

But sternly discarding, shutting our eyes to the glow and grandeur of the general superficial effect, coming down to what is of the only real importance, Personalities, and examining minutely, we question, we ask, Are there, indeed, *men* here worthy the name? Are there athletes? Are there perfect women, to match the generous material luxuriance? Is there a pervading atmosphere of beautiful manners? Are there crops of fine youths, and majestic old persons? Are there arts worthy freedom and a rich people? Is there a great moral and religious civilization—the only justification of a great material one? Confess that to severe eyes, using the moral microscope upon humanity, a sort of dry and flat Sahara appears, these cities, crowded with petty grotesques, malformations, phantoms, playing meaningless antics. Confess that everywhere, in shop, street, church, theatre, bar-room, official chair, are pervading flippancy and vulgarity, low cunning, infidelity—everywhere the youth puny, impudent, foppish, prematurely ripe—everywhere an abnormal libidinousness, unhealthy forms, male, female, painted, padded, dyed, chignon'd, muddy complexions, bad blood, the capacity for good motherhood deceasing or deceas'd, shallow notions of beauty, with a range of manners, or rather lack of manners, (considering the advantages enjoy'd,) probably the meanest to be seen in the world.*

*Of these rapidly-sketch'd hiatuses, the two which seem to me most serious are, for one, the condition, absence, or perhaps the singular abeyance, of moral conscientious fibre all through American society; and, for another, the appalling depletion of women in their powers of sane athletic maternity, their

Of all this, and these lamentable conditions, to breathe into them the breath recuperative of sane and heroic life, I say a new founded literature, not merely to copy and reflect existing surfaces, or pander to what is called taste—not only to amuse, pass away time, celebrate the beautiful, the refined, the past, or exhibit technical, rhythmic, or grammatical dexterity—but a literature underlying life, religious, consistent with science, handling the elements and forces with competent power, teaching and training men—and, as perhaps the most precious of its results, achieving the entire redemption of woman out of these incredible holds and webs of silliness, millinery, and every kind of dyspeptic depletion—and thus insuring to the States a strong and sweet Female Race, a race of perfect Mothers—is what is needed.

And now, in the full conception of these facts and points, and all that they infer, pro and con—with yet unshaken faith in the elements of the American masses, the composites, of both sexes, and even consider'd as individuals—and ever recognizing in them the broadest bases of the best literary and esthetic appreciation—I proceed with my speculations, Vistas.

First, let us see what we can make out of a brief, general, sentimental consideration of political democracy, and whence it has arisen, with regard to some of its current features, as an aggregate, and as the basic structure of our future literature and authorship. We shall, it is true, quickly and continually find the origin-idea of the singleness of man, individualism, asserting itself, and cropping forth, even from the opposite ideas. But the mass, or lump character, for imperative reasons, is to be ever carefully weigh'd, borne in mind, and provided for. Only from it, and from its proper regulation and potency,

---

crowning attribute, and ever making the woman, in loftiest spheres, superior to the man.

I have sometimes thought, indeed, that the sole avenue and means of a reconstructed sociology depended, primarily, on a new birth, elevation, expansion, invigoration of woman, affording, for races to come, (as the conditions that antedate birth are indispensable,) a perfect motherhood. Great, great, indeed, far greater than they know, is the sphere of women. But doubtless the question of such new sociology all goes together, includes many varied and complex influences and premises, and the man as well as the woman, and the woman as well as the man.

comes the other, comes the chance of individualism. The two are contradictory, but our task is to reconcile them.*

The political history of the past may be summ'd up as having grown out of what underlies the words, order, safety, caste, and especially out of the need of some prompt deciding authority, and of cohesion at all cost. Leaping time, we come to the period within the memory of people now living, when, as from some lair where they had slumber'd long, accumulating wrath, sprang up and are yet active, (1790, and on even to the present, 1870,) those noisy eructations, destructive iconoclasms, a fierce sense of wrongs, amid which moves the form, well known in modern history, in the old world, stain'd with much blood, and mark'd by savage reactionary clamors and demands. These bear, mostly, as on one inclosing point of need.

For after the rest is said—after the many time-honor'd and really true things for subordination, experience, rights of property, &c., have been listen'd to and acquiesced in—after the valuable and well-settled statement of our duties and relations in society is thoroughly conn'd over and exhausted—it remains to bring forward and modify everything else with the idea of that Something a man is, (last precious consolation of the drudging poor,) standing apart from all else, divine in his own right, and a woman in hers, sole and untouchable by any canons of authority, or any rule derived from precedent, state-safety, the acts of legislatures, or even from what is called religion, modesty, or art. The radiation of this truth is the key of the most significant doings of our immediately preceding three centuries, and has been the political genesis and life of America. Advancing visibly, it still more advances invisibly. Underneath the fluctuations of the expressions of society, as well as the movements of the politics of the leading nations of the world, we see steadily pressing ahead and strengthening

*The question hinted here is one which time only can answer. Must not the virtue of modern Individualism, continually enlarging, usurping all, seriously affect, perhaps keep down entirely, in America, the like of the ancient virtue of Patriotism, the fervid and absorbing love of general country? I have no doubt myself that the two will merge, and will mutually profit and brace each other, and that from them a greater product, a third, will arise. But I feel that at present they and their oppositions form a serious problem and paradox in the United States.

itself, even in the midst of immense tendencies toward aggregation, this image of completeness in separatism, of individual personal dignity, of a single person, either male or female, characterized in the main, not from extrinsic acquirements or position, but in the pride of himself or herself alone; and, as an eventual conclusion and summing up, (or else the entire scheme of things is aimless, a cheat, a crash,) the simple idea that the last, best dependence is to be upon humanity itself, and its own inherent, normal, full-grown qualities, without any superstitious support whatever. This idea of perfect individualism it is indeed that deepest tinges and gives character to the idea of the aggregate. For it is mainly or altogether to serve independent separatism that we favor a strong generalization, consolidation. As it is to give the best vitality and freedom to the rights of the States, (every bit as important as the right of nationality, the union,) that we insist on the identity of the Union at all hazards.

The purpose of democracy—supplanting old belief in the necessary absoluteness of establish'd dynastic rulership, temporal, ecclesiastical, and scholastic, as furnishing the only security against chaos, crime, and ignorance—is, through many transmigrations, and amid endless ridicules, arguments, and ostensible failures, to illustrate, at all hazards, this doctrine or theory that man, properly train'd in sanest, highest freedom, may and must become a law, and series of laws, unto himself, surrounding and providing for, not only his own personal control, but all his relations to other individuals, and to the State; and that, while other theories, as in the past histories of nations, have proved wise enough, and indispensable perhaps for their conditions, *this*, as matters now stand in our civilized world, is the only scheme worth working from, as warranting results like those of Nature's laws, reliable, when once establish'd, to carry on themselves.

The argument of the matter is extensive, and, we admit, by no means all on one side. What we shall offer will be far, far from sufficient. But while leaving unsaid much that should properly even prepare the way for the treatment of this many-sided question of political liberty, equality, or republicanism—leaving the whole history and consideration of the feudal plan and its products, embodying humanity, its politics and civilization, through the retrospect of past time, (which plan and products, indeed, make up all of the past, and a large part of the present)—leaving unanswer'd, at least by any specific and local answer, many a well-wrought argument and instance, and many a conscientious declamatory cry and warning—as, very lately, from an eminent and venerable person abroad*—things, problems, full of doubt, dread, suspense, (not new to me, but old occupiers of many an anxious hour in city's din, or night's silence,) we still may give a page or so, whose drift is opportune. Time alone can finally answer these things. But as a substitute in passing, let us, even if fragmentarily, throw forth a short direct or indirect suggestion of the premises of that other plan, in the new spirit, under the new forms, started here in our America.

As to the political section of Democracy, which introduces and breaks ground for further and vaster sections, few probably are the minds, even in these republican States, that fully comprehend the aptness of that phrase, "THE GOVERNMENT OF THE PEOPLE, BY THE PEOPLE, FOR THE PEOPLE," which we inherit from the lips of Abraham Lincoln; a formula whose verbal shape is homely wit, but whose scope includes both the totality and all minutiæ of the lesson.

The People! Like our huge earth itself, which, to ordinary scansion, is full of vulgar contradictions and offence, man, viewed in the lump, displeases, and is a constant puzzle and affront to the merely educated classes. The rare, cosmical, artist-mind, lit with the Infinite, alone confronts his manifold and oceanic qualities—but taste, intelligence and culture, (so-called,) have been against the masses, and remain so. There is plenty of glamour about the most damnable crimes and hog-

*"SHOOTING NIAGARA."—I was at first roused to much anger and abuse by this essay from Mr. Carlyle, so insulting to the theory of America—but happening to think afterwards how I had more than once been in the like mood, during which his essay was evidently cast, and seen persons and things in the same light, (indeed some might say there are signs of the same feeling in these Vistas)—I have since read it again, not only as a study, expressing as it does certain judgments from the highest feudal point of view, but have read it with respect as coming from an earnest soul, and as contributing certain sharp-cutting metallic grains, which, if not gold or silver, may be good hard, honest iron.

gish meannesses, special and general, of the feudal and dynastic world over there, with its *personnel* of lords and queens and courts, so well-dress'd and so handsome. But the People are ungrammatical, untidy, and their sins gaunt and ill-bred.

Literature, strictly consider'd, has never recognized the People, and, whatever may be said, does not to-day. Speaking generally, the tendencies of literature, as hitherto pursued, have been to make mostly critical and querulous men. It seems as if, so far, there were some natural repugnance between a literary and professional life, and the rude rank spirit of the democracies. There is, in later literature, a treatment of benevolence, a charity business, rife enough it is true; but I know nothing more rare, even in this country, than a fit scientific estimate and reverent appreciation of the People—of their measureless wealth of latent power and capacity, their vast, artistic contrasts of lights and shades—with, in America, their entire reliability in emergencies, and a certain breadth of historic grandeur, of peace or war, far surpassing all the vaunted samples of book-heroes, or any *haut-ton* coteries, in all the records of the world.

The movements of the late secession war, and their results, to any sense that studies well and comprehends them, show that popular democracy, whatever its faults and dangers, practically justifies itself beyond the proudest claims and wildest hopes of its enthusiasts. Probably no future age can know, but I well know, how the gist of this fiercest and most resolute of the world's war-like contentions resided exclusively in the unnamed, unknown rank and file; and how the brunt of its labor of death was, to all essential purposes, volunteer'd. The People, of their own choice, fighting, dying for their own idea, insolently attack'd by the secession-slave-power, and its very existence imperil'd. Descending to detail, entering any of the armies, and mixing with the private soldiers, we see and have seen august spectacles. We have seen the alacrity with which the American born populace, the peaceablest and most good-natured race in the world, and the most personally independent and intelligent, and the least fitted to submit to the irksomeness and exasperation of regimental discipline, sprang, at the first tap of the drum, to arms—not for gain, nor even glory, nor to repel invasion—but for an emblem, a mere abstraction—for the life, *the safety of the flag.* We have seen the unequal'd docility and obedience of these soldiers. We have seen them tried long and long by hopelessness, mismanagement, and by defeat; have seen the incredible slaughter toward or through which the armies, (as at first Fredericksburg, and afterward at the Wilderness,) still unhesitatingly obey'd orders to advance. We have seen them in trench, or crouching behind breastwork, or tramping in deep mud, or amid pouring rain or thick-falling snow, or under forced marches in hottest summer (as on the road to get to Gettysburg)—vast suffocating swarms, divisions, corps, with every single man so grimed and black with sweat and dust, his own mother would not have known him—his clothes all dirty, stain'd and torn, with sour, accumulated sweat for perfume—many a comrade, perhaps a brother, sun-struck, staggering out, dying, by the roadside, of exhaustion—yet the great bulk bearing steadily on, cheery enough, hollow-bellied from hunger, but sinewy with unconquerable resolution.

We have seen this race proved by wholesale by drearier, yet more fearful tests—the wound, the amputation, the shatter'd face or limb, the slow hot fever, long impatient anchorage in bed, and all the forms of maiming, operation and disease. Alas! America have we seen, though only in her early youth, already to hospital brought. There have we watch'd these soldiers, many of them only boys in years—mark'd their decorum, their religious nature and fortitude, and their sweet affection. Wholesale, truly. For at the front, and through the camps, in countless tents, stood the regimental, brigade and division hospitals; while everywhere amid the land, in or near cities, rose clusters of huge, white-wash'd, crowded, one-story wooden barracks; and there ruled agony with bitter scourge, yet seldom brought a cry; and there stalk'd death by day and night along the narrow aisles between the rows of cots, or by the blankets on the ground, and touch'd lightly many a poor sufferer, often with blessed, welcome touch.

I know not whether I shall be understood, but I realize that it is finally from what I learn'd personally mixing in such scenes that I am now penning these pages. One night in the gloomiest period of the war, in the Patent office hospital in

Washington city, as I stood by the bedside of a Pennsylvania soldier, who lay, conscious of quick approaching death, yet perfectly calm, and with noble, spiritual manner, the veteran surgeon, turning aside, said to me, that though he had witness'd many, many deaths of soldiers, and had been a worker at Bull Run, Antietam, Fredericksburg, &c., he had not seen yet the first case of man or boy that met the approach of dissolution with cowardly qualms or terror. My own observation fully bears out the remark.

What have we here, if not, towering above all talk and argument, the plentifully-supplied, last-needed proof of democracy, in its personalities? Curiously enough, too, the proof on this point comes, I should say, every bit as much from the south, as from the north. Although I have spoken only of the latter, yet I deliberately include all. Grand, common stock! to me the accomplish'd and convincing growth, prophetic of the future; proof undeniable to sharpest sense, of perfect beauty, tenderness and pluck, that never feudal lord, nor Greek, nor Roman breed, yet rival'd. Let no tongue ever speak in disparagement of the American races, north or south, to one who has been through the war in the great army hospitals.

Meantime, general humanity, (for to that we return, as, for our purposes, what it really is, to bear in mind,) has always, in every department, been full of perverse maleficence, and is so yet. In downcast hours the soul thinks it always will be—but soon recovers from such sickly moods. I myself see clearly enough the crude, defective streaks in all the strata of the common people; the specimens and vast collections of the ignorant, the credulous, the unfit and uncouth, the incapable, and the very low and poor. The eminent person just mention'd sneeringly asks whether we expect to elevate and improve a nation's politics by absorbing such morbid collections and qualities therein. The point is a formidable one, and there will doubtless always be numbers of solid and reflective citizens who will never get over it. Our answer is general, and is involved in the scope and letter of this essay. We believe the ulterior object of political and all other government, (having, of course, provided for the police, the safety of life, property, and for the basic statute and common law, and their administration, always first in order,) to be among the rest, not merely to rule, to repress disorder, &c., but to develop, to open up to cultivation, to encourage the possibilities of all beneficent and manly outcroppage, and of that aspiration for independence, and the pride and self-respect latent in all characters. (Or, if there be exceptions, we cannot, fixing our eyes on them alone, make theirs the rule for all.)

I say the mission of government, henceforth, in civilized lands, is not repression alone, and not authority alone, not even of law, nor by that favorite standard of the eminent writer, the rule of the best men, the born heroes and captains of the race, (as if such ever, or one time out of a hundred, get into the big places, elective or dynastic)—but higher than the highest arbitrary rule, to train communities through all their grades, beginning with individuals and ending there again, to rule themselves. What Christ appear'd for in the moral-spiritual field for human-kind, namely, that in respect to the absolute soul, there is in the possession of such by each single individual, something so transcendent, so incapable of gradations, (like life,) that, to that extent, it places all beings on a common level, utterly regardless of the distinctions of intellect, virtue, station, or any height or lowliness whatever—is tallied in like manner, in this other field, by democracy's rule that men, the nation, as a common aggregate of living identities, affording in each a separate and complete subject for freedom, worldly thrift and happiness, and for a fair chance for growth, and for protection in citizenship, &c., must, to the political extent of the suffrage or vote, if no further, be placed, in each and in the whole, on one broad, primary, universal, common platform.

The purpose is not altogether direct; perhaps it is more indirect. For it is not that democracy is of exhaustive account, in itself. Perhaps, indeed, it is, (like Nature,) of no account in itself. It is that, as we see, it is the best, perhaps only, fit and full means, formulater, general caller-forth, trainer, for the million, not for grand material personalities only, but for immortal souls. To be a voter with the rest is not so much; and this, like every institute, will have its imperfections. But to become an enfranchised man, and now, impediments removed, to stand and start without humiliation, and equal with the rest; to commence, or have the road clear'd to commence, the grand experiment of development, whose end, (perhaps requiring several generations,) may be the forming of a full-grown man or woman—that *is* something. To ballast the State is also secured, and in our times is to be secured, in no other way.

We do not, (at any rate I do not,) put it either on the ground that the People, the masses, even the best of them, are, in their latent or exhibited qualities, essentially sensible and good—nor on the ground of their rights; but that good or bad, rights or no rights, the democratic formula is the only safe and preservative one for coming times. We endow the masses with the suffrage for their own sake, no doubt; then, perhaps still more, from another point of view, for community's sake. Leaving the rest to the sentimentalists, we present freedom as sufficient in its scientific aspect, cold as ice, reasoning, deductive, clear and passionless as crystal.

Democracy too is law, and of the strictest, amplest kind. Many suppose, (and often in its own ranks the error,) that it means a throwing aside of law, and running riot. But, briefly, it is the superior law, not alone that of physical force, the body, which, adding to, it supersedes with that of the spirit. Law is the unshakable order of the universe forever; and the law over all, and law of laws, is the law of successions; that of the superior law, in time, gradually supplanting and overwhelming the inferior one. (While, for myself, I would cheerfully agree—first covenanting that the formative tendencies shall be administer'd in favor, or at least not against it, and that this reservation be closely construed—that until the individual or community show due signs, or be so minor and fractional as not to endanger the State, the condition of authoritative tutelage may continue, and self-government must abide its time.) Nor is the esthetic point, always an important one, without fascination for highest aiming souls. The common ambition strains for elevations, to become some privileged exclusive. The master sees greatness and health in being part of the mass; nothing will do as well as common ground. Would you have in yourself the divine, vast, general law? Then merge yourself in it.

And, topping democracy, this most alluring record, that it alone can bind, and ever seeks to bind, all nations, all men, of however various and distant lands, into a brotherhood, a family. It is the old, yet ever-modern dream of earth, out of her eldest and her youngest, her fond philosophers and poets. Not that half only, individualism, which isolates. There is another half, which is adhesiveness or love, that fuses, ties and aggregates, making the races comrades, and fraternizing all. Both are to be vitalized by religion, (sole worthiest elevator of man or State,) breathing into the proud, material tissues, the breath of life. For I say at the core of democracy, finally, is the religious element. All the religions, old and new, are there. Nor may the scheme step forth, clothed in resplendent beauty and command, till these, bearing the best, the latest fruit, the spiritual, shall fully appear.

A portion of our pages we might indite with reference toward Europe, especially the British part of it, more than our own land, perhaps not absolutely needed for the home reader. But the whole question hangs together, and fastens and links all peoples. The liberalist of to-day has this advantage over antique or medieval times, that his doctrine seeks not only to individualize but to universalize. The great word Solidarity has arisen. Of all dangers to a nation, as things exist in our day, there can be no greater one than having certain portions of the people set off from the rest by a line drawn—they not privileged as others, but degraded, humiliated, made of no account. Much quackery teems, of course, even on democracy's side, yet does not really affect the orbic quality of the matter. To work in, if we may so term it, and justify God, his divine aggregate, the People, (or, the veritable horn'd and sharp-tail'd Devil, *his* aggregate, if there be who convulsively insist upon it)—this, I say, is what democracy is for; and this is what our America means, and is doing—may I not say, has done? If not, she means nothing more, and does nothing more, than any other land. And as, by virtue of its kosmical, antiseptic power, Nature's stomach is fully strong enough not only to digest the morbific matter always presented, not to be turn'd aside, and perhaps, indeed, intuitively gravitating thither—but even to change such contributions into nutriment for highest use and life—so American democracy's. That is the lesson we, these days, send over to European lands by every western breeze.

And, truly, whatever may be said in the way of abstract argument, for or against the theory of a wider democratizing of institutions in any civilized country, much trouble might well be saved to all European lands by recognizing this palpable fact, (for a palpable fact it is,) that some form of such democratizing is about the only resource now left. *That,* or chronic dissatisfaction continued, mutterings which grow annually louder and louder, till, in due course, and pretty swiftly in most cases, the inevitable crisis, crash, dynastic ruin. Anything worthy to be call'd statesmanship in the Old World, I should say, among the advanced students, adepts, or men of any brains, does not debate to-day whether to hold on, attempting to lean back and monarchize, or to look forward and democratize—but *how,* and in what degree and part, most prudently to democratize.

The eager and often inconsiderate appeals of reformers and revolutionists are indispensable, to counterbalance the inertness and fossilism making so large a part of human institutions. The latter will always take care of themselves—the danger being that they rapidly tend to ossify us. The former is to be treated with indulgence, and even with respect. As circulation to air, so is agitation and a plentiful degree of speculative license to political and moral sanity. Indirectly, but surely, goodness, virtue, law, (of the very best,) follow freedom. These, to democracy, are what the keel is to the ship, or saltness to the ocean.

The true gravitation-hold of liberalism in the United States will be a more universal ownership of property, general homesteads, general comfort—a vast, intertwining reticulation of wealth. As the human frame, or, indeed, any object in this manifold universe, is best kept together by the simple miracle of its own cohesion, and the necessity, exercise and profit thereof, so a great and varied nationality, occupying millions of square miles, were firmest held and knit by the principle of the safety and endurance of the aggregate of its middling property owners. So that, from another point of view, ungracious as it may sound, and a paradox after what we have been saying, democracy looks with suspicious, ill-satisfied eye upon the very poor, the ignorant, and on those out of business. She asks for men and women with occupations, well-off, owners of houses and acres, and with cash in the bank—and with some cravings for literature, too; and must have them, and hastens to make them. Luckily, the seed is already well-sown, and has taken ineradicable root.*

Huge and mighty are our days, our republican lands—and most in their rapid shiftings, their changes, all in the interest of the cause. As I write this particular passage, (November, 1868,) the din of disputation rages around me. Acrid the temper of the parties, vital the pending questions. Congress convenes; the President sends his message; reconstruction is still in abeyance; the nomination and the contest for the twenty-first Presidentiad draw close, with loudest threat and bustle. Of these, and all the like of these, the eventuations I know not; but well I know that behind them, and whatever their eventuations, the vital things remain safe and certain, and all the needed work goes on. Time, with soon or later superciliousness, disposes of Presidents, Congressmen, party platforms, and such. Anon, it clears the stage of each and any mortal shred that thinks itself so potent to its day; and at and after which, (with precious, golden exceptions once or twice in a century,) all that relates to sir potency is flung to moulder in a burial-vault, and no one bothers himself the least bit about it afterward. But the People ever remain, tendencies continue, and all the idiocratic transfers in unbroken chain go on.

In a few years the dominion-heart of America will be far inland, toward the West. Our future national capital may not be where the present one is. It is possible, nay likely, that in

*For fear of mistake, I may as well distinctly specify, as cheerfully included in the model and standard of these Vistas, a practical, stirring, worldly, money-making, even materialistic character. It is undeniable that our farms, stores, offices, dry-goods, coal and groceries, enginery, cash-accounts, trades, earnings, markets, &c., should be attended to in earnest, and actively pursued, just as if they had a real and permanent existence. I perceive clearly that the extreme business energy, and this almost maniacal appetite for wealth prevalent in the United States, are parts of amelioration and progress, indispensably needed to prepare the very results I demand. My theory includes riches, and the getting of riches, and the amplest products, power, activity, inventions, movements, &c. Upon them, as upon substrata, I raise the edifice design'd in these Vistas.

less than fifty years, it will migrate a thousand or two miles, will be re-founded, and every thing belonging to it made on a different plan, original, far more superb. The main social, political, spine-character of the States will probably run along the Ohio, Missouri and Mississippi rivers, and west and north of them, including Canada. Those regions, with the group of powerful brothers toward the Pacific, (destined to the mastership of that sea and its countless paradises of islands,) will compact and settle the traits of America, with all the old retain'd, but more expanded, grafted on newer, hardier, purely native stock. A giant growth, composite from the rest, getting their contribution, absorbing it, to make it more illustrious. From the north, intellect, the sun of things, also the idea of unswayable justice, anchor amid the last, the wildest tempests. From the south the living soul, the animus of good and bad, haughtily admitting no demonstration but its own. While from the west itself comes solid personality, with blood and brawn, and the deep quality of all-accepting fusion.

Political democracy, as it exists and practically works in America, with all its threatening evils, supplies a training-school for making first-class men. It is life's gymnasium, not of good only, but of all. We try often, though we fall back often. A brave delight, fit for freedom's athletes, fills these arenas, and fully satisfies, out of the action in them, irrespective of success. Whatever we do not attain, we at any rate attain the experiences of the fight, the hardening of the strong campaign, and throb with currents of attempt at least. Time is ample. Let the victors come after us. Not for nothing does evil play its part among us. Judging from the main portions of the history of the world, so far, justice is always in jeopardy, peace walks amid hourly pitfalls, and of slavery, misery, meanness, the craft of tyrants and the credulity of the populace, in some of their protean forms, no voice can at any time say, They are not. The clouds break a little, and the sun shines out—but soon and certain the lowering darkness falls again, as if to last forever. Yet is there an immortal courage and prophecy in every sane soul that cannot, must not, under any circumstances, capitulate. *Vive,* the attack—the perennial assault! *Vive,* the unpopular cause—the spirit that audaciously aims—the never-abandon'd efforts, pursued the same amid opposing proofs and precedents.

Once, before the war, (Alas! I dare not say how many times the mood has come!) I, too, was fill'd with doubt and gloom. A foreigner, an acute and good man, had impressively said to me, that day—putting in form, indeed, my own observations: "I have travel'd much in the United States, and watch'd their politicians, and listen'd to the speeches of the candidates, and read the journals, and gone into the public houses, and heard the unguarded talk of men. And I have found your vaunted America honeycomb'd from top to toe with infidelism, even to itself and its own programme. I have mark'd the brazen hell-faces of secession and slavery gazing defiantly from all the windows and doorways. I have everywhere found, primarily, thieves and scalliwags arranging the nominations to offices, and sometimes filling the offices themselves. I have found the north just as full of bad stuff as the south. Of the holders of public office in the Nation or the States or their municipalities, I have found that not one in a hundred has been chosen by any spontaneous selection of the outsiders, the people, but all have been nominated and put through by little or large caucuses of the politicians, and have got in by corrupt rings and electioneering, not capacity or desert. I have noticed how the millions of sturdy farmers and mechanics are thus the helpless supple-jacks of comparatively few politicians. And I have noticed more and more, the alarming spectacle of parties usurping the government, and openly and shamelessly wielding it for party purposes."

Sad, serious, deep truths. Yet are there other, still deeper, amply confronting, dominating truths. Over those politicians and great and little rings, and over all their insolence and wiles, and over the powerfulest parties, looms a power, too sluggish may-be, but ever holding decisions and decrees in hand, ready, with stern process, to execute them as soon as plainly needed—and at times, indeed, summarily crushing to atoms the mightiest parties, even in the hour of their pride.

In saner hours far different are the amounts of these things from what, at first sight, they appear. Though it is no doubt important who is elected governor, mayor, or legislator, (and full of dismay when incompetent or vile ones get elected, as they sometimes do,) there are other, quieter contingencies, infinitely more important. Shams, &c., will always be the show, like ocean's scum; enough, if waters deep and clear make up the rest. Enough, that while the piled embroider'd shoddy gaud and fraud spreads to the superficial eye, the hidden warp and weft are genuine, and will wear forever. Enough, in short, that the race, the land which could raise such as the late rebellion, could also put it down.

The average man of a land at last only is important. He, in these States, remains immortal owner and boss, deriving good uses, somehow, out of any sort of servant in office, even the basest; (certain universal requisites, and their settled regularity and protection, being first secured,) a nation like ours, in a sort of geological formation state, trying continually new experiments, choosing new delegations, is not served by the best men only, but sometimes more by those that provoke it—by the combats they arouse. Thus national rage, fury, discussion, &c., better than content. Thus, also, the warning signals, invaluable for after times.

What is more dramatic than the spectacle we have seen repeated, and doubtless long shall see—the popular judgment taking the successful candidates on trial in the offices—standing off, as it were, and observing them and their doings for a while, and always giving, finally, the fit, exactly due reward? I think, after all, the sublimest part of political history, and its culmination, is currently issuing from the American people. I know nothing grander, better exercise, better digestion, more positive proof of the past, the triumphant result of faith in human kind, than a well-contested American national election.

Then still the thought returns, (like the thread-passage in overtures,) giving the key and echo to these pages. When I pass to and fro, different latitudes, different seasons, beholding the crowds of the great cities, New York, Boston, Philadelphia, Cincinnati, Chicago, St. Louis, San Francisco, New Orleans, Baltimore—when I mix with these interminable swarms of alert, turbulent, good-natured, independent citizens, mechanics, clerks, young persons—at the idea of this mass of men, so fresh and free, so loving and so proud, a singular awe falls upon me. I feel, with dejection and amazement, that among our geniuses and talented writers or speakers, few or none have yet really spoken to this people, created a single image-making work for them, or absorb'd the central spirit and the idiosyncrasies which are theirs—and which, thus, in highest ranges, so far remain entirely uncelebrated, unexpress'd.

Dominion strong is the body's; dominion stronger is the mind's. What has fill'd, and fills to-day our intellect, our fancy, furnishing the standards therein, is yet foreign. The great poems, Shakspere included, are poisonous to the idea of the pride and dignity of the common people, the life-blood of democracy. The models of our literature, as we get it from other lands, ultramarine, have had their birth in courts, and bask'd and grown in castle sunshine; all smells of princes' favors. Of workers of a certain sort, we have, indeed, plenty, contributing after their kind; many elegant, many learn'd, all complacent. But touch'd by the national test, or tried by the standards of democratic personality, they wither to ashes. I say I have not seen a single writer, artist, lecturer, or what not, that has confronted the voiceless but ever erect and active, pervading, underlying will and typic aspiration of the land, in a spirit kindred to itself. Do you call those genteel little creatures American poets? Do you term that perpetual, pistareen, paste-pot work, American art, American drama, taste, verse? I think I hear, echoed as from some mountain-top afar in the west, the scornful laugh of the Genius of these States.

Democracy, in silence, biding its time, ponders its own ideals, not of literature and art only—not of men only, but of women. The idea of the women of America, (extricated from this daze, this fossil and unhealthy air which hangs about the word *lady,*) develop'd, raised to become the robust equals, workers, and, it may be, even practical and political deciders with the men—greater than man, we may admit, through their divine maternity, always their towering, emblematical attribute—but great, at any rate, as man, in all departments; or, rather, capable of being so, soon as they realize it, and can bring themselves to give up toys and fictions, and launch forth, as men do, amid real, independent, stormy life.

Then, as towards our thought's finalè, (and, in that, over-arching the true scholar's lesson,) we have to say there can be no complete or epical presentation of democracy in the aggregate, or anything like it, at this day, because its doctrines will only be effectually incarnated in any one branch, when, in all, their spirit is at the root and centre. Far, far, indeed, stretch, in distance, our Vistas! How much is still to be disentangled, freed! How long it takes to make this American world see that it is, in itself, the final authority and reliance!

Did you, too, O friend, suppose democracy was only for elections, for politics, and for a party name? I say democracy is only of use there that it may pass on and come to its flower and fruits in manners, in the highest forms of interaction between men, and their beliefs—in religion, literature, colleges, and schools—democracy in all public and private life, and in the army and navy.* I have intimated that, as a paramount scheme, it has yet few or no full realizers and believers. I do not see, either, that it owes any serious thanks to noted propagandists or champions, or has been essentially help'd, though often harm'd, by them. It has been and is carried on by all the moral forces, and by trade, finance, machinery, intercommunications, and, in fact, by all the developments of history, and can no more be stopp'd than the tides, or the earth in its orbit. Doubtless, also, it resides, crude and latent, well down in the hearts of the fair average of the American-born people, mainly in the agricultural regions. But it is not yet, there or anywhere, the fully-receiv'd, the fervid, the absolute faith.

I submit, therefore, that the fruition of democracy, on aught like a grand scale, resides altogether in the future. As, under any profound and comprehensive view of the gorgeous-composite feudal world, we see in it, through the long

*The whole present system of the officering and personnel of the army and navy of these States, and the spirit and letter of their trebly-aristocratic rules and regulations, is a monstrous exotic, a nuisance and revolt, and belong here just as much as orders of nobility, or the Pope's council of cardinals. I say if the present theory of our army and navy is sensible and true, then the rest of America is an unmitigated fraud.

ages and cycles of ages, the results of a deep, integral, human and divine principle, or fountain, from which issued laws, ecclesia, manners, institutes, costumes, personalities, poems, (hitherto unequall'd,) faithfully partaking of their source, and indeed only arising either to betoken it, or to furnish parts of that varied-flowing display, whose centre was one and absolute—so, long ages hence, shall the due historian or critic make at least an equal retrospect, an equal history for the democratic principle. It too must be adorn'd, credited with its results—then, when it, with imperial power, through amplest time, has dominated mankind—has been the source and test of all the moral, esthetic, social, political, and religious expressions and institutes of the civilized world—has begotten them in spirit and in form, and has carried them to its own unprecedented heights—has had, (it is possible,) monastics and ascetics, more numerous, more devout than the monks and priests of all previous creeds—has sway'd the ages with a breadth and rectitude tallying Nature's own—has fashion'd, systematized, and triumphantly finish'd and carried out, in its own interest, and with unparallel'd success, a new earth and a new man.

Thus we presume to write, as it were, upon things that exist not, and travel by maps yet unmade, and a blank. But the throes of birth are upon us; and we have something of this advantage in seasons of strong formations, doubts, suspense—for then the afflatus of such themes haply may fall upon us, more or less; and then, hot from surrounding war and revolution, our speech, though without polish'd coherence, and a failure by the standard called criticism, comes forth, real at least as the lightnings.

And may-be we, these days, have, too, our own reward—(for there are yet some, in all lands, worthy to be so encouraged.) Though not for us the joy of entering at the last the conquer'd city—not ours the chance ever to see with our own eyes the peerless power and splendid *eclat* of the democratic principle, arriv'd at meridian, filling the world with effulgence and majesty far beyond those of past history's kings, or all dynastic sway—there is yet, to whoever is eligible among us, the prophetic vision, the joy of being toss'd in the brave turmoil of these times—the promulgation and the path, obedient, lowly reverent to the voice, the gesture of the god, or holy ghost, which others see not, hear not—with the proud consciousness that amid whatever clouds, seductions, or heart-wearying postponements, we have never deserted, never despair'd, never abandon'd the faith.

So much contributed, to be conn'd well, to help prepare and brace our edifice, our plann'd Idea—we still proceed to give it in another of its aspects—perhaps the main, the high façade of all. For to democracy, the leveler, the unyielding principle of the average, is surely join'd another principle, equally unyielding, closely tracking the first, indispensable to it, opposite, (as the sexes are opposite,) and whose existence, confronting and ever modifying the other, often clashing, paradoxical, yet neither of highest avail without the other, plainly supplies to these grand cosmic politics of ours, and to the launch'd forth mortal dangers of republicanism, to-day or any day, the counterpart and offset whereby Nature restrains the deadly original relentlessness of all her first-class laws. This second principle is individuality, the pride and centripetal isolation of a human being in himself—identity—personalism. Whatever the name, its acceptance and thorough infusion through the organizations of political commonalty now shooting Aurora-like about the world, are of utmost importance, as the principle itself is needed for very life's sake. It forms, in a sort, or is to form, the compensating balance-wheel of the successful working machinery of aggregate America.

And, if we think of it, what does civilization itself rest upon—and what object has it, with its religions, arts, schools, &c., but rich, luxuriant, varied personalism? To that, all bends; and it is because toward such result democracy alone, on anything like Nature's scale, breaks up the limitless fallows of humankind, and plants the seed, and gives fair play, that its claims now precede the rest. The literature, songs, esthetics, &c., of a country are of importance principally because

they furnish the materials and suggestions of personality for the women and men of that country, and enforce them in a thousand effective ways.* As the top-most claim of a strong consolidating of the nationality of these States, is, that only by such powerful compaction can the separate States secure that full and free swing within their spheres, which is becoming to them, each after its kind, so will individuality, with unimpeded branchings, flourish best under imperial republican forms.

Assuming Democracy to be at present in its embryo condition, and that the only large and satisfactory justification of it resides in the future, mainly through the copious production of perfect characters among the people, and through the advent of a sane and pervading religiousness, it is with regard to the atmosphere and spaciousness fit for such characters, and of certain nutriment and cartoon-draftings proper for them, and indicating them for New World purposes, that I continue the present statement—an exploration, as of new ground, wherein, like other primitive surveyors, I must do the best I can, leaving it to those who come after me to do

*After the rest is satiated, all interest culminates in the field of persons, and never flags there. Accordingly in this field have the great poets and literatuses signally toil'd. They too, in all ages, all lands, have been creators, fashioning, making types of men and women, as Adam and Eve are made in the divine fable. Behold, shaped, bred by orientalism, feudalism, through their long growth and culmination, and breeding back in return—(when shall we have an equal series, typical of democracy?)—behold, commencing in primal Asia, (apparently formulated, in what beginning we know, in the gods of the mythologies, and coming down thence,) a few samples out of the countless product, bequeath'd to the moderns, bequeath'd to America as studies. For the men, Yudishtura, Rama, Arjuna, Solomon, most of the Old and New Testament characters; Achilles, Ulysses, Theseus, Prometheus, Hercules, Æneas, Plutarch's heroes; the Merlin of Celtic bards; the Cid, Arthur and his knights, Siegfried and Hagen in the Nibelungen; Roland and Oliver; Roustam in the Shah-Nemah; and so on to Milton's Satan, Cervantes' Don Quixote, Shakspere's Hamlet, Richard II., Lear, Marc Antony, &c., and the modern Faust. These, I say, are models, combined, adjusted to other standards than America's, but of priceless value to her and hers.

Among women, the goddesses of the Egyptian, Indian and Greek mythologies, certain Bible characters, especially the Holy Mother; Cleopatra, Penelope; the portraits of Brunhelde and Chriemhilde in the Nibelungen; Oriana, Una, &c.; the modern Consuelo, Walter Scott's Jeanie and Effie Deans, &c., &c. (Yet woman portray'd or outlin'd at her best, or as perfect human mother, does not hitherto, it seems to me, fully appear in literature.)

much better. (The service, in fact, if any, must be to break a sort of first path or track, no matter how rude and ungeometrical.)

We have frequently printed the word Democracy. Yet I cannot too often repeat that it is a word the real gist of which still sleeps, quite unawaken'd, notwithstanding the resonance and the many angry tempests out of which its syllables have come, from pen or tongue. It is a great word, whose history, I suppose, remains unwritten, because that history has yet to be enacted. It is, in some sort, younger brother of another great and often-used word, Nature, whose history also waits unwritten. As I perceive, the tendencies of our day, in the States, (and I entirely respect them,) are toward those vast and sweeping movements, influences, moral and physical, of humanity, now and always current over the planet, on the scale of the impulses of the elements. Then it is also good to reduce the whole matter to the consideration of a single self, a man, a woman, on permanent grounds. Even for the treatment of the universal, in politics, metaphysics, or anything, sooner or later we come down to one single, solitary soul.

There is, in sanest hours, a consciousness, a thought that rises, independent, lifted out from all else, calm, like the stars, shining eternal. This is the thought of identity—yours for you, whoever you are, as mine for me. Miracle of miracles, beyond statement, most spiritual and vaguest of earth's dreams, yet hardest basic fact, and only entrance to all facts. In such devout hours, in the midst of the significant wonders of heaven and earth, (significant only because of the Me in the centre,) creeds, conventions, fall away and become of no account before this simple idea. Under the luminousness of real vision, it alone takes possession, takes value. Like the shadowy dwarf in the fable, once liberated and look'd upon, it expands over the whole earth, and spreads to the roof of heaven.

The quality of BEING, in the object's self, according to its own central idea and purpose, and of growing therefrom and thereto—not criticism by other standards, and adjustments thereto—is the lesson of Nature. True, the full man wisely gathers, culls, absorbs; but if, engaged disproportionately in that, he slights or overlays the precious idiocrasy and special nativity and intention that he is, the man's self, the main thing, is a failure, however wide his general cultivation. Thus, in our times, refinement and delicatesse are not only attended to sufficiently, but threaten to eat us up, like a cancer. Already, the democratic genius watches, ill-pleased, these tendencies. Provision for a little healthy rudeness, savage virtue, justification of what one has in one's self, whatever it is, is demanded. Negative qualities, even deficiencies, would be a relief. Singleness and normal simplicity and separation, amid this more and more complex, more and more artificialized state of society—how pensively we yearn for them! how we would welcome their return!

In some such direction, then—at any rate enough to preserve the balance—we feel called upon to throw what weight we can, not for absolute reasons, but current ones. To prune, gather, trim, conform, and ever cram and stuff, and be genteel and proper, is the pressure of our days. While aware that much can be said even in behalf of all this, we perceive that we have not now to consider the question of what is demanded to serve a half-starved and barbarous nation, or set of nations, but what is most applicable, most pertinent, for numerous congeries of conventional, over-corpulent societies, already becoming stifled and rotten with flatulent, infidelistic literature, and polite conformity and art. In addition to establish'd sciences, we suggest a science as it were of healthy average personalism, on original-universal grounds, the object of which should be to raise up and supply through the States a copious race of superb American men and women, cheerful, religious, ahead of any yet known.

America has yet morally and artistically originated nothing. She seems singularly unaware that the models of persons, books, manners, &c., appropriate for former conditions and for European lands, are but exiles and exotics here. No current of her life, as shown on the surfaces of what is authoritatively called her society, accepts or runs into social or esthetic democracy; but all the currents set squarely against it. Never, in the Old World, was thoroughly upholster'd exterior appearance and show, mental and other, built entirely on the idea of caste, and on the sufficiency of mere outside acquisition—never were glibness, verbal intellect, more the test, the emulation—more loftily elevated as head and sample—than they are on the surface of our republican States this day. The writers of a time hint the mottoes of its gods. The word of the modern, say these voices, is the word Culture.

We find ourselves abruptly in close quarters with the enemy. This word Culture, or what it has come to represent, involves, by contrast, our whole theme, and has been, indeed, the spur, urging us to engagement. Certain questions arise. As now taught, accepted and carried out, are not the processes of culture rapidly creating a class of supercilious infidels, who believe in nothing? Shall a man lose himself in countless masses of adjustments, and be so shaped with reference to this, that, and the other, that the simply good and healthy and brave parts of him are reduced and clipp'd away, like the bordering of box in a garden? You can cultivate corn and roses and orchards—but who shall cultivate the mountain peaks, the ocean, and the tumbling gorgeousness of the clouds? Lastly—is the readily-given reply that culture only seeks to help, systematize, and put in attitude, the elements of fertility and power, a conclusive reply?

I do not so much object to the name, or word, but I should certainly insist, for the purposes of these States, on a radical change of category, in the distribution of precedence. I should demand a programme of culture, drawn out, not for a single class alone, or for the parlors or lecture-rooms, but with an eye to practical life, the west, the working-men, the facts of farms and jack-planes and engineers, and of the broad range of the women also of the middle and working strata, and with reference to the perfect equality of women, and of a grand and powerful motherhood. I should demand of this programme or theory a scope generous enough to include the widest human area. It must have for its spinal meaning the formation of a typical personality of character, eligible to the uses of the high average of men—and *not* restricted by conditions ineligible to the masses. The best culture will always be that of the manly and courageous instincts, and loving perceptions, and of self-respect—aiming to form, over this continent, an idiocrasy of universalism, which, true child of

America, will bring joy to its mother, returning to her in her own spirit, recruiting myriads of offspring, able, natural, perceptive, tolerant, devout believers in her, America, and with some definite instinct why and for what she has arisen, most vast, most formidable of historic births, and is, now and here, with wonderful step, journeying through Time.

The problem, as it seems to me, presented to the New World, is, under permanent law and order, and after preserving cohesion, (ensemble-Individuality,) at all hazards, to vitalize man's free play of special Personalism, recognizing in it something that calls ever more to be consider'd, fed, and adopted as the substratum for the best that belongs to us, (government indeed is for it,) including the new esthetics of our future.

To formulate beyond this present vagueness—to help line and put before us the species, or a specimen of the species, of the democratic ethnology of the future, is a work toward which the genius of our land, with peculiar encouragement, invites her well-wishers. Already certain limnings, more or less grotesque, more or less fading and watery, have appear'd. We too, (repressing doubts and qualms,) will try our hand.

Attempting, then, however crudely, a basic model or portrait of personality for general use for the manliness of the States, (and doubtless that is most useful which is most simple and comprehensive for all, and toned low enough,) we should prepare the canvas well beforehand. Parentage must consider itself in advance. (Will the time hasten when fatherhood and motherhood shall become a science—and the noblest science?) To our model, a clear-blooded, strong-fibred physique, is indispensable; the questions of food, drink, air, exercise, assimilation, digestion, can never be intermitted. Out of these we descry a well-begotten selfhood—in youth, fresh, ardent, emotional, aspiring, full of adventure; at maturity, brave, perceptive, under control, neither too talkative nor too reticent, neither flippant nor sombre; of the bodily figure, the movements easy, the complexion showing the best blood, somewhat flush'd, breast expanded, an erect attitude, a voice whose sound outvies music, eyes of calm and steady gaze, yet capable also of flashing—and a general presence that holds its own in the company of the highest. (For it is native personality, and that alone, that endows a man to stand before presidents or generals, or in any distinguish'd collection, with *aplomb*—and *not* culture, or any knowledge or intellect whatever.)

With regard to the mental-educational part of our model, enlargement of intellect, stores of cephalic knowledge, &c., the concentration thitherward of all the customs of our age, especially in America, is so overweening, and provides so fully for that part, that, important and necessary as it is, it really needs nothing from us here—except, indeed, a phrase of warning and restraint. Manners, costumes, too, though important, we need not dwell upon here. Like beauty, grace of motion, &c., they are results. Causes, original things, being attended to, the right manners unerringly follow. Much is said, among artists, of "the grand style," as if it were a thing by itself. When a man, artist or whoever, has health, pride, acuteness, noble aspirations, he has the motive-elements of the grandest style. The rest is but manipulation, (yet that is no small matter.)

Leaving still unspecified several sterling parts of any model fit for the future personality of America, I must not fail, again and ever, to pronounce myself on one, probably the least attended to in modern times—a hiatus, indeed, threatening its gloomiest consequences after us. I mean the simple, unsophisticated Conscience, the primary moral element. If I were asked to specify in what quarter lie the grounds of darkest dread, respecting the America of our hopes, I should have to point to this particular. I should demand the invariable application to individuality, this day and any day, of that old, ever-true plumb-rule of persons, eras, nations. Our triumphant modern civilizee, with his all-schooling and his wondrous appliances, will still show himself but an amputation while this deficiency remains. Beyond, (assuming a more hopeful tone,) the vertebration of the manly and womanly personalism of our western world, can only be, and is, indeed, to be, (I hope,) its all penetrating Religiousness.

The ripeness of Religion is doubtless to be looked for in this field of individuality, and is a result that no organization or church can ever achieve. As history is poorly retain'd by what the technists call history, and is not given out from their pages, except the learner has in himself the sense of the well-wrapt, never yet written, perhaps impossible to be written, history—so Religion, although casually arrested, and, after a fashion, preserv'd in the churches and creeds, does not depend at all upon them, but is a part of the identified soul, which, when greatest, knows not bibles in the old way, but in new ways—the identified soul, which can really confront Religion when it extricates itself entirely from the churches, and not before.

Personalism fuses this, and favors it. I should say, indeed, that only in the perfect uncontamination and solitariness of individuality may the spirituality of religion positively come forth at all. Only here, and on such terms, the meditation, the devout ecstasy, the soaring flight. Only here, communion with the mysteries, the eternal problems, whence? whither? Alone, and identity, and the mood—and the soul emerges, and all statements, churches, sermons, melt away like vapors. Alone, and silent thought and awe, and aspiration—and then the interior consciousness, like a hitherto unseen inscription, in magic ink, beams out its wondrous lines to the sense. Bibles may convey, and priests expound, but it is exclusively for the noiseless operation of one's isolated Self, to enter the pure ether of veneration, reach the divine levels, and commune with the unutterable.

To practically enter into politics is an important part of American personalism. To every young man, north and south, earnestly studying these things, I should here, as an offset to what I have said in former pages, now also say, that may-be to views of very largest scope, after all, perhaps the political, (perhaps the literary and sociological,) America goes best about its development its own way—sometimes, to temporary sight, appaling enough. It is the fashion among dillettants and fops (perhaps I myself am not guiltless,) to decry the whole formulation of the active politics of America, as beyond redemption, and to be carefully kept away from. See you that you do not fall into this error. America, it may be, is doing very well upon the whole, notwithstanding these antics of the parties and their leaders, these half-brain'd nominees, the many ignorant ballots, and many elected failures and blatherers. It is the dillettants, and all who shirk their duty, who are not doing well. As for you, I advise you to enter more strongly yet into politics. I advise every young man to do so. Always inform yourself; always do the best you can; always vote. Disengage yourself from parties. They have been useful, and to some extent remain so; but the floating, uncommitted electors, farmers, clerks, mechanics, the masters of parties—watching aloof, inclining victory this side or that side—such are the ones most needed, present and future. For America, if eligible at all to downfall and ruin, is eligible within herself, not without; for I see clearly that the combined foreign world could not beat her down. But these savage, wolfish parties alarm me. Owning no law but their own will, more and more combative, less and less tolerant of the idea of ensemble and of equal brotherhood, the perfect equality of the States, the ever-overarching American ideas, it behooves you to convey yourself implicitly to no party, nor submit blindly to their dictators, but steadily hold yourself judge and master over all of them.

So much, (hastily toss'd together, and leaving far more unsaid,) for an ideal, or intimations of an ideal, toward American manhood. But the other sex, in our land, requires at least a basis of suggestion.

I have seen a young American woman, one of a large family of daughters, who, some years since, migrated from her meagre country home to one of the northern cities, to gain her own support. She soon became an expert seamstress, but finding the employment too confining for health and comfort, she went boldly to work for others, to house-keep, cook, clean, &c. After trying several places, she fell upon one where she was suited. She has told me that she finds nothing degrading in her position; it is not inconsistent with personal dignity, self-respect, and the respect of others. She confers benefits and receives them. She has good health; her presence itself is healthy and bracing; her character is unstain'd; she has made herself understood, and preserves her independence, and has been able to help her parents, and educate and get places for her sisters; and her course of life is not without opportunities for mental improvement, and of much quiet, uncosting happiness and love.

I have seen another woman who, from taste and necessity conjoin'd, has gone into practical affairs, carries on a mechanical business, partly works at it herself, dashes out more and more into real hardy life, is not abash'd by the coarseness of the contact, knows how to be firm and silent at the same time, holds her own with unvarying coolness and decorum, and will compare, any day, with superior carpenters, farmers, and even boatmen and drivers. For all that, she has not lost the charm of the womanly nature, but preserves and bears it fully, though through such rugged presentation.

Then there is the wife of a mechanic, mother of two children, a woman of merely passable English education, but of fine wit, with all her sex's grace and intuitions, who exhibits, indeed, such a noble female personality, that I am fain to record it here. Never abnegating her own proper independence, but always genially preserving it, and what belongs to it—cooking, washing, child-nursing, house-tending—she beams sunshine out of all these duties, and makes them illustrious. Physiologically sweet and sound, loving work, practical, she yet knows that there are intervals, however few, devoted to recreation, music, leisure, hospitality—and affords such intervals. Whatever she does, and wherever she is, that charm, that indescribable perfume of genuine womanhood attends her, goes with her, exhales from her, which belongs of right to all the sex, and is, or ought to be, the invariable atmosphere and common aureola of old as well as young.

My dear mother once described to me a resplendent person, down on Long Island, whom she knew in early days. She was known by the name of the Peacemaker. She was well toward eighty years old, of happy and sunny temperament, had always lived on a farm, and was very neighborly, sensible and discreet, an invariable and welcom'd favorite, especially with young married women. She had numerous children and grandchildren. She was uneducated, but possess'd a native dignity. She had come to be a tacitly agreed upon domestic regulator, judge, settler of difficulties, shepherdess, and reconciler in the land. She was a sight to draw near and look upon, with her large figure, her profuse snow-white hair, (uncoif'd by any head-dress or cap,) dark eyes, clear complexion, sweet breath, and peculiar personal magnetism.

The foregoing portraits, I admit, are frightfully out of line from these imported models of womanly personality—the stock feminine characters of the current novelists, or of the foreign court poems, (Ophelias, Enids, princesses, or ladies of one thing or another,) which fill the envying dreams of so many poor girls, and are accepted by our men, too, as supreme ideals of feminine excellence to be sought after. But I present mine just for a change.

Then there are mutterings, (we will not now stop to heed them here, but they must be heeded,) of something more revolutionary. The day is coming when the deep questions of woman's entrance amid the arenas of practical life, politics, the suffrage, &c., will not only be argued all around us, but may be put to decision, and real experiment.

Of course, in these States, for both man and woman, we must entirely recast the types of highest personality from what the oriental, feudal, ecclesiastical worlds bequeath us, and which yet possess the imaginative and esthetic fields of the United States, pictorial and melodramatic, not without use as studies, but making sad work, and forming a strange anachronism upon the scenes and exigencies around us. Of course, the old undying elements remain. The task is, to successfully adjust them to new combinations, our own days. Nor is this so incredible. I can conceive a community, to-day and here, in which, on a sufficient scale, the perfect personalities, without noise meet; say in some pleasant western settlement or town, where a couple of hundred best men and women, of ordinary worldly status, have by luck been drawn together, with nothing extra of genius or wealth, but virtuous, chaste, industrious, cheerful, resolute, friendly and devout. I can conceive such a community organized in running order, powers judiciously delegated—farming, building, trade, courts, mails, schools, elections, all attended to; and then the rest of life, the main thing, freely branching and blossoming in each individual, and bearing golden fruit. I can see there, in every young and old man, after his kind, and in every woman after hers, a true personality, develop'd, exercised proportionately in body, mind, and spirit. I can imagine this case as one not necessarily rare or difficult, but in buoyant accordance with the municipal and general requirements of our times. And I can realize in it the culmination of something better than any stereotyped *eclat* of history or poems. Perhaps, unsung, undramatized, unput in essays or biographies—perhaps even some such community already exists, in Ohio, Illinois, Missouri, or somewhere, practically fulfilling itself, and thus outvying, in cheapest vulgar life, all that has been hitherto shown in best ideal pictures.

In short, and to sum up, America, betaking herself to formative action, (as it is about time for more solid achievement, and less windy promise,) must, for her purposes, cease to recognize a theory of character grown of feudal aristocracies, or form'd by merely literary standards, or from any ultramarine, full-dress formulas of culture, polish, caste, &c., and must sternly promulgate her own new standard, yet old enough, and accepting the old, the perennial elements, and combining them into groups, unities, appropriate to the modern, the democratic, the west, and to the practical occasions and needs of our own cities, and of the agricultural regions. Ever the most precious in the common. Ever the fresh breeze of field, or hill, or lake, is more than any palpitation of fans, though of ivory, and redolent with perfume; and the air is more than the costliest perfumes.

And now, for fear of mistake, we may not intermit to beg our absolution from all that genuinely is, or goes along with, even Culture. Pardon us, venerable shade! if we have seem'd to speak lightly of your office. The whole civilization of the earth, we know, is yours, with all the glory and the light thereof. It is, indeed, in your own spirit, and seeking to tally the loftiest teachings of it, that we aim these poor utterances. For you, too, mighty minister! know that there is something greater than you, namely, the fresh, eternal qualities of Being. From them, and by them, as you, at your best, we too evoke the last, the needed help, to vitalize our country and our days. Thus we pronounce not so much against the principle of culture; we only supervise it, and promulge along with it, as deep, perhaps a deeper, principle. As we have shown the New World including in itself the all-leveling aggregate of democracy, we show it also including the all-varied, all-permitting, all-free theorem of individuality, and erecting therefor a lofty and hitherto unoccupied framework or platform, broad enough for all, eligible to every farmer and mechanic—to the female equally with the male—a towering self-hood, not physically perfect only—not satisfied with the mere mind's and learning's stores, but religious, possessing the idea of the infinite, (rudder and compass sure amid this troublous voyage, o'er darkest, wildest wave, through stormiest wind, of man's or nation's progress)—realizing, above the rest, that known humanity, in deepest sense, is fair adhesion to itself, for purposes beyond—and that, finally, the personality of mortal life is most important with reference to the immortal, the unknown, the spiritual, the only permanently real, which as the ocean waits for and receives the rivers, waits for us each and all.

Much is there, yet, demanding line and outline in our Vistas, not only on these topics, but others quite unwritten. Indeed, we could talk the matter, and expand it, through lifetime. But it is necessary to return to our original premises. In view of them, we have again pointedly to confess that all the objective grandeurs of the world, for highest purposes, yield themselves up, and depend on mentality alone. Here, and here only, all balances, all rests. For the mind, which alone builds the permanent edifice, haughtily builds it to itself. By it, with what follows it, are convey'd to mortal sense the culminations of the materialistic, the known, and a prophecy of the unknown. To take expression, to incarnate, to endow a literature with grand and archetypal models—to fill with pride and love the utmost capacity, and to achieve spiritual meanings, and suggest the future—these, and these only, satisfy the soul. We must not say one word against real materials; but the wise know that they do not become real till touched by emotions, the mind. Did we call the latter imponderable? Ah, let us rather proclaim that the slightest song-tune, the countless ephemera of passions arous'd by orators and tale-tellers, are more dense, more weighty than the engines there in the great factories, or the granite blocks in their foundations.

Approaching thus the momentous spaces, and considering with reference to a new and greater personalism, the needs and possibilities of American imaginative literature, through the medium-light of what we have already broach'd, it will at once be appreciated that a vast gulf of difference separates the present accepted condition of these spaces, inclusive of what is floating in them, from any condition adjusted to, or fit for, the world, the America, there sought to be indicated, and the copious races of complete men and women, along these Vistas crudely outlined. It is, in some sort, no less a difference than lies between that long-continued nebular state and vagueness of the astronomical worlds, compared with the subsequent state, the definitely-form'd worlds themselves, duly compacted, clustering in systems, hung up there, chandeliers of the universe, beholding and mutually lit by each other's lights, serving for ground of all substantial foothold, all vulgar uses—yet serving still more as an undying chain and echelon of spiritual proofs and shows. A boundless field to fill! A new creation, with needed orbic works launch'd forth, to revolve in free and lawful circuits—to move, self-poised, through the ether, and shine like heaven's own suns! With such, and nothing less, we suggest that New World literature, fit to rise upon, cohere, and signalize in time, these States.

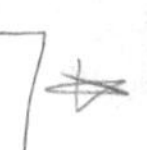

What, however, do we more definitely mean by New World literature? Are we not doing well enough here already? Are not the United States this day busily using, working, more printer's type, more presses, than any other country? uttering and absorbing more publications than any other? Do not our publishers fatten quicker and deeper? (helping themselves, under shelter of a delusive and sneaking law, or rather absence of law, to most of their forage, poetical, pictorial, historical, romantic, even comic, without money and without price—and fiercely resisting the timidest proposal to pay for it.) Many will come under this delusion—but my purpose is to dispel it. I say that a nation may hold and circulate rivers and oceans of very readable print, journals, magazines, novels, library-books, "poetry," &c.—such as the States to-day possess and circulate—of unquestionable aid and value—hundreds of new volumes annually composed and brought out here, respectable enough, indeed unsurpass'd in smartness and erudition—with further hundreds, or rather millions, (as by free forage or theft aforemention'd,) also thrown into the market—and yet, all the while, the said nation, land, strictly speaking, may possess no literature at all.

Repeating our inquiry, what, then, do we mean by real literature? especially the democratic literature of the future? Hard questions to meet. The clues are inferential, and turn us to the past. At best, we can only offer suggestions, comparisons, circuits.

It must still be reiterated, as, for the purpose of these memoranda, the deep lesson of history and time, that all else in the contributions of a nation or age, through its politics, materials, heroic personalities, military eclat, &c., remains crude, and defers, in any close and thorough-going estimate, until vitalized by national, original archetypes in literature. They only put the nation in form, finally tell anything—prove, complete anything—perpetuate anything. Without doubt, some of the richest and most powerful and populous communities of the antique world, and some of the grandest personalities and events, have, to after and present times, left themselves entirely unbequeath'd. Doubtless, greater than any that have come down to us, were among those lands, heroisms, persons, that have not come down to us at all, even by name, date, or location. Others have arrived safely, as from voyages over wide, century-stretching seas. The little ships, the miracles that have buoy'd them, and by incredible chances safely convey'd them, (or the best of them, their meaning and essence,) over long wastes, darkness, lethargy, ignorance, &c., have been a few inscriptions—a few immortal compositions, small in size, yet compassing what measureless values of reminiscence, contemporary portraitures, manners, idioms and beliefs, with deepest inference, hint and thought, to tie and touch forever the old, new body, and the old, new soul! These! and still these! bearing the freight so dear—dearer than pride—dearer than love. All the best experience of humanity, folded, saved, freighted to us here. Some of these tiny ships we call Old and New Testament, Homer, Eschylus, Plato, Juvenal, &c. Precious minims! I think, if we were forced to choose, rather than have you, and the likes of you, and what belongs to, and has grown of you, blotted out and gone, we could better afford, appaling as that would be, to lose all actual ships, this day fasten'd by wharf, or floating on wave, and see them, with all their cargoes, scuttled and sent to the bottom.

Gather'd by geniuses of city, race or age, and put by them in highest of art's forms, namely, the literary form, the peculiar combinations and the outshows of that city, age, or race, its particular modes of the universal attributes and passions, its faiths, heroes, lovers and gods, wars, traditions, struggles, crimes, emotions, joys, (or the subtle spirit of these,) having been pass'd on to us to illumine our own selfhood, and its experiences—what they supply, indispensable and highest, if taken away, nothing else in all the world's boundless storehouses could make up to us, or ever again return.

For us, along the great highways of time, those monuments stand—those forms of majesty and beauty. For us those beacons burn through all the nights. Unknown Egyptians, graving hieroglyphs; Hindus, with hymn and apothegm and endless epic; Hebrew prophet, with spirituality, as in flashes of lightning, conscience like red-hot iron, plaintive songs and screams of vengeance for tyrannies and enslavement; Christ, with bent head, brooding love and peace, like a dove; Greek, creating eternal shapes of physical and esthetic proportion; Roman, lord of satire, the sword, and the codex;—of the figures, some far off and veil'd, others nearer and visible; Dante, stalking with lean form, nothing but fibre, not a grain of superfluous flesh; Angelo, and the great painters, architects, musicians; rich Shakspere, luxuriant as the sun, artist and singer of feudalism in its sunset, with all the gorgeous colors, owner thereof, and using them at will; and so to such as German Kant and Hegel, where they, though near us, leaping over the ages, sit again, impassive, imperturbable, like the Egyptian gods. Of these, and the like of these, is it too much, indeed, to return to our favorite figure, and view them as orbs and systems of orbs, moving in free paths in the spaces of that other heaven, the kosmic intellect, the soul?

Ye powerful and resplendent ones! ye were, in your atmospheres, grown not for America, but rather for her foes, the feudal and the old—while our genius is democratic and modern. Yet could ye, indeed, but breathe your breath of life into our New World's nostrils—not to enslave us, as now, but, for our needs, to breed a spirit like your own—perhaps, (dare we to say it?) to dominate, even destroy, what you yourselves have left! On your plane, and no less, but even higher and wider, must we mete and measure for to-day and here. I demand races of orbic bards, with unconditional uncompromising sway. Come forth, sweet democratic despots of the west!

By points like these we, in reflection, token what we mean by any land's or people's genuine literature. And thus compared and tested, judging amid the influence of loftiest products only, what do our current copious fields of print, covering in manifold forms, the United States, better, for an analogy, present, than, as in certain regions of the sea, those spreading, undulating masses of squid, through which the whale swimming, with head half out, feeds?

Not but that doubtless our current so-called literature, (like an endless supply of small coin,) performs a certain service, and may-be, too, the service needed for the time, (the preparation-service, as children learn to spell.) Everybody reads, and truly nearly everybody writes, either books, or for the magazines or journals. The matter has magnitude, too, after a sort. But is it really advancing? or, has it advanced for a long while? There is something impressive about the huge editions of the dailies and weeklies, the mountain stacks of white paper piled in the press-vaults, and the proud, crashing, ten-cylinder presses, which I can stand and watch any time by the half hour. Then, (though the States in the field of imagination present not a single first-class work, not a single great literatus,) the main objects, to amuse, to titillate, to pass away time, to circulate the news, and rumors of news, to rhyme and read rhyme, are yet attain'd, and on a scale of infinity. To-day, in books, in the rivalry of writers, especially novelists, success, (so-call'd,) is for him or her who strikes the mean flat average, the sensational appetite for stimulus, incident, persiflage, &c., and depicts, to the common calibre, sensual, exterior life. To such, or the luckiest of them, as we see, the audiences are limitless and profitable; but they cease presently. While this day, or any day, to workmen portraying interior or spiritual life, the audiences were limited, and often laggard—but they last forever.

Compared with the past, our modern science soars, and our journals serve—but ideal and even ordinary romantic literature, does not, I think, substantially advance. Behold the prolific brood of the contemporary novel, magazine-tale, theatre-play, &c. The same endless thread of tangled and superlative love-story, inherited, apparently from the Amadises and Palmerins of the 13th, 14th, and 15th centuries over there in Europe. The costumes and associations brought down to date, the seasoning hotter and more varied, the dragons and ogres left out—but the *thing*, I should say, has not advanced—is just as sensational, just as strain'd—remains about the same, nor more, nor less.

What is the reason our time, our lands, that we see no fresh local courage, sanity, of our own—the Mississippi, stalwart Western men, real mental and physical facts, Southerners, &c., in the body of our literature? especially the poetic part of it. But always, instead, a parcel of dandies and ennuyees, dapper little gentlemen from abroad, who flood us with their thin sentiment of parlors, parasols, piano-songs, tinkling rhymes, the five-hundredth importation—or whimpering and crying about something, chasing one aborted conceit after another, and forever occupied in dyspeptic amours with dyspeptic women. While, current and novel, the grandest events and revolutions, and stormiest passions of history, are crossing today with unparallel'd rapidity and magnificence over the stages of our own and all the continents, offering new materials, opening new vistas, with largest needs, inviting the daring launching forth of conceptions in literature, inspired by them, soaring in highest regions, serving art in its highest, (which is only the other name for serving God, and serving humanity,) where is the man of letters, where is the book, with any nobler aim than to follow in the old track, repeat what has been said before—and, as its utmost triumph, sell well, and be erudite or elegant?

Mark the roads, the processes, through which these States have arrived, standing easy, henceforth ever-equal, ever-compact, in their range to-day. European adventures? the most antique? Asiatic or African? old history—miracles—romances? Rather, our own unquestion'd facts. They hasten, incredible, blazing bright as fire. From the deeds and days of Columbus down to the present, and including the present—and especially the late Secession war—when I con them, I feel, every leaf, like stopping to see if I have not made a mistake, and fall'n on the splendid figments of some dream. But it is no dream. We stand, live, move, in the huge flow of our age's materialism—in its spirituality. We have had founded for us the most positive of lands. The founders have pass'd to other spheres—but what are these terrible duties they have left us?

Their politics the United States have, in my opinion, with all their faults, already substantially establish'd, for good, on their own native, sound, long-vista'd principles, never to be overturn'd, offering a sure basis for all the rest. With that, their future religious forms, sociology, literature, teachers, schools, costumes, &c., are of course to make a compact whole, uniform, on tallying principles. For how can we remain, divided, contradicting ourselves, this way?* I say we can only attain harmony and stability by consulting ensemble and the ethic purports, and faithfully building upon them. For the New World, indeed, after two grand stages of preparation-strata, I perceive that now a third stage, being ready for, (and without which the other two were useless,) with unmistakable signs appears. The First stage was the planning and putting on record the political foundation rights of immense masses of people—indeed all people—in the organization of republican National, State, and municipal governments, all con-

*Note, to-day, an instructive, curious spectacle and conflict. Science, (twin, in its fields, of Democracy in its)—Science, testing absolutely all thoughts, all works, has already burst well upon the world—a sun, mounting, most illuminating, most glorious—surely never again to set. But against it, deeply entrench'd, holding possession, yet remains, (not only through the churches and schools, but by imaginative literature, and unregenerate poetry,) the fossil theology of the mythic-materialistic, superstitious, untaught and credulous, fable-loving, primitive ages of humanity.

structed with reference to each, and each to all. This is the American programme, not for classes, but for universal man, and is embodied in the compacts of the Declaration of Independence, and, as it began and has now grown, with its amendments, the Federal Constitution—and in the State governments, with all their interiors, and with general suffrage; those having the sense not only of what is in themselves, but that their certain several things started, planted, hundreds of others in the same direction duly arise and follow. The Second stage relates to material prosperity, wealth, produce, labor-saving machines, iron, cotton, local, State and continental railways, intercommunication and trade with all lands, steamships, mining, general employment, organization of great cities, cheap appliances for comfort, numberless technical schools, books, newspapers, a currency for money circulation, &c. The Third stage, rising out of the previous ones, to make them and all illustrious, I, now, for one, promulge, announcing a native expression-spirit, getting into form, adult, and through mentality, for these States, self-contain'd, different from others, more expansive, more rich and free, to be evidenced by original authors and poets to come, by American personalities, plenty of them, male and female, traversing the States, none excepted—and by native superber tableaux and growths of language, songs, operas, orations, lectures, architecture—and by a sublime and serious Religious Democracy sternly taking command, dissolving the old, sloughing off surfaces, and from its own interior and vital principles, reconstructing, democratizing society.

For America, type of progress, and of essential faith in man, above all his errors and wickedness—few suspect how deep, how deep it really strikes. The world evidently supposes, and we have evidently supposed so too, that the States are merely to achieve the equal franchise, an elective government—to inaugurate the respectability of labor, and become a nation of practical operatives, law-abiding, orderly and well off. Yes, those are indeed parts of the task of America; but they not only do not exhaust the progressive conception, but rather arise, teeming with it, as the mediums of deeper, higher progress. Daughter of a physical revolution—mother of the true revolutions, which are of the interior life, and of the arts. For so long as the spirit is not changed, any change of appearance is of no avail.

The old men, I remember as a boy, were always talking of American independence. What is independence? Freedom from all laws or bonds except those of one's own being, control'd by the universal ones. To lands, to man, to woman, what is there at last to each, but the inherent soul, nativity, idiocrasy, free, highest-poised, soaring its own flight, following out itself?

At present, these States, in their theology and social standards, (of greater importance than their political institutions,) are entirely held possession of by foreign lands. We see the sons and daughters of the New World, ignorant of its genius, not yet inaugurating the native, the universal, and the near, still importing the distant, the partial, and the dead. We see London, Paris, Italy—not original, superb, as where they belong—but second-hand here, where they do not belong. We see the shreds of Hebrews, Romans, Greeks; but where, on her own soil, do we see, in any faithful, highest, proud expression, America herself? I sometimes question whether she has a corner in her own house.

Not but that in one sense, and a very grand one, good theology, good art, or good literature, has certain features shared in common. The combination fraternizes, ties the races—is, in many particulars, under laws applicable indifferently to all, irrespective of climate or date, and, from whatever source, appeals to emotions, pride, love, spirituality, common to humankind. Nevertheless, they touch a man closest, (perhaps only actually touch him,) even in these, in their expression through autochthonic lights and shades, flavors, fondnesses, aversions, specific incidents, illustrations, out of his own nationality, geography, surroundings, antecedents, &c. The spirit and the form are one, and depend far more on association, identity and place, than is supposed. Subtly interwoven with the materiality and personality of a land, a race—Teuton, Turk, Californian, or what not—there is always something—I can hardly tell what it is—history but describes the results of it—it is the same as the untellable look of some human faces. Nature, too, in her stolid forms, is full of it—

but to most it is there a secret. This something is rooted in the invisible roots, the profoundest meanings of that place, race, or nationality; and to absorb and again effuse it, uttering words and products as from its midst, and carrying it into highest regions, is the work, or a main part of the work, of any country's true author, poet, historian, lecturer, and perhaps even priest and philosoph. Here, and here only, are the foundations for our really valuable and permanent verse, drama, &c.

But at present, (judged by any higher scale than that which finds the chief ends of existence to be to feverishly make money during one-half of it, and by some "amusement," or perhaps foreign travel, flippantly kill time, the other half,) and consider'd with reference to purposes of patriotism, health, a noble personality, religion, and the democratic adjustments, all these swarms of poems, literary magazines, dramatic plays, resultant so far from American intellect, and the formation of our best ideas, are useless and a mockery. They strengthen and nourish no one, express nothing characteristic, give decision and purpose to no one, and suffice only the lowest level of vacant minds.

Of what is called the drama, or dramatic presentation in the United States, as now put forth at the theatres, I should say it deserves to be treated with the same gravity, and on a par with the questions of ornamental confectionery at public dinners, or the arrangement of curtains and hangings in a ballroom—nor more, nor less. Of the other, I will not insult the reader's intelligence, (once really entering into the atmosphere of these Vistas,) by supposing it necessary to show, in detail, why the copious dribble, either of our little or well-known rhymesters, does not fulfil, in any respect, the needs and august occasions of this land. America demands a poetry that is bold, modern, and all-surrounding and kosmical, as she is herself. It must in no respect ignore science or the modern, but inspire itself with science and the modern. It must bend its vision toward the future, more than the past. Like America, it must extricate itself from even the greatest models of the past, and, while courteous to them, must have entire faith in itself, and the products of its own democratic spirit only. Like her, it must place in the van, and hold up at all hazards, the banner of the divine pride of man in himself, (the radical foundation of the new religion.) Long enough have the People been listening to poems in which common humanity, deferential, bends low, humiliated, acknowledging superiors. But America listens to no such poems. Erect, inflated, and fully self-esteeming be the chant; and then America will listen with pleased ears.

Nor may the genuine gold, the gems, when brought to light at last, be probably usher'd forth from any of the quarters currently counted on. To-day, doubtless, the infant genius of American poetic expression, (eluding those highly-refined imported and gilt-edged themes, and sentimental and butterfly flights, pleasant to orthodox publishers—causing tender spasms in the coteries, and warranted not to chafe the sensitive cuticle of the most exquisitely artificial gossamer delicacy,) lies sleeping far away, happily unrecognized and uninjur'd by the coteries, the art-writers, the talkers and critics of the saloons, or the lecturers in the colleges—lies sleeping, aside, unrecking itself, in some western idiom, or native Michigan or Tennessee repartee, or stump-speech—or in Kentucky or Georgia, or the Carolinas—or in some slang or local song or allusion of the Manhattan, Boston, Philadelphia or Baltimore mechanic—or up in the Maine woods—or off in the hut of the California miner, or crossing the Rocky mountains, or along the Pacific railroad—or on the breasts of the young farmers of the northwest, or Canada, or boatmen of the lakes. Rude and coarse nursing-beds, these; but only from such beginnings and stocks, indigenous here, may haply arrive, be grafted, and sprout, in time, flowers of genuine American aroma, and fruits truly and fully our own.

I say it were a standing disgrace to these States—I say it were a disgrace to any nation, distinguish'd above others by the variety and vastness of its territories, its materials, its inventive activity, and the splendid practicality of its people, not to rise and soar above others also in its original styles in literature and art, and its own supply of intellectual and esthetic masterpieces, archetypal, and consistent with itself. I know not a land except ours that has not, to some extent, however small, made its title clear. The Scotch have their born ballads, subtly expressing their past and present, and expressing character. The Irish have theirs. England, Italy, France, Spain, theirs. What has America? With exhaustless mines of the richest ore of epic, lyric, tale, tune, picture, &c., in the Four Years' War; with, indeed, I sometimes think, the richest masses of material ever afforded a nation, more variegated, and on a larger scale—the first sign of proportionate, native, imaginative Soul, and first-class works to match, is, (I cannot too often repeat), so far wanting.

Long ere the second centennial arrives, there will be some forty to fifty great States, among them Canada and Cuba. When the present century closes, our population will be sixty or seventy millions. The Pacific will be ours, and the Atlantic mainly ours. There will be daily electric communication with every part of the globe. What an age! What a land! Where, elsewhere, one so great? The individuality of one nation must then, as always, lead the world. Can there be any doubt who the leader ought to be? Bear in mind, though, that nothing less than the mightiest original non-subordinated SOUL has ever really, gloriously led, or ever can lead. (This Soul—its other name, in these Vistas, is LITERATURE.)

In fond fancy leaping those hundred years ahead, let us survey America's works, poems, philosophies, fulfilling prophecies, and giving form and decision to best ideals. Much that is now undream'd of, we might then perhaps see establish'd, luxuriantly cropping forth, richness, vigor of letters and of artistic expression, in whose products character will be a main requirement, and not merely erudition or elegance.

Intense and loving comradeship, the personal and passionate attachment of man to man—which, hard to define, underlies the lessons and ideals of the profound saviours of every land and age, and which seems to promise, when thoroughly develop'd, cultivated and recognized in manners and literature, the most substantial hope and safety of the future of these States, will then be fully express'd.*

*It is to the development, identification, and general prevalence of that fervid comradeship, (the adhesive love, at least rivaling the amative love hitherto possessing imaginative literature, if not going beyond it,) that I look for the counterbalance and offset of our materialistic and vulgar American de-

A strong-fibred joyousness and faith, and the sense of health *al fresco,* may well enter into the preparation of future noble American authorship. Part of the test of a great literatus shall be the absence in him of the idea of the covert, the lurid, the maleficent, the devil, the grim estimates inherited from the Puritans, hell, natural depravity, and the like. The great literatus will be known, among the rest, by his cheerful simplicity, his adherence to natural standards, his limitless faith in God, his reverence, and by the absence in him of doubt, ennui, burlesque, persiflage, or any strain'd and temporary fashion.

Nor must I fail, again and yet again, to clinch, reiterate more plainly still, (O that indeed such survey as we fancy, may show in time this part completed also!) the lofty aim, surely the proudest and the purest, in whose service the future literatus, of whatever field, may gladly labor. As we have intimated, offsetting the material civilization of our race, our nationality, its wealth, territories, factories, population, products, trade, and military and naval strength, and breathing breath of life into all these, and more, must be its moral civilization—the formulation, expression, and aidancy whereof, is the very highest height of literature. The climax of this loftiest range of civilization, rising above all the gorgeous shows and results of wealth, intellect, power, and art, as such—above even theology and religious fervor—is to be its development, from the eternal bases, and the fit expression, of absolute Conscience, moral soundness, Justice. Even in religious fervor there is a touch of animal heat. But moral conscientiousness, crystalline, without flaw, not Godlike only, entirely human, awes and enchants forever. Great is emotional love, even in

---

mocracy, and for the spiritualization thereof. Many will say it is a dream, and will not follow my inferences: but I confidently expect a time when there will be seen, running like a half-hid warp through all the myriad audible and visible worldly interests of America, threads of manly friendship, fond and loving, pure and sweet, strong and life-long, carried to degrees hitherto unknown—not only giving tone to individual character, and making it unprecedently emotional, muscular, heroic, and refined, but having the deepest relations to general politics. I say democracy infers such loving comradeship, as its most inevitable twin or counterpart, without which it will be incomplete, in vain, and incapable of perpetuating itself.

the order of the rational universe. But, if we must make gradations, I am clear there is something greater. Power, love, veneration, products, genius, esthetics, tried by subtlest comparisons, analyses, and in serenest moods, somewhere fail, somehow become vain. Then noiseless, with flowing steps, the lord, the sun, the last ideal comes. By the names right, justice, truth, we suggest, but do not describe it. To the world of men it remains a dream, an idea as they call it. But no dream is it to the wise—but the proudest, almost only solid lasting thing of all. Its analogy in the material universe is what holds together this world, and every object upon it, and carries its dynamics on forever sure and safe. Its lack, and the persistent shirking of it, as in life, sociology, literature, politics, business, and even sermonizing, these times, or any times, still leaves the abysm, the mortal flaw and smutch, mocking civilization to-day, with all its unquestion'd triumphs, and all the civilization so far known.*

Present literature, while magnificently fulfilling certain popular demands, with plenteous knowledge and verbal smartness, is profoundly sophisticated, insane, and its very joy is morbid. It needs tally and express Nature, and the spirit of Nature, and to know and obey the standards. I say the question of Nature, largely consider'd, involves the questions of the esthetic, the emotional, and the religious—and involves happiness. A fitly born and bred race, growing up in right

*I am reminded as I write that out of this very conscience, or idea of conscience, of intense moral right, and in its name and strain'd construction, the worst fanaticisms, wars, persecutions, murders, &c., have yet, in all lands, in the past, been broach'd, and have come to their devilish fruition. Much is to be said—but I may say here, and in response, that side by side with the unflagging stimulation of the elements of religion and conscience must henceforth move with equal sway, science, absolute reason, and the general proportionate development of the whole man. These scientific facts, deductions, are divine too—precious counted parts of moral civilization, and, with physical health, indispensable to it, to prevent fanaticism. For abstract religion, I perceive, is easily led astray, ever credulous, and is capable of devouring, remorseless, like fire and flame. Conscience, too, isolated from all else, and from the emotional nature, may but attain the beauty and purity of glacial, snowy ice. We want, for these States, for the general character, a cheerful, religious fervor, endued with the ever-present modifications of the human emotions, friendship, benevolence, with a fair field for scientific inquiry, the right of individual judgment, and always the cooling influences of material Nature.

conditions of out-door as much as in-door harmony, activity and development, would probably, from and in those conditions, find it enough merely *to live*—and would, in their relations to the sky, air, water, trees, &c., and to the countless common shows, and in the fact of life itself, discover and achieve happiness—with Being suffused night and day by wholesome extasy, surpassing all the pleasures that wealth, amusement, and even gratified intellect, erudition, or the sense of art, can give.

In the prophetic literature of these States (the reader of my speculations will miss their principal stress unless he allows well for the point that a new Literature, perhaps a new Metaphysics, certainly a new Poetry, are to be, in my opinion, the only sure and worthy supports and expressions of the American Democracy,) Nature, true Nature, and the true idea of Nature, long absent, must, above all, become fully restored, enlarged, and must furnish the pervading atmosphere to poems, and the test of all high literary and esthetic compositions. I do not mean the smooth walks, trimm'd hedges, poseys and nightingales of the English poets, but the whole orb, with its geologic history, the kosmos, carrying fire and snow, that rolls through the illimitable areas, light as a feather, though weighing billions of tons. Furthermore, as by what we now partially call Nature is intended, at most, only what is entertainable by the physical conscience, the sense of matter, and of good animal health—on these it must be distinctly accumulated, incorporated, that man, comprehending these, has, in towering superaddition, the moral and spiritual consciences, indicating his destination beyond the ostensible, the mortal.

To the heights of such estimate of Nature indeed ascending, we proceed to make observations for our Vistas, breathing rarest air. What is I believe called Idealism seems to me to suggest, (guarding against extravagance, and ever modified even by its opposite,) the course of inquiry and desert of favor for our New World metaphysics, their foundation of and in literature, giving hue to all.*

*The culmination and fruit of literary artistic expression, and its final fields of pleasure for the human soul, are in metaphysics, including the mysteries of the spiritual world, the soul itself, and the question of the immortal contin-

The elevating and etherealizing ideas of the unknown and of unreality must be brought forward with authority, as they are the legitimate heirs of the known, and of reality, and at least as great as their parents. Fearless of scoffing, and of the ostent, let us take our stand, our ground, and never desert it, to confront the growing excess and arrogance of realism. To

---

uation of our identity. In all ages, the mind of man has brought up here—and always will. Here, at least, of whatever race or era, we stand on common ground. Applause, too, is unanimous, antique or modern. Those authors who work well in this field—though their reward, instead of a handsome percentage, or royalty, may be but simply the laurel-crown of the victors in the great Olympic games—will be dearest to humanity, and their works, however esthetically defective, will be treasur'd forever. The altitude of literature and poetry has always been religion—and always will be. The Indian Vedas, the Nackas of Zoroaster, the Talmud of the Jews, the Old Testament, the Gospel of Christ and his disciples, Plato's works, the Koran of Mohammed, the Edda of Snorro, and so on toward our own day, to Swedenborg, and to the invaluable contributions of Leibnitz, Kant and Hegel—these, with such poems only in which, (while singing well of persons and events, of the passions of man, and the shows of the material universe,) the religious tone, the consciousness of mystery, the recognition of the future, of the unknown, of Deity over and under all, and of the divine purpose, are never absent, but indirectly give tone to all—exhibit literature's real heights and elevations, towering up like the great mountains of the earth.

Standing on this ground—the last, the highest, only permanent ground—and sternly criticising, from it, all works, either of the literary, or any art, we have peremptorily to dismiss every pretensive production, however fine its esthetic or intellectual points, which violates or ignores, or even does not celebrate, the central divine idea of All, suffusing universe, of eternal trains of purpose, in the development, by however slow degrees, of the physical, moral, and spiritual kosmos. I say he has studied, meditated to no profit, whatever may be his mere erudition, who has not absorb'd this simple consciousness and faith. It is not entirely new—but it is for Democracy to elaborate it, and look to build upon and expand from it, with uncompromising reliance. Above the doors of teaching the inscription is to appear, Though little or nothing can be absolutely known, perceiv'd, except from a point of view which is evanescent, yet we know at least one permanency, that Time and Space, in the will of God, furnish successive chains, completions of material births and beginnings, solve all discrepancies, fears and doubts, and eventually fulfil happiness—and that the prophecy of those births, namely spiritual results, throws the true arch over all teaching, all science. The local considerations of sin, disease, deformity, ignorance, death, &c., and their measurement by the superficial mind, and ordinary legislation and theology, are to be met by science, boldly accepting, promulging this faith, and planting the seeds of superber laws—of the explication of the physical universe through the spiritual—and clearing the way for a religion, sweet and unimpugnable alike to little child or great savan.

the cry, now victorious—the cry of sense, science, flesh, incomes, farms, merchandise, logic, intellect, demonstrations, solid perpetuities, buildings of brick and iron, or even the facts of the shows of trees, earth, rocks, &c., fear not, my brethren, my sisters, to sound out with equally determin'd voice, that conviction brooding within the recesses of every envision'd soul—illusions! apparitions! figments all! True, we must not condemn the show, neither absolutely deny it, for the indispensability of its meanings; but how clearly we see that, migrate in soul to what we can already conceive of superior and spiritual points of view, and, palpable as it seems under present relations, it all and several might, nay certainly would, fall apart and vanish.

I hail with joy the oceanic, variegated, intense practical energy, the demand for facts, even the business materialism of the current age, our States. But wo to the age or land in which these things, movements, stopping at themselves, do not tend to ideas. As fuel to flame, and flame to the heavens, so must wealth, science, materialism—even this democracy of which we make so much—unerringly feed the highest mind, the soul. Infinitude the flight: fathomless the mystery. Man, so diminutive, dilates beyond the sensible universe, competes with, outcopes space and time, meditating even one great idea. Thus, and thus only, does a human being, his spirit, ascend above, and justify, objective Nature, which, probably nothing in itself, is incredibly and divinely serviceable, indispensable, real, here. And as the purport of objective Nature is doubtless folded, hidden, somewhere here—as somewhere here is what this globe and its manifold forms, and the light of day, and night's darkness, and life itself, with all its experiences, are for—it is here the great literature, especially verse, must get its inspiration and throbbing blood. Then may we attain to a poetry worthy the immortal soul of man, and which, while absorbing materials, and, in their own sense, the shows of Nature, will, above all, have, both directly and indirectly, a freeing, fluidizing, expanding, religious character, exulting with science, fructifying the moral elements, and stimulating aspirations, and meditations on the unknown.

The process, so far, is indirect and peculiar, and though it may be suggested, cannot be defined. Observing, rapport, and with intuition, the shows and forms presented by Nature, the sensuous luxuriance, the beautiful in living men and women, the actual play of passions, in history and life—and, above all, from those developments either in Nature or human personality in which power, (dearest of all to the sense of the artist,) transacts itself—out of these, and seizing what is in them, the poet, the esthetic worker in any field, by the divine magic of his genius, projects them, their analogies, by curious removes, indirections, in literature and art. (No useless attempt to repeat the material creation, by daguerreotyping the exact likeness by mortal mental means.) This is the image-making faculty, coping with material creation, and rivaling, almost triumphing over it. This alone, when all the other parts of a specimen of literature or art are ready and waiting, can breathe into it the breath of life, and endow it with identity.

"The true question to ask," says the librarian of Congress in a paper read before the Social Science Convention at New York, October, 1869, "The true question to ask respecting a book, is, *has it help'd any human soul?*" This is the hint, statement, not only of the great literatus, his book, but of every great artist. It may be that all works of art are to be first tried by their art qualities, their image-forming talent, and their dramatic, pictorial, plot-constructing, euphonious and other talents. Then, whenever claiming to be first-class works, they are to be strictly and sternly tried by their foundation in, and radiation, in the highest sense, and always indirectly, of the ethic principles, and eligibility to free, arouse, dilate.

As, within the purposes of the Kosmos, and vivifying all meteorology, and all the congeries of the mineral, vegetable and animal worlds—all the physical growth and development of man, and all the history of the race in politics, religions, wars, &c., there is a moral purpose, a visible or invisible intention, certainly underlying all—its results and proof needing to be patiently waited for—needing intuition, faith, idiosyncrasy, to its realization, which many, and especially the intellectual, do not have—so in the product, or congeries of the product, of the greatest literatus. This is the last, profoundest measure and test of a first-class literary or esthetic achievement, and when understood and put in force must fain, I say, lead to works, books, nobler than any hitherto known. Lo! Nature, (the only complete, actual poem,) existing calmly in the divine scheme, containing all, content, careless of the criticisms of a day, or these endless and wordy chatterers. And lo! to the consciousness of the soul, the permanent identity, the thought, the something, before which the magnitude even of democracy, art, literature, &c., dwindles, becomes partial, measurable—something that fully satisfies, (which those do not.) That something is the All, and the idea of All, with the accompanying idea of eternity, and of itself, the soul, buoyant, indestructible, sailing space forever, visiting every region, as a ship the sea. And again lo! the pulsations in all matter, all spirit, throbbing forever—the eternal beats, eternal systole and diastole of life in things—wherefrom I feel and know that death is not the ending, as was thought, but rather the real beginning—and that nothing ever is or can be lost, nor ever die, nor soul, nor matter.

In the future of these States must arise poets immenser far, and make great poems of death. The poems of life are great, but there must be the poems of the purports of life, not only in itself, but beyond itself. I have eulogized Homer, the sacred bards of Jewry, Eschylus, Juvenal, Shakspere, &c., and acknowledged their inestimable value. But, (with perhaps the exception, in some, not all respects, of the second-mention'd,) I say there must, for future and democratic purposes, appear poets, (dare I to say so?) of higher class even than any of those—poets not only possess'd of the religious fire and abandon of Isaiah, luxuriant in the epic talent of Homer, or for proud characters as in Shakspere, but consistent with the Hegelian formulas, and consistent with modern science. America needs, and the world needs, a class of bards who will, now and ever, so link and tally the rational physical being of man, with the ensembles of time and space, and with this vast and multiform show, Nature, surrounding him, ever tantalizing him, equally a part, and yet not a part of him, as to essentially harmonize, satisfy, and put at rest. Faith, very old, now scared away by science, must be restored, brought back by the same power that caused her departure—restored with new sway, deeper, wider, higher than ever. Surely, this universal ennui, this coward fear, this shuddering at death, these low, degrading views, are not always to rule the spirit pervading future society, as it has the past, and does the present. What the Roman Lucretius sought most nobly, yet all too blindly, negatively to do for his age and its successors, must be done positively by some great coming literatus, especially poet, who,—while remaining fully poet, will absorb whatever science indicates, with spiritualism, and out of them, and out of his own genius, will compose the great poem of death. Then will man indeed confront Nature, and confront time and space, both with science, and *con amore,* and take his right place, prepared for life, master of fortune and misfortune. And then that which was long wanted will be supplied, and the ship that had it not before in all her voyages, will have an anchor.

There are still other standards, suggestions, for products of high literatuses. That which really balances and conserves the social and political world is not so much legislation, police, treaties, and dread of punishment, as the latent eternal intuitional sense, in humanity, of fairness, manliness, decorum, &c. Indeed, this perennial regulation, control, and oversight, by self-suppliance, is *sine qua non* to democracy; and a highest widest aim of democratic literature may well be to bring forth, cultivate, brace, and strengthen this sense, in individuals and society. A strong mastership of the general inferior self by the superior self, is to be aided, secured, indirectly, but surely, by the literatus, in his works, shaping, for individual or aggregate democracy, a great passionate body, in and along with which goes a great masterful spirit.

And still, providing for contingencies, I fain confront the fact, the need of powerful native philosophs and orators and bards, these States, as rallying points to come, in times of danger, and to fend off ruin and defection. For history is long, long, long. Shift and turn the combinations of the statement as we may, the problem of the future of America is in certain respects as dark as it is vast. Pride, competition, segregation, vicious wilfulness, and license beyond example, brood already upon us. Unwieldy and immense, who shall hold in behemoth? who bridle leviathan? Flaunt it as we choose, athwart and over the roads of our progress loom huge uncertainty, and dreadful, threatening gloom. It is useless to deny it: Democracy grows rankly up the thickest, noxious, deadliest plants and fruits of all—brings worse and worse invaders—needs newer, larger, stronger, keener compensations and compellers.

Our lands, embracing so much, (embracing indeed the whole, rejecting none,) hold in their breast that flame also, capable of consuming themselves, consuming us all. Short as the span of our national life has been, already have death and downfall crowded close upon us—and will again crowd close, no doubt, even if warded off. Ages to come may never know, but I know, how narrowly during the late secession war—and more than once, and more than twice or thrice—our Nationality, (wherein bound up, as in a ship in a storm, depended, and yet depend, all our best life, all hope, all value,) just grazed, just by a hair escaped destruction. Alas! to think of them! the agony and bloody sweat of certain of those hours! those cruel, sharp, suspended crises!

Even to-day, amid these whirls, incredible flippancy, and blind fury of parties, infidelity, entire lack of first-class captains and leaders, added to the plentiful meanness and vulgarity of the ostensible masses—that problem, the labor question, beginning to open like a yawning gulf, rapidly widening every year—what prospect have we? We sail a dangerous sea of seething currents, cross and under-currents, vortices—all so dark, untried—and whither shall we turn? It seems as if the Almighty had spread before this nation charts of imperial destinies, dazzling as the sun, yet with many a deep intestine difficulty, and human aggregate of cankerous imperfection,—saying, lo! the roads, the only plans of development, long and varied with all terrible balks and ebullitions. You said in your soul, I will be empire of empires, overshadowing all else, past and present, putting the history of old-world dynasties, conquests behind me, as of no account—making a new history, a history of democracy, making old history a dwarf—I alone inaugurating largeness, culminating time. If these, O lands of America, are indeed the prizes, the determinations of your soul, be it so. But behold the cost, and already specimens of the cost. Thought you greatness was to ripen for you like a pear? If you would have greatness, know that you must conquer it through ages, centuries—must pay for it with a proportionate price. For you too, as for all lands, the struggle, the traitor, the wily person in office, scrofulous wealth, the surfeit of prosperity, the demonism of greed, the hell of passion, the decay of faith, the long postponement, the fossil-like lethargy, the ceaseless need of revolutions, prophets, thunderstorms, deaths, births, new projections and invigorations of ideas and men.

Yet I have dream'd, merged in that hidden-tangled problem of our fate, whose long unraveling stretches mysteriously through time—dream'd out, portray'd, hinted already—a little or a larger band—a band of brave and true, unprecedented yet—arm'd and equipt at every point—the members separated, it may be, by different dates and States, or south, or north, or east, or west—Pacific, Atlantic, Southern, Canadian—a year, a century here, and other centuries there—but always one, compact in soul, conscience-conserving, God-inculcating, inspired achievers, not only in literature, the greatest art, but achievers in all art—a new, undying order, dynasty, from age to age transmitted—a band, a class, at least as fit to cope with current years, our dangers, needs, as those who, for their times, so long, so well, in armor or in cowl, upheld and made illustrious, that far-back feudal, priestly world. To offset chivalry, indeed, those vanish'd countless knights, old altars, abbeys, priests, ages and strings of ages, a knightlier and more sacred cause to-day demands, and shall supply, in a New World, to larger, grander work, more than the counterpart and tally of them.

Arrived now, definitely, at an apex for these Vistas, I confess that the promulgation and belief in such a class or institution—a new and greater literatus order—its possibility, (nay certainty,) underlies these entire speculations—and that the rest, the other parts, as superstructures, are all founded upon it. It really seems to me the condition, not only of our future national and democratic development, but of our perpetuation. In the highly artificial and materialistic bases of modern civilization, with the corresponding arrangements and methods of living, the force-infusion of intellect alone, the depraving influences of riches just as much as poverty, the absence of all high ideals in character—with the long series of tendencies, shapings, which few are strong enough to resist, and which now seem, with steam-engine speed, to be everywhere turning out the generations of humanity like uniform iron castings—all of which, as compared with the feudal ages, we can yet do nothing better than accept, make the best of, and even welcome, upon the whole, for their oceanic practical grandeur, and their restless wholesale kneading of the masses—I say of all this tremendous and dominant play of solely materialistic bearings upon current life in the United States, with the results as already seen, accumulating, and reaching far into the future, that they must either be confronted and met by at least an equally subtle and tremendous force-infusion for purposes of spiritualization, for the pure conscience, for genuine esthetics, and for absolute and primal manliness and womanliness—or else our modern civilization, with all its improvements, is in vain, and we are on the road to a destiny, a status, equivalent, in its real world, to that of the fabled damned.

Prospecting thus the coming unsped days, and that new order in them—marking the endless train of exercise, development, unwind, in nation as in man, which life is for—we see, fore-indicated, amid these prospects and hopes, new law-forces of spoken and written language—not merely the pedagogue-forms, correct, regular, familiar with precedents, made for matters of outside propriety, fine words, thoughts definitely told out—but a language fann'd by the breath of Nature, which leaps overhead, cares mostly for impetus and effects, and for what it plants and invigorates to grow—tallies life and character, and seldomer tells a thing than suggests or necessitates it. In fact, a new theory of literary composition for imaginative works of the very first class, and especially for highest poems, is the sole course open to these States. Books are to be call'd for, and supplied, on the assumption that the process of reading is not a half sleep, but, in highest sense, an exercise, a gymnast's struggle; that the reader is to do something for himself, must be on the alert, must himself or herself construct indeed the poem, argument, history, metaphysical essay—the text furnishing the hints, the clue, the start or frame-work. Not the book needs so much to be the complete thing, but the reader of the book does. That were to make a nation of supple and athletic minds, well-train'd, intuitive, used to depend on themselves, and not on a few coteries of writers.

Investigating here, we see, not that it is a little thing we have, in having the bequeath'd libraries, countless shelves of volumes, records, &c.; yet how serious the danger, depending entirely on them, of the bloodless vein, the nerveless arm, the false application, at second or third hand. We see that the real interest of this people of ours in the theology, history, poetry, politics, and personal models of the past, (the British islands, for instance, and indeed all the past,) is not necessarily to mould ourselves or our literature upon them, but to attain fuller, more definite comparisons, warnings, and the insight to ourselves, our own present, and our own far grander, different, future history, religion, social customs, &c. We see that almost everything that has been written, sung, or stated, of old, with reference to humanity under the feudal and oriental institutes, religions, and for other lands, needs to be re-written, re-sung, re-stated, in terms consistent with the institution of these States, and to come in range and obedient uniformity with them.

We see, as in the universes of the material kosmos, after meteorological, vegetable, and animal cycles, man at last arises, born through them, to prove them, concentrate them, to turn upon them with wonder and love—to command them, adorn them, and carry them upward into superior realms—so, out of the series of the preceding social and political universes, now arise these States. We see that while many were supposing things established and completed, really the grandest things always remain; and discover that the work of the New World is not ended, but only fairly begun.

We see our land, America, her literature, esthetics, &c., as, substantially, the getting in form, or effusement and statement, of deepest basic elements and loftiest final meanings, of history and man—and the portrayal, (under the eternal laws and conditions of beauty,) of our own physiognomy, the subjective tie and expression of the objective, as from our own combination, continuation, and points of view—and the deposit and record of the national mentality, character, appeals, heroism, wars, and even liberties—where these, and all, culminate in native literary and artistic formulation, to be perpetuated; and not having which native, first-class formulation, she will flounder about, and her other, however imposing, eminent greatness, prove merely a passing gleam; but truly having which, she will understand herself, live nobly, nobly contribute, emanate, and, swinging, poised safely on herself, illumin'd and illuming, become a full-form'd world, and divine Mother not only of material but spiritual worlds, in ceaseless succession through time—the main thing being the average, the bodily, the concrete, the democratic, the popular, on which all the superstructures of the future are to permanently rest.

Origins of Attempted Secession

Not the whole matter, but some side facts worth conning to-day and any day.

I CONSIDER the war of attempted secession, 1860–65, not as a struggle of two distinct and separate peoples, but a conflict (often happening, and very fierce) between the passions and paradoxes of one and the same identity—perhaps the only terms on which that identity could really become fused, homogeneous and lasting. The origin and conditions out of which it arose, are full of lessons, full of warnings yet to the Republic—and always will be. The underlying and principal of those origins are yet singularly ignored. The Northern States were really just as responsible for that war, (in its precedents, foundations, instigations,) as the South. Let me try to give my view. From the age of 21 to 40, (1840–'60,) I was interested in the political movements of the land, not so much as a participant, but as an observer, and a regular voter at the elections. I think I was conversant with the springs of action, and their workings, not only in New York city and Brooklyn, but understood them in the whole country, as I had made leisurely tours through all the middle States, and partially through the western and southern, and down to New Orleans, in which city I resided for some time. (I was there at the close of the Mexican war—saw and talk'd with General Taylor, and the other generals and officers, who were fêted and detain'd several days on their return victorious from that expedition.)

Of course many and very contradictory things, specialties, developments, constitutional views, &c., went to make up the origin of the war—but the most significant general fact can be best indicated and stated as follows: For twenty-five years previous to the outbreak, the controling "Democratic" nominating conventions of our Republic—starting from their primaries in wards or districts, and so expanding to counties, powerful cities, States, and to the great Presidential nominating conventions—were getting to represent and be composed of more and more putrid and dangerous materials. Let me give a schedule, or list, of one of these representative conventions for a long time before, and inclusive of, that which nominated Buchanan. (Remember they had come to be the fountains and tissues of the American body politic, forming, as it were, the whole blood, legislation, office-holding, &c.) One of these conventions, from 1840 to '60, exhibited a spectacle such as could never be seen except in our own age and in these States. The members who composed it were, seven-eighths of them, the meanest kind of bawling and blowing office-holders, office-seekers, pimps, malignants, conspirators, murderers, fancy-men, custom-house clerks, contractors, kept-editors, spaniels well-train'd to carry and fetch, jobbers, infidels, disunionists, terrorists, mail-riflers, slave-catchers, pushers of slavery, creatures of the President, creatures of would-be Presidents, spies, bribers, compromisers, lobbyers, sponges, ruin'd sports, expell'd gamblers, policy-backers, monte-dealers, duellists, carriers of conceal'd weapons, deaf men, pimpled men, scarr'd inside with vile disease, gaudy outside with gold chains made from the people's money and harlots' money twisted together; crawling, serpentine men, the lousy combings and born freedom-sellers of the earth. And whence came they? From back-yards and bar-rooms; from out of the custom-houses, marshals' offices, post-offices, and gambling-hells; from the President's house, the jail, the station-house; from unnamed by-places, where devilish disunion was hatch'd at midnight; from political hearses, and from the coffins inside, and from the shrouds inside of the coffins; from the tumors and abscesses of the land; from the skeletons and skulls in the vaults of the federal alms-houses; and from the running sores of the great cities. Such, I say, form'd, or absolutely control'd the forming of, the entire personnel, the atmosphere, nutriment and chyle; of our municipal, State, and National politics—substantially permeating, handling, deciding, and wielding everything—legislation, nominations, elections, "public sentiment," &c.—while the great masses of the people, farmers, mechanics, and traders, were helpless in their gripe. These conditions were mostly prevalent in the north and west, and especially in New York and Philadelphia cities; and the southern leaders, (bad enough, but of a far higher order,) struck hands and affiliated with, and used them. Is it strange that a thunder-storm follow'd such morbid and stifling cloud-strata?

I say then, that what, as just outlined, heralded, and made the ground ready for secession revolt, ought to be held up, through all the future, as the most instructive lesson in American political history—the most significant warning and beacon-light to coming generations. I say that the sixteenth, seventeenth and eighteenth terms of the American Presidency have shown that the villainy and shallowness of rulers (back'd by the machinery of great parties) are just as eligible to these States as to any foreign despotism, kingdom, or empire—there is not a bit of difference. History is to record those three Presidentiads, and especially the administrations of Fillmore and Buchanan, as so far our topmost warning and shame. Never were publicly display'd more deform'd, mediocre, snivelling, unreliable, false-hearted men. Never were these States so insulted, and attempted to be betray'd. All the main purposes for which the government was establish'd were openly denied. The perfect equality of slavery with freedom was flauntingly preach'd in the north—nay, the superiority of slavery. The slave trade was proposed to be renew'd. Everywhere frowns and misunderstandings—everywhere exasperations and humiliations. (The slavery contest is settled—and the war is long over—yet do not those putrid conditions, too many of them, still exist? still result in diseases, fevers, wounds—not of war and army hospitals—but the wounds and diseases of peace?)

Out of those generic influences, mainly in New York, Pennsylvania, Ohio, &c., arose the attempt at disunion. To philosophical examination, the malignant fever of that war shows its embryonic sources, and the original nourishment of its life and growth, in the north. I say secession, below the surface, originated and was brought to maturity in the free States. I allude to the score of years preceding 1860. My deliberate opinion is now, that if at the opening of the contest the abstract duality-question of *slavery and quiet* could have been submitted to a direct popular vote, as against their opposite, they would have triumphantly carried the day in a majority of the northern States—in the large cities, leading off with New York and Philadelphia, by tremendous majorities. The events of '61 amazed everybody north and south, and burst all prophecies and calculations like bubbles. But even then, and during the whole war, the stern fact remains that (not only did the north put it down, but) *the secession cause had numerically just as many sympathizers in the free as in the rebel States.*

As to slavery, abstractly and practically, (its idea, and the determination to establish and expand it, especially in the new territories, the future America,) it is too common, I repeat, to identify it exclusively with the south. In fact down to the opening of the war, the whole country had about an equal hand in it. The north had at least been just as guilty, if not more guilty; and the east and west had. The former Presidents and Congresses had been guilty—the governors and legislatures of every northern State had been guilty, and the mayors of New York and other northern cities had all been guilty—their hands were all stain'd. And as the conflict took decided shape, it is hard to tell which class, the leading southern or northern disunionists, was more stunn'd and disappointed at the non-action of the free-state secession element, so largely existing and counted on by those leaders, both sections.

So much for that point, and for the north. As to the inception and direct instigation of the war, in the south itself, I shall not attempt interiors or complications. Behind all, the idea that it was from a resolute and arrogant determination on the part of the extreme slaveholders, the Calhounites, to carry the states rights' portion of the constitutional compact to its farthest verge, and nationalize slavery, or else disrupt the Union, and found a new empire, with slavery for its cornerstone, was and is undoubtedly the true theory. (If successful, this attempt might—I am not sure, but it might—have destroy'd not only our American republic, in anything like first-class proportions, in itself and its prestige, but for ages at least, the cause of Liberty and Equality everywhere—and would have been the greatest triumph of reaction, and the severest blow to political and every other freedom, possible to conceive. Its worst result would have inured to the southern States themselves.) That our national democratic experiment, principle, and machinery, could triumphantly sustain such a shock, and that the Constitution could weather it, like a ship a storm, and come out of it as sound and whole as before, is by far the most signal proof yet of the stability of that experiment, Democracy, and of those principles, and that Constitution.

Of the war itself, we know in the ostent what has been done. The numbers of the dead and wounded can be told or approximated, the debt posted and put on record, the material events narrated, &c. Meantime, elections go on, laws are pass'd, political parties struggle, issue their platforms, &c., just the same as before. But immensest results, not only in politics, but in literature, poems, and sociology, are doubtless waiting yet unform'd in the future. How long they will wait I cannot tell. The pageant of history's retrospect shows us, ages since, all Europe marching on the crusades, those arm'd uprisings of the people, stirr'd by a mere idea, to grandest attempt—and, when once baffled in it, returning, at intervals, twice, thrice, and again. An unsurpass'd series of revolutionary events, influences. Yet it took over two hundred years for the seeds of the crusades to germinate, before beginning even to sprout. Two hundred years they lay, sleeping, not dead, but dormant in the ground. Then, out of them, unerringly, arts, travel, navigation, politics, literature, freedom, the spirit of adventure, inquiry, all arose, grew, and steadily sped on to what we see at present. Far back there, that huge agitation-struggle of the crusades stands, as undoubtedly the embryo, the start, of the high preëminence of experiment, civilization and enterprise which the European nations have since sustain'd, and of which these States are the heirs.

Another illustration—(history is full of them, although the war itself, the victory of the Union, and the relations of our equal States, present features of which there are no precedents in the past.) The conquest of England eight centuries ago, by the Franco-Normans—the obliteration of the old, (in many respects so needing obliteration)—the Domesday Book, and the repartition of the land—the old impedimenta removed, even by blood and ruthless violence, and a new, progressive genesis establish'd, new seeds sown—time has proved plain enough that, bitter as they were, all these were the most salutary series of revolutions that could possibly have happen'd. Out of them, and by them mainly, have come, out of Albic, Roman and Saxon England—and without them could not have come—not only the England of the 500 years down to the present, and of the present—but these States. Nor, except for that terrible dislocation and overturn, would these States, as they are, exist to-day.

It is certain to me that the United States, by virtue of that war and its results, and through that and them only, are now ready to enter, and must certainly enter, upon their genuine career in history, as no more torn and divided in their spinal requisites, but a great homogeneous Nation—free states all—a moral and political unity in variety, such as Nature shows in her grandest physical works, and as much greater than any mere work of Nature, as the moral and political, the work of man, his mind, his soul, are, in their loftiest sense, greater than the merely physical. Out of that war not only has the nationalty of the States escaped from being strangled, but more than any of the rest, and, in my opinion, more than the north itself, the vital heart and breath of the south have escaped as from the pressure of a general nightmare, and are henceforth to enter on a life, development, and active freedom, whose realities are certain in the future, notwithstanding all the southern vexations of the hour—a development which could not possibly have been achiev'd on any less terms, or by any other means than that grim lesson, or something equivalent to it. And I predict that the south is yet to outstrip the north.

PREFACE, 1872,

to "As a Strong Bird on Pinions Free," (now "Thou Mother with thy Equal Brood," in permanent ed'n.)

THE impetus and ideas urging me, for some years past, to an utterance, or attempt at utterance, of New World songs, and an epic of Democracy, having already had their publish'd expression, as well as I can expect to give it, in "Leaves of Grass," the present and any future pieces from me are really but the surplusage forming after that volume, or the wake eddying behind it. I fulfill'd in that an imperious conviction, and the commands of my nature as total and irresistible as those which make the sea flow, or the globe revolve. But of this supplementary volume, I confess I am not so certain. Having from early manhood abandon'd the business pursuits and applications usual in my time and country, and obediently yielded myself up ever since to the impetus mention'd, and to the work of expressing those ideas, it may be that mere habit has got dominion of me, when there is no real need of saying any thing further. But what is life but an experiment? and mortality but an exercise? with reference to results beyond. And so shall my poems be. If incomplete here, and superfluous there, *n'importe*—the earnest trial and persistent exploration shall at least be mine, and other success failing shall be success enough. I have been more anxious, anyhow, to suggest the songs of vital endeavor and manly evolution, and furnish something for races of outdoor athletes, than to make perfect rhymes, or reign in the parlors. I ventur'd from the beginning my own way, taking chances—and would keep on venturing.

I will therefore not conceal from any persons, known or unknown to me, who take an interest in the matter, that I have the ambition of devoting yet a few years to poetic composition. The mighty present age! To absorb and express in poetry, anything of it—of its world—America—cities and States—the years, the events of our Nineteenth century—the rapidity of movement—the violent contrasts, fluctuations of light and shade, of hope and fear—the entire revolution made by science in the poetic method—these great new underlying facts and new ideas rushing and spreading everywhere;—truly a mighty age! As if in some colossal drama, acted again like those of old under the open sun, the Nations of our time, and all the characteristics of Civilization, seem hurrying, stalking across, flitting from wing to wing, gathering, closing up, toward some long-prepared, most tremendous denouement. Not to conclude the infinite scenas of the race's life and toil and happiness and sorrow, but haply that the boards be clear'd from oldest, worst incumbrances, accumulations, and Man resume the eternal play anew, and under happier, freer auspices. To me, the United States are important because in this colossal drama they are unquestionably designated for the leading parts, for many a century to come. In them history and humanity seem to seek to culminate. Our broad areas are even now the busy theatre of plots, passions, interests, and suspended problems, compared to which the intrigues of the past of Europe, the wars of dynasties, the scope of kings and kingdoms, and even the development of peoples, as hitherto, exhibit scales of measurement comparatively narrow and trivial. And on these areas of ours, as on a stage, sooner or later, something like an *eclaircissement* of all the past civilization of Europe and Asia is probably to be evolved.

The leading parts. Not to be acted, emulated here, by us again, that role till now foremost in history—not to become a conqueror nation, or to achieve the glory of mere military, or diplomatic, or commercial superiority—but to become the grand producing land of nobler men and women—of copious races, cheerful, healthy, tolerant, free—to become the most friendly nation, (the United States indeed)—the modern composite nation, form'd from all, with room for all, welcoming all immigrants—accepting the work of our own interior development, as the work fitly filling ages and ages to come;—the leading nation of peace, but neither ignorant nor incapable of being the leading nation of war;—not the man's nation only, but the woman's nation—a land of splendid mothers, daughters, sisters, wives.

Our America to-day I consider in many respects as but indeed a vast seething mass of *materials,* ampler, better, (worse also,) than previously known—eligible to be used to carry towards its crowning stage, and build for good, the great ideal nationality of the future, the nation of the body and the soul,*—no limit here to land, help, opportunities, mines, products, demands, supplies, &c.;—with (I think) our political organization, National, State, and Municipal, permanently establish'd, as far ahead as we can calculate—but, so far, no social, literary, religious, or esthetic organizations, consistent with our politics, or becoming to us—which organizations can only come, in time, through great democratic ideas, religion—through science, which now, like a new sunrise, ascending, begins to illuminate all—and through our own begotten poets and literatuses. (The moral of a late well-written book on civilization seems to be that the only real foundation-walls and bases—and also *sine qua non* afterward—of true and full civilization, is the eligibility and certainty of boundless products for feeding, clothing, sheltering everybody—perennial fountains of physical and domestic comfort, with intercommunication, and with civil and ecclesiastical freedom—and that then the esthetic and mental business will take care of itself. Well, the United States have establish'd this basis, and upon scales of extent, variety, vitality, and continuity, rivaling those of Nature; and have now to proceed to build an edifice upon it. I say this edifice is only to be fitly built by new literatures, especially the poetic. I say a modern image-making creation is indispensable to fuse and express the modern political and scientific creations—and then the trinity will be complete.)

When I commenced, years ago, elaborating the plan of my poems, and continued turning over that plan, and shifting it in my mind through many years, (from the age of twenty-eight to thirty-five,) experimenting much, and writing and abandoning much, one deep purpose underlay the others, and

*The problems of the achievements of this crowning stage through future first-class National Singers, Orators, Artists, and others—of creating in literature an *imaginative* New World, the correspondent and counterpart of the current Scientific and Political New Worlds,—and the perhaps distant, but still delightful prospect, (for our children, if not in our own day,) of delivering

has underlain it and its execution ever since—and that has been the religious purpose. Amid many changes, and a formulation taking far different shape from what I at first supposed, this basic purpose has never been departed from in the composition of my verses. Not of course to exhibit itself in the old ways, as in writing hymns or psalms with an eye to the church-pew, or to express conventional pietism, or the sickly yearnings of devotees, but in new ways, and aiming at the widest sub-bases and inclusions of humanity, and tallying the fresh air of sea and land. I will see, (said I to myself,) whether there is not, for my purposes as poet, a religion, and a sound religious germenancy in the average human race, at least in their modern development in the United States, and in the hardy common fibre and native yearnings and elements, deeper and larger, and affording more profitable returns, than all mere sects or churches—as boundless, joyous, and vital as Nature itself—a germenancy that has too long been unencouraged, unsung, almost unknown. With science, the old theology of the East, long in its dotage, begins evidently to die and disappear. But (to my mind) science—and may be such will prove its principal service—as evidently prepares the way for One indescribably grander—Time's young but perfect offspring—the new theology—heir of the West—lusty and loving, and wondrous beautiful. For America, and for to-day, just the same as any day, the supreme and final science is the science of God—what we call science being only its minister—as Democracy is, or shall be also. And a poet of America (I said) must fill himself with such thoughts, and chant his best out of them. And as those were the convictions and aims, for good or bad, of "Leaves of Grass," they are no less the intention of this volume. As there can be, in my opinion, no sane and complete personality, nor any grand and electric nationality, without the stock element of religion imbuing all the other elements, (like heat in chemistry, invisible itself, but the life of all visible life,) so there can be no poetry worthy the name without that element behind all. The time has cer-

America, and, indeed, all Christian lands everywhere, from the thin moribund and watery, but appallingly extensive nuisance of conventional poetry—by putting something really alive and substantial in its place—I have undertaken to grapple with, and argue, in the preceding "Democratic Vistas."

tainly come to begin to discharge the idea of religion, in the United States, from mere ecclesiasticism, and from Sundays and churches and church-going, and assign it to that general position, chiefest, most indispensable, most exhilarating, to which the others are to be adjusted, inside of all human character, and education, and affairs. The people, especially the young men and women of America, must begin to learn that religion, (like poetry,) is something far, far different from what they supposed. It is, indeed, too important to the power and perpetuity of the New World to be consign'd any longer to the churches, old or new, Catholic or Protestant—Saint this, or Saint that. It must be consign'd henceforth to democracy *en masse,* and to literature. It must enter into the poems of the nation. It must make the nation.

The Four Years' War is over—and in the peaceful, strong, exciting, fresh occasions of to-day, and of the future, that strange, sad war is hurrying even now to be forgotten. The camp, the drill, the lines of sentries, the prisons, the hospitals,—(ah! the hospitals!)—all have passed away—all seem now like a dream. A new race, a young and lusty generation, already sweeps in with oceanic currents, obliterating the war, and all its scars, its mounded graves, and all its reminiscences of hatred, conflict, death. So let it be obliterated. I say the life of the present and the future makes undeniable demands upon us each and all, south, north, east, west. To help put the United States (even if only in imagination) hand in hand, in one unbroken circle in a chant—to rouse them to the unprecedented grandeur of the part they are to play, and are even now playing—to the thought of their great future, and the attitude conform'd to it—especially their great esthetic, moral, scientific future, (of which their vulgar material and political present is but as the preparatory tuning of instruments by an orchestra,) these, as hitherto, are still, for me, among my hopes, ambitions.

"Leaves of Grass," already publish'd, is, in its intentions, the song of a great composite *democratic individual,* male or female. And following on and amplifying the same purpose, I suppose I have in my mind to run through the chants of this volume, (if ever completed,) the thread-voice, more or less audible, of an aggregated, inseparable, unprecedented, vast, composite, electric *democratic nationality.*

Purposing, then, to still fill out, from time to time through years to come, the following volume, (unless prevented,) I conclude this preface to the first instalment of it, pencil'd in the open air, on my fifty-third birth-day, by wafting to you, dear reader, whoever you are, (from amid the fresh scent of the grass, the pleasant coolness of the forenoon breeze, the lights and shades of tree-boughs silently dappling and playing around me, and the notes of the cat-bird for undertone and accompaniment,) my true good-will and love.

Washington, D. C., May 31, 1872. W. W.

PREFACE, 1876,

to the two-volume Centennial Edition of L. of G. and "Two Rivulets."

AT the eleventh hour, under grave illness, I gather up the pieces of prose and poetry left over since publishing, a while since, my first and main volume, "Leaves of Grass"—pieces, here, some new, some old—nearly all of them (sombre as many are, making this almost death's book) composed in by-gone atmospheres of perfect health—and preceded by the freshest collection, the little "Two Rivulets," now send them out, embodied in the present melange, partly as my contribution and outpouring to celebrate, in some sort, the feature of the time, the first centennial of our New World nationality—and then as chyle and nutriment to that moral, indissoluble union, equally representing all, and the mother of many coming centennials.

And e'en for flush and proof of our America—for reminder, just as much, or more, in moods of towering pride and joy, I keep my special chants of death and immortality* to stamp

*PASSAGE TO INDIA.—As in some ancient legend-play, to close the plot and the hero's career, there is a farewell gathering on ship's deck and on shore, a loosing of hawsers and ties, a spreading of sails to the wind—a starting out on unknown seas, to fetch up no one knows whither—to return no more—and the curtain falls, and there is the end of it—so I have reserv'd that poem, with its cluster, to finish and explain much that, without them, would not be explain'd, and to take leave, and escape for good, from all that

the coloring-finish of all, present and past. For terminus and temperer to all, they were originally written; and that shall be their office at the last.

---

has preceded them. (Then probably "Passage to India," and its cluster, are but freer vent and fuller expression to what, from the first, and so on throughout, more or less lurks in my writings, underneath every page, every line, everywhere.)

I am not sure but the last inclosing sublimation of race or poem is, what it thinks of death. After the rest has been comprehended and said, even the grandest—after those contributions to mightiest nationality, or to sweetest song, or to the best personalism, male or female, have been glean'd from the rich and varied themes of tangible life, and have been fully accepted and sung, and the pervading fact of visible existence, with the duty it devolves, is rounded and apparently completed, it still remains to be really completed by suffusing through the whole and several, that other pervading invisible fact, so large a part, (is it not the largest part?) of life here, combining the rest, and furnishing, for person or State, the only permanent and unitary meaning to all, even the meanest life, consistently with the dignity of the universe, in Time. As from the eligibility to this thought, and the cheerful conquest of this fact, flash forth the first distinctive proofs of the soul, so to me, (extending it only a little further,) the ultimate Democratic purports, the ethereal and spiritual ones, are to concentrate here, and as fixed stars, radiate hence. For, in my opinion, it is no less than this idea of immortality, above all other ideas, that is to enter into, and vivify, and give crowning religious stamp, to democracy in the New World.

It was originally my intention, after chanting in "Leaves of Grass" the songs of the body and existence, to then compose a further, equally needed volume, based on those convictions of perpetuity and conservation which, enveloping all precedents, make the unseen soul govern absolutely at last. I meant, while in a sort continuing the theme of my first chants, to shift the slides, and exhibit the problem and paradox of the same ardent and fully appointed personality entering the sphere of the resistless gravitation of spiritual law, and with cheerful face estimating death, not at all as the cessation, but as somehow what I feel it must be, the entrance upon by far the greatest part of existence, and something that life is at least as much for, as it is for itself. But the full construction of such a work is beyond my powers, and must remain for some bard in the future. The physical and the sensuous, in themselves or in their immediate continuations, retain holds upon me which I think are never entirely releas'd; and those holds I have not only not denied, but hardly wish'd to weaken.

Meanwhile, not entirely to give the go-by to my original plan, and far more to avoid a mark'd hiatus in it, than to entirely fulfil it, I end my books with thoughts, or radiations from thoughts, on death, immortality, and a free entrance into the spiritual world. In those thoughts, in a sort, I make the first steps or studies toward the mighty theme, from the point of view necessitated by my foregoing poems, and by modern science. In them I also seek to set

For some reason—not explainable or definite to my own mind, yet secretly pleasing and satisfactory to it—I have not hesitated to embody in, and run through the volume, two altogether distinct veins, or strata—politics for one, and for the other, the pensive thought of immortality. Thus, too, the prose and poetic, the dual forms of the present book. The volume, therefore, after its minor episodes, probably divides into these two, at first sight far diverse, veins of topic and treatment. Three points, in especial, have become very dear to me, and all through I seek to make them again and again, in many forms and repetitions, as will be seen: 1. That the true growth-characteristics of the democracy of the New World are henceforth to radiate in superior literary, artistic and religious expressions, far more than in its republican forms, universal suffrage, and frequent elections, (though

---

the key-stone to my democracy's enduring arch. I recollate them now, for the press, in order to partially occupy and offset days of strange sickness, and the heaviest affliction and bereavement of my life; and I fondly please myself with the notion of leaving that cluster to you, O unknown reader of the future, as "something to remember me by," more especially than all else. Written in former days of perfect health, little did I think the pieces had the purport that now, under present circumstances, opens to me.

[As I write these lines, May 31, 1875, it is again early summer—again my birth-day—now my fifty-sixth. Amid the outside beauty and freshness, the sunlight and verdure of the delightful season, O how different the moral atmosphere amid which I now revise this Volume, from the jocund influence surrounding the growth and advent of "Leaves of Grass." I occupy myself, arranging these pages for publication, still envelopt in thoughts of the death two years since of my dear Mother, the most perfect and magnetic character, the rarest combination of practical, moral and spiritual, and the least selfish, of all and any I have ever known—and by me O so much the most deeply loved—and also under the physical affliction of a tedious attack of paralysis, obstinately lingering and keeping its hold upon me, and quite suspending all bodily activity and comfort.]

Under these influences, therefore, I still feel to keep "Passage to India" for last words even to this centennial dithyramb. Not as, in antiquity, at highest festival of Egypt, the noisome skeleton of death was sent on exhibition to the revelers, for zest and shadow to the occasion's joy and light—but as the marble statue of the normal Greeks at Elis, suggesting death in the form of a beautiful and perfect young man, with closed eyes, leaning on an inverted torch—emblem of rest and aspiration after action—of crown and point which all lives and poems should steadily have reference to, namely, the justified and noble termination of our identity, this grade of it, and outlet-preparation to another grade.

these are unspeakably important.) 2. That the vital political mission of the United States is, to practically solve and settle the problem of two sets of rights—the fusion, thorough compatibility and junction of individual State prerogatives, with the indispensable necessity of centrality and Oneness—the national identity power—the sovereign Union, relentless, permanently comprising all, and over all, and in that never yielding an inch: then 3d. Do we not, amid a general malaria of fogs and vapors, our day, unmistakably see two pillars of promise, with grandest, indestructible indications—one, that the morbid facts of American politics and society everywhere are but passing incidents and flanges of our unbounded impetus of growth? weeds, annuals, of the rank, rich soil—not central, enduring, perennial things? The other, that all the hitherto experience of the States, their first century, has been but preparation, adolescence—and that this Union is only now and henceforth, (*i.e.* since the secession war,) to enter on its full democratic career?

Of the whole, poems and prose, (not attending at all to chronological order, and with original dates and passing allusions in the heat and impression of the hour, left shuffled in, and undisturb'd,) the chants of "Leaves of Grass," my former volume, yet serve as the indispensable deep soil, or basis, out of which, and out of which only, could come the roots and stems more definitely indicated by these later pages. (While that volume radiates physiology alone, the present one, though of the like origin in the main, more palpably doubtless shows the pathology which was pretty sure to come in time from the other.)

In that former and main volume, composed in the flush of my health and strength, from the age of 30 to 50 years, I dwelt on birth and life, clothing my ideas in pictures, days, transactions of my time, to give them positive place, identity—saturating them with that vehemence of pride and audacity of freedom necessary to loosen the mind of still-to-be-form'd America from the accumulated folds, the superstitions, and all the long, tenacious and stifling anti-democratic authorities of the Asiatic and European past—my enclosing purport being to express, above all artificial regulation and aid, the eternal bodily composite, cumulative, natural character of one's self.*

Estimating the American Union as so far, and for some time to come, in its yet formative condition, I bequeath poems and essays as nutriment and influences to help truly assimilate and harden, and especially to furnish something toward what the

*Namely, a character, making most of common and normal elements, to the superstructure of which not only the precious accumulations of the learning and experiences of the Old World, and the settled social and municipal necessities and current requirements, so long a-building, shall still faithfully contribute, but which at its foundations and carried up thence, and receiving its impetus from the democratic spirit, and accepting its gauge in all departments from the democratic formulas, shall again directly be vitalized by the perennial influences of Nature at first hand, and the old heroic stamina of Nature, the strong air of prairie and mountain, the dash of the briny sea, the primary antiseptics—of the passions, in all their fullest heat and potency, of courage, rankness, amativeness, and of immense pride. Not to lose at all, therefore, the benefits of artificial progress and civilization, but to re-occupy for Western tenancy the oldest though ever-fresh fields, and reap from them the savage and sane nourishment indispensable to a hardy nation, and the absence of which, threatening to become worse and worse, is the most serious lack and defect to-day of our New World literature.

Not but what the brawn of "Leaves of Grass" is, I hope, thoroughly spiritualized everywhere, for final estimate, but, from the very subjects, the direct effect is a sense of the life, as it should be, of flesh and blood, and physical urge, and animalism. While there are other themes, and plenty of abstract thoughts and poems in the volume—while I have put in it passing and rapid but actual glimpses of the great struggle between the nation and the slave-power, (1861–'65,) as the fierce and bloody panorama of that contest unroll'd itself: while the whole book, indeed, revolves around that four years' war, which, as I was in the midst of it, becomes, in "Drum-Taps," pivotal to the rest entire—and here and there, before and afterward, not a few episodes and speculations—*that*—namely, to make a type-portrait for living, active, worldly, healthy personality, objective as well as subjective, joyful and potent, and modern and free, distinctively for the use of the United States, male and female, through the long future—has been, I say, my general object. (Probably, indeed, the whole of these varied songs, and all my writings, both volumes, only ring changes in some sort, on the ejaculation, How vast, how eligible, how joyful, how real, is a human being, himself or herself.)

Though from no definite plan at the time, I see now that I have unconsciously sought, by indirections at least as much as directions, to express the whirls and rapid growth and intensity of the United States, the prevailing tendency and events of the Nineteenth century, and largely the spirit of the whole current world, my time; for I feel that I have partaken of that spirit, as I have been deeply interested in all those events, the closing of long-stretch'd eras and ages, and, illustrated in the history of the United States,

States most need of all, and which seems to me yet quite unsupplied in literature, namely, to show them, or begin to show them, themselves distinctively, and what they are for. For though perhaps the main points of all ages and nations are points of resemblance, and, even while granting evolution, are substantially the same, there are some vital things in which this Republic, as to its individualities, and as a compacted Na-

---

the opening of larger ones. (The death of President Lincoln, for instance, fitly, historically closes, in the civilization of feudalism, many old influences—drops on them, suddenly, a vast, gloomy, as it were, separating curtain.)

Since I have been ill, (1873–74–75,) mostly without serious pain, and with plenty of time and frequent inclination to judge my poems, (never composed with eye on the book-market, nor for fame, nor for any pecuniary profit,) I have felt temporary depression more than once, for fear that in "Leaves of Grass" the *moral* parts were not sufficiently pronounc'd. But in my clearest and calmest moods I have realized that as those "Leaves," all and several, surely prepare the way for, and necessitate morals, and are adjusted to them, just the same as Nature does and is, they are what, consistently with my plan, they must and probably should be. (In a certain sense, while the Moral is the purport and last intelligence of all Nature, there is absolutely nothing of the moral in the works, or laws, or shows of Nature. Those only lead inevitably to it—begin and necessitate it.)

Then I meant "Leaves of Grass," as publish'd, to be the Poem of average Identity, (of *yours,* whoever you are, now reading these lines.) A man is not greatest as victor in war, nor inventor or explorer, nor even in science, or in his intellectual or artistic capacity, or exemplar in some vast benevolence. To the highest democratic view, man is most acceptable in living well the practical life and lot which happens to him as ordinary farmer, sea-farer, mechanic, clerk, laborer, or driver—upon and from which position as a central basis or pedestal, while performing its labors, and his duties as citizen, son, husband, father and employ'd person, he preserves his physique, ascends, developing, radiating himself in other regions—and especially where and when, (greatest of all, and nobler than the proudest mere genius or magnate in any field,) he fully realizes the conscience, the spiritual, the divine faculty, cultivated well, exemplified in all his deeds and words, through life, uncompromising to the end—a flight loftier than any of Homer's or Shakspere's—broader than all poems and bibles—namely, Nature's own, and in the midst of it, Yourself, your own Identity, body and soul. (All serves, helps—but in the centre of all, absorbing all, giving, for your purpose, the only meaning and vitality to all, master or mistress of all, under the law, stands Yourself.) To sing the Song of that law of average Identity, and of Yourself, consistently with the divine law of the universal, is a main intention of those "Leaves."

Something more may be added—for, while I am about it, I would make a full confession. I also sent out "Leaves of Grass" to arouse and set flowing in men's and women's hearts, young and old, endless streams of living, pul-

tion, is to specially stand forth, and culminate modern humanity. And these are the very things it least morally and mentally knows—(though, curiously enough, it is at the same time faithfully acting upon them.)

I count with such absolute certainty on the great future of the United States—different from, though founded on, the past—that I have always invoked that future, and surrounded myself with it, before or while singing my songs. (As ever, all tends to followings—America, too, is a prophecy. What, even of the best and most successful, would be justified by itself alone? by the present, or the material ostent alone? Of men or States, few realize how much they live in the future. That, rising like pinnacles, gives its main significance to all You and I are doing to-day. Without it, there were little meaning in lands or poems—little purport in human lives. All ages, all Nations and States, have been such prophecies. But where any former ones with prophecy so broad, so clear, as our times, our lands—as those of the West?)

Without being a scientist, I have thoroughly adopted the conclusions of the great savans and experimentalists of our

---

sating love and friendship, directly from them to myself, now and ever. To this terrible, irrepressible yearning, (surely more or less down underneath in most human souls)—this never-satisfied appetite for sympathy, and this boundless offering of sympathy—this universal democratic comradeship—this old, eternal, yet ever-new interchange of adhesiveness, so fitly emblematic of America—I have given in that book, undisguisedly, declaredly, the openest expression. Besides, important as they are in my purpose as emotional expressions for humanity, the special meaning of the "Calamus" cluster of "Leaves of Grass," (and more or less running through the book, and cropping out in "Drum-Taps,") mainly resides in its political significance. In my opinion, it is by a fervent, accepted development of comradeship, the beautiful and sane affection of man for man, latent in all the young fellows, north and south, east and west—it is by this, I say, and by what goes directly and indirectly along with it, that the United States of the future, (I cannot too often repeat,) are to be most effectually welded together, intercalated, anneal'd into a living union.

Then, for enclosing clue of all, it is imperatively and ever to be borne in mind that "Leaves of Grass" entire is not to be construed as an intellectual or scholastic effort or poem mainly, but more as a radical utterance out of the Emotions and the Physique—an utterance adjusted to, perhaps born of, Democracy and the Modern—in its very nature regardless of the old conventions, and, under the great laws, following only its own impulses.

time, and of the last hundred years, and they have interiorly tinged the chyle of all my verse, for purposes beyond. Following the modern spirit, the real poems of the present, ever solidifying and expanding into the future, must vocalize the vastness and splendor and reality with which scientism has invested man and the universe, (all that is called creation,) and must henceforth launch humanity into new orbits, consonant with that vastness, splendor, and reality, (unknown to the old poems,) like new systems of orbs, balanced upon themselves, revolving in limitless space, more subtle than the stars. Poetry, so largely hitherto and even at present wedded to children's tales, and to mere amorousness, upholstery and superficial rhyme, will have to accept, and, while not denying the past, nor the themes of the past, will be revivified by this tremendous innovation, the kosmic spirit, which must henceforth, in my opinion, be the background and underlying impetus, more or less visible, of all first-class songs.

Only, (for me, at any rate, in all my prose and poetry,) joyfully accepting modern science, and loyally following it without the slightest hesitation, there remains ever recognized still a higher flight, a higher fact, the eternal soul of man, (of all else too,) the spiritual, the religious—which it is to be the greatest office of scientism, in my opinion, and of future poetry also, to free from fables, crudities and superstitions, and launch forth in renew'd faith and scope a hundred fold. To me, the worlds of religiousness, of the conception of the divine, and of the ideal, though mainly latent, are just as absolute in humanity and the universe as the world of chemistry, or anything in the objective worlds. To me

> The prophet and the bard,
> Shall yet maintain themselves—in higher circles yet,
> Shall mediate to the modern, to democracy—
> interpret yet to them,
> God and eidólons.

To me, the crown of savantism is to be, that it surely opens the way for a more splendid theology, and for ampler and diviner songs. No year, nor even century, will settle this. There is a phase of the real, lurking behind the real, which it is all for. There is also in the intellect of man, in time, far in prospective recesses, a judgment, a last appellate court, which will settle it.

In certain parts in these flights, or attempting to depict or suggest them, I have not been afraid of the charge of obscurity, in either of my two volumes—because human thought, poetry or melody, must leave dim escapes and outlets—must possess a certain fluid, aerial character, akin to space itself, obscure to those of little or no imagination, but indispensable to the highest purposes. Poetic style, when address'd to the soul, is less definite form, outline, sculpture, and becomes vista, music, half-tints, and even less than half-tints. True, it may be architecture; but again it may be the forest wild-wood, or the best effect thereof, at twilight, the waving oaks and cedars in the wind, and the impalpable odor.

Finally, as I have lived in fresh lands, inchoate, and in a revolutionary age, future-founding, I have felt to identify the points of that age, these lands, in my recitatives, altogether in my own way. Thus my form has strictly grown from my purports and facts, and is the analogy of them. Within my time the United States have emerged from nebulous vagueness and suspense, to full orbic, (though varied,) decision—have done the deeds and achiev'd the triumphs of half a score of centuries—and are henceforth to enter upon their real history—the way being now, (*i.e.* since the result of the Secession War,) clear'd of death-threatening impedimenta, and the free areas around and ahead of us assured and certain, which were not so before—(the past century being but preparations, trial voyages and experiments of the ship, before her starting out upon deep water.)

In estimating my volumes, the world's current times and deeds, and their spirit, must be first profoundly estimated. Out of the hundred years just ending, (1776–1876,) with their genesis of inevitable wilful events, and new experiments and introductions, and many unprecedented things of war and peace, (to be realized better, perhaps only realized, at the remove of a century hence;) out of that stretch of time, and especially out of the immediately preceding twenty-five years,

(1850–75,) with all their rapid changes, innovations, and audacious movements—and bearing their own inevitable wilful birth-marks—the experiments of my poems too have found genesis. *W. W.*

Poetry To-day in America—Shakspere—The Future

STRANGE as it may seem, the topmost proof of a race is its own born poetry. The presence of that, or the absence, each tells its story. As the flowering rose or lily, as the ripen'd fruit to a tree, the apple or the peach, no matter how fine the trunk, or copious or rich the branches and foliage, here waits *sine qua non* at last. The stamp of entire and finish'd greatness to any nation, to the American Republic among the rest, must be sternly withheld till it has put what it stands for in the blossom of original, first-class poems. No imitations will do.

And though no *esthetik* worthy the present condition or future certainties of the New World seems to have been outlined in men's minds, or has been generally called for, or thought needed, I am clear that until the United States have just such definite and native expressers in the highest artistic fields, their mere political, geographical, wealth-forming, and even intellectual eminence, however astonishing and predominant, will constitute but a more and more expanded and well-appointed body, and perhaps brain, with little or no soul. Sugar-coat the grim truth as we may, and ward off with outward plausible words, denials, explanations, to the mental inward perception of the land this blank is plain; a barren void exists. For the meanings and maturer purposes of these States are not the constructing of a new world of politics merely, and physical comforts for the million, but even more determinedly, in range with science and the modern, of a new world of democratic sociology and imaginative literature. If the latter were not establish'd for the States, to form their only permanent tie and hold, the first-named would be of little avail.

With the poems of a first-class land are twined, as weft with warp, its types of personal character, of individuality, peculiar, native, its own physiognomy, man's and woman's, its own shapes, forms, and manners, fully justified under the eternal laws of all forms, all manners, all times. The hour has come for democracy in America to inaugurate itself in the two directions specified—autochthonic poems and personalities—born expressers of itself, its spirit alone, to radiate in subtle ways, not only in art, but the practical and familiar, in the transactions between employers and employ'd persons, in business and wages, and sternly in the army and navy, and revolutionizing them. I find nowhere a scope profound enough, and radical and objective enough, either for aggregates or individuals. The thought and identity of a poetry in America to fill, and worthily fill, the great void, and enhance these aims, electrifying all and several, involves the essence and integral facts, real and spiritual, of the whole land, the whole body. What the great sympathetic is to the congeries of bones, joints, heart, fluids, nervous system and vitality, constituting, launching forth in time and space a human being—aye, an immortal soul—such relation, and no less, holds true poetry to the single personality, or to the nation.

Here our thirty-eight States stand to-day, the children of past precedents, and, young as they are, heirs of a very old estate. One or two points we will consider, out of the myriads presenting themselves. The feudalism of the British Islands, illustrated by Shakspere—and by his legitimate followers, Walter Scott and Alfred Tennyson—with all its tyrannies, superstitions, evils, had most superb and heroic permeating veins, poems, manners; even its errors fascinating. It almost seems as if only that feudalism in Europe, like slavery in our own South, could outcrop types of tallest, noblest personal character yet—strength and devotion and love better than elsewhere—invincible courage, generosity, aspiration, the spines of all. Here is where Shakspere and the others I have named perform a service incalculably precious to our America. Politics, literature, and everything else, centers at last in perfect *personnel*, (as democracy is to find the same as the rest;) and here feudalism is unrival'd—here the rich and highest-rising lessons it bequeaths us—a mass of foreign nutriment, which we are to work over, and popularize and enlarge, and present again in our own growths.

Still there are pretty grave and anxious drawbacks, jeopardies, fears. Let us give some reflections on the subject, a little fluctuating, but starting from one central thought, and returning there again. Two or three curious results may plow up. As in the astronomical laws, the very power that would seem most deadly and destructive turns out to be latently conservative of longest, vastest future births and lives. We will for once briefly examine the just-named authors solely from a Western point of view. It may be, indeed, that we shall use the sun of English literature, and the brightest current stars of his system, mainly as pegs to hang some cogitations on, for home inspection.

As depicter and dramatist of the passions at their stormiest outstretch, though ranking high, Shakspere (spanning the arch wide enough) is equal'd by several, and excell'd by the best old Greeks, (as Æschylus.) But in portraying mediæval European lords and barons, the arrogant port, so dear to the inmost human heart, (pride! pride! dearest, perhaps, of all—touching us, too, of the States closest of all—closer than love,) he stands alone, and I do not wonder he so witches the world.

From first to last, also, Walter Scott and Tennyson, like Shakspere, exhale that principle of caste which we Americans have come on earth to destroy. Jefferson's verdict on the Waverley novels was that they turn'd and condens'd brilliant but entirely false lights and glamours over the lords, ladies, and aristocratic institutes of Europe, with all their measureless infamies, and then left the bulk of the suffering, down-trodden people contemptuously in the shade. Without stopping to answer this hornet-stinging criticism, or to repay any part of the debt of thanks I owe, in common with every American, to the noblest, healthiest, cheeriest romancer that ever lived, I pass on to Tennyson, his works.

Poetry here of a very high (perhaps the highest) order of verbal melody, exquisitely clean and pure, and almost always perfumed, like the tuberose, to an extreme of sweetness—sometimes not, however, but even then a camellia of the hothouse, never a common flower—the verse of inside elegance and high-life; and yet preserving amid all its super-delicatesse a smack of outdoors and outdoor folk. The old Norman lord-hood quality here, too, cross'd with that Saxon fiber from which twain the best current stock of England springs—poetry that revels above all things in traditions of knights and chivalry, and deeds of derring-do. The odor of English social life in its highest range—a melancholy, affectionate, very manly, but dainty breed—pervading the pages like an invisible scent; the idleness, the traditions, the mannerisms, the stately *ennui;* the yearning of love, like a spinal marrow, inside of all; the costumes, brocade and satin; the old houses and furniture—solid oak, no mere veneering—the moldy secrets everywhere; the verdure, the ivy on the walls, the moat, the English landscape outside, the buzzing fly in the sun inside the window pane. Never one democratic page; nay, not a line, not a word; never free and *naïve* poetry, but involv'd, labor'd, quite sophisticated—even when the theme is ever so simple or rustic, (a shell, a bit of sedge, the commonest love-passage between a lad and lass,) the handling of the rhyme all showing the scholar and conventional gentleman; showing the laureate, too, the *attaché* of the throne, and most excellent, too; nothing better through the volumes than the dedication "to the Queen" at the beginning, and the other fine dedication, "these to his memory" (Prince Albert's,) preceding "Idylls of the King."

Such for an off-hand summary of the mighty three that now, by the women, men, and young folk of the fifty millions given these States by their late census, have been and are more read than all others put together.

We hear it said, both of Tennyson and another current leading literary illustrator of Great Britain, Carlyle—as of Victor Hugo in France—that not one of them is personally friendly or admirant toward America; indeed, quite the reverse. *N'importe.* That they (and more good minds than theirs) cannot span the vast revolutionary arch thrown by the United States over the centuries, fix'd in the present, launch'd to the endless future; that they cannot stomach the high-life-below-stairs coloring all our poetic and genteel social status so far—the measureless viciousness of the great radical Republic, with its ruffianly nominations and elections; its loud, ill-pitch'd voice, utterly regardless whether the verb agrees with the nominative; its fights, errors, eructations, repulsions, dishonesties, audacities; those fearful and varied and long-continued storm and stress stages (so offensive to the well-regulated college-bred mind) wherewith Nature, history, and time block out nationalities more powerful than the past, and to upturn it and press on to the future;—that they cannot understand and fathom all this, I say, is it to be wonder'd at? Fortunately, the gestation of our thirty-eight empires (and plenty more to come) proceeds on its course, on scales of area and velocity immense and absolute as the globe, and, like the globe itself, quite oblivious even of great poets and thinkers. But we can by no means afford to be oblivious of them.

The same of feudalism, its castles, courts, etiquettes, personalities. However they, or the spirits of them hovering in the air, might scowl and glower at such removes as current Kansas or Kentucky life and forms, the latter may by no means repudiate or leave out the former. Allowing all the evil that it did, we get, here and to-day, a balance of good out of its reminiscence almost beyond price.

Am I content, then, that the general interior chyle of our republic should be supplied and nourish'd by wholesale from foreign and antagonistic sources such as these? Let me answer that question briefly:

Years ago I thought Americans ought to strike out separate, and have expressions of their own in highest literature. I think so still, and more decidedly than ever. But those convictions are now strongly temper'd by some additional points, (perhaps the results of advancing age, or the reflections of invalidism.) I see that this world of the West, as part of all, fuses inseparably with the East, and with all, as time does—the ever new, yet old, old human race—"the same subject continued," as the novels of our grandfathers had it for chapter-heads. If we are not to hospitably receive and complete the inaugurations of the old civilizations, and change their small scale to the largest, broadest scale, what on earth are we for?

The currents of practical business in America, the rude, coarse, tussling facts of our lives, and all their daily experiences, need just the precipitation and tincture of this entirely different fancy world of lulling, contrasting, even feudalistic, anti-republican poetry and romance. On the enormous outgrowth of our unloos'd individualities, and the rank self-assertion of humanity here, may well fall these grace-persuading, *recherché* influences. We first require that individuals and communities shall be free; then surely comes a time when it is requisite that they shall not be too free. Although to such results in the future I look mainly for a great poetry native to us, these importations till then will have to be accepted, such as they are, and thankful they are no worse. The inmost spiritual currents of the present time curiously revenge and check their own compell'd tendency to democracy, and absorption in it, by mark'd leanings to the past—by reminiscences in poems, plots, operas, novels, to a far-off, contrary, deceased world, as if they dreaded the great vulgar gulf tides of to-day. Then what has been fifty centuries growing, working in, and accepted as crowns and apices for our kind, is not going to be pulled down and discarded in a hurry.

It is, perhaps, time we paid our respects directly to the honorable party, the real object of these preambles. But we must make *reconnaissance* a little further still. Not the least part of our lesson were to realize the curiosity and interest of friendly foreign experts,* and how our situation looks to them. "American poetry," says the London "Times,"† "is the poetry of apt pupils, but it is afflicted from first to last with a fatal want of raciness. Bryant has been long passed as a poet by Professor Longfellow; but in Longfellow, with all his scholarly grace and tender feeling, the defect is more apparent than it was in Bryant. Mr. Lowell can overflow with American hu-

*A few years ago I saw the question, "Has America produced any great poem?" announced as prize-subject for the competition of some university in Northern Europe. I saw the item in a foreign paper and made a note of it; but being taken down with paralysis, and prostrated for a long season, the matter slipp'd away, and I have never been able since to get hold of any essay presented for the prize, or report of the discussion, nor to learn for certain whether there was any essay or discussion, nor can I now remember the place. It may have been Upsala, or possibly Heidelberg. Perhaps some German or Scandinavian can give particulars. I think it was in 1872.

†In a long and prominent editorial, at the time, on the death of William Cullen Bryant.

mor when politics inspire his muse; but in the realm of pure poetry he is no more American than a Newdigate prize-man. Joaquin Miller's verse has fluency and movement and harmony, but as for the thought, his songs of the sierras might as well have been written in Holland."

Unless in a certain very slight contingency, the "Times" says: "American verse, from its earliest to its latest stages, seems an exotic, with an exuberance of gorgeous blossom, but no principle of reproduction. That is the very note and test of its inherent want. Great poets are tortured and massacred by having their flowers of fancy gathered and gummed down in the *hortus siccus* of an anthology. American poets show better in an anthology than in the collected volumes of their works. Like their audience they have been unable to resist the attraction of the vast orbit of English literature. They may talk of the primeval forest, but it would generally be very hard from internal evidence to detect that they were writing on the banks of the Hudson rather than on those of the Thames. . . . . In fact, they have caught the English tone and air and mood only too faithfully, and are accepted by the superficially cultivated English intelligence as readily as if they were English born. Americans themselves confess to a certain disappointment that a literary curiosity and intelligence so diffused [as in the United States] have not taken up English literature at the point at which America has received it, and carried it forward and developed it with an independent energy. But like reader like poet. Both show the effects of having come into an estate they have not earned. A nation of readers has required of its poets a diction and symmetry of form equal to that of an old literature like that of Great Britain, which is also theirs. No ruggedness, however racy, would be tolerated by circles which, however superficial their culture, read Byron and Tennyson."

The English critic, though a gentleman and a scholar, and friendly withal, is evidently not altogether satisfied, (perhaps he is jealous,) and winds up by saying: "For the English language to have been enriched with a national poetry which was not English but American, would have been a treasure beyond price." With which, as whet and foil, we shall proceed to ventilate more definitely certain no doubt willful opinions.

Leaving unnoticed at present the great masterpieces of the antique, or anything from the middle ages, the prevailing flow of poetry for the last fifty or eighty years, and now at its height, has been and is (like the music) an expression of mere surface melody, within narrow limits, and yet, to give it its due, perfectly satisfying to the demands of the ear, of wondrous charm, of smooth and easy delivery, and the triumph of technical art. Above all things it is fractional and select. It shrinks with aversion from the sturdy, the universal, and the democratic.

The poetry of the future, (a phrase open to sharp criticism, and not satisfactory to me, but significant, and I will use it)—the poetry of the future aims at the free expression of emotion, (which means far, far more than appears at first,) and to arouse and initiate, more than to define or finish. Like all modern tendencies, it has direct or indirect reference continually to the reader, to you or me, to the central identity of everything, the mighty Ego. (Byron's was a vehement dash, with plenty of impatient democracy, but lurid and introverted amid all its magnetism; not at all the fitting, lasting song of a grand, secure, free, sunny race.) It is more akin, likewise, to outside life and landscape, (returning mainly to the antique feeling,) real sun and gale, and woods and shores—to the elements themselves—not sitting at ease in parlor or library listening to a good tale of them, told in good rhyme. Character, a feature far above style or polish—a feature not absent at any time, but now first brought to the fore—gives predominant stamp to advancing poetry. Its born sister, music, already responds to the same influences. "The music of the present, Wagner's, Gounod's, even the later Verdi's, all tends toward this free expression of poetic emotion, and demands a vocalism totally unlike that required for Rossini's splendid roulades, or Bellini's suave melodies."

Is there not even now, indeed, an evolution, a departure from the masters? Venerable and unsurpassable after their kind as are the old works, and always unspeakably precious as studies, (for Americans more than any other people,) is it too much to say that by the shifted combinations of the modern mind the whole underlying theory of first-class verse has changed? "Formerly, during the period term'd classic," says

Sainte-Beuve, "when literature was govern'd by recognized rules, he was consider'd the best poet who had composed the most perfect work, the most beautiful poem, the most intelligible, the most agreeable to read, the most complete in every respect,—the Æneid, the Gerusalemme, a fine tragedy. To-day, something else is wanted. For us the greatest poet is he who in his works most stimulates the reader's imagination and reflection, who excites him the most himself to poetize. The greatest poet is not he who has done the best; it is he who suggests the most; he, not all of whose meaning is at first obvious, and who leaves you much to desire, to explain, to study, much to complete in your turn."

The fatal defects our American singers labor under are subordination of spirit, an absence of the concrete and of real patriotism, and in excess that modern æsthetic contagion a queer friend of mine calls the *beauty disease.* "The immoderate taste for beauty and art," says Charles Baudelaire, "leads men into monstrous excesses. In minds imbued with a frantic greed for the beautiful, all the balances of truth and justice disappear. There is a lust, a disease of the art faculties, which eats up the moral like a cancer."

Of course, by our plentiful verse-writers there is plenty of service perform'd, of a kind. Nor need we go far for a tally. We see, in every polite circle, a class of accomplish'd, good-natured persons, ("society," in fact, could not get on without them,) fully eligible for certain problems, times, and duties—to mix eggnog, to mend the broken spectacles, to decide whether the stew'd eels shall precede the sherry or the sherry the stew'd eels, to eke out Mrs. A. B.'s parlor-tableaux with monk, Jew, lover, Puck, Prospero, Caliban, or what not, and to generally contribute and gracefully adapt their flexibilities and talents, in those ranges, to the world's service. But for real crises, great needs and pulls, moral or physical, they might as well have never been born.

Or the accepted notion of a poet would appear to be a sort of male odalisque, singing or piano-playing a kind of spiced ideas, second-hand reminiscences, or toying late hours at entertainments, in rooms stifling with fashionable scent. I think I haven't seen a new-publish'd, healthy, bracing, simple lyric in ten years. Not long ago, there were verses in each of three fresh monthlies, from leading authors, and in every one the whole central *motif* (perfectly serious) was the melancholiness of a marriageable young woman who didn't get a rich husband, but a poor one!

Besides its tonic and *al fresco* physiology, relieving such as this, the poetry of the future will take on character in a more important respect. Science, having extirpated the old stock-fables and superstitions, is clearing a field for verse, for all the arts, and even for romance, a hundred-fold ampler and more wonderful, with the new principles behind. Republicanism advances over the whole world. Liberty, with Law by her side, will one day be paramount—will at any rate be the central idea. Then only—for all the splendor and beauty of what has been, or the polish of what is—then only will the true poets appear, and the true poems. Not the satin and patchouly of to-day, not the glorification of the butcheries and wars of the past, nor any fight between Deity on one side and somebody else on the other—not Milton, not even Shakspere's plays, grand as they are. Entirely different and hitherto unknown classes of men, being authoritatively called for in imaginative literature, will certainly appear. What is hitherto most lacking, perhaps most absolutely indicates the future. Democracy has been hurried on through time by measureless tides and winds, resistless as the revolution of the globe, and as far-reaching and rapid. But in the highest walks of art it has not yet had a single representative worthy of it anywhere upon the earth.

Never had real bard a task more fit for sublime ardor and genius than to sing worthily the songs these States have already indicated. Their origin, Washington, '76, the picturesqueness of old times, the war of 1812 and the sea-fights; the incredible rapidity of movement and breadth of area—to fuse and compact the South and North, the East and West, to express the native forms, situations, scenes, from Montauk to California, and from the Saguenay to the Rio Grande—the working out on such gigantic scales, and with such a swift and mighty play of changing light and shade, of the great problems of man and freedom,—how far ahead of the stereotyped plots, or gem-cutting, or tales of love, or wars of mere ambition! Our history is so full of spinal, modern, germinal subjects—one above all. What the ancient siege of Ilium, and the puissance of Hector's and Agamemnon's warriors proved to Hellenic art and literature, and all art and literature since, may prove the war of attempted secession of 1861–'65 to the future æsthetics, drama, romance, poems of the United States.

Nor could utility itself provide anything more practically serviceable to the hundred millions who, a couple of generations hence, will inhabit within the limits just named, than the permeation of a sane, sweet, autochthonous national poetry—must I say of a kind that does not now exist? but which, I fully believe, will in time be supplied on scales as free as Nature's elements. (It is acknowledged that we of the States are the most materialistic and money-making people ever known. My own theory, while fully accepting this, is that we are the most emotional, spiritualistic, and poetry-loving people also.)

Infinite are the new and orbic traits waiting to be launch'd forth in the firmament that is, and is to be, America. Lately, I have wonder'd whether the last meaning of this cluster of thirty-eight States is not only practical fraternity among themselves—the only real *union*, (much nearer its accomplishment, too, than appears on the surface)—but for fraternity over the whole globe—that dazzling, pensive dream of ages! Indeed, the peculiar glory of our lands, I have come to see, or expect to see, not in their geographical or republican greatness, nor wealth or products, nor military or naval power, nor special, eminent names in any department, to shine with, or outshine, foreign special names in similar departments,—but more and more in a vaster, saner, more surrounding Comradeship, uniting closer and closer not only the American States, but all nations, and all humanity. That, O poets! is not that a theme worth chanting, striving for? Why not fix your verses henceforth to the gauge of the round globe? the whole race? Perhaps the most illustrious culmination of the modern may thus prove to be a signal growth of joyous, more exalted bards of adhesiveness, identically one in soul, but contributed by every nation, each after its distinctive kind. Let us, audacious, start it. Let the diplomats, as ever, still deeply plan, seeking advantages, proposing treaties between governments, and to bind them, on paper: what I seek is different, simpler. I would inaugurate from America, for this purpose, new formulas—international poems. I have thought that the invisible root out of which the poetry deepest in, and dearest to, humanity grows, is Friendship. I have thought that both in patriotism and song (even amid their grandest shows past) we have adhered too long to petty limits, and that the time has come to enfold the world.

Not only is the human and artificial world we have establish'd in the West a radical departure from anything hitherto known—not only men and politics, and all that goes with them—but Nature itself, in the main sense, its construction, is different. The same old font of type, of course, but set up to a text never composed or issued before. For Nature consists not only in itself, objectively, but at least just as much in its subjective reflection from the person, spirit, age, looking at it, in the midst of it, and absorbing it—faithfully sends back the characteristic beliefs of the time or individual—takes, and readily gives again, the physiognomy of any nation or literature—falls like a great elastic veil on a face, or like the molding plaster on a statue.

What is Nature? What were the elements, the invisible backgrounds and eidólons of it, to Homer's heroes, voyagers, gods? What all through the wanderings of Virgil's Æneas? Then to Shakspere's characters—Hamlet, Lear, the English-Norman kings, the Romans? What was Nature to Rousseau, to Voltaire, to the German Goethe in his little classical court gardens? In those presentments in Tennyson (see the "Idyls of the King"—what sumptuous, perfumed, arras-and-gold Nature, inimitably described, better than any, fit for princes and knights and peerless ladies—wrathful or peaceful, just the same—Vivien and Merlin in their strange dalliance, or the death-float of Elaine, or Geraint and the long journey of his disgraced Enid and himself through the wood, and the wife all day driving the horses,) as in all the great imported artworks, treatises, systems, from Lucretius down, there is a constantly lurking, often pervading something, that will have to be eliminated, as not only unsuited to modern democracy and science in America, but insulting to them, and disproved by them.*

Still, the rule and demesne of poetry will always be not the exterior, but interior; not the macrocosm, but microcosm; not Nature, but Man. I haven't said anything about the imperative need of a race of giant bards in the future, to hold up high to eyes of land and race the eternal antiseptic models, and to dauntlessly confront greed, injustice, and all forms of that wiliness and tyranny whose roots never die—(my opinion is, that after all the rest is advanced, *that* is what first-class poets are for; as, to their days and occasions, the Hebrew lyrists, Roman Juvenal, and doubtless the old singers of India, and the British Druids)—to counteract dangers, immensest ones, already looming in America—measureless corruption in politics—what we call religion, a mere mask of wax or lace;—for *ensemble,* that most cankerous, offensive of all earth's shows—a vast and varied community, prosperous and fat with wealth of money and products and business ventures—plenty of mere intellectuality too—and then utterly without the sound, prevailing, moral and æsthetic health-action beyond all the money and mere intellect of the world.

Is it a dream of mine that, in times to come, west, south, east, north, will silently, surely arise a race of such poets, varied, yet one in soul—nor only poets, and of the best, but newer, larger prophets—larger than Judea's, and more passionate—to meet and penetrate those woes, as shafts of light the darkness?

As I write, the last fifth of the nineteenth century is enter'd upon, and will soon be waning. Now, and for a long time to come, what the United States most need, to give purport,

*Whatever may be said of the few principal poems—or their best passages—it is certain that the overwhelming mass of poetic works, as now absorb'd into human character, exerts a certain constipating, repressing, in-door, and artificial influence, impossible to elude—seldom or never that freeing, dilating, joyous one, with which uncramp'd Nature works on every individual without exception.

definiteness, reason why, to their unprecedented material wealth, industrial products, education by rote merely, great populousness and intellectual activity, is the central, spinal reality, (or even the idea of it,) of such a democratic band of native-born-and-bred teachers, artists, *littérateurs,* tolerant and receptive of importations, but entirely adjusted to the West, to ourselves, to our own days, combinations, differences, superiorities. Indeed, I am fond of thinking that the whole series of concrete and political triumphs of the Republic are mainly as bases and preparations for half a dozen future poets, ideal personalities, referring not to a special class, but to the entire people, four or five millions of square miles.

Long, long are the processes of the development of a nationality. Only to the rapt vision does the seen become the prophecy of the unseen.* Democracy, so far attending only

*Is there not such a thing as the philosophy of American history and politics? And if so, what is it? . . . Wise men say there are two sets of wills to nations and to persons—one set that acts and works from explainable motives—from teaching, intelligence, judgment, circumstance, caprice, emulation, greed, &c.—and then another set, perhaps deep, hidden, unsuspected, yet often more potent than the first, refusing to be argued with, rising as it were out of abysses, resistlessly urging on speakers, doers, communities, unwitting to themselves—the poet to his fieriest words—the race to pursue its loftiest ideal. Indeed, the paradox of a nation's life and career, with all its wondrous contradictions, can probably only be explain'd from these two wills, sometimes conflicting, each operating in its sphere, combining in races or in persons, and producing strangest results.

Let us hope there is (indeed, can there be any doubt there is?) this great unconscious and abysmic second will also running through the average nationality and career of America. Let us hope that, amid all the dangers and defections of the present, and through all the processes of the conscious will, it alone is the permanent and sovereign force, destined to carry on the New World to fulfill its destinies in the future—to resolutely pursue those destinies, age upon age; to build, far, far beyond its past vision, present thought; to form and fashion, and for the general type, men and women more noble, more athletic than the world has yet seen; to gradually, firmly blend, from all the States, with all varieties, a friendly, happy, free, religious nationality—a nationality not only the richest, most inventive, most productive and materialistic the world has yet known, but compacted indissolubly, and out of whose ample and solid bulk, and giving purpose and finish to it, conscience, morals, and all the spiritual attributes, shall surely rise, like spires above some group of edifices, firm-footed on the earth, yet scaling space and heaven.

Great as they are, and greater far to be, the United States, too, are but a series of steps in the eternal process of creative thought. And here is, to my

to the real, is not for the real only, but the grandest ideal—to justify the modern by that, and not only to equal, but to become by that superior to the past. On a comprehensive summing up of the processes and present and hitherto condition of the United States, with reference to their future, and the indispensable precedents to it, my point, below all surfaces, and subsoiling them, is, that the bases and prerequisites of a leading nationality are, first, at all hazards, freedom, worldly wealth and products on the largest and most varied scale, common education and intercommunication, and, in general, the passing through of just the stages and crudities we have passed or are passing through in the United States.

---

mind, their final justification, and certain perpetuity. There is in that sublime process, in the laws of the universe—and, above all, in the moral law—something that would make unsatisfactory, and, even vain and contemptible, all the triumphs of war, the gains of peace, and the proudest worldly grandeur of all the nations that have ever existed, or that (ours included) now exist, except that we constantly see, through all their worldly career, however struggling and blind and lame, attempts, by all ages, all peoples, according to their development, to reach, to press, to progress on, and ever farther on, to more and more advanced ideals.

The glory of the republic of the United States, in my opinion, is to be that, emerging in the light of the modern and the splendor of science, and solidly based on the past, it is to cheerfully range itself, and its politics are henceforth to come, under those universal laws, and embody them, and carry them out, to serve them. And as only that individual becomes truly great who understands well that, while complete in himself in a certain sense, he is but a part of the divine, eternal scheme, and whose special life and laws are adjusted to move in harmonious relations with the general laws of Nature, and especially with the moral law, the deepest and highest of all, and the last vitality of man or state—so the United States may only become the greatest and the most continuous, by understanding well their harmonious relations with entire humanity and history, and all their laws and progress, sublimed with the creative thought of Deity, through all time, past, present, and future. Thus will they expand to the amplitude of their destiny, and become illustrations and culminating parts of the cosmos, and of civilization.

No more considering the States as an incident, or series of incidents, however vast, coming accidentally along the path of time, and shaped by casual emergencies as they happen to arise, and the mere result of modern improvements, vulgar and lucky, ahead of other nations and times, I would finally plant, as seeds, these thoughts or speculations in the growth of our republic—that it is the deliberate culmination and result of all the past—that here, too, as in all departments of the universe, regular laws (slow and sure in planting, slow and sure in ripening) have controll'd and govern'd, and will yet control and govern; and that those laws can no more be baffled or steer'd clear of,

Then, perhaps, as weightiest factor of the whole business, and of the main outgrowths of the future, it remains to be definitely avow'd that the native-born middle-class population of quite all the United States—the average of farmers and mechanics everywhere—the real, though latent and silent bulk of America, city or country, presents a magnificent mass of material, never before equaled on earth. It is this material, quite unexpress'd by literature or art, that in every respect insures the future of the republic. During the Secession War I was with the armies, and saw the rank and file, North and South, and studied them for four years. I have never had the least doubt about the country in its essential future since.

Meantime, we can (perhaps) do no better than to saturate ourselves with, and continue to give imitations, yet awhile, of the æsthetic models, supplies, of that past and of those lands we spring from. Those wondrous stores, reminiscences, floods, currents! Let them flow on, flow hither freely. And let the sources be enlarged, to include not only the works of British origin, as now, but stately and devout Spain, courteous France, profound Germany, the manly Scandinavian lands, Italy's art race, and always the mystic Orient. Remembering that at present, and doubtless long ahead, a certain humility would well become us. The course through time of highest civilization, does it not wait the first glimpse of our contribution to its cosmic train of poems, bibles, first-class structures, perpetuities—Egypt and Palestine and India—Greece and Rome and mediæval Europe—and so onward? The shad-

---

or vitiated, by chance, or any fortune or opposition, than the laws of winter and summer, or darkness and light.

The summing up of the tremendous moral and military perturbations of 1861–5, and their results—and indeed of the entire hundred years of the past of our national experiment, from its inchoate movement down to the present day (1780–1881)—is, that they all now launch the United States fairly forth, consistently with the entirety of civilization and humanity, and in main sort the representative of them, leading the van, leading the fleet of the modern and democratic, on the seas and voyages of the future.

And the real history of the United States—starting from that great convulsive struggle for unity, the secession war, triumphantly concluded, and *the South* victorious after all—is only to be written at the remove of hundreds, perhaps a thousand, years hence.

owy procession is not a meagre one, and the standard not a low one. All that is mighty in our kind seems to have already trod the road. Ah, never may America forget her thanks and reverence for samples, treasures such as these—that other life-blood, inspiration, sunshine, hourly in use to-day, all days, forever, through her broad demesne!

All serves our New World progress, even the bafflers, head-winds, cross-tides. Through many perturbations and squalls, and much backing and filling, the ship, upon the whole, makes unmistakably for her destination. Shakspere has served, and serves, may-be, the best of any.

For conclusion, a passing thought, a contrast, of him who, in my opinion, continues and stands for the Shaksperean cultus at the present day among all English-writing peoples—of Tennyson, his poetry. I find it impossible, as I taste the sweetness of those lines, to escape the flavor, the conviction, the lush-ripening culmination, and last honey of decay (I dare not call it rottenness) of that feudalism which the mighty English dramatist painted in all the splendors of its noon and afternoon. And how they are chanted—both poets! Happy those kings and nobles to be so sung, so told! To run their course—to get their deeds and shapes in lasting pigments—the very pomp and dazzle of the sunset!

Meanwhile, democracy waits the coming of its bards in silence and in twilight—but 'tis the twilight of the dawn.

A Memorandum at a Venture

"All is proper to be express'd, provided our aim is only high enough."—*J. F. Millet.*

"The candor of science is the glory of the modern. It does not hide and repress; it confronts, turns on the light. It alone has perfect faith—faith not in a part only, but all. Does it not undermine the old religious standards? Yes, in God's truth, by excluding the devil from the theory of the universe—by showing that evil is not a law in itself, but a sickness, a perversion of the good, and the other side of the good—that in fact all of humanity, and of everything, is divine in its bases, its eligibilities."

SHALL the mention of such topics as I have briefly but plainly and resolutely broach'd in the "Children of Adam" section of "Leaves of Grass" be admitted in poetry and literature? Ought not the innovation to be put down by opinion and criticism? and, if those fail, by the District Attorney? True, I could not construct a poem which declaredly took, as never before, the complete human identity, physical, moral, emotional, and intellectual, (giving precedence and compass in a certain sense to the first), nor fulfil that *bona fide* candor and entirety of treatment which was a part of my purpose, without comprehending this section also. But I would entrench myself more deeply and widely than that. And while I do not ask any man to indorse my theory, I confess myself anxious that what I sought to write and express, and the ground I built on, shall be at least partially understood, from its own platform. The best way seems to me to confront the question with entire frankness.

There are, generally speaking, two points of view, two conditions of the world's attitude toward these matters; the first, the conventional one of good folks and good print everywhere, repressing any direct statement of them, and making allusions only at second or third hand—(as the Greeks did of death, which, in Hellenic social culture, was not mention'd point-blank, but by euphemisms.) In the civilization of to-day, this condition—without stopping to elaborate the arguments and facts, which are many and varied and perplexing—has led to states of ignorance, repressal, and cover'd over disease and depletion, forming certainly a main factor in the world's woe. A non-scientific, non-æsthetic, and eminently non-religious condition, bequeath'd to us from the past, (its origins diverse, one of them the far-back lessons of benevolent and wise men to restrain the prevalent coarseness and animality of the tribal ages—with Puritanism, or perhaps Protestantism itself for another, and still another specified in the latter part of this memorandum)—to it is probably due most of the ill births, inefficient maturity, snickering pruriency, and of that human pathologic evil and morbidity which is, in my opinion, the keel and reason-why of every evil and morbidity. Its scent, as of something sneaking, furtive, mephitic, seems to lingeringly pervade all modern literature, conversation, and manners.

The second point of view, and by far the largest—as the world in working-day dress vastly exceeds the world in parlor toilette—is the one of common life, from the oldest times down, and especially in England, (see the earlier chapters of "Taine's English Literature," and see Shakspere almost anywhere,) and which our age to-day inherits from riant stock, in the wit, or what passes for wit, of masculine circles, and in erotic stories and talk, to excite, express, and dwell on, that merely sensual voluptuousness which, according to Victor Hugo, is the most universal trait of all ages, all lands. This second condition, however bad, is at any rate like a disease which comes to the surface, and therefore less dangerous than a conceal'd one.

The time seems to me to have arrived, and America to be the place, for a new departure—a third point of view. The same freedom and faith and earnestness which, after centuries of denial, struggle, repression, and martyrdom, the present day brings to the treatment of politics and religion, must work out a plan and standard on this subject, not so much for what is call'd society, as for thoughtfulest men and women, and thoughtfulest literature. The same spirit that marks the physiological author and demonstrator on these topics in his important field, I have thought necessary to be exemplified, for once, in another certainly not less important field.

In the present memorandum I only venture to indicate that plan and view—decided upon more than twenty years ago, for my own literary action, and formulated tangibly in my printed poems—(as Bacon says an abstract thought or theory is of no moment unless it leads to a deed or work done, exemplifying it in the concrete)—that the sexual passion in itself, while normal and unperverted, is inherently legitimate, creditable, not necessarily an improper theme for poet, as confessedly not for scientist—that, with reference to the whole construction, organism, and intentions of "Leaves of Grass," anything short of confronting that theme, and making myself clear upon it, as the enclosing basis of everything, (as the sanity of everything was to be the atmosphere of the poems,) I should beg the question in its most momentous aspect, and the superstructure that follow'd, pretensive as it might assume to be, would all rest on a poor foundation, or no foundation at all. In short, as the assumption of the sanity of birth, Nature and humanity, is the key to any true theory of life and the universe—at any rate, the only theory out of which I wrote—it is, and must inevitably be, the only key to "Leaves of Grass," and every part of it. *That,* (and not a vain consistency or weak pride, as a late "Springfield Republican" charges,) is the reason that I have stood out for these particular verses uncompromisingly for over twenty years, and maintain them to this day. *That* is what I felt in my inmost brain and heart, when I only answer'd Emerson's vehement arguments with silence, under the old elms of Boston Common.

Indeed, might not every physiologist and every good physician pray for the redeeming of this subject from its hitherto relegation to the tongues and pens of blackguards, and boldly putting it for once at least, if no more, in the demesne of poetry and sanity—as something not in itself gross or impure, but entirely consistent with highest manhood and womanhood, and indispensable to both? Might not only every wife and every mother—not only every babe that comes into the world, if that were possible—not only all marriage, the foundation and *sine qua non* of the civilized state—bless and thank the showing, or taking for granted, that motherhood, fatherhood, sexuality, and all that belongs to them, can be asserted, where it comes to question, openly, joyously, proudly, "without shame or the need of shame," from the highest artistic and human considerations—but, with reverence be it written, on such attempt to justify the base and start of the whole divine scheme in humanity, might not the Creative Power itself deign a smile of approval?

To the movement for the eligibility and entrance of women amid new spheres of business, politics, and the suffrage, the current prurient, conventional treatment of sex is the main formidable obstacle. The rising tide of "woman's rights," swelling and every year advancing farther and farther, recoils from it with dismay. There will in my opinion be no general progress in such eligibility till a sensible, philosophic, democratic method is substituted.

The whole question—which strikes far, very far deeper than most people have supposed, (and doubtless, too, something is to be said on all sides,) is peculiarly an important one in art—is first an ethic, and then still more an æsthetic one. I condense from a paper read not long since at Cheltenham, England, before the "Social Science Congress," to the Art Department, by P.H. Rathbone of Liverpool, on the "Undraped Figure in Art," and the discussion that follow'd:

> "When coward Europe suffer'd the unclean Turk to soil the sacred shores of Greece by his polluting presence, civilization and morality receiv'd a blow from which they have never entirely recover'd, and the trail of the serpent has been over European art and European society ever since. The Turk regarded and regards women as animals without soul, toys to be play'd with or broken at pleasure, and to be hidden, partly from shame, but chiefly for the purpose of stimulating exhausted passion. Such is the unholy origin of the objection to the nude as a fit subject for art; it is purely Asiatic, and though not introduced for the first time in the fifteenth century, is yet to be traced to the source of all impurity—the East. Although the source of the prejudice is thoroughly unhealthy and impure, yet it is now shared by many pure-minded and honest, if somewhat uneducated, people. But I am prepared to maintain that it is necessary for the future of English art and of English morality that the right of the nude to a place in our galleries should be boldly asserted; it must, however, be the nude as represented by thoroughly trained artists, and with a pure and noble ethic purpose. The human form, male and female, is the type and standard of all beauty of form and proportion, and it is necessary to be thoroughly familiar with it in order safely to judge of all beauty which consists of form and proportion. To women it is most necessary that they should become thoroughly imbued with the knowledge of the ideal female form, in order that they should recognize the perfection of it at once, and

without effort, and so far as possible avoid deviations from the ideal. Had this been the case in times past, we should not have had to deplore the distortions effected by tight-lacing, which destroy'd the figure and ruin'd the health of so many of the last generation. Nor should we have had the scandalous dresses alike of society and the stage. The extreme development of the low dresses which obtain'd some years ago, when the stays crush'd up the breasts into suggestive prominence, would surely have been check'd, had the eye of the public been properly educated by familiarity with the exquisite beauty of line of a well-shaped bust. I might show how thorough acquaintance with the ideal nude foot would probably have much modified the foot-torturing boots and high heels, which wring the foot out of all beauty of line, and throw the body forward into an awkward and ungainly attitude.

"It is argued that the effect of nude representation of women upon young men is unwholesome, but it would not be so if such works were admitted without question into our galleries, and became thoroughly familiar to them. On the contrary, it would do much to clear away from healthy-hearted lads one of their sorest trials—that prurient curiosity which is bred of prudish concealment. Where there is mystery there is the suggestion of evil, and to go to a theatre, where you have only to look at the stalls to see one-half of the female form, and to the stage to see the other half undraped, is far more pregnant with evil imaginings than the most objectionable of totally undraped figures. In French art there have been questionable nude figures exhibited; but the fault was not that they were nude, but that they were the portraits of ugly immodest women."

Some discussion follow'd. There was a general concurrence in the principle contended for by the reader of the paper. Sir Walter Stirling maintain'd that the perfect male figure, rather than the female, was the model of beauty. After a few remarks from Rev. Mr. Roberts and Colonel Oldfield, the Chairman regretted that no opponent of nude figures had taken part in the discussion. He agreed with Sir Walter Stirling as to the male figure being the most perfect model of proportion. He join'd in defending the exhibition of nude figures, but thought considerable supervision should be exercised over such exhibitions.

No, it is not the picture or nude statue or text, with clear aim, that is indecent; it is the beholder's own thought, inference, distorted construction. True modesty is one of the most precious of attributes, even virtues, but in nothing is there more pretense, more falsity, than the needless assumption of it. Through precept and consciousness, man has long enough realized how bad he is. I would not so much disturb or demolish that conviction, only to resume and keep unerringly with it the spinal meaning of the Scriptural text, *God overlook'd all that He had made,* (including the apex of the whole—humanity—with its elements, passions, appetites,) *and behold, it was very good.*

Does not anything short of that third point of view, when you come to think of it profoundly and with amplitude, impugn Creation from the outset? In fact, however overlaid, or unaware of itself, does not the conviction involv'd in it perennially exist at the centre of all society, and of the sexes, and of marriage? Is it not really an intuition of the human race? For, old as the world is, and beyond statement as are the countless and splendid results of its culture and evolution, perhaps the best and earliest and purest intuitions of the human race have yet to be develop'd.

Death of Abraham Lincoln

LECTURE *deliver'd in New York, April 14, 1879—*
in Philadelphia, '80—in Boston, '81.

How often since that dark and dripping Saturday—that chilly April day, now fifteen years bygone—my heart has entertain'd the dream, the wish, to give of Abraham Lincoln's death, its own special thought and memorial. Yet now the sought-for opportunity offers, I find my notes incompetent, (why, for truly profound themes, is statement so idle? why does the right phrase never offer?) and the fit tribute I dream'd of, waits unprepared as ever. My talk here indeed is less because of itself or anything in it, and nearly altogether because I feel a desire, apart from any talk, to specify the day, the martyrdom. It is for this, my friends, I have call'd you together. Oft as the rolling years bring back this hour, let it again, however briefly, be dwelt upon. For my own part, I hope and desire, till my own dying day, whenever the 14th or 15th of April comes, to annually gather a few friends, and hold its tragic reminiscence. No narrow or sectional reminiscence. It belongs to these States in their entirety—not the North only, but the South—perhaps belongs most tenderly and devoutly to the South, of all; for there, really, this man's birth-stock. There and thence his antecedent stamp. Why should I not say that thence his manliest traits—his universality—his canny, easy ways and words upon the surface—his inflexible determination and courage at heart? Have you never realized it, my friends, that Lincoln, though grafted on the West, is essentially, in personnel and character, a Southern contribution?

And though by no means proposing to resume the Secession war to-night, I would briefly remind you of the public conditions preceding that contest. For twenty years, and especially during the four or five before the war actually began, the aspect of affairs in the United States, though without the flash of military excitement, presents more than the survey of a battle, or any extended campaign, or series, even of Nature's convulsions. The hot passions of the South—the strange mixture at the North of inertia, incredulity, and conscious power—the incendiarism of the abolitionists—the rascality and *grip* of the politicians, unparallel'd in any land, any age. To these I must not omit adding the honesty of the essential bulk of the people everywhere—yet with all the seething fury and contradiction of their natures more arous'd than the Atlantic's waves in wildest equinox. In politics, what can be more ominous, (though generally unappreciated then)—what more significant than the Presidentiads of Fillmore and Buchanan? proving conclusively that the weakness and wickedness of elected rulers are just as likely to afflict us here, as in the countries of the Old World, under their monarchies, emperors, and aristocracies. In that Old World were everywhere heard underground rumblings, that died out, only to again surely return. While in America the volcano, though civic yet, continued to grow more and more convulsive—more and more stormy and threatening.

In the height of all this excitement and chaos, hovering on the edge at first, and then merged in its very midst, and destined to play a leading part, appears a strange and awkward figure. I shall not easily forget the first time I ever saw Abraham Lincoln. It must have been about the 18th or 19th of February, 1861. It was rather a pleasant afternoon, in New York city, as he arrived there from the West, to remain a few hours, and then pass on to Washington, to prepare for his inauguration. I saw him in Broadway, near the site of the present Post-office. He came down, I think from Canal street, to stop at the Astor House. The broad spaces, sidewalks, and street in the neighborhood, and for some distance, were crowded with solid masses of people, many thousands. The omnibuses and other vehicles had all been turn'd off, leaving an unusual hush in that busy part of the city. Presently two or three shabby hack barouches made their way with some difficulty through the crowd, and drew up at the Astor House entrance. A tall figure step'd out of the centre of these barouches, paus'd leisurely on the sidewalk, look'd up at the granite walls and looming architecture of the grand old hotel—then, after a relieving stretch of arms and legs, turn'd round for over a minute to slowly and good-humoredly scan the appearance of the vast and silent crowds. There were no speeches—no compliments—no welcome—as far as I could hear, not a word said. Still much anxiety was conceal'd in that quiet. Cautious persons had fear'd some mark'd insult or indignity to the President-elect—for he possess'd no personal popularity at all in New York city, and very little political. But it was evidently tacitly agreed that if the few political supporters of Mr. Lincoln present would entirely abstain from any demonstration on their side, the immense majority, who were any thing but supporters, would abstain on their side also. The result was a sulky, unbroken silence, such as certainly never before characterized so great a New York crowd.

Almost in the same neighborhood I distinctly remember'd seeing Lafayette on his visit to America in 1825. I had also personally seen and heard, various years afterward, how Andrew Jackson, Clay, Webster, Hungarian Kossuth, Filibuster Walker, the Prince of Wales on his visit, and other celebres, native and foreign, had been welcom'd there—all that indescribable human roar and magnetism, unlike any other sound in the universe—the glad exulting thunder-shouts of countless unloos'd throats of men! But on this occasion, not a voice—not a sound. From the top of an omnibus, (driven up one side, close by, and block'd by the curbstone and the crowds,) I had, I say, a capital view of it all, and especially of Mr. Lincoln, his look and gait—his perfect composure and coolness—his unusual and uncouth height, his dress of complete black, stovepipe hat push'd back on the head, dark-brown complexion, seam'd and wrinkled yet canny-looking face, black, bushy head of hair, disproportionately long neck, and his hands held behind as he stood observing the people. He look'd with curiosity upon that immense sea of faces, and the sea of faces return'd the look with similar curiosity. In both there was a dash of comedy, almost farce, such as Shakspere puts in his blackest tragedies. The crowd that hemm'd around consisted I should think of thirty to forty thousand men, not a single one his personal friend—while I have no doubt, (so frenzied were the ferments of the time,) many an assassin's knife and pistol lurk'd in hip or breast-pocket there, ready, soon as break and riot came.

But no break or riot came. The tall figure gave another relieving stretch or two of arms and legs; then with moderate pace, and accompanied by a few unknown looking persons, ascended the portico-steps of the Astor House, disappear'd through its broad entrance—and the dumb-show ended.

I saw Abraham Lincoln often the four years following that date. He changed rapidly and much during his Presidency—but this scene, and him in it, are indelibly stamped upon my recollection. As I sat on the top of my omnibus, and had a good view of him, the thought, dim and inchoate then, has since come out clear enough, that four sorts of genius, four mighty and primal hands, will be needed to the complete limning of this man's future portrait—the eyes and brains and finger-touch of Plutarch and Eschylus and Michel Angelo, assisted by Rabelais.

And now—(Mr. Lincoln passing on from this scene to Washington, where he was inaugurated, amid armed cavalry, and sharpshooters at every point—the first instance of the kind in our history—and I hope it will be the last)—now the rapid succession of well-known events, (too well known—I believe, these days, we almost hate to hear them mention'd)—the national flag fired on at Sumter—the uprising of the North, in paroxysms of astonishment and rage—the chaos of divided councils—the call for troops—the first Bull Run—the stunning cast-down, shock, and dismay of the North—and so in full flood the Secession war. Four years of lurid, bleeding, murky, murderous war. Who paint those years, with all their scenes?—the hard-fought engagements—the defeats, plans, failures—the gloomy hours, days, when our Nationality seem'd hung in pall of doubt, perhaps death—the Mephistophelean sneers of foreign lands and attachés—the dreaded Scylla of European interference, and the Charybdis of the tremendously dangerous latent strata of secession sympathizers throughout the free States, (far more numerous than is supposed)—the long marches in summer—the hot sweat, and many a sunstroke, as on the rush to Gettysburg in '63—the night battles in the woods, as under Hooker at Chancellorsville—the camps in winter—the military prisons—the hospitals—(alas! alas! the hospitals.)

The Secession war? Nay, let me call it the Union war. Though whatever call'd, it is even yet too near us—too vast and too closely overshadowing—its branches unform'd yet, (but certain,) shooting too far into the future—and the most indicative and mightiest of them yet ungrown. A great literature will yet arise out of the era of those four years, those scenes—era compressing centuries of native passion, first-class pictures, tempests of life and death—an inexhaustible mine for the histories, drama, romance, and even philosophy, of peoples to come—indeed the verteber of poetry and art, (of personal character too,) for all future America—far more grand, in my opinion, to the hands capable of it, than Homer's siege of Troy, or the French wars to Shakspere.

But I must leave these speculations, and come to the theme I have assign'd and limited myself to. Of the actual murder of President Lincoln, though so much has been written, probably the facts are yet very indefinite in most persons' minds. I read from my memoranda, written at the time, and revised frequently and finally since.

The day, April 14, 1865, seems to have been a pleasant one throughout the whole land—the moral atmosphere pleasant too—the long storm, so dark, so fratricidal, full of blood and doubt and gloom, over and ended at last by the sun-rise of such an absolute National victory, and utter break-down of Secessionism—we almost doubted our own senses! Lee had capitulated beneath the apple-tree of Appomattox. The other armies, the flanges of the revolt, swiftly follow'd. And could it really be, then? Out of all the affairs of this world of woe and failure and disorder, was there really come the confirm'd, unerring sign of plan, like a shaft of pure light—of rightful rule—of God? So the day, as I say, was propitious. Early herbage, early flowers, were out. (I remember where I was stopping at the time, the season being advanced, there were many lilacs in full bloom. By one of those caprices that enter and give tinge to events without being at all a part of them, I find myself always reminded of the great tragedy of that day by the sight and odor of these blossoms. It never fails.)

But I must not dwell on accessories. The deed hastens. The popular afternoon paper of Washington, the little "Evening Star," had spatter'd all over its third page, divided among the advertisements in a sensational manner, in a hundred different places, *The President and his Lady will be at the Theatre this evening.* . . . (Lincoln was fond of the theatre. I have myself seen him there several times. I remember thinking how funny it was that he, in some respects the leading actor in the stormiest drama known to real history's stage through centuries, should sit there and be so completely interested and absorb'd in those human jack-straws, moving about with their silly little gestures, foreign spirit, and flatulent text.)

On this occasion the theatre was crowded, many ladies in rich and gay costumes, officers in their uniforms, many well-known citizens, young folks, the usual clusters of gas-lights, the usual magnetism of so many people, cheerful, with perfumes, music of violins and flutes—(and over all, and saturating all, that vast, vague wonder, *Victory,* the nation's victory, the triumph of the Union, filling the air, the thought, the sense, with exhilaration more than all music and perfumes.)

The President came betimes, and, with his wife, witness'd the play from the large stage-boxes of the second tier, two thrown into one, and profusely draped with the national flag. The acts and scenes of the piece—one of those singularly written compositions which have at least the merit of giving entire relief to an audience engaged in mental action or business excitements and cares during the day, as it makes not the slightest call on either the moral, emotional, esthetic, or spiritual nature—a piece, ("Our American Cousin,") in which, among other characters, so call'd, a Yankee, certainly such a one as was never seen, or the least like it ever seen, in North America, is introduced in England, with a varied fol-de-rol of talk, plot, scenery, and such phantasmagoria as goes to make up a modern popular drama—had progress'd through perhaps a couple of its acts, when in the midst of this comedy, or nonsuch, or whatever it is to be call'd, and to offset it, or finish it out, as if in Nature's and the great Muse's mockery of those poor mimes, came interpolated that scene, not really or exactly to be described at all, (for on the many hundreds who were there it seems to this hour to have left a passing blur, a dream, a blotch)—and yet partially to be described as I now proceed to give it. There is a scene in the play representing a modern parlor, in which two unprecedented English ladies are inform'd by the impossible Yankee that he is not a man of fortune, and therefore undesirable for marriage-catching purposes; after which, the comments being finish'd, the dramatic trio make exit, leaving the stage clear for a moment. At this period came the murder of Abraham Lincoln. Great as all its manifold train, circling round it, and stretching into the future for many a century, in the politics, history, art, &c., of the New World, in point of fact the main thing, the actual murder, transpired with the quiet and simplicity of any commonest occurrence—the bursting of a bud or pod in the growth of vegetation, for instance. Through the general hum following the stage pause, with the change of positions, came the muffled sound of a pistol-shot, which not one-hundredth part of the audience heard at the time—and yet a moment's hush—somehow, surely, a vague startled thrill—and then, through the ornamented, draperied, starr'd and striped space-way of the President's box, a sudden figure, a man, raises himself with hands and feet, stands a moment on the railing, leaps below to the stage, (a distance of perhaps fourteen or fifteen feet,) falls out of position, catching his boot-heel in the copious drapery, (the American flag,) falls on one knee, quickly recovers himself, rises as if nothing had happen'd, (he really sprains his ankle, but unfelt then)—and so the figure, Booth, the murderer, dress'd in plain black broadcloth, bare-headed, with full, glossy, raven hair, and his eyes like some mad animal's flashing with light and resolution, yet with a certain strange calmness, holds aloft in one hand a large knife—walks along not much back from the footlights—turns fully toward the audience his face of statuesque beauty, lit by those basilisk eyes, flashing with desperation, perhaps insanity—launches out in a firm and steady voice the words *Sic semper tyrannis*—and then walks with neither slow nor very rapid pace diagonally across to the back of the stage, and disappears. (Had not all this terrible scene—making the mimic ones preposterous—had it not all been rehears'd, in blank, by Booth, beforehand?)

A moment's hush—a scream—the cry of *murder*—Mrs. Lincoln leaning out of the box, with ashy cheeks and lips, with involuntary cry, pointing to the retreating figure, *He has kill'd the President.* And still a moment's strange, incredulous suspense—and then the deluge!—then that mixture of horror, noises, uncertainty—(the sound, somewhere back, of a horse's hoofs clattering with speed)—the people burst through chairs and railings, and break them up—there is inextricable confusion and terror—women faint—quite feeble persons fall, and are trampled on—many cries of agony are heard—the broad stage suddenly fills to suffocation with a dense and motley crowd, like some horrible carnival—the audience rush generally upon it, at least the strong men do—the actors and actresses are all there in their play-costumes and painted faces, with mortal fright showing through the rouge—the screams and calls, confused talk—redoubled, trebled—two or three manage to pass up water from the stage to the President's box—others try to clamber up—&c., &c.

In the midst of all this, the soldiers of the President's guard, with others, suddenly drawn to the scene, burst in—(some two hundred altogether)—they storm the house, through all the tiers, especially the upper ones, inflamed with fury, literally charging the audience with fix'd bayonets, muskets and pistols, shouting *Clear out! clear out! you sons of*—— . . . . . Such the wild scene, or a suggestion of it rather, inside the play-house that night.

Outside, too, in the atmosphere of shock and craze, crowds of people, fill'd with frenzy, ready to seize any outlet for it, come near committing murder several times on innocent individuals. One such case was especially exciting. The infuriated crowd, through some chance, got started against one man, either for words he utter'd, or perhaps without any cause at all, and were proceeding at once to actually hang him on a neighboring lamp-post, when he was rescued by a few heroic policemen, who placed him in their midst, and fought their way slowly and amid great peril toward the station house. It was a fitting episode of the whole affair. The crowd rushing and eddying to and fro—the night, the yells, the pale faces, many frighten'd people trying in vain to extricate themselves—the attack'd man, not yet freed from the jaws of death, looking like a corpse—the silent, resolute, half-dozen policemen, with no weapons but their little clubs, yet stern and steady through all those eddying swarms—made a fitting side-scene to the grand tragedy of the murder. They gain'd the station house with the protected man, whom they placed in security for the night, and discharged him in the morning.

And in the midst of that pandemonium, infuriated soldiers, the audience and the crowd, the stage, and all its actors and actresses, its paint-pots, spangles, and gas-lights—the life blood from those veins, the best and sweetest of the land, drips slowly down, and death's ooze already begins its little bubbles on the lips.

Thus the visible incidents and surroundings of Abraham Lincoln's murder, as they really occur'd. Thus ended the attempted secession of these States; thus the four years' war. But the main things come subtly and invisibly afterward, perhaps long afterward—neither military, political, nor (great as those are,) historical. I say, certain secondary and indirect results, out of the tragedy of this death, are, in my opinion, greatest. Not the event of the murder itself. Not that Mr. Lincoln strings the principal points and personages of the period, like beads, upon the single string of his career. Not that his idiosyncrasy, in its sudden appearance and disappearance, stamps this Republic with a stamp more mark'd and enduring than any yet given by any one man—(more even than Washington's;)—but, join'd with these, the immeasurable value and meaning of that whole tragedy lies, to me, in senses finally dearest to a nation, (and here all our own)—the imaginative and artistic senses—the literary and dramatic ones. Not in any common or low meaning of those terms, but a meaning precious to the race, and to every age. A long and varied series of contradictory events arrives at last at its highest poetic, single, central, pictorial denouement. The whole involved, baffling, multiform whirl of the secession period comes to a head, and is gather'd in one brief flash of lightning-illumination—one simple, fierce deed. Its sharp culmination, and as it were solution, of so many bloody and angry problems, illustrates those climax-moments on the stage of universal Time, where the historic Muse at one entrance, and the tragic Muse at the other, suddenly ringing down the curtain, close an immense act in the long drama of creative thought, and give it radiation, tableau, stranger than fiction. Fit radiation—fit close! How the imagination—how the student loves these things! America, too, is to have them. For not in all great deaths, nor far or near—not Cæsar in the Roman senate-house, or Napoleon passing away in the wild night-storm at St. Helena—not Paleologus, falling, desperately fighting, piled over dozens deep with Grecian corpses—not calm old Socrates, drinking the hemlock—outvies that terminus of the secession war, in one man's life, here in our midst, in our own time—that seal of the emancipation of three million slaves—that parturition and delivery of our at last really free Republic, born again, henceforth to commence its career of genuine homogeneous Union, compact, consistent with itself.

Nor will ever future American Patriots and Unionists, indifferently over the whole land, or North or South, find a better moral to their lesson. The final use of the greatest men of a Nation is, after all, not with reference to their deeds in themselves, or their direct bearing on their times or lands. The final use of a heroic-eminent life—especially of a heroic-eminent death—is its indirect filtering into the nation and the race, and to give, often at many removes, but unerringly, age after age, color and fibre to the personalism of the youth and maturity of that age, and of mankind. Then there is a cement to the whole people, subtler, more underlying, than any thing in written constitution, or courts or armies—namely, the cement of a death identified thoroughly with that people, at its head, and for its sake. Strange, (is it not?) that battles, martyrs, agonies, blood, even assassination, should so condense—perhaps only really, lastingly condense—a Nationality.

I repeat it—the grand deaths of the race—the dramatic deaths of every nationality—are its most important inheritance-value—in some respects beyond its literature and art—(as the hero is beyond his finest portrait, and the battle itself beyond its choicest song or epic.) Is not here indeed the point underlying all tragedy? the famous pieces of the Grecian masters—and all masters? Why, if the old Greeks had had this man, what trilogies of plays—what epics—would have been made out of him! How the rhapsodes would have recited him! How quickly that quaint tall form would have enter'd into the region where men vitalize gods, and gods divinify men! But Lincoln, his times, his death—great as any, any age—belong altogether to our own, and are autochthonic. (Some times indeed I think our American days, our own stage—the actors we know and have shaken hands, or talk'd with—more fateful than any thing in Eschylus—more heroic than the fighters around Troy—afford kings of men for our Democracy prouder than Agamemnon—models of character cute and hardy as Ulysses—deaths more pitiful than Priam's.)

When, centuries hence, (as it must, in my opinion, be centuries hence before the life of these States, or of Democracy, can be really written and illustrated,) the leading historians and dramatists seek for some personage, some special event, incisive enough to mark with deepest cut, and mnemonize, this turbulent Nineteenth century of ours, (not only these

States, but all over the political and social world)—something, perhaps, to close that gorgeous procession of European feudalism, with all its pomp and caste-prejudices, (of whose long train we in America are yet so inextricably the heirs)—something to identify with terrible identification, by far the greatest revolutionary step in the history of the United States, (perhaps the greatest of the world, our century)—the absolute extirpation and erasure of slavery from the States—those historians will seek in vain for any point to serve more thoroughly their purpose, than Abraham Lincoln's death.

Dear to the Muse—thrice dear to Nationality—to the whole human race—precious to this Union—precious to Democracy—unspeakably and forever precious—their first great Martyr Chief.

Two Letters

1.—To——— ——— ——— (London, England.)

CAMDEN, N. J., U. S. AMERICA, *March 17th, 1876.*

DEAR FRIEND:—Yours of the 28th Feb. receiv'd, and indeed welcom'd. I am jogging along still about the same in physical condition—still certainly no worse, and I sometimes lately suspect rather better, or at any rate more adjusted to the situation. Even begin to think of making some move, some change of base, &c.: the doctors have been advising it for over two years, but I haven't felt to do it yet. My paralysis does not lift—I cannot walk any distance—I still have this baffling, obstinate, apparently chronic affection of the stomachic apparatus and liver: yet I get out of doors a little every day—write and read in moderation—appetite sufficiently good—(eat only very plain food, but always did that)—digestion tolerable—spirits unflagging. I have told you most of this before, but suppose you might like to know it all again, up to date. Of course, and pretty darkly coloring the whole, are bad spells, prostrations, some pretty grave ones, intervals—and I have resign'd myself to the certainty of permanent incapacitation from solid work: but things may continue at least in this half-and-half way for months, even years.

My books are out, the new edition; a set of which, immediately on receiving your letter of 28th, I have sent you, (by mail, March 15,) and I suppose you have before this receiv'd them. My dear friend, your offers of help, and those of my other British friends, I think I fully appreciate, in the right spirit, welcome and acceptive—leaving the matter altogether in your and their hands, and to your and their convenience, discretion, leisure, and nicety. Though poor now, even to penury, I have not so far been deprived of any physical thing I need or wish whatever, and I feel confident I shall not in the future. During my employment of seven years or more in Washington after the war (1865–72) I regularly saved part of my wages: and, though the sum has now become about exhausted by my expenses of the last three years, there are already beginning at present welcome dribbles hitherward from the sales of my new edition, which I just job and sell, myself, (all through this illness, my book-agents for three years in New York successively, badly cheated me,) and shall continue to dispose of the books myself. And *that* is the way I should prefer to glean my support. In that way I cheerfully accept all the aid my friends find it convenient to proffer.

To repeat a little, and without undertaking details, understand, dear friend, for yourself and all, that I heartily and most affectionately thank my British friends, and that I accept their sympathetic generosity in the same spirit in which I believe (nay, know) it is offer'd—that though poor I am not in want—that I maintain good heart and cheer; and that by far the most satisfaction to me (and I think it can be done, and believe it will be) will be to live, as long as possible, on the sales, by myself, of my own works, and perhaps, if practicable, by further writings for the press. W. W.

I am prohibited from writing too much, and I must make this candid statement of the situation serve for all my dear friends over there.

2.—To——— ————— (Dresden, Saxony.)

CAMDEN, *New Jersey, U.S.A., Dec. 20, '81.*

DEAR SIR:—Your letter asking definite endorsement to your translation of my *"Leaves of Grass"* into Russian is just received, and I hasten to answer it. Most warmly and willingly

I consent to the translation, and waft a prayerful *God speed* to the enterprise.

You Russians and we Americans! Our countries so distant, so unlike at first glance—such a difference in social and political conditions, and our respective methods of moral and practical development the last hundred years;—and yet in certain features, and vastest ones, so resembling each other. The variety of stock-elements and tongues, to be resolutely fused in a common identity and union at all hazards—the idea, perennial through the ages, that they both have their historic and divine mission—the fervent element of manly friendship throughout the whole people, surpass'd by no other races—the grand expanse of territorial limits and boundaries—the unform'd and nebulous state of many things, not yet permanently settled, but agreed on all hands to be the preparations of an infinitely greater future—the fact that both Peoples have their independent and leading positions to hold, keep, and if necessary, fight for, against the rest of the world—the deathless aspirations at the inmost centre of each great community, so vehement, so mysterious, so abysmic—are certainly features you Russians and we Americans possess in common.

As my dearest dream is for an internationality of poems and poets, binding the lands of the earth closer than all treaties and diplomacy—As the purpose beneath the rest in my book is such hearty comradeship, for individuals to begin with, and for all the nations of the earth as a result—how happy I should be to get the hearing and emotional contact of the great Russian peoples.

To whom, now and here, (addressing you for Russia and Russians, and empowering you, should you see fit, to print the present letter, in your book, as a preface,) I waft affectionate salutation from these shores, in America's name. W.W.

Notes Left Over

Nationality—(And Yet)

It is more and more clear to me that the main sustenance for highest separate personality, these States, is to come from that general sustenance of the aggregate, (as air, earth, rains, give sustenance to a tree)—and that such personality, by democratic standards, will only be fully coherent, grand and free, through the cohesion, grandeur and freedom of the common aggregate, the Union. Thus the existence of the true American continental solidarity of the future, depending on myriads of superb, large-sized, emotional and physically perfect individualities, of one sex just as much as the other, the supply of such individualities, in my opinion, wholly depends on a compacted imperial ensemble. The theory and practice of both sovereignties, contradictory as they are, are necessary. As the centripetal law were fatal alone, or the centrifugal law deadly and destructive alone, but together forming the law of eternal kosmical action, evolution, preservation, and life—so, by itself alone, the fullness of individuality, even the sanest, would surely destroy itself. This is what makes the importance to the identities of these States of the thoroughly fused, relentless, dominating Union—a moral and spiritual idea, subjecting all the parts with remorseless power, more needed by American democracy than by any of history's hitherto empires or feudalities, and the *sine qua non* of carrying out the republican principle to develop itself in the New World through hundreds, thousands of years to come.

Indeed, what most needs fostering through the hundred years to come, in all parts of the United States, north, south, Mississippi valley, and Atlantic and Pacific coasts, is this fused and fervent identity of the individual, whoever he or she may be, and wherever the place, with the idea and fact of American totality, and with what is meant by the Flag, the stars and stripes. We need this conviction of nationality as a faith, to be absorb'd in the blood and belief of the people everywhere, south, north, west, east, to emanate in their life, and in native literature and art. We want the germinal idea that America, inheritor of the past, is the custodian of the future of humanity. Judging from history, it is some such moral and spiritual ideas appropriate to them, (and such ideas only,) that have made the profoundest glory and endurance of nations in the past. The races of Judea, the classic clusters of Greece and Rome, and the feudal and ecclesiastical clusters of the Middle Ages, were each and all vitalized by their separate distinctive ideas, ingrain'd in them, redeeming many sins, and indeed, in a sense, the principal reason why for their whole career.

Then, in the thought of nationality especially for the United States, and making them original, and different from all other countries, another point ever remains to be considered. There are two distinct principles—aye, paradoxes—at the life-fountain and life-continuation of the States; one, the sacred principle of the Union, the right of ensemble, at whatever sacrifice—and yet another, an equally sacred principle, the right of each State, consider'd as a separate sovereign individual, in its own sphere. Some go zealously for one set of these rights, and some as zealously for the other set. We must have both; or rather, bred out of them, as out of mother and father, a third set, the perennial result and combination of both, and neither jeopardized. I say the loss or abdication of one set, in the future, will be ruin to democracy just as much as the loss of the other set. The problem is, to harmoniously adjust the two, and the play of the two. [Observe the lesson of the divinity of Nature, ever checking the excess of one law, by an opposite, or seemingly opposite law—generally the other side of the same law.] For the theory of this Republic is, not that the General government is the fountain of all life and power, dispensing it forth, around, and to the remotest portions of our territory, but that THE PEOPLE are, represented in both, underlying both the General and State governments, and consider'd just as well in their individualities and in their separate aggregates, or States, as consider'd in one vast aggregate, the Union. This was the original dual theory and foundation of the United States, as distinguish'd from the feudal and ecclesiastical single idea of monarchies and papacies, and the divine right of kings. (Kings have been of use, hitherto, as representing the idea of the identity of nations. But, to American democracy, *both* ideas must be fulfill'd, and in my opinion the loss of vitality of either one will indeed be the loss of vitality of the other.)

Emerson's Books, (The Shadows of Them)

In the regions we call Nature, towering beyond all measurement, with infinite spread, infinite depth and height—in those regions, including Man, socially and historically, with his moral-emotional influences—how small a part, (it came in my mind to-day,) has literature really depicted—even summing up all of it, all ages. Seems at its best some little fleet of boats, hugging the shores of a boundless sea, and never venturing, exploring the unmapp'd—never, Columbus-like, sailing out for New Worlds, and to complete the orb's rondure. Emerson writes frequently in the atmosphere of this thought, and his books report one or two things from that very ocean and air, and more legibly address'd to our age and American polity than by any man yet. But I will begin by scarifying him—thus proving that I am not insensible to his deepest lessons. I will consider his books from a democratic and western point of view. I will specify the shadows on these sunny expanses. Somebody has said of heroic character that "wherever the tallest peaks are present, must inevitably be deep chasms and valleys." Mine be the ungracious task (for reasons) of leaving unmention'd both sunny expanses and sky-reaching heights, to dwell on the bare spots and darknesses. I have a theory that no artist or work of the very first class may be or can be without them.

First, then, these pages are perhaps too perfect, too concentrated. (How good, for instance, is good butter, good sugar. But to be eating nothing but sugar and butter all the time! even if ever so good.) And though the author has much to say of freedom and wildness and simplicity and spontaneity, no performance was ever more based on artificial scholarships and decorums at third or fourth removes, (he calls it culture,) and built up from them. It is always a *make*, never an unconscious *growth*. It is the porcelain figure or statuette of lion, or stag, or Indian hunter—and a very choice statuette too—appropriate for the rosewood or marble bracket of parlor or library; never the animal itself, or the hunter himself. Indeed, who wants the real animal or hunter? What would that do amid astral and bric-a-brac and tapestry, and ladies and gentlemen talking in subdued tones of Browning and Longfellow and art? The least suspicion of such actual bull, or Indian, or of Nature carrying out itself, would put all those good people to instant terror and flight.

Emerson, in my opinion, is not most eminent as poet or artist or teacher, though valuable in all those. He is best as critic, or diagnoser. Not passion or imagination or warp or weakness, or any pronounced cause or specialty, dominates him. Cold and bloodless intellectuality dominates him. (I know the fires, emotions, love, egotisms, glow deep, perennial, as in all New Englanders—but the façade hides them well—they give no sign.) He does not see or take one side, one presentation only or mainly, (as all the poets, or most of the fine writers anyhow)—he sees all sides. His final influence is to make his students cease to worship anything—almost cease to believe in anything, outside of themselves. These books will fill, and well fill, certain stretches of life, certain stages of development—are, (like the tenets or theology the author of them preach'd when a young man,) unspeakably serviceable and precious as a stage. But in old or nervous or solemnest or dying hours, when one needs the impalpably soothing and vitalizing influences of abysmic Nature, or its affinities in literature or human society, and the soul resents the keenest mere intellection, they will not be sought for.

For a philosopher, Emerson possesses a singularly dandified theory of manners. He seems to have no notion at all that manners are simply the signs by which the chemist or metallurgist knows his metals. To the profound scientist, all metals are profound, as they really are. The little one, like the conventional world, will make much of gold and silver only. Then to the real artist in humanity, what are called bad manners are often the most picturesque and significant of all. Suppose these books becoming absorb'd, the permanent chyle of American general and particular character—what a well-wash'd and grammatical, but bloodless and helpless, race we should turn out! No, no, dear friend; though the States want scholars, undoubtedly, and perhaps want ladies and gentlemen who use the bath frequently, and never laugh loud, or talk wrong, they don't want scholars, or ladies and gentlemen, at the expense of all the rest. They want good farmers, sailors, mechanics, clerks, citizens—perfect business and social relations—perfect fathers and mothers. If we could only have these, or their approximations, plenty of them, fine and large and sane and generous and patriotic, they might make their verbs disagree from their nominatives, and laugh like volleys of musketeers, if they should please. Of course these are not all America wants, but they are first of all to be provided on a large scale. And, with tremendous errors and escapades, this, substantially, is what the States seem to have an intuition of, and to be mainly aiming at. The plan of a select class, superfined, (demarcated from the rest,) the plan of Old World lands and literatures, is not so objectionable in itself, but because it chokes the true plan for us, and indeed is death to it. As to such special class, the United States can never produce any equal to the splendid show, (far, far beyond comparison or competition here,) of the principal European nations, both in the past and at the present day. But an immense and distinctive commonalty over our vast and varied area, west and east, south and north—in fact, for the first time in history, a great, aggregated, real PEOPLE, worthy the name, and made of develop'd heroic individuals, both sexes—is America's principal, perhaps only, reason for being. If ever accomplish'd, it will be at least as much, (I lately think, doubly as much,) the result of fitting and democratic sociologies, literatures and arts—if we ever get them—as of our democratic politics.

At times it has been doubtful to me if Emerson really knows or feels what Poetry is at its highest, as in the Bible, for instance, or Homer or Shakspere. I see he covertly or plainly likes best superb verbal polish, or something old or odd—Waller's "Go, lovely rose," or Lovelace's lines "to Lucasta"—the quaint conceits of the old French bards, and the like. Of *power* he seems to have a gentleman's admiration—but in his inmost heart the grandest attribute of God and

Poets is always subordinate to the octaves, conceits, polite kinks, and verbs.

The reminiscence that years ago I began like most youngsters to have a touch (though it came late, and was only on the surface) of Emerson-on-the-brain—that I read his writings reverently, and address'd him in print as "Master," and for a month or so thought of him as such—I retain not only with composure, but positive satisfaction. I have noticed that most young people of eager minds pass through this stage of exercise.

The best part of Emersonianism is, it breeds the giant that destroys itself. Who wants to be any man's mere follower? lurks behind every page. No teacher ever taught, that has so provided for his pupil's setting up independently—no truer evolutionist.

Ventures, on an Old Theme

A Dialogue—*One party says*—We arrange our lives—even the best and boldest men and women that exist, just as much as the most limited—with reference to what society conventionally rules and makes right. We retire to our rooms for freedom; to undress, bathe, unloose everything in freedom. These, and much else, would not be proper in society.

Other party answers—Such is the rule of society. Not always so, and considerable exceptions still exist. However, it must be called the general rule, sanction'd by immemorial usage, and will probably always remain so.

First party—Why not, then, respect it in your poems?

Answer—One reason, and to me a profound one, is that the soul of a man or woman demands, enjoys compensation in the highest directions for this very restraint of himself or herself, level'd to the average, or rather mean, low, however eternally practical, requirements of society's intercourse. To balance this indispensable abnegation, the free minds of poets relieve themselves, and strengthen and enrich mankind with free flights in all the directions not tolerated by ordinary society.

First party—But must not outrage or give offence to it.

Answer—No, not in the deepest sense—and do not, and

cannot. The vast averages of time and the race *en masse* settle these things. Only understand that the conventional standards and laws proper enough for ordinary society apply neither to the action of the soul, nor its poets. In fact the latter know no laws but the laws of themselves, planted in them by God, and are themselves the last standards of the law, and its final exponents—responsible to Him directly, and not at all to mere etiquette. Often the best service that can be done to the race, is to lift the veil, at least for a time, from these rules and fossil-etiquettes.

NEW POETRY—*California, Canada, Texas*—In my opinion the time has arrived to essentially break down the barriers of form between prose and poetry. I say the latter is henceforth to win and maintain its character regardless of rhyme, and the measurement-rules of iambic, spondee, dactyl, &c., and that even if rhyme and those measurements continue to furnish the medium for inferior writers and themes, (especially for persiflage and the comic, as there seems henceforward, to the perfect taste, something inevitably comic in rhyme, merely in itself, and anyhow,) the truest and greatest *Poetry,* (while subtly and necessarily always rhythmic, and distinguishable easily enough,) can never again, in the English language, be express'd in arbitrary and rhyming metre, any more than the greatest eloquence, or the truest power and passion. While admitting that the venerable and heavenly forms of chiming versification have in their time play'd great and fitting parts—that the pensive complaint, the ballads, wars, amours, legends of Europe, &c., have, many of them, been inimitably render'd in rhyming verse—that there have been very illustrious poets whose shapes the mantle of such verse has beautifully and appropriately envelopt—and though the mantle has fallen, with perhaps added beauty, on some of our own age—it is, notwithstanding, certain to me, that the day of such conventional rhyme is ended. In America, at any rate, and as a medium of highest æsthetic practical or spiritual expression, present or future, it palpably fails, and must fail, to serve. The Muse of the Prairies, of California, Canada, Texas, and of the peaks of Colorado, dismissing the literary, as well as social etiquette of over-sea feudalism and caste, joyfully enlarging, adapting itself to comprehend the size of the whole people, with the free play, emotions, pride, passions, experiences, that belong to them, body and soul—to the general globe, and all its relations in astronomy, as the savans portray them to us—to the modern, the busy Nineteenth century, (as grandly poetic as any, only different,) with steamships, railroads, factories, electric telegraphs, cylinder presses—to the thought of the solidarity of nations, the brotherhood and sisterhood of the entire earth—to the dignity and heroism of the practical labor of farms, factories, foundries, workshops, mines, or on shipboard, or on lakes and rivers—resumes that other medium of expression, more flexible, more eligible—soars to the freer, vast, diviner heaven of prose.

Of poems of the third or fourth class, (perhaps even some of the second,) it makes little or no difference who writes them—they are good enough for what they are; nor is it necessary that they should be actual emanations from the personality and life of the writers. The very reverse sometimes gives piquancy. But poems of the first class, (poems of the depth, as distinguished from those of the surface,) are to be sternly tallied with the poets themselves, and tried by them and their lives. Who wants a glorification of courage and manly defiance from a coward or a sneak?—a ballad of benevolence or chastity from some rhyming hunks, or lascivious, glib *roué*?

In these States, beyond all precedent, poetry will have to do with actual facts, with the concrete States, and—for we have not much more than begun—with the definitive getting into shape of the Union. Indeed I sometimes think *it* alone is to define the Union, (namely, to give it artistic character, spirituality, dignity.) What American humanity is most in danger of is an overwhelming prosperity, "business" worldliness, materialism: what is most lacking, east, west, north, south, is a fervid and glowing Nationality and patriotism, cohering all the parts into one. Who may fend that danger, and fill that lack in the future, but a class of loftiest poets?

If the United States havn't grown poets, on any scale of grandeur, it is certain they import, print, and read more poetry than any equal number of people elsewhere—probably more than all the rest of the world combined.

Poetry (like a grand personality) is a growth of many generations—many rare combinations.

To have great poets, there must be great audiences, too.

British Literature

To avoid mistake, I would say that I not only commend the study of this literature, but wish our sources of supply and comparison vastly enlarged. American students may well derive from all former lands—from forenoon Greece and Rome, down to the perturb'd medieval times, the Crusades, and so to Italy, the German intellect—all the older literatures, and all the newer ones—from witty and warlike France, and markedly, and in many ways, and at many different periods, from the enterprise and soul of the great Spanish race—bearing ourselves always courteous, always deferential, indebted beyond measure to the mother-world, to all its nations dead, as all its nations living—the offspring, this America of ours, the daughter, not by any means of the British isles exclusively, but of the continent, and all continents. Indeed, it is time we should realize and fully fructify those germs we also hold from Italy, France, Spain, especially in the best imaginative productions of those lands, which are, in many ways, loftier and subtler than the English, or British, and indispensable to complete our service, proportions, education, reminiscences, &c. . . . The British element these States hold, and have always held, enormously beyond its fit proportions. I have already spoken of Shakspere. He seems to me of astral genius, first class, entirely fit for feudalism. His contributions, especially to the literature of the passions, are immense, forever dear to humanity—and his name is always to be reverenced in America. But there is much in him ever offensive to democracy. He is not only the tally of feudalism, but I should say Shakspere is incarnated, uncompromising feudalism, in literature. Then one seems to detect something in him—I hardly know how to describe it—even amid the dazzle of his genius; and, in inferior manifestations, it is found in nearly all leading British authors. (Perhaps we will have to import the words Snob, Snobbish, &c., after all.) While of the great poems of Asian antiquity, the Indian epics, the book of Job, the Ionian

Iliad, the unsurpassedly simple, loving, perfect idyls of the life and death of Christ, in the New Testament, (indeed Homer and the Biblical utterances intertwine familiarly with us, in the main,) and along down, of most of the characteristic, imaginative or romantic relics of the continent, as the Cid, Cervantes' Don Quixote, &c., I should say they substantially adjust themselves to us, and, far off as they are, accord curiously with our bed and board to-day, in New York, Washington, Canada, Ohio, Texas, California—and with our notions, both of seriousness and of fun, and our standards of heroism, manliness, and even the democratic requirements—those requirements are not only not fulfilled in the Shaksperean productions, but are insulted on every page.

I add that—while England is among the greatest of lands in political freedom, or the idea of it, and in stalwart personal character, &c.—the spirit of English literature is not great, at least is not greatest—and its products are no models for us. With the exception of Shakspere, there is no first-class genius in that literature—which, with a truly vast amount of value, and of artificial beauty, (largely from the classics,) is almost always material, sensual, not spiritual—almost always congests, makes plethoric, not frees, expands, dilates—is cold, anti-democratic, loves to be sluggish and stately, and shows much of that characteristic of vulgar persons, the dread of saying or doing something not at all improper in itself, but unconventional, and that may be laugh'd at. In its best, the sombre pervades it; it is moody, melancholy, and, to give it its due, expresses, in characters and plots, those qualities, in an unrival'd manner. Yet not as the black thunder-storms, and in great normal, crashing passions, of the Greek dramatists—clearing the air, refreshing afterward, bracing with power; but as in Hamlet, moping, sick, uncertain, and leaving ever after a secret taste for the blues, the morbid fascination, the luxury of wo. . . .

I strongly recommend all the young men and young women of the United States to whom it may be eligible, to overhaul the well-freighted fleets, the literatures of Italy, Spain, France, Germany, so full of those elements of freedom, self-possession, gay-heartedness, subtlety, dilation, needed in preparations for the future of the States. I only wish we could have really good translations. I rejoice at the feeling for Oriental researches and poetry, and hope it will go on.

Darwinism—(Then Furthermore)

Running through prehistoric ages—coming down from them into the daybreak of our records, founding theology, suffusing literature, and so brought onward—(a sort of verteber and marrow to all the antique races and lands, Egypt, India, Greece, Rome, the Chinese, the Jews, &c., and giving cast and complexion to their art, poems, and their politics as well as ecclesiasticism, all of which we more or less inherit,) appear those venerable claims to origin from God himself, or from gods and goddesses—ancestry from divine beings of vaster beauty, size, and power than ours. But in current and latest times, the theory of human origin that seems to have most made its mark, (curiously reversing the antique,) is that we have come on, originated, developt, from monkeys, baboons—a theory more significant perhaps in its indirections, or what it necessitates, than it is even in itself. (Of the twain, far apart as they seem, and angrily as their conflicting advocates to-day oppose each other, are not both theories to be possibly reconciled, and even blended? Can we, indeed, spare either of them? Better still, out of them is not a third theory, the real one, or suggesting the real one, to arise?)

Of this old theory, evolution, as broach'd anew, trebled, with indeed all-devouring claims, by Darwin, it has so much in it, and is so needed as a counterpoise to yet widely prevailing and unspeakably tenacious, enfeebling superstitions—is fused, by the new man, into such grand, modest, truly scientific accompaniments—that the world of erudition, both moral and physical, cannot but be eventually better'd and broaden'd in its speculations, from the advent of Darwinism. Nevertheless, the problem of origins, human and other, is not the least whit nearer its solution. In due time the Evolution theory will have to abate its vehemence, cannot be allow'd to dominate every thing else, and will have to take its place as a segment of the circle, the cluster—as but one of many theories, many thoughts, of profoundest value—and re-adjusting and differentiating much, yet leaving the divine secrets just as inexplicable and unreachable as before—may-be more so.

Then furthermore—What is finally to be done by priest or poet—and by priest or poet only—amid all the stupendous and dazzling novelties of our century, with the advent of America, and of science and democracy—remains just as indispensable, after all the work of the grand astronomers, chemists, linguists, historians, and explorers of the last hundred years—and the wondrous German and other metaphysicians of that time—and will continue to remain, needed, America and here, just the same as in the world of Europe, or Asia, of a hundred, or a thousand, or several thousand years ago. I think indeed *more* needed, to furnish statements from the present points, the added arriere, and the unspeakably immenser vistas of to-day. Only the priests and poets of the modern, at least as exalted as any in the past, fully absorbing and appreciating the results of the past, in the commonalty of all humanity, all time, (the main results already, for there is perhaps nothing more, or at any rate not much, strictly new, only more important modern combinations, and new relative adjustments,) must indeed recast the old metal, the already achiev'd material, into and through new moulds, current forms.

Meantime, the highest and subtlest and broadest truths of modern science wait for their true assignment and last vivid flashes of light—as Democracy waits for it's—through first-class metaphysicians and speculative philosophs—laying the basements and foundations for those new, more expanded, more harmonious, more melodious, freer American poems.

"Society"

I have myself little or no hope from what is technically called "Society" in our American cities. New York, of which place I have spoken so sharply, still promises something, in time, out of its tremendous and varied materials, with a certain superiority of intuitions, and the advantage of constant agitation, and ever new and rapid dealings of the cards. Of Boston, with its circles of social mummies, swathed in cerements harder than brass—its bloodless religion, (Unitarianism,) its complacent vanity of scientism and literature, lots of grammatical correctness, mere knowledge, (always wearisome, in itself)—its zealous abstractions, ghosts of reforms—I should say, (ever admitting its business powers, its sharp, almost demoniac, intellect, and no lack, in its own way, of courage and generosity)—there is, at present, little of cheering, satisfying sign. In the West, California, &c., "society" is yet unform'd, puerile, seemingly unconscious of anything above a driving business, or to liberally spend the money made by it, in the usual rounds and shows.

Then there is, to the humorous observer of American attempts at fashion, according to the models of foreign courts and saloons, quite a comic side—particularly visible at Washington city—a sort of high-life-below-stairs business. As if any farce could be funnier, for instance, than the scenes of the crowds, winter nights, meandering around our Presidents and their wives, cabinet officers, western or other Senators, Representatives, &c.; born of good laboring mechanic or farmer stock and antecedents, attempting those full-dress receptions, finesse of parlors, foreign ceremonies, etiquettes, &c.

Indeed, consider'd with any sense of propriety, or any sense at all, the whole of this illy-play'd fashionable play and display, with their absorption of the best part of our wealthier citizens' time, money, energies, &c., is ridiculously out of place in the United States. As if our proper man and woman, (far, far greater words than "gentleman" and "lady,") could still fail to see, and presently achieve, not this spectral business, but something truly noble, active, sane, American—by modes, perfections of character, manners, costumes, social relations, &c., adjusted to standards, far, far different from those.

Eminent and liberal foreigners, British or continental, must at times have their faith fearfully tried by what they see of our New World personalities. The shallowest and least American persons seem surest to push abroad, and call without fail on well-known foreigners, who are doubtless affected with indescribable qualms by these queer ones. Then, more than half of our authors and writers evidently think it a great thing to be "aristocratic," and sneer at progress, democracy, revolution, &c. If some international literary snobs' gallery were establish'd, it is certain that America could contribute at least her full share of the portraits, and some very distinguish'd ones. Observe that the most impudent slanders, low insults, &c., on the great revolutionary authors, leaders, poets, &c., of Europe, have their origin and main circulation in certain circles here. The treatment of Victor Hugo living, and Byron dead, are samples. Both deserving so well of America, and both persistently attempted to be soil'd here by unclean birds, male and female.

Meanwhile I must still offset the like of the foregoing, and all it infers, by the recognition of the fact, that while the surfaces of current society here show so much that is dismal, noisome, and vapory, there are, beyond question, inexhaustible supplies, as of true gold ore, in the mines of America's general humanity. Let us, not ignoring the dross, give fit stress to these precious immortal values also. Let it be distinctly admitted, that—whatever may be said of our fashionable society, and of any foul fractions and episodes—only here in America, out of the long history and manifold presentations of the ages, has at last arisen, and now stands, what never before took positive form and sway, *the People*—and that view'd en masse, and while fully acknowledging deficiencies, dangers, faults, this people, inchoate, latent, not yet come to majority, nor to its own religious, literary, or æsthetic expression, yet affords, to-day, an exultant justification of all the faith, all the hopes and prayers and prophecies of good men through the past—the stablest, solidest-based government of the world—the most assured in a future—the beaming Pharos to whose perennial light all earnest eyes, the world over, are tending—and that already, in and from it, the democratic principle, having been mortally tried by severest tests, fatalities of war and peace, now issues from the trial, unharm'd, trebly-invigorated, perhaps to commence forthwith its finally triumphant march around the globe.

The Tramp and Strike Questions

Part of a Lecture proposed, (never deliver'd.)

Two grim and spectral dangers—dangerous to peace, to health, to social security, to progress—long known in concrete to the governments of the Old World, and there eventuating, more than once or twice, in dynastic overturns, bloodshed, days, months, of terror—seem of late years to be nearing the New World, nay, to be gradually establishing themselves among us. What mean these phantoms here? (I personify them in fictitious shapes, but they are very real.) Is the fresh and broad demesne of America destined also to give them foot-hold and lodgment, permanent domicile?

Beneath the whole political world, what most presses and perplexes to-day, sending vastest results affecting the future, is not the abstract question of democracy, but of social and economic organization, the treatment of working-people by employers, and all that goes along with it—not only the wages-payment part, but a certain spirit and principle, to vivify anew these relations; all the questions of progress, strength, tariffs, finance, &c., really evolving themselves more or less directly out of the Poverty Question, ("the Science of Wealth," and a dozen other names are given it, but I prefer the severe one just used.) I will begin by calling the reader's attention to a thought upon the matter which may not have struck you before—the wealth of the civilized world, as contrasted with its poverty—what does it derivatively stand for, and represent? A rich person ought to have a strong stomach. As in Europe the wealth of to-day mainly results from, and represents, the rapine, murder, outrages, treachery, hoggishness, of hundreds of years ago, and onward, later, so in America, after the same token—(not yet so bad, perhaps, or at any rate not so palpable—we have not existed long enough—but we seem to be doing our best to make it up.)

Curious as it may seem, it is in what are call'd the poorest, lowest characters you will sometimes, nay generally, find glints of the most sublime virtues, eligibilities, heroisms. Then it is doubtful whether the State is to be saved, either in the monotonous long run, or in tremendous special crises, by its good people only. When the storm is deadliest, and the disease most imminent, help often comes from strange quarters—(the homœopathic motto, you remember, *cure the bite with a hair of the same dog.*)

The American Revolution of 1776 was simply a great strike, successful for its immediate object—but whether a real success judged by the scale of the centuries, and the long-striking balance of Time, yet remains to be settled. The French Revolution was absolutely a strike, and a very terrible and relentless one, against ages of bad pay, unjust division of wealth-products, and the hoggish monopoly of a few, rolling in superfluity, against the vast bulk of the work-people, living in squalor.

If the United States, like the countries of the Old World, are also to grow vast crops of poor, desperate, dissatisfied, nomadic, miserably-waged populations, such as we see looming upon us of late years—steadily, even if slowly, eating into them like a cancer of lungs or stomach—then our republican experiment, notwithstanding all its surface-successes, is at heart an unhealthy failure.

Feb., '79.—I saw to-day a sight I had never seen before—and it amazed, and made me serious; three quite good-looking American men, of respectable personal presence, two of them young, carrying chiffonier-bags on their shoulders, and the usual long iron hooks in their hands, plodding along, their eyes cast down, spying for scraps, rags, bones, &c.

Democracy in the New World,

estimated and summ'd-up to-day, having thoroughly justified itself the past hundred years, (as far as growth, vitality and power are concern'd,) by severest and most varied trials of peace and war, and having establish'd itself for good, with all its necessities and benefits, for time to come, is now to be seriously consider'd also in its pronounc'd and already develop't dangers. While the battle was raging, and the result suspended, all defections and criticisms were to be hush'd, and everything bent with vehemence unmitigated toward the urge of victory. But that victory settled, new responsibilities advance. I can conceive of no better service in the United States, henceforth, by democrats of thorough and heart-felt faith, than boldly exposing the weakness, liabilities and infinite corruptions of democracy. By the unprecedented opening-up of humanity en-masse in the United States, the last hundred years, under our institutions, not only the good qualities of the race, but just as much the bad ones, are prominently brought forward. Man is about the same, in the main, whether with despotism, or whether with freedom.

"The ideal form of human society," Canon Kingsley declares, "is democracy. A nation—and were it even possible, a whole world—of free men, lifting free foreheads to God and Nature; calling no man master, for One is their master, even God; knowing and doing their duties toward the Maker of the universe, and therefore to each other; not from fear, nor calculation of profit or loss, but because they have seen the beauty of righteousness, and trust, and peace; because the law of God is in their hearts. Such a nation—such a society—what nobler conception of moral existence can we form? Would not that, indeed, be the kingdom of God come on earth?"

To this faith, founded in the ideal, let us hold—and never abandon or lose it. Then what a spectacle is *practically* exhibited by our American democracy to-day!

Foundation Stages—Then Others

Though I think I fully comprehend the absence of moral tone in our current politics and business, and the almost entire futility of absolute and simple honor as a counterpoise against the enormous greed for worldly wealth, with the trickeries of gaining it, all through society our day, I still do not share the depression and despair on the subject which I find possessing many good people. The advent of America, the history of the past century, has been the first general aperture and opening-up to the average human commonalty, on the broadest scale, of the eligibilities to wealth and worldly success and eminence, and has been fully taken advantage of; and the example has spread hence, in ripples, to all nations. To these eligibilities—to this limitless aperture, the race has tended, en-masse, roaring and rushing and crude, and fiercely, turbidly hastening—and we have seen the first stages, and are now in the midst of the result of it all, so far. But there will certainly ensue other stages, and entirely different ones. In nothing is there more evolution than the American mind. Soon, it will be fully realized that ostensible wealth and money-making, show, luxury, &c., imperatively necessitate something beyond—namely, the sane, eternal moral and spiritual-esthetic attributes, elements. (We cannot have even that realization on any less terms than the price we are now paying for it.) Soon, it will be understood clearly, that the State cannot flourish, (nay, cannot exist,) without those elements. They will gradually enter into the chyle of sociology and literature. They will finally make the blood and brawn of the best American individualities of both sexes—and thus, with them, to a certainty, (through these very processes of to-day,) dominate the New World.

General Suffrage, Elections, &c.

It still remains doubtful to me whether these will ever secure, officially, the best wit and capacity—whether, through them, the first-class genius of America will ever personally appear in the high political stations, the Presidency, Congress, the leading State offices, &c. Those offices, or the candidacy for them, arranged, won, by caucusing, money, the favoritism or pecuniary interest of rings, the superior manipulation of the ins over the outs, or the outs over the ins, are, indeed, at best, the mere business agencies of the people, are useful as formulating, neither the best and highest, but the average of the public judgment, sense, justice, (or sometimes want of judgment, sense, justice.) We elect Presidents, Congressmen, &c., not so much to have them consider and decide for us, but as surest practical means of expressing the will of majorities on mooted questions, measures, &c.

As to general suffrage, after all, since we have gone so far, the more general it is, the better. I favor the widest opening of the doors. Let the ventilation and area be wide enough, and all is safe. We can never have a born penitentiary-bird, or panel-thief, or lowest gambling-hell or groggery keeper, for President—though such may not only emulate, but get, high offices from localities—even from the proud and wealthy city of New York.

Who Gets the Plunder?

The protectionists are fond of flashing to the public eye the glittering delusion of great money-results from manufactures, mines, artificial exports—so many millions from this source, and so many from that—such a seductive, unanswerable show—an immense revenue of annual cash from iron, cotton, woollen, leather goods, and a hundred other things, all bolstered up by "protection." But the really important point of all is, *into whose pockets does this plunder really go?* It would be some excuse and satisfaction if even a fair proportion of it went to the masses of laboring-men—resulting in homesteads to such, men, women, children—myriads of actual homes in fee simple, in every State, (not the false glamour of the stunning wealth reported in the census, in the statistics, or tables in the newspapers,) but a fair division and generous average to those workmen and workwomen—*that* would be something. But the fact itself is nothing of the kind. The profits of "protection" go altogether to a few score select persons—who, by favors of Congress, State legislatures, the banks, and other special advantages, are forming a vulgar aristocracy, full as bad as anything in the British or European castes, of blood, or the dynasties there of the past. As Sismondi pointed out, the true prosperity of a nation is not in the great wealth of a special class, but is only to be really attain'd in having the bulk of the people provided with homes or land in fee simple. This may not be the best show, but it is the best reality.

Friendship, (The Real Article)

Though Nature maintains, and must prevail, there will always be plenty of people, and good people, who cannot, or think they cannot, see anything in that last, wisest, most envelop'd of proverbs, "Friendship rules the World." Modern society, in its largest vein, is essentially intellectual, infidelistic—secretly admires, and depends most on, pure compulsion or science, its rule and sovereignty—is, in short, in "cultivated" quarters, deeply Napoleonic.

"Friendship," said Bonaparte, in one of his lightning-flashes of candid garrulity, "Friendship is but a name. I love no one—not even my brothers; Joseph perhaps a little. Still, if I do love him, it is from habit, because he is the eldest of us. Duroc? Ay, him, if any one, I love in a sort—but why? He suits me;

he is cool, undemonstrative, unfeeling—has no weak affections—never embraces any one—never weeps."

I am not sure but the same analogy is to be applied, in cases, often seen, where, with an extra development and acuteness of the intellectual faculties, there is a mark'd absence of the spiritual, affectional, and sometimes, though more rarely, the highest æsthetic and moral elements of cognition.

Lacks and Wants Yet

Of most foreign countries, small or large, from the remotest times known, down to our own, each has contributed after its kind, directly or indirectly, at least one great undying song, to help vitalize and increase the valor, wisdom, and elegance of humanity, from the points of view attain'd by it up to date. The stupendous epics of India, the holy Bible itself, the Homeric canticles, the Nibelungen, the Cid Campeador, the Inferno, Shakspere's dramas of the passions and of the feudal lords, Burns's songs, Goethe's in Germany, Tennyson's poems in England, Victor Hugo's in France, and many more, are the widely various yet integral signs or land-marks, (in certain respects the highest set up by the human mind and soul, beyond science, invention, political amelioration, &c.,) narrating in subtlest, best ways, the long, long routes of history, and giving identity to the stages arrived at by aggregate humanity, and the conclusions assumed in its progressive and varied civilizations. . . . Where is America's art-rendering, in any thing like the spirit worthy of herself and the modern, to these characteristic immortal monuments? So far, our Democratic society, (estimating its various strata, in the mass, as one,) possesses nothing—nor have we contributed any characteristic music, the finest tie of nationality—to make up for that glowing, blood-throbbing, religious, social, emotional, artistic, indefinable, indescribably beautiful charm and hold which fused the separate parts of the old feudal societies together, in their wonderful interpenetration, in Europe and Asia, of love, belief, and loyalty, running one way like a living weft—and picturesque responsibility, duty, and blessedness, running like a warp the other way. (In the Southern States, under slavery, much of the same.) . . . In coincidence, and as things now exist in the States, what is more terrible, more alarming, than the total want of any such fusion and mutuality of love, belief, and rapport of interest, between the comparatively few successful rich, and the great masses of the unsuccessful, the poor? As a mixed political and social question, is not this full of dark significance? Is it not worth considering as a problem and puzzle in our democracy—an indispensable want to be supplied?

Rulers Strictly Out of the Masses

In the talk (which I welcome) about the need of men of training, thoroughly school'd and experienced men, for statesmen, I would present the following as an offset. It was written by me twenty years ago—and has been curiously verified since:

I say no body of men are fit to make Presidents, Judges, and Generals, unless they themselves supply the best specimens of the same; and that supplying one or two such specimens illuminates the whole body for a thousand years. I expect to see the day when the like of the present personnel of the governments, Federal, State, municipal, military, and naval, will be look'd upon with derision, and when qualified mechanics and young men will reach Congress and other official stations, sent in their working costumes, fresh from their benches and tools, and returning to them again with dignity. The young fellows must prepare to do credit to this destiny, for the stuff is in them. Nothing gives place, recollect, and never ought to give place, except to its clean superiors. There is more rude and undevelopt bravery, friendship, conscientiousness, clear-sightedness, and practical genius for any scope of action, even the broadest and highest, now among the American mechanics and young men, than in all the official persons in these States, legislative, executive, judicial, military, and naval, and more than among all the literary persons. I would be much pleased to see some heroic, shrewd, fully-inform'd, healthy-bodied, middle-aged, beard-faced American blacksmith or boatman come down from the West across the Alleghanies, and walk into the Presidency, dress'd in a clean suit of working attire, and with the tan all over his face, breast, and arms; I would certainly vote for that sort of man, possessing the due requirements, before any other candidate.

(The facts of rank-and-file workingmen, mechanics, Lincoln, Johnson, Grant, Garfield, brought forward from the masses and placed in the Presidency, and swaying its mighty powers with firm hand—really with more sway than any king in history, and with better capacity in using that sway—can we not see that these facts have bearings far, far beyond their political or party ones?)

Monuments—The Past and Present

If you go to Europe, (to say nothing of Asia, more ancient and massive still,) you cannot stir without meeting venerable mementos—cathedrals, ruins of temples, castles, monuments of the great, statues and paintings, (far, far beyond anything America can ever expect to produce,) haunts of heroes long dead, saints, poets, divinities, with deepest associations of ages. But here in the New World, while *those* we can never emulate, we have *more* than those to build, and far more greatly to build. (I am not sure but the day for conventional monuments, statues, memorials, &c., has pass'd away—and that they are henceforth superfluous and vulgar.) An enlarged general superior humanity, (partly indeed resulting from those,) we are to build. European, Asiatic greatness are in the past. Vaster and subtler, America, combining, justifying the past, yet works for a grander future, in living democratic forms. (Here too are indicated the paths for our national bards.) Other times, other lands, have had their missions—Art, War, Ecclesiasticism, Literature, Discovery, Trade, Architecture, &c., &c.—but that grand future is the enclosing purport of the United States.

Little or Nothing New, After All

How small were the best thoughts, poems, conclusions, except for a certain invariable resemblance and uniform standard in the final thoughts, theology, poems, &c., of all nations, all civilizations, all centuries and times. Those precious legacies—accumulations! They come to us from the far-off—

from all eras, and all lands—from Egypt, and India, and Greece, and Rome—and along through the middle and later ages, in the grand monarchies of Europe—born under far different institutes and conditions from ours—but out of the insight and inspiration of the same old humanity—the same old heart and brain—the same old countenance yearningly, pensively, looking forth. What we have to do to-day is to receive them cheerfully, and to give them ensemble, and a modern American and democratic physiognomy.

A Lincoln Reminiscence

As is well known, story-telling was often with President Lincoln a weapon which he employ'd with great skill. Very often he could not give a point-blank reply or comment—and these indirections, (sometimes funny, but not always so,) were probably the best responses possible. In the gloomiest period of the war, he had a call from a large delegation of bank presidents. In the talk after business was settled, one of the big Dons asked Mr. Lincoln if his confidence in the permanency of the Union was not beginning to be shaken—whereupon the homely President told a little story: "When I was a young man in Illinois," said he, "I boarded for a time with a deacon of the Presbyterian church. One night I was roused from my sleep by a rap at the door, and I heard the deacon's voice exclaiming, 'Arise, Abraham! the day of judgment has come!' I sprang from my bed and rushed to the window, and saw the stars falling in great showers; but looking back of them in the heavens I saw the grand old constellations, with which I was so well acquainted, fixed and true in their places. Gentlemen, the world did not come to an end then, nor will the Union now."

Freedom

It is not only true that most people entirely misunderstand Freedom, but I sometimes think I have not yet met one person who rightly understands it. The whole Universe is absolute Law. Freedom only opens entire activity and license *under the law*. To the degraded or undevelopt—and even to too many others—the thought of freedom is a thought of escaping from law—which, of course, is impossible. More precious than all worldly riches is Freedom—freedom from the painful constipation and poor narrowness of ecclesiasticism—freedom in manners, habiliments, furniture, from the silliness and tyranny of local fashions—entire freedom from party rings and mere conventions in Politics—and better than all, a general freedom of One's-Self from the tyrannic domination of vices, habits, appetites, under which nearly every man of us, (often the greatest brawler for freedom,) is enslaved. Can we attain such enfranchisement—the true Democracy, and the height of it? While we are from birth to death the subjects of irresistible law, enclosing every movement and minute, we yet escape, by a paradox, into true free will. Strange as it may seem, we only attain to freedom by a knowledge of, and implicit obedience to, Law. Great—unspeakably great—is the Will! the free Soul of man! At its greatest, understanding and obeying the laws, it can then, and then only, maintain true liberty. For there is to the highest, that law as absolute as any—more absolute than any—the Law of Liberty. The shallow, as intimated, consider liberty a release from all law, from every constraint. The wise see in it, on the contrary, the potent Law of Laws, namely, the fusion and combination of the conscious will, or partial individual law, with those universal, eternal, unconscious ones, which run through all Time, pervade history, prove immortality, give moral purpose to the entire objective world, and the last dignity to human life.

Book-Classes—America's Literature

For certain purposes, literary productions through all the recorded ages may be roughly divided into two classes. The first consisting of only a score or two, perhaps less, of typical, primal, representative works, different from any before, and embodying in themselves their own main laws and reasons for being. Then the second class, books and writings innumerable, incessant—to be briefly described as radiations or offshoots, or more or less imitations of the first. The works of the first class, as said, have their own laws, and may indeed be described as making those laws, and amenable only to them. The sharp warning of Margaret Fuller, unquell'd for thirty years, yet sounds in the air; "It does not follow that because the United States print and read more books, magazines, and newspapers than all the rest of the world, that they really have, therefore, a literature."

Our Real Culmination

The final culmination of this vast and varied Republic will be the production and perennial establishment of millions of comfortable city homesteads and moderate-sized farms, healthy and independent, single separate ownership, fee simple, life in them complete but cheap, within reach of all. Exceptional wealth, splendor, countless manufactures, excess of exports, immense capital and capitalists, the five-dollar-a-day hotels well fill'd, artificial improvements, even books, colleges, and the suffrage—all, in many respects, in themselves, (hard as it is to say so, and sharp as a surgeon's lance,) form, more or less, a sort of anti-democratic disease and monstrosity, except as they contribute by curious indirections to that culmination—seem to me mainly of value, or worth consideration, only with reference to it.

There is a subtle something in the common earth, crops, cattle, air, trees, &c., and in having to do at first hand with them, that forms the only purifying and perennial element for individuals and for society. I must confess I want to see the agricultural occupation of America at first hand permanently broaden'd. Its gains are the only ones on which God seems to smile. What others—what business, profit, wealth, without a taint? What fortune else—what dollar—does not stand for, and come from, more or less imposition, lying, unnaturalness?

An American Problem

One of the problems presented in America these times is, how to combine one's duty and policy as a member of associations, societies, brotherhoods or what not, and one's obligations to the State and Nation, with essential freedom as an individual personality, without which freedom a man cannot grow or expand, or be full, modern, heroic, democratic, American. With all the necessities and benefits of association, (and the world cannot get along without it,) the true nobility and satisfaction of a man consist in his thinking and acting for himself. The problem, I say, is to combine the two, so as not to ignore either.

The Last Collective Compaction

I like well our polyglot construction-stamp, and the retention thereof, in the broad, the tolerating, the many-sided, the collective. All nations here—a home for every race on earth. British, German, Scandinavian, Spanish, French, Italian—papers published, plays acted, speeches made, in all languages—on our shores the crowning resultant of those distillations, decantations, compactions of humanity, that have been going on, on trial, over the earth so long.

Pieces in Early Youth

1834–'42.

Dough-Face Song

—Like dough; soft; yielding to pressure; pale.
—*Webster's Dictionary.*

We are all docile dough-faces,
They knead us with the fist,
They, the dashing southern lords,
We labor as they list;
For them we speak—or hold our tongues,
For them we turn and twist.

We join them in their howl against
Free soil and "abolition,"
That firebrand—that assassin knife—
Which risk our land's condition,
And leave no peace of life to any
Dough-faced politician.

To put down "agitation," now,
We think the most judicious;
To damn all "northern fanatics,"
Those "traitors" black and vicious;
The "reg'lar party usages"
For us, and no "new issues."

Things have come to a pretty pass,
When a trifle small as this,
Moving and bartering nigger slaves,
Can open an abyss,
With jaws a-gape for "the two great parties;"
A pretty thought, I wis!

Principle—freedom!—fiddlesticks!
  We know not where they're found.
Rights of the masses—progress!—bah!
  Words that tickle and sound;
But claiming to rule o'er "practical men"
  Is very different ground.

Beyond all such we know a term
  Charming to ears and eyes,
With it we'll stab young Freedom,
  And do it in disguise;
Speak soft, ye wily dough-faces—
  That term is "compromise."

And what if children, growing up,
  In future seasons read
The thing we do? and heart and tongue
  Accurse us for the deed?
The future cannot touch us;
  The present gain we heed.

Then, all together, dough-faces!
  Let's stop the exciting clatter,
And pacify slave-breeding wrath
  By yielding all the matter;
For otherwise, as sure as guns,
  The Union it will shatter.

Besides, to tell the honest truth
  (For us an innovation,)
Keeping in with the slave power
  Is our personal salvation;
We've very little to expect
  From t' other part of the nation.

Besides it's plain at Washington
  Who likeliest wins the race,
What earthly chance has "free soil"
  For any good fat place?
While many a daw has feather'd his nest,
  By his creamy and meek dough-face.

Take heart, then, sweet companions,
  Be steady, Scripture Dick!
Webster, Cooper, Walker,
  To your allegiance stick!
With Brooks, and Briggs and Phœnix,
  Stand up through thin and thick!

We do not ask a bold brave front;
  We never try that game;
'Twould bring the storm upon our heads,
  A huge mad storm of shame;
Evade it, brothers—"compromise"
  Will answer just the same.

PAUMANOK.

DEATH IN THE SCHOOL-ROOM (*A Fact*)

Ting-a-ling-ling-ling! went the little bell on the teacher's desk of a village-school one morning, when the studies of the earlier part of the day were about half completed. It was well understood that this was a command for silence and attention; and when these had been obtain'd, the master spoke. He was a low thick-set man, and his name was Lugare.

"Boys," said he, "I have had a complaint enter'd, that last night some of you were stealing fruit from Mr. Nichols's garden. I rather think I know the thief. Tim Barker, step up here, sir."

The one to whom he spoke came forward. He was a slight, fair-looking boy of about thirteen; and his face had a laughing, good-humor'd expression, which even the charge now preferr'd against him, and the stern tone and threatening look of the teacher, had not entirely dissipated. The countenance of the boy, however, was too unearthly fair for health; it had, notwithstanding its fleshy, cheerful look, a singular cast as if some inward disease, and that a fearful one, were seated within. As the stripling stood before that place of judgment—that place so often made the scene of heartless and coarse brutality, of timid innocence confused, helpless childhood outraged, and gentle feelings crush'd—Lugare looked on him with a frown which plainly told that he felt in no very pleasant mood. (Happily a worthier and more philosophical system is proving to men that schools can be better govern'd than by lashes and tears and sighs. We are waxing toward that consummation when one of the old-fashion'd school-masters, with his cowhide, his heavy birch-rod, and his many ingenious methods of child-torture, will be gazed upon as a scorn'd memento of an ignorant, cruel, and exploded doctrine. May propitious gales speed that day!)

"Were you by Mr. Nichols's garden-fence last night?" said Lugare.

"Yes, sir," answer'd the boy, "I was."

"Well, sir, I'm glad to find you so ready with your confession. And so you thought you could do a little robbing, and enjoy yourself in a manner you ought to be ashamed to own, without being punish'd, did you?"

"I have not been robbing," replied the boy quickly. His face was suffused, whether with resentment or fright, it was difficult to tell. "And I didn't do anything last night, that I am ashamed to own."

"No impudence!" exclaim'd the teacher, passionately, as he grasp'd a long and heavy ratan: "give me none of your sharp speeches, or I'll thrash you till you beg like a dog."

The youngster's face paled a little; his lip quiver'd, but he did not speak.

"And pray, sir," continued Lugare, as the outward signs of wrath disappear'd from his features; "what were you about the garden for? Perhaps you only receiv'd the plunder, and had an accomplice to do the more dangerous part of the job?"

"I went that way because it is on my road home. I was there again afterwards to meet an acquaintance; and—and— But I did not go into the garden, nor take anything away from it. I would not steal,—hardly to save myself from starving."

"You had better have stuck to that last evening. You were seen, Tim Barker, to come from under Mr. Nichols's garden-fence, a little after nine o'clock, with a bag full of something or other over your shoulders. The bag had every appearance of being filled with fruit, and this morning the melon-beds are found to have been completely clear'd. Now, sir, what was there in that bag?"

Like fire itself glow'd the face of the detected lad. He spoke not a word. All the school had their eyes directed at him. The perspiration ran down his white forehead like rain-drops.

"Speak, sir!" exclaimed Lugare, with a loud strike of his ratan on the desk.

The boy look'd as though he would faint. But the unmerciful teacher, confident of having brought to light a criminal, and exulting in the idea of the severe chastisement he should now be justified in inflicting, kept working himself up to a still greater and greater degree of passion. In the meantime, the child seem'd hardly to know what to do with himself. His tongue cleav'd to the roof of his mouth. Either he was very much frighten'd, or he was actually unwell.

"Speak, I say!" again thunder'd Lugare; and his hand, grasping his ratan, tower'd above his head in a very significant manner.

"I hardly can, sir," said the poor fellow faintly. His voice was husky and thick. "I will tell you some—some other time. Please let me go to my seat—I a'n't well."

"Oh yes; that's very likely;" and Mr. Lugare bulged out his nose and cheeks with contempt. "Do you think to make me believe your lies? I've found you out, sir, plainly enough; and I am satisfied that you are as precious a little villain as there is in the State. But I will postpone settling with you for an hour yet. I shall then call you up again; and if you don't tell the whole truth then, I will give you something that'll make you remember Mr. Nichols's melons for many a month to come:—go to your seat."

Glad enough of the ungracious permission, and answering not a sound, the child crept tremblingly to his bench. He felt very strangely, dizzily—more as if he was in a dream than in real life; and laying his arms on his desk, bow'd down his face between them. The pupils turn'd to their accustom'd studies, for during the reign of Lugare in the village-school, they had been so used to scenes of violence and severe chastisement, that such things made but little interruption in the tenor of their way.

Now, while the intervening hour is passing, we will clear up the mystery of the bag, and of young Barker being under the garden fence on the preceding night. The boy's mother was a widow, and they both had to live in the very narrowest limits. His father had died when he was six years old, and little Tim was left a sickly emaciated infant whom no one expected to live many months. To the surprise of all, however, the poor child kept alive, and seem'd to recover his health, as he certainly did his size and good looks. This was owing to the kind offices of an eminent physician who had a country-seat in the neighborhood, and who had been interested in the widow's little family. Tim, the physician said, might possibly outgrow his disease; but everything was uncertain. It was a mysterious and baffling malady; and it would not be wonderful if he should in some moment of apparent health be suddenly taken away. The poor widow was at first in a continual state of uneasiness; but several years had now pass'd, and none of the impending evils had fallen upon the boy's head. His mother seem'd to feel confident that he would live, and be a help and an honor to her old age; and the two struggled on together, mutually happy in each other, and enduring much of poverty and discomfort without repining, each for the other's sake.

Tim's pleasant disposition had made him many friends in the village, and among the rest a young farmer named Jones, who, with his elder brother, work'd a large farm in the neighborhood on shares. Jones very frequently made Tim a present of a bag of potatoes or corn, or some garden vegetables, which he took from his own stock; but as his partner was a parsimonious, high-tempered man, and had often said that Tim was an idle fellow, and ought not to be help'd because he did not work, Jones generally made his gifts in such a manner that no one knew anything about them, except himself and the grateful objects of his kindness. It might be, too, that the widow was loth to have it understood by the neighbors that she received food from anyone; for there is often an excusable pride in people of her condition which makes them shrink from being consider'd as objects of "charity" as they would from the severest pains. On the night in question, Tim had been told that Jones would send them a bag of potatoes, and the place at which they were to be waiting for him was fixed at Mr. Nichols's garden-fence. It was this bag that Tim had been seen staggering under, and which caused the unlucky boy to be accused and convicted by his teacher as a thief. That teacher was one little fitted for his important and responsible office. Hasty to decide, and inflexibly severe, he was the terror of the little world he ruled so despotically. Punishment he seemed to delight in. Knowing little of those sweet fountains which in children's breasts ever open quickly at the call of gentleness and kind words, he was fear'd by all for his sternness, and loved by none. I would that he were an isolated instance in his profession.

The hour of grace had drawn to its close, and the time approach'd at which it was usual for Lugare to give his school a joyfully-receiv'd dismission. Now and then one of the scholars would direct a furtive glance at Tim, sometimes in pity, sometimes in indifference or inquiry. They knew that he would have no mercy shown him, and though most of them loved him, whipping was too common there to exact much sympathy. Every inquiring glance, however, remain'd unsatisfied, for at the end of the hour, Tim remain'd with his face completely hidden, and his head bow'd in his arms, precisely as he had lean'd himself when he first went to his seat. Lugare look'd at the boy occasionally with a scowl which seem'd to bode vengeance for his sullenness. At length the last class had been heard, and the last lesson recited, and Lugare seated himself behind his desk on the platform, with his longest and stoutest ratan before him.

"Now, Barker," he said, "we'll settle that little business of yours. Just step up here."

Tim did not move. The school-room was as still as the grave. Not a sound was to be heard, except occasionally a long-drawn breath.

"Mind me, sir, or it will be the worse for you. Step up here, and take off your jacket!"

The boy did not stir any more than if he had been of wood. Lugare shook with passion. He sat still a minute, as if considering the best way to wreak his vengeance. That minute, passed in death-like silence, was a fearful one to some of the children, for their faces whiten'd with fright. It seem'd, as it slowly dropp'd away, like the minute which precedes the climax of an exquisitely-performed tragedy, when some mighty master of the histrionic art is treading the stage, and you and the multitude around you are waiting, with stretch'd nerves and suspended breath, in expectation of the terrible catastrophe.

"Tim is asleep, sir," at length said one of the boys who sat near him.

Lugare, at this intelligence, allow'd his features to relax from their expression of savage anger into a smile, but that smile look'd more malignant if possible, than his former scowls. It might be that he felt amused at the horror depicted on the faces of those about him; or it might be that he was gloating in pleasure on the way in which he intended to wake the slumberer.

"Asleep! are you, my young gentleman!" said he; "let us see if we can't find something to tickle your eyes open. There's nothing like making the best of a bad case, boys. Tim, here, is determin'd not to be worried in his mind about a little flogging, for the thought of it can't even keep the little scoundrel awake."

Lugare smiled again as he made the last observation. He grasp'd his ratan firmly, and descended from his seat. With light and stealthy steps he cross'd the room, and stood by the unlucky sleeper. The boy was still as unconscious of his impending punishment as ever. He might be dreaming some golden dream of youth and pleasure; perhaps he was far away in the world of fancy, seeing scenes, and feeling delights, which cold reality never can bestow. Lugare lifted his ratan high over his head, and with the true and expert aim which he had acquired by long practice, brought it down on Tim's back with a force and whacking sound which seem'd sufficient to awake a freezing man in his last lethargy. Quick and fast, blow follow'd blow. Without waiting to see the effect of the first cut, the brutal wretch plied his instrument of torture first on one side of the boy's back, and then on the other, and only stopped at the end of two or three minutes from very weariness. But still Tim show'd no signs of motion; and as Lugare, provoked at his torpidity, jerk'd away one of the child's arms, on which he had been leaning over the desk, his head dropp'd down on the board with a dull sound, and his face lay turn'd up and exposed to view. When Lugare saw it, he stood like one transfix'd by a basilisk. His countenance turn'd to a leaden whiteness; the ratan dropp'd from his grasp; and his eyes, stretch'd wide open, glared as at some monstrous spectacle of horror and death. The sweat started in great globules seemingly from every pore in his face; his skinny lips contracted, and show'd his teeth; and when he at length stretch'd forth his arm, and with the end of one of his fingers touch'd the child's cheek, each limb quiver'd like the tongue of a snake; and his strength seemed as though it would momentarily fail him. The boy was dead. He had probably been so for some time, for his eyes were turn'd up, and his body was quite cold. Death was in the school-room, and Lugare had been flogging A CORPSE.

—*Democratic Review, August, 1841.*

One Wicked Impulse!

That section of Nassau street which runs into the great mart of New York brokers and stock-jobbers, has for a long time been much occupied by practitioners of the law. Tolerably well-known amid this class some years since, was Adam Covert, a middle-aged man of rather limited means, who, to tell the truth, gained more by trickery than he did in the legitimate and honorable exercise of his profession. He was a tall, bilious-faced widower; the father of two children; and had lately been seeking to better his fortunes by a rich marriage. But somehow or other his wooing did not seem to thrive well, and, with perhaps one exception, the lawyer's prospects in the matrimonial way were hopelessly gloomy.

Among the early clients of Mr. Covert had been a distant relative named Marsh, who, dying somewhat suddenly, left his son and daughter, and some little property, to the care of Covert, under a will drawn out by that gentleman himself. At no time caught without his eyes open, the cunning lawyer, aided by much sad confusion in the emergency which had caused his services to be called for, and disguising his object under a cloud of technicalities, inserted provisions in the will, giving himself an almost arbitrary control over the property and over those for whom it was designed. This control was even made to extend beyond the time when the children would arrive at mature age. The son, Philip, a spirited and high-temper'd fellow, had some time since pass'd that age. Esther, the girl, a plain, and somewhat devotional young woman, was in her nineteenth year.

Having such power over his wards, Covert did not scruple openly to use his advantage, in pressing his claims as a suitor for Esther's hand. Since the death of Marsh, the property he left, which had been in real estate, and was to be divided equally between the brother and sister, had risen to very considerable value; and Esther's share was to a man in Covert's situation a prize very well worth seeking. All this time, while really owning a respectable income, the young orphans often felt the want of the smallest sum of money—and Esther, on Philip's account, was more than once driven to various contrivances—the pawn-shop, sales of her own little luxuries, and the like, to furnish him with means.

Though she had frequently shown her guardian unequivocal evidence of her aversion, Esther continued to suffer from his persecutions, until one day he proceeded farther and was more pressing than usual. She possess'd some of her brother's mettlesome temper, and gave him an abrupt and most decided refusal. With dignity, she exposed the baseness of his conduct, and forbade him ever again mentioning marriage to her. He retorted bitterly, vaunted his hold on her and Philip, and swore an oath that unless she became his wife, they should both thenceforward become penniless. Losing his habitual self-control in his exasperation, he even added insults such as woman never receives from any one deserving the name of man, and at his own convenience left the house. That day, Philip return'd to New York, after an absence of several weeks on the business of a mercantile house in whose employment he had lately engaged.

Toward the latter part of the same afternoon, Mr. Covert was sitting in his office, in Nassau street, busily at work, when a knock at the door announc'd a visitor, and directly afterward young Marsh enter'd the room. His face exhibited a peculiar pallid appearance that did not strike Covert at all agreeably, and he call'd his clerk from an adjoining room, and gave him something to do at a desk near by.

"I wish to see you alone, Mr. Covert, if convenient," said the new-comer.

"We can talk quite well enough where we are," answer'd the lawyer; "indeed, I don't know that I have any leisure to talk at all, for just now I am very much press'd with business."

"But I *must* speak to you," rejoined Philip sternly, "at least I must say one thing, and that is, Mr. Covert, that you are a villain!"

"Insolent!" exclaimed the lawyer, rising behind the table, and pointing to the door: "Do you see that, sir! Let one minute longer find you the other side, or your feet may reach the landing by quicker method. Begone, sir!"

Such a threat was the more harsh to Philip, for he had rather high-strung feelings of honor. He grew almost livid with suppress'd agitation.

"I will see you again very soon," said he, in a low but distinct manner, his lips trembling as he spoke; and left the office.

The incidents of the rest of that pleasant summer day left little impression on the young man's mind. He roam'd to and fro without any object or destination. Along South street and by Whitehall, he watch'd with curious eyes the movements of the shipping, and the loading and unloading of cargoes; and listen'd to the merry heave-yo of the sailors and stevedores. There are some minds upon which great excitement produces the singular effect of uniting two utterly inconsistent faculties—a sort of cold apathy, and a sharp sensitiveness to all that is going on at the same time. Philip's was one of this sort; he noticed the various differences in the apparel of a gang of wharf-laborers—turn'd over in his brain whether they receiv'd wages enough to keep them comfortable, and their families also—and if they had families or not, which he tried to tell by their looks. In such petty reflections the daylight passed away. And all the while the master wish of Philip's thoughts was a desire to see the lawyer Covert. For what purpose he himself was by no means clear.

Nightfall came at last. Still, however, the young man did not direct his steps homeward. He felt more calm, however, and entering an eating house, order'd something for his supper, which, when it was brought to him, he merely tasted, and stroll'd forth again. There was a kind of gnawing sensation of thirst within him yet, and as he pass'd a hotel, he bethought him that one little glass of spirits would perhaps be just the thing. He drank, and hour after hour wore away unconsciously; he drank not one glass, but three or four, and strong glasses they were to him, for he was habitually abstemious.

It had been a hot day and evening, and when Philip, at an advanced period of the night, emerged from the bar-room into the street, he found that a thunderstorm had just commenced. He resolutely walk'd on, however, although at every step it grew more and more blustering.

The rain now pour'd down a cataract; the shops were all shut; few of the street lamps were lighted; and there was little except the frequent flashes of lightning to show him his way. When about half the length of Chatham street, which lay in the direction he had to take, the momentary fury of the tempest forced him to turn aside into a sort of shelter form'd by the corners of the deep entrance to a Jew pawnbroker's shop there. He had hardly drawn himself in as closely as possible, when the lightning reveal'd to him that the opposite corner of the nook was tenanted also.

"A sharp rain, this," said the other occupant, who simultaneously beheld Philip.

The voice sounded to the young man's ears a note which almost made him sober again. It was certainly the voice of Adam Covert. He made some commonplace reply, and waited for another flash of lightning to show him the stranger's face. It came, and he saw that his companion was indeed his guardian.

Philip Marsh had drank deeply—(let us plead all that may be possible to you, stern moralist.) Upon his mind came swarming, and he could not drive them away, thoughts of all those insults his sister had told him of, and the bitter words Covert had spoken to her; he reflected, too, on the injuries Esther as well as himself had receiv'd, and were still likely to receive, at the hands of that bold, bad man; how mean, selfish, and unprincipled was his character—what base and cruel advantages he had taken of many poor people, entangled in his power, and of how much wrong and suffering he had been the author, and might be again through future years. The very turmoil of the elements, the harsh roll of the thunder, the vindictive beating of the rain, and the fierce glare of the wild fluid that seem'd to riot in the ferocity of the storm around him, kindled a strange sympathetic fury in the young man's mind. Heaven itself (so deranged were his imaginations) appear'd to have provided a fitting scene and time for a deed of retribution, which to his disorder'd passion half wore the semblance of a divine justice. He remember'd not the ready solution to be found in Covert's pressure of business, which had no doubt kept him later than usual; but fancied some mysterious intent in the ordaining that he should be there, and that they two should meet at that untimely hour. All this whirl of influence came over Philip with startling quickness at that horrid moment. He stepp'd to the side of his guardian.

"Ho!" said he, "have we met so soon, Mr. Covert? You traitor to my dead father—robber of his children! I fear to think on *what* I think now!"

The lawyer's natural effrontery did not desert him.

"Unless you'd like to spend a night in the watch-house, young gentleman," said he, after a short pause, "move on. Your father was a weak man, I remember; as for his son, his own wicked heart is his worst foe. I have never done wrong to either—that I can say, and swear it!"

"Insolent liar!" exclaimed Philip, his eye flashing out sparks of fire in the darkness.

Covert made no reply except a cool, contemptuous laugh, which stung the excited young man to double fury. He sprang upon the lawyer, and clutch'd him by the neckcloth.

"Take it, then!" he cried hoarsely, for his throat was impeded by the fiendish rage which in that black hour possess'd him. "You are not fit to live!"

He dragg'd his guardian to the earth and fell crushingly upon him, choking the shriek the poor victim but just began to utter. Then, with monstrous imprecations, he twisted a tight knot around the gasping creature's neck, drew a clasp knife from his pocket, and touching the spring, the long sharp blade, too eager for its bloody work, flew open.

During the lull of the storm, the last strength of the prostrate man burst forth into one short loud cry of agony. At the same instant, the arm of the murderer thrust the blade, once, twice, thrice, deep in his enemy's bosom! Not a minute had passed since that fatal exasperating laugh—but the deed was done, and the instinctive thought which came at once to the guilty one, was a thought of fear and escape.

In the unearthly pause which follow'd, Philip's eyes gave one long searching sweep in every direction, above and around him. *Above!* God of the all-seeing eye! What, and who was that figure there?

"Forbear! In Jehovah's name forbear;" cried a shrill, but clear and melodious voice.

It was as if some accusing spirit had come down to bear witness against the deed of blood. Leaning far out of an open window, appear'd a white draperied shape, its face possess'd of a wonderful youthful beauty. Long vivid glows of lightning gave Philip a full opportunity to see as clearly as though the sun had been shining at noonday. One hand of the figure was raised upward in a deprecating attitude, and his large bright black eyes bent down upon the scene below with an expression of horror and shrinking pain. Such heavenly looks, and the peculiar circumstance of the time, fill'd Philip's heart with awe.

"Oh, if it is not yet too late," spoke the youth again, "spare him. In God's voice, I command, 'Thou shalt do no murder!' "

The words rang like a knell in the ear of the terror-stricken and already remorseful Philip. Springing from the body, he gave a second glance up and down the walk, which was totally lonesome and deserted; then crossing into Reade street, he made his fearful way in a half state of stupor, half-bewilderment, by the nearest avenues to his home.

When the corpse of the murder'd lawyer was found in the morning, and the officers of justice commenced their inquiry, suspicion immediately fell upon Philip, and he was arrested. The most rigorous search, however, brought to light nothing at all implicating the young man, except his visit to Covert's office the evening before, and his angry language there. That was by no means enough to fix so heavy a charge upon him.

The second day afterward, the whole business came before the ordinary judicial tribunal, in order that Philip might be either committed for the crime, or discharged. The testimony of Mr. Covert's clerk stood alone. One of his employers, who, believing in his innocence, had deserted him not in this crisis, had provided him with the ablest criminal counsel in New York. The proof was declared entirely insufficient, and Philip was discharged.

The crowded court-room made way for him as he came out; hundreds of curious looks fixed upon his features, and many a jibe pass'd upon him. But of all that arena of human faces, he saw only *one*—a sad, pale, black-eyed one, cowering in the centre of the rest. He had seen that face twice before—the first time as a warning spectre—the second time in prison, immediately after his arrest—now for the *last* time. This young stranger—the son of a scorn'd race—coming to the court-room to perform an unhappy duty, with the intention of testifying to what he had seen, melted at the sight of Philip's bloodless cheek, and of his sister's convulsive sobs, and forbore witnessing against the murderer. Shall we applaud or condemn him? Let every reader answer the question for himself.

That afternoon Philip left New York. His friendly employer own'd a small farm some miles up the Hudson, and until the excitement of the affair was over, he advised the young man to go thither. Philip thankfully accepted the proposal, made a few preparations, took a hurried leave of Esther, and by nightfall was settled in his new abode.

And how, think you, rested Philip Marsh that night? *Rested* indeed! O, if those who clamor so much for the halter and the scaffold to punish crime, could have seen that sight, they might have learn'd a lesson there! Four days had elapsed since he that lay tossing upon the bed there had slumber'd. Not the slightest intermission had come to his awaken'd and tensely strung sense, during those frightful days.

Disturb'd waking dreams came to him, as he thought what he might do to gain his lost peace. Far, far away would he go! The cold roll of the murder'd man's eye, as it turn'd up its last glance into his face—the shrill exclamation of pain—all the unearthly vividness of the posture, motions, and looks of the dead—the warning voice from above—pursued him like tormenting furies, and were never absent from his mind, asleep or awake, that long weary night. Anything, any place, to escape such horrid companionship! He would travel inland—hire himself to do hard drudgery upon some farm—work incessantly through the wide summer days, and thus force nature to bestow oblivion upon his senses, at least a little while now and then. He would fly on, on, on, until amid different scenes and a new life, the old memories were rubb'd entirely out. He would fight bravely in himself for peace of mind. For peace he would labor and struggle—for peace he would pray!

At length after a feverish slumber of some thirty or forty minutes, the unhappy youth, waking with a nervous start, rais'd himself in bed, and saw the blessed daylight beginning to dawn. He felt the sweat trickling down his naked breast; the sheet where he had lain was quite wet with it. Dragging himself wearily, he open'd the window. Ah! that good morning air—how it refresh'd him—how he lean'd out, and drank in the fragrance of the blossoms below, and almost for the first time in his life felt how beautifully indeed God had made the earth, and that there was wonderful sweetness in mere existence. And amidst the thousand mute mouths and eloquent eyes, which appear'd as it were to look up and speak in every direction, he fancied so many invitations to come among them. Not without effort, for he was very weak, he dress'd himself, and issued forth into the open air.

Clouds of pale gold and transparent crimson draperied the eastern sky, but the sun, whose face gladden'd them into all that glory, was not yet above the horizon. It was a time and place of such rare, such Eden-like beauty! Philip paused at the summit of an upward slope, and gazed around him. Some few miles off he could see a gleam of the Hudson river, and above it a spur of those rugged cliffs scatter'd along its western shores. Nearer by were cultivated fields. The clover grew richly there, the young grain bent to the early breeze, and the air was filled with an intoxicating perfume. At his side was the large well-kept garden of his host, in which were many pretty flowers, grass plots, and a wide avenue of noble trees. As Philip gazed, the holy calming power of Nature—the invisible spirit of so much beauty and so much innocence, melted into his soul. The disturb'd passions and the feverish conflict subsided. He even felt something like envied peace of mind—a sort of joy even in the presence of all the unmarr'd goodness. It was as fair to him, guilty though he had been, as to the purest of the pure. No accusing frowns show'd in the face of the flowers, or in the green shrubs, or the branches of the trees. They, more forgiving than mankind, and distinguishing not between the children of darkness and the children of light—they at least treated him with gentleness. Was he, then a being so accurs'd? Involuntarily, he bent over a branch of red roses, and took them softly between his hands—those murderous, bloody hands! But the red roses neither wither'd nor smell'd less fragrant. And as the young man kiss'd them, and dropp'd a tear upon them, it seem'd to him that he had found pity and sympathy from Heaven itself.

Though against all the rules of story-writing, we continue our narrative of these mainly true incidents (for such they are,) no further. Only to say that *the murderer* soon departed for a new field of action—that he is still living—and that this is but one of thousands of cases of unravel'd, unpunish'd crime—left, not to the tribunals of man, but to a wider power and judgment.

The Last Loyalist

"She came to me last night,
The floor gave back no tread."

The story I am going to tell is a traditional reminiscence of a country place, in my rambles about which I have often passed the house, now unoccupied, and mostly in ruins, that was the scene of the transaction. I cannot, of course, convey to others that particular kind of influence which is derived from my being so familiar with the locality, and with the very people whose grandfathers or fathers were contemporaries of the actors in the drama I shall transcribe. I must hardly expect, therefore, that to those who hear it thro' the medium of my pen, the narration will possess as life-like and interesting a character as it does to myself.

On a large and fertile neck of land that juts out in the Sound, stretching to the east of New York city, there stood, in the latter part of the last century, an old-fashion'd country-residence. It had been built by one of the first settlers of this section of the New World; and its occupant was originally owner of the extensive tract lying adjacent to his house, and pushing into the bosom of the salt waters. It was during the troubled times which mark'd our American Revolution that the incidents occurr'd which are the foundation of my story. Some time before the commencement of the war, the owner, whom I shall call Vanhome, was taken sick and died. For some time before his death he had lived a widower; and his only child, a lad of ten years old, was thus left an orphan. By his father's will this child was placed implicitly under the guardianship of an uncle, a middle-aged man, who had been of late a resident in the family. His care and interest, however, were needed but a little while—not two years elaps'd after the parents were laid away to their last repose before another grave had to be prepared for the son—the child who had been so haplessly deprived of their fostering care.

The period now arrived when the great national convulsion burst forth. Sounds of strife and the clash of arms, and the angry voices of disputants, were borne along by the air, and week after week grew to still louder clamor. Families were divided; adherents to the crown, and ardent upholders of the rebellion, were often found in the bosom of the same domestic circle. Vanhome, the uncle spoken of as guardian to the young heir, was a man who lean'd to the stern, the high-handed and the severe. He soon became known among the most energetic of the loyalists. So decided were his sentiments that, leaving the estate which he had inherited from his brother and nephew, he join'd the forces of the British king. Thenceforward, whenever his old neighbors heard of him, it was as being engaged in the cruelest outrages, the boldest inroads, or the most determin'd attacks upon the army of his countrymen or their peaceful settlements.

Eight years brought the rebel States and their leaders to that glorious epoch when the last remnant of a monarch's rule was to leave their shores—when the last waving of the royal standard was to flutter as it should be haul'd down from the staff, and its place fill'd by the proud testimonial of our warriors' success.

Pleasantly over the autumn fields shone the November sun, when a horseman, of somewhat military look, plodded slowly along the road that led to the old Vanhome farmhouse. There was nothing peculiar in his attire, unless it might be a red scarf which he wore tied round his waist. He was a dark-featured, sullen-eyed man; and as his glance was thrown restlessly to the right and left, his whole manner appear'd to be that of a person moving amid familiar and accustom'd scenes. Occasionally he stopp'd, and looking long and steadily at some object that attracted his attention, mutter'd to himself, like one in whose breast busy thoughts were moving. His course was evidently to the homestead itself, at which in due time he arrived. He dismounted, led his horse to the stables, and then, without knocking, though there were evident signs of occupancy around the building, the traveler made his entrance as composedly and boldly as though he were master of the whole establishment.

Now the house being in a measure deserted for many years, and the successful termination of the strife rendering it probable that the Vanhome estate would be confiscated to the new government, an aged, poverty-stricken couple had been encouraged by the neighbors to take possession as tenants of the place. Their name was Gills; and these people the traveler found upon his entrance were likely to be his host and hostess. Holding their right as they did by so slight a tenure, they ventur'd to offer no opposition when the stranger signified his intention of passing several hours there.

The day wore on, and the sun went down in the west; still the interloper, gloomy and taciturn, made no signs of departing. But as the evening advanced (whether the darkness was congenial to his sombre thoughts, or whether it merely chanced so) he seem'd to grow more affable and communicative, and informed Gills that he should pass the night there, tendering him at the same time ample remuneration, which the latter accepted with many thanks.

"Tell me," said he to his aged host, when they were all sitting around the ample hearth, at the conclusion of their evening meal, "tell me something to while away the hours."

"Ah! sir," answered Gills, "this is no place for new or interesting events. We live here from year to year, and at the end of one we find ourselves at about the same place which we filled in the beginning."

"Can you relate nothing, then?" rejoin'd the guest, and a singular smile pass'd over his features; "can you say nothing about your own place?—this house or its former inhabitants, or former history?"

The old man glanced across to his wife, and a look expressive of sympathetic feeling started in the face of each.

"It is an unfortunate story, sir," said Gills, "and may cast a chill upon you, instead of the pleasant feeling which it would be best to foster when in strange walls."

"Strange walls!" echoed he of the red scarf, and for the first time since his arrival he half laughed, but it was not the laugh which comes from a man's heart.

"You must know, sir," continued Gills, "I am myself a sort of intruder here. The Vanhomes—that was the name of the former residents and owners—I have never seen; for when I came to these parts the last occupant had left to join the red-coat soldiery. I am told that he is to sail with them for foreign lands, now that the war is ended, and his property almost certain to pass into other hands."

As the old man went on, the stranger cast down his eyes, and listen'd with an appearance of great interest, though a transient smile or a brightening of the eye would occasionally disturb the serenity of his deportment.

"The old owners of this place," continued the white-haired narrator, "were well off in the world, and bore a good name among their neighbors. The brother of Sergeant Vanhome, now the only one of the name, died ten or twelve years since, leaving a son—a child so small that the father's will made provision for his being brought up by his uncle, whom I mention'd but now as of the British army. He was a strange man, this uncle; disliked by all who knew him; passionate, vindictive, and, it was said, very avaricious, even from his childhood.

"Well, not long after the death of the parents, dark stories began to be circulated about cruelty and punishment and whippings and starvation inflicted by the new master upon his nephew. People who had business at the homestead would frequently, when they came away, relate the most fearful things of its manager, and how he misused his brother's child. It was half hinted that he strove to get the youngster out of the way in order that the whole estate might fall into his own hands. As I told you before, however, nobody liked the man; and perhaps they judged him too uncharitably.

"After things had gone on in this way for some time, a countryman, a laborer, who was hired to do farm-work upon the place, one evening observed that the little orphan Vanhome was more faint and pale even than usual, for he was always delicate, and that is one reason why I think it possible that his death, of which I am now going to tell you, was but the result of his own weak constitution, and nothing else. The laborer slept that night at the farmhouse. Just before the time at which they usually retired to bed, this person, feeling sleepy with his day's toil, left the kitchen hearth and wended his way to rest. In going to his place of repose he had to pass a chamber—the very chamber where you, sir, are to sleep to-night—and there he heard the voice of the orphan child uttering half-suppress'd exclamations as if in pitiful entreaty. Upon stopping, he heard also the tones of the elder Vanhome, but they were harsh and bitter. The sound of blows followed. As each one fell it was accompanied by a groan or shriek, and so they continued for some time. Shock'd and indignant, the countryman would have burst open the door and interfered to prevent this brutal proceeding, but he bethought him that he might get himself into trouble, and perhaps find that he could do no good after all, and so he passed on to his room.

"Well, sir, the following day the child did not come out among the work-people as usual. He was taken very ill. No physician was sent for until the next afternoon; and though one arrived in the course of the night, it was too late—the poor boy died before morning.

"People talk'd threateningly upon the subject, but nothing could be proved against Vanhome. At one period there were efforts made to have the whole affair investigated. Perhaps that would have taken place, had not every one's attention been swallow'd up by the rumors of difficulty and war, which were then beginning to disturb the country.

"Vanhome joined the army of the king. His enemies said

that he feared to be on the side of the rebels, because if they were routed his property would be taken from him. But events have shown that, if this was indeed what he dreaded, it has happen'd to him from the very means which he took to prevent it."

The old man paused. He had quite wearied himself with so long talking. For some minutes there was unbroken silence.

Presently the stranger signified his intention of retiring for the night. He rose, and his host took a light for the purpose of ushering him to his apartment.

When Gills return'd to his accustom'd situation in the large arm-chair by the chimney hearth, his ancient helpmate had retired to rest. With the simplicity of their times, the bed stood in the same room where the three had been seated during the last few hours; and now the remaining two talk'd together about the singular events of the evening. As the time wore on, Gills show'd no disposition to leave his cosy chair; but sat toasting his feet, and bending over the coals. Gradually the insidious heat and the lateness of the hour began to exercise their influence over the old man. The drowsy indolent feeling which every one has experienced in getting thoroughly heated through by close contact with a glowing fire, spread in each vein and sinew, and relax'd its tone. He lean'd back in his chair and slept.

For a long time his repose went on quietly and soundly. He could not tell how many hours elapsed; but, a while after midnight, the torpid senses of the slumberer were awaken'd by a startling shock. It was a cry as of a strong man in his agony—a shrill, not very loud cry, but fearful, and creeping into the blood like cold, polish'd steel. The old man raised himself in his seat and listen'd, at once fully awake. For a minute, all was the solemn stillness of midnight. Then rose that horrid tone again, wailing and wild, and making the hearer's hair to stand on end. One moment more, and the trampling of hasty feet sounded in the passage outside. The door was thrown open, and the form of the stranger, more like a corpse than living man, rushed into the room.

"All white!" yell'd the conscience-stricken creature—"all white, and with the grave-clothes around him. One shoulder was bare, and I saw," he whisper'd, "I saw blue streaks upon it. It was horrible, and I cried aloud. He stepp'd toward me! He came to my very bedside; his small hand almost touch'd my face. I could not bear it, and fled."

The miserable man bent his head down upon his bosom; convulsive rattlings shook his throat; and his whole frame waver'd to and fro like a tree in a storm. Bewilder'd and shock'd, Gills look'd at his apparently deranged guest, and knew not what answer to make, or what course of conduct to pursue.

Thrusting out his arms and his extended fingers, and bending down his eyes, as men do when shading them from a glare of lightning, the stranger stagger'd from the door, and, in a moment further, dash'd madly through the passage which led through the kitchen into the outer road. The old man heard the noise of his falling footsteps, sounding fainter and fainter in the distance, and then, retreating, dropp'd his own exhausted limbs into the chair from which he had been arous'd so terribly. It was many minutes before his energies recover'd their accustomed tone again. Strangely enough, his wife, unawaken'd by the stranger's ravings, still slumber'd on as profoundly as ever.

Pass we on to a far different scene—the embarkation of the British troops for the distant land whose monarch was never more to wield the sceptre over a kingdom lost by his imprudence and tyranny. With frowning brow and sullen pace the martial ranks moved on. Boat after boat was filled, and, as each discharged its complement in the ships that lay heaving their anchors in the stream, it return'd, and was soon filled with another load. And at length it became time for the last soldier to lift his eye and take a last glance at the broad banner of England's pride, which flapp'd its folds from the top of the highest staff on the Battery.

As the warning sound of a trumpet called together all who were laggards—those taking leave of friends, and those who were arranging their own private affairs, left until the last moment—a single horseman was seen furiously dashing down the street. A red scarf tightly encircled his waist. He made directly for the shore, and the crowd there gather'd started back in wonderment as they beheld his dishevel'd appearance and ghastly face. Throwing himself violently from his saddle, he flung the bridle over the animal's neck, and gave him a sharp cut with a small riding whip. He made for the boat; one minute later, and he had been left. They were pushing the keel from the landing—the stranger sprang—a space of two or three feet already intervened—he struck on the gunwale—and the Last Soldier of King George had left the American shores.

Wild Frank's Return

As the sun, one August day some fifty years ago, had just pass'd the meridian of a country town in the eastern section of Long Island, a single traveler came up to the quaint low-roof'd village tavern, open'd its half-door, and enter'd the common room. Dust cover'd the clothes of the wayfarer, and his brow was moist with sweat. He trod in a lagging, weary way; though his form and features told of an age not more than nineteen or twenty years. Over one shoulder was slung a sailor's jacket, and in his hand he carried a little bundle. Sitting down on a rude bench, he told a female who made her appearance behind the bar, that he would have a glass of brandy and sugar. He took off the liquor at a draught: after which he lit and began to smoke a cigar, with which he supplied himself from his pocket—stretching out one leg, and leaning his elbow down on the bench, in the attitude of a man who takes an indolent lounge.

"Do you know one Richard Hall that lives somewhere here among you?" said he.

"Mr. Hall's is down the lane that turns off by that big locust tree," answer'd the woman, pointing to the direction through the open door; "it's about half a mile from here to his house."

The youth, for a minute or two, puff'd the smoke from his mouth very leisurely in silence. His manner had an air of vacant self-sufficiency, rather strange in one of so few years.

"I wish to see Mr. Hall," he said at length—"Here's a silver sixpence, for any one who will carry a message to him."

"The folks are all away. It's but a short walk, and your limbs are young," replied the female, who was not altogether pleased with the easy way of making himself at home, which mark'd her shabby-looking customer. That individual, however, seem'd to give small attention to the hint, but lean'd and puff'd his cigar-smoke as leisurely as before.

"Unless," continued the woman, catching a second glance at the sixpence; "unless old Joe is at the stable, as he's very likely to be. I'll go and find out for you." And she push'd open a door at her back, stepp'd through an adjoining room into a yard, whence her voice was the next moment heard calling the person she had mention'd, in accents by no means remarkable for their melody or softness.

Her search was successful. She soon return'd with him who was to act as messenger—a little, wither'd, ragged old man—a hanger-on there, whose unshaven face told plainly enough the story of his intemperate habits—those deeply seated habits, now too late to be uprooted, that would ere long lay him in a drunkard's grave. The youth inform'd him what the required service was, and promised him the reward as soon as he should return.

"Tell Richard Hall that I am going to his father's house this afternoon. If he asks who it is that wishes him here, say the person sent no name," continued the stranger, sitting up from his indolent posture, as the feet of old Joe were about leaving the door-stone, and his blear'd eyes turned to catch the last sentence of the mandate.

"And yet, perhaps you may as well," added he, communing a moment with himself: "you may tell him his brother Frank, Wild Frank, it is, who wishes him to come."

The old man departed on his errand, and he who call'd himself Wild Frank, toss'd his nearly smoked cigar out of the window, and folded his arms in thought.

No better place than this, probably, will occur to give a brief account of some former events in the life of the young stranger, resting and waiting at the village inn. Fifteen miles east of that inn lived a farmer named Hall, a man of good repute, well-off in the world, and head of a large family. He was fond of gain—required all his boys to labor in proportion to their age; and his right hand man, if he might not be called favorite, was his eldest son Richard. This eldest son, an industrious, sober-faced young fellow, was invested by his father with the powers of second in command; and as strict and swift obedience was a prime tenet in the farmer's domestic government, the children all tacitly submitted to their brother's sway—all but one, and that was Frank. The farmer's wife was a quiet woman, in rather tender health; and though for all her offspring she had a mother's love, Frank's kiss ever seem'd sweetest to her lips. She favor'd him more than the rest—perhaps, as in a hundred similar instances, for his being so often at fault, and so often blamed. In truth, however, he seldom receiv'd more blame than he deserv'd, for he was a capricious, high-temper'd lad, and up to all kinds of mischief. From these traits he was known in the neighborhood by the name of Wild Frank.

Among the farmer's stock there was a fine young blood mare—a beautiful creature, large and graceful, with eyes like dark-hued jewels, and her color that of the deep night. It being the custom of the farmer to let his boys have something about the farm that they could call their own, and take care of as such, Black Nell, as the mare was called, had somehow or other fallen to Frank's share. He was very proud of her, and thought as much of her comfort as his own. The elder brother, however, saw fit to claim for himself, and several times to exercise, a privilege of managing and using Black Nell, notwithstanding what Frank consider'd his prerogative. On one of these occasions a hot dispute arose, and after much angry blood, it was referr'd to the farmer for settlement. He decided in favor of Richard, and added a harsh lecture to his other son. The farmer was really unjust; and Wild Frank's face paled with rage and mortification. That furious temper which he had never been taught to curb, now swell'd like an overflowing torrent. With difficulty restraining the exhibition of his passions, as soon as he got by himself he swore that not another sun should roll by and find him under that roof. Late at night he silently arose, and turning his back on what he thought an inhospitable home, in mood in which the child should never leave the parental roof, bent his steps toward the city.

It may well be imagined that alarm and grief pervaded the whole of the family, on discovering Frank's departure. And as week after week melted away and brought no tidings of him, his poor mother's heart grew wearier and wearier. She spoke not much, but was evidently sick in spirit. Nearly two years had elaps'd when about a week before the incidents at the commencement of this story, the farmer's family were joyfully surprised by receiving a letter from the long absent son. He had been to sea, and was then in New York, at which port his vessel had just arrived. He wrote in a gay strain; appear'd to have lost the angry feeling which had caused his flight from home; and said he heard in the city that Richard had married, and settled several miles distant, where he wished him all good luck and happiness. Wild Frank wound up his letter by promising, as soon as he could get through the imperative business of his ship, to pay a visit to his parents and native place. On Tuesday of the succeeding week, he said he would be with them.

Within half an hour after the departure of old Joe, the form of that ancient personage was seen slowly wheeling round the locust-tree at the end of the lane, accompanied by a stout young man in primitive homespun apparel. The meeting between Wild Frank and his brother Richard, though hardly of that kind which generally takes place between persons so closely related, could not exactly be call'd distant or cool either. Richard press'd his brother to go with him to the farm house, and refresh and repose himself for some hours at least, but Frank declined.

"They will all expect me home this afternoon," he said, "I wrote to them I would be there to-day."

"But you must be very tired, Frank," rejoin'd the other; "won't you let some of us harness up and carry you? Or if you like—" he stopp'd a moment, and a trifling suffusion spread over his face; "if you like, I'll put the saddle on Black Nell—she's here at my place now, and you can ride home like a lord."

Frank's face color'd a little, too. He paused for a moment in thought—he was really foot-sore, and exhausted with his journey that hot day—so he accepted his brother's offer.

"You know the speed of Nell, as well as I," said Richard; "I'll warrant when I bring her here you'll say she's in good order as ever." So telling him to amuse himself for a few minutes as well as he could, Richard left the tavern.

Could it be that Black Nell knew her early master? She

neigh'd and rubb'd her nose on his shoulder; and as he put his foot in the stirrup and rose on her back, it was evident that they were both highly pleased with their meeting. Bidding his brother farewell, and not forgetting old Joe, the young man set forth on his journey to his father's house. As he left the village behind, and came upon the long monotonous road before him, he thought on the circumstances of his leaving home—and he thought, too, on his course of life, how it was being frittered away and lost. Very gentle influences, doubtless, came over Wild Frank's mind then, and he yearn'd to show his parents that he was sorry for the trouble he had cost them. He blamed himself for his former follies, and even felt remorse that he had not acted more kindly to Richard, and gone to his house. Oh, it had been a sad mistake of the farmer that he did not teach his children to love one another. It was a foolish thing that he prided himself on governing his little flock well, when sweet affection, gentle forbearance, and brotherly faith, were almost unknown among them.

The day was now advanced, though the heat pour'd down with a strength little less oppressive than at noon. Frank had accomplish'd the greater part of his journey; he was within two miles of his home. The road here led over a high, tiresome hill, and he determined to stop on the top of it and rest himself, as well as give the animal he rode a few minutes' breath. How well he knew the place! And that mighty oak, standing just outside the fence on the very summit of the hill, often had he reposed under its shade. It would be pleasant for a few minutes to stretch his limbs there again as of old, he thought to himself; and he dismounted from the saddle and led Black Nell under the tree. Mindful of the comfort of his favorite, he took from his little bundle, which he had strapped behind him on the mare's back, a piece of strong cord, four or five yards in length, which he tied to the bridle, and wound and tied the other end, for security, over his own wrist; then throwing himself at full length upon the ground, Black Nell was at liberty to graze around him, without danger of straying away.

It was a calm scene, and a pleasant. There was no rude sound—hardly even a chirping insect—to break the sleepy silence of the place. The atmosphere had a dim, hazy cast, and was impregnated with overpowering heat. The young man lay there minute after minute, as time glided away unnoticed; for he was very tired, and his repose was sweet to him. Occasionally he raised himself and cast a listless look at the distant landscape, veil'd as it was by the slight mist. At length his repose was without such interruptions. His eyes closed, and though at first they open'd languidly again at intervals, after a while they shut altogether. Could it be that he slept? It was so indeed. Yielding to the drowsy influences about him, and to his prolong'd weariness of travel, he had fallen into a deep, sound slumber. Thus he lay; and Black Nell, the original cause of his departure from his home—by a singular chance, the companion of his return—quietly cropp'd the grass at his side.

An hour nearly pass'd away, and yet the young man slept on. The light and heat were not glaring now; a change had come over earth and heaven. There were signs of one of those thunderstorms that in our climate spring up and pass over so quickly and so terribly. Masses of vapor loom'd up in the horizon, and a dark shadow settled on the woods and fields. The leaves of the great oak rustled together over the youth's head. Clouds flitted swiftly in the sky, like bodies of armed men coming up to battle at the call of their leader's trumpet. A thick rain-drop fell now and then, while occasionally hoarse mutterings of thunder sounded in the distance; yet the slumberer was not arous'd. It was strange that Wild Frank did not awake. Perhaps his ocean life had taught him to rest undisturbed amid the jarring of elements. Though the storm was now coming on its fury, he slept like a babe in its cradle.

Black Nell had ceased grazing, and stood by her sleeping master with ears erect, and her long mane and tail waving in the wind. It seem'd quite dark, so heavy were the clouds. The blast blew sweepingly, the lightning flash'd, and the rain fell in torrents. Crash after crash of thunder seem'd to shake the solid earth. And Black Nell, she stood now, an image of beautiful terror, with her fore feet thrust out, her neck arch'd, and her eyes glaring balls of fear. At length, after a dazzling and lurid glare, there came a peal—a deafening crash—as if the great axle was rent. God of Spirits! the startled mare sprang off like a ship in an ocean-storm! Her eyes were blinded with light; she dashed madly down the hill, and plunge after plunge—far, far away—swift as an arrow—dragging the hapless body of the youth behind her!

In the low, old-fashion'd dwelling of the farmer there was a large family group. The men and boys had gather'd under shelter at the approach of the storm; and the subject of their talk was the return of the long absent son. The mother spoke of him, too, and her eyes brighten'd with pleasure as she spoke. She made all the little domestic preparations—cook'd his favorite dishes—and arranged for him his own bed, in its own old place. As the tempest mounted to its fury they discuss'd the probability of his getting soak'd by it; and the provident dame had already selected some dry garments for a change. But the rain was soon over, and nature smiled again in her invigorated beauty. The sun shone out as it was dipping in the west. Drops sparkled on the leaf-tips—coolness and clearness were in the air.

The clattering of a horse's hoofs came to the ears of those who were gather'd there. It was on the other side of the house that the wagon road led; and they open'd the door and rush'd in a tumult of glad anticipations, through the adjoining room to the porch. What a sight it was that met them there! Black Nell stood a few feet from the door, with her neck crouch'd down; she drew her breath long and deep, and vapor rose from every part of her reeking body. And with eyes starting from their sockets, and mouths agape with stupefying terror, they beheld on the ground near her a mangled, hideous mass—the rough semblance of a human form—all batter'd and cut, and bloody. Attach'd to it was the fatal cord, dabbled over with gore. And as the mother gazed—for she could not withdraw her eyes—and the appalling truth came upon her mind, she sank down without shriek or utterance, into a deep, deathly swoon.

The Boy Lover

Listen, and the old will speak a chronicle for the young. Ah, youth! thou art one day coming to be old, too. And let me tell thee how thou mayest get a useful lesson. For an hour, *dream thyself old.* Realize, in thy thoughts and consciousness, that vigor and strength are subdued in thy sinews—that the color of the shroud is liken'd in thy very hairs—that all those leaping desires, luxurious hopes, beautiful aspirations, and proud confidences, of thy younger life, have long been buried (a funeral for the better part of thee) in that grave which must soon close over thy tottering limbs. Look back, then, through the long track of the past years. How has it been with thee? Are there bright beacons of happiness enjoy'd, and of good done by the way? Glimmer gentle rays of what was scatter'd from a holy heart? Have benevolence, and love, and undeviating honesty left tokens on which thy eyes can rest sweetly? Is it well with thee, thus? Answerest thou, it is? Or answerest thou, I see nothing but gloom and shatter'd hours, and the wreck of good resolves, and a broken heart, filled with sickness, and troubled among its ruined chambers with the phantoms of many follies?

O, youth! youth! this dream will one day be a *reality*—a reality, either of heavenly peace or agonizing sorrow.

And yet not for all is it decreed to attain the neighborhood of the three-score and ten years—the span of life. I am to speak of one who died young. Very awkward was his childhood—but most fragile and sensitive! So delicate a nature may exist in a rough, unnoticed plant! Let the boy rest;—he was not beautiful, and dropp'd away betimes. But for the cause—it is a singular story, to which let crusted worldings pay the tribute of a light laugh—light and empty as their own hollow hearts.

Love! which with its cankerseed of decay within, has sent young men and maidens to a long'd-for, but too premature burial. Love! the child-monarch that Death itself cannot conquer; that has its tokens on slabs at the head of grass-cover'd tombs—tokens more visible to the eye of the stranger, yet not so deeply graven as the face and the remembrances cut upon the heart of the living. Love! the sweet, the pure, the innocent; yet the causer of fierce hate, of wishes for deadly revenge, of bloody deeds, and madness, and the horrors of hell. Love! that wanders over battlefields, turning up mangled human trunks, and parting back the hair from gory faces, and daring the points of swords and the thunder of artillery, without a fear or a thought of danger.

Words! words! I begin to see I am, indeed, an old man, and garrulous! Let me go back—yes, I see it must be many years!

It was at the close of the last century. I was at that time studying law, the profession my father follow'd. One of his clients was an elderly widow, a foreigner, who kept a little ale-house, on the banks of the North River, at about two miles from what is now the centre of the city. *Then* the spot was quite out of town and surrounded by fields and green trees. The widow often invited me to come and pay her a visit, when I had a leisure afternoon—including also in the invitation my brother and two other students who were in my father's office. Matthew, the brother I mention, was a boy of sixteen; he was troubled with an inward illness—though it had no power over his temper, which ever retain'd the most admirable placidity and gentleness. He was cheerful, but never boisterous, and everybody loved him; his mind seem'd more develop'd than is usual for his age, though his personal appearance was exceedingly plain. Wheaton and Brown, the names of the other students, were spirited, clever young fellows, with most of the traits that those in their position of life generally possess. The first was as generous and brave as any man I ever knew. He was very passionate, too, but the whirlwind soon blew over, and left everything quiet again. Frank Brown was slim, graceful, and handsome. He profess'd to be fond of sentiment, and used to fall regularly in love once a month.

The half of every Wednesday we four youths had to ourselves, and were in the habit of taking a sail, a ride, or a walk together. One of these afternoons, of a pleasant day in April, the sun shining, and the air clear, I bethought myself of the widow and her beer—about which latter article I had made inquiries, and heard it spoken of in terms of high commendation. I mention'd the matter to Matthew and to my fellow-students, and we agreed to fill up our holiday by a jaunt to the ale-house. Accordingly, we set forth, and, after a fine walk, arrived in glorious spirits at our destination.

Ah! how shall I describe the quiet beauties of the spot, with its long, low piazza looking out upon the river, and its clean homely tables, and the tankards of real silver in which the ale was given us, and the flavor of that excellent liquor itself. There was the widow; and there was a sober, stately old woman, half companion, half servant, Margery by name; and there was (good God! my fingers quiver yet as I write the word!) young Ninon, the daughter of the widow.

O, through the years that live no more, my memory strays back, and that whole scene comes up before me once again—and the brightest part of the picture is the strange ethereal beauty of that young girl! She was apparently about the age of my brother Matthew, and the most fascinating, artless creature I had ever beheld. She had blue eyes and light hair, and an expression of childish simplicity which was charming indeed. I have no doubt that ere half an hour had elapsed from the time we enter'd the tavern and saw Ninon, every one of the four of us loved the girl to the very depth of passion.

We neither spent so much money, nor drank as much beer, as we had intended before starting from home. The widow was very civil, being pleased to see us, and Margery served our wants with a deal of politeness—but it was to Ninon that the afternoon's pleasure was attributable; for though we were strangers, we became acquainted at once—the manners of the girl, merry as she was, putting entirely out of view the most distant imputation of indecorum—and the presence of the widow and Margery, (for we were all in the common room together, there being no other company,) serving to make us all disembarass'd and at ease.

It was not until quite a while after sunset that we started on our return to the city. We made several attempts to revive the mirth and lively talk that usually signalized our rambles, but they seem'd forced and discordant, like laughter in a sick-room. My brother was the only one who preserved his usual tenor of temper and conduct.

I need hardly say that thenceforward every Wednesday afternoon was spent at the widow's tavern. Strangely, neither Matthew or my two friends, or myself, spoke to each other of the sentiment that filled us in reference to Ninon. Yet we all knew the thoughts and feelings of the others; and each, perhaps, felt confident that his love alone was unsuspected by his companions.

The story of the widow was a touching yet simple one. She was by birth a Swiss. In one of the cantons of her native land, she had grown up, and married, and lived for a time in happy comfort. A son was born to her, and a daughter, the beautiful Ninon. By some reverse of fortune, the father and head of the family had the greater portion of his possessions swept from him. He struggled for a time against the evil influence, but it press'd upon him harder and harder. He had heard of a people in the western world—a new and swarming land—where the stranger was welcom'd, and peace and the protection of the strong arm thrown around him. He had not heart to stay and struggle amid the scenes of his former prosperity, and he determin'd to go and make his home in that distant republic of the west. So with his wife and children, and the proceeds of what little property was left, he took passage for New York. He was never to reach his journey's end. Either the cares that weigh'd upon his mind, or some other cause, consign'd him to a sick hammock, from which he only found relief through the Great Dismisser. He was buried in the sea, and in due time his family arrived at the American emporium. But there, the son too sicken'd—died, ere long, and was buried likewise. They would not bury him in the city, but away—by the solitary banks of the Hudson; on which the widow soon afterwards took up her abode.

Ninon was too young to feel much grief at these sad occurrences; and the mother, whatever she might have suffer'd inwardly, had a good deal of phlegm and patience, and set about making herself and her remaining child as comfortable as might be. They had still a respectable sum in cash, and after due deliberation, the widow purchas'd the little quiet tavern, not far from the grave of her boy; and of Sundays and holidays she took in considerable money—enough to make a decent support for them in their humble way of living. French and Germans visited the house frequently, and quite a number of young Americans too. Probably the greatest attraction to the latter was the sweet face of Ninon.

Spring passed, and summer crept in and wasted away, and autumn had arrived. Every New Yorker knows what delicious weather we have, in these regions, of the early October days; how calm, clear, and divested of sultriness, is the air, and how decently nature seems preparing for her winter sleep.

Thus it was the last Wednesday we started on our accustomed excursion. Six months had elapsed since our first visit, and, as then, we were full of the exuberance of young and joyful hearts. Frequent and hearty were our jokes, by no means particular about the theme or the method, and long and loud the peals of laughter that rang over the fields or along the shore.

We took our seats round the same clean, white table, and received our favorite beverage in the same bright tankards. They were set before us by the sober Margery, no one else being visible. As frequently happen'd, we were the only company. Walking and breathing the keen, fine air had made us dry, and we soon drain'd the foaming vessels, and call'd for more. I remember well an animated chat we had about some poems that had just made their appearance from a great British author, and were creating quite a public stir. There was one, a tale of passion and despair, which Wheaton had read, and of which he gave us a transcript. Wild, startling, and dreamy, perhaps it threw over our minds its peculiar cast.

An hour moved off, and we began to think it strange that neither Ninon or the widow came into the room. One of us gave a hint to that effect to Margery; but she made no answer, and went on in her usual way as before.

"The grim old thing," said Wheaton, "if she were in Spain, they'd make her a premier duenna!"

I ask'd the woman about Ninon and the widow. She seemed disturb'd, I thought; but, making no reply to the first part of my question, said that her mistress was in another part of the house, and did not wish to be with company.

"Then be kind enough, Mrs. Vinegar," resumed Wheaton, good-naturedly, "be kind enough to go and ask the widow if we can see Ninon."

Our attendant's face turn'd as pale as ashes, and she precipitately left the apartment. We laugh'd at her agitation, which Frank Brown assigned to our merry ridicule.

Quite a quarter of an hour elaps'd before Margery's return. When she appear'd she told us briefly that the widow had bidden her obey our behest, and now, if we desired, she would conduct us to the daughter's presence. There was a singular expression in the woman's eyes, and the whole affair began to strike us as somewhat odd; but we arose, and taking our caps, follow'd her as she stepp'd through the door. Back of the house were some fields, and a path leading into clumps of trees. At some thirty rods distant from the tavern, nigh one of those clumps, the larger tree whereof was a willow, Margery stopp'd, and pausing a minute, while we came up, spoke in tones calm and low:

"Ninon is there!"

She pointed downward with her finger. Great God! There was a *grave,* new made, and with the sods loosely join'd, and a rough brown stone at each extremity! Some earth yet lay upon the grass near by. If we had look'd, we might have seen the resting-place of the widow's son, Ninon's brother—for it was close at hand. But amid the whole scene our eyes took in nothing except that horrible covering of death—the oven-shaped mound. My sight seemed to waver, my head felt dizzy, and a feeling of deadly sickness came over me. I heard a stifled exclamation, and looking round, saw Frank Brown leaning against the nearest tree, great sweat upon his forehead, and his cheeks bloodless as chalk. Wheaton gave way to his agony more fully than ever I had known a man before; he had fallen—sobbing like a child, and wringing his hands. It is impossible to describe the suddenness and fearfulness of the sickening truth that came upon us like a stroke of thunder.

Of all of us, my brother Matthew neither shed tears, or turned pale, or fainted, or exposed any other evidence of inward depth of pain. His quiet, pleasant voice was indeed a tone lower, but it was that which recall'd us, after the lapse of many long minutes, to ourselves.

So the girl had died and been buried. We were told of an illness that had seized her the very day after our last preceding visit; but we inquired not into the particulars.

And now come I to the conclusion of my story, and to the most singular part of it. The evening of the third day afterward, Wheaton, who had wept scalding tears, and Brown, whose cheeks had recover'd their color, and myself, that for an hour thought my heart would never rebound again from the fearful shock—that evening, I say, we three were seated around a table in another tavern, drinking other beer, and laughing but a little less cheerfully, and as though we had never known the widow or her daughter—neither of whom, I venture to affirm, came into our minds once the whole night, or but to be dismiss'd again, carelessly, like the remembrance of faces seen in a crowd.

Strange are the contradictions of the things of life! The seventh day after that dreadful visit saw my brother Matthew—the delicate one, who, while bold men writhed in torture, had kept the same placid face, and the same untrembling fingers—him that seventh day saw a clay-cold corpse, carried to the repose of the churchyard. The shaft, rankling far down and within, wrought a poison too great for show, and the youth died.

The Child and the Profligate

Just after sunset, one evening in summer—that pleasant hour when the air is balmy, the light loses its glare, and all around is imbued with soothing quiet—on the door-step of a house there sat an elderly woman waiting the arrival of her son. The house was in a straggling village some fifty miles from New York city. She who sat on the door step was a widow; her white cap cover'd locks of gray, and her dress, though clean, was exceedingly homely. Her house—for the tenement she occupied was her own—was very little and very old. Trees cluster'd around it so thickly as almost to hide its color—that blackish gray color which belongs to old wooden houses that have never been painted; and to get in it you had to enter a little rickety gate and walk through a short path, border'd by carrot beds and beets and other vegetables. The son whom she was expecting was her only child. About a year before he had been bound apprentice to a rich farmer in the place, and after finishing his daily task he was in the habit of spending half an hour at his mother's. On the present occasion the shadows of night had settled heavily before the youth made his appearance. When he did, his walk was slow and dragging, and all his motions were languid, as if from great weariness. He open'd the gate, came through the path, and sat down by his mother in silence.

"You are sullen to-night, Charley," said the widow, after a moment's pause, when she found that he return'd no answer to her greeting.

As she spoke she put her hand fondly on his head; it seem'd moist as if it had been dipp'd in the water. His shirt, too, was soak'd; and as she pass'd her fingers down his shoulder she felt a sharp twinge in her heart, for she knew that moisture to be the hard wrung sweat of severe toil, exacted from her young child (he was but thirteen years old) by an unyielding task-master.

"You have work'd hard to-day, my son."

"I've been mowing."

The widow's heart felt another pang.

"Not *all day,* Charley?" she said, in a low voice; and there was a slight quiver in it.

"Yes, mother, all day," replied the boy; "Mr. Ellis said he couldn't afford to hire men, for wages are so high. I've swung the scythe ever since an hour before sunrise. Feel of my hands."

There were blisters on them like great lumps. Tears started in the widow's eyes. She dared not trust herself with a reply, though her heart was bursting with the thought that she could not better his condition. There was no earthly means of support on which she had dependence enough to encourage her child in the wish she knew he was forming—the wish not utter'd for the first time—to be freed from his bondage.

"Mother," at length said the boy, "I can stand it no longer. I cannot and will not stay at Mr. Ellis's. Ever since the day I first went into his house I've been a slave; and if I have to work so much longer I know I shall run off and go to sea or somewhere else. I'd as leave be in my grave as there." And the child burst into a passionate fit of weeping.

His mother was silent, for she was in deep grief herself. After some minutes had flown, however, she gather'd sufficient self-possession to speak to her son in a soothing tone, endeavoring to win him from his sorrows and cheer up his heart. She told him that time was swift—that in the course of a few years he would be his own master—that all people have their troubles—with many other ready arguments which, though they had little effect in calming her own distress, she hoped would act as a solace to the disturb'd temper of the boy. And as the half hour to which he was limited had now elaps'd, she took him by the hand and led him to the gate, to set forth on his return. The youth seemed pacified, though occasionally one of those convulsive sighs that remain after a fit of weeping, would break from his throat. At the gate he threw his arms about his mother's neck; each press'd a long kiss on the lips of the other, and the youngster bent his steps towards his master's house.

As her child pass'd out of sight the widow return'd, shut the gate and enter'd her lonely room. There was no light in the old cottage that night—the heart of its occupant was dark and cheerless. Love, agony, and grief, and tears and convulsive wrestlings were there. The thought of a beloved son condemned to labor—labor that would break down a man—struggling from day to day under the hard rule of a soulless gold-worshipper; the knowledge that years must pass thus; the sickening idea of her own poverty, and of living mainly on the grudged charity of neighbors—thoughts, too, of former happy days—these rack'd the widow's heart, and made her bed a sleepless one without repose.

The boy bent his steps to his employer's, as has been said. In his way down the village street he had to pass a public house, the only one the place contain'd; and when he came off against it he heard the sound of a fiddle—drown'd, however, at intervals, by much laughter and talking. The windows were up, and, the house standing close to the road, Charles thought it no harm to take a look and see what was going on within. Half a dozen footsteps brought him to the low casement, on which he lean'd his elbow, and where he had a full view of the room and its occupants. In one corner was an old man, known in the village as Black Dave—he it was whose musical performances had a moment before drawn Charles's attention to the tavern; and he it was who now exerted himself in a violent manner to give, with divers flourishes and extra twangs, a tune very popular among that thick-lipp'd race whose fondness for melody is so well known. In the middle of the room were five or six sailors, some of them quite drunk, and others in the earlier stages of that process, while on benches around were more sailors, and here and there a person dress'd in landsman's attire. The men in the middle of the room were dancing; that is, they were going through certain contortions and shufflings, varied occasionally by exceedingly hearty stamps upon the sanded floor. In short the whole party were engaged in a drunken frolic, which was in no respect different from a thousand other drunken frolics, except, perhaps, that there was less than the ordinary amount of anger and quarreling. Indeed everyone seem'd in remarkably good humor.

But what excited the boy's attention more than any other object was an individual, seated on one of the benches opposite, who, though evidently enjoying the spree as much as if he were an old hand at such business, seem'd in every other particular to be far out of his element. His appearance was youthful. He might have been twenty-one or two years old. His countenance was intelligent, and had the air of city life and society. He was dress'd not gaudily, but in every respect fashionably; his coat being of the finest broadcloth, his linen delicate and spotless as snow, and his whole aspect that of one whose counterpart may now and then be seen upon the pave in Broadway of a fine afternoon. He laugh'd and talk'd with the rest, and it must be confess'd his jokes—like the most of those that pass'd current there—were by no means distinguish'd for their refinement or purity. Near the door was a small table, cover'd with decanters and glasses, some of which had been used, but were used again indiscriminately, and a box of very thick and very long cigars.

One of the sailors—and it was he who made the largest share of the hubbub—had but one eye. His chin and cheeks were cover'd with huge, bushy whiskers, and altogether he had quite a brutal appearance. "Come, boys," said this gentleman, "come, let us take a drink. I know you're all a getting dry;" and he clench'd his invitation with an appalling oath.

This politeness was responded to by a general moving of the company toward the table holding the before-mention'd decanters and glasses. Clustering there around, each one help'd himself to a very handsome portion of that particular liquor which suited his fancy; and steadiness and accuracy being at that moment by no means distinguishing traits of the arms and legs of the party, a goodly amount of the fluid was spill'd upon the floor. This piece of extravagance excited the ire of the personage who gave the "treat;" and that ire was still further increas'd when he discover'd two or three loiterers who seem'd disposed to slight his request to drink. Charles, as we have before mention'd, was looking in at the window.

"Walk up, boys! walk up! If there be any skulker among us, blast my eyes if he shan't go down on his marrow bones and taste the liquor we have spilt! Hallo!" he exclaim'd as he spied Charles; "hallo, you chap in the window, come here and take a sup."

As he spoke he stepp'd to the open casement, put his brawny hands under the boy's arms, and lifted him into the room bodily.

"There, my lads," said he, turning to his companions, "there's a new recruit for you. Not so coarse a one, either," he added as he took a fair view of the boy, who, though not what is called pretty, was fresh and manly looking, and large for his age.

"Come, youngster, take a glass," he continued. And he pour'd one nearly full of strong brandy.

Now Charles was not exactly frighten'd, for he was a lively fellow, and had often been at the country merry-makings, and at the parties of the place; but he was certainly rather abash'd at his abrupt introduction to the midst of strangers. So, putting the glass aside, he look'd up with a pleasant smile in his new acquaintance's face.

"I've no need for anything now," he said, "but I'm just as much obliged to you as if I was."

"Poh! man, drink it down," rejoin'd the sailor, "drink it down—it won't hurt you."

And, by way of showing its excellence, the one-eyed worthy drain'd it himself to the last drop. Then filling it again, he renew'd his efforts to make the lad go through the same operation.

"I've no occasion. Besides, *my mother has often pray'd me not to drink*, and I promised to obey her."

A little irritated by his continued refusal, the sailor, with a loud oath, declared that Charles should swallow the brandy, whether he would or no. Placing one of his tremendous paws on the back of the boy's head, with the other he thrust the edge of the glass to his lips, swearing at the same time, that if he shook it so as to spill its contents the consequences would be of a nature by no means agreeable to his back and shoulders. Disliking the liquor, and angry at the attempt to overbear him, the undaunted child lifted his hand and struck the arm of the sailor with a blow so sudden that the glass fell and was smash'd to pieces on the floor; while the brandy was about equally divided between the face of Charles, the clothes of the sailor, and the sand. By this time the whole of the company had their attention drawn to the scene. Some of them laugh'd when they saw Charles's undisguised antipathy to the drink; but they laugh'd still more heartily when he discomfited the sailor. All of them, however, were content to let the matter go as chance would have it—all but the young man of the black coat, who has been spoken of.

What was there in the words which Charles had spoken that carried the mind of the young man back to former times—to a period when he was more pure and innocent than now? *"My mother has often pray'd me not to drink!"* Ah, how the mist of months roll'd aside, and presented to his soul's eye the picture of *his* mother, and a prayer of exactly similar purport! Why was it, too, that the young man's heart moved with a feeling of kindness toward the harshly treated child?

Charles stood, his cheek flush'd and his heart throbbing, wiping the trickling drops from his face with a handkerchief. At first the sailor, between his drunkenness and his surprise, was much in the condition of one suddenly awaken'd out of a deep sleep, who cannot call his consciousness about him. When he saw the state of things, however, and heard the jeering laugh of his companions, his dull eye lighting up with anger, fell upon the boy who had withstood him. He seized Charles with a grip of iron, and with the side of his heavy boot gave him a sharp and solid kick. He was about repeating the performance—for the child hung like a rag in his grasp—but all of a sudden his ears rang, as if pistols were snapp'd close to them; lights of various hues flicker'd in his eye, (he had but one, it will be remember'd,) and a strong propelling power caused him to move from his position, and keep moving until he was brought up by the wall. A blow, a cuff given in such a scientific manner that the hand from which it proceeded was evidently no stranger to the pugilistic art, had been suddenly planted in the ear of the sailor. It was planted by the young man of the black coat. He had watch'd with interest the proceeding of the sailor and the boy—two or three times he was on the point of interfering; but when the kick was given, his rage was uncontrollable. He sprang from his seat in the attitude of a boxer—struck the sailor in a manner to cause those unpleasant sensations which have been described—and would probably have follow'd up the attack, had not Charles, now thoroughly terrified, clung around his legs and prevented his advancing.

The scene was a strange one, and for the time quite a silent one. The company had started from their seats, and for a moment held breathless but strain'd positions. In the middle of the room stood the young man, in his not at all ungraceful attitude—every nerve out, and his eyes flashing brilliantly. He seem'd rooted like a rock; and clasping him, with an appearance of confidence in his protection, clung the boy.

"You scoundrel!" cried the young man, his voice thick with passion, "dare to touch the boy again, and I'll thrash you till no sense is left in your body."

The sailor, now partially recover'd, made some gestures of a belligerent nature.

"Come on, drunken brute!" continued the angry youth; "I wish you would! You've not had half what you deserve!"

Upon sobriety and sense more fully taking their power in the brains of the one-eyed mariner, however, that worthy determined in his own mind that it would be most prudent to let the matter drop. Expressing therefore his conviction to that effect, adding certain remarks to the purport that he "meant no harm to the lad," that he was surprised at such a gentleman being angry at "a little piece of fun," and so forth—he proposed that the company should go on with their jollity just as if nothing had happen'd. In truth, he of the single eye was not a bad fellow at heart, after all; the fiery enemy whose advances he had so often courted that night, had stolen away his good feelings, and set busy devils at work within him, that might have made his hands do some dreadful deed, had not the stranger interposed.

In a few minutes the frolic of the party was upon its former footing. The young man sat down upon one of the benches, with the boy by his side, and while the rest were loudly laughing and talking, they two convers'd together. The stranger learn'd from Charles all the particulars of his simple story—how his father had died years since—how his mother work'd hard for a bare living—and how he himself, for many dreary months, had been the servant of a hard-hearted, avaricious master. More and more interested, drawing the child close to his side, the young man listen'd to his plainly told history—and thus an hour pass'd away.

It was now past midnight. The young man told Charles that on the morrow he would take steps to relieve him from his servitude—that for the present night the landlord would probably give him a lodging at the inn—and little persuading did the host need for that.

As he retired to sleep, very pleasant thoughts filled the mind of the young man—thoughts of a worthy action perform'd—thoughts, too, newly awakened ones, of walking in a steadier and wiser path than formerly.

That roof, then, sheltered two beings that night—one of them innocent and sinless of all wrong—the other—oh, to that other what evil had not been present, either in action or to his desires!

Who was the stranger? To those that, from ties of relationship or otherwise, felt an interest in him, the answer to that question was not pleasant to dwell upon. His name was Langton—parentless—a dissipated young man—a brawler—one whose too frequent companions were rowdies, blacklegs, and swindlers. The New York police offices were not strangers to his countenance. He had been bred to the profession of medicine; besides, he had a very respectable income, and his house was in a pleasant street on the west side of the city. Little of his time, however, did Mr. John Langton spend at his domestic hearth; and the elderly lady who officiated as his housekeeper was by no means surprised to have him gone for a week or a month at a time, and she knowing nothing of his whereabouts.

Living as he did, the young man was an unhappy being. It was not so much that his associates were below his own capacity—for Langton, though sensible and well bred, was not highly talented or refined—but that he lived without any steady purpose, that he had no one to attract him to his home, that he too easily allow'd himself to be tempted—which caused his life to be, of late, one continued scene of dissatisfaction. This dissatisfaction he sought to drive away by the brandy bottle, and mixing in all kinds of parties where the object was pleasure. On the present occasion he had left the city a few days before, and was passing his time at a place near the village where Charles and his mother lived. He fell in, during the day, with those who were his companions of the tavern spree; and thus it happen'd that they were all together. Langton hesitated not to make himself at home with any associate that suited his fancy.

The next morning the poor widow rose from her sleepless cot; and from that lucky trait in our nature which makes one extreme follow another, she set about her toil with a lighten'd heart. Ellis, the farmer, rose, too, short as the nights were, an hour before day; for his god was gain, and a prime article of his creed was to get as much work as possible from every one around him. In the course of the day Ellis was called upon by young Langton, and never perhaps in his life was the farmer puzzled more than at the young man's proposal—his desire to provide for the widow's family, a family that could do him no pecuniary good, and his willingness to disburse money for that purpose. The widow, too, was called upon, not only on that day, but the next and the next.

It needs not that I should particularize the subsequent events of Langton's and the boy's history—how the reformation of the profligate might be dated to begin from that time—how he gradually sever'd the guilty ties that had so long gall'd him—how he enjoy'd his own home again—how the friendship of Charles and himself grew not slack with time—and how, when in the course of seasons he became head of a family of his own, he would shudder at the remembrance of his early dangers and his escapes.

Lingave's Temptation

"Another day," utter'd the poet Lingave, as he awoke in the morning, and turn'd him drowsily on his hard pallet, "another day comes out, burthen'd with its weight of woes. Of what use is existence to me? Crush'd down beneath the merciless heel of poverty, and no promise of hope to cheer me on, what have I in prospect but a life neglected, and a death of misery?"

The youth paused; but receiving no answer to his questions, thought proper to continue the peevish soliloquy. "I am a genius, they say," and the speaker smiled bitterly, "but genius is not apparel and food. Why should I exist in the world, unknown, unloved, press'd with cares, while so many around me have all their souls can desire? I behold the splendid equipages roll by—I see the respectful bow at the presence of pride—and I curse the contrast between my own lot, and the fortune of the rich. The lofty air—the show of dress—the aristocratic demeanor—the glitter of jewels—dazzle my eyes; and sharp-tooth'd envy works within me. I hate these haughty and favor'd ones. Why should my path be so much rougher than theirs? Pitiable, unfortunate man that I am! to be placed beneath those whom in my heart I despise—and to be constantly tantalized with the presence of that wealth I cannot enjoy!" And the poet cover'd his eyes with his hands, and wept from very passion and fretfulness.

O, Lingave! be more of a man! Have you not the treasures of health and untainted propensities, which many of those you envy never enjoy? Are you not their superior in mental power, in liberal views of mankind, and in comprehensive intellect? And even allowing you the choice, how would you shudder at changing, in total, conditions with them! Besides, were you willing to devote all your time and energies, you could gain property too: squeeze, and toil, and worry, and twist everything into a matter of profit, and you can become a great man, as far as money goes to make greatness.

Retreat, then, man of the polish'd soul, from those irritable complaints against your lot—those longings for wealth and puerile distinction, not worthy your class. Do justice, philosopher, to your own powers. While the world runs after its shadows and its bubbles, (thus commune in your own mind,) we will fold ourselves in our circle of understanding, and look with an eye of apathy on those things it considers so mighty and so enviable. Let the proud man pass with his pompous glance—let the gay flutter in finery—let the foolish enjoy his folly, and the beautiful move on in his perishing glory; we will gaze without desire on all their possessions, and all their pleasures. Our destiny is different from theirs. Not for such as we, the lowly flights of their crippled wings. We acknowledge no fellowship with them in ambition. We composedly look down on the paths where they walk, and pursue our own, without uttering a wish to descend, and be as they. What is it to us that the mass pay us not that deference which wealth commands? We desire no applause, save the applause of the good and discriminating—the choice spirits among men. Our intellect would be sullied, were the vulgar to approximate to it, by professing to readily enter in, and praising it. Our pride is a towering, and thrice refined pride.

When Lingave had given way to his temper some half hour, or thereabout, he grew more calm, and bethought himself that he was acting a very silly part. He listen'd a moment to the clatter of the carts, and the tramp of early passengers on the pave below, as they wended along to commence their daily toil. It was just sunrise, and the season was summer. A little canary bird, the only pet poor Lingave could afford to keep, chirp'd merrily in its cage on the wall. How slight a circumstance will sometimes change the whole current of our thoughts! The music of that bird abstracting the mind of the poet but a moment from his sorrows, gave a chance for his natural buoyancy to act again.

Lingave sprang lightly from his bed, and perform'd his ablutions and his simple toilet—then hanging the cage on a nail outside the window, and speaking an endearment to the songster, which brought a perfect flood of melody in return—he slowly passed through his door, descended the long narrow turnings of the stairs, and stood in the open street. Undetermin'd as to any particular destination, he folded his hands behind him, cast his glance upon the ground, and moved listlessly onward.

Hour after hour the poet walk'd along—up this street and down that—he reck'd not how or where. And as crowded thoroughfares are hardly the most fit places for a man to let his fancy soar in the clouds—many a push and shove and curse did the dreamer get bestow'd upon him.

The booming of the city clock sounded forth the hour twelve—high noon.

"Ho! Lingave!" cried a voice from an open basement window as the poet pass'd.

He stopp'd, and then unwittingly would have walked on still, not fully awaken'd from his reverie.

"Lingave, I say!" cried the voice again, and the person to whom the voice belong'd stretch'd his head quite out into the area in front, "Stop man. Have you forgotten your appointment?"

"Oh! ah!" said the poet, and he smiled unmeaningly, and descending the steps, went into the office of Ridman, whose call it was that had startled him in his walk.

Who was Ridman? While the poet is waiting the convenience of that personage, it may be as well to describe him.

Ridman was a *money-maker*. He had much penetration, considerable knowledge of the world, and a disposition to be constantly in the midst of enterprise, excitement, and stir. His schemes for gaining wealth were various; he had dipp'd into almost every branch and channel of business. A slight acquaintance of several years' standing subsisted between him and the poet. The day previous a boy had call'd with a note from Ridman to Lingave, desiring the presence of the latter at the money-maker's room. The poet return'd for answer that he would be there. This was the engagement which he came near breaking.

Ridman had a smooth tongue. All his ingenuity was needed in the explanation to his companion of why and wherefore the latter had been sent for.

It is not requisite to state specifically the offer made by the man of wealth to the poet. Ridman, in one of his enterprises, found it necessary to procure the aid of such a person as Lingave—a writer of power, a master of elegant diction, of fine taste, in style passionate yet pure, and of the delicate imagery that belongs to the children of song. The youth was absolutely startled at the magnificent and permanent remuneration which was held out to him for a moderate exercise of his talents.

But the *nature* of the service required! All the sophistry and art of Ridman could not veil its repulsiveness. The poet was to labor for the advancement of what he felt to be unholy—he was to inculcate what would lower the perfection of man. He promised to give an answer to the proposal the succeeding day, and left the place.

Now during the many hours there was a war going on in the heart of the poor poet. He was indeed *poor;* often, he had no certainty whether he should be able to procure the next day's meals. And the poet knew the beauty of truth, and adored, not in the abstract merely, but in practice, the excellence of upright principles.

Night came. Lingave, wearied, lay upon his pallet again and slept. The misty veil thrown over him, the spirit of poesy came to his visions, and stood beside him, and look'd down pleasantly with her large eyes, which were bright and liquid like the reflection of stars in a lake.

Virtue, (such imagining, then, seem'd conscious to the soul of the dreamer,) is ever the sinew of true genius. Together, the two in one, they are endow'd with immortal strength, and approach loftily to Him from whom both spring. Yet there are those that having great powers, bend them to the slavery of wrong. God forgive them! for they surely do it ignorantly or heedlessly. Oh, could he who lightly tosses around him the seeds of evil in his writings, or his enduring thoughts, or his chance words—could he see how, haply, they are to spring up in distant time and poison the air, and putrefy, and cause to sicken—would he not shrink back in horror? A bad principle, jestingly spoken—a falsehood, but of a word—may taint a whole nation! Let the man to whom the great Master has given the might of mind, beware how he uses that might. If for the furtherance of bad ends, what can be expected but that, as the hour of the closing scene draws nigh, thoughts of harm done, and capacities distorted from their proper aim, and strength so laid out that men must be worse instead of better, through the exertion of that strength—will come and swarm like spectres around him?

"Be and continue poor, young man," so taught one whose counsels should be graven on the heart of every youth, "while others around you grow rich by fraud and disloyalty. Be without place and power, while others beg their way upward. Bear the pain of disappointed hopes, while others gain the accomplishment of their flattery. Forego the gracious pressure of a hand, for which others cringe and crawl. Wrap yourself in your own virtue, and seek a friend and your daily bread. If you have, in such a course, grown gray with unblench'd honor, bless God and die."

When Lingave awoke the next morning, he despatch'd his answer to his wealthy friend, and then plodded on as in the days before.

Little Jane

"Lift up!" was ejaculated as a signal!—and click! went the glasses in the hands of a party of tipsy men, drinking one night at the bar of one of the middling order of taverns. And many a wild gibe was utter'd, and many a terrible blasphemy, and many an impure phrase sounded out the pollution of the hearts of these half-crazed creatures, as they toss'd down their liquor, and made the walls echo with their uproar. The first and foremost in recklessness was a girlish-faced, fair-hair'd fellow of twenty-two or three years. They called him Mike. He seemed to be look'd upon by the others as a sort of prompter, from whom they were to take cue. And if the brazen wickedness evinced by him in a hundred freaks and remarks to his companions, during their stay in that place, were any test of his capacity—there might hardly be one more fit to go forward as a guide on the road to destruction. From the conversation of the party, it appear'd that they had been spending the early part of the evening in a gambling house.

A second, third and fourth time were the glasses fill'd; and the effect thereof began to be perceiv'd in a still higher degree of noise and loquacity among the revellers. One of the serving-men came in at this moment, and whisper'd the bar-keeper, who went out, and in a moment return'd again.

"A person," he said, "wish'd to speak with Mr. Michael. He waited on the walk in front."

The individual whose name was mention'd, made his excuses to the others, telling them he would be back in a moment, and left the room. As he shut the door behind him, and stepp'd into the open air, he saw one of his brothers—his elder by eight or ten years—pacing to and fro with rapid and uneven steps. As the man turn'd in his walk, and the glare of the street lamp fell upon his face, the youth, half-benumb'd as his senses were, was somewhat startled at its paleness and evident perturbation.

"Come with me!" said the elder brother, hurriedly, "the illness of our little Jane is worse, and I have been sent for you."

"Poh!" answered the young drunkard, very composedly, "is that all? I shall be home by-and-by," and he turn'd back again.

"But, brother, she is worse than ever before. Perhaps when you arrive she may be *dead*."

The tipsy one paus'd in his retreat, perhaps alarm'd at the utterance of that dread word, which seldom fails to shoot a chill to the hearts of mortals. But he soon calm'd himself, and waving his hand to the other:

"Why, see," said he, "a score of times at least, have I been call'd away to the last sickness of our good little sister; and each time, it proves to be nothing worse than some whim of the nurse or the physician. Three years has the girl been able to live very heartily under her disease; and I'll be bound she'll stay on the earth three years longer."

And as he concluded this wicked and most brutal reply, the speaker open'd the door and went into the bar-room. But in his intoxication, during the hour that follow'd, Mike was far from being at ease. At the end of that hour, the words, "perhaps when you arrive she may be *dead*," were not effaced from his hearing yet, and he started for home. The elder brother had wended his way back in sorrow.

Let me go before the younger one, awhile, to a room in that home. A little girl lay there dying. She had been ill a long time; so it was no sudden thing for her parents, and her brethren and sisters, to be called for the witness of the death agony. The girl was not what might be called beautiful. And yet, there is a solemn kind of loveliness that always surrounds a sick child. The sympathy for the weak and helpless sufferer, perhaps, increases it in our own ideas. The ashiness and the moisture on the brow, and the film over the eye-balls—what man can look upon the sight, and not feel his heart awed within him? Children, I have sometimes fancied too, increase in beauty as their illness deepens.

Besides the nearest relatives of little Jane, standing round her bedside, was the family doctor. He had just laid her wrist down upon the coverlet, and the look he gave the mother, was a look in which there was no hope.

"My child!" she cried, in uncontrollable agony, "O! my child!"

And the father, and the sons and daughters, were bowed down in grief, and thick tears rippled between the fingers held before their eyes.

Then there was silence awhile. During the hour just bygone, Jane had, in her childish way, bestow'd a little gift upon each of her kindred, as a remembrancer when she should be dead and buried in the grave. And there was one of these simple tokens which had not reach'd its destination. She held it in her hand now. It was a very small much-thumbed book—a religious story for infants, given her by her mother when she had first learn'd to read.

While they were all keeping this solemn stillness—broken only by the suppress'd sobs of those who stood and watch'd for the passing away of the girl's soul—a confusion of some one entering rudely, and speaking in a turbulent voice, was heard in an adjoining apartment. Again the voice roughly sounded out; it was the voice of the drunkard Mike, and the father bade one of his sons go and quiet the intruder.

"If nought else will do," said he sternly, "put him forth by strength. We want no tipsy brawlers here, to disturb such a scene as this."

For what moved the sick girl uneasily on her pillow, and raised her neck, and motion'd to her mother? She would that Mike should be brought to her side. And it was enjoin'd on him whom the father had bade to eject the noisy one, that he should tell Mike his sister's request, and beg him to come to her.

He came. The inebriate—his mind sober'd by the deep solemnity of the scene—stood there, and leaned over to catch the last accounts of one who soon was to be with the spirits of heaven. All was the silence of the deepest night. The dying child held the young man's hand in one of hers; with the other she slowly lifted the trifling memorial she had assigned especially for him, aloft in the air. Her arm shook—her eyes, now becoming glassy with the death-damps, were cast toward her brother's face. She smiled pleasantly, and as an indistinct gurgle came from her throat, the uplifted hand fell suddenly into the open palm of her brother's, depositing the tiny volume there. Little Jane was dead.

From that night, the young man stepped no more in his wild courses, but was reform'd.

Dumb Kate

Not many years since—and yet long enough to have been before the abundance of railroads, and similar speedy modes of conveyance—the travelers from Amboy village to the metropolis of our republic were permitted to refresh themselves, and the horses of the stage had a breathing spell, at a certain old-fashion'd tavern, about half way between the two places. It was a quaint, comfortable, ancient house, that tavern. Huge buttonwood trees embower'd it round about, and there was a long porch in front, the trellis'd work whereof, though old and moulder'd, had been, and promised still to be for years, held together by the tangled folds of a grape vine wreath'd about it like a tremendous serpent.

How clean and fragrant everything was there! How bright the pewter tankards wherefrom cider or ale went into the parch'd throat of the thirsty man! How pleasing to look into the expressive eyes of Kate, the landlord's lovely daughter, who kept everything so clean and bright!

Now the reason why Kate's eyes had become so expressive was, that, besides their proper and natural office, they stood to the poor girl in the place of tongue and ears also. Kate had been dumb from her birth. Everybody loved the helpless creature when she was a child. Gentle, timid, and affectionate was she, and beautiful as the lilies of which she loved to cultivate so many every summer in her garden. Her light hair, and the like-color'd lashes, so long and silky, that droop'd over her blue eyes of such uncommon size and softtness—her rounded shape, well set off by a little modest art of dress—her smile—the graceful ease of her motions, always attracted the admiration of the strangers who stopped there, and were quite a pride to her parents and friends.

How could it happen that so beautiful and inoffensive a being should taste, even to its dregs, the bitterest unhappiness? Oh, there must indeed be a mysterious, unfathomable meaning in the decrees of Providence which is beyond the comprehension of man; for no one on earth less deserved or needed 'the uses of adversity' than Dumb Kate. Love, the mighty and lawless passion, came into the sanctuary of the maid's pure breast, and the dove of peace fled away forever.

One of the persons who had occasion to stop most frequently at the tavern kept by Dumb Kate's parents was a young man, the son of a wealthy farmer, who own'd an estate in the neighborhood. He saw Kate, and was struck with her natural elegance. Though not of thoroughly wicked propensities, the fascination of so fine a prize made this youth determine to gain her love, and, if possible, to win her to himself. At first he hardly dared, even amid the depths of his own soul, to entertain thoughts of vileness against one so confiding and childlike. But in a short time such feelings wore away, and he made up his mind to become the betrayer of poor Kate. He was a good-looking fellow, and made but too sure of his victim. Kate was lost!

The villain came to New York soon after, and engaged in a business which prosper'd well, and which has no doubt by this time made him what is call'd a man of fortune.

Not long did sickness of the heart wear into the life and happiness of Dumb Kate. One pleasant spring day, the neighbors having been called by a notice the previous morning, the old churchyard was thrown open, and a coffin was borne over the early grass that seem'd so delicate with its light green hue. There was a new made grave, and by its side the bier was rested—while they paused a moment until holy words had been said. An idle boy, call'd there by curiosity, saw something lying on the fresh earth thrown out from the grave, which attracted his attention. A little blossom, the only one to be seen around, had grown exactly on the spot where the sexton chose to dig poor Kate's last resting-place. It was a weak but lovely flower, and now lay where it had been carelessly toss'd amid the coarse gravel. The boy twirl'd it a moment in his fingers—the bruis'd fragments gave out a momentary perfume, and then fell to the edge of the pit, over which the child at that moment lean'd and gazed in his inquisitiveness. As they dropp'd, they were wafted to the bottom of the grave. The last look was bestow'd on the dead girl's face by those who loved her so well in life, and then she was softly laid away to her sleep beneath that green grass covering.

Yet in the churchyard on the hill is Kate's grave. There stands a little white stone at the head, and verdure grows richly there; and gossips, sometimes of a Sabbath afternoon, rambling over that gathering-place of the gone from earth, stop a while, and con over the dumb girl's hapless story.

Talk to an Art-Union

(A Brooklyn fragment.)

It is a beautiful truth that all men contain something of the artist in them. And perhaps it is the case that the greatest artists live and die, the world and themselves alike ignorant what they possess. Who would not mourn that an ample palace, of surpassingly graceful architecture, fill'd with luxuries, and embellish'd with fine pictures and sculpture, should stand cold and still and vacant, and never be known or enjoy'd by its owner? Would such a fact as this cause your sadness? Then be sad. For there is a palace, to which the courts of the most sumptuous kings are but a frivolous patch, and, though it is always waiting for them, not one of its owners ever enters there with any genuine sense of its grandeur and glory.

I think of few heroic actions, which cannot be traced to the artistical impulse. He who does great deeds, does them from his innate sensitiveness to moral beauty. Such men are not merely artists, they are also artistic material. Washington in some great crisis, Lawrence on the bloody deck of the Chesapeake, Mary Stuart at the block, Kossuth in captivity, and Mazzini in exile—all great rebels and innovators, exhibit the highest phases of the artist spirit. The painter, the sculptor, the poet, express heroic beauty better in description; but the others *are* heroic beauty, the best belov'd of art.

Talk not so much, then, young artist, of the great old masters, who but painted and chisell'd. Study not only their productions. There is a still higher school for him who would kindle his fire with coal from the altar of the loftiest and purest art. It is the school of all grand actions and grand virtues, of heroism, of the death of patriots and martyrs—of all the mighty deeds written in the pages of history—deeds of daring, and enthusiasm, devotion, and fortitude.

Blood-Money

"Guilty of the body and the blood of Christ."

I.

Of olden time, when it came to pass
That the beautiful god, Jesus, should finish his work on
earth,
Then went Judas, and sold the divine youth,
And took pay for his body.

Curs'd was the deed, even before the sweat of the clutching
hand grew dry;
And darkness frown'd upon the seller of the like of God,
Where, as though earth lifted her breast to throw him from
her, and heaven refused him,
He hung in the air, self-slaughter'd.

The cycles, with their long shadows, have stalk'd silently
forward,
Since those ancient days—many a pouch enwrapping
meanwhile
Its fee, like that paid for the son of Mary.

And still goes one, saying,
"What will ye give me, and I will deliver this man unto
you?"
And they make the covenant, and pay the pieces of silver.

II.

Look forth, deliverer,
Look forth, first-born of the dead,

Over the tree-tops of Paradise;
See thyself in yet-continued bonds,
Toilsome and poor, thou bear'st man's form again,
Thou art reviled, scourged, put into prison,
Hunted from the arrogant equality of the rest;
With staves and swords throng the willing servants of
authority,
Again they surround thee, mad with devilish spite;
Toward thee stretch the hands of a multitude, like vultures'
talons,
The meanest spit in thy face, they smite thee with their
palms;
Bruised, bloody, and pinion'd is thy body,
More sorrowful than death is thy soul.

Witness of anguish, brother of slaves,
Not with thy price closed the price of thine image:
And still Iscariot plies his trade.

PAUMANOK. *April, 1843.*

WOUNDED IN THE HOUSE OF FRIENDS

"And one shall say unto him, What are these wounds in thy hands? Then he shall answer, These with which I was wounded in the house of my friends."
—Zechariah, xiii.6

If thou art balk'd, O Freedom,
The victory is not to thy manlier foes;
From the house of friends comes the death stab.

Virginia, mother of greatness,
Blush not for being also mother of slaves;
You might have borne deeper slaves—
Doughfaces, crawlers, lice of humanity—
Terrific screamers of freedom,
Who roar and bawl, and get hot i' the face,
But were they not incapable of august crime,
Would quench the hopes of ages for a drink—
Muck-worms, creeping flat to the ground,
A dollar dearer to them than Christ's blessing;

All loves, all hopes, less than the thought of gain,
In life walking in that as in a shroud;
Men whom the throes of heroes,
Great deeds at which the gods might stand appal'd,
The shriek of the drown'd, the appeal of women,
The exulting laugh of untied empires,
Would touch them never in the heart,
But only in the pocket.

Hot-headed Carolina,
Well may you curl your lip;
With all your bondsmen, bless the destiny
Which brings you no such breed as this.

Arise, young North!
Our elder blood flows in the veins of cowards:
The gray-hair'd sneak, the blanch'd poltroon,
The feign'd or real shiverer at tongues
That nursing babes need hardly cry the less for—
Are they to be our tokens always?

Sailing the Mississippi at Midnight

Vast and starless, the pall of heaven
  Laps on the trailing pall below;
And forward, forward, in solemn darkness,
  As if to the sea of the lost we go.

Now drawn nigh the edge of the river,
  Weird-like creatures suddenly rise;
Shapes that fade, dissolving outlines
  Baffle the gazer's straining eyes.

Towering upward and bending forward,
  Wild and wide their arms are thrown,
Ready to pierce with forked fingers
  Him who touches their realm upon.

Tide of youth, thus thickly planted,

While in the eddies onward you swim,
Thus on the shore stands a phantom army,
Lining forever the channel's rim.

Steady, helmsman! you guide the immortal;
Many a wreck is beneath you piled,
Many a brave yet unwary sailor
Over these waters has been beguiled.

Nor is it the storm or the scowling midnight,
Cold, or sickness, or fire's dismay—
Nor is it the reef, or treacherous quicksand,
Will peril you most on your twisted way.

But when there comes a voluptuous languor,
Soft the sunshine, silent the air,
Bewitching your craft with safety and sweetness,
Then, young pilot of life, beware.

November Boughs

Our Eminent Visitors, Past, Present and Future

Welcome to them each and all! They do good—the deepest, widest, most needed good—though quite certainly not in the ways attempted—which have, at times, something irresistibly comic. What can be more farcical, for instance, than the sight of a worthy gentleman coming three or four thousand miles through wet and wind to speak complacently and at great length on matters of which he both entirely mistakes or knows nothing—before crowds of auditors equally complacent, and equally at fault?

Yet welcome and thanks, we say, to those visitors we have, and have had, from abroad among us—and may the procession continue! We have had Dickens and Thackeray, Froude, Herbert Spencer, Oscar Wilde, Lord Coleridge—soldiers, savants, poets—and now Matthew Arnold and Irving the actor. Some have come to make money—some for a "good time"—some to help us along and give us advice—and some undoubtedly to investigate, *bona fide,* this great problem, democratic America, looming upon the world with such cumulative power through a hundred years, now with the evident intention (since the Secession War) to stay, and take a leading hand, for many a century to come, in civilization's and humanity's eternal game. But alas! that very investigation—the method of that investigation—is where the deficit most surely and helplessly comes in. Let not Lord Coleridge and Mr. Arnold (to say nothing of the illustrious actor) imagine that when they have met and survey'd the etiquettical gatherings of our wealthy, distinguish'd and sure-to-be-put-forward-on-such-occasions citizens (New York, Boston, Philadelphia, &c., have certain stereotyped strings of them, continually lined and paraded like the lists of dishes at hotel tables—you are sure to get the same over and over again—it is very amusing)—and the bowing and introducing, the receptions at the swell clubs, the eating and drinking and praising and praising back—and the next day riding about Central Park, or doing the "Public Institutions"—and so passing through, one after another, the full-dress coteries of the Atlantic cities, all grammatical and cultured and correct, with the toned-down manners of the gentlemen, and the kid-gloves, and luncheons and finger-glasses—Let not our eminent visitors, we say, suppose that, by means of these experiences, they have "seen America," or captur'd any distinctive clew or purport thereof. Not a bit of it. Of the pulse-beats that lie within and vitalize this Commonweal to-day—of the hard-pan purports and idiosyncrasies pursued faithfully and triumphantly by its bulk of men North and South, generation after generation, superficially unconscious of their own aims, yet none the less pressing onward with deathless intuition—those coteries do not furnish the faintest scintilla. In the Old World the best flavor and significance of a race may possibly need to be look'd for in its "upper classes," its gentries, its court, its *état major*. In the United States the rule is revers'd. Besides (and a point, this, perhaps deepest of all,) the special marks of our grouping and design are not going to be understood in a hurry. The lesson and scanning right on the ground are difficult; I was going to say they are impossible to foreigners—but I have occasionally found the clearest appreciation of all, coming from far-off quarters. Surely nothing could be more apt, not only for our eminent visitors present and to come, but for home study, than the following editorial criticism of the London *Times* on Mr. Froude's visit and lectures here a few years ago, and the culminating dinner given at Delmonico's, with its brilliant array of guests:

> "We read the list," says the *Times,* "of those who assembled to do honor to Mr. Froude: there were Mr. Emerson, Mr. Beecher, Mr. Curtis, Mr. Bryant; we add the names of those who sent letters of regret that they could not attend in person—Mr. Longfellow, Mr. Whittier. They are names which are well known—almost as well known and as much honor'd in England as in America; and yet what must we say in the end? The American people outside this assemblage of writers is something vaster and greater than they,

singly or together, can comprehend. It cannot be said of any or all of them that they can speak for their nation. We who look on at this distance are able perhaps on that account to see the more clearly that there are qualities of the American people which find no representation, no voice, among these their spokesmen. And what is true of them is true of the English class of whom Mr. Froude may be said to be the ambassador. Mr. Froude is master of a charming style. He has the gift of grace and the gift of sympathy. Taking any single character as the subject of his study, he may succeed after a very short time in so comprehending its workings as to be able to present a living figure to the intelligence and memory of his readers. But the movements of a nation, *the voiceless purpose of a people which cannot put its own thoughts into words, yet acts upon them in each successive generation*—these things do not lie within his grasp. . . . The functions of literature such as he represents are limited in their action; the influence he can wield is artificial and restricted, and, while he and his hearers please and are pleas'd with pleasant periods, the great mass of national life will flow around them unmov'd in its tides by action as powerless as that of the dwellers by the shore to direct the currents of the ocean."

A thought, here, that needs to be echoed, expanded, permanently treasur'd by our literary classes and educators. (The gestation, the youth, the knitting preparations, are now over, and it is full time for definite purpose, result.) How few think of it, though it is the impetus and background of our whole Nationality and popular life. In the present brief memorandum I very likely for the first time awake "the intelligent reader" to the idea and inquiry whether there isn't such a thing as the distinctive genius of our democratic New World, universal, immanent, bringing to a head the best experience of the past—not specially literary or intellectual—not merely "good," (in the Sunday School and Temperance Society sense,)—some invisible spine and great sympathetic to these States, resident only in the average people, in their practical life, in their physiology, in their emotions, in their nebulous yet fiery patriotism, in the armies (both sides) through the whole Secession War—an identity and character which indeed so far "finds no voice among their spokesmen."

To my mind America, vast and fruitful as it appears to-day, is even yet, for its most important results, entirely in the tentative state; its very formation-stir and whirling trials and essays more splendid and picturesque, to my thinking, than the accomplish'd growths and shows of other lands, through European history, or Greece, or all the past. Surely a New World literature, worthy the name, is not to be, if it ever comes, some fiction, or fancy, or bit of sentimentalism or polish'd work merely by itself, or in abstraction. So long as such literature is no born branch and offshoot of the Nationality, rooted and grown from its roots, and fibred with its fibre, it can never answer any deep call or perennial need. Perhaps the untaught Republic is wiser than its teachers. The best literature is always a result of something far greater than itself—not the hero, but the portrait of the hero. Before there can be recorded history or poem there must be the transaction. Beyond the old masterpieces, the Iliad, the interminable Hindu epics, the Greek tragedies, even the Bible itself, range the immense facts of what must have preceded them, their *sine qua non*—the veritable poems and masterpieces, of which, grand as they are, the word-statements are but shreds and cartoons.

For to-day and the States, I think the vividest, rapidest, most stupendous processes ever known, ever perform'd by man or nation, on the largest scales and in countless varieties, are now and here presented. Not as our poets and preachers are always conventionally putting it—but quite different. Some colossal foundry, the flaming of the fire, the melted metal, the pounding trip-hammers, the surging crowds of workmen shifting from point to point, the murky shadows, the rolling haze, the discord, the crudeness, the deafening din, the disorder, the dross and clouds of dust, the waste and extravagance of material, the shafts of darted sunshine through the vast open roof-scuttles aloft—the mighty castings, many of them not yet fitted, perhaps delay'd long, yet each in its due time, with definite place and use and meaning—Such, more like, is a symbol of America.

After all of which, returning to our starting-point, we reiterate, and in the whole Land's name, a welcome to our eminent guests. Visits like theirs, and hospitalities, and hand-shaking, and face meeting face, and the distant brought near—what divine solvents they are! Travel, reciprocity, "interviewing," intercommunion of lands—what are they but Democracy's and the highest Law's best aids? O that our own country—that every land in the world—could annually, continually, receive the poets, thinkers, scientists, even the official magnates, of other lands, as honor'd guests. O that the United States, especially the West, could have had a good long visit and explorative jaunt, from the noble and melancholy Tourguéneff, before he died—or from Victor Hugo—or Thomas Carlyle. Castelar, Tennyson, any of the two or three great Parisian essayists—were they and we to come face to face, how is it possible but that the right understanding would ensue?

The Bible as Poetry

I SUPPOSE one cannot at this day say anything new, from a literary point of view, about those autochthonic bequests of Asia—the Hebrew Bible, the mighty Hindu epics, and a hundred lesser but typical works; (not now definitely including the Iliad—though that work was certainly of Asiatic genesis, as Homer himself was—considerations which seem curiously ignored.) But will there ever be a time or place—ever a student, however modern, of the grand art, to whom those compositions will not afford profounder lessons than all else of their kind in the garnerage of the past? Could there be any more opportune suggestion, to the current popular writer and reader of verse, what the office of poet was in primeval times—and is yet capable of being, anew, adjusted entirely to the modern?

All the poems of Orientalism, with the Old and New Testaments at the centre, tend to deep and wide, (I don't know but the deepest and widest,) psychological development—with little, or nothing at all, of the mere æsthetic, the principal verse-requirement of our day. Very late, but unerringly, comes to every capable student the perception that it is not in beauty, it is not in art, it is not even in science, that the profoundest laws of the case have their eternal sway and outcropping.

In his discourse on "Hebrew Poets" De Sola Mendes said: "The fundamental feature of Judaism, of the Hebrew nationality, was religion; its poetry was naturally religious. Its subjects, God and Providence, the covenants with Israel, God in Nature, and as reveal'd, God the Creator and Governor, Nature in her majesty and beauty, inspired hymns and odes to Nature's God. And then the checker'd history of the nation furnish'd allusions, illustrations, and subjects for epic display—the glory of the sanctuary, the offerings, the splendid ritual, the Holy City, and lov'd Palestine with its pleasant valleys and wild tracts." Dr. Mendes said "that rhyming was not a characteristic of Hebrew poetry at all. Metre was not a necessary mark of poetry. Great poets discarded it; the early Jewish poets knew it not."

Compared with the famed epics of Greece, and lesser ones since, the spinal supports of the Bible are simple and meagre. All its history, biography, narratives, etc., are as beads, strung on and indicating the eternal thread of the Deific purpose and power. Yet with only deepest faith for impetus, and such Deific purpose for palpable or impalpable theme, it often transcends the masterpieces of Hellas, and all masterpieces. The metaphors daring beyond account, the lawless soul, extravagant by our standards, the glow of love and friendship, the fervent kiss—nothing in argument or logic, but unsurpass'd in proverbs, in religious ecstacy, in suggestions of common mortality and death, man's great equalizers—the spirit everything, the ceremonies and forms of the churches nothing, faith limitless, its immense sensuousness immensely spiritual—an incredible, all-inclusive non-worldliness and dew-scented illiteracy (the antipodes of our Nineteenth Century business absorption and morbid refinement)—no hair-splitting doubts, no sickly sulking and sniffling, no "Hamlet," no "Adonais," no "Thanatopsis," no "In Memoriam."

The culminated proof of the poetry of a country is the quality of its personnel, which, in any race, can never be really superior without superior poems. The finest blending of individuality with universality (in my opinion nothing out of the galaxies of the "Iliad," or Shakspere's heroes, or from the Tennysonian "Idyls," so lofty, devoted and starlike,) typified in the songs of those old Asiatic lands. Men and women as great columnar trees. Nowhere else the abnegation of self towering in such quaint sublimity; nowhere else the simplest human emotions conquering the gods of heaven, and fate itself. (The episode, for instance, toward the close of the "Mahabharata"—the journey of the wife Savitri with the god of death, Yama,

> "One terrible to see—blood-red his garb,
> His body huge and dark, bloodshot his eyes,
> Which flamed like suns beneath his turban cloth,
> Arm'd was he with a noose,"

who carries off the soul of the dead husband, the wife tenaciously following, and—by the resistless charm of perfect poetic recitation!—eventually redeeming her captive mate.)

I remember how enthusiastically William H. Seward, in his last days, once expatiated on these themes, from his travels in Turkey, Egypt, and Asia Minor, finding the oldest Biblical narratives exactly illustrated there to-day with apparently no break or change along three thousand years—the veil'd women, the costumes, the gravity and simplicity, all the manners just the same. The veteran Trelawney said he found the only real *nobleman* of the world in a good average specimen of the mid-aged or elderly Oriental. In the East the grand figure, always leading, is the *old man,* majestic, with flowing beard, paternal, etc. In Europe and America, it is, as we know, the young fellow—in novels, a handsome and interesting hero, more or less juvenile—in operas, a tenor with blooming cheeks, black mustache, superficial animation, and perhaps good lungs, but no more depth than skim-milk. But reading folks probably get their information of those Bible areas and current peoples, as depicted in print by English and French cads, the most shallow, impudent, supercilious brood on earth.

I have said nothing yet of the cumulus of associations (perfectly legitimate parts of its influence, and finally in many respects the dominant parts,) of the Bible as a poetic entity, and of every portion of it. Not the old edifice only—the congeries also of events and struggles and surroundings, of which it has been the scene and motive—even the horrors, dreads, deaths. How many ages and generations have brooded and wept and agonized over this book! What untellable joys and ecstasies—what support to martyrs at the stake—from it. (No really great song can ever attain full purport till long after the death of its singer—till it has accrued and incorporated the many passions, many joys and sorrows, it has itself arous'd.) To what myriads has it been the shore and rock of safety—the refuge from driving tempest and wreck! Translated in all languages, how it has united this diverse world! Of civilized lands to-day, whose of our retrospects has it not interwoven and link'd and permeated? Not only does it bring us what is clasp'd within its covers; nay, that is the least of what it brings. Of its thousands, there is not a verse, not a word, but is thick-studded with human emotions, successions of fathers and sons, mothers and daughters, of our own antecedents, inseparable from that background of us, on which, phantasmal as it is, all that we are to-day inevitably depends—our ancestry, our past.

Strange, but true, that the principal factor in cohering the nations, eras and paradoxes of the globe, by giving them a common platform of two or three great ideas, a commonalty of origin, and projecting cosmic brotherhood, the dream of all hope, all time—that the long trains, gestations, attempts and failures, resulting in the New World, and in modern solidarity and politics—are to be identified and resolv'd back into a collection of old poetic lore, which, more than any one thing else, has been the axis of civilization and history through thousands of years—and except for which this America of ours, with its polity and essentials, could not now be existing.

No true bard will ever contravene the Bible. If the time ever comes when iconoclasm does its extremest in one direction against the Books of the Bible in its present form, the collection must still survive in another, and dominate just as much as hitherto, or more than hitherto, through its divine and primal poetic structure. To me, that is the living and definite element-principle of the work, evolving everything else. Then the continuity; the oldest and newest Asiatic utterance and character, and all between, holding together, like the apparition of the sky, and coming to us the same. Even to our Nineteenth Century here are the fountain heads of song.

Father Taylor (and Oratory)

I HAVE never heard but one essentially perfect orator—one who satisfied those depths of the emotional nature that in most cases go through life quite untouch'd, unfed—who held every hearer by spells which no conventionalist, high or low—nor any pride or composure, nor resistance of intellect—could stand against for ten minutes.

And by the way, is it not strange, of this first-class genius in the rarest and most profound of humanity's arts, that it will be necessary, (so nearly forgotten and rubb'd out is his name by the rushing whirl of the last twenty-five years,) to first inform current readers that he was an orthodox minister, of no particular celebrity, who during a long life preach'd especially to Yankee sailors in an old fourth-class church down by the wharves in Boston—had practically been a sea-faring man through his earlier years—and died April 6, 1871, "just as the tide turn'd, going out with the ebb as an old salt should"? His name is now comparatively unknown, outside of Boston—and even there, (though Dickens, Mr. Jameson, Dr. Bartol and Bishop Haven have commemorated him,) is mostly but a reminiscence.

During my visits to "the Hub," in 1859 and '60 I several times saw and heard Father Taylor. In the spring or autumn, quiet Sunday forenoons, I liked to go down early to the quaint ship-cabin-looking church where the old man minister'd—to enter and leisurely scan the building, the low ceiling, everything strongly timber'd (polish'd and rubb'd apparently,) the dark rich colors, the gallery, all in half-light—and smell the aroma of old wood—to watch the auditors, sailors, mates, "matlows," officers, singly or in groups, as they came in—their physiognomies, forms, dress, gait, as they walk'd along the aisles,—their postures, seating themselves in the rude, roomy, undoor'd, uncushion'd pews—and the evident effect upon them of the place, occasion, and atmosphere.

The pulpit, rising ten or twelve feet high, against the rear wall, was back'd by a significant mural painting, in oil—

showing out its bold lines and strong hues through the subdued light of the building—of a stormy sea, the waves high-rolling, and amid them an old-style ship, all bent over, driving through the gale, and in great peril—a vivid and effectual piece of limning, not meant for the criticism of artists (though I think it had merit even from that standpoint,) but for its effect upon the congregation, and what it would convey to them.

Father Taylor was a moderate-sized man, indeed almost small, (reminded me of old Booth, the great actor, and my favorite of those and preceding days,) well advanced in years, but alert, with mild blue or gray eyes, and good presence and voice. Soon as he open'd his mouth I ceas'd to pay any attention to church or audience, or pictures or lights and shades; a far more potent charm entirely sway'd me. In the course of the sermon, (there was no sign of any MS., or reading from notes,) some of the parts would be in the highest degree majestic and picturesque. Colloquial in a severe sense, it often lean'd to Biblical and oriental forms. Especially were all allusions to ships and the ocean and sailors' lives, of unrival'd power and life-likeness. Sometimes there were passages of fine language and composition, even from the purist's point of view. A few arguments, and of the best, but always brief and simple. One realized what grip there might have been in such words-of-mouth talk as that of Socrates and Epictetus. In the main, I should say, of any of these discourses, that the old Demosthenean rule and requirement of "action, action, action," first in its inward and then (very moderate and restrain'd) its outward sense, was the quality that had leading fulfilment.

I remember I felt the deepest impression from the old man's prayers, which invariably affected me to tears. Never, on similar or any other occasions, have I heard such impassion'd pleading—such human-harassing reproach (like Hamlet to his mother, in the closet)—such probing to the very depths of that latent conscience and remorse which probably lie somewhere in the background of every life, every soul. For when Father Taylor preach'd or pray'd, the rhetoric and art, the mere words, (which usually play such a big part) seem'd altogether to disappear, and the *live feeling* advanced upon you and seiz'd you with a power before unknown. Everybody felt this marvelous and awful influence. One young sailor, a Rhode Islander, (who came every Sunday, and I got acquainted with, and talk'd to once or twice as we went away,) told me, "that must be the Holy Ghost we read of in the Testament."

I should be at a loss to make any comparison with other preachers or public speakers. When a child I had heard Elias Hicks—and Father Taylor (though so different in personal appearance, for Elias was of tall and most shapely form, with black eyes that blazed at times like meteors,) always reminded me of him. Both had the same inner, apparently inexhaustible, fund of latent volcanic passion—the same tenderness, blended with a curious remorseless firmness, as of some surgeon operating on a belov'd patient. Hearing such men sends to the winds all the books, and formulas, and polish'd speaking, and rules of oratory.

Talking of oratory, why is it that the unsophisticated practices often strike deeper than the train'd ones? Why do our experiences perhaps of some local country exhorter—or often in the West or South at political meetings—bring the most definite results? In my time I have heard Webster, Clay, Edward Everett, Phillips, and such *célébrès;* yet I recall the minor but life-eloquence of men like John P. Hale, Cassius Clay, and one or two of the old abolition "fanatics" ahead of all those stereotyped fames. Is not—I sometimes question—the first, last, and most important quality of all, in training for a "finish'd speaker," generally unsought, unreck'd of, both by teacher and pupil? Though maybe it cannot be taught, anyhow. At any rate, we need to clearly understand the distinction between oratory and elocution. Under the latter art, including some of high order, there is indeed no scarcity in the United States, preachers, lawyers, actors, lecturers, &c. With all, there seem to be few real orators—almost none.

I repeat, and would dwell upon it (more as suggestion than mere fact)—among all the brilliant lights of bar or stage I have heard in my time (for years in New York and other cities I haunted the courts to witness notable trials, and have heard all the famous actors and actresses that have been in America the past fifty years) though I recall marvellous effects from one or other of them, I never had anything in the way of vocal utterance to shake me through and through, and become fix'd, with its accompaniments, in my memory, like those prayers and sermons—like Father Taylor's personal electricity and the whole scene there—the prone ship in the gale, and dashing wave and foam for background—in the little old sea-church in Boston, those summer Sundays just before the Secession War broke out.

The Spanish Element in Our Nationality

[Our friends at Santa Fé, New Mexico, have just finish'd their long drawn out anniversary of the 333d year of the settlement of their city by the Spanish. The good, gray Walt Whitman was asked to write them a poem in commemoration. Instead he wrote them a letter as follows:—*Philadelphia Press,* August 5, 1883.]

CAMDEN, NEW JERSEY, *July 20, 1883.*

To Messrs. Griffin, Martinez, Prince, and other Gentlemen at Santa Fé:

DEAR SIRS:—Your kind invitation to visit you and deliver a poem for the 333d Anniversary of founding Santa Fé has reach'd me so late that I have to decline, with sincere regret. But I will say a few words off hand.

We Americans have yet to really learn our own antecedents, and sort them, to unify them. They will be found ampler than has been supposed, and in widely different sources. Thus far, impress'd by New England writers and schoolmasters, we tacitly abandon ourselves to the notion that our United States have been fashion'd from the British Islands only, and essentially form a second England only—which is a very great mistake. Many leading traits for our future national personality, and some of the best ones, will certainly prove to have originated from other than British stock. As it is, the British and German, valuable as they are in the concrete, already threaten excess. Or rather, I should say, they have certainly reach'd that excess. To-day, something outside of them, and to counterbalance them, is seriously needed.

The seething materialistic and business vortices of the United States, in their present devouring relations, controlling and belittling everything else, are, in my opinion, but a vast and indispensable stage in the new world's development, and are certainly to be follow'd by something entirely different—at least by immense modifications. Character, literature, a society worthy the name, are yet to be establish'd, through a nationality of noblest spiritual, heroic and democratic attributes—not one of which at present definitely exists—entirely different from the past, though unerringly founded on it, and to justify it.

To that composite American identity of the future, Spanish character will supply some of the most needed parts. No stock shows a grander historic retrospect—grander in religiousness and loyalty, or for patriotism, courage, decorum, gravity and honor. (It is time to dismiss utterly the illusion-compound, half raw-head-and-bloody-bones and half Mysteries-of-Udolpho, inherited from the English writers of the past 200 years. It is time to realize—for it is certainly true—that there will not be found any more cruelty, tyranny, superstition, &c., in the *résumé* of past Spanish history than in the corresponding *résumé* of Anglo-Norman history. Nay, I think there will not be found so much.)

Then another point, relating to American ethnology, past and to come, I will here touch upon at a venture. As to our aboriginal or Indian population—the Aztec in the South, and many a tribe in the North and West—I know it seems to be agreed that they must gradually dwindle as time rolls on, and in a few generations more leave only a reminiscence, a blank. But I am not at all clear about that. As America, from its many far-back sources and current supplies, develops, adapts, entwines, faithfully identifies its own—are we to see it cheerfully accepting and using all the contributions of foreign lands from the whole outside globe—and then rejecting the only ones distinctively its own—the autochthonic ones?

As to the Spanish stock of our Southwest, it is certain to me that we do not begin to appreciate the splendor and sterling value of its race element. Who knows but that element, like the course of some subterranean river, dipping invisibly for a hundred or two years, is now to emerge in broadest flow and permanent action?

If I might assume to do so, I would like to send you the

most cordial, heartfelt congratulations of your American fellow-countrymen here. You have more friends in the Northern and Atlantic regions than you suppose, and they are deeply interested in the development of the great Southwestern interior, and in what your festival would arouse to public attention.

Very respectfully, &c.,

WALT WHITMAN.

WHAT LURKS BEHIND SHAKSPERE'S HISTORICAL PLAYS?

WE all know how much *mythus* there is in the Shakspere question as it stands to-day. Beneath a few foundations of proved facts are certainly engulf'd far more dim and elusive ones, of deepest importance—tantalizing and half suspected—suggesting explanations that one dare not put in plain statement. But coming at once to the point, the English historical plays are to me not only the most eminent as dramatic performances (my maturest judgment confirming the impressions of my early years, that the distinctiveness and glory of the Poet reside not in his vaunted dramas of the passions, but those founded on the contests of English dynasties, and the French wars,) but form, as we get it all, the chief in a complexity of puzzles. Conceiv'd out of the fullest heat and pulse of European feudalism—personifying in unparallel'd ways the mediæval aristocracy, its towering spirit of ruthless and gigantic caste, with its own peculiar air and arrogance (no mere imitation)—only one of the "wolfish earls" so plenteous in the plays themselves, or some born descendant and knower, might seem to be the true author of those amazing works—works in some respects greater than anything else in recorded literature.

The start and germ-stock of the pieces on which the present speculation is founded are undoubtedly (with, at the outset, no small amount of bungling work) in "Henry VI." It is plain to me that as profound and forecasting a brain and pen as ever appear'd in literature, after floundering somewhat in the first part of that trilogy—or perhaps draughting it more or less experimentally or by accident—afterward developed and defined his plan in the Second and Third Parts, and from time to time, thenceforward, systematically enlarged it to majestic and mature proportions in "Richard II," "Richard III," "King John," "Henry IV," "Henry V," and even in "Macbeth," "Coriolanus" and "Lear." For it is impossible to grasp the whole cluster of those plays, however wide the intervals and different circumstances of their composition, without thinking of them as, in a free sense, the result of an *essentially controling plan*. What was that plan? Or, rather, what was veil'd behind it?—for to me there was certainly something so veil'd. Even the episodes of Cade, Joan of Arc, and the like (which sometimes seem to me like interpolations allow'd,) may be meant to foil the possible sleuth, and throw any too 'cute pursuer off the scent. In the whole matter I should specially dwell on, and make much of, that inexplicable element of every highest poetic nature which causes it to cover up and involve its real purpose and meanings in folded removes and far recesses. Of this trait—hiding the nest where common seekers may never find it—the Shaksperean works afford the most numerous and mark'd illustrations known to me. I would even call that trait the leading one through the whole of those works.

All the foregoing to premise a brief statement of how and where I get my new light on Shakspere. Speaking of the special English plays, my friend William O'Connor says:

> They seem simply and rudely historical in their motive, as aiming to give in the rough a tableau of warring dynasties,—and carry to me a lurking sense of being in aid of some ulterior design, probably well enough understood in that age, which perhaps time and criticism will reveal. . . . . Their atmosphere is one of barbarous and tumultuous gloom,—they do not make us love the times they limn, ... and it is impossible to believe that the greatest of the Elizabethan men could have sought to indoctrinate the age with the love of feudalism which his own drama in its entirety, if the view taken of it herein be true, certainly and subtly saps and mines.

Reading the just-specified plays in the light of Mr. O'Connor's suggestion, I defy any one to escape such new and deep utterance-meanings, like magic ink, warm'd by the fire, and previously invisible. Will it not indeed be strange if the author of "Othello" and "Hamlet" is destin'd to live in America, in a generation or two, less as the cunning draughtsman of the passions, and more as putting on record the first full exposé—and by far the most vivid one, immeasurably ahead of doctrinaires and economists—of the political theory and results, or the reason-why and necessity for them which America has come on earth to abnegate and replace?

The summary of my suggestion would be, therefore, that while the more the rich and tangled jungle of the Shaksperean area is travers'd and studied, and the more baffled and mix'd, as so far appears, becomes the exploring student (who at last surmises everything, and remains certain of nothing,) it is possible a future age of criticism, diving deeper, mapping the land and lines freer, completer than hitherto, may discover in the plays named the scientific (Baconian?) inauguration of modern Democracy—furnishing realistic and first-class artistic portraitures of the mediæval world, the feudal personalties, institutes, in their morbid accumulations, deposits, upon politics and sociology,—may penetrate to that hard-pan, far down and back of the ostent of to-day, on which (and on which only) the progressism of the last two centuries has built this Democracy which now holds secure lodgment over the whole civilized world.

Whether such was the unconscious, or (as I think likely) the more or less conscious, purpose of him who fashion'd those marvellous architectonics, is a secondary question.

A Thought on Shakspere

THE most distinctive poems—the most permanently rooted and with heartiest reason for being—the copious cycle of Arthurian legends, or the almost equally copious Charlemagne cycle, or the poems of the Cid, or Scandinavian Eddas, or Nibelungen, or Chaucer, or Spenser, or *bona fide* Ossian, or Inferno—probably had their rise in the great historic perturbations, which they came in to sum up and confirm, indirectly embodying results to date. Then however precious to "culture," the grandest of those poems, it may be said, preserve and typify results offensive to the modern spirit, and long past away. To state it briefly, and taking the strongest examples, in Homer lives the ruthless military prowess of Greece, and of its special god-descended dynastic houses; in Shakspere the dragon-rancors and stormy feudal splendor of mediæval caste.

Poetry, largely consider'd, is an evolution, sending out improved and ever-expanded types—in one sense, the past, even the best of it, necessarily giving place, and dying out. For our existing world, the bases on which all the grand old poems were built have become vacuums—and even those of many comparatively modern ones are broken and half-gone. For us to-day, not their own intrinsic value, vast as that is, backs and maintains those poems—but a mountain-high growth of associations, the layers of successive ages. Everywhere—their own lands included—(is there not something terrible in the tenacity with which the one book out of millions holds its grip?)—the Homeric and Virgilian works, the interminable ballad-romances of the middle ages, the utterances of Dante, Spenser, and others, are upheld by their cumulus-entrenchment in scholarship, and as precious, always welcome, unspeakably valuable reminiscences.

Even the one who at present reigns unquestion'd—of Shakspere—for all he stands for so much in modern literature, he stands entirely for the mighty æsthetic sceptres of the past, not for the spiritual and democratic, the sceptres of the future. The inward and outward characteristics of Shakspere are his vast and rich variety of persons and themes, with his wondrous delineation of each and all—not only limitless funds of verbal and pictorial resource, but great excess, superfœtation—mannerism, like a fine, aristocratic perfume, holding a touch of musk (Euphues, his mark)—with boundless sumptuousness and adornment, real velvet and gems, not shoddy nor paste—but a good deal of bombast and fustian—(certainly some terrific mouthing in Shakspere!)

Superb and inimitable as all is, it is mostly an objective and physiological kind of power and beauty the soul finds in Shakspere—a style supremely grand of the sort, but in my opinion stopping short of the grandest sort, at any rate for fulfilling and satisfying modern and scientific and democratic American purposes. Think, not of growths as forests primeval, or Yellowstone geysers, or Colorado ravines, but of costly marble palaces, and palace rooms, and the noblest fixings and furniture, and noble owners and occupants to correspond—think of carefully built gardens from the beautiful but sophisticated gardening art at its best, with walks and bowers and artificial lakes, and appropriate statue-groups and the finest cultivated roses and lilies and japonicas in plenty—and you have the tally of Shakspere. The low characters, mechanics, even the loyal henchmen—all in themselves nothing—serve as capital foils to the aristocracy. The comedies (exquisite as they certainly are) bringing in admirably portray'd common characters, have the unmistakable hue of plays, portraits, made for the divertisement only of the élite of the castle, and from its point of view. The comedies are altogether non-acceptable to America and Democracy.

But to the deepest soul, it seems a shame to pick and choose from the riches Shakspere has left us—to criticise his infinitely royal, multiform quality—to gauge, with optic glasses, the dazzle of his sun-like beams.

The best poetic utterance, after all, can merely hint, or remind, often very indirectly, or at distant removes. Aught of real perfection, or the solution of any deep problem, or any completed statement of the moral, the true, the beautiful, eludes the greatest, deftest poet—flies away like an always uncaught bird.

Robert Burns as Poet and Person

What the future will decide about Robert Burns and his works—what place will be assign'd them on that great roster of geniuses and genius which can only be finish'd by the slow but sure balancing of the centuries with their ample average—I of course cannot tell. But as we know him, from his recorded utterances, and after nearly one century, and its diligence of collections, songs, letters, anecdotes, presenting the figure of the canny Scotchman in a fullness and detail wonderfully complete, and the lines mainly by his own hand, he forms to-day, in some respects, the most interesting personality among singers. Then there are many things in Burns's poems and character that specially endear him to America. He was essentially a Republican—would have been at home in the Western United States, and probably become eminent there. He was an average sample of the good-natured, warm-blooded, proud-spirited, amative, alimentive, convivial, young and early-middle-aged man of the decent-born middle classes everywhere and any how. Without the race of which he is a distinct specimen, (and perhaps his poems) America and her powerful Democracy could not exist to-day—could not project with unparallel'd historic sway into the future.

Perhaps the peculiar coloring of the era of Burns needs always first to be consider'd. It included the times of the '76–'83 Revolution in America, of the French Revolution, and an unparallel'd chaos development in Europe and elsewhere. In every department, shining and strange names, like stars, some rising, some in meridian, some declining—Voltaire, Franklin, Washington, Kant, Goethe, Fulton, Napoleon, mark the era. And while so much, and of grandest moment, fit for the trumpet of the world's fame, was being transacted—that little tragi-comedy of R. B.'s life and death was going on in a country by-place in Scotland!

Burns's correspondence, generally collected and publish'd since his death, gives wonderful glints into both the amiable and weak (and worse than weak) parts of his portraiture, habits, good and bad luck, ambition and associations. His letters to Mrs. Dunlop, Mrs. McLehose, (Clarinda,) Mr. Thompson, Dr. Moore, Robert Muir, Mr. Cunningham, Miss Margaret Chalmers, Peter Hill, Richard Brown, Mrs. Riddel, Robert Ainslie, and Robert Graham, afford valuable lights and shades to the outline, and with numerous others, help to a touch here, and fill-in there, of poet and poems. There are suspicions, it is true, of "the Genteel Letter-Writer," with scraps and words from "the Manual of French Quotations," and, in the love-letters, some hollow mouthings. Yet we wouldn't on any account lack the letters. A full and true portrait is always what is wanted; veracity at every hazard. Besides, do we not all see by this time that the story of Burns, even for its own sake, requires the record of the whole and several, with nothing left out? Completely and every point minutely told out its fullest, explains and justifies itself—(as perhaps almost any life does.) He is very close to the earth. He pick'd up his best words and tunes directly from the Scotch home-singers, but tells Thompson they would not please his, T's, "learn'd lugs," adding, "I call them simple—you would pronounce them silly." Yes, indeed; the idiom was undoubtedly his happiest hit. Yet Dr. Moore, in 1789, writes to Burns, "If I were to offer an opinion, it would be that in your future productions you should abandon the Scotch stanza and dialect, and adopt the measure and language of modern English poetry"!

As the 128th birth-anniversary of the poet draws on, (January, 1887,) with its increasing club-suppers, vehement celebrations, letters, speeches, and so on—(mostly, as William O'Connor says, from people who would not have noticed R. B. at all during his actual life, nor kept his company, or read his verses, on any account)—it may be opportune to print some leisurely-jotted notes I find in my budget. I take my observation of the Scottish bard by considering him as an individual amid the crowded clusters, galaxies, of the old world—and fairly inquiring and suggesting what out of these myriads he too may be to the Western Republic. In the first place no poet on record so fully bequeaths his own personal magnetism,* nor illustrates more pointedly how one's verses, by time and reading, can so curiously fuse with the versifier's own life and death, and give final light and shade to all.

I would say a large part of the fascination of Burns's homely, simple dialect-melodies is due, for all current and future readers, to the poet's personal "errors," the general

*Probably no man that ever lived—a friend has made the statement—was so fondly loved, both by men and women, as Robert Burns. The reason is not hard to find: he had a real heart of flesh and blood beating in his bosom; you could almost hear it throb. "Some one said, that if you had shaken hands with him his hand would have burnt yours. The gods, indeed, made him poetical, but Nature had a hand in him first. His heart was in the right place; he did not pile up cantos of poetic diction; he pluck'd the mountain daisy under his feet; he wrote of field-mouse hurrying from its ruin'd dwelling. He held the plough or the pen with the same firm, manly grasp. And he was loved. The simple roll of the women who gave him their affection and their sympathy would make a long manuscript; and most of these were of such noble worth that, as Robert Chambers says, 'their character may stand as a testimony in favor of that of Burns.' " [As I understand, the foregoing is from an extremely rare book publish'd by M'Kie, in Kilmarnock. I find the whole beautiful paragraph is a capital paper on Burns, by Amelia Barr.]

bleakness of his lot, his ingrain'd pensiveness, his brief dash into dazzling, tantalizing, evanescent sunshine—finally culminating in those last years of his life, his being taboo'd and in debt, sick and sore, yaw'd as by contending gales, deeply dissatisfied with everything, most of all with himself—high-spirited too—(no man ever really higher-spirited than Robert Burns.) I think it a perfectly legitimate part too. At any rate it has come to be an impalpable aroma through which only both the songs and their singer must henceforth be read and absorb'd. Through that view-medium of misfortune—of a noble spirit in low environments, and of a squalid and premature death—we view the undoubted facts, (giving, as we read them now, a sad kind of pungency,) that Burns's were, before all else, the lyrics of illicit loves and carousing intoxication. Perhaps even it is this strange, impalpable *post mortem* comment and influence referr'd to, that gives them their contrast, attraction, making the zest of their author's after fame. If he had lived steady, fat, moral, comfortable, well-to-do years, on his own grade, (let alone, what of course was out of the question, the ease and velvet and rosewood and copious royalties of Tennyson or Victor Hugo or Longfellow,) and died well-ripen'd and respectable, where could have come in that burst of passionate sobbing and remorse which well'd forth instantly and generally in Scotland, and soon follow'd everywhere among English-speaking races, on the announcement of his death? and which, with no sign of stopping, only regulated and vein'd with fitting appreciation, flows deeply, widely yet?

Dear Rob! manly, witty, fond, friendly, full of weak spots as well as strong ones—essential type of so many thousands—perhaps the average, as just said, of the decent-born young men and the early mid-aged, not only of the British Isles, but America, too, North and South, just the same. I think, indeed, one best part of Burns is the unquestionable proof he presents of the perennial existence among the laboring classes, especially farmers, of the finest latent poetic elements in their blood. (How clear it is to me that the common soil has always been, and is now, thickly strewn with just such gems.) He is well-called the *Ploughman*. "Holding the plough," said his brother Gilbert, "was the favorite situation with Robert for poetic compositions; and some of his best verses were produced while he was at that exercise." "I must return to my humble station, and woo my rustic muse in my wonted way, at the plough-tail." 1787, to the Earl of Buchan. He has no high ideal of the poet or the poet's office; indeed quite a low and contracted notion of both:

> "Fortune! if thou'll but gie me still
> Hale breeks, a scone, and whiskey gill,
> An' rowth o' rhyme to rave at will,
> Tak' a' the rest."

See also his rhym'd letters to Robert Graham invoking patronage; "one stronghold," Lord Glencairn, being dead, now these appeals to "Fintra, my other stay," (with in one letter a copious shower of vituperation generally.) In his collected poems there is no particular unity, nothing that can be called a leading theory, no unmistakable spine or skeleton. Perhaps, indeed, their very desultoriness is the charm of his songs: "I take up one or another," he says in a letter to Thompson, "just as the bee of the moment buzzes in my bonnet-lug."

Consonantly with the customs of the time—yet markedly inconsistent in spirit with Burns's own case, (and not a little painful as it remains on record, as depicting some features of the bard himself,) the relation called *patronage* existed between the nobility and gentry on one side, and literary people on the other, and gives one of the strongest side-lights to the general coloring of poems and poets. It crops out a good deal in Burns's Letters, and even necessitated a certain flunkeyism on occasions, through life. It probably, with its requirements, (while it help'd in money and countenance) did as much as any one cause in making that life a chafed and unhappy one, ended by a premature and miserable death.

Yes, there is something about Burns peculiarly acceptable to the concrete, human points of view. He poetizes work-a-day agricultural labor and life, (whose spirit and sympathies, as well as practicalities, are much the same everywhere,) and treats fresh, often coarse, natural occurrences, loves, persons, not like many new and some old poets in a genteel style of gilt and china, or at second or third removes, but in their own born atmosphere, laughter, sweat, unction. Perhaps no one ever sang "lads and lasses"—that universal race, mainly the same, too, all ages, all lands—down on their own plane, as he has. He exhibits no philosophy worth mentioning; his morality is hardly more than parrot-talk—not bad or deficient, but cheap, shopworn, the platitudes of old aunts and uncles to the youngsters (be good boys and keep your noses clean.) Only when he gets at Poosie Nansie's, celebrating the "barley bree," or among tramps, or democratic bouts and drinking generally,

("Freedom and whiskey gang thegither,")

we have, in his own unmistakable color and warmth, those interiors of rake-helly life and tavern fun—the cantabile of jolly beggars in highest jinks—lights and groupings of rank glee and brawny amorousness, outvying the best painted pictures of the Dutch school, or any school.

By America and her democracy such a poet, I cannot too often repeat, must be kept in loving remembrance; but it is best that discriminations be made. His admirers (as at those anniversary suppers, over the "hot Scotch") will not accept for their favorite anything less than the highest rank, alongside of Homer, Shakspere, etc. Such, in candor, are not the true friends of the Ayrshire bard, who really needs a different place quite by himself. The Iliad and the Odyssey express courage, craft, full-grown heroism in situations of danger, the sense of command and leadership, emulation, the last and fullest evolution of self-poise as in kings, and god-like even while animal appetites. The Shaksperean compositions, on vertebers and framework of the primary passions, portray (essentially the same as Homer's,) the spirit and letter of the feudal world, the Norman lord, ambitious and arrogant, taller and nobler than common men—with much underplay and gusts of heat and cold, volcanoes and stormy seas. Burns (and some will say to his credit) attempts none of these themes. He poetizes the humor, riotous blood, sulks, amorous torments, fondness for the tavern and for cheap objective nature, with disgust at the grim and narrow ecclesiasticism of his time and land, of a young farmer on a bleak and hired farm in Scotland, through the years and under the circumstances of the British politics of that time, and of his short personal career as author, from 1783 to 1796. He is intuitive and affectionate, and just emerged or emerging from the shackles of the kirk, from poverty, ignorance, and from his own rank appetites—(out of which later, however, he never extricated himself.) It is to be said that amid not a little smoke and gas in his poems, there is in almost every piece a spark of fire, and now and then the real afflatus. He has been applauded as democratic, and with some warrant; while Shakspere, and with the greatest warrant, has been called monarchical or aristocratic (which he certainly is.) But the splendid personalizations of Shakspere, formulated on the largest, freest, most heroic, most artistic mould, are to me far dearer as lessons, and more precious even as models for Democracy, than the humdrum samples Burns presents. The motives of some of his effusions are certainly discreditable personally—one or two of them markedly so. He has, moreover, little or no spirituality. This last is his mortal flaw and defect, tried by highest standards. The ideal he never reach'd (and yet I think he leads the way to it.) He gives melodies, and now and then the simplest and sweetest ones; but harmonies, complications, oratorios in words, never. (I do not speak this in any deprecatory sense. Blessed be the memory of the warm-hearted Scotchman for what he has left us, just as it is!) He likewise did not know himself, in more ways than one. Though so really free and independent, he prided himself in his songs on being a reactionist and a Jacobite—on persistent sentimental adherency to the cause of the Stuarts—the weakest, thinnest, most faithless, brainless dynasty that ever held a throne.

Thus, while Burns is not at all great for New World study, in the sense that Isaiah and Eschylus and the book of Job are unquestionably great—is not to be mention'd with Shakspere—hardly even with current Tennyson or our Emerson—he has a nestling niche of his own, all fragrant, fond, and quaint and homely—a lodge built near but outside the mighty temple of the gods of song and art—those universal strivers, through their works of harmony and melody and power, to ever show or intimate man's crowning, last, victorious fusion in himself of Real and Ideal. Precious, too—fit and precious beyond all singers, high or low—will Burns ever be to the native Scotch, especially to the working-classes of North Britain; so intensely one of them, and so racy of the soil, sights, and local customs. He often apostrophizes Scotland, and is, or would be, enthusiastically patriotic. His country has lately commemorated him in a statue.* His aim is declaredly to be 'a Rustic Bard.' His poems were all written in youth or young manhood, (he was little more than a young man when he died.) His collected works in giving everything, are nearly one half first drafts. His brightest hit is his use of the Scotch patois, so full of terms flavor'd like wild fruits or berries. Then I should make an allowance to Burns which cannot be made for any other poet. Curiously even the frequent crudeness, haste, deficiencies, (flatness and puerilities by no means absent) prove upon the whole not out of keeping in any comprehensive collection of his works, heroically printed, 'following copy,' every piece, every line according to originals. Other poets might tremble for such boldness, such rawness. In 'this odd-kind chiel' such points hardly mar the rest. Not only are they in consonance with the underlying spirit of the pieces, but complete the full abandon and veracity of the farm-fields and the home-brew'd flavor of the Scotch vernacular. (Is there not often something in the very neglect, unfinish, careless nudity, slovenly hiatus, coming from intrinsic genius, and not 'put on,' that secretly pleases the soul more than the wrought and re-wrought polish of the most perfect verse?) Mark the native spice and untranslatable twang in the very names of his songs—"O for ane and twenty, Tam," "John Barleycorn," "Last May a braw Wooer,"

*The Dumfries statue of Robert Burns was successfully unveil'd April 1881 by Lord Roseberry, the occasion having been made national in its character. Before the ceremony, a large procession paraded the streets of the town, all the trades and societies of that part of Scotland being represented, at the head of which went dairymen and ploughmen, the former driving their carts and being accompanied by their maids. The statute is of Sicilian marble. It rests on a pedestal of gray stone five feet high. The poet is represented as sitting easily on an old tree root, holding in his left hand a cluster of daisies. His face is turn'd toward the right shoulder, and the eyes gaze into the distance. Near by lie a collie dog, a broad bonnet half covering a well-thumb'd song-book, and a rustic flageolet. The costume is taken from the Nasmyth portrait, which has been follow'd for the features of the face.

"Rattlin roarin Willie," "O wert thou in the cauld, cauld blast," "Gude e'en to you, Kimmer," "Merry hae I been teething a Heckle," "O lay thy loof in mine, lass," and others.

The longer and more elaborated poems of Burns are just such as would please a natural but homely taste, and cute but average intellect, and are inimitable in their way. The "Twa Dogs," (one of the best) with the conversation between Cesar and Luath, the "Brigs of Ayr," "the Cotter's Saturday Night," "Tam O'Shanter"—all will be long read and re-read and admired, and ever deserve to be. With nothing profound in any of them, what there is of moral and plot has an inimitably fresh and racy flavor. If it came to question, Literature could well afford to send adrift many a pretensive poem, and even book of poems, before it could spare these compositions.

Never indeed was there truer utterance in a certain range of idiosyncracy than by this poet. Hardly a piece of his, large or small, but has "snap" and raciness. He puts in cantering rhyme (often doggerel) much cutting irony and idiomatic ear-cuffing of the kirk-deacons—drily good-natured addresses to his cronies, (he certainly would not stop us if he were here this moment, from classing that "to the De'il" among them)—"to Mailie and her Lambs," "to auld Mare Maggie," "to a Mouse,"

"Wee, sleekit, cowrin, tim'rous beastie:"

"to a Mountain Daisy," "to a Haggis," "to a Louse," "to the Toothache," etc.—and occasionally to his brother bards and lady or gentleman patrons, often with strokes of tenderest sensibility, idiopathic humor, and genuine poetic imagination—still oftener with shrewd, original, sheeny, steel-flashes of wit, home-spun sense, or lance-blade puncturing. Then, strangely, the basis of Burns's character, with all its fun and manliness, was hypochondria, the blues, palpable enough in "Despondency," "Man was made to Mourn," "Address to Ruin," a "Bard's Epitaph," &c. From such deep-down elements sprout up, in very contrast and paradox, those riant utterances of which a superficial reading will not detect the hidden foundation. Yet nothing is clearer to me than the black and desperate background behind those pieces—as I shall now specify them. I find his most characteristic, Nature's masterly touch and luxuriant life-blood, color and heat, not in "Tam O'Shanter," "the Cotter's Saturday Night," "Scots who hae," "Highland Mary," "the Twa Dogs," and the like, but in "the Jolly Beggars," "Rigs of Barley," "Scotch Drink," "the Epistle to John Rankine," "Holy Willie's Prayer," and in "Halloween," (to say nothing of a certain cluster, known still to a small inner circle in Scotland, but, for good reasons, not published anywhere.) In these compositions, especially the first, there is much indelicacy (some editions flatly leave it out,) but the composer reigns alone, with handling free and broad and true, and is an artist. You may see and feel the man indirectly in his other verses, all of them, with more or less life-likeness—but these I have named last call out pronouncedly in his own voice,

"I, Rob, am here."

Finally, in any summing-up of Burns, though so much is to be said in the way of fault-finding, drawing black marks, and doubtless severe literary criticism—(in the present outpouring I have 'kept myself in,' rather than allow'd any free flow)—after full retrospect of his works and life, the aforesaid 'odd-kind chiel' remains to my heart and brain as almost the tenderest, manliest, and (even if contradictory) dearest flesh-and-blood figure in all the streams and clusters of by-gone poets.

A Word about Tennyson

Beautiful as the song was, the original 'Locksley Hall' of half a century ago was essentially morbid, heart-broken, finding fault with everything, especially the fact of money's being made (as it ever must be, and perhaps should be) the paramount matter in worldly affairs;

> Every door is barr'd with gold, and opens but to golden keys.

First, a father, having fallen in battle, his child (the singer)

> Was left a trampled orphan, and a selfish uncle's ward.

Of course love ensues. The woman in the chant or monologue proves a false one; and as far as appears the ideal of woman, in the poet's reflections, is a false one—at any rate for America. Woman is *not* 'the lesser man.' (The heart is not the brain.) The best of the piece of fifty years since is its concluding line:

> For the mighty wind arises roaring seaward and I go.

Then for this current 1886–7, a just-out sequel, which (as an apparently authentic summary says) 'reviews the life of mankind during the past sixty years, and comes to the conclusion that its boasted progress is of doubtful credit to the world in general and to England in particular. A cynical vein of denunciation of democratic opinions and aspirations runs throughout the poem in mark'd contrast with the spirit of the poet's youth.' Among the most striking lines of this sequel are the following:

> Envy wears the mask of love, and, laughing sober fact to scorn,
> Cries to weakest as to strongest, 'Ye are equals, equal born,'
> Equal-born! Oh yes, if yonder hill be level with the flat.
> Charm us, orator, till the lion look no larger than the cat:
> Till the cat, through that mirage of overheated language, loom
> Larger than the lion Demo—end in working its own doom.
> Tumble Nature heel o'er head, and, yelling with the yelling street,
> Set the feet above the brain, and swear the brain is in the feet.
> Bring the old dark ages back, without the faith, without the hope
> Beneath the State, the Church, the Throne, and roll their ruins down the slope.

I should say that all this is a legitimate consequence of the tone and convictions of the earlier standards and points of view. Then some reflections, down to the hard-pan of this sort of thing.

The course of progressive politics (democracy) is so certain and resistless, not only in America but in Europe, that we can well afford the warning calls, threats, checks, neutralizings, in imaginative literature, or any department, of such deep-sounding and high-soaring voices as Carlyle's and Tennyson's. Nay, the blindness, excesses, of the prevalent tendency—the dangers of the urgent trends of our times—in my opinion, need such voices almost more than any. I should, too, call it a signal instance of democratic humanity's luck that it has such enemies to contend with—so candid, so fervid, so heroic. But why do I say enemies? Upon the whole is not Tennyson—and was not Carlyle (like an honest and stern physician)—the true friend of our age?

Let me assume to pass verdict, or perhaps momentary judgment, for the United States on this poet—a remov'd and distant position giving some advantages over a nigh one. What is Tennyson's service to his race, times, and especially to America? First, I should say—or at least not forget—his personal character. He is not to be mention'd as a rugged, evolutionary, aboriginal force—but (and a great lesson is in it) he has been consistent throughout with the native, healthy, patriotic spinal element and promptings of himself. His moral line is local and conventional, but it is vital and genuine. He reflects the upper-crust of his time, its pale cast of thought—even its *ennui*. Then the simile of my friend John Burroughs is entirely true, 'his glove is a glove of silk, but the hand is a hand of iron.' He shows how one can be a royal laureate, quite elegant and 'aristocratic,' and a little queer and affected, and at the same time perfectly manly and natural. As to his non-democracy, it fits him well, and I like him the better for it. I guess we all like to have (I am sure I do) some one who presents those sides of a thought, or possibility, different from our own—different and yet with a sort of home-likeness—a tartness and contradiction offsetting the theory as we view it, and construed from tastes and proclivities not at all his own.

To me, Tennyson shows more than any poet I know (perhaps has been a warning to me) how much there is in finest verbalism. There is such a latent charm in mere words, cunning collocations, and in the voice ringing them, which he has caught and brought out, beyond all others—as in the line,

> And hollow, hollow, hollow, all delight,

in 'The Passing of Arthur,' and evidenced in 'The Lady of Shalott,' 'The Deserted House,' and many other pieces. Among the best (I often linger over them again and again) are 'Lucretius,' 'The Lotos Eaters,' and 'The Northern Farmer.' His mannerism is great, but it is a noble and welcome mannerism. His very best work, to me, is contain'd in the books of 'The Idyls of the King,' and all that has grown out of them. Though indeed we could spare nothing of Tennyson, however small or however peculiar—not 'Break, Break,' nor 'Flower in the Crannied Wall,' nor the old, eternally-told passion of 'Edward Gray:'

> Love may come and love may go,
> And fly like a bird from tree to tree.
> But I will love no more, no more
> Till Ellen Adair come back to me.

Yes, Alfred Tennyson's is a superb character, and will help give illustriousness, through the long roll of time, to our Nineteenth Century. In its bunch of orbic names, shining like a constellation of stars, his will be one of the brightest. His very faults, doubts, swervings, doublings upon himself, have been typical of our age. We are like the voyagers of a ship, casting off for new seas, distant shores. We would still dwell in the old suffocating and dead haunts, remembering and magnifying their pleasant experiences only, and more than once impell'd to jump ashore before it is too late, and stay where our fathers stay'd, and live as they lived.

May-be I am non-literary and non-decorous (let me at least be human, and pay part of my debt) in this word about Tennyson. I want him to realize that here is a great and ardent Nation that absorbs his songs, and has a respect and affection for him personally, as almost for no other foreigner. I want this word to go to the old man at Farringford as conveying no more than the simple truth; and that truth (a little Christmas gift) no slight one either. I have written impromptu, and shall let it all go at that. The readers of more than fifty millions of people in the New World not only owe to him some of their most agreeable and harmless and healthy hours, but he has enter'd into the formative influences of character here, not only in the Atlantic cities, but inland and far West, out in Missouri, in Kansas, and away in Oregon, in farmer's house and miner's cabin.

Best thanks, anyhow, to Alfred Tennyson—thanks and appreciation in America's name.

Slang in America

View'd freely, the English language is the accretion and growth of every dialect, race, and range of time, and is both the free and compacted composition of all. From this point of view, it stands for Language in the largest sense, and is really the greatest of studies. It involves so much; is indeed a sort of universal absorber, combiner, and conqueror. The scope of its etymologies is the scope not only of man and civilization, but the history of Nature in all departments, and of the organic Universe, brought up to date; for all are comprehended in words, and their backgrounds. This is when words become vitaliz'd, and stand for things, as they unerringly and soon come to do, in the mind that enters on their study with fitting spirit, grasp, and appreciation.

Slang, profoundly consider'd, is the lawless germinal element, below all words and sentences, and behind all poetry, and proves a certain perennial rankness and protestantism in speech. As the United States inherit by far their most precious possession—the language they talk and write—from the Old World, under and out of its feudal institutes, I will allow myself to borrow a simile even of those forms farthest removed from American Democracy. Considering Language then as some mighty potentate, into the majestic audience-hall of the monarch ever enters a personage like one of Shakspere's clowns, and takes position there, and plays a part even in the stateliest ceremonies. Such is Slang, or indirection, an attempt of common humanity to escape from bald literalism, and express itself illimitably, which in highest walks produces poets and poems, and doubtless in pre-historic times gave the start to, and perfected, the whole immense tangle of the old mythologies. For, curious as it may appear, it is strictly the same impulse-source, the same thing. Slang, too, is the wholesome fermentation or eructation of those processes eternally active in language, by which froth and specks are thrown up, mostly to pass away; though occasionally to settle and permanently chrystallize.

To make it plainer, it is certain that many of the oldest and solidest words we use, were originally generated from the daring and license of slang. In the processes of word-formation, myriads die, but here and there the attempt attracts superior meanings, becomes valuable and indispensable, and lives forever. Thus the term *right* means literally only straight. *Wrong* primarily meant twisted, distorted. *Integrity* meant oneness. *Spirit* meant breath, or flame. A *supercilious* person was one who rais'd his eyebrows. To *insult* was to leap against. If you *influenc'd* a man, you but flow'd into him. The Hebrew word which is translated *prophesy* meant to bubble up and pour forth as a fountain. The enthusiast bubbles up with the Spirit of God within him, and it pours forth from him like a fountain. The word prophecy is misunderstood. Many suppose that it is limited to mere prediction; that is but the lesser portion of prophecy. The greater work is to reveal God. Every true religious enthusiast is a prophet.

Language, be it remember'd, is not an abstract construction of the learn'd, or of dictionary-makers, but is something arising out of the work, needs, ties, joys, affections, tastes, of long generations of humanity, and has its bases broad and low, close to the ground. Its final decisions are made by the masses, people nearest the concrete, having most to do with actual land and sea. It impermeates all, the Past as well as the Present, and is the grandest triumph of the human intellect. "Those mighty works of art," says Addington Symonds, "which we call languages, in the construction of which whole peoples unconsciously co-operated, the forms of which were determin'd not by individual genius, but by the instincts of successive generations, acting to one end, inherent in the nature of the race—Those poems of pure thought and fancy, cadenced not in words, but in living imagery, fountainheads of inspiration, mirrors of the mind of nascent nations, which we call Mythologies—these surely are more marvellous in their infantine spontaneity than any more mature production of the races which evolv'd them. Yet we are utterly ignorant of their embryology; the true science of Origins is yet in its cradle."

Daring as it is to say so, in the growth of Language it is certain that the retrospect of slang from the start would be the recalling from their nebulous conditions of all that is poetical in the stories of human utterance. Moreover, the honest delving, as of late years, by the German and British workers in comparative philology, has pierc'd and dispers'd many of the falsest bubbles of centuries; and will disperse many more. It was long recorded that in Scandinavian mythology the heroes in the Norse Paradise drank out of the skulls of their slain enemies. Later investigation proves the word taken for skulls to mean *horns* of beasts slain in the hunt. And what reader had not been exercis'd over the traces of that feudal custom, by which *seigneurs* warm'd their feet in the bowels of serfs, the abdomen being open'd for the purpose? It now is made to appear that the serf was only required to submit his unharm'd abdomen as a foot cushion while his lord supp'd, and was required to chafe the legs of the seigneur with his hands.

It is curiously in embryons and childhood, and among the illiterate, we always find the groundwork and start, of this great science, and its noblest products. What a relief most people have in speaking of a man not by his true and formal name, with a "Mister" to it, but by some odd or homely appellative. The propensity to approach a meaning not directly and squarely, but by circuitous styles of expression, seems indeed a born quality of the common people everywhere, evidenced by nick-names, and the inveterate determination of the masses to bestow sub-titles, sometimes ridiculous, sometimes very apt. Always among the soldiers during the Secession War, one heard of "Little Mac" (Gen. McClellan), or of "Uncle Billy" (Gen. Sherman.) "The old man" was, of course, very common. Among the rank and file, both armies, it was very general to speak of the different States they came from by their slang names. Those from Maine were call'd Foxes; New Hampshire, Granite Boys; Massachusetts, Bay Staters; Vermont, Green Mountain Boys; Rhode Island, Gun Flints; Connecticut, Wooden Nutmegs; New York, Knickerbockers; New Jersey, Clam Catchers; Pennsylvania, Logher Heads; Delaware, Muskrats; Maryland, Claw Thumpers; Virginia, Beagles; North Carolina, Tar Boilers; South Carolina, Weasels; Georgia, Buzzards; Louisiana, Creoles; Alabama, Lizzards; Kentucky, Corn Crackers; Ohio, Buckeyes; Michigan, Wolverines; Indiana, Hoosiers; Illinois, Suckers; Missouri, Pukes; Mississippi, Tad Poles; Florida, Fly up the Creeks; Wisconsin, Badgers; Iowa, Hawkeyes; Oregon, Hard Cases. Indeed I am not sure but slang names have more than once made Presidents. "Old Hickory," (Gen. Jackson) is one case in point. "Tippecanoe, and Tyler too," another.

I find the same rule in the people's conversations everywhere. I heard this among the men of the city horse-cars, where the conductor is often call'd a "snatcher" (i. e. because his characteristic duty is to constantly pull or snatch the bell-strap, to stop or go on.) Two young fellows are having a friendly talk, amid which, says 1st conductor, "What did you do before you was a snatcher?" Answer of 2d conductor, "Nail'd." (Translation of answer: "I work'd as carpenter.") What is a "boom"? says one editor to another. "Esteem'd contemporary," says the other, "a boom is a bulge." "Barefoot whiskey" is the Tennessee name for the undiluted stimulant. In the slang of the New York common restaurant waiters a plate of ham and beans is known as "stars and stripes," codfish balls as "sleeve-buttons," and hash as "mystery."

The Western States of the Union are, however, as may be supposed, the special areas of slang, not only in conversation, but in names of localities, towns, rivers, etc. A late Oregon traveller says:

> "On your way to Olympia by rail, you cross a river called the Shookum-Chuck; your train stops at places named Newaukum, Tumwater, and Toutle; and if you seek further you will hear of whole counties labell'd Wahkiakum, or Snohomish, or Kutsar, or Klikatat; and Cowlitz, Hookium, and Nenolelops greet and offend you. They complain in

Olympia that Washington Territory gets but little immigration; but what wonder? What man, having the whole American continent to choose from, would willingly date his letters from the county of Snohomish or bring up his children in the city of Nenolelops? The village of Tumwater is, as I am ready to bear witness, very pretty indeed; but surely an emigrant would think twice before he establish'd himself either there or at Toutle. Seattle is sufficiently barbarous; Stelicoom is no better; and I suspect that the Northern Pacific Railroad terminus has been fixed at Tacoma because it is one of the few places on Puget Sound whose name does not inspire horror."

Then a Nevada paper chronicles the departure of a mining party from Reno: "The toughest set of roosters that ever shook the dust off any town left Reno yesterday for the new mining district of Cornucopia. They came here from Virginia. Among the crowd were four New York cock-fighters, two Chicago murderers, three Baltimore bruisers, one Philadelphia prize-fighter, four San Francisco hoodlums, three Virginia beats, two Union Pacific roughs, and two check guerrillas." Among the far-west newspapers, have been, or are, *The Fairplay* (Colorado) *Flume, The Solid Muldoon,* of Ouray, *The Tombstone Epitaph,* of Nevada, *The Jimplecute,* of Texas, and *The Bazoo,* of Missouri. Shirttail Bend, Whiskey Flat, Puppytown, Wild Yankee Ranch, Squaw Flat, Rawhide Ranch, Loafer's Ravine, Squitch Gulch, Toenail Lake, are a few of the names of places in Butte county, Cal.

Perhaps indeed no place or term gives more luxuriant illustrations of the fermentation processes I have mention'd, and their froth and specks, than those Mississippi and Pacific coast regions, at the present day. Hasty and grotesque as are some of the names, others are of an appropriateness and originality unsurpassable. This applies to the Indian words, which are often perfect. Oklahoma is proposed in Congress for the name of one of our new Territories. Hog-eye, Lick-skillet, Rake-pocket and Steal-easy are the names of some Texan towns. Miss Bremer found among the aborigines the following names: *Men's,* Horn-point; Round-Wind; Stand-and-look-out; The-Cloud-that-goes-aside; Iron-toe; Seek-the-sun;

Iron-flash; Red-bottle; White-spindle; Black-dog; Two-feathers-of-honor; Gray-grass; Bushy-tail; Thunder-face; Go-on-the-burning-sod; Spirits-of-the-dead. *Women's,* Keep-the-fire; Spiritual-woman; Second-daughter-of-the-house; Blue-bird.

Certainly philologists have not given enough attention to this element and its results, which, I repeat, can probably be found working every where to-day, amid modern conditions, with as much life and activity as in far-back Greece or India, under prehistoric ones. Then the wit—the rich flashes of humor and genius and poetry—darting out often from a gang of laborers, railroad-men, miners, drivers or boatmen! How often have I hover'd at the edge of a crowd of them, to hear their repartees and impromptus! You get more real fun from half an hour with them than from the books of all "the American humorists."

The science of language has large and close analogies in geological science, with its ceaseless evolution, its fossils, and its numberless submerged layers and hidden strata, the infinite go-before of the present. Or, perhaps Language is more like some vast living body, or perennial body of bodies. And slang not only brings the first feeders of it, but is afterward the start of fancy, imagination and humor, breathing into its nostrils the breath of life.

An Indian Bureau Reminiscence

After the close of the Secession War in 1865, I work'd several months (until Mr. Harlan turn'd me out for having written "Leaves of Grass") in the Interior Department at Washington, in the Indian Bureau. Along this time there came to see their Great Father an unusual number of aboriginal visitors, delegations for treaties, settlement of lands, &c.—some young or middle-aged, but mainly old men, from the West, North, and occasionally from the South—parties of from five to twenty each—the most wonderful proofs of what Nature can produce, (the survival of the fittest, no doubt—all the frailer samples dropt, sorted out by death)—as if to show how the earth and woods, the attrition of storms and elements, and the exigencies of life at first hand, can train and fashion men, indeed *chiefs,* in heroic massiveness, imperturbability, muscle, and that last and highest beauty consisting of strength—the full exploitation and fruitage of a human identity, not from the culmination-points of "culture" and artificial civilization, but tallying our race, as it were, with giant, vital, gnarl'd, enduring trees, or monoliths of separate hardiest rocks, and humanity holding its own with the best of the said trees or rocks, and outdoing them.

There were Omahas, Poncas, Winnebagoes, Cheyennes, Navahos, Apaches, and many others. Let me give a running account of what I see and hear through one of these conference collections at the Indian Bureau, going back to the present tense. Every head and face is impressive, even artistic; Nature redeems herself out of her crudest recesses. Most have red paint on their cheeks, however, or some other paint. ("Little Hill" makes the opening speech, which the interpreter translates by scraps.) Many wear head tires of gaudy-color'd braid, wound around thickly—some with circlets of eagles' feathers. Necklaces of bears' claws are plenty around their necks. Most of the chiefs are wrapt in large blankets of the brightest scarlet. Two or three have blue, and I see one black. (A wise man call'd "the Flesh" now makes a short speech, apparently asking something. Indian Commissioner Dole answers him, and the interpreter translates in scraps again.) All the principal chiefs have tomahawks or hatchets, some of them very richly ornamented and costly. Plaid shirts are to be observ'd—none too clean. Now a tall fellow, "Hole-in-the-Day," is speaking. He has a copious head-dress composed of feathers and narrow ribbon, under which appears a countenance painted all over a bilious yellow. Let us note this young chief. For all his paint, "Hole-in-the-Day" is a handsome Indian, mild and calm, dress'd in drab buckskin leggings, dark gray surtout, and a soft black hat. His costume will bear full observation, and even fashion would accept him. His apparel is worn loose and scant enough to show his superb physique, especially in neck, chest, and legs. ("The Apollo Belvidere!" was the involuntary exclamation of a famous European artist when he first saw a full-grown young Choctaw.)

One of the red visitors—a wild, lean-looking Indian, the one in the black woolen wrapper—has an empty buffalo head, with the horns on, for his personal surmounting. I see a markedly Bourbonish countenance among the chiefs—(it is not very uncommon among them, I am told.) Most of them avoided resting on chairs during the hour of their "talk" in the Commissioner's office; they would sit around on the floor, leaning against something, or stand up by the walls, partially wrapt in their blankets. Though some of the young fellows were, as I have said, magnificent and beautiful animals, I think the palm of unique picturesqueness, in body, limb, physiognomy, etc., was borne by the old or elderly chiefs, and the wise men.

My here-alluded-to experience in the Indian Bureau produced one very definite conviction, as follows: There is something about these aboriginal Americans, in their highest characteristic representations, essential traits, and the ensemble of their physique and physiognomy—something very remote, very lofty, arousing comparisons with our own civilized ideals—something that our literature, portrait painting, etc., have never caught, and that will almost certainly never be transmitted to the future, even as a reminiscence. No biographer, no historian, no artist, has grasp'd it—perhaps could not grasp it. It is so different, so far outside our standards of eminent humanity. Their feathers, paint—even the empty buffalo skull—did not, to say the least, seem any more ludicrous to me that many of the fashions I have seen in civilized society. I should not apply the word savage (at any rate, in the usual sense) as a leading word in the description of those great aboriginal specimens, of whom I certainly saw many of the best. There were moments, as I look'd at them or studied them, when our own exemplification of personality, dignity, heroic presentation anyhow (as in the conventions of society, or even in the accepted poems and plays,) seem'd sickly, puny, inferior.

The interpreters, agents of the Indian Department, or other whites accompanying the bands, in positions of responsibility, were always interesting to me; I had many talks with them. Occasionally I would go to the hotels where the bands were quarter'd, and spend an hour or two informally. Of course we could not have much conversation—though (through the interpreters) more of this than might be supposed—sometimes quite animated and significant. I had the good luck to be invariably receiv'd and treated by all of them in their most cordial manner.

[Letter to W. W. from an artist, B. H., who has been much among the American Indians:]

"I have just receiv'd your little paper on the Indian delegations. In the fourth paragraph you say that there is something about the essential traits of our aborigines which 'will almost certainly never be transmitted to the future.' If I am so fortunate as to regain my health I hope to weaken the force of that statement, at least in so far as my talent and training will permit. I intend to spend some years among them, and shall endeavor to perpetuate on canvas some of the finer types, both men and women, and some of the characteristic features of their life. It will certainly be well worth the while. My artistic enthusiasm was never so thoroughly stirr'd up as by the Indians. They certainly have more of beauty, dignity and nobility mingled with their own wild individuality, than any of the other indigenous types of man. Neither black nor Afghan, Arab nor Malay (and I know them all pretty well) can hold a candle to the Indian. All of the other aboriginal types seem to be more or less distorted from the model of perfect human form—as we know it—the blacks, thin-hipped, with bulbous limbs, not well mark'd; the Arabs large-jointed, &c. But I have seen many a young Indian as perfect in form and feature as a Greek statue—very different from a Greek statue, of course, but as satisfying to the artistic perceptions and demand.

"And the worst, or perhaps the best of it all is that it will require an artist—and a good one—to record the real facts and impressions. Ten thousand photographs would not have the value of one really finely felt painting. Color is all-important. No one but an artist knows how much. An Indian is only half an Indian without the blue-black hair and the brilliant eyes shining out of the wonderful dusky ochre and rose complexion."

Some Diary Notes at Random

Negro Slaves in New York.—I can myself almost remember negro slaves in New York State, as my grandfather and great-grandfather (at West Hills, Suffolk County, New York) own'd a number. The hard labor of the farm was mostly done by them, and on the floor of the big kitchen, toward sundown, would be squatting a circle of twelve or fourteen "pickaninnies," eating their supper of pudding (Indian corn mush) and milk. A friend of my grandfather, named Wortman, of Oyster Bay, died in 1810, leaving ten slaves. Jeanette Treadwell, the last of them, died suddenly in Flushing last Summer (1884,) at the age of ninety-four years. I remember "old Mose," one of the liberated West Hills slaves, well. He was very genial, correct, manly, and cute, and a great friend of my childhood.

CANADA NIGHTS.—*Late in August.*—Three wondrous nights. Effects of moon, clouds, stars, and night-sheen, never surpass'd. I am out every night, enjoying all. The sunset begins it. (I have said already how long evening lingers here.) The moon, an hour high just after eight, is past her half, and looks somehow more like a human face up there than ever before. As it grows later, we have such gorgeous and broad cloud-effects, with Luna's tawny halos, silver edgings—great fleeces, depths of blue-black in patches, and occasionally long, low bars hanging silently a while, and then gray bulging masses rolling along stately, sometimes in long procession. The moon travels in Scorpion to-night, and dims all the stars of that constellation except fiery Antares, who keeps on shining just to the big one's side.

COUNTRY DAYS AND NIGHTS.—*Sept. 30, '82, 4.30 A. M.*—I am down in Camden County, New Jersey, at the farm-house of the Staffords—have been looking a long while at the comet—have in my time seen longer-tail'd ones, but never one so pronounc'd in cometary character, and so spectral-fierce—so like some great, pale, living monster of the air or sea. The atmosphere and sky, an hour or so before sunrise, so cool, still, translucent, give the whole apparition to great advantage. It is low in the east. The head shows about as big as an ordinary good-sized saucer—is a perfectly round and defined disk—the tail some sixty or seventy feet—not a stripe, but quite broad, and gradually expanding. Impress'd with the silent, inexplicably emotional sight, I linger and look till all begins to weaken in the break of day.

October 2.—The third day of mellow, delicious, sunshiny weather. I am writing this in the recesses of the old woods, my seat on a big pine log, my back against a tree. Am down here a few days for a change, to bask in the Autumn sun, to idle lusciously and simply, and to eat hearty meals, especially my breakfast. Warm mid-days—the other hours of the twenty-four delightfully fresh and mild—cool evenings, and early mornings perfect. The scent of the woods, and the peculiar aroma of a great yet unreap'd maize-field near by—the white butterflies in every direction by day—the golden-rod, the wild asters, and sunflowers—the song of the katydid all night.

Every day in Cooper's Woods, enjoying simple existence and the passing hours—taking short walks—exercising arms and chest with the saplings, or my voice with army songs or recitations. A perfect week for weather; seven continuous days bright and dry and cool and sunny. The nights splendid, with full moon—about 10 the grandest of star-shows up in the east and south, Jupiter, Saturn, Capella, Aldebaran, and great Orion. Am feeling pretty well—am outdoors most of the time, absorbing the days and nights all I can.

CENTRAL PARK NOTES.—*American Society from a Park Policeman's Point of View.*—Am in New York City, upper part—visit Central Park almost every day (and have for the last three weeks) off and on, taking observations or short rambles, and sometimes riding around. I talk quite a good deal with one of the Park policemen, C. C., up toward the Ninetieth street entrance. One day in particular I got him a-going, and it proved deeply interesting to me. Our talk floated into sociology and politics. I was curious to find how these things appear'd on their surfaces to my friend, for he plainly possess'd sharp wits and good nature, and had been seeing, for years, broad streaks of humanity somewhat out of my latitude. I found that as he took such appearances the inward caste-spirit of European "aristocracy" pervaded rich America, with cynicism and artificiality at the fore. Of the bulk of official persons, Executives, Congressmen, Legislators, Aldermen,

Department heads, etc., etc., or the candidates for those positions, nineteen in twenty, in the policeman's judgment, were just players in a game. Liberty, Equality, Union, and all the grand words of the Republic, were, in their mouths, but lures, decoys, chisel'd likenesses of dead wood, to catch the masses. Of fine afternoons, along the broad tracks of the Park, for many years, had swept by my friend, as he stood on guard, the carriages, etc., of American Gentility, not by dozens and scores, but by hundreds and thousands. Lucky brokers, capitalists, contractors, grocery-men, successful political strikers, rich butchers, dry goods' folk, &c. And on a large proportion of these vehicles, on panels or horse-trappings, were conspicuously borne *heraldic family crests.* (Can this really be true?) In wish and willingness (and if that were so, what matter about the reality?) titles of nobility, with a court and spheres fit for the capitalists, the highly educated, and the carriage-riding classes—to fence them off from "the common people"—were the heart's desire of the "good society" of our great cities—aye, of North and South.

So much for my police friend's speculations—which rather took me aback—and which I have thought I would just print as he gave them (as a doctor records symptoms.)

PLATE GLASS NOTES.—*St. Louis, Missouri, November, '79.*—What do you think I find manufactur'd out here—and of a kind the clearest and largest, best, and the most finish'd and luxurious in the world—and with ample demand for it too? *Plate glass!* One would suppose that was the last dainty outcome of an old, almost effete-growing civilization; and yet here it is, a few miles from St. Louis, on a charming little river, in the wilds of the West, near the Mississippi. I went down that way to-day by the Iron Mountain Railroad—was switch'd off on a side-track four miles through woods and ravines, to Swash Creek, so-call'd, and there found Crystal City, and immense Glass Works, built (and evidently built to stay) right in the pleasant rolling forest. Spent most of the day, and examin'd the inexhaustible and peculiar sand the glass is made of—the original whity-gray stuff in the banks—saw the melting in the pots (a wondrous process, a real poem)—saw the delicate preparation the clay material undergoes for these great pots (it has to be kneaded finally by human feet, no machinery answering, and I watch'd the picturesque bare-legged Africans treading it)—saw the molten stuff (a great mass of a glowing pale yellow color) taken out of the furnaces (I shall never forget that Pot, shape, color, concomitants, more beautiful than any antique statue,) pass'd into the adjoining casting-room, lifted by powerful machinery, pour'd out on its bed (all glowing, a newer, vaster study for colorists, indescribable, a pale red-tinged yellow, of tarry consistence, all lambent,) roll'd by a heavy roller into rough plate glass, I should say ten feet by fourteen, then rapidly shov'd into the annealing oven, which stood ready for it. The polishing and grinding rooms afterward—the great glass slabs, hundreds of them, on their flat beds, and the see-saw music of the steam machinery constantly at work polishing them—the myriads of human figures (the works employ'd 400 men) moving about, with swart arms and necks, and no superfluous clothing—the vast, rude halls, with immense play of shifting shade, and slow-moving currents of smoke and steam, and shafts of light, sometimes sun, striking in from above with effects that would have fill'd Michel Angelo with rapture.

Coming back to St. Louis this evening, at sundown, and for over an hour afterward, we follow'd the Mississippi, close by its western bank, giving me an ampler view of the river, and with effects a little different from any yet. In the eastern sky hung the planet Mars, just up, and of a very clear and vivid yellow. It was a soothing and pensive hour—the spread of the river off there in the half-light—the glints of the down-bound steamboats plodding along—and that yellow orb (apparently twice as large and significant as usual) above the Illinois shore. (All along, these nights, nothing can exceed the calm, fierce, golden, glistening domination of Mars over all the stars in the sky.)

As we came nearer St. Louis, the night having well set in, I saw some (to me) novel effects in the zinc smelting establishments, the tall chimneys belching flames at the top, while inside through the openings at the façades of the great tanks burst forth (in regular position) hundreds of fierce tufts of a peculiar blue (or green) flame, of a purity and intensity, like electric lights—illuminating not only the great buildings themselves, but far and near outside, like hues of the aurora borealis, only more vivid. (So that—remembering the Pot from the crystal furnace—my jaunt seem'd to give me new revelations in the color line.)

Some War Memoranda

JOTTED DOWN AT THE TIME

I FIND this incident in my notes (I suppose from "chinning" in hospital with some sick or wounded soldier who knew of it):

When Kilpatrick and his forces were cut off at Brandy Station (last of September, '63, or thereabouts,) and the bands struck up "Yankee Doodle," there were not cannon enough in the Southern Confederacy to keep him and them "in." It was when Meade fell back. K. had his large cavalry division (perhaps 5000 men,) but the rebs, in superior force, had surrounded them. Things look'd exceedingly desperate. K. had two fine bands, and order'd them up immediately; they join'd and play'd "Yankee Doodle" with a will! It went through the men like lightning—but to inspire, not to unnerve. Every man seem'd a giant. They charged like a cyclone, and cut their way out. Their loss was but 20. It was about two in the afternoon.

WASHINGTON STREET SCENES

April 7, 1864.—WALKING DOWN PENNSYLVANIA AVENUE.—Warmish forenoon, after the storm of the past few days. I see, passing up, in the broad space between the curbs, a big squad of a couple of hundred conscripts, surrounded by a strong cordon of arm'd guards, and others interspers'd between the ranks. The government has learn'd caution from its experiences; there are many hundreds of "bounty jumpers," and already, as I am told, eighty thousand deserters! Next (also passing up the Avenue,) a cavalry company, young, but evidently well drill'd and service-harden'd men. Mark the upright posture in their saddles, the bronz'd and bearded young faces, the easy swaying to the motions of the horses, and the carbines by their right knees; handsome and reckless, some eighty of them, riding with rapid gait, clattering along. Then the tinkling bells of passing cars, the many shops (some with large show-windows, some with swords, straps for the shoulders of different ranks, hat-cords with acorns, or other insignia,) the military patrol marching along, with the orderly or second-lieutenant stopping different ones to examine passes—the forms, the faces, all sorts crowded together, the worn and pale, the pleas'd, some on their way to the railroad depot going home, the cripples, the darkeys, the long trains of government wagons, or the sad strings of ambulances conveying wounded—the many officers' horses tied in front of the drinking or oyster saloons, or held by black men or boys, or orderlies.

THE 195TH PENNSYLVANIA

Tuesday, Aug. 1, 1865.—About 3 o'clock this afternoon (sun broiling hot) in Fifteenth street, by the Treasury building, a large and handsome regiment, 195th Pennsylvania, were marching by—as it happen'd, receiv'd orders just here to halt and break ranks, so that they might rest themselves awhile. I thought I never saw a finer set of men—so hardy, candid, bright American looks, all weather-beaten, and with warm clothes. Every man was home-born. My heart was much drawn toward them. They seem'd very tired, red, and streaming with sweat. It is a one-year regiment, mostly from Lancaster County, Pa.; have been in Shenandoah Valley. On halting, the men unhitch'd their knapsacks, and sat down to rest themselves. Some lay flat on the pavement or under trees. The fine physical appearance of the whole body was remarkable. Great, very great, must be the State where such young farmers and mechanics are the practical average. I went around for half an hour and talk'd with several of them, sometimes squatting down with the groups.

LEFT-HAND WRITING BY SOLDIERS

April 30, 1866.—Here is a single significant fact, from which one may judge of the character of the American soldiers in this just concluded war: A gentleman in New York City, a while since, took it into his head to collect specimens of writing from soldiers who had lost their right hands in battle, and afterwards learn'd to use the left. He gave public notice of his desire, and offer'd prizes for the best of these specimens. Pretty soon they began to come in, and by the time specified for awarding the prizes three hundred samples of such left-hand writing by maim'd soldiers had arrived.

I have just been looking over some of this writing. A great many of the specimens are written in a beautiful manner. All are good. The writing in nearly all cases slants backward instead of forward. One piece of writing, from a soldier who had lost both arms, was made by holding the pen in his mouth.

CENTRAL VIRGINIA IN '64

CULPEPER, where I am stopping, looks like a place of two or three thousand inhabitants. Must be one of the pleasantest towns in Virginia. Even now, dilapidated fences, all broken down, windows out, it has the remains of much beauty. I am standing on an eminence overlooking the town, though within its limits. To the west the long Blue Mountain range is very plain, looks quite near, though from 30 to 50 miles distant, with some gray splashes of snow yet visible. The show is varied and fascinating. I see a great eagle up there in the air sailing with pois'd wings, quite low. Squads of red-legged soldiers are drilling; I suppose some of the new men of the Brooklyn 14th; they march off presently with muskets on their shoulders. In another place, just below me, are some soldiers squaring off logs to build a shanty—chopping away, and the noise of the axes sounding sharp. I hear the bellowing, unmusical screech of the mule. I mark the thin blue smoke rising from camp fires. Just below me is a collection of hospital tents, with a yellow flag elevated on a stick, and moving languidly in the breeze. Two discharged men (I know them both) are just leaving. One is so weak he can hardly walk; the other is stronger, and carries his comrade's musket. They move slowly along the muddy road toward the depot. The scenery is full of breadth, and spread on the most generous scale (everywhere in Virginia this thought fill'd me.) The sights, the scenes, the groups, have been varied and picturesque here beyond description, and remain so.

I heard the men return in force the other night—heard the shouting, and got up and went out to hear what was the matter. That night scene of so many hundred tramping steadily by, through the mud (some big flaring torches of pine knots,) I shall never forget. I like to go to the paymaster's tent, and watch the men getting paid off. Some have furloughs, and start at once for home, sometimes amid great chaffing and blarneying. There is every day the sound of the wood-chopping axe, and the plentiful sight of negroes, crows, and mud. I note large droves and pens of cattle. The teamsters have camps of their own, and I go often among them. The officers occasionally invite me to dinner or supper at headquarters. The fare is plain, but you get something good to drink, and plenty of it. Gen. Meade is absent; Sedgwick is in command.

PAYING THE 1ST U.S.C.T.

ONE of my war time reminiscences comprises the quiet side scene of a visit I made to the First Regiment U.S. Color'd Troops, at their encampment, and on the occasion of their first paying off, July 11, 1863. Though there is now no difference of opinion worth mentioning, there was a powerful opposition to enlisting blacks during the earlier years of the secession war. Even then, however, they had their champions. "That the color'd race," said a good authority, "is capable of military training and efficiency, is demonstrated by the testimony of numberless witnesses, and by the eagerness display'd in the raising, organizing, and drilling of African troops. Few white regiments make a better appearance on parade than the First and Second Louisiana Native Guards. The same remark is true of other color'd regiments. At Milliken's Bend, at Vicksburg, at Port Hudson, on Morris Island, and wherever tested, they have exhibited determin'd bravery, and compell'd the plaudits alike of the thoughtful and thoughtless soldiery. During the siege of Port Hudson the question was often ask'd those who beheld their resolute charges, how the 'niggers' behav'd under fire; and without exception the answer was complimentary to them. 'O, tip-top!' 'first-rate!' 'bully!' were the usual replies." But I did not start out to argue the case—

only to give my reminiscence literally, as jotted on the spot at the time.

I write this on Mason's (otherwise Analostan) Island, under the fine shade trees of an old white stucco house, with big rooms; the white stucco house, originally a fine country seat (tradition says the famous Virginia Mason, author of the Fugitive Slave Law, was born here.) I reach'd the spot from my Washington quarters by ambulance up Pennsylvania avenue, through Georgetown, across the Aqueduct bridge, and around through a cut and winding road, with rocks and many bad gullies not lacking. After reaching the island, we get presently in the midst of the camp of the 1st Regiment U.S.C.T. The tents look clean and good; indeed, altogether, in locality especially, the pleasantest camp I have yet seen. The spot is umbrageous, high and dry, with distant sounds of the city, and the puffing steamers of the Potomac, up to Georgetown and back again. Birds are singing in the trees, the warmth is endurable here in this moist shade, with the fragrance and freshness. A hundred rods across is Georgetown. The river between is swell'd and muddy from the late rains up country. So quiet here, yet full of vitality, all around in the far distance glimpses, as I sweep my eye, of hills, verdure-clad, and with plenteous trees; right where I sit, locust, sassafras, spice, and many other trees, a few with huge parasitic vines; just at hand the banks sloping to the river, wild with beautiful, free vegetation, superb weeds, better, in their natural growth and forms, than the best garden. Lots of luxuriant grape vines and trumpet flowers; the river flowing far down in the distance.

Now the paying is to begin. The Major (paymaster) with his clerk seat themselves at a table—the rolls are before them—the money box is open'd—there are packages of five, ten, twenty-five cent pieces. Here comes the first Company (B), some 82 men, all blacks. Certes, we cannot find fault with the appearance of this crowd—negroes though they be. They are manly enough, bright enough, look as if they had the soldier-stuff in them, look hardy, patient, many of them real handsome young fellows. The paying, I say, has begun. The men are march'd up in close proximity. The clerk calls off name after name, and each walks up, receives his money, and passes along out of the way. It is a real study, both to see them come close, and to see them pass away, stand counting their cash—(nearly all of this company get ten dollars and three cents each.) The clerk calls George Washington. That distinguish'd personage steps from the ranks, in the shape of a very black man, good sized and shaped, and aged about 30, with a military moustache; he takes his "ten three," and goes off evidently well pleas'd. (There are about a dozen Washingtons in the company. Let us hope they will do honor to the name.) At the table, how quickly the Major handles the bills, counts without trouble, everything going on smoothly and quickly. The regiment numbers to-day about 1,000 men (including 20 officers, the only whites.)

Now another company. These get $5.36 each. The men look well. They, too, have great names; besides the Washingtons aforesaid, John Quincy Adams, Daniel Webster, Calhoun, James Madison, Alfred Tennyson, John Brown, Benj. G. Tucker, Horace Greeley, etc. The men step off aside, count their money with a pleas'd, half-puzzled look. Occasionally, but not often, there are some thoroughly African physiognomies, very black in color, large, protruding lips, low forehead, etc. But I have to say that I do not see one utterly revolting face.

Then another company, each man of this getting $10.03 also. The pay proceeds very rapidly (the calculation, roll-signing, etc., having been arranged before hand.) Then some trouble. One company, by the rigid rules of official computation, gets only 23 cents each man. The company (K) is indignant, and after two or three are paid, the refusal to take the paltry sum is universal, and the company marches off to quarters unpaid.

Another company (I) gets only 70 cents. The sullen, lowering, disappointed look is general. Half refuse it in this case. Company G, in full dress, with brass scales on shoulders, look'd, perhaps, as well as any of the companies—the men had an unusually alert look.

These, then, are the black troops,—or the beginning of them. Well, no one can see them, even under these circumstances—their military career in its novitiate—without feeling well pleas'd with them.

As we enter'd the island, we saw scores at a little distance, bathing, washing their clothes, etc. The officers, as far as looks go, have a fine appearance, have good faces, and the air military. Altogether it is a significant show, and brings up some "abolition" thoughts. The scene, the porch of an Old Virginia slave-owner's house, the Potomac rippling near, the Capitol just down three or four miles there, seen through the pleasant blue haze of this July day.

After a couple of hours I get tired, and go off for a ramble. I write these concluding lines on a rock, under the shade of a tree on the banks of the island. It is solitary here, the birds singing, the sluggish muddy-yellow waters pouring down from the late rains of the upper Potomac; the green heights on the south side of the river before me. The single cannon from a neighboring fort has just been fired, to signal high noon. I have walk'd all around Analostan, enjoying its luxuriant wildness, and stopt in this solitary spot. A water snake wriggles down the bank, disturb'd, into the water. The bank near by is fringed with a dense growth of shrubbery, vines, etc.

Five Thousand Poems

There have been collected in a cluster nearly five thousand big and little American poems—all that diligent and long-continued research could lay hands on! The author of 'Old Grimes is Dead' commenced it, more than fifty years ago; then the cluster was pass'd on and accumulated by C. F. Harris; then further pass'd on and added to by the late Senator Anthony, from whom the whole collection has been bequeath'd to Brown University. A catalogue (such as it is) has been made and publish'd of these five thousand poems—and is probably the most curious and suggestive part of the whole affair. At any rate it has led me to some abstract reflection like the following.

I should like, for myself, to put on record my devout acknowledgment not only of the great masterpieces of the past, but of the benefit of *all* poets, past and present, and of *all* poetic utterance—in its entirety the dominant moral factor of humanity's progress. In view of that progress, and of evolution, the religious and æsthetic elements, the distinctive and most important of any, seem to me more indebted to poetry than to all other means and influences combined. In a very profound sense *religion is the poetry of humanity.* Then the points of union and rapport among all the poems and poets of the world, however wide their separations of time and place and theme, are much more numerous and weighty than the points of contrast. Without relation as they may seem at first sight, the whole earth's poets and poetry—*en masse*—the Oriental, the Greek, and what there is of Roman—the oldest myths—the interminable ballad-romances of the Middle Ages—the hymns and psalms of worship—the epics, plays, swarms of lyrics of the British Islands, or the Teutonic old or new—or modern French—or what there is in America, Bryant's, for instance, or Whittier's or Longfellow's—the verse of all tongues and ages, all forms, all subjects, from primitive times to our own day inclusive—really combine in one aggregate and electric globe or universe, with all its numberless parts and radiations held together by a common centre or verteber. To repeat it, all poetry thus has (to the point of view comprehensive enough) more features of resemblance than difference, and becomes essentially, like the planetary globe itself, compact and orbic and whole. Nature seems to sow countless seeds—makes incessant crude attempts—thankful to get now and then, even at rare and long intervals, something approximately good.

The Old Bowery

A Reminiscence of New York Plays and Acting Fifty Years Ago.

In an article not long since, "Mrs. Siddons as Lady Macbeth," in "The Nineteenth Century," after describing the bitter regretfulness to mankind from the loss of those first-class poems, temples, pictures, gone and vanish'd from any record of men, the writer (Fleeming Jenkin) continues:

> If this be our feeling as to the more durable works of art, what shall we say of those triumphs which, by their very nature, last no longer than the action which creates them—the triumphs of the orator, the singer or the actor? There

is an anodyne in the words, "must be so," "inevitable," and there is even some absurdity in longing for the impossible. This anodyne and our sense of humor temper the unhappiness we feel when, after hearing some great performance, we leave the theatre and think, "Well, this great thing has been, and all that is now left of it is the feeble print upon my brain, the little thrill which memory will send along my nerves, mine and my neighbors, as we live longer the print and thrill must be feebler, and when we pass away the impress of the great artist will vanish from the world." The regret that a great art should in its nature be transitory, explains the lively interest which many feel in reading anecdotes or descriptions of a great actor.

All this is emphatically my own feeling and reminiscence about the best dramatic and lyric artists I have seen in bygone days—for instance, Marietta Alboni, the elder Booth, Forrest, the tenor Bettini, the baritone Badiali, "old man Clarke"—(I could write a whole paper on the latter's peerless rendering of the Ghost in "Hamlet" at the Park, when I was a young fellow)—an actor named Ranger, who appear'd in America forty years ago in *genre* characters; Henry Placide, and many others. But I will make a few memoranda at least of the best one I knew.

For the elderly New Yorker of to-day, perhaps, nothing were more likely to start up memories of his early manhood than the mention of the Bowery and the elder Booth. At the date given, the more stylish and select theatre (prices, 50 cents pit, $1 boxes) was "The Park," a large and well-appointed house on Park Row, opposite the present Post-office. English opera and the old comedies were often given in capital style; the principal foreign stars appear'd here, with Italian opera at wide intervals. The Park held a large part in my boyhood's and young manhood's life. Here I heard the English actor, Anderson, in "Charles de Moor," and in the fine part of "Gisippus." Here I heard Fanny Kemble, Charlotte Cushman, the Seguins, Daddy Rice, Hackett as Falstaff, Nimrod Wildfire, Rip Van Winkle, and in his Yankee characters. (See pages 727, 728, *Specimen Days.*) It was here (some years later than the date in the headline) I also heard Mario many times, and at his best. In such parts as Gennaro, in "Lucrezia Borgia," he was inimitable—the sweetest of voices, a pure tenor, of considerable compass and respectable power. His wife, Grisi, was with him, no longer first-class or young—a fine Norma, though, to the last.

Perhaps my dearest amusement reminiscences are those musical ones. I doubt if ever the senses and emotions of the future will be thrill'd as were the auditors of a generation ago by the deep passion of Alboni's contralto (at the Broadway Theatre, south side, near Pearl street)—or by the trumpet notes of Badiali's baritone, or Bettini's pensive and incomparable tenor in Fernando in "Favorita," or Marini's bass in "Faliero," among the Havana troupe, Castle Garden.

But getting back more specifically to the date and theme I started from—the heavy tragedy business prevail'd more decidedly at the Bowery Theatre, where Booth and Forrest were frequently to be heard. Though Booth *pere,* then in his prime, ranging in age from 40 to 44 years (he was born in 1796,) was the loyal child and continuer of the traditions of orthodox English play-acting, he stood out "himself alone" in many respects beyond any of his kind on record, and with effects and ways that broke through all rules and all traditions. He has been well describ'd as an actor "whose instant and tremendous concentration of passion in his delineations overwhelm'd his audience, and wrought into it such enthusiasm that it partook of the fever of inspiration surging through his own veins." He seems to have been of beautiful private character, very honorable, affectionate, good-natured, no arrogance, glad to give the other actors the best chances. He knew all stage points thoroughly, and curiously ignored the mere dignities. I once talk'd with a man who had seen him do the Second Actor in the mock play to Charles Kean's Hamlet in Baltimore. He was a marvellous linguist. He play'd Shylock once in London, giving the dialogue in Hebrew, and in New Orleans Oreste (Racine's "Andromaque") in French. One trait of his habits, I have heard, was strict vegetarianism. He was exceptionally kind to the brute creation. Every once in a while he would make a break for solitude or wild freedom, sometimes for a few hours, sometimes for days. (He illustrated Plato's rule that to the forming an artist of the very highest rank a dash of insanity or what the world calls insanity is indispensable.) He was a small-sized man—yet sharp observers noticed that however crowded the stage might be in certain scenes, Booth never seem'd overtopt or hidden. He was singularly spontaneous and fluctuating; in the same part each rendering differ'd from any and all others. He had no stereotyped positions and made no arbitrary requirements on his fellow-performers.

As is well known to old play-goers, Booth's most effective part was Richard III. Either that, or Iago, or Shylock, or Pescara in "The Apostate," was sure to draw a crowded house. (Remember heavy pieces were much more in demand those days than now.) He was also unapproachably grand in Sir Giles Overreach, in "A New Way to Pay Old Debts," and the principal character in "The Iron Chest."

In any portraiture of Booth, those years, the Bowery Theatre, with its leading lights, and the lessee and manager, Thomas Hamblin, cannot be left out. It was at the Bowery I first saw Edwin Forrest (the play was John Howard Payne's "Brutus, or the Fall of Tarquin," and it affected me for weeks; or rather I might say permanently filter'd into my whole nature,) then in the zenith of his fame and ability. Sometimes (perhaps a veteran's benefit night,) the Bowery would group together five or six of the first-class actors of those days—Booth, Forrest, Cooper, Hamblin, and John R. Scott, for instance. At that time and here George Jones ("Count Joannes") was a young, handsome actor, and quite a favorite. I remember seeing him in the title role in "Julius Cæsar," and a capital performance it was.

To return specially to the manager. Thomas Hamblin made a first-rate foil to Booth, and was frequently cast with him. He had a large, shapely, imposing presence, and dark and flashing eyes. I remember well his rendering of the main role in Maturin's "Bertram, or the Castle of St. Aldobrand." But I thought Tom Hamblin's best acting was in the comparatively minor part of Faulconbridge in "King John"—he himself evidently revell'd in the part, and took away the house's applause from young Kean (the King) and Ellen Tree (Constance,) and everybody else on the stage—some time afterward at the Park. Some of the Bowery actresses were remarkably good. I remember Mrs. Pritchard in "Tour de Nesle," and Mrs. McClure in "Fatal Curiosity," and as Millwood in "George Barnwell." (I wonder what old fellow reading these lines will recall the fine comedietta of "The Youth That Never Saw a Woman," and the jolly acting in it of Mrs. Herring and old Gates.)

The Bowery, now and then, was the place, too, for spectacular pieces, such as "The Last Days of Pompeii," "The Lion- Doom'd" and the yet undying "Mazeppa." At one time "Jonathan Bradford, or the Murder at the Roadside Inn," had a long and crowded run; John Sefton and his brother William acted in it. I remember well the Frenchwoman Celeste, a splendid pantomimist, and her emotional "Wept of the Wish-ton-Wish." But certainly the main "reason for being" of the Bowery Theatre those years was to furnish the public with Forrest's and Booth's performances—the latter having a popularity and circles of enthusiastic admirers and critics fully equal to the former—though people were divided as always. For some reason or other, neither Forrest nor Booth would accept engagements at the more fashionable theatre, the Park. And it is a curious reminiscence, but a true one, that both these great actors and their performances were taboo'd by "polite society" in New York and Boston at the time—probably as being too robustuous. But no such scruples affected the Bowery.

Recalling from that period the occasion of either Forrest or Booth, any good night at the old Bowery, pack'd from ceiling to pit with its audience mainly of alert, well dress'd, full-blooded young and middle-aged men, the best average of American-born mechanics—the emotional nature of the whole mass arous'd by the power and magnetism of as mighty mimes as ever trod the stage—the whole crowded auditorium, and what seeth'd in it, and flush'd from its faces and eyes, to me as much a part of the show as any—bursting forth in one of those long-kept-up tempests of hand-clapping peculiar to the Bowery—no dainty kid-glove business, but electric force and muscle from perhaps 2000 full-sinew'd men—(the inimitable and chromatic tempest of one of those ovations to Edwin Forrest, welcoming him back after an absence, comes up to me this moment)—Such sounds and scenes as here resumed will surely afford to many old New Yorkers some fruitful recollections.

I can yet remember (for I always scann'd an audience as rigidly as a play) the faces of the leading authors, poets, editors, of those times—Fenimore Cooper, Bryant, Paulding, Irving, Charles King, Watson Webb, N. P. Willis, Hoffman, Halleck, Mumford, Morris, Leggett, L. G. Clarke, R. A. Locke and others, occasionally peering from the first tier boxes; and even the great National Eminences, Presidents Adams, Jackson, Van Buren and Tyler, all made short visits there on their Eastern tours.

Awhile after 1840 the character of the Bowery as hitherto described completely changed. Cheap prices and vulgar programmes came in. People who of after years saw the pandemonium of the pit and the doings on the boards must not gauge by them the times and characters I am describing. Not but what there was more or less rankness in the crowd even then. For types of sectional New York those days—the streets East of the Bowery, that intersect Division, Grand, and up to Third Avenue—types that never found their Dickens, or Hogarth, or Balzac, and have pass'd away unportraitured—the young ship-builders, cartmen, butchers, firemen (the old-time "soap-lock" or exaggerated "Mose" or "Sikesey," of Chanfrau's plays,) they, too, were always to be seen in these audiences, racy of the East River and the Dry Dock. Slang, wit, occasional shirt sleeves, and a picturesque freedom of looks and manners, with a rude good-nature and restless movement, were generally noticeable. Yet there never were audiences that paid a good actor or an interesting play the compliment of more sustain'd attention or quicker rapport. Then at times came the exceptionally decorous and intellectual congregations I have hinted at; for the Bowery really furnish'd plays and players you could get nowhere else. Notably, Booth always drew the best hearers; and to a specimen of his acting I will now attend in some detail.

I happen'd to see what has been reckon'd by experts one of the most marvelous pieces of histrionism ever known. It must have been about 1834 or '35. A favorite comedian and actress at the Bowery, Thomas Flynn and his wife, were to have a joint benefit, and, securing Booth for Richard, advertised the fact many days before-hand. The house fill'd early from top to bottom. There was some uneasiness behind the scenes, for the afternoon arrived, and Booth had not come from down in Maryland, where he lived. However, a few minutes before ringing-up time he made his appearance in lively condition.

After a one-act farce over, as contrast and prelude, the curtain rising for the tragedy, I can, from my good seat in the pit, pretty well front, see again Booth's quiet entrance from the side, as, with head bent, he slowly and in silence, (amid the tempest of boisterous hand-clapping,) walks down the stage to the footlights with that peculiar and abstracted gesture, musingly kicking his sword, which he holds off from him by its sash. Though fifty years have pass'd since then, I can hear the clank, and feel the perfect following hush of perhaps three thousand people waiting. (I never saw an actor who could make more of the said hush or wait, and hold the audience in an indescribable, half-delicious, half-irritating suspense.) And so throughout the entire play, all parts, voice, atmosphere, magnetism, from

"Now is the winter of our discontent,"

to the closing death fight with Richmond, were of the finest and grandest. The latter character was play'd by a stalwart young fellow named Ingersoll. Indeed, all the renderings were wonderfully good. But the great spell cast upon the mass of hearers came from Booth. Especially was the dream scene very impressive. A shudder went through every nervous system in the audience; it certainly did through mine.

Without question Booth was royal heir and legitimate representative of the Garrick-Kemble-Siddons dramatic traditions; but he vitalized and gave an unnamable *race* to those traditions with his own electric personal idiosyncrasy. (As in all art-utterance it was the subtle and powerful something *special to the individual* that really conquer'd.)

To me, too, Booth stands for much else besides theatricals. I consider that my seeing the man those years glimps'd for me, beyond all else, that inner spirit and form—the unquestionable charm and vivacity, but intrinsic sophistication and artificiality—crystallizing rapidly upon the English stage and literature at and after Shakspere's time, and coming on accumulatively through the seventeenth and eighteenth centuries to the beginning, fifty or forty years ago, of those disintegrating, decomposing processes now authoritatively going on. Yes; although Booth must be class'd in that antique, almost extinct school, inflated, stagy, rendering Shakspere (perhaps inevitably, appropriately) from the growth of arbitrary and often cockney conventions, his genius was to me one of the grandest revelations of my life, a lesson of artistic expression. The words fire, energy, *abandon,* found in him unprecedented meanings. I never heard a speaker or actor who could give such a sting to hauteur or the taunt. I never heard from any other the charm of unswervingly perfect vocalization without trenching at all on mere melody, the province of music.

So much for a Thespian temple of New York fifty years since, where "sceptred tragedy went trailing by" under the gaze of the Dry Dock youth, and both players and auditors were of a character and like we shall never see again. And so much for the grandest histrion of modern times, as near as I can deliberately judge (and the phrenologists put my "caution" at 7)—grander, I believe, than Kean in the expression of electric passion, the prime eligibility of the tragic artist. For though those brilliant years had many fine and even magnificent actors, undoubtedly at Booth's death (in 1852) went the last and by far the noblest Roman of them all.

Notes to Late English Books

"SPECIMEN DAYS IN AMERICA," LONDON EDITION, JUNE, 1887. PREFACE TO THE READER IN THE BRITISH ISLANDS

If you will only take the following pages, as you do some long and gossippy letter written for you by a relative or friend traveling through distant scenes and incidents, and jotting them down lazily and informally, but ever veraciously (with occasional diversions of critical thought about somebody or something,) it might remove all formal or literary impediments at once, and bring you and me close together in the spirit in which the jottings were collated to be read. You have had, and have, plenty of public events and facts and general statistics of America;—in the following book is a common individual New World *private life,* its birth and growth, its struggles for a living, its goings and comings and observations (or representative portions of them) amid the United States of America the last thirty or forty years, with their varied war and peace, their local coloring, the unavoidable egotism, and the lights and shades and sights and joys and pains and sympathies common to humanity. Further introductory light may be found in the paragraph, "A Happy Hour's Command," and the bottom note belonging to it, at the beginning of the book. I have said in the text that if I were required to give good reason-for-being of "Specimen Days," I should be unable to do so. Let me fondly hope that it has at least the reason and excuse of such off-hand gossippy letter as just alluded to, portraying American life-sights and incidents as they actually occurred—their presentation, making additions as far as it goes, to the simple experience and association of your soul, from a comrade soul;—and that also, in the volume, as below any page of mine, anywhere, ever remains, for seen or unseen basis-phrase, GOOD-WILL BETWEEN THE COMMON PEOPLE OF ALL NATIONS.

ADDITIONAL NOTE, 1887, TO ENGLISH EDITION "SPECIMEN DAYS"

As I write these lines I still continue living in Camden, New Jersey, America. Coming this way from Washington City, on my road to the sea-shore (and a temporary rest, as I supposed) in the early summer of 1873, I broke down disabled, and have dwelt here, as my central residence, all the time since—almost 14 years. In the preceding pages I have described how, during those years, I partially recuperated (in 1876) from my worst paralysis by going down to Timber Creek, living close to Nature, and domiciling with my dear friends, George and Susan Stafford. From 1877 or '8 to '83 or '4 I was well enough to travel around, considerably—journey'd westward to Kansas, leisurely exploring the Prairies, and on to Denver and the Rocky Mountains; another time north to Canada, where I spent most of the summer with my friend Dr. Bucke, and jaunted along the great lakes, and the St. Lawrence and Saguenay rivers; another time to Boston, to properly print the final edition of my poems (I was there over two months, and had a "good time.") I have so brought out the completed "Leaves of Grass" during this period; also "Specimen Days," of which the foregoing is a transcript; collected and re-edited the "Democratic Vistas" cluster (see companion volume to the present)—commemorated Abraham Lincoln's death, on the successive anniversaries of its occurrence, by delivering my lecture on it ten or twelve times; and "put in," through many a month and season, the aimless and resultless ways of most human lives.

Thus the last 14 years have pass'd. At present (end-days of March, 1887—I am nigh entering my 69th year) I find myself continuing on here, quite dilapidated and even wreck'd bodily from the paralysis, &c.—but in *good heart* (to use a Long Island country phrase,) and with about the same mentality as ever. The worst of it is, I have been growing feebler quite rapidly for a year, and now can't walk around—hardly from one room to the next. I am forced to stay in-doors and in my big chair nearly all the time. We have had a sharp, dreary winter too, and it has pinch'd me. I am alone most of the time; every week, indeed almost every day, write some—reminiscences, essays, sketches, for the magazines; and read, or rather I should say dawdle over books and papers a good deal—spend half the day at that.

Nor can I finish this note without putting on record—wafting over sea from hence—my deepest thanks to certain friends and helpers (I would specify them all and each by name, but imperative reasons, outside of my own wishes, forbid,) in the British Islands, as well as in America. Dear, even in the abstract, is such flattering unction always no doubt to the soul! Nigher still, if possible, I myself have been, and am to-day indebted to such help for my very sustenance, clothing, shelter, and continuity. And I would not go to the grave without briefly, but plainly, as I here do, acknowledging—may I not say even glorying in it?

PREFACE TO "DEMOCRATIC VISTAS" WITH OTHER PAPERS.—ENGLISH EDITION

MAINLY I think I should base the request to weigh the following pages on the assumption that they present, however indirectly, some views of the West and Modern, or of a distinctly western and modern (American) tendency, about certain matters.

Then, too, the pages include (by attempting to illustrate it,) a theory herein immediately mentioned. For another and different point of the issue, the Enlightenment, Democracy and Fair-show of the bulk, the common people of America (from sources representing not only the British Islands, but all the world,) means, at least, eligibility to Enlightenment, Democracy and Fair-show for the bulk, the common people of all civilized nations.

That positively "the dry land has appeared," at any rate, is an important fact.

America is really the great test or trial case for all the problems and promises and speculations of humanity, and of the past and present.

I say, too, we* are not to look so much to changes, ameliorations, and adaptations in Politics as to those of Literature and (thence) domestic Sociology. I have accordingly in the following melange introduced many themes besides political ones.

Several of the pieces are ostensibly in explanation of my own writings; but in that very process they best include and set forth their side of principles and generalities pressing vehemently for consideration our age.

Upon the whole, it is on the atmosphere they are born in, and, (I hope) give out, more than any specific piece or trait, I would care to rest.

I think Literature—a new, superb, democratic literature—is to be the medicine and lever, and (with Art) the chief influence in modern civilization. I have myself not so much made a dead set at this theory, or attempted to present it directly,

*We who, in many departments, ways, make *the building up of the masses,* by *building up grand individuals,* our shibboleth: and in brief that is the marrow of this book.

as admitted it to color and sometimes dominate what I had to say. In both Europe and America we have serried phalanxes who promulge and defend the political claims: I go for an equal force to uphold the other.

WALT WHITMAN.

CAMDEN, NEW JERSEY, *April, 1888*.

ABRAHAM LINCOLN

GLAD am I to give—were anything better lacking—even the most brief and shorn testimony of Abraham Lincoln. Everything I heard about him authentically, and every time I saw him (and it was my fortune through 1862 to '65 to see, or pass a word with, or watch him, personally, perhaps twenty or thirty times,) added to and anneal'd my respect and love at the moment. And as I dwell on what I myself heard or saw of the mighty Westerner, and blend it with the history and literature of my age, and of what I can get of all ages, and conclude it with his death, it seems like some tragic play, superior to all else I know—vaster and fierier and more convulsionary, for this America of ours, than Eschylus or Shakspere ever drew for Athens or for England. And then the Moral permeating, underlying all! the Lesson that none so remote—none so illiterate—no age, no class—but may directly or indirectly read!

Abraham Lincoln's was really one of those characters, the best of which is the result of long trains of cause and effect—needing a certain spaciousness of time, and perhaps even remoteness, to properly enclose them—having unequal'd influence on the shaping of this Republic (and therefore the world) as to-day, and then far more important in the future. Thus the time has by no means yet come for a thorough measurement of him. Nevertheless, we who live in his era—who have seen him, and heard him, face to face, and are in the midst of, or just parting from, the strong and strange events which he and we have had to do with—can in some respects bear valuable, perhaps indispensable testimony concerning him.

I should first like to give a very fair and characteristic likeness of Lincoln, as I saw him and watch'd him one afternoon in Washington, for nearly half an hour, not long before his death. It was as he stood on the balcony of the National Hotel, Pennsylvania Avenue, making a short speech to the crowd in front, on the occasion either of a set of new colors presented to a famous Illinois regiment, or of the daring capture, by the Western men, of some flags from "the enemy," (which latter phrase, by the by, was not used by him at all in his remarks.) How the picture happen'd to be made I do not know, but I bought it a few days afterward in Washington, and it was endors'd by every one to whom I show'd it. Though hundreds of portraits have been made, by painters and photographers, (many to pass on, by copies, to future times,) I have never seen one yet that in my opinion deserv'd to be called a perfectly *good likeness;* nor do I believe there is really such a one in existence. May I not say too, that, as there is no entirely competent and emblematic likeness of Abraham Lincoln in picture or statue, there is not—perhaps cannot be—any fully appropriate literary statement or summing-up of him yet in existence?

The best way to estimate the value of Lincoln is to think what the condition of America would be to-day, if he had never lived—never been President. His nomination and first election were mainly accidents, experiments. Severely view'd, one cannot think very much of American Political Parties, from the beginning, after the Revolutionary War, down to the present time. Doubtless, while they have had their uses—have been and are "the grass on which the cow feeds"—and indispensable economies of growth—it is undeniable that under flippant names they have merely identified temporary passions, or freaks, or sometimes prejudice, ignorance, or hatred. The only thing like a great and worthy idea vitalizing a party, and making it heroic, was the enthusiasm in '64 for re-electing Abraham Lincoln, and the reason behind that enthusiasm.

How does this man compare with the acknowledg'd "Father of his country?" Washington was model'd on the best Saxon, and Franklin—of the age of the Stuarts (rooted in the Elizabethan period)—was essentially a noble Englishman, and just the kind needed for the occasions and the times of 1776–'83. Lincoln, underneath his practicality, was far less European, was quite thoroughly Western, original, essentially non-conventional, and had a certain sort of out-door or prairie stamp. One of the best of the late commentators on Shakspere, (Professor Dowden,) makes the height and aggregate of his quality as a poet to be, that he thoroughly blended the ideal with the practical or realistic. If this be so, I should say that what Shakspere did in poetic expression, Abraham Lincoln essentially did in his personal and official life. I should say the invisible foundations and vertebra of his character, more than any man's in history, were mystical, abstract, moral and spiritual—while upon all of them was built, and out of all of them radiated, under the control of the average of circumstances, what the vulgar call *horse-sense,* and a life often bent by temporary but most urgent materialistic and political reasons.

He seems to have been a man of indomitable firmness (even obstinacy) on rare occasions, involving great points; but he was generally very easy, flexible, tolerant, almost slouchy, respecting minor matters. I note that even those reports and anecdotes intended to level him down, all leave the tinge of a favorable impression of him. As to his religious nature, it seems to me to have certainly been of the amplest, deepest-rooted, loftiest kind.

Already a new generation begins to tread the stage, since the persons and events of the Secession War. I have more than once fancied to myself the time when the present century has closed, and a new one open'd, and the men and deeds of that contest have become somewhat vague and mythical—fancied perhaps in some great Western city, or group collected together, or public festival, where the days of old, of 1863 and '4 and '5 are discuss'd—some ancient soldier sitting in the background as the talk goes on, and betraying himself by his emotion and moist eyes—like the journeying Ithacan at the banquet of King Alcinoüs, when the bard sings the contending warriors and their battles on the plains of Troy:

> "So from the sluices of Ulysses' eyes
> Fast fell the tears, and sighs succeeded sighs."

I have fancied, I say, some such venerable relic of this time of ours, preserv'd to the next or still the next generation of

America. I have fancied, on such occasion, the young men gathering around; the awe, the eager questions: "What! have you seen Abraham Lincoln—and heard him speak—and touch'd his hand? Have you, with your own eyes, look'd on Grant, and Lee, and Sherman?"

Dear to Democracy, to the very last! And among the paradoxes generated by America, not the least curious was that spectacle of all the kings and queens and emperors of the earth, many from remote distances, sending tributes of condolence and sorrow in memory of one rais'd through the commonest average of life—a rail-splitter and flat-boatman!

Consider'd from contemporary points of view—who knows what the future may decide?—and from the points of view of current Democracy and The Union, (the only thing like passion or infatuation in the man was the passion for the Union of These States,) Abraham Lincoln seems to me the grandest figure yet, on all the crowded canvas of the Nineteenth Century.

[*From the New Orleans Picayune, Jan. 25, 1887.*]

New Orleans in 1848

WALT WHITMAN GOSSIPS OF HIS SOJOURN HERE YEARS AGO AS A NEWSPAPER WRITER. NOTES OF HIS TRIP UP THE MISSISSIPPI AND TO NEW YORK

Among the letters brought this morning (Camden, New Jersey, Jan. 15, 1887,) by my faithful post-office carrier, J. G., is one as follows:

> "New Orleans, Jan. 11, '87.—We have been informed that when you were younger and less famous than now, you were in New Orleans and perhaps have helped on the *Picayune*. If you have any remembrance of the *Picayune's* young days, or of journalism in New Orleans of that era, and would put it in writing (verse or prose) for the *Picayune's* fiftieth year edition, Jan. 25, we shall be pleased," etc.

In response to which: I went down to New Orleans early in 1848 to work on a daily newspaper, but it was not the

Picayune, though I saw quite a good deal of the editors of that paper, and knew its personnel and ways. But let me indulge my pen in some gossipy recollections of that time and place, with extracts from my journal up the Mississippi and across the great lakes to the Hudson.

Probably the influence most deeply pervading everything at that time through the United States, both in physical facts and in sentiment, was the Mexican War, then just ended. Following a brilliant campaign (in which our troops had march'd to the capital city, Mexico, and taken full possession,) we were returning after our victory. From the situation of the country, the city of New Orleans had been our channel and *entrepot* for everything, going and returning. It had the best news and war correspondents; it had the most to say, through its leading papers, the *Picayune* and *Delta* especially, and its voice was readiest listen'd to; from it "Chapparal" had gone out, and his army and battle letters were copied everywhere, not only in the United States, but in Europe. Then the social cast and results; no one who has never seen the society of a city under similar circumstances can understand what a strange vivacity and *rattle* were given throughout by such a situation. I remember the crowds of soldiers, the gay young officers, going or coming, the receipt of important news, the many discussions, the returning wounded, and so on.

I remember very well seeing Gen. Taylor with his staff and other officers at the St. Charles Theatre one evening (after talking with them during the day.) There was a short play on the stage, but the principal performance was of Dr. Colyer's troupe of "Model Artists," then in the full tide of their popularity. They gave many fine groups and solo shows. The house was crowded with uniforms and shoulder-straps. Gen. T. himself, if I remember right, was almost the only officer in civilian clothes; he was a jovial, old, rather stout, plain man, with a wrinkled and dark-yellow face, and, in ways and manners, show'd the least of conventional ceremony or etiquette I ever saw; he laugh'd unrestrainedly at everything comical. (He had a great personal resemblance to Fenimore Cooper, the novelist, of New York.) I remember Gen. Pillow and quite a cluster of other militaires also present.

One of my choice amusements during my stay in New Orleans was going down to the old French Market, especially of a Sunday morning. The show was a varied and curious one; among the rest, the Indian and negro hucksters with their wares. For there were always fine specimens of Indians, both men and women, young and old. I remember I nearly always on these occasions got a large cup of delicious coffee with a biscuit, for my breakfast, from the immense shining copper kettle of a great Creole mulatto woman (I believe she weigh'd 230 pounds.) I never have had such coffee since. About nice drinks, anyhow, my recollection of the "cobblers" (with strawberries and snow on top of the large tumblers,) and also the exquisite wines, and the perfect and mild French brandy, help the regretful reminiscence of my New Orleans experiences of those days. And what splendid and roomy and leisurely bar-rooms! particularly the grand ones of the St. Charles and St. Louis. Bargains, auctions, appointments, business conferences, &c., were generally held in the spaces or recesses of these bar-rooms.

I used to wander a midday hour or two now and then for amusement on the crowded and bustling levees, on the banks of the river. The diagonally wedg'd-in boats, the stevedores, the piles of cotton and other merchandise, the carts, mules, negroes, etc., afforded never-ending studies and sights to me. I made acquaintances among the captains, boatmen, or other characters, and often had long talks with them—sometimes finding a real rough diamond among my chance encounters. Sundays I sometimes went forenoons to the old Catholic Cathedral in the French quarter. I used to walk a good deal in this arrondissement; and I have deeply regretted since that I did not cultivate, while I had such a good opportunity, the chance of better knowledge of French and Spanish Creole New Orleans people. (I have an idea that there is much and of importance about the Latin race contributions to American nationality in the South and Southwest that will never be put with sympathetic understanding and tact on record.)

Let me say, for better detail, that through several months (1848) I work'd on a new daily paper, *The Crescent;* my situation rather a pleasant one. My young brother, Jeff, was with me; and he not only grew very homesick, but the climate of the place, and especially the water, seriously disagreed with him. From this and other reasons (although I was quite happily fix'd) I made no very long stay in the South. In due time we took passage northward for St. Louis in the "Pride of the West" steamer, which left her wharf just at dusk. My brother was unwell, and lay in his berth from the moment we left till the next morning; he seem'd to me to be in a fever, and I felt alarm'd. However, the next morning he was all right again, much to my relief.

Our voyage up the Mississippi was after the same sort as the voyage, some months before, down it. The shores of this great river are very monotonous and dull—one continuous and rank flat, with the exception of a meagre stretch of bluff, about the neighborhood of Natchez, Memphis, etc. Fortunately we had good weather, and not a great crowd of passengers, though the berths were all full. The "Pride" jogg'd along pretty well, and put us into St. Louis about noon Saturday. After looking around a little I secured passage on the steamer "Prairie Bird," (to leave late in the afternoon,) bound up the Illinois River to La Salle, where we were to take canal for Chicago. During the day I rambled with my brother over a large portion of the town, search'd after a refectory, and, after much trouble, succeeded in getting some dinner.

Our "Prairie Bird" started out at dark, and a couple of hours after there was quite a rain and blow, which made them haul in along shore and tie fast. We made but thirty miles the whole night. The boat was excessively crowded with passengers, and had withal so much freight that we could hardly turn around. I slept on the floor, and the night was uncomfortable enough. The Illinois River is spotted with little villages with big names, Marseilles, Naples, etc.; its banks are low, and the vegetation excessively rank. Peoria, some distance up, is a pleasant town; I went over the place; the country back is all rich land, for sale cheap. Three or four miles from P., land of the first quality can be bought for $3 or $4 an acre. (I am transcribing from my notes written at the time.)

Arriving at La Salle Tuesday morning, we went on board a canal-boat, had a detention by sticking on a mud bar, and then jogg'd along at a slow trot, some seventy of us, on a moderate-sized boat. (If the weather hadn't been rather cool, particularly at night, it would have been insufferable.) Illinois is the most splendid agricultural country I ever saw; the land is of surpassing richness; the place par excellence for farmers. We stopt at various points along the canal, some of them pretty villages.

It was 10 o'clock A.M. when we got in Chicago, too late for the steamer; so we went to an excellent public house, the "American Temperance," and I spent the time that day and till next morning, looking around Chicago.

At 9 the next forenoon we started on the "Griffith" (on board of which I am now inditing these memoranda,) up the blue waters of Lake Michigan. I was delighted with the appearance of the towns along Wisconsin. At Milwaukee I went on shore, and walk'd around the place. They say the country back is beautiful and rich. (It seems to me that if we should ever remove from Long Island, Wisconsin would be the proper place to come to.) The towns have a remarkable appearance of good living, without any penury or want. The country is so good naturally, and labor is in such demand.

About 5 o'clock one afternoon I heard the cry of "a woman overboard." It proved to be a crazy lady, who had become so from the loss of her son a couple of weeks before. The small boat put off, and succeeded in picking her up, though she had been in the water 15 minutes. She was dead. Her husband was on board. They went off at the next stopping place. While she lay in the water she probably recover'd her reason, as she toss'd up her arms and lifted her face toward the boat.

Sunday Morning, June 11.—We pass'd down Lake Huron yesterday and last night, and between 4 and 5 o'clock this morning we ran on the "flats," and have been vainly trying, with the aid of a steam tug and a lumbering lighter, to get clear again. The day is beautiful and the water clear and calm. Night before last we stopt at Mackinaw, (the island and town,) and I went up on the old fort, one of the oldest stations in the Northwest. We expect to get to Buffalo by to-morrow. The tug has fasten'd lines to us, but some have been snapt and the others have no effect. We seem to be firmly imbedded in the sand. (With the exception of a larger boat and better accommodations, it amounts to about the same thing as a becalmment I underwent on the Montauk voyage,

East Long Island, last summer.) Later.—We are off again—expect to reach Detroit before dinner.

We did not stop at Detroit. We are now on Lake Erie, jogging along at a good round pace. A couple of hours since we were on the river above. Detroit seem'd to me a pretty place and thrifty. I especially liked the looks of the Canadian shore opposite and of the little village of Windsor, and, indeed, all along the banks of the river. From the shrubbery and the neat appearance of some of the cottages, I think it must have been settled by the French. While I now write we can see a little distance ahead the scene of the battle between Perry's fleet and the British during the last war with England. The lake looks to me a fine sheet of water. We are having a beautiful day.

June 12.—We stopt last evening at Cleveland, and though it was dark, I took the opportunity of rambling about the place; went up in the heart of the city and back to what appear'd to be the court-house. The streets are unusually wide, and the buildings appear to be substantial and comfortable. We went down through Main Street and found, some distance along, several squares of ground very prettily planted with trees and looking attractive enough. Return'd to the boat by way of the light-house on the hill.

This morning we are making for Buffalo, being, I imagine, a little more than half across Lake Erie. The water is rougher than on Michigan or Huron. (On St. Clair it was smooth as glass.) The day is bright and dry, with a stiff head wind.

We arriv'd in Buffalo on Monday evening; spent that night and a portion of next day going round the city exploring. Then got in the cars and went to Niagara; went under the falls—saw the whirlpool and all the other sights.

Tuesday night started for Albany; travel'd all night. From the time daylight afforded us a view of the country all seem'd very rich and well cultivated. Every few miles were large towns or villages.

Wednesday late we arriv'd at Albany. Spent the evening in exploring. There was a political meeting (Hunker) at the capitol, but I pass'd it by. Next morning I started down the Hudson in the "Alida;" arriv'd safely in New York that evening.

Small Memoranda

Thousands lost—here one or two preserv'd.

Attorney General's Office, *Washington, Aug. 22, 1865.*—As I write this, about noon, the suite of rooms here is fill'd with southerners, standing in squads, or streaming in and out, some talking with the Pardon Clerk, some waiting to see the Attorney General, others discussing in low tones among themselves. All are mainly anxious about their pardons. The famous 13th exception of the President's Amnesty Proclamation of————, makes it necessary that every secessionist, whose property is worth $20,000 or over, shall get a special pardon, before he can transact any legal purchase, sale, &c. So hundreds and thousands of such property owners have either sent up here, for the last two months, or have been, or are now coming personally here, to get their pardons. They are from Virginia, Georgia, Alabama, Mississippi, North and South Carolina, and every southern State. Some of their written petitions are very abject. Secession officers of the rank of Brigadier General, or higher, also need these special pardons. They also come here. I see streams of the $20,000 men, (and some women,) every day. I talk now and then with them, and learn much that is interesting and significant. All the southern women that come (some splendid specimens, mothers, &c.) are dress'd in deep black.

Immense numbers (several thousands) of these pardons have been pass'd upon favorably; the Pardon Warrants (like great deeds) have been issued from the State Department, on the requisition of this office. But for some reason or other, they nearly all yet lie awaiting the President's signature. He seems to be in no hurry about it, but lets them wait.

The crowds that come here make a curious study for me. I get along, very sociably, with any of them—as I let them do all the talking; only now and then I have a long confab, or ask a suggestive question or two.

If the thing continues as at present, the property and wealth of the Southern States is going to legally rest, for the future, on these pardons. Every single one is made out with the condition that the grantee shall respect the abolition of slavery, and never make an attempt to restore it.

Washington, Sept. 8, 9, &c., 1865.—The arrivals, swarms, &c., of the $20,000 men seeking pardons, still continue with increas'd numbers and pertinacity. I yesterday (I am a clerk in the U. S. Attorney General's office here) made out a long list from Alabama, nearly 200, recommended for pardon by the Provisional Governor. This list, in the shape of a requisition from the Attorney General, goes to the State Department. There the Pardon Warrants are made out, brought back here, and then sent to the President, where they await his signature. He is signing them very freely of late.

The President, indeed, as at present appears, has fix'd his mind on a very generous and forgiving course toward the return'd secessionists. He will not countenance at all the demand of the extreme Philo-African element of the North, to make the right of negro voting at elections a condition and *sine qua non* of the reconstruction of the United States south, and of their resumption of co-equality in the Union.

A glint inside of Abraham Lincoln's Cabinet appointments. One item of many.—While it was hanging in suspense who should be appointed Secretary of the Interior, (to take the place of Caleb Smith,) the choice was very close between Mr. Harlan and Col. Jesse K. Dubois, of Illinois. The latter had many friends. He was competent, he was honest, and he was a *man*. Mr. Harlan, in the race, finally gain'd the Methodist interest, and got himself to be consider'd as identified with it; and his appointment was apparently ask'd for by that powerful body. Bishop Simpson, of Philadelphia, came on and spoke for the selection. The President was much perplex'd. The reasons for appointing Col. Dubois were very strong, almost insuperable—yet the argument for Mr. Harlan, under the adroit position he had plac'd himself, was heavy. Those who press'd him adduc'd the magnitude of the Methodists as a body, their loyalty, more general and genuine than any other sect—that they represented the West, and had a right to be heard—that all or nearly all the other great denominations had their representatives in the heads of the government—that they as a body and the great sectarian power of the West, formally ask'd Mr. Harlan's appointment—that he was of them, having been a Methodist minister—that it would not do to offend them, but was highly necessary to propitiate them.

Mr. Lincoln thought deeply over the whole matter. He was in more than usual tribulation on the subject. Let it be enough to say that though Mr. Harlan finally receiv'd the Secretaryship, Col. Dubois came as near being appointed as a man could, and not be. The decision was finally made one night about 10 o'clock. Bishop Simpson and other clergymen and leading persons in Mr. Harlan's behalf, had been talking long and vehemently with the President. A member of Congress who was pressing Col. Dubois's claims, was in waiting. The President had told the Bishop that he would make a decision that evening, and that he thought it unnecessary to be press'd any more on the subject. That night he call'd in the M. C. above alluded to, and said to him: "Tell Uncle Jesse that I want to give him this appointment, and yet I cannot. I will do almost anything else in the world for him I am able. I have thought the matter all over, and under the circumstances think the Methodists too good and too great a body to be slighted. They have stood by the government, and help'd us their very best. I have had no better friends; and as the case stands, I have decided to appoint Mr. Harlan."

NOTE TO A FRIEND

[*Written on the fly-leaf of a copy of "Specimen Days," sent to Peter Doyle, at Washington, June, 1883.*]

PETE, do you remember—(of course you do—I do well)—those great long jovial walks we had at times for years, (1866–'72) out of Washington City—often moonlight nights—'way to "Good Hope";—or, Sundays, up and down the Potomac shores, one side or the other, sometimes ten miles at a stretch? Or when you work'd on the horse-cars, and I waited for you, coming home late together—or resting and chatting at the Market, corner 7th Street and the Avenue, and eating those nice musk or watermelons? Or during my tedious sickness and first paralysis ('73) how you used to come to my solitary garret-room and make up my bed, and enliven me, and chat for an hour or so—or perhaps go out and get the medicines Dr. Drinkard had order'd for me—before you went on duty? . . . . Give my love to dear Mrs. and Mr. Nash, and tell them I have not forgotten them, and never will.

W. W.

WRITTEN IMPROMPTU IN AN ALBUM

GERMANTOWN, PHILA., *Dec. 26, '83.*

IN memory of these merry Christmas days and nights—to my friends Mr. and Mrs. Williams, Churchie, May, Gurney, and little Aubrey. . . . . A heavy snow-storm blocking up everything, and keeping us in. But souls, hearts, thoughts, unloos'd. And so—one and all, little and big—hav'n't we had a good time?

W. W.

From the Philadelphia Press, Nov. 27, *1884,* (*Thanksgiving number.*)

THE PLACE GRATITUDE FILLS IN A FINE CHARACTER

Scene.—A large family supper party, a night or two ago, with voices and laughter of the young, mellow faces of the old, and a by-and-by pause in the general joviality. "Now, Mr. Whitman," spoke up one of the girls, "what have you to say about Thanksgiving? Won't you give us a sermon in advance, to sober us down?" The sage nodded smilingly, look'd a moment at the blaze of the great wood fire, ran his forefinger right and left through the heavy white moustache that might have otherwise impeded his voice, and began: "Thanksgiving goes probably far deeper than you folks suppose. I am not sure but it is the source of the highest poetry—as in parts of the Bible. Ruskin, indeed, makes the central source of all great art to be praise (gratitude) to the Almighty for life, and the universe with its objects and play of action.

"We Americans devote an official day to it every year; yet I sometimes fear the real article is almost dead or dying in our self-sufficient, independent Republic. Gratitude, anyhow, has never been made half enough of by the moralists; it is indispensable to a complete character, man's or woman's—the disposition to be appreciative, thankful. That is the main matter, the element, inclination—what geologists call the *trend*. Of my own life and writings I estimate the giving thanks part, with what it infers, as essentially the best item. I should say the quality of gratitude rounds the whole emotional nature; I should say love and faith would quite lack vitality without it. There are people—shall I call them even religious people, as things go?—who have no such trend to their disposition."

Last of the War Cases

Memorandized at the time, Washington, 1865–'66.

[Of reminiscences of the Secession War, after the rest is said, I have thought it remains to give a few special words—in some respects at the time the typical words of all, and most definite—of the samples of the kill'd and wounded in action, and of soldiers who linger'd afterward, from these wounds, or were laid up by obstinate disease or prostration. The general statistics have been printed already, but can bear to be briefly stated again. There were over 3,000,000 men (for all periods of enlistment, large and small) furnish'd to the Union army during the war, New York State furnishing over 500,000, which was the greatest number of any one State. The losses by disease, wounds, kill'd in action, accidents, &c., were altogether about 600,000, or approximating to that number. Over 4,000,000 cases were treated in the main and adjudicatory army hospitals. The number sounds strange, but it is true. More than two-thirds of the deaths were from prostration or disease. To-day there lie buried over 300,000 soldiers in the various National Army Cemeteries, more than half of them (and that is really the most significant and eloquent bequest of the War) mark'd "unknown." In full mortuary statistics of the war, the greatest deficiency arises from our not having the rolls, even as far as they were kept, of most of the Southern military prisons—a gap which probably both adds to, and helps conceal, the indescribable horrors of those places; it is, however, (restricting one vivid point only) certain that over 30,000 Union soldiers died, largely of actual starvation, in them. And now, leaving all figures and their "sum totals," I feel sure a few genuine memoranda of such things—

some cases jotted down '64, '65, and '66—made at the time and on the spot, with all the associations of those scenes and places brought back, will not only go directest to the right spot, but give a clearer and more actual sight of that period, than anything else. Before I give the last cases I begin with verbatim extracts from letters home to my mother in Brooklyn, the second year of the war.—W. W.]

Washington, Oct. 13, 1863.—There has been a new lot of wounded and sick arriving for the last three days. The first and second days, long strings of ambulances with the sick. Yesterday the worst, many with bad and bloody wounds, inevitably long neglected. I thought I was cooler and more used to it, but the sight of some cases brought tears into my eyes. I had the luck yesterday, however, to do lots of good. Had provided many nourishing articles for the men for another quarter, but, fortunately, had my stores where I could use them at once for these new-comers, as they arrived, faint, hungry, fagg'd out from their journey, with soil'd clothes, and all bloody. I distributed these articles, gave partly to the nurses I knew, or to those in charge. As many as possible I fed myself. Then I found a lot of oyster soup handy, and bought it all at once.

It is the most pitiful sight, this, when the men are first brought in, from some camp hospital broke up, or a part of the army moving. These who arrived yesterday are cavalry men. Our troops had fought like devils, but got the worst of it. They were Kilpatrick's cavalry; were in the rear, part of Meade's retreat, and the reb cavalry, knowing the ground and taking a favorable opportunity, dash'd in between, cut them off, and shell'd them terribly. But Kilpatrick turn'd and brought them out mostly. It was last Sunday. (One of the most terrible sights and tasks is of such receptions.)

Oct. 27, 1863.—If any of the soldiers I know (or their parents or folks) should call upon you—as they are often anxious to have my address in Brooklyn—you just use them as you know how, and if you happen to have pot-luck, and feel to ask them to take a bite, don't be afraid to do so. I have a friend, Thomas Neat, 2d N. Y. Cavalry, wounded in leg, now home in Jamaica, on furlough; he will probably call. Then possibly a Mr.

Haskell, or some of his folks, from western New York: he had a son died here, and I was with the boy a good deal. The old man and his wife have written me and ask'd me my Brooklyn address; he said he had children in New York, and was occasionally down there. (When I come home I will show you some of the letters I get from mothers, sisters, fathers, &c. They will make you cry.)

How the time passes away! To think it is over a year since I left home suddenly—and have mostly been down in front since. The year has vanish'd swiftly, and oh, what scenes I have witness'd during that time! And the war is not settled yet; and one does not see anything certain, or even promising, of a settlement. But I do not lose the solid feeling, in myself, that the Union triumph is assured, whether it be sooner or whether it be later, or whatever roundabout way we may be led there; and I find I don't change that conviction from any reverses we meet, nor delays, nor blunders. One realizes here in Washington the great labors, even the negative ones, of Lincoln; that it is a big thing to have just kept the United States from being thrown down and having its throat cut. I have not waver'd or had any doubt of the issue, since Gettysburg.

8th September, '63.—Here, now, is a specimen army hospital case: Lorenzo Strong, Co. A, 9th United States Cavalry, shot by a shell last Sunday; right leg amputated on the field. Sent up here Monday night, 14th. Seem'd to be doing pretty well till Wednesday noon, 16th, when he took a turn for the worse, and a strangely rapid and fatal termination ensued. Though I had much to do, I staid and saw all. It was a death-picture characteristic of these soldiers' hospitals—the perfect specimen of physique, one of the most magnificent I ever saw—the convulsive spasms and working of muscles, mouth, and throat. There are two good women nurses, one on each side. The doctor comes in and gives him a little chloroform. One of the nurses constantly fans him, for it is fearfully hot. He asks to be rais'd up, and they put him in a half-sitting posture. He call'd for "Mark" repeatedly, half-deliriously, all day. Life ebbs, runs now with the speed of a mill race; his splendid neck, as it lays all open, works still, slightly; his eyes turn back. A religious person coming in offers a prayer, in subdued tones, bent at the foot of the bed; and in the space of the aisle, a crowd, including two or three doctors, several students, and many soldiers, has silently gather'd. It is very still and warm, as the struggle goes on, and dwindles, a little more, and a little more—and then welcome oblivion, painlessness, death. A pause, the crowd drops away, a white bandage is bound around and under the jaw, the propping pillows are removed, the limpsy head falls down, the arms are softly placed by the side, all composed, all still,—and the broad white sheet is thrown over everything.

April 10, 1864.—Unusual agitation all around concentrated here. Exciting times in Congress. The Copperheads are getting furious, and want to recognize the Southern Confederacy. "This is a pretty time to talk of recognizing such——," said a Pennsylvania officer in hospital to me to-day, "after what has transpired the last three years." After first Fredericksburg I felt discouraged myself, and doubted whether our rulers could carry on the war. But that had pass'd away. The war *must* be carried on. I would willingly go in the ranks myself if I thought it would profit more than as at present, and I don't know sometimes but I shall, as it is. Then there is certainly a strange, deep, fervid feeling form'd or arous'd in the land, hard to describe or name; it is not a majority feeling, but it will make itself felt. M., you don't know what a nature a fellow gets, not only after being a soldier a while, but after living in the sights and influences of the camps, the wounded, &c.—a nature he never experienced before. The stars and stripes, the tune of Yankee Doodle, and similar things, produce such an effect on a fellow as never before. I have seen them bring tears on some men's cheeks, and others turn pale with emotion. I have a little flag (it belong'd to one of our cavalry regiments,) presented to me by one of the wounded; it was taken by the secesh in a fight, and rescued by our men in a bloody skirmish following. It cost three men's lives to get back that four-by-three flag—to tear it from the breast of a dead rebel—for *the name* of getting their little "rag" back again. The man that secured it was very badly wounded, and they let him keep it. I was with him a good deal; he wanted to give me some keepsake, he said,—he didn't expect to live,—so he gave me that flag. The best of it all is, dear M., there isn't a regiment, cavalry or infantry, that wouldn't do the like, on the like occasion.

April 12.—I will finish my letter this morning; it is a beautiful day. I was up in Congress very late last night. The House had a very excited night session about expelling the men that proposed recognizing the Southern Confederacy. You ought to hear (as I do) the soldiers talk; they are excited to madness. We shall probably have hot times here, not in the military fields alone. The body of the army is true and firm as the North Star.

May 6, '64.—M., the poor soldier with diarrhœa, is still living, but, oh, what a looking object! Death would be a relief to him—he cannot last many hours. Cunningham, the Ohio soldier, with leg amputated at thigh, has pick'd up beyond expectation; now looks indeed like getting well. (He died a few weeks afterward.) The hospitals are very full. I am very well indeed. Hot here to-day.

May 23, '64.—Sometimes I think that should it come when it *must*, to fall in battle, one's anguish over a son or brother kill'd might be temper'd with much to take the edge off. Lingering and extreme suffering from wounds or sickness seem to me far worse than death in battle. I can honestly say the latter has no terrors for me, as far as I myself am concern'd. Then I should say, too, about death in war, that our feelings and imaginations make a thousand times too much of the whole matter. Of the many I have seen die, or known of, the past year, I have not seen or known one who met death with terror. In most cases I should say it was a welcome relief and release.

Yesterday I spent a good part of the afternoon with a young soldier of seventeen, Charles Cutter, of Lawrence City, Massachusetts, 1st Massachusetts Heavy Artillery, Battery M. He was brought to one of the hospitals mortally wounded in abdomen. Well, I thought to myself, as I sat looking at him, it ought to be a relief to his folks if they could see how little he really suffer'd. He lay very placid, in a half lethargy, with his eyes closed. As it was extremely hot, and I sat a good while silently fanning him, and wiping the sweat, at length he open'd his eyes quite wide and clear, and look'd inquiringly around. I said, "What is it, my boy? Do you want anything?"

He answer'd quietly, with a good-natured smile, "Oh, nothing; I was only looking around to see who was with me." His mind was somewhat wandering, yet he lay in an evident peacefulness that sanity and health might have envied. I had to leave for other engagements. He died, I heard afterward, without any special agitation, in the course of the night.

Washington, May 26, '63.—M., I think something of commencing a series of lectures, readings, talks, &c., through the cities of the North, to supply myself with funds for hospital ministrations. I do not like to be so beholden to others; I need a pretty free supply of money, and the work grows upon me, and fascinates me. It is the most magnetic as well as terrible sight: the lots of poor wounded and helpless men depending so much, in one ward or another, upon my soothing or talking to them, or rousing them up a little, or perhaps petting, or feeding them their dinner or supper (here is a patient, for instance, wounded in both arms,) or giving some trifle for a novelty or change—anything, however trivial, to break the monotony of those hospital hours.

It is curious: when I am present at the most appalling scenes, deaths, operations, sickening wounds (perhaps full of maggots,) I keep cool and do not give out or budge, although my sympathies are very much excited; but often, hours afterward, perhaps when I am home, or out walking alone, I feel sick, and actually tremble, when I recall the case again before me.

Sunday afternoon, opening of 1865.—Pass'd this afternoon among a collection of unusually bad cases, wounded and sick Secession soldiers, left upon our hands. I spent the previous Sunday afternoon there also. At that time two were dying. Two others have died during the week. Several of them are partly deranged. I went around among them elaborately. Poor boys, they all needed to be cheer'd up. As I sat down by any particular one, the eyes of all the rest in the neighboring cots would fix upon me, and remain steadily riveted as long as I sat within their sight. Nobody seem'd to wish anything special to eat or drink. The main thing ask'd for was postage stamps, and paper for writing. I distributed all the stamps I had. Tobacco was wanted by some.

One call'd me over to him and ask'd me in a low tone what

denomination I belong'd to. He said he was a Catholic—wish'd to find some one of the same faith—wanted some good reading. I gave him something to read, and sat down by him a few minutes. Moved around with a word for each. They were hardly any of them personally attractive cases, and no visitors come here. Of course they were all destitute of money. I gave small sums to two or three, apparently the most needy. The men are from quite all the Southern States, Georgia, Mississippi, Louisiana, &c.

Wrote several letters. One for a young fellow named Thomas J. Byrd, with a bad wound and diarrhœa. Was from Russell county, Alabama; been out four years. Wrote to his mother; had neither heard from her nor written to her in nine months. Was taken prisoner last Christmas, in Tennessee; sent to Nashville, then to Camp Chase, Ohio, and kept there a long time; all the while not money enough to get paper and postage stamps. Was paroled, but on his way home the wound took gangrene; had diarrhœa also; had evidently been very low. Demeanor cool, and patient. A dark-skinn'd, quaint young fellow, with strong Southern idiom; no education.

Another letter for John W. Morgan, aged 18, from Shellot, Brunswick county, North Carolina; been out nine months; gunshot wound in right leg, above knee; also diarrhœa; wound getting along well; quite a gentle, affectionate boy; wish'd me to put in the letter for his mother to kiss his little brother and sister for him. [I put strong envelopes on these, and two or three other letters, directed them plainly and fully, and dropt them in the Washington post-office the next morning myself.]

The large ward I am in is used for Secession soldiers exclusively. One man, about forty years of age, emaciated with diarrhœa, I was attracted to, as he lay with his eyes turn'd up, looking like death. His weakness was so extreme that it took a minute or so, every time, for him to talk with anything like consecutive meaning; yet he was evidently a man of good intelligence and education. As I said anything, he would lie a moment perfectly still, then, with closed eyes, answer in a low, very slow voice, quite correct and sensible, but in a way and tone that wrung my heart. He had a mother, wife, and child living (or probably living) in his home in Mississippi. It was long, long since he had seen them. Had he caus'd a letter to be sent them since he got here in Washington? No answer. I repeated the question, very slowly and soothingly. He could not tell whether he had or not—things of late seem'd to him like a dream. After waiting a moment, I said: "Well, I am going to walk down the ward a moment, and when I come back you can tell me. If you have not written, I will sit down and write." A few minutes after I return'd; he said he remember'd now that some one had written for him two or three days before. The presence of this man impress'd me profoundly. The flesh was all sunken on face and arms; the eyes low in their sockets and glassy, and with purple rings around them. Two or three great tears silently flow'd out from the eyes, and roll'd down his temples (he was doubtless unused to be spoken to as I was speaking to him.) Sickness, imprisonment, exhaustion, &c., had conquer'd the body, yet the mind held mastery still, and call'd even wandering remembrance back.

There are some fifty Southern soldiers here; all sad, sad cases. There is a good deal of scurvy. I distributed some paper, envelopes, and postage stamps, and wrote addresses full and plain on many of the envelopes.

I return'd again Tuesday, August 1, and moved around in the same manner a couple of hours.

September 22, '65.—Afternoon and evening at Douglas Hospital to see a friend belonging to 2d New York Artillery (Hiram W. Frazee, Serg't,) down with an obstinate compound fracture of left leg receiv'd in one of the last battles near Petersburg. After sitting a while with him, went through several neighboring wards. In one of them found an old acquaintance transferr'd here lately, a rebel prisoner, in a dying condition. Poor fellow, the look was already on his face. He gazed long at me. I ask'd him if he knew me. After a moment he utter'd something, but inarticulately. I have seen him off and on for the last five months. He has suffer'd very much; a bad wound in left leg, severely fractured, several operations, cuttings, extractions of bone, splinters, &c. I remember he seem'd to me, as I used to talk with him, a fair specimen of the main strata of the Southerners, those without property or education, but still with the stamp which comes from freedom and equality. I liked him; Jonathan Wallace, of Hurd Co., Georgia, age 30 (wife, Susan F. Wallace, Houston, Hurd Co., Georgia.) [If any good soul of that county should see this, I hope he will send her this word.] Had a family; had not heard from them since taken prisoner, now six months. I had written for him, and done trifles for him, before he came here. He made no outward show, was mild in his talk and behavior, but I knew he worried much inwardly. But now all would be over very soon. I half sat upon the little stand near the head of the bed. Wallace was somewhat restless. I placed my hand lightly on his forehead and face, just sliding it over the surface. In a moment or so he fell into a calm, regular-breathing lethargy or sleep, and remain'd so while I sat there. It was dark, and the lights were lit. I hardly know why (death seem'd hovering near,) but I stay'd nearly an hour. A Sister of Charity, dress'd in black, with a broad white linen bandage around her head and under her chin, and a black crape over all and flowing down from her head in long wide pieces, came to him, and moved around the bed. She bow'd low and solemn to me. For some time she moved around there noiseless as a ghost, doing little things for the dying man.

December, '65.—The only remaining hospital is now "Harewood," out in the woods, northwest of the city. I have been visiting there regularly every Sunday, during these two months.

January 24, '66.—Went out to Harewood early to-day, and remain'd all day.

Sunday, February 4, 1866.—Harewood Hospital again. Walk'd out this afternoon (bright, dry, ground frozen hard) through the woods. Ward 6 is fill'd with blacks, some with wounds, some ill, two or three with limbs frozen. The boys made quite a picture sitting round the stove. Hardly any can read or write. I write for three or four, direct envelopes, give some tobacco, &c.

Joseph Winder, a likely boy, aged twenty-three, belongs to 10th Color'd Infantry (now in Texas;) is from Eastville, Virginia. Was a slave; belong'd to Lafayette Homeston. The master was quite willing he should leave. Join'd the army two years ago; has been in one or two battles. Was sent to hospital with rheumatism. Has since been employ'd as cook. His parents at Eastville; he gets letters from them, and has letters written to them by a friend. Many black boys left that part of Virginia and join'd the army; the 10th, in fact, was made up of Virginia blacks from thereabouts. As soon as discharged is going back to Eastville to his parents and home, and intends to stay there.

Thomas King, formerly 2d District Color'd Regiment, discharged soldier, Company E, lay in a dying condition; his disease was consumption. A Catholic priest was administering extreme unction to him. (I have seen this kind of sight several times in the hospitals; it is very impressive.)

Harewood, April 29, 1866. *Sunday afternoon.*—Poor Joseph Swiers, Company H, 155th Pennsylvania, a mere lad (only eighteen years of age;) his folks living in Reedsburgh, Pennsylvania. I have known him now for nearly a year, transferr'd from hospital to hospital. He was badly wounded in the thigh at Hatcher's Run, February 6, '65.

James E. Ragan, Atlanta, Georgia; 2d United States Infantry. Union folks. Brother impress'd, deserted, died; now no folks, left alone in the world, is in a singularly nervous state; came in hospital with intermittent fever.

Walk slowly around the ward, observing, and to see if I can do anything. Two or three are lying very low with consumption, cannot recover; some with old wounds; one with both feet frozen off, so that on one only the heel remains. The supper is being given out; the liquid call'd tea, a thick slice of bread, and some stew'd apples.

That was about the last I saw of the regular army hospitals.

HERE is a portrait of E. H. from life, by Henry Inman, in New York, about 1827 or '28. The painting was finely copper-plated in 1830, and the present is a fac simile. Looks as I saw him in the following narrative.

The time was signalized by the *separation* of the Society of Friends, so greatly talked of—and continuing yet—but so little really explain'd. (All I give of this separation is in a Note following.)

BORN . . . . MARCH 19, 1748.
DIED . . . . FEBRUARY 20, 1830.

NOTES (*such as they are*) *founded on*

ELIAS HICKS

Prefatory Note.—As myself a little boy hearing so much of E. H., at that time, long ago, in Suffolk and Queens and Kings Counties—and more than once personally seeing the old man—and my dear, dear father and mother faithful listeners to him at the meetings—I remember how I dream'd to write perhaps a piece about E. H. and his look and discourses, however long afterward—for my parents' sake—and the dear Friends too! And the following is what has at last but all come out of it—the feeling and intention never forgotten yet!

There is a sort of nature of persons I have compared to little rills of water, fresh, from perennial springs—(and the comparison is indeed an appropriate one)—persons not so very plenty, yet some few certainly of them running over the surface and area of humanity, all times, all lands. It is a specimen of this class, I would now present. I would sum up in E. H., and make his case stand for the class, the sort, in all ages, all lands, sparse, not numerous, yet enough to irrigate the soil—enough to prove the inherent moral stock and irrepressible devotional aspirations growing indigenously of themselves, always advancing, and never utterly gone under or lost.

Always E. H. gives the service of pointing to the fountain of all naked theology, all religion, all worship, all the truth to which you are possibly eligible—namely in *yourself* and your inherent relations. Others talk of Bibles, saints, churches, exhortations, vicarious atonements—the canons outside of yourself and apart from man—E. H. to the religion inside of man's very own nature. This he incessantly labors to kindle, nourish, educate, bring forward and strengthen. He is the most *democratic* of the religionists—the prophets.

I have no doubt that both the curious fate and death of his four sons, and the facts (and dwelling on them) of George Fox's strange early life, and permanent "conversion," had much to do with the peculiar and sombre ministry and style of E. H. from the first, and confirmed him all through. One must not be dominated by the man's almost absurd saturation in cut and dried biblical phraseology, and in ways, talk, and standard, regardful mainly of the one need he dwelt on, above all the rest. This main need he drove home to the soul; the canting and sermonizing soon exhale away to any auditor that realizes what E. H. is for and after. The present paper, (a broken memorandum of his formation, his earlier life,) is the cross-notch that rude wanderers make in the woods, to remind them afterward of some matter of first-rate importance and full investigation. (Remember too, that E. H. was *a thorough believer in the Hebrew Scriptures,* in his way.)

The following are really but disjointed fragments recall'd to serve and eke out here the lank printed pages of what I commenc'd unwittingly two months ago. Now, as I am well in for it, comes an old attack, the sixth or seventh recurrence, of my war-paralysis, dulling me from putting the notes in shape, and threatening any further action, head or body.

—W. W., Camden, N. J., July, 1888.

TO begin with, my theme is comparatively featureless. The great historian has pass'd by the life of Elias Hicks quite without glance or touch. Yet a man might commence and overhaul it as furnishing one of the amplest historic and biography's backgrounds. While the foremost actors and events from 1750 to 1830 both in Europe and America were crowding each other on the world's stage—While so many kings, queens, soldiers, philosophs, musicians, voyagers, littérateurs, enter one side, cross the boards, and disappear—amid loudest reverberating names—Frederick the Great, Swedenborg, Junius, Voltaire, Rousseau, Linneus, Herschel—curiously contemporary with the long life of Goethe—through the occupancy of the British throne by George the Third—amid stupendous visible political and social revolutions, and far more stupendous invisible moral ones—while the many quarto volumes of the Encyclopædia Française are being published at fits and intervals, by Diderot, in Paris—while Haydn and Beethoven and Mozart and Weber are working out their harmonic compositions—while Mrs. Siddons and Talma and Kean are acting—while Mungo Park explores Africa, and Capt. Cook circumnavigates the globe—through all the fortunes of the

American Revolution, the beginning, continuation and end, the battle of Brooklyn, the surrender at Saratoga, the final peace of '83—through the lurid tempest of the French Revolution, the execution of the king and queen, and the Reign of Terror—through the whole of the meteor-career of Napoleon—through all Washington's, Adams's, Jefferson's, Madison's, and Monroe's Presidentiads—amid so many flashing lists of names, (indeed there seems hardly, in any department, any end to them, Old World or New,) Franklin, Sir Joshua Reynolds, Mirabeau, Fox, Nelson, Paul Jones, Kant, Fichte, and Hegel, Fulton, Walter Scott, Byron, Mesmer, Champollion—Amid pictures that dart upon me even as I speak, and glow and mix and coruscate and fade like aurora boreales—Louis the 16th threaten'd by the mob, the trial of Warren Hastings, the death-bed of Robert Burns, Wellington at Waterloo, Decatur capturing the Macedonian, or the sea-fight between the Chesapeake and the Shannon—During all these whiles, I say, and though on a far different grade, running parallel and contemporary with all—a curious quiet yet busy life centred in a little country village on Long Island, and within sound on still nights of the mystic surf-beat of the sea. About this life, this Personality—neither soldier, nor scientist, nor littérateur—I propose to occupy a few minutes in fragmentary talk, to give some few melanges, disconnected impressions, statistics, resultant groups, pictures, thoughts of him, or radiating from him.

Elias Hicks was born March 19, 1748, in Hempstead township, Queens county, Long Island, New York State, near a village bearing the old Scripture name of Jericho, (a mile or so north and east of the present Hicksville, on the L. I. Railroad.) His father and mother were Friends, of that class working with their own hands, and mark'd by neither riches nor actual poverty. Elias as a child and youth had small education from letters, but largely learn'd from Nature's schooling. He grew up even in his ladhood a thorough gunner and fisherman. The farm of his parents lay on the south or sea-shore side of Long Island, (they had early removed from Jericho,) one of the best regions in the world for wild fowl and for fishing. Elias became a good horseman, too, and knew the animal well, riding races; also a singer, fond of "vain songs," as he afterwards calls them; a dancer, too, at the country balls. When a boy of 13 he had gone to live with an elder brother; and when about 17 he changed again and went as apprentice to the carpenter's trade. The time of all this was before the Revolutionary War, and the locality 30 to 40 miles from New York city. My great-grandfather, Whitman, was often with Elias at these periods, and at merry-makings and sleigh-rides in winter over "the plains."

How well I remember the region—the flat plains of the middle of Long Island, as then, with their prairie-like vistas and grassy patches in every direction, and the 'kill-calf' and herds of cattle and sheep. Then the South Bay and shores and the salt meadows, and the sedgy smell, and numberless little bayous and hummock-islands in the waters, the habitat of every sort of fish and aquatic fowl of North America. And the bay men—a strong, wild, peculiar race—now extinct, or rather entirely changed. And the beach outside the sandy bars, sometimes many miles at a stretch, with their old history of wrecks and storms—the weird, white-gray beach—not without its tales of pathos—tales, too, of grandest heroes and heroisms.

In such scenes and elements and influences—in the midst of Nature and along the shores of the sea—Elias Hicks was fashion'd through boyhood and early manhood, to maturity. But a moral and mental and emotional change was imminent. Along at this time he says:

> My apprenticeship being now expir'd, I gradually withdrew from the company of my former associates, became more acquainted with Friends, and was more frequent in my attendance of meetings; and although this was in some degree profitable to me, yet I made but slow progress in my religious improvement. The occupation of part of my time in fishing and fowling had frequently tended to preserve me from falling into hurtful associations; but through the rising intimations and reproofs of divine grace in my heart, I now began to feel that the manner in which I sometimes amus'd myself with my gun was not without sin; for although I mostly preferr'd going alone, and while waiting in stillness for the coming of the fowl, my mind was at times

so taken up in divine meditations, that the opportunities were seasons of instruction and comfort to me; yet, on other occasions, when accompanied by some of my acquaintances, and when no fowls appear'd which would be useful to us after being obtain'd, we sometimes, from wantonness or for mere diversion, would destroy the small birds which could be of no service to us. This cruel procedure affects my heart while penning these lines.

In his 23d year Elias was married, by the Friends' ceremony, to Jemima Seaman. His wife was an only child; the parents were well off for common people, and at their request the son-in-law mov'd home with them and carried on the farm—which at their decease became his own, and he liv'd there all his remaining life. Of this matrimonial part of his career, (it continued, and with unusual happiness, for 58 years,) he says, giving the account of his marriage:

On this important occasion, we felt the clear and consoling evidence of divine truth, and it remain'd with us as a seal upon our spirits, strengthening us mutually to bear, with becoming fortitude, the vicissitudes and trials which fell to our lot, and of which we had a large share in passing through this probationary state. My wife, although not of a very strong constitution, liv'd to be the mother of eleven children, four sons and seven daughters. Our second daughter, a very lovely, promising child, died when young, with the small-pox, and the youngest was not living at its birth. The rest all arriv'd to years of discretion, and afforded us considerable comfort, as they prov'd to be in a good degree dutiful children. All our sons, however, were of weak constitutions, and were not able to take care of themselves, being so enfeebl'd as not to be able to walk after the ninth or tenth year of their age. The two eldest died in the fifteenth year of their age, the third in his seventeenth year, and the youngest was nearly nineteen when he died. But, although thus helpless, the innocency of their lives, and the resign'd cheerfulness of their dispositions to their allotments, made the labor and toil of taking care of them agreeable and pleasant; and I trust we were preserv'd from murmuring or repining, believing the dispensation to be in wisdom, and according to the will and gracious disposing of an all-wise providence, for purposes best known to himself. And when I have observ'd the great anxiety and affliction which many parents have with undutiful children who are favor'd with health, especially their sons, I could perceive very few whose troubles and exercises, on that account, did not far exceed ours. The weakness and bodily infirmity of our sons tended to keep them much out of the way of the troubles and temptations of the world; and we believ'd that in their death they were happy, and admitted into the realms of peace and joy: a reflection, the most comfortable and joyous that parents can have in regard to their tender offspring.

Of a serious and reflective turn, by nature, and from his reading and surroundings, Elias had more than once markedly devotional inward intimations. These feelings increas'd in frequency and strength, until soon the following:

About the twenty-sixth year of my age I was again brought, by the operative influence of divine grace, under deep concern of mind; and was led, through adorable mercy, to see, that although I had ceas'd from many sins and vanities of my youth, yet there were many remaining that I was still guilty of, which were not yet aton'd for, and for which I now felt the judgments of God to rest upon me. This caus'd me to cry earnestly to the Most High for pardon and redemption, and he graciously condescended to hear my cry, and to open a way before me, wherein I must walk, in order to experience reconciliation with him; and as I abode in watchfulness and deep humiliation before him, light broke forth out of obscurity, and my darkness became as the noon-day. I began to have openings leading to the ministry, which brought me under close exercise and deep travail of spirit; for although I had for some time spoken on subjects of business in monthly and preparative meetings, yet the prospect of opening my mouth in public meetings was a close trial; but I endeavor'd to keep my mind quiet and resign'd to the heavenly call, if it should be made clear to me to be my duty. Nevertheless, as I was, soon after, sitting in a meeting, in much weightiness of spirit, a secret, though clear, intimation accompanied me to speak a few words, which were then given to me to utter, yet fear so prevail'd, that I did not yield to the intimation. For this omission, I felt close rebuke, and judgment seem'd, for some time, to cover my mind; but as I humbl'd myself under the Lord's mighty hand, he again lifted up the light of his countenance upon me, and enabl'd me to renew covenant with him, that if he would pass by this my offence, I would, in future, be faithful, if he should again require such a service of me.

The Revolutionary War following, tried the sect of Friends more than any. The difficulty was to steer between their convictions as patriots, and their pledges of non-warring peace. Here is the way they solv'd the problem:

A war, with all its cruel and destructive effects, having raged for several years between the British Colonies in North America and the mother country, Friends, as well as others, were expos'd to many severe trials and sufferings; yet, in the colony of New York, Friends, who stood faithful to their principles, and did not meddle in the controversy, had, after a short period at first, considerable favor allow'd them. The yearly meeting was held steadily, during the war, on Long Island, where the king's party had the rule; yet Friends from the Main, where the American army ruled, had free passage through both armies to attend it, and any other meetings they were desirous of attending, except in a few instances. This was a favor which the parties would not grant to their best friends, who were of a warlike disposition; which shows what great advantages would redound to mankind, were they all of this pacific spirit. I pass'd myself through the lines of both armies six times during the war, without molestation, both parties generally receiving me with openness and civility; and although I had to pass over a tract of country, between the two armies, sometimes more than thirty miles in extent, and which was much frequented by robbers, a set, in general, of cruel, unprincipled banditti, issuing out from both parties, yet, excepting once, I met with no interruption even from them. But although Friends in general experienc'd many favors and deliverances, yet those scenes of war and confusion occasion'd many trials and provings in various ways to the faithful. One circumstance I am willing to mention, as it caus'd me considerable exercise and concern. There was a large cellar under the new meeting-house belonging to Friends in New York, which was generally let as a store. When the king's troops enter'd the city, they took possession of it for the purpose of depositing their warlike stores; and ascertaining what Friends had the care of letting it, their commissary came forward and offer'd to pay the rent; and those Friends, for want of due consideration, accepted it. This caus'd great uneasiness to the concern'd part of the Society, who apprehended it not consistent with our peaceable principles to receive payment for the depositing of military stores in our houses. The subject was brought before the yearly meeting in 1779, and engag'd its careful attention; but those Friends, who had been active in the reception of the money, and some few others, were not willing to acknowledge their proceedings to be inconsistent, nor to return the money to those from whom it was receiv'd; and in order to justify themselves therein, they referr'd to the conduct of Friends in Philadelphia in similar cases. Matters thus appearing very difficult and embarrassing, it was unitedly concluded to refer the final determination thereof to the yearly meeting of Pennsylvania; and several Friends were appointed to attend that meeting in relation thereto, among whom I was one of the number. We accordingly set out on the 9th day of the 9th month, 1779, and I was accompanied from home by my beloved friend John Willis, who was likewise on the appointment. We took a solemn leave of our families, they feeling much anxiety at parting with us, on account of the dangers we were expos'd to, having to pass not only the lines of the two armies, but the deserted and almost uninhabited country that lay between them, in many places the grass being grown up in the streets, and many houses desolate and empty. Believing it, however, my duty to proceed in the service, my mind was so settled and trust-fix'd in the divine arm of power, that faith seem'd to banish all fear, and cheerfulness and quiet resignation were, I believe, my constant companions during the journey. We got permission, with but little difficulty, to pass the outguards of the king's army at Kingsbridge, and proceeded to Westchester. We afterwards attended meetings at Harrison's Purchase, and Oblong, having the concurrence of our monthly meeting to take some meetings in our way, a concern leading thereto having for some time previously attended my mind. We pass'd from thence to Nine Partners, and attended their monthly meeting, and then turn'd our faces towards Philadelphia, being join'd by several others of the Committee. We attended New Marlborough, Hardwick, and Kingswood meetings on our journey, and arriv'd at Philadelphia on the 7th day of the week, and 25th of 9th month, on which day we attended the yearly meeting of Ministers and Elders, which began at the eleventh hour. I also attended all the sittings of the yearly meeting until the 4th day of the next week, and was then so indispos'd with a fever, which had been increasing on me for several days, that I was not able to attend after that time. I was therefore not present when the subject was discuss'd, which came from our yearly meeting; but I was inform'd by my companion, that it was a very solemn opportunity, and the matter was resulted in advising that the money should be return'd into the office from whence it was receiv'd, accompanied with our reasons for so doing: and this was accordingly done by the direction of our yearly meeting the next year.

Then, season after season, when peace and independence reign'd, year following year, this remains to be (1791) a specimen of his personal labors:

I was from home on this journey four months and eleven days; rode about one thousand five hundred miles, and attended forty-nine particular meetings among Friends, three quarterly meetings, six monthly meetings, and forty meetings among other people.

And again another experience:

In the forepart of this meeting, my mind was reduc'd into such a state of great weakness and depression, that my faith was almost ready to fail, which produc'd great searchings of heart, so that I was led to call in question all that I had ever before experienc'd. In this state of doubting, I was ready to wish myself at home, from an apprehension that I should only expose myself to reproach, and wound the cause I was embark'd in; for the heavens seem'd like brass, and the earth as iron; such coldness and hardness, I thought, could scarcely have ever been experienc'd before by any creature, so great was the depth of my baptism at this time; nevertheless, as I endeavor'd to quiet my mind, in this conflicting dispensation, and be resign'd to my allotment, however distressing, towards the latter part of the meeting a ray of light broke through the surrounding darkness, in which the Shepherd of Israel was pleas'd to arise, and by the light of his glorious countenance, to scatter those clouds of opposition. Then ability was receiv'd, and utterance given, to speak of his marvellous works in the redemption of souls, and to open the way of life and salvation, and the mysteries of his glorious kingdom, which are hid from the wise and prudent of this world, and reveal'd only unto those who are reduc'd into the state of little children and babes in Christ.

And concluding another jaunt in 1794:

I was from home in this journey about five months, and travell'd by land and water about two thousand two hundred and eighty-three miles; having visited all the meetings of Friends in the New England states, and many meetings amongst those of other professions; and also visited many meetings, among Friends and others, in the upper part of our own yearly meeting; and found real peace in my labors.

Another 'tramp' in 1798:

I was absent from home in this journey about five months and two weeks, and rode about sixteen hundred miles, and attended about one hundred and forty-three meetings.

Here are some memoranda of 1813, near home:

First day. Our meeting this day pass'd in silent labor. The cloud rested on the tabernacle; and, although it was a day of much rain outwardly, yet very little of the dew of Hermon appear'd to distil among us. Nevertheless, a comfortable calm was witness'd towards the close, which we must render to the account of unmerited mercy and love.

Second day. Most of this day was occupied in a visit to a sick friend, who appear'd comforted therewith. Spent part of the evening in reading part of Paul's Epistle to the Romans.

Third day. I was busied most of this day in my common vocations. Spent the evening principally in reading Paul. Found considerable satisfaction in his first epistle to the Corinthians; in which he shows the danger of some in setting too high a value on those who were instrumental in bringing them to the knowledge of the truth, without looking through and beyond the instrument, to the great first cause and Author of every blessing, to whom all the praise and honor are due.

Fifth day, 1st of 4th month. At our meeting to-day found it, as usual, a very close steady exercise to keep the mind center'd where it ought to be. What a multitude of intruding thoughts imperceptibly, as it were, steal into the mind, and turn it from its proper object, whenever it relaxes its vigilance in watching against them. Felt a little strength, just at the close, to remind Friends of the necessity of a steady perseverance, by a recapitulation of the parable of the unjust judge, showing how men ought always to pray, and not to faint.

Sixth day. Nothing material occurr'd, but a fear lest the cares of the world should engross too much of my time.

Seventh day. Had an agreeable visit from two ancient friends, whom I have long lov'd. The rest of the day I employ'd in manual labor, mostly in gardening.

But we find if we attend to records and details, we shall lay out an endless task. We can briefly say, summarily, that his whole life was a long religious missionary life of method, practicality, sincerity, earnestness, and pure piety—as near to his time here, as one in Judea, far back—or in any life, any age. The reader who feels interested must get—with all its dryness and mere dates, absence of emotionality or literary quality, and whatever abstract attraction (with even a suspicion of cant, sniffling,) the "Journal of the Life and Religious Labours of Elias Hicks, written by himself," at some Quaker book-store. (It is from this headquarters I have extracted the preceding quotations.) During E. H.'s matured life, continued from fifty to sixty years—while working steadily, earning his living and paying his way without intermission—he makes, as previously memorandised, several hundred preaching visits, not only through Long Island, but some of them away into the Middle or Southern States, or north into Canada, or the then far West—extending to thousands of miles, or filling several weeks and sometimes months. These religious journeys—scrupulously accepting in payment only his transportation from place to place, with his own food and shelter, and never receiving a dollar of money for "salary" or preaching—Elias, through good bodily health and strength, continues till quite the age of eighty. It was thus at one of his latest jaunts in Brooklyn city I saw and heard him. This sight and hearing shall now be described.

Elias Hicks was at this period in the latter part (November or December) of 1829. It was the last tour of the many missions of the old man's life. He was in the 81st year of his age, and a few months before he had lost by death a beloved wife with whom he had lived in unalloyed affection and esteem for 58 years. (But a few months after this meeting Elias was paralyzed and died.) Though it is sixty years ago since—and I a little boy at the time in Brooklyn, New York—I can remember my father coming home toward sunset from his day's work as carpenter, and saying briefly, as he throws down his armful of kindling-blocks with a bounce on the kitchen floor, "Come, mother, Elias preaches to-night." Then my mother, hastening the supper and the table-cleaning afterward, gets a neighboring young woman, a friend of the family, to step in and keep house for an hour or so—puts the two little ones to bed—and as I had been behaving well that day, as a special reward I was allow'd to go also.

We start for the meeting. Though, as I said, the stretch of more than half a century has pass'd over me since then, with its war and peace, and all its joys and sins and deaths (and what a half century! how it comes up sometimes for an instant, like the lightning flash in a storm at night!) I can recall that meeting yet. It is a strange place for religious devotions. Elias preaches anywhere—no respect to buildings—private or public houses, school-rooms, barns, even theatres—anything that will accommodate. This time it is in a handsome ball-room, on Brooklyn Heights, overlooking New York, and in full sight of that great city, and its North and East Rivers fill'd with ships—is (to specify more particularly) the second story of "Morrison's Hotel," used for the most genteel concerts, balls, and assemblies—a large, cheerful, gay-color'd room, with glass chandeliers bearing myriads of sparkling pendants, plenty of settees and chairs, and a sort of velvet divan running all round the side-walls. Before long the divan and all the settees and chairs are fill'd; many fashionables out of curiosity; all the principal dignitaries of the town, Gen. Jeremiah Johnson, Judge Furman, George Hall, Mr. Willoughby, Mr. Pierrepont, N. B. Morse, Cyrus P. Smith, and F. C. Tucker. Many young folks too; some richly dress'd women; I remember I noticed with one party of ladies a group of uniform'd officers, either from the U. S. Navy Yard, or some ship in the stream, or some adjacent fort. On a slightly elevated platform at the head of the room, facing the audience, sit a dozen or more Friends, most of them elderly, grim, and with their broad-brimm'd hats on their heads. Three or four women, too, in their characteristic Quaker costumes and bonnets. All still as the grave.

At length after a pause and stillness becoming almost painful, Elias rises and stands for a moment or two without a word. A tall, straight figure, neither stout nor very thin, dress'd in drab cloth, clean-shaved face, forehead of great expanse, and large and clear black eyes,* long or middling-long white hair; he was at this time between 80 and 81 years of age, his head still wearing the broad-brim. A moment looking around the audience with those piercing eyes, amid the perfect stillness. (I can almost see him and the whole scene now.) Then the words come from his lips, very emphatically and slowly pronounc'd, in a resonant, grave, melodious voice, *What is the chief end of man?* I was told in my early youth, *it was to glorify God, and seek and enjoy him forever.*

*In Walter Scott's reminiscences he speaks of Burns as having the most eloquent, glowing, flashing, illuminated dark-orbed eyes he ever beheld in a human face; and I think Elias Hicks's must have been like them.

I cannot follow the discourse. It presently becomes very fervid, and in the midst of its fervor he takes the broad-brim hat from his head, and almost dashing it down with violence on the seat behind, continues with uninterrupted earnestness. But, I say, I cannot repeat, hardly suggest his sermon. Though the differences and disputes of the formal division of the Society of Friends were even then under way, he did not allude to them at all. A pleading, tender, nearly agonizing conviction, and magnetic stream of natural eloquence, before which all minds and natures, all emotions, high or low, gentle or simple, yielded entirely without exception, was its cause, method, and effect. Many, very many were in tears. Years afterward in Boston, I heard Father Taylor, the sailor's preacher, and found in his passionate unstudied oratory the resemblance to Elias Hicks's—not argumentative or intellectual, but so penetrating—so different from anything in the books—(different as the fresh air of a May morning or sea-shore breeze from the atmosphere of a perfumer's shop.) While he goes on he falls into the nasality and sing-song tone sometimes heard in such meetings; but in a moment or two more, as if recollecting himself, he breaks off, stops, and resumes in a natural tone. This occurs three or four times during the talk of the evening, till all concludes.

Now and then, at the many scores and hundreds—even thousands—of his discourses—as at this one—he was very mystical and radical,* and had much to say of "the light within." Very likely this same *inner light,* (so dwelt upon by

*The true Christian religion, (such was the teaching of Elias Hicks,) consists neither in rites or Bibles or sermons or Sundays—but in noiseless secret ecstasy and unremitted aspiration, in purity, in a good practical life, in charity to the poor and toleration to all. He said, "A man may keep the Sabbath, may belong to a church and attend all the observances, have regular family prayer, keep a well-bound copy of the Hebrew Scriptures in a conspicuous place in his house, and yet not be a truly religious person at all." E. believ'd little in a church as organiz'd—even his own—with houses, ministers, or with salaries, creeds, Sundays, saints, Bibles, holy festivals, &c. But he believ'd always in the universal church, in the soul of man, invisibly rapt, ever-waiting, ever-responding to universal truths.—He was fond of pithy proverbs. He said, "It matters not where you live, but how you live." He said once to my father. "They talk of the devil—I tell thee, Walter, there is no worse devil than man."

newer men, as by Fox and Barclay at the beginning, and all Friends and deep thinkers since and now,) is perhaps only another name for the religious conscience. In my opinion they have all diagnos'd, like superior doctors, the real inmost disease of our times, probably any times. Amid the huge inflammation call'd society, and that other inflammation call'd politics, what is there to-day of moral power and ethic sanity as antiseptic to them and all? Though I think the essential elements of the moral nature exist latent in the good average people of the United States of to-day, and sometimes break out strongly, it is certain that any mark'd or dominating National Morality (if I may use the phrase) has not only not yet been develop'd, but that—at any rate when the point of view is turn'd on business, politics, competition, practical life, and in character and manners in our New World—there seems to be a hideous depletion, almost absence, of such moral nature. Elias taught throughout, as George Fox began it, or rather reiterated and verified it, the Platonic doctrine that the ideals of character, of justice, of religious action, whenever the highest is at stake, are to be conform'd to no outside doctrine of creeds, Bibles, legislative enactments, conventionalities, or even decorums, but are to follow the inward Deity-planted law of the emotional soul. In this only the true Quaker, or Friend, has faith; and it is from rigidly, perhaps strainingly carrying it out, that both the Old and New England records of Quakerdom show some unseemly and insane acts.

In one of the lives of Ralph Waldo Emerson is a list of lessons or instructions, ("seal'd orders" the biographer calls them,) prepar'd by the sage himself for his own guidance. Here is one:

> Go forth with thy message among thy fellow-creatures; teach them that they must trust themselves as guided by that inner light which dwells with the pure in heart, to whom it was promis'd of old that they shall see God.

How thoroughly it fits the life and theory of Elias Hicks. Then in Omar Khayyam:

> I sent my soul through the Invisible,
> Some letter of that after-life to spell,

And by-and-by my soul return'd to me,
And answer'd, "I myself am Heaven and Hell."

Indeed, of this important element of the theory and practice of Quakerism, the difficult-to-describe "Light within" or "Inward Law, by which all must be either justified or condemn'd," I will not undertake where so many have fail'd—the task of making the statement of it for the average comprehension. We will give, partly for the matter and partly as specimen of his speaking and writing style, what Elias Hicks himself says in allusion to it—one or two of very many passages. Most of his discourses, like those of Epictetus and the ancient peripatetics, have left no record remaining—they were extempore, and those were not the times of reporters. Of one, however, deliver'd in Chester, Pa., toward the latter part of his career, there is a careful transcript; and from it (even if presenting you a sheaf of hidden wheat that may need to be pick'd and thrash'd out several times before you get the grain,) we give the following extract:

"I don't want to express a great many words; but I want you to be call'd home to the substance. For the Scriptures, and all the books in the world, can do no more; Jesus could do no more than to recommend to this Comforter, which was the light in him. 'God is light, and in him is no darkness at all; and if we walk in the light, as he is in the light, we have fellowship one with another.' Because the light is one in all, and therefore it binds us together in the bonds of love; for it is not only light, but love—that love which casts out all fear. So that they who dwell in God dwell in love, and they are constrain'd to walk in it; and if they 'walk in it, they have fellowship one with another, and the blood of Jesus Christ his Son cleanseth us from all sin.'

"But what blood, my friends? Did Jesus Christ, the Saviour, ever have any material blood? Not a drop of it, my friends—not a drop of it. That blood which cleanseth from the life of all sin, was the life of the soul of Jesus. The soul of man has no material blood; but as the outward material blood, created from the dust of the earth, is the life of these bodies of flesh, so with respect to the soul, the immortal and invisible spirit, its blood is that life which God breath'd into it.

"As we read, in the beginning, that 'God form'd man of the dust of the ground, and breath'd into him the breath of life, and man became a living soul.' He breath'd into that soul, and it became alive to God."

Then, from one of his many letters, for he seems to have delighted in correspondence:

"Some may query, What is the cross of Christ? To these I answer, It is the perfect law of God, written on the tablet of the heart, and in the heart of every rational creature, in such indelible characters that all the power of mortals cannot erase nor obliterate it. Neither is there any power or means given or dispens'd to the children of men, but this inward law and light, by which the true and saving knowledge of God can be obtain'd. And by this inward law and light, all will be either justified or condemn'd, and all made to know God for themselves, and be left without excuse, agreeably to the prophecy of Jeremiah, and the corroborating testimony of Jesus in his last counsel and command to his disciples, not to depart from Jerusalem till they should receive power from on high; assuring them that they should receive power, when they had receiv'd the pouring forth of the spirit upon them, which would qualify them to bear witness of him in Judea, Jerusalem, Samaria, and to the uttermost parts of the earth; which was verified in a marvellous manner on the day of Pentecost, when thousands were converted to the Christian faith in one day.

"By which it is evident that nothing but this inward light and law, as it is heeded and obey'd, ever did, or ever can, make a true and real Christian and child of God. And until the professors of Christianity agree to lay aside all their non-essentials in religion, and rally to this unchangeable foundation and standard of truth, wars and fightings, confusion and error, will prevail, and the angelic song cannot be heard in our land—that of 'glory to God in the highest, and on earth peace and good will to men.'

"But when all nations are made willing to make this inward law and light the rule and standard of all their faith and works, then we shall be brought to know and believe alike, that there is but one Lord, one faith, and but one baptism; one God and Father, that is above all, through all, and in all.

"And then will all those glorious and consoling prophecies recorded in the scriptures of truth be fulfill'd—'He,' the Lord, 'shall judge among the nations, and shall rebuke many people; and they shall beat their swords into ploughshares, and their spears into pruning-hooks; nation shall not lift up the sword against nation, neither shall they learn war any more. The wolf also shall dwell with the lamb; and the cow and the bear shall feed; and the lion shall eat straw like the ox; and the sucking child shall play on the hole of the asp, and the wean'd child put his hand on the cockatrice's den. They shall not hurt nor destroy in all my holy mountain; for the earth,' that is our earthly tabernacle, 'shall be full of the knowledge of the Lord, as the waters cover the sea.' "

The exposition in the last sentence, that the terms of the texts are not to be taken in their literal meaning, but in their spiritual one, and allude to a certain wondrous exaltation of the body, through religious influences, is significant, and is but one of a great number of instances of much that is obscure, to "the world's people," in the preachings of this remarkable man.

Then a word about his physical oratory, connected with the preceding. If there is, as doubtless there is, an unnameable something behind oratory, a fund within or atmosphere without, deeper than art, deeper even than proof, that unnameable constitutional something Elias Hicks emanated from his very heart to the hearts of his audience, or carried with him, or probed into, and shook and arous'd in them—a sympathetic germ, probably rapport, lurking in every human eligiblity, which no book, no rule, no statement has given or can give inherent knowledge, intuition—not even the best speech, or best put forth, but launch'd out only by powerful human magnetism:

Unheard by sharpest ear—unform'd in clearest eye, or cunningest mind,
Nor lore, nor fame, nor happiness, nor wealth,

And yet the pulse of every heart and life throughout the
  world, incessantly,
Which you and I, and all, pursuing ever, ever miss;
Open, but still a secret—the real of the real—an illusion;
Costless, vouchsafed to each, yet never man the owner;
Which poets vainly seek to put in rhyme—historians in
  prose;
Which sculptor never chisel'd yet, nor painter painted;
Which vocalist never sung, nor orator nor actor ever utter'd.

That remorse, too, for a mere worldly life—that aspiration towards the ideal, which, however overlaid, lies folded latent, hidden, in perhaps every character. More definitely, as near as I remember (aided by my dear mother long afterward,) Elias Hicks's discourse there in the Brooklyn ball-room, was one of his old never-remitted appeals to that moral mystical portion of human nature, *the inner light.* But it is mainly for the scene itself, and Elias's *personnel,* that I recall the incident.

Soon afterward the old man died:

> On first day morning, the 14th of 2d month (February, 1830,) he was engaged in his room, writing to a friend, until a little after ten o'clock, when he return'd to that occupied by the family, apparently just attack'd by a paralytic affection, which nearly deprived him of the use of his right side, and of the power of speech. Being assisted to a chair near the fire, he manifested by signs, that the letter which he had just finish'd, and which had been dropp'd by the way, should be taken care of; and on its being brought to him, appear'd satisfied, and manifested a desire that all should sit down and be still, seemingly sensible that his labours were brought to a close, and only desirous of quietly waiting the final change. The solemn composure at this time manifest in his countenance, was very impressive, indicating that he was sensible the time of his departure was at hand, and that the prospect of death brought no terrors with it. During his last illness, his mental faculties were occasionally obscured, yet he was at times enabled to give satisfactory evidence to those around him, that all was well, and that he felt nothing in his way.

His funeral took place on fourth day, the 3d of 3d month. It was attended by a large concourse of Friends and others, and a solid meeting was held on the occasion; after which, his remains were interr'd in Friends' burial-ground at this place (Jericho, Queens County, New York.)

I have thought (even presented so incompletely, with such fearful hiatuses, and in my own feebleness and waning life) one might well memorize this life of Elias Hicks. Though not eminent in literature or politics or inventions or business, it is a token of not a few, and is significant. Such men do not cope with statesmen or soldiers—but I have thought they deserve to be recorded and kept up as a sample—that this one specially does. I have already compared it to a little flowing liquid rill of Nature's life, maintaining freshness. As if, indeed, under the smoke of battles, the blare of trumpets, and the madness of contending hosts—the screams of passion, the groans of the suffering, the parching of struggles of money and politics, and all hell's heat and noise and competition above and around—should come melting down from the mountains from sources of unpolluted snows, far up there in God's hidden, untrodden recesses, and so rippling along among us low in the ground, at men's very feet, a curious little brook of clear and cool, and ever-healthy, ever-living water.

Note.—The Separation.—The division vulgarly call'd between Orthodox and Hicksites in the Society of Friends took place in 1827, '8 and '9. Probably it had been preparing some time. One who was present has since described to me the climax, at a meeting of Friends in Philadelphia crowded by a great attendance of both sexes, with Elias as principal speaker. In the course of his utterance or argument he made use of these words: "The blood of Christ—the blood of Christ—why, my friends, the actual blood of Christ in itself was no more effectual than the blood of bulls and goats—not a bit more—not a bit." At these words, after a momentary hush, commenced a great tumult. Hundreds rose to their feet. . . . Canes were thump'd upon the floor. From all parts of the house angry mutterings. Some left the place, but more remain'd, with exclamations, flush'd faces and eyes. This was the definite utterance, the overt act, which led to the separation. Families diverg'd—even husbands and wives, parents and children, were separated.

Of course what Elias promulg'd spread a great commotion among the Friends. Sometimes when he presented himself to speak in the meeting, there would be opposition—this led to angry words, gestures, unseemly noises, recriminations. Elias, at such times, was deeply affected—the tears roll'd in streams down his cheeks—he silently waited the close of the dispute. "Let the Friend speak; let the Friend speak!" he would say when his supporters in the meeting tried to bluff off some violent orthodox person objecting to the new doctrinaire. But he never recanted.

A reviewer of the old dispute and separation made the following comments on them in a paper ten years ago: "It was in America, where there had been no persecution worth mentioning since Mary Dyer was hang'd on Boston Common, that about fifty years ago differences arose, singularly enough upon doctrinal points of the divinity of Christ and the nature of the atonement. Whoever would know how bitter was the controversy, and how much of human infirmity was found to be still lurking under broad-brim hats and drab coats, must seek for the information in the Lives of Elias Hicks and of Thomas Shillitoe, the latter an English Friend, who visited us at this unfortunate time, and who exercised his gifts as a peacemaker with but little success. The meetings, according to his testimony, were sometimes turn'd into mobs. The disruption was wide, and seems to have been final. Six of the ten yearly meetings were divided; and since that time various subdivisions have come, four or five in number. There has never, however, been anything like a repetition of the excitement of the Hicksite controversy; and Friends of all kinds at present appear to have settled down into a solid, steady, comfortable state, and to be working in their own way without troubling other Friends whose ways are different."

Note.—Old persons, who heard this man in his day, and who glean'd impressions from what they saw of him, (judg'd from their own points of view,) have, in their conversation with me, dwelt on another point. They think Elias Hicks had a large element of personal ambition, the pride of leadership, of establishing perhaps a sect that should reflect his own name, and to which he should give especial form and character. Very likely. Such indeed seems the means, all through progress and civilization, by which strong men and strong convictions achieve anything definite. But the basic foundation of Elias was undoubtedly genuine religious fervor. He was like an old Hebrew prophet. He had the spirit of one, and in his later years look'd like one. What Carlyle says of John Knox will apply to him:

> "He is an instance to us how a man, by sincerity itself, becomes heroic; it is the grand gift he has. We find in him a good, honest, intellectual talent, no transcendent one;—a narrow, inconsiderable man, as compared with Luther; but in heartfelt instinctive adherence to truth, in *sincerity* as we say, he has no superior; nay, one might ask, What equal he has? The heart of him is of the true Prophet cast. 'He lies there,' said the Earl of Morton at Knox's grave, 'who never fear'd the face of man.' He resembles, more than any of the moderns, an old Hebrew Prophet. The same inflexibility, intolerance, rigid, narrow-looking adherence to God's truth."

A Note yet. The United States to-day.—While under all previous conditions (even convictions) of society, Oriental, Feudal, Ecclesiastical, and in all past (or present) Despotisms, through the entire past, there existed, and exists yet, in ally and fusion with them, and frequently forming the main part of them, certain churches, institutes, priesthoods, fervid beliefs, &c., practically promoting religious and moral action to the fullest degrees of which humanity there under circumstances was capable, and often conserving all there was of justice, art, literature, and good manners—it is clear I say, that, under the Democratic Institutes of the United States, now and henceforth, there are no equally genuine fountains of fervid beliefs, adapted to produce similar moral and religious results, according to our circumstances. I consider that the churches, sects, pulpits, of the present day, in the United States, exist not by any solid convictions, but by a sort of tacit, supercilious, scornful sufferance. Few speak openly—none officially—against them. But the ostent continuously imposing, who is not aware that any such living fountains of belief in them are now utterly ceas'd and departed from the minds of men?

A Lingering Note.—In the making of a full man, all the other consciences, (the emotional, courageous, intellectual, esthetic, &c.,) are to be crown'd and effused by the religious conscience. In the higher structure of a human self, or of community, the Moral, the Religious, the Spiritual, is strictly analogous to the subtle vitalization and antiseptic play call'd Health in the physiologic structure. To person or State, the main verteber (or rather *the* verteber) is Morality. That is indeed the only real vitalization of character, and of all the supersensual, even heroic and artistic portions of man or nationality. It is to run through and knit the superior parts, and keep man or State vital and upright, as health keeps the body straight and blooming. Of course a really grand and strong and beautiful character is probably to be slowly grown, and adjusted strictly with reference to itself, its own personal and social sphere—with (paradox though it may be) the clear understanding that the conventional theories of life, worldly ambition, wealth, office, fame, &c., are essentially but glittering mayas, delusions.

Doubtless the greatest scientists and theologians will sometimes find themselves saying, It isn't only those who know most, who contribute most to God's glory. Doubtless these very scientists at times stand with bared heads before the humblest lives and personalities. For there is something greater (is there not?) than all the science and poems of the world—above all else, like the stars shining eternal—above Shakspere's plays, or Concord philosophy, or art of Angelo or Raphael—something that shines elusive, like beams of Hesperus at evening—high above all the vaunted wealth and pride—prov'd by its practical outcropping in life, each case after its own concomitants—the intuitive blending of divine love and faith in a human emotional character—blending for all, for the unlearn'd, the common, and the poor.

I don't know in what book I once read, (possibly the remark has been made in books, all ages,) that no life ever lived, even the most uneventful, but, probed to its centre, would be found in itself as subtle a drama as any that poets have ever sung, or playwrights fabled. Often, too, in size and weight, that life suppos'd obscure. For it isn't only the palpable stars; astronomers say there are dark, or almost dark, unnotic'd orbs and suns, (like the dusky companion of Sirius, seven times as large as our own sun,) rolling through space, real and potent as any—perhaps the most real and potent. Yet none recks of them. In the bright lexicon we give the spreading heavens, they have not even names. Amid ceaseless sophistications all times, the soul would seem to glance yearningly around for such contrasts—such cool, still offsets.

George Fox (and Shakspere)

While we are about it, we must almost inevitably go back to the origin of the Society of which Elias Hicks has so far prov'd to be the most mark'd individual result. We must revert to the latter part of the 16th, and all, or nearly all of that 17th century, crowded with so many important historical events, changes, and personages. Throughout Europe, and especially in what we call our Mother Country, men were unusually arous'd—(some would say demented.) It was a special age of the insanity of witch-trials and witch-hangings. In one year 60 were hung for witchcraft in one English county alone. It was peculiarly an age of military-religious conflict. Protestantism and Catholicism were wrestling like giants for the mastery, straining every nerve. Only to think of it—that age! its events, persons—Shakspere just dead, (his folios publish'd, complete)—Charles 1st, the shadowy spirit and the solid block! To sum up all, it was *the age of Cromwell!*

As indispensable foreground, indeed, for Elias Hicks, and perhaps *sine qua non* to an estimate of the kind of man, we must briefly transport ourselves back to the England of that period. As I say, it is the time of tremendous moral and political agitation; ideas of conflicting forms, governments, theologies, seethe and dash like ocean storms, and ebb and flow like mighty tides. It was, or had been, the time of the long feud between the Parliament and the Crown. In the midst of the sprouts, began George Fox—born eight years after the death of Shakspere. He was the son of a weaver, himself a shoemaker, and was "converted" before the age of 20. But O the sufferings, mental and physical, through which those years of the strange youth pass'd! He claim'd to be sent by God to fulfil a mission. "I come," he said, "to direct people to the spirit that gave forth the Scriptures." The range of his thought, even then, cover'd almost every important subject of after times, anti-slavery, women's rights, &c. Though in a low sphere, and among the masses, he forms a mark'd feature in the age.

And how, indeed, beyond all any, that stormy and perturb'd age! The foundations of the old, the superstitious, the conventionally poetic, the credulous, all breaking—the light of the new, and of science and democracy, definitely beginning—a mad, fierce, almost crazy age! The political struggles of the reigns of the Charleses, and of the Protectorate of Cromwell, heated to frenzy by theological struggles. Those were the years following the advent and practical working of the Reformation—but Catholicism is yet strong, and yet seeks supremacy. We think our age full of the flush of men and doings, and culminations of war and peace; and so it is. But there could hardly be a grander and more picturesque and varied age than that.

Born out of and in this age, when Milton, Bunyan, Dryden and John Locke were still living—amid the memories of Queen Elizabeth and James First, and the events of their reigns—when the radiance of that galaxy of poets, warriors, statesmen, captains, lords, explorers, wits and gentlemen, that crowded the courts and times of these sovereigns still fill'd the atmosphere—when America commencing to be explor'd and settled commenc'd also to be suspected as destin'd to overthrow the old standards and calculations—when Feudalism, like a sunset, seem'd to gather all its glories, reminiscences, personalisms, in one last gorgeous effort, before the advance of a new day, a new incipient genius—amid the social and domestic circles of that period—indifferent to reverberations that seem'd enough to wake the dead, and in a sphere far from the pageants of the court, the awe of any personal rank or charm of intellect, or literature, or the varying excitement of Parliamentarian or Royalist fortunes—this curious young rustic goes wandering up and down England.

George Fox, born 1624, was of decent stock, in ordinary lower life—as he grew along toward manhood, work'd at shoemaking, also at farm labors—loved to be much by himself, half-hidden in the woods, reading the Bible—went about from town to town, dress'd in leather clothes—walk'd much at night, solitary, deeply troubled ("the inward divine teaching of the Lord")—sometimes goes among the ecclesiastical gatherings of the great professors, and though a mere youth bears bold testimony—goes to and fro disputing—(must have had great personality)—heard the voice of the Lord speaking articulately to him, as he walk'd in the fields—feels resistless commands not to be explain'd, but follow'd, to abstain from taking off his hat, to say *Thee* and *Thou,* and not bid others Good morning or Good evening—was illiterate, could just read and write—testifies against shows, games, and frivolous pleasures—enters the courts and warns the judges that they see to doing justice—goes into public houses and market-places, with denunciations of drunkenness and money-making—rises in the midst of the church-services, and gives his own explanations of the ministers' explanations, and of Bible passages and texts—sometimes for such things put in prison, sometimes struck fiercely on the mouth on the spot, or knock'd down, and lying there beaten and bloody—was of keen wit, ready to any question with the most apropos of answers—was sometimes press'd for a soldier, (*him* for a soldier!)—was indeed terribly buffeted; but goes, goes, goes—often sleeping out-doors, under hedges, or hay stacks—forever taken before justices—improving such, and all occasions, to *bear testimony,* and give good advice—still enters the "steeple-houses," (as he calls churches,) and though often dragg'd out and whipt till he faints away, and lies like one dead, when he comes-to—stands up again, and offering himself all bruis'd and bloody, cries out to his tormenters, "Strike—strike again, here where you have not yet touch'd! my arms, my head, my cheeks."—Is at length arrested and sent up to London, confers with the Protector, Cromwell,—is set at liberty, and holds great meetings in London.

Thus going on, there is something in him that fascinates

one or two here, and three or four there, until gradually there were others who went about in the same spirit, and by degrees the Society of Friends took shape, and stood among the thousand religious sects of the world. Women also catch the contagion, and go round, often shamefully misused. By such contagion these ministerings, by scores, almost hundreds of poor travelling men and women, keep on year after year, through ridicule, whipping, imprisonment, &c.—some of the Friend-ministers emigrate to New England—where their treatment makes the blackest part of the early annals of the New World. Some were executed, others maim'd, par-burnt, and scourg'd—two hundred die in prison—some on the gallows, or at the stake.

George Fox himself visited America, and found a refuge and hearers, and preach'd many times on Long Island, New York State. In the village of Oysterbay they will show you the rock on which he stood, (1672,) addressing the multitude, in the open air—thus rigidly following the fashion of apostolic times.—(I have heard myself many reminiscences of him.) Flushing also contains (or contain'd—I have seen them) memorials of Fox, and his son, in two aged white-oak trees, that shaded him while he bore his testimony to people gather'd in the highway.—Yes, the American Quakers were much persecuted—almost as much, by a sort of consent of all the other sects, as the Jews were in Europe in the middle ages. In New England, the cruelest laws were pass'd, and put in execution against them. As said, some were whipt—women the same as men. Some had their ears cut off—others their tongues pierc'd with hot irons—others their faces branded. Worse still, a woman and three men had been hang'd, (1660.)—Public opinion, and the statutes, join'd together, in an odious union, Quakers, Baptists, Roman Catholics and Witches.—Such a fragmentary sketch of George Fox and his time—and the advent of 'the Society of Friends' in America.

Strange as it may sound, Shakspere and George Fox, (think of them! compare them!) were born and bred of similar stock, in much the same surroundings and station in life—from the same England—and at a similar period. One to radiate all of art's, all literature's splendor—a splendor so dazzling that he himself is almost lost in it, and his contemporaries the same—his fictitious Othello, Romeo, Hamlet, Lear, as real as any lords of England or Europe then and there—more real to us, the mind sometimes thinks, than the man Shakspere himself. Then the other—may we indeed name him the same day? What is poor plain George Fox compared to William Shakspere—to fancy's lord, imagination's heir? Yet George Fox stands for something too—a thought—the thought that wakes in silent hours—perhaps the deepest, most eternal thought latent in the human soul. This is the thought of God, merged in the thoughts of moral right and the immortality of identity. Great, great is this thought—aye, greater than all else. When the gorgeous pageant of Art, refulgent in the sunshine, color'd with roses and gold—with all the richest mere poetry, old or new, (even Shakspere's)—with all that statue, play, painting, music, architecture, oratory, can effect, ceases to satisfy and please—When the eager chase after wealth flags, and beauty itself becomes a loathing—and when all worldly or carnal or esthetic, or even scientific values, having done their office to the human character, and minister'd their part to its development—then, if not before, comes forward this over-arching thought, and brings its eligibilities, germinations. Most neglected in life of all humanity's attributes, easily cover'd with crust, deluded and abused, rejected, yet the only certain source of what all are seeking, but few or none find—in it I for myself clearly see the first, the last, the deepest depths and highest heights of art, of literature, and of the purposes of life. I say whoever labors here, makes contributions here, or best of all sets an incarnated example here, of life or death, is dearest to humanity—remains after the rest are gone. And here, for these purposes, and up to the light that was in him, the man Elias Hicks—as the man George Fox had done years before him—lived long, and died, faithful in life, and faithful in death.

Good-Bye my Fancy

An Old Man's Rejoinder

In the domain of Literature loftily consider'd (an accomplish'd and veteran critic in his just out work* now says,) 'the kingdom of the Father has pass'd; the kingdom of the Son is passing; the kingdom of the Spirit begins.' Leaving the reader to chew on and extract the juice and meaning of this, I will proceed to say in melanged form what I have had brought out by the English author's essay (he discusses the poetic art mostly) on my own, real, or by him supposed, views and purports. If I give any answers to him, or explanations of what my books intend, they will be not direct but indirect and derivative. Of course this brief jotting is personal. Something very like querulous egotism and growling may break through the narrative (for I have been and am rejected by all the great magazines, carry now my 72d annual burden, and have been a paralytic for 18 years.)

No great poem or other literary or artistic work of any scope, old or new, can be essentially consider'd without weighing first the age, politics (or want of politics) and aim, visible forms, unseen soul, and current times, out of the midst of which it rises and is formulated: as the Biblic canticles and their days and spirit—as the Homeric, or Dante's utterance, or Shakspere's, or the old Scotch or Irish ballads, or Ossian, or Omar Khayyam. So I have conceiv'd and launch'd, and work'd for years at, my 'Leaves of Grass'—personal emanations only at best, but with specialty of emergence and background—the ripening of the nineteenth century, the thought and fact and radiation of individuality, of America, the Secession war, and showing the democratic conditions supplanting everything that insults them or impedes their aggregate way.

*Two new volumes, 'Essays Speculative and Suggestive,' by John Addington Symonds. One of the Essays is on 'Democratic Art,' in which I and my books are largely alluded to and cited and dissected. It is this part of the vols. that has caused the off-hand lines above—(first thanking Mr. S. for his invariable courtesy of personal treatment).

Doubtless my poems illustrate (one of novel thousands to come for a long period) those conditions; but 'democratic art' will have to wait long before it is satisfactorily formulated and defined—if it ever is.

I will now for one indicative moment lock horns with what many think the greatest thing, the question of art, so-call'd. I have not seen without learning something therefrom, how, with hardly an exception, the poets of this age devote themselves, always mainly, sometimes altogether, to fine rhyme, spicy verbalism, the fabric and cut of the garment, jewelry, *concetti*, style, art. To-day these adjuncts are certainly the effort, beyond all else. Yet the lesson of Nature undoubtedly is, to proceed with single purpose toward the result necessitated, and for which the time has arrived, utterly regardless of the outputs of shape, appearance or criticism, which are always left to settle themselves. I have not only not bother'd much about style, form, art, etc., but confess to more or less apathy (I believe I have sometimes caught myself in decided aversion) toward them throughout, asking nothing of them but negative advantages—that they should never impede me, and never under any circumstances, or for their own purposes only, assume any mastery over me.

From the beginning I have watch'd the sharp and sometimes heavy and deep-penetrating objections and reviews against my work, and I hope entertain'd and audited them; (for I have probably had an advantage in constructing from a central and unitary principle since the first, but at long intervals and stages—sometimes lapses of five or six years, or peace or war.) Ruskin, the Englishman, charges as a fearful and serious lack that my poems have no humor. A profound German critic complains that, compared with the luxuriant and well-accepted songs of the world, there is about my verse a certain coldness, severity, absence of spice, polish, or of consecutive meaning and plot. (The book is autobiographic at bottom, and may-be I do not exhibit and make ado about the stock passions: I am partly of Quaker stock.) Then E. C. Stedman finds (or found) mark'd fault with me because while celebrating the common people *en masse,* I do not allow enough heroism and moral merit and good intentions to the choicer classes, the college-bred, the *état-major*. It is quite probable that S. is right in the matter. In the main I myself look, and have from the first look'd, to the bulky democratic *torso* of the United States even for esthetic and moral attributes of serious account—and refused to aim at or accept anything less. If America is only for the rule and fashion and small typicality of other lands (the rule of the *état-major*) it is not the land I take it for, and should to-day feel that my literary aim and theory had been blanks and misdirections. Strictly judged, most modern poems are but larger or smaller lumps of sugar, or slices of toothsome sweet cake—even the banqueters dwelling on those glucose flavors as a main part of the dish. Which perhaps leads to something: to have great heroic poetry we need great readers—a heroic appetite and audience. Have we at present any such?

Then the thought at the centre, never too often repeated. Boundless material wealth, free political organization, immense geographic area, and unprecedented 'business' and products—even the most active intellect and 'culture'—will not place this Commonwealth of ours on the topmost range of history and humanity—or any eminence of 'democratic art'—to say nothing of its pinnacle. Only the production (and on the most copious scale) of loftiest moral, spiritual and heroic personal illustrations—a great native Literature headed with a Poetry stronger and sweeter than any yet. If there can be any such thing as a kosmic modern and original song, America needs it, and is worthy of it.

In my opinion to-day (bitter as it is to say so) the outputs through civilized nations everywhere from the great words Literature, Art, Religion, etc., with their conventional administerers, stand squarely in the way of what the vitalities of those great words signify, more than they really prepare the soil for them—or plant the seeds, or cultivate or garner the crop. My own opinion has long been, that for New World service our ideas of beauty (inherited from the Greeks, and so on to Shakspere—*query*—perverted from them?) need to be radically changed, and made anew for to-day's purposes and finer standards. But if so, it will all come in due time—the real change will be an autochthonic, interior, constitutional, even local one, from which our notions of beauty (lines and colors are wondrous lovely, but character is lovelier) will branch or offshoot.

So much have I now rattled off (old age's garrulity,) that there is not space for explaining the most important and pregnant principle of all, *viz.*, that *Art is one,* is not partial, but includes all times and forms and sorts—is not exclusively aristocratic or democratic, or oriental or occidental. My favorite symbol would be a good font of type, where the impeccable long-primer rejects nothing. Or the old Dutch flour-miller who said, 'I never bother myself what road the folks come—I only want good wheat and rye.'

The font is about the same forever. Democratic art results of democratic development, from tinge, true nationality, belief, in the one setting up from it.

Old Poets

Poetry (I am clear) is eligible of something far more ripen'd and ample, our lands and pending days, than it has yet produced from any utterance old or new. Modern or new poetry, too, (viewing or challenging it with severe criticism,) is largely a void—while the very cognizance, or even suspicion of that void, and the need of filling it, proves a certainty of the hidden and waiting supply. Leaving other lands and languages to speak for themselves, we can abruptly but deeply suggest it best from our own—going first to oversea illustrations, and standing on them. Think of Byron, Burns, Shelley, Keats, (even first-raters, "the brothers of the radiant summit," as William O'Connor calls them,) as having done only their precursory and 'prentice work, and all their best and real poems being left yet unwrought, untouch'd. Is it difficult to imagine ahead of us and them, evolv'd from them, poesy completer far than any they themselves fulfill'd? One has in his eye and mind some very large, very old, entirely sound and vital tree or vine, like certain hardy, ever-fruitful specimens in California and Canada, or down in Mexico, (and indeed in all lands) beyond the chronological records—illustrations of growth, continuity, power, amplitude and *exploitation,* almost beyond statement, but proving fact and possibility, outside of argument.

Perhaps, indeed, the rarest and most blessed quality of transcendent noble poetry—as of law, and of the profoundest wisdom and æstheticism—is, (I would suggest,) from sane, completed, vital, capable old age. The final proof of song or personality is a sort of matured, accreted, superb, evoluted, almost divine, impalpable diffuseness and atmosphere or invisible magnetism, dissolving and embracing all—and not any special achievement of passion, pride, metrical form, epigram, plot, thought, or what is call'd beauty. The bud of the rose or the half-blown flower is beautiful, of course, but only the perfected bloom or apple or finish'd wheat-head is beyond the rest. Completed fruitage like this comes (in my opinion) to a grand age, in man or woman, through an essentially sound continuated physiology and psychology (both important) and is the culminating glorious aureole of all and several preceding. Like the tree or vine just mention'd, it stands at last in a beauty, power and productiveness of its own, above all others, and of a sort and style uniting all criticisms, proofs and adherences.

Let us diversify the matter a little by portraying some of the American poets from our own point of view.

Longfellow, reminiscent, polish'd, elegant, with the air of finest conventional library, picture-gallery or parlor, with ladies and gentlemen in them, and plush and rosewood, and ground-glass lamps, and mahogany and ebony furniture, and a silver inkstand and scented satin paper to write on.

Whittier stands for morality (not in any all-accepting philosophic or Hegelian sense, but) filter'd through a Puritanical or Quaker filter—is incalculably valuable as a genuine utterance, (and the finest,)—with many local and Yankee and *genre* bits—all hued with anti-slavery coloring—(the *genre* and anti-slavery contributions all precious—all help.) Whittier's is rather a grand figure, but pretty lean and ascetic—no Greek—not universal and composite enough (don't try—don't wish to be) for ideal Americanism. Ideal Americanism would take the Greek spirit and law, and democratize and scientize and (thence) truly Christianize them for the whole, the globe, all history, all ranks and lands, all facts, all good and bad. (Ah this *bad*—this nineteen-twentieths of us all! What a stumbling-block it remains for poets and metaphysicians—what a chance (the strange, clear-as-ever inscription on the old dug-up tablet) it offers yet for being translated—what can be its purpose in the God-scheme of this universe, and all?)

Then William Cullen Bryant—meditative, serious, from first to last tending to threnodies—his genius mainly lyrical—when reading his pieces who could expect or ask for more magnificent ones than such as "The Battle-Field," and "A Forest Hymn"? Bryant, unrolling, prairie-like, notwithstanding his mountains and lakes—moral enough (yet worldly and conventional)—a naturalist, pedestrian, gardener and fruiter—well aware of books, but mixing to the last in cities and society. I am not sure but his name ought to lead the list of American bards. Years ago I thought Emerson pre-eminent (and as to the last polish and intellectual cuteness may-be I think so still)—but, for reasons, I have been gradually tending to give the file-leading place for American native poesy to W. C. B.

Of Emerson I have to confirm my already avow'd opinion regarding his highest bardic and personal attitude. Of the galaxy of the past—of Poe, Halleck, Mrs. Sigourney, Allston, Willis, Dana, John Pierpont, W. G. Simms, Robert Sands, Drake, Hillhouse, Theodore Fay, Margaret Fuller, Epes Sargent, Boker, Paul Hayne, Lanier, and others, I fitly in essaying such a theme as this, and reverence for their memories, may at least give a heart-benison on the list of their names.

Time and New World humanity having the venerable resemblances more than anything else, and being "the same subject continued," just here in 1890, one gets a curious nourishment and lift (I do) from all those grand old veterans, Bancroft, Kossuth, von Moltke—and such typical specimen-reminiscences as Sophocles and Goethe, genius, health, beauty of person, riches, rank, renown and length of days, all combining and centering in one case.

Above everything, what could humanity and literature do without the mellow, last-justifying, averaging, bringing-up of many, many years—a great old age amplified? Every really first-class production has likely to pass through the crucial tests of a generation, perhaps several generations. Lord Bacon says the first sight of any work really new and first-rate in beauty and originality always arouses something disagreeable and repulsive. Voltaire term'd the Shaksperean works, "a huge dunghill"; Hamlet he described (to the Academy, whose members listen'd with approbation) as "the dream of a drunken savage, with a few flashes of beautiful thoughts." And not the Ferney sage alone; the orthodox judges and law-givers of France, such as La Harpe, J. L. Geoffroy, and Chateaubriand, either join'd in Voltaire's verdict, or went further. Indeed the classicists and regulars there still hold to it. The lesson is very significant in all departments. People resent anything new as a personal insult. When umbrellas were first used in England, those who carried them were hooted and pelted so furiously that their lives were endanger'd. The same rage encounter'd the attempt in theatricals to perform women's parts by real women, which was publicly consider'd disgusting and outrageous. Byron thought Pope's verse incomparably ahead of Homer and Shakspere. One of the prevalent objections, in the days of Columbus was, the learn'd men boldly asserted that if a ship should reach India she would never get back again, because the rotundity of the globe would present a kind of mountain, up which it would be impossible to sail even with the most favorable wind.

"Modern poets," says a leading Boston journal, "enjoy longevity. Browning lived to be seventy-seven. Wordsworth, Bryant, Emerson, and Longfellow were old men. Whittier, Tennyson, and Walt Whitman still live." Started out by that item on Old Poets and Poetry for chyle to inner American sustenance—I have thus gossipp'd about it all, and treated it from my own point of view, taking the privilege of rambling wherever the talk carried me. Browning is lately dead; Bryant, Emerson and Longfellow have not long pass'd away; and yes, Whittier and Tennyson remain, over eighty years old—the latter having sent out not long since a fresh volume, which the English-speaking Old and New Worlds are yet reading. I have already put on record my notions of T. and his effusions: they are very attractive and flowery to me—but flowers, too, are at least as profound as anything; and by common consent T. is settled as the poetic cream-skimmer of our age's melody, *ennui* and polish—a verdict in which I agree, and should say that nobody (not even Shakspere) goes deeper in those exquisitely touch'd and half-hidden hints and indirections left like faint perfumes in the crevices of his lines. Of Browning I don't know enough to say much; he must be studied deeply out, too, and quite certainly repays the trouble—but I am old and indolent, and cannot study (and never did.)

Grand as to-day's accumulative fund of poetry is, there is certainly something unborn, not yet come forth, different from anything now formulated in any verse, or contributed by the past in any land—something waited for, craved, hitherto non-express'd. What it will be, and how, no one knows. It will probably have to prove itself by itself and its readers. One thing, it must run through entire humanity (this new word and meaning Solidarity has arisen to us moderns) twining all lands like a divine thread, stringing all beads, pebbles or gold, from God and the soul, and like God's dynamics and sunshine illustrating all and having reference to all. From anything like a cosmical point of view, the entirety of imaginative literature's themes and results as we get them to-day seems painfully narrow. All that has been put in statement, tremendous as it is, what is it compared with the vast fields and values and varieties left unreap'd? Of our own country, the splendid races North or South, and especially of the Western and Pacific regions, it sometimes seems to me their myriad noblest Homeric and Biblic elements are all untouch'd, left as if ashamed of, and only certain very minor occasional *delirium tremens* glints studiously sought and put in print, in short tales, "poetry" or books.

I give these speculations, or notions, in all their audacity, for the comfort of thousands—perhaps a majority of ardent minds, women's and young men's—who stand in awe and despair before the immensity of suns and stars already in the firmament. Even in the Iliad and Shakspere there is (is there not?) a certain humiliation produced to us by the absorption of them, unless we sound in equality, or above them, the songs due our own democratic era and surroundings, and the full assertion of ourselves. And in vain (such is my opinion) will America seek successfully to tune any superb national song unless the heart-strings of the people start it from their own breasts—to be return'd and echoed there again.

Ship Ahoy!

In dreams I was a ship, and sail'd the boundless seas,
Sailing and ever sailing—all seas and into every port, or out
upon the offing,
Saluting, cheerily hailing each mate, met or pass'd, little or
big,
"Ship ahoy!" thro' trumpet or by voice—if nothing more,
some friendly merry word at least,
For companionship and good will for ever to all and each.

For Queen Victoria's Birthday

An American arbutus bunch to be put in a little vase on the royal breakfast table, May 24th, 1890.

Lady, accept a birth-day thought—haply an idle gift and
token,
Right from the scented soil's May-utterance here,
(Smelling of countless blessings, prayers, and old-time
thanks,)*
A bunch of white and pink arbutus, silent, spicy, shy,
From Hudson's, Delaware's, or Potomac's woody banks.

*Note—Very little, as we Americans stand this day, with our sixty-five or seventy millions of population, an immense surplus in the treasury, and all that actual power or reserve power (land and sea) so dear to nations—very little I say do we realize that curious crawling national shudder when the "Trent affair" promis'd to bring upon us a war with Great Britain—follow'd unquestionably, as that war would have, by recognition of the Southern Confederacy from all the leading European nations. It is now certain that all this then inevitable train of calamity hung on arrogant and peremptory phrases in the prepared and written missive of the British Minister, to America, which the Queen (and Prince Albert latent) positively and promptly cancell'd; and which her firm attitude did alone actually erase and leave out, against all the other official prestige and Court of St. James's. On such minor and personal incidents (so to call them,) often depend the great growths and turns of civilization. This moment of a woman and a queen surely swung the grandest oscillation of modern history's pendulum. Many sayings and doings of that period, from foreign potentates and powers, might well be dropt in oblivion by America—but never *this,* if I could have my way. W. W.

AMERICAN NATIONAL LITERATURE

Is there any such thing—or can there ever be?

So you want an essay about American National Literature, (tremendous and fearful subject!) do you?* Well, if you will let me put down some melanged cogitations regarding the matter, hap-hazard, and from my own points of view, I will try. Horace Greeley wrote a book named "Hints toward Reforms," and the title-line was consider'd the best part of all. In the present case I will give a few thoughts and suggestions, of good and ambitious intent enough anyhow—first reiterating the question right out plainly: American National Literature—is there distinctively any such thing, or can there ever be? First to me comes an almost indescribably august form, the People, with varied typical shapes and attitudes—then the divine mirror, Literature.

As things are, probably no more puzzling question ever offer'd itself than (going back to old Nile for a trope,) What bread-seeds of printed mentality shall we cast upon America's waters, to grow and return after many days? Is there for the future authorship of the United States any better way than submission to the teeming facts, events, activities, and importations already vital through and beneath them all? I have often ponder'd it, and felt myself disposed to let it go at that. Indeed, are not those facts and activities and importations potent and certain to fulfil themselves all through our Commonwealth, irrespective of any attempt from individual guidance? But allowing all, and even at that, a good part of the matter being honest discussion, examination, and earnest personal presentation, we may even for sanitary exercise and contact plunge boldly into the spread of the many waves and cross-tides, as follows. Or, to change the figure, I will present my varied little collation (what is our Country itself but an infinitely vast and varied collation?) in the hope that the show itself indicates a duty getting more and more incumbent every day.

In general, civilization's totality or real representative National Literature formates itself (like language, or "the

*The essay was for the *North American Review,* in answer to the formal request of the editor. It appear'd in March, 1891.

weather") not from two or three influences, however important, nor from any learned syllabus, or criticism, or what ought to be, nor from any minds or advice of toploftical quarters—and indeed not at all from the influences and ways ostensibly supposed (though they too are adopted, after a sort)—but slowly, slowly, curiously, from many more and more, deeper mixings and siftings (especially in America) and generations and years and races, and what largely appears to be chance—but is not chance at all. First of all, for future National Literature in America, New England (the technically moral and schoolmaster region, as a cynical fellow I know calls it) and the three or four great Atlantic-coast cities, highly as they to-day suppose they dominate the whole, will have to haul in their horns. *Ensemble* is the tap-root of National Literature. America is become already a huge world of peoples, rounded and orbic climates, idiocrasies, and geographies—forty-four Nations curiously and irresistibly blent and aggregated in ONE NATION, with one imperial language, and one unitary set of social and legal standards over all—and (I predict) a yet to be National Literature. (In my mind this last, if it ever comes, is to prove grander and more important for the Commonwealth than its politics and material wealth and trade, vast and indispensable as those are.)

Think a moment what must, beyond peradventure, be the real permanent sub-bases, or lack of them. Books profoundly consider'd show a great nation more than anything else—more than laws or manners. (This is, of course, probably the deep-down meaning of that well-buried but ever-vital platitude, Let me sing the people's songs, and I don't care who makes their laws.) Books too reflect humanity *en masse,* and surely show them splendidly, or the reverse, and prove or celebrate their prevalent traits (these last the main things.) Homer grew out of and has held the ages, and holds to-day, by the universal admiration for personal prowess, courage, rankness, *amour propre,* leadership, inherent in the whole human race. Shakspere concentrates the brilliancy of the centuries of feudalism on the proud personalities they produced, and paints the amorous passion. The books of the Bible stand for the final superiority of devout emotions over the rest, and of religious adoration, and ultimate absolute justice, more powerful than haughtiest kings or millionaires or majorities.

What the United States are working out and establishing needs imperatively the connivance of something subtler than ballots and legislators. The Goethean theory and lesson (if I may briefly state it so) of the exclusive sufficiency of artistic, scientific, literary equipment to the character, irrespective of any strong claims of the political ties of nation, state, or city, could have answer'd under the conventionality and pettiness of Weimar, or the Germany, or even Europe, of those times; but it will not do for America to-day at all. We have not only to exploit our own theory above any that has preceded us, but we have entirely different, and deeper-rooted, and infinitely broader themes.

When I have had a chance to see and observe a sufficient crowd of American boys or maturer youths or well-grown men, all the States, as in my experiences in the Secession War among the soldiers, or west, east, north, or south, or my wanderings and loiterings through cities (especially New York and in Washington,) I have invariably found coming to the front three prevailing personal traits, to be named here for brevity's sake under the heads Good-Nature, Decorum, and Intelligence. (I make Good-Nature first, as it deserves to be—it is a splendid resultant of all the rest, like health or fine weather.) Essentially these lead the inherent list of the high average personal born and bred qualities of the young fellows everywhere through the United States, as any sharp observer can find out for himself. Surely these make the vertebral stock of superbest and noblest nations! May the destinies show it so forthcoming. I mainly confide the whole future of our Commonwealth to the fact of these three bases. Need I say I demand the same in the elements and spirit and fruitage of National Literature?

Another, perhaps a born root or branch, comes under the words *Noblesse Oblige*, even for a national rule or motto. My opinion is that this foregoing phrase, and its spirit, should influence and permeate official America and its representatives in Congress, the Executive Departments, the Presidency, and the individual States—should be one of their chiefest mottoes, and be carried out practically. (I got the idea from my dear friend the democratic Englishwoman, Mrs. Anne Gilchrist, now dead. "The beautiful words *Noblesse Oblige*," said she to me once, "are not best for some develop'd gentleman or lord, but some rich and develop'd nation—and especially for your America.")

Then another and very grave point (for this discussion is deep, deep—not for trifles, or pretty seemings.) I am not sure but the establish'd and old (and superb and profound, and, one may say, needed as old) conception of Deity as mainly of moral constituency (goodness, purity, sinlessness, &c.) has been undermined by nineteenth-century ideas and science. What does this immense and almost abnormal development of Philanthropy mean among the moderns? One doubts if there ever will come a day when the moral laws and moral standards will be supplanted as over all: while time proceeds (I find it so myself) they will probably be intrench'd deeper and expanded wider. Then the expanded scientific and democratic and truly philosophic and poetic quality of modernism demands a Deific identity and scope superior to all limitations, and essentially including just as well the so-call'd evil and crime and criminals—all the malformations, the defective and abortions of the universe.

Sometimes the bulk of the common people (who are far more 'cute than the critics suppose) relish a well-hidden allusion or hint carelessly dropt, faintly indicated, and left to be disinterr'd or not. Some of the very old ballads have delicious morsels of this kind. Greek Aristophanes and Pindar abounded in them. (I sometimes fancy the old Hellenic audiences must have been as generally keen and knowing as any of their poets.) Shakspere is full of them. Tennyson has them. It is always a capital compliment from author to reader, and worthy the peering brains of America. The mere smartness of the common folks, however, does not need encouraging, but qualities more solid and opportune.

What are now deepest wanted in the States as roots for their literature are Patriotism, Nationality, Ensemble, or the ideas of these, and the uncompromising genesis and saturation of these. Not the mere bawling and braggadocio of them, but the radical emotion-facts, the fervor and perennial fructifying spirit at fountain-head. And at the risk of being misunderstood

I should dwell on and repeat that a great imaginative *literatus* for America can never be merely good and moral in the conventional method. Puritanism and what radiates from it must always be mention'd by me with respect; then I should say, for this vast and varied Commonwealth, geographically and artistically, the puritanical standards are constipated, narrow, and non-philosophic.

In the main I adhere to my positions in "Democratic Vistas," and especially to my summing-up of American literature as far as to-day is concern'd. In Scientism, the Medical Profession, Practical Inventions, and Journalism, the United States have press'd forward to the glorious front rank of advanced civilized lands, as also in the popular dissemination of printed matter (of a superficial nature perhaps, but that is an indispensable preparatory stage,) and have gone in common education, so-call'd, far beyond any other land or age. Yet the high-pitch'd taunt of Margaret Fuller, forty years ago, still sounds in the air: "It does not follow, because the United States print and read more books, magazines, and newspapers than all the rest of the world, that they really have therefore a literature." For perhaps it is not alone the free schools and newspapers, nor railroads and factories, nor all the iron, cotton, wheat, pork, and petroleum, nor the gold and silver, nor the surplus of a hundred or several hundred millions, nor the Fourteenth and Fifteenth Amendments, nor the last national census, that can put this Commonweal high or highest on the cosmical scale of history. Something else is indispensable. All that record is lofty, but there is a loftier.

The great current points are perhaps simple, after all: first, that the highest developments of the New World and Democracy, and probably the best society of the civilized world all over, are to be only reach'd and spinally nourish'd (in my notion) by a new evolutionary sense and treatment; and, secondly, that the evolution-principle, which is the greatest law through nature, and of course in these States, has now reach'd us markedly for and in our literature.

In other writings I have tried to show how vital to any aspiring Nationality must ever be its autochthonic song, and how for a really great people there can be no complete and glorious Name, short of emerging out of and even rais'd on such born poetic expression, coming from its own soil and soul, its area, spread, idiosyncrasies, and (like showers of rain, originally rising impalpably, distill'd from land and sea,) duly returning there again. Nor do I forget what we all owe to our ancestry; though perhaps we are apt to forgive and bear too much for that alone.

One part of the national American literatus's task is (and it is not an easy one) to treat the old hereditaments, legends, poems, theologies, and even customs, with fitting respect and toleration, and at the same time clearly understand and justify, and be devoted to and exploit our own day, its diffused light, freedom, responsibilities, with all it necessitates, and that our New-World circumstances and stages of development demand and make proper. For American literature we want mighty authors, *not* even Carlyle- and Heine-like, born and brought up in (and more or less essentially partaking and giving out) that vast abnormal ward or hysterical sick-chamber which in many respects Europe, with all its glories, would seem to be. The greatest feature in current poetry (perhaps in literature anyhow) is the almost total lack of first-class power, and simple, natural health, flourishing and produced at first hand, typifying our own era. Modern verse generally lacks quite altogether the modern, and is oftener possess'd in spirit with the past and feudal, dressed may-be in late fashions. For novels and plays often the plots and surfaces are contemporary—but the spirit, even the fun, is morbid and effete.

There is an essential difference between the Old and New. The poems of Asia and Europe are rooted in the long past. They celebrate man and his intellections and relativenesses as they have been. But America, in as high a strain as ever, is to sing them all as they are and are to be. (I know, of course, that the past is probably a main factor in what we are and know and must be.) At present the States are absorb'd in business, money-making, politics, agriculture, the development of mines, intercommunications, and other material attents—which all shove forward and appear at their height—as, consistently with modern civilization, they must be and should be. Then even these are but the inevitable precedents and providers for home-born, transcendent, democratic literature—to be shown in superior, more heroic, more spiritual, more emotional, personalities and songs. A national literature is, of course, in one sense, a great mirror or reflector. There must however be something before—something to reflect. I should say now, since the Secession War, there has been, and to-day unquestionably exists, that something.

Certainly, anyhow, the United States do not so far utter poetry, first-rate literature, or any of the so-call'd arts, to any lofty admiration or advantage—are not dominated or penetrated from actual inherence or plain bent to the said poetry and arts. Other work, other needs, current inventions, productions, have occupied and to-day mainly occupy them. They are very 'cute and imitative and proud—can't bear being left too glaringly away far behind the other high-class nations—and so we set up some home "poets," "artists," painters, musicians, *literati*, and so forth, all our own (thus claim'd.) The whole matter has gone on, and exists to-day, probably as it should have been, and should be; as, for the present, it must be. To all which we conclude, and repeat the terrible query: American National Literature—is there distinctively any such thing, or can there ever be?

Gathering the Corn

Last of October.—Now mellow, crisp Autumn days, bright moonlight nights, and gathering the corn—"cutting up," as the farmers call it. Now, or of late, all over the country, a certain green and brown-drab eloquence seeming to call out, "You that pretend to give the news, and all that's going, why not give us a notice?" Truly, O fields, as for the notice,

"Take, we give it willingly."

Only we must do it our own way. Leaving the domestic, dietary, and commercial parts of the question (which are enormous, in fact, hardly second to those of any other of our great soil-products), we will just saunter down a lane we know, on an average West Jersey farm, and let the fancy of the hour itemize America's most typical agricultural show and specialty.

Gathering the Corn—the British call it Maize, the old Yankee farmer Indian Corn. The great plumes, the ears well-envelop'd in their husks, the long and pointed leaves, in summer, like green or purple ribands, with a yellow stem-line in the middle, all now turn'd dingy; the sturdy stalks, and the rustling in the breeze—the breeze itself well tempering the sunny noon—The varied reminiscences recall'd—the ploughing and planting in spring—(the whole family in the field, even the little girls and boys dropping seed in the hill)—the gorgeous sight through July and August—the walk and observation early in the day—the cheery call of the robin, and the low whirr of insects in the grass—the Western husking party, when ripe—the November moonlight gathering, and the calls, songs, laughter of the young fellows.

Not to forget, hereabouts, in the Middle States, the old worm fences, with the gray rails and their scabs of moss and lichen—those old rails, weather beaten, but strong yet. Why not come down from literary dignity, and confess we are sitting on one now, under the shade of a great walnut tree? Why not confide that these lines are pencill'd on the edge of a woody bank, with a glistening pond and creek seen through the trees south, and the corn we are writing about close at hand on the north? Why not put in the delicious scent of the "life everlasting" that yet lingers so profusely in every direction—the chromatic song of the one persevering locust (the insect is scarcer this fall and the past summer than for many years) beginning slowly, rising and swelling to much emphasis, and then abruptly falling—so appropriate to the scene, so quaint, so racy and suggestive in the warm sunbeams, we could sit here and look and listen for an hour? Why not even the tiny, turtle-shaped, yellow-back'd, black-spotted lady-bug that has lit on the shirt-sleeve of the arm inditing this? Ending our list with the fall-drying grass, the Autumn days themselves,

"Sweet days; so cool, so calm, so bright,"

(yet not so cool either, about noon)—the horse-mint, the wild carrot, the mullein, and the bumble-bee.

How the half-mad vision of William Blake—how the far freer, far firmer fantasy that wrote "Midsummer Night's

Dream"—would have revell'd night or day, and beyond stint, in one of our American corn fields! Truly, in color, outline, material and spiritual suggestiveness, where any more inclosing theme for idealist, poet, literary artist?

What we have written has been at noon day—but perhaps better still (for this collation,) to steal off by yourself these fine nights, and go slowly, musingly down the lane, when the dry and green-gray frost-touch'd leaves seem whisper-gossipping all over the field in low tones, as if every hill had something to say—and you sit or lean recluse near by, and inhale that rare, rich, ripe and peculiar odor of the gather'd plant which comes out best only to the night air. The complex impressions of the far-spread fields and woods in the night, are blended mystically, soothingly, indefinitely, and yet palpably to you (appealing curiously, perhaps mostly, to the sense of smell.) All is comparative silence and clear-shadow below, and the stars are up there with Jupiter lording it over westward; sulky Saturn in the east, and over head the moon. A rare well-shadow'd hour! By no means the least of the eligibilities of the gather'd corn!

A Death-Bouquet

Pick'd Noontime, Early January, 1890.

Death—too great a subject to be treated so—indeed the greatest subject—and yet I am giving you but a few random lines about it—as one writes hurriedly the last part of a letter to catch the closing mail. Only I trust the lines, especially the poetic bits quoted, may leave a lingering odor of spiritual heroism afterward. For I am probably fond of viewing all really great themes indirectly, and by side-ways and suggestions. Certain music from wondrous voices or skilful players—then poetic glints still more—put the soul in rapport with death, or toward it. Hear a strain from Tennyson's late "Crossing the Bar":

"Twilight and evening bell,
  And after that the dark!
And may there be no sadness of farewell,
  When I embark;

"For tho' from out our bourne of Time and Place
The floods may bear me far,
I hope to see my Pilot face to face
When I have crost the bar."

Am I starting the sail-craft of poets in line? Here then a quatrain of Phrynichus long ago to one of old Athens' favorites:

"Thrice-happy Sophocles! in good old age,
Bless'd as a man, and as a craftsman bless'd,
He died; his many tragedies were fair,
And fair his end, nor knew he any sorrow."

Certain music, indeed, especially voluntaries by a good player, at twilight—or idle rambles alone by the shore, or over prairie or on mountain road, for that matter—favor the right mood. Words are difficult—even impossible. No doubt any one will recall ballads or songs or hymns (may-be instrumental performances) that have arous'd so curiously, yet definitely, the thought of death, the mystic, the after-realm, as no statement or sermon could—and brought it hovering near.

A happy (to call it so) and easy death is at least as much a physiological result as a psychological one. The foundation of it really begins before birth, and is thence directly or indirectly shaped and affected, even constituted, (the base stomachic) by every thing from that minute till the time of its occurrence. And yet here is something (Whittier's "Burning Driftwood") of an opposite coloring:

"I know the solemn monotone
Of waters calling unto me;
I know from whence the airs have blown,
That whisper of the Eternal Sea;
As low my fires of driftwood burn,
I hear that sea's deep sounds increase,
And, fair in sunset light, discern
Its mirage-lifted Isles of Peace."

Like an invisible breeze after a long and sultry day, death sometimes sets in at last, soothingly and refreshingly, almost vitally. In not a few cases the termination even appears to be a sort of ecstasy. Of course there are painful deaths, but I do not believe such is at all the general rule. Of the many hundreds I myself saw die in the fields and hospitals during the Secession War the cases of mark'd suffering or agony *in extremis* were very rare. (It is a curious suggestion of immortality that the mental and emotional powers remain to their clearest through all, while the senses of pain and flesh-volition are blunted or even gone.)

Then to give the following, and cease before the thought gets threadbare:

"Now, land and life, finalè, and farewell!
Now Voyager depart! (much, much for thee is yet
in store;)
Often enough hast thou adventur'd o'er the seas,
Cautiously cruising, studying the charts,
Duly again to port and hawser's tie returning.
—But now obey thy cherish'd, secret wish,
Embrace thy friends—leave all in order;
To port and hawser's tie no more returning,
Depart upon thy endless cruise, old Sailor!"

Some Laggards Yet

THE PERFECT HUMAN VOICE

STATING it briefly and pointedly I should suggest that the human voice is a cultivation or form'd growth on a fair native foundation. This foundation probably exists in nine cases out of ten. Sometimes nature affords the vocal organ in perfection, or rather I would say near enough to whet one's appreciation and appetite for a voice that might be truly call'd perfection. To me the grand voice is mainly physiological—(by which I by no means ignore the mental help, but wish to keep the emphasis where it belongs.) Emerson says *manners* form the representative apex and final charm and captivation of humanity: but he might as well have changed the typicality to voice.

Of course there is much taught and written about elocution, the best reading, speaking, etc., but it finally settles down to *best* human vocalization. Beyond all other power and beauty, there is something in the quality and power of the right voice (*timbre* the schools call it) that touches the soul, the abysms. It was not for nothing that the Greeks depended, at their highest, on poetry's and wisdom's vocal utterance by *tete-a-tete* lectures—(indeed all the ancients did.)

Of celebrated people possessing this wonderful vocal power, patent to me, in former days, I should specify the contralto Alboni, Elias Hicks, Father Taylor, the tenor Bettini, Fanny Kemble, and the old actor Booth, and in private life many cases, often women. I sometimes wonder whether the best philosophy and poetry, or something like the best, after all these centuries, perhaps waits to be rous'd out yet, or suggested, by the perfect physiological human voice.

SHAKSPERE FOR AMERICA

LET me send you a supplementary word to that "view" of Shakspere attributed to me, publish'd in your July number,*

*This bit was in "Poet-lore" monthly for September, 1890.

so courteously worded by the reviewer (thanks! dear friend.) But you have left out what, perhaps, is the main point, as follows:

"Even the one who at present reigns unquestion'd—of Shakspere—for all he stands for so much in modern literature, he stands entirely for the mighty æsthetic sceptres of the past, not for the spiritual and democratic, the sceptres of the future." (See p. 1175 in "November Boughs," and also some of my further notions on Shakspere.)

The Old World (Europe and Asia) is the region of the poetry of concrete and real things,—the past, the æsthetic, palaces, etiquette, the literature of war and love, the mythological gods, and the myths anyhow. But the New World (America) is the region of the future, and its poetry must be spiritual and democratic. Evolution is not the rule in Nature, in Politics, and Inventions only, but in Verse. I know our age is greatly materialistic, but it is greatly spiritual, too, and the future will be, too. Even what we moderns have come to mean by *spirituality* (while including what the Hebraic utterers, and mainly perhaps all the Greek and other old typical poets, and also the later ones, meant) has so expanded and color'd and vivified the comprehension of the term, that it is quite a different one from the past. Then science, the final critic of all, has the casting vote for future poetry.

"UNASSAIL'D RENOWN"

THE N. Y. *Critic*, Nov. 24, 1889, propounded a circular to several persons, and giving the responses, says, "Walt Whitman's views [as follow] are, naturally, more radical than those of any other contributor to the discussion":

Briefly to answer impromptu your request of Oct. 19—the question whether I think any American poet not now living deserves a place among the thirteen "English inheritors of unassail'd renown" (Chaucer, Spenser, Shakspere, Milton, Dryden, Pope, Gray, Burns, Wordsworth, Coleridge, Byron, Shelley and Keats,)—and which American poets would be truly worthy, &c. Though to me the *deep* of the matter goes down, down beneath. I remember the London *Times* at the time, in opportune, profound and friendly articles on Bryant's and Longfellow's deaths, spoke of the embarrassment, warping effect, and confusion on America (her poets and poetic students) "coming in possession of a great estate they had never lifted a hand to form or earn"; and the further contingency of "the English language ever having annex'd to it a lot of first-class Poetry that would be American, not European"—proving then something precious over all, and beyond valuation. But perhaps that is venturing outside the question. Of the thirteen British immortals mention'd—after placing Shakspere on a sort of pre-eminence of fame not to be invaded yet—the names of Bryant, Emerson, Whittier and Longfellow (with even added names, sometimes Southerners, sometimes Western or other writers of only one or two pieces,) deserve in my opinion an equally high niche of renown as belongs to any on the dozen of that glorious list.

INSCRIPTION FOR A LITTLE BOOK ON GIORDANO BRUNO

As America's mental courage (the thought comes to me to-day) is so indebted, above all current lands and peoples, to the noble army of Old-World martyrs past, how incumbent on us that we clear those martyrs' lives and names, and hold them up for reverent admiration, as well as beacons. And typical of this, and standing for it and all perhaps, Giordano Bruno may well be put, to-day and to come, in our New World's thankfulest heart and memory. W. W.

February 24th, 1890. Camden, N. J.

SPLINTERS

WHILE I stand in reverence before the fact of Humanity, the People, I will confess, in writing my L of G, the least consideration out of all that has had to do with it has been the consideration of "the public"—at any rate as it now exists. Strange as it may sound for a democrat to say so, I am clear that no free and original and lofty-soaring poem, or one ambitious of those achievements, can possibly be fulfill'd by any writer who has largely in his thought *the public*—or the question, What will establish'd literature—What will the current authorities say about it?

As far as I have sought any, not the best laid out garden or parterre has been my model—but Nature has been. I know that in a sense the garden is nature too, but I had to choose—I could not give both. Besides the gardens are well represented in poetry; while Nature (in letter and in spirit, in the divine essence,) little if at all.

Certainly, (while I have not hit it by a long shot,) I have aim'd at the most ambitious, the best—and sometimes feel to advance that aim (even with all its arrogance) as the most redeeming part of my books. I have never so much cared to feed the esthetic or intellectual palates—but if I could arouse from its slumbers that eligibility in every soul for its own true exercise! if I could only wield that lever!

Out from the well-tended concrete and the physical—and in them and from them only—radiate the spiritual and heroic.

Undoubtedly many points belonging to this essay—perhaps of the greatest necessity, fitness and importance to it—have been left out or forgotten. But the amount of the whole matter—poems, preface and everything—is merely to make one of those little punctures or eye-lets the actors possess in the theatre-curtains to look out upon "the house"—one brief, honest, living glance.

HEALTH, (OLD STYLE)

In that condition the whole body is elevated to a state by others unknown—inwardly and outwardly illuminated, purified, made solid, strong, yet buoyant. A singular charm, more than beauty, flickers out of, and over, the face—a curious transparency beams in the eyes, both in the iris and the white—the temper partakes also. Nothing that happens—no event, rencontre, weather, etc.—but it is confronted—nothing but is subdued into sustenance—such is the marvellous transformation from the old timorousness and the old process of causes and effects. Sorrows and disappointments cease—there is no more borrowing trouble in advance. A man realizes the venerable myth—he is a god walking the earth, he sees new eligibilities, powers and beauties everywhere; he himself has a new eyesight and hearing. The play of the body in motion takes a previously unknown grace. Merely *to move* is then a happiness, a pleasure—to breathe, to see, is also. All the beforehand gratifications, drink, spirits, coffee, grease, stimulants, mixtures, late hours, luxuries, deeds of the night, seem as vexatious dreams, and now the awakening;—many fall into their natural places, wholesome, conveying diviner joys.

What I append—Health, old style—I have long treasur'd—found originally in some scrap-book fifty years ago—a favorite of mine (but quite a glaring contrast to my present bodily state:)

On a high rock above the vast abyss,
  Whose solid base tumultuous waters lave;
Whose airy high-top balmy breezes kiss,
  Fresh from the white foam of the circling wave—

There ruddy Health, in rude majestic state,
  His clust'ring forelock combatting the winds—
Bares to each season's change his breast elate,
  And still fresh vigor from th' encounter finds:

With mighty mind to every fortune braced,
  To every climate each corporeal power,
And high-proof heart, impenetrably cased,
  He mocks the quick transitions of the hour.

Now could he hug bleak Zembla's bolted snow,
  Now to Arabia's heated deserts turn,
Yet bids the biting blast more fiercely blow,
  The scorching sun without abatement burn.

There this bold Outlaw, rising with the morn,
  His sinewy functions fitted for the toil,
Pursues, with tireless steps, the rapturous horn,
  And bears in triumph back the shaggy spoil.

Or, on his rugged range of towering hills,
  Turns the stiff glebe behind his hardy team;

His wide-spread heaths to blithest measures tills,
And boasts the joys of life are not a dream!

Then to his airy hut, at eve, retires,
Clasps to his open breast his buxom spouse,
Basks in his faggot's blaze, his passions fires,
And strait supine to rest unbroken bows.

On his smooth forehead, Time's old annual score,
Tho' left to furrow, yet disdains to lie;
He bids weak sorrow tantalize no more,
And puts the cup of care contemptuous by.

If, from some inland height, that, skirting, bears
Its rude encroachments far into the vale,
He views where poor dishonor'd nature wears
On her soft cheek alone the lily pale;

How will he scorn alliance with the race,
Those aspin shoots that shiver at a breath;
Children of sloth, that danger dare not face,
And find in life but an extended death:

Then from the silken reptiles will he fly,
To the bold cliff in bounding transports run,
And stretch'd o'er many a wave his ardent eye,
Embrace the enduring Sea-Boy as his son!

Yes! thine alone—from pain, from sorrow free,
The lengthen'd life with peerless joys replete;
Then let me, Lord of Mountains, share with thee
The hard, the early toil—the relaxation sweet.

GAY-HEARTEDNESS

WALKING on the old Navy Yard bridge, Washington, D. C., once with a companion, Mr. Marshall, from England, a great traveler and observer, as a squad of laughing young black girls pass'd us—then two copper-color'd boys, one good-looking lad 15 or 16, barefoot, running after—"What *gay creatures* they all appear to be," said Mr. M. Then we fell to talking about the general lack of buoyant animal spirits. "I think," said Mr. M., "that in all my travels, and all my intercourse with people of every and any class, especially the cultivated ones, (the literary and fashionable folks,) I have never yet come across what I should call a really GAY-HEARTED MAN."

It was a terrible criticism—cut into me like a surgeon's lance. Made me silent the whole walk home.

AS IN A SWOON

As in a swoon, one instant,
Another sun, ineffable, full-dazzles me,
And all the orbs I knew—and brighter, unknown orbs;
One instant of the future land, Heaven's land.

L. OF G.

THOUGHTS, suggestions, aspirations, pictures,
Cities and farms—by day and night—book of peace and war,
Of platitudes and of the commonplace.

For out-door health, the land and sea—for good will,
For America—for all the earth, all nations, the common
people,
(Not of one nation only—not America only.)

In it each claim, ideal, line, by all lines, claims, ideals,
temper'd;
Each right and wish by other wishes, rights.

AFTER THE ARGUMENT

A GROUP of little children with their ways and chatter
flow in,
Like welcome rippling water o'er my heated nerves and flesh.

FOR US TWO, READER DEAR

SIMPLE, spontaneous, curious, two souls interchanging,
With the original testimony for us continued to the last.

Memoranda

[Let me indeed turn upon myself a little of the light I have been so fond of casting on others.

Of course these few exceptional later mems are far far short of one's concluding history or thoughts or life-giving—only a hap-hazard pinch of all. But the old Greek proverb put it, "Anybody who really has a good quality" (or bad one either, I guess) "has *all*." There's something in the proverb; but you mustn't carry it too far.

I will not reject any theme or subject because the treatment is too personal. As my stuff settles into shape, I am told (and sometimes myself discover, uneasily, but feel all right about it in calmer moments) it is mainly autobiographic, and even egotistic after all—which I finally accept, and am contented so.

If this little volume betrays, as it doubtless does, a weakening hand, and decrepitude, remember it is knit together out of accumulated sickness, inertia, physical disablement, acute pain, and listlessness. My fear will be that at last my pieces show indooredness, and being chain'd to a chair—as never before. Only the resolve to keep up, and on, and to add a remnant, and even perhaps obstinately see what failing powers and decay may contribute too, have produced it.

And now as from some fisherman's net hauling all sorts, and disbursing the same.]

A WORLD'S SHOW

New York, Great Exposition open'd in 1853.—I went a long time (nearly a year)—days and nights—especially the latter—as it was finely lighted, and had a very large and copious exhibition gallery of paintings (shown at best at night, I tho't)—hundreds of pictures from Europe, many masterpieces—all an exhaustless study—and, scatter'd thro' the building, sculptures, single figures or groups—among the rest, Thorwaldsen's "Apostles," colossal in size—and very many fine bronzes, pieces of plate from English silversmiths, and curios from everywhere abroad—with woods from all lands of the earth—all sorts of fabrics and products and handiwork from the workers of all nations.

NEW YORK—THE BAY—THE OLD NAME

Commencement of a gossipy travelling letter in a New York city paper, May 10, 1879.—My month's visit is about up; but before I get back to Camden let me print some jottings of the last four weeks. Have you not, reader dear, among your intimate friends, some one, temporarily absent, whose letters to you, avoiding all the big topics and disquisitions, give only minor, gossipy sights and scenes—just as they come—subjects disdain'd by solid writers, but interesting to you because they were such as happen to everybody, and were the moving entourage to your friend—to his or her steps, eyes, mentality? Well, with an idea something of that kind, I suppose, I set out on the following hurrygraphs of a breezy early-summer visit to New-York City and up the North River—especially at present of some hours along Broadway.

What I came to New York for.—To try the experiment of a lecture—to see whether I could stand it, and whether an audience could—was my specific object. Some friends had invited me—it was by no means clear how it would end—I stipulated that they should get only a third-rate hall, and not sound the advertising trumpets a bit—and so I started. I much wanted something to do for occupation, consistent with my limping and paralyzed state. And now, since it came off, and since neither my hearers nor I myself really collaps'd at the aforesaid lecture, I intend to go up and down the land (in moderation,) seeking whom I may devour, with lectures, and reading of my own poems—short pulls, however—never exceeding an hour.

Crossing from Jersey City, 5 to 6 p. m.—The city part of the North River with its life, breadth, peculiarities—the amplitude of sea and wharf, cargo and commerce—one don't realize them till one has been away a long time and, as now returning, (crossing from Jersey City to Desbrosses-st.,) gazes on the unrivall'd panorama, and far down the thin-vapor'd vistas of the bay, toward the Narrows—or northward up the Hudson—or on the ample spread and infinite variety, free and floating, of the more immediate views—a countless river series—everything moving, yet so easy, and such plenty of room! Little, I say, do folks here appreciate the most ample, eligible, picturesque bay and estuary surroundings in the world! This is the third time such a conviction has come to me after absence, returning to New-York, dwelling on its magnificent entrances—approaching the city by them from any point.

More and more, too, the *old name* absorbs into me—MANNAHATTA, "the place encircled by many swift tides and sparkling waters." How fit a name for America's great democratic island city! The word itself, how beautiful! how aboriginal! how it seems to rise with tall spires, glistening in sunshine, with such New World atmosphere, vista and action!

A SICK SPELL

Christmas Day, 25th Dec., 1888.—Am somewhat easier and freer to-day and the last three days—sit up most of the time—read and write, and receive my visitors. Have now been indoors sick for seven months—half of the time bad, bad, vertigo, indigestion, bladder, gastric, head trouble, inertia—Dr. Bucke, Dr. Osler, Drs. Wharton and Walsh—now Edward Wilkins my help and nurse. A fine, splendid, sunny day. My "November Boughs" is printed and out; and my "Complete Works, Poems and Prose," a big volume, 900 pages, also. It is ab't noon, and I sit here pretty comfortable.

TO BE PRESENT ONLY

At the Complimentary Dinner, Camden, New Jersey, May 31, 1889.—Walt Whitman said:

My friends, though announced to give an address, there is no such intention. Following the impulse of the spirit, (for I am at least half of Quaker stock) I have obey'd the command to come and look at you, for a minute, and show myself, face to face; which is probably the best I can do. But I have felt no command to make a speech; and shall not therefore attempt any. All I have felt the imperative conviction to say I have already printed in my books of poems or prose; to which I refer any who may be curious. And so, hail and farewell. Deeply acknowledging this deep compliment, with my best respects and love to you personally—to Camden—to New-Jersey, and to all represented here—you must excuse me from any word further.

F'm Pall-Mall Gazette, London, England, Feb. 8, 1890.

"INTESTINAL AGITATION"

MR. Ernest Rhys has just receiv'd an interesting letter from Walt Whitman, dated "Camden, January 22, 1890." The following is an extract from it:

> I am still here—no very mark'd or significant change or happening—fairly buoyant spirits, &c.—but surely, slowly ebbing. At this moment sitting here, in my den, Mickle Street, by the oakwood fire, in the same big strong old chair with wolf-skin spread over back—bright sun, cold, dry winter day. America continues—is generally busy enough all over her vast demesnes (intestinal agitation I call it,) talking, plodding, making money, every one trying to get on—perhaps to get towards the top—but no special individual signalism—(just as well, I guess.)

"WALT WHITMAN'S LAST 'PUBLIC' "

THE gay and crowded audience at the Art Rooms, Philadelphia, Tuesday night, April 15, 1890, says a correspondent of the Boston *Transcript*, April 19, might not have thought that W. W. crawl'd out of a sick bed a few hours before, crying,

> Dangers retreat when boldly they're confronted,

and went over, hoarse and half blind, to deliver his memoranda and essay on the death of Abraham Lincoln, on the twenty-fifth anniversary of that tragedy. He led off with the following new paragraph:

> "Of Abraham Lincoln, bearing testimony twenty-five years after his death—and of that death—I am now my friends before you. Few realize the days, the great historic and esthetic personalities, with him in the centre, we pass'd

through. Abraham Lincoln, familiar, our own, an Illinoisian, modern, yet tallying ancient Moses, Joshua, Ulysses, or later Cromwell, and grander in some respects than any of them; Abraham Lincoln, that makes the like of Homer, Plutarch, Shakspere, eligible our day or any day. My subject this evening for forty or fifty minutes' talk is the death of this man, and how that death will really filter into America. I am not going to tell you anything new; and it is doubtless nearly altogether because I ardently wish to commemorate the hour and martyrdom and name I am here. Oft as the rolling years bring back this hour, let it again, however briefly, be dwelt upon. For my own part I hope and intend till my own dying day, whenever the 14th or 15th of April comes, to annually gather a few friends and hold its tragic reminiscence. No narrow or sectional reminiscence. It belongs to these States in their entirety—not the North only, but the South—perhaps belongs most tenderly and devoutly to the South, of all; for there really this man's birthstock; there and then his antecedent stamp. Why should I not say that thence his manliest traits, his universality, his canny, easy ways and words upon the surface—his inflexible determination at heart? Have you ever realized it, my friends, that Lincoln, though grafted on the West, is essentially in personnel and character a Southern contribution?"

The most of the poet's address was devoted to the actual occurrences and details of the murder. We believe the delivery on Tuesday was Whitman's thirteenth of it. The old poet is now physically wreck'd. But his voice and magnetism are the same. For the last month he has been under a severe attack of the lately prevailing influenza, the grip, in accumulation upon his previous ailments, and, above all, that terrible paralysis, the bequest of Secession War times. He was dress'd last Tuesday night in an entire suit of French Canadian grey wool cloth, with broad shirt collar, with no necktie; long white hair, red face, full beard and moustache, and look'd as though he might weigh two hundred pounds. He had to be help'd and led every step. In five weeks more he will begin his seventy-second year. He is still writing a little.

From the Camden Post, N.J., June 2, 1890.

INGERSOLL'S SPEECH

He attends and makes a speech at the celebration of Walt Whitman's birthday.—Walt Whitman is now in his seventy-second year. His younger friends, literary and personal, men and women, gave him a complimentary supper last Saturday night, to note the close of his seventy-first year, and the late curious and unquestionable "boom" of the old man's wide-spreading popularity, and that of his "Leaves of Grass." There were thirty-five in the room, mostly young, but some old, or beginning to be. The great feature was Ingersoll's utterance. It was probably, in its way, the most admirable specimen of modern oratory hitherto delivered in the English language, immense as such praise may sound. It was 40 to 50 minutes long, altogether without notes, in a good voice, low enough and not too low, style easy, rather colloquial (over and over again saying "you" to Whitman who sat opposite,) sometimes markedly impassion'd, once or twice humorous—amid his whole speech, from interior fires and volition, pulsating and swaying like a first-class Andalusian dancer.

And such a critical dissection, and flattering summary! The Whitmanites for the first time in their lives were fully satisfied; and that is saying a good deal, for they have not put their claims low, by a long shot. Indeed it was a tremendous talk! Physically and mentally Ingersoll (he had been working all day in New York, talking in court and in his office,) is now at his best, like mellow'd wine, or a just ripe apple; to the artist-sense, too, looks at his best—not merely like a bequeath'd Roman bust or fine smooth marble Cicero-head, or even Greek Plato; for he is modern and vital and vein'd and American, and (far more than the age knows,) justifies us all.

We cannot give a full report of this most remarkable talk and supper (which was curiously conversational and Greek-like) but must add the following significant bit of it.

After the speaking, and just before the close, Mr. Whitman reverted to Colonel Ingersoll's tribute to his poems, pronouncing it the cap-sheaf of all commendation that he had ever receiv'd. Then, his mind still dwelling upon the Colonel's religious doubts, he went on to say that what he himself had in his mind when he wrote "Leaves of Grass" was not only to depict American life, as it existed, and to show the triumphs of science, and the poetry in common things, and the full of an individual democratic humanity, for the aggregate, but also to show that there was behind all something which rounded and completed it. "For what," he ask'd, "would this life be without immortality? It would be as a locomotive, the greatest triumph of modern science, with no train to draw after it. If the spiritual is not behind the material, to what purpose is the material? What is this world without a further Divine purpose in it all?"

Colonel Ingersoll repeated his former argument in reply.

FEELING FAIRLY

Friday, July 27, 1890.—Feeling fairly these days, and even jovial—sleep and appetite good enough to be thankful for—had a dish of Maryland blackberries, some good rye bread and a cup of tea, for my breakfast—relish'd all—fine weather—bright sun to-day—pleasant north-west breeze blowing in the open window as I sit here in my big rattan chair—two great fine roses (white and red, blooming, fragrant, sent by mail by W. S. K. and wife, Mass.) are in a glass of water on the table before me.

Am now in my 72d year.

OLD BROOKLYN DAYS

It must have been in 1822 or '3 that I first came to live in Brooklyn. Lived first in Front street, not far from what was then call'd "the New Ferry," wending the river from the foot of Catharine (or Main) street to New York City.

I was a little child (was born in 1819,) but tramp'd freely about the neighborhood and town, even then; was often on the aforesaid New Ferry; remember how I was petted and deadheaded by the gatekeepers and deckhands (all such fellows are kind to little children,) and remember the horses that seem'd to me so queer as they trudg'd around in the central houses of the boats, making the water-power. (For it was just on the eve of the steam-engine, which was soon after introduced on the ferries.) Edward Copeland (afterward Mayor) had a grocery store then at the corner of Front and Catharine streets.

Presently we Whitmans all moved up to Tillary street, near Adams, where my father, who was a carpenter, built a house for himself and us all. It was from here I 'assisted' the personal coming of Lafayette in 1824–5 to Brooklyn. He came over the Old Ferry, as the now Fulton Ferry (partly navigated quite up to that day by 'horse boats,' though the first steamer had begun to be used hereabouts) was then call'd, and was receiv'd at the foot of Fulton street. It was on that occasion that the corner-stone of the Apprentices' Library, at the corner of Cranberry and Henry streets—since pull'd down—was laid by Lafayette's own hands. Numerous children arrived on the grounds, of whom I was one, and were assisted by several gentlemen to safe spots to view the ceremony. Among others, Lafayette, also helping the children, took me up—I was five years old, press'd me a moment to his breast—gave me a kiss and set me down in a safe spot. Lafayette was at that time between sixty-five and seventy years of age, with a manly figure and a kind face.

TWO QUESTIONS

AN editor of (or in) a leading monthly magazine (Harper's Monthly, July, 1890,) asks: "A hundred years from now will W. W. be popularly rated a great poet—or will he be forgotten?" . . . A mighty ticklish question—which can only be left for a hundred years hence—perhaps more than that. But whether W. W. has been mainly rejected by his own times is an easier question to answer.

All along from 1860 to '91, many of the pieces in L of G, and its annexes, were first sent to publishers or magazine editors before being printed in the L, and were premptorily rejected by them, and sent back to their author. The "Eidōlons" was sent back by Dr. H., of "Scribner's Monthly" with a lengthy, very insulting and contemptuous letter. "To the Sun-Set Breeze," was rejected by the editor of "Harper's Monthly" as being "an improvisation" only. "On, on ye jocund twain" was rejected by the "Century" editor as being personal merely. Several of the pieces went the rounds of all the monthlies, to be thus summarily rejected.

June, '90.—The———rejects and sends back my little poem, so I am now set out in the cold by every big magazine and publisher, and may as well understand and admit it—which is just as well, for I find I am palpably losing my sight and ratiocination.

PREFACE

to a volume of essays and tales by Wm. D. O'Connor, pub'd posthumously in 1891

A HASTY memorandum, not particularly for Preface to the following tales, but to put on record my respect and affection for as sane, beautiful, cute, tolerant, loving, candid and free and fair-intention'd a nature as ever vivified our race.

In Boston, 1860, I first met WILLIAM DOUGLAS O'CONNOR.* As I saw and knew him then, in his 29th year, and for twenty-five further years along, he was a gallant, handsome, gay-hearted, fine-voiced, glowing-eyed man; lithe-moving on his feet, of healthy and magnetic atmosphere and presence, and the most welcome company in the world. He was a thorough-going anti-slavery believer, speaker and writer, (doctrinaire,) and though I took a fancy to him from the first, I remember I fear'd his ardent abolitionism—was afraid it would probably keep us apart. (I was a decided and out-spoken anti-slavery believer myself, then and always; but shy'd from the extremists, the red-hot fellows of those times.) O'C. was then correcting the proofs of *Harrington,* an eloquent and fiery novel he had written, and which was printed just before the commencement of the Secession War. He was already married, the father of two fine little children, and was personally and intellectually the most attractive man I had ever met.

Last of '62 I found myself led towards the war-field—went

*Born Jan. 2d, 1832. When grown, lived several years in Boston, and edited journals and magazines there—went about 1861 to Washington, D. C., and became a U. S. clerk, first in the Light-House Bureau, and then in the U. S. Life-Saving Service, in which branch he was Assistant Superintendent for many years—sicken'd in 1887—died there at Washington, May 9th, 1889.

to Washington City—(to become absorb'd in the armies, and in the big hospitals, and to get work in one of the Departments,)—and there I met and resumed friendship, and found warm hospitality from O'C. and his noble New England wife. They had just lost by death their little child-boy, Philip; and O'C. was yet feeling serious about it. The youngster had been vaccinated against the threatening of small-pox which alarm'd the city; but somehow it led to worse results than it was intended to ward off—or at any rate O'C. thought that proved the cause of the boy's death. He had one child left, a fine bright little daughter, and a great comfort to her parents. (Dear Jeannie! She grew up a most accomplish'd and superior young woman—declined in health, and died about 1881.)

On through for months and years to '73 I saw and talk'd with O'C. almost daily. I had soon got employment, first for a short time in the Indian Bureau (in the Interior Department,) and then for a long while in the Attorney General's Office. The Secession War, with its tide of varying fortunes, excitements—President Lincoln and the daily sight of him—the doings in Congress and at the State Capitals—the news from the fields and campaigns, and from foreign governments—my visits to the Army Hospitals, daily and nightly, soon absorbing everything else,—with a hundred matters, occurrences, personalities,—(Greeley, Wendell Phillips, the parties, the Abolitionists, &c.)—were the subjects of our talk and discussion. I am not sure from what I heard then, but O'C. was cut out for a first-class public speaker or forensic advocate. No audience or jury could have stood out against him. He had a strange charm of physiologic voice. He had a power and sharp-cut faculty of statement and persuasiveness beyond any man's else. I know it well, for I have felt it many a time. If not as orator, his forte was as critic, newer, deeper than any: also, as literary author. One of his traits was that while he knew all, and welcom'd all sorts of great *genre* literature, all lands and times, from all writers and artists, and not only tolerated each, and defended every attack'd literary person with a skill or heart-catholicism that I never saw equal'd—invariably advocated and excused them—he kept an idiosyncrasy and identity of his own very mark'd, and without special tinge or undue color from any source. He always applauded the freedom of the masters, whence and whoever. I remember his special defences of Byron, Burns, Poe, Rabelais, Victor Hugo, George Sand, and others. There was always a little touch of pensive cadence in his superb voice; and I think there was something of the same sadness in his temperament and nature. Perhaps, too, in his literary structure. But he was a very buoyant, jovial, good-natured companion.

So much for a hasty melanged reminiscence and note of William O'Connor, my dear, dear friend, and staunch, (probably my staunchest) literary believer and champion from the first, and throughout without halt or demur, for twenty-five years. No better friend—none more reliable through this life of one's ups and downs. On the occurrence of the latter he would be sure to make his appearance on the scene, eager, hopeful, full of fight like a perfect knight of chivalry. For he was a born sample here in the 19th century of the flower and symbol of olden time first-class knighthood. Thrice blessed be his memory! W. W.

F'm the Engineering Record, New York, Dec. 13, 1890.

AN ENGINEER'S OBITUARY

THOMAS JEFFERSON WHITMAN was born July 18, 1833, in Brooklyn, N. Y., from a father of English stock, and mother (Louisa Van Velsor) descended from Dutch (Holland) immigration. His early years were spent on Long Island, either in the country or Brooklyn. As a lad he show'd a tendency for surveying and civil engineering, and about at 19 went with Chief Kirkwood, who was then prospecting and outlining for the great city water-works. He remain'd at that construction throughout, was a favorite and confidant of the Chief, and was successively promoted. He continued also under Chief Moses Lane. He married in 1859, and not long after was invited by the Board of Public Works of St. Louis, Missouri, to come there and plan and build a new and fitting water-works for that great city. Whitman accepted the call, and moved and settled there, and had been a resident of St. Louis ever since. He plann'd and built the works, which were very successful, and remain'd as superintendent and chief for nearly 20 years.

Of the last six years he has been largely occupied as consulting engineer (divested of his cares and position in St. Louis,) and has engaged in public constructions, bridges, sewers, &c., West and Southwest, and especially the Memphis, Tenn., city water-works.

Thomas J. Whitman was a theoretical and practical mechanic of superior order, founded in the soundest personal and professional integrity. He was a great favorite among the young engineers and students; not a few of them yet remaining in Kings and Queens Counties, and New York City, will remember "Jeff," with old-time good-will and affection. He was mostly self-taught, and was a hard student.

He had been troubled of late years from a bad throat and from gastric affection, tending on typhoid, and had been rather seriously ill with the last malady, but was getting over the worst of it, when he succumb'd under a sudden and severe attack of the heart. He died at St. Louis, November 25, 1890, in his 58th year. Of his family, the wife died in 1873, and a daughter, Mannahatta, died two years ago. Another daughter, Jessie Louisa, the only child left, is now living in St. Louis.

[When Jeff was born I was in my 15th year, and had much care of him for many years afterward, and he did not separate from me. He was a very handsome, healthy, affectionate, smart child, and would sit on my lap or hang on my neck half an hour at a time. As he grew a big boy he liked outdoor and water sports, especially boating. We would often go down summers to Peconic Bay, east end of Long Island, and over to Shelter Island. I loved long rambles, and he carried his fowling-piece. O, what happy times, weeks! Then in Brooklyn and New York City he learn'd printing, and work'd awhile at it; but eventually (with my approval) he went to employment at land surveying, and merged in the studies and work of topographical engineer; this satisfied him, and he continued at it. He was of noble nature from the first; very good-natured, very plain, very friendly. O, how we loved each other—how many jovial good times we had! Once we made a long trip from New York City down over the Allegheny Mountains (the National Road) and via the Ohio and Mississippi Rivers, from Cairo to New Orleans.]

God's blessing on your name and memory, dear brother Jeff! W. W.

OLD ACTORS, SINGERS, SHOWS, &C., IN NEW YORK

Flitting mention—(with much left out.)

SEEMS to me I ought acknowledge my debt to actors, singers, public speakers, conventions, and the Stage in New York, my youthful days, from 1835 onward—say to '60 or '61—and to plays and operas generally. (Which nudges a pretty big disquisition: of course it should be all elaborated and penetrated more deeply—but I will here give only some flitting mentionings of my youth.) Seems to me now when I look back, the Italian contralto Marietta Alboni (she is living yet, in Paris, 1891, in good condition, good voice yet, considering) with the then prominent histrions Booth, Edwin Forrest, and Fanny Kemble and the Italian singer Bettini, have had the deepest and most lasting effect upon me. I should like well if Madame Alboni and the old composer Verdi, (and Bettini the tenor, if he is living) could know how much noble pleasure and happiness they gave me, and how deeply I always remember them and thank them to this day. For theatricals in literature and doubtless upon me personally, including opera, have been of course serious factors. (The experts and musicians of my present friends claim that the new Wagner and his pieces belong far more truly to me, and I to them. Very likely. But I was fed and bred under the Italian dispensation, and absorb'd it, and doubtless show it.)

As a young fellow, when possible I always studied a play or libretto quite carefully over, by myself, (sometimes twice through) before seeing it on the stage; read it the day or two days before. Tried both ways—not reading some beforehand; but I found I gain'd most by getting that sort of mastery first, if the piece had depth. (Surface effects and glitter were much less thought of I am sure those times.) There were many fine old plays, neither tragedies nor comedies—the names of them quite unknown to to-day's current audiences. "All is not Gold that Glitters," in which Charlotte Cushman had a superbly enacted part, was of that kind. C. C., who revel'd in them, was great in such pieces; I think better than in the heavy popular rôles.

We had some fine music those days. We had the English opera of "Cinderella" (with Henry Placide as the pompous old father, an unsurpassable bit of comedy and music.) We had Bombastes Furioso. Must have been in 1844 (or '5) I saw Charles Kean and Mrs. Kean (Ellen Tree)—saw them in the Park in Shakspere's "King John." He, of course, was the chief character. She play'd *Queen Constance.* Tom Hamblin was *Faulconbridge,* and probably the best ever on the stage. It was an immense show-piece, too; lots of grand set scenes and fine armor-suits and all kinds of appointments imported from London (where it had been first render'd.) The large brass bands—the three or four hundred "supes"—the interviews between the French and English armies—the talk with *Hubert* (and the hot irons) the delicious acting of *Prince Arthur* (Mrs. Richardson, I think)—and all the fine *blare* and court pomp—I remember to this hour. The death-scene of the King in the orchard of Swinstead Abbey, was very effective. Kean rush'd in, gray-pale and yellow, and threw himself on a lounge in the open. His pangs were horribly realistic. (He must have taken lessons in some hospital.)

Fanny Kemble play'd to wonderful effect in such pieces as "Fazio, or the Italian wife." The turning-point was jealousy. It was a rapid-running, yet heavy-timber'd, tremendous wrenching, passionate play. Such old pieces always seem'd to me built like an ancient ship of the line, solid and lock'd from keel up—oak and metal and knots. One of the finest characters was a great court lady, *Aldabella,* enacted by Mrs. Sharpe. O how it all entranced us, and knock'd us about, as the scenes swept on like a cyclone!

Saw Hackett at the old Park many times, and remember him well. His renderings were first-rate in everything. He inaugurated the true "Rip Van Winkle," and look'd and acted and dialogued it to perfection (he was of Dutch breed, and brought up among old Holland descendants in Kings and Queens counties, Long Island.) The play and the acting of it have been adjusted to please popular audiences since; but there was in that original performance certainly something of a far higher order, more art, more reality, more resemblance, a bit of fine pathos, a lofty *brogue,* beyond anything afterward.

One of my big treats was the rendering at the old Park of Shakspere's "Tempest" in musical version. There was a very fine instrumental band, not numerous, but with a capital leader. Mrs. Austin was the *Ariel,* and Peter Richings the *Caliban;* both excellent. The drunken song of the latter has probably been never equal'd. The perfect actor Clarke (old Clarke) was *Prospero.*

Yes; there were in New York and Brooklyn some fine non-technical singing performances, concerts, such as the Hutchinson band, three brothers, and the sister, the red-cheek'd New England carnation, sweet Abby; sometimes plaintive and balladic—sometimes anti-slavery, anti-calomel, and comic. There were concerts by Templeton, Russell, Dempster, the old Alleghanian band, and many others. Then we had lots of "negro minstrels," with capital character songs and voices. I often saw Rice the original "Jim Crow" at the old Park Theatre filling up the gap in some short bill—and the wild chants and dances were admirable—probably ahead of anything since. Every theatre had some superior voice, and it was common to give a favorite song between the acts. "The Sea" at the bijou Olympic, (Broadway near Grand,) was always welcome from a little Englishman named Edwin, a good balladist. At the Bowery the loves of "Sweet William,"

"When on the Downs the fleet was moor'd,"

always bro't an encore, and sometimes a treble.

I remember Jenny Lind and heard her (1850 I think) several times. She had the most brilliant, captivating, popular musical style and expression of any one known; (the canary, and several other sweet birds are wondrous fine—but there is something in song that goes deeper—isn't there?)

The great "Egyptian Collection" was well up in Broadway, and I got quite acquainted with Dr. Abbott, the proprietor—paid many visits there, and had long talks with him, in connection with my readings of many books and reports on Egypt—its antiquities, history, and how things and the scenes really look, and what the old relics stand for, as near as we can now get. (Dr. A. was an Englishman of say 54—had been settled in Cairo as physician for 25 years, and all that time was collecting these relics, and sparing no time or money seeking and getting them. By advice and for a change of base for himself, he brought the collection to America. But the whole enterprise was a fearful disappointment, in the pay and commercial part.) As said, I went to the Egyptian Museum many many times; sometimes had it all to myself—delved at the formidable catalogue—and on several occasions had the invaluable personal talk, correction, illustration and guidance of Dr. A. himself. He was very kind and helpful to me in those studies and examinations; once, by appointment, he appear'd in full and exact Turkish (Cairo) costume, which long usage there had made habitual to him.

One of the choice places of New York to me then was the "Phrenological Cabinet" of Fowler & Wells, Nassau street near Beekman. Here were all the busts, examples, curios and books of that study obtainable. I went there often, and once for myself had a very elaborate and leisurely examination and "chart of bumps" written out (I have it yet,) by Nelson Fowler (or was it Sizer?) there.

And who remembers the renown'd New York "Tabernacle" of those days "before the war"? It was on the east side of Broadway, near Pearl street—was a great turtle-shaped hall, and you had to walk back from the street entrance, thro' a long wide corridor to get to it—was very strong—had an immense gallery—altogether held three or four thousand people. Here the huge annual conventions of the windy and cyclonic "reformatory societies" of those times were held—especially the tumultuous Anti-Slavery ones. I remember hearing Wendell Phillips, Emerson, Cassius Clay, John P. Hale, Beecher, Fred Douglas, the Burleighs, Garrison, and others. Sometimes the Hutchinsons would sing—very fine. Sometimes there were angry rows. A chap named Isaiah Rhynders, a fierce politician of those days, with a band of robust supporters, would attempt to contradict the speakers and break up the meetings. But the Anti-Slavery, and Quaker, and Temperance, and Missionary and other conventicles and speakers were tough, tough, and always maintained their ground, and carried out their programs fully. I went frequently to these meetings, May after May—learn'd much from them—was sure to be on hand when J. P. Hale or Cash Clay made speeches.

There were also the smaller and handsome halls of the Historical and Athenæum Societies up on Broadway. I very well remember W. C. Bryant lecturing on Homœopathy in one of them, and attending two or three addresses by R. W. Emerson in the other.

There was a series of plays and dramatic *genre* characters by a gentleman bill'd as Ranger—very fine, better than merely technical, full of exquisite shades, like the light touches of the violin in the hands of a master. There was the actor Anderson, who brought us Gerald Griffin's "Gisippus," and play'd it to admiration. Among the actors of those times I recall: Cooper, Wallack, Tom Hamblin, Adams (several), Old Gates, Scott, Wm. Sefton, John Sefton, Geo. Jones, Mitchell, Seguin, Old Clarke, Richings, Fisher, H. Placide, T. Placide, Thorne, Ingersoll, Gale (Mazeppa) Edwin, Horncastle. Some of the women hastily remember'd were: Mrs. Vernon, Mrs. Pritchard, Mrs. McClure, Mary Taylor, Clara Fisher, Mrs. Richardson, Mrs. Flynn. Then the singers, English, Italian and other: Mrs. Wood, Mrs. Seguin, Mrs. Austin, Grisi, La Grange, Steffanone, Bosio, Truffi, Parodi, Vestvali, Bertucca, Jenny Lind, Gazzaniga, Laborde. And the opera men: Bettini, Badiali, Marini, Mario, Brignoli, Amodio, Beneventano, and many, many others whose names I do not at this moment recall.

In another paper I have described the elder Booth, and the Bowery Theatre of those times. Afterward there was the Chatham. The elder Thorne, Mrs. Thorne, William and John Sefton, Kirby, Brougham, and sometimes Edwin Forrest himself play'd there. I remember them all, and many more, and especially the fine theatre on Broadway near Pearl, in 1855 and '6.

There were very good circus performances, or horsemanship, in New York and Brooklyn. Every winter in the first-named city, a regular place in the Bowery, nearly opposite the old theatre; fine animals and fine riding, which I often witness'd. (Remember seeing near here, a young, fierce, splendid lion, presented by an African Barbary Sultan to President Andrew Jackson. The gift comprised also a lot of jewels, a fine steel sword, and an Arab stallion; and the lion was made over to a show-man.)

If it is worth while I might add that there was a small but well-appointed amateur-theatre up Broadway, with the usual stage, orchestra, pit, boxes, &c., and that I was myself a member for some time, and acted parts in it several times—"second parts" as they were call'd. Perhaps it too was a lesson, or help'd that way; at any rate it was full of fun and enjoyment.

And so let us turn off the gas. Out in the brilliancy of the footlights—filling the attention of perhaps a crowded audience, and making many a breath and pulse swell and rise—O so much passion and imparted life!—over and over again, the season through—walking, gesticulating, singing, reciting his or her part—But then sooner or later inevitably wending to the flies or exit door—vanishing to sight and ear—and never materializing on this earth's stage again!

SOME PERSONAL AND OLD-AGE JOTTINGS

ANYTHING like unmitigated acceptance of my *Leaves of Grass* book, and heart-felt response to it, in a popular however faint degree, bubbled forth as a fresh spring from the ground in England in 1876. The time was a critical and turning point in my personal and literary life. Let me revert to my memorandum book, Camden, New Jersey, that year, fill'd with addresses, receipts, purchases, &c., of the two volumes pub'd then by myself—the *Leaves,* and the *Two Rivulets*—some home customers for them, but mostly from the British Islands. I was seriously paralyzed from the Secession war, poor, in debt, was expecting death, (the doctors put four chances out of five against me,)—and I had the books printed during the lingering interim to occupy the tediousness of glum days and nights. Curiously, the sale abroad proved prompt, and what one might call copious: the names came in lists and the money with them, by foreign mail. The price was $10 a set. Both the cash and the emotional cheer were deep medicines; many paid double or treble price, (Tennyson and Ruskin did,) and many sent kind and eulogistic letters; ladies, clergymen, social leaders, persons of rank, and high officials.

Those blessed gales from the British Islands probably (certainly) saved me. Here are some of the names, for I w'd like to preserve them: Wm. M. and D. G. Rossetti, Lord Houghton, Edwd. Dowden, Mrs. Ann Gilchrist, Keningale Cook, Edwd. Carpenter, Therese Simpson, Rob't Buchanan, Alfred Tennyson, John Ruskin, C. G. Oates, E. T. Wilkinson, T. L. Warren, C. W. Reynell, W. B. Scott, A. G. Dew Smith, E. W. Gosse, T. W. Rolleston, Geo. Wallis, Rafe Leicester, Thos. Dixon, N. MacColl, Mrs. Matthews, R. Hannah, Geo. Saintsbury, R. S. Watson, Godfrey and Vernon Lushington, G. H. Lewes, G. H. Boughton, Geo. Fraser, W. T. Arnold, A. Ireland, Mrs. M. Taylor, M. D. Conway, Benj. Eyre, E. Dannreather, Rev. T. E. Brown, C. W. Sheppard, E. J. A. Balfour, P. B. Marston, A. C. De Burgh, J. H. McCarthy, J. H. Ingram, Rev. R. P. Graves, Lady Mount-temple, F. S. Ellis, W. Brockie, Rev. A. B. Grosart, Lady Hardy, Hubert Herkomer, Francis Hueffer, H. G. Dakyns, R. L. Nettleship, W. J. Stillman, Miss Blind, Madox Brown, H. R. Ricardo, Messrs. O'Grady and Tyrrel; and many, many more.

Severely scann'd, it was perhaps no very great or vehement success; but the tide had palpably shifted at any rate, and the sluices were turn'd into my own veins and pockets. That emotional, audacious, open-handed, friendly-mouth'd just-opportune English action, I say, pluck'd me like a brand from the burning, and gave me life again, to finish my book, since ab't completed. I do not forget it, and shall not; and if I ever have a biographer I charge him to put it in the narrative. I have had the noblest friends and backers in America; Wm. O'Connor, Dr. R. M. Bucke, John Burroughs, Geo. W. Childs, good ones in Boston, and Carnegie and R. G. Ingersoll in New York; and yet perhaps the tenderest and gratefulest breath of my heart has gone, and ever goes, over the sea-gales across the big pond.

About myself at present. I will soon enter upon my 73d year, if I live—have pass'd an active life, as country school-teacher, gardener, printer, carpenter, author and journalist, domicil'd in nearly all the United States and principal cities, North and South—went to the front (moving about and occupied as army nurse and missionary) during the Secession war, 1861 to '65, and in the Virginia hospitals and after the battles of that time, tending the Northern and Southern wounded alike—work'd down South and in Washington city arduously three years—contracted the paralysis which I have suffer'd ever since—and now live in a little cottage of my own, near the Delaware in New Jersey. My chief book, unrhym'd and unmetrical (it has taken thirty years, peace and war, "a borning") has its aim as once said, "to utter the same old human *critter*—but now in Democratic American modern and scientific conditions." Then I have publish'd two prose works "Specimen Days," and a late one "November Boughs." (A little volume "Good-Bye my Fancy" is soon to be out, wh' will finish the matter.) I do not propose here to enter the much-fought field of the literary criticism of any of those works.

But for a few portraiture or descriptive bits. To-day in the upper of a little wooden house of two stories near the Delaware river, east shore, sixty miles up from the sea, is a rather large 20-by-20 low ceiling'd room something like a big old ship's cabin. The floor, three quarters of it with an ingrain carpet, is half cover'd by a deep litter of books, papers, magazines, thrown-down letters and circulars, rejected manuscripts, memoranda, bits of light or strong twine, a bundle to be "express'd," and two or three venerable scrap books. In the room stand two large tables (one of ancient St. Domingo mahogany with immense leaves) cover'd by a jumble of more papers, a varied and copious array of writing materials, several glass and china vessels or jars, some with cologne-water, others with real honey, granulated sugar, a large bunch of beautiful fresh yellow chrysanthemums, some letters and envelopt papers ready for the post office, many photographs, and a hundred indescribable things besides. There are all around many books, some quite handsome editions, some half cover'd by dust, some within reach, evidently used, (good-sized print, no type less than long primer,) some maps, the Bible, (the strong cheap edition of the English crown,) Homer, Shakspere, Walter Scott, Emerson, Ticknor's "Spanish Literature," John Carlyle's Dante, Felton's Greece, George Sand's Consuelo, a very choice little Epictetus, some novels, the latest foreign and American monthlies, quarterlies, and so on. There being quite a strew of printer's proofs and slips, and the daily papers, the place with its quaint old fashion'd calmness has also a smack of something alert and of current work. There are several trunks and depositaries back'd up at the walls; (one well-bound and big box came by express lately from Washington city, after storage there for nearly twenty years.) Indeed the whole room is a sort of result and storage collection of my own past life. I have here various editions of my own writings, and sell them upon request; one is a big volume of complete poems and prose, 1000 pages, autograph, essays, speeches, portraits from life, &c. Another is a little *Leaves of Grass,* latest date, six portraits, morocco bound, in pocket-book form.

Fortunately the apartment is quite roomy. There are three windows in front. At one side is the stove, with a cheerful fire of oak wood, near by a good supply of fresh sticks, whose faint aroma is plain. On another side is the bed with white coverlid and woollen blankets. Toward the windows is a huge arm-chair, (a Christmas present from Thomas Donaldson's young daughter and son, Philadelphia) timber'd as by some stout ship's spars, yellow polish'd, ample, with rattan-woven seat and back, and over the latter a great wide wolf-skin of hairy black and silver, spread to guard against cold and draught. A time-worn look and scent of old oak attach both to the chair and the person occupying it.

But probably (even at the charge of parrot talk) I can give no more authentic brief sketch than "from an old remembrance copy," where I have lately put myself on record as follows: Was born May 31, 1819, in my father's farm-house, at West Hills, L. I., New York State. My parents' folks mostly farmers and sailors—on my father's side, of English—on my mother's, (Van Velsor's) from Hollandic immigration. There was, first and last, a large family of children; (I was the second.) We moved to Brooklyn while I was still a little one in frocks—and there in B. I grew up out of frocks—then as child and boy went to the public schools—then to work in a printing office. When only sixteen or seventeen years old, and for three years afterward, I went to teaching country schools down in Queens and Suffolk counties, Long Island, and "boarded round." Then, returning to New York, work'd as printer and writer, (with an occasional shy at "poetry.")

1848–'9.—About this time—after ten or twelve years of experiences and work and lots of fun in New York and Brooklyn—went off on a leisurely journey and working expedition (my brother Jeff with me) through all the Middle States, and down the Ohio and Mississippi rivers. Lived a while in New Orleans, and work'd there. (Have lived quite a good deal in the Southern States.) After a time, plodded back northward, up the Mississippi, the Missouri, &c., and around to, and by way of, the great lakes, Michigan, Huron and Erie, to Niagara Falls and Lower Canada—finally returning through Central New York, and down the Hudson. 1852–'54—Occupied in house-building in Brooklyn. (For a little while of the first part of that time in printing a daily and weekly paper.)

1855.—Lost my dear father this year by death. . . . Commenced putting *Leaves of Grass* to press, for good—after many MSS. doings and undoings—(I had great trouble in leaving out the stock "poetical" touches—but succeeded at last.) The book has since had some eight hitches or stages of growth, with one annex, (and another to come out in 1891, which will complete it.)

1862.—In December of this year went down to the field of war in Virginia. My brother George reported badly wounded in the Fredericksburg fight. (For 1863 and '64, see *Specimen Days.*) 1865 to '71—Had a place as clerk (till well on in '73) in the Attorney General's Office, Washington. (New York and Brooklyn seem more like *home,* as I was born near, and brought up in them, and lived, man and boy, for 30 years. But I lived some years in Washington, and have visited, and partially lived, in most of the Western and Eastern cities.)

1873.—This year lost, by death, my dear dear mother—and, just before, my sister Martha—the two best and sweetest women I have ever seen or known, or ever expect to see. Same year, February, a sudden climax and prostration from paralysis. Had been simmering inside for several years; broke out during those times temporarily, and then went over. But now a serious attack, beyond cure. Dr. Drinkard, my Washington physician, (and a first-rate one,) said it was the result of too extreme bodily and emotional strain continued at Washington and "down in front," in 1863, '4 and '5. I doubt if a heartier, stronger, healthier physique, more balanced upon itself, or more unconscious, more sound, ever lived, from 1835 to '72. My greatest call (Quaker) to go around and do what I could there in those war-scenes where I had fallen, among the sick and wounded, was, that I seem'd to be *so strong and well.* (I consider'd myself invulnerable.) But this last attack shatter'd me completely. Quit work at Washington, and moved to Camden, New Jersey—where I have lived since, receiving many buffets and some precious caresses—and now write these lines. Since then, (1874–'91) a long stretch of illness, or half-illness, with occasional lulls. During these latter, have revised and printed over all my books—Bro't out "November Boughs"—and at intervals leisurely and exploringly travel'd to the Prairie States, the Rocky Mountains, Canada, to New York, to my birthplace in Long Island, and to Boston. But physical disability and the war-paralysis above alluded to have settled upon me more and more, the last year or so. Am now (1891) domicil'd, and have been for some years, in this little old cottage and lot in Mickle Street, Camden, with a house-keeper and man nurse. Bodily I am completely disabled, but still write for publication. I keep generally buoyant spirits, write often as there comes any lull in physical sufferings, get in the sun and down to the river whenever I can, retain fair appetite, assimilation and digestion, sensibilities acute as ever, the strength and volition of my right arm good, eyesight dimming, but brain normal, and retain my heart's and soul's unmitigated faith not only in their own original literary plans, but in the essential bulk of American humanity east and west, north and south, city and country, through thick and thin, to the last. Nor must I forget, in conclusion, a special, prayerful, thankful God's blessing to my dear firm friends and personal helpers, men and women, home and foreign, old and young.

From the Camden Post, April 16, '91.

OUT IN THE OPEN AGAIN

WALT WHITMAN got out in the mid-April sun and warmth of yesterday, propelled in his wheel chair, the first time after four months of imprisonment in his sick room. He has had the worst winter yet, mainly from grippe and gastric troubles, and threaten'd blindness; but keeps good spirits, and has a new little forthcoming book in the printer's hands.

AMERICA'S BULK AVERAGE

IF I were ask'd *persona* to specify the one point of America's people on which I mainly rely, I should say the final average or bulk quality of the whole.

Happy indeed w'd I consider myself to give a fair reflection and representation of even a portion of shows, questions, humanity, events, unfoldings, thoughts, &c. &c. my age in these States.

The great social, political, historic function of my time has been of course the attempted Secession War.

And was there not something grand, and an inside proof of perennial grandeur, in that war! We talk of our age's and the States' materialism—and it is too true. But how amid the whole sordidness—the entire devotion of America, at any price, to pecuniary success, merchandise—disregarding all but business and profit—this war for a bare idea and abstraction—a mere, at bottom, heroic dream and reminiscence—burst forth in its great devouring flame and conflagration quickly and fiercely spreading and raging, and enveloping all, defining in two conflicting ideas—first the Union cause—second *the other,* a strange deadly interrogation point, hard to define—Can we not now safely confess it? with magnificent rays, streaks of noblest heroism, fortitude, perseverance, and even conscientiousness, through its pervadingly malignant darkness.

What an area and rounded field, upon the whole—the spirit, arrogance, grim tenacity of the South—the long stretches of murky gloom—the general National Will below and behind and comprehending all—not once really wavering, not a day, not an hour—What could be, or ever can be, grander?

As in that war, its four years—as through the whole history and development of the New World—these States through all trials, processes, eruptions, deepest dilemmas, (often straining, tugging at society's heart-strings, as if some divine curiosity would find out how much this democracy could stand,) have so far finally and for more than a century best justified themselves by the average impalpable quality and personality of the bulk, the People *en masse*. . . . I am not sure but my main and chief however indefinite claim for any page of mine w'd be its derivation, or seeking to derive itself, f'm that average quality of the American bulk, the people, and getting back to it again.

LAST SAVED ITEMS

f'm a vast batch left to oblivion.

IN its highest aspect, and striking its grandest average, essential Poetry expresses and goes along with essential Religion—has been and is more the adjunct, and more serviceable to that true religion (for of course there is a false one and plenty of it,) than all the priests and creeds and churches that now exist or have ever existed—Even while the temporary prevalent theory and practice of poetry is merely one-side and ornamental and dainty—a love-sigh, a bit of jewelry, a feudal conceit, an ingenious tale or intellectual *finesse,* adjusted to the low taste and calibre that will always sufficiently generally prevail—(ranges of stairs necessary to ascend the higher.)

The sectarian, church and doctrinal, follies, crimes, fanaticisms, aggregate and individual, so rife all thro' history, are proofs of the radicalness and universality of the indestructible element of humanity's Religion, just as much as any, and are the other side of it. Just as disease proves health, and is the other side of it. . . . . The philosophy of Greece taught normality and the beauty of life. Christianity teaches how to endure illness and death. I have wonder'd whether a third philosophy fusing both, and doing full justice to both, might not be outlined.

It will not be enough to say that no Nation ever achiev'd materialistic, political and money-making successes, with general physical comfort, as fully as the United States of America are to-day achieving them. I know very well that those are the indispensable foundations—the *sine qua non* of moral and heroic (poetic) fruitions to come. For if those pre-successes were all—if they ended at that—if nothing more were yielded than so far appears—a gross materialistic prosperity only—America, tried by subtlest tests, were a failure—has not advanced the standard of humanity a bit further than other nations. Or, in plain terms, has but inherited and enjoy'd the results of ordinary claims and preceding ages.

Nature seem'd to use me a long while—myself all well able, strong and happy—to portray power, freedom, health. But after a while she seems to fancy, may-be I can see and understand it all better by being deprived of most of those.

How difficult it is to add anything more to literature—and how unsatisfactory for any earnest spirit to serve merely the amusement of the multitude! (It even seems to me, said H. Heine, more invigorating to accomplish something bad than something empty.)

The Highest said: Don't let us begin so low—isn't our range too coarse—too gross? . . . . The Soul answer'd: No, not when we consider what it is all for—the end involved in Time and Space.

Essentially my own printed records, all my volumes, are doubtless but off-hand utterances f'm Personality, spontaneous, following implicitly the inscrutable command, dominated by that Personality, vaguely even if decidedly, and with little or nothing of plan, art, erudition, &c. If I have chosen to hold the reins, the mastery, it has mainly been to give the way, the power, the road, to the invisible steeds. (I wanted to see how a Person of America, the last half of the 19th century, w'd appear, put quite freely and fairly in honest type.)

Haven't I given specimen clues, if no more? At any rate I have written enough to weary myself—and I will dispatch it to the printers, and cease. But how much—how many topics, of the greatest point and cogency, I am leaving untouch'd!

SUPPLEMENTARY PROSE

Contents

Supplementary Prose

The Eighteenth Presidency!

Voice of Walt Whitman to each Young Man in the Nation, North, South, East, and West

FIRST, WHO ARE THE NATION?

Before the American era, the programme of the classes of a nation read thus, first the king, second the noblemen and gentry, third the great mass of mechanics, farmers, men following the water, and all laboring persons. The first and second classes are unknown to the theory of the government of These States; the likes of the class rated third on the old programme were intended to be, and are in fact, and to all intents and purposes, the American nation, the people.

Mechanics, farmers, sailors, &c., constitute some six millions of the inhabitants of These States; merchants, lawyers, doctors, teachers, and priests, count up as high as five hundred thousand; the owners of slaves number three hundred and fifty thousand; the population of The States being altogether about thirty millions, seven tenths of whom are women and children. At present, the personnel of the government of these thirty millions, in executives and elsewhere, is drawn from limber-tongued lawyers, very fluent but empty, feeble old men, professional politicians, dandies, dyspeptics, and so forth, and rarely drawn from the solid body of the people; the effects now seen, and more to come. Of course the fault, if it be a fault, is for reasons, and is of the people themselves, and will mend when it should mend.

HAS MUCH BEEN DONE IN THE THEORY OF THESE STATES?

Very good; more remains. Who is satisfied with the theory, or a parade of the theory? I say, delay not, come quickly to its most courageous facts and illustrations. I say no body of men are fit to make Presidents, Judges, and Generals, unless they themselves supply the best specimens of the same, and that supplying one or two such specimens illuminates the whole body for a thousand years.

I expect to see the day when the like of the present personnel of the governments, federal, state, municipal, military, and naval, will be looked upon with derision, and when qualified mechanics and young men will reach Congress and other official stations, sent in their working costumes, fresh from their benches and tools, and returning to them again with dignity. The young fellows must prepare to do credit to this destiny, for the stuff is in them. Nothing gives place, recollect, and never ought to give place except to its clean superiors. There is more rude and undeveloped bravery, friendship, conscientiousness, clear-sightedness, and practical genius for any scope of action, even the broadest and highest, now among the American mechanics and young men, than in all the official persons in These States, legislative, executive, judicial, military, and naval, and more than among all the literary persons. I would be much pleased to see some heroic, shrewd, fully-informed, healthy-bodied, middle-aged, beard-faced American blacksmith or boatman come down from the West across the Alleghanies, and walk into the Presidency, dressed in a clean suit of working attire, and with the tan all over his face, breast, and arms; I would certainly vote for that sort of man, possessing the due requirements, before any other candidate. Such is the thought that must become familiar to you, whoever you are, and to the people of These States; and must eventually take shape in action.

At present, we are environed with nonsense under the name of respectability. Everywhere lowers that stifling atmosphere that makes all the millions of farmers and mechanics of These States and helpless supple-jacks of a comparatively few politicians. Somebody must make a bold push. The people, credulous, generous, deferential, allow the American government to be managed in many respects as is only proper under the personnel of a king and hereditary lords; or, more truly, not proper under any decent men anywhere. If this were to go on, we ought to change the title of the President, and issue patents of nobility. Of course it is not to go on; the Americans are no fools. I perceive meanwhile that nothing less than marked inconsistencies and usurpations will arouse a nation, and make ready for better things afterwards.

BUT WHAT AILS THE PRESENT WAY OF FILLING THE OFFICES OF THE STATES? IS IT NOT GOOD ENOUGH?

I should say it was not. To-day, of all the persons in public office in These States, not one in a thousand has been chosen by any spontaneous movement of the people, nor is attending to the interests of the people; all have been nominated and put through by great or small caucuses of the politicians, or appointed as rewards for electioneering; and all consign themselves to personal and party interests. Neither in the Presidency, nor in Congress, nor in the foreign ambassadorships, nor in the governorships of The States, nor in legislatures, nor in the mayoralities of cities, nor the aldermanships, nor among the police, nor on the benches of judges, do I observe a single bold, muscular, young, well-informed, well-beloved, resolute American man, bound to do a man's duty, aloof from all parties, and with a manly scorn of all parties. Instead of that, every trustee of the people is a traitor, looking only to his own gain, and to boost up his party. The berths, the Presidency included, are bought, sold, electioneered for, prostituted, and filled with prostitutes. In the North and East, swarms of dough-faces, office-vermin, kept-editors, clerks, attaches of the ten thousand officers and their parties, aware of nothing further than the drip and spoil of politics—ignorant of principles, the true glory of a man. In the South, no end of blusterers, braggarts, windy, melodramatic, continually screaming in falsetto, a nuisance to These States, their own just as much as any; altogether the most impudent persons that have yet appeared in the history of lands, and with the most incredible successes, having pistol'd, bludgeoned, yelled and threatened America, the past twenty years into one long train of cowardly concessions, and still not through, but rather at the commencement. Their cherished secret scheme is to dissolve the union of These States.

WELL, WHAT MORE?

Is nothing but breed upon breed like these to be represented in the Presidency? Are parties to forever usurp the government? Are lawyers, dough-faces, and the three hundred and fifty thousand owners of slaves, to sponge the mastership of thirty millions? Where is the real America? Where are the laboring persons, ploughmen, men with axes, spades, scythes, flails? Where are the carpenters, masons, machinists, drivers of horses, workmen in factories? Where is the spirit of the manliness and common-sense of These States? It does not appear in the government. It does not appear at all in the Presidency.

LESSON OF THE SIXTEENTH AND SEVENTEENTH TERMS OF THE PRESIDENCY.

The sixteenth and seventeenth terms of the American Presidency have shown that the villainy and shallowness of great rulers are just as eligible to These States as to any foreign despotism, kingdom, or empire—there is not a bit of difference. History is to record these two Presidencies as so far our topmost warning and shame. Never were publicly displayed more deformed, mediocre, snivelling, unreliable, false-hearted men! Never were These States so insulted, and attempted to be betrayed! All the main purposes for which the government was established are openly denied. The perfect equality of slavery with freedom is flauntingly preached in the North—nay, the superiority of slavery. The slave trade is proposed to be renewed. Everywhere frowns and misunderstandings—everywhere exasperations and humiliations. The President eats dirt and excrement for his daily meals, likes it, and tries to force it on The States. The cushions of the Presidency are nothing but filth and blood. The pavements of Congress are also bloody. The land that flushed amazed at the basest outrage of our times, grows pale with a far different feeling to see the outrage unanimously commended back again to those who only half rejected it. The national tendency toward populating the territories full of free work-people, established by the organic compacts of These States, promulged by the fathers, the Presidents, the old warriors, and the earlier Congresses, a tendency vital to the life and thrift of the masses of the citizens, is violently put back under the feet of slavery, and against the free people the masters of slaves are everywhere held up by the President by the red hand. In fifteen of The States the three hundred and fifty thousand masters keep down the true people, the millions of white citizens, mechanics, farmers, boatmen, manufacturers, and the like, excluding them from politics and from office, and punishing by the lash, by tar and feathers, binding fast to rafts on the rivers or trees in the woods, and sometimes by death, all attempts to discuss the evils of slavery in its relations to the whites. The people of the territories are denied the power to form State governments unless they consent to fasten upon them the slave-hopple, the iron wristlet, and the neck-spike. For refusing such consent, the governor and part of the legislature of the State of Kansas are chased, seized, chained, by the creatures of the President, and are to-day in chains. Over the vast continental tracts of unorganized American territory, equal in extent to all the present organized States, and in future to give the law to all, the whole executive, judicial, military and naval power of These States is foresworn to the people, the rightful owners, and sworn to the help of the three hundred and fifty thousand masters of slaves, to put them through this continent, with their successors, at their pleasure, and to maintain by force their mastership over their slave men and women, slave-farmers, slave-miners, slave-blacksmiths, slave-carpenters, slave-cartmen, slave-sailors, and the like. Slavery is adopted as an American institution, superior, national, constitutional, right in itself, and under no circumstances to take any less than freedom takes. Nor is that all; to-day, to-night, the constables and commissioners of the President can by law step into any part of These States and pick out whom they please, deciding which man or woman they will allow to be free, and which shall be a slave, no jury to intervene, but the commissioner's mandate to be enforced by the federal troops and cannon, and has been actually so enforced.

ARE THE STATES RETARDED THEN?

No; while all is drowned and desperate that the government has had to do with, all outside the influence of government, (for ever the largest part,) thrives and smiles. The sun shines, corn grows, men go merrily about their affairs, houses are built, ships arrive and depart. Through evil and through good, the republic stands, and is for centuries yet to stand, immovable from its foundations. No, no; out of dastards and disgraces, fortunate are the wrongs that call forth stout and angry men; then is shown what stuff there is in a nation.

The young genius of America is not going to be emasculated and strangled just as it arrives toward manly age. It shall live, and yet baffle the politicians and the three hundred and fifty thousand masters of slaves.

NOMINEES OF THE POLITICIANS.

Now the term of the seventeenth Presidency passing hooted and spurned to its close, the delegates of the politicians have nominated for the eighteenth term, Buchanan of Pennsylvania, and Fillmore of New York, separate tickets, but men both patterned to follow and match the seventeenth term, both disunionists, both old politicians, both sworn down to the theories of special parties, and of all others the theories that balk and reverse the main purposes of the founders of These States. Such are the nominees that have arisen out of the power of the politicians; but another power has also arisen.

COUNTERACTION OF A NEW RACE OF YOUNG MEN.

A new race copiously appears, with resolute tread, soon to confront Presidents, Congresses and parties, to look them sternly in the face, to stand no nonsense; American young men, the offspring and proof of These States, the West the same as the East, and the South alike with the North.

America sends these young men in good time, for they were needed. Much waits to be done. First, people need to realize who are poisoning the politics of These States.

WHENCE THE DELEGATES OF THE POLITICIANS? WHENCE THE BUCHANAN AND FILLMORE CONVENTIONS?

Not from sturdy American freemen; not from industrious homes; not from thrifty farms; not from the ranks of fresh-bodied young men; not from among teachers, poets, savans, learned persons, beloved persons, temperate persons; not from among ship-builders, engineers, agriculturists, scythe-swingers, corn-hoers; not from the race of mechanics; not from that great strong stock of Southerners that supplied the land in old times; not from the real West, the log-hut, the clearing, the woods, the prairie, the hill-side; not from the sensible, generous, rude Californian miners; nor from the best specimens of Massachusetts, Maine, New Jersey, Pennsylvania, Ohio, Illinois, Wisconsin, Indiana, nor from the untainted unpolitical citizens of the cities.

WHENCE THEN DO THESE NOMINATING DICTATORS OF AMERICA YEAR AFTER YEAR START OUT?

From lawyers' offices, secret lodges, back-yards, bed-houses, and bar-rooms; from out of the custom-houses, marshals' offices, post-offices, and gambling hells; from the President's house, the jail, the venereal hospital, the station-house; from unnamed by-places where devilish disunion is hatched at midnight; from political hearses, and from the coffins inside, and from the shrouds inside of the coffins; from the tumors and abscesses of the land; from the skeletons and skulls in the vaults of the federal almshouses; from the running sores of the great cities; thence to the national, state, city, and district nominating conventions of These States, come the most numerous and controlling delegates.

WHO ARE THEY PERSONALLY?

Office-holders, office-seekers, robbers, pimps, exclusives, malignants, conspirators, murderers, fancy-men, post-masters, custom-house clerks, contractors, kept-editors, spaniels well-trained to carry and fetch, jobbers, infidels, disunionists, terrorists, mail-riflers, slave-catchers, pushers of slavery, creatures of the President, creatures of would-be Presidents, spies, blowers, electioneerers, body-snatchers, bawlers, bribers, compromisers, runaways, lobbyers, sponges, ruined sports, expelled gamblers, policy backers, monte-dealers, duelists, carriers of concealed weapons, blind men, deaf men, pimpled men, scarred inside with the vile disorder, gaudy outside with gold chains made from the people's money and harlot's money twisted together; crawling, serpentine men, the lousy combings and born freedom sellers of the earth.

STRIPT OF PADDING AND PAINT, WHO ARE BUCHANAN AND FILLMORE? WHAT HAS THIS AGE TO DO WITH THEM?

Two galvanized old men, close on the summons to depart this life, their early contemporaries long since gone, only they two left, relics and proofs of the little political bargains, chances, combinations, resentments of a past age, having nothing in common with this age, standing for the first crop of political graves and grave-stones planted in These States, but in no sort standing for the lusty young growth of the modern times of The States. It is clear from all these two men say and do, that their hearts have not been touched in the least by the flowing fire of the humanitarianism of the new world, its best glory yet, and a moral control stronger than all its governments. It is clear that neither of these nominees of the politicians has thus far reached an inkling of the real scope and character of the contest of the day, probably now only well begun, to stretch through years, with varied temporary successes and reverses. Still the two old men live in respectable little spots, with respectable little wants. Still their eyes stop at the edges of the tables of committees and cabinets, beholding not the great round world beyond. What has this age to do with them?

You Americans who travel with such men, or who are nominated on tickets any where with them, or who support them at popular meetings, or write for them in the newspapers, or who believe that any good can come out of them, you also understand not the present age, the fibre of it, the countless currents it brings of American young men, a different superior race. All this effervescence is not for nothing; the friendlier, vaster, more vital modern spirit, hardly yet arrived at definite proportions, or to the knowledge of itself, will have the mastery. The like turmoil prevails in the expressions of literature, manners, trade, and other departments.

TO BUTCHERS, SAILORS, STEVEDORES, AND DRIVERS OF HORSES—TO PLOUGHMEN, WOOD-CUTTERS, MARKETMEN, CARPENTERS, MASONS, AND LABORERS—TO WORKMEN IN FACTORIES—AND TO ALL IN THESE STATES WHO LIVE BY THEIR DAILY TOIL.

Mechanics! A parcel of windy northern liars are bawling in your ears the easily-spoken words Democracy and the democratic party. Others are making a great ado with the word Americanism, a solemn and great word. What the so-called democracy are now sworn to perform would eat the faces off the succeeding generations of common people worse than the most horrible disease. The others are contributing to the like performance, and are using the great word Americanism without yet feeling the first aspiration of it, as the great word Religion has been used, probably loudest and oftenest used, by men that made indiscriminate massacres at night, and filled the world so full with hatreds, horrors, partialities, exclusions, bloody revenges, penal conscience laws and test-oaths. To the virtue of Americanism is happening to-day, what happens many days to many virtues, namely, the masses who possess them but do not understand them are sought to be sold by that very means to those who neither possess them nor understand them. What are the young men suspicious of? I will tell them what it stands them in hand to be suspicious of, and that is American craft; it is subtler than Italian craft; I guess it is about the subtlest craft upon the earth.

WHAT IS THERE IN PROSPECT FOR FREE FARMERS AND WORK PEOPLE?

A few generations ago, the general run of farmers and work-people like us were slaves, serfs, deprived of their liberty by law; they are still so deprived on some parts of the continent of Europe. To-day, those who are free here, and free in the British islands and elsewhere, are free through deeds that were done, and men that lived, some of them an age or so ago, and some of them many ages ago. The men and deeds of these days also decide for generations ahead, as past men and deeds decided for us.

As the broad fat States of The West, the largest and best parts of the inheritance of the American farmers and mechanics, were ordained to common people and workmen long in advance by Jefferson, Washington, and the earlier Congresses, now a far ampler west is to be ordained. Is it to be ordained to workmen, or to the masters of workmen? Shall the future mechanics of America be serfs? Shall labor be degraded, and women be whipt in the fields for not performing their tasks? If slaves are not prohibited from all national American territory by law, as prohibited in the beginning, as the organic compacts authorize and require, and if, on the contrary, the entrance and establishment of slave labor through the continent is secured, there will steadily wheel into this Union, for centuries to come, slave state after slave state, the entire surface of the land owned by great proprietors, in plantations of thousands of acres, showing no more sight for free races of farmers and work-people than there is now in any European despotism or aristocracy; and the existence of our present Free States put in jeopardy, because out of that vast territory are to come states enough to overbalance all.

Workmen! Workwomen! Those immense national American tracts belong to you; they are in trust with you; they are latent with the populous cities, numberless farms, herds, granaries, groves, golden gardens, and inalienable homesteads, of your successors. The base political blowers and kept-editors of the North are raising a fog of prevarications around you. But the manlier Southern disunionists, the chieftains among the three hundred and fifty thousand masters, clearly distinguish the issue, and the principle it rests upon. McDuffie, disunionist governor, lays it down with candid boldness that the workingmen of a state are unsafe depositaries of political powers and rights, and that a republic can not permanently exist unless those who ply the mechanical trades and attend to the farm-work are slaves, subordinated by strict laws to their masters. Calhoun, disunionist senator, denounces and denies, in the presence of the world, the main article of the organic compact of These States, that all men are born free and equal, and bequeaths to his followers, at present leaders of the three hundred and fifty thousand masters, guides of the so-called democracy, counsellors of Presidents, and getters-up of the nominations of Buchanan and Fillmore, his deliberate charge, to be carried out against that main article, that it is the most false and dangerous of all political errors; such being the words of that charge, spoken in the summer of the 73d year of These States, and, indeed, carried out since in the spirit of congressional legislation, executive action, and the candidates offered by the political parties to the people.

ARE NOT POLITICAL PARTIES ABOUT PLAYED OUT?

I say they are, all round. America has outgrown parties; henceforth it is too large, and they too small. They habitually make common cause just as soon in advocacy of the worst deeds and men as the best, or probably a little sooner for the worst. I place no reliance upon any old party, nor upon any new party. Suppose one to be formed under the noblest auspices, and getting into power with the noblest intentions, how long would it remain so? How many years? Would it remain so one year? As soon as it becomes successful, and there are offices to be bestowed, the politicians leave the unsuccessful parties, and rush toward it, and it ripens and rots with the rest.

WHAT RIGHT HAS ANY ONE POLITICAL PARTY, NO MATTER WHICH, TO WIELD THE AMERICAN GOVERNMENT?

No right at all. Not the so-called democratic, not abolition, opposition to foreigners, nor any other party, should be permitted the exclusive use of the Presidency; and every American young man must have sense enough to comprehend this. I have said the old parties are defunct; but there remains of them empty flesh, putrid mouths, mumbling and squeaking the tones of these conventions, the politicians standing back in shadow, telling lies, trying to delude and frighten the people; and nominating such candidates as Fillmore and Buchanan.

PARTY PLATFORMS, SECTIONS, CREEDS.

What impudence! for any one platform, section, creed, no matter which, to expect to subordinate all the rest, and rule the immense diversity of These free and equal States! Platforms are of no account. The right man is every thing. With the downfall of parties go the platforms they are forever putting up, lowering, turning, repainting, and changing.

THE UNCHANGEABLE AMERICAN PLATFORMS.

The platforms for the Presidency of These States are simply the organic compacts of The States, the Declaration of Independence, the Federal Constitution, the action of the earlier Congresses, the spirit of the fathers and warriors, the official lives of Washington, Jefferson, Madison, and the now well-understood and morally established rights of man, wherever the sun shines, the rain falls, and the grass grows.

THE FEDERAL CONSTITUTION.

Much babble will always be heard in the land about the Federal Constitution, this, that, and the other concerning it. The Federal Constitution is a perfect and entire thing, an edifice put together, not for the accommodation of a few persons, but for the whole human race; not for a day or a year, but for many years, perhaps a thousand, perhaps many thousand. Its architecture is not a single brick, a beam, an apartment, but only the whole. It is the grandest piece of moral building ever constructed; I believe its architects were some mighty prophets and gods. Few appreciate it, Americans just as few as any. Like all perfect works or persons, time only is great enough to give it area. Five or six centuries hence, it will be better understood from results, growths.

The Federal Constitution is the second of the American organic compacts. The premises, outworks, guard, defense, entrance of the Federal Constitution, is the primary compact of These States, sometimes called the Declaration of Independence; and the groundwork, feet, understratum of that again, is its deliberate engagement, in behalf of the States, thenceforward to consider all men to be born free and equal into the world, each one possessed of inalienable rights to his life and liberty, (namely, that no laws passed by any government could be considered to alienate or take away those born rights, the penalties upon criminals being, of course, for the very purpose of preserving those rights.) This is the covenant of the Republic from the beginning, now and forever. It is not a mere opinion; it is the most venerable pledge, with all the forms observed, signed by the commissioners, ratified by The States, and sworn to by Washington at the head of his army, with his hand upon the Bible. It is supreme over all American law, and greater than Presidents, Congresses, elections, and what not, for they hurry out of the way, but it remains. Above all, it is carefully to be observed in all that relates to the continental territories. When they are organized into States, it is to be passed over to the good faith of those States.

ONE OR TWO RADICAL PARTS OF THE AMERICAN THEORY OF GOVERNMENT.

Man can not hold property in man. As soon as there are clear-brained original American judges, this saying will be simplified by their judgments, and no State out of the whole confederacy but will confirm and approve those judgments.

Any one of These States is perfect mistress of itself; and each additional State the same. When States organize themselves, the Federal government withdraws, absolved from its duties, except certain specific ones under the Constitution, and only in behalf of them can it interfere in The States.

The true government is much simpler than is supposed, and abstains from much more. Nine tenths of the laws passed every winter at the Federal Capitol, and all the State Capitols, are not only unneeded laws, but positive nuisances, jobs got up for the service of special classes or persons.

Every rational uncriminal person, twenty-one years old, should be eligible to vote, on actual residence, no other requirement needed. The day will come when this will prevail.

The whole American government is itself simply a compact with each individual of the thirty millions of persons now inhabitants of These States, and prospectively with each individual of the hundred millions and five hundred millions that are in time to become inhabitants, to protect each one's life, liberty, industry, acquisitions, without excepting one single individual out of the whole number, and without making ignominious distinctions. Thus is government sublime; thus is it equal; otherwise it is a government of castes, on exactly the same principles with the kingdoms of Europe.

I said the national obligation is passed over to The States. Then if they are false to it, and impose upon certain persons, can the national government interfere? It can not, under any circumstances whatever. We must wait, no matter how long. There is no remedy, except in The State itself. A corner-stone of the organic compacts of America is that a State is perfect mistress of itself. If that is taken away, all the rest may just as well be taken away. When that is taken away, this Union is dissolved.

MUST RUNAWAY SLAVES BE DELIVERED BACK?

They must. Many things may have the go-by, but good faith shall never have the go-by.

By a section of the fourth article of the Federal Constitution, These States compact each with the other, that any person held to service or labor in one State under its laws, and escaping into another State, shall not be absolved from service by any law of that other State, but shall be delivered up to the persons to whom such service or labor is due. This part of the second organic compact between the original States should be carried out by themselves in their usual forms, but in spirit and in letter. Congress has no business to pass any law upon the subject, any more than upon the hundred other of the compacts between the States, left to be carried out by their good faith. Why should Congress pick out this particular one? I had quite as lief depend on the good faith of any of These States, as on the laws of Congress and the President. Good faith is irresistible among men, and friendship is; which lawyers can not understand, thinking nothing but compulsion will do.

But cannot that requirement of the fourth article of the Second Compact be evaded, on any plea whatever, even the plea of its unrighteousness? Nay, I perceive it is not to be evaded on any plea whatever, not even the plea of its unrighteousness. It should be observed by The States, in spirit and in letter, whether it is pleasant to them or unpleasant, beholding in it one item among many items, each of the rest as important as it, and each to be so carried out as not to contravene the rest. As to what is called the Fugitive Slave Law, insolently put over the people by their Congress and President, it contravenes the whole of the organic compacts, and is at all times to be defied in all parts of These States, South or North, by speech, by pen, and, if need be, by the bullet and the sword.

Shall we determine upon such things, then, and not leave them to the great judges and the scholars? Yes, it is best that we determine upon such things.

TO FREMONT, OF NEW YORK.

Whenever the day comes for him to appear, the man who shall be the Redeemer President of These States, is to be the one that fullest realizes the rights of individuals, signified by the impregnable rights of The States, the substratum of this Union. The Redeemer President of These States is not to be exclusive, but inclusive. In both physical and political America there is plenty of room for the whole human race; if not, more room can be provided.

TO THE AMERICAN YOUNG MEN, MECHANICS, FARMERS, BOATMEN, MANUFACTURERS, &C., OF VIRGINIA, DELAWARE, MARYLAND, THE CAROLINAS, KENTUCKY, TENNESSEE, GEORGIA, ALABAMA, FLORIDA, MISSISSIPPI, ARKANSAS, MISSOURI, LOUISIANA AND TEXAS.

How much longer do you intend to submit to the espionage and terrorism of the three hundred and fifty thousand owners of slaves? Are you too their slaves, and their most obedient slaves? Shall no one among you dare open his mouth to say he is opposed to slavery, as a man should be, on account of the whites, and wants it abolished for their sake? Is not a writer, speaker, teacher to be left alive, but those who lick up the spit that drops from the mouths of the three hundred and fifty thousand masters? Is there hardly one free, courageous soul left in fifteen large and populous States? Do the ranks of the owners of slaves themselves contain no men desperate and tired of that service and sweat of the mind, worse than any service in sugar-fields or corn-fields, under the eyes of overseers? Do the three hundred and fifty thousand expect to bar off forever all preachers, poets, philosophers—all that makes the brain of These States, free literature, free thought, the good old cause of liberty? Are they blind? Do they not see those unrelaxed circles of death narrowing and narrowing every hour around them?

You young men of the Southern States! is the word Abolitionist so hateful to you, then? Do you not know that Washington, Jefferson, Madison, and all the great Presidents and primal warriors and sages were declared abolitionists?

You young men! American mechanics, farmers, boatmen, manufacturers, and all work-people of the South, the same as the North! you are either to abolish slavery, or it will abolish you.

TO THE THREE HUNDRED AND FIFTY THOUSAND OWNERS OF SLAVES.

Suppose you get Kansas, do you think it would be ended? Suppose you and the politicians put Buchanan into the Eighteenth Presidency, or Fillmore into the Presidency, do you think it would be ended? I know nothing more desirable for those who contend against you than that you should get Kansas. Then would the melt begin in These States that would not cool till Kansas should be redeemed, as of course it would be.

O gentlemen, you do not know whom Liberty has nursed in These States, and depends on in time of need. You have not received any report of the Free States, but have received only the reports of the trustees who have betrayed the Free States. Do you suppose they will betray many thousand men, and stick at betraying a few men like you? Raised on plantations or in towns full of menial workmen and workwomen, you do not know, as I know, these fierce and turbulent races that fill the Northeast, the East, the West, the Northwest, the Pacific shores, the great cities, Manhattan Island, Brooklyn,

Newark, Boston, Worcester, Hartford, New Haven, Providence, Portland, Bangor, Augusta, Albany, Buffalo, Rochester, Syracuse, Lockport, Cleaveland, Detroit, Milwaukee, Racine, Sheboygan, Madison, Galena, Burlington, Iowa City, Chicago, St. Louis, Cincinnati, Columbus, Pittsburgh, Philadelphia, San Francisco, Sacramento, and many more. From my mouth hear the will of These States taking form in the great cities. Where slavery is, there it is. The American compacts, common sense, all things unite to make it the affair of the States diseased with it, to cherish the same as long as they see fit, and to apply the remedy when they see fit. But not one square mile of continental territory shall henceforward be given to slavery, to slaves, or to the masters of slaves—not one square foot. If any laws are passed giving up such territory, those laws will be repealed. In organizing the territories, what laws are good enough for the American freeman must be good enough for you; if you come in under the said laws, well and good; if not, stay away. What is done, is done; henceforth there is no further compromise. All this is now being cast in the stuff that makes the tough national resolves of These States, that every hour only anneals tougher. It is not that putty you see in Congress and in the Presidency; it is iron—it is the undissuadable swift metal of death.

TO EDITORS OF THE INDEPENDENT PRESS, AND TO RICH PERSONS.

Circulate and reprint this Voice of mine for the workingmen's sake. I hereby permit and invite any rich person, anywhere, to stereotype it, or re-produce it in any form, to deluge the cities of The States with it, North, South, East and West. It is those millions of mechanics you want; the writers, thinkers, learned and benevolent persons, merchants, are already secured almost to a man. But the great masses of the mechanics, and a large portion of the farmers, are unsettled, hardly know whom to vote for, or whom to believe. I am not afraid to say that among them I seek to initiate my name, Walt Whitman, and that I shall in future have much to say to them. I perceive that the best thoughts they have wait unspoken, impatient to be put in shape; also that the character, power, pride, friendship, conscience of America have yet to be proved to the remainder of the world.

THE WORLD'S PORTENTS, ISSUES, THE 80TH YEAR OF THESE STATES.

The times are full of great portents in These States and in the whole world. Freedom against slavery is not issuing here alone, but is issuing everywhere. The horizon rises, it divides I perceive, for a more august drama than any of the past. Old men have played their parts, the act suitable to them is closed, and if they will not withdraw voluntarily, must be bid to do so with unmistakeable voice. Landmarks of masters, slaves, kings, aristocracies, are moth-eaten, and the peoples of the earth are planting new vast landmarks for themselves. Frontiers and boundaries are less and less able to divide men. The modern inventions, the wholesale engines of war, the world-spreading instruments of peace, the steamship, the locomotive, the electric telegraph, the common newspaper, the cheap book, the ocean mail, are interlinking the inhabitants of the earth together as groups of one family—America standing, and for ages to stand, as the host and champion of the same, the most welcome spectacle ever presented among nations. Every thing indicates unparalleled reforms. Races are marching and countermarching by swift millions and tens of millions. Never was justice so mighty amid injustice; never did the idea of equality erect itself so haughty and uncompromising amid inequality, as to-day. Never were such sharp questions asked as to-day. Never was there more eagerness to know. Never was the representative man more energetic, more like a god, than to-day. He urges on the myriads before him, he crowds them aside, his daring step approaches the arctic and the antarctic poles, he colonizes the shores of the Pacific, the Asiatic Indias, the birthplace of languages and of races, the archipelagoes, Australia; he explores Africa, he unearths Assyria and Egypt, he re-states history, he enlarges morality, he speculates anew upon the soul, upon original premises; nothing is left quiet, nothing but he will settle by demonstrations for himself. What whispers are these running through the eastern continents, and crossing the Atlantic and Pacific?

What historic denouements are these we are approaching? On all sides tyrants tremble, crowns are unsteady, the human race restive, on the watch for some better era, some divine war. No man knows what will happen next, but all know that some such things are to happen as mark the greatest moral convulsions of the earth. Who shall play the hand for America in these tremendous games? A pretty time to put up two debauched old disunionist politicians, the lees and dregs of more than sixty years! A pretty time for two dead corpses to go walking up and down the earth, to guide by feebleness and ashes a proud, young, friendly, fresh, heroic nation of thirty millions of live and electric men!

Appendix to Leaves of Grass, 1856

Letter to Walt Whitman

Concord, Massachusetts, *21 July, 1855.*

DEAR SIR—I am not blind to the worth of the wonderful gift of "LEAVES OF GRASS." I find it the most extraordinary piece of wit and wisdom that America has yet contributed. I am very happy in reading it, as great power makes us happy. It meets the demand I am always making of what seemed the sterile and stingy nature, as if too much handiwork, or too much lymph in the temperament, were making our western wits fat and mean.

I give you joy of your free and brave thought. I have great joy in it. I find incomparable things said incomparably well, as they must be. I find the courage of treatment which so delights us, and which large perception only can inspire.

I greet you at the beginning of a great career, which yet must have had a long foreground somewhere, for such a start. I rubbed my eyes a little, to see if this sunbeam were no illusion; but the solid sense of the book is a sober certainty. It has the best merits, namely, of fortifying and encouraging.

I did not know until I last night saw the book advertised in a newspaper that I could trust the name as real and available for a post-office. I wish to see my benefactor, and have felt much like striking my tasks and visiting New York to pay you my respects.

R. W. Emerson.

Letter to Ralph Waldo Emerson

Brooklyn, *August, 1856.*

Here are thirty-two Poems, which I send you, dear Friend and Master, not having found how I could satisfy myself with sending any usual acknowledgment of your letter. The first edition, on which you mailed me that till now unanswered letter, was twelve poems—I printed a thousand copies, and they readily sold; these thirty-two Poems I stereotype, to print several thousand copies of. I much enjoy making poems. Other work I have set for myself to do, to meet people and The States face to face, to confront them with an American rude tongue; but the work of my life is making poems. I keep on till I make a hundred, and then several hundred—perhaps a thousand. The way is clear to me. A few years, and the average annual call for my Poems is ten or twenty thousand copies—more, quite likely. Why should I hurry or compromise? In poems or in speeches I say the word or two that has got to be said, adhere to the body, step with the countless common footsteps, and remind every man and woman of something.

Master, I am a man who has perfect faith. Master, we have not come through centuries, caste, heroisms, fables, to halt in this land today. Or I think it is to collect a ten-fold impetus that any halt is made. As nature, inexorable, onward, resistless, impassive amid the threats and screams of disputants, so America. Let all defer. Let all attend respectfully the leisure of These States, their politics, poems, literature, manners, and their free-handed modes of training their own offspring. Their own comes, just matured, certain, numerous and capable enough, with egotistical tongues, with sinewed wrists, seizing openly what belongs to them. They resume Personality, too long left out of mind. Their shadows are projected in employments, in books, in the cities, in trade; their feet are on the flights of the steps of the Capitol; they dilate, a larger, brawnier, more candid, more democratic, lawless, positive native to The States, sweet-bodied, completer, dauntless, flowing, masterful, beard-faced, new race of men.

Swiftly, on limitless foundations, the United States too are founding a literature. It is all as well done, in my opinion, as could be practicable. Each element here is in condition. Every day I go among the people of Manhattan Island, Brooklyn, and other cities, and among the young men, to discover the spirit of them, and to refresh myself. These are to be attended to; I am myself more drawn here than to those authors, publishers, importations, reprints, and so forth. I pass coolly through those, understanding them perfectly well, and that they do the indispensable service, outside of men like me, which nothing else could do. In poems, the young men of

The States shall be represented, for they out-rival the best of the rest of the earth.

The lists of ready-made literature which America inherits by the mighty inheritance of the English language—all the rich repertoire of traditions, poems, histories, metaphysics, plays, classics, translations, have made, and still continue, magnificent preparations for that other plainly signified literature, to be our own, to be electric, fresh, lusty, to express the full-sized body, male and female—to give the modern meanings of things, to grow up beautiful, lasting, commensurate with America, with all the passions of home, with the inimitable sympathies of having been boys and girls together, and of parents who were with our parents.

What else can happen The States, even in their own despite? That huge English flow, so sweet, so undeniable, has done incalculable good here, and is to be spoken of for its own sake with generous praise and with gratitude. Yet the price The States have had to lie under for the same has not been a small price. Payment prevails; a nation can never take the issues of the needs of other nations for nothing. America, grandest of lands in the theory of its politics, in popular reading, in hospitality, breadth, animal beauty, cities, ships, machines, money, credit, collapses quick as lightning at the repeated, admonishing, stern words, Where are any mental expressions from you, beyond what you have copied or stolen? Where the born throngs of poets, literats, orators, you promised? Will you but tag after other nations? They struggled long for their literature, painfully working their way, some with deficient languages, some with priest-craft, some in the endeavor just to live—yet achieved for their times, works, poems, perhaps the only solid consolation left to them through ages afterward of shame and decay. You are young, have the perfectest of dialects, a free press, a free government, the world forwarding its best to be with you. As justice has been strictly done to you, from this hour do strict justice to yourself. Strangle the singers who will not sing you loud and strong. Open the doors of The West. Call for new great masters to comprehend new arts, new perfections, new wants. Submit to the most robust bard till he remedy your barrenness. Then you will not need to adopt the heirs of others; you will have true heirs, begotten of yourself, blooded with your own blood.

With composure I see such propositions, seeing more and more every day of the answers that serve. Expressions do not yet serve, for sufficient reasons; but that is getting ready, beyond what the earth has hitherto known, to take home the expressions when they come, and to identify them with the populace of The States, which is the schooling cheaply procured by any outlay any number of years. Such schooling The States extract from the swarms of reprints, and from the current authors and editors. Such service and extract are done after enormous, reckless, free modes, characteristic of The States. Here are to be attained results never elsewhere thought possible; the modes are very grand too. The instincts of the American people are all perfect, and tend to make heroes. It is a rare thing in a man here to understand The States.

All current nourishments to literature serve. Of authors and editors I do not know how many there are in The States, but there are thousands, each one building his or her step to the stairs by which giants shall mount. Of the twenty-four modern mammoth two-double, three-double, and four-double cylinder presses now in the world, printing by steam, twenty-one of them are in These States. The twelve thousand large and small shops for dispensing books and newspapers—the same number of public libraries, any one of which has all the reading wanted to equip a man or woman for American reading—the three thousand different newspapers, the nutriment of the imperfect ones coming in just as usefully as any—the story papers, various, full of strong-flavored romances, widely circulated—the one-cent and two-cent journals—the political ones, no matter what side—the weeklies in the country—the sporting and pictorial papers—the monthly magazines, with plentiful imported feed—the sentimental novels, numberless copies of them—the low-priced flaring tales, adventures, biographies—all are prophetic; all waft rapidly on. I see that they swell wide, for reasons. I am not troubled at the movement of them, but greatly pleased. I see plying shuttles, the active ephemeral myriads of books also, faithfully weaving the garments of a generation of men, and a generation of women, they do not perceive or know. What a progress popular reading and writing has made in fifty years! What a progress fifty years hence! The time is at hand when inherent literature will be a main part of These States, as general and real as steam-power, iron, corn, beef, fish. First-rate American persons are to be supplied. Our perennial materials for fresh thoughts, histories, poems, music, orations, religions, recitations, amusements, will then not be disregarded, any more than our perennial fields, mines, rivers, seas. Certain things are established, and are immovable; in those things millions of years stand justified. The mothers and fathers of whom modern centuries have come, have not existed for nothing; they too had brains and hearts. Of course all literature, in all nations and years, will share marked attributes in common, as we all, of all ages, share the common human attributes. America is to be kept coarse and broad. What is to be done is to withdraw from precedents, and be directed to men and women—also to The States in their federalness; for the union of the parts of the body is not more necessary to their life than the union of These States is to their life.

A profound person can easily know more of the people than they know of themselves. Always waiting untold in the souls of the armies of common people, is stuff better than anything that can possibly appear in the leadership of the same. That gives final verdicts. In every department of These States, he who travels with a coterie, or with selected persons, or with imitators, or with infidels, or with the owners of slaves, or with that which is ashamed of the body of a man, or with that which is ashamed of the body of a woman, or with any thing less than the bravest and the openest, travels straight for the slopes of dissolution. The genius of all foreign literature is clipped and cut small, compared to our genius, and is essentially insulting to our usages, and to the organic compacts of These States. Old forms, old poems, majestic and proper in their own lands here in this land are exiles; the air here is very strong. Much that stands well and has a little enough place provided for it in the small scales of European kingdoms, empires, and the like, here stands haggard, dwarfed, ludicrous, or has no place little enough provided for it. Authorities, poems, models, laws, names, imported into America, are useful to America today to destroy them, and so move disencumbered to great works, great days.

Just so long, in our country or any country, as no revolutionists advance, and are backed by the people, sweeping off the swarms of routine representatives, officers in power, bookmakers, teachers, ecclesiastics, politicians, just so long, I perceive, do they who are in power fairly represent that country, and remain of use, probably of very great use. To supersede them, when it is the pleasure of These States, full provision is made; and I say the time has arrived to use it with a strong hand. Here also the souls of the armies have not only overtaken the souls of the officers, but passed on, and left the souls of the officers behind out of sight many week's journey; and the souls of the armies now go en-masse without officers. Here also formulas, glosses, blanks, minutiæ, are choking the throats of the spokesmen to death. Those things most listened for, certainly those are the things least said. There is not a single History of the World. There is not one of America, or of the organic compacts of These States, or of Washington, or of Jefferson, nor of Language, nor any Dictionary of the English Language. There is no great author; every one has demeaned himself to some etiquette or some impotence. There is no manhood or life-power in poems; there are shoats and geldings more like. Or literature will be dressed up, a fine gentleman, distasteful to our instincts, foreign to our soil. Its neck bends right and left wherever it goes. Its costumes and jewelry prove how little it knows Nature. Its flesh is soft; it shows less and less of the indefinable hard something that is Nature. Where is any thing but the shaved Nature of synods and schools? Where is a savage and luxuriant man? Where is an overseer? In lives, in poems, in codes of law, in Congress, in tuitions, theatres, conversations, argumentations, not a single head lifts itself clean out, with proof that it is their master, and has subordinated them to itself, and is ready to try their superiors. None believes in These States, boldly illustrating them in himself. Not a man faces round at the rest with terrible negative voice, refusing all terms to be bought off from his own eye-sight, or from the soul that he is, or from friendship, or from the body that he is, or from the soil and sea. To creeds, literature, art, the army, the navy, the executive, life is hardly proposed, but the sick and dying are proposed to cure the sick and dying. The churches are one vast lie; the people do not believe them, and they do not believe themselves; the priests are continually telling what they know well enough is not so, and keeping back what they know is so. The spectacle is a pitiful one. I think there can never be again upon the festive earth more bad-disordered persons deliberately taking seats, as of late in These States, at the heads of the public tables—such corpses' eyes for judges—such a rascal and thief in the Presidency.

Up to the present, as helps best, the people, like a lot of large boys, have no determined tastes, are quite unaware of the grandeur of themselves, and of their destiny, and of their immense strides—accept with voracity whatever is presented them in novels, histories, newspapers, poems, schools, lectures, every thing. Pretty soon, through these and other means, their development makes the fibre that is capable of itself, and will assume determined tastes. The young men will be clear what they want, and will have it. They will follow none except him whose spirit leads them in the like spirit with themselves. Any such man will be welcome as the flowers of May. Others will be put out without ceremony. How much is there anyhow, to the young men of These States, in a parcel of helpless dandies, who can neither fight, work, shoot, ride, run, command—some of them devout, some quite insane, some castrated—all second-hand, or third, fourth, or fifth hand—waited upon by waiters, putting not this land first, but always other lands first, talking of art, doing the most ridiculous things for fear of being called ridiculous, smirking and skipping along, continually taking off their hats—no one behaving, dressing, writing, talking, loving, out of any natural and manly tastes of his own, but each one looking cautiously to see how the rest behave, dress, write, talk, love—pressing the noses of dead books upon themselves and upon their country—favoring no poets, philosophs, literats here, but dog-like danglers at the heels of the poets, philosophs, literats, of enemies' lands—favoring mental expressions, models of gentlemen and ladies, social habitudes in These States, to grow up in sneaking defiance of the popular substratums of

The States? Of course they and the likes of them can never justify the strong poems of America. Of course no feed of theirs is to stop and be made welcome to muscle the bodies, male and female, for Manhattan Island, Brooklyn, Boston, Worcester, Hartford, Portland, Montreal, Detroit, Buffalo, Cleaveland, Milwaukee, St. Louis, Indianapolis, Chicago, Cincinnati, Iowa City, Philadelphia, Baltimore, Raleigh, Savannah, Charleston, Mobile, New Orleans, Galveston, Brownsville, San Francisco, Havana, and a thousand equal cities, present and to come. Of course what they and the likes of them have been used for, draws toward its close, after which they will all be discharged, and not one of them will ever be heard of any more.

America, having duly conceived, bears out of herself offspring of her own to do the workmanship wanted. To freedom, to strength, to poems, to personal greatness, it is never permitted to rest, not a generation or part of a generation. To be ripe beyond further increase is to prepare to die. The architects of These States laid their foundations, and passed to further spheres. What they laid is a work done; as much more remains. Now are needed other architects, whose duty is not less difficult, but perhaps more difficult. Each age forever needs architects. America is not finished, perhaps never will be; now America is a divine true sketch. There are Thirty-Two States sketched—the population thirty millions. In a few years there will be Fifty States. Again in a few years there will be A Hundred States, the population hundreds of millions, the freshest and freest of men. Of course such men stand to nothing less than the freshest and freest expression.

Poets here, literats here, are to rest on organic different bases from other countries; not a class set apart, circling only in the circle of themselves, modest and pretty, desperately scratching for rhymes, pallid with white paper, shut off, aware of the old pictures and traditions of the race, but unaware of the actual race around them—not breeding in and in among each other till they all have the scrofula. Lands of ensemble, bards of ensemble! Walking freely out from the old traditions, as our politics has walked out, American poets and literats recognize nothing behind them superior to what is present with them—recognize with joy the sturdy living forms of the men and women of These States, the divinity of sex, the perfect eligibility of the female with the male, all The States, liberty and equality, real articles, the different trades, mechanics, the young fellows of Manhattan Island, customs, instincts, slang, Wisconsin, Georgia, the noble Southern heart, the hot blood, the spirit that will be nothing less than master, the filibuster spirit, the Western man, native-born perceptions, the eye for forms, the perfect models of made things, the wild smack of freedom, California, money, electric-telegraphs, free-trade, iron and the iron mines—recognize without demur those splendid resistless black poems, the steam-ships of the sea-board states, and those other resistless splendid poems, the locomotives, followed through the interior states by trains of rail-road cars.

A word remains to be said, as of one ever present, not yet permitted to be acknowledged, discarded or made dumb by literature, and the results apparent. To the lack of an avowed, empowered, unabashed development of sex, (the only salvation for the same,) and to the fact of speakers and writers fraudulently assuming as always dead what every one knows to be always alive, is attributable the remarkable non-personality and indistinctness of modern productions in books, art, talk; also that in the scanned lives of men and women most of them appear to have been for some time past of the neuter gender; and also the stinging fact that in orthodox society today, if the dresses were changed, the men might easily pass for women and the women for men.

Infidelism usurps most with fœtid polite face; among the rest infidelism about sex. By silence or obedience the pens of savans, poets, historians, biographers, and the rest, have long connived at the filthy law, and books enslaved to it, that what makes the manhood of a man, that sex, womanhood, maternity, desires, lusty animations, organs, acts, are unmentionable and to be ashamed of, to be driven to skulk out of literature with whatever belongs to them. This filthy law has to be repealed—it stands in the way of great reforms. Of women just as much as men, it is the interest that there should not be infidelism about sex, but perfect faith. Women in These States approach the day of that organic equality with men, without which, I see, men cannot have organic equality among themselves. This empty dish, gallantry, will then be filled with something. This tepid wash, this diluted deferential love, as in songs, fictions, and so forth, is enough to make a man vomit; as to manly friendship, everywhere observed in The States, there is not the first breath of it to be observed in print. I say that the body of a man or woman, the main matter, is so far quite unexpressed in poems; but that the body is to be expressed, and sex is. Of bards for These States, if it come to a question, it is whether they shall celebrate in poems the eternal decency of the amativeness of Nature, the motherhood of all, or whether they shall be the bards of the fashionable delusion of the inherent nastiness of sex, and of the feeble and querulous modesty of deprivation. This is important in poems, because the whole of the other expressions of a nation are but flanges out of its great poems. To me, henceforth, that theory of any thing, no matter what, stagnates in its vitals, cowardly and rotten, while it cannot publicly accept, and publicly name, with specific words, the things on which all existence, all souls, all realization, all decency, all health, all that is worth being here for, all of woman and of man, all beauty, all purity, all sweetness, all friendship, all strength, all life, all immortality depend. The courageous soul, for a year or two to come, may be proved by faith in sex, and by disdaining concessions.

To poets and literats—to every woman and man, today or any day, the conditions of the present, needs, dangers, prejudices, and the like, are the perfect conditions on which we are here, and the conditions for wording the future with undissuadable words. These States, receivers of the stamina of past ages and lands, initiate the outlines of repayment a thousand fold. They fetch the American great masters, waited for by old worlds and new, who accept evil as well as good, ignorance as well as erudition, black as soon as white, foreign-born materials as well as home-born, reject none, force discrepancies into range, surround the whole, concentrate them on present periods and places, show the application to each and any one's body and soul, and show the true use of precedents. Always America will be agitated and turbulent. This day it is taking shape, not to be less so, but to be more so, stormily, capriciously, on native principles, with such vast proportions of parts! As for me, I love screaming, wrestling, boiling-hot days.

Of course, we shall have a national character, an identity. As it ought to be, and as soon as it ought to be, it will be. That, with much else, takes care of itself, is a result, and the cause of greater results. With Ohio, Illinois, Missouri, Oregon—with the states around the Mexican sea—with cheerfully welcomed immigrants from Europe, Asia, Africa—with Connecticut, Vermont, New Hampshire, Rhode Island—with all varied interests, facts, beliefs, parties, genesis—there is being fused a determined character, fit for the broadest use for the freewomen and freemen of The States, accomplished and to be accomplished, without any exception whatever—each indeed free, each idiomatic, as becomes live states and men, but each adhering to one enclosing general form of politics, manners, talk, personal style, as the plenteous varieties of the race adhere to one physical form. Such character is the brain and spine to all, including literature, including poems. Such character, strong, limber, just, open-mouthed, American-blooded, full of pride, full of ease, of passionate friendliness, is to stand compact upon that vast basis of the supremacy of Individuality—that new moral American continent without which, I see, the physical continent remained incomplete, may-be a carcass, a bloat—that newer America, answering face to face with The States, with ever-satisfying and ever-unsurveyable seas and shores.

Those shores you found. I say you have led The States there—have led Me there. I say that none has ever done, or ever can do, a greater deed for The States, than your deed. Others may line out the lines, build cities, work mines, break up farms; it is yours to have been the original true Captain who put to sea, intuitive, positive, rendering the first report, to be told less by any report, and more by the mariners of a thousand bays, in each tack of their arriving and departing, many years after you.

Receive, dear Master, these statements and assurances through me, for all the young men, and for an earnest that we know none before you, but the best following you; and that we demand to take your name into our keeping, and that we understand what you have indicated, and find the same indicated in ourselves, and that we will stick to it and enlarge upon it through These States.

Walt Whitman.

Note at Beginning

The following volume contains

LEAVES OF GRASS,
with the brief Annex, SANDS AT SEVENTY, *in November Boughs,*

SPECIMEN DAYS AND COLLECT . . . . and

NOVEMBER BOUGHS,

Revised, corrected, &c., down to date.

(When I had got this volume well under way, I was quite suddenly prostrated by illness—paralysis, continued yet—which will have to serve as excuse for many faults both of omission and commission in it.)

But I would not let the great and momentous Era of these years, these States, slip away without attempting to arrest in a special printed book (as much in spirit as letter, and may-be for the future more than the present,) some few specimens—even vital throbs, breaths—as representations of it all—from my point of view, and right from the midst of it, jotted at the time.

There is a tally-stamp and stage-result of periods and nations, elusive, at second or third hand, often escaping the historian of matter-of-fact—in some sort the nation's spiritual formative ferment or chaos—the getting in of its essence, formulating identity—a law of it, and significant part of its progress. (Of the best of events and facts, even the most important, there are finally not the events and facts only, but something flashing out and fluctuating like tuft-flames or eidólons, from all.) My going up and down amidst these years, and the impromptu jottings of their sights and thoughts, of war and peace, have been in accordance with that law, and probably a result of it. . . . In certain respects, (emotionality, passions, spirituality, the invisible trend,) I therefore launch forth the divisions of the following book as not only a consequent of that period and its influences, but in one sort a History of America, the past 35 years, after the rest, after the adjuncts of that history have been studied and attended to.

Note at End of Complete Poems and Prose

As I conclude—and (to get typographical correctness,) after running my eyes diligently through the three big divisions of the preceding volume—the interrogative wonder-fancy rises in me whether (if it be not too arrogant to even state it,) the 33 years of my current time, 1855–1888, with their aggregate of our New World doings and people, have not, indeed, created and formulated the foregoing leaves—forcing their utterance as the pages stand—coming actually from the direct urge and developments of those years, and not from any individual epic or lyrical attempts whatever, or from my pen or voice, or any body's special voice. Out of that supposition, the book might assume to be consider'd an autochthonic record and expression, freely render'd, of and out of these 30 to 35 years—of the soul and evolution of America—and of course, by reflection, not ours only, but more or less of the common people of the world. . . . . Seems to me I may dare to claim a deep native tap-root for the book, too, in some sort. I came on the stage too late for personally knowing much of even the lingering Revolutionary worthies—the men of '76. Yet, as a little boy, I have been press'd tightly and lovingly to the breast of Lafayette, (Brooklyn, 1825,) and have talk'd with old Aaron Burr, and also with those who knew Washington and his surroundings, and with original Jeffersonians, and more than one very old soldier and sailor. And in my own day and maturity, my eyes have seen, and ears heard, Lincoln, Grant and Emerson, and my hands have been grasp'd by their hands. Though in a different field and range from most of theirs, I give the foregoing pages as perfectly legitimate, resultant, evolutionary and consistent with them. If these lines should ever reach some reader of a far off future age, let him take them as a missive sent from Abraham Lincoln's fateful age. . . . Repeating, parrot-like, what in the preceding divisions has been already said, and must serve as a great reason-why of this whole book—1st, That the main part about pronounc'd events and shows, (poems and persons also,) is the point of view from which they are view'd and estimated—and 2d, That I cannot let my momentous, stormy, peculiar Era of peace and war, these States, these years, slip away without arresting some of its specimen events—even its vital breaths—to be portray'd and inscribed from out of the midst of it, from its own days and nights—not so much in themselves, (statistically and descriptively our times are copiously noted and memorandized with an industrial zeal)—but to give from them here their flame-like results in imaginative and spiritual suggestiveness—as they present themselves to me, at any rate, from the point of view alluded to.

Then a few additional words yet to this hurried farewell note. In another sense (the warp crossing the woof, and knitted in,) the book is probably a sort of autobiography; an element I have not attempted to specially restrain or erase. As alluded to at beginning, I had about got the volume well started by the printers, when a sixth recurrent attack of my war-paralysis fell upon me. It has proved the most serious and continued of the whole. I am now uttering *November Boughs,* and printing this book, in my 70th year. To get out the collection—mainly the born results of health, flush life, buoyancy, and happy out-door volition—and to prepare the *Boughs*—have beguiled my invalid months the past summer and fall. ("Are we to be beaten down in our old age?" says one white-hair'd fellow remonstratingly to another in a budget of letters I read last night.) . . . Then I have wanted to leave something markedly *personal.* I have put my name with pen-and-ink with my own hand in the present volume. And from engraved or photo'd portraits taken from life, I have selected some, of different stages, which please me best, (or at any rate displease me least,) and bequeath them at a venture to you, reader, with my love.

W. W., *Nov. 13, '88.*

May 31, 1889

CAMDEN, NEW JERSEY, U. S. AMERICA.

To-day completes my three-score-and-ten years—rounds and coheres the successive growths and stages of L. of G. with the following essay and (sort of) testament—my hurried epilogue of intentions-bequest—and gives me the crowning content, (for these lines are written at the last,) of feeling and definitely, perhaps boastfully, reiterating, For good or bad, plain or not-plain, I have held out and now concluded my utterance, entirely its own way; the main wonder being to me, of the foregoing 404 pages entire, amid their many faults and omissions, that (after looking over them leisurely and critically, as the last week, night and day,) they have adhered faithfully to, and carried out, for nearly 40 years, over many gaps, through thick and thin, peace and war, sickness and health, clouds and sunshine, my latent purposes, &c., even as measurably well and far as they do between these covers. (Nature evidently achieves specimens only—plants the seeds of suggestions—is not so intolerant of what is call'd evil—relies on *law* and *character* more than special cases or partialities; and in my little scope I have follow'd or tried to follow the lesson: . . Probably that is about all.)

Yes, to-day finishes my 70th year; and even if but the merest additional preface, (and not plain what tie-together it has with the following *Backward Glance,*) I suppose I must reel out something to celebrate my old birthday anniversary, and for this special edition of the latest completest L. of G. utterance.* Printers send word, too, there is a blank here to be written up—and what with? . . . Probably I may as well transcribe and eke out this note by the following lines of a letter last week to a valued friend who demands to know my current

*As there are now several editions of L. of G., different texts and dates, I wish to say that I prefer and recommend the present one, complete, for future printing, if there should be any; a copy and fac-simile, indeed, of the text of these 422 pages. The subsequent interval which is so important to form'd and launch'd works, books especially, has pass'd; and waiting till fully after that, I give these concluding words.

personal condition: . . . "First asking pardon for long neglect—The perfect physical health, strength, buoyancy, (and inward impetus to back them,) which were vouchsafed during my whole life, and especially throughout the Secession War period, (1860 to '66,) seem'd to wane after those years, and were closely track'd by a stunning paralytic seizure, and following physical debility and inertia, (laggardness, torpor, indifference, perhaps laziness,) which put me low in 1873 and '4 and '5—then lifted a little, but have essentially remain'd ever since; several spirts or attacks—five or six of them, one time or another from 1876 onward, but gradually mainly overcome—till now, 1888 and '9, the worst and most obstinate seizure of all. . . . Upon the whole, however, and even at this, and though old and sick, I keep up, maintain fair spirits, partially read and write—have publish'd last and full and revised editions of my poems and prose (records and results of youth and early and mid age—of absolute strength and health—o'erseen now during a lingering ill spell)—But have had a bad year, this last one—have run a varied gauntlet, chronic constipation, and then vertigo, bladder and gastric troubles, and the foremention'd steady disability and inertia; bequests of the serious paralysis at Washington, D. C., closing the Secession War—that seizure indeed the culmination of much that preceded, and real source of all my woes since. During the past year, and now, with all these, (a body and brain-action dull'd, while the spirit is perhaps willing and live enough,) I get along more contentedly and comfortably than you might suppose—sit here all day in my big, high, strong, rattan-bottom'd chair, (with great wolf-skin spread on the back in cool weather)—as writing to you now on a tablet on my lap, may-be my last missives of love, memories and cheer."

The Old Man Himself

from Horace Traubel, "Walt Whitman: Poet and Philosopher and Man,"
Lippincott's Magazine, *March 1891.*

A POSTSCRIPT

Walt Whitman has a way of putting in his own special word of thanks, his own way, for kindly demonstrations, and may now be considered as appearing on the scene, wheeled at last in his invalid chair, and saying, *propria persona*, Thank you, thank you, my friends all. The living face and voice and emotional pulse only at last hold humanity together; even old poets and their listeners and critics too. One of my dearest objects in my poetic expression has been to combine these Forty-Four United States into One Identity, fused, equal, and independent. My attempt has been mainly of suggestion, atmosphere, reminder, the native and common spirit of all, and perennial heroism.

Walt Whitman.

Walt Whitman's Last

from Lippincott's Magazine, *August, 1891*

"Good-Bye my Fancy"—concluding Annex to Leaves of Grass.

"The Highest said: Don't let us begin so low—isn't our range too coarse—too gross? . . . . The Soul answer'd: No, not when we consider what it is all for—the end involved is Time and Space."—*An item from last page of "Good-Bye."*

H. Heine's first principle of criticising a book was, What motive is the author trying to carry out, or express or accomplish? and the second, Has he achiev'd it?

The theory of my "Leaves of Grass" as a composition of verses has been from first to last, (if I am to give impromptu a hint of the spinal marrow of the business, and sign it with my name,) to thoroughly possess the mind, memory, cognizance of the author himself, with everything beforehand—a full armory of concrete actualities, observations, humanity, past poems, ballads, facts, technique, war and peace, politics, North and South, East and West, nothing too large or too small, the sciences as far as possible—and above all America and the present—after and out of which the subject of the poem, long or short, has been invariably turned over to his Emotionality, even Personality, to be shaped thence; and emerges strictly therefrom, with all its merits and demerits on its head. Every page of my poetic or attempt at poetic utterance therefore smacks of the living physical identity, date, environment, individuality, probably beyond anything known, and in style often offensive to the conventions.

This new last cluster, "Good-Bye my Fancy" follows suit, and yet with a difference. The clef is here changed to its lowest, and the little book is a lot of tremolos about old age, death, and faith. The physical just lingers, but almost vanishes. The book is garrulous, irascible (like old Lear) and has various breaks and even tricks to avoid monotony. It will have to be ciphered and ciphered out long—and is probably in some respects the most curious part of its author's baffling works.

Walt Whitman.

Chronology

1819 Walter Whitman born (May 31) at West Hills, Huntington Township, New York, the second child (and second son) of Walter Whitman, housebuilder, and Louisa Van Velsor, both descended from early settlers on Long Island. Of the seven other Whitman children who survived infancy, Jesse (b. 1818) was unstable and died (1870) in a lunatic asylum; Hannah Louisa (b. 1823) may have been psychotic; Andrew (b. 1827) became an alcoholic; and Edward (b. 1835) was feebleminded.

1823 The senior Walter Whitman moves his family to Brooklyn, where he hopes to prosper from a building boom.

1825 The Marquis de Lafayette visits Brooklyn and, according to Walt Whitman's cherished recollection, embraces him. Walt Whitman attends public school in Brooklyn (until about 1830).

1830–31 Works as an office boy.

1831–35 Learns printing trade on *Patriot* and *Star* in Brooklyn; remains there after family moves back to Long Island (1833).

1835–36 Works as a printer in New York City but is unable to find employment after the printing district is devastated by fire.

1836–38 Teaches school on Long Island at East Norwich, Hempstead, Babylon, Long Swamp, and Smithtown (where he is active in local debating society).

1838–39 Founds, publishes, and edits a weekly newspaper, *Long-Islander*, at Huntington; works on *Democrat* (Jamaica); writes poetry and literary prose.

1840–41 Electioneers for Martin Van Buren; teaches school again; publishes poetry in *Democrat.*

1841 Moves to New York City (May) and works as compositor for *New World*; addresses Democratic party rally in City Hall Park (July); publishes "Death in the School-Room (a Fact)" in *Democratic Review* (August) and other stories.

1842–45 Works for *Aurora*, *Evening Tattler*, and other papers in New York City. Publishes a "temperance novel," *Franklin Evans* (Nov. 1842), and over fifteen stories and sketches.

1845–48 Returns to Brooklyn and works for *Star* (1845–46) and *Daily Eagle*; becomes a devotee of grand opera.

1848 Leaves for New Orleans (February) with brother Jeff to edit *Daily Crescent*; resigns (May) and returns to Brooklyn by way of the Mississippi, the Great Lakes, and the Hudson.

1848–49 Founds (September 1848) and edits *Brooklyn Freeman*, a "free-soil" newspaper. The phrenologist Lorenzo N. Fowler reads his bumps (July 1849) and gives him a favorable analysis of character and abilities.

1849–54 Runs job-printing office, bookstore, and housebuilding business; writes freelance journalism. Revisits West Hills with his father (1850). Publishes four topical poems (1850), one of which ("Europe") will appear in *Leaves of Grass* (along with a later topical poem, "A Boston Ballad," referring to the 1854 rendition of the fugitive slave Anthony Burns). Addresses Brooklyn Art Union (1851); writes "Pictures" (1853) and notebook fragments anticipating the final manner of *Leaves of Grass.*

1855 Takes out copyright (May 15) on first edition (795 copies) of *Leaves of Grass* (twelve untitled poems and a preface), which he publishes himself during first week of July. Father dies (July 11). Ralph Waldo Emerson sends a letter (July 21) saluting *Leaves of Grass.*

1856 Publishes the second edition of *Leaves of Grass*—it contains thirty-three poems, Emerson's letter, and a long open letter by Whitman in answer to it. Completes and runs off proof sheets of his political tract, "The Eighteenth Presidency!" Henry David Thoreau and Bronson Alcott visit him in Brooklyn.

1857–59 Edits Brooklyn *Times.* Envisions "the Great Construction of the New Bible" (*Leaves of Grass* in a fulfilled form) but falls into an emotional "slough."

1860 Frequents Pfaff's restaurant on Broadway, meeting place for New York's literary bohemia. Goes to Boston (March) to oversee third edition of *Leaves of Grass*, published by Thayer and Eldridge. Walks on Boston Common with Emerson, who urges him to "expurgate" the "Children of Adam" poems—"I said no, no."

1861–62 At outbreak of Civil War vows to live a "purged" and "cleansed" life. Writes freelance journalism; visits the sick, injured, and wounded at New-York Hospital. Goes to the war front in Virginia (December 1862) when he learns his brother George has been wounded.

1863–64 Settles in Washington, D.C., as a visitor ("Wound-Dresser") in the military hospitals, supporting himself by part-time clerical work in Army Paymaster's office. Becomes an intimate friend of William Douglas O'Connor and family. Returns to Brooklyn (June 1864) on extended sick leave.

1865 Returns to Washington after appointment (January) to Department of Interior clerkship; fired by Secretary James Harlan (June), supposedly because of authorship of *Leaves of Grass*, and transferred to clerkship in Attorney General's office. Writes "When Lilacs Last in the Dooryard Bloom'd" (summer) in response to the assassination of Lincoln; published in *Drum-Taps and Sequel* (October). Meets Peter Doyle, eighteen, a conductor on Washington street railway.

1866 Enraged by the Harlan firing, O'Connor publishes *The Good Gray Poet*, a vindictive tract, and joins forces with John Burroughs, another of Whitman's fervent admirers.

1867 Fourth edition of *Leaves of Grass*; publishes "Democracy," first part of *Democratic Vistas*, in *Galaxy* (New York). Published appreciations by William Michael Rossetti, "Walt Whitman's Poems," in *Chronicle* (London), and by John Burroughs, *Notes on Walt Whitman as Poet and Person*.

1868 Rossetti's *Poems of Walt Whitman*, a selection, published in London. "Personalism," second part of *Democratic Vistas*, published in *Galaxy*.

1870 Prints fifth edition of *Leaves of Grass*, *Democratic Vistas*, and *Passage to India*, all dated 1871. The widow of William Blake's biographer, Mrs. Anne Gilchrist, who had fallen in love with Whitman after reading the Rossetti edition, publishes "An Englishwoman's Estimate of Walt Whitman" in *The Radical* (Boston).

1871 Receives an adulatory poem from Swinburne, a fraternal letter from Tennyson, and a declaration of love from Anne

Gilchrist. Reads "After All Not to Create Only" at American Institute Exhibition, New York City.

1872 Reads "As a Strong Bird on Pinions Free" at Dartmouth College commencement; becomes "real ill" after suffering heat prostration; has serious falling-out with O'Connor over personal and public issues; makes his will.

1873 Has paralytic stroke (January). Depressed by deaths of his brother Jeff's wife, Martha (February), and his mother (May). An invalid, leaves Washington and moves in with brother George in Camden, New Jersey (June).

1874 Publishes "Song of the Redwood-Tree" and "Prayer of Columbus" (with apparent self-portrait as "a batter'd, wreck'd old man") in *Harper's Magazine*; discharged from government clerkship.

1876 Publishes "Author's" or "Centennial" edition of *Leaves of Grass* (a reprint of the 1871 edition); *Two Rivulets*; *Memoranda During the War*; and "Walt Whitman's Actual American Position" (in *West Jersey Press*, Camden), an unsigned article that generates international controversy, book sales, and cash gifts. Becomes intimate with young Harry Stafford, printers' employee; pays frequent visits to Stafford family farm ("Timber Creek"). Hoping to marry Whitman, Anne Gilchrist arrives in the U.S. with her children.

1877 Lectures on Thomas Paine in Philadelphia; with Harry Stafford visits John Burroughs in Esopus, New York.

1879 Lectures on Abraham Lincoln in New York (April); travels west (September) as far as Colorado; falls ill and stays with brother Jeff in St. Louis (October–January 1880).

1880 Travels in Canada (June–October), where he visits his admirer and future biographer, Dr. R.M. Bucke.

1881 Pays last visit to family birthplaces and graveyards on Long Island; goes to Boston (August–October) to supervise new edition of *Leaves of Grass* (293 poems) published (November) by James R. Osgood and Co. Visits Emerson in Concord.

1882 Oscar Wilde calls on Whitman in Camden (January). Osgood withdraws edition of *Leaves of Grass* (April) after warning from Boston District Attorney that certain poems fall within provisions of "Public Statutes respecting obscene literature." Rees Welsh and Co. (later David McKay) reprints Osgood edition in Philadelphia and also issues *Specimen Days and Collect.* Largely as result of publicity associated with Boston "banning," Whitman earns $1,439.30 in royalties (as against $25.00 in 1881 and $329.66 in 1883).

1883 McKay publishes Bucke's *Walt Whitman*, a discipular study closely supervised by Whitman.

1884 Moves (March) to 328 Mickle Street, Camden, "a little old shanty of my own," for which he pays $1,750.

1885 Friends and supporters present him with a horse and buggy for outings.

1886 Receives an $800 subscription fund for the purchase of a summer house; sits for portrait by Thomas Eakins.

1888 Suffers another paralytic stroke (June) followed by severe illness; draws up a new will naming Bucke, Thomas B. Harned, and Horace L. Traubel as literary executors. Publishes *November Boughs* and *Complete Poems and Prose.*

1889 Goes outdoors in his wheelchair (May) after nearly a year of being "cabin'd" with illness. The proceedings at his seventieth birthday party are published as *Camden's Compliment to Walt Whitman.*

1890 Delivers "Death of Abraham Lincoln" lecture for the last time (April), in Philadelphia. Writes letter to John Addington Symonds (August) rejecting as "damnable" Symonds' homosexual interpretation of "Calamus" and claiming, "Tho' always unmarried I have had six children." Signs $4,000 contract (October) for construction, after his own design, of a granite "burial house" in Harleigh Cemetery, Camden.

1891 Publishes *Good-Bye my Fancy* and "deathbed" edition of *Leaves of Grass* ("supercedes them all by far"). Prepares *Complete Prose Works* (published 1892).

1892 Dies (March 26) at Mickle Street; buried (March 30) in Harleigh Cemetery.

Note on the Texts

This volume reprints three books that Walt Whitman saw through the press: the first edition of *Leaves of Grass* (Brooklyn, 1855); the final ("authorized," or "deathbed") edition of *Leaves of Grass* (Philadelphia, 1891–92); and *Complete Prose Works* (Philadelphia, 1892). It also contains a supplement (or "annex," to use one of Whitman's preferred terms) of fugitive prose pieces, and a number of poems not included in the deathbed edition. (The sources for the texts of these poems are provided in the Notes; "The Eighteenth Presidency!" is printed here from proof sheets in the Manuscript Division, Library of Congress.) Obvious typographical errors found in the originals have been corrected in the text and are accounted for below. The Notes, for the most part, record significant textual variants.

Two months before his death in 1892, Whitman announced in a promotional statement that *Leaves of Grass*, "which he has been working on at great intervals and partially issued for the past thirty-five or forty years, is now completed, so to call it, and he would like this new 1892 edition to absolutely supercede all previous ones." One obeys this injunction by here reprinting Whitman's lifework—which he compared, fancifully, with a modern city, a cathedral, an eldest child, or something found in nature, a tree with many growth rings—in its "completed" form. But from several standpoints it also seems desirable to reprint his 1855 edition as well, even at the cost of some repetitions and overlappings.

The first *Leaves of Grass*, comprising a preface and twelve untitled poems (the titles Whitman ultimately gave them are supplied here in the Table of Contents), is a turning-point document in American literary history. Whitman was its (anonymous) author, its publisher, and to some extent, its printer as well. This was the edition in which Ralph Waldo Emerson discovered, as he wrote to Whitman, "the most extraordinary piece of wit and wisdom America has yet contributed." Whitman spent the rest of his life expanding, articulating, and rearranging his book of poems, but the 1855 *Leaves of Grass* retains a formal, substantive, and genetic character that sets it apart from subsequent editions, some more than four times its page bulk.

Whitman's preface to the 1855 *Leaves of Grass*, here reprinted in its functional position, was the most decisive of all his critical declarations. Yet when he brought out a second, enlarged edition in 1856 he replaced this preface with a "dear Friend and Master" letter to Emerson (reprinted here among the supplementary prose) and then allowed it to slide into neglect. The shortened version of the 1855 preface which he included in *Complete Prose Works* has been omitted from this edition.

Whitman was also casual about "Pieces in Early Youth," which he included, selectively and arbitrarily, in *Complete Prose Works* "with some qualms," as he explained, "in order to avoid the annoyance of their surreptitious issue." Readers who, like the present editor, find in these "crude and boyish pieces" suggestive anticipations, in theme and trope, of Whitman's mature manner should consult *The Early Poems and Fiction*, edited by Thomas L. Brasher (New York, 1963). This is a volume in the New York University Press series, *The Collected Writings of Walt Whitman* (1963–), the authoritative modern edition, which now includes the three-volume *Leaves of Grass: A Textual Variorum of the Printed Poems*, edited by Sculley Bradley, Harold W. Blodgett, Arthur Golden, and William White (1980).

The standards for American English continue to fluctuate and in some ways were conspicuously different in earlier periods from what they are now. In nineteenth-century writings, for example, a word might be spelled in more than one way, even in the same work, and such variations might be carried into print. Commas were sometimes used expressively to suggest the movements of voice, and capitals were sometimes meant to give significances to a word beyond those it might have in its uncapitalized form. Since modernization would remove such effects, this volume has preserved the spelling, punctuation, capitalization, and wording of the editions reprinted here.

The present edition is concerned only with representing the *texts* of the three Whitman books; with the exception of the display capitalization of the 1855 *Leaves of Grass*, it does not attempt to reproduce features of typographic design.

Some changes, however, have been made. Whitman's references to page numbers have been changed to conform to the pages in this volume. Typographical errors have also been corrected. The following is a list of those errors, cited by page and line numbers: 11.28, re examine; 14.13, sooth; 15.9, secresy; 15.39, it president; 16.6, sufficent; 42.3, abode; 62.6, furs; 67.13, aud; 88.9, me me; 145.4, administrations,; 490.25, machines; 831.15, havn't; 902.1–2, Bethlehem; 997.2, if were; 1010.8, nether; 1078.37-38, Lucusta; 1161.20, his; 1173.38, play; 1188.2, collocutions; 1276.20, a-void; 1284.1–2, millionares; 1335.19, Fifty.

List of the pages where a stanza concludes on the last line

27, 28, 31, 32, 34, 36, 38, 44, 46, 50, 51, 52, 55, 65, 66, 67, 68, 71, 72, 77, 78, 81, 82, 83, 85, 86, 87, 91, 103, 104, 105, 107, 110, 111, 113, 114, 116, 122, 123, 125, 130, 136, 138, 140, 142, 143, 179, 182, 183, 191, 192, 193, 194, 197, 198, 199, 204, 205, 206, 207, 208, 209, 210, 212, 213, 214, 217, 228, 230, 232, 234, 235, 238, 239, 240, 241, 243, 245, 246, 253, 255, 256, 259, 290, 299, 305, 307, 314, 317, 323, 325, 328, 329, 334, 336, 337, 338, 341, 345, 348, 352, 356, 357, 358, 364, 366, 369, 371, 373, 375, 382, 383, 386, 389, 390, 391, 392, 395, 404, 405, 406, 408, 432, 434, 437, 441, 444, 447, 451, 459, 465, 466, 469, 470, 474, 478, 482, 487, 488, 489, 490, 500, 503, 506, 509, 511, 517, 519, 529, 531, 537, 539, 541, 542, 543, 552, 554, 556, 575, 576, 579, 592, 599, 600, 609, 618, 652, 682, 684, 686, 687, 1100, 1101.

Notes

In the notes below, the reference numbers denote page and line of the present volume (the line count includes chapter headings). Notes printed at the foot of pages within the text are by Whitman.

Abbreviations:

CPW	*Complete Prose Works*, Philadelphia, 1892.
LG—1855	*Leaves of Grass*, Brooklyn, 1855.
LG—1856	*Leaves of Grass*, Brooklyn, 1856.
LG—1860	*Leaves of Grass*, Boston, 1860.
LG—1867	*Leaves of Grass*, New York, 1867.
LG—1871	*Leaves of Grass*, Washington, 1871.
LG—1876	*Leaves of Grass*, Camden, N. J., 1876.
LG—1881	*Leaves of Grass*, Boston, 1881.
LG—1891–92	*Leaves of Grass*, Philadelphia, 1891–92.

LEAVES OF GRASS (1855)

23.32 semitic muscle] Seminal muscle.

25.36–37 proud beyond] Later editions read "proud, beyond".

109.26–110.12 O hotcheeked . . . best liquor afterward.] These lines were deleted in *LG—1881* and subsequent editions.

LEAVES OF GRASS (1891–92)

148.2 present one] *LG—1891–92* has 438 pages. The page numbers given here conform to the present volume.

171.8 When I Read the Book] In *LG—1867* this was a five-line poem, the concluding two lines of which read:

(As if any man really knew aught of my life,
As if you, O cunning Soul, did not keep your secret well!)

172.29 Cantatrice] Whitman encountered this word, meaning a female professional singer, in the Francis G. Shaw translation (Boston, 1846) of George Sand's novel, *Consuelo.*

173.13 Mannahatta] Whitman preferred the Indian name to New York, which, he said, merely commemorated the British occupation of the island.

176.1 Paumanok] Long Island, from the Algonquian. Whitman used Paumanok as a nom de plume (see page 1156).

176.21 heard at dawn] In some preceding editions: "heard at dusk". The earlier reading is consistent with Whitman's notes on the hermit thrush: "Sings oftener after sundown."

191.4–6 As the hugging . . . tread,] Compare *LG—1855*:

As God comes a loving bedfellow and sleeps at my side
all night and close on the peep of day,

206.29 carlacue] Curlicue.

212.7 sweet-flag] Calamus. See note, 268.1.

257.6–258.26 O my body! . . . the soul!] This entire concluding section was added in *LG—1856*.

266.4 Once I . . . City] The manuscript reads:

Once I passed through a populous celebrated city, imprinting on
my brain for future use, its shows, with its shows, architecture,
customs and traditions
But now of all that city I remember only the man who wandered
with me, there, for love of me,
Day by day, and night by night, we were together,
All else has long been forgotten by me—I remember, I say, only
one rude and ignorant man who, when I departed, long and
long held me by the hand, with silent lip, sad and tremulous.—

(Fredson Bowers, ed., *Whitman's Manuscripts: "Leaves of Grass" [1860]* [Chicago, 1955], p. 64.)

268.1 Calamus] Whitman provided this partial explanation: "It is the very large & aromatic grass, or rush, growing about water-ponds in the valleys . . . often called 'sweet flag' . . . The recherché or ethereal sense of the terms, as used in my book, arises probably from the actual Calamus presenting the biggest & hardiest kind of spears of grass—and their fresh, aquatic, pungent bouquet." (Edwin Haviland Miller, ed., *The Correspondence* [New York, 1961], I, 347.) But the sexually symbolic context Whitman provided for "sweet flag" in "Song of Myself" (page 212) is more illuminating.

275.33 Recorders ages hence,] In *LG—1860*, this line read:

You bards of ages hence! when you refer to me, mind not so much
my poems,
Nor speak of me that I prophesied of The States, and led them the
way of their glories;

279.28 live-oak] In the Whitman manuscripts, "Live Oak with Moss" preceded "Calamus" as basic symbol and series title.

285.20–22 (I loved . . . these songs.)] In *LG—1860* the poem ended with the single line:

Doubtless I could not have perceived the universe, or written one of
my poems, if I had not freely given myself to comrades, to love.

293.23 10] Sections 8–10 were much revised, and in this edition, there is no section 9.

307.30 Crossing Brooklyn Ferry] Titled "Sun-Down Poem" on first publication in *LG—1856*.

388.2 Out of the Cradle Endlessly Rocking] Earlier titles were "A Child's Reminiscence" and "A WORD OUT OF THE SEA."

396.19–20 (See, from my dead lips . . . and rolling,)] On the urging of the *Atlantic Monthly*'s editor, James Russell Lowell, Whitman deleted these lines from the text printed in the magazine (April 1860) under the title "Bardic Symbols."

416.1 Drum-Taps] *LG—1871* and *LG—1876* printed this four-line epigraph (now three lines in "The Wound-Dresser," pages 442.32–443.4):

Aroused and angry,
I thought to beat the alarum, and urge relentless war;
But soon my fingers fail'd me, my face droop'd, and I resign'd myself,
To sit by the wounded and soothe them, or silently watch the dead.

467.14 O Captain! My Captain!] "I'm almost sorry I ever wrote the poem," Whitman said. "It had certain emotional immediate reasons for being."

586.8–12 A million people . . . my city!] In *LG—1860* the following passage took the place of these lines:

The parades, processions, bugles playing, flags flying, drums beating;
A million people—manners free and superb—open voices—hospitality—the most courageous and friendly young men;
The free city! no slaves! no owners of slaves!
The beautiful city! the city of hurried and sparkling waters! the city of spires and masts!
The city nested in bays! my city!
The city of such women, I am mad to be with them! I will return after death to be with them.
The city of such young men, I swear I cannot live happy, without I often go talk, walk, eat, drink, sleep with them!

605.13–15 Yet certain remembrances . . . bundle of songs.] In *LG—1871* and *LG—1876* these lines read:

Only these Souvenirs of Democracy—In them—in all my songs—behind me leaving,
To You, whoever you are, (bathing, leavening this leaf especially with my breath—pressing on it a moment with my own hands;
—Here! feel how the pulse beats in my wrists!—how my heart's-blood is swelling, contracting!)
I will You, in all, Myself, with promise to never desert you,
To which I sign my name, *Walt Whitman*

609.8 So Long!] In Whitman's design this is the concluding poem of *Leaves of Grass* proper. He arranged the poems that follow it into two "annexes."

SUPPLEMENTARY POEMS

677.6–678.3 33. His shape . . . his.] In revisions after 1860, this stanza was dropped and poem "2" of the "Chants Democratic" group became "Song of the Broad-Axe" (page 330.24 in this volume).

678.4 5] Versions of the poem also appeared in *LG—1856* ("Poem of the Propositions of Nakedness"), *LG—1867* ("Respondez!"), and *LG—1871–LG—1876* ("Respondez!"). Some of the revisions are noted below. For *LG—1881*, Whitman used lines from the poem to form "Reversals," page 484.1, and "Transpositions," page 551.7, in this volume.

678.5 RESPONDEZ! / Let every] In 1871, Whitman inserted between these lines:

(The war is completed—the price is paid—the title is settled beyond recall;)

678.34–35 love! / Let the theory] In 1871, Whitman inserted:

(Stifled, O days! O lands! in every public and private corruption!
Smother'd in thievery, impotence, shamelessness, mountain-high!
Brazen effrontery, scheming, rolling like ocean's waves around and upon you, O my days! my lands!
For not even those thunderstorms, nor fiercest lightnings of the war, have purified the atmosphere;)

679.36–37 Let every . . . man!] Excluded after 1867.

681.5–7 Let the preachers of . . . lost!)] Appears only in 1860.

681.25 6] In *LG—1856*, the poem lacked the present opening line and was titled "Poem of Remembrances for A Girl or A Boy of These States." After 1860, Whitman eliminated the first 44 lines of the present poem, and the remaining lines (682.27–683.26), slightly revised, continued as a separate poem, "Think of the Soul," in *LG—1867–LG—1876*.

683.28 24] "24" concluded the "Leaves of Grass" group of poems in *LG—1860*. After that, Whitman revised the poem, titled it "Now Lift me Close," and used it to conclude *LG—1867*. He then revised it once more, and it became the penultimate poem in *Passage to India* (1871–1876), where it read:

TO THE READER AT PARTING

Now, dearest comrade, lift me to your face,
We must separate awhile—Here! take from my lips this kiss;
Whoever you are, I give it especially to you;
So long!—And I hope we shall meet again.

684.6 5] For later editions, Whitman used lines from this poem to form "Over the Carnage Rose Prophetic a Voice," page 449.1, and "For You O Democracy," page 272.1, in this volume.

688.15–16 story, / Tell me] After 1860, Whitman inserted: "Let us talk of death—unbosom all freely,". The five-line version appeared in *Passage to India* (1871–1876).

688.19 1] Published once more, in *LG—1867*.

689.1 *Says*] When Whitman revised the poem for *LG—1867*, he eliminated sections 2–4 and 6. The second version was further revised and, titled "Suggestions," appeared in *LG—1871–LG—1876*.

690.24 *Debris*] After 1860, various passages appeared as separate poems or parts of poems. Some are noted below.

691.4–8 Have you learned . . . passage with you?] Cf. "Stronger Lessons," page 631.30–35 in this volume.

691.9–20 Despairing . . . *escape?*] Cf. "Yet, Yet, Ye Downcast Hours," page 562.4–14 in this volume.

691.21–23 A thousand . . . offerings.] Cf. "Offerings," page 414.27–29 in this volume.

691.26–29 A mask . . . sleeps.] Cf. "Visor'd," page 413.20–23 in this volume.

692.13–15 Women . . . young.] Cf. "Beautiful Women," page 413.7–9 in this volume.

693.15–22 Not . . . hence.] Cf. "Not the Pilot," page 442.9–15 in this volume.

693.23–28 I thought . . . me.] Cf. "As If a Phantom Caress'd Me," page 562.17–22 in this volume.

694.4–5 flag! / O to hear you] After 1865, Whitman inserted: "(Should the days needing armies, needing fleets, come again,)." The seven-line version was incorporated in *LG—1871–LG—1876*.

695.5–32 Or, from . . . sail.] Whitman rearranged and somewhat revised these lines to form stanzas 5–8 of "As Consequent, Etc.," pages 485.20–486.11 in this volume.

COMPLETE PROSE WORKS (1892)

718.23 two samples] With some changes and deletions, Whitman is quoting here from John Burroughs, *Notes on Walt Whitman as Poet and Person* (New York, 1867).

860.28 As we walk'd] From "When Lilacs Last in the Dooryard Bloom'd," *LG—1867*.

1024.4 Preface, 1872] In *CPW* this was preceded by a revised text of the Preface to *LG—1855*. It has been omitted from this edition; see Note on the Texts.

1071.15 Two Letters] Addressed, respectively, to William Michael Rossetti and Dr. John Fitzgerald Lee. The letters are printed in full in Edwin Haviland Miller, ed., *Correspondence* (New York, 1964), 3:28–30 and 259–60.

1100.3 Dough-Face Song] Titled "Song for Certain Congressmen" when first published in New York *Evening Post*, March 2, 1850.

1102.14 Death in the School-Room (*A Fact*)] First published in *Democratic Review* (New York), August 1841.

1108.14 One Wicked Impulse!] Titled "Revenge and Requital: A Tale of a Murderer Escaped" when first published in *Democratic Review*, July-August 1845.

1116.21 The Last Loyalist] Titled "The Child-Ghost; a Story of the Last Loyalist" when first published in *Democratic Review*, May 1842.

1123.8 Wild Frank's Return] First published in *Democratic Review*, November 1841, with this note: "The main incidents of this and another story, 'Death in the School-Room,' contributed by the same writer to a preceding number of the *Democratic Review*, were of actual occurrence; and in the native town of the author, the relation of them often beguiles the farmer's winter-fireside."

1129.35 The Boy Lover] First published in *American Review* (New York), May 1845.

1136.16 The Child and the Profligate] Titled "The Child's Champion" when first published in *New World* (New York), November 29, 1841.

1144.37 Lingave's Temptation] First publication unknown.

1149.9 Little Jane] First published in chapter 14 of Whitman's "temperance novel," *Franklin Evans*, in *New World*, November 1842.

1152.8 Dumb Kate] Titled "Dumb Kate.—An Early Death" when first published in *Columbian Magazine* (New York), May 1844.

1154.11 Talk to an Art-Union] A lecture before the Brooklyn Art Union, March 31, 1851. A fuller text appeared in Brooklyn *Daily Advertizer*, April 3, 1851, and is reprinted in Emory Holloway, ed., *The Uncollected Poetry and Prose of Walt Whitman* (New York, 1921), 1:241–47.

1155.7 Blood-Money] Contrary to Whitman's dating (page 1156), probably first published in New York *Tribune Supplement*, March 22, 1850.

1156.19 Wounded in the House of Friends] Titled "The House of Friends" when first published, in a fuller version, in New York *Tribune*, June 14, 1850.

1157.19 Sailing the Mississippi at Midnight] Titled "The Mississippi at Midnight" when first published, in a somewhat different form, in New Orleans *Crescent*, March 6, 1848.

1186.25 lion Demo— . . . doom.] The line from Tennyson's "Locksley Hall Sixty Years After," should read: "Larger than the Lion,—Demos end in working its own doom." Tennyson capitalized the words Love, Weakest, Strongest, Orator, Cat, and Nature. Whitman omits twenty lines after the word "doom."

1292.14 "Now, land and life,] With the first line omitted and minor variations, this is Whitman's poem "Now Finalè to the Shore" (page 608).

1308.8 Preface] The O'Connor collection is titled *Three Tales* (Boston, 1892).

SUPPLEMENTARY PROSE

1366.1 May 31, 1889] This untitled note immediately precedes "A Backward Glance o'er Travel'd Roads" in the 1889 edition of *Leaves of Grass.*

1369.1 *Walt Whitman's Last*] The editor's note accompanying this piece reads:

> With "Good-Bye my Fancy" Walt Whitman has rounded out his life-work. This book is his last message, and of course a great deal will be said about it by critics all over the world both in praise and dispraise; but probably nothing that the critics will say will be as interesting as this characteristic utterance upon the book by the poet himself. It is the subjective view as opposed to the objective views of the critics. Briefly Whitman gives as he puts it "a hint of the spinal marrow of the business," not only of "Good-Bye my Fancy" but also of the "Leaves of Grass."
>
> It was only after considerable persuasion on the editor's part that Mr. Whitman consented to write the above. As a concise explanation of the poet's life-work it must have great value to his readers and admirers. After the critics "have ciphered and ciphered out long" they will probably have nothing better to say.

Poetry Title Index

Asterisks indicate the untitled poems of Leaves of Grass (1855). *They are listed by the titles Whitman eventually gave to them. Double asterisks indicate first lines, or parts of them, for poems Whitman never titled.*

Index of First Lines

Cataloging Information

Whitman, Walt, 1819–1892.
[Works. 1996]
Poetry and prose / Walt Whitman.—1st Library of America college ed.
p. cm.—(Library of America college editions)
Rev. ed. of: Complete poetry and collected prose. New York, N.Y.: Literary Classics of the United States; Distributed by Viking Press, ©1982.
Includes index.
Contents: Leaves of grass (1855)—Leaves of grass (1891–92)—Supplementary poems—Complete prose works (1892)—Supplementary prose.
I. Whitman, Walt, 1819–1892. Works. 1982. II. Title. III. Title: Leaves of grass (1855) IV. Title: Leaves of grass (1891–92) V. Series.
PS3200.F96 1996 95-52466
811'.3—dc20
ISBN 1-883011-35-3

ABOUT THE LIBRARY OF AMERICA

THE LIBRARY OF AMERICA is an award-winning, nonprofit publisher dedicated to preserving America's best and most significant writing in handsome, enduring volumes, featuring authoritative texts. Founded in 1979 with initial funding from the National Endowment for the Humanities and the Ford Foundation, the series, which now numbers over a hundred volumes, has been called "the most important book-publishing project in the nation's history."

For the first time, the full range of outstanding American writing will be permanently available in uniform, hardcover volumes, priced to reach a wide audience. Each volume contains up to 1600 pages and includes a number of works by our country's foremost novelists, historians, poets, essayists, journalists, philosophers, and statesmen. Authoritative, unabridged, scrupulously accurate texts are a hallmark of the volumes, which also feature a handsomely designed page, high-quality, acid-free paper bound in a cloth cover and sewn to lie flat when opened, a ribbon marker, and printed endpapers. The series includes acknowledged classics and neglected masterpieces, and new volumes are added each year.

Library of America hardcover volumes are available singly or by subscription. A jacketed edition, available in bookstores, is priced between $30.00 and $47.50. A slipcased edition is available by subscription at $24.95.

Library of America College Editions bring these authoritative and comprehensive editions to teachers and students for the first time in an affordable paperback format.

For more information, a complete list of titles, or to place an order, contact:

The Library of America
14 East 60th Street
New York, New York 10022
Telephone: (212) 308-3360
Fax: (212) 750-8352
E-Mail: LibAmerica@aol.com
Website: www.loa.org

LIBRARY OF AMERICA COLLEGE EDITIONS

American Poetry: The Nineteenth Century
John Hollander, editor
ISBN 1-883011-36-1 $14.95 1040 pages

Willa Cather • NOVELS AND STORIES 1905–1918
Sharon O'Brien, editor
The Troll Garden, O Pioneers!, The Song of the Lark, My Ántonia
ISBN 1-883011-74-4 $13.95 975 pages

Stephen Crane • PROSE AND POETRY
J. C. Levenson, editor
Maggie: A Girl of the Streets; The Red Badge of Courage; Stories; Journalism; Poetry
ISBN 1-883011-39-6 $15.95 1379 pages

Frederick Douglass • AUTOBIOGRAPHIES
Henry Louis Gates, Jr., editor
Narrative of the Life; My Bondage and My Freedom; Life and Times
ISBN 1-883011-30-2 $13.95 1126 pages

W.E.B. Du Bois • WRITINGS
Nathan I. Huggins, editor
The Suppression of the African Slave-Trade; The Souls of Black Folk; Dusk of Dawn; Essays & Articles from The Crisis
ISBN 1-883011-31-0 $15.95 1334 pages

Ralph Waldo Emerson • ESSAYS AND POEMS
Joel Porte, Harold Bloom, and Paul Kane, editors
Nature; Addresses, and Lectures; Essays: First and Second Series; Representative Men; The Conduct of Life; Poems 1847; May-Day and Other Poems; Uncollected Poems
ISBN 1-883011-32-9 $15.95 1360 pages

Nathaniel Hawthorne • TALES AND SKETCHES
Roy Harvey Pearce, editor
Twice-told Tales; Mosses from an Old Manse; The Snow Image
ISBN 1-883011-33-7 $13.95 1181 pages

Henry James • MAJOR STORIES AND ESSAYS
ISBN 1-883011-75-2 $11.95 705 pages

Sarah Orne Jewett • NOVELS AND STORIES
Michael Davitt Bell, editor
Deephaven; A Country Doctor; The Country of the Pointed Firs; Stories and Sketches
ISBN 1-883011-34-5 $11.95 937 pages

Herman Melville • MOBY-DICK, BILLY BUDD, AND OTHER WRITINGS
G. Thomas Tanselle, Harrison Hayford, John Hollander, editors
Moby-Dick, Bartleby, The Scrivener, Benito Cereno, The Encantadas, Billy Budd, Hawthorne and His Mosses, Selected Poems
ISBN 1-883011-89-2 $13.95 996 pages

Edgar Allan Poe • POETRY, TALES, AND SELECTED ESSAYS
Patrick F. Quinn and G. R. Thompson, editors
ISBN 1-883011-38-8 $16.95 1506 pages

Mark Twain • HUCK FINN; PUDD'NHEAD WILSON; NO. 44, THE MYSTERIOUS STRANGER; AND OTHER WRITINGS
Guy Cardwell and Louis J. Budd, editors
ISBN 1-883011-88-4 $12.95 808 pages

Edith Wharton • FOUR NOVELS
R.W.B. Lewis and Cynthia Griffin Wolff, editors
The House of Mirth; Ethan Frome; The Custom of the Country; The Age of Innocence
ISBN 1-883011-37-X $13.95 1156 pages

Walt Whitman • POETRY AND PROSE
Justin Kaplan, editor
Leaves of Grass 1855; Leaves of Grass 1891–92; Supplementary Poems; Complete Prose
ISBN 1-883011-35-3 $17.95 1407 pages